Human Rights and World Public Order

OF RELATED INTEREST

Harold D. Lasswell and Abraham Kaplan
POWER AND SOCIETY: A Framework for Political Inquiry. 1950

Myres S. McDougal and Associates
STUDIES IN WORLD PUBLIC ORDER. 1960

Myres S. McDougal and Florentino P. Feliciano
LAW AND MINIMUM WORLD PUBLIC ORDER: The Legal Regulation of International Coercion. 1961

Myres S. McDougal and William T. Burke
THE PUBLIC ORDER OF THE OCEANS: A Contemporary International Law of the Sea. 1962

Myres S. McDougal, Harold D. Lasswell, and Ivan A. Vlasic
LAW AND PUBLIC ORDER IN SPACE. 1963

Douglas M. Johnston
THE INTERNATIONAL LAW OF FISHERIES: A Framework for Policy-Oriented Inquiries. 1965.

B. S. Murty
PROPAGANDA AND WORLD PUBLIC ORDER: The Legal Regulation of the Ideological Instrument of Coercion. 1968

Myres S. McDougal, Harold D. Lasswell, and James C. Miller
THE INTERPRETATION OF AGREEMENTS AND WORLD PUBLIC ORDER: Principles of Content and Procedure. 1967

W. Michael Reisman
NULLITY AND REVISION: The Review and Enforcement of International Judgments and Awards. 1971

Human Rights and World Public Order

The Basic Policies of an International Law of Human Dignity

by Myres S. McDougal, Harold D. Lasswell,
and Lung-chu Chen

New Haven and London, Yale University Press, 1980

Set in Baskerville type. Printed in the United States of America by The Vail-Ballou Press, Inc., Binghamton, New York.

Published in Great Britain, Europe, Africa, and Asia (except Japan) by Yale University Press, Ltd., London. Distributed in Australia and New Zealand by Book & Film Services, Artarmon, N.S.W., Australia; and in Japan by Harper & Row, Publishers, Tokyo Office.

Library of Congress Cataloging in Publication Data

McDougal, Myres Smith, 1906–
Human rights and world public order.
Includes indexes.
1. Civil rights (International law)
I. Lasswell, Harold Dwight, 1902–1978 joint author.
II. Chen, Lung-chu, 1935– joint author.
III. Title.
K3240.4.M27 341.48′1 79-18149
ISBN 0-300-02344-8

TO

FRANCES LEE McDOUGAL

SU-TON CHEN

LAI-CHU HUANG CHEN

CONTENTS

PREFACE

This book is designed to outline a comprehensive framework for inquiry about human rights and to suggest certain preliminary clarifications of such rights by criteria appropriate to a world public order of human dignity. It recommends a conception of human rights in terms of the shaping and sharing of values in community process and seeks to locate such rights in their most comprehensive community context and in relation to all relevant processes of authoritative decision. It explores the conditions affecting human rights in the contemporary world community and recommends intellectual procedures for relating the more fundamental, but necessarily complementary, policies about human rights to particular instances of choice. The general framework of inquiry proposed is illustrated by its detailed application to certain important problems concerning the value of respect, regarded as the core value of all human rights.

The observational standpoint to which we aspire is that of citizens of the larger community of humankind who identify with the whole community, rather than with the primacy of particular groups, and who are committed to clarifying and securing the common interests of all individuals in realizing human dignity on the widest possible scale.

The conception of human rights which we recommend, in terms of the interactions of individuals in the shaping and sharing of values, can be made to transcend all differences in the subjectivities and practices of peoples, not merely across nation-state lines, but as between the different cultures of the larger community. By a combination of value references, taken from ethical philosophers—such as respect, power, enlightenment, well-being, wealth, skill, affection, and rectitude—and of institutional or practice references, taken from cultural anthropologists—such as participation, perspectives (demands, identifications, expectations), situations, bases of power, strategies, and outcomes—the description of individual interactions in the shaping and sharing of values can be made as comprehensive and as precisely detailed, through time and across boundaries, as inquiry and decision may require. Detailed operational indices may be assigned to both value and institutional terms

ıake necessary. For exploration of the outcomes of any process, thus, we recommend such subcategorizations as:

sic share of participation and enjoyment;

sitive opportunity for further participation and enjoyment, ree from discrimination for reasons irrelevant to capabilities;

Further recognition or reward for actual contributions to the common interest; and

4. The largest possible aggregate shaping and sharing.

It is the aggregate of these outcomes in all value processes that determines in any community the kind and quantum of human rights that its members enjoy. From the standpoint we recommend, all differentiations between values, sanctifying some as components of "human rights" and ascribing to others a lesser status, become not merely irrelevant, but invidious; because of the interdependences of peoples everywhere, both within any particular value process and as between different value processes, there is a human rights dimension to every interaction in the shaping and sharing of values, and this dimension includes in varying constellations effects upon the outcomes of all values.

The value that we here emphasize as the core value of all human rights is, however, that of *respect,* in its most extensive sense of an interrelation among human beings in which they reciprocally recognize and honor each other's freedom of choice about participation in other value processes. In this sense respect includes not only the perspectives and symbols of recognition and worth by which individuals reciprocally characterize each other, but also the translation of these perspectives and symbols into the operative facts of freedom of choice in social process. One important outcome of the respect process in any community is in determining the access of its members to all other value processes.

It is common observation that both the more comprehensive transnational social processes and the internal social processes of different particular communities are today, as historically, characterized by a continuous flow of deprivations and nonfulfillments for individuals in the shaping and sharing of values. The contemporary processes as a whole exhibit grave and immense disparities between the growing common demands of the peoples of the world for a greater production and wider sharing of human dignity values and the actual production and distribution of such values. In consequence, both individuals and groups are making increasingly intense claims upon established authoritative decision makers, both transcending particular communities and within particular communities, for the minimization of such deprivations and nonfulfillments and for the better securing and protection of their asserted human rights. The various particular claims that different individuals and groups make to authoritative decision relate both to every phase of every value process comprised within the global and particular community processes and to every feature and aspect of the processes of authoritative decision to which claim is made.

The framework of inquiry we recommend seeks, accordingly, to suggest the broad outlines of a comprehensive map of the global community and social processes in which deprivations and nonfulfillments of human rights are effected, to specify the different kinds of claims that are made to authoritative decision in empirical terms that will facilitate performance of all the intellectual tasks necessary to rational decision, and to delineate, comprehensively, the various features of the constitutive processes of authoritative decision that the global community maintains for response to such claims. Any framework of inquiry which makes sharp distinctions between the national and transnational dimensions of human rights creates illusion by ignoring the transnational interdependences of all social processes, including the interpenetration across geographic boundaries of the expectations and facts of authority and control.

It is observed in our study, as others have observed before us, that the contemporary world arena exhibits an increasingly viable constitutive process of authoritative decision which, though it has not yet achieved that high stability in expectations about authority and in degree of control over constituent members that characterizes the internal processes of certain national communities, still offers in more than rudimentary form all the basic features essential to the effective making and application of law on a global scale. In recent decades, this emerging constitutive process has been expanding and improving itself at an accelerating rate and, judged in the light of long historical perspective, rapidly making itself much more adequate to cope with human rights, as well as other, problems. One most significant feature of this developing process is the emergence, in response to the ever intensifying demands from peoples everywhere for the greater production and wider sharing of human dignity values, of a growing body of prescriptions—beginning with the United Nations Charter and extending through the Universal Declaration of Human Rights to the two international covenants and a whole host of more specialized conventions and ancillary expressions—which are taking on both the substance and form of the basic bills of rights long established and maintained in some national communities. It needs to be emphasized, however, that human rights are at stake not only in the modalities by which the different constitutive processes of the global community regulate and protect access to the various value processes, but also in the functioning of every feature of the constitutive processes themselves.

This intellectual procedures we recommend for relating the more fundamental, but complementary, policies about human rights to particular instances of choice require the explicit postulation, as distinguished from syntactic derivation, of a comprehensive set of policy preferences, formulated at necessarily high levels of abstraction, and the systematic employment of certain distinctive, yet interrelated, intellectual tasks in the accommodation of preferred policies. These more specific intellectual tasks include the detailed clarification of goals, the description of past decisions in terms of approximation to preferred policies, the analysis of conditions affecting decision, the projection of probable future developments, and the invention and evaluation of policy alternatives in decision. For the better performance of these different tasks we recommend the deliberate and systematic employment of certain principles of content, which indicate the features of the processes of deprivation, claim, and decision relevant to choice, and of procedure, which outline an order and modalities for effective inquiry.

The public order goals we recommend for postulation are, as indicated, those which are today commonly characterized as the basic values of human dignity, or of a free society, and which have been authoritatively incorporated, as *ius cogens* of high level abstraction, in the newly emerged global bill of human rights. The contemporary image of man as capable of respecting himself and others, and of constructively participating in the shaping and sharing of all human dignity values, is, we suggest, the culmination of many different trends in thought, secular as well as religious, with origins extending far back into antiquity and coming down through the centuries with vast cultural and geographic reach. The intensifying demands of peoples for these values are fortified by an increasing recognition that the most fundamental policies underlying all law, in any community that seeks a genuine clarification and implementation of the common interests of its members, are those which today are described as of human rights. In a very realistic sense the recently achieved global bill of rights is an immense, authoritative postulation of demanded values by the whole of humankind.

We write in full recognition that the fundamental policies of the new global bill of rights are being but slowly put into controlling practice. Among the most important factors in contemporary global processes of effective power are, however, the rising common demands of individual human beings, irrespective of community and transcending all communities, for the greater production and wider sharing of all values and the increasing participation by individuals through many different groups, functional as well as governmental, in value processes transcending nation-state lines. The nation-state and other territorial associations, like the functional groupings, are but patterns of perspectives and operations of individual human beings and instruments by which they seek to clarify and secure their common interests. In a world in which peoples enjoy ever increasing enlightenment about the conditions affecting their common interests, a concern for human rights may not be utopianism but rather hard-bitten realism. Unhappily, much of the contemporary concern for human rights is confined to what is described as "implementation," characterized by a scattering of recommendations for change in institution or practice. The difficulty with most of these recommendations is that they are proffered in fragmented and anecdotal form, without clear and systematic relation either to the comprehensive constitutive decision process which they are designed to affect or to the effective power processes which condition change in authoritative decision. The urgent challenge to contemporary scholarship is to supply a framework for inquiry, or a model, which will facilitate both the detailed clarification of the most fundamental public order policies and the design of appropriate constitutive processes, at all necessary geographic levels, for putting such policies into effect. It is in beginning response to such challenge that our book has been constructed.

It remains briefly to indicate the organization of the book:

Chapter 1 establishes our conception of human rights and sets forth a broad framework of inquiry—deliberately policy oriented, contextual, problem solving, and multimethod—for the location of human rights in their most comprehensive context.

Chapter 2 outlines, and illustrates, a way of describing the comprehensive global social process in which the continuous flow of deprivations and nonfulfillment of human rights occurs.

Chapter 3 formulates the recurrent types of claims made to authoritative decision, in relation both to deprivations and nonfulfillments in the different value processes and to features of the constitutive process, in categorizations designed to facilitate performance of all relevant intellectual tasks.

Chapter 4 offers a comprehensive outline of the contemporary global constitutive process of authoritative decision and spotlights the emergence of the global bill of human rights.

Chapter 5 postulates some of the basic policies of a comprehensive public order of human dignity and specifies the intellectual procedures we recommend for the clarification and application of fundamental policies in particular instances.

Chapters 6 to 16 offer illustration of the application of the framework of inquiry to some of the more important outcomes of the respect value.

Chapter 16, the concluding chapter, while focusing upon the aggregate dimensions of shared respect and the necessities of accommodation, suggests a direction for future development toward a world civic order in which the individual enjoys the utmost possible freedom of choice in the shaping and sharing of values compatible with common interest.

It may be noted that different segments of the book had to be prepared at different times. We have not sought to bring the documentation of the book uniformly up to date. Our interest has been more in outlining a comprehensive frame of reference and in specifying intellectual procedures for the clarification of policy in particular instances than in the detail of documentation.

When we first began our study, we had hoped to explore in detail the human rights dimensions of all the eight major values with which we customarily work. It has already been observed that this volume contains only a general introduction to such a comprehensive inquiry and a detailed study of the outcome features of the respect value. It proved impossible, unhappily, to secure the resources necessary to a more comprehensive study.

The appendix was designed to be a part of a comprehensive study of human rights in relation to the value of power. We include it in this volume partly because of the importance of the problems of nationality and partly to suggest a model for the study of other claims in relation to power.

Our debts for generous assistance in the preparation of this book are many. Our deepest gratitude is to H. Peter Stern, who offered intellectual stimulus, moral encouragement, and financial assistance from the inception of the book until its completion. W. Michael Reisman was characteristically helpful, participating in most of our group discussions and critically reading most of the chapters; in chapter 4 we draw heavily upon collaborative work with him. Charles Runyon supplied information, ideas, and encouragement. John E. Claydon read chapters 6–9, 11, and 13. Thomas I. Emerson read chapters 12 and 16. Robert H. Miller and Winston P. Nagan read chapters 6 to 9. Barbara D. Underwood and Kreszentia M. Duer read chapter 10. Irving I. Zaretsky read chapters 11 and 13. Robert M. Cover assisted in guiding us through the literature relating to slavery. Lung-Fong Chen afforded significant assistance in securing research materials. K. N. Nayak very graciously undertook the laborious task of preparing the indexes. Stephen A. Jarowski assisted in proofreading the footnotes of chapter 4. Several generations of our students contributed to our enterprise by critical response to preliminary drafts.

The principal source of financial support, apart from the Yale Law School, in the preparation of our book has been the Ralph E. Ogden Foundation of Mountainville, New York, of which H. Peter Stern is president. The officers of this foundation have been consistently generous. A grant from the National Science Foundation (Grant No. SOC 76-22335), for which we would especially thank Professor David C. Baldus, was helpful in the preparation of chapter 4. A grant from the Torrey H. Webb Charitable Trust of Los Angeles, California, for which we would especially thank Professor Carl M. Franklin, was indispensable to the final preparation of the manuscript and in seeing the book through the press.

For bearing difficult secretarial burdens we are grateful to Elise Kelso, Edna Scott, Maureen Morris, Mary Kozlowski, Isabel Poludnewycz, Mary Ellen Kennedy, the late Myra Brunswick, Pamela Carter, and Eileen Quinn. Arthur A. Charpentier and various members of the Yale Law Library staff, including especially Gene Coakley, Frances Woods, Carl F. Lamers, Robert E. Brooks, and J. Michael Hughes, and Michele F. Sullivan and Carol Park of the Yale University Library were graciously helpful in maintaining a flow of books and other documentation.

Our appreciation is extended to the editors of a number of law journals for their earlier separate publication of some of the chapters, their assistance in editing and checking these chapters, and their consent to our making use of the materials in their originally published form. These journals include the *American Journal of International Law,* the *American University Law Review, Michigan Law Review, New York Law School Law Review, Northwestern University Law Review, Revista Juridica de la Universidad de Puerto Rico* (in which chapter 2 will appear), *Southern Illinois University Law Journal, University of Florida Law Review,* the *Yale Law Journal,* and *Yale Studies in World Public Order.*

We would also thank Deans Abraham S. Goldstein and Harry H. Wellington of Yale Law School, and Dean E. Donald Shapiro of New York Law School, for strong and consistent support.

The officers of the Yale University Press have been as always generous in encouragement and support. It is not possible to find words adequate to indicate our debt to Chester Kerr and Marian Ash for their indispensable assistance with respect to this book, as well as to the earlier books in our series. Janis Bolster was excellent in her role as copy editor.

Lung-chu Chen would like to thank his parents, to whom the book is dedicated, his wife and children, and extended family, for all their encouragement, patience, and support.

Myres S. McDougal
Harold D. Lasswell
Lung-chu Chen

New Haven, Conn.
New York, N.Y.

The death on December 18, 1978, of Harold Dwight Lasswell deprived us of a friend, colleague, and mentor and the world of an extraordinarily gifted scholar whose contribution to human rights and international law has been immense. The principal thrust of the "policy sciences," the conception of which was the summation of Lasswell's achievements, is in explicit and deliberate emphasis upon policy, and the basic content of the policy postulated and recommended by Lasswell is the autonomy of the individual human being and his freedom of choice about participation in the shaping and sharing of all cherished values. The purpose Lasswell had in the conception and writing of this book was that of indicating how people who cherish the values of human dignity can clarify in detail an international law, and other relevant law, which reflect and secure such values. It is our deep sorrow that he is not able to join us in the dedication of this book. He not only believed in and wrote about the values of human dignity, he practiced such values. His dedication was to humanity and all living forms.*

M.S.M.
L.C.

June 1, 1979

*A more detailed commemorative statement appears in *Harold Dwight Lasswell, 1902–1978,* 88 YALE L.J. 675 (1979). *See also* POLITICS, PERSONALITY, AND SOCIAL SCIENCE IN THE TWENTIETH CENTURY (A. Rogow ed. 1969); H. LASSWELL ON POLITICAL SOCIOLOGY (D. Marvick ed. 1977).

PART I

Delimitation of the Problem

1. HUMAN RIGHTS IN COMPREHENSIVE CONTEXT

The demands for human rights being made today around the world are heir to all the great historic movements for human freedom, equality, and solidarity—including the English, American, French, Russian, and Chinese revolutions and the events they set in train. They derive also from the more enduring elements in the traditions both of natural law and natural rights and of most of the world's great religions and philosophies. They achieve support, further, from the findings of modern science about the close link between simple respect for human dignity and the shaping and sharing of all other values.[1] It has been

---

In slightly different form this chapter first appeared as *Human Rights and World Public Order: Human Rights in Comprehensive Context,* 72 Nw. U. L. Rev. 227 (1977).

1. *See generally* Fundamental Rights (J. Bridge, D. Lasok, D. Perrott, & R. Plender eds. 1973); J. Carey, UN Protection of Civil and Political Rights (1970); Comparative Human Rights (R. Claude ed. 1976) [hereinafter cited as Comparative Human Rights]; Commission to Study the Organization of Peace, The United Nations and Human Rights (1968); Cornell Law School, Human Rights: Protection of the Individual under International Law (1970) (Proceedings of the Fifth Summer Conference on International Law); M. Cranston, What Are Human Rights? (1973) [hereinafter cited as M. Cranston]; A. Del Russo, International Protection of Human Rights (1971); P. Drost, Human Rights as Legal Rights (1951) [hereinafter cited as P. Drost]; I. Duchacek, Rights & Liberties in the World Today: Constitutional Promise & Reality (1973); International Protection of Human Rights (A. Eide & A. Schou eds. 1968) (Nobel Symposium 7) [hereinafter cited as Nobel Symposium on Human Rights]; M. Ganji, International Protection of Human Rights (1962) [hereinafter cited as M. Ganji]; M. Ganji, The Realization of Economic, Social and Cultural Rights: Problems, Policies, Progress, U.N. Doc. E/CN.4/1108/Rev. 1 and 30 U.N. ESCOR (Provisional Agenda Item 7), U.N. Doc. E/CN.4/1131/Rev. 1 (1975) [hereinafter cited as Economic, Social and Cultural Rights]; Human Dignity: This Century and the Next (R. Gotesky & E. Laszlo eds. 1970) [hereinafter cited as Human Dignity]; Human Rights, Federalism and Minorities (A. Gotlieb ed. 1970); J. Green, The United Nations and Human Rights (1956); E. Haas, Human Rights and International Action (1970); Socialist Concept of Human Rights (J. Halasz ed. 1966) [hereinafter cited as Socialist Concept of Human Rights]; T. Hesburgh, The Human Imperative 23–37 (1974); A. Holcombe, Human Rights in the Modern World (1948); René Cassin, Amicorum Discipulorumque Liber (Institut International des Droits de l'Homme ed. 1969–72) (4 vols.)

many times observed how rudimentary demands for freedom from despotic executive tyranny have gradually been transformed into demands for protection against not only the executive but all institutions or functions of government and all private coercion. Early demands for the barest "civil liberties," inherent in the most primitive conception of rule by law, have burgeoned into insistence upon comprehensive "human

---

[hereinafter cited as RENÉ CASSIN]; INTERNATIONAL LABOUR OFFICE, SOCIAL POLICY IN A CHANGING WORLD: THE ILO RESPONSE (1976) (Selected Speeches by Wilfred Jenks); G. JELLINEK, THE DECLARATION OF THE RIGHTS OF MAN AND OF CITIZENS: A CONTRIBUTION TO MODERN CONSTITUTIONAL HISTORY (M. Farrand trans. 1901); THE HUMAN RIGHT TO INDIVIDUAL FREEDOM (L. Kutner ed. 1970); H. LAUTERPACHT, AN INTERNATIONAL BILL OF THE RIGHTS OF MAN (1945); H. LAUTERPACHT, INTERNATIONAL LAW AND HUMAN RIGHTS (1950) [hereinafter cited as H. LAUTERPACHT, 1950]; THE INTERNATIONAL PROTECTION OF HUMAN RIGHTS (E. Luard ed. 1967) [hereinafter cited as E. LUARD]; J. MARITAIN, THE RIGHTS OF MAN AND NATURAL LAW (D. Anson trans. 1943); HUMAN RIGHTS (A. Melden ed. 1970); M. MOSKOWITZ, INTERNATIONAL CONCERN WITH HUMAN RIGHTS (1974) [hereinafter cited as M. MOSKOWITZ, 1974]; M. MOSKOWITZ, THE POLITICS AND DYNAMICS OF HUMAN RIGHTS (1968) [hereinafter cited as M. MOSKOWITZ, 1968]; HUMAN RIGHTS (E. Pollack ed. 1971) [hereinafter cited as HUMAN RIGHTS]; POLITICAL THEORY AND THE RIGHTS OF MAN (D. Raphael ed. 1967); A. ROBERTSON, HUMAN RIGHTS IN THE WORLD (1972) [hereinafter cited as A. ROBERTSON]; HUMAN RIGHTS IN NATIONAL AND INTERNATIONAL LAW (A. Robertson ed. 1968); D. SANDIFER & L. SCHEMAN, THE FOUNDATIONS OF FREEDOM: THE INTERRELATIONSHIP BETWEEN DEMOCRACY AND HUMAN RIGHTS (1966); E. SCHWELB, HUMAN RIGHTS AND THE INTERNATIONAL COMMUNITY (1964); N. SINGH, HUMAN RIGHTS AND INTERNATIONAL COOPERATION (1969); L. SINGHVI, HORIZONS OF FREEDOM (1969); L. SOHN & T. BUERGENTHAL, INTERNATIONAL PROTECTION OF HUMAN RIGHTS (1973); UNITED NATIONS, UNITED NATIONS ACTION IN THE FIELD OF HUMAN RIGHTS, U.N. Doc. ST/HR/2 (1974); UNITED NATIONS EDUCATIONAL, SCIENTIFIC AND CULTURAL ORGANIZATION, BIRTHRIGHT OF MAN (1969) [hereinafter cited as BIRTHRIGHT OF MAN]; HUMAN RIGHTS (UNESCO ed. 1949); AN INTRODUCTION TO THE STUDY OF HUMAN RIGHTS (F. Vallat ed. 1972); V. VAN DYKE, HUMAN RIGHTS, THE UNITED STATES, AND WORLD COMMUNITY (1970); *Hearings on International Protection of Human Rights before the Subcomm. on International Organization and Movements of the House Comm. on Foreign Affairs,* 93d Cong., 1st Sess. (1974) [hereinafter cited as *Hearings*]; Bilder, *Rethinking International Human Rights: Some Basic Questions,* 1969 WIS. L. REV. 170; Humphrey, *The International Law of Human Rights in the Middle Twentieth Century,* in THE PRESENT STATE OF INTERNATIONAL LAW AND OTHER ESSAYS 75 (M. Bos ed. 1973).

On the regional level, *see* R. BEDDARD, HUMAN RIGHTS AND EUROPE (1973); BRITISH INSTITUTE OF INTERNATIONAL AND COMPARATIVE LAW, THE EUROPEAN CONVENTION ON HUMAN RIGHTS (1965) (International Law Series No. 5); F. CASTBERG, THE EUROPEAN CONVENTION ON HUMAN RIGHTS (T. Opsahl & T. Ouchterlony eds. 1974); HUMAN RIGHTS AND THE LIBERATION OF MAN IN THE AMERICAS (L. Colonnese ed. 1970); J. FAWCETT, THE APPLICATION OF THE EUROPEAN CONVENTION ON HUMAN RIGHTS (1969); F. Jacob, THE EUROPEAN CONVENTION ON HUMAN RIGHTS (1975); MELANGES OFFERTS À POLYS MODINOS (1968); C. MORRISON, THE DEVELOPING EUROPEAN LAW OF HUMAN RIGHTS (1967); A. SCHREIBER, THE INTER-AMERICAN COMMISSION ON HUMAN RIGHTS (1970); SECRETARIAT OF THE INTER-AMERICAN COMMISSION ON HUMAN RIGHTS, THE ORGANIZATION OF AMERICAN STATES AND HUMAN RIGHTS, 1960–1967 (1972); G. WEIL, THE EUROPEAN CONVENTION ON HUMAN RIGHTS (1963).

rights"—that is, into demands for effective participation in all community value processes and for wide sharing in all the values upon which even minimum civil liberties depend.[2] This history can be traced in the changing relation of the individual to the state: from the absolutist state through the liberal or laissez-faire state to the welfare or socialist state, with an increasing perception of political organization as an instrument of all values, and of the importance of government of, by, and for all people.[3] From demands for physical security and inviolability of the person, with freedom from cruel and inhuman treatment and freedom from arbitrary arrest and confinement, a progression may be noted to demands for freedom of conscience and religion, of opinion and expression, and of association and assembly.[4] With the impact of industrialization, massive concentration of wealth, sprawling urbanization, accelerating change, and the attendant ills of exploitation, disparities in wealth distribution, unemployment, inadequate housing, medical care, education, skills, and so on have come not unnaturally demands for fair and adequate wages, basic income, improved working and health conditions, access to education and skill acquisition, and protection against the hazards of unemployment, sickness, old age, and the like.[5]

Different peoples located in different parts of the world, conditioned by varying cultural traditions and employing divergent modes of social organization, may of course assert these fundamental demands in many different modalities and nuances of institutional practice. There would appear, however, to be an overriding insistence, transcending all cultures and climes, upon the greater production and wider distribution of

---

2. For an excellent, succinct account, *see* Claude, *The Classical Model of Human Rights Development,* in COMPARATIVE HUMAN RIGHTS, *supra* note 1, at 6–50.

3. *See* E. BARKER, PRINCIPLES OF SOCIAL AND POLITICAL THEORY 244–52 (1951); K. MANNHEIM, MAN AND SOCIETY IN AN AGE OF RECONSTRUCTION 336 (1940).

4. *See* E. CORWIN, LIBERTY AGAINST GOVERNMENT (1948).

5. *See* R. MACIVER, DEMOCRACY AND THE ECONOMIC CHALLENGE 29 (1952); Lasswell, *The Interrelations of World Organization and Society,* 55 YALE L.J. 889 (1946), *reprinted in* THE POLICY SCIENCES 102 (D. Lerner & H. Lasswell eds. 1951). *See also* E. BARKER, THE DEVELOPMENT OF PUBLIC SERVICES IN WESTERN EUROPE, 1660–1930 (1945); M. BEER, SOCIAL STRUGGLES IN ANTIQUITY (1922); M. BEER, SOCIAL STRUGGLES IN THE MIDDLE AGES (1924); B. GILBERT, THE EVOLUTION OF NATIONAL INSURANCE IN GREAT BRITAIN: THE ORIGINS OF THE WELFARE STATE (1966); INTERNATIONAL LABOUR OFFICE, SOCIAL POLICY IN A CHANGING WORLD: THE ILO RESPONSE (1976) (Selected Speeches by Wilfred Jenks); C. JENKS, LAW, FREEDOM AND WELFARE 1–31, 101–36 (1963); J. ROMANYSHYN, SOCIAL WELFARE: CHARITY TO JUSTICE (1971); SOCIAL WELFARE AND HUMAN RIGHTS: PROCEEDINGS OF THE XIVTH INTERNATIONAL CONFERENCE ON SOCIAL WELFARE, HELSINKI, FINLAND, AUGUST 18–24, 1968 (1969); W. TRATTNER, FROM POOR LAW TO WELFARE STATE: A HISTORY OF SOCIAL WELFARE IN AMERICA (1974); E. WITTE, THE DEVELOPMENT OF THE SOCIAL SECURITY ACT (1962).

all basic values,[6] accompanied by increasing recognition that a world public order of human dignity can tolerate wide differences in the specific practices by which values are shaped and shared, so long as all demands and practices are effectively appraised and accommodated in terms of common interest. The important fact is that the peoples of the world, whatever their differences in cultural traditions and styles of justification, are today increasingly demanding the enhanced protection of all those basic rights, commonly characterized in empirical reference as those of human dignity, by the processes of law in all the different communities of which they are members, including especially the international or world community.[7]

---

6. For specification of the value terms with which we work, *see* H. LASSWELL & A. KAPLAN, POWER AND SOCIETY (1950); Lasswell & Holmberg, *Toward a General Theory of Directed Value Accumulation and Institutional Development,* in COMPARATIVE THEORIES OF SOCIAL CHANGE 12 (H. Peter ed. 1966).

7. Thus, President Carter in his address to the United Nations stated: "The basic thrust of human affairs points toward a more universal demand for fundamental human rights." *Peace, Arms Control, World Economic Progress, Human Rights: Basic Priorities of U.S. Foreign Policy,* 76 DEP'T STATE BULL. 329, 332 (1977); N.Y. Times, Mar. 18, 1977, at A10, col. 6 (city ed.).

For an abundant collection of expressions of the common demands of peoples for values across cultures and through time, *see* BIRTHRIGHT OF MAN *supra* note 1. On a more formal level, demands for all important values have been eloquently articulated and summarized in the Universal Declaration of Human Rights, the International Covenants on Human Rights and their ancillary expressions, the regional human rights conventions, and the bills of rights embodied in various national constitutions. Useful compilations include: BASIC DOCUMENTS ON HUMAN RIGHTS (I. Brownlie ed. 1971); BASIC DOCUMENTS ON INTERNATIONAL PROTECTION OF HUMAN RIGHTS (L. Sohn & T. Buergenthal eds. 1973); UNITED NATIONS, HUMAN RIGHTS: A COMPILATION OF INTERNATIONAL INSTRUMENTS OF THE UNITED NATIONS, U.N. Doc. ST/HR/1 (1973).

On a less formal level, *see* M. ADLER, THE COMMON SENSE OF POLITICS (1971); C. BAY, THE STRUCTURE OF FREEDOM (1966); H. CANTRIL, THE PATTERN OF HUMAN CONCERNS 315–22 (1965); N. COHN, THE PURSUIT OF THE MILLENNIUM (rev. & expanded ed. 1970); R. FALK, A STUDY OF FUTURE WORLDS 11–32 (1975); G. FEINBERG, THE PROMETHEUS PROJECT: MANKIND'S SEARCH FOR LONG-RANGE GOALS (1968); K. FOX, SOCIAL INDICATORS AND SOCIAL THEORY 8–28 (1974); E. HOBSBAWM, THE AGE OF REVOLUTION, 1789–1848, at 81, 218–37, 278–79, 303, 327 (1962); B. MOORE, REFLECTIONS ON THE CAUSES OF HUMAN MISERY AND UPON CERTAIN PROPOSALS TO ELIMINATE THEM (1972); Galtung, *Towards New Indicators of Development,* 8 FUTURES 261 (1976); Toth, *Human Rights and World Peace,* in 1 RENÉ CASSIN, *supra* note 1, at 362–82.

Ralph Linton characterizes demands for values in terms of "biological needs," "social needs," and "psychic needs." R. LINTON, THE STUDY OF MAN 394–96, 412–17 (1937). In his words: "While human needs, in the abstract, are probably constant, the forms in which they present themselves to the members of societies are rarely twice the same." *Id.* at 414.

In Abraham Maslow's postulation, the demands of human beings find expression in a hierarchy of needs, and the lower level needs must be fulfilled before the higher ones. *See* A. MASLOW, MOTIVATION AND PERSONALITY, 97–104 (2d ed. 1970); A. MASLOW, THE

THE RISING COMMON DEMANDS

For a systematic, though necessarily synoptic and impressionistic, review of the empirical content of the demands commonly described as of "human rights," we offer an itemization in terms of the principal features of a number of representative value processes, believed to be indigenous in varying forms of equivalency in most contemporary cultures. Because of its critical importance, we begin with the value of respect. When respect is conceived as the reciprocal honoring of freedom of choice about participation in value processes, it is an indispensable component and determinant in all human rights.[8] With regard to each value, we itemize in comparable pattern:

Demands Relating to Respect

For a fundamental freedom of choice for all individuals regarding participation in all value processes;

For an effective equality of opportunity that precludes discriminations based on race (color), sex, religion, political opinion, language, or other grounds irrelevant to capability, and a social environment that affords conditions enabling people to enjoy a wide range of effective choice in their interactions with others;

For distinctive recognition of preeminent contribution to the common interest;

For an aggregate pattern of social interactions in which all individuals and groups are protected in the utmost freedom of choice and subjected to the least possible coercion, governmental or private;

For effective participation in the shaping and sharing of respect, both individually and through groups;

Farther Reaches of Human Nature 299–340, 370–90 (1971). We find it unnecessary and counter-productive to indulge in debate about a hierarchy in demands. It suffices to say that the overall trend is clearly toward demands for a wider shaping and sharing of all values.

In his book Ends and Means (1937), Aldous Huxley observed: "About the ideal goal of human effort there exists in our civilization and, for nearly thirty centuries, there has existed, a very general agreement." *Quoted in* Reston, *The Condition of the Press in the World Today (1)*, 7 Human Rights J. 593, 595 (1974). Similarly, the late Secretary-General U Thant:

> A gradual development is taking place within the United Nations of a common philosophy regarding the right of every individual, without distinction as to race, sex, language or religion, to secure respect for his dignity as a human being whether in the political and civil, or the economic, social and cultural fields.

Quoted in Nobel Symposium on Human Rights, *supra* note 1, at 267–68.

8. *See* chapter 6 *infra*.

For freedom to acquire a demand for respect, with appropriate opportunity to discover latent capabilities and to exercise such capabilities;

For freedom to establish and change identifications;

For opportunity to achieve realism in expectations;

For freedom to initiate and constitute institutions specialized to respect;

For freedom of access to institutions specialized to respect;

For freedom of access to institutions not specialized to respect;

For protection of respect even under conditions of crisis;

For the availability of processes of authoritative decision and effective power to defend and fulfill respect;

For special assistance to overcome handicaps not attributable to merit;

For freedom to employ the different instruments of policy (diplomatic, ideological, economic, military) in the protection of respect;

For freedom from imposition of disrespect by the use of the different instruments of policy;

For freedom from forced labor and from imprisonment for debt;

For freedom from terrorist activities and other acts of violence.

Demands Relating to Power

For recognition as a human being;

For admission to group membership (nationality);

For fullest participation in both the processes of government (including voting and officeholding) and effective power;

For freedom from discrimination in participation;

For freedom to establish and join groups (including political parties, pressure groups, and private associations);

For protection of minority associations;

For freedom to change rulers of groups;

For freedom to constitute a new entity;

For freedom from coercion external to the group;

For freedom to acquire a demand for power;

For freedom of access to, movement within, and egress from territory (including asylum);

For stability of expectations about continuation of rights;

For freedom to initiate and constitute power and other value institutions;

For freedom of access to adequate power and other value institutions;

For freedom from deprivations disproportionate to crisis;

For the availability of processes of authoritative decision adequate to defend and fulfill all rights;

For the comparable availability of processes of effective power;

For freedom to employ the diplomatic and other instruments to enhance the shaping and sharing of power;

For freedom from arbitrary restrains in the employment of the diplomatic, ideological, economic, and military instruments of strategy;

For freedom from coercive employment of the diplomatic and other instruments;

For freedom from arbitrary seizure and confinement;

For the maintenance of, and access to, adequate institutions for making and applying law;

For protection of equality before the law;

For the establishment and maintenance of a community that effectively, responsibly, and responsively performs all essential decision functions (intelligence, promotion, prescription, invocation, application, termination, and appraisal).

Demands Relating to Enlightenment

For achievement of an optimum aggregate in the shaping and sharing of enlightenment (in the gathering, dissemination, and enjoyment of knowledge and information);

For the provision of a basic enlightenment to all individuals;

For additional access to enlightenment on the basis of capability and contribution;

For general participation in the giving and receiving of enlightenment (knowledge and information);

For freedom from discrimination in the acquisition, use, and communication of knowledge and information;

For group participation in opportunity to acquire and disseminate knowledge;

For freedom to acquire the demand for enlightenment;

For freedom from state or private conditioning;

For freedom from distorted communications (misinformation);

For disclosure of special interests;

For freedom to initiate and constitute institutions specialized to enlightenment;

For freedom of access to adequate enlightenment and other value institutions;

For freedom from deprivations of enlightenment disproportionate to crisis;

For the availability of processes of authoritative decision adequate to defend and fulfill demands for enlightenment;

For the comparable availability of processes of effective power;

For freedom to acquire and employ appropriate language;

For freedom in both small group and mass communications;

For freedom in the assembly of appropriate resources for enlightenment;

For freedom from coerced deprivations of enlightenment (censorship, indoctrination, distortion).

Demands Relating to Well-Being

For an optimum aggregate in the shaping and sharing of well-being;

For the right to life;

For a basic minimum in safety, health, and comfort, and for additional opportunities in accordance with choice;

For progress toward optimum somatic and psychological development throughout life;

For a merciful euthanasia (for freedom to depart or continue life);

For general participation in the realization of bodily and mental health and development;

For freedom from restrictions for reasons irrelevant to individual capabilities and contributions;

For group survival and development;

For an environment that is conducive to survival and development;

For freedom to initiate and constitute institutions specialized to well-being;

For freedom of access to adequate well-being and other value institutions;

For the availability of processes of authoritative decision adequate to defend and fulfill demands for well-being;

For the comparable availability of processes of effective power;

For being a beneficiary of pertinent science and technology;

For the employment of appropriate strategies in relation to health for prevention, deterrence, restoration, rehabilitation, reconstruction, and correction;

For freedom from coerced experimentation and other deprivations;

For freedom to accept or reject medical service;

For freedom to accept or reject transplantation and repair;

For freedom to employ specific strategies in birth control;

For the employment of genetic engineering.

Demands Relating to Wealth

For the maintenance of high levels of productivity;

For a basic minimum of benefits from the wealth process (guaranteed income, social security, abolition of poverty);

For the enjoyment of benefits on the basis of contribution;

For general participation in wealth shaping and sharing (working, investing, employing resources, enjoying, etc.);

For freedom from restrictions irrelevant to capabilities for contribution;

For freedom of association in group shaping and sharing (producers, entrepreneurs, laborers, consumers, investors);

For freedom to acquire (or reject) a demand to participate in the wealth process;

For freedom to initiate and constitute, and freedom of access to, institutions specialized to wealth;

For freedom from deprivations of wealth disproportionate to crisis;

For the availability of processes of authoritative decision and effective power to defend and fulfill wealth demands (including the right to property);

For freedom to accumulate and employ resources for productive purposes;

For freedom from wasteful use of resources;

For freedom to employ all relevant strategies, without coercion or discrimination, in production, conservation, distribution, and consumption.

Demands Relating to Skill

For an optimum aggregate in the acquisition and exercise of skills;

For acquisition of a basic minimum of skills relevant to effective participation in all value processes;

For additional acquisition in terms of talent and motivation;

For unrestricted opportunity to acquire and exercise socially acceptable skill;

For opportunity to have talent discovered;

For opportunity to acquire and exercise skill without discrimination;

For accordance of skill to groups;

For acquisition of a demand for, and capability of, skill expression;

For freedom to initiate and constitute, and freedom of access to, institutions specialized to skill;

For the availability of processes of authoritative decision and effective power to defend and fulfill demands for the acquisition and exercise of skills;

For special assistance to overcome handicaps;

For exposure to training, both in content and method, appropriate to a culture of science and technology;

For freedom from coercive strategies other than those inherent in compulsory education;

For exposure to a socialization process that enables the individual to acquire the motivations and capabilities appropriate to the performance of adult roles in value processes.

Demands Relating to Affection

For an optimum aggregate in the shaping and sharing of affection (loyalties, positive sentiments);

For the basic acceptance necessary for individuals to acquire the motivations and capabilities of functioning effectively in the shaping and sharing of values;

For additional affection in terms of capability and contribution;

For giving and receiving affection on a reciprocal basis, free from restrictions irrelevant to capabilities;

For freedom to give and receive loyalty to groups of one's choice;

For freedom of association;

For freedom to acquire (or reject) a demand to participate in the affection process;

For freedom to initiate and constitute intimate and congenial personal relationships;

For freedom of access to institutions specialized to affection (adoption, legitimacy, proper spouse);

For recognition of membership in specialized groups;

For the availability of processes of authoritative decision and effective power to defend and facilitate affection demand;

For freedom in the cultivation of positive sentiments and loyalty, free from coercive and discriminatory strategies.

Demands Relating to Rectitude

For the maintenance of public and civic order in which individuals demand of themselves and others that they act responsibly for common interest;

For a minimum opportunity to receive positive evaluation of rectitude;

For movement toward a fuller participation of all in responsible conduct;

For freedom to participate in the formulation and application of standards of responsibility (religious and secular);

For freedom from discrimination in the shaping and sharing of rectitude;

For freedom of association for rectitude purposes;

For freedom to acquire a demand on the self to act responsibly;

For freedom to choose among justifications of responsible conduct (secular and religious, transempirical and empirical, etc.);

For freedom to initiate and constitute, and freedom of access to, institutions specialized to rectitude;

For the availability of processes of authoritative decision and effective power to defend and fulfill rectitude demands;

For freedom to employ all relevant strategies, without coercion or discrimination, in the pursuit of rectitude.

INADEQUATE RESPONSES—DEPRIVATIONS AND NONFULFILLMENT OF HUMAN RIGHTS

All this cumulative upsurge in common demands for human rights has not, in common knowledge, been matched by the effective realization of such rights in the public and civic orders about the world. The responses of both transnational and national processes of authoritative decision to these rising common demands have been most halting and inadequate.

Whether one looks with difficulty back into the remote past or considers the more clearly recorded world picture of the last two hundred years, the condition of the great mass of people in terms of the protection of their demands for values has not been good. Even a cursory look at daily events on a global scale leaves no doubt, further, that nonfulfillment of human dignity values still characterizes all cultures and that large-scale deprivations of individuals and groups continue to prevail everywhere.[9] Though the nature, scope, and magnitude of values at stake may differ from one community to another and from occasion to occasion, the nonfulfillments and deprivations encompass every value sector. We offer selective itemizations:

---

9. For example, the New York Times of Oct. 31, 1976, included the following headings:

U.S. Study Links Rise in Jobless to Deaths, Murders and Suicides, N.Y. Times, Oct. 31, 1976, § 1, at 1, col. 1;

State Department Said to Have Urged Korea Inquiry in '75: Investigation of Park Tong Sun Followed Testimony in Senate on Payment by Gulf Oil, id.;

Protection of Alaska's Wilderness New Priority of Conservationists, id. § 1, at 1, col. 3;

Human Rights Group Reports Repression in South America, id. § 1, at 3, col. 3;

Lebanese Fight On as Factions Quarrel over Peace Plan Terms, id. § 1, at 3, col. 1;

Devaluation Adding to Mexico's Unrest, id. § 1, at 4, col. 1;

China Posters Link Left to Killing Plot, id. § 1, at 7, col. 1;

Three Investigations Begun in Bizarre Tokyo Case Involving Miki, a Judge and a Midnight Telephone Call, id. § 1, at 8, col. 1;

India Puts Off Parliament Election, id. § 1, at 10, col. 1;

Indira Gandhi's Aunt Says She Is "Profoundly Troubled" at Direction India is Taking, id. § 1, at 11, col. 2;

Increase in Crime Worries Hungary, id. § 1, at 12, col. 3;

Thai Purge Results in Climate of Fear: With More Than 5,000 Arrested by the Military Junta, Roundups and Searches Continue Daily, id. § 1, at 13, col. 1;

Separatists in Quebec May Profit as Popularity of Liberals Declines, id. § 1, at 20, col. 3;

Military Institute Told to Admit Girls, id. § 1, at 25, col. 1;

Children's Rights Drive Centered in Courtroom, id. § 1, at 26, col. 1;

Lower East Side Churches Mobilize against Vandalism and Fires, id. § 1, at 58, col. 3.

In an unpublicized report to Congress, prepared in connection with the Foreign Assistance Act of 1975, the Department of State indicated: "Repressive laws and actions, arbitrary arrest and prolonged detention, torture or cruel, inhuman or degrading treatment or punishment, unfair trials or other flagrant denials of rights of life, liberty and the security of the person are not extraordinary events in the world community." *Id.,* Nov. 19, 1975, at 14, col. 7.

Emphasizing that "[h]uman rights abuses follow no pattern," the report further pointed out: "They are not limited to types of political regimes or political philosophies. Abuses take place in both the Western and Eastern Hemispheres. They are carried out by and against persons of virtually all races and major religions of the world." *Id.*

The annual comparative survey of freedom (with country-by-country rating) undertaken under the auspices of Freedom House is a valuable source of reference. *See* Gastil, *The Comparative Survey of Freedom VI,* 34 FREEDOM AT ISSUE 11 (1976). For previous surveys, see 29 FREEDOM AT ISSUE 5 (1975); 26 *id.* 15 (1974); 23 *id.* 8 (1974); 20 *id.* 14 (1973); 17 *id.* 4 (1973).

DEPRIVATIONS RELATING TO RESPECT

Widespread denial of individual freedom of choice regarding participation in value processes, including the comprehensive and systematic deprivations inherent in slavery, caste, apartheid, and equivalents;[10]

Persistent discrimination on such invidious grounds as race (racism), sex (sexism), religion, political opinion, language, alienage, and age;[11]

Bestowal or withholding of honor (symbolic recognition) in disregard of actual contribution to common interest;

Massive encroachments upon the zone of individual autonomy, especially privacy, as a consequence of the trends toward militarization, concentration of power, governmentalization, regimentation, and high bureaucratization;[12]

Suppression of demands for respect by denying opportunity to discover latent capabilities for participation and to acquire and exercise such capabilities;

Denial of freedom to initiate and constitute, and of freedom of access to, institutions specialized to respect (*e.g.*, suppression of civil rights organizations);[13]

Inability of processes of authoritative decision and effective power to defend and fulfill respect;

Controversies and difficulties about programs of affirmative action;[14]

---

10. *See* chapter 7 *infra,* at notes 27–78, 303–22, and 387–439, and accompanying text. *See generally Conférence Internationale de Dakar sur la Namibie et les Droits de l'Homme: d'hier a demain,* 9 HUMAN RIGHTS J. 209 (1976).

11. *See* chapters 8–15 *infra. See also* CASE STUDIES ON HUMAN RIGHTS AND FUNDAMENTAL FREEDOMS: A WORLD SURVEY (W. Veenhoven ed. 1975) [hereinafter cited as CASE STUDIES]; E. VIERDAG, THE CONCEPT OF DISCRIMINATION IN INTERNATIONAL LAW (1973).

12. *See* chapter 16 *infra.*

Of a burgeoning literature concerning encroachments upon privacy, *see* Z. MEDVEDEV, THE MEDVEDEV PAPERS 293–470 (V. Rich trans. 1971); A. MILLER, THE ASSAULT ON PRIVACY: COMPUTERS, DATA BANKS, AND DOSSIERS (1971); PRIVACY AND HUMAN RIGHTS (A. Robertson ed. 1973); A. WESTIN, PRIVACY AND FREEDOM (1968); A. WESTIN & M. BAKER, DATABANKS IN A FREE SOCIETY: COMPUTERS, RECORD-KEEPING AND PRIVACY (1972). More detailed references are contained in chapter 16 *infra.*

13. *See, e.g.,* N.Y. Times, Apr. 19, 1975, at 7, col. 2 (arrest of members of the small Soviet chapter of Amnesty International by the Soviet security police [KGB]).

14. The controversy has generated extraordinary interest in the academic community, as well as proliferation of debate among legal commentators. *See* B. BITTKER, THE CASE FOR BLACK REPARATIONS (1973); DE FUNIS VERSUS ODEGAARD AND THE UNIVERSITY OF

Widespread practices of forced labor, debt bondage, and so on;[15]
Occurrences or threats of terrorist activities endangering innocent people (*e.g.*, kidnapping, hijacking, terror bombs, etc.).[16]

WASHINGTON (A. Ginger ed. 1974); N. GLAZER, AFFIRMATIVE DISCRIMINATION: ETHNIC INEQUALITY AND PUBLIC POLICY (1975); R. O'NEIL, DISCRIMINATING AGAINST DISCRIMINATION (1975); Askin, *Eliminating Racial Inequality in a Racist World,* 2 CIV. LIB. REV. 96 (Spring 1975); Bell, *Black Students in White Schools: The Ordeal and the Opportunity,* 1970 U. TOL. L. REV. 539; Cohen, *The De Funis Case: Race and the Constitution,* THE NATION, Feb. 8, 1975, at 135; *De Funis Symposium,* 75 COLUM. L. REV. 483 (1975); Ely, *The Constitutionality of Reverse Racial Discrimination,* 41 U. CHI. L. REV. 723 (1974); Graglia, *Special Admission of the "Culturally Deprived" to Law School,* 119 U. PA. L. REV. 351 (1970); Kaplan, *Equal Justice in an Unequal World: Equality for the Negro—The Problem of Special Treatment,* 61 NW. U.L. REV. 363 (1966); Karst & Horowitz, *Affirmative Action and Equal Protection,* 60 VA. L. REV. 955 (1974); Morris, *Equal Protection, Affirmative Action and Racial Preferences in Law Admission: DeFunis v. Odegaard,* 49 WASH. L. REV. 1 (1973); O'Neill, *Racial Preference and Higher Education: The Larger Context,* 60 VA. L. REV. 925 (1974); O'Neill, *Preferential Admissions: Equalizing the Access of Minority Groups to Higher Education,* 80 YALE L.J. 699 (1971); Pelikan, *Quality and Equality,* N.Y. Times, Mar. 29, 1976, at 29, col. 2; Pollock, *On Academic Quotas, id.,* Mar. 4, 1975, at 33, col. 3; Posner, *The DeFunis Case and the Constitutionality of Preferential Treatment of Racial Minorities,* 1974 SUP. CT. REV. 1; Redish, *Preferential Law Admissions,* 22 U.C.L.A. L. REV. 343 (1974); *"Reverse Discrimination": Has It Gone Too Far?* U.S. NEWS & WORLD REPORT, Mar. 29, 1976, at 26–29; Rosen, *Equalizing Access to Legal Education: Special Programs for Law Students Who Are Not Admissible by Traditional Standards,* 1970 U. TOL. L. REV. 321; Sandalow, *Racial Preferences in Higher Education: Political Responsibility and the Judical Role,* 42 U. CHI. L. REV. 653 (1975); Sowell, *Black Conservative Dissents,* N.Y. Times, Aug. 8, 1976, § 6 (Magazine), at 14–15 *et seq.;* Summers, *Preferential Admissions: An Unreal Solution to a Real Problem,* 1970 U. TOL. L. REV. 377; *Symposium—DeFunis: The Road Not Taken,* 60 VA. L. REV. 917 (1974); *Symposium—Disadvantaged Students and Legal Education—Programs for Affirmative Action,* 1970 U. TOL. L. REV. 277; Totenberg, *Discriminating to End Discrimination,* N.Y. Times, Apr. 14, 1974, § 6 (Magazine), at 9; Bakke v. The Regents of the Univ. of Cal., 18 Cal. 3d 34, 553 P.2d 1152, 132 Cal. Rptr. 680 (1976) (en banc), *cert. granted,* 97 S. Ct. 1098 (1977).

15. *See* C. GREENIDGE, SLAVERY 66–73 (1958); G. MYRDAL, ASIAN DRAMA: AN INQUIRY INTO THE POVERTY OF NATIONS 273–81, 745–49 (1971); UNITED NATIONS & INTERNATIONAL LABOUR OFFICE, REPORT OF THE AD HOC COMMITTEE ON FORCED LABOUR, U.N. Doc. E/2431 (1953); AD HOC COMMITTEE ON SLAVERY AND SERVITUDE, FORMS OF INVOLUNTARY SERVITUDE IN ASIA, OCEANIA AND AUSTRALIA, U.N. Doc. E/AC.33/R.11 (1951); Gullick, *Debt Bondage in Malaya,* in SLAVERY: A COMPARATIVE PERSPECTIVE 51–57 (R. Winks ed. 1972); N.Y. Times, Oct. 5, 1973, at 10, col. 1; *id.,* Dec. 8, 1968, § 1, at 7, col. 1.

16. *See* J. AREY, THE SKY PIRATES (1972); C. BAUMANN, THE DIPLOMATIC KIDNAPPINGS: A REVOLUTIONARY TACTIC OF URBAN TERRORISM (1973); J. BELL, TRANSNATIONAL TERROR (1975); INTERNATIONAL TERRORISM AND WORLD SECURITY (D. Carlton & C. Schaerf eds. 1975); R. CLUTTERBUCK, LIVING WITH TERRORISM (1975); P. CLYDE, AN ANATOMY OF SKYJACKING (1973); R. GAUCHER, THE TERRORISTS: FROM TSARIST RUSSIA TO THE O.A.S. (1968); E. HYAMS, TERRORISTS AND TERRORISM (1975); B. JENKINS, INTERNATIONAL TERRORISM: A NEW MODE OF CONFLICT (1975); REPORT OF THE AD HOC COMMITTEE ON INTERNATIONAL TERRORISM, 28 U.N. GAOR, Supp. (No. 28), U.N. Doc. A/9028 (1973); UNITED NATIONS, DEP'T OF ECONOMIC AND SOCIAL AFFAIRS, FIFTH UNITED NATIONS CONGRESS ON THE PREVENTION OF CRIME AND THE TREATMENT OF OFFENDERS, GENEVA, 1–12, SEPTEMBER 1975, at 1,3,15–16,52, U.N. Doc. A/CONF.56/10 (1976) (report prepared by the Sec-

DEPRIVATIONS RELATING TO POWER

Arbitrary denial or deprivation of nationality causing numerous unprotected, stateless persons;[17]

Denial of full participation in the processes of government by exclusion from voting and officeholding;[18]

Manipulation of elective machinery through various devices, making elections a mockery of democracy;[19]

Suspension of elections in the guise of national emergency;[20]

---

retariat) [hereinafter cited as THE PREVENTION OF CRIME]; U.S. FEDERAL BUREAU OF INVESTIGATION, NATIONAL BOMB DATA CENTER, BOMB SUMMARY: A COMPREHENSIVE REPORT OF INCIDENTS INVOLVING EXPLOSIVE AND INCENDIARY DEVICES IN THE NATION, 1974 (1975); Measures to Prevent International Terrorism Which Endangers or Takes Innocent Human Lives or Jeopardizes Fundamental Freedoms, and Study of the Underlying Causes of Those Forms of Terrorism and Acts of Violence Which Lie in Misery, Frustration, Grievance and Despair and Which Cause Some People to Sacrifice Human Lives, Including Their Own, in an Attempt to Effect Radical Changes, 27 U.N. GAOR (Agenda Item 92), U.N. Doc. A/C.6/418 (1972) (study prepared by the Secretariat); Alexander, *Some Perspectives on International Terrorism,* 14 INT'L PROBLEMS 24 (Fall 1975); *Around the Globe: Outbreaks of Terror,* U.S. NEWS & WORLD REPORT, Sept. 29, 1975, at 76–79; Franck & Lockwood, *Preliminary Thoughts towards an International Convention on Terrorism,* 68 AM. J. INT'L L. 69 (1974); Howard, *Terrorists: How They Operate a Worldwide Network,* PARADE, Jan. 18, 1976, at 12; Jenkins, *Do What They Ask and Don't Worry. They May Kill Me but They Are Not Evil Men,* N.Y. Times, Oct. 3, 1975, at 35, col. 2; Rovine, *The Contemporary International Legal Attack on Terrorism,* 3 ISRAEL Y.B. HUMAN RIGHTS 9 (1973); *Terrorism and Political Crimes in International Law,* 1973 PROC., AM. SOC'Y INT'L L. 87; *World Terrorism Flares Anew,* U.S. NEWS & WORLD REPORT, Mar. 17, 1975, at 25–26; N.Y. Times, July 16, 1976, at 1, col. 1 (the arming and training of world terrorists by Libyans); *id.,* July 23, 1976, at A2, col. 3 (improvement of terrorists' techniques).

17. *See* the appendix *infra,* at notes 160–386 and accompanying text.

The denationalization and forcible exile on February 13, 1974, of Alexander I. Solzhenitsyn by the Soviet Union for the publication in December 1973 in the West of his book THE GULAG ARCHIPELAGO, 1918–1956, is a most dramatic recent example. For further detail and pertinent references, *see* the appendix *infra,* at note 280.

18. *See* H. SANTA CRUZ, RACIAL DISCRIMINATION 45–48, U.N. Doc. E/CN.4/Sub. 2/307/Rev. 1 (1971) [hereinafter cited as RACIAL DISCRIMINATION]; H. SANTA CRUZ, STUDY OF DISCRIMINATION IN THE MATTER OF POLITICAL RIGHTS 26–42, U.N. Doc. E/CN.4/Sub. 2/213/Rev. 1 (1962) [hereinafter cited as H. SANTA CRUZ].

For an attempt by a distinguished political scientist at classifying and rating countries (114 in total) according to "eligibility to participate in elections and degree of opportunity for public opposition," *see* R. DAHL, POLYARCHY: PARTICIPATION AND OPPOSITION 231–45 (1971).

19. *See, e.g.,* the practice of the Nationalist Chinese regime in Taiwan: L. CHEN & H. LASSWELL, FORMOSA, CHINA AND THE UNITED NATIONS 132–36, 151, 164–65, 170–73, 251–53, 275–77 (1967); Axelbank, *Chiang Kai-shek's Silent Enemies,* HARPER'S MAGAZINE, Sept. 1963, at 46–53.

20. *See, e.g.,* N.Y. Times, Oct. 31, 1976, § 1, at 10, col. 1 (India); *id.,* Nov. 6, 1976, at 3, col. 1 (India); *id.,* Nov. 8, 1976, at 1, col. 1 (India); *id.,* Oct. 14, 1976, at 8, col. 1 (Thailand).

Denial of full participation in the process of effective power because of disparities in the distribution of base values among members of the community;

Denial or severe restrictions on participation in the power process on invidious grounds, especially through intolerance of political nonconformists;

Prevalence of one-party rule, de jure or de facto;

Total suppression of opposition parties or toleration only of token opposition parties;

Denial or severe restrictions on freedom of association and assembly;

Suppression of minority groups;

Severe sanctions against efforts to change incumbent power elites or to form a new entity;

Denial or severe restrictions on freedom of access to, movement within, and egress from territory (*e.g.*, emigration of minorities, restrictive immigration policies);[21]

---

21. *See* J. Ingles, Study of Discrimination in Respect of the Right of Everyone to Leave Any Country, Including His Own, and to Return to His Country 18–63, U.N. Doc. E/CN.4/Sub. 2/229/Rev. 1 (1963); *Expulsion and Expatriation in International Law: The Right to Leave, to Stay, and to Return,* 1973 Proc. Am. Soc'y Int'l L. 122–40; Higgins, *The Right in International Law of an Individual to Enter, Stay In and Leave a Country,* 49 Int'l Affairs 341 (1973); Partsch, *The Right to Leave and to Return in the Countries of the Council of Europe,* 5 Israel Y.B. Human Rights 215 (1975); Pettiti, *The Right to Leave and to Return in the USSR,* 5 Israel Y.B. Human Rights 264 (1975); Plender, *The Ugandan Crisis and the Right of Expulsion under International Law,* 9 Rev. Int'l Comm'n Jurists 19 (Dec. 1972); Silverstein, *Emigration: A Policy Oriented Inquiry,* 2 Syracuse J. Int'l L. & Com. 149 (1974); Toman, *The Right to Leave and to Return in Eastern Europe,* 5 Israel Y.B. Human Rights 276 (1975); Weis, *The Right to Leave and to Return in the Middle East,* 5 Israel Y.B. Human Rights 322 (1975); N.Y. Times, Nov. 19, 1976, at A1, col. 4 (restrictions on emigration to the West by East Germans); *id.,* Dec. 26, 1974, at 8, col. 3 (the new internal passport system in the Soviet Union); *id.,* Dec. 27, 1974, at 4, col. 6.

Recently, the principal focus of attention has centered upon the problem of emigration of Soviet Jews. *See* V. Chalidze, To Defend These Rights: Human Rights and the Soviet Union 92–114 (1974); W. Korey, The Soviet Cage: Anti-Semitism in Russia 184–200 (1973); Z. Medvedev, *supra* note 12, at 173–270; A. Sakharov, My Country and the World 51–61 (G. Daniels trans. 1975); A. Sakharov, Sakharov Speaks 159–63 (H. Salisbury ed. 1974); T. Taylor, Courts of Terror: Soviet Criminal Justice and Jewish Emigration (1976); *Anti-Semitism and Reprisals against Jewish Emigration in the Soviet Union: Hearing before the Subcomm. on International Organizations of the House Comm. on International Relations,* 94th Cong., 2d Sess. (1976); Dinstein, *Freedom of Emigration and Soviet Jewry,* 4 Israel Y.B. Human Rights 266 (1974); Higgins, *Human Right of Soviet Jews to Leave: Violations and Obstacles,* 4 Israel Y.B. Human Rights 275 (1974); Knisbacher, *Aliyah of Soviet Jews: Protection of the Right of Emigration Under International Law,* 14 Harv. Int'l L.J. 89 (1973); Pettiti, *The Administrative Practice, the Measures Taken and the Harassments Applied Following the Request for a Visa,* 4 Israel Y.B. Human Rights 288 (1974); Shroeter, *How*

Mass expulsion of resident aliens (expulsion of Asians in Uganda);

Vast numbers of refugees fleeing persecution amidst deterioration of the practices of asylum;

Imposition of restrictions on freedom to initiate and constitute, and freedom of access to institutions specialized to power;[22]

Governmental institutions closed to free access;

Deprivation or suspension of important human rights through spurious invocation or abusive application of national security, as through declarations of martial law (state of siege);[23]

They Left: Varieties of Soviet Jewish Exit Experience, 2 SOVIET JEWISH AFFAIRS 3 (1972); Vazquez, *The Soviet Jewish Minority and the Right to Leave,* 4 ISRAEL Y.B. HUMAN RIGHTS 302 (1974); N.Y. Times, Feb. 17, 1976, at 6, col. 2; *id.,* Oct. 20, 1976, at 1, col. 1; *id.,* Oct. 22, 1976, at A2, col. 3; *id.,* Oct. 26, 1976, at 16, col. 1.

A dramatic recent example of suppression of freedom to travel abroad is the denial of such freedom to Andrei D. Sakharov by the Soviet government for acceptance in person of the 1975 Nobel Peace Prize. *See* N.Y. Times, Oct. 11, 1975, at 1, col. 2; *id.,* Dec. 11, 1975, at 10, col. 1; *id.,* Dec. 13, 1975, at 6, col. 3.

22. *See* C. FRIEDRICH & Z. BRZEZINSKI, TOTALITARIAN DICTATORSHIP AND AUTOCRACY 27–39 (1961) [hereinafter cited as C. FRIEDRICH & Z. BRZEZINSKI]; H. SANTA CRUZ, *supra* note 18. *See generally* REGIMES AND OPPOSITIONS (R. Dahl ed. 1973); AUTHORITARIAN POLITICS IN MODERN SOCIETY: THE DYNAMICS OF ESTABLISHED ONE-PARTY SYSTEMS (S. Huntington & C. Moore eds. 1970). *See also* R. DAHL, *supra* note 18; N.Y. Times, Dec. 3, 1974, at 6, col. 1; *id.,* June 10, 1976, 8, col. 1; *id.,* July 15, 1976, at 11, col. 3 (from the strict ban of political parties to legalization of political parties in Spain).

23. INTERNATIONAL COMMISSION OF JURISTS, THE HUNGARIAN SITUATION AND THE RULE OF LAW (1957); UNITED NATIONS, 1959 SEMINAR ON JUDICIAL AND OTHER REMEDIES AGAINST THE ILLEGAL EXERCISE OR ABUSE OF ADMINISTRATIVE AUTHORITY, U.N. DOC. ST/TAO/HR/6 (1960); UNITED NATIONS, REMEDIES AGAINST THE ABUSE OF ADMINISTRATIVE AUTHORITY, SELECTED STUDIES (1964); Azad, *A Letter from Mrs. Gandhi's India,* THE NEW REPUBLIC, Aug. 7 & 14, 1976, at 19–23; Butler, *Political Repression in South Korea—1974,* 13 REV. INT'L COMM'N JURISTS 37 (1974); *Human Rights in the World, Uruguay,* 16 REV. INT'L COMM'N JURISTS 19–22 (June 1976); *Indira's Next Decade,* NEWSWEEK, Feb. 16, 1976, at 37; N.Y. Times, July 4, 1975, at 3, col. 1 (city ed.); *id.,* Sept. 8, 1975, at 1, col. 1 (late city ed.); *id.,* Dec. 26, 1975, at 1, col. 1; *id.,* Sept. 15, 1976, at 18, col. 1; *id.,* Nov. 3, 1976, at 45, col. 8 (India). *But see* Kaul, *In Which Reasons for the State of Emergency Are Explained and Defended, id.,* July 28, 1975, at 21, col. 1; *Prime Minister Indira Gandhi Responds to Charges That Democracy in India Is Dead,* SATURDAY REV., Aug. 9, 1975, at 10.

For abuse of power under pretext of national security in connection with the Watergate scandal, see WATERGATE: SPECIAL PROSECUTION FORCE REPORT (Oct. 1975) (containing a detailed bibliography of Watergate source materials at 265–73); *Hearings and Final Reports, Pursuant to H. Res. 803, of the House Comm. on the Judiciary,* 93d Cong., 2d Sess. (1974) (Impeachment Hearings). *See also* J. DEAN, BLIND AMBITION: THE WHITE HOUSE YEARS (1976); L. JAWORSKI, THE RIGHT AND THE POWER: THE PROSECUTION OF WATERGATE (1976); E. RICHARDSON, THE CREATIVE BALANCE: GOVERNMENT, POLITICS, AND THE INDIVIDUAL IN AMERICA'S THIRD CENTURY 1–47 (1976).

Abuse of governmental power is the common thread that runs through the composite experience of the deceptions which made possible the drift into Vietnam, the long

Subverting the normal civilian processes of government by declarations of martial law (or state of siege);[24]

Inability of the processes of authoritative decision and effective power to defend and fulfill particular rights;[25]

---

contempt for the law by the Federal Bureau of Investigation under its late director J. Edgar Hoover, the persistent violations of its own charter and of fundamental civil liberties by the Central Intelligence Agency and similar transgressions by the Internal Revenue Service.

Above the Law, N.Y. Times, Dec. 28, 1975, § 4, at 10, col. 1 (editorial). *See* FINAL REPORT OF THE SENATE SELECT COMMITTEE TO STUDY GOVERNMENTAL OPERATIONS WITH RESPECT TO INTELLIGENCE ACTIVITIES, S. REP. NO. 755, 94th Cong., 2d Sess. (1976); P. AGEE, INSIDE THE COMPANY: CIA DIARY (1976); N. BLACKSTOCK, COINTELPRO: THE FBI'S SECRET WAR ON POLITICAL FREEDOM (1976); M. HALPERIN, THE LAWLESS STATE: THE CRIME OF THE U.S. INTELLIGENCE AGENCIES (1976); V. MARCHETTI & J. MARKS, THE CIA AND THE CULT OF INTELLIGENCE (1974); REPORT TO THE PRESIDENT BY THE COMMISSION ON CIA ACTIVITIES WITHIN THE UNITED STATES (June, 1975) (Rockefeller Commission Report); S. UNGAR, FBI (1976); Calamaro, *The Way the Government Is Going,* N.Y. Times, Mar. 17, 1976, at 41, col. 2; Donner, *Electronic Surveillance: The National Security Game,* 2 CIVIL LIB. REV. 15–47 (Summer 1975); Halperin, *National Security and Civil Liberties,* 21 FOREIGN POLICY 125 (1975); Ungar, *The Intelligence Tangle: The CIA and the FBI Face the Moment of Truth,* THE ATLANTIC, Apr. 1976, at 31–42; *Summary of Rockefeller Panel's C.I.A. Report,* N.Y. Times, June 11, 1975, at 18–20; *id.,* Mar. 29, 1976, at 1, col. 1 (FBI's burglarization of the offices of the Socialist Workers Party); *id.,* June 27, 1976, § 1, at 16, col. 3.

24. *See generally* J. HUREWITZ, MIDDLE EAST POLITICS: THE MILITARY DIMENSION (1969); M. JANOWITZ, THE MILITARY IN THE POLITICAL DEVELOPMENT OF NEW NATIONS (1964); THE ROLE OF THE MILITARY IN UNDERDEVELOPED COUNTRIES (J. Johnson ed. 1962); G. KENNEDY, THE MILITARY IN THE THIRD WORLD (1975) (containing an appendix on "Military Interventions in the Third World 1945–72," at 337–44); MILITARY PROFESSION AND MILITARY REGIMES (J. Van Doorn ed. 1969); Lerner, *Military Rule—Can It Spark a New Latin Self-Reliance?* SATURDAY REV./WORLD, Oct. 23, 1973, at 12–15.

See also De Onis, *Latin America, the Growing Graveyard for Democracies,* N.Y. Times, Mar. 28, 1976, § 4, at 1, col. 4; *Human Rights in the World, Argentina,* 16 REV. INT'L COMM'N JURISTS 1–4 (June 1976); *In 10th Year, Brazil Regime Gives No Sign of Restoring Civil Rule,* N.Y. Times, Apr. 4, 1973, at 8, col. 1 (city ed.); *Chile: The System of Military Justice,* 15 REV. INT'L COMM'N JURISTS 1 (Dec. 1975); *The Legal System in Chile,* 13 REV. INT'L COMM'N JURISTS 45 (Dec. 1974); Zalaguett, *Human Rights in Chile,* N.Y. Times, May 26, 1976, at 39, col. 2; *Chile Gives Free Rein to Secret Police, id.,* May 12, 1975, at 1, col. 5; *Chile Junta Resisting Critics, id.,* Sept. 21, 1975, at 1, col. 3; George, *For Marcos, The Lesser Danger,* FAR EASTERN ECONOMIC REV., Jan. 8, 1973, at 23–25; Kattenburg, *Marcos Said They "Chose to Stay" in Prison,* N.Y. Times, July 24, 1974, at 41, col. 1; *Marcos Says He Must Keep Martial Law, id.,* June 17, 1974, at 7, col. 1; *Troubles for Marcos, id.,* July 5, 1974, at 3, col. 1 (city ed.); *High Court in Philippines Upholds Marcos's Martial-Law Regime, id.,* Feb. 2, 1975, § 1, at 12, col. 4; *Marcos Says Martial Law Stands Despite Gains, id.,* Aug. 28, 1976, at 2, col. 4; *One More Infant Democracy Dies in the Cradle,* THE ECONOMIST, Oct. 9, 1976, at 55 (Thailand); N.Y. Times, Oct. 7, 1976, at 1, col. 1 (Thailand); *id.,* Oct. 8, 1976, at A1, col. 2 (Thailand); *id.,* Oct. 9, 1976, at 3, col. 4 (Thailand); *id.,* Oct. 23, 1976, at 2, col. 3 (Thailand).

25. *See* INTERNATIONAL COMMISSION OF JURISTS, JUSTICE ENSLAVED: A COLLECTION OF DOCUMENTS ON THE ABUSE OF JUSTICE FOR POLITICAL ENDS (1955) [hereinafter cited as JUSTICE ENSLAVED].

Total breakdown of the process of authoritative decision (no rule of law);[26]

Oppressive or totalitarian character of the processes of authoritative decision and effective power;

Controversies about proportional representation or quota representation in the power process;[27]

Monopolization by a particular "class" or caste of the processes of both authoritative decision and effective power, because of disparities in the distribution of base values;

Imposition of arbitrary restraints upon the employment of the relevant instruments of policy;

Prevalence of the reign of terror, as sustained by monopoly of the means of violence (secret police, military and para-military organizations, etc.);

Widespread practices of arbitrary arrest, detention, imprisonment and torture;[28]

---

26. *See* H. Arendt, The Origins of Totalitarianism (1958); B. Chapman, Police State (1970); Totalitarianism (C. Friedrich ed. 1964); C. Friedrich & Z. Brzezinski, *supra* note 22; F. Hayek, The Road to Serfdom (1950); J. Talmon, The Origins of Totalitarian Democracy (1960).

27. *See generally* J. Laponce, The Protection of Minorities 111–31 (1960).

28. *See* United Nations, Study of the Right of Everyone to be Free from Arbitrary Arrest, Detention and Exile, U.N. Doc. E/CN.4/826/Rev. 1 (1964); *Freedom from Arbitrary Arrest, Detention and Exile,* [1955] Y.B. on Human Rights (United Nations) (1st Supp. Vol. 1959).

See also W. Butler & G. Levasseur, Human Rights and the Legal System in Iran (1976); *Hearings on Human Rights in South Korea: Implications for U.S. Policy before the Subcomms. on Asian and Pacific Affairs and on International Organizations and Movements of the House Comm. on Foreign Affairs,* 93d Cong., 2d Sess. (1974); Amalrik, *Arrest on Suspicion of Courage: Detention by the KGB,* Harper's Magazine, Aug. 1976, at 37–44, 49–56; Shelton, *The Geography of Disgrace: A World Survey of Political Prisoners,* Saturday Rev./World, June 15, 1974, at 14; N.Y. Times, Oct. 12, 1975, § 1, at 1, col. 2 (Ethiopia); *id.,* Oct. 16, 1976, at 1, col. 6 (Thailand); *id.,* Oct. 21, 1976, at 1, col. 2 (Thailand); *id.,* Nov. 22, 1975, at 6, col. 3 (political prisoners around the world).

For the recent tragic events, including the large-scale arrest and imprisonment of opposing political leaders in the name of national security and emergency, in India, once the world's most populous democracy, *see id.,* June 13, 1975, at 1, col. 1; *id.,* June 27, 1975, at 1, col. 6; *id.,* June 28, 1975, at 1, col. 6; *id.,* Aug. 5, 1975, at 10, col. 3.

On perversion of judicial systems, *see* L. Downie, Justice Denied: The Case for Reform of the Courts (1972); C. Goodell, Political Prisoners in America (1973); O. Kirchheimer, Political Justice: The Use of Legal Procedure for Political Ends (1961); J. Lieberman, How the Government Breaks the Law (1972); The Trial of the Four: A Collection of Materials on the Case of Galanskov, Ginzburg, Dobrovolsky & Lashkova, 1967–68 (P. Litvinov comp. & P. Reddaway ed. 1972); J. Newfield, Cruel and Unusual Justice (1974); With Justice for Some: An Indictment of the Law by

Subversion of the procedures of due process and of fair and public trial;

Subjection of civilians to court-martial;

Arbitrary arrest and detention of individuals, kept incommunicado, without the filing of charges;

Widespread failure to establish and maintain community structures that effectively and responsibly perform all essential decision functions.

DEPRIVATIONS RELATING TO ENLIGHTENMENT

Continuing high illiteracy rate in many communities around the world;[29]

YOUNG ADVOCATES (B. Wasserstein & M. Green eds. 1970); P. ZIMROTH, PERVERSIONS OF JUSTICE: THE PROSECUTION AND ACQUITTAL OF THE PANTHER 21 (1974).

29. According to the Final Act of the International Conference on Human Rights, adopted in Teheran, "over 700 million persons in the world" were, in 1968, "still illiterate." FINAL ACT OF THE INTERNATIONAL CONFERENCE ON HUMAN RIGHTS, TEHERAN, 22 APRIL TO 13 MAY 1968, at 12, U.N. Doc. A/CONF.32/41 (1968). According to a recent United Nations report:

> The literacy situation varies considerably from one country to another; whereas in some countries a relatively high level of literacy has been achieved, in others, the existing low percentage of literates is not rising fast enough to keep pace with the increase in population. The over-all percentage of adults, i.e., persons of 15 years of age or over, who are illiterate declined from 39 per cent in 1960 to 34 per cent in 1970 (table 140). The number of literate adults in the world rose by over 370 million. However, because the total adult population grew during the same period by some 420 million, the actual number of illiterates also increased by nearly 50 million. The illiteracy rate among females is higher than among males. The present male illiteracy rate is 28 per cent, whereas the female illiteracy rate stands at 40 per cent. The highest illiteracy rates are found in Africa (74 per cent) and the Arab States (73 per cent) followed by Asia (47 per cent) and Latin America (24 per cent) and this order has not changed between 1960 and 1970.

UNITED NATIONS, DEP'T OF ECONOMIC AND SOCIAL AFFAIRS, 1974 REPORT ON THE WORLD SOCIAL SITUATION 224–25, U.N. Doc. E/CN.5/512/Rev. 1 (ST/ESA/24) (1975) [hereinafter cited as 1974 REPORT ON THE WORLD SOCIAL SITUATION].

See also L. BROWN, IN THE HUMAN INTEREST: A STRATEGY TO STABILIZE WORLD POPULATION 104–05 (1974) [hereinafter cited as IN THE HUMAN INTEREST]; L. BROWN, WORLD WITHOUT BORDERS 116 (1972) [hereinafter cited as WORLD WITHOUT BORDERS]; LITERACY IN TRADITIONAL SOCIETIES (J. Goody ed. 1968); B. RUSSETT, H. ALKER, K. DEUTSCH, & H. LASSWELL, WORLD HANDBOOK OF POLITICAL AND SOCIAL INDICATORS 221–26 (1964) [hereinafter cited as B. RUSSETT, et al.]; C. TAYLOR & M. HUDSON, WORLD HANDBOOK OF POLITICAL AND SOCIAL INDICATORS 323–35 (2d ed. 1972) [hereinafter cited as C. TAYLOR & M. HUDSON]; UNITED NATIONS, DEP'T OF ECONOMIC AND SOCIAL AFFAIRS, 1970 REPORT ON THE WORLD SOCIAL SITUATION 198–99, U.N. Doc. E/CN.5/456/Rev. 1 (ST/SOA/110) (1971) [hereinafter cited as 1970 REPORT ON THE WORLD SOCIAL SITUATION]; UNESCO, LITERACY

Unequal and limited opportunity in access to institutions of higher learning;[30]

Wholesale indoctrination (thought control, brainwashing, conditioning);[31]

Deliberate fabrication and dissemination of misinformation (distorted information), especially by the government;[32]

Politicization of enlightenment;[33]

Withholding or suppression of information essential to independent appraisal of governmental policies and decisions;[34]

1969–1971: PROGRESS ACHIEVED IN LITERACY THROUGHOUT THE WORLD (1972); N.Y. Times, Sept. 4, 1975, at 12, col. 4.

30. *See* C. AMMOUN, STUDY OF DISCRIMINATION IN EDUCATION 1–89, U.N. DOC. E/CN.4/Sub. 2/181/Rev. 1 (1957); ECONOMIC, SOCIAL AND CULTURAL RIGHTS, *supra* note 1, at 81–86. *See also* HARVARD EDUCATIONAL REVIEW, EQUAL EDUCATIONAL OPPORTUNITY (1969); C. JENCKS, INEQUALITY; A REASSESSMENT OF THE EFFECT OF FAMILY AND SCHOOLING IN AMERICA (1972).

31. *See generally* T. CHEN, THOUGHT REFORM OF THE CHINESE INTELLECTUALS (1960); A. DALLIN & G. BRESLAUER, POLITICAL TERROR IN COMMUNIST SYSTEMS (1970); R. LIFTON, THOUGHT REFORM AND THE PSYCHOLOGY OF TOTALISM: A STUDY OF "BRAINWASHING" IN CHINA (1961); A. MEERLOO, THE RAPE OF THE MIND: THE PSYCHOLOGY OF THOUGHT CONTROL, MENTICIDE, AND BRAINWASHING (1956); S. NEUMANN, PERMANENT REVOLUTION: TOTALITARIANISM IN THE AGE OF INTERNATIONAL CIVIL WAR 205–29 (2d ed. 1965); W. SARGANT, BATTLE FOR THE MIND: A PHYSIOLOGY OF CONVERSION AND BRAINWASHING (1957); T. YU, MASS PERSUASION IN COMMUNIST CHINA (1964).

32. *See* D. WISE, THE POLITICS OF LYING: GOVERNMENT DECEPTION, SECRECY, AND POWER (1973).

33. For attempts by the Third World nations to pool their government-controlled news agencies in order to replace coverage by the existing major news gathering and disseminating organizations and to liberate "information and mass media from the colonial legacy," *see* N.Y. Times, July 14, 1976, at 3, col. 5. *See also id.*, Jan. 25, 1976, § 1, at 13, col. 1; *id.*, Aug. 2, 1976, at 20, col. 4. For a reaction to such an attempt, *see Muzzling the World's Press,* Wall St. J., July 23, 1976, at 10, col. 1 (editorial).

34. For vivid illustration, *see* H. SMITH, THE RUSSIANS 344–74 (1976). Smith observes: "The absence of such routine and obviously necessary information is typical. Russians take it as a fact of life that much of the information they need to know just to get along day by day does not appear in their press." *Id.* at 345. Smith further states:

> In the West, Soviet censorship has a reputation for suppressing bad news like airplane crashes or political purges, or for turning Trotsky, Khrushchev, and other foes of the regime into nonpersons. But what is more important is that on behalf of the Soviet elite, the system of censorship suppresses the facts of life in many areas that seem to have no obvious connection with national security or the political secrets of Soviet rulers—and this cripples independent public discussion of almost any serious issue.

Id. at 373.

The profound consequence of withholding or suppressing information was explored by one of the authors many years ago:

Dissemination of information calculated to win blind public support rather than create public enlightenment;

Monopoly of the instruments of public enlightenment (the media of mass communication) by the ruling power elites;[35]

Politicization and governmental domination of universities and denial of academic freedom;[36]

Excessive concentration in private ownership of the instruments of mass communication;

Systematic undertaking of drastic measures to curb freedom of opinions and expression (freedom to acquire, use, and communicate knowledge and information) under the pretext of national security and internal order;[37]

Exploitation of the process of authoritative decision to support and defend practices suppressing freedom of expression;[38]

Suppression of nondominant languages;[39]

> Cut off from the means by which statements can be tested in reality, cut off from the quickening support of institutions of genuine inquiry, independent minds are cast adrift from their moorings. They are no longer in a position to exercise the kind of criticisms which they themselves most respect; for mature independent minds respect information and inquiry. The impoverished pabulum available to the ego first weakens the ego and typically ends in transforming the conscience. The ego is constrained to admit that given the miserable sources of current intelligence, the individual has little more than his suspicions to contribute to the consideration of public policy. And the coercive menaces of the ruling regime provide strong incentives against speaking up and demanding wider access to intelligence sources.

Lasswell, *Propaganda and Mass Insecurity,* in PERSONALITY AND POLITICAL CRISIS 21 (A. Stanton & E. Perry eds. 1951).

35. Needless to say, totalitarian regimes distinguish themselves by monopolizing the media of mass communication. *See* C. FRIEDRICH & Z. BRZEZINSKI, *supra* note 22, at 107–17; F. HOUN, TO CHANGE A NATION (1961) (China); A. INKELES, PUBLIC OPINION IN SOVIET RUSSIA 150–56 (1951); B. MURTY, PROPAGANDA AND WORLD PUBLIC ORDER: THE LEGAL REGULATION OF THE IDEOLOGICAL INSTRUMENT OF COERCION 39–44 (1968); THE PRESS IN AUTHORITARIAN COUNTRIES 28–43 (International Press Institute Survey No. 5, 1959).

36. *See, e.g., Human Rights in the World, Uruguay,* 16 REV. INT'L COMM'N JURISTS 19–22 (June 1976); *400 Professors Ousted in Korea: Seoul Forces Resignations or Dismissals under New Tenure Law,* N.Y. Times, Mar. 14, 1976, § 1, at 1, col. 2; *id.,* Nov. 30, 1976, at 1, col. 1 (Latin American universities).

37. *See, e.g.,* Irani, *The Indian Press under Pressure,* 30 FREEDOM AT ISSUE 7 (1975). *See also* notes 23–24 *supra.*

38. *See* N.Y. Times, June 2, 1974, § 1, at 18, col. 1 (Singapore); *id.,* Sept. 6, 1974, at 8, col. 4 (Peru); *id.,* Apr. 11, 1976, § 1, at 2, col. 3 (Nigeria); *id.,* Aug. 15, 1976, § 1, at 1, col. 3 (South Africa); *id.,* Oct. 26, 1975, § 1, at 14, col. 4 (Latin America).

39. *See* chapter 13 *infra,* at notes 2–18 and accompanying text. *See also Spanish Regions Bitter at Ruling on Languages,* N.Y. Times, Nov. 17, 1975, at 1, col. 6; *Seoul, to "Purify" Language, Acts against Foreign Words, id.,* May 21, 1976, at A6, col. 4.

Keeping people ignorant and content, by severe restrictions on travel abroad and contact with foreigners, and by constant surveillance, jamming of transnational radio broadcasting and control over access to foreign publications (books, periodicals and dailies);[40]

Suppression of dissenters and nonconformists through coercive measures;[41]

Manipulated standardization (requisitioning) of taste and style to suppress diversity and innovation;[42]

Widespread practices of censorship.[43]

---

40. *See, e.g.*, N.Y. Times, Sept. 28, 1975, § 1, at 23, col. 1 (Soviet curbs on import of Western publications).

41. Such activities are increasingly carried out transnationally as well as internally. For transnational operations by South Korean governmental agents against Koreans residing in the United States and against Korean-Americans, see *id.*, Oct. 29, 1976, at A1, col. 3; *id.*, Oct. 30, 1976, at 1, col. 2. For coercive suppression of dissidents within South Korea, see Falk, *Seoul's Repression, id.*, Apr. 25, 1976, § 4, at 15, col. 2; Kim, *From a Seoul Prison, id.*, Dec. 17, 1975, at 45, col. 3; *25 Years after War South Korea Mixes Progress and Repression, id.*, June 25, 1975, at 10, col. 1; *Curbs Are Tighter on South Koreans, id.*, Sept. 22, 1975, at 1, col. 4; *11 Critics of Regime Are Seized in Seoul, id.*, Mar. 11, 1976, at 1, col. 1; *South Korea Dissidents Tell of Threats and Fear in Days of Nonstop Grilling by Intelligence Agents, id.*, Mar. 12, 1976, at 7, col. 1; *South Korea Begins Trial of 18 Opposition Leaders, id.*, May 5, 1976, at 3, col. 5; *12 in Clergy Are Reported Detained in South Korea, id.*, June 25, 1976, at A3, col. 3; *Seoul Adamant over Dissidents, id.*, Aug. 23, 1976, at 7, col. 1; *Seoul Sentences Expected to Intimidate Park's Foes, id.*, Aug. 29, 1976, § 1, at 3, col. 1.

Regarding India, *see* Borders, *India's Usual Dissenters Fall Silent, id.*, Aug. 10, 1975, § 4, at 3, col. 3; X, *Dismay in India, id.*, Apr. 9, 1976, at 37, col. 2; *id.*, July 5, 1975, at 1, col. 4; *id.*, May 26, 1976, at 1, col. 1; *id.*, Aug. 25, 1976, at 4, col. 4.

See also C. BELFRAGE, THE AMERICAN INQUISITION, 1945–1960 (1973); THIRTY YEARS OF TREASON: EXCERPTS FROM HEARINGS BEFORE THE HOUSE COMMITTEE ON UN-AMERICAN ACTIVITIES, 1938–1968 (E. Bentley ed. 1971); C. MEE, THE INTERNMENT OF SOVIET DISSENTERS IN MENTAL HOSPITALS (1971); Jacoby & Astracham, *Soviet Dissent: An Ebb Tide*, WORLD, June 19, 1973, at 13–19; *Human Rights in the World, Yugoslavia*, 16 REV. INT'L COMM'N JURISTS 17–19 (June 1976); N.Y. Times, May 10, 1976, at 7, col. 1 (city ed.) (imprisonment of journalists in seventeen countries); *East Germany Tightening Curbs, But Dissidents Say They'll Fight On, id.*, Nov. 30, 1976, at 3, col. 2; *id.*, Sept. 16, 1974, at 1, col. 5 (late city ed.) (disruption of a nonconformist modern art show by the Soviet government through bulldozers, dump trucks and water-spraying trucks); *id.*, Sept. 14, 1975, § 1, at 15, col. 1 (arrest of Andrei Amalrik, a dissident writer, by the Soviet police); *id.*, Oct. 10, 1976, § 1, at 3, col. 4 (Thailand); *id.*, Feb. 16, 1975, § 1, at 12, col. 3 (purge of academic dissidents in Yugoslavia).

42. This has been most vividly illustrated by Mao's China. *See* A. SAKHAROV, PROGRESS, COEXISTENCE, AND INTELLECTUAL FREEDOM 59–62 (The New York Times trans. 1968) [hereinafter cited as A. SAKHAROV].

43. "A recent study of the world's press has concluded that only 16 of the 132 nations now represented in the United Nations have a press that can be said to be 'free to a degree.'" Reston, *The Condition of the Press in the World Today* (1), 7 HUMAN RIGHTS J. 593, 596 (1974).

Deprivations Relating to Well-Being

Persistence of human misery from disease and hunger (starvation);[44]

High mortality rate and low life expectancy in many parts of the world;[45]

Frequent occurrences of death by violence;

Continued employment of death penalty;[46]

See A. Sakharov, *supra* note 42, at 62–65; *Press Freedom 1970–1975,* 16 Rev. Int'l Comm'n Jurists 45 (June 1976) (covering many countries); *Human Rights in the World, Brazil, id.,* at 7.

Regarding India, *see Censorship in India: Grim Editors, Lifeless Papers,* N.Y. Times, July 3, 1975, at 4, col. 5; *Indian Censorship Upsets U.S. Press, id.,* July 22, 1975, at 7, col. 1; *India Parliament Approves Curbs, id.,* July 24, 1975, at 1, col. 7; *India Seeking to Tighten Control over the Press, id.,* Dec. 21, 1975, § 1, at 1, col. 1; *Permanent Censorship Approved in Indian Parliament, id.,* Jan. 30, 1976, at 3, col. 5.

44. *See* G. Borgstrom, The Hungry Planet: The Modern World at the Edge of Famine (rev. ed. 1970); G. Borgstrom, Too Many: A Study of Earth's Biological Limitations (1969); L. Brown, By Bread Alone (1974); J. Shepherd, The Politics of Starvation (1975); A. Simon, Bread for the World (1975); Transnational Institute, World Hunger: Causes and Remedies (1974); *Africa's Other Crisis: Ethiopia's Right to Famine,* The Interdependent, Feb. 1976, at 1 *et seq.; Forecast: Famine? CIA Report,* Time, May 17, 1976, at 85 *et seq.;* Johnson, *Hunger: A Historical Perspective,* The Interdependent, Apr. 1975, at 1, 3; Rothschild, *Food Politics,* 54 Foreign Affairs 285 (1976).

See also Maloney, *The Ghost of Malthus in South Asia,* N.Y. Times, Feb. 14, 1974, at 41, col. 1; Murphy, *Starving Children and the Catholic Church, id.,* May 31, 1974, at 33, col. 2; Rensberger, *32 Nations Close to Starvation, id.,* Oct. 20, 1974, § 4, at 4, col. 1; Silver, *Sub-Sahara Africa Waits for Help, id.,* Sept. 22, 1974, § 4, at 17, col. 1; Weinraub, *Bangladesh, The Hungriest of Them All, id.,* Dec. 29, 1974, § 4, at 4, col. 4 (city ed.); *I—Hunger in America, id.,* July 8, 1974, at 28, col. 1 (editorial); *II—Hunger in the World, id.,* July 9, 1974, at 36, col. 1; *Ethiopian Famine Hits Millions, id.,* Feb. 15, 1974, at 1, col. 2; *Food an Obsession in Misery-Ridden Calcutta, id.,* Sept. 5, 1974, at 39, col. 1; *id.,* Sept. 19, 1974, at 1, col. 6; *Bangladesh Is Faced with Large-Scale Deaths from Starvation, id.,* Oct. 11, 1974, at 3, col. 1; *Anguish of the Hungry Spreading Across India, id.,* Oct. 27, 1974, § 1, at 1, col. 5 (city ed.); *World Food Crisis: Basic Ways of Life Face Upheaval, id.,* Nov. 5, 1974, at 1, col. 3.

45. *See* B. Russett, et al., *supra* note 29, at 196–201; C. Taylor & M. Hudson, *supra* note 29, at 253–55.

46. *See* The Death Penalty in America: An Anthology (H. Bedau ed. rev. ed. 1967); C. Black, Jr., Capital Punishment: The Inevitability of Caprice and Mistake (1974); The Hanging Question: Essays on the Death Penalty (L Blom-Cooper ed. 1969); Canada, Dept. of Justice, Capital Punishment: New Material: 1965–1972 (1972); B. Cohen, Law without Order: Capital Punishment and the Liberals (1970); E. Fattah, A Study of the Deterrent Effect of Capital Punishment with Special Reference to the Canadian Situation (1972); The Penalty Is Death (B. Jones comp. 1968); J. Joyce, Capital Punishment: A World View (1961); J. McCafferty, Capital Punishment (1972); M. Meltsner, Cruel and Unusual: The Supreme Court and Capital Punishment (1973); Capital Punishment (T. Sellin ed. 1967); N. St. John-Stevas, The Right to Life (1964); Bedau, *Problem of Capital Punishment,* 71 Current History 14 (1976); *Death Penalty Rebounds,* The Interdependent, Mar. 1976, at 1, 6.

Inadequate provision for safety, health, and comfort;

Unhealthy psychosomatic development because of malnutrition;[47]

Recurrences of communicable diseases in parts of the world;[48]

High incidences of mental and emotional disturbances in stress-laden societies;[49]

Intense anxieties generated by threats of violence, both large-scale and small-scale;

Indiscriminate mass killings in armed conflict and other situations;[50]

Deliberate destruction of group members (genocide);[51]

---

47. Protein malnutrition is an important cause of infant and young child mortality, stunted physical growth, low work output, premature aging and reduced life span in the developing world. Recent research has also revealed a link between malnutrition in infancy and early childhood and impaired learning and behaviour in later life. The widespread occurrence of protein malnutrition especially among infants, pre-school children, and expectant and nursing mothers in many developing nations spells grave danger to the full expression of the genetic potential of the population of large sections of the world community.

United Nations, Dep't of Economic and Social Affairs, Strategy Statement on Action to Avert the Protein Crisis in the Developing Countries 7, U.N. Doc. E/5018/Rev. 1 (ST/ECA/144) (1971).

See Food and Agriculture Organization, Lives in Peril: Protein and the Child (1970); 1975 Report on the World Social Situation, *supra* note 29, at 211–12; *Hunger's Lifelong Effects,* N.Y. Times, May 5, 1974, § 4, at 5, col. 3; *Malnutrition Is Up Sharply among World's Children, id.,* Oct. 6, 1974, § 1, at 1, col. 6.

48. *See* 1970 Report on the World Social Situation, *supra* note 29, at 164–67.

49. 1974 Report on the World Social Situation, *supra* note 29, at 221–22. The Report indicates:

> The conflicts and contradictions inherent in rapid social change, urbanization and the difficulties in adapting to the urban style of life, crowding, the increased pace and stress of life, changing social structures and a growing proportion of old persons are factors responsible for an increasingly heavy toll of mental disorders in the developed and developing world.

Id. at 221.

50. *See, e.g.,* J. Goldstein, B. Marshall, & J. Schwartz, The My Lai Massacre and Its Cover-up: Beyond the Reach of Law? (1976); C. Taylor & M. Hudson, *supra* note 29, at 110–15; Emerson, *The Fate of Human Rights in the Third World,* 27 World Politics 201, 213–21 (1975); *Argentine Extremists Kill 46 in 2 Mass Executions,* N.Y. Times, Aug. 21, 1976, at 1, col. 1.

51. Undoubtedly the Third Reich remains the archetype of genocide, but events of the recent years in Tibet, Indonesia, Nigeria, Burundi, Rwanda, East Pakistan (now Bangladesh), the Middle East, and other areas suggest that genocidal practices are far from a thing of the past. *See* C. Aguolu, Biafra: Its Case for Independence (1969); N. Akpan, The Struggle for Secession, 1966–1970 (1972); M. Bowen, G. Freeman, & K. Miller, Passing By: The United States and Genocide in Burundi, 1972 (1973); L. Dawidowicz,

Globalization of torture as a deliberate instrument of policy;[52]

Inadequate medical care and services, especially for the handicapped and the aged;[53]

Poor and overcrowded housing and other living conditions (*e.g.*, poor sanitation);[54]

THE WAR AGAINST THE JEWS, 1933–1945 (1975); R. HILBERG, THE DESTRUCTION OF THE EUROPEAN JEWS (1967); R. HILBERG, DOCUMENTS OF DESTRUCTION: GERMANY AND JEWRY 1933–1945 (1971); A. KIRK-GREENE, CRISIS AND CONFLICT IN NIGERIA (1971); J. OYNIBO, NIGERIA: CRISIS AND BEYOND (1971); J. PAUST & A. BLAUSTEIN, WAR CRIMES TRIALS AND HUMAN RIGHTS: THE CASE OF BANGLADESH (1974); THE SECRETARIAT OF THE INTERNATIONAL COMMISSION OF JURISTS, THE EVENTS IN EAST PAKISTAN, 1971 (1972); S. SLOAN, A STUDY IN POLITICAL VIOLENCE: THE INDONESIAN EXPERIENCE 13 (1971); Melady, *Death in Burundi, and U.S. Power,* N.Y. Times, Oct. 27, 1974, § 4, at 17, col. 3; Salzberg, *U.N. Prevention of Human Rights Violations: The Bangladesh Case,* 27 INT'L ORG. 115 (1973).

52. Amnesty International has rendered important contributions in undertaking a world survey of torture and exposing the growing barbarism of contemporary practices country by country. *See* AMNESTY INTERNATIONAL, ANNUAL REPORT, 1974–75 (1975); AMNESTY INTERNATIONAL, REPORT ON TORTURE (1975).

See Hearings on Human Rights in Chile before the Subcomm. on Inter-American Affairs and on International Organizations and Movements of the House Comm. on Foreign Affairs, 93d Cong., 2d Sess. (1974); *Hearing on Torture and Oppression in Brazil before the Subcomm. on International Organizations and Movements of the House Comm. on Foreign Affairs,* 93d Cong., 2d Sess. (1974); Baraheni, *Terror in Iran,* N.Y. REV. BOOKS, Oct. 28, 1976, at 21–25; Buckley, *Colonels' Torture: Use in Greece,* NATIONAL REV., July 23, 1976, at 803; Colligan, *New Science of Torture,* SCIENCE DIGEST, July 1976, at 44–49; Dolan & van den Assum, *Torture and the 5th UN Congress on Crime Prevention,* 14 REV. INT'L COMM'N JURISTS 55 (June 1975); *Human Rights in the World: Torture Continues,* 10 REV. INT'L COMM'N JURISTS 10 (June 1973); *Lawyers against Torture,* 16 REV. INT'L COMM'N JURISTS 29 (June 1976); McCarthy, *Complicity in Torture,* 103 COMMONWEALTH 200 (1976); Styron, *Torture in Chile,* THE NEW REPUBLIC, Mar. 20, 1976, at 15–17; Styron, *Uruguay: The Oriental Republic,* THE NATION, Aug. 14, 1976, at 107–11; *Torture as Policy: The Network of Evil,* TIME, Aug. 16, 1976, at 31–34.

See also Baraheni, *Torture in Iran: It Is a Hell Made by One Man for Another Man,* N.Y. Times, Apr. 21, 1976, at 37, col. 2; Laber, *Torture and Death in Uruguay, id.,* Mar. 10, 1976, at 39, col. 1; Lewis, *The Meaning of Torture, id.,* May 30, 1974, at 37, col. 5; Majuda, *Torture and Harassment in Brazil, id.,* July 11, 1975, at 29, col. 2; Solomon, *Torture in Spain, id.,* Nov. 25, 1974, at 31, col. 2; *id.,* Nov. 4, 1974, at 2, col. 4 (Brazil); *id.,* Nov. 20, 1976, at 1, col. 1 (Brazil); *id.,* July 28, 1974, § 1, at 2, col. 3 (Chile); *id.,* Sept. 11, 1974, at 15, col. 1 (Chile); *id.,* Oct. 24, 1974, at 11, col. 1 (Chile); *id.,* Dec. 10, 1974, at 8, col. 3 (Chile); *id.,* Oct. 19, 1975, § 1, at 3, col. 4 (Chile); *id.,* June 8, 1976, at 1, col. 1 (Chile); *id.,* Feb. 29, 1976, § 1, at 5, col. 1 (Iran); *id.,* Sept. 3, 1976, at A4, col. 6 (finding by the European Commission on Human Rights that the British government was guilty of torturing suspected terrorists in Northern Ireland in 1971).

53. *See* 1974 REPORT ON THE WORLD SOCIAL SITUATION, *supra* note 29, at 218–20.

54. *See id.,* at 232–35; UNITED NATIONS, DEP'T OF ECONOMIC AND SOCIAL AFFAIRS, WORLD HOUSING SURVEY 1974, at 5–7, 28–57, U.N. Doc. ST/ESA/30 (1976) [hereinafter cited as WORLD HOUSING SURVEY 1974].

See generally D. HUNTER, THE SLUMS: CHALLENGE AND RESPONSE (1964). *See also* N.Y. Times, Nov. 6, 1976, at 1, col. 4 (Latin America); *id.,* Oct. 20, 1974, § 1, at 21, col. 1 (city ed.); *id.,* May 31, 1976, at 3, col. 1; *id.,* June 9, 1976, at 4, col. 4.

Deterioration of the environment that endangers health and human survival (ecocide);[55]

Unequal access to the benefits of modern medical science and technology;

Inability to anticipate and cope with natural disasters;[56]

Inadequacy in community performance of the tasks of prevention, deterrence, restoration, rehabilitation, reconstruction, and correction in regard to well-being;[57]

Human experimentation without informed consent;[58]

---

55. *See* R. CARSON, SILENT SPRING (1962); THE ENVIRONMENTAL HANDBOOK (G. De Bell ed. 1970); P. EHRLICH & A. EHRLICH, POPULATION, RESOURCES, ENVIRONMENT 117–97 (1970); R. FALK, THIS ENDANGERED PLANET 21–36 (1971); F. GRAHAM, SINCE SILENT SPRING (1970); LAW, INSTITUTIONS AND THE GLOBAL ENVIRONMENT (J. Hargrove ed. 1972); THE ENVIRONMENTAL CRISIS: MAN'S STRUGGLE TO LIVE WITH HIMSELF (H. Helfrich ed. 1970); WORLD ECO-CRISIS: INTERNATIONAL ORGANIZATIONS IN RESPONSE (D. Kay & E. Skolnikoff eds. 1972); MAN'S IMPACT ON THE GLOBAL ENVIRONMENT (Report of the Study of Critical Environmental Problems) (1970); THE ENDANGERED ENVIRONMENT (A. Montagu comp. 1974); M. NICHOLSON, THE ENVIRONMENTAL REVOLUTION (1970); H. SPROUT & M. SPROUT, TOWARD A POLITICS OF THE PLANET EARTH (1971); STOCKHOLM AND BEYOND (Report of the Secretary of State's Advisory Committee on the 1972 United Nations Conference on the Human Environment) (1972); B. WARD, et al., WHO SPEAKS FOR EARTH? (1973); B. WARD & R. DUBOS, ONLY ONE EARTH: THE CARE AND MAINTENANCE OF A SMALL PLANET (1972); Problems of the Human Environment (report of the secretary-general), 47 U.N. GAOR, Annex (Agenda Item 10), U.N. Doc. E/4667 (1969); Report of the United Nations Conference on the Human Environment, U.N. Doc. A/CONF.48/14 (1972); J. Schneider, World Public Order of the Environment: Toward an International Ecological Law and Organization, 1975 (unpublished Ph.D. dissertation, Yale University Library); McDougal & Schneider, *The Protection of the Environment and World Public Order: Some Recent Developments,* 45 MISS. L.J. 1085 (1974); Strong, *One Year after Stockholm: An Ecological Approach to Management,* 51 FOREIGN AFFAIRS 690 (1973); *The Concorde Furor,* NEWSWEEK, Feb. 16, 1976, at 16–21; Hill, *A Look at the Man-Made Mess,* N.Y. Times, May 30, 1976, § 4, at 7, col. 4.

56. Recent examples include the disastrous earthquakes in China and Turkey. *See China'sKiller Quake,* NEWSWEEK, Aug. 9, 1976, at 30–32; N.Y. Times, Nov. 26, 1976, at 2, col. 3; *Turkish Quake Toll Passes 3,000 Mark, id.,* Nov. 26, 1976, at A1, col. 6.

57. *See* 1974 REPORT ON THE WORLD SOCIAL SITUATION, *supra* note 29, at 222–23; 1970 REPORT ON THE WORLD SOCIAL SITUATION, *supra* note 29, at 167–71.

58. *See* B. BARBER, RESEARCH ON HUMAN SUBJECTS: PROBLEMS OF SOCIAL CONTROL IN MEDICAL EXPERIMENTATION (1973); C. LEVY, THE HUMAN BODY AND THE LAW: LEGAL AND ETHICAL CONSIDERATIONS IN HUMAN EXPERIMENTATION (1975); EXPERIMENTATION WITH HUMAN SUBJECTS (P. Freund ed. 1970); B. GRAY, HUMAN SUBJECTS IN MEDICAL EXPERIMENTATION: A. SOCIOLOGICAL STUDY OF THE CONDUCT AND REGULATION OF CLINICAL RESEARCH (1975); N. HERSHEY & R. MILLER, HUMAN EXPERIMENTATION AND THE LAW (1976); J. KATZ, EXPERIMENTATION WITH HUMAN BEINGS: THE AUTHORITY OF THE INVESTIGATOR, SUBJECT, PROFESSIONS, AND STATE IN THE HUMAN EXPERIMENTATION PROCESS (1972); NATIONAL ACADEMY OF SCIENCE, EXPERIMENTS AND RESEARCH WITH HUMANS: VALUES IN CONFLICT (1975); M. PAPPWORTH, HUMAN GUINEA PIGS (1967); U.S. DEP'T OF

Difficulties associated with family planning and restrictions on birth control;[59]

Controversy about genetic engineering, euthanasia, etc.[60]

Health, Education, and Welfare, Public Health Service, Final Report of the Tuskegee Syphilis Study Ad Hoc Advisory Panel (1973); *Hearings on Quality of Health Care—Human Experimentation before the Subcomm. on Health of the Senate Comm. on Labor and Public Welfare,* 93d Cong., 1st Sess. (1973); Adams & Cowan, *The Human Guinea Pig: How We Test New Drugs,* World, Dec. 5, 1972, at 20–24; Capron, *Informed Consent in Catastrophic Disease Research and Treatment,* 123 U. Pa. L. Rev. 340 (1974); Katz, *Experiments on Humans,* N.Y. Times, Feb. 20, 1975, at 33, col. 2; *Symposium: Medical Experimentation on Human Subjects,* 25 Case W. Res. L. Rev. 431 (1975).

59. *See* R. Gardner, Abortion: The Personal Dilemma (1972); R. Gorney, The Human Agenda 197–312 (1972); Abortion in a Changing World (R. Hall ed. 1970); D. Kennedy, Birth Control in America: The Career of Margaret Sanger (1970); D. Lowe, Abortion and the Law (1966); The Morality of Abortion: Legal and Historical Perspectives (J. Noonan ed. 1970); G. Taylor, The Biological Time Bomb (1968); United Nations, Dep't of Economic and Social Affairs, Human Fertility and National Development: A Challenge to Science and Technology, U.N. Doc. ST/ECA/138 (1971); United Nations, Dep't of Economic and Social Affairs, Social Welfare and Family Planning, U.N. Doc. ST/ESA/27 (1976); United Nations, Dep't of Economic and Social Affairs, Status of Women and Family Planning: Report of the Special Rapporteur Appointed by the Economic and Social Council under Resolution 1326 (XLIV), U.N. Doc. E/CN.6/575/Rev. 1 (1975); Kutner, *Due Process of Abortion,* 53 Minn. L. Rev. 1 (1968); Peterson, *Family Planning in Poor Nations,* N.Y. Times, Aug. 2, 1976, at 23, col. 2; Prescott, *Abortion or the Unwanted Child: A Choice for a Humanistic Society,* The Humanist, Mar./Apr. 1975, at 11–15; Peterson, *Family Planning in Poor Nations,* N.Y. Times, Aug. 2, 1976, at 23, col. 2; *Text of Pope Paul's Encyclical Reaffirming the Prohibition against Birth Control, id.,* July 30, 1968, at 20, col. 1; *id.,* Oct. 28, 1976, at 14, col. 3 (deaths resulting from riots connected with compulsory sterilization in India).

60. *See* J. Fletcher, The Ethics of Genetic Control: Ending Reproductive Roulette (1974); P. Ramsey, The Ethics of Fetal Research (1975); P. Ramsey, Fabricated Man: The Ethics of Genetic Control (1970); P. Ramsey, The Patient as Person: Exploration in Medical Ethics (1970); Genetics and the Future of Man (J. Roslansky ed. 1966); Capron, *Legal Considerations Affecting Clinical Pharmacological Studies in Children,* Clinical Research, Feb. 1973, at 141–50; Note, *Fetal Experimentation: Moral, Legal, and Medical Implications,* 26 Stan. L. Rev. 1191 (1974).

On the controversy concerning euthanasia, *see* a comprehensive bibliography: C. Triche & D. Triche, The Euthanasia Controversy, 1812–1974: A Bibliography with Select Annotations (1975). *See also* Euthanasia and the Right to Death: The Case for Voluntary Euthanasia (A. Downing ed. 1970); Group for the Advancement of Psychiatry, The Right to Die: Decision and Decision Makers (1974); E. Kluge, The Practice of Death (1975); M. Kohl, The Morality of Killing, Euthanasia, Abortion and Transplants (1974); M. Mannes, Last Rights (1974); G. Williams, The Sanctity of Life and the Criminal Law (1957); Kutner, *Due Process of Euthanasia: The Living Will, A Proposal,* 44 Ind. L.J. 539 (1969); Morris, *Voluntary Euthanasia,* 45 Wash. L. Rev. 239 (1970); Silving, *Euthanasia: A Study in Comparative Criminal Law,* 103 U. Pa. L. Rev. 350 (1954); Williams, *Euthanasia and Abortion,* 38 U. Colo. L. Rev. 178 (1966).

Deprivations Relating to Wealth

Prevalence of poverty around the globe, except in some pockets of affluence;[61]

Inadequate provision of a basic income and social security;[62]

Enjoyment of benefits of goods and services disproportionate to actual contribution;[63]

Serious problems of mass unemployment;[64]

---

61. *See* E. Eames & J. Goode, Urban Povery in a Cross-Cultural Context (1973); G. Meier, Studies in International Poverty (2d ed. 1970); G. Myrdal, Asian Drama: An Inquiry into the Poverty of Nations (1968); G. Myrdal, The Challenge of World Poverty (1970); 1970 Report on the World Social Situation, *supra* note 29, at 211–19; 1974 Report on the World Social Situation, *supra* note 29, at 202–06; Organization for Economic Co-operation and Development, Development Co-operation: Efforts and Policies of the Members of the Development Assistance Committee 52–54 (1975) (report by Maurice J. Williams) [hereinafter cited as Development Co-operation]; B. Schiller, The Economics of Poverty and Discrimination (2d ed. 1976); A. Shonfield, The Attack on World Poverty (1960); The Concept of Poverty: Working Papers on Methods of Investigation and Life-Styles of the Poor in Different Countries (P. Townsend ed. 1970); United Nations, Dep't of Economic and Social Affairs, Attack on Mass Poverty and Unemployment: Views and Recommendations of the Committee for Development Planning, U.N. Doc. ST/ECA/162 (1972) [hereinafter cited as Attack on Mass Poverty]; U.S. Dep't of Health, Education, and Welfare, Social Security Administration, Social Security Programs throughout the World (1969) (Research Report No. 31); Daniel, *Can World Poverty Be Abolished?* 12 World Justice 31 (1970); Simpson, *The Dimensions of World Poverty,* Scientific American, Nov. 1964, at 27.

Even in what is commonly regarded as the most affluent country—the United States—poverty has not disappeared. For the classic that exposed poverty in the United States and was instrumental in the initiation of the "war on poverty," *see* M. Harrington, The Other America: Poverty in the United States (1962).

In the same vein, Peter Drucker observes:

> What impresses the outside world about the United States today is not how our rich men live—the world has seen riches before, and on a larger and more ostentatious scale. What impresses the outside world is how the poor of this country live.
>
> "Up to Poverty" is the proper slogan. . . .

P. Drucker, Landmarks of Tommorrow 160–61 (1959).

Concerning the extent and distribution of poverty in the United States, *see* M. Arnold & G. Rosenbaum, The Crime of Poverty (1973); A. Batchelder, The Economics of Poverty (1966); Poverty in America (L. Ferman, J. Kornbluh, & A. Haber eds. rev. ed. 1968); Poverty Amid Affluence (L. Fishman ed. 1966); L. Galloway, Poverty in America (1973); Poverty in the Affluent Society (H. Meissner ed. 1966).

62. *See* Economic, Social and Cultural Rights, *supra* note 1, at 94–97.

63. *See id.* at 67–78.

64. *See* Attack on Mass Poverty, *supra* note 61; 1970 Report on the World Social Situation, *supra* note 29, at 200–04; 1974 Report on the World Social Situation, *supra* note 29, at 39–41, 62–63, 137–40, 153–57, 194–97; N.Y. Times, Nov. 6, 1976, at 1, col. 6.

Lack of freedom in seeking and changing employment, especially in completely state-controlled economies;

Limitations on freedom of association in group shaping and sharing of wealth (*e.g.*, restrictions on laborers' right to organize, purge of "capitalists");[65]

Denial of private ownership;

Arbitrary deprivations of wealth, especially at times of crisis;

Lack of or inadequate protection of the rights of property;

Rampant inflation;[66]

Denial of freedom to accumulate and employ resources for productive purposes;

Disparities in the distribution of wealth;[67]

Overconcentration of wealth in a few private hands;

---

65. *See* Allegations Regarding Infringements of Trade Union Rights, 54 U.N. ESCOR ANNEX (AGENDA ITEM 18(b)), U.N. Doc. E/5245 (1973). *See generally,* E. HAAS, HUMAN RIGHTS AND INTERNATIONAL ACTION: THE CASE OF FREEDOM OF ASSOCIATION (1970); C. JENKS, HUMAN RIGHTS AND INTERNATIONAL LABOUR STANDARDS 49–69 (1960).

66. *See* Chapman, *Inflation around the World,* SATURDAY REV./WORLD, July 27, 1974, at 14; Rolfe, *The Great Inflation,* SATURDAY REV./WORLD, July 27, 1974, at 12; N.Y. Times, July 7, 1974, § 4, at 1, col. 3 (inflation around the world, including a map of rising world inflation rates).

67. The enormous differential between the world's rich and poor is widening rather than narrowing. In 1970, an individual living in the richest part of the world (defined so as to include one tenth of the world's population) had 13 times more real income than an individual living in the poorest part (defined in a similar way).

REVIEWING THE INTERNATIONAL ORDER (RIO): INTERIM REPORT 5 (June 1975). The RIO project was initiated in response to increasing demands for a New Economic Order by Dr. Aurelio Peccei, Chairman of the Club of Rome, in February 1974. Professor Jan Tinbergen was the project coordinator. *See also* the group's final report: RIO: RESHAPING THE INTERNATIONAL ORDER 86–88 (1976) (A Report to the Club of Rome) [hereinafter cited as RIO].

Disparities in the distribution of wealth are manifested between states as well as within states. *See* DEVELOPMENT CO-OPERATION, *supra* note 61, at 55–56, 61–63; ECONOMIC, SOCIAL, AND CULTURAL RIGHTS, *supra* note 1, at 114–16; THE GAP BETWEEN RICH AND POOR NATIONS (G. Ranis ed. 1972); J. REES, EQUALITY 28–36 (1971); 1974 REPORT ON THE WORLD SOCIAL SITUATION, *supra* note 29, at 46–53, 64–70, 80–89, 106–12, 123–28, 140–43, 157–60, 175–77; B. WARD, THE RICH NATIONS AND THE POOR NATIONS (1962); Barraclough, *The Haves and the Have-Nots,* N.Y. REV. BOOKS, May 13, 1976, at 31–41; Kravis, *A World of Unequal Incomes,* 409 ANNALS 61 (1973); Kuznets, *Economic Growth and Income Inequality,* 45 AM. ECON. REV. 1 (1955); Grant, *While We Fertilize Golf Courses,* N.Y. Times, Aug. 28, 1974, at 31, col. 1; *id.,* Dec. 12, 1975, § 1, at 18, col. 3 (city ed.); Hofman, *The Misnamed "Third World" Has Divisions All Its Own, id.,* May 23, 1976, § 4, at 3, col. 4; *id.,* Sept. 26, 1976, § 1, at 1, col. 4.

Wasteful use of resources;

Depletion of available and potential resources without adequate regard for future generations;

Massive diversion of resources for destructive purposes (for military overkill or for suppression of internal opposition);[68]

Severe restrictions on the employment of relevant strategies in production, conservation, distribution, and consumption;

Continuing practices of forced labor;[69]

---

68. "World Military expenditures are now approaching $300 billion a year—nearly $35 million every hour of every day—and they continue to rise. . . . The net transfer of financial resources from rich to poor countries amounts to about one thirtieth of world military expenditures and they are 163 times more than the sum spent on peace and development through the United Nations system." RIO, *supra* note 67, at 25.

See THE MILITARY BALANCE, published annually by the Institute for Strategic Studies; R. SIVARD, WORLD MILITARY AND SOCIAL EXPENDITURES (1976); UNITED NATIONS, ECONOMIC AND SOCIAL CONSEQUENCES OF THE ARMS RACE AND OF MILITARY EXPENDITURES (Report of the Secretary-General), U.N. GAOR, U.N. Doc. A/8469/Rev. 1 (1972); UNITED NATIONS, REDUCTION OF THE MILITARY BUDGETS OF STATES PERMANENT MEMBERS OF THE SECURITY COUNCIL BY 10 PER CENT AND UTILIZATION OF PART OF THE FUNDS THUS SAVED TO PROVIDE ASSISTANCE TO DEVELOPING COUNTRIES (Report of the Secretary-General), U.N. GAOR, U.N. Doc. A/9770/Rev. 1 (1975); WORLD MILITARY EXPENDITURES, published annually by United States Arms Control and Disarmament Agency; Benoit & Lubell, *World Defense Expenditures,* 3 J. PEACE RESEARCH 97 (1966); Epstein, *The Disarmament Hoax,* WORLD, Apr. 10, 1973, at 24–29. *See also* N.Y. Times, Mar. 1, 1976, at 1, col. 1 ("World's Spending on Arms Reported at Record Levels: Study Places Annual Outlay at $300 Billion—Fastest Rise in Developing Lands"); *id.,* Mar. 7, 1976, § 4, at 4, col. 1 (containing the comparative figures of per capita 1973 expenditures in dollars by governments of 128 nations in the military, educational and health fields).

On the global arms trade, *see* J. STANLEY & M. PEARTON, THE INTERNATIONAL TRADE IN ARMS (1972); STOCKHOLM INTERNATIONAL PEACE RESEARCH INSTITUTE, THE ARMS TRADE WITH THE THIRD WORLD (1971); STOCKHOLM INTERNATIONAL PEACE RESEARCH INSTITUTE, THE ARMS TRADE WITH THE THIRD WORLD (rev. & abr. ed. 1975); G. THAYER, THE WAR BUSINESS: THE INTERNATIONAL TRADE IN ARMAMENTS (1969); *Anatomy of the Arms Trade,* NEWSWEEK, Sept. 6, 1976, at 39; Luck, *The New Regional Arms Merchants,* THE INTERDEPENDENT, Jan. 1976, at 1, 3. *See also* Vance, *Controlling U.S. Arms Sales,* N.Y. Times, May 13, 1976, at 35, col. 2; *Mindless Arms Sales, id.,* Aug. 11, 1976, at 34, col. 1 (editorial); *id.,* Oct. 19, 1975, § 1, at 1, col. 2 ("U.S. Arms-Sale Rise Stirs Capital Concern") (the rise of American arms sales abroad from $2 billion in 1967 to about $11 billion in the 1974 fiscal year); *id.,* Aug. 8, 1976, § 1, at 1, col. 1 ("Iranians Plan to Purchase $10 Billion in U.S. Arms").

For a penetrating study of the pervasive impacts of the American military establishment on American society, *see* A. YARMOLINSKY, THE MILITARY ESTABLISHMENT: ITS IMPACTS ON AMERICAN SOCIETY (1971). *See also* R. BARNET, THE ECONOMY OF DEATH (1969); R. LAPP, THE WEAPONS CULTURE (1968); THE WAR ECONOMY OF THE UNITED STATES: READINGS IN MILITARY INDUSTRY AND ECONOMY (S. Melman ed. 1971).

69. *See* W. KLOOSTERBOER, INVOLUNTARY LABOUR SINCE THE ABOLITION OF SLAVERY (1960).

Expropriation without adequate compensation.[70]

DEPRIVATIONS RELATING TO SKILL

The requisitioning of talent and skill;

Compulsory assignment of skill training to fit a particular role and reduction of the freedom of job choice;

Alienation from work—intense feelings of meaninglessness because of high degree of automation in modern process of production;[71]

Restrictions on freedoms of skill groups to organize and function;

Inadequacy in overcoming hardships caused by rapid obsolescence of skills amid accelerating change in science-based technology;[72]

Lack of exposure to training, in both content and method, appropriate to a culture of science and technology;

The problem of the brain drain.[73]

DEPRIVATIONS RELATING TO AFFECTION

The requisitioning of loyalty in the name of the state;

Intense demands for submission to regimentation on behalf of the institutions of power;

---

70. *See* Weston, *International Law and the Deprivation of Foreign Wealth: A Framework for Future Inquiry,* in 2 THE FUTURE OF THE INTERNATIONAL LEGAL ORDER 36–182 (R. Falk & C. Black eds. 1970). For further references, *see* chapter 14 *infra,* at note 13.

71. *See* R. BLAUNER, ALIENATION AND FREEDOM: THE FACTORY WORKER AND HIS INDUSTRY (1964); D. JENKINS, JOB POWER: BLUE AND WHITE COLLAR DEMOCRACY 36–61 (1st ed. 1973); J. LOPREATO & L. HAZELRIGG, CLASS, CONFLICT, AND MOBILITY: THEORIES AND STUDIES OF CLASS STRUCTURE 303–38 (1972); B. MURCHLAND, THE AGE OF ALIENATION 14–23 (1971); R. SCHACHT, ALIENATION 168–73 (1970); MAN AGAINST WORK (L. Zimpel ed. 1974).

72. *See* AUTOMATION AND TECHNOLOGICAL CHANGE (J. Dunlop ed. 1962); G. FRIEDMANN, THE ANATOMY OF WORK: LABOR, LEISURE, AND THE IMPLICATIONS OF AUTOMATION (W. Rawson trans. 1961); L. GOODMAN, MAN AND AUTOMATION (1957); INTERNATIONAL LABOR OFFICE, AUTOMATION AND NON-MANUAL WORKERS (1967); A. JAFFE & J. FROOMKIN, TECHNOLOGY AND JOBS: AUTOMATION IN PERSPECTIVE (1968); R. MACMILLAN, AUTOMATION: FRIEND OR FOE? (1956); F. MANN & R. HOFFMAN, AUTOMATION AND THE WORKER (1960); F. POLLOCK, AUTOMATION: A STUDY OF ITS ECONOMIC AND SOCIAL CONSEQUENCES (W. Henderson & W. Chaloner trans. 1957); C. SILBERMAN, THE MYTHS OF AUTOMATION (1966); C. WALKER, TECHNOLOGY, INDUSTRY, AND MAN: THE AGE OF ACCELERATION (1968); Hoffer, *Automation Is Here to Liberate Us,* in TECHNOLOGY AND SOCIAL CHANGE 64–74 (W. Moore ed. 1972); Perrucci, *Work in the Cybernetic State,* in THE TRIPLE REVOLUTION EMERGING 174–94 (2d ed. R. Perrucci & M. Pilisuk eds. 1971); Raskin, *Pattern for Tomorrow's Industry?* in TECHNOLOGY AND SOCIAL CHANGE 54–63 (W. Moore ed. 1972).

73. *See* THE BRAIN DRAIN (W. Adams ed. 1968); THE BRAIN DRAIN AND TAXATION: THEORY AND EMPIRICAL ANALYSIS (J. Bhagwati ed. 1975); ECONOMIC, SOCIAL, AND CULTURAL RIGHTS, *supra* note 1, at 121–22; Kannappan, *The Brain Drain and Developing Countries,* 98 INT'L LAB. REV. 1 (1968); Watanabe, *The Brain Drain from Developing to Developed*

Undermining or weakening of rival groups competing for loyal service of the individual;

Calculated administration of hate;

Denial or severe restrictions on freedom of association;

The family in crisis at a time of rapid social change;[74]

Practices of involuntary or disguised marriage and sham adoption;[75]

Prohibition of interracial marriages or interreligious marriages;[76]

Confusion and difficulties associated with the search for alternative modes of affection in lieu of the traditional affection unit—the nuclear family;[77]

Unreasonable limitations on freedom to terminate uncongenial personal relationships;[78]

Countries, 99 INT'L LAB. REV. 401 (1969); N.Y. Times, Nov. 1, 1976, at 14, col. 3 (Nigeria's effort to stop an African "brain drain").

74. *See* J. BERNARD, THE FUTURE OF MARRIAGE (1972); D. COOPER, THE DEATH OF THE FAMILY (1971); THE NUCLEAR FAMILY IN CRISIS: THE SEARCH FOR AN ALTERNATIVE (M. Gordon ed. 1972); B. MOORE, POLITICAL POWER AND SOCIAL THEORY 160–78 (1958); THE FAMILY IN SEARCH OF A FUTURE: ALTERNATIVE MODELS FOR MODERNS (H. Otto ed. 1970); FAMILY IN TRANSITION (A. Skolnick & J. Skolnick eds. 1971); B. YORBURG, THE CHANGING FAMILY: A SOCIOLOGICAL PERSPECTIVE (1973); Goode, *Family Disorganization,* in CONTEMPORARY SOCIAL PROBLEMS 479–522 (2d ed. R. Merton & R. Nisbet eds. 1966); Keller, *Does the Family Have a Future?* in INTIMACY, FAMILY, AND SOCIETY 114–28 (A. Skolnick & J. Skolnick eds. 1974); Hendin, *The Ties Don't Bind,* N.Y. Times, Aug. 26, 1976, at 33, col. 1. *See also* Crosby, *The Death of the Family—Revisited,* THE HUMANIST, May/June 1975, at 12–14; Mace, *In Defense of the Nuclear Family, id.,* at 27–29; Pickett, *The American Family: An Embattled Institution, id.,* at 5–8; Whitehurst, *Alternative Life-Styles, id.,* at 23–26.

75. *See* C. GREENIDGE, *supra* note 15, at 94–116; J. GULLICK, DEBT BONDAGE IN MALAYA (1958). *See generally* M. WOLF, WOMAN AND THE FAMILY IN RURAL TAIWAN (1972).

76. *See* S. ANANT, THE CHANGING CONCEPT OF CASTE IN INDIA 104–18 (1972); G. CARTER, THE POLITICS OF INEQUALITY: SOUTH AFRICA SINCE 1948, at 76–81 (rev. ed. 1962); L. DUMONT, HOMO HIERARCHICUS: AN ESSAY ON THE CASTE SYSTEM 109–29 (M. Sainsbury trans. 1970); R. SICKELS, RACE, MARRIAGE AND THE LAW 10–91 (1972); L. THOMPSON, POLITICS IN THE REPUBLIC OF SOUTH AFRICA 32 (1966).

See generally N.Y. Times, June 8, 1976, at 19, col. 1 (a joint Roman Catholic-Anglican report on mixed marriages urging relaxation of the requirements for recognition of such marriages).

77. *See* M. CARDEN, ONEIDA: FROM UTOPIAN COMMUNITY TO MODERN CORPORATION (1969); W. HEDGEPETH & D. STOCK, THE ALTERNATIVES: COMMUNAL LIFE IN NEW AMERICA (1970); R. KANTER, COMMITMENT AND COMMUNITY: COMMUNES AND UTOPIAS IN SOCIOLOGICAL PERSPECTIVE (1972); R. KANTER, COMMUNES: CREATING AND MANAGING THE COLLECTIVE LIFE (1973); C. NORDHOFF, THE COMMUNISTIC SOCIETIES OF THE UNITED STATES (1965); B. ZABLOCKI, THE JOYFUL COMMUNITY (1971); N.Y. Times, Sept. 2, 1976, at 26, col. 1 ("Cohabitation and the Courts: The Stigma Begins to Fade").

78. *See* N.Y. Times, May 6, 1975, at 44, col. 1 ("Divorce around the World: Even When Easy, It Carries a Stigma").

Social ostracism by tactics of presuming "guilt by association";[79]

Frustration (stifling) of congenial personal relationships, by manipulating fear and anxiety in a pervasive atmosphere of mutual suspicion sustained by a network of the secret police and informers.[80]

Deprivations Relating to Rectitude

The politicization of rectitude;[81]

Widespread tactics of ostentatious conformity in evading individual responsibility of conscience;

Denial of freedom to worship;[82]

Adoption of atheism as a national policy;[83]

Intolerance and persecution of heretics or nonbelievers;

Intolerance and persecution of religious minorities;[84]

Discrimination regarding participation in value processes on religious grounds;[85]

---

79. *See* chapter 12 *infra,* at note 33 and accompanying text.

80. *See generally* C. Friedrich & Z. Brzezinski, *supra* note 22, at 239–89; J. Hazard, The Soviet System of Government 136–52 (3d ed. 1964); S. Neumann, *supra* note 31, at 142–204; A. Solzhenitsyn, The Gulag Archipelago, 1918–1956 (T. Whitney trans. 1974); A. Solzhenitsyn, The Gulag Archipelago, Two (1975).

81. *See* N.Y. Times, Aug. 28, 1976, at 2, col. 3 ("Church-State Conflict Troubles Latin Lands").

82. *See* Jancar, *Religious Dissent in the Soviet Union,* in Dissent in the USSR: Politics, Ideology, and People 191 (R. Tokes ed. 1975); Reddaway, *Freedom of Worship and the Law,* in In Quest of Justice: Protest and Dissent in the Soviet Union Today 62 (A. Brumberg ed. 1970); *Religions in the Soviet Union (1960–71),* in The Fourth World: Victims of Group Oppression 218–68 (B. Whitaker ed. 1972).

83. This is characteristic of communist societies. *See* J. Bennett, Christianity and Communism Today (rev. ed. 1970); R. Bush, Religion in Communist China (1970); H. Chambre, Christianity and Communism (R. Trevett trans. 1960); M. D'Arcy, Communism and Christianity (1957); A. Galter, The Red Book of the Persecuted Church (2d ed. 1957); G. MacEoin, The Communist War on Religion (1951); D. MacInnis, Religious Policy and Practice in Communist China (1972).

84. At the fifth assembly of the World Council of Churches held in Dec. 1975, in Nairobi, Kenya, the enduring problem of religious persecution was "the most nettlesome issue." Allegations of religious persecution came from every part of the world, ranging from "restrictions on preaching to outright physical punishment of believers," and affecting Protestants, Catholics and Jews. N.Y. Times, Dec. 13, 1975, at 13, col. 3.

See chapter 11 *infra,* at notes 24–38 and accompanying text; N.Y. Times, Dec. 22, 1975, at 3, col. 1 (organized religion branded by Yugoslav Communist leaders as "a dangerous domestic enemy"). *See also Religious Persecution in El Salvador: Hearings before the Subcomm. on International Organizations of the House Comm. on International Relations,* 95th Cong., 1st Sess. (1977).

85. *See* chapter 11 *infra,* at notes 1–47 and accompanying text.

Restrictions on formation of association for rectitude purposes;

Warfare over religious conflicts;[86]

Coercion to worship and compulsory conversion;[87]

Imposition of religious or atheistic instruction;

Arbitrary restrictions on modalities of worship, places of worship, and the performance of rites;

Caprice in recognizing or rejecting conscientious objection to military service.[88]

CONDITIONS AFFECTING DEPRIVATIONS AND NONFULFILLMENT

The conditions which have resulted in these great disparities between the rising common demands of people for human dignity values and the degree of achievement of these values are both environmental and predispositional. The relevance of the environmental factors derives from the limitations which such factors impose upon peoples' achievements, irrespective of their predispositions. The relevance of predispositional factors derives from the maximization postulate—that human beings act in social process in such a way as to maximize all basic values, conscious

---

86. It is a dismal truth that probably half or more of the wars now being fought around the world are either openly religious conflicts or involved with religious disputes. And, since virtually all formerly organized creeds are monotheistic, this means that at this very instant men are killing other men in the name of an identical, if variously named, God.

Sulzberger, *Death in the Name of God,* N.Y. Times, Jan. 24, 1976, at 27, col. 2. Examples include: the conflict between Christians and Moslems in Lebanon, the conflict between Protestants and Catholics in Northern Ireland, the Arab-Israeli conflict, the conflict between Turkey and Greece on Cyprus, intermittent civil conflicts involving Christian tribesmen in Burma, occasional outbursts between largely Hindu India and Moslem Pakistan, the guerrilla campaign of Moslems in the southern Philippines seeking freedom from Catholic Manila's control.

See R. Hull, The Irish Triangle: Conflict in Northern Ireland (1976); C. O'Brien, States of Ireland (1972); D. Smith, Religion, Politics, and Social Change in the Third World 170–93 (1971); Jackson, *The Two Irelands: The Problem of the Double Minority—A Dual Study in Inter-Group Tensions,* in The Fourth World: Victims of Group Oppression 187–216 (B. Whitaker ed. 1973). *See also* Markham, *Lebanon: The Insane War,* N.Y. Times, Aug. 15, 1976, § 6 (Magazine), at 6–7 *et seq.;* Weinraub, *The Violence in Ulster Never Ends, id.,* July 25, 1976, § 4, at 3, col. 3; *id.,* Sept. 11, 1975, at 1, col. 3 (the Moslems rebel in the southern Philippines).

87. *See* chapter 11 *infra,* at note 8 and accompanying text; N.Y. Times, Sept. 18, 1974, at 12, col. 1 (charges of compulsory conversion to Islam in Malaysia).

88. *See* Council of Europe, Consultative Assembly, The Right to Conscientious Objection (1967); A Conflict of Loyalties: The Case for Selective Conscientious Objection (J. Finn ed. 1968); W. Gaylin, In the Service of Their Country: War

and unconscious. Though the predispositional factors and significant features of the environment are in constant interaction, it is useful for the present purpose to recognize and highlight their relative distinctiveness.[89]

Environmental Factors

From a comprehensive perspective, the environmental factors relate to every feature of social process. Among the most important are, of course, population, resources, and institutional arrangements and practices.

The explosive growth of the population is one of the most salient trends in human history.[90] Though population increase has in various

---

Resisters in Prison (1970); E. Long, War and Conscience in America (1968); M. Pusey, The Way We Go to War (1969); J. Rae, Conscience and Politics: The British Government and the Conscientious Objector to Military Service, 1916–1919 (1970); J. Rohr, Prophets without Honor: Public Policy and the Selective Conscientious Objector (1971); Conscience in America: A Documentary History of Conscientious Objection in America, 1757–1967 (L. Schlissel ed. 1968); Handbook for Conscientious Objectors (A. Tatum ed. 1972); Law and Resistance (L. Veysey ed. 1970); R. Williams, The New Exiles: American War Resisters in Canada (1971); H. Zinn, Disobedience and Democracy: Nine Fallacies on Law and Order (1968).

89. The principal thrust of B.F. Skinner, Beyond Freedom and Dignity (1971), would not appear to affect our thesis. Skinner emphasizes the tremendous importance of environmental variables in affecting behavior but continues himself to make reference to subjectivities. *Id.* at 62, 199. At times, he seems largely to be quibbling about the appropriate words for referring to subjectivities. *Id.* at 94–95, 107. The references he makes to "genetic endowment" and "environmental circumstances" are not always accorded clear indices. His conception of "autonomous man" or "an autonomous controlling agent," *id.* at 20, 101, would appear a factitious dummy. He too often uses "control" as an absolute, with no continuum between "control" and "non-control." *Id.* at 82. For establishing the importance of environmental variables that affect behavior, it would scarcely appear necessary to belittle the role of predispositional variables. There are more indices for subjectivities than Skinner recognizes and more different ways of referring to and generalizing these indices than he seems to understand. His vague references to Freud indicate a minimal conception of man's subjective events. *Id.* at 62–63, 85, 211–12.

In contrast, for a more realistic approach to the problem, *see* F. Alexander, Our Age of Unreason (1942); T. Dobzhansky, Mankind Evolving: The Evolution of the Human Species (1962); R. Dubos, Beast or Angel? Choices That Make Us Human (1974); R. Dubos, So Human an Animal (1968); E. Fromm, Escape from Freedom (1963).

Contemporary psychoanalytic thought, while continuing to emphasize predispositional factors, certainly gives prominent attention to environmental factors. *See, e.g.,* E. Erikson, Childhood and Society (1950); K. Horney, The Neurotic Personality of Our Time (1937); A. Kardiner, The Psychological Frontiers of Society (1945); H. Sullivan, The Interpersonal Theory of Psychiatry (1953).

90. Of the burgeoning literature on population, useful citations include: Population: The Vital Revolution (R. Freedman ed. 1964); The Study of Population: An Inventory and Appraisal (P. Hauser & O. Duncan eds. 1959); D. Heer, Society and Popula-

contexts served to promote development and fulfill human rights, it is causing considerable difficulties in the contemporary worldwide context. The more people for whom human rights have to be secured and maintained, the greater the difficulties. The world population problem today is characterized by large numbers, continuing high rates of growth (given present limitations of the earth's resources in the perspective of contemporary technology), and uneven distribution, both globally and nationally.[91] Prior to 1800, the population grew sporadically, and it took at least a million years for human numbers to reach the billion mark. The second billion took only 130 years and the third billion took only 30 years.[92] In 1976, there were approximately four billion people on this finite planet, with an expected annual increase of some seventy million persons. Despite recent efforts at family planning and fertility control, the population growth rate remains intolerably high when evaluated in terms of developments in technology during at least the immediate future. Given the prevailing rate, the world population is projected to double in 35 years. The rates of population growth differ from region to region and from state to state. What exacerbates the present population dilemma is that high growth rates concentrate in the areas that are already congested and have the least capacity to absorb increased population. Of the total world population of four billion, more than two-thirds inhabit the developing countries, which are characterized by low per capita income and poverty. With very few habitable open spaces remaining, given current and prospective levels of demand and production, and with the universal erection of national barriers to immigration, the present disparities in the distribution of the world population are likely to continue for the foreseeable future. Within particular territorial communities, there have been overwhelming trends toward rapid

---

TION (2d ed. 1975); POLICY SCIENCES AND POPULATION (W. Ilchman, H. Lasswell, J. Montgomery, & M. Weiner eds. 1975); 1, 2, & 3 WORLD POPULATION: BASIC DOCUMENTS (J. Joyce ed. 1975–76); POPULATION: A CLASH OF PROPHETS (E. Pohlman ed. 1973); THE WORLD POPULATION CRISIS: POLICY IMPLICATIONS AND THE ROLE OF LAW (Proc., Am. Soc'y Int'l L. & John Bassett Moore Soc'y Int'l L. Symposium 1971).

On the history of population growth, *see* A. CARR-SAUNDERS, WORLD POPULATION: PAST GROWTH AND PRESENT TRENDS (2d ed. 1964); POPULATION IN HISTORY: ESSAYS IN HISTORICAL DEMOGRAPHY (D. Eversley & D. Glass eds. 1965); POPULATION AND SOCIAL CHANGE (D. Glass & R. Revelle eds. 1972); UNITED NATIONS, THE DETERMINANTS AND CONSEQUENCES OF POPULATION TRENDS (1953); E. WRIGLEY, POPULATION AND HISTORY (1969).

91. *See* G. BREESE, URBANIZATION IN NEWLY DEVELOPING COUNTRIES (1966); J. CLARKE, POPULATION GEOGRAPHY (1965); THE STUDY OF URBANIZATION (P. Hauser & L. Schnore eds. 1965).

92. UNITED NATIONS, HUMAN FERTILITY AND NATIONAL DEVELOPMENT: A CHALLENGE TO SCIENCE AND TECHNOLOGY 11, U.N. Doc. ST/ECA/138 (1971).

urbanization—a continuous, swelling flow of people from the rural to the urban area—culminating in overconcentration and overcrowding.[93]

The present world population problem, as manifested in its various dimensions, has profound implications for the protection and fulfillment of human rights. The situation is perceived as alarming by many outspoken world leaders. In the words of Robert S. McNamara, president of the World Bank:

> The end desired by the Church and by all men of good will is the enhancement of human dignity. That is what development is all about. Human dignity is threatened by the population explosion—more severely, more completely, more certainly threatened than it has been by any catastrophe the world has yet endured.[94]

The problem is not confined to the Malthusian dimension of food supply. It affects the entire quality of life, or the shaping and sharing of all important values. In brief illustration, the population-resource-technology imbalances have significantly contributed to the deprivations and nonfulfillment of human rights: widespread hunger and malnutrition; the existence of slums and shantytowns, poor housing, crowded living conditions; the spread of disease and emotional stress; poor health and leisure facilities and services; the deterioration of the environment (well-being); the widening gap between the rich and the poor (both individually and nationally); depletion of finite resources; widespread poverty; substandard living conditions (wealth); rising levels of unemployment and underemployment (skill); persisting widespread illiteracy and inadequate educational facilities and opportunities (enlightenment); practices of discrimination, especially racism (respect); confusion in rectitude standards and the rising rate of crime (rectitude); the pervasive sense of loneliness and dislocation of families (affection); the popularity of political extremism; the propensity toward recourse to violence (internal and external); the increasing potential for transnational conflicts (power and security).[95]

---

93. *See* note 91 *supra. See also* L. Brown, World without Borders 73–87 (1972); T. Chandler & G. Fox, 3000 Years of Urban Growth (1973); 2 K. Davis, World Urbanization, 1950–1970 (1972); H. Hoyt, World Urbanization: Expanding Population in a Shrinking World (1962); 1974 Report on the World Social Situation, *supra* note 29, at 58–62, 83–85; World Housing Survey 1974, *supra* note 54, at 5–6, 16–17; Davis, *The Urbanization of the Human Population,* in Cities 3–25 (1969) (a Scientific American book).

94. R. McNamara, One Hundred Countries, Two Billion People: The Dimensions of Development 46 (1973).

95. *See* R. McNamara, The Essence of Security 141–58 (1968); Caldwell, *Population,* in 4 The Future of the International Legal Order 32, 34–53 (C. Black & R. Falk eds. 1972); Dyckman, *Some Aspects of Civic Order in an Urbanized World,* Daedalus, Summer

In relation to the burgeoning population, the resources of the world appear to diminish in quantity, to deteriorate in quality because of misexploitation, and to distribute themselves unevenly globe-wide.[96] A salient reality of the earth, given the levels of technology at hand or in immediate prospect, is the apparently finite quantity of resources essential to human existence and fulfillment. The resources of the earth can be divided into three categories: renewable resources, nonrenewable resources, and spatial-extension resources.[97] Until quite recently, it was generally assumed that our planet had ample carrying capacity to accommodate any number of people, and very little attention was given to "the limits of the earth."[98] Because of the continuing debate concerning "the limits to growth,"[99] especially in the wake of the energy crisis, it has increasingly been recognized that, on certain assumptions about the relationship of the earth to its solar and trans-solar environment, the earth is

---

1966, at 797–812; Falk, *World Population and International Law,* 63 AM. J. INT'L L. 514 (1969).

See also Lee, *Law, Human Rights and Population: A Strategy for Action,* 12 VA. J. INT'L L. 309 (1972); Sipila, *Population and Human Rights,* 7 HUMAN RIGHTS J. 222 (1974).

96. On the relation between population and resources, *see* RESOURCES AND POPULATION (B. Benjamin, P. Cox, & J. Peel eds. 1973); G. BORGSTROM, THE HUNGRY PLANET: THE MODERN WORLD AT THE EDGE OF FAMINE (1965); H. BROWN, THE CHALLENGE OF MAN'S FUTURE (1954); L. BROWN, IN THE HUMAN INTEREST: A STRATEGY TO STABILIZE WORLD POPULATION 28–98 (1974); P. CONNELLY & R. PERLMAN, THE POLITICS OF SCARCITY: RESOURCE CONFLICTS IN INTERNATIONAL RELATIONS (1975); P. EHRLICH & A. EHRLICH, *supra* note 55.

See A Symposium on Primary Resource Scarcity Effects on Trade and Investment, 24 AM. U.L. REV. 1087 (1975).

97. *See* M. MCDOUGAL, H. LASSWELL, & I. VLASIC, LAW AND PUBLIC ORDER IN SPACE 776–81 (1963). *See also* S. CIRIACY-WANTRUP, RESOURCE CONSERVATION: ECONOMICS AND POLICIES 35 (1952); COMMITTEE ON RESOURCES AND MAN, NATIONAL ACADEMY OF SCIENCES—NATIONAL RESEARCH COUNCIL, RESOURCES AND MAN (1969).

98. F. OSBORN, THE LIMITS OF THE EARTH (1953).

99. *See* D. MEADOWS, THE LIMITS TO GROWTH (1972) (A Report for the Club of Rome's Project on the Predicament of Mankind). *See* W. OLTMANS, ON GROWTH (1974), and W. OLTMANS, ON GROWTH II (1975), for a divergence of views. *See generally* J. MADDOX, THE DOOMSDAY SYNDROME (1972); M. MESAROVIC & E. PESTEL, MANKIND AT THE TURNING POINT (1974) (The Second Report to the Club of Rome); E. SCHUMACHER, SMALL IS BEAUTIFUL: ECONOMICS AS IF PEOPLE MATTERED (1975); *The Limits to Growth Controversy,* 5 FUTURES, NOS. 1–2 (1973); *The No-Growth Society,* DAEDALUS, Fall 1973 (entire issue); *The Ups and Downs of "Growth is Good,"* THE INTERDEPENDENT, Dec. 1975, at 1. *See also* Dubos, *On Growth,* N.Y. Times, Nov. 11, 1975, at 31, col. 1; Esfandiary, *Homo Sapiens, the Manna Maker, id.,* Aug. 9, 1975, at 17, col. 2; *Scientist Sees World Ready for "New Mode of Life," id.,* Oct. 17, 1974, at 14, col. 1; *Scholars Rebut Computer View That Disaster Awaits Mankind, id.,* Oct. 18, 1974, at 4, col. 3; *Conference Debates the Limiting of Economic Growth to Conserve Resources, id.,* Oct. 21, 1975, at 18, col. 3; *Scholars Favor Global Growth: Members of Club of Rome Say Further Rise Is Needed to Fight World Poverty, id.,* Apr. 13, 1976, at 1, col. 5.

finite and some currently vital resources are not inexhaustible. With the expansion and acceleration of industrialization and development, the depletion of resources presently perceived as essential quickens at an alarming rate. Despite divergent forecasts, it would appear that many of the key resources may in the not too distant future be depleted, or become too costly to exploit, given the present rate of resource consumption within existing frameworks of knowledge and technique.

In addition, the existing miseries of nonfulfillment are due in significant measure to mismanagement and misuse of available resources. Because of the continuing ascendancy within the global military arena of contending blocs, sustained by persisting expectations of violence and war, a disproportionately large share of world's resources has continued to be diverted for military purposes.[100] Barriers of various kinds have been erected to restrict the free flow of people, ideas, technology, goods, and services across national boundaries. Consequently, the management of resources (both sharable and nonsharable) tends to be so fragmented and impaired as to fail to achieve maximum efficiency.

The mismanagement of resources has, further, helped to create an ecological crisis of world proportions that seriously threatens the quality of life on this planet.[101] The nature, degree, and tempo of environmental deterioration differ from region to region and from community to community, but the crisis is global in scope and impact. This unprecedented crisis is characterized by the combined scourges of "the population bomb";[102] air, water, noise, and other pollution; the shrinkage of open spaces; the deterioration of agricultural lands; urban congestion; the growing danger of extinction of many forms of nonhuman life; destruction of natural beauty; and the poor integration of advanced technology with environmental requirements. The plants, homo sapiens and other animals, and microorganisms that inhabit the planet are united with each other and with their nonliving surroundings by a network of complex and interdependent natural and cultural components which comprise a planetary ecosystem.[103] But this delicate ecological

---

100. *See* note 68 *supra.*

101. On the ecological crisis, *see* note 55 *supra. See also* ORGANIZATION FOR ECONOMIC CO-OPERATION AND DEVELOPMENT, ECONOMICS OF TRANSFRONTIER POLLUTION (1976); ORGANIZATION FOR ECONOMIC CO-OPERATION AND DEVELOPMENT, PROBLEMS IN TRANSFRONTIER POLLUTION (1974); McDougal & Schneider, *Priorities for Public Order of the Environment,* in ENVIRONMENT AND SOCIETY IN TRANSITION: WORLD PRIORITIES 81–114 (B. Pregel, H. Lasswell, & J. McHale eds. 1975) (Annals of the New York Academy of Sciences, Vol. 261).

102. P. EHRLICH, THE POPULATION BOMB (1968). *See also* P. APPLEMAN, THE SILENT EXPLOSION (1965).

103. In the words of Ward and Dubos:

unity of the entire earth-space environment is widely believed by many competent experts to be in grave jeopardy today.[104]

The available resources of the world, like the populations, are unevenly distributed, with glaring discrepancies in the pattern of resource consumption.[105] While arable land; fresh water (including rainfall); fossil fuels (coal, oil, and natural gas); ferrous, nonferrous, and nonmetallic minerals; and other natural resources are relatively abundant in some areas of the world, they are either absent or scarce in other areas. Similar disparities also characterize the distribution of the knowledge of science, technology, skills, and machinery, resulting in varying stages of development and different levels of productivity and consumption.[106] When the prospects of "limitless growth" appear to run high, "growth" is the global catchword: with patience and effort, it is counseled, the less developed areas would sooner or later enjoy the benefits of growth. However, as the finiteness of critical resources and the limits to growth (including knowledge) are taken with increasing seriousness, the focus of attention is expected to shift markedly from enlarging the aggregate pie to dividing the existing pie, with possible "wars of redistribution"[107] becoming characteristic of the global arena.[108] Although the importance of any particular resource is a function of many other factors, including the state of technology, available manpower, and efficiency in social organization, it is clear that the competition for scarce resources of all kinds—land, water, air, food, energy, materials and so on—will accentuate unless populations are brought rather promptly into balance and

---

> There is a profound paradox in the fact that four centuries of intense scientific work, focused on the dissection of the seamless web of existence and resulting in ever more precise but highly specialized knowledge, has led to a new and unexpected vision of the total unity, continuity, and interdependence of the entire cosmos.

B. WARD & R. DUBOS, *supra* note 55, at 30. *See also* J. MCHALE, THE ECOLOGICAL CONTEXT (1970); H. SPROUT & M. SPROUT, *supra* note 55, at 13–31.

104. Sauvy compiled an inventory of some current book titles: *"The Hungry Future, Standing Room Only, Born to Starve, Our Polluted World, Murderous Providence, Beyond Repair, Timetable for Disaster, The Vanishing Air, We Can't Breathe."* A. SAUVY, ZERO GROWTH? 137 (1975).

105. *See* note 67 *supra. See also* C. HENSMAN, RICH AGAINST POOR: THE REALITY OF AID (1971); THE WIDENING GAP: DEVELOPMENT IN THE 1970'S (B. Ward, J. Runnalls, & L. D'anjou eds. 1971); L. ZIMMERMAN, POOR LANDS, RICH LANDS: THE WIDENING GAP (1965); Spengler, *Allocation and Development, Economic and Political,* In POLITICAL AND ADMINISTRATIVE DEVELOPMENT 588–637 (R. Braibanti ed. 1969).

106. *See* W. ROSTOW, THE STAGES OF ECONOMIC GROWTH (1960). *See generally* W. ROSTOW, HOW IT ALL BEGAN: THE ORIGINS OF THE MODERN ECONOMY (1975). *See also* A. ORGANSKI, STAGES OF POLITICAL DEVELOPMENT (1965).

107. R. HEILBRONER, AN INQUIRY INTO THE HUMAN PROSPECT 43 (1974).

108. *See* W. OLTMANS, ON GROWTH 285 (1974) (remark of Noam Chomsky).

scientific expansion is maintained. All this will carry ominous implications for the general fulfillment of human rights.

Confronted with the unprecedented challenges of our planetary ecosystem that require integrated global solutions, the value institutions and practices of humankind appear to be inadequate and faltering. The human institutions and practices are, geographically, too state-centered and, functionally, too tradition-bound to make timely responses and adjustments to the accelerating pace and dimensions of change generated by the universalization of science and technology and the ever-increasing global interdependences. There appears to be a lack of appropriate balance in institutional arrangements and activities at the national, regional, and global levels. Ever since the rise of the modern state system in the mid-seventeenth century, the world arena has been characterized by the predominance of territorially organized nation-states. The quality of transnational interaction has largely been shaped by the pattern of cooperation and coercion among elites representing states of varying sizes, capabilities and orientation. Despite the increasingly varied and important roles played by a multiplicity of nonstate participants, especially international organizations (both governmental and functional), the nation-states (especially the large ones) continue to dominate the world arena. Anchored in the nation-state system, the organizations that pursue specific power objectives, or that concentrate on values other than power, adjust themselves to the territorial context. The ascendancy of the nation-state has been such that it has built into the perspectives of the world community a bias in favor of perceiving advantages and disadvantages in terms of the individual nation-state. Because of this, both the search for and the discovery of common interests are impaired. The emphasis on state "sovereignty" in expression of excessive "nationalism" has further been exacerbated by the rival ideologies representing the contending systems of public order. The centrality of the state affects and is manifested in every feature of the world constitutive process of authoritative decision (with which we propose to deal in detail later).[109]

---

109. *See* chapter 4 *infra*. For preliminary indication, *see* McDougal, Lasswell & Chen, *Human Rights and World Public Order: A Framework for Policy-Oriented Inquiry*, 63 AM. J. INT'L L. 237, 258–64 (1969); McDougal, *Human Rights and World Public Order: Principles of Content and Procedure for Clarifying General Community Policies*, 14 VA. J. INT'L L. 387, 415–19 (1974). *See generally* McDougal, Lasswell, & Reisman, *The World Constitutive Process of Authoritative Decision*, in 1 THE FUTURE OF THE INTERNATIONAL LEGAL ORDER 73–154 (R. Falk & C. Black eds. 1969) [hereinafter cited as *World Constitutive Process of Authoritative Decision*].

Predispositional Factors

Closely linked to the inadequacies of the institutional arrangements and practices in meeting the contemporary challenges for the defense and fulfillment of human rights are basic predispositional factors. In constant interaction with the environmental factors, the predispositional variables include the more fundamental demands, identifications and expectations of the peoples of the world. Too often and too intensely they continue to demand special interests at the expense of common interests. Their identifications are fragmented, testifying to the continuing vigor of the syndrome of national parochialism.[110] It is generally perceived that special interest demands will continue to pay off in the contemporary unorganized world arena without necessity for paying heed to long-term aggregate consequences.

As previously indicated, common demands for human dignity values have been rising on a world scale. Nevertheless, the actual patterns of demand vary in kind and in scope from community to community and from culture to culture. Many of the demands that are most intensely promoted are often less than comprehensive. Divided by the contending ideologies and systems of public order (especially in the wealth process), conditioned by many variations of parochialism, and oriented toward the calculation of short-term payoffs, the constellation of effective demands gives emphatic priority to the assertion of special interests in defiance of the common interests that give expression to human dignity values.

Attenuated conceptions of common interest are sustained by, and in turn foster, systems of identification that give primacy to national loyalties that fall short of embracing the whole of humankind. In a dynamically interactive world community, human beings cannot fail to be partially linked to one another and to many territorial and pluralized groups; and under various circumstances priorities may vary among different identities. At times conflicts of loyalty arise, especially when the claims of larger and smaller entities seem to be incompatible with one another. Although the accelerating pace of global intercourse would seem to pave the way toward greater identification with a universal vision and with realistic programs of common humanity, the countervailing trends associated with national parochialism retain their strength.[111]

---

110. *See* Lasswell, *Introduction: Universality versus Parochialism,* in M. McDougal & F. Feliciano, Law and Minimum World Public Order xix–xxvi (1961).

111. For detailed elaboration, *see* Lasswell, *Future Systems of Identity in the World Community,* in 4 The Future of the International Legal Order 3–31 (C. Black & R. Falk eds. 1972). *See also* Taylor, *Strangers in the World Community,* World, July 17, 1973, at 30-31.

It is often noted that in a world of growing communication and interdependence, the sharing of common sets of identifying symbols makes it possible for larger numbers of people to act together more quickly than ever before—even people possessing different backgrounds of culture, class, interest, personality, and crisis experience. The sheer fact of interaction does not signify the automatic expansion of primary identities from the national to the world community of humankind. In a divided world the increasing interdependence does not necessarily undermine parochialism during the initial period of contact. On the contrary, contacts with contrasting ways of life not infrequently enhance preoccupation with the self, as distinct from the other.[112] Interacting with and counteracting the trend toward universalization and inclusivity, the syndrome of parochialism, ultimately inherited from folk society, continues to flourish in the present epoch of nationalism and nation building. This syndrome is characterized by apprehensive expectations about the intentions and capabilities of strangers (aliens, others) and an intense demand to fight if required to defend the value position of the collective self.[113] In short, it appears that the identifications are characteristically ambivalent, simultaneously exhibiting both expanding and contracting identifications with the inclusive community. We refer to ourselves and others with labels (such as race, color) having no rational relation to basic humanity or to potential contributions to the common interest.

Fragmented identifications have been sustained and fortified by persisting expectations of violence and other coercions that are widely shared by leaders and the led.[114] Coercive expectations profoundly af-

---

112. Harold Isaacs observes:

> This fragmentation of human society is a pervasive fact in human affairs and always has been. It persists and increases in our own time as part of an ironic, painful, and dangerous paradox: the more global our science and technology, the more tribal our politics; the more universal our system of communications, the less we know what to communicate; the closer we get to other planets, the less able we become to lead a tolerable existence on our own; the more it becomes apparent that human beings cannot decently survive with their separateness, the more separate they become. In the face of an ever more urgent need to pool the world's resources and its powers, human society is splitting itself into smaller and smaller fragments.

H. Isaacs, Idols of the Tribe: Group Identity and Political Change 2 (1975).

113. *See* Lasswell, *supra* note 110, at xxi–xxvi.

114. *See generally* R. Barnet, The Roots of War (1972); 3 The Future of the International Legal Order (C. Black & R. Falk eds. 1971) ("Conflict Management"); G. Cochran, The War System (1965); R. Falk, Legal Order in a Violent World (1968); T. Gurr, Why Men Rebel (1970); C. Johnson, Revolutionary Change (1966); C. Leiden & K. Schmitt, The Politics of Violence: Revolution in the Modern World (1968); Law and Civil War in the Modern World (J. Moore ed. 1974); Lasswell, *The Garrison*

fect the pattern of cooperative activities implicated in the shaping and sharing of values. The expectation of violence is the assumption that, whether we like it or not, many conflicts are going to be settled by recourse to large-scale organized violence. It remains true in the world arena that the power elites do not expect to be as well off by making the sacrifices required to change the situation as they are by allowing it to continue. Perceiving the expectation of violence (and hence the institution of war) as a basic fact of life and knowing their own vulnerability, the effective elites are hypersensitive about openly initiating a change in world public order that would appear to subordinate them to other powers. Amid the unceasing anxieties of a global war system, with its popular socialization of risk, the balancing of police and military power continues to dominate policy.[115] The paramount objective of maintaining national security (freedom from external coercion and dictation) necessitates the perpetual appraisal and reappraisal of all social values and institutional practices with fighting effectiveness in view.[116] Many deprivations or nonfulfillments of human rights occur as a consequence of the general preoccupation with the real or imagined needs of national security and internal order.

The expectations of the peoples of the world differ markedly in the realism with which they perceive the conditions that affect the achievement of human dignity. Accustomed to calculations of short-term payoff rather than long-term aggregate consequences, the effective elites of the world, wittingly or unwittingly, share the perceptions of monopoly advantage by affording the rank and file only a minimal opportunity necessary to the maintenance of minimum order. Instead of clarifying and implementing common interests, people assert special interests that are destructive of the common interest. In sum, there is a failure in understanding—and taking seriously—the interdependences of the world social process.

INTERDEPENDENCES

The most striking fact about the global social process in which contemporary man pursues his basic values is in its comprehensive and ineradicable interdependences.[117] These interdependences are of two

---

State Hypothesis Today, in CHANGING PATTERNS OF MILITARY POLITICS (S. Huntington ed. 1962).

115. *See* Reisman, *Private Armies in a Global War System: Prologue to Decision,* in LAW AND CIVIL WAR IN THE MODERN WORLD 252–303 (J. Moore ed. 1974).

116. *See* H. LASSWELL, NATIONAL SECURITY AND INDIVIDUAL FREEDOM (1950).

117. Nearly two centuries ago, Kant wrote: "The intercourse, more or less close, which has been everywhere steadily increasing between the nations of the earth, has now ex-

distinct kinds: first, the interdependences of peoples transnationally within a particular value process; and second, the interdependences of peoples everywhere between different value processes. The growth of these various interdependences has established that if any peoples are to realize their values over time, these values must be achieved on a transnational scale. Sustained global interaction renders the stable existence and the quality of life of every individual dependent upon numerous factors operating beyond his local community and national boundaries and, hence, affecting what others can achieve.

The most decisive value process in the world community is the world *power* process, in which the state is still the predominant participant. How power is structured internally in a state—how the individual human being is related to centrally organized coercion—affects importantly how that state seeks to exercise power in the world arena, whether by violent or peaceful procedures. All too recent history makes it clear that elites who come to power and maintain internal rule by violence are also prone to regard violence as the principal instrument of change in

---

tended so enormously that a violation of right in one part of the world is felt all over it." I. KANT, PERPETUAL PEACE 142 (M. Smith trans. 1903).

In the words of Bloomfield and Bloomfield:

> What is interdependence? What do we mean when we use that word? Usually the emphasis is on economic relationships. But interdependence exists in other relationships as well—political, strategic, military, environmental and cultural. Indeed, some of the most difficult problems of our age are posed by the linkages between or among these relationships.

L. BLOOMFIELD & I. BLOOMFIELD, THE U.S., INTERDEPENDENCE AND WORLD ORDER 10 (1975) (Foreign Policy Association Headline Series No. 228).

For an eloquent statement on global interdependence, *see An Introduction by R. Buckminster Fuller,* in E. HIGBEE, A QUESTION OF PRIORITIES: NEW STRATEGIES FOR OUR URBANIZED WORLD xviii–xxxiv (1970). *See also* ASPEN INSTITUTE FOR HUMANISTIC STUDIES PROGRAM IN INTERNATIONAL AFFAIRS, COPING WITH INTERDEPENDENCE: A COMMISSION REPORT (1976); L. BROWN, THE INTERDEPENDENCE OF NATIONS (1972) (Foreign Policy Association Headline Series No. 212); M. CAMPS, THE MANAGEMENT OF INTERDEPENDENCE: A PRELIMINARY VIEW (1974); R. COOPER, THE ECONOMICS OF INTERDEPENDENCE: ECONOMIC POLICY IN THE ATLANTIC COMMUNITY (1968); A DECLARATION OF INTERDEPENDENCE: AN AMERICAN RESPONSE TO NEW GLOBAL IMPERATIVES (1976) (a program of The World Affairs Council of Philadelphia for the Bicentennial Era: 1976–1989); A. ETZIONI, THE ACTIVE SOCIETY: A THEORY OF SOCIETAL AND POLITICAL PROCESSES 553–78 (1968); Cooper, *Economic Interdependence and Foreign Policy in the Seventies,* 24 WORLD POLITICS 159 (1972); Katzenstein, *International Interdependence: Some Long-Term Trends and Recent Changes,* 29 INT'L ORG. 1021 (1975); Keohane & Nye, *International Interdependence and Integration,* 8 HANDBOOK OF POLITICAL SCIENCE 363–414 (F. Greenstein & N. Polsby eds. 1975); Morse, *The Politics of Interdependence,* 23 INT'L ORG. 311 (1969); Rosecrance & Stein, *Interdependence: Myth or Reality?,* 26 WORLD POLITICS 1 (1973); Waldheim, *Toward Global Interdependence,* SATURDAY REV./WORLD, Aug. 24, 1974, at 63–64 *et seq.;* Waltz, *The Myth of National Interdependence,* in THE INTERNATIONAL CORPORATION: A SYMPOSIUM 205–23 (C. Kindleberger ed. 1970).

the external arena. Complementarily, their intimidated masses are all too ready to turn their repressed and accumulated hatreds against their fellow men across some arbitrary boundary line.[118] Conversely, the respect for individual human dignity which even a democratic state is able to maintain is in large measure a function of the state's position in an inclusive world arena. When expectations of violence and war are high, the requirements of self-preservation may move even the best-intentioned individuals and groups toward a garrison police state, which carries with it wholesale trampling of human rights. On examination it is apparent that the power of every state or transnational political party is tied to the changing levels of discontent in the emerging nations as well as in the "internal proletariat" of the historic powers. In an earth-space arena in which humankind is intimidated and threatened by mass destructive means, and in which state elites are so obsessed by expectations of impending violence that they calculate every proposed measure of cooperation about wealth, enlightenment, or other values in terms of possible effects on fighting power and defense capability, it takes no great insight to know that no people can be fully secure unless all peoples are secure.

The world *wealth* process manifests a similarly high degree of interdependence.[119] No contemporary state can achieve or sustain a desired level of economic activity as a self-sufficient unit: it needs and seeks

---

118. Franz Alexander offered this incisive analysis:

> A peculiarly vicious circle in socio-dynamics can be observed here. An authoritarian state is created which deprives its citizens of self-expression in the interests of economic competition with other nations. This injury to self-esteem requires aggressive action and war becomes an inevitable compensation. Diplomatic victories achieved by compromise no longer suffice, for the heroic life of conquest and domination for their own sake and the myth of the superior race are incompatible with anything but martial victory. In order to make some compensation to those who have lost their normal means of self-expression, the ideology of the victorious super-race was invented. This was an appeal to the destructive emotional forces in human nature, especially hate, which had been simmering for years in an impoverished and overdisciplined people who had been forced to sacrifice butter for guns, individual expression for cringing subordination, self-esteem for awe, and conscience for blind obedience. This hate was generated in the barracks under the sadistic drill of the sergeants, in the factories by the abolition of recently acquired political rights, in a demoralized middle-class which had sunk to the level of the proletariat and needed someone to look down upon as inferior. The awakened Frankenstein's monster of hate must move against the rest of humanity to save the Fuhrer and his small camarilla from destruction. Hate once mobilized knows no barriers and cares little who are its victims. If an object is lacking, it may even react against the hater himself and occasion suicide.

F. ALEXANDER, *supra* note 89, at 268–69.

119. For an exposition of economic interdependence, see RIO, *supra* note 67, at 43–45. For interdependencies between development policies, *see* UNITED NATIONS, DEP'T OF ECO-

resources, skill, labor, goods, and markets beyond its borders. The unsettling impact precipitated by the energy crisis continues to reverberate around the globe after the gradual subsidence of the initial shock.[120] The economic cycle is global in its impact: depression or protracted recession in any significant area of the world makes it correspondingly difficult in all other areas to maintain high levels in the production and sharing of goods and, hence, in the conditions under which liberty and human personality can fourish. The economic welfare of the peasant, the farmer, the factory worker, as of every category of producer, is affected by the fluctuating level of prices at the principal trading centers and especially by the rise and fall of the dollar, the pound, and other mone-

---

NOMIC AND SOCIAL AFFAIRS, CONTINUITY AND CHANGE: DEVELOPMENT AT MID-DECADE 11-14, U.N. Doc. ST/ESA/25 (1975) (comments and recommendations of the Committee for Development Planning). *See* note 117 *supra;* Rose, *Third World "Commodity Power" Is a Costly Illusion,* FORTUNE, Nov. 1976, at 147-50.

120. Michael Field characterizes the oil crisis unfolding during the weekend of Oct. 6-7, 1973, as the "twelve days that changed the world." M. FIELD, A HUNDRED MILLION DOLLARS A DAY 9 (1975).

See M. ADELMAN, THE WORLD PETROLEUM MARKET (1972); THE WORLD ECONOMIC CRISIS (W. Bundy ed. 1975); B. COMMONER, THE POVERTY OF POWER: ENERGY AND THE ECONOMIC CRISIS (1976); C. CONCONCI, D. OSTERHOUT, & S. UDALL, THE ENERGY BALLOON (1974); G. CRAWLEY, ENERGY (1975); DIALOGUE ON WORLD OIL: HIGHLIGHTS OF A CONFERENCE ON WORLD OIL PROBLEMS (E. Mitchell ed. 1974); THE ENERGY QUESTION: AN INTERNATIONAL FAILURE OF POLICY (E. Erickson & L. Waverman eds. 1974); S. FREEMAN, ENERGY: THE NEW ERA (1974); HIGHER OIL PRICES AND THE WORLD ECONOMY: THE ADJUSTMENT PROBLEM (E. Fried & C. Schultze eds. 1975); R. GARDNER, THE WORLD FOOD AND ENERGY CRISES (1974); A. HAMMOND, W. METZ, & T. MAUGH II, ENERGY AND THE FUTURE (1973); N. JACOBY, MULTINATIONAL OIL: A STUDY IN INDUSTRIAL DYNAMICS (1974); J. MADDOX, BEYOND THE ENERGY CRISIS (1975); ENERGY AND DEVELOPMENT: PROCEEDINGS OF THE INTERNATIONAL CONFERENCE ON THE ECONOMICS OF ENERGY AND DEVELOPMENT (R. Mallakh & C. McGuire eds. 1974); R. MANCKE, THE FAILURE OF U.S. ENERGY POLICY (1974); L. MOSLEY, POWER PLAY: OIL IN THE MIDDLE EAST (1973); P. ODELL, OIL AND WORLD POWER: BACKGROUND TO THE OIL CRISIS (1975); ORGANIZATION FOR ECONOMIC CO-OPERATION AND DEVELOPMENT, ENERGY BALANCES OF OECD COUNTRIES, 1960-74 (1976); T. RIFAI, THE PRICING OF CRUDE OIL: ECONOMIC AND STRATEGIC GUIDELINES FOR AN INTERNATIONAL ENERGY POLICY (1974); L. ROCKS & R. RUNYON, THE ENERGY CRISIS (1972); A. SAMPSON, THE SEVEN SISTERS: THE GREAT OIL COMPANIES AND THE WORLD THEY MADE (1975); E. STEINBERG & J. YAGER, ENERGY AND U.S. FOREIGN POLICY (1974); T. SZULC, THE ENERGY CRISIS (1974); M. TANZER, THE ENERGY CRISIS: WORLD STRUGGLE FOR POWER AND WEALTH (1975); A TIME TO CHOOSE: AMERICA'S ENERGY FUTURE (Final Report by the Energy Policy Project of the Ford Foundation) (1974); UNITED NATIONS, DEP'T OF ECONOMIC AND SOCIAL AFFAIRS, PETROLEUM IN THE 1970s, U.N. Doc. ST/ECA/179 (1974); UNITED NATIONS, DEP'T OF ECONOMIC AND SOCIAL AFFAIRS, WORLD ECONOMIC SURVEY, 1975; FLUCTUATIONS AND DEVELOPMENT IN THE WORLD ECONOMY 23-27, U.N. Doc. E/5790/Rev. 1 (ST/ESA/49) (1976); THE OIL CRISIS (R. Vernon ed. 1976); M. WILLRICH, ENERGY AND WORLD POLITICS (1975); Barraclough, *The Great World Crisis I,* N.Y. REV. BOOKS, Jan. 23, 1975, at 20-29; Barraclough, *Wealth and Power: The Politics of Food and Oil,* N.Y. REV. BOOKS, Aug. 7, 1975, at 23-30.

tary units. The intricacies of global economic interdependences have been aptly described[121] as a "formidable agenda of complex, interrelated and well-nigh impossible questions:"

> They include nothing less than the reorganization of the international monetary system, the role of the dollar and special drawing rights and perhaps of gold, essential questions of multinational trade, trade blocks, incentives, preferences, reciprocity, tariff and nontariff barriers for both industrial and agricultural products, questions of government procurement and discrimination against foreign bidders, balance of payments, international investments, capital movements, fiscal policies, burden sharing of defense costs, harmonization of antipollution standards and regulations, and the operation and future of the multinational enterprise—plus many other collateral issues, and of course the question of the overall aid needed by the less-developed nations.[122]

Physical *well-being* depends upon the efficiency of the health services of the globe in spotting the origin of epidemics and in adopting measures to prevent their spread along the routes of traffic by land, sea, and air. Effective control of narcotics cannot be achieved merely by tight border surveillance and other internal measures—it requires transnational coordination and cooperation in coming to grips with all of the associated problems, including illicit production, manufacture, transport, sale, and use.[123] Polluted air and water know no national boundary. Hunger cannot be coped with without mobilizing the total food production and supply of the world.[124]

---

121. W. Oltmans, On Growth 478 (1974) (remarks by Aurelio Peccei, chairman of the Club of Rome).

122. *Id.* at 478–79.

123. *See generally* P. Lowes, The Genesis of International Narcotics Control (1966); Comments by Governments on the Draft Protocol on Psychotropic Substances, U.N. Doc. E/CN.7/525 (1969) (note by the secretary-general); The Prevention of Crime, *supra* note 16, at 2–3, 7, 12–15, 54; United Nations Office of Public Information, The United Nations and the Fight against Drug Abuse (1972); *The Drug Vigilantes,* Newsweek, Aug. 16, 1976, at 56–57; Fooner, *Cocaine: The South American Connection,* World, Feb. 27, 1973, at 22–26; *Latins Now Leaders of Hard-Drug Trade: Operators of Rings Supplying U.S. Virtually Immune from Prosecution,* N.Y. Times, Apr. 21, 1975, at 1, col. 1; *Argentine Filled Key Role in Latins' Drugs Network, id.,* Apr. 23, 1975, at 1, col. 6; *Lack of Treaties Hinders Drug Control Effort Here, id.,* Apr. 24, 1975, at 1, col. 4.

124. *See* The World Food Situation: Problems and Prospects to 1985 (J. Willett comp. 1976); UNWFC, Assessment of the World Food Situation—Present and Future, Rome, 5–16 November 1974, U.N. Doc. E/CONF.65/3 (1974) (staff report); UNWFC, Report of the World Food Conference, Rome, 5–16 November 1974, U.N. Doc. E/CONF.65/20 (1975). *See also* G. Borgstrom, Focal Points: A Global Food

With regard to *enlightenment,* accurate knowledge of other peoples' demands, identifications, and expectations and a clear understanding of worldwide interdependences are indispensable to rational decisions about security, power, and other values. No scientific or advanced educational enterprise can maintain its creativity or keep its integrity without keeping in touch with the transnational network of laboratories, periodicals, and books. The elite newspapers (or radio-TV programs) cover Washington, Moscow, and the other world capitals and create transnational expectations as a regular routine.[125] The broad category of professional intellectuals in each society can no longer comment accurately, usefully, and creatively on any aspect of a domestic scene without a thorough appreciation of the comprehensive global arena which affects and is affected by each of its component parts. The lay citizen, a role common to all, is increasingly alive to the fact that world events affect his life and that the mundane events of his immediate existence affect the world.

In a world of universalizing science and technology, new technologies and *skills* developed in one community have application far beyond its borders; they travel with the increasing tempo throughout the globe. Although there are recognized centers of creativity, no single state has the monopoly of innovation in technology and skill. Hence, programs for transfer of technology and skill (technical exchange or assistance) flourish.

As transnational mobility grows, families are widely dispersed across boundary lines for purposes of work, travel, or study; and the continuity of the family unit is influenced by speed of communication and visitation. Increasingly, especially among the elites in different sectors, the network of friendship (*affection*) is established transnationally, with circles of friends scattered in different parts of the globe. As the life styles of the elite everywhere in the world continue to converge, more and more people (top managers, engineers, scientists, public figures, and so on) appear to have more major contacts in the principal cities of the world than within the territorial communities to which they belong.

The crisis in *rectitude* does not stop at national borders. Much armed conflict about the world today exhibits a deep religious motivation. The ecumenical movement, with its zigs and zags, is global in scope.[126] To

---

STRATEGY (1973); G. BORGSTROM, THE FOOD AND PEOPLE DILEMMA (1974); L. BROWN & E. ECKHOLM, BY BREAD ALONE (1974); *International Law and the Food Crisis,* 1975 PROC., AM. SOC'Y INT'L L. 39–63 (1975); Note, *World Hunger and International Trade: An Analysis and a Proposal for Action,* 84 YALE L.J. 1046 (1975).

125. *See* J. MERRILL, THE ELITE PRESS: GREAT NEWSPAPERS OF THE WORLD (1968).

126. *See* chapter 11 *infra,* at notes 179–89 and accompanying text; *A World Council of Churches Founder Says the Ecumenical Movement Is Still Viable as a Religious Force,* N.Y. Times,

the devout Muslim the transnational pilgrimage to Mecca remains the crowning experience of this life. Indeed, a world public order of human dignity can be a feasible hope only if people's perspectives of responsibility are global in scope.

Finally, coming explicitly to the value of *respect* itself, recent scientific studies confirm the commonsense notion that the degree to which individuals are treated with simple human dignity affects all their responses, predisposing them either to violence, war, and revolution or to their utmost exertion in the peaceful production of values.[127] One of the major factors in world politics today, affecting every decision, is the accumulated resentment of countless millions of people, and even whole nations, arising from long-endured discriminations, deprivations, and humiliations—a resentment capable of being discharged against many targets, internal and external.[128] It may be recalled also that aggression, brutality, and violations of human dignity, such as devised by the Nazis, are as contagious as germs. Models of disrespect for human dignity anywhere in the world can be copied everywhere. It is not too much, therefore, to say in summary that because of man's deep, rising demands for consideration and because of all these interdependences, it is questionable whether a world half-slave and half-free can endure.

The ever-intensifying transnational interdependences *within* particular value processes are fully matched by the interdependences of peoples everywhere *between* value processes. In constant interaction with all other value processes, each particular process affects and is affected by the others.

Thus, the *power* of any participant in the world arena is obviously influenced by the levels of physical and mental *well-being* within its own community and in other communities. Since rational decision making is unattainable without access to a flow of comprehensive, dependable, and pertinent knowledge and information, the dependence of *power* upon the production and distribution of *enlightenment* is evident. The influence of *wealth* on *power* is indicated by the changing roles of industri-

---

May 11, 1975, § 1, at 35, col. 1; *id.*, Dec. 1, 1975, at 14, col. 4; *id.*, Oct. 21, 1975, at 39, col. 1. *See* TWENTIETH CENTURY THEOLOGY IN THE MAKING: 3, ECUMENICITY AND RENEWAL (J. Pelikan ed. 1971).

127. *See* the classic work: J. DOLLARD, FRUSTRATION AND AGGRESSION (1939). *See also* E. FROMM, ESCAPE FROM FREEDOM (1941); A. KARDINER, THE PSYCHOLOGICAL FRONTIERS OF SOCIETY (1945); H. LASSWELL, POWER AND PERSONALITY (1966); E. MAYO, THE SOCIAL PROBLEMS OF AN INDUSTRIAL CIVILIZATION (1945); H. SULLIVAN, CONCEPTIONS OF MODERN PSYCHIATRY (1947).

128. *See* H. LASSWELL, WORLD POLITICS AND PERSONAL INSECURITY 23–104 (1965). *See generally* O. KLINEBERG, THE HUMAN DIMENSION IN INTERNATIONAL RELATIONS (1964); R. WEST, INTERNATIONAL LAW AND PSYCHOLOGY (1974).

alism and the allocation of resources in the contemporary world, as exemplified by the dramatic upsurge of the influence on the part of OPEC countries in the wake of the global energy crisis.[129] The impact of *respect* on *power* has been cogently demonstrated by the postwar movements of decolonization and nation building. The breakdown of traditional systems of society has upset former respect relationships and engendered the respect revolution of our time. Intense demands for equality (not merely for nondiscrimination, but also for effective opportunities in the shaping and sharing of values) are widely distributed throughout the world community.[130] Demands for individual fulfillment are particularly pronounced wherever conditions favoring social mobility are found. The effect of *skill* is occasionally decisive and always significant. In modern polities the dissolution of traditional patterns of authority and control created vast audiences of conflict-ridden persons eager to find a new world view.[131] Hence specialists in mass communication are able to exploit their propaganda skills on behalf of nationalism, proletarianism, anarchism, and other rival ideologies. *Power* is, similarly, affected by the pattern of *affection* and loyalties in society. The component groupings in society often conflict with one another to control the sentiments of the individual. Excessive loyalty to the family or to the tribe, coupled with preoccupation with the fulfillment of family or tribal obligations, is a frequent barrier to modernization and national development.[132] Finally, *power* is modified by effective conceptions of *rectitude.* Unhappy recent events make it clear that confrontations and confusions in *rectitude* standards (*e.g.,* whether waging a particular war is morally just or unjust) can frustrate the fighting will and capability of a great power to conduct a war.[133]

---

129. *See* note 120 *supra.*

130. *See* Z. BRZEZINSKI, BETWEEN TWO AGES: AMERICA'S ROLE IN THE TECHNETRONIC ERA 111–15 (1970); H. GANS, MORE EQUALITY (1973); J. REES, *supra* note 67.

131. *See* THE EMERGING NATIONS: THEIR GROWTH AND UNITED STATES POLICY 3–90 (M. Millikan & D. Blackmer eds. 1961). *See generally* THE POLITICS OF THE DEVELOPING AREAS (G. Almond & J. Coleman eds. 1960); D. APTER, POLITICS OF MODERNIZATION (1965); C. BLACK, THE DYNAMICS OF MODERNIZATION: A STUDY IN COMPARATIVE HISTORY (1966); A. INKELES & D. SMITH, BECOMING MODERN: INDIVIDUAL CHANGE IN SIX DEVELOPING COUNTRIES (1974); D. LERNER, THE PASSING OF TRADITIONAL SOCIETY: MODERNIZING THE MIDDLE EAST (1958); M. LEVY, MODERNIZATION AND THE STRUCTURE OF SOCIETY: A SETTING FOR INTERNATIONAL AFFAIRS (1966); L. PYE, ASPECTS OF POLITICAL DEVELOPMENT (1966); MODERNIZATION: THE DYNAMICS OF GROWTH (M. Weiner ed. 1966).

132. For example, in traditional Chinese civilization family obligations frequently stood in rather direct opposition to impersonal administration. Another example is found in Burma. *See* L. PYE, POLITICS, PERSONALITY, AND NATION BUILDING: BURMA'S SEARCH FOR IDENTITY 177–86 (1962).

133. The antiwar movement against the involvement of the United States in the Vietnam War is a case in point. For the ambiguities of the legal, moral, and other issues

The distribution of *respect* in any society is affected by *power* factors. The alteration of *respect* relations in the course of social revolution is one of the conspicuous features of the process as a whole. The history of radical socialist and communist movements in modern times shows that the systematic inculcation of disrespect for the older generation, for the ruling classes, and for the law is a deliberate strategy of successful revolutionaries. After the seizure of power, active manifestations of contempt for the vestiges of the old regime are mobilized to consolidate the revolutionary order. It is evident on reflection and study that *respect* relations are deeply affected by the prevailing degree of *enlightenment.* The *respect* systems of the globe evolved under circumstances in which parochial assumptions about the past, present, and future were unchecked by broader perspectives. Many traditional biases have been sustained through generations simply because they have never been challenged by contradictory experience. *Wealth* has a profound influence on the structure of *respect* in the national communities and in the world community. Obviously, in many cultures the control of material instruments of production and consumption does not confer the highest claim to *respect.* However, with the rise and spread of modern methods of production, high premiums have been put upon the control of material resources. The distribution of *respect* is influenced by demonstrations of *skill.* Demonstrations of excellence in sports, in music, in arts, and in other spheres have modified some stereotyped derogatory images of national and ethnic groups. *Respect* is subject to changes rooted in *affection.* In an epoch of expanding nationalism, the older structures of *respect* are greatly modified as traditional barriers are relaxed and social intercourse is greatly simplified. The same process appears among co-revolutionaries and among those who come to share a positive tie with any collective symbols of identification. *Rectitude* factors enter into the patterning of *respect* relationships. The vision of common humanity, as projected by the great religions and philosophies, has been a driving force in the contemporary movement for human dignity and human rights.[134] Finally, we note that *respect* is affected by *well-being.* Apart from the state of health, physiological factors (*e.g.*, pigmentation) are continually seized upon to justify and guide the allocation of respect to the self and others.[135]

Enlightenment is affected by *power.* When the gathering and dissemination of information are in the hands of governments and political parties,

---

involved, *see* THE VIETNAM WAR AND INTERNATIONAL LAW (R. Falk ed. 1968–1976) (4 vols.). *See also* R. HULL & J. NOVOGROD, LAW AND VIETNAM (1968); J. MOORE, LAW AND THE INDO-CHINA WAR (1972).

134. *See* authorities cited in note 1 *supra,* especially BIRTHRIGHT OF MAN.

135. *See* chapter 9 *infra,* at notes 1–53 and accompanying text.

the content of the stream is decisively affected by power calculations. Totalitarian elites appraise and control every phase of the gathering, processing, and dissemination of information in terms of its political usefulness to them.[136] Besides power considerations, *enlightenment* is also influenced by *wealth.* Where the media of communication are owned and operated for private profit, characteristic distortions occur. News and editorial policy are greatly influenced by calculated interests in obtaining advertisement, promoting circulation, and cutting production costs.[137] Where the press is not monopolized, the competitive structure of the communications industry permits a great deal of freedom in news coverage and editorial outlook. Where competitive news gathering and dissemination are possible through these diversified channels, the result is likely to be a realistic public image. *Respect* factors affect the sources and interpretations of information. For instance, lower classes may be overlooked entirely as sources of information; contemptuous attitudes toward other peoples may result in gross distortions of reality.[138] An

136. *See* C. Friedrich & Z. Brzezinski, *supra* note 22, at 107–15.

137. As George Kennan sharply stated:

> [The] phenomenon of American advertising . . . has been permitted to dominate and exploit the entire process of public communication in our country. It is to be positively inconceivable that the whole great, infinitely responsible function of mass communication, including very important phases of the educational process, should be farmed out—as something to be mined for whatever profit there may be in it—to people whose function and responsibility have nothing to do with the truth—whose function and responsibility, in fact, are concerned with the peddling of what is, by definition, untruth, and the peddling of it in trivial, inane forms that are positively debauching in their effect on the human understanding. After the heedless destruction of natural environment, I regard this—not advertising as such, but the consignment to the advertiser of the entire mass communication process, as a concession to be exploited by it for commercial gain—as probably the greatest evil of our national life. We will not, I think, have a healthy intellectual climate in this country, a successful system of education, a sound press, or a proper vitality of artistic and recreational life, until advertising is rigorously separated from every form of legitimate cultural and intellectual communication. . . .

G. Kennan, Democracy and the Student Left 231–32 (1968).

See generally N. Johnson, How to Talk Back to Your Television Set (1970); J. Merrill & R. Lowenstein, Media, Messages and Men: New Perspectives in Communication 79–88 (1971); E. Turner, The Shocking History of Advertising (1953); Editors of the Atlantic Monthly, *The American Media Baronies,* The Atlantic, July 1969, at 82–86, *reprinted in* Sociology in the World Today 89–96 (J. Kinch ed. 1971).

138. As late as 1937, for example, some American officers were so biased against the Japanese that they kept reiterating the idea that the Japanese would never make first-class airplane pilots "because of their eyes." This was reminiscent of the appraisals made on the eve of the Russo-Japanese War by Russian officers.

Conversely, respect factors may work to give added resonance to realistic evaluation of the situation. When Herman Rauschning published his disillusioned estimate of the Nazis, much of its impact on official circles in Great Britain was not unrelated to the fact that the

important factor in *enlightenment* is the pattern of *skills* for obtaining and evaluating information. Given appropriate access, journalists are enabled to make indispensable contributions to the appraisal of national and world affairs.[139]

The role of journalistic skill becomes much less, however, when "curtains" descend and shut off the sources indispensable to the reporter. Positive and negative sentiments (*affection*) affect the sources and interpretations of information. It is notorious that love distorts an image in one direction, while hatred distorts it another way. The inculcation of group loyalties (and group enmities) results in the false perception of the target objects.[140] Finally, standards of *rectitude* affect the stream of intelligence available in national and world affairs. It is demonstrable that common codes of conduct affect the flow of intelligence in many direct and indirect ways. If the world itself is perceived as the scene of the triumph of evil over good, the result may be extreme pessimism about the political prospects of the righteous. By contrast, some communities emphasize the impending triumph of good and cast politics into a moralizing approach that maintains a tone in public life in which emphases upon difficulties or limitations are unwelcome, even if seriously proposed by competent observers.

The level of mental and physical *well-being* is influenced by *power* factors. Aside from the direct effect of destructive weapons, wars and other political crises tend to foster anxiety and to upset the personality equilibrium of the individual.[141] Health is influenced by national and world economic conditions (*wealth*). A striking demonstration of the impact of economic fluctuations and health is the relation between prosperity, depression, and suicide. There are direct correlations between high unemployment and the incidence of mental problems and suicide.[142] Health is also affected by the distribution of *enlightenment*.

---

author was no "mere journalist" or even a scholar, but a man with a substantial official career.

139. The role played by the press in the unfolding drama of Watergate is a vivid testimony. For insight into a team of reporters that played the key role, see C. BERNSTEIN & B. WOODWARD, ALL THE PRESIDENT'S MEN (1974).

140. *See* B. EPSTEIN & A. FORSTER, THE NEW ANTI-SEMITISM (1974); B. EPSTEIN & A. FORSTER, "SOME OF MY BEST FRIENDS . . ." (1962); O. KLINEBERG, *supra* note 128, at 3–57. *See also* G. ALLPORT, THE NATURE OF PREJUDICE (1958); PREJUDICE U.S.A. (C. Glock & E. Siegelman eds. 1969); M. HERSKOVITS, THE MYTH OF THE NEGRO PAST (1958); A. MONTAGU, MAN'S MOST DANGEROUS MYTH: THE FALLACY OF RACE (5th ed. 1974); G. SELZNICK & S. STEINBERG, THE TENACITY OF PREJUDICE: ANTI-SEMITISM IN CONTEMPORARY AMERICA (1969).

141. *See, e.g.,* C. LIMPKIN, THE BATTLE OF BOGSIDE (1972); W. VAN VORIS, VIOLENCE IN ULSTER (1975).

142. A recent congressional study for the Joint Economic Committee suggests that a significant number of suicides, deaths and murders from 1970 to 1975 were related to a

Modern efforts to control epidemics have frequently encountered local beliefs that have stood in the way of immediate success. Health is likewise influenced by the patterns of *respect.* Deprivations of respect (*e.g.,* the humiliation of failure resulting from bankruptcy or protracted unemployment) often lead the individual to turn his destructive tendencies against himself.[143] Health is directly affected by the world distribution of *skill*; this is particularly obvious among peoples who lack medical and sanitation experts. Health is also affected by whatever influences the congeniality of the immediate environment. The dependence of human beings on the continuing exchange of *affection* in intimate groups is a matter of fundamental importance for mental and physical health. Health is, finally, affected by the distribution of *rectitude* standards. One striking result of modern research on psychosomatic disorders has been the discovery of the frequent connection between illness and guilt. When the individual suffers from "guilt feelings," components of his personality are in conflict.

Wealth is affected by the world *power* process. The degree of concern about national security affects the armament race, and the burden of armaments is reflected in the degree to which the potential standard of living of the entire population is sacrificed. The speedy universalization of modern production patterns is due in no small measure to political factors.[144] *Enlightenment* affects the continuity and levels of economic life which were formerly dependent upon interactions that were poorly reported and, hence, inadequately understood. Today vast fact-gathering

---

sharp increase in unemployment in 1970. The study stresses that "actions which influence national economic activity—especially unemployment rate—have substantial bearing on physical health, mental health and criminal aggression. . . ." N.Y. Times, Oct. 31, 1976, § 1, at 1, col. 1.

See E. DURKHEIM, SUICIDE, A STUDY IN SOCIOLOGY (J. Spaulding & G. Simpson trans., G. Simpson ed. 1951); POVERTY AND MENTAL HEALTH (M. Greenblatt, P. Emery, & B. Glueck, Jr. eds. 1967); R. HURLEY, POVERTY AND MENTAL RETARDATION: A CAUSAL RELATIONSHIP (1970); POVERTY AND HEALTH: A SOCIOLOGICAL ANALYSIS (rev. ed. J. Kosa & I. Sola 1975).

143. This is affected by the values of a highly competitive society in which "strive and succeed" is the maxim and in which respect is accorded or withheld on the basis of success or failure. In Japanese civilization suicide is a well-established escape from situations in which honor is imperiled or lost. In the case of people who have been suddenly deprived of all self-respect and who are left impotent, aggressions may be directed against the self. *See* R. BENEDICT, THE CHRYSANTHEMUM AND THE SWORD: PATTERNS OF JAPANESE CULTURE 151, 166–68, 199–205 (1974).

144. The old elites of ancient civilizations (like China and Japan) tried to block the penetration of their territories by the products and the processes of the West. They failed, mainly because the governments of Western nations stood behind their traders, miners, and planters. It was superior coercive power that led to the comparatively rapid spread of modern technology throughout the globe.

agencies survey crop conditions, industrial output, employment, consumption standards, saving, investment, public revenue and expenditures, and related activities whose economic character is obvious. Under these circumstances the fluctuations in economic life are less unanticipated, and the effectiveness of measures of prevention and recovery can be continually appraised. *Respect* factors influence the direction and magnitude of economic activity. Advertising, through which consumer demand is managed,[145] relies largely on respect appeal.[146] And advertising is a major business function in a system of free private enterprise. The inventive exuberance of modern science and technology has not resulted in complete self-sufficiency for even the largest states. *Affection* influences wealth production and consumption. The importance of congenial human relationships upon the maintenance of high levels of productivity cannot be overemphasized.[147] A pervasive sense of alienation impedes productivity.[148] *Rectitude* also influences the economic process. Though not uncontroverted, the impact of "the Protestant ethic" on the evolution of modern capitalistic economies has gained wide recognition.[149] Finally, *well-being* also has an impact on wealth. The deviations from health to be found in a given population put an obvious limit upon the productive potential of the economy. Lack of physical vitality may also act as a drag on the growth of new levels of aspiration for goods and services.

In regard to *skill, power* relations play an influential and occasionally a decisive role. Power considerations have affected skill development in the areas most closely related to the balancing of power: the control of energy (nuclear and other). The correlation of total power with power over energy is very close. The overriding need of national security and the institution of war have led to the introduction and improvement of various skills and technologies, many of which have much wider application than to the specific tasks of fighting. *Skill* is affected by the state of *enlightenment*. Dramatic illustration of the significance of unrestricted intellectual exchange as the basis of scientific development has been

145. For a brilliant exposition of the management of specific consumer demand, see J. Galbraith, The New Industrial State 198–212 (2d ed. 1971). *See generally* E. Burton, Promise Them Anything: The Inside Story of the Madison Avenue Power Struggle (1972).

146. For instance, this is very much evident in cigarette advertising.

147. In his famous experiments, Elton Mayo made convincing demonstrations of the importance of the primary group upon output, as well as upon enjoyment in work. *See* E. Mayo, The Human Problems of an Industrial Civilization (1933).

148. *See* note 71 *supra.*

149. *See* M. Weber, The Protestant Ethic and the Spirit of Capitalism (T. Parsons trans. 1958).

provided by twentieth-century examples of the effect of censorship in the reduction of scientific "give and take." Censorship practices result in extensive scientific and cultural impoverishment.[150] *Wealth* affects the pattern and the pace of *skill* development. The development of modern techno-scientific culture requires the investment of vast sums. As the division of labor grows more complex, the skills connected with science, engineering, and management become more numerous and refined. Without a great economic base, it is impracticable for any community to keep pace with the evolution of the wealthier centers. *Respect* factors, too, modify the distribution of skills. The introduction of modern industrial society over the globe is affected by the respect patterns that prevail in many cultures and classes. It is notorious, for instance, that nomadic hunters and herders are averse to "demeaning" themselves by becoming "mere peasants" or "petty tradesmen." And in some cultures, manual skill has no place in the life of the intellectual.[151] The cultivation of meditative skill has been a principal feature of civilizations with strong internalizing trends.[152] Skills are modified by the prevailing patterns of *affection* and loyalties. The expansion of nationalistic sentiment has typically resulted in mobilizing the younger generation to serve the cause of national liberation and development. And the pursuit of modernization leads to the study of all the skills believed to be part of the culture of an advanced society. Finally, the development of *skill* is influenced by *rectitude* factors. In every known area of human experience, the enforce-

---

150. Censorship in the services of the Nazi orthodoxy culminated in the decisive decline of German science. State withdrawal of "non-Aryan" sources of enlightenment from the main stream of scientific communication seriously impaired research in such fields as psychology and physics, which could perforce resort to Freud and Einstein only by indirection. More serious results flowed from the increasing imposition of the practice of secrecy in research, stifling free exchanges among the German scientists.

In regard to such phenomena in contemporary Russia, *see* H. Smith, The Russians 361–68 (1976). Smith writes:

> Soviet science is hurt, they [Soviet scientists] said, by poor communications among Soviet scientists who are terribly compartmentalized. Normally it takes a year or two for new findings to get into scholarly journals, a process that in the West can be cut to weeks or days for important breakthroughs and thus speed scientific progress. The ferment and fast moving exchange of ideas prevalent in Western science, I was told, is largely absent in Soviet science.

Id. at 363.

151. In pre-Communist China the life of the scholarly official found no place for manual skill; hence it was difficult to give practical as well as theoretical training to engineers. The enormous prestige of passing literary examinations turned the energies of bright and ambitious young people toward sedentary reading, memorizing, and recalling.

152. Deference has thus gone to the withdrawn Holy Man.

ment of standards of orthodoxy or secrecy has been seen to be inimical to an untrammeled scientific development dependent upon a wide exchange of information.[153]

Affection is influenced by *power* factors. The power-balancing process in any arena often creates difficulties in the adjustment of loyalties and friendships to new conditions. The consequences of power for family life and friendship have often been reviewed, especially in their more tragic aspects. Military service reaches into the home and may disrupt family circles for a long period of time. We know, of course, of the perpetual complaint of those in high positions of authority and control who find themselves suffering from loneliness. *Affection* is influenced by the sources and content of *enlightenment.* The influence of information on the formation of attitudes has been studied from many points of view. The single most immediate factor that guides the sentiments of humankind is the limitations upon enlightenment that are very largely a function of parochialism. *Wealth* modifies the distribution of sentiment patterns. When traders and merchants are in no position to intimidate potential customers, they find that the cultivation of amicable relationships is good business.[154] *Respect* factors influence the distribution of *affection.* The narrowing effect of social class upon the permissible range of friendship and marriage are well known in all societies. *Skill* is a factor in the distribution of friendly attitudes. Many of the skills connected with modern science and technology are developed and applied by practitioners who identify with one another and keep in close association (within politically feasible limits). *Rectitude* is a factor shaping the distribution of *affection.* Worshiping the same god, especially in the same church or temple, helps to forge a tie of affection. Finally, *well-being* influences the distribution of *affection.* Tensions in world affairs and in human relations are caused in part by many neurotic, psychopathic, and

---

153. Medieval Christendom stifled a widespread development of learning under a variety of vicissitudes, not least of which was the suppression of "heresy." The reign of the Holy Inquisition did little to encourage the utilization of records of experience which diverged from the contemporary models of orthodoxy. Avicenna's and Averroes's interpretations of Aristotle were consigned to temporary oblivion; contact with the scientific achievements of the Arab world was fraught with danger; science could be equated with magic in the official mind; and scientific development languished in this atmosphere. In contrast, the neighboring Moslem civilization encouraged the unrestricted absorption of all available skill models—and witnessed a flourishing era of scientific development. The result was the development of eleventh-century Arab medicine, to take one example, to a height not reached by its European counterpart until the late Renaissance.

154. On the other hand, when markets can be obtained by force, the calculation of economic advantage may lead to an unfriendly attitude toward commercial rivals and a positive attitude toward partners.

even psychotic factors that operate in the lives of elites and members of the rank and file.[155]

Conceptions of *rectitude* frequently adjust themselves to the prevailing patterns of *power*. Power and rectitude myths are in constant interplay. Clearly, *enlightenment* based upon scientific methods of verification undermines traditional justifications of *rectitude* patterns. The search for standards of responsibility has led from theological doctrines to the growth of "man-centered" conception.[156] Economic relations (*wealth*) modify *rectitude* standards.[157] *Respect* factors influence the patterns of *rectitude*. The "internal proletariats" of great empires have been the cradles in which many new ideologies have taken root in the name of protests against injustice.[158] The propagandists of religious or secular cults have worked from the "top" when the upper elite has been judged to be strong enough to carry the whole community in their wake in case of

---

155. Historically, this has been most apparent in the lives of certain outstanding personages. The grandiosity or the suspiciousness of a ruler or of a ruling clique may bring about policies that provoke crises of such intensity that the result is disastrous. On the other hand, the "tendency to love masochistically" may carry with it an urge to give in to the aggressor; decision makers possessing such personality systems may temporize.

See generally K. HORNEY, THE NEUROTIC PERSONALITY OF OUR TIME (1937); K. HORNEY, OUR INNER CONFLICTS: A CONSTRUCTIVE THEORY OF NEUROSIS (1945); R. MAY, THE MEANING OF ANXIETY (1950).

156. *See generally* R. BAKER, THE DIGNITY OF MAN (1947); E. CASSIRER, THE INDIVIDUAL AND THE COSMOS IN RENAISSANCE PHILOSOPHY (M. Domandi trans. 1972); P. GAY, THE ENLIGHTENMENT: AN INTERPRETATION: 2, THE SCIENCE OF FREEDOM (1969); G. MIRANDOLA, ORATION ON THE DIGNITY OF MAN (A. Caponigri trans. 1956).

157. At one time, advocates of free world trade were confident that the way to a peaceful and prosperous world was by the expansion of commerce. It is true that the seller has a continuing interest in the buyer if he expects to do business with him again. And it is also true that the buyer is interested in sellers in order to maintain healthy price and quality competition. Traders are notoriously "broadminded" in the sense that "money talks" whether it comes from Christian or Jew, white man or black man, rich or poor. The common concern for a peaceful exchange has resulted in the holding of great fairs at accessible centers and the development of codes of conduct suitable to the perpetuation of the institution. Procedures of arbitration and settlement were devised to cover the many differences of claim between sellers and buyers. "Client nursing" is an ancient custom, and this means binding the prospect by catering to his whims and tastes, even when such whims and tastes are in many ways offensive to the traditional code in which the trader was reared.

For McNamara's theory of the close link between the level of violence and the level of poverty, *see* Rosenfeld, *Robert S. McNamara and the Wiser Use of Power*, WORLD, July 3, 1973, at 18, 24.

158. The "proletariat" in the sense described by Toynbee is recruited from the lower levels of the social structure and, therefore, includes those who suffer in physical health and who endure poverty and other experiences connected with a lowly status. But the accelerating factor appears to be connected in particular with respect considerations. An examination of the spread of the Christian cult in the Roman world indicates that it spread,

conversion. And social revolutions typically occur where the upper class is divided, having lost a unified sense of mission. Conceptions of *rectitude,* moreover, are continually modified by *skill* factors. Religious and moral sentiment have given rise to many works of art which have contributed to the consolidation of established orders. Conversely, factors of skill and taste have contributed to the undermining of entrenched codes. *Affection* factors also influence *rectitude* standards. It has often been assumed that the ties of a primary circle are the dominant ones and take precedence over such formal obligations as obedience to law. It is devotion to large secondary groups that creates a demand to act for their preservation and extension, and this becomes crystallized into rectitude standards by enlarging the established rectitude patterns to include the "true" interests of the lesser groups. Finally, it may be noted that the intensity with which considerations of *rectitude* enter into world and national affairs may be influenced by the mental health (*well-being*) of significant figures in decision process.

The facts outlined above clearly establish interdetermination on a global scale in the sense that everybody affects everybody else. The degree to which any particular individual can, in the long run, secure and maintain enjoyment in any particular value process is a function of the degree to which other individuals differentially situated about the globe can secure and maintain a corresponding enjoyment both in that process and other processes. No one can achieve security—when security is defined as high position, expectancy, and potential with regard to all values—unless others do.[159] When John Donne asked for whom the bell tolled, he rightly answered that it tolled for one and all alike.

INADEQUACIES IN INQUIRY: THE INTELLECTUAL CONFUSION ABOUT HUMAN RIGHTS

One of the most important of the many conditions affecting the transnational community's failures in securing the protection of human rights may be described as that of simple intellectual confusion.[160] Scholars and

---

in part, among persons of position who were disaffected with their society. Persons of lower status were greatly encouraged by recruits from the upper classes and found corroboration of their resentment against discrimination.

159. In a letter sent to the New York Times from Novosibirsk, U.S.S.R., in support of Andrei Sakharov, Victor D. Kurdin stressed: "If today you do not energetically put an end to aggression wherever it takes place and if you do not energetically support human rights of any person anywhere in the world—then, soon enough you'll have aggression and servitude in your homes." N.Y. Times, Aug. 22, 1976, § 4, at 16, col. 5.

160. Moskowitz has issued a formidable challenge:

> [I]nternational human rights is still waiting for its theoretician to systematize the thoughts and speculations on the subject and to define desirable goals. Intelligent

others charged with performance of the intelligence function have not adequately formulated the more fundamental problems or performed the necessary intellectual tasks for assisting in establishing and maintaining appropriate constitutive processes and public order policies. They have neither adequately clarified a common interest in the greater production and wider sharing of all human rights values nor created among community members the appropriate perceptions of such common interest. They have not met their responsibilities for clarifying and promoting the demands, identifications, and expectations among the peoples of the world which are an essential precondition of a public order of human dignity.

It is in the substantive definition of human rights that the greatest confusion and inadequacy prevail. Little effort has been made to create a comprehensive map of the totality of human rights, and there has been little discussion of the detailed content of particular rights.[161] Often even

---

> truisms do not necessarily add up to a theory. No one has yet arisen to draw together into a positive synthesis the facts and fancies which emerge daily from events of bewildering complexity and to carry on an authentic debate. International concern with human rights is still very much a theme begging for a writer. And the scholar has not yet appeared to redress the distortions through a calm and systematic application of facts, to ground abstractions in the specific, and to define the limits of discourse. In the absence of a definite body of doctrine, as well as of deeply rooted convictions, international human rights have been dealt with on the basis of the shifts and vagaries of daily affairs and of evocations of daily events. There is a great need for technical resources and ability to channel the facts to greater effect. Human rights as a matter of international concern is an untrodden area of systematic research. But still a greater need is for superlative virtuosity to deal with international human rights in their multiple human dimensions.

M. Moskowitz, 1968, *supra* note 1, at 98–99.

See also M. Moskowitz, 1974, *supra* note 1, at 1–37; Cohn, *A Human Rights Theory of Law: Prolegomena to a Methodology of Instruction,* in 4 René Cassin, *supra* note 1, at 31–60; Devall, *Social Science Research on Support of Human Rights,* in Comparative Human Rights, *supra* note 1, at 326, 329–33; Moskowitz, *Toward an Integrated Approach to International Human Rights,* in 4 René Cassin, *supra* note 1, at 61–68; Toth, *Les Droits de l'Homme et la Theorie du Droit,* in 4 René Cassin, *supra* note 1, at 69–90; Vegleris, *Preliminaire à la Methodologie des Droits de l'Homme,* 4 René Cassin, *supra* note 1, at 19–30.

161. The importance of definition is appropriately emphasized by Bilder: "The issue of definition is not trivial. For what we think human rights really are will inevitably influence not only our judgment as to which types of claims to recognize as human rights, but also our expectations and programs for implementation and compliance with these standards." Bilder, *supra* note 1, at 174.

Similarly, Walter Weyrauch writes:

> A difficulty with definitions, for example efforts to define universal human rights, might be that they purport to reveal something *essential* about the matter under consideration. Yet the definitions often fail to yield the clarification we thought was attainable. There is a tautological quality in many definitions, which in the last analysis

the very conception of human rights is left obscure. Sometimes no specification is offered of what is meant by human rights.[162] When specification is attempted, it commonly exhibits a broad range of confusions.[163] Sometimes human rights are conceived in terms of natural law absolutes and buttressed by transempirical justifications, both theological and metaphysical.[164] At other times human rights are confined to the demands which particular peoples make at particular times in their particular, unique communities.[165] Still again, human rights are often conceived as merely the rights which a particular system of law in a particular state in fact protects.[166] Sometimes this positivist conception is not even ex-

---

> can reduce them to cryptic circular statements—in our context, human rights are human rights. The reason may be in part that definitions, as well as more lengthy explanations, equate certain words with other groups of words.

Weyrauch, *On Definitions, Tautologies, and Ethnocentrism in Regard to Universal Human Rights*, in HUMAN RIGHTS, *supra* note 1, at 198.

162. *E.g.*, M. GANJI, *supra* note 1; L. SOHN & T. BUERGENTHAL, *supra* note 1; V. VAN DYKE, *supra* note 1.

163. In the words of Maurice Cranston: "Human rights is a twentieth-century name for what has been traditionally known as natural rights or, in a more exhilarating phrase, the rights of man. Much has been said about them, and yet one may still be left wondering what they are." M. CRANSTON, *supra* note 1, at 1.

Similarly, Claude observes:

> [T]he scope of the field of human rights remains in dispute. Must the expression of a human need be translated into a legally enforceable claim before we can properly call it a right? Is a legal demand entitled to the designation of human right only if we can somehow philosophically justify it in terms of human dignity? We do not believe such difficult questions need to be finally answered before enlisting the term, human rights, as a worthy generic title for cross-national comparative study of various moral and politico-legal claims.

Editor's Introduction, in COMPARATIVE HUMAN RIGHTS, *supra* note 1, at 71-72.

For a diversity of perspectives, *see* HUMAN RIGHTS: COMMENTS AND INTERPRETATIONS (UNESCO ed. 1949); Bilder, *supra* note 1, at 173-76. *See also* Edel, *Some Reflections on the Concept of Human Rights,* in HUMAN RIGHTS, *supra* note 1, at 1; Nagel, *The Social Consequences of Basic Legal Rights,* in *id.* at 306; Pollack, *What Are Human Rights?* in *id.* at 82; Weyrauch, *supra* note 161.

164. *See* M. CRANSTON, WHAT ARE HUMAN RIGHTS? 36 (1962); Bilder, *supra* note 1, at 173; Castberg, *Natural Law and Human Rights: An Idea-Historical Survey,* in NOBEL SYMPOSIUM ON HUMAN RIGHTS, *supra* note 1, at 13-14 [hereinafter cited as Castberg]. *See also* Blackstone, *The Justification of Human Rights,* in HUMAN RIGHTS, *supra* note 1, at 90-103; De Cervera, *Natural Law Restated: An Analysis of Liberty,* in *id.* at 55-79; Edel, *Some Reflections on the Concept of Human Rights,* in *id.* at 1-13.

165. In the words of Cranston: "A right presupposes a claim; if the claim is not made, the question of right does not arise." M. CRANSTON, *supra* note 1, at 81. *See* Doyle, *Personal Claims, Human Rights, and Social Justice,* in HUMAN RIGHTS, *supra* note 1, at 38-39; Edel, *supra* note 164, at 6-9.

166. *See* M. CRANSTON, *supra* note 1, at 4-7; P. DROST, *supra* note 1, at 11-13, 39; Bilder, *supra* note 1, at 173-74.

tended to all individual rights, but is limited only to certain specified rights distinguished by arbitrary criteria.[167] Characteristically, the particular rights regarded as human rights are not explicitly related to the value features and institutional features of social process, and no procedures are specified for ascribing an empirical reference to the different categories of rights.[168] Human rights are, further, often discussed as operative within a national or subnational context, without appropriate reference being made to any relevant larger community context, global or regional. Similarly, it is not always recognized that the honoring of certain rights may require limitations of other rights. No intellectual procedures are devised, much less employed, for calculating the costs and benefits in terms of value consequences of a particular option in decision. The assumption is far too common that inherited technical, legal terms for the description of human rights can carry a reasonably precise and consistent empirical reference ascertainable by all.

The principal focus of attention, in a vast literature, has been upon what is called the problem of implementation.[169] Even upon this problem, however, the range of alternatives considered has been highly partial and fragmented. The major emphasis in most recommendations for improvement in implementation has been upon isolated features of rule and procedure, without appropriate relation to the larger processes of effective and authoritative power which condition the impact of all changes in rules and procedures. The literature affords little recognition of the comprehensive, interpenetrating constitutive processes (global, regional, national, local) which identify authoritative decision makers, specify basic community policies, establish necessary structures of authority, allocate bases of power, authorize appropriate procedures, and make provision for many different, indispensable types of decisions.[170]

---

167. Cranston contends that economic and social rights are not "universal human rights" since they "cannot be transformed into positive rights" for failing "the test of practicability." M. CRANSTON, *supra* note 1, at 54, 66. For his detailed argument, *see id.* at 65–71. *See also* Cranston, *Human Rights, Real and Supposed,* in POLITICAL THEORY AND THE RIGHTS OF MAN 43–53 (D. Raphael ed. 1967).

168. It could be suggested that even the emphasis on "rights" is a misleading focus since that suggests a reference only to an application of law in a particular instance. A comprehensive perspective must require a concern not merely for application but for all the other functions (prescription, intelligence, promotion, invocation, appraisal, and termination) of the constitutive process of authoritative decision. A more relevant term might be "human interest" if interests are conceived as demands for values plus supporting expectations about the conditions under which such demands can be secured and fulfilled.

169. *See, e.g.,* J. CAREY, *supra* note 1; M. GANJI, *supra* note 1; E. HAAS, *supra* note 1; M. MOSKOWITZ, 1974, *supra* note 1; A. ROBERTSON, *supra* note 1; L. SOHN & T. BUERGENTHAL, *supra* note 1; V. VAN DYKE, *supra* note 1.

170. *See* note 169 *supra.*

Similarly, very little effort has been made to inquire into the processes of effective power that establish and maintain such constitutive processes and, hence, into how the predispositions of effective elites may be managed to cause them to demand or accept the changes in constitutive processes necessary to the better protection of human rights.

The failure of inquiry, with regard to both the definition of substantive content and the implementation of human rights, to adopt a configurative, problem-solving approach, employing all relevant intellectual skills, is as conspicuous as it is unfortunate.[171] In the absence of an explicit relation of particular rights to specific value processes and of a comprehensive conception of global constitutive processes, it has not been possible to formulate problems precisely in terms either of factual disparities in the achievement of demanded values or of rational and available options in effecting improvements in decision. This failure in the appropriate formulation of problems has in turn made difficult the performance of the various intellectual tasks of relevant inquiry. There has been little successful effort to postulate and clarify basic general community policies at all the necessary levels of abstraction or to devise and employ appropriate principles of content and procedure for relating high-level abstractions to the unique circumstances of particular instances of application. The description of past trends in decision has been highly anecdotal rather than in terms of approximation to clarified policies, permitting little effective comparison of successes and failures at different times and places. Performance of the scientific task of identifying the factors affecting decision has built more upon intuition than upon systematic inquiry about both environmental and predispositional variables. Anticipations of the future have consisted more of pessimistic forebodings and utopian fantasies than of disciplined developmental constructs, designed to promote creativity in the choice of decision options. As indicated above, the invention and evaluation of alternatives in process and decision have been—because of all these underlying failures in performance—most limited and halting, confined to relatively few of the many features of effective power and constitutive process.

For a more detailed exposition of the inadequacies in intellectual in-

171. The overriding emphasis is on logical derivation. This reflects the legacy of the major traditional jurisprudential approaches. *See generally* E. Bodenheimer, Jurisprudence: The Philosophy and Method of the Law (rev. ed. 1974); A. Brecht, Political Theory: The Foundations of Twentieth Century Political Thought (1959); H. Cairns, Legal Philosophy from Plato to Hegel (1949); W. Friedmann, Legal Theory (5th ed. 1967); C. Friedrich, The Philosophy of Law in Historical Perspective (2d. ed. 1963); G. Paton, A Textbook of Jurisprudence (4th ed. 1972); 1 R. Pound, Jurisprudence (1959) [hereinafter cited as R. Pound]; G. Sabine, A History of Political Theory (3d ed. 1961); J. Stone, Human Law and Human Justice (1965).

quiry which appear importantly to have conditioned the general community's failures in achievement of human rights, we make reference to the unique emphases about and contributions to human rights theory proffered by certain major jurisprudential approaches.

The Natural Law Approach

The natural law approach begins with the assumption that there are natural laws, both theological and metaphysical, which confer certain particular rights upon individual human beings.[172] These rights find their authority either in divine will or in specified metaphysical absolutes. The natural law constitutes a "higher law" which is "the ultimate standard of fitness of all positive law, whether national or international";[173] decisions by state elites which are taken contrary to this law are regarded as mere exercises of naked power.

The great historic contribution of the natural law emphasis has been in the affording of this appeal from the realities of naked power to a higher authority which is asserted to require the protection of individual rights.[174] The observational standpoint assumed by those who take this

---

172. *See* C. Becker, The Declaration of Independence 24–79 (1942); A. Passerin d'Entreves, Natural Law: An Introduction to Legal Philosophy 51–64 (2d ed. 1970); J. Maritain, Man and the State 76–107 (1951); J. Maritain, *supra* note 1; 4 R. Pound, *supra* note 171, at 61; D. Ritchie, Natural Rights (1895) [hereinafter cited as D. Ritchie]; H. Rommen, The Natural Law, A Study in Legal and Social History and Philosophy (T. Hanley trans. 1948) [hereinafter cited as H. Rommen]; L. Strauss, Natural Right and History (1953); Midgley, *Natural Law and Fundamental Rights,* 21 Am. J. Juris. 144 (1976).

For the classic exposition of the impact of natural law upon the American Declaration of Independence and the United States Constitution, *see* E. Corwin, The Higher Law Background of American Constitutional Law (1955) [hereinafter cited as E. Corwin].

In the words of Jacques Maritain:

> The human person possesses rights because of the very fact that it is a person, a whole, master of itself and of its acts, and which consequently is not merely a means to an end, but an end, an end which must be treated as such. The dignity of the human person? The expression means nothing if it does not signify that by virtue of natural law, the human person has the right to be respected, is the subject of rights, possesses rights. There are things which are owed to man because of the very fact that he is man.

J. Maritain, *supra* note 1, at 65.

173. H. Lauterpacht, 1950, *supra* note 1, at 74. Castberg writes: "There is one eternal and immutable law, which will apply to all peoples at all times. God is the source of this law." Castberg, *supra* note 164, at 14.

174. Ritchie offered this observation nearly a century ago:

> The appeal to natural rights, which has filled a noble place in history, is only a safe form of appeal if it be interpreted, as just explained, as an appeal to what is socially

approach has commonly been that of identification with the whole of humanity. A principal emphasis has been upon a common human nature that implies comparable rights and equality for all. For many centuries this approach has been an unfailing source of articulated demand and of theoretical justification for human rights. Its preeminent contribution to both constitutional and international law, and especially to the protection of individual rights within these interpenetrating processes of authoritative decision, has been many times recorded.[175]

The principal inadequacies of the natural law approach stem from its conception of authority.[176] When authority is conceived in terms of divine will or metaphysical absolutes, little encouragement is given to that comprehensive and selective inquiry about empirical processes which is indispensable to the management of the variables that in fact affect decision.[177] It is not to be expected, further, that scholars and decision makers, whose primary concern is to put into effect on earth either divine will or the import of transcendental essences, will devote much attention to the formulation of human rights problems in terms of the shaping and sharing of values or to the location of such problems in the larger community processes which affect their solution. Similarly, the establishment of the most basic, overriding, and abstract goals of the community by the use of exercises in faith, rather than by the empirical exploration of common interest, can only provoke the assertion of different, and perhaps opposing, goals by those who profess a different faith.

> useful, account being taken not only of immediate convenience to the existing members of a particular society, but of the future welfare of the society in relation, so far as possible, to the whole of humanity.

D. Ritchie, *supra* note 172, at 103. *See also* E. Corwin, *supra* note 172, at 20.

175. *See* E. Bodenheimer, *supra* note 171, at 57–59; E. Corwin, *supra* note 172; H. Lauterpacht, 1950, *supra* note 1, at 94–141.

176. *See generally* C. Becker, The Heavenly City of the Eighteenth Century Philosophers (1932); A. Passerin d'Entreves, *supra* note 172; L. Fuller, The Morality of Law (rev. ed. 1969); H. Rommen, *supra* note 172; Chroust, *On the Nature of Natural Law*, in Interpretations of Modern Legal Philosophies 70–84 (P. Sayre ed. 1947); Northrup, *Naturalistic and Cultural Foundations for a More Effective International Law*, 59 Yale L.J. 1430 (1950).

177. *See* M. Cranston, *supra* note 1, at 13. In the words of Ritchie:

> And the voice of God and Nature in the heart of every mortal is thought of as a universal revelation: it professes to mean, not what any chance person happens to feel, but what approves itself to calm, reflective reason, and what can be shown to be in accordance with the essential nature of things.

D. Ritchie, *supra* note 172, at 86.

The intellectual task most relied upon in the natural law approach is syntactic derivation.[178] Though appropriate concern is exhibited for the establishment and clarification of goals, the method by which clarification is sought for decision in particular instances is not by the disciplined, systematic employment of a variety of relevant intellectual skills, but rather by derivation from postulated norms achieved by techniques such as the revelation of divine will, messages obtained by consultation of oracles or entrails, transcendental cognition of absolutes, and participation in natural reason.[179] In a frame of reference so inexplicitly and anecdotally related to human choice and empirical decision, it would be incongruous to expect more than a modest orientation toward the other intellectual tasks—such as the descriptive, scientific, predictive, and inventive—which are required for effective inquiry and rational decision. The abiding difficulty with the natural law approach is that its assumptions, intellectual procedures, and modalities of justification can

---

178. This emphasis pervades, for example, HUMAN RIGHTS, *supra* note 1.

For an example of a natural law approach fused with linguistic analysis, *see* Hart, *Are There Any Natural Rights?* in HUMAN RIGHTS 61–75 (A. Melden ed. 1970). *See* H. HART, THE CONCEPT OF LAW 181–207 (1961). For criticism of Hart from another natural law perspective, *see* L. FULLER, *supra* note 176, at 184–86.

179. For an excellent demonstration of the irrelevance of philosophical derivation, see Munster, *A Critique of Blackstone's Human Right and Human Dignity,* in HUMAN DIGNITY, *supra* note 1, at 65–94, especially at 65, 70.

Rights considered to be natural differ widely from author to author, depending upon their conceptions of nature. In the words of Ritchie: "The words 'nature' and 'natural' are constantly bandied about in controversy as if they settled quarrels, whereas they only provoke them by their ambiguity." D. RITCHIE, *supra* note 172, at 20.

Similarly, Patterson observed:

> The ambiguity of 'nature' has been the chief source of the fertility of natural law theories. Sometimes nature is physical nature in general, either as a model of the kind of order, stability and universality which men should seek to attain in their political laws. . . . , or as a part of man's environment setting inexorable limitations upon what human laws can do. . . . Sometimes nature has meant the biological make-up of man, as in Ulpian's famous passage.

E. PATTERSON, JURISPRUDENCE: MEN AND IDEAS OF THE LAW 362 (1953).

Patterson continued: "The peculiarly human attributes or qualities of man are the ones which most natural-law theories refer to and rely upon. Now men have long differed as to the basic traits of human nature, and assumptions about human nature often give a natural-law theory its basic slant." *Id.* at 363.

Hugo Grotius is "said to have marked the transition from the metaphysical to the rationalist natural law." H. ROMMEN, *supra* note 172, at 70.

Insofar as natural lawyers purport to build upon the nature of man and to use scientific inquiry to ascertain the nature of man, we would not quarrel. The difficulty is that too many natural lawyers tend to ground their concepts of authority in theological or metaphysical sources.

be employed equally by the proponents of human dignity and the proponents of human indignity in support of diametrically opposed empirical specifications of rights, and neither set of proponents has at its disposal any means of confirming the one claim or of disconfirming the other.[180]

THE HISTORICAL APPROACH

In the frame of reference known as the "historical approach" human rights are conceived in terms of the factual demands of community members for participation in different value processes. This approach finds "authority" in the finite perspectives—the "living law"—of the members of a particular community and emphasizes that the human rights demanded and protected within any given community are a function of many cultural and environmental variables unique to that community.[181]

The major contribution of the historical approach has been to provide a framework of theory for the realistic and contextual examination of particular situations in which the degree of protection of human rights is under challenge or at stake. It has stressed the importance of the time and space dimensions of human rights problems and afforded knowledge of trends in degrees of realization through time and in different communities. It has also presented a modest, preliminary approximation of the causal analysis that is characteristic of social science.

The principal difficulty with the historical approach has been in the almost total immersion of inquiry within an undifferentiated community process. Some exponents of this approach do not distinguish the demands of the individual human being from the demands made in the name of the aggregate of community members. Further, many propo-

---

180. Ritchie wrote:

> And all abstract theories about human society admit of divergent and conflicting application. Thus the theory of social contract is used by Hobbes to condemn rebellion, and by Locke to justify it. The conception of social organism is used by Plato to justify the extremist interference with individual liberty, and by Mr. Herbert Spencer to condemn a very moderate amount of State control. And so the theory of natural rights is used by Anarchists to condemn the existing inequalities of social conditions, and by Conservatives to check attempts on the part of governments to remedy these inequalities. . . .

D. RITCHIE, *supra* note 172, at 14–15. *See* A. ROSS, ON LAW AND JUSTICE 261–62 (1959); L. STRAUSS, *supra* note 172, at 185–86.

181. *See* J. CARTER, LAW: ITS ORIGIN, GROWTH, AND FUNCTION (1907); H. MAINE, ANCIENT LAW (1963); R. POUND, INTERPRETATIONS OF LEGAL HISTORY (1923); 1 R. POUND, *supra* note 171, at 8–87; P. VINOGRADOFF, OUTLINES OF HISTORICAL JURISPRUDENCE (1920–22); Kantorowicz, *Savigny and the Historical School of Law*, 53 LAW Q. REV. 326 (1937).

nents do not isolate the authoritative decision or constitutive process from the whole flow of particular choices by which values are shaped and shared in the community. Thus, it is sometimes said that the collectivity has "a real mind, a real will and a real power of action"[182] and that the rights of the individual find expression only through this collectivity. The individual is subsumed within the state and has no rights apart from the state.[183] Similarly, authority is often found not so much in the actual perspectives of particular community members about the course of future decision as in some mythical *geist,* which is said to emanate out of the people like language, religion, poetry, and music, and to be unique to every community.[184]

The deep and pervasive determinism in the historical approach has made difficult the adequate performance of all the relevant intellectual tasks. The deference to mysterious and ineluctable social forces is completely inimical to deliberate postulation and detailed clarification of policies about human rights. Sole emphasis upon the demands of community members as the empirical content of human rights ignores the fact that individuals may be conditioned to demand even the values of human indignity. The not infrequent assertion that the individual achieves his rights only through the state ignores the point that states

---

182. G. Paton, *supra* note 171, at 414.

Maitland offered this summation of Gierke's group theory:

> [O]ur German Fellowship is no fiction, no symbol, no piece of the State's machinery, no collective name for individuals, but a living organism and a real person, with body and members and a will of its own. Itself can will, itself can act; it wills and acts by the men who are its organs as a man wills and acts by brain, mouth and hand. It is not a fictitious person; it is a *Gesammtperson,* and its will is *Gesammtwille;* it is a group-person, and its will is a group-will.

Translator's Introduction, in O. Gierke, Political Theories of the Middle Age xxvi (F. Maitland trans. 1900). Maitland's introduction is an excellent account of Otto Von Gierke's theory of group personality and group association. *See id.* at vii–xiv.

For further elaboration of Von Gierke's theory, *see* S. Mogi, Otto Von Gierke: His Political Teaching and Jurisprudence 107–221 (1932); G. Paton, *supra* note 171, at 414–19; 1 R. Pound, *supra* note 171, at 313–18; Coker, *Pluralistic Theories and the Attack upon State Sovereignty,* in A History of Political Theories: Recent Times 80, 89–98 (C. Merriam & H. Barnes eds. 1924). *See generally* O. Von Gierke, The Development of Political Theory (B. Freyd trans. 1939); O. Von Gierke, Natural Law and the Theory of Society, 1500–1800 (E. Barker trans. 1934).

183. The historical approach is highly nationalistic in perspective. *See* McDougal, Lasswell, & Reisman, *Theories about International Law: Prologue to a Configurative Jurisprudence,* 8 Va. J. Int'l L. 188, 230–33, 241 (1968) [hereinafter cited as McDougal, Lasswell, & Reisman]. *See also* 1 F. Savigny, System of the Modern Roman Law 68–72 (W. Holloway trans. 1867).

184. *See* C. Allen, Law in the Making 87–151 (7th ed. 1964); D. Lloyd, The Idea of Law 251–55 (1964); F. Savigny, *supra* note 183, at 16–17.

may be in varying degree totalitarian, and that, even in a public order of human dignity, the accommodation of the rights of the individual with the rights of the groups of which he is a member is a difficult and delicate task. In the absence of a clear focus upon authoritative decision, as both affecting and being affected by specific value processes, the spokesmen of the historical approach have devised a largely anecdotal method which fails to perform the historical, much less the scientific, task. An approach so deeply passive could hardly be expected to muster the courage to undertake the tasks of deliberately forecasting decisions or of inventing new policy options. The emphasis, finally, upon the uniqueness of every community vastly underplays the universal character of problems of human rights and tends to minimize the importance of transnational concern for and experience with the protection of these rights.

The Positivist Approach

The positivist approach assumes that the most important measure of human rights is to be found in the authoritative enactment of a system of law sustained by organized community coercion.[185] Within this approach authority is found in the perspectives of established officials, and any appeal to a "higher law" for the protection of individual rights is regarded as utopian or at least as a meta-legal aspiration.[186] The explicit emphasis is upon the institutions of the modern state, and it is inspired by and inflated with exaggerated notions of sovereignty. It is this viewpoint whose champions have most strenuously insisted that only nation-states, and not individual human beings, are appropriate subjects of international law.[187]

The great contribution of the positivists has been in recognizing the importance of bringing organized community coercion, the state's established processes of authoritative decision, to bear upon the protection of

---

185. P. Drost, *supra* note 1; H. Lauterpacht, 1950, *supra* note 1, at 75.

Positivists base "obligation simply upon the external authority of the State. In this 'sophistic' theory, custom or usage becomes explicit as the mere arbitrary will of the sovereign." D. Ritchie, *supra* note 172, at 85.

186. *See* J. Austin, The Province of Jurisprudence Determined and the Uses of the Study of Jurisprudence (1954) (introduction by H. L. A. Hart and bibliographical note); J. Gray, The Nature and Source of Law (2d ed. 1931); H. Hart, The Concept of Law (1961); T. Holland, The Elements of Jurisprudence 1–13 (13th ed. 1924); H. Kelsen, General Theory of Law and State (1945); E. Patterson, *supra* note 179.

187. *See* H. Lauterpacht, 1950, *supra* note 1, at 75–77; Castberg, *supra* note 164, at 30; Manner, *The Object Theory of the Individual in International Law,* 46 Am. J. Int'l L. 428 (1952); Szabo, *The Theoretical Foundations of Human Rights,* in Nobel Symposium on Human Rights, *supra* note 1, at 35, 38; Tucker, *Has the Individual Become the Subject of International Law?* 34 U. Cin. L. Rev. 341 (1965).

human rights. By focusing upon deprivations in concrete situations and by stressing the importance of structures and procedures, as well as prescriptions, at phases of implementation, the positivists have enhanced the protection of many particular rights and strengthened explicit concern for more comprehensive means of fulfillment.

The fatal weakness of the positivist approach is in its location of authority in the perspective of established officials. The rules of law expressing these perspectives are commonly assumed to have a largely autonomous reference, different from community policy in context. The same rules are supposed to describe what past decisions have been, to predict what future decisions will be and to state what future decisions ought to be.[188] From this standpoint, the deliberate postulation and clarification of basic community policies about human rights are perceived as superfluous or as tasks to be performed by inexplicit intuition, rather than by systematic inquiry.[189] Actually, in the positivist approach the task of specifying the detailed content of the human rights protected in a community goes forward very much as in the natural law approach—by logical, syntactic derivation.[190] The difference is that, while the natural lawyer takes off from theological or metaphysical abso-

---

188. Hohfeld's book, W. Hohfeld, Fundamental Legal Conceptions as Applied in Judicial Reasoning, and Other Legal Essays (W. Cook ed. 1919), is a dramatic demonstration of the tautology of "rights" and comparable concepts (immunities, powers, privileges).

As Judge (formerly Dean) Hardy Dillard pointed out:

> To ask, however tentatively, "what are rules?" Is unwittingly to endow them with a kind of reality or existence, even a metaphysical existence, which is illusory. Rules of law do not "exist" in the sense in which a tree or a stone or the planet Mars might be said to exist. True, they may be articulated and put on paper and in that form they exist, but, whatever their form, they are expressed in words which are merely signs mediating human subjectivities. They represent and arouse expectations which are capable of being explored scientifically. The "law" is thus not a "something" impelling obedience; it is a constantly evolving process of decision making and the way it evolves will depend on the knowledge and insights of the decision makers. So viewed, norms of laws should be considered less as compulsive commands than as tools of thought or instruments of analysis. Their impelling quality will vary greatly depending on the context of application, and, since the need for stability is recognized, the norms may frequently provide a high order of predictability. But this is referable back to the expectations entertained and is not attributable to some existential quality attaching to the norms themselves. In other words, our concept of "law" needs to be liberated from the cramping assumption that it "exists" as a kind of "entity" imposing restraints on the decision maker.

Dillard, *The Policy-Oriented Approach to Law,* 40 Va. Q. Rev. 626, 629 (1964).

189. *See* A. Ross, *supra* note 180, at 253.

190. *See* note 171 *supra.*

lutes, the positivist takes off from assumptions about the empirical reference of traditional legal concepts.

The difficulties inherent in clarifying the content of human rights, either as a whole or in particular, by relying on logical derivation from highly abstract and traditional legal concepts are multiple. The most obvious difficulty is that the inherited concepts may embody not the values of human dignity, but those of human indignity.[191] A second difficulty is that traditional legal conceptions and principles commonly travel in pairs of opposites from which only antithetical conclusions can be drawn.[192] Even in a legal system whose content is predominantly that of a free society, the over-elaborate manipulation of doctrinal technicalities may produce consequences inimical to the realization of human dignity. Still another difficulty is that one-sided stress put upon derivations from legal technicalities emphasizing the role of the nation-state can produce the intolerable view that the individual has no rights under international law.[193]

The positivistic conception of authority is equally incompatible with the performances of other problem-oriented tasks pertinent to human rights. The elaborate presentation of accumulated systems of legal technicality, allegedly describing the perspectives of established officials, falls far short of carefully describing past uniformities in the decision of comparable cases according to degrees of approximation toward clarified community goals. The tragic facts of human deprivation in consequence of inadequate decision may be left unexposed. Similarly, when it is assumed that formal rules are the factors that predominantly affect decision, the effort expended in search of other factors in predisposition and environment tends to be insubstantial. Again, when decision makers are asserted to be under an "obligation" to align future decisions with the rules employed in justifying past decisions, the prediction of future outcomes becomes mere extrapolation, as simpleminded as it is unreliable. The ultimate, integrative task of inventing and evaluating new practices and institutions that are better designed to protect and fulfill human rights is not likely to succeed if attempted in the absence of the adequate performance of the other relevant tasks.

---

191. Note, for example, the "legality" of the apartheid policy and practice in today's South Africa and of the anti-Semitic measures under the Third Reich.

192. *See* McDougal, *The Ethics of Applying Systems of Authority: The Balanced Opposites of a Legal System,* in THE ETHICS OF POWER 221 (H. Lasswell & H. Cleveland eds. 1962).

193. Lauterpacht observed that "the recognition, by the State, of fundamental human rights must remain precarious and incomplete, in fact and in law, unless such recognition is supported by the twin sanction of the law of nature and the law of nations." H. LAUTERPACHT, 1950, *supra* note 1, at 94.

The Marxist (Communist) Approach

The Marxist approach projects human rights as the inevitable realization of a metaphysical determinism that proceeds in harmony with the laws of dialectical materialism.[194] In this frame of reference the world social process is conceived as a continuing class struggle generated by the concentrated control of production in a comparatively few hands.[195] In a society in which the bourgeois class monopolizes the means of production, human rights are alleged to be little more than illusion.[196] Only in a society where the means of production are publicly owned, it is asserted, can human rights become a reality.[197] The ultimate achievement of a commonwealth of free men (defined as a classless society enjoying communal ownership of the instruments of production) is perceived as depending on the inevitable processes of history which mobilize and pass through the proletarian revolution. In its more detailed theories about human rights, the Marxist framework incorporates various elements (including inadequacies) from the natural law, positivist, and historical systems.[198]

---

194. On the socialist approach to human rights, *see* V. Chalidze, *supra* note 21, at 3–49; Socialist Concept OF Human Rights, *supra* note 1; G. Tunkin, Theory of International Law 79–83 (W. Butler trans. 1974) [hereinafter cited as G. Tunkin]; *Fundamental Rights*, in 4 Marxism, Communism, and Western Society: A Comparative Encyclopedia 55 (C. Kernig ed. 1972) [hereinafter cited as *Fundamental Rights*]; Movchan, *The Human Rights Problem in Present-Day International Law,* in Contemporary International Law 233 (G. Tunkin ed., G. Ivanov-Mumjiev trans. 1969) [hereinafter cited as Movchan]; Przetacznik, *The Socialist Concept of Protection of Human Rights,* 38 Social Research 337 (1971) [hereinafter cited as Przetacznik].

For an excellent history of human rights from a Marxist perspective, *see* Szabo, *Fundamental Questions Concerning the Theory and History of Citizens' Rights,* in Socialist Concept of Human Rights, *supra* note 1, at 2–81 [hereinafter cited as Szabo]. *See also* I. Lapenna, State and Law: Soviet and Yugoslav Theory (1964); Douglas, *Proletarian Political Theory,* in A History of Political Theories: Recent Times 178 (C. Merriam & H. Barnes eds. 1924); Hazard, *Soviet Law and Its Assumptions,* in Ideological Differences and World Order 192 (F. Northrop ed. 1949); Murphy, *Ideological Interpretations of Human Rights,* 21 De Paul L. Rev. 286 (1971); Panczuk, *Human Rights and the Soviet Union,* 10 World Justice 224 (1968).

195. C. Friedrich, *supra* note 171, at 143–53.

196. M. Cranston, *supra* note 1, at 3; *Fundamental Rights, supra* note 194, at 61; Peteri, *Citizen's Rights and the Natural Law Theory,* in Socialist Concept of Human Rights, *supra* note 1, at 83, 85, 97; Szabo, *supra* note 194, at 34, 37–38.

197. W. Friedman, *supra* note 171, at 367; *Fundamental Rights, supra* note 194, at 60; Kóvacs, *General Problems of Rights,* in Socialist Concept of Human Rights, *supra* note 1, at 7, 16; Szabo, *supra* note 194, at 53–81.

198. In the words of Szabo:

> The third main trend concerning human rights—to be outlined here—is the socialist concept based on Marxism. This concept is alternately branded as being of the

The enduring contribution of the Marxist theory has been its initial intense concern for human dignity. The theory and the movement evolved in the nineteenth century in response to a sense of injustice brought into being by a highly exploitative, industrial society. Marxists sought to extend certain human rights to the vast numbers of a hitherto deprived group, the working class. The manifest content of the theory, whatever its covert uses, was directed toward the promotion of human dignity and the realization of free men. Irrespective of its limitations, the movement sought to relate human rights to causal constellation in social process and to confer operational meaning upon protected claims of right. Underscoring the interdetermination among empirical variables in social process, attention was drawn to the importance of material values in the defense and fulfillment of human rights. By reiterating the crucial role of the sharing of material values (especially wealth, well-being, and skill), Marxists have defined an indispensable agenda for the enlargement of human rights everywhere.

Nevertheless, this approach, certainly as exemplified in some contemporary states, is seriously afflicted with inadequacies, unique and otherwise. In some perspectives it can be interpreted as denying even the most fundamental notion of human rights. A persistent theme in Marxist-Communist literature is that human rights appertain not to the individual person but to the collectivity, and especially to that collectivity known as the nation-state. Apart from the state, it is often asserted, there are no human rights.[199] The concern of this literature for humanity extends to the human being conceived as an abstract "species being";[200] it does not run to particular "individuals with separate inalienable rights."[201] As the chosen instrument for subordinating the individual to the collectivity, the Communist state and the ruling party are charged

---

> natural-law or the positivist type, although in fact it is neither. A few analogous elements may be found in it, but basically it is a radically new, different theory.

Szabo, *The Theoretical Foundations of Human Rights,* in NOBEL SYMPOSIUM ON HUMAN RIGHTS, *supra* note 1, at 39.

For the affinity of the Marxist approach to the historical approach, *see* McDougal, Lasswell, & Reisman, *supra* note 183, at 229–30.

199. *See* J. COHEN & H. CHIU, PEOPLE'S CHINA AND INTERNATIONAL LAW 97–98 (1974); E. HAAS, *supra* note 1, at 15; J. HAZARD, COMMUNISTS AND THEIR LAW: A SEARCH FOR THE COMMON CORE OF THE LEGAL SYSTEMS OF THE MARXIAN SOCIALIST STATES 139 (1969); J. HAZARD & I. SHAPIRO, THE SOVIET LEGAL SYSTEM 13–58 (1962); H. KELSEN, THE COMMUNIST THEORY OF LAW 179–82 (1955); S. LENG, JUSTICE IN COMMUNIST CHINA 171 (1967); G. TUNKIN, *supra* note 194, at 82–83; Movchan, *supra* note 194, at 239–40; Przetacznik, *supra* note 194, at 338–41; Tsou, *The Values of the Chinese Revolution,* in CHINA'S DEVELOPMENTAL EXPERIENCE 27–32 (M. Oksenberg ed. 1973).

200. M. CRANSTON, *supra* note 1, at 3.

201. *Id. See also Fundamental Rights, supra* note 194, at 63.

with playing a strong parental role in every value sector. The party is regarded as an embodiment of infallible wisdom in every domain.[202]

Similarly, even though the Marxist approach does purport to relate human rights to empirical social process, the distorting effects of the dialectical dogma are so severe that the resulting map of society seems a caricatured resemblance to a disciplined scientific product. The primacy accorded materialistic over symbolic values is so exaggerated that values other than wealth, and especially power, are not adequately appraised for their impacts upon the achievement of human rights.[203]

By asserting that human rights are an illusion unless they are brought under the protection of the state, the theorists of Marxism have borrowed heavily from the positivist approach. In fact, though Marxists sometimes disparage law as a superstructure of verbalisms depending on an economic base, the notion of law that is actually used is largely positivistic. The emphasis upon rules is inordinate. The conception of authority is formulated more in terms of the expectations of established elites than of community members, and the idea of effective control is warped by the overwhelming stress laid upon the variable of wealth.

In much Marxist theory about human rights the attempt is made to confine the global constitutive process of authoritative decision to the prescribing of high-level norms. Communist writers characteristically insist that by its nature the detailed protection of human rights is a matter of domestic jurisdiction, lying within the exclusive domain of a particular nation-state and involving no matter of international concern.[204] While the larger community of humankind is accorded competence to formulate high-level prescriptions outlining a transnational interest in human rights, the detailed application of these norms is held to be a matter of exclusive national concern and competence.[205] The

---

202. It is apparent that the Soviet emphasis on the educational role of law presupposes a new conception of man. The Soviet citizen is considered to be a member of a growing, unfinished, still immature society, which is moving toward a new and higher phase of development. As a subject of law, or a litigant in court, he is like a child or youth to be trained, guided, disciplined, protected. The judge plays the part of a parent or guardian; indeed, the whole legal system is parental.

H. Berman, Justice in the U.S.S.R.: An Interpretation of Soviet Law 284 (rev. ed. 1963). *See also* L. Lloyd, Introduction to Jurisprudence 643–46 (3d ed. 1972); *Fundamental Rights, supra* note 194, at 62–63.

203. *See* V. Chalidze, *supra* note 21, at 41.

204. *See* J. Cohen & H. Chiu, *supra* note 199, at 97–98, 607–10; G. Tunkin, *supra* note 194, at 82–83; Movchan, *supra* note 194, at 239–40; Przetacznik, *supra* note 194, at 351; Tedin, *The Development* [*of*] *the Soviet Attitude toward Implementing Human Rights Un* [*sic*] *Under the Charter,* 5 Human Rights J. 399 (1972).

205. Przetacznik, *supra* note 194, at 351–59. *See* M. Moskowitz, 1974, *supra* note 1, at 4.

Communist doctrine of peaceful coexistence, which projects one system of international law to govern relations between Communist states and another system for governing relations between Communist and non-Communist states, is a further hindrance to the acceptance of a comprehensive global decision process designed to protect human rights.[206]

The Marxist approach, finally, contributes very little to the performance of the relevant intellectual tasks. The deliberate postulation and detailed clarification of goals is as incompatible with this as it is with any natural law theory. The specification of policy is more a function of philosophical derivation from metaphysical absolutes than a disciplined, configurative examination of context. Further, trends in past decisions are described more in relation to class struggle than according to the degree of approximation to more comprehensive policies that affect the shaping and sharing of all values. The adequate performance of the scientific task is thwarted by exaggerated deference to the weight of the economic variable. Explanations that stress the predominating significance of a single causal factor are in a peculiarly vulnerable position as knowledge advances, and it has become increasingly clumsy to divide all factors in psychological and social processes into the "material" and the "nonmaterial." A two-term system can, of course, be made to serve some purposes of investigation. However, its utility is modest in any case, and the hazards of rigidifying an entire approach into empty verbal dialectic are greatly increased in such a limited system. Since the dogma of dialectical materialism is not open to challenge or continuing assessment, the future course of human rights development is not acknowledged to be problematic. Rather, future events are affirmed to be inevitable. The eventual realization of a commonwealth of free men is cast in categorical, inevitable terms rather than in the language of alternative constructs that concede a wide range of potential developments.[207] In a world so fixed and certain there is little scope for the invention, evaluation, and recommendation of policy alternatives in the defense and fulfillment of human rights at national, much less transnational, levels.

---

206. *See generally* E. McWhinney, "Peaceful Coexistence" and Soviet-Western International Law (1964); G. Tunkin, *supra* note 194, at 21–87; Hazard, *Codifying Peaceful Coexistence,* 55 Am. J. Int'l L. 109 (1961); Kartashkin, *Human Rights and Peaceful Coexistence,* 9 Human Rights J. 5 (1976); Lipson, *International Law,* in 8 Handbook of Political Science 415, 430–32 (F. Greenstein & N. Polsby eds. 1975); Lipson, *Peaceful Coexistence,* 29 Law & Contemp. Prob. 871 (1964); Tunkin, *Peaceful Coexistence and International Law,* in Contemporary International Law 5–35 (G. Tunkin ed., G. Ivanov-Mumjiev trans. 1969).

207. Our approach toward the future is that of developmental constructs. For comparison with the Marxist model, see H. Lasswell, A Pre-View of Policy Sciences 67–69 (1971).

The Social Science Approach

The contemporary social science approach builds upon the theories and techniques of modern science to enhance our knowledge of the factors that affect failures and successes in the protection of human rights. This approach seeks to formulate relevant theories and techniques for investigating cause and effect in relation to human rights in the larger social process context. It gives prominence to theoretical models and empirical procedures by which data can be gathered and processed to supplement the more traditional philosophical and historical inquiries.[208]

The principal contributions of this approach are its concern for the whole process of community interaction in which human rights are shaped and shared and its invention of procedures potentially capable of wider application in performance of other relevant tasks of inquiry. Many of its efforts to improve the performance of the scientific task and, in general, to specify the empirical components of human rights protection anticipate research methods employed more recently to aid broader and more policy-oriented inquiry.[209]

---

208. COMPARATIVE HUMAN RIGHTS, *supra* note 1 (edited by Richard P. Claude), represents the most ambitious attempt yet to achieve a larger map of human rights in the social process context which would facilitate performance of all the relevant intellectual tasks, especially the scientific task, by devising categories and identifying variables.

See also I. DUCHACEK, supra note 1; E. HAAS, *supra* note 1; S. SCHEINGOLD, THE POLITICS OF RIGHTS: LAWYERS, PUBLIC POLICY, AND POLITICAL CHANGE (1974); Danelski, *A Behavioral Conception of Human Rights,* 3 LAW IN TRANSITION Q. 63 (1966) [hereinafter cited as Danelski]. *See generally* Feeley, *The Concept of Laws in Social Science: A Critique and Notes on an Expanded View,* 10 LAW & SOC'Y REV. 497 (1976); Nonet, *For Jurisprudential Sociology,* 10 LAW & SOC'Y REV. 525 (1976).

Some of these books, such as that by Scheingold, misconceive law, power, and authority. Law is conceived as a body of rules distinct from political process; power as naked power only, including no element of authority; and authority as the perspectives of established officials only, and not of community members. It is small wonder that little fruitful inquiry is achieved.

The various emphases subsumed under "sociological jurisprudence" and "the sociology of law," all inspired by accelerating developments in the natural and social sciences, have sought to bring inquiry about law, as well as law itself, into a more realistic relation to the facts of social process. For our present purposes, these emphases can be properly subsumed under "the social science approach." The classic presentation of the sociological approach is of course that of Dean Pound: 1 R. POUND, *supra* note 171, at 289–358. *See also* E. EHRLICH, FUNDAMENTAL PRINCIPLES OF THE SOCIOLOGY OF LAW (W. Moll trans. 1912); N. TIMASHEFF, AN INTRODUCTION TO THE SOCIOLOGY OF LAW (1939).

209. *See* Claude, *Comparative Rights Research: Some Intersections between Law and the Social Sciences,* in COMPARATIVE HUMAN RIGHTS, *supra* note 1, at 382–407 [hereinafter cited as Claude]; Strouse & Claude, *Empirical Comparative Rights Research: Some Preliminary Tests of Development Hypotheses,* in *id.* at 51–67. *See also* Danelski, *supra* note 208, at 72.

The major failure of those who rely on the scientific approach is that they have been slow in evolving a comprehensive map of or framework of inquiry about human rights in social process. Thus far, the social science approach offers neither precise, empirical definitions of particular human rights, nor a comprehensive categorization of all the important rights, together with needed indications of how particular rights are interrelated.[210] Users of scientific methods are too often confounded by abiding misconceptions about the more fundamental interconnections of law and social process. A clear focus has not emerged on the role of authoritative decision in the protection of human rights. In consequence, there is disproportionate emphasis upon legal rules and insufficient regard for the often complementary and ambiguous reference of such rules to actual outcomes in decision. Authority is often defined, after the manner of the positivists, in reference to the perspectives of official elites rather than to those of community members.[211] The distinction between the degree of control that is indispensable to authoritative decision and the exercise of mere naked power is not always maintained. In general, there is a sense of pessimism about the potential role of authority.[212] The concept of control may be left unclarified in terms of the variables that actually affect decision, and there appears to be little notion of a comprehensive process of constitutive decision that both reflects and affects the value outcomes of human dignity or indignity. Too often the focus of inquiry about relevant community processes is confined to nation-states and neglects the hierarchy of interpenetrating communities from local and national to transnational and global levels.

The exponents of the social science approach characteristically underestimate the importance of deliberately postulating and clarifying human rights goals, as distinct from justifying those goals by transempirical postulates of faith or by outright incorporation of community preferences. Some existing studies assume that the only sources of goals are community acknowledgment[213] or preferences acceptable to nation-state elites.[214] In the absence of clear and explicit postulation of goals, it is not surprising to find that little attention is paid to the detailed specification of recommended policies. Goal clarification may itself be eschewed as an unscientific operation and may be permitted to regress toward unalleviated adoption of traditional modes of philosophical speculation. Fur-

210. For an attempt, see Claude, *supra* note 209, at 392–93. The categories of rights Claude offers, though comprehensive, are less than homogeneous.

211. *See, e.g.*, E. Haas, *supra* note 1, at vii–viii, 127–31.

212. *See id.* at 120–21, 127–29.

213. Danelski, *supra* note 208, at 66–68.

214. *E.g.*, E. Haas, *supra* note 1, at 4, 130–33.

ther, in the absence of detailed specification of particular rights, there is no adequate performance of the task of describing historic flows of decision in terms of varying degrees of approximation to clarified goals. Obviously, the most conspicuous task is that of scientific inquiry, but lacking a comprehensive map of human rights and a realistic conception of the interrelations between law and social process, it is impossible to perform even this task adequately.[215] Certainly no viable, overall theory has been developed that includes both predispositional and environmental variables as they relate to human rights. Sometimes the search for conditions has degenerated into a miscellaneous search for the "natural laws" of social interaction. It is difficult to relate the part to the whole and vice versa when the part and the whole are not clearly identified. Much scientific speculation is devoted to relating high-level "ought" statements to high-level "is" statements, with a minimum intermediate specification.[216] Even when attempted, many projections of future events have been unsystematic and elliptical, often confined to fantasies of future horror.[217] The range of policy invention, evaluation, and recommendation has been relatively circumscribed and commonplace. In the absence of realistic notions either of the constitutive process or of the effective power process that maintains the constitutive process, the performance of these tasks, if they are performed at all, is necessarily left to others.

HUMAN RIGHTS IN POLICY-ORIENTED PERSPECTIVE

The framework of inquiry that appears necessary to escape our inherited confusions about human rights and to meet the enormous contemporary challenge to scholarship is one that would: (1) offer a comprehensive map of what is meant by human rights in terms of the shaping and sharing of all values; (2) relate such rights to all community contexts which affect their achievement; (3) specify in detail the past and potential role of processes of authoritative decision at all community levels in clarifying and securing such rights; and (4) mobilize and integrate all appropriate intellectual skills for the better clarification and

---

215. *See* Claude *supra* note 209, at 401–05.

216. E. Haas, *supra* note 1, offers no comprehensive map of rights and no detailed procedures for description in particular instances. There is, further, a complete underestimation of the role of authority in the implementation of human rights and of the role of custom in creating authority. No effort is made to clarify goals; values must, apparently, be taken from the "consent" of established elites.

The Claude book Comparative Human Rights, *supra* note 1, seeks to improve performance of the scientific task but offers little specification of the other intellectual tasks necessary to the deliberate use of law as an instrument of policy.

217. Claude, *supra* note 209, at 398.

protection of all rights. The broad outlines of such a deliberately policy-oriented, contextual, and multi-method approach may be indicated in terms of four major features:

The establishment of the observational standpoint;

The delimitation of the focus of inquiry;

The explicit postulation of basic public order goals; and

The performance of intellectual tasks.[218]

The Establishment of the Observational Standpoint

The necessary observational standpoint is that of a citizen of the largest earth-space community who identifies with the whole of humankind. In this largest community the human rights that any one individual can enjoy are, as we have indicated above, a function of what others can enjoy, and the greater protection of certain particular rights may upon occasion require the lesser protection of other rights. The responsibility of the scholar who is concerned with enlightenment, as well as of the decision maker who is concerned for all the consequences of his decisions through time, is that of ascertaining and specifying the common interests of all peoples—in all their interpenetrating communities, both territorial and functional—in the better protection of the whole range of individual rights. It is indispensable that both the scholarly inquirer and the established decision maker achieve an observational standpoint, as free as possible from parochial interests and biases, which will enable them to ascertain and clarify for the active participants in the different communities common interests that they themselves have not been able to perceive. The clarity and fidelity with which this standpoint is maintained affects every other feature of inquiry: how problems are defined, what goals are postulated, and what intellectual skills are employed.

The Delimitation of the Focus of Inquiry

An appropriate focus for a policy-relevant inquiry about human rights will be both comprehensive and selective.[219] The comprehensiveness and the realism in detail with which a focus is delimited may affect both

---

218. For general formulation of this approach, *see* Lasswell & McDougal, *Criteria for a Theory about Law,* 44 S. Cal. L. Rev. 362 (1971). For detailed development of this approach in reference to international law in general, *see* McDougal, Lasswell, & Reisman, *supra* note 183. *See also* Lasswell & McDougal, *Jurisprudence in Policy-Oriented Perspective,* 19 U. Fla. L. Rev. 486 (1966–67); McDougal, *Jurisprudence for a Free Society,* 1 Ga. L. Rev. 1 (1966).

219. In referring to the Ptolemaic paradigm, Thomas Kuhn observes: "What a man sees depends both upon what he looks at and also what his previous visual-conceptual experience has taught him to see." T. Kuhn, The Structure of Scientific Revolutions 113 (1962).

how particular problems are formulated and the dependability and economy with which the different relevant intellectual tasks can be brought to bear on inquiry. The broadest reach of an appropriately contextual, configurative approach will relate human rights to the whole of the social and community processes in which they are demanded and in which authoritative decision is invoked for their protection. Yet a viable theory must offer concepts and procedures which will facilitate a focus, with whatever precision may be necessary, upon both value interactions in social process and particular decisions or flows of decisions.

We outline a possible focus of inquiry in terms of the following emphases.

THE RELATION OF HUMAN RIGHTS TO SOCIAL PROCESS

An appropriate, empirical conception of human rights must refer to the interactions in social process by which values are shaped and shared. In any community the interdeterminations between different particular values in the shaping and sharing of all values are such that whatever the basic preferences of community members about the honoring of individual freedom of choice, some human rights dimension would appear to be at stake in every particular instance of interaction in social process.[220] A deliberately policy-oriented framework of inquiry which would concern itself with all the human rights of all individuals must, accordingly, seek a comprehensive map of social process that will permit the precise location of particular rights in their larger context. It is only by the aid of such a map that problems in disparities between aspiration and achievement can be formulated in ways to facilitate performance of the various relevant intellectual tasks and to afford comparisons through time and across boundaries.[221]

It may be noted that the conception of human rights outlined by Secretary of State Vance, in an address on "Human Rights and Foreign Policy" to the University of Georgia School of Law, embraces all values. *See Human Rights and Foreign Policy,* 76 DEP'T STATE BULL. 505 (1977).

220. As James Coolidge Carter stated more than half a century ago:

> Law, Custom, Conduct, Life—different names for almost the same thing—true names for different aspects of the same thing—are so inseparably blended together that one cannot even be thought of without the other. No improvement can be effected in one without improving the other, and no retrogression can take place in one without a corresponding decline in the other.

J. CARTER, *supra* note 181, at 320.

221. For the comprehensive map we have outlined, *see* McDougal, Lasswell, & Chen, *Human Rights and World Public Order: A Framework for Policy-Oriented Inquiry,* 63 AM. J. INT'L L. 237, 246–57 (1969); McDougal, *Human Rights and World Public Order: Principles of Content and Procedure for Clarifying General Community Policies,* 14 VA. J. INT'L L. 387, 406–21 (1974).

The most general conceptualization of social process we recommend is in terms of certain value and institutional categories which can be given detailed operational indices that refer to specific empirical relations between human beings in the shaping and sharing of values. The value terms we employ, though any comprehensive set of equivalents would suffice, are as follows:

Respect:	Freedom of choice, equality, and recognition
Power:	Making and influencing community decisions
Enlightenment:	Gathering, processing, and disseminating information and knowledge
Well-being:	Safety, health, and comfort
Wealth:	Production, distribution, and consumption of goods and services; control of resources
Skill:	Acquisition and exercise of capabilities in vocations, professions, and the arts
Affection:	Intimacy, friendship, loyalty; positive sentiments
Rectitude:	Participation in forming and applying norms of responsible conduct

The categorizations of institutional practices we recommend for the detailed description of any and all particular value processes include:

Participation (individual and group, governmental and nongovernmental);

Perspectives (demands, identifications, and expectations);

Situations (geographic, temporal, institutional, and crisis);

Bases of power (authoritative, controlling);

Strategies (diplomatic, ideological, economic, military); and

Outcomes (shaping and sharing values).

By appropriate subcategorizations and refinement, these categorizations may be made to serve the purposes of description of whatever comprehensiveness and precision may be necessary.

Given the dynamic nature of human rights and the continuing gap between aspiration and achievement, the provisional map we have outlined is, as in any other comparable attempt, subject to constant review. As Georges Burdeau points out: "[I]n any given society at any given time, the dominant sociopolitical thought results in reinforced weighting of certain rights as these rights become reflected in the legal value structure by which they are enforced. Consequently, the listing of rights appears to be contingent and subject to constant revision." *Editor's Introduction,* in COMPARATIVE HUMAN RIGHTS, *supra* note 1, at 71, 72 (quoting Georges Burdeau).

The most useful subcategorization, for human rights inquiry, of the outcomes of each particular value process would appear to be as follows:

1. A basic share of participation and enjoyment;
2. Positive opportunity for further participation and enjoyment free from discrimination for reasons irrelevant to capabilities;
3. Further recognition or reward for actual meritorious contribution; and
4. The largest possible aggregate shaping and sharing.[222]

The degree to which any particular community, whether global or local, achieves these outcomes in any particular value process is a function not only of the other institutional features of *that* process but of such features in all other processes and especially of the features of all relevant constitutive processes of authoritative decision.

THE CONCEPTION OF AUTHORITATIVE DECISION

In any community the application of organized, community-wide coercion is, as the positivists rightly insist, an indispensable component of the effective protection of human rights, however broadly or narrowly such rights may be conceived. A deliberately policy-oriented approach will, accordingly, characterize law not as mere rules embodying ambiguously ascribed perspectives, but as *decision* which embodies both perspectives (the subjectivities attending choice) and operations (the choices actually made and enforced by threats of severe deprivations or promises of extreme indulgences). The most realistic inquiry requires a focus upon both technical myth and actual practice. A policy-oriented approach will be concerned, further, not with effective decision alone, but with *authoritative decision,* that is, decision in which elements of authority and control are appropriately balanced. By authority, we refer to the expectations of community members about who is to make what decisions, in what structures, by what procedures, and in accordance with what criteria. By control, we refer to effective participation in the choices that are in fact put into community practice. In the absence of decision characterized by authority, human rights are left dependent upon mere naked power or arbitrary whim. When control does not accompany decision, the protection of human rights may become mere illusion and mockery, as in some modern constitutions.

COMPREHENSIVENESS IN CONCEPTION OF PROCESSES OF AUTHORITATIVE DECISION

It is not, further, mere occasional or isolated decisions which, in any community, determine the aggregate protection of human rights, but

222. For its application to the respect value, *see* chapters 6–16 *infra.*

rather a comprehensive and continuous flow of authoritative decisions. In any community the process of authoritative decision, as an integral part of a more comprehensive process of effective power, may be observed to comprise two very different kinds of decisions. The first, or constitutive decisions, are those which establish and maintain a comprehensive and continuing process of authoritative decision. The second, or public order decisions, are those which, continuously emerging from constitutive process, shape and maintain the protected features of the community's various value processes (respect, enlightenment, wealth, well-being, and so on).

It is easily observable in any community that there is a human rights dimension—that human rights are at stake—in every authoritative decision, whether constitutive or public order. The decisions by which the constitutive process is established and maintained must in all their features and modalities reflect in varying degree basic human rights policies; thus, the "due process" of procedures for the making of different types of decisions is always relevant. The character and economy of the constitutive process as a whole, further, most directly affect the character and comprehensiveness of the public order protection it affords. Human rights are, finally, most explicitly at stake in the particular public order decisions emerging from the constitutive process for regulating the shaping and sharing of each particular value.

The appropriate general description of a community's constitutive process must, as with any social process, make reference to all its features and component practices. The basic outline of constitutive process we recommend is, thus, in terms of established authoritative decision makers, the basic perspectives (demands, identifications, and expectations) for which the process is maintained, the structures of authority provided, the bases of power (in authority and control) placed at the disposal of different decision makers, the procedures authorized for the making of different kinds of decisions, and the various kinds of decision functions regarded as necessary to the making and administering of general community policy. These necessary decision functions are commonly described in conventional terms as "legislative," "executive," "judicial," and "administrative," but these words appear to refer more to structures of authority than to functions. For more comprehensive and precise description we distinguish the following:

Intelligence:	Obtaining information about the past, making estimates of the future, planning
Promoting:	Advocating general policies, urging proposals
Prescribing:	Projecting authoritative community policies
Invoking:	Making a provisional characterization of a concrete situation in terms of a prescription

Applying:	Making a final characterization and executing prescriptions in a concrete situation
Terminating:	Ending a prescription or arrangement within the scope of a prescription
Appraising:	Comparing goals and performance in the decision process.[223]

The most comprehensive and economic description of public order decisions—the decisions which most directly express the human rights achieved or not achieved in a community—may, as anticipated above, be sought in terms of both the basic values and the detailed institutional practices affected. The categorizations we recommend are the same as for such values and practices: for values in terms of respect, power, enlightenment, well-being, wealth, skill, affection, and rectitude, or their equivalents; and for institutional practices in relation to each such value in terms of participation, perspectives, situations, bases of power, strategies, and outcomes, or their equivalents. Such categorizations may be expanded or made more precise by ascription of appropriate operational indices to serve the purposes of all relevant intellectual tasks.

THE RELATION TO COMMUNITY PROCESSES

The net aggregate in protection of human rights that a particular individual can achieve today is observably a function, not merely of the operation of social and decision processes within any single territorial community, but of the operation of such processes within a whole hierarchy of interpenetrating communities—from local, regional, and national to hemispheric and global or earth-space. The contemporary accelerating intensity of global interaction, not to mention the spectre of nuclear holocaust, renders even the life and stable existence of every human being dependent upon a multitude of factors beyond the boundaries of any single territorial community.

From an anthropological perspective, the whole of humankind presently constitutes, in the sense of interdetermination with regard to all values, a single community, however primitively organized. This largest community of humankind operates through and has impacts upon all the lesser communities, both territorial and functional, and these lesser communities reciprocally affect one another and the character of the most comprehensive process of interaction. The ultimate actor in all social interaction is the individual human being, but individuals identify

223. For elaboration on these seven decision functions, *see* H. LASSWELL, THE DECISION PROCESS: SEVEN CATEGORIES OF FUNCTIONAL ANALYSIS (1956); *World Constitutive Process of Authoritative Decision, supra* note 109, at 131–54.

and affiliate with and make demands upon and on behalf of a whole range of groups and associations—including not merely nation-states, but also the lesser territorial communities, international governmental organizations, political parties, pressure groups, tribes, families, and private associations of all kinds. A most important component of this largest community process of humankind is an effective power process, entirely global or earth-space in its reach, in which decisions are in fact taken and enforced by severe deprivations or high indulgences irrespective of the wishes of particular individuals and groups. Observable within this comprehensive process of effective power is, further, a transnational process of authoritative decision in the sense of a continuous flow of decisions made from perspectives of authority—that is, made by the people who are expected to make them, in accordance with community expectations about how they should be made, in established structures, and by authorized procedures. This transnational process of authoritative decision includes both constitutive and public order decisions and, like its embracing transnational social processes, is maintained at many different community levels and in many different interpenetrating patterns of perspectives and operations and of authority and control, affecting and being affected by the value and decision processes in all the component communities of the larger earth-space community.

The public order established and maintained by this most comprehensive process of transnational authoritative decision affects the internal public order of all its constituent communities. The internal public order of each constituent community, in turn, affects the global public order. In such a context, the effective securing of human rights must depend, not merely upon the protection afforded by and within national communities, but also upon that afforded by and within transnational communities, regional and global, as well as by functional and pluralistic organizations of the greatest range and variety. When matters of "international concern," regarded as appropriate for transnational decision, are considered factual questions dependent upon the interdetermination of value processes transcending nation-state boundaries, there can be few matters in the contemporary world relating to human rights which can be accurately described as of "domestic jurisdiction" only, confined exclusively to the competence of nation-state officials.[224] Any relevant conception of the implementation of human rights in the con-

224. *See* McDougal & Reisman, *Rhodesia and the United Nations: The Lawfulness of International Concern*, 62 AM. J. INT'L L. 1 (1968). *See also* R. HIGGINS, THE DEVELOPMENT OF INTERNATIONAL LAW THROUGH THE POLITICAL ORGANS OF THE UNITED NATIONS 58–130 (1963); H. LAUTERPACHT, 1950, *supra* note 1, at 166–220; M. RAJAN, UNITED NATIONS AND DOMESTIC JURISDICTION (2d ed. 1961); V. VAN DYKE, *supra* note 1, at 105–56; Chen, *Self-Determination as a Human Right*, in TOWARD WORLD ORDER AND HUMAN DIGNITY 198,

temporary world will extend to the configurative, deliberate management of all features of the whole hierarchy of interpenetrating effective power and constitutive processes, as well as of the features of the affected, and affecting, social processes.

A viable, policy-oriented framework of inquiry about human rights will employ theories such as we have recommended above, or their equivalents, for investigation of all these complex transnational interrelationships.

THE EXPLICIT POSTULATION OF BASIC PUBLIC ORDER GOALS

The comprehensive set of goal values we recommend for postulation, clarification, and implementation are those which today are commonly characterized as the basic values of human dignity or of a free society. This is not an idiosyncratic or arbitrary choice, but a product of many heritages. These values are, as indicated above, those which have been bequeathed to us by all the great democratic movements of humankind and which are being ever more insistently expressed in the rising common demands and expectations of peoples everywhere.[225] As projected in the United Nations Charter, the International Bill of Human Rights (the Universal Declaration of Human Rights, the International Covenant on Civil and Political Rights and its Protocol, and the International Covenant on Economic, Social, and Cultural Rights), and their host of ancillary expressions, these values are formulated at many different levels of abstraction and in many different cultural and institutional modalities.[226] The basic thrust of all such formulations is, however, toward the greatest production and widest possible distribution of all important values, with a high priority accorded persuasion rather than coercion in such production and distribution.

The basic goal values postulated for clarification of human rights in the largest community of humankind cannot of course be representative only of the exclusive, parochial values of some particular segment of the larger community of humankind, but must admit a very great diversity in the institutional practices by which they are sought and secured. In different particular communities and cultures, very different institutional practices may contribute equally to overriding goals for the increased production and sharing of values. When appropriate overriding goals

---

219–24 (M. Reisman & B. Weston eds. 1976); Ermacora, *Human Rights and Domestic Jurisdiction (Article 2, § 7, of the Charter),* 124 HAGUE RECUEIL DES COURS 375 (1968); Fawcett, *Human Rights and Domestic Jurisdiction,* in THE INTERNATIONAL PROTECTION OF HUMAN RIGHTS 286–303 (E. Luard ed. 1967).

225. *See* notes 1–8 *supra* and accompanying text.

226. *See* note 7 *supra.*

are accepted, experimentation and creativity may be encouraged by the honoring of a wide range of functional equivalents in the institutional practices by which values are sought.

It may be noted that the postulation of basic goal values we recommend differs from a mere exercise in faith. We do not expect to acquire new knowledge by postulation alone. It is only by the systematic and disciplined exercise of the various relevant intellectual skills that new knowledge can be acquired. The more comprehensive the map of basic goal values and the more it admits of refinements and equivalences at different levels of abstraction, the more effective can be the exercise of the different intellectual skills. We emphasize the postulation and clarification of public order goals in contradistinction to their derivation. Infinitely regressive logical derivations from premises of theological, metaphysical, or other highly ambiguous references contribute little to the detailed specification of human rights in the designative sense of demanded relations between human beings which is required for rational decision. Peoples subscribing to very different styles in derivation have long demonstrated that they can cooperate for promotion of the values of human dignity, irrespective of the faiths or creeds which they employ for justification. The importance of a deliberate, explicit postulation of a comprehensive set of goals about human rights lies in its possible facilitation of the performance of all the intellectual tasks relevant to policy-oriented inquiry.

The Performance of Intellectual Tasks

The intellectual tasks requisite to a policy-oriented framework of inquiry about human rights extend beyond the derivational exercises and restrictive conceptions of science to a whole series of interrelated activities, indispensable both to effective inquiry and to rational choice in decision. These tasks include the detailed clarification of goals, the description of past trends in decision, the analysis of conditions affecting decision, the projection of future trends in decision, and the invention and evaluation of policy alternatives. It is our recommendation that all these tasks be performed systematically and configuratively in relation to specified problems in context. The rational employment of any particular task requires both the disciplined location of specific problems in human rights in their larger context and the systematic testing of the formulations and findings achieved in the performance of that particular task against the formulations and findings achieved by the other tasks with respect to every significant feature of the context. The performance of all tasks must, thus, relate to the same events in the shaping and sharing of values and in measure go forward concurrently, but with clear discrimination in purpose of observation and particular skill employed.

THE CLARIFICATION OF COMMUNITY POLICIES

The detailed specification of preferred policies about human rights, in terms that make a clear empirical reference to the shaping and sharing of values in social process, is necessary both to relate broad postulated goals to specific instances and to facilitate performance of other relevant intellectual tasks. To the degree that economy permits, every choice in alternatives recommended will be related to its larger community context and to all important community interests which may be affected. The time dimensions of clarification will be made explicit, where appropriate, by distinguishing short-range, middle-range, and long-range objectives. Efforts at clarification will build upon the concurrent and systematic performance of all the other relevant intellectual tasks and will employ the knowledge so acquired about past trends in decision, past conditioning factors, future probabilities, and possible alternative solutions.

THE DESCRIPTION OF PAST TRENDS IN DECISION

The description of past trends in decision about human rights, in approximation to preferred policies about both the constitutive process and public order, is indispensable to ascertaining where any particular community stands at any given time in achievement and also to drawing upon the wisdom of the past for future guidance. For the most effective comparison of decisions and their consequences through time and across community boundaries, the events about human rights which precipitate recourse to authoritative decision, the detailed claims which participants make to such decision, the factors which appear to condition decision, and the immediate and longer-term consequences of decision for the participants and others must, as we have recommended above, all be categorized factually in terms of value-institution processes, including all the different detailed phases of such processes. A comprehensive map of the community process in which values are shaped and shared is as necessary for the descriptive as for the other intellectual tasks.

THE ANALYSIS OF FACTORS AFFECTING DECISION

Knowledge of the factors affecting past trends in decision is important, not merely for understanding the past, but for the projection of future developments and alternatives. In a policy-relevant performance of the scientific task, inquiry will be made for the interplay of the multiple factors affecting decision: overwhelming importance will not be ascribed to any one factor or category of factors (such as those relating to wealth). Guided by the "optimalization postulate" that all responses are, within the limits of capabilities, a function of net value expectation, emphasis will be placed upon both predispositional and environmental variables. The significance of factors deriving from culture, class, interest, personality, and previous exposure to crisis will be explicitly examined. Many different vantage points and both extensive and intensive procedures will be employed in data gathering and processing.

THE PROJECTION OF FUTURE TRENDS

The projection of possible future developments in decision about human rights is important for stimulating creativity in the invention and evaluation of alternatives. In policy-relevant inquiry, expectations about the future will be made as conscious, explicit, comprehensive, and realistic as possible. Developmental constructs, embodying varying alternative anticipations of the future, will be deliberately formulated and tested in the light of all available information. The simple linear or chronological extrapolations made in conventional theory will be subjected to the discipline of knowledge about conditioning factors and past changes in the composition of trends.

THE INVENTION AND EVALUATION OF POLICY ALTERNATIVES

The final task of policy-relevant inquiry, toward which all the others are cumulative, relates to the deliberate invention, assessment, and recommendation of new alternatives in policy, institutional structures, and procedures for the better protection or optimal realization of human rights. In such an inquiry, every phase of decision process, whether constitutive or relating to public order, and every facet of conditioning context will be examined for opportunities in innovation which may influence decision toward greater conformity with clarified goals. Assessment of particular alternatives will be made in terms of gains and losses with regard to all clarified goals, and disciplined by the knowledge acquired of trends, conditioning factors, and future probabilities. All the other intellectual tasks will be synthesized and brought to bear upon the search for and promotion of integrative solutions characterized by maximum gains and minimum losses.

2. THE SOCIAL SETTING OF HUMAN RIGHTS: THE PROCESS OF DEPRIVATION AND NONFULFILLMENT OF VALUES

The existence in fact of a world community, in the sense of the long-term interdetermination of all individuals with regard to all values, is today commonly recognized. This larger community of humankind may be observed to comprise a whole hierarchy of interpenetrating lesser communities, of many different sizes and characteristics, with the larger communities affecting the lesser communities contained within them, and the lesser communities, in turn, affecting the larger communities which they compose. In the comprehensive social process which transcends all these different communities, individual human beings, affected by constantly changing environmental and predispositional factors, are continuously engaged in the shaping and sharing of all values, with achievement of many different outcomes in deprivation and fulfillment. It is these outcomes in deprivation and fulfillment in the shaping and sharing of values which constitute, in an empirical and policy-oriented conception, the human rights which the larger community of humankind protects or fails to protect.

The first indispensable step in relevant and effective inquiry must be that of creating a map or model of world social process, as the larger context of human rights, which will permit empirical reference to human rights problems in whatever degrees of comprehensiveness and precision performance of the necessary intellectual tasks may require. It is this most comprehensive social process which affects, not merely degrees in the achievement of human rights, but also the kinds of claims that are made to authoritative decision for redress of deprivations and nonfulfillments, as well as the responding outcomes in decision. With a map of world social process, which both exhibits broad outlines and points to relevant detail, a scholarly observer may be able to formulate the claims which participants make to authoritative decision in factual terms of discrepancy between community aspiration and achievement and, hence, may be able to facilitate comparisons in flows of authoritative decisions through time and across community boundaries.

The map of comprehensive world social process we recommend, in expansion of the generalized image of "man" striving to maximize "values" by applying "institutions" to "resources," includes, as previously noted, a number of distinguishable, but interrelated, features:

1. Participation. Individual and group actors.
2. Perspectives. The subjectivities of the actors that give direction and intelligibility to interaction.
3. Situations. The geographic, temporal, institutional, and crisis features of interaction.
4. Base values. The values and resources (potential values) available to different actors in shaping interactions.
5. Strategies. The modalities employed in managing base values.
6. Outcomes. The shapings and sharings of values achieved.[1]

In more detailed exposition of the reference and potential significance of these features, we emphasize items that may especially affect deprivations and nonfulfillments in the achievement of values.

---

1. For exposition of the theoretical system *see* H. Lasswell & A. Kaplan, Power and Society: A Framework for Political Inquiry (1950). For preliminary applications of the theory in various fields, *see,* for instance, R. Arens & H. Lasswell, In Defense of Public Order: The Emerging Field of Sanction Law (1961); L. Chen & H. Lasswell, Formosa, China, and the United Nations (1967); D. Johnston, The International Law of Fisheries: A Framework for Policy-Oriented Inquiries (1965); M. McDougal & W. Burke, The Public Order of the Oceans: A Contemporary International Law of the Sea (1962); M. McDougal & F. Feliciano, Law and Minimum World Public Order: The Legal Regulation of International Coercion (1961); M. McDougal, H. Lasswell, & J. Miller, The Interpretation of Agreements and World Public Order: Principles of Content and Procedure (1967); M. McDougal, H. Lasswell, & I. Vlasic, Law and Public Order in Space (1963); B. Murty, Propaganda and World Public Order: The Legal Regulation of the Ideological Instrument of Coercion (1968); W. Reisman, Nullity and Revision (1971); Toward World Order and Human Dignity: Essays in Honor of Myres S. McDougal (W. Reisman & B. Weston eds. 1976) [hereinafter cited as Toward World Order and Human Dignity]; A. Rogow & H. Lasswell, Power, Corruption, and Rectitude (1963).

For comparable maps by other social scientists, *see* Political Development and Change: A Policy Approach (G. Brewer & R. Brunner eds. 1975); A. Etzioni, The Active Society: A Theory of Societal and Political Processes (1968); J. Galtung, Theory and Methods of Society Research (1967); P. Kelvin, The Basis of Social Behaviour (1970); R. Merton, Social Theory and Social Structure (3d ed. 1968); R. Nisbet, The Social Bond: An Introduction to the Study of Society (1970); G. Mead, Mind, Self, and Society (C. Morris ed. 1943); T. Parsons, The Social System (1951); N. Smelser, Theory of Collective Behavior (1971).

PARTICIPANTS

The principal participants in the world social process, in which human rights are both deprived and fulfilled, are individual human beings with all their many different group identifications. Individual human beings are the ultimate actors in any social process; but they affiliate, voluntarily or involuntarily, with many different groups (both territorial and functional) and act through the form of, or play roles in, organizations of the greatest variety, including not only nation-states but also international governmental organizations, political parties, pressure groups, and private associations of all kinds. Individuals operate through all these groups in many different interacting circles (which may or may not overlap one another), playing multiple roles under dynamically changing circumstances, either in their own behalf or on behalf of groups, and increasingly with transnational consequences.[2] Aside from prominent figures who make headlines, millions and millions of human beings daily make their own choices regarding participation in different value processes, travel beyond particular territorial communities, and communicate and collaborate, transnationally as well as nationally, in pursuit of all values.

The individual human being, as the basic actor in all interactions, is always potentially both a depriver and a deprivee of human rights. The extent to which particular individuals become deprivers or deprivees relates importantly to the broader features of the context: the roles they play (governmental or private), the perspectives they entertain (human dignity or anti-human dignity), the situational dynamics (crisis or noncrisis), the authority and other base values at their disposal (concentrated or nonconcentrated), and the strategies employable (persuasive or coercive). With the vast increases in population described above, the number of people with the predispositions to impose and capabilities of imposing deprivations has increased enormously, along with cumulating tension and conflict in human relations.[3] Similarly, as more and more individuals have become available as targets, the number of people who in fact sustain deprivations and cannot secure fulfillment of important values has significantly multiplied.

Because of an enormous diversity in both cultural environment and biological endowment, individuals exhibit a comparable diversity in the detailed patterns of activities by which they pursue different cherished

---

2. For the many roles individuals play in everyday life, *see* the brilliant works by Erving Goffman, including: E. Goffman, Encounters (1961); E. Goffman, The Presentation of Self in Everyday Life (1959). *See also* P. Kelvin, *supra* note 1, at 139–67; R. Nisbet, *supra* note 1, at 148–80.

3. *See* chapter 1 *supra.*

values. While this diversity undoubtedly enriches the quality of life and culture, it has simultaneously contributed to the present state of deprivation and nonfulfillment of values. Consider, for example, the various grounds in the name of which discriminatory deprivations are commonly imposed, including biological characteristics (race, sex, age), culture (nationality), class (in reference to wealth, power, respect, rectitude, and all other values), interest (group memberships), and personality.[4]

The groups which individuals create in the pursuit of values, like the individuals themselves, today proliferate in great abundance. Group interactions are those in which, in the pursuit of collective activities, individuals identify with other persons and concurrently establish relatively stable patterns of subjectivity and operation. The interaction between one individual and another typically results in value indulgence and deprivation. Viewed in the perspective of group-to-group interaction—which is typically a multi-individual to multi-individual phenomenon—the results are both value indulgent and value deprivational.[5]

Organized Groups

The significant groups in the world context are *organized* and *unorganized* (or partially organized). The organized groups are conspicuous in the processes specialized to government, law, and politics (political power) because the organizations involved include all the members and are comparatively easy to identify as participants. The unorganized groups do not completely coincide with persons who share the common characteristics that define the groups.

We employ five categories of organized groups whose interactions of

---

4. *See* chapters 8–15 *infra.*

See also The Fourth World: the Imprisoned, the Poor, the Sick, the Elderly and Underaged in America (L. Hamlian & F. Karl eds. 1976); P. Van den Berghe, Man in Society: A Biosocial View 93–124 (1975); 1 & 2 Case Studies on Human Rights and Fundamental Freedoms: A World Survey (W. Veenhoven ed. 1975); E. Vierdag, The Concept of Discrimination in International Law (1973); The Fourth World: Victims of Group Oppression (B. Whitaker ed. 1973).

5. On group interaction, *see* R. Bales, Interaction Process Analysis: A Method for the Study of Small Groups (1952); C. Cooley, Social Organization: A Study of the Larger Mind (1909); G. Homans, The Human Group (1964); Group Relations and Group Antagonisms (R. MacIver ed. 1944); E. Malecki & H. Mahood, Group Politics (1972); M. Olson, The Logic of Collective Action: Public Goods and the Theory of Groups (rev. ed. 1971); G. Simmel, The Sociology of George Simmel (K. Wolff ed. & trans. 1950); S. Stoljar, Groups and Entities: An Inquiry into Corporate Theory (1973).

For convenient summaries of various group theories, *see* Greenstone, *Group Theories,* in 2 Handbook of Political Science 243–318 (F. Greenstein & N. Polsby eds. 1975); Homans, et al., *Groups,* 6 Int'l Encyc. Soc. Sc. 259 (1968).

value indulgence and deprivation can be described in detail. We identify nation-states, international governmental organizations, political parties, pressure groups, and private organizations. In addition, we single out terror groups and gangs for special attention.

NATION-STATES

In a territorially organized world, the nation-state remains, despite the growing roles of other groups, a dominant participant in the shaping and sharing of all values. The kinds and magnitudes of deprivations and nonfulfillments of human rights to which individuals are today subjected are largely determined by the nation-states of which they are members. Subject to certain reservations to be specified as we proceed, the degree to which demands for human dignity values are fulfilled is still largely dependent upon the performance of governmental functions within territorially organized communities.

In spite of the myth of formal equality, the nation-states of the world are far from congruent with one another. Nation-states vary tremendously in size, population (number and composition), resources, complex matrix of institutions, and stages of development measured by science and technology.[6] It is noteworthy that political boundaries are far from congruous with ethnic, linguistic, cultural, religious, and other boundaries.[7] In terms of the public order system demanded and projected, particularly in the structure of power shaping and sharing, states differ profoundly in characteristics that range from totalitarian or authoritarian to the patterns of democracy.

At the end of World War I a rapid proliferation of nation-states occurred as the ancient empires of Europe divided their continental domains. World War II initiated a fantastically accelerated process which was mainly characterized by the breakup of extra-European empires.[8]

---

6. *See* B. RUSSETT, et al., WORLD HANDBOOK OF POLITICAL AND SOCIAL INDICATORS 293–303 (1964), for quantitative comparison.

7. *See* L. DOOB, COMMUNICATION IN AFRICA: A SEARCH FOR BOUNDARIES (1961); ETHNICITY: THEORY AND EXPERIENCE (N. Glazer & D. Moynihan eds. 1975) [hereinafter cited as ETHNICITY]; Claydon, *The Transnational Protection of Ethnic Minorities: A Tentative Framework for Inquiry,* 13 CANADIAN Y.B. INT'L L. 25 (1975); Connor, *Ethnology and the Peace of South Asia,* 22 WORLD POLITICS 51 (1969); Connor, *Nation-Building or Nation-Destroying?* 24 WORLD POLITICS 319 (1972); Connor, *The Politics of Ethnonationalism,* 27 J. INT'L AFFAIRS 1 (1973); Possony, *Nationalism and the Ethnic Factor,* 10 ORBIS 1218 (1967); Hughes, *The Real Boundaries in Africa Are Ethnic, Not Lines on a Map,* N.Y. Times, June 15, 1975, § 4, at 4, col. 4.

8. *See* Chen, *Self-Determination as a Human Right,* in TOWARD WORLD ORDER AND HUMAN DIGNITY, *supra* note 1, at 198–261. *See also* A. COBBAN, THE NATION STATE AND NATIONAL SELF-DETERMINATION (1969); R. EMERSON, FROM EMPIRE TO NATION (1960); R. EMERSON, SELF-DETERMINATION REVISITED IN THE ERA OF DECOLONIZATION (Occasional Paper No. 9,

At the same time the numerous demands to bring into effective being a transnational network of effective cooperation fell far short of the dreams and challenges of the world political arena. Failing to achieve sufficient agreement on common purposes, nation-states, like private groups, often give expression to special interests. The massive transformation of ex-colonies into independent states has typically failed to combine nationalism, democracy, and development into coherent and effective programs.[9] The world community is sensitized to a generation of "petty tyrants," who are determined to hold onto power at all cost.[10] Sheltered behind the relative indifference of many elements in the outside world, local rulers have given effect to measures of deprivation and nonfulfillment.

Parallel tendencies have made their presence felt in the older nation-states, some of which were commonly assumed to be insulated from the impact of factors that undermine authority and control. The growing role of government in society, which has frequently gone hand in hand with the centralization of power and the concentration of effective decision making in a few hands, has often led to bureaucratic rigidity and regimentation, corruption, and loss of confidence in the body politic.[11]

Harvard University Center for International Affairs, 1964); D. GORDON, SELF-DETERMINATION AND HISTORY IN THE THIRD WORLD (1971); H. JOHNSON, SELF-DETERMINATION WITHIN THE COMMUNITY OF NATIONS (1967); A. SUREDA, THE EVOLUTION OF THE RIGHT OF SELF-DETERMINATION (1973); U. UMOZURIKE, SELF-DETERMINATION IN INTERNATIONAL LAW (1972).

9. For difficulties associated with contemporary nation building, *see* D. APTER, THE POLITICS OF MODERNIZATION (1965); L. BINDER, et al., CRISES AND SEQUENCES IN POLITICAL DEVELOPMENT (1971) (other contributors are: James S. Coleman, Joseph LaPalombara, Lucian W. Pye, Sidney Verba, & Myron Weiner); C. BLACK, THE DYNAMICS OF MODERNIZATION (1966); S. HUNTINGTON, POLITICAL ORDER IN CHANGING SOCIETIES (1968); A. INKELES & D. SMITH, BECOMING MODERN: INDIVIDUAL CHANGE IN SIX DEVELOPING COUNTRIES (1974); D. LERNER, THE PASSING OF TRADITIONAL SOCIETY: MODERNIZING THE MIDDLE EAST (1963); M. LEVY, MODERNIZATION AND THE STRUCTURE OF SOCIETY: A SETTING FOR INTERNATIONAL AFFAIRS (1966); Lasswell, *The Policy Sciences of Development,* 17 WORLD POLITICS 286 (1965).

10. *See, e.g.,* Hills, *Amin Is a Tyrant, but Not without Admirers,* N.Y. Times, July 11, 1976, § 4, at 3, col. 3; Sulzberger, *No Antidote to 'Big Daddy,' id.,* June 29, 1975, § 4, at 15, col. 2; *Africa Can't Afford Him, id.,* July 12, 1975, at 24, col. 1 (editorial); *id.,* July 10, 1976, at 3, col. 1; *id.,* Oct. 5, 1975, § 1, at 2, col. 3 (Ambassador Daniel Moynihan's criticism of Amin).

See also Uganda: Amin vs. the World, NEWSWEEK, Aug. 9, 1976, at 35–36; N.Y. Times, Dec. 5, 1976, § 1, at 15, col. 1 (city ed.) (the transformation of the Central African Republic to the Central African Empire and of Salah Eddine Ahmed Bokassa from president for life to Emperor Bokassa I).

11. *See* M. HALPERIN, et al., THE LAWLESS STATE: THE CRIME OF THE U.S. INTELLIGENCE AGENCIES (1976); J. LIEBERMAN, HOW THE GOVERNMENT BREAKS THE LAW (1972); D. WISE, THE POLITICS OF LYING: GOVERNMENT DECEPTION, SECRECY, AND POWER (1973); A. WOLFE, THE SEAMY SIDE OF DEMOCRACY: REPRESSION IN AMERICA (1973).

INTERNATIONAL GOVERNMENTAL ORGANIZATIONS

Under the pressures generated by interdependence, nation-states have found it expedient to organize a network of transnational intergovernmental structures to accomplish a range of specific objectives. Being creatures of nation-states, these organizations are generally handicapped in activities relating to human rights by the acute concern of the most influential elements in particular nation-states with avoiding either a formal or an effective loss of power. Though formal competences for the promotion or protection of human rights may be conferred upon those organizations, their actual capacity for furthering value fulfillment is commonly curtailed by the limited resources made available to them.[12]

The disappointing developments to which brief allusion has been made are especially painful to the large number of articulate spokesmen of human interest values in the nontotalitarian or ex-colonial powers who cooperated to achieve international or local treaties and statutes that put into authoritative language the aspirations of many generations of humanizing and revolutionary politicians and lawyers. The Charter of the United Nations and the many accompanying declarations and conventions about human rights are the most influential and conspicuous and therefore the most important sources of hope, action, and partial disappointment.[13]

As we shall have occasion to demonstrate, the turbulence, confusion, and conflict connected with human rights have created a state of affairs that multiplies participants in the world (including local) processes of politics, which are more dynamic than ever before as factors in issues pertaining to human dignity.

Whatever the words of authority that authorize action on behalf of human rights, the somber story is that, so far, the resources of manpower, facilities, and support have been insufficient to take advantage of the growing complexities of the situation.

---

12. The 1972 budget of the United Nations was $213 million. N.Y. Times, Dec. 2, 1972, at 13, col. 4. In U.N. circles, the U.N. budget is compared to that of the Fire Department of New York City. According to Professor Karl W. Deutsch's estimate, as based on data in B. RUSSETT, *supra* note 6, at 56–68, the total governmental expenditures (governments at all levels—national, state or provincial, and local) of all the nation-states are between approximately one-quarter and one-third of the GNP of the non-Communist countries. On the other hand, the total expenditures of all the international organizations are roughly 1 percent of the GNP of these same countries. Deutsch, *The Probability of International Law,* in THE RELEVANCE OF INTERNATIONAL LAW 60 (K. Deutsch & S. Hoffmann eds. 1968).

13. Relevant human rights prescriptions are conveniently collected in BASIC DOCUMENTS ON HUMAN RIGHTS (I. Brownlie ed. 1971); BASIC DOCUMENTS ON INTERNATIONAL PROTECTION OF HUMAN RIGHTS (L. Sohn & T. Buergenthal eds. 1973); UNITED NATIONS, HUMAN RIGHTS: A COMPILATION OF INTERNATIONAL INSTRUMENTS OF THE UNITED NATIONS, U.N. Doc. ST/HR/1 (1973).

POLITICAL PARTIES

The world situation relevant to human dignity is affected by the positive, negative, or indifferent roles played by political parties that cooperate or coordinate across national lines.[14] In totalitarian states that share the tradition of international socialism, the language of the constitution is consonant with the doctrines and procedures of human rights. When the actual situations in such societies are investigated, however, it is far from obvious that the prescriptive norms are put into effect. Underground political parties include organizations that protest as vigorously as they can under the circumstances against the contradictions between proclamation and practice. However, it is not to be taken for granted that every vestige has disappeared of sociopolitical orders that were pushed aside by revolutionary programs championing the cause of human dignity. Underground movements continue in the hope of reinstating as much as possible of previous systems. These residual fragments make common cause with one another, and with the reactionary elites of the world arena. These party programs may speak in the name of ancient programs of caste and class, and of value and religion. On the whole, however, it is correct to affirm that political parties are more heavily weighted in favor of than in opposition to human rights.

It is worth taking note of a distinction that can usefully be made between genuine political parties and monopoly organizations that may be called political parties. The latter are more properly known as political orders. Political parties are institutions that evolved in arenas where organized participation in the decision process of the nation-state is relatively open.

PRESSURE GROUPS

Unlike political parties, many organizations concentrate on a single demand rather than upon comprehensive programs of public order.

---

14. *See generally* W. Chambers, Political Parties in a New Nation (1963); R. Dahl, Political Oppositions in Western Democracies (1966); Regimes and Oppositions (R. Dahl ed. 1973); M. Duverger, Political Parties (1954); V. Key, Politics, Parties, and Pressure Groups (5th ed. 1964); Political Parties and Political Development (J. LaPalombara & M. Weiner eds. 1966); H. Lasswell & A. Kaplan, *supra* note 1, at 169-73; D. MacRae, Parliament Parties, and Society in France, 1946–1958 (1967); S. Neuman, Modern Political Parties (1956); J. Saloma & F. Sontag, Parties: The Real Opportunity for Effective Citizen Politics (1972); Epstein, *Political Parties,* in 4 Handbook of Political Science 229–77 (F. Greenstein & N. Polsby eds. 1975).

See also Laqueur, *Eurocommunism and Its Friends,* 62 Commentary 25 (Aug. 1976); Seligman, *Communism's Crisis of Authority,* Fortune, Feb. 1976, at 92–95 *et seq.;* Seligman, *Communists in Democratic Clothing,* Fortune, Mar. 1976, at 116–19 *et seq.;* Birnbaum, *The New European Socialism,* N.Y. Times, May 15, 1976, at 25, col. 2 (city ed.); Gordon, *Changes in Communist Parties in Developed Capitalist Nations,* N.Y. Times, Mar. 21, 1976, § 4, at 17, col. 1.

Socialism or liberalism, for instance, is translated into inclusive conceptions of governmental structure and function by political parties. Pressure groups concentrate on particular details, such as the abolition of slavery, the graduated income tax, women's suffrage, free public education, and so on, through scores of proposals.[15] Almost every measure that has a recognized relation to human dignity has been, or is currently, a target of pressure group action. Sometimes the political system permits a "one-issue group" to call itself a political party and to nominate candidates. Strictly speaking, the "conventional" labels are misleading. In a functional sense, these are pressure groups.

It is not to be overlooked that pressure groups, like political parties, may operate on all sides of an issue. We are not surprised to find that collective action is directed *against* as well as *for* human rights. In practice, the true orientation of a group may be disguised by the rhetoric of "liberalism," "moderation," or "progressivism."

PRIVATE ASSOCIATIONS

A comprehensive inventory of organizations with transnational impact quickly establishes that political power is only one of the value outcomes that are pursued chiefly by private or mixed public and private associations. Nation-states, political parties, and pressure groups emphasize power. Yet it is apparent that their distinctive accent on political power in no way implies that their impacts on enlightenment, wealth, or any other value-institution sector are trivial. The same pattern is present in associations that are primarily private (in the civic order). Scientific societies, both local and transnational, are distinctively aimed at the cultivation and dissemination of knowledge. At the same time it is perceived that they require funds and manpower to get on with their goals, and that they contribute to the economy of the territories where they are based.

15. *See* J. LADOR-LEDERER, INTERNATIONAL GROUP PROTECTION 373–417 (1968); L. WHITE, INTERNATIONAL NON-GOVERNMENTAL ORGANIZATIONS (1951); *Interest Groups in International Perspective,* 413 ANNALS 1 (May 1974); *Non-Governmental Organizations,* U.N. Doc. E/4476 (1968) (report of the secretary-general).

See more generally C. ASTIZ, PRESSURE GROUPS AND POWER ELITES IN PERUVIAN POLITICS (1969); H. ECKSTEIN, PRESSURE GROUP POLITICS: THE CASE OF THE BRITISH MEDICAL ASSOCIATION (1960); INTEREST GROUPS ON FOUR CONTINENTS (H. Ehrmann ed. 1958); A. HOLTZMAN, INTEREST GROUPS AND LOBBYING (1966); V. KEY, *supra* note 14; PRIVATE GOVERNMENT: INTRODUCTORY READINGS (S. Lakoff ed. 1973); J. LAPALOMBARA, INTEREST GROUPS IN ITALIAN POLITICS (1964); G. MCCONNELL, PRIVATE POWER AND AMERICAN DEMOCRACY (1966); VOLUNTARY ASSOCIATIONS (J. Pennock & J. Chapman eds. 1969); H. ZIEGLER & G. PEAK, INTEREST GROUPS IN AMERICAN SOCIETY (2d ed. 1972); *Pressure and Interest Groups,* in COMPARATIVE POLITICS 388–430 (H. Eckstein & D. Apter eds. 1963) (articles by Almond, Eckstein, and LaPalombara); Salisbury, *Interest Groups,* 4 HANDBOOK OF POLITICAL SCIENCE 171–228 (F. Greenstein & N. Polsby eds. 1975).

The point is especially evident when we consider the multinational corporations, i.e., those transnational corporations and associations that frequently operate in finance, transportation, communication, mining, fishing, agriculture, manufacturing, wholesaling, retailing, and other branches of economic life. They employ a wide variety of modern technologies, in activities ranging from production and marketing to financing and management. Thanks to these new technological developments, new management techniques, and the transnational network of communication and transportation, multinational corporations have grown in number, size, activities, and importance. As they operate across many state boundaries, they serve as a global vehicle for the transfer and dissemination of capital and skill, as well as of technology. They have greatly contributed to the internationalization of production, finance, and ownership, and to the growing integration of national economies into a world economy.[16]

Multinational corporations, since they may possess more resources than many nation-states, have sometimes been seen as posing threats to nation-states.[17] Their actual and potential impact on deprivations and

---

16. The increasing attention accorded the roles of multinational corporations is clearly demonstrated by the rapid proliferation of literature. *See* The Multinational Corporation and Social Change (D. Apter & L. Goodman eds. 1976); Global Companies: The Political Economy of World Business (G. Ball ed. 1975) [hereinafter cited as Global Companies]; World Business: Promise and Problems (C. Brown ed. 1970) [hereinafter cited as World Business]; The Multinational Enterprise (J. Dunning ed. 1971); N. Fatemi, G. Williams, & T. DeSaint-Phalle, Multinational Corporatons (2d ed. 1976); B. Ganguli, Multinational Corporations (1974); International Labour Office, Multinational Enterprises and Social Policy (1973); The Multinational Corporation (C. Kindleberger ed. 1970); E. Kolde, The Multinational Company (1974); J. Stopford & L. Wells, Managing the Multinational Enterprise (1972); C. Tugendhat, The Multinationals (1972); L. Turner, Multinational Companies and the Third World (1973); United Nations, Department of Economic and Social Affairs, The Impact of Multinational Corporations on Development and on International Relations, U.N. Doc. E/5500/Rev. 1 (ST/ESA/6) (1974) [hereinafter cited as The Impact]; United Nations, Department of Economic and Social Affairs, Multinational Corporations in World Development, U.N. Doc. ST/ECA/190 (1973) [hereinafter cited as Multinational Corporations in World Development]; United Nations, Department of Economic and Social Affairs, Summary of the Hearings Before the Group of Eminent Persons to Study the Impact of Multinational Corporations on Development and on International Relations, U.N. Doc. ST/ESA/15 (1974); R. Vernon, Sovereignty at Bay: The Multinational Spread of United States Enterprises (1971); Seidl-Hohenveldern, *Multinational Enterprises and the International Law of the Future,* [1975] Y.B. World Affairs 301; Cary, *Multinational Corporations as Development Partners,* N.Y. Times, Nov. 8, 1975, at 27, col. 2 (city ed.).

17. Starting from the assumption that "The men who run the global corporations are the first in history with the organization, technology, money, and ideology to make a credible try at managing the world as an integrated unit," Barnet and Muller argue that "the goal of corporate diplomacy is nothing less than the replacement of national loyalty

nonfulfillment in the shaping and sharing of values has provoked increasing alarm. Multinational corporations, profit-oriented as they have to be, are variously perceived as exploiters of the labor and physical resources of the developing countries, practitioners of corrupt business practices, environmental polluters, manipulators of currencies and commodities, tax dodgers, instruments of their national governments, and supporters of reactionary regimes.[18] In recent times they have achieved notoriety by the exposure of the widespread business practice of bribery, regarded as corrupting and conspiring with power elites to the detriment of the masses of the population.[19]

---

with corporate loyalty. If they are to succeed in integrating the planet, loyalty to the global enterprise must take precedence over all other political loyalties." R. BARNET & R. MULLER, GLOBAL REACH: THE POWER OF THE MULTINATIONAL CORPORATIONS 13, 89 (1974). For detail, see *id.* at 72–104.

Raymond Vernon dramatizes the threat of the multinational enterprises in these words: "Suddenly, it seems, the sovereign states are feeling naked. Concepts such as national sovereignty and national economic strength appear curiously drained of meaning." R. VERNON, *supra* note 16, at 3.

See also J. BEHRMAN, NATIONAL INTERESTS AND THE INTERNATIONAL ENTERPRISE: TENSIONS AMONG THE NORTH ATLANTIC COUNTRIES (1970); THE NATION-STATE AND TRANSACTIONAL CORPORATIONS IN CONFLICT, WITH SPECIAL REFERENCE TO LATIN AMERICA (J. Gunnemann ed. 1975); T. MORAN, MULTINATIONAL CORPORATIONS AND THE POLITICS OF DEPENDENCE: COPPER IN CHILE (1974); Ball, *Introduction,* in GLOBAL COMPANIES, *supra* note 16, at 1–2; Behrman, Multination Corporations and National Sovereignty, in WORLD BUSINESS, *supra* note 16, at 114–25; Barnet & Muller, *Planet Earth, A Wholly-Owned Subsidiary,* N.Y. Times, Jan. 23, 1975, at 33, col. 1.

18. *See* R. BARNET & R. MULLER, *supra* note 17, at 123–84, 278–83, 334–62. For a case study, *see* A. SAMPSON, THE SOVEREIGN STATE OF ITT (1973).

As Katzenbach points out:

> The earlier literature tended to regard the so-called multinational corporation as a new form of internationalism which would have beneficent results in terms of rationalizing the world economic order irrespective of political boundaries, of transferring technology from the haves to the have-nots, and being a sort of great engine for economic development in the post-war period.

"More recently," he continues, "for a variety of reasons, multinational corporations have been viewed as instruments of a new imperialism in which the rich exploit the poor and the haves exploit the have-nots." Katzenbach, *Law-Making for Multinational Corporations,* in C. BLACK, et al., A NEW WORLD ORDER? 25 (World Order Studies Program Occasional Paper No. 1, Princeton University, Center of International Studies, 1975).

On tax problems involving multinational corporations, *see* a study prepared by Carl S. Shoup for the United Nations: UNITED NATIONS, DEPARTMENT OF ECONOMIC AND SOCIAL AFFAIRS, THE IMPACT OF MULTINATIONAL CORPORATIONS ON DEVELOPMENT AND ON INTERNATIONAL RELATIONS—TECHNICAL PAPERS: TAXATION, U.N. Doc. ST/ESA/11 (1974).

19. *See* W. REISMAN, FOLDED LIES: BRIBERY, CRUSADES, AND REFORMS (1978); N.Y. Times, Feb. 15, 1976, § 3, at 1, col. 1 (containing a compilation of reported payments abroad by American corporations for bribes, political contributions, sales commissions, and other purposes); *id.,* May 5, 1975, at 1, col. 1 (city ed.) (*U.S. Company Payoffs Way of Life*

The foregoing examples of private groups have dealt chiefly with *power* and *wealth*, with a brief allusion to scientific *enlightenment*. Specialized operations connected with the gathering, processing, and dissemination of current information are often in the hands of news associations. These activities are especially germane to the focusing of attention on, or distraction of attention from, matters that pertain to human rights. The number of topics that may arouse the curiosity of human beings, and that initiate the formation of groups, is infinite. In an important sense, a long-range drive is to explore the total environment of mankind, and—almost as a by-product—to discover the interconnectedness of human lives.

Private as well as governmental groups are absorbed with all aspects of *well-being*. These range from the survey of health threats and opportunities to the cultivation of diversions that counteract any tendency toward boredom. Another enormously variegated sector of value and institutional practice is related to *skill*. Skills are occupational and professional; and they include all manner of artistic expression, since a relatively distinctive use of skill implies the completion of acts and of physical arrangements in ways that emphasize the pattern of internal adjustment, rather than the impact on wealth, power, or other discussions of social process. The "human right to enjoy and pursue excellence in the arts" is a manifestation of deep-lying initiatives in human personality.

Unquestionably the institutions related to intimacy and loyalty are deeply intertwined with human rights. Wherever there is human contact, it is probable that friendship and intimacy will appear; and these commitments are frequently such that barriers that seek to block these culminations are pushed aside.

With the intensification of association on a global scale it is clear that the interplay of admiration and contempt are differentiated, and that the giving and receiving of respect become major demands that affect the patterns of respect. In the same way global exposure modifies targets and judgments of decency and belief (rectitude). These are among the parameters that define the content and significance of human rights.

We note that the linkages between public and civic order are subtle, and hence visible only when special procedures are used to bring them to the focus of an observer's attention. Complex socialist societies give relative prominence to the role of government, and hence to public order. As a rule, the official doctrine attempts to modulate the passage of public into private and of private into explicitly public activities. The pattern of

---

Overseas); Cohen, *Lockheed Cover-Up? id.*, Mar. 29, 1976, at 29, col. 2; Barnet, *Not Just Your Corner Drugstore, id.*, June 19, 1975, at 35, col. 1. *See also* POLITICAL CORRUPTION: READINGS IN COMPARATIVE ANALYSIS (A. Heidenheimer comp. 1970).

ultimate regimentation on a world scale would approximate a global prison camp in which the top hierarchy would do everything it could to specify in detail the daily calendar of individual and small-group, as well as large-group, contact and to mobilize every means for the purpose of regimenting behavior in conformity with these detailed prescriptions.[20] Thus far, at least, regimentation of this kind is rarely approximated.

TERROR GROUPS AND GANGS

We single out for special mention terror groups and gangs. Depending as they do on the use of violent coercion, they obviously are functionally related to power and can be thought of as closely akin to pressure groups. They differ, however, in that although they rely on a form of power, they do not necessarily limit themselves to the pursuit of power as the principal value toward which their efforts are directed.[21] Some terror gangs are focused on wealth, as in the notorious instance of the slave trade,[22] or that of the organized criminal associations whose dealings in drugs or prostitution, for example, penetrate the boundaries of many countries. Value objectives other than power or wealth are seldom of major importance. We know of tribal societies in the past, however, whose members engaged in mutual raiding that was principally a matter of respect. It was a necessary act to demonstrate the readiness of a youth to become a man.

In the contemporary world, terror gangs have become particularly

---

20. This garrison-state hypothesis was originally presented by one of the authors in 1937. *See* Lasswell, *Sino-Japanese Crisis: The Garrison State versus the Civilian State,* 2 CHINA Q. 643 (1937); Lasswell, *The Garrison State,* 46 AM. J. SOCIOLOGY 455 (1941); Lasswell, *The Garrison State Hypothesis Today,* in CHANGING PATTERNS OF MILITARY POLITICS 51–70 (S. Huntington ed. 1962). *See also* Fox, *Harold D. Lasswell and the Study of World Politics: Configurative Analysis, Garrison State, and World Commonwealth,* in POLITICS, PERSONALITY, AND SOCIAL SCIENCE IN THE TWENTIETH CENTURY: ESSAYS IN HONOR OF HAROLD D. LASSWELL 367–81 (A. Rogow ed. 1969).

Cf. A. HUXLEY, BRAVE NEW WORLD (Bantam classic ed. 1958); A. HUXLEY, BRAVE NEW WORLD REVISITED (1965); G. ORWELL, 1984 (1949); 1984 REVISITED: PROSPECTS FOR AMERICAN POLITICS (R. Wolff ed. 1973).

21. *See* UNITED NATIONS, DEPARTMENT OF ECONOMIC AND SOCIAL AFFAIRS, FIFTH UNITED NATIONS CONGRESS ON THE PREVENTION OF CRIME AND THE TREATMENT OF OFFENDERS, GENEVA, 1–12 SEPTEMBER 1975 (report prepared by the Secretariat) 10–15, U.N. Doc. A/CONF.56/10 (1976); W. WHYTE, STREET CORNER SOCIETY (1943); Tyler, *The Roots of Organized Crime,* 8 CRIME AND DELINQUENCY 325 (1962), *reprinted in* SOCIAL PROBLEMS IN A CHANGING WORLD 198–214 (W. Gerson ed. 1969); N.Y. Times, Nov. 7, 1976, § 1, at 1, col. 4 (city ed.).

22. *See* B. DAVIDSON, BLACK MOTHER: THE YEARS OF THE AFRICAN SLAVE TRADE (1961); C. GREENIDGE, SLAVERY 49–57 (1958); S. O'CALLAGHAN, THE SLAVE TRADE TODAY (1961); Schakteton, *The Slave Trade Today,* in SLAVERY: A COMPARATIVE PERSPECTIVE 188 (R. Winks ed. 1972).

prominent participants in the processes of politics, reflecting a complex constellation of factors that condition, and in turn are conditioned by, the social process as a whole.[23]

Unorganized Groups

The organizations mentioned heretofore include in their membership those who by formally binding themselves together share significant traits. Unorganized participants in the world social process share certain common characteristics, even though they are not typically joined together for joint operations. We consider culture, class, interest, personality, and crisis groups, and give particular attention to the fact that they interact as conditioning factors with the organized groups enumerated above.

CULTURE

The term "culture" is employed to designate distinctive and stable patterns of values and institutions that are deployed around the globe.[24] Each culture may assign value priorities in a somewhat distinctive manner, as when we find that nomadic tribesmen glorify power, whereas neighboring agriculturalists emphasize the production of wealth and the gratifications of peace. Institutional practices vary greatly from culture to culture and from value to value.

In earlier times—notably in the fourth or fifth millennium B.C.—the urban division of labor supplemented tribal cultures with civilization. In more recent years science and technology have moved toward universality, with the result that communities throughout the globe are exhibit-

---

23. *See* J. Bell, Transnational Terror (1975); International Terrorism and World Security (D. Carlton & C. Schaerf eds. 1975); E. Hyams, Terrorists and Terrorism (1975); B. Jenkins, International Terrorism: A New Mode of Conflict (1975); Report of the Ad Hoc Committee on International Terrorism, 28 U.N. GAOR, Supp. (No. 28), U.N. Doc. A/9028 (1973); Rovine, *The Contemporary International Legal Attack on Terrorism,* 3 Israel Y.B. Human Rights 9 (1973); *Terrorism and Political Crimes in International Law,* [1973] Proc., Am. Soc'y Int'l L. 87.

See also Organized Crime Reaps Huge Profits from Dealing in Pornographic Films, N.Y. Times, Oct. 12, 1975, § 1, at 1, col. 1; *Key Mafia Figure Tells of 'Wars' and Gallo-Colombo Peace Talks, id.,* July 7, 1975, at 1, col. 1; *Kidnapping a Lucrative Crime in Argentina, id.,* May 29, 1974, at 53, col. 1 (city ed.).

24. *See* H. Lasswell & A. Kaplan, *supra* note 1, at 47–51. *See generally* B. Malinowski, A Scientific Theory of Culture, and Other Essays (1960); R. Benedict, Patterns of Culture (1959); J. Honingmann, Understanding Culture (1963); A. Kroeber, The Nature of Culture (1952); The Science of Man in the World Crisis (R. Linton ed. 1945) especially articles by Clyde Kluckhohn and William H. Kelly and by Abram Kardiner); E. Tylor, Primitive Culture (1871); L. White, The Science of Culture: A Study of Man and Civilization (1949).

ing an enormous variety of transitional patterns. This distinctiveness has been described in many different ways: "primitive, archaic, historic, pre-modern, or modern";[25] traditional or modern; nomadic, agricultural, industrial, or postindustrial.[26] The accent may be on traditional collectivities or upon a multitude of functional (pluralized) groups. The class structure may be limited to a two-class model or diversified into a multiple-class system. There may be low or high social mobility.[27]

In an increasingly interactive world, the cultural factors play complicating and contradictory roles. It is easy to recognize the trends toward instantaneous news, transnational travel, or world science, for example. At the same time, observant individuals perceive that the trend toward technological universalization has not meant peace, understanding, and cooperation for the common interest; rather, it often signifies the use of universal cultural traits to enhance parochial demands and identities, accompanied by partial adaptation to a limited number of common activities. Abiding parochialism has meant that surviving or novel practices are not always tolerated as functional equivalents. Conflicts arise over different ways of doing the same thing, and the aggregate common interest is not discovered.

It may be worth emphasizing that urban civilization evolved only seven or eight thousand years ago, and that prior to that time, prodigious

---

25. J. PEACOCK & A. KIRSCH, THE HUMAN DIRECTION: AN EVOLUTIONARY APPROACH TO SOCIAL AND CULTURAL ANTHROPOLOGY vi (1970).

In his analysis of religious evolution, Bellah conceptualizes in terms of five stages: "primitive religion," "archaic religion," "historic religion," "early modern religion," and "modern religion." Bellah, *Religious Evolution,* 29 AM. SOCIOLOGICAL REV. 358 (1964). *See also* R. BELLAH, BEYOND BELIEF: ESSAYS ON RELIGION IN A POST-TRADITIONAL WORLD 20–50 (1976).

26. The classic work on the "stages" theory of economic growth, W. ROSTOW, THE STAGES OF ECONOMIC GROWTH: A NON-COMMUNIST MANIFESTO (1960), characterizes the stages as "the traditional society, the preconditions for take-off, the take-off, the drive to maturity, and the age of high mass consumption" (at 4). *Cf.* A. HIRSCHMAN, THE STRATEGY OF ECONOMIC DEVELOPMENT (1968), which suggests the limitations of Rostow's theories. *Cf. also* A. ORGANSKI, THE STAGES OF POLITICAL DEVELOPMENT (1965).

The term "postindustrial" is employed, and made popular, by Daniel Bell. For a comprehensive treatment, *see* D. BELL, THE COMING OF POST-IINDUSTRIAL SOCIETY: A VENTURE IN SOCIAL FORECASTING (1973). Other scholars prefer other designations. For example, Brzezinski prefers "technetronic." Z. BRZEZINSKI, BETWEEN TWO AGES: AMERICA'S ROLE IN THE TECHNETRONIC ERA 9 (1971).

27. For an outstanding account of different approaches to class and mobility in contemporary societies, *see* R. DAHRENDORF, CLASS AND CLASS CONFLICT IN INDUSTRIAL SOCIETY (1959).

For a standard work on this subject, *see* S. LIPSET & R. BENDIX, SOCIAL MOBILITY IN INDUSTRIAL SOCIETY (1959). Also, *cf.* T. BOTTOMORE, CLASSES IN MODERN SOCIETY (1966).

emphasis was put on identifying with small groups.[28] This was a necessary means of socializing individuals to incorporate the demands of others, and prepared the way for cooperation on a much larger scale. In civilization, writing and other modes of transmitting knowledge become dynamic factors in accelerating the evolution of social institutions.[29]

Anxieties are generated by the unceasing challenge to change by modifying value priorities and institutional arrangements.[30] "Culture shock" is a continuing cost of innovation and complicates the task of those who strive for effective action in the field of human rights.[31]

CLASS

Within any given society, classes are formed according to the degree of control individuals exercise over values. All known societies are more or less class-ridden, although the character and magnitude of stratification differ from one community to another.[32] Rigidity of stratification exhibits a wide spectrum that ranges from a highly hierarchized, closed society to an open society that is highly mobile.[33]

---

28. V. Gordon Childe stresses the central importance of the creation of cities for the emergence of civilization. The invention is tentatively located in a few river valleys (notably the Nile, the Tigris-Euphrates, and the Indus) about seven thousand years ago. *See* V. Childe, New Light on the Most Ancient East (1935). *See also* R. Redfield, The Primitive World and Its Transformations (1953).

29. *Cf.* L. Mumford, The City in History (1961); L. Mumford, The Culture of Cities (1938).

30. This theme has been dramatically popularized by a recent best seller: A. Toffler, Future Shock (Bantam ed. 1971). *Cf.* C. Walker, Technology, Industry, and Man: The Age of Acceleration (1968).

31. *See* A. Toffler, *supra* note 30, at 10–11, 347–48.

32. A valuable anthology that combines fragments of many of the classics and empirical studies is Class, Status, and Power (R. Bendix & S. Lipset eds. 2d ed. 1966). For a critique of the class system in Communist countries by a top Yugoslav official in disgrace, *see* M. Djilas, The New Class: An Analysis of the Communist System (1959).

See also B. Bernard, Social Stratification: A Comparative Analysis of Structure and Process (1957); Social Inequality (A. Beteille ed. 1969); The Impact of Social Class (P. Blumberg ed. 1971); R. Brown, Social Psychology 101–51 (1965); A. Hollingshead & F. Reblich, Social Class and Mental Illness (1958); Comparative Perspectives on Stratification: Mexico, Great Britain, Japan (J. Kahl ed. 1968); G. Lenski, Power and Privilege: A Theory of Social Stratification (1966); J. Lopreato & L. Hazelrigg, Class, Conflict and Mobility (1972); J. Schumpeter, Social Classes (1951); A. Tuden & L. Plotnicov, Social Stratification in Africa (1970); T. Tumin, Social Stratification: The Forms and Functions of Inequality (1972).

33. Highly hierarchized, closed societies are exemplified by societies in which the caste system or the practice of apartheid prevails. For further factual background and pertinent references, *see* chapter 7 *infra,* at notes 303–598 and accompanying text.

Concerning open, mobile, societies, *see, e.g.,* G. Carlsson, Social Mobility and Class

From the time of their first appearance, urban civilizations have accentuated class differences with special reference to wealth and power. The rich and the poor, the strong and the weak, became the criteria of identification, superseding family and kinship as bases of loyalty.

The class divisions of modern urban and industrial society combined with the structure of feudalism to lend plausibility to political movements in the name of class. Class distinctions, however, continue to clash with other perspectives. Upper-, middle-, and lower-class attitudes are often in conflict with conceptions of equal opportunity for all.[34]

INTEREST

The factor of interest cuts across both culture and class lines. Less comprehensive than either culture or class groupings, interest groups are formed in reference to particular values, institutional perspectives, and operations. In a modern technological society a great number of interest groups is continually generated as a consequence of the division of labor and the multiplication of patterns of both symbols and operations. Consequently, perspectives about interest have tended to cut across and dissolve large cultural and class groupings. The result is to increase the frequency and fluidity of the coalitions involved in the shaping and sharing of values.[35] The individuals who constitute the core of an interest group may be widely distributed over the globe. Typically, they are surrounded by persons whose perspectives are nebulous and whose conduct is little influenced by the central perspective. Contemporary processes, dynamic as they are, confront individuals with a bewildering variety of interests. Collective programs—focused on human rights, for example—suffer corresponding difficulties.

PERSONALITY

The conception of personality is not to be confused with that of the individual as a biological entity.[36] The biological entity that appears at

---

STRUCTURE (1958); SOCIAL MOBILITY IN BRITAIN (D. Glass ed. 1955); S. LIPSET & R. BENDIX, *supra* note 27.

34. Systematic inquiry on class has owed significantly to Lloyd Warner and associates, who stressed upper-class exemptions from law enforcement. On middle- and upper-class violations in general, *see* D. CRESSEY, OTHER PEOPLE'S MONEY (1953); A. SUTHERLAND, WHITE COLLAR CRIME (1949). The late Svend Ranulf employed quantitative methods to investigate the impact of changes in class structure upon the scope and severity of criminal legislation. *See* S. RANULF, MORAL INDIGNATION AND MIDDLE CLASS PSYCHOLOGY: A SOCIOLOGICAL STUDY (1964). Research on class remains relatively undifferentiated, focusing largely upon wealth, respect, and skill.

35. *See* H. LASSWELL & A. KAPLAN, *supra* note 1, at 40–45. *Cf.* note 15 *supra.*

36. Personality has been given a wide range of references. A useful compendium of articles on this subject is PERSONALITY IN NATURE, SOCIETY, AND CULTURE (C. Kluckhohn & H. Murray eds. 2d ed. 1953).

birth is equipped with dispositions to initiate and to respond to the various components of the body and also of the surrounding environment. The physical individual becomes a "person" in the process of interaction. When an act is rewarded by a value indulgence—such as food and cuddling—the result is to strengthen the tendency to initiate or complete the rewarded act. If the completed act is met with value deprivations rather than indulgences, the resulting tendency is for the person to avoid or cut short the act. Taken as a whole, the dispositions of the person to interact in a discernible manner are "personality."

Without going into detail, it is nevertheless useful to recognize that a personality system, viewed as an entirety, includes three categories of acts. The "ego" covers all the moods and images that are fully conscious. The "superego" includes the norms that are automatically implied to bar the completion of acts or to expedite completion as a compulsive or obsessional occurrence. The "id" refers to basic impulses, especially to those that are denied expression by the superego.[37]

Personality structures are formed in interaction with patterns of culture. The exposure of the person to the value indulgences or deprivations of the culture environment results in the formation of an ego and superego system that incorporates the value priorities and practices. To the degree that "socialization" is successful, personalities monitor themselves in accordance with the identities, demands, and expectations of the culture.[38]

It is apparent that if violations of human rights are component ele-

---

The major theoretical positions are well described in M. DEUTSCH & R. KRAUSS, THEORIES IN SOCIAL PSYCHOLOGY (1965). *See also* G. ALLPORT, BECOMING: BASIC CONSIDERATIONS FOR A PSYCHOLOGY OF PERSONALITY (1955); G. ALLPORT, PERSONALITY AND SOCIAL ENCOUNTER (1960); G. HALL & G. LINDZEY, THEORIES OF PERSONALITY (1957); R. LAZARUS, PERSONALITY (1963); A. MASLOW, MOTIVATION AND PERSONALITY (1954).

37. *See* S. FREUD, THE COMPLETE INTRODUCTORY LECTURES ON PSYCHOANALYSIS 521–75 (J. Strachey trans. 1966) [hereinafter cited as S. FREUD]; S. FREUD, THE EGO AND THE ID (J. Riviere trans., J. Strachey ed. 1962). *See also* C. BRENNER, AN ELEMENTARY TEXTBOOK OF PSYCHOANALYSIS (rev. ed. 1974); H. LASSWELL, & A. KAPLAN, *supra* note 1, at 10–15.

38. An excellent overview of socialization and personality development is SOCIALIZATION AND PERSONALITY DEVELOPMENT (E. Zigler & I. Child eds. 1973) (containing a comprehensive bibliography). *See also* R. BROWN, *supra* note 32, at 193–417; F. GREENSTEIN, CHILDREN AND POLITICS (1965); PERSONALITY AND SOCIALIZATION (D. Heise ed. 1972); H. HYMAN, POLITICAL SOCIALIZATION (1959); G. MEAD, *supra* note 1; P. MUSSEN, J. CONGER, & J. KAGAN, CHILD DEVELOPMENT AND PERSONALITY (1963); T. PARSONS & R. BATES, FAMILY: SOCIALIZATION AND INTERACTION PROCESS (1955); PERSONALITY AND SOCIAL SYSTEMS (N. Smelser & W. Smelser eds. 1963); Sears, *Political Socialization,* in 2 HANDBOOK OF POLITICAL SCIENCE 93–153 (F. Greenstein & N. Polsby eds. 1975).

For an understanding of the different worlds of childhood, *see* P. ARIES, CENTURIES OF CHILDHOOD (1962). *See also* U. BRONFENBRENNER, TWO WORLDS OF CHILDHOOD (1972) (an interesting comparative study); CHILDHOOD IN CHINA (W. Kessen ed. 1975); J. WHITING & I. CHILD, CHILD TRAINING AND PERSONALITY: A CROSS-CULTURAL STUDY (1953).

ments of a culture, it is essential to bring about the reconstruction of culture before the norms compatible with human rights can be effectively realized. Within the broad framework of a culture, many of the established class and interest group differences must be changed before human rights can become embedded in the culture.

It has often been argued that human beings include natural "slaves" and that the demand to move toward a public and civic order of human dignity is a chimera. Much evidence has accumulated to show that the biological inheritance is relatively plastic, and that persons who are subjected to a culture of slavery will conform to their socialization. However, there is ample evidence that the culture of slavery is not an inevitable outcome.[39] The varieties of human motivations are such that varying degrees of rejection have culminated in "slave revolts" and in the substitution of cultures of freedom. In particular, there is evidence that personalities who are totally power indulged or power deprived exhibit characteristics that limit the potential creativity of the persons concerned.

The personality structure of the oppressor (depriver) is of particularly direct concern to the analyst of human rights and of the circumstances in which cultures are altered in ways that discourage the formation of value deprivers. The modern study of personality growth recognizes the important consequences of early experiences of deprivation of affection, respect, and other significant outcome opportunities.[40] Persons who occupy an advantaged social position often respond to the ordinary misadventures of life by intense overreactions that seize every occasion to reaffirm the significance of the weakened ego by attacking the self-respect of other human beings, and especially by adopting an intransigent attitude toward anyone who, occupying an inferior position in society, attempts to improve his status or to alter the established routines of the social structure. These truly "reactionary" personalities stand in the way of relatively peaceful readjustment of the system of value shaping and sharing, and therefore seek to block the spread of effective adoption and enforcement of norms compatible with human rights.[41]

---

39. *Cf.* A. Kardiner & L. Ovesey, The Mark of Oppression (1951).

40. *Cf.* O. Fenichel, The Psychoanalytic Theory of Neurosis (1945); K. Horney, Our Inner Conflicts: A Constructive Theory of Neurosis (1945); H. Lasswell, Power and Personality (1962).

41. For broad, sometimes questionable, expositions of the basic point, *see* R. Ardrey, The Territorial Imperative (1966); K. Lorenz, On Aggression (1966); D. Morris, The Naked Ape: A Zoologist's Study of the Human Animal (1967).

For more hopeful views of human nature, *see* A. Alland, The Human Imperative (1972); R. Dubos, So Human an Animal (1968); R. Dubos, Beast or Angel? (1974); E. Fromm, The Anatomy of Human Destructiveness (1973).

CRISIS

The connotations of a crisis include stress generated by conflict and the likelihood that at least some members of a group will suffer value deprivation. Among the most evident factors in the study of world change are the crises that are internal or external to organized or unorganized groups. Many crises fail to correspond to any definite line of demarcation, since they involve participants who are widely scattered in accord with culture, class, or similar characteristics.

The recurring crises among organized groups receive the greatest attention, whether the value frame of reference is power, wealth, or other. Among the more subtle crises are the tensions elicited between traditional and innovative sharers of an established culture, or between the compulsive-obsessional mechanisms and the innovative mechanisms at the disposal of personalities in decision-making elites.[42]

Studies of crisis tend to confirm the view that a moderate level of tension is a valuable incentive for well-considered change. The fact of crisis is enough to open many minds to the probability that prevailing values and institutions are less than perfect; and the modesty of the crisis permits the rational use of the mind—and of collective policy processes—in the search for solutions.[43]

PERSPECTIVES

It is the perspectives of the individuals who participate in the world social process that constitute the predispositional variables which in interaction with the environmental factors affect the flow of deprivations and fulfillment of values. These perspectives may be described in terms of demands for values, the identities of those for whom such values are demanded, and expectations about the conditions affecting the fulfillment or nonfulfillment of values.

---

42. See, for instance, a brilliant case study probing the tension between tradition and modernity among the Dinka, a Nilotic people in the Republic of the Sudan: F. Deng, Tradition and Modernization: A Challenge for Law among the Dinka of the Sudan (1971).

43. In the words of Dubos:

> Crises are practically always a source of enrichment and of renewal because they encourage the search for new solutions. These solutions cannot come from a transformation of human nature, because it is not possible to change the genetic endowment of the human species. But they can come from the manipulation of social structures, because these affect the quality of behavior and of the environment, and therefore the quality of life.

Dubos, *The Humanizing of Humans,* Saturday Rev./World, Dec. 14, 1974, at 76, 80.

Demands

The demands people make for preferred events in the contemporary world cover a wide range of values, whatever the particular characterizations employed, and embrace every variety of nuance in institutional practice in the shaping and sharing of values. It has already been shown that in many parts of the world people increasingly share rising common demands for human dignity values.[44] In other parts of the globe countertrends may predominate. The different demands that are made for values are sometimes inclusive, in the sense that they affect many people, and are linked with expectations of reciprocity for all who are comparably situated. Sometimes demands are exclusive, in the sense that they are made on behalf of rather limited identities and actually affect very few participants in the world process. On occasion demands may be special rather than common, since they are made without regard for the value consequences affecting others, whether they are few or many. Similarly, demands may be constructive and expansionist, designed to increase aggregate values for all, or defensive, intended to protect existing values, whether of all or of relatively exclusive groups. In chosen modality, demands may vary from the most manifest and explicit to the latent and the covert.[45]

In most of the world today, there is, as a consequence of socialization, a high and continuing acquiescence in the prevailing pattern of equality or inequality in the shaping and sharing of values. Millions of the earth's population are socialized to acquiesce in whatever plight of deprivation and nonfulfillment they have come to know in their cultural environment. Established deprivations and nonfulfillments tend to be internalized and tolerated by the middle and lower classes.[46] Many people are

---

44. In very recent times, as decolonization, nation building, and the expanding role of government have gone hand in hand, hitherto deprived groups and peoples in every continent have made insistent demands for wider participation in the shaping and sharing of values. Contemporary demands for human rights, especially freedom and equality, are made in both positive and negative terms, in both individual and collective terms, and in both national and transnational terms. For further elaboration, *see* chapter 1 *supra*.

Long ago Tocqueville pointed out the distinctively dynamic and expanding character of the demand for equality. Once human beings achieve equality in some respects, their quest becomes "totalistic," moving toward equality in all respects. *See* A. de Toqueville, Democracy in America (J. Mayer ed. 1969). *See also* T. Marshall, Class, Citizenship, and Social Development 65–122 (1964); Fallers, *Equality, Modernity, and Democracy in the New States,* in Old Societies and New States: The Quest for Modernity in Asia and Africa 158, 204–19 (C. Geertz ed. 1963).

45. *Cf.* R. Brown, *supra* note 32, at 358–59; S. Freud, *supra* note 37, at 113–25; R. Merton, On Theoretical Sociology 73–138 (1967).

46. A miscellany of researches tends to corroborate the broad hypothesis that "the lower the value position of the participant who suffers a value deprivation the less probable the resort to official arenas; and, once there, the less likely to obtain a value-indulgent result."

so cut off from the outside world, and so conditioned by internal routines, that their latent demands for greater participation in the shaping and sharing of values are suppressed or repressed. This continues to characterize the world scene in spite of growing discontent based on widened experience and exposure to agitational activity.[47]

The demand for total subordination to a governing elite continues in many localities and among many functional groups. Many elites are trained to take no notice of the fact that they are imposing deprivations on others or denying the fulfillment of values. In part, this seeming callousness is to be understood as a standard result of a process of socialization that displaces private motives onto public objects and rationalizes these objectives in terms of common interest.[48]

Identifications

People demand values for particular identities, with various levels of inclusiveness. Changing perspectives of demand and expectation bring about changes in conceptions of the self. The self-system of each individual is composed of the primary ego symbol (of the "I," "me") and the symbols of reference singly or collectively to those egos who are included in a common "we."[49] The self-system also includes symbols that identify the "nonself other," such as members of other nation-states. It is clear on analysis that individuals have multiple identifications, some of which may crosscut and latently conflict with one another.[50] While some iden-

---

We need remind ourselves only of the continuing deprivations to which the powerless, the uninformed, the poor, the weak, the untrained, the unloved, the disrespected, and the heretics are subjected. For a preliminary approach to an appraisal of the working of our "criminal" and "civil" codes, *see* R. Arens & H. Lasswell, *supra* note 1. On other dimensions, *see* A. Rogow & H. Lasswell, *supra* note 1.

47. Since Plato and Aristotle, attention has focused explicitly upon the problem of maintaining public order by fostering an appropriate "character." The problem is that of creating self-systems in which the primary ego identifies with the body politic sufficiently to demand of the self and others that behavior conform to what is required to defend and extend the value position of the body politic. In industrialized societies failures of political socialization in the early years are alleged to encourage "alienation." Transition from traditional to industrial societies is alleged to depend on "empathetic" personalities and on "achievement" orientation. The pertinent context is sketched in G. Almond & S. Verba, Civic Culture (1963); F. Greenstein, *supra* note 38; E. Hagen, The Theory of Social Change (1962); D. Lerner, *supra* note 9; D. McClelland, The Achieving Society (1961).

48. *See* H. Lasswell, *supra* note 40, at 20–38.

49. An outstanding compendium containing various theories about the self-system is The Self in Social Interaction (C. Gordon & K. Gergen eds. 1968). *See also* R. Merton, *supra* note 1; P. Rose, They and We (1965); S. Schachter, The Psychology of Affiliation (1959).

50. *See* H. Guetzkow, Multiple Loyalties (1955); G. Simmel, Conflict and the Web of Group-Affiliation (K. Wolff & R. Bendix trans. 1955).

tifications are ascriptive, and reflect the traditional routines of a social context, more and more identifications appear to be matters of individual choice.

As indicated above, the identifications of many individuals express high ambivalence, exhibiting both expanding and contracting empathy with the inclusive community.[51] Sometimes human dignity demands are made on behalf of lesser groups, even tiny localities and small functional groups.

In an epoch of exacerbated nationalism and accelerated nation building, it must be recognized that dominant identities (loyalties) remain parochial, not universal. Sentiment on behalf of "spaceship earth" remains scattered and weak.[52] It is relatively unusual for people to evolve a system of identities that ranges from the importance of the individual human being to the whole of mankind.

Exaggerated images of the difference between the "self" and "other" help to account for the continuing vogue of large-scale deprivation. How the depriver perceives and identifies the deprivee (target) is crucial. The deprivee may be perceived as possessing common humanity, or as a "subhuman" "thing." When human beings are perceived as subhuman, it is easy to magnify perspectives of hatred and contempt, and to further denigrate the "humanity" of the target.[53]

In the early stages, at least, of a rapidly expanding technological society, local symbols of identity may weaken. However, this is usually for the benefit of entities (like nation-states) that are intermediate between the older territory and the inclusive world community.[54]

A persisting residue of the ancient past and of more recent conflict is

---

51. *See* chapter 1 *supra.*

52. *Cf.* B. Ward, Spaceship Earth (1966).

53. Reflecting upon the Nazi atrocities against the Jews, Yosal Rogat suggests that "to be capable of ultimate cruelty men must first cut off sympathy for and identification with their victims by perceiving them as beings fundamentally different in kind from themselves; or, perhaps more accurately, not as beings at all, but as *things*." Y. Rogat, The Eichmann Trial and Rule of Law 9 (1961).

Similarly, Chief Albert Luthuli observes:

> We Africans are depersonalised by the whites; our humanity and dignity is reduced in their imaginations to a minimum. We are "boys," "girls," "Kaffirs," "good natives" and "bad natives." But we are not, to them, really quite people, scarcely more than units in a labour force and parts of a "Native Problem."

A. Luthuli, Let My People Go 155 (1962).

Cf. M. Buber, I and Thou (W. Kaufmann trans. 1970); O. Klineberg, The Human Dimension in International Relations 33–48 (1965); Berkowitz & Green, *The Stimulus Qualities of the Scapegoat,* 64 J. Abnormal & Social Psychology 293 (1962).

54. *See* Lasswell, *Future Systems of Identity in the World Community,* in 4 The Future of the International Legal Order 3–31 (C. Black & R. Falk eds. 1972).

the practice of imaging both the self and other in terms of characteristics that bear no rational relation to basic humanity and to potential contributions to the common interest. Random characteristics, having no relation to capability, are seized upon to justify deprivations, to exclude participation, and to deny fulfillment. Notable examples are phrased in reference to race, color, sex, religion, political or other opinion, language, nationality, age, and life-style.[55]

Expectations

The degree to which peoples can attain their demanded values is deeply affected by the comprehensiveness and realism of their expectations about the conditions under which these values can be secured. It cannot be denied that the peoples of today's world exhibit almost every conceivable degree of comprehensiveness and realism in their expectations about the circumstances that determine the realization of human dignity.

The expectations of the great bulk of humankind are still fragmented and uninformed. Few individuals have a cognitive map of the world social process of value shaping and sharing. Relatively few have access to the information (intelligence) essential to the attainment of such a map. Comparable to the absence of inclusive identification with the global community, there is a failure to achieve a shared vision of the conditions and potentialities of a comprehensive, concerted program for the realization of dignified, humane existence for humankind as a whole.

Despite a growing perception of interdependence, the significant facts of global interdependence are not widely understood. The intimate interdependences that condition the inner and external relations of particular value processes at all levels of geographic and functional interaction are rarely explored and articulated with the necessary comprehensiveness and realism.[56] Even when common values are objects of demand, the effort to clarify and implement common interest falters, with the result that participants in the total interaction do not necessarily recognize their common interests, both inclusive and exclusive. In consequence, assertions of special interest are often made that are destructive of the common interest.[57] Further, participants exhibit varying degrees of willingness or unwillingness to engage in the task of clarifying, articulating, and implementing the common interest. Too many individuals, living in

55. *See* chapters 8–15 *infra.*

56. For an attempt at articulation of interdependences, *see* chapter 1 *supra*, at notes 117–59 and accompanying text.

57. For our concepts on interests, *see* M. McDougal, H. Lasswell, & I. Vlasic, *supra* note 1, at 145–67.

too many parts of the world, continue to expect to gain more by perpetuating the practices of human indignity than by transforming the routines of the world community by promoting human dignity through cooperative activities.

In a divided world where pervasive expectations of violence generate chronic anxiety and personal insecurity, many individuals and groups still expect to be better off by strategies of violence than by those of peaceful cooperation. Many governing elites, preoccupied with the consolidation and expansion of power, are determined to exclude most of the population from participating effectively in important value processes. They therefore continue to impart a distorted world view to their people. They not infrequently mobilize the masses in ways that encourage docility despite persisting circumstances of deprivation and nonfulfillment. They cultivate international tension as a means of deflecting latent hostility toward foreign targets.[58]

There are, more happily, increasing numbers of people who realistically perceive the interdependences of the world, and who expect to achieve human dignity values through peaceful cooperation. Closely connected with this perception of interdependence is the revolution of "rising expectations," with its frequent accompaniment of "rising frustrations." A view that distinguishes the contemporary world from the outlook of traditional societies is the assumption that, within ever widening limits, it is possible for human beings to control their destinies. This view is attributable in part to the explosive expansion of scientific knowledge and in part to the realization that historic inequalities have no anchorage in an immutable decree of nature. In consequence, the middle and lower strata of the global community, such as the undeveloped nations, are stirred by a spark of hope that is fanned by a sense of injustice at their traditional predicament. Despite elite efforts to hold the rank and file of the population in check, more people are coming to entertain the expectation that the endurance of deprivation and nonfulfillment of values is no rational answer to deprivation, and that things can be changed for the better.[59]

---

58. *Cf.* Wicker, *Jobs and Crimes,* N.Y. Times, Apr. 4, 1975, at 33, col. 5 (city ed.).

For development of the theme that revolutionary elites, once in power, seek scapegoats to lower people's expectations, because of limited resources available for fulfilling popular aspirations for equitable distribution, *see* H. Arendt, On Revolution (1963).

59. *See* J. Skolnick, The Politics of Protest (1969); Williams, *The Rise of Middle Class Activism: Fighting "City Hall,"* Saturday Rev., Mar. 8, 1975, at 12–16; *New Militance Bringing Gains for Japan's "Outcasts,"* N.Y. Times, Dec. 11, 1974, at 18, col. 4 (city ed.); *id.,* Dec. 9, 1976, at 1, col. 5 (city ed.) (growing and intense demands for land by Mexican peons).

CONTENDING SYSTEMS OF PUBLIC ORDER

All these competing demands, ambivalent identifications, and conflicting expectations of individuals and groups today interact and culminate in contending systems of public order. It is the great diversity in the demands, identifications, and expectations of peoples that underlies the contemporary contention of different systems of world public order, a contention which renders the fulfillment of human dignity values increasingly difficult.

Rhetorically, the major contending systems are in many fundamental respects already unified. All systems proclaim the dignity of the human individual and the ideal of a worldwide public order in which dignity is authoritatively pursued and effectively approximated. They differ, however, in many details of the institutionalized patterns of practice by which they seek to achieve such goals, both in specific areas and in the world as a whole.[60]

Universal words in praise of human dignity obviously do not imply universal deeds in harmony with the rhetoric. The crux of the matter is that operational practices in the shaping and sharing of values diverge widely from professed goals. Special interests continue to assert themselves in effective sabotage of proclaimed objectives. There remains chronic tension among competing common interests, interests whose accommodation is always necessary.[61] The realization of the overriding prescriptions of an authoritative legal system depends upon compatible structures in the decision process as a whole, and in the everyday mustering of support in coalitions that give effect to aspiration.

SITUATIONS

The fundamental dimensions of the social process set the parameters within which the shaping and sharing of values must proceed. These parameters are not immutable. Even the geographic constraints that

60. *See* McDougal & Lasswell, *The Identification and Appraisal of Diverse Systems of Public Order,* 53 Am. J. Int'l L. (1959), *reprinted in* International Law in the Twentieth Century 169-97 (L. Gross ed. 1969). *Cf.* K. Boulding, The Meaning of the Twentieth Century 156-79 (1965); W. Friedmann, The Changing Structure of International Law 325-40 (1964); R. Higgins, Conflict of Interests: International Law in a Divided World (1965); C. Jenks, The Common Law of Mankind, ch. 2 (1958); Lissitzyn, *International Law in a Divided World,* 542 Int'l Conciliation (1963); Pachter, *The Meaning of Peaceful Coexistence,* Problems of Communism, Jan.-Feb. 1961, at 1-8.

61. *See* McDougal, *Human Rights and World Public Order: Principles of Content and Procedure for Clarifying General Community Policies,* 14 Va. J. Int'l L. 387 (1974); chapter 16 *infra.* *See also* M. McDougal, H. Lasswell, & J. Miller, *supra* note 1, at 35-77.

affect life on this planet are in flux, and the temporal sequences and juxtapositions of interactive factors are of decisive significance. We have made previous references to the tangle of institutional practice and the levels of crisis action that circumscribe results.

Geographic Features

The geographical ramifications of value deprivations and nonfulfillment may be universal, regional, national, or subnational in either origin or impact. Within particular communities, further, these impacts may be central or peripheral, omnipresent or occasional. The global scene has never before been the stage for interactive events of such frequency, intensity, and impact. More and more occurrences ignore state boundaries and generate repercussions beyond the limits of a single state.[62] The movements of people, goods, services, and ideas involve several nation-states. The cumulative impact of even the most local-seeming event may be transnational in scope. Parallel events may be observable on a worldwide scale. This means that, in contrast to previous times, when the shock wave generated by war, natural disaster, or other significant events could be contained within a particular locality (or the adjacent area), at the present time events tend to reverberate with great rapidity throughout the globe. In actuality, the transnational community is a complex matrix of situations whose spatial limits have begun to transcend "habitat earth" and to implicate other components of the solar system.[63] To take one another into account is the most enlightened form of interaction; and it is evident today that the inhabitants of the globe constitute a whole that takes its elements progressively into consideration.

We must not, however, exaggerate the degree to which awareness has been universally achieved. Many peoples remain outside the major forums of interaction; they are, for one reason or another, anchored in their localities without significant contact with the outside environment. Even now there are large blocs and pockets that permit little penetration by "outsiders." As a result, the world at large is totally uninformed about the deprivations and nonfulfillments that persist in those areas.[64] We

---

62. *See* United Nations, Department of Economic and Social Affairs, 1974 Report on the World Social Situations 8–13, U.N. Doc. E/CN.5/512/Rev. 1 (ST/ESA/24) (1975).

63. *See* M. McDougal, H. Lasswell, & I. Vlasic, *supra* note 1.

64. For example, the tight control exercised by the Soviet elite over all forms of communication made it possible to conceal from most Russians, as well as the outside world, the true scope of the famine of 1932–33. Rumors could not be confirmed because of the restriction upon freedom of movement inside the Soviet Union. Foreign correspondents stationed in Moscow could not hold their posts if they tried to send out dispatches at

cannot therefore assume that parochialism is overcome as a direct consequence of accelerated communication. It is, in fact, typical to find that symbols of local references have multiplied so rapidly at the focus of attention that wider aspects of the world are effectively excluded.

Over a longer interval it is to be assumed that the annihilation of distance by modern technology will accentuate the sense of relative deprivation in a particular area and magnify the importance of nonfulfillment everywhere. In the words of McNamara:

> For centuries stagnating societies and deprived peoples remained content with their lot because they were unaware that life was really any better elsewhere. Their very remoteness saved them from odious comparisons. The technological revolution changed all that. Today, the transistor radio and the television tube in remote corners of the world dramatize the disparities in the equality of life. What was tolerable in the past provokes turbulence today.[65]

Temporal Features

Value deprivation and nonfulfillment have temporal dimensions. The duration of a particular practice may be temporary or permanent, and its manifestation may be sporadic or continuous. The more permanent

---

variance with Soviet policy. To smuggle such reports out of the country opened the correspondent to retaliation by the government (withdrawal of visa and other essential privileges). Persistent filing of dispatches with censorable material simply meant that the home paper received nothing from its correspondent, since the censors interfered with transmission. Hence the home newspaper or press association was confronted by the dilemma of encouraging foreign staffs to conform to the official line, or of ceasing to maintain a news contact.

For more recent examples in the Soviet Union, *see* H. Smith, The Russians 344–74 (1976). After providing a list of examples, Smith concludes: "What is striking about such a list is that the Soviet people are being denied an accurate general picture of their own life and their own society, let alone a chance to compare it with other societies. Censorship prevents that." *Id.* at 374.

Comparable problems exist in China and other relatively closed societies. As Marva Shearer writes: "Since 1969, more Americans have landed on the moon than have visited Tibet in the People's Republic of China." Shearer, *A Journey to the Roof of the World*, Parade, Dec. 12, 1976, at 6.

Similarly, after a massive earthquake (the initial shock measured at 8.2 on the Richter scale, "the world's worst earthquake in twelve years") struck Tangshan in northern China (a thriving coal and steel city inhabited by more than one million people) in July 1976, no casualty figures were released. It was only in January 1977, more than five months later, that "Peking confirmed for the first time that the quake had taken as many as 700,000 lives." *Hua's Crackdown*, Newsweek, Jan. 17, 1977, at 33. *See China's Killer Quake*, *id.*, Aug. 9, 1976, at 30–32.

65. R. McNamara, One Hundred Countries, Two Billion People 90 (1973).

and continuous the deprivation, the greater is the destruction of human dignity values and the danger of destructive response.

Instantaneous global communication informs the world about itself. The world community is in effect becoming an open forum in constant session on matters of value deprivation and indulgence.[66] When deprivations occur it is no longer necessary—in a host of specific instances—to wait for days or weeks before hearing, for example, of imprisonment without a trial.[67]

It is important, however, to recognize that, while instantaneity in communication has grown, many interferences prevent realization of the full potential of instantaneity. Countering the growing demand that information be spread quickly is the no less intense demand by many elites that information be stifled. Trapped in a pervasive sense of insecurity, many power elites attempt to maintain their ascendancy by keeping the levels of aspiration of their peoples low and attempt to accomplish this by insulating the rank and file of the population from open exposure to the outside world. Messages that originate in the outside community are carefully scrutinized and tightly controlled in the hope of forestalling any "contamination" of established perspectives.[68]

More positively, it seems to be impracticable for apprehensive ruling classes to prevent "leakage" of information from the outside world into

---

66. In the words of Marshall McLuhan: "Today, after more than a century of electric technology, we have extended our central nervous system itself in a global embrace, abolishing both space and time as far as our planet is concerned." M. McLuhan, Understanding Media: The Extensions of Man 3 (1964).

Similarly, Cater observes: "The Gutenberg communicator—for the past 500 years patiently transmitting experience line by line, usually left to right, down the printed page—is no longer relevant. TV man has become conditioned to a total communication environment, to constant stimuli which he shares with everyone else in society." Cater, *The Intellectual in Videoland,* Saturday Rev., May 31, 1975, at 12, 15.

For a perceptive analysis of the instantaneity and totality of contemporary communication as revolutionalized by television, *see* T. Schwartz, The Responsive Chord (1973).

For an interesting study of humankind's temporal environment from historical and comparative perspectives, *see* The Future of Time: Man's Temporal Environment (H. Yaker, H. Osmond, & F. Cheek eds. 1971).

67. In reporting upon the closed nature of the Soviet society, Hedrick Smith wrote: "It [the Soviet government] has stopped jamming selected Western radio stations but has kept sufficient controls at home to prevent the contamination of free ideas from stirring new creativity among the intelligentsia, many of whose members seem more interested in the latest Western fashions than in dissident ideas." N.Y. Times, Dec. 23, 1974, at 1, col. 1, col. 4; at 16, col. 1 (city ed.).

He continued: "Censorship remains tight. Except for brief, chance encounters, foreigners are allowed to mingle with only a selected segment of society." *Id.,* at 16, col. 1.

68. Recently, for instance, most Eastern European countries have intensified efforts to curb the "bourgeois ideological plague." N.Y. Times, Dec. 12, 1976, § 1, at 6, col. 1 (city ed.).

their domains. This leakage occurs as an incident to any contact in the spheres of science, music, sport, medicine, and so on. Further, modern instruments enable compatible political persons and groups to maintain covert, if not overt, communication with one another and to coordinate strategies of change.[69]

Institutionalization

As the intensity of contact increases in space and time, institutional changes are initiated, diffused, or restricted as means of protecting or extending the value positions of participants. The cultural matrix of deprivations and nonfulfillment may or may not be institutionalized. Deprivations or nonfulfillment may be organized or unorganized, patterned or unpatterned, centralized or decentralized, secret or open. The pattern of deprivation and nonfulfillment may be occasional or systematic and routinized.[70] Sometimes deprivations and nonfulfillment are so deeply ingrained in cultural practices that members of the community are hardly conscious of their existence.[71] At other times, in contrast, deprivations and nonfulfillment may be made a deliberate and manifest instrument of oppression and of monopoly.[72]

In a technologically differentiated society, both public and private activities have become highly complex and institutionalized. Organizational complexity in government, in the corporate world, and in other

---

69. In the words of Claydon: "Recent improvements in transportation and communications have enabled groups in different parts of the world to recognize their common inferior status, have facilitated their mobilization into organizations capable of pressing effectively for remedial action, and have secured the dissemination of potentially useful methods for rectifying such situations." Claydon, *supra* note 7, at 29.

70. Both apartheid and caste epitomize a pattern of systematic, routinized deprivation. *See* chapter 7 *infra,* at notes 303–22 and 387–439 and accompanying text.

71. For instance, it may seem paradoxical that, despite the liberation movement, many of the sex-based deprivations continue to be accepted, consciously or unconsciously, as an inescapable fact of life by vast segments of the female population around the world. *See* chapter 10 *infra,* at notes 6–75 and accompanying text.

72. Amnesty International's country-by-country survey indicates that torture is increasingly becoming a deliberate instrument of policy in many communities:

> Policemen, soldiers, doctors, scientists, judges, civil servants, politicians are involved in torture, whether in direct beating, examining victims, inventing new devices and techniques, sentencing prisoners on extorted false confessions, officially denying the existence of torture, or using torture as a means of maintaining their power. And torture is not simply an indigenous activity, it is international; foreign experts are sent from one country to another, schools of torture explain and demonstrate methods, and modern torture equipment used in torture is exported from one country to another.

Amnesty International, Report on Torture 21 (1975) [hereinafter cited as Report on Torture].

sectors of life is subjecting people to intense organizational pressures. They respond by feeling like cogs in a machine, or simple accessories to the technology and organization. Their autonomy, integrity, and spontaneity as human beings are in jeopardy. It is quite evident that big organizations follow a logic of their own. Stressing the purposes and efficiency of the organization as paramount, they tend to adopt a purely instrumental view of the human beings at their disposal. In extreme cases, they have practically taken possession of the lives of their members, directing their basic political orientation, controlling the information that reaches their focus of attention, and decisively influencing their opportunities for work and livelihood, education, health, recreation, recognition, friendship, family activities, and religious observances.[73]

The psychological impacts of large-scale organization are compounded by the tensions that have been generated by changes in the relations between the public and private sectors of society. In a divided and militarized world where expectations of violence persist, there has been a persistent trend toward greater govermentalization, centralization, concentration, bureaucratization, and regimentation.[74] Governments multiply functions in response to intensifying demands upon public authorities. The tendency accelerates even in societies which have traditionally been resistant to "encroachment" by the state. Within nation-states the centralized decisions are taken and implemented at the top level of highly concentrated authority and control. This does not, however, imply that a direct trend exists to centralize decisions in a world-inclusive political organization. Since effective power in the global arena is monopolized in the hands of nation-states, vested and sentimental interests oppose further centralization, which would involve supranational entities. Within any nation-state the concentration of authority and control in the hands of a few officials or structures at a given level varies from one entity to another. The most concentrated structure in a political arena is a hierarchy in which effective decisions are made by one person and a limited number of advisors.

When there is a relatively low circulation of officials through a hierarchy, we speak of bureaucracy. Govermentalizing, centralizing, and concentrating tendencies foster hierarchy; and the stabilization of large hierarchies is almost certain to spell bureaucracy.[75] Bureaucratization is

---

73. *See* R. Presthus, The Organizational Society (1962); The Dilemma of Organizational Society (H. Ruitenbeek ed. 1963); W. Whyte, The Organization Man (1958).

74. *See* H. Lasswell, National Security and Individual Freedom (1950); Lasswell, *The Garrison-State Hypothesis Today,* in Changing Patterns of Military Politics 51–70 (S. Huntington ed. 1962).

75. *See generally* P. Blau, The Dynamics of Bureaucracy (2d ed. 1963); P. Blau & M. Meyer, Bureaucracy in Modern Society (2d ed. 1971); M. Crozier, The Bureaucratic

typically followed by regimentation, meaning that the state seeks to restrict all areas of private and individual as well as organized choice by using measures that depend on varying degrees of coerciveness. It is often alleged that a new "organization man" has emerged, a dedicated person who submerges his individuality to fit the requirements of large-scale action programs.[76] The trend toward govermentalization—which is sustained by the associated syndromes of centralization, concentration, bureaucratization, and regimentation—has upset the traditional balance between the public and the private sector, and the change is largely at the expense of civic order and personal autonomy.[77] In the extreme case, such as a totalitarian regime, society is practically swallowed up by government.[78]

PHENOMENON (1964); A SOCIOLOGICAL READER ON COMPLEX ORGANIZATIONS (A. Etzioni ed. 1969); H. JACOBY, THE BUREAUCRATIZATION OF THE WORLD (E. Kanes trans. 1976); BUREAUCRACY AND POLITICAL DEVELOPMENT (J. LaPalombara ed. 2d ed. 1967); R. MERTON, *supra* note 1, at 249–60; F. MORSTEIN-MARX, THE ADMINISTRATIVE STATE: AN INTRODUCTION TO BUREAUCRACY (1957); D. SILVERMAN, THE THEORY OF ORGANIZATIONS (1971); Weber, *Bureaucracy,* in FROM MAX WEBER: ESSAYS IN SOCIOLOGY 214 (H. Gerth & C. Mills eds. 1958); *Bureaucracy Explosion,* U.S. NEWS & WORLD REP., Aug. 16, 1976, at 22–26.

76. *See* W. WHYTE, *supra* note 73.

In his analysis of the social structure of bureaucracy, Robert Merton indicates that "the bureaucratic social structure exerts a constant pressure upon the individual to be methodical, prudent, disciplined." As a consequence, "discipline, readily interpreted as conformance with regulations, whatever the situation, is seen not as a measure designed for specific purposes but becomes an immediate value in the life-organization of the bureaucrat . . . develop[ing] into rigidities and an inability to adjust readily." R. MERTON, SOCIAL THEORY AND SOCIAL STRUCTURE 198, 199 (rev. ed. 1957).

The changing significance of bureaucratization is articulated by Daniel Bell in these words:

> In the broadest sense, the most besetting dilemma confronting all modern society is bureaucratization, or the "rule of rules." Historically, bureaucratization was in part an advance of freedom. Against the arbitrary and capricious power, say, of a foreman, the adoption of impersonal rules was a guarantee of rights. But when an entire world becomes impersonal, and bureaucratic organizations are run by mechanical rules (and often for the benefit and convenience of the bureaucratic staff), then inevitably the principle has swung too far.

D. BELL, *supra* note 26, at 119.

77. For the threat to personal autonomy posed by growing bureaucratization resulting from the expanding role of government in various value-institutional sectors, *see* R. NISBET, TWILIGHT OF AUTHORITY (1975). *See also* chapter 16 *infra.*

78. As Bracher puts it:

> Another important feature also distinguishing totalitarian systems from older forms of dictatorship, is the degree to which individual and private life is controlled and subjugated to a "new morality" of collective behavior. The regime demands quite openly the complete politicizing of all realms of life, and its success in performing this

Confronted with the frontal assaults of large scale organization and especially of expanding governmentalization (with its associated syndromes), various countermovements are set in motion. Popular demands are for less governmentalization, less bureaucratization, and less regimentation and for more decentralization and deconcentration, more spontaneity, and more personal autonomy. People demand more widespread and effective participation, through various strategies, in power and other value processes intended to make government responsive and responsible. Where private organizations are fortified by traditions of social diversity, the drift toward "big government" is rather successfully opposed by vigorous private organizations. Wherever the established political practice favors decentralization within government—as in a federal system—any fundamental change in the structural balance is achieved with difficulty. In consequence, the tension between the public and the private sector persists; and the balance between the two is fluid, dynamic, and shifting.[79]

Crisis

The direction and rapidity of institutional change are closely linked to the spread and intensity of the crises that accompany the evolution of an interdependent world. Crises are situations in which impending large-scale value deprivations are expected, and in which acute stress toward action is generated. Crises exhibit many differing degrees in intensity of expectation about the threat of damage. In security crises all values are critically at stake. Obviously, the growing militarization of the world arena has pervasive and far-reaching impacts upon the fulfillment and nonfulfillment of every value. It is commonplace to acknowledge that

---

> part of totalitarian control reveals the degree to which the regime is able to realize its claim to fuse state and society, party and people, individual and collective into the ideal of total unity.

Bracher, *Totalitarianism,* 4 Dictionary of the History of Ideas 406, 410 (P. Wiener ed. 1974).

79. Within the Soviet world, on the other hand, while the elite structure has remained tenaciously in favor of the formal principle of civilian supremacy, the Party continues to be the major ladder up the authority and control pyramid. Within the Party, of course, it is the specialist on the political-police function who has a distinct advantage, because central power elements look to the police to protect them from the challenges that arise in a totalitarian system. Established elites in such a system typically perceive themselves as threatened by demands for decentralization, deconcentration, democratization, pluralization, and deregimentation. *See* M. Fainsod, Smolensk under Soviet Rule (1958); N. Leites & E. Bernaut, Ritual of Liquidation (1954); B. Meissner & J. Reshetar, The Communist Party of the Soviet Union (1956); The Soviet Secret Police (S. Wolin & R. Slusser eds. 1957).

humankind is today living in the shadow of nuclear war and the possible annihilation of humanity and civilization.[80] Reflective minds recognize that the commonplaceness of this perception should in no way dull the sense of the reality of danger.[81] A partial consequence of the delicate balance of nuclear terror is that limited violence by private armies and private groups has increased tremendously, and the destructive potentiality of chemical and biological weapons are not neglected.[82]

The more important crises in the contemporary world can be analytically related to every important value. Such an itemization would include:

> Power—war, internal violence, breakdown in internal order;
>
> Wealth—depression, speculative booms, rampant inflation, acute and widespread poverty, acute shortage of food and other goods;

---

80. In the words of a Nobel laureate: "We live—while that is permitted us—in a balance of terror. The United States and the Soviet Union together have already stockpiled nuclear weapons with the explosive force of ten tons of TNT for every man, woman and child on the earth." Wald, *It Is Too Late for Declarations, for Popular Appeals,* N.Y. Times, Aug. 17, 1974, at 23, col. 1 (city ed.).

Cf. THE ABSOLUTE WEAPON: ATOMIC POWER AND WORLD ORDER (B. Brodie ed. 1946); THE EFFECTS OF NUCLEAR WEAPONS (S. Glasstone ed. 1962); M. HALPERIN, LIMITED WAR IN THE NUCLEAR AGE (1963); H. KAHN, ON THERMONUCLEAR WAR (1960); H. KISSINGER, NUCLEAR WEAPONS AND FOREIGN POLICY (1957); H. KISSINGER, THE NECESSITY FOR CHOICE: PROSPECTS OF AMERICAN FOREIGN POLICY (1962); T. SCHELLING & M. HALPERIN, STRATEGY AND ARMS CONTROL (1961); ARMS, DEFENSE POLICY AND ARMS CONTROL, DAEDALUS, Summer 1975 (including articles by Graham T. Allison, Les Aspin, Harvey Brooks, Barry Carter, Abram Chayes, Paul Doty, Richard A. Falk, F. A. Long, Frederic A. Morris, G.W. Rathjens, Thomas C. Schelling, Marshall D. Shulman, John Steinbruner, R. James Woolsey); Ikle, *Can Nuclear Deterrence Last Out the Century?* 51 FOREIGN AFFAIRS 272 (1973); *Note, The SALT Process and Its Use in Regulating Mobile ICBM's,* 84 YALE L.J. 1078 (1975).

81. For the continuing community concern for disarmament, *see* UNITED NATIONS, DEPARTMENT OF POLITICAL AND SECURITY COUNCIL AFFAIRS, THE UNITED NATIONS AND DISARMAMENT, 1945–1970 (1970); UNITED NATIONS, DEPARTMENT OF POLITICAL AND SECURITY COUNCIL AFFAIRS, THE UNITED NATIONS AND DISARMAMENT, 1970–1975 (1976); UNITED NATIONS, OFFICE OF PUBLIC INFORMATION, DISARMAMENT: PROGRESS TOWARDS PEACE (1974); UNITED NATIONS, COMPREHENSIVE STUDY OF THE QUESTION OF NUCLEAR-WEAPON-FREE ZONES IN ALL ITS ASPECTS: SPECIAL REPORT OF THE CONFERENCE OF THE COMMITTEE ON DISARMAMENT, U.N. Doc. A/10027/Add. 1 (1976).

82. *See* J. COOKSON & J. NOTTINGHAM, A SURVEY OF CHEMICAL AND BIOLOGICAL WARFARE (1969); CBW—CHEMICAL AND BIOLOGICAL WARFARE (S. Rose & D. Pavett eds. 1969); UNITED NATIONS, CHEMICAL AND BACTERIOLOGICAL (BIOLOGICAL) WEAPONS AND THE EFFECTS OF THEIR POSSIBLE USE (1969); UNITED NATIONS, DEPARTMENT OF POLITICAL AND SECURITY COUNCIL AFFAIRS, NAPALM AND OTHER INCENDIARY WEAPONS AND ALL ASPECTS OF THEIR POSSIBLE USE (report of the secretary-general), U.N. Doc. A/8803/Rev. 1 (1973); Larson, *Biological Warfare: Model 1967,* 46 MILITARY REV. 31 (1966); Meselson, *Chemical and Biological Weapons,* SCIENTIFIC AMERICAN, May 1970, at 15–25.

Well-being—epidemics, famines, and other natural disasters, and stress created by overcrowding;

Enlightenment—the communications revolution, exposing many people to the stress of new maps of man, environment, and nature; large-scale breakdown in communication; systematic manipulation of information;

Skill—the rapid obsolescence of skill because of the technical revolution, excessive automation and sudden displacement, critical shortages in educational facilities and manpower, the brain drain;

Affection—the massive dislocations of the family caused by refugee movements and by mass migration from rural to urban areas; vast increase in unwanted children precipitated by the disintegration of the family;

Respect—confrontations between castes, classes, and ethnic groups; collective defamation;

Rectitude—conflicts between the church and the state; conflicts between different religions.

In the contemporary world, crises in different value sectors (such as expansion and contraction in wealth processes) become more severe and rapid. Millions of human beings are exposed to contrasting life styles, conjoined with the possibility of obtaining at least short-range advantage by experimenting with variations from the culture norms in which they were socialized. Subcultures of mutual approbation spring into ephemeral and excited existence, only to recluster around a new and equally transient model. Thousands of individuals shift from one religious belief to another or from one secular ideology to another. Millions have been soldiers, gangsters, refugees, prisoners, vagabonds, and drifters. Millions have been unemployed, forced out of jobs by technological change, converted to new and uncomprehended tasks, uprooted from homes and shelters, jammed into crowded vehicles, and moved in and out of confinement. The weapons of the nuclear age contribute to the death threat that is permanently symbolized in the mushroom cloud over Hiroshima.[83]

Critical to crises are the perceptions of the people involved. People must be aware of intense demands and of the necessity to act before situations become full-blown crises. The elites and the rank and file may diverge radically in their perceptions of the same situation. Elite members are disposed to use crisis terms prematurely in a developing situation

83. *See* R. Lifton, Death in Life: Survivors of Hiroshima (1968). *See also* Lifton, *The Hiroshima Connection,* The Atlantic, Nov. 1975, at 83–88.

as they attempt to secure popular support and maintain their ascendancy. Real or imagined crises impel ruling elites to take disproportionately severe measures. Elite overreactions take various forms: initially justifiable measures of deprivations may be retained long after the alleged crisis is over; excessive measures cause more destruction than conservation of values; arbitrary measures may bear no rational relation whatever to the actual dangers involved in the alleged crisis.[84] Preoccupied with the task of maintaining their ascendancy in a highly insecure world, elites may go beyond the exploitation of crises to the fabrication of crises for exploitation. It is not uncommon for harsh measures of deprivation and nonfulfillment to be justified in the name of national security. It is notorious that many dictatorial regimes have arbitrarily declared and maintained martial law (a "state of siege" or a "state of emergency") as an excuse to suppress and liquidate dissenters and to consolidate the regime.[85]

In a world of instantaneous communication, crises are generated by the mass media themselves through sensationalism or over-reporting.[86] While genuine crises may positively affect the mobilization of public support and collective action,[87] the perpetual pseudo-crises fabricated by hyperactive mass media may become so routinized as to interfere with the future capacity of the media to arouse attention. Audiences may be so overwhelmed by sensational trivialization as to become numbed,

---

84. For instance, in India, what began in June 1975 as "temporary" authoritarian measures adopted in the name of national security were, after sixteen months, becoming "permanent." These measures included tight press censorship, concentration of power, suppression of dissents, and suspension of a parliamentary election. N.Y. Times, Nov. 8, 1976, at 1, col. 1 (city ed.).

For further background, *see* N.Y. Times, July 4, 1975, at 3, col. 1 (city ed.); *id.*, Sept. 8, 1975, at 1, col. 1; *id.*, Dec. 26, 1975, at 1, col. 1; *id.*, Sept. 15, 1976, at 18, col. 1; *id.*, Nov. 3, 1976, at 45, col. 6. *See also* Nanda, *The Constitutional Framework and the Current Political Crisis in India,* 2 HASTINGS CONST. L. Q. 859 (1975); *Indira's Next Decade,* NEWSWEEK, Feb. 16, 1976, at 37–41.

85. *See* G. KENNEDY, THE MILITARY IN THE THIRD WORLD (1974); MILITARY PROFESSION AND MILITARY REGIMES (J. Van Doorn ed. 1969); *Chile: The System of Military Justice,* 15 REV. INT'L COMM'N JURISTS 1 (1975); George, *For Marcos, the Lesser Danger,* FAR EASTERN ECONOMIC REV., Jan. 8, 1973, at 23–25; *One More Infant Democracy Dies in the Cradle,* THE ECONOMIST, Oct. 9, 1976, at 55; De Onis, *Latin America, the Growing Graveyard for Democracies,* N.Y. Times, Mar. 28, 1976, § 4, at 1, col. 4.

86. Boorstin has characterized this as "a flood of pseudo-events." *See* D. BOORSTIN, THE IMAGE, OR WHAT HAPPENED TO THE AMERICAN DREAM 7–44 (1962). *Cf.* Tannenbaum & Lynch, *Sensationalism: The Concept and Its Measurement,* 37 JOURNALISM Q. 381 (1960).

87. The positive or negative effect of a crisis to an individual often depends upon whether he experiences it singly or collectively. Such communal disasters as a flood or an earthquake can have various beneficial effects upon individuals involved. For instance, physical illnesses may suddenly disappear and altruism may prevail upon selfishness.

apathetic, impotent, and immobilized; they may lose a legitimate sense of outrage, withdrawing effective identity with the larger self, and may remain unresponsive in times of genuine crisis.[88]

BASE VALUES

Potentially, all values—respect, power, enlightenment, well-being, wealth, skill, affection, and rectitude—may be bases of power affecting deprivations and fulfillments. In different contexts different participants in world social process may employ any one or all of these values in imposing deprivation or seeking fulfillment of human rights. The degree to which any given value is important in a particular instance is a function of context.

Power is a principal base for nation-state officials, who typically utilize both authority and effective control. The effective control at the disposal of these officials is a combination of all values. Differences in the internal constitutive processes of states bear directly upon the configuration of authority and effective control. The degree to which authority and effective control are concentrated or nonconcentrated (totalitarian or democratic) affects the patterns of deprivation and fulfillment. In recent times there has been a tremendous expansion of totalitarian and authoritarian regimes. By their nature, totalitarianism and authoritarianism involve the employment of authority in deprivation of human rights. Totalitarian regimes are notorious for arrogating all choices into the sphere of public order, and for exercising practically unlimited authority over the value deprivation of individuals.[89] It must be recognized that in polities

---

88. Given the complexities of contemporary life and the media overload, people, including the educated, may become so bewildered as to be indifferent and lose the capacity for outrage and commitment in the face of massive atrocities and deprivations. This state of affairs is in turn apt for exploitation by ruling elites. Similarly, there is danger, amidst abiding parochialism, of contributing to the strength of a local development by magnifying its significance, and hence enhancing its appeal to other local elements who share nothing more tangible than a generalized resentment against outsiders, and the assumption that whatever worries the foreigners deserves support.

Cf. Baker, *Stomach-Bulge Defense,* N.Y. Times, Apr. 5, 1975, at 29, col. 1 (city ed.); Baker, *After the Flood, id.,* Apr. 19, 1975, at 31, col. 1.

For assessment of the implications of "communication overload," *see* D. BELL, *supra* note 26, at 316–17; A. TOFFLER, *supra* note 30, at 350–55.

89. On totalitarianism, *see generally* H. ARENDT, THE ORIGINS OF TOTALITARIANISM (1958); K. BRACHER, THE GERMAN DICTATORSHIP (1970); H. BUCHHEIM, TOTALITARIAN RULE: ITS NATURE AND CHARACTERISTICS (R. Hein trans. 1968); B. CHAPMAN, POLICE STATE (1970); C. FRIEDRICH & Z. BRZEZINSKI, TOTALITARIAN DICTATORSHIP AND AUTOCRACY (1961); C. FRIEDRICH, M. CURTIS, & B. BARBER, TOTALITARIANISM IN PERSPECTIVE: THREE VIEWS (1969); E. FROMM, ESCAPE FROM FREEDOM (1941; 1965); F. HAYEK, THE ROAD TO SERFDOM (1944); S. NEUMANN, PERMANENT REVOLUTION: TOTALITARIANISM IN THE AGE OF INTERNATIONAL CIVIL WAR (2d ed. 1965); W. REICH, THE MASS PSYCHOLOGY OF FACISM

that proclaim themselves to be democracies individuals may at times be victimized by the misuse and abuse of authority. Governmental officials may act without authority, under pretended authority, or under authority incompatible with human dignity; they may exercise authority arbitrarily to impose deprivations and deny fulfillment.[90] In extreme cases, law may be perverted into an instrument of oppression.

Participants in the world social process who are not state officials may, of course, draw upon authoritative decisions as power assets in support of their activities. Primarily, however, nongovernmental participants depend on values other than power (notably wealth, knowledge, and skill). The degree to which individuals are vulnerable to deprivation and are capable of achieving the fulfillment of their human rights depends largely upon the kind of public order system—totalitarian, authoritarian, or democratic—in which they live and upon the base values at their disposal. The degree to which authority is available for the defense of human rights, especially in challenge of deprivations, varies substantially from community to community.[91]

The distribution of base values within the world social process obviously conditions the deprivation and fulfillment of values. The influence extends to the distribution *among* and *within* states. As between states, the distribution is glaringly discrepant. Within a particular state, discrepancy extends not only to power and wealth but also to all other values which comprise effective power. Many countries have an abundance of resources and potential values, while others appear almost hopelessly deprived. Thus, important technology is still monopolized by the developed countries; nuclear power and other technology are still closely held. New scientific discoveries, technological developments, and access to outer space are bases for only a few communities. There has been

---

(1946); L. Schapiro, Totalitarianism (1972); J. Talmon, The Origins of Totalitarian Democracy (1960); E. Tannenbaum, The Facist Experience: Italian Society and Culture 1922–1945 (1972); Totalitarianism (C. Friedrich ed. 1964); World Revolutionary Elites: Studies in Coercive Ideological Movements (H. Lasswell & D. Lerner eds. 1966).

90. For abuse of power associated with the Watergate syndrome, *see* Watergate: Special Prosecution Force Report (Oct. 1975) (containing a detailed bibliography of Watergate source materials); *Hearings and Final Reports pursuant to H. Res. 803, of the House Comm. on the Judiciary,* 93d Cong., 2d Sess. (1974) (Impeachment Hearings). *See also* J. Dean, Blind Ambition: The White House Years (1976); L. Jaworski, The Right and the Power: The Prosectuion of Watergate (1976); E. Richardson, The Creative Balance: Government, Politics, and the Individual in America's Third Century 1–47 (1976). *See also* note 11 *supra.*

91. *Cf., e.g.,* V. Chalidze, To Defend These Rights: Human Rights and the Soviet Union (G. Daniels trans. 1974); T. Taylor, et al., Courts of Terror: Soviet Criminal Justice and Jewish Emigration (1976).

increasing recognition of the importance of knowledge and skill as bases of power; but these values are not widely and evenly spread about the globe. The cumulative result is the deep disparities between have and have-not countries (as summarized in North-South division).[92] Consequently, such countries differ in priority and direction in their respective programs for facilitating various human rights.[93]

The uneven distribution of values and resources between territorial communities is carried forward within even the best of states. Within many national communities, disparities in the distribution of wealth and other values are a commonplace phenomenon. The disparity is especially pronounced in the relationship between the power elite and the rank and file. While ruling elites tend to achieve overwhelming power, the masses of people remain powerless. The masses, in whose name the elite rules, become more often than not mere objects of deprivation rather than subjects of fulfillment, whatever the official rhetoric may allege.

In the light of the structure of effective power in the contemporary world, it is certain that no individual can control sufficient base values to be immune from deprivations emanating from various sources and to achieve the utmost fulfillment of values. Every individual depends upon the groups (nation-state, political party, union, trade association, educational institution, church, family, and so on) of which he is a member for his value position.

---

92. In the words of Lester Brown:

> In effect, our world today is in reality two worlds, one rich, one poor; one literate, one largely illiterate; one industrial and urban, one agrarian and rural; one overfed and overweight, one hungry and malnourished; one affluent and consumption-oriented, one poverty-stricken and survival-oriented. North of this line, life expectancy at birth closely approaches the Biblical threescore and ten; south of it, many do not survive infancy. In the North, economic opportunities are plentiful and social mobility is high. In the South, economic opportunities are scarce and societies are rigidly stratified.

L. Brown, World without Borders 41 (1973).

See generally C. Hensman, Rich against Poor: The Reality of Aid (1971); J. Pincus, Trade, Aid and Development: The Rich and Poor Nations (1967); The Gap between Rich and Poor Nations (G. Ranis ed. 1972); P. Uri, Development Without Dependence (1976); B. Ward, The Rich Nations and the Poor Nations (1962); The Widening Gap: Development in the 1970's (B. Ward, J. Runnalls, & L. D'Anjou eds. 1971). Barraclough, *The Haves and the Have Nots,* N.Y. Rev. Books, May 13, 1976, at 31–41; Hansen, *The Political Economy of North-South Relations: How Much Change?* 29 Int'l Org. 921 (1975); Reisman, *The Third World's Fading Dream,* The Nation, June 12, 1976, at 716–20.

93. For some of the pertinent issues raised, see the statements and comments made at the panel on *Economic Development and Human Rights: Brazil, Chile, and Cuba,* [1973] Proc., Am. Soc'y Int'l L. 198. *See also* M. Ganji, The Realization of Economic, Social and Cultural Rights: Problems, Policies, Progress, U.N. Doc. E/CN.4/1108/Rev. 1 (E/CN.4/1131/Rev. 1) (1975); *Human Rights and the "Single Standard"* (editorial), N.Y. Times, Jan. 11, 1977, at 32, col. 1 (city ed.).

In examining the entire spectrum of base values available for value deprivations and indulgences, special attention must be given to the unique position of science-based technology. The impact of technology on the fulfillment and deprivations of values is widely felt and appreciated. Great contributions have of course been made to human rights by the technology which has eliminated so much physical labor (depending upon political power and social structure) and released tremendous manpower and leisure for creative and rich pursuits of values. On the other hand, increasing threats to human rights have obviously come from the spectacular developments of modern science and technology. These threats may be exemplified in multiple detail, including such items as the sophisticated techniques of physical, psychological, and data surveillance that penetrate the traditional zones of privacy and jeopardize the very core of personal autonomy;[94] the reign of terror made possible by modern weapons; the horrible techniques of torture that dehumanize, intimidate, and oppress;[95] the routinization of work caused by widespread automation;[96] the obsolescence of skill caused by the technical revolution; and the ambivalent potentialities of the burgeoning science and technology of genetic engineering.[97]

---

94. *See* A. Miller, The Assault on Privacy: Computers, Data Banks, and Dossiers (1971); Privacy and Human Rights (A. Robertson ed. 1973); A. Westin, Privacy and Freedom (1968); A. Westin & M. Baker, Databanks in a Free Society: Computers, Record-Keeping and Privacy (1972). For further references, *see* chapter 16 *infra.*

In his classic study, Edward T. Hall observes that a person exists, in effect, within an invisible bubble of "personal space," which varies in size from individual to individual, depending upon his personality, his culture, and other situational factors in a particular context. *See* E. Hall, The Hidden Dimension (1966).

95. *See* Report on Torture, *supra* note 72, at 39–69. *See also Hearings on Human Rights in Chile before the Subcomm. on Inter-American Affairs and on International Organizations and Movements of the House Comm. on Foreign Affairs,* 93d Cong., 2d Sess. (1974); *Hearings on Torture and Oppression in Brazil before the Subcomm. on International Organizations and Movements of the House Comm. on Foreign Affairs,* 93d Cong., 2d Sess. (1974); Baraheni, *Terror in Iran,* N.Y. Rev. Books, Oct. 28, 1976, at 21–25; Colligan, *New Science of Torture,* Science Digest, July 1976, at 44–49; *Human Rights in the World: Torture Continues,* 10 Rev. Int'l Comm'n Jurists 10 (1973); Shelton, *The Geography of Disgrace: A World Survey of Political Prisoners,* Saturday Rev./World, June 15, 1974, at 14 *et seq.;* Styron, *Torture in Chile,* The New Republic, March 20, 1976, at 15–17; Styron, *Uruguay: The Oriental Republic,* The Nation, Aug. 14, 1976, at 107–11; *Torture as Policy: The Network of Evil,* Time, Aug. 16, 1976, at 31–34.

96. *See* Automation and Technological Change (J. Dunlop ed. 1962); International Labor Office, Automation and Non-Manual Workers (1967); A. Jaffe & J. Froomkin, Technology and Jobs: Automation in Perspective (1968); C. Silberman, et al., The Myths of Automation (1966); Hoffer, *Automation Is Here to Liberate Us,* in Technology and Social Change 64–74 (W. Moore ed. 1972).

97. *Cf.* J. Fletcher, The Ethics of Genetic Control: Ending Reproductive Roulette (1974); P. Ramsey, The Ethics of Fetal Research (1975); P. Ramsey, Fabricated Man (1971); Genetics and the Future of Man (J. Roslansky ed. 1966); Human

As modern science and technology move toward universality, certain uniformities are imposed upon world attention, and attitudes are molded in similar ways. Long a monopoly of Western Europe, modern science and technology are spreading throughout the globe, although at present inhibited by factors that find expression through the contending systems of public order. Certain consequences follow inexorably from the appearance in a community of the "machine," or modern techno-scientific complex. The machine, with all the problems it brings, confers a sense of mastery. Even those who at first are mastered do not fail to observe and presently to admire the impersonal strength and precision of mechanical, electrical, and other forms of energy applied to production. On the basis of direct experience, certain inferences sprout into belief and harden into faith, such as the speculation that if the brain of man can grasp and shape the hidden dynamics of nature, man is capable of controlling himself and his gadgets for the common good. This inference comes not from propaganda or pedagogy alone, or even principally; rather, it rises from indelible impressions left by association with man's handiwork. From glimpses of the possible develop demands that authority be induced or coerced to make whatever provision is necessary to share the fruits of knowledge with the "common man." However supine the traditional outlook of any culture, contact with the machine touches off a dynamic approach to life.[98]

RIGHTS AND SCIENTIFIC AND TECHNOLOGICAL DEVELOPMENT, U.N. DOC. E/CN.4/1173 (1975) (report of the World Health Organization to U.N. Commission on Human Rights).

98. For a provocative, penetrating analysis of the contemporary technical civilization that borders on "technological determinism," *see* J. ELLUL, THE TECHNOLOGICAL SOCIETY (J. Wilkinson trans. 1964). In Ellul's words:

> Technique has penetrated the deepest recesses of the human being. The machine tends not only to create a new human environment, but also to modify man's very essence. The milieu in which he lives is no longer his. He must adapt himself, as though the world were new, to a universe for which he was not created.

Id. at 325.

For differing views, *see* V. FERKISS, TECHNOLOGICAL MAN: THE MYTH AND THE REALITY (1969); H. MULLER, THE CHILDREN OF FRANKENSTEIN: A PRIMER ON MODERN TECHNOLOGY AND HUMAN VALUES (1970); L. MUMFORD, THE PENTAGON OF POWER (1970).

See also L. BERKNER, THE SCIENTIFIC AGE: THE IMPACT OF SCIENCE ON SOCIETY (1964); G. FOSTER, TRADITIONAL CULTURES AND THE IMPACT OF TECHNOLOGICAL CHANGE (1962); TECHNOLOGY AND SOCIAL CHANGE (W. Moore ed. 1972); L. MUMFORD, THE MYTH OF THE MACHINE: TECHNICS AND HUMAN DEVELOPMENT (1967); L. MUMFORD, TECHNICS AND CIVILIZATION (1963); C. HASKINS, THE SCIENTIFIC REVOLUTION AND WORLD POLITICS (1964); D. LOTH & M. ERNST, THE TAMING OF TECHNOLOGY (1972); MODERN TECHNOLOGY AND CIVILIZATION (C. Walker ed. 1962); Lasswell, *The Political Science of Science: An Inquiry into the Possible Reconciliation of Mastery and Freedom,* 50 AM. POL. SC. REV. 961 (1956).

STRATEGIES

The strategies employed by both deprivers and deprivees to manage base values in the pursuit of their objectives in the shaping and sharing of values embrace the whole range of possible instruments of policy. All the different types of strategy—commonly characterized as diplomatic, ideological, economic, and military—are employed, singly and in varying combinations, with many differing degrees of coerciveness and persuasiveness.[99]

Each particular type of strategy differs from the others in the degree to which it relies upon symbols or material resources. Diplomacy in the broadest sense depends primarily upon symbols in the form of offers, counter-offers, and agreements (deals) among elite figures. Ideological strategy also uses symbols as the principal means of action, its distinctiveness being communications directed to large audiences.[100] Economic instruments involve goods and services; military strategy employs means of violence and destruction. While diplomacy and ideology are especially concerned with perspectives, economic and military instruments are based upon capabilities. No instrument, however, is restricted to its most distinctive modality. Similarly, any organization primarily specialized to one instrument finds it expedient to make use of all. Every strategy can be employed, singly or in combination with other strategies, for productive, constructive purposes as well as for deprivational, destructive purposes.

Agreements (deals) of various types are made by group participants as well as individuals with varying degrees of explicitness and reciprocity. Deals are frequently made by governmental officials, business tycoons, gang leaders, and so on. As interaction accelerates about the

---

99. Some violence may be done to ordinary usage when we speak of the diplomatic, ideological, economic, and military strategies of some of the participants whom we have identified in the world arena, or when we refer to the internal rather than to external arenas. The most obvious discrepancies are in reference to the strategies of an individual. We do not usually think of a person as engaged in diplomacy when he is negotiating a deal on his own behalf. Nor do we speak of the use of propaganda by an individual to advance a private project as an example of "ideological" strategy. It is more in tune with everyday discourse to assess someone's private "economic" policies. Moreover, use of the term "military" seems to overstate the degree of control the individual exercises over destructive instruments which he employs for private purposes. We accept these inconveniences to underscore that strategies operate with the same values as bases whether the objectives sought are identified with the "primary ego" or with the larger self shared by a collectivity.

100. *Cf.* L. Fraser, Propaganda (1957); B. Murty, Propaganda and World Public Order: The Legal Regulation of the Ideological Instrument of Coercion (1968); J. Whitton & A. Larson, Propaganda: Towards Disarmament in the War of Words (1963); Lasswell, *Propaganda,* 12 Encyc. Soc. Sc. 521 (1934).

globe, there would appear a new intensity in the use of agreements of all kinds to promote the shaping and sharing of values. Given the ubiquity of the effective power processes operating at all levels of communities and organizations, it is no surprise that practices of deprivations and nonfulfillment are frequently effected through secret, as well as overt, deals of one kind or another. Among the elite who engage in such practices there is of course a shared expectation of silence and reciprocity—a consensus about not asking too many questions.

Improved techniques in communication enhance potential not only for a richer and wider fulfillment of values but also for deprivations. Such deprivational potentiality has been manifested in various ways. In many communities in which the media of mass communication are more or less monopolized by power elites, the gathering, processing, and dissemination of information are made a deliberate and vital instrument of thought conditioning and coerced conformity; generally, censorship prevails; information may be fabricated, distorted, restricted, and blocked out; and nonconforming opinions are suppressed.[101] In parallel, in some communities in which the media of mass communication are concentrated in the hands of wealth elites, the gathering, processing, and dissemination of information tend to be dominated by profit considerations and colored by inordinate commercialism, thereby debasing the quality of enlightenment.[102] Under contemporary conditions, the ideological instrument is often closely associated with instruments of physical destruction. It has, further, accentuated the sense of relative deprivation and nonfulfillment.[103] To minimize the deepening sense of relative deprivation and nonfulfillment, power elites in relatively closed societies take measures to prevent and interfere with the flow of information from dangerous or "undesirable" sources (both internal and external) and to restrict the free movement of people both beyond and within national boundaries.[104]

---

101. *See* C. FRIEDRICH & Z. BRZEZINSKI, *supra* note 89, at 107–17; A SAKHAROV, PROGRESS, COEXISTENCE, AND INTELLECTUAL FREEDOM 62–65 (The New York Times trans. 1968); H. SMITH, *supra* note 64, at 344–74; *Press Freedom 1970–1975,* 16 REV. INT'L COMM'N JURISTS 45 (1976); Reston, *The Condition of the Press in the World Today (1),* 7 HUMAN RIGHTS J. 593 (1974).

102. *See* E. EPSTEIN, NEWS FROM NOWHERE: TELEVISION AND THE NEWS 78–130 (1973); N. JOHNSON, HOW TO TALK BACK TO YOUR TELEVISION SET (1970); J. MERRILL & R. LOWENSTEIN, MEDIA, MESSAGES AND MEN: NEW PERSPECTIVES IN COMMUNICATION 79–88 (1971); Editors of the Atlantic Monthly, *The American Media Baronies,* in SOCIOLOGY IN THE WORLD TODAY 89–96 (J. Kinch ed. 1971).

103. For development of the theme of relative deprivation, *see* T. GURR, WHY MEN REBEL (1971).

104. *See* V. CHALIDZE, *supra* note 91, at 92–114; W. KOREY, THE SOVIET CAGE: ANTI-SEMITISM IN RUSSIA 184–200 (1973); Z. MEDVEDEV, THE MEDVEDEV PAPERS 173–270 (V.

It may be noted that, despite the difficulty in gaining effective access to the mass media, deprivees have increasingly resorted to the ideological instrument (the mass media of communication) to dramatize their grievances and aspirations and to gain wider attention (locally, nationally, regionally, or globally).[105] The politically persecuted, when denied internal channels of attention, seek to gain attention and support through the available media abroad.[106]

Goods and services may of course be managed to impose deprivations not only of wealth, but also of all other values. Individuals are highly vulnerable to deprivations stemming from the manipulation and withholding of goods and services. The breakup of family and traditional organizations in the production of goods and services (especially rural organizations) makes the individual largely dependent upon a new economic system against which the lone individual is commonly powerless.[107] The damage that can be done by mismanagement of goods and services has been recently exemplified by rampant corrupt practices of bribery in many parts of the world.[108]

In an insecure world of persisting expectations of violence, many people (elite and nonelite alike) not only expect violence but preach violence as the key to solution of human miseries, injustices, and inequalities (transnationally and nationally).[109] Convinced that their ascendancy depends upon a monopoly of the organization and means of

---

Rich trans. 1971); A. Sakharov, My Country and the World 51-61 (G. Daniels trans. 1975); H. Smith, *supra* note 64, at 344-74, 464-88.

105. *See* Protest and Discontent (B. Crick & W. Robson eds. 1970); S. Eisenstadt, Modernization: Protest and Change 31-35, 61-64, 74-75, 104-09 (1966); The Politics of Confrontation (S. Hendel ed. 1971).

106. The controversy concerning the emigration of Soviet Jews is a well-known example.

Cf. Amnesty International, Annual Report 1974/75 (1975); P. Litvinov, The Trial of the Four (P. Reddaway ed. 1972); T. Taylor, *supra* note 91; Scoble & Wiseberg, *Human Rights and Amnesty International,* 413 Annals 11 (1974).

107. Karl Polanyi maintains that the emergence of the "market mentality" under the laissez-faire climate of the Industrial Revolution led to a fundamental change in the relationship between the public and the private sector. *See* K. Polanyi, The Great Transformation (1944).

108. *See* note 19 *supra.*

109. A well-worn quotation of Mao Tse-tung typifies this expectation: "Political power grows out of the barrel of a gun."

Cf. K. Lang, Military Institutions and the Sociology of War (1972). *Cf. also* American Violence (R. Brown ed. 1970); Assassination and Political Violence (J. Kirkham, S. Levy, & W. Crotty eds. 1970) (a report to the National Commission on the Causes and Prevention of Violence); G. Sorel, Reflections on Violence (1961); Violence: An Element of American Life (K. Taylor & F. Soady eds. 1972); F. von der Mehden, Comparative Political Violence (1973).

violence and destruction, power elites in many communities have achieved high degrees of concentration and control. It is such monopoly that enables many dictatorial regimes and military juntas to stay in power despite intense popular resentment and opposition; overwhelmed by a vast network of terror, buttressed by the modern military, para-military, and police organizations of the state, individuals have little choice but to conform and be silent.[110]

Despite widespread attempts by power elites to monopolize the means of violence, the fact remains that the cheapness and easy availability of military hardware has put violence and terror at the disposal, not merely of state elites, but of individuals and small groups as well. This has made possible a transnational network of terror and has enhanced the danger and range of deprivation and destruction.[111]

OUTCOMES

The outcomes of the process of interaction are a continuing flow of deprivations and fulfillment with regard to all values, as manifested in variable patterns of value accumulation and distribution. From a long historical perspective, it would appear that just as science and technology move toward universalization, so the overall trend is toward the wider shaping and sharing of major values, despite zigzag patterns occurring at different times and in different communities. Yet the contemporary world has scarcely begun to mobilize its full potential to fulfill the rising common demands of humankind; though the nature, scope, and magnitude of the values at stake differ from one community to another and from one occasion to another, large-scale value deprivations and nonfulfillments of individuals and pluralistic groups continue to prevail. Deprivation and nonfulfillment appear to characterize the value-institutional processes of vast segments of the world's population, and a rich flow of fulfillment is enjoyed by only a small segment of that population. In the previous chapter, we itemized in summary outline the flow of de-

---

110. See E. Bramstedt, Dictatorship and Political Police: The Technique of Control by Fear (1945). *See also* note 89 *supra.*

111. *See* note 23 *supra. See also* M. Willrich & T. Taylor, Nuclear Theft: Risks and Safeguards (1974); Howard, *Terrorists: How They Operate a Worldwide Network,* Parade, Jan. 18, 1976, at 14 *et seq.;* Laqueur, *The Futility of Terrorism,* Harper's Magazine, Mar. 1976, at 99–105; *Terrorists with Atomic Bomb Could Hold World for Ransom,* New Haven Register, Sept. 17, 1972, at 24G, col. 1.

See also Fisk, *The World's Terrorists Sometimes Are United,* N.Y. Times, Aug. 17, 1975, § 4, at 3, col. 3; Middleton, *Could a U.S. Atom Bomb Be Stolen? id.,* Sept. 22, 1974, § 4, at 3, col. 3; *id.,* July 23, 1976, at A2, col. 3 ("Terrorists' Techniques Improve, and So Do Efforts to Block Them"); *id.,* July 16, 1976, at 1, col. 1 (city ed.) ("Libyans Arm and Train World Terrorists").

privations and nonfulfillment in regard to all values, by reference to the distinctive features of each of the value processes.[112]

Because of the interdependences brought about by accelerating changes in science and technology (particularly in communication), in population growth, in the demands and identifications of peoples, and in techniques of organization, there continue to be rising, common demands among peoples about the world for the greater production and wider sharing of all the basic values and an increasing perception by them of their inescapable interdependence in the shaping and sharing of all such demanded values.[113] Peoples everywhere (elites and nonelites alike), while cherishing parochial identifications, are also exhibiting increasing identifications with larger and larger groups, gradually extending to the whole of humankind. In an earth-space arena in which predispositional and environmental factors are in constant interplay, and in which mass destructive means intimidate and threaten humankind and civilization, no people can fully be secure unless all peoples are secure.

Even in these days of wars and revolution, and of genocide and arbitrary internal violence, the basic interrelationship of human rights and security (peace) is not difficult to discern: that interrelationship is one, not of contraposition or indifference, but rather of an interdependence so comprehensive and intense as to approximate identity.[114] In increasingly common conception, human rights and peace (security) are today regarded, not as static and independent absolutes or vague and utopian goals, but rather as the shared aspirations of peoples engaged in a cooperative community enterprise and inspired both by identifications with the whole of humankind and by realistic perceptions of a complete interdetermination in the achievement of such aspirations. Even when conceived in the minimal sense of freedom from the fact and expectation of arbitrary violence and coercion, peace is increasingly observed to be dependent upon maintaining people's expectations that the processes of effective decision in public order will be responsive to their demands for a reasonable access to all the values commonly characterized as those

---

112. *See* chapter 1 *supra,* at notes 9–88 and accompanying text.

113. For further elaboration, *see* chapter 1 *supra,* at notes 117–59 and accompanying text. An eloquent statement on global interdependences is *An Introduction by R. Buckminster Fuller,* in E. Higbee, A Question of Priorities: New Strategies for Our Urbanized World xvii–xxxiv (1970).

114. *See* note 113 *supra. See also* McDougal & Leighton, *The Rights of Man in the World Community: Constitutional Illusions versus Rational Action,* 14 Law & Contemp. Prob. 490 (1949), *reprinted in* M. McDougal, et al., Studies in World Public Order 335, 335–43 (1960); McDougal & Bebr, *Human Rights in the United Nations,* 58 Am. J. Int'l L. 603, 603–08 (1964); Toth, *Human Rights and World Peace,* in 1 Rene Cassin, Amicorum Discipulorumque Liber 362–82 (Institut International des Droits de l'Homme ed. 1969).

of human dignity or of a free society.[115] When peace is more broadly conceived as security in position, expectation, and potential with regard to all basic community values, the interrelationship of peace and human rights quite obviously passes beyond that of interdependence and, as suggested, approaches that of identity. To President John F. Kennedy's question "Is not peace, in the last analysis, basically a matter of human rights?" there can be but one rational answer. In the light of all the pervasive interconnections of both predispositional and environmental factors, as previously elaborated, it would appear incontestable that in today's world, without a more secure peace and continuing expectations of peace, there can be little hope of an improved and sustained protection of human rights and, conversely, that without a more extensive protection of human rights, there can be little realistic hope of a better peace.

The comprehensive world social process, which includes the processes of all its component communities from local to global and which determines the degree to which individuals can achieve their demanded values through time, is a dynamic and changing, not static and changeless, process. It embraces the whole manifold of historic events, extending from the past to the present and to the future. In this comprehensive process, each feature is constantly changing and interacting with the other features:

> Participants are constantly changing in characteristics, as they affect, and are affected by, the changing variables of culture, class, interest, personality, and crisis;
>
> The perspectives of participants are in continuous flux and revision in the light of changing conditions—they shift in the intensity and scope of their demands, expand or contract their identifications, and modify their world views and maps of reality;
>
> Changing dimensions of time, space, institutionalization, and crisis exert constant pressures on the situation of interaction;

---

115. Dismissing the trap of "a semantic jungle" that tends to "identify security with exclusively military phenomena and most particularly with military hardware," McNamara conceives security in broad terms of "development" in the contemporary modernizing context:

> In a modernizing society security means development. Security is not military hardware, though it may involve it; security is not traditional military activity, though it may encompass it. Security is development, and without development there can be no security. A developing nation that does not, in fact, develop simply cannot remain secure for the intractable reason that its own citizenry cannot shed its human nature.

R. McNamara, The Essence of Security, 150, 149 (1968).

The significance of resources and other base values, extending from the earth to outer space, continues to change under the impact of science and technology;

Strategies are employed and manipulated in varying combinations to cope with ever changing contexts; and

The varied outcomes find expression in changing aggregate patterns of value accumulation and distribution and in differing impacts on different individuals, groups, and communities.

The impacts of this ongoing process of deprivation and fulfillment of values reach beyond immediate deprivees and deprivers, affecting in the long run the aggregate patterns in innovation, diffusion, and restriction of value-institutional practices at all levels of communities (local, national, regional, and global) in the earth-space arena. Beyond even living generations, impacts extend to all future generations of humankind; ultimately at stake is the entire pattern of balance or imbalance among people, institutions, resources, technology, and the ecosystem.[116]

Given this dynamism of change inherent in the world social process, with its constant feedback of the flow of continuing events, immediate value outcomes, and long-term consequences, it is apparent that rational inquiry about world social process requires a continuing, systematic monitoring by reference to each of its main features.[117] This monitoring and appraising task is indispensable to the creation and maintenance

---

116. In the words of Secretary-General Kurt Waldheim:

> One of the most unfortunate aspects of modern society is the increasing tendency to see problems solely in immediate terms. We are fascinated and obsessed by the suddenness and drama of events; we seldom look deeply into their causes, and hardly ever into those elements which could lead to future crises. Yet the Roman adage that great disputes often result from small events but never from small causes remains absolutely valid. The majority of the great issues that confront mankind are profound, complex, and, above all, long-term problems. They cannot be resolved swiftly or dramatically; they are closely interrelated; and they bear directly upon the lives of all. For the great problems are the global problems, and they require a concerted global approach.

Waldheim, *Toward Global Interdependence,* SATURDAY REV./WORLD, Aug. 24, 1974, at 63.

117. *See* Snyder, Hermann, & Lasswell, *A Global Monitoring System: Appraising the Effects of Government on Human Dignity,* 20 INT'L STUDIES Q. 221 (1976). *Cf.* Lasswell, *Toward Continuing Appraisal of the Impact of Law on Society,* 21 RUTGERS L. REV. 645 (1967).

To keep abreast of the changing context of world social process, it is vital to improve the coverage provided by surveys of trends that use relatively "extensive" methods of continuous observation. More "intensive" studies need to be made periodically to disclose changing "predispositions" in depth. For a research design of the kind required, though adapted to another field, *see* Brodbeck & Jones, *Television Viewing and Norm-Violating Practices and Perspectives of Adolescents: A Synchronized Depth and Scope Program of Policy Research,* in TELEVISION AND HUMAN BEHAVIOR 98–135 (L. Arons & M. May eds. 1963).

of a continuing map of the interactions that constitute the events from which claims for freedom from deprivations and for value fulfillments emanate, and to which the process of authoritative decision responds. A continuing monitoring of the world social process which would present a dynamic world map with adequate comprehensiveness, selectivity, and realism would enhance effective performance of all the necessary intellectual tasks—clarification of goals, description of trends, analysis of conditioning factors, future projection, and recommendation of alternatives—necessary to facilitate and optimalize the defense and fulfillment of human rights.

3. CLAIMS MADE TO AUTHORITY FOR THE PROTECTION OF HUMAN RIGHTS

In preceding pages we have observed the continuous flow of deprivations and nonfulfillments in the shaping and sharing of values which characterizes both the internal social processes of different particular communities and the more comprehensive social process of the larger global community. It has been emphasized that there are human rights dimensions and policies at stake in all social interaction and in all authoritative decision by which such interaction is regulated. One consequence of the continuous flow of deprivations and nonfulfillments is that many different participants in social process, in equal constancy, make claims to established general community decision makers for the minimization of such deprivations and nonfulfillments and for the better securing and protection of their human rights.

The various particular claims that different participants make to authoritative decision relate both to every phase of every value process comprised within social or community process and to every aspect of the processes of authoritative decision to which claim is made.

It has already been noted that a comprehensive and detailed map of value shaping and sharing in the global community, and in its component communities, can be obtained by employing a selected list of value categories (such as our recommended categories of respect, power, enlightenment, well-being, wealth, skill, affection, and rectitude), accompanied by a detailed specification of the content of these categories in terms of particular institutional practices (as in terms of participation, perspectives, situations, bases of power, strategies, and outcomes). Some such mode of description would appear to be indispensable to an adequate categorization of the different substantive claims that participants make about the shaping and sharing of particular values.

An opportunity to challenge unlawful deprivations before authoritative decision is often said to be a minimum condition for the protection of human rights. As important as is such opportunity for challenge, it is indeed but a minimum condition. The most comprehensive claim is of course for the constitution and maintenance of an adequate and continuous process of authoritative decision in all relevant communities. When specified in detail, this most comprehensive claim includes more particular claims relating to the establishment and identification of authorized decision makers, the statement of overriding goals of community public order, the creation of structures of authority in which claims can be heard and decisions taken, the allocation of appropriate bases of power in authority and other values in support of decision, and the provision and management of necessary strategies and procedures for the making and management of many different types of decisions. These relevant types of decision include not merely those specifying the opportunity to challenge unlawfulness (an effective invocation function), but also those constituting the intelligence, promoting, prescribing, applying, appraising, and terminating functions.

The appropriate characterization of claims is important because it affects the comprehensiveness and realism with which both observers and decision makers can perform the various intellectual tasks indispensable to inquiry about, and the making of, the authoritative decisions relevant to the protection of human rights. When closely examined, any particular claim may be seen to include the participants' versions of the events (value shapings and sharings) which precipitated the claim to decision, demands that relate to allegedly relevant community policies, and demands for specific remedial or other appropriate action by authoritative decision. Scholarly observers and authoritative decision makers may of course have perceptions of the relevant events, of appropriate community policies, and of economic remedies very different from those of the parties. The explicitness, comprehensiveness, and sharpness with which claims are formulated in terms of social process events, comparable through time and across community boundaries, must, thus, importantly affect the detailed clarification of basic community policies and their relation to specific instances, the appraisal of past trends in decision in terms of the degree of their approximation to preferred policies, the economy with which environmental and predispositional factors affecting decision are specified, the estimation of the probable costs and benefits of different options to decision to both the parties and the common interest, and the devising of new alternatives in authoritative decision better designed to secure preferred community policies.

For convenience in more detailed inquiry, we may generalize a process of claim, comparable to the processes of interaction and decision, and consider briefly the different claimants, their perspectives, the specific types of controversies, and the conditions which peculiarly affect claims.

CLAIMANTS

The participants in world social process who make claims to established decision makers for the prescription and application of community policies in protecting human rights include the whole gamut, from governmental officials and agencies (national and transnational) through political parties, pressure groups, and private associations, to individual human beings. The increasing democratization of effective participation in power processes, with a vast rise in the number and power of different geographic and functional groupings, has brought a rapid proliferation in the number of entities making claims to established authority. Most importantly, what are commonly known as "nongovernmental organizations" (NGOs) (including both pressure groups and some private associations) have become active in making various claims to authority in the defense and fulfillment of human rights. These nongovernmental organizations may be generally observant or may be specialized to a wide range of human rights, in a particular value sector or in a particular problem area. Their voices, activities, and resources are especially significant because victims of deprivation and nonfulfillment are not always in positions to make effective claims to authority.

Individual human beings are claimants both in their own right and as representatives of groups. While individuals are of course always the ultimate deprivees, they do not necessarily become active, or effective, claimants in seeking remedy against deprivation or nonfulfillment. They may be too intimidated, uninformed, powerless, or resourceless to make claims; hence the great importance of the nongovernmental organizations. For the same reason, official invokers (e.g., ombudsmen, attorneys general, etc.) are being increasingly recommended and established to enhance the protection of human rights. Such official claimants, endowed with formal authority and effective power, and capable of reaching beyond what is achievable by private initiatives and activities, are vital to enhancement of the aggregate common interest.

PERSPECTIVES

The most general objective of claimants is of course to secure the prescription and application of general community policies for the better protection of human rights. The range of values and institutional practices for which protection is demanded, the sense of realism about conditioning factors, and the intensity with which claims are put forward vary according to context. What appear as manifest demands for the protection of human rights may upon occasion be disguised strategies for the attainment of other objectives, such as the mere harassment or embarrassment of an adversary. Conversely, what appear to be very specific, immediate demands may sometimes be disguised strategies for the attainment of long-term interests.

In terms of identification, claimants make demands either for themselves, or for others (*e.g.*, racial, religious, or linguistic minorities, or certain individual victims), or in the name of humanity or the common interest. The range of identifications of claimants with territorial and functional groups, and the contradictory trends toward both parochialism and universalism, are as evident here as among participants in social process more generally. It has already been noted that in many communities many people who suffer deprivations or nonfulfillments are conditioned or forced to endure them in silence; their claims must perforce stimulate the formal and effective identifications of surrogates.

The more detailed objectives of claimants to authoritative decision may be most economically described in terms of particular types of controversy. Any categorization of types of controversies that even aspires toward comprehensiveness must make reference to every value process and every phase of each process, to contexts of many different kinds of crises and differing intensities in crisis, and to all the different features of the process of authoritative decision to which claim is made. The special relevance of careful categorization of types of controversy resides in the fact that the general community, quite appropriately, prescribes very different policies and remedies for application, dependent upon differences in type of controversy. An appropriate categorization of specific types of claims, with insightful relation of the part to the whole, may facilitate systematic inquiry that is contextual, problem-oriented, and multi-method.

SPECIFIC TYPES OF CLAIM

The more important recurrent types of claim can be classified under three main headings: first, claims relating to the process of deprivation and nonfulfillment of values; second, claims relating to official demands for derogation under crisis conditions; and third, claims relating to the constitutive process of authoritative decision. Itemization of these recurrent types of claim in detail follows.

Claims Relating to the Process of Deprivation and Nonfulfillment of Values

I. Claims Relating to Respect

A. *Claims relating to outcomes*
  1. Claims for a basic degree of respect as individual human beings
     (a) Fundamental freedom of choice in value participation

(b) Elimination of slavery
(c) Elimination of caste
(d) Elimination of apartheid

2. Claims relating to a basic equality of opportunity in the enjoyment of all values, that is, freedom from discrimination for reasons irrelevant to capability, in terms of:
   (a) Race (color; national, ethnic, or social origin; birth, descent, or other status)
   (b) Sex
   (c) Religion
   (d) Political or other opinion
   (e) Language
   (f) Alienage
   (g) Age
   (h) Other factors
3. Claims for further rewards in respect for meritorious contribution
   (a) Recognition
   (b) Honor
   (c) Reputation
4. Claims relating to the aggregate interest in respect
   (a) Comprehensive public order
   (b) Civic order (including privacy)

B. *Claims relating to participation*
1. Claims in relation to participation in the shaping of respect
   (a) Governmental deprivations
      (i) In conformity with law
      (ii) Not in conformity with law
   (b) Nongovernmental deprivations
2. Claims in relation to participation in the sharing of respect
   (a) Individuals
   (b) Groups (minority protection)

C. *Claims relating to perspectives*
1. Claims relating to permissibility or impermissibility of purposes
   (a) Range of values included within impermissible purposes
   (b) Relevance of grounds alleged for deprivations to common interests
   (c) Discriminatory purpose per se constituting deprivation
2. Claims to be free to acquire a demand for respect—the opportunity to have experiences that will facilitate capabilities (claims to freedom from indoctrination)
   (a) Opportunity to discover latent capabilities for participation
   (b) Opportunity to acquire capabilities

        (c) Opportunity to exercise capabilities
    3. Claims for freedom to establish and change identification
    4. Claims for opportunity to achieve realism in expectations

D. *Claims relating to situations—freedom of access to all social interactions in which respect is shaped and shared*
    1. Claims relating to institutions specialized to respect
        (a) Freedom to initiate and constitute institutions specialized to respect
        (b) Freedom of access to institutions specialized to respect
        (c) Prohibition of organizations or institutions inimical to respect (*e.g.*, racist organizations)
    2. Claims relating to institutions not specialized to respect (equality in association)—freedom of access to institutions not specialized to respect (access to public accommodations, etc.)
    3. Claims relating to geographic separation
    4. Claims relating to crisis
        (a) Impact of crises upon differentiation
        (b) The accordance of respect proportionately despite crises

E. *Claims relating to base values*
    1. Claims relating to authority—the availability of the process of authoritative decision to defend and fulfill respect
        (a) Equality of access to authority (invocation)
        (b) Impartiality in the application of law (application)
        (c) Equality in law or legal interests (prescription)
    2. Claims relating to control
        (a) Availability of participation in each of the other value processes to defend and fulfill respect
        (b) Impartial allocation of participation in value processes
    3. Claims for special assistance to overcome handicaps not attributable to merit ("compensatory differentiation")

F. *Claims relating to strategies*
    1. Claims for employment of the diplomatic instrument for affecting respect: enforcing agreements, prohibiting discriminatory agreements, minimizing deprivations, protecting reputation, etc.
    2. Claims relating to the use of the ideological instrument for affecting respect
        (a) Prohibition of race-mongering
        (b) Education for the enjoyment of equality
    3. Claims relating to the management of goods and services for affecting respect
        (a) Prohibition of slavery, forced labor, imprisonment for debt, etc.
        (b) Employment of monetary rewards

4. Claims relating to the use of the military instrument for affecting respect
   (a) Terrorist activities
   (b) Use of the military instrument for the protection of groups (martial law, etc.)

II. Claims Relating to Power

A. *Claims relating to participation*
   1. Claims for individual participation
      (a) Claims to be recognized as a person
      (b) Claims to be protected in external interactions (nationality)
      (c) Claims to participate in the internal constitutive process (citizenship)
         (i) Authoritative
            a) Officeholding
            b) Voting
         (ii) Controlling—participation in all other value processes
      (d) Claims not to be denied participation for reasons irrelevant to merit (race, etc.)
   2. Claims for association in groups (freedom to establish and join groups)
      (a) Claims in relation to political parties
      (b) Claims in relation to pressure groups
      (c) Claims in relation to private associations
      (d) Claims in relation to protection for minorities
      (e) Claims to change rulers of groups (right of revolution)
      (f) Claims to constitute a new entity (self-determination)
      (g) Claims to be free from external coercion

B. *Claims relating to perspectives*
   1. Claims to be free (after exposure to adequate enlightenment) to acquire, or not to acquire, a demand for power
      (a) Claims to discover latent capabilities for participation
      (b) Claims to acquire capabilities
      (c) Claims to exercise capabilities
   2. Claims for freedom to establish and change identification
   3. Claims for opportunity to achieve realism in expectations

C. *Claims relating to arenas*
   1. Geographical
      (a) Claims for freedom of transnational movement
         (i) Claims for freedom to enter
            a) Nationals
            b) Nonnationals
               i) Ordinary aliens

ii) Refugees
(ii) Claims for freedom to stay
a) Nationals
b) Nonnationals
i) Ordinary aliens
ii) Refugees
(iii) Claims for freedom to leave
a) Nationals
b) Nonnationals
i) Ordinary aliens
ii) Refugees
(b) Claims for freedom of internal movement
(i) Nationals
(ii) Nonnationals
a) Ordinary aliens
b) Refugees
2. Temporal—claims to continuation of rights
3. Authoritative institutions (freedom to establish internal constitutive process of groups)
(a) Claims to freedom to initiate and constitute institutions specialized to power
(b) Claims to freedom of access to adequate institutions specialized to power
4. Controlling institutions
(a) Claims for freedom to initiate and constitute institutions specialized to values other than power
(b) Claims for freedom of access to adequate institutions specialized to values other than power
5. Crisis—claims to receive a proportionate degree of public support despite crises (in security, power, respect, enlightenment, well-being, wealth, skill, affection, and rectitude)

D. *Claims relating to base values*
1. Authoritative—claims that the processes of authoritative decision, at all community levels, be available to defend and fulfill all rights
2. Controlling
(a) Claims that participation in each of the other value processes be available to defend and fulfill all rights
(b) Claims for special assistance to overcome handicaps

E. *Claims relating to strategies*
1. Claims relating to the diplomatic instrument
(a) Claims to freedom to employ
(b) Claims to freedom from coercive employment

2. Claims relating to the ideological instrument
    (a) Claims to freedom to employ
    (b) Claims to freedom from coercive employment
3. Claims relating to the economic instrument
    (a) Claims to freedom to employ
    (b) Claims to freedom from coercive employment
4. Claims relating to the military instrument
    (a) Claims to freedom to employ
    (b) Claims to freedom from coercive employment

F. *Claims relating to outcomes*

1. General
    (a) Claims for a civic domain (freedom from both official and effective power)
    (b) Claims to freedom from arbitrary seizure and confinement (freedom from arbitrary power of government)
    (c) Claims to widest possible sharing of power
2. Particular—claims that the community maintain and afford appropriate access to institutions specialized to each of seven functions:
    (a) Intelligence (access to information relating to decision process)
    (b) Promotion (freedom to organize and participate in pressure groups and parties)
    (c) Prescription (voting)
    (d) Invocation (open access and effectiveness)
    (e) Application (fair trials, etc.)
    (f) Termination (referendum, assertion of unconstitutionality)
    (g) Appraisal (participation in commission of inquiry)

III. Claims Relating to Enlightenment

A. *Claims relating to outcomes*

1. Claims to an optimum aggregate in the shaping and sharing of enlightenment (gathering, disseminating, enjoying)
2. Claims to basic enlightenment
3. Claims to additional enlightenment on merit

B. *Claims relating to participation*

1. Claims to general participation in receiving and giving enlightenment
2. Claims to be free of restrictions for reasons irrelevant to merit (race, etc.)
3. Claims for group participation in opportunity to acquire and disseminate knowledge

C. *Claims relating to perspectives*
   1. Claims for freedom to acquire the demand for enlightenment
   2. Claims to be free from conditioning with regard to thought process
      (a) Claims to be free from state conditioning
      (b) Claims to be free from private conditioning
   3. Claims to be free from distorted communications
   4. Claims for disclosure of special interests

D. *Claims relating to situations*
   1. Institutions specialized to enlightenment
      (a) Claims for freedom to initiate and constitute institutions of enlightenment
      (b) Claims for freedom of access to institutions of enlightenment
   2. Institutions not specialized to enlightenment—claims for freedom of access to institutions not specialized to enlightenment
   3. Crisis—claims that enlightenment not be denied disproportionately to crisis

E. *Claims relating to base values*
   1. Authoritative—claims that the process of authoritative decision be available to defend and fulfill participation in the enlightenment process
   2. Controlling
      (a) Claims that participation in each of the other value processes be available to the extent necessary to enlightenment (no monopoly in governmental or private sources)
      (b) Claims for special assistance
      (c) Claims for freedom to acquire and employ appropriate language

F. *Claims relating to strategies*
   1. Singly
      (a) Claims for freedom in small-group communication
      (b) Claims for freedom in access to and employment of mass communication
      (c) Claims for freedom in the assembly of appropriate resources for enlightenment
      (d) Claims for freedom to employ the military instrument to preserve enlightenment
   2. In combination—claims to freedom from coerced deprivation of enlightenment (censorship)

IV. Claims Relating to Well-Being

A. *Claims relating to outcomes*
   1. Claims to an optimum aggregate in the shaping and sharing of well-being

   2. Claims for the right to life
   3. Claims to a basic minimum in safety, health, and comfort
   4. Claims for additional opportunities in accordance with choice—the range of choice: body form (cosmetic surgery); choice of sex; choice of organs (mechanical and human transplantation); choice of children (number, sex, and other genetic characteristics)
   5. Claims for progress toward optimum somatic and psychological development through life
   6. Claims to a merciful euthanasia

B. *Claims relating to participation*
   1. Claims for general participation in the realization of bodily and mental health and development
   2. Claims to be free of restrictions for reasons irrelevant to merit (race, etc.)
   3. Claims for group survival and development (no genocide)

C. *Claims relating to perspectives*—claims for freedom to acquire the demand for life and its full development

D. *Claims relating to situations*
   1. Geographical—claims for an environment that is conducive to survival and development
   2. Institutions specialized to well-being
      (a) Claims for freedom to initiate and constitute institutions specialized to well-being
      (b) Claims for freedom of access to institutions specialized to well-being
   3. Institutions not specialized to well-being—claims for freedom of access to institutions not specialized to well-being
   4. Crisis—claims not to be denied well-being disproportionately to crisis

E. *Claims relating to base values*
   1. Authoritative—claims that the process of authoritative decision be available to defend and fulfill well-being
   2. Controlling
      (a) Claims that participation in each of the other value processes be available to defend and fulfill well-being
      (b) Claims for special assistance
      (c) Claims to be a beneficiary of pertinent science and technology

F. *Claims relating to strategies*
   1. Claims for the employment of appropriate strategies in relation to health for
      (a) Prevention
      (b) Deterrence
      (c) Restoration
      (d) Rehabilitation

(e) Reconstruction
(f) Correction
2. Claims for freedom from coercive strategies
3. Claims to be free to accept or reject medical service (right to die)
4. Claims for freedom to accept or reject transplantation and repair (surgical intervention, drugs, communicative therapy, situation therapy)
5. Claims to employ specified strategies in birth control (family planning, abortion)
6. Claims for the employment of genetic engineering (artificial insemination, incubation outside the body, choice of psychophysical pattern)

V. Claims Relating to Wealth

A. *Claims relating to outcomes*
1. Claims to the maintenance of a high level of productivity (rising standard of living)
2. Claims to a basic minimum of benefits from the wealth process (guaranteed income, social security, abolition of poverty)
3. Claims to the enjoyment of benefits on the basis of contribution and merit

B. *Claims relating to participation*
1. Claims for general participation in wealth shaping and sharing (right to work, right to invest and employ resources, right to enjoy)
2. Claims for freedom from restrictions irrelevant to capabilities for contribution (race, etc.)
3. Claims for freedom of association and group shaping and sharing of wealth

C. *Claims relating to perspectives*—claims for freedom to acquire (or reject) a demand to participate in the wealth process

D. *Claims relating to situations*
1. Institutions specialized to wealth
(a) Claims for freedom to initiate and constitute institutions specialized to wealth
(b) Claims for freedom of access to institutions specialized to wealth
2. Institutions not specialized to wealth—claims for freedom of access to institutions not specialized to wealth
3. Crisis—claims that wealth not be denied disproportionately to crisis

E. *Claims relating to base values*
1. Authoritative

(a) Claims that the process of authoritative decision be available to defend and fulfill wealth demands
(b) Claims for a degree of protection in the employment of resources in the wealth process
(c) Claims to the continuing accumulation of assets

2. Controlling
(a) Claims that participation in each of the other value processes be available to defend and fulfill wealth demands
(b) Claims for special assistance
(c) Claims to employ resources for productive purposes (claims for freedom from wasteful use of resources)
(d) Claims that resources be open to exploitation and development ("economic self-determination," "permanent sovereignty over natural wealth and resources")

F. *Claims relating to strategies*
1. Claims for freedom to employ all relevant strategies in the shaping and sharing of wealth
2. Claims to be free from coercive strategies
3. Claims to be free from discriminatory strategies (*e.g.*, discriminatory wages)
4. Claims to be free from capricious and arbitrary management

VI. Claims Relating to Skill

A. *Claims relating to outcomes*
1. Claims to an optimum aggregate in the acquisition and exercise of skills
2. Claims for a basic minimum of skills relevant to effective participation in all value processes
3. Claims for additional acquisition of skill in terms of talent and motivation

B. *Claims relating to participation*
1. Claims for unrestricted opportunity to acquire and exercise socially acceptable skill
2. Claims for opportunity to have latent talent discovered
3. Claims not to be denied opportunity to acquire and exercise skill for reasons irrelevant to merit (race, etc.)
4. Claims that groups be accorded skill

C. *Claims relating to perspectives*—claims to acquire a demand for, and capability of, skill expression

D. *Claims relating to situations*
1. Institutions specialized to skill
(a) Claims for freedom to initiate and constitute institutions specialized to skill

(b) Claims for freedom of access to institutions specialized to skill
2. Institutions not specialized to skill—claims for freedom of access to institutions not specialized to skill
3. Crisis—claims that skill not be denied disproportionately to crisis

E. *Claims relating to base values*
1. Authoritative—claims that the process of authoritative decision be available to defend and fulfill participation in the skill process
2. Controlling
(a) Claims that participation in each of the other value processes be available to the extent necessary to skill
(b) Claims for special assistance

F. *Claims relating to strategies*
1. Claims for exposure to a training of a content appropriate to a culture of science and technology
2. Claims for exposure to strategies in training relevant to a culture of science and technology (claims for exposure to good teaching)
3. Claims to be free from coercive strategies (other than those inherent in the process of compulsory education)
4. Claims for exposure to a socialization process that enables the individual to acquire the motivations and capabilities appropriate to the performance of adult roles in value processes

VII. Claims Relating to Affection

A. *Claims relating to outcomes*
1. Claims to an optimum aggregate in the shaping and sharing of affection (loyalties, positive sentiments)
2. Claims to a basic minimum of love as a human being (that necessary for individuals to acquire the motivations and capabilities to function effectively in shaping and sharing values)
3. Claims for additional affection in terms of capability and contribution

B. *Claims relating to participation*
1. Claims to give and receive affection
2. Claims for freedom from restrictions irrelevant to capabilities (race, etc.)
3. Claims to give and receive loyalty to groups of one's choice
4. Claims for freedom of association

C. *Claims relating to perspectives*—claims for freedom to acquire (or reject) a demand to participate in the affection process

D. *Claims relating to situations*
1. Institutions specialized to affection
(a) Claims to initiate and constitute intimate and congenial personal relationships

(b) Claims for freedom of access to institutions specialized to affection (adoption, legitimacy, proper spouse)
(c) Claims for recognition of membership in specialized groups
2. Institutions not specialized to affection—claims for freedom of access to institutions not specialized to affection
3. Crisis—claims that affection not be denied disproportionately to crisis

E. *Claims relating to base values*
1. Authoritative—claims that the process of authoritative decision be available to defend and facilitate affection demand
2. Controlling
(a) Claims that participation in each of the other value processes be available to defend and facilitate affection demand
(b) Claims for special assistance (capability of loving and being loved)

F. *Claims relating to strategies*
1. Claims for freedom in the cultivation of love and loyalty
2. Claims to be free from coercive strategies
3. Claims to be free from discriminatory strategies

VIII. Claims Relating to Rectitude

A. *Claims relating to outcomes*
1. Claims for the maintenance of an order in which individuals demand of themselves and others that they act responsibly
2. Claims to a minimum opportunity to receive positive evaluation of rectitude as a human being
3. Claims for movement toward a more perfect participation of all in responsible conduct

B. *Claims relating to participation*
1. Claims for freedom to participate in the formulation and application of standards of responsibility (norms of responsible conduct)
2. Claims for freedom from restrictions irrelevant to capabilities (race, etc.)
3. Claims for freedom of association for rectitude purposes

C. *Claims relating to perspectives*
1. Claims for freedom to acquire a demand on the self to act responsibly
2. Claims for freedom to choose among justifications of responsible conduct (secular and religious justifications, and empirical, transempirical, or metaphysical justifications)

D. *Claims relating to situations*
1. Institutions specialized to rectitude
(a) Claims for freedom to initiate and constitute institutions

specialized to rectitude
 (b) Claims for freedom of access to institutions specialized to rectitude
 2. Institutions not specialized to rectitude—claims for freedom of access to institutions not specialized to rectitude
 3. Crisis—claims that rectitude not be denied disproportionately to crisis

E. *Claims relating to base values*
 1. Authoritative—claims that the process of authoritative decision be available to defend and facilitate freedom of choice in rectitude
 2. Controlling
 (a) Claims that participation in each of the other value processes be available to defend and facilitate freedom of choice in rectitude
 (b) Claims for special assistance

F. *Claims relating to strategies*
 1. Claims for freedom to employ all relevant strategies in the pursuit of rectitude
 2. Claims to be free from coercive strategies
 3. Claims to be free from discriminatory strategies

Claims Relating to Permissible Derogation from Established Standards

I. *Claims relating to crises in security*
(External security—threats of force, war, invasion, occupation; internal security—revolution, coup d'etat, insurrection, internal violence, civil disobedience)

II. *Claims relating to crises in power*
(Governmental breakdown, strikes by governmental employees, strife for succession, fraudulent election)

III. *Claims relating to crises in respect*
(Wholesale denial of human dignity, genocide, confrontations among classes and castes, collective defamation)

IV. *Claims relating to crises in enlightenment*
(Large-scale breakdown in communication, seizure of facilities)

V. *Claims relating to crises in well-being*
(Epidemics and natural disasters such as earthquakes and floods, famines, population explosion)

VI. *Claims relating to crises in wealth*
(Depression, speculative booms, monopolization of resources, deficit in balance of payments, acute shortage of food and other goods)

VII. *Claims relating to crises in skill*
(Drastic shortages, sudden displacement, excessive automation)

VIII. *Claims relating to crises in affection*
(Withdrawal of loyalties and commitment, large-scale dislocations in family patterns, mass migration)

IX. *Claims relating to crises in rectitude*
(Conflicts among religions, conflicting secular ideologies, dissolution of the sense of responsibility)

Claims Relating to the Constitutive Process of Authoritative Decision

I. *Claims relating to participation*
II. *Claims relating to perspectives*
III. *Claims relating to situations*
IV. *Claims relating to base values*
V. *Claims relating to strategies*
VI. *Claims relating to outcomes*
   A. Intelligence
   B. Promotion (Recommendation)
   C. Prescription
   D. Invocation
   E. Application
   F. Termination
   G. Appraisal
VII. *Claims relating to effects*

THE CONTEXT OF CONDITIONS

The conditions under which claims about human rights are, and will be, made to authoritative decision include, as elaborated above, both environmental and predispositional factors and their dynamic interplay, in a world of growing interaction and interdependences. Among the important environmental factors are the global population explosion, the scarcity, disparity in distribution, and mismanagement of certain vital resources, and continuing manifestations of inordinately state-centered institutional arrangements and practices. Among the important predispositional factors are the growing demands of peoples everywhere for the wider shaping and sharing of values; the continuing tension between an inclusive concern for the whole of humanity and the exclusive obsession of national parochialism; and the aroused, and often frustrated, expectations of peoples about the conditions under which their values can be secured. Such frustrated expectations have been exacerbated by the sense of futility inspired by a highly decentralized world constitutive process of authoritative decision which has been unable even to minimize unlawful violence, much less to maximize the shaping and sharing of demanded values, and which remains colored by widespread elite concern for short-term payoffs rather than longer-term aggregate interests.

In such a context the confidence of potential claimants in the efficacy of appeals to authoritative decision is, not irrationally, weak. An important consequence is that both deprivees and their surrogates increasingly take to the modern mass media of instantaneous communication in order insistently to demand the better protection of particular rights. When denied authoritative protection and effective remedy, deprivees and others tend to band in groups, organized and unorganized, and to engage in nonviolent (sometimes violent) demonstrations and other strategies to dramatize their grievances and to appeal to world attention. This strategy of desperation, though often falling short of achieving immediate gains, is increasingly adopted because of the expectation that unceasing provocation (agitation, confrontation) is necessary to move reluctant elites toward a better protection and fulfillment of demanded rights.

4. The Global Constitutive Process of Authoritative Decision

It is sometimes complained that, while most of humankind's problems—including those of human rights—are global in their reach, the processes of law maintained to cope with these problems are not. This would appear a profound misperception. The contemporary world arena does exhibit a comprehensive process of authoritative decision which, though it has not yet achieved that high stability in expectations about authority and in degree of control over constituent members characterizing the internal processes of mature national communities, still offers in somewhat more than rudimentary form all the basic features essential to the effective making and application of law on a global scale.[1] In recent decades, this emerging comprehensive process of authoritative decision has, further, been expanding and improving itself at an accelerating rate and, in the light of long historical perspective, rapidly making itself much more adequate to cope with human rights, as well as other, problems. The development of this comprehensive process of authoritative decision entirely parallels, and is an integral part of, the larger development of world social process.

In the most comprehensive view, humankind as a whole today presents, as we have documented elsewhere, both the aspect and fact of a global community, entirely comparable to the internal communities of lesser territorial groupings, in the sense of interdetermination and interdependences in the shaping and sharing of all values.[2] One vital component value process within this larger community process is, observably, an ongoing process of effective power, also global in its reach, in

1. *See* McDougal, Lasswell, & Reisman, *The World Constitutive Process of Authoritative Decision,* in 1 THE FUTURE OF THE INTERNATIONAL LEGAL ORDER 73–154 (R. Falk & C. Black eds. 1969) [hereinafter cited as McDougal, Lasswell, & Reisman]. In making this study, we have drawn upon unpublished, collaborative work with our colleague Professor W. Michael Reisman.

2. This is developed in M. MCDOUGAL, H. LASSWELL, & I. VLASIC, LAW AND PUBLIC ORDER IN SPACE (1963).

which decisions are in fact taken and enforced by severe deprivations or high indulgences, irrespective of the wishes of any particular participant. Operating within this global process of effective power is, further, a comprehensive process of authoritative decision, in the sense of a continuous flow of decisions made by the persons who are expected to make them, in accordance with criteria expected by community members, in established structures of authority, with enough bases in power to secure consequential control, and by authorized procedures. Upon close examination, this comprehensive process of authoritative decision can be observed, again, to be composed of two distinct, though interrelated, kinds of decisions: first, the constitutive decisions which establish and maintain the most comprehensive process of authoritative decision; and, secondly, the public order decisions which emerge from such constitutive process in regulation of all other community value processes. By "constitutive process" we refer, in detail, to those decisions which identify and characterize authoritative decision makers, postulate and specify basic community policies, establish appropriate structures of authority, allocate bases of power for sanctioning purposes, authorize procedures for the making of different kinds of decisions, and secure performance of all the different decision functions (intelligence, promotion, prescription, etc.) necessary to the maintenance and administration of general community policy. By the "public order" decisions we refer, more specifically, to those decisions, emerging as outcomes of the established constitutive process, which shape and maintain the protected features of the community's various value processes, including the value processes embodied within human rights.[3] It is with the emergence and continuing development of a constitutive process of global dimensions, and with the bearing of that process upon the protection of human rights, that we are here concerned.

It can be no cause for surprise that the basic features of a global constitutive process have been clearly delineated only within relatively recent times. For millennia the conditions essential to the establishment and maintenance of a larger community and appropriate decision processes did not exist; the peoples of the world lived in isolated groupings with little physical contact, much less cooperative interaction in the shaping and sharing of values. As populations increased and interactions became more frequent and differentiated, specialized institutional practices began to appear, culminating in decision processes capable of sus-

3. *See* Lasswell & McDougal, *Criteria for a Theory about Law,* 44 S. Cal. L. Rev. 362 (1971); Lasswell & McDougal, *Trends in Theories about Law: Comprehensiveness in Conceptions of Constitutive Process,* 41 Geo. Wash. L. Rev. 1 (1972) [hereinafter cited as *Comprehensiveness in Conceptions of Constitutive Process*]; chapter 1 *supra.*

taining stable contact and of restoring severed relations. Thus, the civilizations of China, India, Greece, and Rome all recognized expectations of authority and control shared between different territorial communities as important instrumentalities for the clarification and maintenance of common interest;[4] indeed, the conceptions of the Greeks of a natural law shared by all humankind and of the Romans of a *jus naturale* and a *jus gentium* shared by many peoples have for centuries been among the most influential factors affecting the development of what is regarded as contemporary international law.[5] Over many millennia the skeletonized practices in cooperation that were in the beginning barely more than exchanges of intermediaries have developed into a highly complex system of bilateral and multilateral arrangements and organized decision making. Many predispositions shaped in the primitive, pre-global arrangements of humankind continue, unhappily, to affect the configuration of contemporary decision making.[6]

The universal decision institutions of the contemporary world are commonly regarded as having been shaped most directly by the internal and external dynamisms of a Western Europe recovering from the centuries that followed the collapse of feudalism and of the Roman Empire in the West. As the aggregate impact of Europe on peoples external to it gained momentum, and international interactions increased in breadth and intensity, the world began to be shaped into a single system of public order. In the seventeenth century, the relatively unipolar European system built upon the paramountcy of the pope and Christian unity began to be transformed into a multipolar state system. The loyalties of individuals were in measure shifted from family, church, guild, and local community to the state, and the state assumed a new supreme authority to discharge security and other functions without elaborate external arrangements. This process of transformation reached its climax in 1648,

---

4. *See* Lasswell & McDougal, *Trends in Theories about Law: Maintaining Observational Standpoint and Delimiting the Focus of Inquiry,* 8 U. Tol. L. Rev. 1 (1976); McDougal, Lasswell, & Reisman, *Theories about International Law: Prologue to a Configurative Jurisprudence,* 8 Va. J. Int'l L. 188, 202–04 (1968) [hereinafter cited as McDougal, Lasswell, & Reisman, *Theories about International Law*]. *See also* A. Bozeman, Politics and Culture in International History 118 (1960); D. Brown, The White Umbrella: Indian Political Thought from Manu to Gandhi (1953); E. Havelock, The Liberal Temper in Greek Politics (1957); M. Levi, Political Power in the Ancient World (1965); 2 J. Needham, Science and Civilization in China 526 (1969); P. Sen, The General Principles of Hindu Jurisprudence 24 *et seq.* (1918).

5. *See* A. Nussbaum, A Concise History of the Law of Nations 5–16 (rev. ed. 1954).

6. *See* M. Barkun, Law Without Sanctions: Order in Primitive Societies and the World Community (1968); S. Edmunds, The Lawless Law of Nations (1925); G. Niemeyer, Law Without Force: The Function of Politics in International Law (1941).

when the Peace of Westphalia formally terminated the Thirty Years' War.[7] Born of the spiritual disunity in Christendom, the Peace of Westphalia marked the shift in the locus of power from the church to the secular authority of the nation-state. What had been a relatively centralized system of public order became a highly decentralized system, with many contending centers of power. Under the new, decentralized system, a continuous balancing of power, with ever-changing alliances, became the cornerstone for maintaining minimum public order and for fostering the general functioning of the system. The important contribution of the great writers regarded as the founding fathers of contemporary international law was in their creation of a conception of a law of nations appropriate to this new role of the state and of a decentralized, relatively unorganized community of states. This they achieved by drawing upon both the law of nature and custom as sources of substantive policy and by conceptualizing a process of decision, built upon actual and potential reciprocities and retaliations, in which particular states were alternately both claimants and decision makers, thus insuring that claims would be based upon at least a modicum of common interest.[8] The result was that, though the peoples of the world lived under the immediate authority and control of different territorial communities, they were nevertheless "united in a larger legal community under the rule of a law higher in kind than the law of those bodies."[9]

The development of "formal, continuing institutional structures"[10] within the European-based constitutive process came somewhat slowly. Following the settlement of Vienna of 1815 and the Congress of Aix-la-

---

7. *See* R. Falk, A Study of Future Worlds 59–69 (1975); P. Reuter, International Institutions 35–52 (J. Chapman trans. 1955); Gross, *The Peace of Westphalia, 1648–1948,* 42 Am. J. Int'l L. 20 (1948), *reprinted in* International Law in the Twentieth Century 25–46 (L. Gross ed. 1969).

8. *See* M. Kaplan & N. Katzenbach, The Political Foundations of International Law (1961); W. Schiffer, The Legal Community of Mankind (1954). *See also* L. Henkin, How Nations Behave (1968); H. Kelsen, Principles of International Law (1952); A. Nussbaum, *supra* note 5; P. Reuter, *supra* note 7; Dickinson, *Changing Concepts and the Doctrine of Incorporation,* 26 Am. J. Int'l L. 239 (1932); Gross, *States as Organs of International Law and the Problem of Autointerpretation,* in Law and Politics in the World Community 59 (G. Lipsky ed. 1953); Scelle, *Le Phenomene juridique du dedoublement fonctionnel,* in Rechtsfragen der Internationalen Organisation: Festschrift für Hans Wehberg 324 (1956).

For development of the notion of law as based upon conceptions of common interest, reciprocity, and retaliation, *see* B. Malinowski, Crime and Custom in Savage Society (1926); B. Malinowski, Freedom and Civilization (1944); L. Pospisil, Anthropology of Law: A Comparative Theory (1974).

9. W. Schiffer, *supra* note 8, at 46.

10. Claude, *International Organization: The Process and the Institutions,* in 8 Int'l Encyc. Soc. Sc. 33 (1968).

Chapelle of 1818, a loose system of consultation among the great powers, known as the Concert of Europe, was inaugurated to manage a delicate balancing of power in maintenance of a precarious peace.[11] While the Concert of Europe failed to institutionalize permanent structures of authority, it did provide a framework for occasional great-power consultations and conferences, giving substance to the fact that the European states shared a larger community interest. This community, with its constitutive process, widened as the European colonization expanded, and its growth found further impetus in the Hague Conferences of 1899 and 1907, which included small states as well as great powers, and non-European as well as European states.[12] With the establishment of the Pan American Union near the end of the nineteenth century and the initiation of a series of inter-American conferences, the states of the Western Hemisphere clearly emerged as "a distinct subgroup within the larger multi-state system."[13] Meanwhile, various nation-states, in response to the new needs generated by the spread of science and technology and the new methods of transnational communication and transportation, cooperated to create intergovernmental organizations specialized to particular values other than power. The establishment and growth of both geographic and functional structures of authority thus moved gradually beyond the confines of the European territorial context to a larger world.

The beginnings of structures of authority appropriate to a global constitutive process appear only with the advent of the short-lived League of Nations and with its hopefully more enduring successor, the United Nations. The Covenant of the League of Nations sought, without success, to establish a permanent, relatively universal, multipurposed constitutional structure for the larger community of humankind. The reasons for the League's failure and the lessons to be gained from its experience have been many times recounted.[14] The successor United Nations offers, in still higher aspiration, a vast and complex network of

---

11. *See* I. Claude, Swords into Plowshares: The Problems and Progress of International Organization 24–28 (4th ed. 1971); G. Mangone, A Short History of International Organization (1954); H. Nicolson, The Congress of Vienna (1946); P. Reuter, *supra* note 7, at 52–56; C. Webster, The Congress of Vienna (1919).

12. *See* J. Choate, The Two Hague Conferences (1913); The Reports to the Hague Conferences of 1899 and 1907 (J. Scott ed. 1917).

13. Claude, *supra* note 10, at 33.

14. *See* G. Scott, The Rise and Fall of the League of Nations (1973); F. Walters, A History of the League of Nations (1952); C. Webster & S. Herbert, The League of Nations in Theory and Practice (1933); A. Zimmern, The League of Nations and the Rule of Law, 1918–1935 (1936); Walters, *The League of Nations,* in The Evolution of International Organizations 25–41 (E. Luard ed. 1966) [hereinafter cited as The Evolution of International Organizations].

institutions exhibiting both highly centralized components designed to facilitate the making and application of law for multiple and universal purposes and more dispersed components designed to guide and coordinate the workings of a whole host of regional and functional organizations for more limited purposes. It is this immense maze of institutions within the United Nations, augmented by many other relatively independent intergovernmental organizations, that comprises the core structures of authority giving form to contemporary global constitutive process.

The more recent trends in decision suggest some modest movement toward greater adequacy in global constitutive process.[15] The number of states has greatly multiplied, with continuing expansion from European to non-European states, and movement toward universality in participation. Nonstate participants, including private associations dedicated to many values, have vastly proliferated and play increasingly important roles. The perspectives of participants exhibit demands not merely for a historic minimum public order (minimization of unauthorized coercion) but also for an optimum public order (in the sense of the maximum production and widest possible sharing of all values). There would appear a gradual expansion of identifications with the most inclusive community of humankind and deepening perception of common interest in

---

15. This development is well described in a series of books by Jenks: C. Jenks, The Common Law of Mankind (1968); C. Jenks, The Proper Law of International Organisations (1962); C. Jenks, The Prospects of International Adjudication (1964) [hereinafter cited as C. Jenks, International Adjudication]; C. Jenks, The World Beyond the Charter (1969). *See also* C. De Visscher, Théories et Réalités en Droit International Public (4th ed. 1970); W. Friedmann, The Changing Structure of International Law (1964); A. Ross, The United Nations: Peace and Progress (1966); International Organization: Politics and Process (L. Goodrich & D. Kay eds. 1973); G. Schwarzenberger, International Law as Applied by International Courts and Tribunals: 3, International Constitutional Law (1976) [hereinafter cited as G. Schwarzenberger, International Constitutional Law]; I. Seidl-Hohenveldern, Das Recht der Internationalen Organisationen eninschliesslich der Supranationalen Gemeinschaften (1967); Mosler, *The International Society as a Legal Community,* 140 Hague Recueil des Cours 1 (1974).

For a review indicating that Friedmann's book (W. Friedmann, *supra*) did not present a sufficiently comprehensive conception of global constitutive process, *see* McDougal & Reisman, *"The Changing Structure of International Law": Unchanging Theory for Inquiry,* 65 Colum. L. Rev. 810 (1965).

For a treatment from the human rights perspective, *see* Vasak, *Le Droit International des Droits de l'Homme,* 140 Hague Recueil des Cours 333 (1974). For a brief overview from the perspective of the international law of development, *see* Schachter, *The Evolving International Law of Development,* 15 Colum. J. Transn'l L. 1 (1976).

For a pessimistic view of the development of the notion of "international constitutional law," with many references to earlier notions, *see* Opsahl, *An "International Constitutional Law"?* 10 Int'l & Comp. L.Q. 760 (1961). Opsahl appears to have inadequate conceptions of authority and control and little notion of law as a process of decision.

a world of growing interdependences. The arenas of decision have moved from loose institutionalization to a high degree of institutionalization and from unorganized to organized; diplomatic and diplomatic-parliamentary arenas have been augmented by parliamentary, adjudicative, and executive arenas; sporadic, occasional interactions have been replaced by permanent, continuous structures of authority; and, finally, the geographic distribution of arenas has been improved, with a range from local and national, through regional, to global. In terms of bases of power, the trend has been from exclusive to inclusive authority, with erosion of the concept of domestic jurisdiction and the expansion of the scope of international concern, and from exclusive effective control over other values to more inclusive effective control. In terms of strategies, the customary modalities of creating expectations about authority and control by reciprocal, cooperative behavior have been supplemented by more deliberate law making through explicit agreement, and ultimately by parliamentary procedures. In terms of outcomes, the pristine unity of undifferentiated functions has evolved into highly differentiated decision functions (intelligence, promotion, prescription, invocation, application, appraisal, termination), each of which is distinctive though interrelated with the others.

For examining contemporary global constitutive process in detail, with special reference to the protection and fulfillment accorded human rights, we propose to explore each basic feature of such process and, in conclusion, to note the clear emergence of a global bill of rights. Some consideration will be given also to factors that may affect future constitutive process.

THE MAJOR FEATURES OF CONTEMPORARY CONSTITUTIVE PROCESS

Participation

In recent decades, participation in the world constitutive process, as in its sustaining process of effective power, has been tremendously democratized. All the participants in world social process—conveniently categorized as nation-states, international governmental organizations, political parties, pressure groups, private associations, and individual human beings—now play important roles and perform many varying functions in the global processes of decision.[16] Nation-states historically have played, and continue to play, a predominant role. International

---

16. *See* McDougal, *International Law, Power, and Policy: A Contemporary Conception,* 82 Hague Recueil des Cours 133, 192–256 (1953). *See also* W. Friedmann, *supra* note 15, at 213–49; P. Jessup, A Modern Law of Nations—An Introduction 15–42 (1968); Lauterpacht, *The Subjects of the Law of Nations,* 63 Law Q. Rev. 438 (1947) and 64 Law Q. Rev. 97 (1948).

governmental organizations have more recently come to be recognized as appropriate "subjects" of international law, participating in all functions. Political parties, though not always recognized in authoritative myth, in fact affect many decisions. Pressure groups are formed primarily with a view to promoting and influencing the making of decisions. Multiplying hosts of private associations, operating within the larger constitutive framework, are increasingly transnational in membership, goals, areas of activity, and power impacts. Individual human beings, acting both as individuals and as representatives of groups, have abundant opportunity to participate in all aspects of making and applying law.

NATION-STATES

Since the rise of the modern system in the seventeenth century, the nation-state—with its unique control of a territorial base—has been the overwhelmingly dominant participant in world constitutive process.[17] The officials of nation-states are still by far the most important participants in the performance of all decision functions. Thus, they make and apply, or participate in the making and applying of, all law that affects human rights.

In origin a response to demands for the better protection of the individual in the chaos of feudalism, the nation-state has long been the principal framework within which demands for the shaping and sharing of values (respect, power, enlightenment, wealth, and so on) are expressed and fulfilled. With nation-states representing both the symbol and the fact of accumulated respect, power, wealth, and so on, individuals have sought many of their values through close identification with the nation-states of which they are members. At a time when the degree of transnational interdependence was relatively low, this emphasis upon the nation-state as a principal instrument of value shaping and sharing and decision making was not irrational. Insofar as the nation-state system can be made to reflect a rational geographic organization of the world, it may still serve as an economic allocation of responsibility for the development of resources and the protection of human rights.

In recent years, the number of nation-states has been greatly multi-

---

17. *See* Herz, *Rise and Demise of the Territorial State,* 9 World Politics 473 (1957), *reprinted in* Power, Action, and Interaction: Readings on International Politics 159–80 (G. Quester ed. 1971); Herz, *The Territorial State Revisited: Reflections on the Future of the Nation-State,* 1 Polity 12 (1968), *reprinted in* International Politics and Foreign Policy: A Reader in Research and Theory 76–89 (rev. ed. J. Rosenau ed. 1969); F. Hinsley, Power and the Pursuit of Peace 153–271 (1967); Hinsley, *The Development of the European States System since the Eighteenth Century,* 11 Transactions of the Royal Historical Society 69 (1961), *reprinted in* Power, Action, and Interaction, *supra,* at 284–94.

plied as a consequence of the disintegration of former empires and the transformation of ex-colonies into independent states.[18] In a move toward universalization of the form, the European-centered, Christian-oriented state system has been extended to embrace every continent and every culture. This rapid proliferation of nation-states has brought some measure of democratization to the making and applying of international law. Since decisions are taken by numerical majority in many transnational arenas, effective power has shifted significantly to coalitions of the African-Asian states or of the Third World.[19]

This trend toward broader participation has not, however, always been accompanied by appropriate regard for the capabilities of new states to assume a responsible role in world constitutive process. The proliferation of many "mini-states," while reflecting a trend toward democratization, does give rise to serious constitutive problems in responsibility and enforcement.[20]

The states of the world differ widely in size, population, resources, institutions, and projected public order systems. Hence, it is important to pierce the veil of the nominal "equality" of states for participating in a law of human dignity. The internal processes of decision within states,

---

18. *See* UNITED NATIONS, THE UNITED NATIONS AND DECOLONIZATION: HIGHLIGHTS OF THIRTY YEARS OF UNITED NATIONS EFFORTS ON BEHALF OF COLONIAL COUNTRIES AND PEOPLES, U.N. Doc. OPI/573 (1977); Chen, *Self-Determination as a Human Right,* in TOWARD WORLD ORDER AND HUMAN DIGNITY: ESSAYS IN HONOR OF MYRES S. MCDOUGAL 198–261 (W. Reisman & B. Weston eds. 1976), and relevant references therein.

See also ASIAN STATES AND THE DEVELOPMENT OF UNIVERSAL INTERNATIONAL LAW (R. Anand ed. 1972); R. ANAND, NEW STATES AND INTERNATIONAL LAW (1972); H. BOKOR-SZEGO, NEW STATES AND INTERNATIONAL LAW (1970); KEESING'S RESEARCH REPORT, AFRICA INDEPENDENT: A SURVEY OF POLITICAL DEVELOPMENTS (1972); J. SYATAUW, SOME NEWLY ESTABLISHED ASIAN STATES AND THE DEVELOPMENT OF INTERNATIONAL LAW (1961); Fatouros, *The Participation of the "New" States in the International Legal Order,* in 1 THE FUTURE OF THE INTERNATIONAL LEGAL ORDER 317–71 (R. Falk & C. Black eds. 1969); Suzuki, *Self-Determination and World Public Order: Community Response to Territorial Separation,* 16 VA. J. INT'L L. 779 (1976).

19. *See* H. ALKER & B. RUSSETT, WORLD POLITICS IN THE GENERAL ASSEMBLY (1965); AFRICA AND INTERNATIONAL ORGANIZATION (Y. El-Ayouty & H. Brooks eds. 1974), especially the article by Hovet at 11–17; T. HOVET, BLOC POLITICS IN THE UNITED NATIONS (1960); RIO: RESHAPING THE INTERNATIONAL ORDER: A REPORT TO THE CLUB OF ROME 11–24 (1976) (Jan Tinbergen coordinator, Antony J. Dolman ed., Jan van Ettinger director) [hereinafter cited as RIO]; Keohane, *Political Influence in the General Assembly,* 557 INT'L CONCILIATION (1966).

20. *See* P. BLAIR, THE MINISTATE DILEMMA (1967); PROBLEMS OF SMALLER TERRITORIES (B. Benedict ed. 1967); S. DE SMITH, MICROSTATES AND MICRONESIA (1970); D. MCHENRY, MICRONESIA: TRUST BETRAYED (1975); UNITED NATIONS INSTITUTE FOR TRAINING AND RESEARCH, SMALL STATES AND TERRITORIES: STATUS AND PROBLEMS (1971); Emerson, *Self-Determination,* 65 AM. J. INT'L L. 459, 469–73 (1971); Fisher, *The Participation of Microstates in International Affairs,* 1968 PROC., AM. SOC'Y INT'L L. 164.

as manifested in complex institutions with varying degrees of centralization and pluralization, affect the total configuration of authority and effective control. As totalitarian and authoritarian regimes grow in number, many nation-states are not organized to encourage democratic participation in constitutive process, whether national or transnational.

In the meantime, as global interdependences intensify and more and more human rights problems require global solutions, the existing state system appears increasingly inadequate for decision making that will fulfill demands for human dignity values on a global scale. Departing from their appropriate roles as providers and protectors of human rights, nation-states themselves become the most important deprivers.[21] Given their wide preoccupation with maintenance of their ascendancy in power, the effective elites of many communities tend to become oppressive of, or insensitive to, rising demands for human rights. So preoccupied, they make vehement assertions, highly archaic in the contemporary world, of a large domain of domestic jurisdiction for exercise of exclusive competence regarding human rights.[22] In sum, the existing predominance of nation-states in world constitutive process would appear to be less than rationally designed, both geographically and functionally, to fulfill the rising common demands of peoples everywhere for human dignity values.

INTERNATIONAL GOVERNMENTAL ORGANIZATIONS

International governmental organizations serve for human rights purposes, as for other purposes, a dual function in global constitutive process: they both offer indispensable structures of authority for other participants and themselves become unique, distinguishable participants in decision making. Such organizations, proliferating even more rapidly than nation-states within recent years and exhibiting many differing degrees of comprehensiveness and specialization, engage in or facilitate the collective performance of many different decision functions, such as intelligence, promotion, prescription, and application.[23] They may be general in the sense of being designed to affect all values, or specialized

---

21. *See* chapter 2 *supra.*

22. For further treatment of this question, *see* notes 147–71 *infra* and accompanying text.

23. *See generally* A. Bennett, International Organizations: Principles and Issues (1977); D. Bowett, The Law of International Institutions (2d ed. 1970) [hereinafter cited as D. Bowett]; I. Claude, *supra* note 10; R. Cox & H. Jacobson, et al., The Anatomy of Influence: Decision Making in International Organization (1974) [hereinafter cited as R. Cox & H. Jacobson]; M. Elmandjra, The United Nations System: An Analysis (1973); The Evolution of International Organizations, *supra* note 14; S. Goodspeed, The Nature and Function of International Organizations (1958); E.

to different values or aspects of value processes; they may be global or regional or local in their geographic reach.

The United Nations is, of course, the general-purpose organization, supplying the backbone structures of authority for the whole global constitutive process, which aspires to affect all values, including those of both minimum and optimum public order. Since its founding in 1945, the United Nations has undergone significant constitutive development; its own activities have tremendously increased its membership and democratized decision. The General Assembly shortly became the focal point for the intense aspirations for change deriving from both developed and developing states, and over the years it has greatly expanded its base in authority.[24] The Security Council has been transformed, through broad conceptions of minimum order, into an agency for the more general application of policies. Most importantly, the transnational protection of human rights, whose scope was only dimly perceived in 1945, has become a principal, ongoing enterprise of the entire organization.

Notable among the regional organizations of sufficiently general purposes to include human rights objectives are the Organization of American States (OAS), the Organization of African Unity (OAU), the complex of European community organizations, and the League of Arab States.[25] Each of these organizations projects a value program of broad spectrum, and seeks to bring to bear local initiatives, resources, and potentials in the pursuit of regional cooperation for established goals.

Haas, Beyond the Nation-State: Functionalism and International Organization (1964) [hereinafter cited as E. Haas]; International Organization: Politics and Process, *supra* note 15; E. Luard, International Agencies: The Emerging Framework of Interdependence (1977) [hereinafter cited as E. Luard]; P. Reuter, *supra* note 7.

24. *See* S. Bailey, The General Assembly of the United Nations: A Study of Procedure and Practice (1964); I. Claude, *supra* note 11, at 163–90; B. Cohen, The United Nations: Constitutional Developments, Growth, and Possibilities (1961); E. Gross, The United Nations: Structure for Peace (1962); H. Haviland, The Political Role of the General Assembly (1951); H. Nicholas, The United Nations as a Political Institution 41–63 (2d ed. 1963); Goodwin, *The General Assembly of the United Nations,* in The Evolution of International Organizations, *supra* note 14, at 42–67.

25. *See generally* B. Andemicael, The OAU and the UN: Relations between the Organization of African Unity and the United Nations (1976) (UNITAR Regional Study No. 2); Z. Cervenka, The Organisation of African Unity and Its Charter (1969); M. el-Khatib, The Status of the League of Arab States in the International Community (1958); Regional Politics and World Order (R. Falk & S. Mendlovitz eds. 1973); Basic Documents of Asian Regional Organizations (M. Haas ed. 1974) (4 vols.); M. Khalil, The Arab States and the Arab League (1962); R. MacDonald, The League of Arab States (1965); J. Nye, International Regionalism—Readings (1968); A. Robertson, The Relations between the Council of Europe and the United Nations (1972) (UNITAR Regional Study No. 1); B. Russett, International Regions and the International System (1967); Basic Documents of African Regional Organizations (L. Sohn ed. 1971–72) (4 vols.); P. Tharp, Regional International Organizations:

The various functional organizations, i.e., international governmental organizations specialized to a particular value or cluster of values, may of course also make, or participate in, decisions which affect the degree of achievement of human rights in different communities. Well-known examples of such specialized organizations include the United Nations Educational, Scientific, and Cultural Organization (UNESCO); the World Health Organization (WHO); the United Nations International Children's Emergency Fund (UNICEF); the Food and Agriculture Organization (FAO); the International Labor Organization (ILO); the International Bank for Reconstruction and Development (the World Bank); the International Monetary Fund (IMF); the Universal Postal Union (UPU); and the International Telecommunications Union (ITU).[26]

The sustained growth of international governmental organizations reflects both the increasing vigor of transnational interactions and the shared perception of participants in world social process that many of their preferred values are practicably obtainable only through collaborative transnational action. As such organizations cope with problems of transnational magnitude and impact, they serve to dilute the importance of historic, somewhat arbitrary, national boundaries. In growing measure, they provide alternatives to the arbitrary power of nation-state officials. In increasing degree they open up what is going on within nation-states for observation by outsiders. They begin to constitute an organized conscience of the world and to bring a world public opinion to bear on furtherance of the defense and fulfillment of human rights. In addition, the international civil servants who staff such organizations

---

Structures and Functions (1971); I. Wallerstein, Africa: The Politics of Unity (1967); J. Woronoff, Organizing African Unity (1970); Bebr, *Regional Organizations: A United Nations Problem,* 49 Am. J. Int'l L. 166 (1955); Elias, *The Charter of the Organization of African Unity,* 59 Am. J. Int'l L. 243 (1965); Langley & Okolo, *Organization of African Unity and Apartheid: Constraints on Resolution,* 137 World Affairs 206 (1975); Nanda, *Implementation of Human Rights by the United Nations and Regional Organizations,* 21 De Paul L. Rev. 307 (1971); Padelford, *The Organization of African Unity,* 18 Int'l Org. 521 (1964); Wilcox, *Regionalism and the United Nations,* 19 Int'l Org. 789 (1965).

26. *See* C. Alexandrowicz, World Economic Agencies: Law and Practice (1962); R. Asher, et al., The United Nations and Promotion of the General Welfare (1957); H. Aufricht, The International Monetary Fund: Legal Aspects, Structure, Functions, 1945–1964 (1964); R. Berkov, The World Health Organisation: A Study in Decentralised International Administration (1957); T. Buergenthal & J. Torney, International Human Rights and International Education (1976); G. Codding, The Universal Postal Union (1964); R. Cox & H. Jacobson, *supra* note 23; Functionalism: Theory and Practice in International Relations (A. Groom & P. Taylor eds. 1975); W. Laves & C. Thomson, UNESCO: Purpose, Progress, Prospects (1958); E. Luard, *supra* note 23; Herzog & Juvigny, *UNESCO and the Struggle for Human Rights,* 26 UNESCO Courier 4 (Oct. 1973).

increasingly develop loyalties to the organizations themselves and seek, in various ways, to strengthen their viability as instruments of inclusive goals.[27]

Although in terms of numbers the proliferation of international governmental organizations has been impressive, the aggregate contribution of such organizations to global decision making has not been equally impressive. The resources, independent of state control, made available to such organizations have not been adequate. The structures of the organizations are kept primitive, without appropriate regional or functional balance. Their technical procedures remain unsystematized and uneconomic. Particular national elites still too often perceive such organizations as instruments of their own national policy rather than of the clarification and implementation of genuine common interest.

POLITICAL PARTIES

Political parties, as organized groups which present comprehensive programs of policy and put forward candidates in elections, both play an important role in global processes of effective power and directly affect the performance of many different functions in authoritative decisions.[28] The most intensive impact of political parties is of course in the organization and management of particular nation-states. Political party representatives achieve access to the public organs of the nation-state, not only by election, but also by patronage and infiltration at all levels of government into executive, legislative, judicial, and administrative institutions.

The way any particular state is molded by political parties has of course its external impact. Modern techniques of mass communication and transportation make it possible for political parties to effect a high degree of organization, to centralize their command, to coordinate their national and international forces, and to participate with striking effectiveness in power processes, both in and out of government and within and beyond the boundaries of any particular nation-state. Some political parties deliberately seek transnational effects and play roles in intelli-

---

27. *See generally* S. BAILEY, THE SECRETARIAT OF THE UNITED NATIONS (2d ed. 1964); D. HAMMARSKJOLD, THE INTERNATIONAL CIVIL SERVANT IN LAW AND IN FACT (1961); G. LANGROD, THE INTERNATIONAL CIVIL SERVICE (1963); S. SCHWEBEL, THE SECRETARY-GENERAL OF THE UNITED NATIONS (1952); ANDREW A. STARK (Under-Secretary-General for Administration and Management), THE SECRETARIAT—TWENTY-FIVE YEARS AFTER, U.N. Doc. OPI/419 (1970); Cox, *The Executive Head: An Essay on Leadership in International Organization,* in INTERNATIONAL ORGANIZATION: POLITICS AND PROCESS, *supra* note 15, at 155–80; Scott, *The World's Civil Service,* 496 INT'L CONCILIATION (1954).

28. *See* authorities cited in chapter 2 *supra,* at note 14 and accompanying text. *See also* R. MICHELS, POLITICAL PARTIES (1949).

gence, recommending, prescribing, and appraising functions, with important effects upon the formulation and application of global policies. One important contribution of political parties is in affording channels, other than official, for the initiation and communication of policies.

The same individual human being may be a key actor both within a political party and within the structures of authority of a state. Though international governmental organizations may make no provision for access by political parties as such, representatives of parties do in fact obtain access through other identifications, including those of the state.

The greatest threat to shared power in global decision making from political parties is that they may degenerate into political orders, monopolizing power and destroying freedom.[29] In lesser threat, parties may become parochial and nationalistic, with scant identification with the whole range of troubled humanity.

PRESSURE GROUPS

Pressure groups, that is, organized groups which seek particular power objectives but do not present comprehensive programs and candidates for office, play an increasingly important role in transnational decision making. Notable among the nongovernmental organizations concerned with human rights are the International Commission of Jurists, the International League for Human Rights, Amnesty International, the International Council of Women, the Anti-Slavery Society, and the World Jewish Congress.[30] Many such organizations achieve consultative status with the United Nations, notably the Economic and Social Council. Depending upon the particular status achieved, such organizations may be permitted to be present at the Council's deliberations, or even to enter items on the provisional agenda. In fact, many of the human rights recommendations and decisions within the United Nations have resulted, directly or indirectly, from the initiatives and efforts of transnational pressure groups.[31]

---

29. *See, e.g.*, W. EBENSTEIN, THE NAZI STATE (1943).

30. For further detail, *see* notes 296–300 and 306–14 *infra* and accompanying text. *See also* HUMAN RIGHTS: TOWARD AN NGO STRATEGY FOR THE ADVANCEMENT OF HUMAN RIGHTS (1968) (final report of the International NGO Conference, Paris, September 16–20, 1968) [hereinafter cited as NGO STRATEGY]; J. LADOR-LEDERER, INTERNATIONAL GROUP PROTECTION (1968); J. LADOR-LEDERER, INTERNATIONAL NON-GOVERNMENTAL ORGANIZATIONS AND ECONOMIC ENTITIES: A STUDY IN AUTONOMOUS ORGANIZATION AND IUS GENTIUM (1963); L. WHITE, INTERNATIONAL NON-GOVERNMENTAL ORGANIZATIONS (1951); *Interest Groups in International Perspective*, 413 ANNALS 1 (1974); Shestack, *Sisyphus Endures: The International Human Rights NGO*, 24 N.Y.L.S.L. REV. 89 (1978); Weissbrodt, *The Role of International Nongovernmental Organizations in the Implementation of Human Rights*, 12 TEXAS INT'L L.J. 293 (1977); *Non-Governmental Organizations*, U.N. Doc. E/4476 (1968) (report of the secretary-general).

31. For further elaboration, *see* notes 306–14 *infra* and accompanying text.

The influence of pressure groups upon decision making has greatly increased within recent years. Such groups circulate the globe and employ all media of communication to pursue and achieve their particular power purposes. They are able to operate with a minimum regard for national boundaries, and the communications revolution gives them practically unlimited geographic reach. Problems in human rights afford a peculiarly effective focus for their activities.

Pressure groups bring their influence to bear upon a variety of decision functions, including especially intelligence, promoting, invoking, and appraising. Such groups are able to take stands which state officials cannot take or are unwilling to risk. They are able also, without concern for total policy considerations, to engage in intense campaigns for their particular purposes. The danger they create is that their preoccupation with particular concerns may blind them and others to the common interest.

PRIVATE ASSOCIATIONS

Multiplying hosts of private associations, that is, organized groups primarily dedicated to the shaping and sharing of values other than power, are increasingly transnational in membership, goals, areas of activity, resources, and strategies. These private associations relate in abundance to many different values, such as wealth, enlightenment, well-being, and so on. Those which relate to wealth, as symbolized by multinational corporations, establish and maintain a global economy that affects the production and distribution of goods and services everywhere. Those which relate to enlightenment, as exemplified by the International Press Institute and the International Law Association,[32] gather, process, and disseminate information and knowledge transnationally. Those which relate to well-being, as exemplified by the International Red Cross,[33] seek to improve health, safety, and comfort transna-

32. *See* Olmstead, *The International Law Association: A World-Wide Organization for Development and Promotion of International Law,* in THE PRESENT STATE OF INTERNATIONAL LAW AND OTHER ESSAYS: WRITTEN IN HONOUR OF THE CENTENARY CELEBRATION OF THE INTERNATIONAL LAW ASSOCIATION, 1873–1973, at 3–9 (M. Bos ed. 1973) [hereinafter cited as THE PRESENT STATE OF INTERNATIONAL LAW]; Wilberforce, *The Daily Life and Administration of the International Law Association,* in *id.* at 11–22; Munch, *L'influence de l'International Law Association sur la doctrine et la pratique du droit international,* in *id.* at 23–36.

See also Dupuy, *La Contribution de l'Académie au Développement du Droit International,* 138 HAGUE RECUEIL DES COURS 44 (1973); Fitzmaurice, *The Contribution of the Institute of International Law to the Development of International Law, id.* at 203–60; Van Roijen, *Holland and the Hague Academy of International Law, id.* at 27–43.

33. *See* J. JOYCE, RED CROSS INTERNATIONAL AND THE STRATEGY OF PEACE (1959); Bissell, *International Committee of the Red Cross and the Protection of Human Rights,* 1 HUMAN RIGHTS J.

tionally. Those which relate to skill, as exemplified by labor unions and various professional associations, seek to maintain professional ties and collaboration transnationally.[34] Those which relate to affection, as based upon ethnic, religious, linguistic, kinship, and other ties, seek to establish and maintain congenial relationships, group identifications, and collaboration transnationally. Those which relate to rectitude, as symbolized by the Roman Catholic Church, the World Council of Churches, and other religious organizations, seek to formulate and express norms of responsible conduct transnationally.[35] Those which relate to respect, as exemplified by the Nobel Foundation and other honorific societies, seek to recognize and bestow honor for distinctive contributions to the common interest transnationally.[36]

The important point of present concern is that all of these associations, whatever the values to which they are especially dedicated, characteristically seek, and obtain, effects upon transnational decision making. They achieve important impacts both directly upon constitutive process, in the making and application of law, and upon all the features of effective power and public order which sustain constitutive process. The wealth, enlightenment, skill, well-being, and so on that they control give them highly significant bases in effective power. By supplying many of the structures of interaction through which global society is established and maintained, they have an effect on the production and distribution of all public order values, which effect in turn affects the quality and direction of constitutive process. The danger from private associations, comparable to that from pressure groups, is that, concerned primarily with one value or only a few values, they may bring their resources to bear in pursuit of effects incompatible with genuine, long-term common interest.

THE INDIVIDUAL

Individual human beings, acting through all the organizations and associations itemized above, continuously communicate and collaborate

---

255 (1968); *The International Committee of the Red Cross and Torture,* 16 Int'l Red Cross 610 (1976); Rosenne, *The Red Cross, Red Crescent, Red Lion and Sun and the Red Shield of David*, 5 Israel Y.B. Human Rights 9 (1975).

34. *See* R. Beever, European Unity and the Trade Union Movements (1960); L. Lorwin, The International Labor Movement (1953); W. Schevenels, Forty-Five Years, 1901–1945: International Federation of Trade Unions, A Historical Précis (1956); Berg & Schmidhauser, *American Bar Association and the Human Rights Conventions: The Political Significance of Private Professional Associations,* 38 Social Research 362 (1971).

35. *See* chapter 11 *infra,* at notes 179–86 and accompanying text. *See also* Grubb & Booth, *The Church and International Relations,* 17 Y.B. World Affairs 219 (1963).

36. *See* Nobel Lectures: Peace (F. Haberman ed. 1972) (3 vols.).

both in every phase of effective and authoritative decision and in the shaping and sharing of all values. Individuals may act not only in the name of, or as representatives of, the different organizations and associations, but simply in their own right as individuals qua individuals. Whatever their identifications, individuals are the ultimate actors in all social process. Individuals have always played significant roles in effective power. They are increasingly achieving recognized roles in the process of authoritative decision.

The decision functions in which individuals, qua individuals, have long played important roles transnationally include the intelligence, promoting, and appraising functions. Through the concept of "custom," that is, of law created by uniformities in peoples' behavior and other communications, individuals and their private associations have always participated in the prescribing function.[37] For invoking the authoritative application of transnational prescriptions, individuals continue to have access, for what it is worth, to national courts; they are, further, being increasingly accorded access to transnational arenas of authority, such as United Nations Commission on Human Rights, the European Commission on Human Rights, and the Inter-American Commission on Human Rights.[38]

Historically, one of the great difficulties in the transnational protection of human rights has been the notion that only states, and not individuals or their other associations, are appropriate "subjects" of international law.[39] An individual human being, the myth dictated, could secure transnational protection only through a nation-state protector. This

---

37. *See* notes 315–20 and 347–57 *infra* and accompanying text.

38. *See* notes 79–108 and 389–405 *infra* and accompanying text.

39. On the controversy whether the individual is a subject of international law, *see* P. Corbett, The Individual and World Society (1953); P. Jessup, *supra* note 16, at 15–42; H. Lauterpacht, International Law and Human Rights 27–72 (1950) [hereinafter cited as H. Lauterpacht]; C. Norgaard, The Position of the Individual in International Law (1962); R. Pollack, The Individual's Rights and International Organization (1966); P. Remec, The Position of the Individual in International Law according to Grotius and Vattel (1960); L. Sohn & T. Buergenthal, International Protection of Human Rights 1–21 (1973); J. Jefferies, The Individual and International Law, 1954 (unpublished J.S.D. dissertation, Yale Law School Library); Amon, *Individual in International Law,* 13 Far Eastern L. Rev. 185 (1966); Cohen, *Human Rights, the Individual, and International Law,* in 3 René Cassin, Amicorum Discipulorumque Liber 69 (Institut International des Droits de l'Homme ed. 1971) [hereinafter cited as René Cassin]; Higgins, *Conceptual Thinking about the Individual in International Law,* 24 N.Y.L.S.L. Rev. 11 (1978); MacBride, *Conference of European Jurists on "The Individual and the State,"* 3 Int'l Lawyer 603 (1969); Manner, *The Object Theory of the Individual in International Law,* 46 Am. J. Int'l L. 428 (1952); Parry, *Some Considerations upon the Protection of Individuals in International Law,* 90 Hague Recueil des Cours 653 (1956); Tucker, *Has the Individual Become the Subject of International Law?* 34 U. Cin. L. Rev. 341 (1965).

formulation raises of course all the ambiguities inherent in the concept of nationality and makes the security of the individual dependent upon the willingness of his state to protect him. Enjoying a high degree of discretion, nation-state officials have tended to decide whether or not to espouse claims against external entities on behalf of their nationals on the basis of considerations of putative "national interest" rather than of concern for the protection of the deprived person.[40]

The notion that states are the only appropriate "subjects" of international law is belied by all the contemporary facts, recited above, about participation in the global processes of effective power and authoritative decision. This notion, unknown to the founding fathers and deriving from certain parochial misconceptions of the late nineteenth century, lingers on to impede the protection of human rights merely because it sometimes serves the power purposes of state elites. One important factor in contemporary effective power is that many state elites cannot endure their nationals complaining to other state elites or the larger community of humankind about the deprivations within their particular communities.

Historically, the greatest difficulty concerning participation in the world constitutive process has been this exaggeration of the role of the nation-state as the principal subject of international law. Because of the overwhelming emphasis on the "sovereignty" of nation-states, there has been a great reluctance to recognize other participants in world social process as in fact active subjects of international law. For a time even international governmental organizations were denied acceptance as subjects of international law; their factual role was obscured and their separate legal personality was questioned. The role of nongovernmental participants—political parties, pressure groups, and private associations—was considered a matter more of sociology than of law. Individual human beings were regarded as objects, not subjects, of international law. In a world in which individuals often had minimal participation even in their own governmental processes, it was possible to deny their frequent participation in the processes of transnational decision making.

While the dominant role of the nation-state remains a fact today, it is important to recall that the "omnipotent" nation-state is but one of many structures that human beings design and employ to protect and fulfill their interests. Originally formed to protect individual human beings from the tyranny and exploitation of feudal lords, the nation-state was then widely perceived to be the structure most adequate to protect and fulfill the demands of individuals for a greater production and sharing of values. Like all other human institutions, when the nation-state fails to

---

40. *See* the appendix *infra,* at notes 4–42 and accompanying text.

serve such common interest, it can be expected to wane and be succeeded by other institutions. The nation-state is in fact today a most important depriver, as well as protector, of human rights. Confronted with the ever-growing pressures of global interdependences that defy artificial and arbitrary national boundaries, and the growing perception of these interdependences, the contemporary state system can be expected to be under increasingly severe challenge.[41]

The alternatives in world constitutive process of authoritative decision open to individuals who aspire toward a better protection of human rights need not be misconceived. The choice in features of world constitutive process is not one of simple dichotomy: either of a world controlled solely by "sovereign" nation-states or of a world government supplanting all the existing nation-states.[42] Ours is a world of pluralism and diversity, a global arena in which various participants—groups (territorial and functional, governmental and nongovernmental) and individual human beings—constantly interact under ever-changing conditions. All of the above-mentioned group participants—nation-states, international governmental organizations, political parties, pressure groups, and private associations—are forms of associations through which individuals cooperate to achieve fulfillment of their demands. They are, in the ultimate analysis, highly malleable instruments created and maintained by individual human beings to clarify and secure the basic human rights of themselves and others. They offer an almost infinite spectrum of potentiality in the arrangement and rearrangement of functional and geographic structures and practices toward this end.

Perspectives

The perspectives of the effective elites of the world, which infuse the global processes of authoritative and controlling decision, would appear to exhibit both an increasing stability and a turgid, but perceptible, movement toward the demands, identifications, and expectations appropriate to a public order of human dignity. The rising common demands of the peoples of the world for a greater production and wider sharing of all basic values—respect, power, enlightenment, well-being, wealth, skill, affection, and rectitude—are rapidly being incorporated into authoritative prescription. Beginning with the United Nations Charter, extending through the Universal Declaration of Human Rights, to the International Covenants on Human Rights and a host of

---

41. *See* chapter 1 *supra*.

42. One defect in an otherwise deeply insightful book, W. Schiffer, *supra* note 8, is in its emphasis upon this dichotomy and its failure to see that potential patterns in the distribution of transnational authority and control are almost infinite.

more specialized conventions and ancillary expressions about human rights, a growing body of prescriptions makes comprehensive and detailed reference to the same basic values that are found in the bills of rights of the more mature nation-states. In projecting the protection of human rights as one of its major goals, the Charter of the United Nations repeatedly stresses the importance of "universal respect for, and observance of, human rights and fundamental freedoms"[43] as indispensable to "the creation of conditions of stability and well-being which are necessary for peaceful and friendly relations among states."[44] The Universal Declaration of Human Rights,[45] which when adopted in 1948 was regarded as merely "a common standard of achievement" devoid of legal enforceability, has become widely accepted as customary international law binding upon all nation-states.[46] The International Covenant on Economic, Social, and Cultural Rights[47] and the International Covenant on Civil and Political Rights[48] (and its Optional Protocol)[49] have, despite considerable doubts and misgivings expressed over the years, been in effect since early 1976. The Universal Declaration and the two Covenants, taken together, are widely regarded, as will be developed below, as an International Bill of Human Rights.[50] These demands for human dignity values, thus formally articulated and prescribed in this International Bill of Human Rights, are given further detailed specifications in the multitude of specialized human rights conventions and other ancillary expressions that seek to protect a particular category of individual or deal with a particular value.[51]

---

43. U.N. Charter, Art. 55 (opening sentence).

44. U.N. Charter, Art. 55c.

45. Universal Declaration of Human Rights, *adopted* Dec. 10, 1948, G.A. Res. 217, U.N. Doc. A/810 at 71 (1948) [hereinafter cited as Universal Declaration].

46. *See* notes 363–67 and 583–610 *infra* and accompanying text.

47. International Covenant on Economic, Social, and Cultural Rights, *adopted* Dec. 16, 1966, G.A. Res. 2200A, 21 U.N. GAOR, Supp. (No. 16) 49, U.N. Doc. A/6316 (1966) (entered into force Jan. 3, 1976) [hereinafter cited as Covenant on Economic, Social, and Cultural Rights].

48. International Covenant on Civil and Political Rights, *adopted* Dec. 16, 1966, G.A. Res. 2200A, 21 U.N. GAOR, Supp. (No. 16) 49, U.N. Doc. A/6316 (1966) (entered into force Mar. 23, 1976) [hereinafter cited as Covenant on Civil and Political Rights].

49. Optional Protocol to the International Covenant on Civil and Political Rights, *adopted* Dec. 16, 1966, G.A. Res. 2200A, 21 U.N. GAOR, Supp. (No. 16) 49, U.N. Doc. A/6316 (1966) (entered into force Mar. 23, 1976) [hereinafter cited as Optional Protocol].

50. *See* notes 558–610 *infra* and accompanying text.

51. For a convenient collection of these instruments, *see* United Nations, Human Rights: A Compilation of International Instruments of the United Nations, U.N. Doc. ST/HR/1 (1973) [hereinafter cited as U.N. Human Rights Instruments]. Other useful collections include Basic Documents on Human Rights (I. Brownlie ed. 1971); Documentary Supplement to Cases and Materials on the International

Despite this great bulk of recent prescription, the movement toward making the transnational protection of human rights a fundamental policy in world constitutive process developed rather slowly. Basically elite-centered between states, international law was for a long time preoccupied with the interrelations of states as entities. Human rights problems were generally considered to raise "political questions," beyond the realm of law. When human rights problems were considered to fall within the province of law, they were regarded as within the "domestic jurisdiction" of particular states.[52] How a state treated its own nationals was regarded as beyond the domain of international law, precluding interference by other states.

Demands for the transnational protection of individual rights found their most comprehensive initial expression in an evolving body of customary international law about the responsibility of states with regard to treatment of aliens.[53] The development of customary international law in this area was in the beginning shaped primarily by the shared concerns of state elites both with consolidating their bases of power by controlling their nationals (abroad as well as at home) and with minimizing frictions and conflicts in their interrelations. This law rapidly became, however, an important source of transnational protection of human rights for a particular category of people (aliens) in an era when the nation-state was still regarded as the only subject in international law. Further demands for the transnational protection of human rights were manifested in connection with the efforts to abolish slavery,[54] the development of humanitarianism in the law of war (as expressed in the delicate balancing between the principles of military necessity and humanity),[55] the doctrine of humanitarian intervention for remedying

---

LEGAL SYSTEM (N. Leech, C. Oliver, & J. Sweeney eds. 1973) [hereinafter cited as DOCUMENTARY SUPPLEMENT]; BASIC DOCUMENTS ON INTERNATIONAL PROTECTION OF HUMAN RIGHTS (L. Sohn & T. Buergenthal eds. 1973) [hereinafter cited as BASIC DOCUMENTS].

52. *See* notes 145–71 *infra* and accompanying text.

53. *See* chapter 14 *infra.*

54. *See* chapter 7 *infra*, at notes 84–282 and accompanying text.

55. *See* M. McDOUGAL & F. FELICIANO, LAW AND MINIMUM WORLD PUBLIC ORDER 521–30 (1961). *See also* J. PICTET, THE PRINCIPLES OF INTERNATIONAL HUMANITARIAN LAW (1967); J. STONE, LEGAL CONTROLS OF INTERNATIONAL CONFLICT (rev. ed. 1959) [hereinafter cited as J. STONE, LEGAL CONTROLS]; *Respect for Human Rights in Armed Conflicts: Existing Rules of International Law Concerning the Prohibition or Restriction of Use of Specific Weapons,* U.N. Doc. A/9215 (Vols. 1 and 2) (1973); Baxter, *The Law of War,* in THE PRESENT STATE OF INTERNATIONAL LAW, *supra* note 32, at 107–24; Draper, *Human Rights and the Law of War,* 12 VA. J. INT'L L. 326 (1972); Draper, *The Relationship between the Human Rights Regime and the Law of Armed Conflict,* 1 ISRAEL Y.B. HUMAN RIGHTS 191 (1971); Greenspan, *The Protection of Human Rights in Time of Warfare,* 1 ISRAEL Y.B. HUMAN RIGHTS 228 (1971); Hewitt,

deprivations of human rights within particular states that outrage the conscience of humankind,[56] and an international regime for the protection of minorities under the League of Nations.[57]

It was the establishment of the United Nations that ushered in, in the wake of the Nazi atrocities, a new epoch in international protection of human rights. Like its predecessor, the United Nations seeks, as its primary goal, to maintain world minimum public order (peace and security). From the Westphalian concept that tolerated and condoned the use of force as an instrument of change, through the Hague Conferences, the League of Nations, and the Kellogg-Briand Pact, there developed an ever more insistent demand for outlawing the use of force save for purposes of conservation. This demand was crystallized and incorpo-

---

Respect for Human Rights in Armed Conflicts, 4 N.Y.U. Int'l L. & Politics 41 (1971); Paust, *An International Structure for Implementation of the 1949 Geneva Conventions: Needs and Function Analysis,* 1 Yale Studies in World Public Order 148 (1974); Schwarzenberger, *Human Rights and Guerrilla Warfare,* 1 Israel Y.B. Human Rights 246 (1971); Von Glahn, *The Protection of Human Rights in Time of Armed Conflict,* 1 Israel Y.B. Human Rights 208 (1971).

56. *See* notes 232–65 *infra* and accompanying text.

57. *See* League of Nations, Protection of Linguistic, Racial and Religious Minorities by the League of Nations: Provisions Contained in the Various International Instruments at Present in Force, League of Nations Publications 1927.I.B.2 (1927). *See also* I. Claude, National Minorities: An International Problem (1955); O. Janowski, The Jews and Minority Rights, 1898–1919 (1933); C. Macartney, National States and National Minorities (1934); T. Modeen, The International Protection of National Minorities in Europe 47–65 (1969); L. Sohn & T. Buergenthal, *supra* note 39, at 213–335; J. Stone, International Guarantee of Minority Rights (1932); J. Stone, Regional Guarantee of Minority Rights: A Study of Minority Procedure in Upper Silesia (1933); Green, *Protection of Minorities in the League of Nations and the United Nations,* in Human Rights, Federalism, and Minorities 180 (A. Gotlieb ed. 1970); Macartney, *League of Nations' Protection of Minority Rights,* in The International Protection of Human Rights 22–38 (E. Luard ed. 1967) [hereinafter cited as E. Luard, International Protection].

For contemporary concern for the protection of minorities, *see* U. Haksar, Minority Protection and International Bill of Human Rights (1974); United Nations, Definition and Classification of Minorities, U.N. Doc. E/CN.4/Sub. 2/85 (1950) (memorandum submitted by the secretary-general); *Progress Reports on the Study on the Rights of Persons Belonging to Ethnic, Religious and Linguistic Minorities,* U.N. Doc. E/CN.4/Sub. 2/L.582 (1973), E/CN.4/Sub. 2/L.595 (1974), and E/CN.4/Sub. 2/L.621 (1975); Bruegel, *A Neglected Field: The Protection of Minorities,* 4 Human Rights J. 413 (1971); De Nova, *Human Rights and the Protection of Minorities,* 11 How. L.J. 275 (1965); Galey, *Indigenous Peoples, International Consciousness Raising and the Development of International Law on Human Rights,* 8 Human Rights J. 21 (1975); Green, *Canadian Bill of Rights, Indian Rights, and the United Nations,* 22 Chitty's L.J. 22 (1974); Kunz, *The Present Status of the International Law for the Protection of Minorities,* 48 Am. J. Int'l L. 282 (1954); Lannung, *The Rights of Minorities,* in Melanges Offerts à Polys Modinos 181–95 (1968); O'Brien, *On the Rights of Minorities,*

rated in the Charter of the United Nations.[58] The provisions of the Charter, including Article 2(4) and various ancillary provisions, have made a tremendous contribution to the clarification, if not consistent implementation, of this most intense demand for minimum order.[59] The most important purpose for which the global constitutive process of authoritative decision is established and maintained today is widely recognized as that of securing a basic public order both by minimizing unauthorized coercion and by protecting the reasonable expectations created by agreement and customary behavior. The comprehensiveness of this purpose reflects a shared perception that only when minimum public order is secured can optimum public order (in the sense of the greatest production and widest possible sharing of all values) be seriously pursued and achieved. Conversely, there is comparable recognition that, in a global context of intensifying interdependence, minimum order cannot be established and maintained without the supporting conditions of a viable optimum order.[60] Hence the importance of the protection of human rights extends, beyond mere aspirations toward a greater production and wider distribution of values, to the necessities for maintaining a secure base for the enjoyment of any rights. Both minimum order and optimum order are in constant interaction: they affect and reinforce each other, both positively and negatively.

The identifications of the effective elites which establish and maintain the global constitutive process, like those of peoples more generally,

---

55 COMMENTARY 46 (June, 1973); Vukas, *General International Law and the Protection of Minorities,* 8 HUMAN RIGHTS J. 41 (1975).

For a brilliant analysis of the nature of contemporary minority problems, *see* Claydon, *The Transnational Protection of Ethnic Minorities: A Tentative Framework for Inquiry,* 13 CANADIAN Y.B. INT'L L. 25 (1975). *See also* Claydon, *Internationally Uprooted People and the Transnational Protection of Minority Culture,* 24 N.Y.L.S.L. REV. 125 (1978).

58. *See* M. McDOUGAL & F. FELICIANO, *supra* note 55, at 121–260. *See also* D. BOWETT, SELF-DEFENSE IN INTERNATIONAL LAW (1958); I. BROWNLIE, INTERNATIONAL LAW AND THE USE OF FORCE BY STATES (1963) [hereinafter cited as I. BROWNLIE, USE OF FORCE]; B. FERENCZ, DEFINING INTERNATIONAL AGGRESSION: THE SEARCH FOR WORLD PEACE: A DOCUMENTARY HISTORY AND ANALYSIS (1975); J. STONE, AGGRESSION AND WORLD ORDER: A CRITIQUE OF UNITED NATIONS THEORIES OF AGGRESSION (1958) [hereinafter cited as J. STONE, AGGRESSION AND WORLD ORDER]; J. STONE, LEGAL CONTROLS, *supra* note 55; Q. WRIGHT, THE ROLE OF INTERNATIONAL LAW IN THE ELIMINATION OF WAR (1962); Higgins, *The Legal Limits of the Use of Force by Sovereign States: United Nations Practice,* 37 BRIT. Y.B. INT'L L. 269 (1961); Waldock, *The Regulation of the Use of Force by Individual States in International Law,* 81 HAGUE RECUEIL DES COURS 455 (1952).

59. Art. 2(4) of the United Nations Charter reads, "All Members shall refrain in their international relations from the threat or use of force against the territorial integrity or political independence of any state, or in any other manner inconsistent with the Purposes of the United Nations."

60. *See* chapter 1 *supra.*

remain multiple and ambivalent, exhibiting tendencies toward both expansion and contraction.[61] In a global social process characterized by both increasing perceptions of comprehensive interdependences and rising demands for self-determination and autonomy among different groups, it can only be expected that the identifications of effective and authoritative decision makers will waver between a rational concern for the whole of humankind and less constructive parochial concerns. The best promise of the future is that an accelerating understanding of the conditions of both security and human rights will promote and stabilize a better balance between inclusive and exclusive identifications.

The expectations of peoples which affect constitutive process would in fact appear, because of the ineluctable spread of a civilization of science and technology, to include an increasingly common and realistic map of world social process. Until relatively recent times, expectations were quite unrealistic. There were few modes of communication, education was poor, and few interchanges occurred across state borders. Whatever the interdependences, these were not realistically perceived. With increasing communication, increased and widespread literacy, and wider use of science and technology, peoples everywhere are acquiring much more comprehensive and realistic maps of the world. With regard to human rights, and social process more generally, expectations are becoming more contextual and rational. Though expectations of violence and of continuing deprivation of human rights in a world of real and perceived scarcity are still widely shared, there is an increasing recognition of the conditions of interdependence under which individuals and groups can fulfill their demands for values.

The increasing perception by peoples of a global interdependence happily conditions also an ever more realistic recognition that a principal goal of global constitutive process must be that of protecting the common interests of peoples, while rejecting all claims of special interest. By an interest is meant a value demand formulated in the name of an identity and sustained by expectations about the conditions under which the demand can be fulfilled. Common interests refer to demands shared by the great bulk of community members and whose fulfillment is affected by the same or comparable conditions. Common interests comprise a continuum of inclusive and exclusive interests: the former affect two or more members of a community; the latter predominantly affect only a single member. Special interests are those destructive of common interests, in the sense defined, which are asserted by one member irre-

---

61. *See* Lasswell, *Future Systems of Identity in the World Community*, in 4 THE FUTURE OF THE INTERNATIONAL LEGAL ORDER 3-31 (C. Black & R. Falk eds. 1972); Lasswell, *Introduction: Universality versus Parochialism*, in M. McDOUGAL & F. FELICIANO, *supra* note 55, at xix–xxvi.

spective of the consequences for others. It has of course long been recognized that among the continuing goals of any viable constitutive process are those of framing the interests of particular individuals and groups with due regard for the comparable interests of other individuals and groups and of accommodating in times of crisis even the most intensely demanded interests of individuals and groups with long-term common interests in the larger communities of which they are members.[62]

In consequence of many recent developments—the rising common demands of peoples for human dignity values, the expanding identities for whom these values are being demanded, the increasingly realistic perception of the conditions of interdependence, and the growing insistence that a principal goal of global constitutive process is the protection of common interest—there would appear to be today a growing recognition and acceptance, even demand, that the protection and fulfillment of human rights be regarded as matters of "international concern," for the employment of all constitutive functions, rather than as matters of "domestic jurisdiction," exclusively within the competence of particular territorial communities.[63] Indeed many of the policies about human rights would appear to be so intensely demanded that they are acquiring, as will be developed below, not merely the status of "international concern," but in addition that of *jus cogens* or of a global bill of rights.[64]

ARENAS

The structures of authority and other situations in which the participants in world constitutive process interact have exhibited in recent years both an enormous expansion and a modest movement toward organized, inclusive form. A principal contribution of the United Nations and of the great host of specialized agencies and regional organizations has been in the supply of a new abundance of diplomatic, parliamentary, diplomatic-parliamentary, adjudicative, and executive arenas in which all the effective participants in world power process can interact. A comparable increase has occurred in the patterns of interaction established by burgeoning private, nongovernmental associations primarily dedicated to values other than power. In consequence, the interactions of the decision makers whose choices in sum create global policy have become more timely and continuous, that is, less episodic and more alert and responsive to crisis.

Similarly, though some official arenas remain closed to some effective

62. *See* McDougal, *Human Rights and World Public Order: Principles of Content and Procedure for Clarifying General Community Policies,* 14 VA. J. INT'L L. 387 (1974); chapter 16 *infra.*

63. *See* notes 147–71 *infra* and accompanying text.

64. *See* notes 539–767 *infra* and accompanying text.

participants, there has been a general trend toward openness in arenas and a parallel movement toward making appearance compulsory for participants whose choices in fact affect community policy. Both openness and compulsoriness are promoted by increasing interdependences in effective power.

ESTABLISHMENT

The institutional structures, in which both official and unofficial interactions recur and which exhibit varying degrees of organization, may be described in terms of five different patterns of interaction.[65]

Diplomatic

The diplomatic arena, characterized by interelite communications, has a long tradition and is the most frequent locus of human rights controversies. In recent years there has been a tremendous increase in diplomatic activities regarding human rights matters from foreign office to foreign office. The successive statements and comments made by the Carter administration in regard to human rights within the Soviet Union and the responses by Soviet officials offer excellent illustration.[66]

---

65. These five categories are described in McDougal, Lasswell, & Reisman, *supra* note 1, at 100–02.

66. A chronicle of events will illumine the dynamics and complexities involved in human rights diplomacy: *Response Favorable to Carter in Soviet: His Inaugural Address Received "With Deep Satisfaction," Says Specialist in U.S. Affairs,* N.Y. Times, Jan. 22, 1977, at 11, col. 4 (city ed.); *Sakharov Is Warned about His Accusing K.G.B. in Explosion, id.,* Jan. 26, 1977, at A7, col. 1; *U.S. Cautions Soviet on Sakharov Curbs, id.,* Jan. 28, 1977, at A1, col. 3; *Sakharov Sends Letter to Carter Urging Help on Rights in Soviet, id.,* Jan. 29, 1977, at 1, col. 1; Smith, *U.S. Policy on Soviet: A Two-Edged Attitude, id.,* Jan. 29, 1977, at 3, col. 1; *Hunger for Rights in Soviet Bloc Spurs Open Protest and Criticism, id.,* Jan. 31, 1977, at 1, col. 1; *Carter Says Warning on a Soviet Dissident Reflected His View, id.,* Jan. 31, 1977, at 1, col. 1; *Soviet, Undeterred on Dissidents, Seeks Improved U.S. Ties, id.,* Feb. 1, 1977, at 1, col. 6; *Vance Says the U.S. Won't Be Strident over Rights Abroad, id.,* Feb. 1, 1977, at 1, col. 6; *Carter Discusses Human Rights and Arms Issues with Dobrynin, id.,* Feb. 2, 1977, at A1, col. 1; Lewis, *Repression and Response, id.,* Feb. 7, 1977, at 23, col. 5; *U.S. Again Comments on Soviet Dissident, id.,* Feb. 8, 1977, at 1, col. 2; *Soviet Seizes a Dissident Who Saw Safety in U.S. Statement of Support, id.,* Feb. 11, 1977, at A1, col. 2; Shipler, *Soviet Drive against Dissidents and the Carter Response, id.,* Feb. 12, 1977, at 7, col. 1; *Sakharov Receives Carter Letter Affirming Commitment on Rights, id.,* Feb. 18, 1977, at A3, col. 1; *U.S. Stoutly Defends Letter That Carter Wrote to Sakharov, id.,* Feb. 19, 1977, at 1, col. 6; Smith, *Few but Resolute: The Dissidents Cast a Long Shadow, id.,* Feb. 20, § 4, at 1, col. 1; Reston, *The Sakharov Letter, id.,* Feb. 20, 1977, § 4, at 15, col. 1; Sulzberger, *Where Do We Go Now? id.,* Feb. 20, 1977, § 4, at 15, col. 2; Gusev, *Moscow, on Sakharov, id.,* Feb. 23, 1977, at A29, col. 3; *Soviet Said to Fear Dissident Issue May Damage Relations with West, id.,* Feb. 25, 1977, at A3, col. 1; *Carter and Mondale See Bukovsky, a Soviet Dissident, id.,* Mar. 2, 1977, at 1, col. 4; *Vance Says Moscow Still Seeks Detente Despite Rights Rift, id.,* Mar. 5, 1977, at 1, col. 1; Gwertzman, *Human Rights: The Rest of the World Sees Them Differently, id.,* Mar. 6, 1977, § 4, at 5, col. 1; *Soviet Concern on Human Rights Criticism Subsides, id.,* Mar. 11, 1977, at A3, col. 4;

Parliamentary-Diplomatic

Occasional conferences dealing with a broad range of human rights concerns have grown in frequency and importance. Among the more important recent conferences are: the International Conference on Human Rights held in Teheran in 1968,[67] the United Nations Confer-

---

Pravda Cautions U.S. on Rights Criticism, id., Mar. 14, 1977, at 1, col. 5; *Soviet Expert on U.S. Asserts Rights Issue May Cloud Arms Talk, id.,* Mar. 17, 1977, at A2, col. 3; *Carter Urges U.N. to Step up Efforts for Human Rights, id.,* Mar. 18, 1977, at A1, col. 6; *Brezhnev Criticizes U.S. Stand on Rights; Warns on Relations, id.,* Mar. 22, 1977, at 1, col. 3; *Carter Encouraged by Soviet on Arms; Adamant on Rights, id.,* Mar. 23, 1977, at 1, col. 1; Reston, *Gesundheit! id.,* Mar. 23, 1977, at A25, col. 1; *The Sneeze from Moscow* (editorial), *id.,* Mar. 23, 1977, at A24, col. 1; *Amalrik on Human Rights and U.S. Flexibility* (letter), *id.,* Mar. 26, 1977, at 18, col. 3; *58 in Senate Send Letter of Support to Carter on Rights, id.,* Mar. 26, 1977, at 1, col. 1; *Human Rights and Soviet Reactions* (letters), *id.,* Mar. 27, 1977, § 4, at 16, col. 3; *Andrei D. Sakharov, on 'This Frightful Situation,' id.,* Mar. 29, 1977, at 31, col. 2; *Arms Talks Break Off as Soviet Rejects 2 Key Proposals by U.S.; Carter Says He Isn't Discouraged, id.,* Mar. 31, 1977, at A1, col. 6; *After a Rebuff in Moscow, Detente Is Put to the Test, id.,* Apr. 1, 1977, at A1, col. 4; Reston, *Kennan on Carter's Diplomacy, id.,* Apr. 3, 1977, § 1, at 17, col. 1; *Soviet Indicates U.S. Must Take Initiative in Mending Relations, id.,* Apr. 4, 1977, at 1, col. 6; *Soviet Denies Human Rights Issue Led to Rejection of U.S. Arms Plans, id.,* Apr. 7, 1977, at A10, col. 4; *Vance Asks Realism in U.S. Rights Policy, id.,* May 1, 1977, § 1, at 1, col. 4; *Carter Stresses His Commitment to Human Rights, id.,* May 3, 1977, at 1, col. 2; *Carter Appears to Have Adopted Quieter Human Rights Approach, id.,* May 11, 1977, at A1, col. 6; Gwertzman, *The Limits of an Activist U.S. Approach to Promoting Respect for Human Rights Abroad, id.,* May 18, 1977, at A14, col. 1; *Soviet Charges a Key Jewish Human Rights Activist with Treason, id.,* June 2, 1977, at A14, col. 3; *Soviet Makes No Legal Changes on Human Rights in New Charter, id.,* June 5, 1977, § 1, at 1, col. 4; *Soviet Steps Up Propaganda against Carter on Rights, id.,* June 9, 1977, at A3, col. 4; Reston, *Carter and Communism, id.,* June 10, 1977, at A27, col. 5; *K.G.B. Questions U.S. Reporter about Shcharansky, id.,* June 16, 1977, at A8, col. 1; *Vance Concedes Certain "Strains" in Ties to Soviet, id.,* June 25, 1977, at 1, col. 5; *Soviet Bars U.S. Envoy's TV Talk with Rights Remark, id.,* July 3, 1977, at 1, col. 4; *Brezhnev Lectures U.S. Envoy on Policy, id.,* July 6, 1977, at A1, col. 3; *Soviet Jews Deliver Challenge on Rights, id.,* July 12, 1977, at 1, col. 1. *See also* HUMAN RIGHTS AND AMERICAN DIPLOMACY: 1975–77 (J. Buncher ed. 1977).

For appraisals of U.S. human rights policy, *see Symposium on Human Rights and United States Foreign Policy,* 14 VA. J. INT'L L. 591 (1974) (containing articles by Richard B. Lillich, Richard B. Bilder, Thomas A. Buergenthal, Tom J. Farer, Louis Henkin, Jerome J. Shestack, and Roberta Cohen); Schachter, *International Law Implications of U.S. Human Rights Policies,* 24 N.Y.L.S.L. REV. 63 (1978). *See also* FOREIGN AFFAIRS AND NATIONAL DEFENSE DIVISION, CONGRESSIONAL RESEARCH SERVICE, LIBRARY OF CONGRESS, HUMAN RIGHTS IN THE INTERNATIONAL COMMUNITY AND IN U.S. FOREIGN POLICY, 1945–76: PREPARED FOR THE SUBCOMM. ON INTERNATIONAL ORGANIZATIONS OF THE HOUSE COMM. ON INTERNATIONAL RELATIONS (Comm. Print 1977); *Human Rights and United States Foreign Policy: A Review of the Administration's Record: Hearing before the Subcomm. on International Organizations of the House Comm. on International Relations,* 95th Cong., 1st Sess. (1977).

67. *See* UNITED NATIONS, FINAL ACT OF THE INTERNATIONAL CONFERENCE ON HUMAN RIGHTS, TEHERAN, 22 APRIL TO 13 MAY 1968, U.N. Doc. A/CONF.32/41 (1968) [hereinafter cited as FINAL ACT OF THE TEHERAN CONFERENCE]. *See also* M. MOSKOWITZ, INTERNATIONAL CONCERN WITH HUMAN RIGHTS 13–23 (1974) [hereinafter cited as M. MOSKOWITZ]; *International Conference on Human Rights,* Y.B.U.N. 1968, at 538–48.

ence on the Human Environment held in Stockholm in 1972,[68] the World Population Conference held in Bucharest in 1974,[69] the World Food Conference held in Rome in 1974,[70] the World Conference of the International Women's Year held in Mexico City in 1975,[71] and the United Nations Conference-Exposition on Human Settlements held in Vancouver in 1976.[72] These conferences, touching upon various value sectors and dimensions of human rights (the quality of life) on a global scale, contribute in various ways to the protection and fulfillment of human rights. They have greatly facilitated the performance of such important functions as intelligence (gathering and exchange of information and knowledge) and planning, appraisal (evaluating past and existing inadequacies), and promotion (suggesting concrete proposals and advocating future courses of action). Although they may exude "more rhetoric than action," they are vital to generating and crystallizing expectations of the members of the world community in the defense and fulfillment of the quality of life characterized by human dignity values.

Parliamentary

Guided more or less by doctrines of majority rule and of equality in representation, parliamentary arenas are, as compared to the two previous arenas, characterized by a higher level of organization and continuity. On the global level, the principal parliamentary arenas are the General Assembly of the United Nations and its subsidiary entities (*e.g.*, the Third, First, and Fourth Committees, the Special Committee of

68. *See* REPORT OF THE UNITED NATIONS CONFERENCE ON THE HUMAN ENVIRONMENT, U.N. Doc. A/CONF.48/14 (1972); STOCKHOLM AND BEYOND: REPORT OF THE SECRETARY OF STATE'S ADVISORY COMMITTEE ON THE 1972 UNITED NATIONS CONFERENCE ON THE HUMAN ENVIRONMENT (1972). *See also* WORLD ECO-CRISIS (D. Kay & E. Skolnikoff eds. 1972); Feraru, *Transnational Political Interests and the Global Environment,* 28 INT'L ORG. 31 (1974); Hardy, *The United Nations Environment Program,* 13 NATURAL RESOURCES J. 235 (1973); McDougal & Schneider, *The Protection of the Environment and World Public Order: Some Recent Developments,* 45 MISS. L.J. 1085 (1974); Sohn, *Stockholm Declaration on the Human Environment,* 14 HARV. INT'L L.J. 423 (1973).

69. *See* 1, 2, & 3 WORLD POPULATION: BASIC DOCUMENTS (J. Joyce ed. 1975–76).

70. *See Report of the World Food Conference,* U.N. Doc. E/CONF.65/20 (1974), reprinted in 1 THE WORLD FOOD SITUATION 455–522 (J. Willett comp. 1976). *See also* Note, *World Hunger and International Trade: An Analysis and a Proposal for Action,* 84 YALE L.J. 1046 (1975).

71. *See* UNITED NATIONS, MEETING IN MEXICO: THE STORY OF THE WORLD CONFERENCE OF THE INTERNATIONAL WOMEN'S YEAR (MEXICO CITY, 19 JUNE–2 JULY 1975) (1975) [here inafter cited as MEETING IN MEXICO].

72. *See* HABITAT: UNITED NATIONS CONFERENCE ON HUMAN SETTLEMENTS, VANCOUVER, 31 MAY TO 11 JUNE 1976, U.N. Doc. A/CONF.70/A/1–4 (1976); *Conference Adopts Recommendations for Action on Human Settlements Problem,* 13 UN MONTHLY CHRONICLE 50 (July 1976).

Twenty-four on Decolonization, and the Special Committee on Apartheid) and the Economic and Social Council and its functional commissions (the Commission on Human Rights and the Commission on the Status of Women).[73] Other important arenas include the Security Council and the Trusteeship Council. As human rights are closely linked to peace and security, the Security Council plays a very important role in cases of gross human rights violations, as illustrated by its roles in regard to Southern Rhodesia, Namibia, and South Africa.[74]

The emergence of institutions having the characteristics of parliamentary bodies is not confined to the United Nations. It extends to specialized agencies and regional organizations as well. Note, for example, the International Labor Conference of the ILO (characterized by the tripartite system of representation), the General Conference of UNESCO, the World Health Assembly of WHO, the Board of Governors of IMF (characterized by the principle of one state, one governor, wielding unequal votes based on a system of quotas), the Consultative Assembly of the Council of Europe, the General Assembly of OAS, the General Council of the League of Arab States, and the Assembly of Heads of State and Government of the Organization of African Unity.[75] These arenas provide forums for discussing virtually any problem relating to human rights.

Adjudicative

Adjudicative arenas, characterized by third-party decision as well as by distinctive procedures and criteria of decision, include tribunals of all degrees of organization. Typical examples are the International Court

---

Concerning the 1974 Diplomatic Conference on Humanitarian Law, *see* Baxter, *Humanitarian Law or Humanitarian Politics? The 1974 Diplomatic Conference on Humanitarian Law,* 16 HARV. INT'L L.J. 1 (1975); Forsythe, *1974 Diplomatic Conference on Humanitarian Law: Some Observations,* 69 AM. J. INT'L L. 77 (1975); Graham, *1974 Diplomatic Conference on the Law of War: A Victory for Political Causes and a Return to the "Just War" Concept of the Eleventh Century,* 32 WASH. & LEE L. REV. 25 (1975).

73. *See* UNITED NATIONS, UNITED NATIONS ACTION IN THE FIELD OF HUMAN RIGHTS 129-51, U.N. Doc. ST/HR/2 (1974) [hereinafter cited as UNITED NATIONS ACTION]. *See also* Hoare, *The UN Commission on Human Rights,* in E. LUARD, INTERNATIONAL PROTECTION, *supra* note 57, at 59-98; Humphrey, *United Nations Commission on Human Rights and Its Parent Body,* 1 RENÉ CASSIN, *supra* note 39, at 108-13; Humphrey, *United Nations Sub-Commission on the Prevention of Discrimination and the Protection of Minorities,* 62 AM. J. INT'L L. 869 (1968); *Review of the United Nations 33d Commission on Human Rights: Hearing before the Subcomm. on International Organizations of the House Comm. on International Relations,* 95th Cong., 1st Sess. (1977).

74. *See* notes 216-24 *infra* and accompanying text. *See also* chapter 7 *infra*, at notes 449-598 and accompanying text.

75. *See* notes 25 and 26 *supra.*

of Justice, numerous arbitral tribunals, the Human Rights Committee under the International Covenant on Civil and Political Rights, the Committee on the Elimination of Racial Discrimination, the European Commission of Human Rights, the European Court of Human Rights, and the Inter-American Commission on Human Rights.[76] On the national level, more and more recourse is made to judicial tribunals for the protection of human rights.

Executive

Executive arenas include the international secretariats of both official and nonofficial participants and the executive arenas of nation-states. Official international secretariats concerned with human rights include the United Nations Secretariat, the Office of the United Nations High Commissioner for Refugees,[77] the International Labor Office of ILO, and the secretariats of UNESCO, WHO, FAO, and so on. The office of the secretary-general of the United Nations, though particular incumbents may be ambivalent, offers high potentialities for the protection of human rights.

In terms of geographical range, institutional structures can be classified as universal, general, plurilateral, regional, and bilateral. The scope of participation may encompass the entire earth-space arena, or be confined to small groups of actors.

In terms of historical development, all these different types of arenas

---

76. *See* notes 424–90 *infra* and accompanying text.

77. *See* L. Holborn, Refugees, A Problem of Our Time: The Work of the United Nations High Commissioner for Refugees, 1951–1972 (1975); United Nations High Commissioner for Refugees, A Mandate to Protect and Assist Refugees (1971); Fowler, *The Developing Jurisdiction of the United Nations High Commissioner for Refugees,* 7 Human Rights J. 119 (1974); Weis, *The Office of the United Nations High Commissioner for Refugees and Human Rights,* 1 Human Rights J. 243 (1968).

See also 1 & 2 A. Grahl-Madsen, The Status of Refugees in International Law (1966–72); L. Holborn, The International Refugee Organization (1956); F. Norwood, Strangers and Exiles (1969); J. Schechtman, The Refugee in the World (1963); J. Stoessinger, The Refugee and the World Community (1956); J. Veranant, The Refugee in the Post-War World (1953); Evans, *The Political Refugee in United States Immigration Law and Practice,* 3 Int'l Lawyer 205 (1969); Krenz, *The Refugee as a Subject of International Law,* 15 Int'l & Comp. L.Q. 90 (1966); Read, *The United Nations and Refugees: Changing Concepts,* 537 Int'l Conciliation (1962); Rees, *Century of the Homeless Man,* 515 Int'l Conciliation (1957); Weis, *The Concept of the Refugee in International Law,* [1960] Journal du Droit International 928; Weis, *The International Protection of Refugees,* 48 Am. J. Int'l L. 193 (1954).

On a related refugee agency, the United Nations Relief and Works Agency for Palestine Refugees in the Near East (UNRWA), *see* E. Buehrig, The UN and the Palestine Refugees (1971); Dale, *UNRWA—A Subsidiary Organ of the United Nations,* 23 Int'l & Comp. L.Q. 576 (1974).

could be described as exhibiting many, not always compatible, trends, such as: from unorganized interactions to organized structures of decision; from a low to a high degree of institutionalization; from the relatively simple diplomatic and diplomatic-parliamentary arenas to the more complex parliamentary, adjudicative, and executive arenas; from sporadic and occasional to relatively permanent and continuous structures of authority; and from imbalanced geographic and functional structures toward balanced development of both territorial (national, regional, and global) and functional (value-specialized) organizations. The structuring of arenas per se does not guarantee the content and quality of human rights protection. Nevertheless, the more varied and pluralistic the structures, the more likely it will be that different interests are protected. As a wide range of structures of authority becomes available, different participants with differing bases of power may take advantage of opportunities to enhance the protection accorded to many different individuals and groups.

In a state-centered world, the global arena is still characterized by an absence of centralized institutions specialized to the decision functions essential to a better protection and fulfillment of human rights. The centralization of structures of authority is no more adequate for human rights problems than for other transnational problems. In terms of geographical diffusion, there has been some modest movement toward appropriate regionalism, as exemplified by the European Convention on Human Rights and the Inter-American Commission on Human Rights under the Organization of American States. This movement falls far short, however, of appropriate and effective regionalism. Wide gaps continue to exist between the structures of national communities and those of the global community.

In temporal terms, many decision activities are still far from continuous and permanent. Even the United Nations Commission on Human Rights and its Sub-Commission on Prevention of Discrimination and Protection of Minorities meet for only a few weeks each year. In addition, much of the protection of aliens is still carried out by sporadic negotiations and arbitrations between states. When appraised for responsiveness to crisis, existing structures of authority appear less than alert. There is commonly a long delay between the imposition of deprivations and a consideration of legal problems and remedies. The procedures for handling complaints about human rights violations before the United Nations Commission on Human Rights are, for example, extremely slow and cumbersome.[78]

---

78. *See* notes 389–96 *infra* and accompanying text.

ACCESS

In terms of access, many of the established arenas of authority remain closed to individuals and private groups. Most notably, such claimants still have no access to the International Court of Justice. Article 34(1) of the Statute of the Court provides: "Only States may be parties in cases before the Court." Similarly, the individual is still highly dependent upon a protecting state for access to other transnational arenas. Unless the state of which he is a national is willing to sponsor his case, he may get little succor.

Individuals have, however, always enjoyed access to municipal and national courts under varying conditions. In addition, in recent years, the access of individuals and groups of persons to transnational arenas of authority appears to be increasing.[79] In the context of decolonization, the right of individual petition has been well established. To facilitate the process of decolonization, individuals and groups in colonial territories are given ample access to the Trusteeship Council, the Committee of Twenty-Four on Decolonization, the Council of Namibia, and so on. In a comparable development, on a regional scale, the Court of Justice of the European Communities is established to serve the specified objectives of the Communities—i.e., the European Economic Community, the European Coal and Steel Community, and the European Atomic Energy Community. In addition to member states of the Communities, individuals, firms, and institutions of the Communities are afforded access, under prescribed conditions, to the Court.[80]

In the more specific context of human rights, the trend would appear to be toward according the individual a fuller access for the protection of his own rights. This trend may be noted particularly in relation to developments within the United Nations Commission on Human Rights, the Optional Protocol to the International Covenant on Civil and Political Rights, the International Convention on the Elimination of Racial Discrimination, the European Convention on Human Rights, and the Inter-American Commission on Human Rights.[81] The importance of this trend can scarcely be overemphasized. The fundamental point is made by Robertson:

---

79. *See* W. Gormley, Procedural Status of the Individual before International and Supranational Tribunals (1966); R. Pollack, *supra* note 39; J. Jefferies, *supra* note 39; C. Norgaard, *supra* note 39.

80. *See* D. Bowett, *supra* note 23, at 274–75; E. Stein, P. Hay, & M. Waelbroeck, European Community Law and Institutions in Perspective: Text, Cases and Readings 158–71 (1976). For a comprehensive treatment, *see* D. Valentine, The Court of Justice of the European Communities (1965).

81. *See* notes 83–108 and 389–405 *infra* and accompanying text.

> The real party in interest, if a violation occurs, is the individual whose rights have been denied; and the violation will in all probability have been the act of the authorities of his own government. Under the classic concept of international law the individual has no *locus standi,* on the theory that his rights will be championed by his government. But how can his government be his champion, when it is *ex hypothesi* the offender? What is necessary therefore, is to give the individual a right of appeal to an international organ which is competent to call the offending party to account.[82]

The trend toward the right of individual petition within the United Nations first found expression under the trusteeship system. Article 87(b) of the Charter provides that the General Assembly and the Trusteeship Council may "accept petitions and examine them in consultation with the administering authority." The Council's Rules of Procedure adopted under Article 90 of the Charter contained detailed provisions for dealing with petitions.[83] As the process of decolonization accelerates, the right of individual petitions has been extended from the trust territories to non-self-governing territories. The Committee of Twenty-Four on Decolonization, the Special Committee on the Policies of Apartheid of the Government of the Republic of South Africa, and the Council of Namibia have, consequently, played increasingly important roles in receiving and acting on individual petitions.[84]

The development of access for individuals and groups to the Commission on Human Rights has been more tortuous.[85] Initially, in 1947, the

---

82. A. Robertson, Human Rights in the World 72–73 (1972) [hereinafter cited as A. Robertson].

In the same vein, Vasak writes:

> It is now recognised that, in order to protect human rights, it is not always necessary to put a State on trial and then condemn it: the right of an individual to file a petition in law to a court may become a right to ordinary petition without thereby lessening the effectiveness of the protection.

Vasak, *National, Regional and Universal Institutions for the Promotion and Protection of Human Rights,* 1 Human Rights J. 165, 171 (1968) [hereinafter cited as Vasak].

83. Rules of Procedure of the Trusteeship Council (as amended up to and during its 29th session) 13–17, U.N. Doc. T/1/Rev. 6 (1962) (Rules 76–92).

84. *See* Khol, *The "Committee of Twenty-Four" and the Implementation of the Declaration on the Granting of Independence to Colonial Countries and Peoples,* 3 Human Rights J. 21 (1970); chapter 7 *infra,* at notes 559–94 and accompanying text.

85. *See* L. Sohn & T. Buergenthal, *supra* note 39, at 739–856; United Nations Actions, *supra* note 73, at 177–84; Carey, *Progress on Human Rights at the UN,* 66 Am. J. Int'l L. 107 (1972); Cassese, *The Admissibility of Communications to the United Nations on Human Rights Violations,* 5 Human Rights J. 375 (1972); Ermacora, *Procedure to Deal with Human Rights Violations: A Hopeful Start in the United Nations?* 7 Human Rights J. 670

Commission on Human Rights declared that it had "no power to take any action in regard to any complaints concerning human rights."[86] This declaration was promptly confirmed by the Economic and Social Council in its Resolution 75(V).[87] Thus, for the next two decades, the many thousands of complaints made annually by individuals and groups to the United Nations received virtually no attention, unless such complaints related to a colony or to Southern Africa. The only step characteristically taken within the United Nations was to forward the "communication" to the government concerned.

Repeated attempts to change or ameliorate this self-denying rule—amidst growing apprehension about apartheid, racial discrimination, and other human rights deprivations—led the General Assembly, in 1966, to urge the Economic and Social Council and the Commission on Human Rights to "give urgent consideration to ways and means of improving the capacity of the United Nations to put a stop to violations of human rights *wherever they may occur.*"[88] In 1967, the Economic and Social Council, by Resolution 1235, authorized the Commission on Human Rights and the Sub-Commission on Prevention of Discrimination and Protection of Minorities to examine communications received by the United Nations for information relevant to gross violations of human rights.[89] The Sub-Commission was instructed to prepare a report containing information on violations of human rights from all available sources. The Commission was authorized, after careful consideration of the available information, to make a thorough study of situations revealing a consistent pattern of violations of human rights.

In 1970 the Council, by Resolution 1503, established procedures for the Sub-Commission and the Commission to deal with "communications relating to violations of human rights and fundamental freedoms" and authorized the Sub-Commission to adopt rules on the admissibility of

---

(1974); Humphrey, *The Right of Petition in the UN,* 4 HUMAN RIGHTS J. 463 (1971); Newman, *The New U.N. Procedures for Human Rights Complaints: Reform, Status Quo, or Chambers of Horror?* in *Hearings on International Protection of Human Rights before the Subcomm. on International Organizations and Movements of the House Comm. on Foreign Affairs,* 93d Cong., 1st Sess. 715–22 (1974) [hereinafter cited as *Hearings*]; Schwelb, *Complaints by Individuals to the Commission on Human Rights: 25 Years of an Uphill Struggle, in* THE CHANGING INTERNATIONAL COMMUNITY 119–39 (C. Boasson & M. Nurock eds. 1973); Van Boven, *The United Nations Commission on Human Rights and Violations of Human Rights and Fundamental Freedoms,* 15 NEDERLANDS TIJDSCHRIFT VOOR INTERNATIONAAL RECHT 374 (1968).

86. REPORT OF THE COMMISSION ON HUMAN RIGHTS, FIRST SESSION, JAN.-FEB. 1947, 4 U.N. ESCOR, Supp. (No. 3) 5–6, U.N. Doc. E/259 (1947).

87. E.S.C. Res. 75, U.N. Doc. E/573 at 20 (1947).

88. G.A. Res. 2144A, 21 U.N. GAOR, Supp. (No. 16) 46, U.N. Doc. A/6316 (1966) (italics added).

89. E.S.C. Res. 1235, 42 U.N. ESCOR, Supp. (No. 1) 17, U.N. Doc. E/4393 (1967).

communications.[90] Under these procedures a working group of five members of the Sub-Commission is empowered to make the initial examination of all communications, and of replies by governments, received by the United Nations and handled under ECOSOC Resolution 728f (XXVIII) and to decide which communications are to be referred to the full Sub-Commission. According to the provisional procedures for dealing with the question on admissibility of communications, "admissible communications may originate from a person or group of persons" who are "victims" of "a consistent pattern of gross and reliably attested violations of human rights and fundamental freedoms," from "any person or group of persons who have direct and reliable knowledge of those violations, or non-governmental organizations acting in good faith . . . and having direct and reliable knowledge of such violations."[91] The Sub-Commission then receives the communications brought before it by the working group and decides whether to refer to the Commission on Human Rights particular situations "which appear to reveal a consistent pattern of gross and reliably attested violations of human rights and fundamental freedoms within the terms of reference of the Sub-Commission."[92]

The Commission on Human Rights reviews those situations referred to it by the Sub-Commission and decides whether a particular situation requires "a thorough study" by the Commission or an investigation by an ad hoc committee to be appointed by the Commission. Such an investigation requires "the express consent of the state concerned" and "constant cooperation" with that state.[93] Upon completion of the study or the investigation, the Commission decides whether to make recommendations to the Economic and Social Council.

Although this access to the Commission by individuals and groups of individuals is indirect and limited,[94] it is of the utmost importance. The

---

90. E.S.C. Res. 1503, 48 U.N. ESCOR, Supp. (No. 1A) 8, U.N. Doc. E/4832/Add. 1 (1970).

91. Res. 1 (XXIV) of the Sub-Commission on Prevention of Discrimination and Protection of Minorities, August 13, 1971, *Report of the Twenty-Fourth Session of the Sub-Commission on Prevention of Discrimination and Protection of Minorities to the Commission on Human Rights, New York, 2-20 August 1971,* at 50–52, U.N. Doc. E/CN.4/1070 (E/CN.4/Sub. 2/323) (1971).

92. E.S.C. Res. 1503, *supra* note 90.

93. *Id.*

94. Ambassador Scranton stated before the Third Committee of the General Assembly:

> We are all familiar with the procedures which were authorized by the Economic and Social Council in 1970 in Resolution 1503. These procedures marked what we then hoped would be a major step forward in improving the capability of the United Nations to deal with situations of serious human rights violations. They authorized action on human rights petitions which "reveal a consistent pattern of gross and reliably attested violations. . . . "

Commission is practically the only official forum open to all the individuals of the world for bringing complaints about human rights violations. Unlike the Human Rights Committee under the Covenant on Civil and Political Rights and its Optional Protocol, and unlike the Committee on the Elimination of Racial Discrimination, the Commission is potentially open to all and not confined to particular individuals and groups identified through the jurisdiction of a particular ratifying state. The promise of this access, even as encumbered by procedural niceties, is indicated by recent attempts to undercut it, on the pretext that the future operation of the Covenant on Civil and Political Rights and of its Optional Protocol may render such access unnecessary.[95]

Under the International Covenant on Civil and Political Rights, the right of individual petition is not provided for in the Covenant itself, but is included in the Optional Protocol to the Covenant. According to the Optional Protocol, any state contracting to the Covenant that becomes a party to this Protocol recognizes the competence of the Human Rights Committee "to receive and consider communications from individuals subject to its jurisdiction who claim to be victims of a violation by that State Party of any of the rights set forth in the Covenant."[96]

Under the International Convention on the Elimination of All Forms of Racial Discrimination, the Committee on the Elimination of Racial Discrimination is authorized to handle complaints brought by one state party against another and petitions by individuals under the conditions stipulated in Article 14. Unlike the state-to-state complaint procedure, the procedure of individual petitions is made subject to the option of state parties to the Convention. Article 14(1) provides that "A State Party may at any time declare that it recognizes the competence of the Committee to receive and consider communications from individuals or groups of individuals within its jurisdiction claiming to be victims of a violation by that State Party of any of the rights set forth in this Conven-

---

> But the record of Human Rights Commission actions under these procedures has been one of nonperformance. One basic reason for the dismal record is the procedures themselves. They virtually assure that complaints of violations will die in a bureaucratic maze. For example, after the receipt of the complaint, long delays occur before there is any possibility of action by the Commission.
>
> Eighteen months must pass before a complaint is first reviewed—a complaint that evidences "a consistent pattern of gross violations." By the time a complaint is considered, it needs updating, and an update must go through the same delay-plagued process.

Scranton, *Human Rights: Let's Mean What We Say,* 75 DEP'T STATE BULL. 745, 748 (1976).

95. *See UN Commission on Human Rights,* 18 REV. INT'L COMM'N JURISTS 25, 25–26 (1977).

96. Optional Protocol, *supra* note 49, Art. 1.

tion."[97] The same provision, however, immediately adds: "No communication shall be received by the Committee if it concerns a State Party which has not made such a declaration."[98] Furthermore, the competence of the Committee regarding individual petitions is operative "only when at least ten States Parties" have made the requisite declarations of acceptance, a condition yet to be fulfilled.[99]

The greatest success in developing a right of individual petition is of course exhibited by the system, many times described, of the European Convention of Human Rights. Individuals may, under Article 25 of the European Convention, bring complaints before the European Commission on Human Rights (even against their own governments).[100] Understandably, not all governments found such a radical innovation in international law readily acceptable. The right of individual petition was hence made optional and the relevant provisions applicable only to those states which by specific declarations (for an indefinite or specified period) expressly recognized "the competence of the Commission to receive such petitions."[101] Such individual petitions may be submitted to the secretary-general of the Council of Europe by "any person, non-governmental organization or group of individuals claiming to be the victim of a violation by one of the High Contracting Parties of the rights set forth in [the] Convention."[102] Complaints may be lodged without regard to nationality or domicile of the petitioner, provided that the petitioner was within the jurisdiction of the respondent government when the alleged violation occurred. It is noteworthy that thirteen of the eighteen contracting states have accepted this novel procedure of individual petitions.[103] Compared to about a dozen cases brought under the interstate complaint system, some 7,200 petitions were brought against states by individuals and/or groups of individuals during the two decades

---

97. International Convention on the Elimination of All Forms of Racial Discrimination, *opened for signature* Mar. 7, 1966, Art. 14(1), 660 U.N.T.S. 195 (entered into force Jan. 4, 1969) [hereinafter cited as Convention on the Elimination of Racial Discrimination].

98. *Id.*

99. *Id.,* Art. 14(9).

100. Convention for the Protection of Human Rights and Fundamental Freedoms, *adopted* Nov. 4, 1950, 1950 Europ. T.S. No. 5, 213 U.N.T.S. 221 (entered into force Sept. 3, 1953), *reprinted in* Council of Europe, European Convention on Human Rights: Collected Texts 101–15 (11th ed. 1976) [hereinafter cited as European Convention and Collected Texts, respectively].

101. European Convention, *supra* note 100, Art. 25(1).

102. *Id.*

103. These thirteen states are Austria, Belgium, Denmark, Federal Republic of Germany, Iceland, Ireland, Italy, Luxembourg, the Netherlands, Norway, Sweden, Switzerland, and the United Kingdom (including twenty-one overseas territories). The remaining five states are Cyprus, Greece, France, Malta, and Turkey.

after the European Commission became competent, in 1955, to receive individual petitions.[104] Under the rigid, multiple requirements of admissibility, only 129 of the some 7,200 petitions were declared admissible, and this figure includes several groups of cases involving the same legal issues.[105] Needless to say, the cumulative impact of these cases goes far beyond the number.

As far as the European Court of Human Rights is concerned, only state parties to the Convention and the European Commission on Human Rights can bring cases before the Court.[106] Individuals are denied access to the Court. This, however, does not altogether preclude the individual applicant (who is, in substance, the interested party) from having his views brought before the Court. Judging from the practice of the Court, it would appear that while the individual applicant cannot participate personally (through written or oral submissions) in the proceedings, the Court may, if it finds advisable, permit the Commission to present to the Court any comments that an individual applicant may make upon the Commission's Report.[107]

When it first came into operation in 1960, the Inter-American Commission on Human Rights created by the Organization of American States had no authority to act on individual petitions. In 1965, the Commission was authorized to examine individual petitions complaining of violations of certain rights provided for in the American Declaration of the Rights and Duties of Man of 1948. Subsequently, as a consequence of a protocol amending the Charter of the OAS, adopted in Buenos Aires in 1967 and coming into effect in February 1970, the Commission has been elevated in status from "an autonomous entity" to a principal organ of the OAS; and its authority in dealing with individual petitions and other functions has been greatly fortified.[108]

---

104. THE SECRETARY TO THE EUROPEAN COMMISSION ON HUMAN RIGHTS (MR. A.B. MCNULTY), STOCK-TAKING ON THE EUROPEAN CONVENTION ON HUMAN RIGHTS 4–5, Doc. DH(75)4 (Oct. 1, 1975) [hereinafter cited as STOCK-TAKING].

105. *Id.*

106. European Convention, *supra* note 100, Art. 44, provides that "Only the High Contracting Parties and the Commission shall have the right to bring a case before the Court."

107. *See* F. CASTBERG, THE EUROPEAN CONVENTION ON HUMAN RIGHTS (T. Opsahl & T. Ouchterlony eds. 1974); J. FAWCETT, THE APPLICATION OF THE EUROPEAN CONVENTION ON HUMAN RIGHTS (1969); F. JACOBS, THE EUROPEAN CONVENTION ON HUMAN RIGHTS (1975); MacBride, *The European Court of Human Rights,* 3 N.Y.U.J. INT'L L. & POLITICS 1 (1970).

108. *See* A. SCHREIBER, THE INTER-AMERICAN COMMISSION ON HUMAN RIGHTS (1970); SECRETARIAT OF THE INTER-AMERICAN COMMISSION ON HUMAN RIGHTS, THE ORGANIZATION OF AMERICAN STATES AND HUMAN RIGHTS, 1960–1967, at 10–11, 36–39, 52–54 (1972); Buergenthal, *The Revised OAS Charter and the Protection of Human Rights,* 69 AM. J. INT'L L. 828 (1975).

COMPULSORINESS

A problem no less important and difficult than that of access by petitioners is that of bringing recalcitrant respondent states into contentious proceedings. Generally speaking, there is still no way to insure the attendance of defendant states before transnational tribunals. Suits brought before the International Court of Justice are still largely dependent upon the consent of the state being charged. Although a fair number of states have, pursuant to the Optional Clause of the Statute of the Court (Article 36, paragraph 2),[109] accepted compulsory jurisdiction of the Court, so many reservations (as exemplified by the self-serving Connally Reservation) have been attached to their acceptances as greatly to diminish that compulsory jurisdiction. The difficulty caused by reservations is further compounded by the fact that the Optional Clause is generally made to operate on a *reciprocal* basis: each state accepts compulsory jurisdiction vis-à-vis another state only to the extent that the obligations undertaken in their respective declarations mutually correspond. The consequence is that the Court can acquire compulsory jurisdiction over a particular dispute only when both plaintiff and defendant states made declarations which include that dispute within the compass of the Court's jurisdiction.[110] In more promising development, a number of the specialized human rights conventions accord the Interna-

---

109. Art. 36(2) of the Statute of the International Court of Justice reads:

> The states parties to the present Statute may at any time declare that they recognize as compulsory *ipso facto* and without special agreement, in relation to any other state accepting the same obligation, the jurisdiction of the Court in all legal disputes concerning:
>
> a. the interpretation of a treaty;
>
> b. any question of international law;
>
> c. the existence of any fact which, if established, would constitute a breach of an international obligation;
>
> d. the nature or extent of the reparation to be made for the breach of an international obligation.

110. *See* R. ANAND, COMPULSORY JURISDICTION OF THE INTERNATIONAL COURT OF JUSTICE (1961); R. ANAND, INTERNATIONAL COURTS AND CONTEMPORARY CONFLICTS (1974); THE FUTURE OF THE INTERNATIONAL COURT OF JUSTICE (L. Gross ed. 1976); M. HUDSON, THE PERMANENT COURT OF INTERNATIONAL JUSTICE (1934); C. JENKS, INTERNATIONAL ADJUDICATION, *supra* note 15, at 13–118; DOCUMENTS ON THE INTERNATIONAL COURT OF JUSTICE (S. Rosenne ed. 1974); S. ROSENNE, THE INTERNATIONAL COURT OF JUSTICE (1957); S. ROSENNE, THE WORLD COURT (3d rev. ed. 1973); J. STONE, THE INTERNATIONAL COURT AND WORLD CRISIS (1962); Briggs, *Reservations to the Acceptance of Compulsory Jurisdiction of the International Court of Justice,* 93 HAGUE RECUEIL DES COURS 223 (1958); Gross, *Some Observations on the International Court of Justice,* 56 AM. J. INT'L L. (1962); Hambro, *The Jurisdiction of the International Court of Justice,* 76 HAGUE RECUEIL DES COURS 121 (1950); Hambro, *Some*

tional Court of Justice jurisdiction over disputes concerning interpretation and application of such conventions. An illustrative list includes: the Convention on the Prevention and Punishment of the Crime of Genocide, 1948 (Article 9);[111] the Supplementary Convention on the Abolition of Slavery, the Slave Trade and Institutions and Practices Similar to Slavery, 1956 (Article 10);[112] the Convention on the Political Rights of Women, 1953 (Article 9);[113] the Convention relating to the Status of Refugees, 1951 (Article 38);[114] the Convention of the Reduction of Statelessness, 1961 (Article 14).[115] A typical formulation runs like this:

> Any dispute which may arise between any two or more Contracting States concerning the interpretation or application of this Convention, which is not settled by negotiation, shall at the request of any one of the parties to the dispute be referred to the International Court of Justice for decision, unless they agree to another mode of settlement.[116]

The settlement of disputes by occasionally established arbitral tribunals is as dependent upon state consent as is judicial settlement. It is indeed not unknown for states even to refuse to participate in arbitral proceedings to which they have previously agreed.[117] Although arbitration was a popular method of settling international disputes in medieval

---

Observations on the Compulsory Jurisdiction of the International Court of Justice, 25 BRIT. Y.B. INT'L L. 133 (1948); McClure, *World Rule of Law: The Jurisdiction of the International Court of Justice,* 1960 DUKE L.J. 56; Wagner, *Is a Compulsory Adjudication of International Legal Disputes Possible?* 47 NW. U.L. REV. 21 (1952); Waldock, *The Decline of the Optional Clause,* 32 BRIT. Y.B. INT'L L. 244 (1957).

111. Convention on the Prevention and Punishment of the Crime of Genocide, *adopted* Dec. 9, 1948, 78 U.N.T.S. 277 (entered into force Jan. 12, 1951), *reprinted in* U.N. HUMAN RIGHTS INSTRUMENTS, *supra* note 51, at 41–42 [hereinafter cited as Genocide Convention].

112. Supplementary Convention on the Abolition of Slavery, the Slave Trade, and Institutions and Practices Similar to Slavery, *done* Sept. 7, 1956, [1967] 3 U.S.T. 3201, T.I.A.S. No. 6418, 266 U.N.T.S. 3 (entered into force Apr. 30, 1957), *reprinted in* U.N. HUMAN RIGHTS INSTRUMENTS, *supra* note 51, at 47–51 [hereinafter cited as Supplementary Convention on Abolition of Slavery].

113. Convention on the Political Rights of Women, *opened for signature* Mar. 31, 1953, 193 U.N.T.S. 135 (entered into force July 7, 1954), *reprinted in* U.N. HUMAN RIGHTS INSTRUMENTS, *supra* note 51, at 90–91.

114. Convention Relating to the Status of Refugees, *signed* July 28, 1951, 189 U.N.T.S. 137 (entered into force Apr. 22, 1954), *reprinted in* U.N. HUMAN RIGHTS INSTRUMENTS, *supra* note 51, at 66–75.

115. Convention on the Reduction of Statelessness, *adopted* Aug. 30, 1961, U.N. Doc. A/Conf.9/15 (1961) (United Nations Conference on the Elimination or Reduction of Future Statelessness) (entered into force Dec. 13, 1975), *reprinted in* U.N. HUMAN RIGHTS INSTRUMENTS, *supra* note 51, at 57–61.

116. Convention on the Political Rights of Women, *supra* note 113, Art. 9.

117. *See, e.g.,* Lalive, *Un Grand Arbitrage Pétrolier entre un Gouvernement et Deux Sociétés Privées Étrangères,* 104 JOURNAL DU DROIT INTERNATIONAL 319 (1977).

times, it fell into disuse with the rise of the modern state system because of the overriding emphasis upon the sovereign equality of states. Thanks largely to the series of Jay Treaties concluded by the United States with Great Britain and other powers, and to the Alabama Arbitration established by Great Britain and the United States in 1871, arbitration as a method of third-party decision was revived in the nineteenth century.[118] This revival led to the creation of the Permanent Court of Arbitration by the Hague Convention for the Pacific Settlement of International Disputes, made in 1899, amended in 1907, and still in force. The name "Permanent Court" appears to be a misnomer. The entity consists of little more than a permanent panel from which arbitrators can be chosen, and the Court itself has to be constituted on an ad hoc basis—from case to case. There is no machinery whatsoever for compulsory jurisdiction.[119] Evidently, few states are willing to commit themselves unequivocally in advance to arbitrate potential disputes. Recourse to arbitration (through mixed tribunals, etc.) waxed in the decade after World War I and and has waned since the end of World War II. In recent years the Permanent Court of Arbitration has had very little business, and important occasional arbitrations have been rare.[120]

An excellent example of how even an obligation to compulsory arbitration may be frustrated is offered by the case of *Interpretation of Peace Treaties with Bulgaria, Hungary, and Roumania.* The peace treaties that were concluded, in February 1947 in Paris, by the Allied powers with Bulgaria, Hungary, and Roumania, respectively, and that went into effect in September 1947, contained certain provisions for observance of human rights.[121] Upon the insistence of the Soviet Union, they provided also that disputes arising under the treaties should be referred to arbitral

---

118. *See* S. Bemis, Jay's Treaty: A Study in Commerce and Diplomacy (rev. ed. 1962); P. Corbett, Law in Diplomacy 136-86 (1959); C. Jenks, International Adjudication, *supra* note 15, at 343-57, 412-27; H. Lauterpacht, Private Law Sources and Analogies of International Law 215-43 (1927) [hereinafter cited as H. Lauterpacht, Private Law Sources]; J. Moore, International Arbitration, chapter 1 (1898); J. Ralston, International Arbitration, from Athens to Locarno (1929); J. Ralston, The Law and Procedure of International Tribunals (rev. ed. 1926); J. Ralston, A Quest for International Order 169-71 (1941); Sohn, *The Function of International Arbitration Today,* 108 Hague Recueil des Cours 1 (1963).

119. M. Hudson, The Permanent Court of International Justice, 1920-42, at 11 (1943). For a comprehensive treatment, *see* François, *La Cour Permanente d'Arbitrage, son Origine, sa Jurisprudence, son Avenir,* 87 Hague Recueil des Cours 457 (1955).

120. *See* W. Jenks, International Adjudication, *supra* note 15, at 336-43; W. Reisman, Nullity and Revision: The Review and Enforcement of International Judgments and Awards 222-23 (1971) [hereinafter cited as W. Reisman].

121. *See* Bulgarian Peace Treaty, 1947, Arts. 2-6, in 4 Major Peace Treaties of Modern History, 1648-1967, at 2525, 2526-27 (F. Israel ed. 1967); Hungarian Peace Treaty, 1947, Arts. 2-6, in *id.* at 2553, 2555-57; Roumanian Peace Treaty, 1947, Arts. 3-6, in *id.* at 2585, 2586-88.

tribunals ("conciliation commissions") rather than to the International Court of Justice.[122] Subsequently, in 1949, the United States and the United Kingdom brought charges before the General Assembly of the United Nations, accusing the governments of Bulgaria, Hungary, and Roumania of having violated the human rights obligations stipulated in the peace treaties.[123] As the United States and the United Kingdom had duly followed and exhausted the treaty procedure for the settlement of the disputes, Bulgaria, Hungary, and Roumania were in August 1949 requested to join in constituting the conciliation commissions contemplated in the treaties. Bulgaria, Hungary, and Roumania were, however, able to frustrate the arbitration of these disputes simply by refusing to appoint an arbitrator on their behalf. In response to a request of the General Assembly, the International Court of Justice declared in an advisory opinion that, unless and until both parties to the dispute had appointed their arbitrators, the secretary general of the United Nations was not authorized to appoint a third arbitrator.[124]

---

122. Art. 36 of the Bulgarian Peace Treaty provides:

> 1) Except where another procedure is specifically provided under any Article of the present Treaty, any dispute concerning the interpretation or execution of the Treaty, which is not settled by direct diplomatic negotiations, shall be referred to the Three Heads of Mission acting under Article 35, except that in this case the Heads of Mission will not be restricted by the time limit provided in that Article. Any such dispute not resolved by them within a period of two months shall, unless the parties to the dispute mutually agree upon another means of settlement, be referred at the request of either party to the dispute to a Commission composed of one representative of each party and a third member selected by mutual agreement of the two parties from nationals of a third country. Should the two parties fail to agree within a period of one month upon the appointment of the third member, the Secretary-General of the United Nations may be requested by either party to make the appointment.
>
> 2) The decision of the majority of the members of the Commission shall be the decision of the Commission, and shall be accepted by the parties as definitive and binding.

4 Major Peace Treaties of Modern History, 1648–1967, at 2542.

See also Hungarian Peace Treaty, Art. 40, *id.* at 2573; Roumanian Peace Treaty, Art. 38, *id.* at 2603.

123. *See Observance of Human Rights and Fundamental Freedoms: Bulgaria, Hungary and Romania,* in Y.B.U.N. 1948–49, at 316–33; *Observance in Bulgaria, Hungary and Romania of Human Rights and Fundamental Freedoms,* in Y.B.U.N. 1950, at 385–97.

124. Advisory Opinion on Interpretation of Peace Treaties with Bulgaria, Hungary and Romania (Second Phase), [1950] I.C.J. 221. *See also* Advisory Opinion on Interpretation of Peace Treaties, [1950] I.C.J. 65.

For commentaries, *see* J. Green, The United Nations and Human Rights 147–53 (1956); H. Lauterpacht, The Development of International Law by the International Court 284–93 (1958); M. McDougal, H. Lasswell, & J. Miller, The Interpre-

Fortunately, both in matters not relating to human rights and in matters directly related to human rights, in recognition of the critical importance in a decentralized world of compulsory third-party decision for the settling of disputes, a slow trend can be observed toward the establishment of such decision.

The first important attempt in the post–World War II era to improve compulsory third-party decision making, in matters not directly relating to human rights, was the effort of the International Law Commission to codify a comprehensive draft convention on arbitral procedure. In 1949, at its first sesssion, the International Law Commission selected arbitral procedure regarding international disputes as one of the topics for codification. The overriding issue confronting the Commission was whether every phase of arbitral procedure should reflect some degree of compulsoriness in order to ensure its effectiveness. Building upon the latter emphasis, the Commission prepared a draft convention and presented it to the General Assembly in 1953.[125] According to the draft, an undertaking to arbitrate would entail the consequence of empowering the International Court of Justice to pass upon the arbitrability of the dispute, so as to prevent one of the parties from evading arbitration by claiming the dispute to be beyond the scope of the agreement.[126] The Court would further be empowered to maintain the immutability of the

---

TATION OF AGREEMENTS AND WORLD PUBLIC ORDER: PRINCIPLES OF CONTENT AND PROCEDURE 168–86 (1967); L. SOHN & T. BUERGENTHAL, *supra* note 39, at 617–34; Carlston, *Interpretation of Peace Treaties with Bulgaria, Hungary and Romania,* 44 AM. J. INT'L L. 728 (1950); Lalive, *Interpretation of Peace Treaties Signed with Bulgaria, Hungary and Romania,* 77 JOURNAL DU DROIT INTERNATIONAL 1228 (1950); Tamm, *Observance of Human Rights and Fundamental Freedoms in Bulgaria, Romania and Hungary in Relation to the Peace Treaties and the United Nations' Charter,* 1 JUS GENTIUM: NORDIS TIDSSKRIFT FOR INTERNATIONAL RET 359 (1949).

125. *See* [1953] 2 Y.B. INT'L L. COMM'N 201–12. For a detailed analysis of the Draft Convention on Arbitral Procedure, *see* COMMENTARY ON THE DRAFT CONVENTION ON ARBITRAL PROCEDURE ADOPTED BY THE INTERNATIONAL LAW COMMISSION AT ITS FIFTH SESSION, U.N. Doc. A/CN.4/92 (1955) (prepared by the Secretariat) [hereinafter cited as COMMENTARY ON THE DRAFT CONVENTION ON ARBITRAL PROCEDURE].

126. The Draft Convention on Arbitral Procedure, in Article 2, provides:

> 1. If, prior to the constitution of an arbitral tribunal, the parties to an undertaking to arbitrate disagree as to the existence of a dispute, or as to whether an existing dispute is within the scope of the obligation to have recourse to arbitration, such preliminary question may, in the absence of agreement between the parties upon another procedure, be brought before the International Court of Justice by application of either party. The decision rendered by the Court shall be final.
>
> 2. In its decision on the question, the Court may prescribe the provisional measures to be taken for the protection of the respective interests of the parties pending the constitution of the arbitral tribunal.

tribunal, once formed, even if one of the parties should choose to withdraw its arbitrator.[127]

The draft received a critical audience in the General Assembly. The features of "a quasi-compulsory jurisdictional procedure" and the Commission's recommendation for concluding a convention on arbitral procedure were especially criticized. In 1955, the Assembly decided to send the draft back to the Commission for further consideration, taking into account the comments of governments and the discussion in the Sixth Committee of the Assembly. In 1957, instead of undertaking a thorough revision of the draft, the Commission decided to keep the substance of the draft intact and to submit it to the Assembly as a set of draft articles that could serve as model rules for states in particular arbitrations. "[N]o longer presented in the form of a potential general treaty of arbitration,"[128] the "Model Rules on Arbitral Procedure" prepared by the Commission were submitted, in 1958, to the General Assembly. The General Assembly voted to bring these Model Rules to "the attention of Member States for their consideration and use, in such cases and to such extent as they consider appropriate, in drawing up treaties of arbitration or *compromis.*"[129]

Another significant attempt toward establishing compulsory third-party decision took place at the United Nations Conference on the Law of the Sea held in Geneva in 1958. In addition to the four Conventions (dealing with the territorial sea and the contiguous zone, the high seas, fisheries, and the continental shelf), the Conference adopted an Optional Protocol of Signature concerning the Compulsory Settlement of Disputes (going into force on September 30, 1962), which provides for the compulsory jurisdiction of the International Court of Justice regarding "disputes arising out of the interpretation or application of any Convention on the Law of the Sea" (except the one on fisheries).[130] Hence, any party to the Optional Protocol may bring a dispute before the Court or, if the parties so prefer, submit the dispute to conciliation or arbitration. The 1958 Convention on Fishing and Conservation of the Living

---

[1953] 2 Y.B. INT'L L. COMM'N 208–09. *See* COMMENTARY ON THE DRAFT CONVENTION ON ARBITRAL PROCEDURE, *supra* note 125, at 13–16.

127. *See* Draft Convention on Arbitral Procedure, Arts. 3–8, [1953] 2 Y.B. INT'L L. COMM'N 209; COMMENTARY ON DRAFT CONVENTION ON ARBITRAL PROCEDURE, *supra* note 125, at 17–33.

128. UNITED NATIONS, OFFICE OF PUBLIC INFORMATION, THE WORK OF THE INTERNATIONAL LAW COMMISSION 37 (1967).

129. G.A. Res. 1262, 13 U.N. GAOR, Supp. (No. 18) 53, U.N. Doc. A/4090 (1958).

130. Optional Protocol of Signature concerning the Compulsory Settlement of Disputes, *adopted* and *opened for signature* Apr. 29, 1958, Art. 1, 450 U.N.T.S. 169 (entered into force Sept. 30, 1962).

Resources of the High Seas stipulates its own procedure of compulsory third-party decision.[131] Article 9(1) provides:

> Any dispute which may arise between States under articles 4, 5, 6, 7 and 8 shall, at the request of any of the parties, be submitted for settlement to a special commission of five members, unless the parties agree to seek a solution by another method of peaceful settlement, as provided for in Article 33 of the Charter of the United Nations.[132]

The movement toward compulsory third-party decision was reinforced in conjunction with the Vienna Convention on Diplomatic Relations of 1961 and the Vienna Convention on Consular Relations of 1963. There was an Optional Protocol concerning the Compulsory Settlement of Disputes in relation to each of the two Conventions.[133] Article 1 of each of the Optional Protocols, in identical words, provides:

> Disputes arising out of the interpretation or application of the Convention shall lie within the compulsory jurisdiction of the International Court of Justice and may accordingly be brought before the Court by an application made by any party to the dispute being a party to the present Protocol.[134]

The next significant step in reinforcement came with the Vienna Convention on the Law of Treaties of 1969.[135] The concern for compulsory third-party decision finds expression in Article 66 of the Convention and the Annex to the Convention. Article 66 and the Annex were adopted not without painstaking efforts.[136] According to Article 66, any party to

---

131. Convention on Fishing and Conservation of the Living Resources of the High Seas, *done* Apr. 29, 1958, 559 U.N.T.S. 285 (entered into force Mar. 20, 1966).

132. Art. 9(1), *id.*

133. Optional Protocol to the Vienna Convention on Diplomatic Relations, concerning the Compulsory Settlement of Disputes, *done* Apr. 18, 1961, 500 U.N.T.S. 241 (entered into force Apr. 24, 1964); Optional Protocol to the Vienna Convention on Consular Relations, concerning the Compulsory Settlement of Disputes, *done* Apr. 24, 1963, 596 U.N.T.S. 487 (entered into force Mar. 19, 1967).

134. 500 U.N.T.S. 241, 242; 596 U.N.T.S. 487, 488.

135. Vienna Convention on the Law of Treaties, U.N. Doc. A/CONF.39/27, in UNITED NATIONS, UNITED NATIONS CONFERENCE ON THE LAW OF TREATIES, FIRST AND SECOND SESSIONS, VIENNA, 26 MARCH–24 MAY 1968 AND 9 APRIL–22 MAY 1969, OFFICIAL RECORDS: DOCUMENTS OF THE CONFERENCE 287–301, U.N. Doc. A/CONF.39/11/Add. 2 (1971) [hereinafter cited as Vienna Convention and DOCUMENTS OF THE TREATY CONFERENCE, respectively].

136. *See* Kearney & Dalton, *The Treaty of Treaties,* 64 AM. J. INT'L L. 495, 545–57 (1970). *See also* T. ELIAS, THE MODERN LAW OF TREATIES 188–98 (1974); S. ROSENNE, THE LAW OF TREATIES: A GUIDE TO THE LEGISLATIVE HISTORY OF THE VIENNA CONVENTION 336–49 (1970) [hereinafter cited as S. ROSENNE]; I. SINCLAIR, THE VIENNA CONVENTION ON THE

a dispute arising under the *jus cogens* articles of the Convention may submit the disputes to the International Court of Justice for adjudication whenever the procedures in Article 33 of the United Nations Charter have failed to reach a solution within twelve months and unless the parties have agreed instead to refer the dispute to arbitration.[137] A party to a dispute regarding "the application or the interpretation of any of the other articles in Part V" of the Convention may set in motion certain conciliation procedures provided in the Annex to the Convention through a request to the secretary-general of the United Nations.[138]

There has similarly been a gradual movement toward compulsory third-party decision in matters relating to human rights. While under the existing human rights conventions, global and regional, the right of individual petition is provided for on an optional basis, the state-to-state complaint system is made compulsory under both the International Convention on the Elimination of All Forms of Racial Discrimination and the European Convention on Human Rights. Article 11(1) of the Convention on the Elimination of Racial Discrimination provides in part: "If a State Party considers that another State Party is not giving effect to the provisions of this Convention, it may bring the matter to the attention of the Committee [on the Elimination of Racial Discrimination]. The Committee shall then transmit the communication to the State Party concerned."[139] The detailed procedures for dealing with such a state-to-state complaint are spelled out in the remainder of Article 11 and in Articles 12 and 13.[140] In comparable fashion the European Convention on Human Rights provides for a compulsory state-to-state system in Article 24: "Any High Contracting Party may refer to the Commission, through the Secretary General of the Council of Europe, any alleged breach of the provisions of the Convention by another High

---

LAW OF TREATIES 131–44 (1973); McDougal, *Third-Party Decision,* 63 AM. J. INT'L L. 685 (1969).

137. Vienna Convention, *supra* note 135, Art. 66.

138. *Id.*

In the current conferences on the law of seas, the question of compulsory settlement of disputes has been seriously proposed and considered. The profound recognition of its importance and the complexities involved are well reflected in the arduous negotiations so far. *See* Adede, *Settlement of Disputes Arising under the Law of the Sea Convention,* 69 AM. J. INT'L L. 798 (1975); Adede, *Law of the Sea: The Scope of the Third-Party, Compulsory Procedures for Settlement of Disputes,* 71 AM. J. INT'L L. 305 (1977); Sohn, *Settlement of Disputes Arising out of the Law of the Sea Convention,* 12 SAN DIEGO L. REV. 495 (1975).

139. Convention on the Elimination of Racial Discrimination, *supra* note 97, Art. 11(1).

140. *Id.,* Arts. 11–13. *See* chapter 9 *infra,* at notes 250–68 and accompanying text; Schwelb, *The International Convention on the Elimination of All Forms of Racial Discrimination,* 15 INT'L & COMP. L.Q. 996, 1037–41 (1966); N. LERNER, THE U.N. CONVENTION ON THE ELIMINATION OF ALL FORMS OF RACIAL DISCRIMINATION 87–90 (1970).

Contracting Party."[141] In a decentralized world in which reciprocity sometimes prevails, states are, understandably, highly reluctant to resort to such complaint procedures against other states in regard to human rights violations, as attested by the experiences under these two Conventions.[142] Nevertheless, the availability of these compulsory state-to-state complaint procedures does contribute immensely, since the abiding impact of prevention and deterrence cannot be underestimated, to the protection of human rights of the individual. It may be noted that under the International Covenant on Civil and Political Rights and the American Convention on Human Rights, the state-to-state complaint system is made optional rather than automatic (or compulsory). According to Article 41 of the Covenant, the state-to-state complaint procedure will apply, upon acceptance by at least ten states, only to states which have expressly accepted it.[143] Article 45 of the American Convention contains comparable optional features.[144]

Base Values

While many of the more important base values for influencing decision remain under the relatively exclusive control of nation-states, there appears to be a modest trend toward allocating to representatives of the inclusive community the authority and effective control required for the better protection and fulfillment of human rights. We document this trend first in relation to authority and secondly in relation to effective control.

AUTHORITY

Authority, in the sense of the expectations of the members of a community about who will decide what and how, has always been an important base of power. Lord Acton was but one of many who have recognized that authority in this sense builds upon itself and constitutes a most effective base of power for any decision maker. A comparable concep-

141. European Convention, *supra* note 100, Art. 24.

142. *See* notes 374–88 *infra* and accompanying text.

Cf. Brand, *Avoidance of the Traditional Machinery of Adjudication: A World-Wide Trend?* 38 Social Research 268 (1971).

143. Covenant on Civil and Political Rights, *supra* note 48, Art. 41.

144. American Convention on Human Rights, *signed* Nov. 22, 1969, Art. 45, O.A.S. Official Records OEA/Ser. K/XVI/1.1, Doc. 65, Rev. 1, Corr. 1 (Jan. 7, 1970), *reprinted in* 9 Int'l Legal Materials 99 (1970) [hereinafter cited as American Convention].

The European Convention on the Suppression of Terrorism, adopted by the Committee of Ministers of the Council of Europe on Nov. 10, 1976, provides for compulsory arbitration in case any dispute between contracting states about the interpretation and application of the Convention fails to reach "a friendly settlement" (Art. 10). *Reprinted in* 15 Int'l Legal Materials 1272, 1274 (1976).

tion of authority and of its role in decision making is apparent, in various equivalent forms, in the notions of customary law prevalent in primitive societies, ancient China, India, Greece, Rome, Western Europe, and the Americas.[145] This conception is, also, the descriptive component in the great, historic, insistent demands made by many peoples down through the centuries, with regard to deliberately created as well as customary law, and enduring into the constitutions of contemporary democratic communities, that authority rightfully comes from the whole people.[146] The importance of such a conception in a global constitutive process which increasingly emphasizes the basic human rights of the individual person and private groups is easily demonstrable.

In the necessary allocation of authority between the general community and particular states, one most encouraging development is the continuing expansion of the concept of "international concern," along with the concomitant erosion of the concept of "domestic jurisdiction." As both the transnational impacts of human rights deprivations within particular states and the ineradicable interdependences of peoples everywhere are better perceived, the organized general community, through what we call the global constitutive process, is increasingly accorded both the general authority and the particular competences essential to the protection of human rights.

The dichotomy between matters of "international concern" and those of "domestic jurisdiction" or more local concern is inherent in the very conception of international law, even of a world rationally organized on a geographic basis. It reflects the necessity of a continuing allocation and balancing of competences between the center, or general community, and its component territorial communities—states or regions—in a way best designed to serve the common interest. The technical terms "international concern" and "domestic jurisdiction," and their equivalents, are merely two polar concepts, like the blades of a scissors, designed to indicate an appropriate balancing between inclusive and exclusive competences.[147] Thus, what is meant by "international concern" is that cer-

145. *See* notes 4, 5, and 8 *supra.*

146. *See Comprehensiveness in Conceptions of Constitutive Process, supra* note 3.

147. On the controversy of domestic jurisdiction versus international concern, *see* R. Higgins, The Development of International Law through the Political Organs of the United Nations 5–130 (1963) [hereinafter cited as R. Higgins]; H. Lauterpacht, *supra* note 39, at 166–220; M. Rajan, United Nations and Domestic Jurisdiction (2d ed. 1961); The Status of Domestic Jurisdiction (1962) (Proceedings of the Fourth Summer Conference on International Law, Cornell Law School); V. Van Dyke, Human Rights, the United States, and World Community 105–56 (1970); Bilder, *Rethinking International Human Rights: Some Basic Questions,* 1969 Wis. L. Rev. 170, 180–93 (1969); Chen,

tain matters, though including events occurring within the territorial boundaries of particular states, are of such importance to a general, transnational community that such community can make or apply law to such matters in protection of the common interests of all peoples affected by those matters. One function of international law is, hence, to permit external decision makers to intercede in matters which would otherwise be regarded as internal to a particular state. What is meant by "domestic jurisdiction," in contrast, is that certain matters are regarded as of predominant importance only to a particular state. Ever since the rise of the modern state system, animated by the notion of the sovereign equality of all states, particular states have always enjoyed, and insisted upon, a large domain of exclusive competence. This demand for exclusive competence has been asserted, and protected, under many different, but equivalent, technical concepts, such as "sovereignty," "independence," "equality of states," and "nonintervention"; taken together, these concepts have served largely to insulate internal elites from external regulation.

The employment of the technical term "domestic jurisdiction" to protect the exclusive competence of internal elites is of relatively recent origin. Its use in formal prescription first appeared in the Covenant of the League of Nations. Article 15(8) of the Covenant read:

> If the dispute between the parties is claimed by one of them, and is found by the Council, to arise out of a matter which by international law is solely within the domestic jurisdiction of that party, the Council shall so report, and shall make no recommendation as to its settlement.[148]

---

supra note 18, at 219–24, 253–55; Ermacora, *Human Rights and Domestic Jurisdiction (Article 2, § 7, of the Charter)*, 124 Hague Recueil des Cours 371 (1968); Fawcett, *Human Rights and Domestic Jurisdiction,* in E. Luard, International Protection, *supra* note 57, at 286–303; Ghatate, *Human Rights and the Domestic Jurisdiction Clause of the U.N. Charter,* in Horizons of Freedom 122–34 (L. Singhvi ed. 1969); Markovic, *Implementation of Human Rights and the Domestic Jurisdiction of States,* in International Protection of Human Rights 47–68 (A. Eide & A. Schou eds. 1968) (Nobel Symposium 7) [hereinafter cited as Nobel Symposium on Human Rights]; McDougal & Reisman, *Rhodesia and the United Nations: The Lawfulness of International Concern,* 62 Am. J. Int'l L. 1 (1968); Preuss, *Article 2, Paragraph 7 of the Charter of the United Nations and Matters of Domestic Jurisdiction,* 74 Hague Recueil des Cours 547 (1949); Verdross, *Domestic Jurisdiction under International Law* 1971 U. Tol. L. Rev. 119; Waldock, *The Plea of Domestic Jurisdiction before International Legal Tribunals,* 31 Brit. Y.B. Int'l L. 96 (1954); Watson, *Autointerpretation, Competence, and the Continuing Validity of Article 2(7) of the UN Charter,* 71 Am. J. Int'l L. 60 (1977); Wright, *Domestic Jurisdiction as a Limit on National and Supra-National Action,* 56 Nw. U.L. Rev. 11 (1961).

148. This clause was included at the insistence of the U.S. delegation to the Paris Peace Conference of 1919. 1 D. Miller, The Drafting of the Covenant 276–77 (1928).

This formulation of the Covenant, with slight modification, has been incorporated into the Charter of the United Nations.[149] Article 2(7) provides:

> Nothing contained in the present Charter shall authorize the United Nations to intervene in matters which are essentially within the domestic jurisdiction of any state or shall require the Members to submit such matters to settlement under the present Charter; but this principle shall not prejudice the application of enforcement measures under Chapter VII.

In consequence of this explicit constitutional formulation, the label "domestic jurisdiction" has in recent years largely superseded its many historic equivalents for the assertion of exclusive competence.

In particular instances of controversy, the critical question confronting decision makers, identifying with the larger community of humankind, is of course that of how best to relate options in the allocation of inclusive and exclusive competence to the more fundamental policies of the larger community. Happily, the intellectual task involved in making a rational choice among options in the allocation of those competences was early recognized as requiring a careful, configurative examination of the facts of interdependence in a particular context. The immensely authoritative exposition of this view came in 1923 from the Permanent Court of International Justice in the *Tunis-Morocco* case.[150] In that case the Court was requested by the League Council to give an advisory opinion on whether a dispute between France and Great Britain over the applicability to British subjects of certain French nationality decrees, promulgated in 1921 in Tunis and the French zone of Morocco (both under French protection), came under Article 15(8) and, hence, could not be dealt with by the League Council. The Court held that, while questions of nationality are "in principle" within a state's "reserved domain," certain treaties concerning Tunis and Morocco to which France and Great Britain were respectively parties rendered the immediate dispute over the nationality decrees an international dispute.[151] The Court affirmed that the question of treaty obligation "does not, according to international law, fall solely within the domestic jurisdiction of a single

149. The Charter changes the key wording—from "solely within the domestic jurisdiction" to "essentially within the domestic jurisdiction" of a state. Applied contextually, this change does not appear to make a real difference in actual and potential application. *See* Preuss, *supra* note 147, at 597–604.

150. Advisory Opinion on Tunis-Morocco Nationality Decrees, [1923] P.C.I.J., Ser. B, No. 4.

151. *Id.* at 24–32.

State."[152] In words that have since become well-worn, the Court enunciated a broad test: "The question whether a certain matter is or is not solely within the domestic jurisdiction of a state is an essentially relative question; it depends upon the development of international relations."[153] The choice between "international concern" and "domestic jurisdiction" was thus made to depend not only upon fact, but upon changing fact, permitting a continuing readjustment of inclusive and exclusive competences as conditions might require.

The problems of human rights have always caused special difficulties in the allocation of authoritative competences between the general community and particular states. Historically, since the emergence of the modern system of nation-states, particular states have been accorded a high degree of exclusive competence over people, resources, and events within their boundaries. How a state treats its own nationals was long regarded as an internal affair of the particular state, beyond the reach of international law. The very essence of the contemporary international law of human rights is, however, precisely to shatter this traditional insulation of competence. The general community is made competent to inquire into how a particular state treats, not merely aliens, but all individuals within its boundaries, including its own nationals. Indeed, given the facts of global interdependences and the intimate links between peace and human rights, much of humankind appears today to have come to the opinion that nothing could be of greater "international concern" than the "human rights" of all individuals.

The trend in authoritative decision within the United Nations toward expansion of "international concern" has been facilitated, in interpreting Article 2(7) of the Charter, by clarification of what is meant by "intervention." A definition given by Lauterpacht has been widely accepted:

> Intervention is a technical term of, on the whole, unequivocal connotation. It signifies dictatorial interference in the sense of action amounting to a denial of the independence of the State. It implies a demand which, if not complied with, involves a threat of or recourse to compulsion, though not necessarily physical compulsion, in some form.[154]

From this conception of intervention, it is but a short step to recognition that there is a vast difference between the unilateral interference by one state in the internal affairs of another state and the general community's

---

152. *Id.* at 30.
153. *Id.* at 24.
154. H. Lauterpacht, *supra* note 39, at 167.

inclusive making and application of law for protecting the rights of individuals within all states. The one is forbidden by law; the other is the establishment of law.

The expansion of "international concern" in United Nations practice is exhibited in all decision functions. Thus, in performance of the intelligence function (that is, the gathering, processing, and dissemination of information), it appears that Article 2(7) does not bar inscription in the agenda of, and debate on, any issue having an "undeniable international impact, even if there is no consensus over the degree to which international law does or should regulate the matter."[155] The United Nations is perfectly competent, the Repertory of Practice summarizes, "to talk about a situation, to discuss it, to debate, to persuade, to negotiate,"[156] without such activity amounting to intervention in internal affairs. Similarly, with respect to the promoting function (advocacy and recommendations of proposals), the various organs and agencies of the United Nations, as abundantly illustrated in countless resolutions, have shown little hesitation in making recommendation because of claimed limitations upon the subject matter of their competence. The exercise of the prescribing function (that is, the projection and communication of authoritative policies) has, further, been without easily identifiable limit. The Universal Declaration of Human Rights, the two Covenants on Human Rights, and the host of specialized conventions and related expressions encompass practically every aspect of human life, including the shaping and sharing of all important values. Clearly, there has been a "diminishing willingness to insulate internationally important activity from international legal control by deference to the dogma of domestic jurisdiction."[157]

The invoking of authoritative decision (through the provisional characterization of concrete circumstances in terms of human rights prescriptions) has found little impediment in Article 2(7), whether invocation is made by state complaint or by individual petition. In the more definitive characterization of particular events in terms of prescriptions, that is, in the application function, the inclusive competence of the United Nations has been debated most extensively in connection with the policies of racial discrimination and apartheid in South Africa. Though the issue was first raised about the treatment by South Africa of its nationals of Indian origin, the focus of attention soon shifted to the

---

155. H. STEINER & D. VAGTS, TRANSNATIONAL LEGAL PROBLEMS: MATERIALS AND TEXT 324 (2d ed. 1976).

156. 1 UNITED NATIONS, REPERTORY OF PRACTICE OF UNITED NATIONS ORGANS, SUPPLEMENT No. 3, at 109 (1972) [hereinafter cited as U.N. REPERTORY].

157. Falk, *On the Quasi-Legislative Competence of the General Assembly,* 60 AM. J. INT'L L. 782, 785 (1966).

entire apartheid policies and practices of South Africa. Year after year and resolution after resolution, the various United Nations organs have not been deterred by the persisting objections of the government of South Africa, invoking Article 2(7) of the Charter.[158] The United Nations organs have, similarly, overruled the plea of domestic jurisdiction in numerous cases relating to self-determination and to threats to peace and security, in contexts having obvious human rights implications.[159] Other notable cases rejecting the domestic jurisdiction plea include the question of observance of human rights in the Soviet Union (the Russian wives case);[160] the question of observance of human rights in Bulgaria, Hungary, and Roumania;[161] the Austro-Italian dispute regarding the status of the German-speaking minority in the Province of Bolzano (South Tyrol);[162] the question of Tibet;[163] the situation in Angola;[164] the question of Southern Rhodesia;[165] Israeli practices affecting the human rights of the population of the occupied territories;[166] and violations of

---

158. *See* chapter 7 *infra,* at notes 449–598 and accompanying text.

159. *See* R. Higgins, *supra* note 147, at 90–106; Chen, *supra* note 18, at 220–24, 253–55.

160. *See* Y.B.U.N. 1948–49, at 327–33.

161. *See* notes 121–24 *supra* and accompanying text.

162. *See* U.N. Repertory, *supra* note 156, at 91–92; Ermacora, *supra* note 147, at 414–15.

For a comprehensive treatment of this issue, *see* A. Alcock, The History of the South Tyrol Question (1970).

163. U.N. Repertory, *supra* note 156, at 84–85; *The Question of Tibet,* Y.B.U.N. 1959, at 67–70; *The Question of Tibet,* Y.B.U.N. 1961, at 138–40; *The Question of Tibet,* Y.B.U.N. 1965, at 191–94.

For further background, *see* International Commission of Jurists, The Question of Tibet and the Rule of Law (1959); International Commission of Jurists, Tibet and the Chinese People's Republic (1960).

164. U.N. Repertory, *supra* note 156, at 92–94; *The Situation in Angola,* Y.B.U.N. 1961, at 89–96; *The Situation in Angola,* Y.B.U.N. 1962, at 88–93.

165. *See* U.N. Repertory, *supra* note 156, at 87–91; McDougal & Reisman, *supra* note 147.

166. *See Questions Concerning Treatment of Civilian Populations in Israeli-Occupied Territories,* Y.B.U.N. 1969, at 209–21; *Treatment of Civilian Populations in Israeli-Occupied Territories and Related Matters,* Y.B.U.N. 1970, at 244–52; *The Treatment of the Civilian Population in Israeli-Occupied Territories and Related Matters,* Y.B.U.N. 1971, at 187–95; *The Treatment of the Civilian Population in Israeli-Occupied Territories and Related Matters,* Y.B.U.N. 1972, at 182–90; *Treatment of the Civilian Population in Israeli-Occupied Territories and Related Matters,* Y.B.U.N. 1973, at 225–34; H. Amerasinghe, The Work of the Special Committee to Investigate Israeli Practices Affecting the Human Rights of the Population of the Occupied Territories, U.N. Doc. OPI/495 (1973); *Report on Israeli Practices: Safeguards Urged for Protection of Human Rights in Occupied Territories,* 13 UN Monthly Chronicle 63 (Dec. 1976); *Human Rights Commission Acts on Situations in Southern Africa and Israeli-Occupied Territories,* 14 UN Monthly Chronicle 44, 44–46 (Apr. 1977).

See also Alderson, et al., *Protection of Human Rights in the Israeli-Occupied Territories,* 15 Harv. Int'l L.J. 470 (1974); Greenspan, *Human Rights in the Territories Occupied by Israel,* 12

human rights in Chile.[167] With reference to the terminating function (the ending of prescription and other arrangements) and the appraising function (that is, the evaluation of decision process), the general community is generally assumed to have the same broad inclusive competence, free of domestic jurisdiction, that it has in relation to the prescribing and intelligence functions.[168]

It may bear emphasis that it is the general community, the global constitutive process, which determines what matters are within international concern and what within domestic jurisdiction. As peoples' perceptions of their interdependences deepen and become more realistic, and as understanding of the intimate interrelations of peace and human rights widens,[169] the established processes of authoritative decision can be expected to have less and less difficulty in bringing all problems relating to human rights within the compass of inclusive competence. Events occurring within the boundaries of one state with appreciable deprivatory effects upon others have always been subject to claim and decision on the international plane. The frequent invocation by defendant states of the doctrine of domestic jurisdiction has rarely resulted, when transnational impacts are clearly generated, in precluding effective accommodations in keeping with inclusive interest. Domestic jurisdiction means little more than a concession by the general community to particular states of a primary, but not necessarily wholly exclusive, competence over matters arising within the boundaries, and predominantly affecting the internal public order, of such states. When particular events precipitate significant inclusive deprivations, the general community can be expected to internationalize jurisdiction and to authorize appropriate inclusive decision and action.[170] In President Carter's concise exposition before the United Nations on March 17, 1977:

Santa Clara Lawyer 377 (1972); Grunis, *United Nations and Human Rights in the Israel Occupied Territories,* 7 Int'l Lawyer 271 (1973); Liskofsky, *Coping with the "Question of the Violation of Human Rights and Fundamental Freedoms": Highlights of 31st Session of the United Nations Commission of Human Rights,* 8 Human Rights J. 883, 887–90 (1975); Meguid, *Israeli Practices and Human Rights in Occupied Arab Territories,* 7 Int'l Lawyer 279 (1973).

167. *See* Report of the Economic and Social Council: Protection of Human Rights in Chile, U.N. Doc. A/10285 (1975) (note by the secretary-general); *Human Rights Commission Acts on Situations in Southern Africa and Israeli-Occupied Territories,* 14 UN Monthly Chronicle 44, 47 (Apr. 1977); *Assembly Calls on Chile to End Torture; Re-examine Basis of State of Siege,* 14 UN Monthly Chronicle 62 (Jan. 1977); *Rights Group Adopts Decisions on Chile, Uganda, Argentina, Mozambique,* 13 UN Monthly Chronicle 31 (Oct. 1976); Liskofsky, *supra* note 166, at 890–91.

168. *See* notes 491–538 *infra* and accompanying text.

169. *See* chapter 1 *supra.*

170. *See* McDougal & Reisman, *supra* note 147, at 13–18.

> The search for peace and justice also means respect for human dignity. All the signatories of the United Nations Charter have pledged themselves to observe and respect basic human rights. Thus, no member of the United Nations can claim that mistreatment of its citizens is solely its own business. Equally, no member can avoid its responsibilities to review and to speak when torture or unwarranted deprivation of freedom occurs in any part of the world.[171]

Turning from the allocation of competences between the general community and particular states to the allocation of the competences within "domestic jurisdiction" between states, it is easily obvious that in the state-centered world of today most authority over individual human beings is still exercised at the national level. In an inherited, horizontal legal order, this authority of states is allocated under certain reciprocally honored principles of jurisdiction—namely, the principle of territoriality, the principle of nationality, the protective principle (overlapping in part the principle of impact territoriality), the principle of passive personality, and the principle of universality.[172] The principle of territoriality authorizes states to prescribe and apply law to all events occurring within their boundaries, irrespective of whether such events involve nationals or nonnationals. The nationality principle authorizes states to make and apply law to their own nationals, wherever they may interact or be. The protective principle (including that of impact territoriality) authorizes a state to take measures against direct attack upon its security and other values, though the events occur abroad. Under the principle of passive personality, states are authorized to make and apply law to people who injure their nationals, wherever the events may occur. The principle of universality, regarding certain events (such as those involved in piracy, war crimes, slave trading, and genocide) as threatening the common interests of all humanity, authorizes any state securing effective control over the actors to apply certain inclusive prescriptions. Taken in sum, these principles confer upon any state the competence to make and

---

171. *Peace, Arms Control, World Economic Progress, Human Rights: Basic Priorities of U.S. Foreign Policy,* 76 DEP'T STATE BULL. 329, 332 (1977); N.Y. Times, Mar. 18, 1977, at A10, cols. 5–6 (city ed.). *See also The Violation of Our Common Humanity Is Nobody's Internal Affairs,* 63 COMMENTARY 29 (May 1977); Cleveland, *In International Affairs, One Thing Leads to Another,* N.Y. Times, June 11, 1977, at 19, col. 2 (city ed.).

172. *See* M. MCDOUGAL, H. LASSWELL, & I. VLASIC, LAW AND PUBLIC ORDER IN SPACE 646–748 (1963) [hereinafter cited as M. MCDOUGAL, H. LASSWELL, & I. VLASIC]; McDougal, *Jurisdiction,* NAVAL WAR COLLEGE REV., Jan. 1957, at 1–22. *See also* I. BROWNLIE, PRINCIPLES OF PUBLIC INTERNATIONAL LAW 292–98 (2d ed. 1973) [hereinafter cited as I. BROWNLIE]; F. MANN, STUDIES IN INTERNATIONAL LAW [hereinafter cited as F. MANN].

apply law in relation to any events by which it is substantially affected. In an interdependent world, in which everything affects everything else, such broad grants of competence must often overlap and conflict, subjecting individuals to many different competences.

The competences over individuals achieved by states under all these primary principles of jurisdiction are not lessened by certain secondary allocations of competence under such doctrines as those of "act of state" and "sovereign immunity."[173] In a global social process in which people and goods are in constant movement, the primary principles of jurisdiction could not serve their appropriate ordering purpose if states did not in substantial measure honor each other's excercises of authority. Thus, states which have effective control over persons and resources are often required, under these doctrines about a secondary allocation of competence, to forgo the exercise of their own authority in deference to the prior legislative, executive, and judicial acts of other states or because of immunities accorded heads of state, diplomats, public ships, public corporations, and state agencies. The operation of these doctrines about secondary allocation may, consequently, quite often result in immunizing state officials from responsibility for human rights deprivations and thus compound and exacerbate the original wrong. A different result could not be expected from principles designed more to protect the interests of state elites in controlling peoples as bases of power than to protect the fundamental rights of the individuals being controlled.

---

173. *See* McDougal, *Act of State in Policy Perspective: The International Law of an International Economy,* in SOUTHWESTERN LEGAL FOUNDATIONS, SYMPOSIUM, PRIVATE INVESTORS ABROAD, STRUCTURES AND SAFEGUARDS 327–59 (1966). *See also* R. FALK, THE ROLE OF DOMESTIC COURTS IN THE INTERNATIONAL LEGAL ORDER (1964); T. GIUTTARI, THE AMERICAN LAW OF SOVEREIGN IMMUNITY (1970); RESTATEMENT (SECOND), FOREIGN RELATIONS LAW OF THE UNITED STATES §§ 62–82 (1965); R. LILLICH, THE PROTECTION OF FOREIGN INVESTMENT, chapter 3 (1965); H. STEINER & D. VAGTS, *supra* note 155, at 637–728; SUCHARITKUL, STATE IMMUNITIES AND STATE TRADING ACTIVITIES IN INTERNATIONAL LAW (1959); Brower, *Litigation of Sovereign Immunity before a State Administrative Body and the Department of State: The Japanese Uranium Tax Case,* 71 AM. J. INT'L L. 438 (1977); Cardozo, *Judicial Deference to State Department Suggestions: Recognition of Prerogative or Abdication to Usurper,* 48 CORNELL L.Q. 461 (1963); Delaume, *Public Debt and Sovereign Immunity: The Foreign Sovereign Immunities Act of 1976,* 71 AM. J. INT'L L. 399 (1977); Delson, *The Act of State Doctrine—Judicial Deference or Abstention,* 66 AM. J. INT'L L. 82 (1972); Dunbar, *Controversial Aspect of Sovereign Immunity in the Case of Law of Some States,* 132 HAGUE RECUEIL DES COURS 197 (1971); Higgins, *Recent Developments in the Law of Sovereign Immunity in the United Kingdom,* 71 AM. J. INT'L L. 423 (1977); Lowenfeld, *Claims against Foreign States—A Proposal for Reform of United States Law,* 44 N.Y.U.L. REV. 901 (1969); Markesinis, *A "Breeze" of Change in the Law of Sovereign Immunity,* 1976 CAMB. L.J. 198; Sinclair, *The European Convention on State Immunity,* 22 INT'L & COMP. L.Q. 254 (1973); Weber, *The Foreign Sovereign Immunities Act of 1976: Its Origin, Meaning and Effect,* 3 YALE STUDIES IN WORLD PUBLIC ORDER 1 (1976); *Note, Sovereign Immunity,* 15 HARV. INT'L L.J. 157 (1974).

EFFECTIVE CONTROL

It is maldistribution in the effective controls over peoples and resources (potential values) required to establish and maintain authoritative decision that today most significantly impedes global constitutive process both in the maintenance of security and in the promotion of human rights. Individual states, with large inherited controls over both peoples and resources, are highly reluctant to yield any genuine controls to the organized agencies of the general community. Among the individual states themselves, there are such disproportionate aggregations and concentrations of effective controls over peoples and territories as to make difficult any organized cooperation which reflects a sharing both of power and of responsibility. Within particular states, further, a high concentration and maldistribution of effective controls often enables state officials to persist in practices of deprivation and nonfulfillment, maintaining an impoverished and regimented social process.

A most important failure in global constitutive process is in the lack of allocation to the organized general community of the resources adequate to the effective pursuit of its major goals. Thus, the organized general community lacks any direct control over wealth and is, hence, dependent upon the good will of states for financing its human rights and other activities. This is a persisting difficulty plaguing all international governmental organizations.[174] The United Nations, for example, has no resource base of its own (even among the shareable resources of the oceans and outer space), and must rely upon annual contributions of members in order to implement its human rights and other programs. Thus, wealthy member states possess a de facto veto power over any decisions and activities to which they object, and may, in varying ways and degrees, frustrate the functioning of the organization.[175] The ab-

---

174. *See* Rowe, *Financial Support for the United Nations: The Evolution of Member Contributions, 1946–1969,* 26 INT'L ORG. 619 (1972).

For an innovative proposal for improvement, *see* Taubenfeld & Taubenfeld, *Independent Revenue for the United Nations,* 18 INT'L ORG. 241 (1964).

If proposals for an international seabed authority supervising license and exploration of deep sea resources come to fruition, it would greatly augment the effective power of the inclusive community in dealing with human rights and other matters. *See* Adede, *The System for Exploration of the "Common Heritage of Mankind" at the Caracas Conference,* 69 AM. J. INT'L L. 31 (1975); Stevenson & Oxman, *The Preparations for the Law of the Sea Conference,* 68 AM. J. INT'L L. 1, 4–8 (1974); Stevenson & Oxman, *The Third United Nations Conference on the Law of the Sea: The 1974 Caracas Session,* 69 AM. J. INT'L L. 1, 6–12 (1975); Stevenson & Oxman, *The Third United Nations Conference on the Law of the Sea: The 1975 Geneva Session,* 69 AM. J. INT'L L. 763, 765–69 (1975); Oxman, *The Third United Nations Conference on the Law of the Sea: The 1976 New York Sessions,* 71 AM. J. INT'L L. 247, 251–59 (1977).

175. This is dramatized by the paralysis caused by the controversy relating to the *Expenses* case, Advisory Opinion on Certain Expenses of the United Nations (Article 17,

sence of an independent control over base values continues as a great constraint upon all international governmental organizations for all shared purposes.

There would, however, in very recent times appear to be some modest movement toward a greater inclusivity in the allocation of the effective controls necessary to sustain authoritative decision. There would appear some increasing diffusion of the bases of effective power (including especially wealth, enlightenment, and skill) among the peoples of the world. A more pluralistic distribution of effective bases of power among a wide range of participants, operating under ever-changing constellations of conditions and in varying coalitions of groups and interests, could of course greatly enhance the potentialities of the general community for effective protection of human rights.

The worldwide spread of enlightenment and skills, facilitating perception of interdependences and common interests, along with contemporary instrumentalities of instantaneous communication, is beginning to place more appropriate assets in the hands of inclusive decision makers.

---

paragraph 2, of the Charter), [1962] I.C.J. 151.

For discussions, *see* G. SCHWARZENBERGER, INTERNATIONAL CONSTITUTIONAL LAW, *supra* note 15, at 291–99; Gross, *Expenses of the United Nations for Peace-Keeping Operations: The Advisory Opinion of the International Court of Justice,* 17 INT'L ORG. 27 (1963); Jennings, *International Court of Justice, Advisory Opinion of July 20, 1962, Certain Expenses of the United Nations (Article 17, paragraph 2 of the Charter),* 11 INT'L & COMP. L.Q. 1169 (1962); Lauterpacht, *The Legal Effect of Illegal Acts of International Organisations,* in CAMBRIDGE ESSAYS IN INTERNATIONAL LAW: ESSAYS IN HONOUR OF LORD MCNAIR 88, 106–14 (1965) [hereinafter cited as Lauterpacht and CAMBRIDGE ESSAYS, respectively]; Simmonds, *The U.N. Assessments Advisory Opinion,* 13 INT'L & COMP. L.Q. 854 (1964).

For further background, *see* L. GOODRICH, E. HAMBRO, & A. SIMONS, CHARTER OF THE UNITED NATIONS: COMMENTARY AND DOCUMENTS 148–67 (3d & rev. ed. 1969) [hereinafter cited as L. GOODRICH, E. HAMBRO & A. SIMONS]; J. SINGER, FINANCING INTERNATIONAL ORGANIZATION: THE UNITED NATIONS BUDGET PROCESS (1961); J. STOESSINGER, FINANCING THE UNITED NATIONS SYSTEM (1964); Claude, *The Political Framework of the United Nations' Financial Problems,* in INTERNATIONAL ORGANIZATION: POLITICS AND PROCESS, *supra* note 15, at 107–35; Meron, *Budget Approval by the General Assembly of the United Nations: Duty or Discretion?* 42 BRIT. Y.B. INT'L L. 91 (1967).

In November 1975, the United States formally informed the International Labor Organization of the U.S. intention of withdrawing from the organization unless it "depoliticized" its activities within the mandatory two-year waiting period. On this controversy, *see Two Key I.L.O. Votes Encouraging to U.S.: Governing Body Approves Request to Drop Israel Inquiry—Change of Rules Is Also Favored,* N.Y. Times, Mar. 6, 1977, § 1, at 8, col. 1 (city ed.); Raskin, *The Nearing Showdown on Effort to Change I.L.O., id.,* May 4, 1977, at D5, col. 1; *Secretary of Labor Terms U.S. Likely to Quit I.L.O. Soon, id.,* June 23, 1977, at A8, col. 1; Raskin, *The Tripartism Element If U.S. Quits the I.L.O., id.,* July 13, 1977, at D9, col. 1; *Why Stay in the I.L.O.?* (editorial), *id.,* Aug. 14, 1977, § 4, at 16, col. 1; *Why We Ought to Withdraw from the I.L.O., id.,* Aug. 27, 1977, at 20, col. 1 (letter of Phil Baum, Associate Executive Director, American Jewish Congress). *Cf.* Schwebel, *United States Assaults the I.L.O.*, 65 AM. J. INT'L L. 136 (1971).

The expanding identities and loyalties of peoples, as transnational interactions accelerate, and the increasing internationalization of standards of rectitude and of respect for human rights similarly add to the strength of inclusive decision. As the modern revolution in communication establishes a global forum for human rights and other discourses, mobilization of world public opinion promises to be, in the long run, the most effective means for the defense and fulfillment of human rights. Both the private and the public sectors of social process can be expected increasingly to join in such mobilization. While world public opinion may at times appear to be elusive, it is an indispensable weapon in exposing facts of deprivation and nonfulfillment of values, in articulating the shared aspirations for the greater shaping and wider sharing of values, and in generating and crystallizing the necessary support for a better implementation of human rights.[176]

Strategies

The strategies employed in global constitutive process, when considered most comprehensively, include the procedures in all arenas of authority. In this sense, the procedures on the global level for the protection of human rights appear to be still highly rudimentary. Nevertheless, improvements in communication, expanding scientific knowledge and skills in observation, and accumulating experience in large-scale administration have all combined in recent years to facilitate a gradual rationalization of the procedures by which decision makers manage base values in performance of the different policy functions necessary to the making and application of law. In all arenas the exploration of potential facts and potential community policies is being made more dependable, contextual, selective, and creative; the final characterization of facts and policies in prescriptive or applicative decision is being made more deliberate, rational, and nonprovocative; and the communication of the shared subjectivities indispensable to legal process is being made more effective. It will be convenient to consider these different trends below in relation to each of the seven different types of decision function.[177]

---

176. In the words of Ambassador Scranton:

> Human Rights are destroyed in little moves that flourish in darkness and quiet—destructive steps, each so minor that one seems able to justify not putting up a defense, not just yet. Only exposure—precise, unrelenting, and complete exposure—will prevail against that destructive process.
>
> The conscience of mankind can ignore injustice in the dark. When the lights are on, few men of conscience can remain quiet.

Scranton, *supra* note 94, at 749.

For further elaboration, *see* notes 185–205 *infra* and accompanying text.

177. *See* notes 266–538 *infra* and accompanying text.

Here we propose to examine certain more fundamental instruments of policy—namely, the diplomatic, the ideological, the economic, and the military—which may affect the economy and effectiveness of all particular procedures. These different instruments, or strategies, involve the management of two critical components—communications (symbols) and resources. The diplomatic instrument refers to communications from elite to elite, while the ideological instrument refers to communications directed to general audiences. The economic instrument involves the management of goods and services, and the military instrument involves resources specialized to violence. All these instruments are available to decision makers in global constitutive process for the protection (or nonprotection) of human rights, as for other purposes. They may be employed either singly or in varying combinations.

THE DIPLOMATIC INSTRUMENT

Historically, the diplomatic instrument has often been employed by states for the purposes of protecting their nationals abroad. Elite-centered, from foreign office to foreign office, this diplomatic remedy, called "diplomatic protection," is still slow and cumbersome.[178] Under

178. For a comprehensive summary of technical theories of that body of law known sometimes as diplomatic protection of citizens abroad and sometimes as responsibility of states, *see* C. AMERASINGHE, STATE RESPONSIBILITY FOR INJURIES TO ALIENS (1967) [hereinafter cited as C. AMERASINGHE]; E. BORCHARD, THE DIPLOMATIC PROTECTION OF CITIZENS ABROAD OR THE LAW OF INTERNATIONAL CLAIMS (1922) [hereinafter cited as E. BORCHARD]; F. DUNN, THE PROTECTION OF NATIONALS (1932) [hereinafter cited as F. DUNN]; C. EAGLETON, THE RESPONSIBILITY OF STATES IN INTERNATIONAL LAW (1928); F. GARCIA-AMADOR, L. SOHN, & R. BAXTER, RECENT CODIFICATION OF THE LAW OF STATE RESPONSIBILITY FOR INJURIES TO ALIENS (1974) [hereinafter cited as F. GARCIA-AMADOR, L. SOHN, & R. BAXTER]. For more detailed references, *see* chapter 14 *infra*. *See also* Kerley, *Nationality of Claims—A Vista,* 1969 PROC., AM. SOC'Y INT'L L. 35; Leigh, *Nationality and Diplomatic Protection,* 20 INT'L & COMP. L.Q. 453 (1971); Weis, *Diplomatic Protection of Nationals and International Protection of Human Rights,* 4 HUMAN RIGHTS J. 643 (1971).

For employment of the diplomatic instrument more generally, *see* D. ACHESON, MEETINGS AT THE SUMMIT: A STUDY IN DIPLOMATIC METHOD (1958); G. BALL, DIPLOMACY FOR A CROWDED WORLD: AN AMERICAN FOREIGN POLICY (1976); J. BURTON, SYSTEMS, STATES, DIPLOMACY AND RULES (1968); M. CARDOZO, DIPLOMATS IN INTERNATIONAL COOPERATION: STEPCHILDREN OF THE FOREIGN SERVICE (1962); F. IKLÉ, HOW NATIONS NEGOTIATE (1967); DIPLOMACY IN A CHANGING WORLD (S. Kertesz & M. Fritzsimons eds. 1959); H. KISSINGER, THE NECESSITY FOR CHOICE (1960); H. NICOLSON, THE EVOLUTION OF DIPLOMATIC METHOD (1954); L. PEARSON, DIPLOMACY IN THE NUCLEAR AGE (1959); INTERNATIONAL POLITICS AND FOREIGN POLICY (J. Rosenau ed. rev. ed. 1969); E. SATOW, A GUIDE TO DIPLOMATIC PRACTICE (rev. ed. 1958); H. WESTERFIELD, THE INSTRUMENTS OF AMERICA'S FOREIGN POLICY (1963); A. WOLFERS, DISCORD AND COLLABORATION: ESSAYS ON INTERNATIONAL POLITICS (1962); C. YOST, THE CONDUCT AND MISCONDUCT OF FOREIGN AFFAIRS (1972); Murty, *International Diplomacy in Perspective—A Contextual Analysis,* 3 YALE STUDIES IN WORLD PUBLIC ORDER 123 (1976).

the long-prevailing, and still lingering, myth that the individual human being is not an appropriate subject of international law, the individual must in principle rely for protection upon the state of his nationality. It is only through the "nationality" link that the individual secures much of what access he has to transnational arenas of authority vis-à-vis external entities.

Operating under Vattel's fiction that an injury to the individual is an injury to the state of his nationality, traditional international law regards a state's right to protect its nationals as independent of the individual's interest.[179] The state enjoys complete discretion—and bears no duty—to decide whether or not to espouse claims against external entities on behalf of its nationals. Because of their paramount concern for a comprehensive "national" interest, state elites tend to exaggerate the state interest at the expense of individual deprivees. The total policy considerations of the state may even prompt state officials to take action in contravention of the interests and wishes of the individual concerned. The individual is, hence, largely at the mercy of state officials.

In its specific application, the nationality test requires "continuity" of nationality. An individual claimant must possess the nationality of the espousing state from the instant of deprivation, through the presentation of the claim, and perhaps even to the time of final settlement. Thus, an individual claimant who loses or changes his nationality after having sustained a deprivation may not be able to secure remedy. His state of nationality at the time of deprivation is barred from espousing his claim because he is no longer its national; and his new state of nationality is disqualified because he was not its national at the time of deprivation. Such technical restrictiveness has resulted in the rejection of innumerable claims by arbitral tribunals.[180]

Further, the core reference of the concept of nationality itself is sometimes questioned or distorted in ways that deny protection to individual persons. States are accorded, under contemporary international law, a broad competence in the conferment of nationality upon individuals, and commonly bestow reciprocal deference on each other's conferments

---

179. Vattel's classic exposition reads as follows:

> Whoever ill-treats a citizen indirectly injures the State, which must protect that citizen. The sovereign of the injured citizen must avenge the deed and, if possible, force the aggressor to give full satisfaction or punish him, since otherwise the citizen will not obtain the chief end of civil society, which is protection.

3 E. de Vattel, The Classics of International Law: The Law of Nations or the Principles of Natural Law 136 (J. Scott ed., C. Fenwick trans. 1916) [hereinafter cited as E. de Vattel].

180. *See* the appendix *infra*, at notes 12–15 and accompanying text.

in accordance with customary criteria. Individuals are, however, occasionally deprived of a protecting state and of a hearing upon the merits of their claims because of invocation of ambiguous and spurious conceptions of nationality or imposition of tests over and beyond any traditional conception. A number of famous cases dramatically illustrate such miscarriages of justice.[181]

It may be noted, further, that diplomatic remedies for the protection of human rights are subject to all the limitations inherent in decentralized law making and application. When considerations of reciprocity and effective power dominate decision, the mere fact that a state is willing to act as a protector is no guarantee that the individual national will actually receive effective protection and fulfillment of human rights. Vacillation, trade-offs, and compromises among state elites are all too common.

In very recent times, as perception of the transnational impact of human rights deprivations has become more realistic, states have begun to employ the diplomatic instrument for the protection, not merely of their own nationals, but of all persons. The diplomatic instrument lends itself easily to inquiries about alleged violations, to expressions of general and particular concerns, to suggestions about the discontinuation of certain practices, to recommendations of measures of amelioration (*e.g.*, release of particular political prisoners), to intimations of possible consequences of continuing practices of deprivation, and so on. In reciprocal deference to sensitivities, such communications ordinarily go forward in what is called "quiet diplomacy." In a pervasive air of confidentiality, such "quiet diplomacy" too often tends, unhappily, to become a "silent" diplomacy, degenerating into mere cover for indifference and inaction.[182]

Most importantly, with the multiplication of new, more stable, and more continuous inclusive arenas, the old diplomacy of episodic official or elite communication is being transformed, as in the United Nations, into a kind of parliamentary representation and activity.[183] Important

---

181. *See* Nottebohm Case, [1955] I.C.J. 4; Flegenheimer Claim, 25 I.L.R. 91 (Italian-United States Conciliation Commission 1963); Case Concerning the Barcelona Traction, Light and Power Company, Limited, Second Phase, [1970] I.C.J. 4. For comments upon these cases, *see* the appendix *infra,* at notes 16–42 and accompanying text.

182. *Cf.* International League for Human Rights, Report of the Conference on Implementing a Human Rights Commitment in United States Foreign Policy 5 (Feb. 1977) [hereinafter cited as the ILHR Conference Report].

183. *See* Jessup, *Parliamentary Diplomacy,* 89 Hague Recueil des Cours 185 (1956). *See also* A. Lall, Modern International Negotiation: Principles and Practice (1966); Hambro, *Some Notes on Parliamentary Diplomacy,* in Transnational Law in a Changing Society: Essays in Honor of Philip C. Jessup 280–97 (W. Friedmann, L. Henkin, & O. Lissitzyn eds. 1972) [hereinafter cited as Transnational Law in a Changing Society].

new multilateral conventions have been formulated and accepted for guiding and assisting diplomatic interactions and for the making and performance of agreements. New procedures are constantly being devised and tested for executive and administrative arenas. This new parliamentary diplomacy, by increasing the intensity, frequency, and openness of contact, adds a new dimension to the diplomatic instrument for the protection of human rights.[184] The availability of collective, permanent, and continuous forums affords new opportunities for state officials to air grievances, to express aspirations, and to engage in reciprocal influence and education. Whether it is a debate about the inscription of a particular human rights matter in an agenda, a general debate, or a debate about a specific controversy, and notwithstanding all the polemics of self-righteousness and of condemnation of others, the long-term salutary effect upon the protection of human rights can scarcely be questioned.

THE IDEOLOGICAL INSTRUMENT

The special significance of the ideological instrument is in its potentialities for mobilizing world public opinion, not merely against particular instances of barbarism, but also in support of sustained programs in continuing, long-term protection.[185] It involves the mobilization both of enlightenment and of transnational identifications and loyalties as bases of power. Humphrey realistically observes that the "ordinary if not the ultimate sanction of the international law of human rights is the force of world opinion."[186] Similarly, Fawcett emphasizes "the aspect of publicity because, though its effect may be slow and unspectacular, often even unremarked, it is the medium through which human rights come to be understood, recognised and elaborated, and their denial, where it occurs, made known; it is therefore a real and essential mode of implemen-

---

184. *See* notes 358–71 *infra* and accompanying text. *Cf.* Bissell, *Negotiation by International Bodies and the Protection of Human Rights,* 7 COLUM. J. TRANSN'L L. 90 (1968).

185. On the ideological instrument generally, *see* B. MURTY, PROPAGANDA AND WORLD PUBLIC ORDER: THE LEGAL REGULATION OF THE IDEOLOGICAL INSTRUMENT OF COERCION (1968). *See also* READER IN PUBLIC OPINION AND COMMUNICATION (2d ed. B. Berelson & M. Janowitz eds. 1966); S. CHAKHOTIN, THE RAPE OF THE MASSES (E. Dickes trans. 1940); W. DAUGHERTY, A PSYCHOLOGICAL WARFARE CASEBOOK (1958); F. DUNN, WAR AND THE MINDS OF MEN (1950); L. FRASER, PROPAGANDA (1957); L. MARTIN, INTERNATIONAL PROPAGANDA: ITS LEGAL AND DIPLOMATIC CONTROL (1958); MASS COMMUNICATIONS (2d ed., W. Schramm ed. 1960); J. WHITTON & A. LARSON, PROPAGANDA: TOWARDS DISARMAMENT IN THE WAR OF WORDS (1963); *International Control of Propaganda,* 31 LAW & CONTEMP. PROB. 437 (1966).

186. *Quoted* in *First Interim Report of the Sub-Committee on the International Protection of Human Rights by the Mobilisation of Public Opinion to International Law Association, Madrid Conference (1976),* at 1 (1976) [hereinafter cited as *Report of the Sub-Committee*].

tation."[187] The potentialities for the management of world public opinion in the improved protection of human rights have, however, hardly begun to be realized. There have been momentary outbursts of indignation against Nazism, apartheid, racial discrimination, discrimination against women, and so on. Yet there has been no sustained management of public opinion against the less dramatic, but continuous, flow of deprivations and nonfulfillments more generally.

The potentialities of instantaneous communication about the globe, to mass audiences beyond elite groups, promise both greatly to increase participation in global constitutive process and profoundly to affect performance of many policy functions, such as—especially—promotion, prescription, and application. The ideological instrument is of peculiar importance for international government organizations in performance of their various functions. Because of their limited resources, international governmental organizations have tended to emphasize the use of symbols to expose glaring human rights deprivations and nonfulfillments, to focus world attention on human rights problems, and to enlighten and stimulate members of the public as vanguards in protection. It is the ideological instrument, emphasizing contemporary communication technology and skills, that enables these organizations to utilize bases of power that would otherwise not be at their disposal. In the words of the late U.N. Secretary-General U Thant, "a purposeful and universal programme of public information is, in fact, a programme of implementation—an essential counterpart of the substantive activities of the Organization."[188] Similarly, Holder and Sharma observe in their report to the International Law Association: "Throughout UN programmes, in particular, runs an assumption that communication of the world at large—whether neutral "news" or the exhortations of members and officers—will counteract destructive trends and prod and ambarrass [sic] particular States."[189]

The principal weapon relied upon by the United Nations in combatting the policies and practices of apartheid in South Africa, for example, has been the sustained employment of the ideological instrument.[190] A protracted world war of "publicity" has been undertaken to enlighten

187. Fawcett, *The Protection of Human Rights on a Universal Basis: Recent Experience and Proposals,* in HUMAN RIGHTS IN NATIONAL AND INTERNATIONAL LAW 289, 292 (A. Robertson ed. 1968).

188. INTRODUCTION TO THE ANNUAL REPORT OF THE SECRETARY-GENERAL ON THE WORK OF THE ORGANIZATION, 16 JUNE 1965–15 JUNE 1966, 21 U.N. GAOR, Supp. (No. 1A) 2, U.N. Doc. A/6301/Add. 1 (1966).

189. *Report of the Sub-Committee, supra* note 186, at 12.

190. J. CAREY, UN PROTECTION OF CIVIL AND POLITICAL RIGHTS 154–58 (1970) [hereinafter cited as J. CAREY].

"public opinion" on "the evils of apartheid" and, ultimately, to overcome the vehement resistance of the South African government. The use of publicity has, further, been extended from the anti-apartheid crusade to other human rights matters, including the efforts to eradicate slavery and slavelike practices; to eliminate racial discrimination; to foster equality of men and women; to minimize arbitrary arrest, detention, and imprisonment; to eradicate the practice of torture; to combat terrorism; to eradicate illiteracy; to eliminate communicable diseases; to secure a healthy environment; to wipe out poverty and accelerate development; to achieve rational control of population; to seek freedom from hunger; to foster the transfer of technology and skills; to assist the homeless and children; and to eradicate religious discrimination and intolerance. With its global constituency, the United Nations has employed a strategy of selective attention—relying heavily upon publicity—by commemorating a particular day, year, or decade in reference to a particular human rights matter or a particular category of people. The list includes:

> Human Rights Day (December 10 of each year, in commemoration of the adoption of the Universal Declaration of Human Rights);[191]
>
> The International Year for Human Rights in 1968;[192]
>
> International Day for the Elimination of Racial Discrimination (March 21 of each year, the anniversary of the Sharpeville incident);[193]
>
> The International Year for Action to Combat Racism and Racial Discrimination (1971);[194]
>
> The Decade for Action to Combat Racism and Racial Discrimination (beginning on December 10, 1973);[195]

---

191. G.A. Res. 423, 5 U.N. GAOR, Supp. (No. 20) 43, U.N. Doc. A/1775 (1950).

192. G.A. Res. 1961, 18 U.N. GAOR, Supp. (No. 15) 43, U.N. Doc. A/5515 (1963). *See also* G.A. Res. 2081, 20 U.N. GAOR, Supp. (No. 14) 44, U.N. Doc. A/6014 (1965); G.A. Res. 2217A, 21 U.N. GAOR, Supp. (No. 16) 61, U.N. Doc. A/6316 (1966); G.A. Res. 2307, 22 U.N. GAOR, Supp. (No. 16) 19, U.N. Doc. A/6716 (1967); G.A. Res. 2588A, 24 U.N. GAOR, Supp. (No. 30) 60, U.N. Doc. A/7630 (1969). *See also* Final Act of the Teheran Conference, *supra* note 67; United Nations, International Conference on Human Rights, Teheran, Iran, 22 April–13 May 1968, U.N. Doc. OPI/336 (1968).

193. G.A. Res. 2307, 22 U.N. GAOR, Supp. (No. 16) 19, U.N. Doc. A/6716 (1967). *See* United Nations, International Day for the Elimination of Racial Discrimination, U.N. Doc. OPI/383 (1970); Y.B.U.N. 1967, at 94–95.

194. G.A. Res. 2544, 24 U.N. GAOR, Supp. (No. 30) 53, U.N. Doc. A/7630 (1969).

195. G.A. Res. 2919, 27 U.N. GAOR, Supp. (No. 30) 62, U.N. Doc. A/8730 (1972); G.A. Res. 3057, 28 U.N. GAOR, Supp. (No. 30) 70, U.N. Doc. A/9030 (1973).

International Women's Year (1975);[196]

The United Nations Decade for Women: Equality, Development and Peace (1975–85);[197]

International Year of the Child (1979);[198]

World Refugee Year (1959–60);[199]

World Population Year (1974);[200]

The First United Nations Development Decade (1960–70);[201]

The Second United Nations Development Decade (1970–80).[202]

The ideological instrument is, similarly, available to private groups and individuals, making it possible to mobilize a wide range of effective participants in both the private and the public sectors. As Holder and Sharma put it: "In competing in the international market place of ideas, NGOs and individuals often rely largely on communication to awaken, educate, engage and enrage public opinion. In so doing they emphasize the adversary nature of the human rights campaign."[203] In the race to

---

196. G.A. Res. 3275, 29 U.N. GAOR, Supp. (No. 31) 93, U.N. Doc. A/9631 (1974); G.A. Res. 3010, 27 U.N. GAOR, Supp. (No. 30) 66, U.N. Doc. A/8730 (1972).

See Chen, *International Women's Year: Law and Women,* PROCEEDINGS AND COMMITTEE REPORTS OF THE AMERICAN BRANCH OF THE INTERNATIONAL LAW ASSOCIATION, 1975–1976, at 72–82 (1976); Swift, *International Women's Year: The Mexico City Conference, id.* at 82–92; chapter 10 *infra.*

197. *See* UNITED NATIONS, WORLD CONFERENCE ON THE INTERNATIONAL WOMEN'S YEAR, 19 JUNE–2 JULY 1975: DECLARATION OF MEXICO, PLANS OF ACTION (1975); MEETING IN MEXICO, *supra* note 71; *Mexico Conference Launches Plan of Action for Women,* 12 U.N. MONTHLY CHRONICLE 44 (July 1975).

198. G.A. Res. 31/169, U.N. Doc. A/Res./31/169 (14 Feb. 1977) (*adopted* Dec. 21, 1976). *See 1979 Proclaimed International Year of the Child by Assembly,* 14 UN MONTHLY CHRONICLE 55 (Jan. 1977).

199. G.A. Res. 1285, 13 U.N. GAOR, Supp. (No. 18) 25, U.N. Doc. A/4090 (1958); G.A. Res. 1390, 14 U.N. GAOR, Supp. (No. 16) 21, U.N. Doc. A/4354 (1960). *See also* G.A. Res. 1388, 14 U.N. GAOR, Supp. (No. 16) 20, U.N. Doc. A/4354 (1959); G.A. Res. 1502, 15 U.N. GAOR, Supp. (No. 16) 20, U.N. Doc. A/4684 (1960).

200. G.A. Res. 2683, 25 U.N. GAOR, Supp. (No. 28) 55, U.N. Doc. A/8028 (1970). *See* UNITED NATIONS FUND FOR POPULATION ACTIVITIES, WORLD POPULATION YEAR 1974: PURPOSES, PRINCIPLES, PROGRAMMES (1973).

201. G.A. Res. 1710, 16 U.N. GAOR, Supp. (No. 17) 17, U.N. Doc. A/5100 (1961); G.A. Res. 1715, 16 U.N. GAOR, Supp. (No. 17) 23, U.N. Doc. A/5100 (1961). *See* UNITED NATIONS, THE UNITED NATIONS DEVELOPMENT DECADE: PROPOSALS FOR ACTION (1962); UNITED NATIONS, THE UNITED NATIONS DEVELOPMENT DECADE AT MID-POINT: AN APPRAISAL BY THE SECRETARY-GENERAL (1965).

202. G.A. Res. 2305, 22 U.N. GAOR, Supp. (No. 16) 29, U.N. Doc. A/6716 (1967); G. A. Res. 2626, 25 U.N. GAOR, Supp. (No. 28) 39, U.N. Doc. A/8028 (1970). *See* UNITED NATIONS, CONTINUITY AND CHANGE: DEVELOPMENT AT MID-DECADE, U.N. Doc. ST/ESA/25 (1975).

203. *Report of the Sub-Committee, supra* note 186, at 12.

win the hearts and minds of the world's population, private groups and individuals constitute a formidable force, despite their limited resources and the handicaps of governmental regulation. The nongovernmental sector has the distinct advantages of offering more inclusive identifications to the whole of humankind and of not being inhibited by such parochial notions as sovereignty and domestic jurisdiction. It is somewhat freer to tell the truth as it is. With appropriate skill, the ideological instrument can be mobilized to reach a worldwide audience and to build a global constituency in support of the defense and fulfillment of human rights.[204]

Rhetoric has long proved itself to be far from cheap and meaningless. More and more rhetoric in support of human rights can help to generate, cultivate, sustain, and strengthen the expectations of the peoples about the globe in the direction of human dignity.[205] Constant clarification and reaffirmation are indispensable components of an enduring program for the protection and fulfillment of human rights.

THE ECONOMIC INSTRUMENT

The economic instrument may be employed to affect all phases of wealth processes—production, conservation, distribution, and consumption—as well as other value processes. It involves methods of and facilities for managing a flow of capital, goods, and services across state

---

204. *See* Report of the Regional Conference of Non-Governmental Organizations Organized by the United Nations Office of Public Information at the Invitation of the Government of Argentina, Buenos Aires, 21 to 25 August 1972, U.N. Doc. OPI/NGO/2 (1973); Jenks, *Law and Opinion in the International Protection of Human Rights,* in 1 René Cassin, *supra* note 39, at 114-20.

Concerning public opinion and law more generally, *see* a classic, A. Dicey, Lectures on the Relation between Law and Public Opinion in England during the Nineteenth Century (1905).

205. As President Carter recently stated:

> I understand fully the limits of moral suasion. I have no illusion that changes will come easily or soon. But I also believe that it is a mistake to undervalue the power of words and of the ideas that words embody. . . .
>
> In the life of the human spirit, words are action—much more so than many of us realize who live in countries where freedom of expression is taken for granted.
>
> The leaders of totalitarian countries understand this very well. The proof is that words are precisely the action for which dissidents in those countries are being persecuted.

N.Y. Times, May 23, 1977, at 12, cols. 4-5 (city ed.).

At a recent conference on implementing a human rights commitment in United States foreign policy, sponsored by the International League for Human Rights, Professor Louis Henkin urged "a plea for more, not less rhetoric." The ILHR Conference Report, *supra* note 182, at 7. *See also* The White House Commemoration of the 30th Anniversary of the Universal Declaration of Human Rights (Dec. 1978).

borders. The economic instrument can be used by the general community of states through a growing network of international governmental organizations (both general and functional). It can also be used by individual states to promote aggregate interests. The economic instrument can be employed positively to foster fulfillment of wealth and other values and negatively as a sanctioning measure against deprivations of human rights. Given the enormous importance of wealth (control and access to capital, goods, and services) as a base for all other values, the economic instrument is clearly important for multiple purposes.

The positive use of the economic instrument by the general community has been enormously increased through a global network of organizations, consisting of the United Nations, its subsidiary organs, and many specialized agencies. This growing network of agencies has employed the economic instrument in promoting what is known as "development" and in maximizing the production and distribution of all important values.[206] This network is established and maintained, in the words of the Preamble of the United Nations Charter, "to promote social progress and better standards of life in larger freedom" and "to employ international machinery for the promotion of the economic and social advancement of all peoples." Notable in this expanding network are the Economic and Social Council (including its four regional economic commissions and a number of functional commissions), the United Nations Conference on Trade and Development (UNCTAD), the United Nations Development Program (UNDP), the World Bank Group (the International Bank for Reconstruction and Development, the International Finance Corporation, and the International Development Association), and the International Monetary Fund (IMF).[207] The range of con-

206. *See generally* R. ASHER, DEVELOPMENT ASSISTANCE IN THE SEVENTIES (1970); R. ASHER, et al., *supra* note 26; E. BLACK, THE DIPLOMACY OF ECONOMIC DEVELOPMENT (1960); INTERNATIONAL ORGANIZATION: WORLD POLITICS (R. Cox ed. 1969); U.S. AND WORLD DEVELOPMENT: AGENDA FOR ACTION (J. Howe ed. 1975); INTERNATIONAL COMMISSION ON DEVELOPMENT (PEARSON COMMISSION), PARTNERS IN DEVELOPMENT (1969); W. LEONTIEF, THE FUTURE OF THE WORLD ECONOMY (1977) (a United Nations study); RESHAPING THE INTERNATIONAL ORDER (a report to the Club of Rome) (1976) [hereinafter cited as RIO]; O. SCHACHTER, SHARING THE WORLD'S RESOURCES (1977); W. SHARP, FIELD ADMINISTRATION IN THE UNITED NATIONS SYSTEM (1961); A. SHONFIELD, THE ATTACK ON WORLD POVERTY (1960); R. TOWNLEY, DEVELOPING INTERNATIONAL INSTITUTIONS (1966); G. VERBIT, TRADE AGREEMENTS FOR DEVELOPING COUNTRIES (1969); Friedmann, *The Relevance of International Law to the Processes of Economic and Social Development,* in 2 THE FUTURE OF THE INTERNATIONAL LEGAL ORDER 3–35 (R. Falk & C. Black eds. 1970).

207. In addition to the sources cited in note 26 *supra*, *see generally* M. DE VRIES, THE INTERNATIONAL MONETARY FUND, 1966–1971 (1976); K. HAGRAS, UNITED NATIONS CONFERENCE ON TRADE AND DEVELOPMENT (1965); S. HORIE, THE INTERNATIONAL MONETARY

cern includes international investment, monetary policy, manpower, health, education, food and agriculture, and transportation and communication of all kinds.

The widening gap between the more developed and the less developed communities in an interdependent world has caused the general community in recent years to pay special attention to the less developed communities. Economic strategies for facilitating the development of these communities include programs for pooling and making available technological and managerial skills. An equally important component is provision for a continuing and expanded flow of international capital into the less developed communities. Scarcely less important are the reorganization of archaic patterns in agriculture, the achievement of high and stable levels of employment, the integration of production potential into the global economy, and avoidance of widespread depressions. Still another aspect is the coordination of the expanding number of national and transnational agencies engaged in economic assistance and financing programs.

Frustrated by the slow pace of development and the persistence of glaring gaps, the less developed communities (the Third World) have crystallized their demands into insistence upon the establishment of "a New International Economic Order."[208] This insistence finds formal expression in the Declaration of the Establishment of a New International Economic Order adopted by the United Nations General Assembly on May 1, 1974,[209] and in the Charter of Economic Rights and Duties of States adopted by the Assembly on December 12, 1974.[210] The emerging New International Economic Order vividly reflects a conspicuous power

---

FUND (1964); R. JACKSON, A STUDY OF THE CAPACITY OF THE UN DEVELOPMENT SYSTEM (1969); E. LUARD, *supra* note 23; E. MASON & R. ASHER, THE WORLD BANK SINCE BRETTON WOODS (1973); J. MORRIS, THE WORLD BANK (1963); W. SCAMMELL, INTERNATIONAL MONETARY POLICY (1957); R. TRIFFIN, GOLD AND THE DOLLAR CRISIS (1960); THE FUTURE OF INTERNATIONAL ECONOMIC ORGANIZATIONS (D. Wallace & H. Escobar eds. 1977); ECONOMIC COOPERATION IN LATIN AMERICA, AFRICA AND ASIA: A HANDBOOK OF DOCUMENTS (M. Wionczek ed. 1969); Singh, *Regional Development Banks,* 576 INT'L CONCILIATION (Jan. 1970).

208. *See* O. SCHACHTER, *supra* note 206, at 3-34; Hudes, *Towards a New International Economic Order,* 2 YALE STUDIES IN WORLD PUBLIC ORDER 88 (1975); Reisman, *Trade Helps the Traders: The Third World's Fading Dream,* THE NATION, June 12, 1976, at 716-20; Tucker, *A New International Order?* COMMENTARY, Feb. 1975, at 38-50; *Recent Developments, The General Assembly's International Economics,* 16 HARV. INT'L L.J. 670 (1975); Gardner, *Economic Warfare: "All Can Play,"* Washington Post, Dec. 14, 1973, at A30, col. 5; Reston, *A New Economic Order,* N.Y. Times, May 30, 1975, at 31, col. 5; *U.N. Adopts Plan for Poor Nations,* N.Y. Times, Sept. 16, 1975, at 9, col. 1.

209. G.A. Res. 3201 (S-VI), May 1, 1974, U.N. GAOR, 6 Spec. Sess., Supp. (No. 1) 3, U.N. Doc. A/9559 (1974); G.A. Res. 3202 (S-VI), May 1, 1974, *id.* at 6.

210. G.A. Res. 3281, 29 U.N. GAOR, Supp. (No. 31) 50, U.N. Doc. A/9631 (1974).

shift to the Third World. The thrust of the new order is to effect fundamental changes in world economic relations, and especially to redress past deprivations and injustices by developing a new world trade pattern favoring developing countries. Its far-reaching implications are not confined to the reshaping of world economic relations; they involve ultimately the reshaping of the entire global constitutive process of authoritative decision.[211] Unsettling as they may appear, these demands for a New International Economic Order are in a profound sense demands for human rights—demands for better employment of the economic instrument to facilitate greater fulfillment worldwide of wealth and other values, especially for the vast segment of the world's population that have hitherto been deprived and underfulfilled.

The employment of the economic instrument as a measure of sanction against human rights deprivations encounters formidable difficulties. When the economic instrument is employed as a means of sanction, it may take the form of isolating the violator state from access to the flow of outside resources and services, upsetting its economic influence in third states, and hampering the efficient use of its internal resources. Among economic measures designed to sanction the violator state are commodity and financial controls.[212] Commodity controls seek to sever or regulate the trade both of the sanctioners and of third states with the violator state. They may involve the imposition of an embargo on direct exports from the sanctioners to the violator state and on direct imports by the sanctioners from the violator, and the prevention of reexportation or transshipment from third states of goods from the sanctioners to the violator state or vice versa. An embargo on exports, whether total or selective, is calculated to weaken the violator state directly by withholding strategic and other critical supplies from it; and an embargo on

---

211. *See* RIO, *supra* note 206; Barraclough, *The Great World Crisis I,* N.Y. REV. BOOKS, Jan. 23, 1975, at 20–29; Barraclough, *Wealth and Power: The Politics of Food and Oil,* N.Y. REV. BOOKS, Aug. 7, 1975, at 23–30; Cooper, *A New International Economic Order for Mutual Gain,* 26 FOREIGN POLICY 65 (1977); Leff, *The New Economic Order—Bad Economics, Worse Politics,* 24 FOREIGN POLICY 202 (1976); Reisman, *supra* note 208; Tinbergen, *A New International Order,* NATO REV., Dec. 1975, at 9.

See also Alzamora, *Reshaping World Economics,* N.Y. Times, May 7, 1977, at 25, col. 6 (city ed.); Peterson, *A New International Economic Order: Helping Others—and Ourselves, id.,* May 13, 1977, at A27, col. 4.

212. *See* ECONOMIC COERCION AND THE NEW INTERNATIONAL ECONOMIC ORDER (R. Lillich ed. 1976) (containing articles by Bowett, Buchheit, Lillich, Paust & Blaustein, Shihata, Smith, Boorman, Brosche, Franck & Chesler, & Schachter) [hereinafter cited as ECONOMIC COERCION]; A. LOWENFELD, TRADE CONTROLS FOR POLITICAL ENDS (1977); M. MCDOUGAL & F. FELICIANO, *supra* note 55, at 30–32, 322–29; Y. WU, ECONOMIC WARFARE (1952); L. Chen, The Legal Regulation of Minor International Coercion, 1964, at 131–210, 430–49 (unpublished J.S.D. dissertation, Yale Law School Library) [hereinafter cited as L. Chen].

imports (boycott) is designed to deprive the violator state of the foreign exchange needed for financing its purchases from abroad. Embargoes may be enforced and supplemented by ancillary controls on communications and trsnsportation (land, sea, and air) lines and facilities, and by such other measures as blacklisting.[213]

Financial controls may take the form of halting the flow of capital to the violator state by such measures as the denial of grants (aid), loans, and credits and the suspension of payments. Other measures include blocking or freezing assets of the violator state and its nationals. Like the import embargo (boycott), the measures of financial control are calculated to curtail the purchasing power abroad of the violator state.

The effectiveness of economic sanctioning strategies is, of course, a function of many variables relevant to a particular context. Among the important factors affecting such effectiveness are the vulnerability of the violator state to economic sanctions, the costs of such sanctions, capabilities for bearing costs, the requirements of coordination, and time factors.[214] The relative vulnerability of the violator state to the impact of particular measures of economic sanction is affected by such interrelated factors as the degree of its industrial development and the degree of its dependence upon foreign trade. A state that is highly industrialized may

---

213. The impact of commodity control was of course dramatized by the oil crisis of October precipitated in Oct. 1973. For two contrasting views on the lawfulness of the oil embargo, *see* Paust & Blaustein, *The Arab Oil Weapon—A Threat to International Peace,* 68 AM. J. INT'L L. 410 (1974), and Shihata, *Destination Embargo: Its Legality under International Law,* 68 AM. J. INT'L L. 591 (1974); both articles are reprinted in ECONOMIC COERCION, *supra* note 212, at 123–91. For their further exchanges, and other views, *see* ECONOMIC COERCION, *supra* note 212, at 195–317.

On the Arab boycott of Israel and antiboycott measures, *see* A. LOWENFELD, *supra* note 212, at 1–258; *Foreign Investment and Arab Boycott Legislation: Hearings before Subcomm. on International Finance of Senate Comm. on Banking, Housing, and Urban Affairs,* 94th Cong., 1st Sess. (1975); *Secretary Vance Discusses Antiboycott Legislation and Nuclear Non-Proliferation,* 76 DEP'T STATE BULL. 267 (1977).

See also Nolte, *The Saudi Connection and the Arab Boycott,* N.Y. Times, Feb. 18, 1977, at A27, col. 2 (city ed.); *One Boycott Is Enough* (editorial), *id.,* Feb. 24, 1977, at 34, col. 1; *The Arab Boycott and the Ex-Ambassador* (letters), *id.,* Feb. 28, 1977, at 26, col. 3; *Carter Seeks Bill to Thwart Intent of Arab Boycott, id.,* Mar. 1, 1977, at 1, col. 2; *Bill to Bar Americans' Role in Boycott of Israel Ready, id.,* Mar. 21, 1977, at 43, col. 5; *Vance Is Seeking Changes in Bill on Arab Boycott, id.,* Mar. 25, 1977, at D1, col. 5; *Fine-Tuning the Boycott Bill* (editorial), *id.,* Apr. 14, 1977, at A24, col. 1; *U.S. Business Opens Campaign to Amend Anti-Boycott Bills, id.,* Apr. 19, 1977, at 51, col. 1; *House Votes to Bar Compliance in U.S. with Arab Boycott, id.,* Apr. 21, 1977, at A1, col. 1; *Anti-Boycott Legislation: "One Narrow Point"* (letters), *id.,* Apr. 22, 1977, at A26, col. 3; *Arab League Adds 5 U.S. Concerns to Boycott List for the First Time, id.,* June 21, 1977, at 41, col. 5; *Carter Signs Compromise Bill on Arab Boycott, id.,* June 23, 1977, at D1, col. 1; *Hundreds of Concerns in France Cooperate with Arab Boycott of Israel, id.,* Aug. 8, 1977, at 8, col. 3; Salpukas, *How Business Grappled with the Arab Boycott, id.,* Aug. 21, § 3, at 1, col. 5.

214. *See* L. Chen, *supra* note 212, at 143–52.

rely heavily upon foreign trade for markets or energy and other raw materials, or both, and thus may be particularly vulnerable to imposition of embargoes. A state with a larger agrarian sector may be only slightly affected by an embargo on food or raw materials, but its capabilities for maintaining internal order by coercion may be significantly weakened by the cutting off of its access to arms and strategic materials. Conversely, an arms embargo may be ineffective against a highly industrialized state. Further, it is possible for the violator (offending) state to offset the adverse effect of economic sanctions through its network of established or potential trading partners and through recourse to such remedial measures as stockpiling, substitutes, rationing of commodities, and reallocation of resources.

It may be noted, further, that economic measures of sanction are not without cost to the sanctioning states that employ them. The damage done to the violator state may ultimately be matched by a corresponding loss spilled over into the economies of the sanctioning states. Unless the burden is widely shared and sanctions are collectively applied, the costs may simply become prohibitive to the sanctioning states. The efficiency of economic sanctions maintained for a protracted period of time against states capable of economic endurance gradually tend to diminish. Unless economic sanctions are well coordinated among the sanctioning states and effectively applied in conjunction with other strategies, defections among the sanctioning states tend to spread as time passes.[215]

The consequence is that, since the wealth of the world is still largely controlled by particular nation-states, the general community cannot hope to employ the economic instrument effectively as a sanction against human rights deprivations without the cooperation of many nation-states. Since any use of the economic instrument is so deeply intertwined in the welfare of particular states, it is, further, extremely difficult to persuade states to undertake and coordinate economic sanctions to protect human rights.

The ineffectiveness of economic sanctions against Rhodesia and against South Africa is instructive.[216] In response to the unilateral decla-

---

215. *See generally* C. BROWN-JOHN, MULTILATERAL SANCTIONS IN INTERNATIONAL LAW, A COMPARATIVE ANALYSIS (1975); M. DOXEY, ECONOMIC SANCTIONS AND INTERNATIONAL ENFORCEMENT (1971); INTERNATIONAL SANCTIONS (1938) (a report by a group of members for the Royal Institute of International Affairs); Hoffman, *The Function of Economic Sanctions: A Comparative Analysis,* 2 J. PEACE RESEARCH 140 (1967); MacDonald, *Economic Sanctions in the International System,* 7 CANADIAN Y.B. INT'L L. 61 (1969); Taubenfeld & Taubenfeld, *The "Economic Weapon": The League and the United Nations,* 1964 PROC., AM. SOC'Y INT'L L. 183.

216. Regarding sanctions against Southern Rhodesia, *see* R. GOOD, U.D.I., THE INTERNATIONAL POLITICS OF THE RHODESIAN REBELLION (1973); L. KAPUNGO, THE UNITED NATIONS AND ECONOMIC SANCTIONS AGAINST RHODESIA (1973); A. LOWENFELD, *supra* note 212, at 259–319, 697–869; C. PALLEY, THE CCONSTITUTIONAL HISTORY AND LAW OF SOUTH-

ration of independence of Southern Rhodesia by the minority regime of Ian Smith on November 11, 1965, the Security Council for the first time in U.N. history, acting under Chapter VII of the Charter, imposed mandatory, though selective, sanctions against Southern Rhodesia under Resolution 232 of December 16, 1966.[217] Urging "all States to do their utmost to break off economic relations with Southern Rhodesia,"[218] the Security Council mandates, among other things, that all member states of the United Nations impose import and export embargoes against Southern Rhodesia and refuse financial or other economic aid to the Smith regime.[219] The record of compliance has been dismal and is dramatized, in open defiance of the United Nations mandatory sanctions, by the congressional enactment and belated repeal of the Byrd Amendment for importation of Rhodesian chrome to the United States.[220] Similarly, in response to South Africa's policies and practices of

---

ERN RHODESIA, 1888-1965 (1966) (for background history prior to the Unilateral Declaration of Independence); K. YOUNG, RHODESIA AND INDEPENDENCE: A STUDY IN BRITISH COLONIAL POLICY (1969); Doxey, *The Rhodesian Sanctions Experiment,* 25 Y.B. WORLD AFFAIRS 142 (1971); Fawcett, *Security Council Resolutions on Rhodesia,* 41 BRIT. Y.B. INT'L L. 103 (1968); Galtung, *On the Effects of International Economic Sanctions with Examples from the Case of Rhodesia,* 19 WORLD POLITICS 378 (1967); McDougal & Reisman, *supra* note 147.

Regarding sanctions against South Africa, *see* chapter 7 *infra*, at notes 559–98 and accompanying text. *See also* SANCTIONS AGAINST SOUTH AFRICA (R. Segal ed. 1964); J. SPENCE, REPUBLIC UNDER PRESSURE (1965); Dale, *South Africa and the International Community,* 18 WORLD POLITICS 297 (1966); Doxey, *International Sanctions: A Framework for Analysis with Special Reference to the UN and Southern Africa,* 26 INT'L ORG. 527 (1972); Mudge, *Domestic Policies and UN Activities: the Cases of Rhodesia and the Republic of South Africa,* 21 INT'L ORG. 55 (1967).

217. S.C. Res. 232 (1966), *Resolutions and Decisions of the Security Council, 1966,* 7, 21 U.N. SCOR, U.N. Doc. 5/INF/21/Rev. 1 (1966).

218. *Id.*

219. *Id.*

220. *See* A. LAKE, THE "TAR BABY" OPTION, AMERICAN POLICY TOWARD SOUTHERN RHODESIA (1976); *U.N. Sanctions against Rhodesia-Chrome: Hearings on S. 1404 before the Senate Comm. on Foreign Relations,* 92d Cong., 1st Sess. (1971); *Sanctions as an Instrumentality of the United Nations—Rhodesia as a Case Study: Hearings before the Subcomm. on International Organizations and Movements of House Comm. on Foreign Affairs,* 92d Cong., 2d Sess. (1972); *Hearings on Rhodesian Sanctions Bill before Subcomm. on International Organizations and Movements of House Comm. on Foreign Affairs,* 94th Cong., 1st Sess. (1975); *Rhodesian Sanctions: Hearings on S. 174 before the Subcomm. on African Affairs of the Senate Comm. on Foreign Relations,* 95th Cong., 1st Sess. (1977) (dealing with a bill to amend the United Nations Participation Act of 1945 to halt the importation of Rhodesian chrome); *Ambassador Young Testifies on Rhodesian Sanctions Bill,* 76 DEP'T STATE BULL. 271 (1977); *Department Urges Passage of Bill to Halt Importation of Rhodesian Chrome,* 76 DEP'T STATE BULL. 170 (1977) (statements by Secretary Vance and Assistant Secretary Katz); Note, *The Rhodesian Chrome Statute: The Congressional Response to United Nations Economic Sanctions against Southern Rhodesia,* 58 VA. L. REV. 511 (1972); *Vance Begins Drive to End U.S. Imports of Rhodesian Chrome,* N.Y. Times, Feb. 11, 1977, at A1, col. 1 (city ed.); *House Votes, 250–146, to Stop Importing Rhodesian Chrome, id.*, Mar. 15, 1977, at 1, col. 6.

apartheid and its "illegal occupation" of Namibia, both the General Assembly and the Security Council have passed numerous resolutions urging member states of the United Nations to undertake, inter alia, embargoes on arms and other goods (both export and import) and measures of financial control.[221] These resolutions seek especially to "dissuade the main trading partners of South Africa and economic and financial interests from collaborating with the Government of South Africa and companies registered in South Africa."[222] The result to date has been as negligible as in regard to Rhodesia. As noted by the Special Committee on Apartheid, the main trading partners of South Africa have ignored the United Nations resolutions and, consequently, "the United Nations action on *apartheid* has remained far from effective."[223] Reisman has sharply pointed out:

> In a world of fragmented and selfish loyalties, there is a scant possibility of a united front against Pretoria. One of the sad ironies of the struggle for freedom in Africa has been that a number of African states, vociferous in their condemnation of racism, have slipped under the economic dam which they themselves erected against white minority regimes in southern Africa.[224]

The general difficulties with mobilizing effective economic sanctions do not mean that the economic instrument is under all circumstances ineffective as a sanctioning measure against human rights deprivations. Given a wide range of potential sanctioners and the intricate division of labor in the contemporary world, there is selective vulnerability that can be exploited by skillful management. In its recent amendments to the Foreign Assistance Act, the Congress has made it the policy of the United States to refuse "security assistance" (both military and economic) to "any country the government of which engages in a consistent pattern of gross violations of internationally recognized human rights."[225] While a blanket application of this provision may not produce desired results

---

221. *See* chapter 7 *infra,* at notes 449–511 and 555–98 and accompanying text.

222. G.A. Res. 2506, para. 5, 24 U.N. GAOR Supp. (No. 30) 23, U.N. Doc. A/7630 (1969). For other, related, resolutions, see chapter 7 *infra,* at notes 561–79 and accompanying text.

223. *Policies of Apartheid of the Government of South Africa: Implementation by States of United Nations Resolutions on Apartheid* 5, U.N. Doc. A/9168 (1973) (report of the Special Committee on Apartheid).

224. Reisman, *Polaroid Power: Taxing Business for Human Rights,* 4 FOREIGN POLICY 101, 103–04 (1971).

225. International Security Assistance and Arms Export Control Act of 1976, Public Law 94-329, § 301(a) (amending § 502B of the Foreign Assistance Act of 1961). *See* HUMAN RIGHTS REPORTS PREPARED BY THE DEPARTMENT OF STATE IN ACCORDANCE WITH SECTION 502(B) OF THE FOREIGN ASSISTANCE ACT, AS AMENDED, SUBMITTED TO THE SUBCOMM. ON

(or may even be counter-productive) in the short term, its long-term aggregate effect promises to be beneficial to the defense and fulfillment of human rights.[226] Comparable observations could be made in regard to attempts by multilateral lending agencies, such as the World Bank, at withholding international loans from states violating human rights.[227] Sanctions conducted by private groups can sometimes be quite effective, as demonstrated by the boycott of travel to Mexico organized by Jewish groups in the United States in protest against Mexico's endorsement of the United Nations Zionism resolution.[228]

FOREIGN ASSISTANCE OF THE SENATE COMM. ON FOREIGN RELATIONS, 95TH CONG., 1ST SESS. (Comm. Print 1977) [hereinafter cited as HUMAN RIGHTS REPORTS].

See also DEPARTMENT OF STATE, HUMAN RIGHTS PRACTICES IN COUNTRIES RECEIVING U.S. SECURITY ASSISTANCE : REPORT SUBMITTED TO THE HOUSE COMMITTEE ON INTERNATIONAL RELATIONS, 95th Cong., 1st Sess. (Comm. Print 1977); DEPARTMENT OF STATE, COUNTRY REPORTS ON HUMAN RIGHTS PRACTICES: REPORT SUBMITTED TO THE HOUSE COMM. ON INTERNATIONAL RELATIONS AND THE SENATE COMM. ON FOREIGN RELATIONS, 95th Cong., 2d Sess. (Joint Comm. Print 1978); FOREIGN AFFAIRS AND NATIONAL DEFENSE DIVISION, CONGRESSIONAL RESEARCH SERVICE, LIBRARY OF CONGRESS, THE STATUS OF HUMAN RIGHTS IN SELECTED COUNTRIES AND THE U.S. RESPONSE: PREPARED FOR THE SUBCOMM. ON INTERNATIONAL ORGANIZATIONS OF THE HOUSE COMM. ON INTERNATIONAL RELATIONS, 95th Cong., 1st Sess. (Comm. Print 1977); FOREIGN AFFAIRS AND NATIONAL DEFENSE DIVISION, CONGRESSIONAL RESEARCH SERVICE, LIBRARY OF CONGRESS, HUMAN RIGHTS CONDITIONS IN SELECTED COUNTRIES AND THE U.S. RESPONSE: PREPARED FOR THE SUBCOMM. ON INTERNATIONAL ORGANIZATIONS OF THE HOUSE COMM. ON INTERNATIONAL RELATIONS, 95th Cong., 2d Sess. (Comm. Print 1978); *Foreign Assistance Legislation for Fiscal Year 1979 (part 4): Hearings before the Subcomm. on International Organizations of the House Comm. on International Relations,* 95th Cong., 2d Sess. (1978).

For a nonofficial appraisal, *see* CENTER FOR INTERNATIONAL POLICY, HUMAN RIGHTS AND THE U.S. FOREIGN ASSISTANCE PROGRAM, FISCAL YEAR 1978, PART 1—LATIN AMERICA (1977). *See also* Salzberg & Young, *The Parliamentary Role in Implementing International Human Rights: A U.S. Example,* 12 TEXAS INT'L L.J. 251 (1977).

226. The abolition of the secret security agency by the government of Chile in Aug. 1977, in response to the pressures of the United States, is quite instructive. *See Secret Police Agency Is Abolished in Chile,* N.Y. Times, Aug. 13, 1977, at 1, col. 4 (city ed.); *U.S. Aides in Chile Find Shift on Rights, id.,* Aug. 12, 1977, at A5, col. 1.

Cf. Chile: The Status of Human Rights and Its Relationship to U.S. Economic Assistance Programs: Hearings before the Subcomm. on International Organizations of the House Comm. on International Relations, 94th Cong., 2d Sess. (1976).

227. *See International Development Institutions Authorizations—1977: Hearings on H.R. 5262 before the Subcomm. on International Development Institutions and Finance of House Comm. on Banking, Finance and Urban Affairs,* 95th Cong., 1st Sess. (1977). *See also U.S. for Rights Curb on World Bank Loan,* N.Y. Times, Mar. 24, 1977, at A1, col. 5 (city ed.); *Rights Move Tied to World Bank Funds Defeated, id.,* June 15, 1977, at D5, col. 1; Farnsworth, *Linking Aid Plans to Human Rights, id.,* June 19, 1977, § 3, at 5, col. 1.

228. The reference is to G.A. Res. 3379, 30 U.N. GAOR, Supp. (No. 34) 83, U.N. Doc. A/10034 (1975). This resolution characterizes "Zionism" as a form of racism, without defining what is meant by Zionism. The indignation aroused by this resolution, especially among the Jewish community, was immediate and widespread. As a means of protest, the

Though direct control over resources and the management of wealth processes are still largely reserved to the exclusive competence of nation-states, the organized general community is acquiring an increasing experience in the promotion of economic development and in the management of credit and monetary policies. As the elites of nation-states come to grips with the perception that their own prosperity depends upon the prosperity of all lands, especially those less developed, a critical dimension is added to the global program of development and fulfillment of human rights. The positive employment of the economic instrument could facilitate an integrated solution to the global problems of development, augmenting aggregate production and fulfillment of wealth and other values. The expansion of this constructive role, built upon rich experience, could greatly enhance the potential of the economic instrument in promoting a desired world public order of human dignity.

THE MILITARY INSTRUMENT

The military instrument, involving implements of desctruction, is commonly associated with coercion and the destruction of human rights. Even this instrument, however, may be employed, by either the organized general community or by individual states, to protect human rights. Thus, the constructive use of the military instrument for collective security—for the maintenance of minimum public order—does bear directly upon the defense and fulfillment of human rights. Minimum public order is indispensable to human rights in the broadest sense of the optimum shaping and sharing of all values.[229]

The employment of violence and other intense coercion against the human person is, however, basically incompatible with human dignity. Hence, a general community aspiring toward human dignity values must seek to minimize the employment of such violence and coercion as an instrument of change in the shaping and sharing of values. The employment of violence and coercion in authoritative sanctioning measures can only be a last resort.

It must be recognized that the employment of the military instrument

---

Jewish community in the United States undertook selective measures against selected targets, attempting, for example, to influence the Mexican government by boycotting travel to Mexico. For further background, *see* chapter 11 *infra,* at note 189 and accompanying text.

229. The point was eloquently made by President Kennedy: "Is not peace, in the last analysis, basically a matter of human rights?" Address at the American University, June 10, 1963.

For a perceptive analysis, *see* Toth, *Human Rights and World Peace,* in 1 René Cassin, *supra* note 39, at 362–82.

for the purpose of maintaining minimum public order (peace and security) has not been very effective. This is a large unsolved problem in the global constitutive process of authoritative decision. Control over the implements of military strategy remains in the nation-state. Efforts to transfer to the general community the sole privilege of permissible employment of force have not been successful. The original plan to establish within the United Nations a permanent international military force for the maintenance of minimum order was stillborn.[230]

The fundamental general community policies commonly postulated, in customary international law and in the United Nations Charter, as constituting minimum public order are complementary in nature. In a world arena in which authoritative and effective power is still largely unorganized and decentralized, it cannot be expected that the various lesser communities of humankind can achieve even a minimum security, much less optimal fulfillment of human rights, if they are completely denied appropriate measures in, and capabilities of, self-help. The authoritative prescriptions of customary international law and the United Nations Charter thus, quite rationally, distinguish between impermissible coercion ("acts of aggression," "threats to the peace," "breach of the peace," "intervention," and so on) and permissible coercion ("self-defense," "collective self-defense," "police action," "humanitarian intervention," "reprisals," and so on) and simultaneously demand, in further complementarity, the promotion of human rights, self-determination, and economic development.[231] As difficult as it has been for the general community to regulate employment of the military instrument for the maintenance of minimum order, it has been even more difficult to regulate such employment for the protection of human rights.

---

230. *See* U.N. Charter, Arts. 43, 45, 46, and 47.

On United Nations peacekeeping, *see generally* L. Bloomfield, et al., International Military Forces (1964); D. Bowett, United Nations Forces (1964); J. Boyd, United Nations Peace-Keeping Operations: A Military and Political Appraisal (1972); A. Burns & N. Heathcote, Peace-Keeping by UN Forces (1962); Canadian Institute of International Affairs, Peacekeeping: International Challenge and Canadian Response (1968); A. Cox, Prospects for Peacekeeping (1967); L. Fabian, Soldiers without Enemies: Preparing the United Nations for Peacekeeping (1971); P. Frydenberg, Peace-Keeping: Experience and Evaluation (1964); W. Frye, United Nations Peace Force (1957); L. Goodrich & A. Simons, The United Nations and the Maintenance of International Peace and Security (1955); R. Higgins, United Nations Peacekeeping, 1946–1967: Documents and Commentary (1969–70); A. James, The Politics of Peace-Keeping (1969); G. Rosner, The United Nations Emergency Force (1963); R. Russell, United Nations Experience with Military Forces: Political and Legal Aspects (1964).

231. *See* McDougal, *Foreword,* in J. Moore, Law and the Indo-China War vii–xiv (1972). *See also* J. Moore, *supra,* at 163–73.

Historically, when states have employed the military instrument to protect human rights within other states, their action has been described and justified under the label of "humanitarian intervention."[232] In keeping with the natural law traditions and more secular perceptions of humanitarian responsibilities transcending geographical boundaries, the doctrine of humanitarian intervention is asserted to express humankind's abiding concern for the survival and sanctity of human life and for a basic human solidarity.[233] The employment of the military instrument for humanitarian purposes has traditionally been related to the protection of two different groups of victims. First, such protection has been extended to nationals abroad in order to secure compliance with the minimum standards for the treatment of aliens under customary international law.[234] The use of force for this purpose was fully permissible prior to the United Nations Charter, because at that time even war itself was a permissible instrument for change in interstate relations. Secondly, protection through the military instrument has upon occasion been extended to nonnationals in order to deter and terminate atrocious deprivations of human rights by a particular state against its own nation-

232. On humanitarian intervention, *see* M. GANJI, INTERNATIONAL PROTECTION OF HUMAN RIGHTS 9–44 (1962) [hereinafter cited as M. GANJI]; HUMANITARIAN INTERVENTION AND THE UNITED NATIONS (R. Lillich ed. 1973) (including conference proceedings, and papers by Brownlie, Farer, Reisman [with the collaboration of McDougal], and Fonteyne) [hereinafter cited as HUMANITARIAN INTERVENTION]; L. SOHN & T. BUERGENTHAL, *supra* note 39, at 137–211; Brownlie, *Humanitarian Intervention,* in LAW AND CIVIL WAR IN THE MODERN WORLD 217–28 (J. Moore ed. 1974) [hereinafter cited as Brownlie]; *Chilstrom, Humanitarian Intervention under Contemporary International Law: A Policy-Oriented Approach,* 1 YALE STUDIES IN WORLD PUBLIC ORDER 93 (1974); Claydon, *Humanitarian Intervention and International Law,* 1 QUEENS INTRAMURAL L.J. 36 (1969); Fonteyne, *The Customary International Law Doctrine of Humanitarian Intervention: Its Current Validity under the U.N. Charter,* 4 CALIF. WESTERN INT'L L.J. 203 (1974); Franck & Rodley, *After Bangladesh: The Law of Humanitarian Intervention by Military Force,* 67 AM. J. INT'L L. 275 (1973); *The International Protection of Human Rights by General International Law,* in INTERNATIONAL LAW ASSOCIATION, REPORT OF THE FIFTH CONFERENCE, NEW YORK 608–24 (1972); Lillich, *Forcible Self-Help to Protect Human Rights,* 53 IOWA L. REV. 325 (1967) [hereinafter cited as Lillich, *Forcible Self-Help*]; Lillich, *Humanitarian Intervention: A Reply to Dr. Brownlie and a Plea for Constructive Alternatives,* in LAW AND CIVIL WAR IN THE MODERN WORLD 229–51 (J. Moore ed. 1974) [hereinafter cited as Lillich]; Lillich, *Intervention to Protect Human Rights,* 15 MCGILL L.J. 205 (1969); McDougal & Reisman, *Response,* 3 INT'L LAWYER 438 (1969); Wiseberg, *Humanitarian Intervention: Lessons from the Nigerian Civil War,* 7 HUMAN RIGHTS J. 61 (1974).

233. *See* M. GANJI, *supra* note 232, at 9–14; A. THOMAS & A. THOMAS, NON-INTERVENTION: THE LAW AND ITS IMPORT IN THE AMERICAS 372–73 (1956) [hereinafter cited as A. THOMAS & A. THOMAS]; Reisman, *Humanitarian Intervention to Protect the Ibos,* in HUMANITARIAN INTERVENTION, *supra* note 232, at 167, 168–70 [hereinafter cited as Reisman].

234. *See* E. BORCHARD, *supra* note 178, at 445–56; A. THOMAS & A. THOMAS, *supra* note 233, at 303–58.

als or the nationals of third states. In a restrictive sense, the label "humanitarian intervention" is sometimes made to refer only to this type of situation.[235] The doctrine stipulates, in more detailed specification, that where egregious violations of human rights are occurring within a state whose government will not or cannot stop them, the general community, or in exigent circumstances a single state, may enter into the territory of the defaulting state for the purposes of terminating the outrage and securing compliance with a minimum international standard of human rights.

A classic statement of this doctrine, cutting so deeply into parochial notions of sovereignty, is offered by Borchard:

> [W]here a state under exceptional circumstances disregards certain rights of its own citizens, over whom presumably it has absolute sovereignty, the other states of the family of nations are authorized by international law to intervene on grounds of humanity. When these "human" rights are habitually violated, one or more states may intervene in the name of the society of nations and may take such measures as to substitute at least temporarily, if not permanently, its own sovereignty for that of the state thus controlled. Whatever the origin, therefore, of the rights of the individual, it seems assured that these essential rights rest upon the ultimate sanction of international law, and will be protected, in last resort, by the most appropriate organ of the international community. . . .[236]

The practice commonly invoked to establish the community expectations making humanitarian intervention lawful has been subjected to varying interpretations. A number of important historical examples would appear, however, to vindicate the remedy when employed under appropriate circumstances of necessity and proportionality. Among the more notable of these examples are the intervention on behalf of the Greeks in 1830;[237] the intervention in 1860–61 by Austria, France, Great Britain, Prussia, and Russia on behalf of the persecuted Christian population in Syria;[238] the intervention in 1866–68 on behalf of the oppressed Christian population in Crete;[239] the Russian intervention against Tur-

---

235. Such restrictive reference is offered in Oppenheim-Lauterpacht: "[W]hen a State renders itself guilty of cruelties against and persecution of its nationals in such a way as to deny their fundamental human rights and to shock the conscience of mankind, intervention in the interest of humanity is legally permissible." 1 L. OPPENHEIM, INTERNATIONAL LAW 312 (8th ed. H. Lauterpacht ed. 1955).

236. E. BORCHARD, *supra* note 178, at 14.

237. *See* M. GANJI, *supra* note 232, at 22–24; Reisman, *supra* note 233, at 179–80.

238. *See* M. GANJI, *supra* note 232, at 24–26; L. SOHN & T. BUERGENTHAL, *supra* note 39, at 143–78; Reisman, *supra* note 233, at 180–81.

239. *See* M. GANJI, *supra* note 232, at 26–29; Reisman, *supra* note 233, at 181.

key concerning Bosnia, Herzegovina, and Bulgaria in 1877–78;[240] the intervention in 1903–08 by Austria, France, Great Britain, Italy, and Russia against Turkey for its misrule of Macedonia;[241] and the humanitarian intercession with Turkey by the United States and others on behalf of Armenians in 1904–16.[242]

The advent of the United Nations, with all its fundamental changes in community prescriptions about the use of force, has generated considerable controversy about the continuing permissibility of humanitarian intervention. Discarding the confused term "war," the Charter has prohibited the deliberate use of coercion in terms of "threat or use of force," "threat to the peace," "breach of the peace," and "act of aggression." These references, taken as a whole, could be made to cover not only "war" in the sense of comprehensive and highly intense use of the military instrument, but also those applications of force of a lesser intensity and magnitude previously labeled as "short of war."[243] Article 2(4), the cornerstone of the Charter system, stipulates: "All Members shall refrain in their international relations from the threat or use of force against the territorial integrity or political independence of any state, or in any manner inconsistent with the Purposes of the United Nations." The ambiguities in this language are obviously multiple.

One view takes the position that humanitarian intervention is now impermissible.[244] The arguments for this view may be summarized, perhaps somewhat cryptically and unsympathetically, as follows: (1) projecting the basic policies of promoting peaceful change and of minimizing unauthorized coercion, the United Nations Charter as a whole prohibits the use of military force save for self-defense and community police action; (2) the blanket prohibition of the use of force embodied in Article 2(4) of the Charter suggests that humanitarian intervention is inconsistent with the purposes of the United Nations and, hence, impermissible; and (3) highly susceptible to abuse, humanitarian intervention is an instrument of naked power for aggrandizement of the powerful against the weak.

A contraposed view, which appears more persuasive, maintains that the remedy of humanitarian intervention is still not only permissible but

---

240. *See* M. Ganji, *supra* note 232, at 29–33; Reisman, *supra* note 233, at 182.

241. *See* M. Ganji, *supra* note 232, at 33–37; Reisman, *supra* note 233, at 183.

242. *See* L. Sohn & T. Buergenthal, *supra* note 39, at 181–94.

243. *See* F. Grob, The Relativity of War and Peace (1949); A. Hindmarsh, Force in Peace (1933).

244. *See, e.g.*, I. Brownlie, Use of Force, *supra* note 58, at 340–41; Brownlie, *supra* note 232; Franck & Rodley, *supra* note 232; Henkin, *Remarks*, 1972 Proc., Am. Soc'y Int'l L. 95–97.

even strengthened under contemporary international law.[245] The nub of this view is that a Charter which has as one of its two principal purposes improvement in the protection of human rights can scarcely be interpreted, in the absence of unmistakable direction, as having abolished a most potent remedy for the protection of such rights. Because of its overriding commitment to the protection and fulfillment of human rights, the Charter would appear, on the contrary, to have fortified the customary remedy of humanitarian intervention. The overriding commitment to the protection and fulfillment of human rights, coequal with that of the maintenance of peace and security, is made manifest throughout the Charter.[246] To achieve the goal of "universal respect for, and observance of, human rights and fundamental freedoms for all without distinction as to race, sex, language, or religion," all member states are obliged, under Article 56, to "take joint and separate action in co-operation with the Organization." This overriding commitment has found further expression in the vast flow of ancillary prescriptions, including the Universal Declaration of Human Rights; the International Covenant on Civil and Political Rights (and its Protocol); the International Covenant on Economic, Social, and Cultural Rights; and a multiplying host of related instruments.[247] Because of this overriding commitment to human rights—a goal intimately interdependent with that of maintaining peace and security—the Charter prohibition of the use of armed force must be interpreted in a way to take this commitment into account. Given the reality and widespread perception of the intimate link between human rights and international peace and security, the use of armed force in defense of human rights may be emphatically in the common interest as a mode of maintaining international peace and security.

Even a literal reading of Article 2(4) of the Charter indicates that the prohibition extends, not to the use of force per se, but to the use of force for specified unlawful purposes—i.e., "against the territorial integrity or political independence of any state, or in any other manner inconsistent with the Purposes of the United Nations." When it seeks neither a territorial change nor a challenge to the political independence of the state concerned, an act of humanitarian intervention not only is not inconsistent with the purposes of the United Nations but rather is in conformity

---

245. *See, e.g.*, J. Stone, Aggression and World Order, *supra* note 58, at 92–103; Chilstrom, *supra* note 232; the articles by Lillich cited in note 232 *supra*; Reisman, *supra* note 233.

246. Recall U.N. Charter, Preamble, Arts. 1(3), 13(1), 55, 56, 62(2), and 76.

247. *See* notes 325–46 *infra* and accompanying text.

with the major purposes and norms of the Charter.[248] Article 2(4) is, therefore, no necessary bar to an otherwise appropriate act of humanitarian intervention.

In the absence of effective centralized decision and enforcement, the remedy of humanitarian intervention may continue to have rational place. The general ban in the Charter on the use of force was predicated upon the establishment within the United Nations of effective centralized decision and enforcement. So long as this projected condition remains unfulfilled, the general community cannot afford a paralysis which invites particular states to violate grossly the rights of individuals. In circumstances in which the organized general community (through an authoritative organ of the United Nations or a relevant regional organization) either cannot act or cannot act with sufficient dispatch, the intervention of particular states—whether acting individually or in coordination—may offer the only alternative for defense of the common interest in human rights. Hence, insofar as a humanitarian intervention is precipitated by egregious human rights deprivations and conforms rigorously to the international legal regulations governing the use of force—notably the principles of necessity and proportionality—such intervention constitutes a vindication and functional enforcement of the international law of human rights.[249]

The continued availability in general community expectation of the remedy of humanitarian intervention would appear confirmed by recent practice. Three important examples of such practice include the Congo rescue operation, the Indian activities in Bangladesh, and the Entebee operation undertaken by Israel to rescue the hostages held in the Entebee airport in Uganda.[250] The salient features of these examples may be indicated.

The Congo Case

In late 1964, a rebel group in the Congo seized thousands of civilians and held them as hostages, in contravention of the Geneva Conventions,

---

248. *See* J. Stone, Aggression and World Order, *supra* note 58, at 95–96; Reisman, *supra* note 233, at 176–78.

249. Reisman, *supra* note 233, at 177. *See* Scelle, *supra* note 8; Reisman, *Sanctions and Enforcement,* in 3 The Future of the International Legal Order 273–335 (C. Black & R. Falk eds. 1971).

250. A more controversial case relates to United States intervention, to rescue U.S. nationals and other nationals, in the Dominican Republic in 1965. *See* A. Thomas & A. Thomas, The Dominican Republic Crisis, 1965 (J. Carey ed. Hammarskjold Forum 1967); Dupuy, *Les Etats-Unis, l'O.E.A. et l'O.N.U. à Saint-Dominque,* 11 Annuaire Français de Droit International 71 (1965); Meeker, *The Dominican Situation in Perspective of International Law,* 53 Dep't State Bull. 60 (1965); Nanda, *The United States Action in the Dominican Crisis: Impact on World Order,* 43 Denver L.J. 439 (1966).

in order to extract concessions from the central government. While the concessions were being denied, forty-five of the civilian hostages were slaughtered. The situation was further exacerbated by the imminent threat that the rest of the hostages would be massacred, a threat confirmed by an intercepted telegram from a rebel general to a field officer. A Belgian paratroop battalion, transported by United States planes and supported by British facilities, was first moved to the Ascension Islands. When further negotiations for the release of the hostages came to naught, the paratroopers were dropped at Stanleyville in an emergency rescue mission, in which some two thousand persons (of nineteen different nationalities) were evacuated in four days.

Undertaken with the consent of the central government of the Congo, the operation was discontinued as soon as the rescue had been completed. The Department of State had offered this explanation:

> [T]his operation is humanitarian—not military. It is designed to avoid bloodshed—not to engage the rebel forces in combat. Its purpose is to accomplish its task quickly and withdraw—not to seize or hold territory. Personnel are engaged under order to use force only in their own defense or in the defense of the foreign or Congolese civilians. They will depart from the scene as soon as their evacuation mission is accomplished.[251]

The rescue operation was attacked in the Security Council by several African states and the Soviet Union largely in terms of encroachment upon domestic jurisdiction. Significantly, the fact that the mission had been executed by individual states rather than United Nations forces did not give rise to serious challenge, and the Security Council did not condemn the action. The majority of the scholars who have appraised the operation have concluded that it was permissible.[252]

The Bangladesh Case

In the general elections held in December 1970 and January 1971, the Awami League (the East Pakistani political party led by Sheik Mujib Rahman) won a majority of the seats in the National Assembly of Pakistan. The government of Pakistan refused, however, to convene the National Assembly in order to prevent a power shift from West to East Pakistan and to frustrate the East Pakistan demand for autonomy. While the negotiations for a political settlement between the government and the Awami League were supposedly in progress, the Pakistan army,

---

251. 51 Dep't State Bull. 842 (1964).

252. *See, e.g.*, J. Brierly, The Law of Nations 427–28 (6th ed. H. Waldock ed. 1963); Lillich, *Forcible Self-Help, supra* note 232, at 340; Reisman, *supra* note 233, at 185–86.

without warning, struck the civilian population of East Pakistan on the night of March 25, 1971. The Pakistan army employed excessive force and repressive measures to "pacify" the population, causing a heavy loss of life and a mass destruction of villages, towns, and property. Amid a continuing stream of reports and allegations of "genocide," "brutal atrocities," "horrors," rapes, and so on, millions of refugees fled from East Pakistan into India. India intervened militarily, and the atrocities were terminated upon the fall of Dacca on December 16, 1971.[253]

While the atrocities were rampant for nine months, the general organized community (notably the United Nations) displayed its stark inaction and impotence (except for assumption of part of the burden of the refugees pouring into India).[254] The United Nations broke its protracted silence only after the outbreak of a full-scale Indo-Pakistani war, when the Security Council was convened on December 4, 1971. As the Security Council was paralyzed by the Soviet vetoes, the matter was referred to the General Assembly. On December 7, 1971, the Assembly promptly adopted a resolution calling for an immediate cease-fire and withdrawal of troops.[255] Subsequently, when the Security Council was reconvened on December 12, 1971, it was able to adopt a resolution only on December 21, after the fall of Dacca (and the birth of the Republic of Bangladesh) and the cessation of hostilities, calling for strict observance of the cease-fire and withdrawal of troops "as soon as practicable."[256]

While the Assembly resolution calling for an immediate cease-fire was adopted by an overwhelming majority, none of the U.N. organs con-

---

253. For a detailed factual account, *see* THE SECRETARIAT OF THE INTERNATIONAL COMMISSION OF JURISTS, THE EVENTS IN EAST PAKISTAN, 1971, at 15–45 (1972) [hereinafter cited as THE EVENTS IN EAST PAKISTAN]. For an abbreviated version of this study, see *East Pakistan Staff Study,* 8 REV. INT'L COMM'N JURISTS 23 (1972).

A comprehensive collection of documents relating to this crisis was compiled in 1971 by the Ministry of External Affairs, India, entitled BANGLA DESH: DOCUMENTS. *See also Documents: Civil War in Pakistan,* 4 N.Y.U.J. INT'L L. & POLITICS 524 (1971).

See also Franck & Rodley, *The Law, the United Nations and Bangla Desh,* 2 ISRAEL Y.B. HUMAN RIGHTS 142 (1972); Heck, *East Pakistan Refugees,* 584 INT'L CONCILIATION 201 (1971); La Porte, *Pakistan in 1971: The Disintegration of a Nation,* 12 ASIAN SURVEY 87 (1972); MacDermot, *Crimes against Humanity in Bangladesh,* 7 INT'L LAWYER 476 (1973); Nanda, *Self-Determination in International Law: The Tragic Tale of Two Cities—Islamabad (West Pakistan) and Dacca (East Pakistan),* 66 AM. J. INT'L L. 321 (1972); Schanberg, *Pakistan Divided,* 50 FOREIGN AFFAIRS 125 (1971).

254. *See The Situation in the India-Pakistan Subcontinent,* Y.B.U.N. 1971, at 137–43. For critical observations of this inaction of the general organized community, *see* THE EVENTS IN EAST PAKISTAN, *supra* note 223, at 76–84; Nanda, *A Critique of the United Nations Inaction in the Bangladesh Crisis,* 49 DENVER L.J. 53 (1972); Salzberg, *UN Prevention of Human Rights Violations: The Bangladesh Case,* 27 INT'L ORG. 115 (1973).

255. G.A. Res. 2793, 26 U.N. GAOR, Supp. (No. 29) 3, U.N. Doc. A/8429 (1971).

256. S.C. Res. 307 (1971), Dec. 21, 1971.

demned India for its military intervention in East Pakistan.[257] Although the Indian government justified its action largely in terms of self-defense,[258] it would appear that its action could have been more appropriately justified under the doctrine of humanitarian intervention. Given the egregious deprivations of life and other human rights, the mass influx of refugees to India, the protracted impotence of the general organized community amid the exigencies of the mounting military crisis, it would appear that India's action fulfilled the requirements of necessity and proportionality and constituted a lawful exercise of humanitarian intervention.[259] It is not without significance that Bangladesh quickly secured an overwhelming record of recognition by other states, notwithstanding the vital role played by India's military intervention.[260]

The Entebbe Rescue Operation

On the night of July 3–4, 1976, following the highjacking several days earlier at Athens of an Air France plane to Entebee Airport in Uganda the Israeli military forces landed at Entebbe to rescue some one hundred hostages and return them to Israel. The operation came only hours before the deadline of agonizing, fruitless negotiations for the release of the hostages, and lasted for only about ninety minutes. The Israel rescue mission left some people dead and caused some damage to Ugandan property.[261] When the Security Council met in an emergency session, Uganda and its supporters charged that Israel had violated the sovereignty and territorial integrity of Uganda. But the Security Council failed to adopt any resolution.[262] The Israeli operation would, among other things, appear justified as a humanitarian intervention permitted under contemporary international law. One contemporary appraisal reads:

> In a context of the most inhumane deprivations and the failure of the Ugandan government to give protection, it can only be Op-

257. *See Communications concerning India-Pakistan Question,* Y.B.U.N. 1971, at 143–61.

258. *See* 26 U.N. SCOR (1606th mtg.) 14–18, U.N. Doc. S/PV 1606 (1971); 26 U.N. SCOR (1608th mtg.) 7–10, 14, 27–28, U.N. Doc. S/PV 1608 (1971); 26 U.N. SCOR (1611th mtg.) 4–14, U.N. Doc. S/PV 1611 (1971).

259. The study undertaken by the International Commission of Jurists arrived at the same conclusion. THE EVENTS IN EAST PAKISTAN, *supra* note 223, at 96, 98. For a contrary appraisal, *see* Franck & Rodley, *supra* note 232.

260. *See Recognition of Bangladesh: Hearings on S. Con. Res. 55, S. Con. Res. 58, and S. Res. 242 before the Senate Comm. on Foreign Relations,* 92d Cong., 2d Sess. (1972), especially at 49.

261. For a detailed, though somewhat romanticized, factual account, *see* W. STEVENSON, 90 MINUTES AT ENTEBBE (1976).

262. *See Council Fails to Adopt Draft Resolution after Considering Uganda Hijacking Issue,* 13 UN MONTHLY CHRONICLE 15 (Aug.–Sept. 1976).

> posite-speak to describe the rescue operation as an act of aggression against Uganda. The action of the Israelis could not possibly have had the effect of threatening the territorial integrity or political independence of Uganda. This action, on the contrary, was entirely necessary and proportionate to the lawful purposes of the rescue.[263]

While the remedy of humanitarian intervention may continue to have a place under contemporary international law, it is important to recognize that, in a decentralized world in which the effective power of state participants is patently discrepant, this remedy is highly susceptible to abuse. Any particular state, further, undertakes humanitarian intervention at its own peril. The characterization by an intervening state of particular acitivities as requiring humanitarian intervention partakes of the nature of a provisional determination in precisely the same way as a claim of self-defense, and remains subject both to the contemporaneous appraisal of other states and to any subsequent review the organized community may eventually exercise.[264]

There can of course be no easy and dogmatic intellectual procedures for distinguishing between genuine and spurious acts of humanitarian intervention. Any serious review of a particular instance from general community perspectives of the conditions of necessity and proportionality must require a careful contextual scrutiny, appraising systematically and rigorously many features of the particular context. Lawfulness or unlawfulness must depend upon the answers to many questions about each feature of the context, with the significance of any one feature being dependent upon the total configuration.[265] Some of the more important questions about relevant features may be briefly indicated:

Participants

Is the intervention by or against a recognized government, or by or against segments only of a community? Is it on behalf of a substantial segment of an oppressed population? Is it on behalf of nationals or nonnationals of the intervening state? How many states participate in the intervention? Is the general community (collectivity) represented in the action?

---

263. *The Entebbe Rescue and International Law,* N.Y. Times, July 16, 1976, at A20, col. 3 (letter of Myres S. McDougal and Michael Reisman). For a comparable appraisal, *see* Green, *Rescue at Entebbe—Legal Aspects,* 6 Israel Y.B. Human Rights 312 (1976).

264. For such characterization in the context of aggression and self-defense, *see* M. McDougal & F. Feliciano, *supra* note 55, at 143–260.

265. For an excellent comparable analysis, *see* Chilstrom, *supra* note 232, at 134–47.

Perspectives

Are both manifest and genuine objectives related to the preservation of human rights? Is the action being taken to save lives, to rescue from arbitrary incarceration or torture? How are the actions of the intervening state related to the aggregate interest of all states?

Situation

How intense are expectations of irremediable loss in the absence of the immediate use of the military instrument? With regard to what values are deprivations threatened and in what degree of intensity and magnitude? Are the deprivations systematic and of long duration, or sporadic and occasional?

Base Values

What are the disparities in relative strength of the intervening state and the target state? Do differing degrees in strength suggest duress for nonhumanitarian purposes?

Strategies

Have the diplomatic, ideological, and economic instruments been mobilized and employed prior to the use of the military instrument? Has recourse to available remedies through organized collective action been exhausted?

Outcomes

With what intensity and destruction has the military instrument been used? What values were conserved? Was the use of the military instrument in proportion to the intensity of the threats of deprivation? Did the host state or segments of the host state invite military intervention? Was the military intervention terminated as soon as its manifest objectives were accomplished?

In a better-organized world, humankind might be able to dispense with a doctrine of humanitarian intervention which permits a state unilaterally to employ the military instrument against another state for the purpose of securing a minimum international standard of human rights. Until that better organization is more nearly achieved, the task for those who are genuinely committed to human dignity values is, however, that of clarifying and applying a conception of humanitarian intervention which will best serve the common interests of all in achieving at least the minimum conditions of dignified human existence.

OUTCOMES

The outcomes of the comprehensive world constitutive process of authoritative decision are the various types of decisions which are taken in the making and application of law to human rights problems. These different types of decisions are conveniently categorized in terms of seven functions—intelligence, promotion, prescription, invocation, application, termination, and appraisal.[266] The effectiveness and the economy with which all these different functions are performed directly affect the quality of the protection of human rights achieved. It may be noted that in consequence of continuous improvement of all the varying features of the constitutive process described below, there has been observable improvement in the performance of all the different functions. The relevant decisions appear to be becoming more comprehensive, in the sense of embracing all necessary policy functions; more inclusive, in the sense of extension toward participants and interactions affecting common interests; more rational, in the sense of conformity to the basic public order demands and expectations of the peoples of the world; and more integrative, in the sense of molding the potentially divisive claims of peoples into the perception and fact of common interest.

All these decision functions, though distinctive, are of course interrelated. Each decision function contributes to, and is affected by, the performance of every other function.[267] We propose to outline, seriatim, developments with respect to each function.

THE INTELLIGENCE FUNCTION

The intelligence function includes the gathering, processing, and dissemination of information essential to decision making.[268] The impor-

---

266. *See* H. LASSWELL, THE DECISION PROCESS: SEVEN CATEGORIES OF FUNCTIONAL ANALYSIS (1956); H. LASSWELL, A. PRE-VIEW OF POLICY SCIENCES 85-97 (1971); M. MCDOUGAL, H. LASSWELL, & I. VLASIC, *supra* note 172, at 113-27; McDougal, Lasswell, & Reisman, *supra* note 1, at 131-54.

267. *See* McDougal, Lasswell, & Reisman, *supra* note 1, at 131-54.

268. On the intelligence function, *see* Lasswell, *Research in Policy Analysis: The Intelligence and Appraisal Functions,* in 6 HANDBOOK OF POLITICAL SCIENCE 1-22 (F. Greenstein & N. Polsby eds. 1975); McDougal, Lasswell, & Reisman, *The Intelligence Function and World Public Order,* 46 TEMPLE L.Q. 365 (1973) [hereinafter cited as McDougal, Lasswell, & Reisman, *The Intelligence Function*].

More generally, *see* K. DEUTSCH, THE NERVES OF GOVERNMENT: MODELS OF POLITICAL COMMUNICATION AND CONTROL (1966); H. WILENSKY, ORGANIZATIONAL INTELLIGENCE: KNOWLEDGE AND POLICY IN GOVERNMENT AND INDUSTRY (1967); A. DULLES, THE CRAFT OF INTELLIGENCE (1963); R. HILSMAN, STRATEGIC INTELLIGENCE AND NATIONAL DECISIONS (1956); L. KIRKPATRICK, THE U.S. INTELLIGENCE COMMUNITY: FOREIGN POLICY AND DOMESTIC ACTIVITIES (1973); F. MACHLUP, THE PRODUCTION AND DISTRIBUTION OF KNOWLEDGE IN THE UNITED STATES (1962); H. RANSOM, CENTRAL INTELLIGENCE AND NA-

tance of this function inheres in the indispensability of an exploration of the facts as a first step in the performance of every decision function. How well the intelligence function is performed thus bears directly upon the performance of all the other functions. The availability of a continuing flow of dependable, comprehensive, and relevant information is essential to the task of recommending concrete proposals in the common interest, generating rational prescriptions, initiating a timely invocation against a threatened or actual violation of human rights, securing effective application of human rights norms with a minimal recourse to coercion, facilitating timely termination of obsolete prescriptions, and undertaking a critical yet constructive appraisal. In a decentralized, state-centered world in which mobilization of world public opinion plays a most crucial and abiding role in the defense and fulfillment of human rights, effective and continuing exposure of the facts of deprivations and nonfulfillments in every community is instrumental to minimizing deprivations and maximizing fulfillments.

Traditionally, most intelligence gathering is done by the officials of nation-states. This is one of the oldest activities in which governments engage. Some of these activities have been legal and some illegal.[269] States have, however, long employed the cloak of domestic jurisdiction (noninterference in internal affairs) to resist inquiries about what is happening within their borders.[270] More recently, international governmental organizations have participated more and more in gathering information, making studies, and sending missions for fact-finding, despite reluctance to cooperate on the part of states. Similarly, the role of private associations in such activities has been increased. These associations operate both within states and beyond their borders. Nongovernmental organizations, such as the International Commission of Jurists and Amnesty International, have undertaken many intelligence tasks.[271]

TIONAL SECURITY (1958); H. RANSOM, THE INTELLIGENCE ESTABLISHMENT (1970); Colby, *The Developing International Law on Gathering and Sharing Security Intelligence,* 1 YALE STUDIES IN WORLD PUBLIC ORDER 49 (1974); De Sola Pool, *Content Analysis and the Intelligence Function,* in POLITICS, PERSONALITY, AND SOCIAL SCIENCE IN THE TWENTIETH CENTURY: ESSAYS IN HONOR OF HAROLD D. LASSWELL 197–223 (A. Rogow ed. 1969). *See also* Berger, *To Insure Reliable Human-Rights Information,* N.Y. Times, June 4, 1977, at 19, col. 2 (city ed.); McGovern, *The Information Age, id.,* June 9, 1977, at A21, col. 2.

269. *See* M. HALPERIN, et al., THE LAWLESS STATE: THE CRIMES OF THE U.S. INTELLIGENCE AGENCIES (1976); V. MARCHETTI & J. MARKS, THE CIA AND THE CULT OF INTELLIGENCE (1974); T. ROSS & D. WISE, THE INVISIBLE GOVERNMENT (1974); ESSAYS ON ESPIONAGE AND INTERNATIONAL LAW (R. Stanger ed. 1962). *See also* J. BARRON, KGB (1974); R. CONQUEST, THE GREAT TERROR (1968); D. DALLIN, SOVIET ESPIONAGE (1955).

270. *See* notes 147–71 *supra* and accompanying text.

271. Recent Staff Studies of the International Commission of Jurists include THE

In recent times there have been increasing demands for better information about human rights. Many voices are raised in international organizations and private associations. The geographic range of demands is increasing, extending to remote corners of the globe. There is agitation from West to East and from North to South for information about the conditions that affect human rights. Many intelligence activities must of necessity go beyond the boundaries of a single state. The process of disseminating information is facilitated by a global network of the media of communication. As a result, there has been a tremendous flow of information about the shaping and sharing of values around the globe, and about the conditions under which human rights can be protected and fulfilled.

Increasingly, international governmental organizations have played an immensely important role in the gathering, processing, and dissemination of information through their bureaucratic structures. Specific authority is conferred upon various United Nations structures and other international governmental bodies. The General Assembly is empowered, under Article 13 of the Charter, to "initiate studies" for the purpose of "promoting international cooperation in the economic, social, cultural, educational, and health fields, and assisting in the realization of human rights and fundamental freedoms for all without distinction as to race, sex, language, or religion." "The Economic and Social Council," according to Article 62(1) of the Charter, "may make or initiate studies and reports with respect to international economic, social, cultural, educational, health, and related matters." The Council may, further, under Article 64(1) of the Charter,

> take appropriate steps to obtain regular reports from the specialized agencies. It may make arrangements with the Members of the United Nations and with the specialized agencies to obtain reports on the steps taken to give effect to its own recommendations and to

---

EVENTS IN EAST PAKISTAN, 1971 (1972); REPORT OF MISSION TO URUGUAY (1974); REPORT OF MISSION TO CHILE (1974); ASYLUM IN LATIN AMERICA (1975); RACIAL DISCRIMINATION AND REPRESSION IN SOUTHERN RHODESIA (1976); HUMAN RIGHTS AND THE LEGAL SYSTEM IN IRAN (1976) (by William J. Butler & Georges Levasseur). *See Rights Group Assails Philippines Regime,* N.Y. Times, July 31, 1977, § 1, at 9, col. 1 (city ed.).

Amnesty International is especially noted for its worldwide surveys of torture. *See* AMNESTY INTERNATIONAL, REPORT ON TORTURE (1975); AMNESTY INTERNATIONAL, ANNUAL REPORTS, 1974/75 (1975). *See also* AMNESTY INTERNATIONAL, REPORT OF AN AMNESTY INTERNATIONAL MISSION TO THE REPUBLIC OF THE PHILIPPINES, 22 NOVEMBER–5 DECEMBER 1975 (1976); AMNESTY INTERNATIONAL, TAIWAN (REPUBLIC OF CHINA) (1976) (Briefing Paper No. 6); *Amnesty International Lists Over 100 Journalists Held in 25 Countries,* N.Y. Times, Apr. 29, 1977, at A12, col. 3 (city ed.); *Rights Organization Accuses Nicaragua of Widespread Abuses, id.,* Aug. 16, 1977, at 6, col. 1.

recommendations on matters falling within its competence made by the General Assembly.

In actual performance, the great variety of intelligence activities includes seminars (interregional and regional), fellowship programs, advisory services of experts, special studies, exchanges of information and documentation, technical assistance, press and information services, the reporting system, presence of observers, fact-finding missions, and investigation.[272] The Secretariat of the United Nations provides formally within its cellular bureaucracy for the gathering, processing, and dissemination of information about human rights and other problems. As Bailey points out,

> Information reaches the United Nations Secretariat in a continuous stream from a variety of sources: speeches made in the general debate of the General Assembly and in other United Nations bodies, written reports from inter-governmental agencies, governments, and non-governmental organizations, conversations between United Nations officials and national representatives, reports from UNDP resident representatives, information centers, field missions, observation and findings of visiting missions and United Nations committees, research by United Nations officials derived from published sources, and so on.[273]

Under the auspices of the secretary-general, many international seminars have been held in various parts of the world with regard to a wide range of subjects concerning human rights, contributing significantly to the assembling and circulation of human rights information.[274] Many studies have been undertaken, especially by the Commission on Human Rights and its Sub-Commission on Prevention of Discrimination and Protection of Minorities, to provide United Nations organs and others with information concerning a variety of human rights questions.[275] The Economic and Social Council and its network of regional economic commissions, GATT, UNCTAD, and UNDP, are engaged in numerous intelligence activities regarding transnational wealth processes. The World Bank group and the International Monetary Fund collect, process, and disseminate information about the fluctuations of national economies and transnational monetary trends.UNESCO's intelligence

---

272. *See* A. Szalai, M. Croke, & Associates, The United Nations and the News Media (UNITAR, 1972); United Nations Actions, *supra* note 73, at 190–200.

273. S. Bailey, Peaceful Settlement of Disputes: Ideas and Proposals for Research 34–35 (1970).

274. For detail, *see* United Nations Action, *supra* note 73, at 193–95.

275. A recent list can be found in *id.* at 191–92.

activities relate mainly to trends in enlightenment and skills. The concern of the International Labor Organization extends to human rights in the wealth, skill, and well-being sectors. The World Health Organization collects and disseminates information about health and safety conditions around the world, and the FAO assembles and disseminates information about the world's food resources and supply. The United Nations Environment Programme (UNEP) collects and disseminates information concerning the world's environmental conditions. And the United Nations High Commissioner for Refugees (UNHCR) is an important source of information about the plight and conditions of the refugees about the globe. This rather comprehensive flow of information, as exemplified by these examples and further supplemented and fortified by various regional organizations, extends to every value sector.

In performing the intelligence function, international governmental organizations rely heavily upon the cooperation of nation-states. As states remain the primary gatherers and disseminators of information, the world constitutive process must rely extensively in human rights matters, as in so many other matters, upon government reports. Under the League of Nations, the government reporting system was instituted in relation to mandated territories and the international regime of minority protection.[276] Under the United Nations system, governmental reports on trust territories and non-self-governing territories are mandated by the Charter.[277] The Economic and Social Council may, as indicated above, "make arrangements with the Members of the United Nations" to "obtain reports on the steps taken to give effect to its own recommendations and to recommendations on matters falling within its competence made by the General Assembly."[278]

A periodic reporting system on human rights matters was inaugurated, in 1956, by the Economic and Social Council, requiring governments (and also specialized agencies and some nongovernmental organizations) to submit reports to the Commission on Human Rights.[279] In 1965 the reporting system was modified to require submission of information on a continuing three-year cycle: the subject in the first year being civil and political rights; the second year economic, social, and cultural rights; and the third year freedom of information.[280] Although this reporting system not only has served "as a source of information" but also has "furnished a valuable incentive to Governments to promote

---

276. *See* Q. Wright, Mandates under the League of Nations 159–89 (1930).
277. U.N. Charter, Arts. 73(e), 87(a), and 88.
278. U.N. Charter, Art. 64(1).
279. ECOSOC Res. 624B (XXII) (1956); ECOSOC Res. 888B (XXXIV) (1962).
280. ECOSOC Res. 1074c (XXXIX) (1965).

and protect those rights,"[281] it has been less than adequate. Many states have simply ignored repeated requests for reports; when reports are submitted, they tend to be perfunctory and self-serving and to avoid the core problem of the actual behavior of governments concerned.[282]

The reporting system is an important feature in most of the transnational human rights instruments, notably the two International Covenants on Human Rights,[283] the International Convention on the Elimination of All Forms of Racial Discrimination,[284] the Convention on the Political Rights of Women, the Convention Relating to the Status of Refugees of 1951,[285] the Protocol Relating to the Status of Refugees of 1966,[286] the Convention Relating to the Status of Stateless Persons of 1954,[287] and the Supplementary Convention on the Abolition of Slavery, the Slave Trade, and Institutions and Practices Similar to Slavery.[288]

An important method for obtaining dependable information is of course on-the-spot investigations in the form of fact-finding commissions (commissions of inquiry).[289] Such a practice antedates the rise of contemporary international organization, and has long been employed by nation-states, bilaterally or multilaterally, gaining wide acceptance at the 1899 Hague Convention.[290] Subsequently, international organiza-

---

281. *Draft Report of the Ad Hoc Committee on Periodic Reports* 17, U.N. Doc. E/CN.4/AC.20/L.19 (1969). *See also Periodic Reports on Human Rights,* U.N. Doc. E/CN.4/980/Rev. 1 (1969).

282. *See, e.g., Periodic Reports on Human Rights: Analytical Summary of Reports and Other Material on Economic, Social and Cultural Rights for the Period 1 July 1969 to 30 June 1973, Received under Economic and Social Council Resolution 1974C (XXXIX),* U.N. Doc. E/CN.4/1164 (1974).

283. Covenant on Civil and Political Rights, *supra* note 48, Art. 40; Covenant on Economic, Social, and Cultural Rights, *supra* note 47, Arts. 16–22.

284. Convention on the Elimination of Racial Discrimination, *supra* note 97, Art. 9. *See* Das, *Measures of Implementation of the International Convention on the Elimination of All Forms of Racial Discrimination with Special Reference to the Provisions concerning Reports from States Parties to the Convention,* 4 HUMAN RIGHTS J. 213 (1971).

285. Convention Relating to the Status of Refugees, *supra* note 114, Arts. 35 and 36.

286. Protocol Relating to the Status of Refugees, Arts. 2 and 3, 606 U.N.T.S. 267 (entered into force Oct. 4, 1967).

287. Convention Relating to the Status of Stateless Persons, 360 U.N.T.S. 117, Art. 33 (adopted Sept. 28, 1954 and entered into force June 6, 1960), *reprinted in* U.N. HUMAN RIGHTS INSTRUMENTS, *supra* note 51, at 61–66.

288. Supplementary Convention on the Abolition of Slavery, *supra* note 112, Art. 8.

289. *See* Bailey, *U.N. Fact-Finding and Human Rights Complaints,* 48 INT'L AFFAIRS 250 (1972); Ermacora, *International Enquiry Commissions in the Field of Human Rights,* 1 HUMAN RIGHTS J. 180 (1968); Ermacora, *Partiality and Impartiality of Human Rights Enquiry Commissions of International Organisations,* in 1 RENÉ CASSIN, *supra* note 39, at 64–74.

290. *See* N. BAR-YAACOV, THE HANDLING OF INTERNATIONAL DISPUTES BY MEANS OF INQUIRY 20–44 (1974) [hereinafter cited as N. BAR-YAACOV]; W. SHORE, FACT-FINDING IN THE MAINTENANCE OF INTERNATIONAL PEACE 12–19 (1970) [hereinafter cited as W. SHORE].

tions have adopted this technique and put it to use in various contexts. For example, the General Assembly of the United Nations has created commissions of inquiry and directed them into the field to collect information relating to a variety of questions.[291] The technique is similarly employed by the International Labor Organization in the form of the Committee of Experts, instituted in 1957. The Committee not only receives the formal national reports submitted to the ILO, but also solicits information from both local employer and worker organizations. This fact-finding method has proved to be quite effective.[292]

The common resistance of nation-states to on-the-spot investigations of human rights violations is notorious. In United Nations history, the human rights mission dispatched in 1963 by the General Assembly to investigate the oppression of the Buddhists in South Vietnam stands out as a notable exception, because of a combination of factors unique to that situation.[293] Subsequently, in 1968, the secretary-general sent to Nigeria a Representative on Humanitarian Activities, who visited the southern and western fronts.[294] Elsewhere, as in southern Africa, the Israeli-occupied territories, and Chile, efforts for on-the-spot investigations have been frustrated.[295]

---

291. *See* N. BAR-YAACOV, *supra* note 290, at 248–321; W. SHORE, *supra* note 290, at 83–133.

292. For further detail *see* notes 526–31 *infra* and accompanying text. *See also* E. HAAS, *supra* note 23, at 250–52; E. LANDY, THE EFFECTIVENESS OF INTERNATIONAL SUPERVISION 19–34 (1966) [hereinafter cited as E. LANDY]; INTERNATIONAL LABOUR OFFICE, THE IMPACT OF INTERNATIONAL LABOUR CONVENTIONS AND RECOMMENDATIONS 47–63 (1976) [hereinafter cited as THE IMPACT]; C. JENKS, SOCIAL JUSTICE IN THE LAW OF NATIONS: THE ILO IMPACT AFTER FIFTY YEARS 33–44 (1970).

With specific reference to the case of freedom of association, *see* E. HAAS, HUMAN RIGHTS AND INTERNATIONAL ACTION: THE CASE OF FREEDOM OF ASSOCIATION (1970); Nafziger, *International Labor Organization and Social Change: The Fact-Finding and Conciliation Commission on Freedom of Association,* 2 N.Y.U.J. INT'L L. & POLITICS 1 (1969).

293. *See The Violations of Human Rights in South Viet-Nam,* Y.B.U.N. 1963, at 47–50; *The Violation of Human Rights in South Viet-Nam: Report of the United Nations Fact-Finding Mission to South Viet-Nam,* U.N. Doc. A/5630 (1963); Volio-Jimenez, *International Protection of Human Rights: Balance Sheet of a Promising Action,* 1 UN MONTHLY CHRONICLE 75 (Dec. 1964).

294. *See* UNITED NATIONS, OFFICE OF PUBLIC INFORMATION, EVERYMAN'S UNITED NATIONS: A SUMMARY OF THE ACTIVITIES OF THE UNITED NATIONS DURING THE FIVE-YEAR PERIOD 1966–1970, at 62–63 (1971).

295. *See* J. CAREY, *supra* note 190, at 84–126; Res. 6 (XXV) of the Commission on Human Rights, COMMISSION ON HUMAN RIGHTS, REPORT ON THE TWENTY-FIFTH SESSION, 46 U.N. ESCOR 183, U.N. Doc. E/4621 (E/CN.4/1007) (1969).

See also G.A. Res. 2443, 23 U.N. GAOR, Supp. (No. 18) 50, U.N. Doc. A/7218 (1968); G.A. Res. 2727, 25 U.N. GAOR, Supp. (No. 28) 36, U.N. Doc. A/8028 (1970); *Human Rights Commission Acts on Situations in Southern Africa and Israeli-Occupied Territories,* 14 UN MONTHLY CHRONICLE 44 (Apr. 1977); *Report of the Special Committee to Investigate Israeli*

The growing role of pressure groups and private associations in the world constitutive process makes them an important source of information about human rights. The attention of these nongovernmental organizations tends to be confined to the particular value process in which they specialize, but within this limit they frequently possess a tremendous wealth of information and knowledge, as exemplified by Amnesty International's global surveys of torture.[296] A growing number of nongovernmental organizations (NGOs) have sought and obtained consultative status in relation to the Economic and Social Council of the United Nations,[297] and from this position disseminate information to the world community in the value sectors with which they are particularly concerned. Other nongovernmental organizations, national and transnational, collect and disseminate information through nonofficial communication channels which ultimately reach both transnational and national decision makers. These organizations, representing every value sector, provide a critically needed dimension in the entire intelligence function, furnishing and disseminating information that would otherwise be unavailable from the governmental source. Diverse, and at times conflicting, as these organizations may be, the aggregate flow of information generated and disseminated by them is likely to facilitate the sifting of fact from falsehood or fantasy. And their very diversities probably help to police special interests in terms of the common interest of a more inclusive community.

The recent proliferation of international governmental organizations and the enhanced participation in constitutive process of political parties, pressure groups, and private associations have, thus, immensely increased facilities for the gathering, processing, and dissemination on a global scale of the intelligence necessary to rational decision. The developing technology of observation and communication through various instrumentalities offers still further augmentation of potentialities.[298] The massive and complex intelligence required for effective protection and fulfillment of human rights appears to be well within reach. Nonetheless, its organization throughout the entire constitutive process will require cooperation on a larger scale than heretofore.

Despite such potentialities, the fact remains that it is difficult to secure

---

Practices Affecting the Human Rights of the Population of the Occupied Territories, U.N. Doc. A/8389 (1971) (note by the secretary-general); *Report of the Special Committee to Investigate Israeli Practices Affecting the Human Rights of the Population of the Occupied Territories,* U.N. Doc. A/8089 (1971) (note by the secretary-general).

296. *See* note 271 *supra.*

297. *See* notes 306–11 *infra* and accompanying text.

298. *See generally* McDougal, Lasswell, & Reisman, *The Intelligence Function, supra* note 268.

a continuing flow of dependable and comprehensive information relevant to rational decision making for the defense and fulfillment of human rights. That the nation-state remains unwilling to subject itself to effective external scrutiny is a commonplace. A greater difficulty, perhaps, inheres in the appropriate processing and use of the information that can be obtained. "The world," in the words of Bailey, "is not short of facts; it is suffering from an information explosion, of which the fall-out is the printed word."[299] What is critical is that the mass of information be assembled, processed, and disseminated in such a way as to meet effectively and promptly the ongoing, and often pressing, needs of rational decision. The notable, contemporary shortcomings relate to the lack of a comprehensive conception of the goals and ramifications in the gathering, processing, and dissemination of information, and to the absence of a centralized clearing house procedure capable of absorbing and consolidating the many fragmented items of information into a coherent, contextual, and comprehensive whole essential to the effective functioning of the entire constitutive process. Without such a comprehensive frame of reference, the real relevance and significance of individual intelligence efforts are lost. Hence dissemination becomes untimely and uneconomical.[300]

THE PROMOTING FUNCTION

The promoting function refers to the advocacy of policy alternatives, including the taking of initiatives to secure the enactment of prescriptions.[301] It adds intensity of demand to expectation. Three sequences are often involved: the exploration of possible promotions; the detailed formulation of demands; and the propagation of demands by mobilizing resources and managing people to obtain necessary commitments. It is by exercising this function that effective power is distinctively able to bring its influence to bear upon authoritative community policy.

The promoting function has, historically, been performed by all groups and individuals having effective power. Sometimes these participants are government officials, but often they are active in political par-

---

299. S. Bailey, *supra* note 273, at 35.

300. *Cf.* McDougal, Lasswell, & Reisman, *The Intelligence Function, supra* note 268, at 370–78.

301. It may be noted that what we mean by "promotion" is more limited than what is meant in the United Nations Charter and in U.N. parlance more generally. The broader reference appears to be to the progressive achievement of human rights. *See* Schwelb, *Some Aspects of the International Covenants on Human Rights of December 1966,* in Nobel Symposium on Human Rights, *supra* note 147, at 103, 107–08 [hereinafter cited as Schwelb, *Some Aspects*]; Vasak, *National, Regional and Universal Institutions for the Promotion and Protection of Human Rights,* 1 Human Rights J. 165, 165–69 (1968) [hereinafter cited as Vasak].

ties, pressure groups, and private associations. A primary function of political parties is to organize and promote explicit programs. Pressure groups are directed toward both general and particular policy purposes. Private associations, specialized to values other than power, commonly seek power effects in relation to the particular value to which they are specialized. These groups and individuals operate through a great variety of organizational techniques and a diversified range of mass communication media. Promotional messages are directed to official and effective elites and also to wide general audiences. Promoters create and maintain an ever-expanding network of organizations and contacts around the globe. Besides small-group bargaining, they generate a massive flow of propaganda and agitation. Their cumulative activities, day in and day out, year in and year out, are vital to managing and mobilizing world public opinion and to the transformation of policy alternatives into authoritative prescription and application.

The increasing democratization of participation in world processes of effective power, the availability and openness of the new structures of authority, and the contemporary instrumentalities for communication have brought a new comprehensiveness and intensity to the active advocacy of conflicting policy alternatives before authoritative decision makers. The ease with which demands can be formulated and propagated, and support mobilized, for the enactment and application of new authoritative prescriptions is dramatically demonstrated on a global scale in the field of human rights.

The nation-state, with its concentration of effective power, has traditionally played a leading role in transnational promotional activities. For such activities nation-state officials do not require any particular authorization; the whole framework of international law is their charter. The role of nation-states in the promotion of human rights is, however, somewhat ambivalent. Highly jealous of their prerogatives in controlling their own people and conscious of the importance of reciprocal deference, state elites tend to be wary of open involvement in human rights matters within other states. The active role played by President Jimmy Carter (with its far-reaching potential ramifications upon the internal constitutive process of the United States) is a promising exception.[302]

---

302. *See Carter's Human Rights Policy: A Sword Aimed at Our Friends,* 37 HUMAN EVENTS 1 (4 June 1977); Fraser, *Freedom and Foreign Policy,* 26 FOREIGN POLICY 140 (1977); *Human Rights and Foreign Relations: Is Jimmy Carter a Wilsonian or a Moral Realist?* 123 CONG. REC. H5738 (June 10, 1977) (commencement address by Dr. Edward J. Blaustein, president, Rutgers State University, at Hebrew Union College, Cincinnati, Ohio); *Human Rights—How Deep Is Our Commitment?* 123 CONG. REC. H5496 (June 6, 1977) (Congressman Marc Marks's commencement address at Pennsylvania State University); Lacquer, *The Issue of Human Rights,* 63 COMMENTARY 29 (May 1977); Reisman, *Diplomacy of the Possible: The*

In open, democratic polities where freedom of association and assembly is honored, private groups and individuals are relatively free, and even encouraged, to undertake a variety of activities in the promotion of human rights. In totalitarian polities, however, where freedom of association and assembly is a farce, private groups and individuals who seek to promote human rights often find themselves incapacitated by drastic measures;[303] hence the critical importance of transnational concern and promotion.

The increasing importance of the promotional role conferred upon international governmental organizations gives clear recognition to the imperative need of transnational cooperation. For instance, the General Assembly, under Article 13(1) of the Charter, is authorized to "make recommendations" for the purposes of "promoting international co-operation in the economic, social, cultural, educational, and health fields, and assisting in the realization of human rights and fundamental freedoms for all without distinction as to race, sex, language, or religion." Similarly, the Economic and Social Council, according to Article 62(2) of the Charter, "may make recommendations for the purpose of promoting respect for, and observance of, human rights and fundamental freedoms for all." The General Assembly and the Economic and Social Council, and various specialized agencies have of course made innumerable recommendations, extending to a wide range of values and problems. Many of these recommendations have matured, further, into either multilateral treaties (*e.g.*, the International Convention on the Elimination of All Forms of Racial Discrimination)[304] or customary in-

---

Pragmatism of Human Rights, THE NATION, May 7, 1977, at 554–58; Steel, *Motherhood, Apple Pie and Human Rights,* 176 THE NEW REPUBLIC 14 (June 4, 1977); *Where Are the President, the Secretary of State, and Ambassador Young When Human Rights Need Them?* 123 CONG. REC. S9543 (June 13, 1977).

For more general background, *see* HUMAN RIGHTS IN THE WORLD COMMUNITY: A CALL FOR U.S. LEADERSHIP, REPORT OF THE SUBCOMM. ON INTERNATIONAL ORGANIZATIONS AND MOVEMENTS OF HOUSE COMM. ON FOREIGN AFFAIRS, 93d Cong., 2d Sess. (Comm. Print 1974); *International Protection of Human Rights: The Work of International Organizations and the Role of U.S. Foreign Policy: Hearings before the Subcomm. on International Organizations and Movements of the House Comm. on Foreign Affairs,* 93d Cong., 1st Sess. (1973) [hereinafter cited as *Hearings*]; *Symposium: Human Rights and United States Foreign Policy,* 14 VA. J. INT'L L. 591 (1974) (including aritcles by Lillich, Bilder, Buergenthal, Farer, Henkin, Shestack, & Cohen).

303. *See* F. BARGHOORN, DETENTE AND THE DEMOCRATIC MOVEMENT IN THE USSR (1976); V. CHALIDZE, TO DEFEND THESE RIGHTS: HUMAN RIGHTS AND THE SOVIET UNION (G. Daniels trans. 1974); L. GREENBERG, THE JEWS IN RUSSIA: THE STRUGGLE FOR EMANCIPATION (M. Wischnitzer ed. 1976); W. KOREY, THE SOVIET CAGE: ANTI-SEMITISM IN RUSSIA (1973).

304. Convention on the Elimination of Racial Discrimination, *supra* note 97. *See* chapter 9 *infra,* at notes 89–284 and accompanying text.

ternational law (*e.g.*, the Universal Declaration of Human Rights).[305]

Increasingly evident, also, is the prominent role presently played by nongovernmental organizations (pressure groups and private associations) in promoting the transnational protection and fulfillment of human rights. The importance of nongovernmental organizations is formally recognized in Article 71 of the United Nations Charter, which authorizes the Economic and Social Council to "make suitable arrangements for consultation with non-governmental organizations which are concerned with matters within its competence." Thus, effective power obtains a formal voice in the process of authoritative decision, with the result that the special knowledge and expertise of nongovernmental organizations are made available to serve the common interest.

The Economic and Social Council has established three categories of nongovernmental organization in consultative status. Category I comprises organizations which

> are concerned with most of the activities of the Council and can demonstrate to the satisfaction of the Council that they have marked and sustained contributions to make to the achievement of the objectives of the United Nations [with regard to international economic, social, cultural, educational, health, scientific, technological, and related matters and to questions of human rights] and are closely involved with the economic and social life of the peoples of the areas they represent and whose membership, which should be considerable, is broadly representative of major segments of population in a large number of countries.[306]

Category II comprises those organizations which "have a special competence in, and are concerned specifically with, only a few of the fields of activity covered by the Council."[307] Category III is described as "Roster" with this specification:

> Other organizations which do not have general or special consultative status but which the Council, or the Secretary-General of the United Nations, in consultation with the Council or its Committee on Non-Governmental Organizations, considers can make occasional and useful contributions to the work of the Council or its subsidiary bodies or other United Nations bodies within their competence.[308]

---

305. *See* notes 347–67 *infra* and accompanying text.

306. *Consultative Status Urged for 18 Non-Govt. Organizations,* 14 UN MONTHLY CHRONICLE 34 (Mar. 1977).

307. *Id.*

308. *Id.*

The total numbers of nongovernmental organizations comprised within these three categories in 1977 were 26, 207, and 478, respectively.[309]

The nongovernmental organizations may send representatives to sit as observers, and to speak, at public meetings of the Council and its subsidiary bodies. They may submit memoranda relating to the work of the Council and its subsidiary bodies and have such memoranda circulated as United Nations documents. They may further consult with the United Nations Secretariat on matters of mutual concern.[310] In addition, the organizations in Category I may submit proposals for the Council's agenda.[311]

In regard to human rights matters, many of the nongovernmental organizations have participated very actively in specialized seminars, established and maintained close contacts with governmental delegates, and on occasion supplied the initiative to prepare draft conventions. At the San Francisco conference, the campaign waged by a number of nongovernmental organizations, notably from the United States, was instrumental in the ultimate incorporation of the rather comprehensive human rights provisions in the Charter.[312] Another example of effective action relates to the adoption in 1966 of the Optional Protocol to the International Covenant on Civil and Political Rights, which provides the remedy of individual petitions with regard to the rights protected in the Covenant on Civil and Political Rights. As Cassin pointed out: "[I]t is well known . . . that but for the counsel given by the competent non-governmental organizations to the governmental delegations to the Assembly, the protocol, inadequate though it is, would never have been adopted."[313] "It is impossible," in the words of Cassin, "to say how many problems involving Human Rights would never have got on to the agendas of these

309. *Id. See also Report of the Committee on Non-Governmental Organizations,* U.N. Doc. E/5934 (1977).

310. *See* United Nations, Rules of Procedure of the Economic and Social Council 20–22, U.N. Doc. E/5715 (1975) (Rules 80–84).

311. *Id.* at 3 (Rule 9, para. 3).

312. *See* Charter of the United Nations: Report to the President on the Results of the San Francisco Conference by the Chairman of the United States Delegation 114 (1945) (Dep't of State Pub. 2349). *See also* J. Blaustein, *Human Rights—A Challenge to the United Nations and to Our Generation* 6–7 (Dag Hammarskjold Memorial Lecture, Columbia University, December 4, 1963), *reprinted in* The Quest for Peace: The Dag Hammarskjold Memorial Lectures 315, 318–19 (A. Cordier & W. Foote eds. 1965); L. Goodrich, The United Nations 245–47 (1959); L. White, *supra* note 30, at 262.

313. Cassin, *Twenty Years of NGO Effort on Behalf of Human Rights,* in NGO Strategy, *supra* note 30, at 20, 21.

bodies but for the initiative or indirect action of non-governmental organizations."[314]

The promise of the promoting function resides in the ease, in the context of the present communications revolution, by which private groups and individuals who entertain strong demands about human rights can organize groups (including transnational groups) to take the initiative, to agitate, and to propose alternatives. A most important task is that of finding and forging sufficiently inclusive symbols to attract, manage, and mobilize world public opinion. Fortunately, in an interdependent, dynamically changing world, effective power groups are increasingly mobile and changing. Hence it is increasingly possible to assemble the resources and to organize the activities necessary to change peoples' perceptions of common interest.

The less promising aspect of promotion in reference to human rights is that promotional activities are still too often carried forward from parochial and fragmented, rather than inclusive, perspectives. A frequent limitation on adequate performance of the promoting function appears to be the common domination of public channels of communication by agents of special interests. Too often degenerating into propaganda for special interests, promotional activities may be exclusively perceived as a means of interbloc warfare—East against West, North against South, etc. Within bodies politic which stifle freedoms of communication and association, it is no news that transnational activities for the promotion of human rights continue to encounter vast resistance.

THE PRESCRIBING FUNCTION

Inquiry about the prescribing function has commonly gone forward in terms of quests for the "bases of obligation" or the "binding nature of law" or of efforts to identify certain ambiguously conceived "sources" of international law.[315] These bases and sources are located sometimes in

---

314. *Id.* For increasing recognition of the importance of nongovernmental organizations devoted to human rights, *see Human Rights Groups Riding a Wave of Popularity,* N.Y. Times, Feb. 28, 1977, at 2, col. 3 (city ed.).

315. *See generally* J. Brierly, The Basis of Obligation in International Law (1958); B. Cheng, General Principles of Law as Applied by International Courts and Tribunals (1953); A. D'Amato, The Concept of Custom in International Law (1971); G. Finch, The Sources of International Law (1937); H. Lauterpacht, Private Law Sources, *supra* note 118; 2 International Law: Being the Collected Papers of Hersch Lauterpacht 173–303 (E. Lauterpacht ed. 1975); C. Parry, The Sources and Evidences of International Law (1965); H. Thirlway, International Customary Law and Codification (1972); G. Tunkin, Theory of International Law 89–203 (W. Butler trans. 1974) [hereinafter cited as G. Tunkin]; K. Wolfke, Custom in Present Interna-

transempirical absolutes, sometimes in the express consent of personal sovereigns or state entities, and sometimes in transnational group expectations. Some of the ambiguities involved in the employment of the term "sources" are well summarized by Briggs. He finds four major, though shifting, references: (1) the "*basis* of international law," which includes derivational exercises from assumed premises about the nature of international law; (2) the *causes* of international law, including such factors as "reason, convenience, tradition, policy, necessity, and concepts of justice or of social solidarity," which influence "the development of international law," but which are said, curiously, to be irrelevant to providing "working criteria by which to distinguish law from practice or from opinions of what the law should be"; (3) the "evidences of international law," sometimes referring to "substantive rules" and sometimes to the "documentary sources" in which such rules find expression; and, finally, most appropriately, (4) the "methods or procedures by which international law is created."[316]

When attention is clearly focused upon the methods and procedures by which international law is created, it is tropistic to begin with Article 38 of the Statute of the International Court of Justice. This article is commonly regarded as of the highest authority in specifying the "sources" to which any tribunal must turn in search of international law. It reads:

> 1. The Court, whose function is to decide in accordance with international law such disputes as are submitted to it, shall apply:
>   a. international conventions, whether general or particular, establishing rules expressly recognized by the contesting states;
>   b. international custom, as evidence of a general practice accepted as law;

TIONAL LAW (1964); Corbett, *The Consent of States and the Sources of the Law of Nations,* 6 BRIT. Y.B. INT'L L. 20 (1925); Elias, *Modern Sources of International Law,* in TRANSNATIONAL LAW IN A CHANGING SOCIETY, *supra* note 183, at 34–69; Erickson, *Soviet Theory of the Legal Nature of Customary International Law,* 7 CASE W. RES. J. INT'L L. 148 (1975); Fitzmaurice, *The Foundations of the Authority of International Law and the Problem of Enforcement,* 19 MODERN L. REV. 1 (1956); Fitzmaurice, *The Law and Procedure of the International Court of Justice, 1951–54: General Principles and Sources of Law,* 30 BRIT. Y.B. INT'L L. 1 (1953); Kopelmanas, *Custom as a Means of the Creation of International Law,* 18 BRIT. Y.B. INT'L L. 127 (1937); Kunz, *The Nature of Customary International Law,* 47 AM. J. INT'L L. 662 (1953); MacGibbon, *Customary International Law and Acquiescence,* 33 BRIT. Y.B. INT'L L. 115 (1957); Silving, *"Customary Law": Continuity in Municipal and International Law,* 31 IOWA L. REV. 614 (1946); Starke, *Treaties as a "Source" of International Law,* 23 BRIT. Y.B. INT'L L. 341 (1946); Tunkin, *Remarks on the Judicial Nature of Customary Norms of International Law,* 49 CALIF. L. REV. 419 (1961).

316. H. BRIGGS, THE LAW OF NATIONS 44 (2d ed. 1952) [hereinafter cited as H. BRIGGS].

c. the general principles of law recognized by civilized nations;
d. subject to the provisions of Article 59, judicial decisions and the teachings of the most highly qualified publicists of the various nations, as subsidiary means for the determination of rules of law.

2. This provision shall not prejudice the power of the Court to decide a case *ex aequo et bono,* if the parties agree thereto.[317]

It scarcely requires close examination to observe that this itemization of possible sources of international law is neither comprehensive nor homogeneous and that it offers little assistance in the relation of the different itemized sources to particular instances of controversy. Most importantly, this itemization offers little guidance when the inferences to be drawn from different sources are ambiguous, incomplete, and contradictory or indicate clear expectations that are inimical to more basic community policy.

What has been ostensibly deficient in inquiry about the prescribing function is the failure to grasp the true nature of that function. From the appropriate perspective, the particular itemizations embodied in Article 38 are merely component parts of a more comprehensive, ongoing flow of communication and collaboration; the significance of the particular itemizations derives from the services they perform as indices of community expectation. It is the function of the more comprehensive process of communication to create the expectations about policy, authority, and control characteristic of law.

Prescription, thus conceived, refers to the projection of a policy about the shaping and sharing of values as authoritative community policy. It is the outcome of a process of communication which proceeds on three levels: the designation of the content of a policy in terms of the shaping and sharing of values under specified factual contingencies; the creation of expectations about the authority of the policy so designated; and the creation of expectations that this policy will in fact be put into controlling practice.[318] In the global community, as in its lesser component communities, the processes of communication by which prescriptions are shaped range from the most deliberate, formal and organized through many gradations to the least deliberate, formal, and organized. When prescriptive processes are most deliberate, formal, and organized, they may be conveniently analyzed in terms of four distinctive sequential phases: the initiation of the process; the exploration of relevant facts and potential policies; the formulation of the policy to be projected as au-

317. *Reprinted in* Documentary Supplement, *supra* note 51, at 26, 33.
318. *See* McDougal, Lasswell, & Reisman, *supra* note 1, at 139–40.

thoritative for the community; and the communication of the prescriptive content and expectations about authority and control to the target audience. Even when a prescriptive process is highly informal and unorganized, some rough approximation to, or functional equivalence of, these sequential phases may be observed.

The diversity and abundance of the processes of communication by which prescriptions are created in the contemporary world arena are staggering. The peoples of the world communicate to one another expectations about policy, authority, and control, not merely through state or intergovernmental entities, but through reciprocal claims and mutual tolerances in all their interactions. The participants in the relevant processes of communication (the communicators and the communicatees) exhibit a wide spectrum of specialization to the prescribing function, ranging from the most specialized to the least specialized. They include not only the officials of states and intergovernmental organizations but also the representatives of political parties, pressure groups and private associations, and the individual human being qua individual, with all his identifications. The perspectives of participants, ranging from the most deliberate to the least deliberate in relation to prescriptive purposes, display demands, identifications, and expectations with differing degrees of compatibility or incompatibility with common interests and fundamental general community policies.[319] The situations of communicative interaction are both official and nonofficial, and organized and unorganized; the organized situations include the familiar types of arenas mentioned above (i.e., diplomatic, parliamentary-diplomatic, parliamentary, adjudicative, and executive arenas),[320] and all situations may be characterized in terms of geographic range, temporal features, degrees of institutionalization, and expectations of crisis. The different participants bring many varying base values in terms of authority and effective control to bear upon particular interactions. The strategies employed by participants in the management of their base values exhibit varying degrees of explicitness or implicitness in relation to prescription and a wide continuum of coercion and persuasion; they extend from the modalities suggested in Article 38 of the Statute of the International Court of Justice to the whole complex of procedures employed in the different types of arenas and all the strategies characteristic of the different value processes. The culminating outcomes of all this communication, as expressed in a continuing flow of words and behavior, exhibit

319. The deliberateness of prescriptive intent may be highly ambiguous even in an explicit agreement. *See, e.g.,* Schachter, *The Twilight Existence of Nonbinding International Agreements,* 71 AM. J. INT'L L. 296 (1977).

320. See notes 65–77 *supra* and accompanying text.

wide diversities both in the facts about shared perspectives in relation to policy, authority, and control and in the evidences of such perspectives in the form of explicit formulations and unarticulated assumptions. The important point is that the outcomes in shared expectations, in whatever degree they approach prescription and however they may be evidenced, are a function of the entire configuration of variables in the whole process of communication.

It is a process of communication in this comprehensive sense which creates and maintains the contemporary human rights prescriptions. All the different historic modes of international law making—including explicit formulations in agreements and official declarations and implicit communications through uniformities in behavior—are as available for human rights as for other problems.

The most deliberate form of prescription, in which governments cooperate with one another explicitly in formulating and undertaking commitments, is of course the international agreement in all its many manifestations.[321] The Vienna Convention on the Law of Treaties, in Article 2(1)(a), defines "treaty" as "an international agreement concluded between States in written form and governed by international law, whether embodied in a single instrument or in two or more related instruments and whatever its particular designation."[322] In the absence of centralized legislative institutions in the world arena, international agreements offer the closest approach to the considered and deliberate prescription of future policies, which is the characteristic function of legislative institutions in national arenas. It is sometimes rather futilely debated what agreements between nation-states are "law making" and what are not.[323] From our perspective all agreements between nation-states project policies into the future, and the number of participants affected by such projections is a matter, not for dogmatic conclusion from implicit assumptions about the nature of law or the nature of agreement, but rather for empirical inquiry and rational decision, taking into accourt all the values at stake.

The process of agreement, like the prescribing process in general, can be realistically understood only by reference to the participants, their perspectives (including demands, identifications, and expectations), situations of interaction, base values, modalities in expression of commitment, outcomes in shared expectations, and effects upon different

321. For an excellent introduction, see M. HUDSON, 1 INTERNATIONAL LEGISLATION xiii–lx (1931).

322. Vienna Convention, *supra* note 135, Art. 2(1)(a).

323. *See* I. BROWNLIE, *supra* note 172, at 11–15; D. O'CONNELL, INTERNATIONAL LAW 22–25 (2d ed. 1970) [hereinafter cited as D. O'CONNELL].

value processes. The relevant participants are of course state officials and the other participants with whom they interact. Their demands, identifications, and expectations are shaped by the differences and nuances in culture, class, interest, personality, and crisis. The most general objective of parties in making an international agreement is to project a common policy regarding a future distribution of values. The more detailed objectives of the parties may relate to any value category (respect, power, enlightenment, well-being, wealth, skill, affection, and rectitude) or to any phase of a particular value process (participation, situations, base values, strategies, and outcomes). The great range of values sought in international agreements may be illustrated by quick reference to some of the more important types of agreements made by states: agreements concerning human rights, including the protection of minorities (respect); treaties of alliance (power); agreements relating to communications and exchange of knowledge (enlightenment); sanitary conventions (well-being); treaties of friendship, commerce, and navigation (wealth); agreements for the transfer of technology and for the exchange of technical personnel (skill); agreements for the protection of marital and family rights (affection); and treaties guaranteeing freedom of religion (rectitude). The situations in which international agreements are negotiated and performed differ measurably in features relevant to the communication of demands and expectations about commitment. Such differences can be observed in terms of spatial position, time, degree of institutionalization, and intensities in exposures to crisis. Potentially, all values may be employed as base values in processes of negotiation, and the relative positions of the parties in control over particular base values bear significantly upon both the degree and content of their commitment. The sequence of negotiations and other activities by which the parties mediate their subjectivities to achieve outcomes in shared commitment may be direct and explicit or indirect and implicit, expressed in both words and deeds. Agreements between states differ in the number of parties sharing commitment, in the scope and detail of policies projected, and in the expectations of permanence or impermanence attending commitment.[324]

It may be noted, in minor paradox, that agreements between states play a most important role in the development of customary international law. Because of the dual function of state officials in the world arena, as both claimants and judges, agreements may both express the demands or claims of certain states against the general community of

---

324. *See* M. McDougal, H. Lasswell, & J. Miller, The Interpretation of Agreements and World Public Order: Principles of Content and Procedure 13–21 (1967).

states and establish the uniformities in expectation which ultimately add up to lawfulness. The fact that many uniform agreements have been made, and tolerated without protest, over a period of time is often adduced as good evidence of customary international law. It is for this reason that the core content of the contemporary agreements and declarations has become a part of authoritative general community expectation.[325]

Since the establishment of the United Nations, many transnational prescriptions concerning human rights have been effected by multilateral agreement. Among the most important of these agreements are:

The International Covenant on Economic, Social and Cultural Rights;[326]

The International Covenant on Civil and Political Rights;[327]

The Optional Protocol to the International Covenant on Civil and Political Rights;[328]

The International Convention on the Elimination of All Forms of Racial Discrimination;[329]

The Convention on the Prevention and Punishment of the Crime of Genocide;[330]

The International Convention on the Suppression and Punishment of the Crime of Apartheid;[331]

The Supplementary Convention on the Abolition of Slavery, the Slave Trade, and Institutions and Practices Similar to Slavery;[332]

The Convention on the Nationality of Married Women;[333]

The Convention on the Reduction of Statelessness;[334]

The Convention Relating to the Status of Refugees;[335]

---

325. *See* notes 558–610 *infra* and accompanying text.

326. Covenant on Economic, Social, and Cultural Rights, *supra* note 47.

327. Covenant on Civil and Political Rights, *supra* note 48.

328. Optional Protocol, *supra* note 49.

329. Convention on the Elimination of Racial Discrimination, *supra* note 97.

330. Genocide Convention, *supra* note 111.

331. International Convention on the Suppression and Punishment of the Crime of Apartheid, *adopted* Nov. 30, 1973, G.A. Res. 3068, 28 U.N. GAOR, Supp. (No. 30) 75, U.N. Doc. A/9030 (1973) [hereinafter cited as Apartheid Convention]. For an analysis of this Convention, *see* chapter 7 *infra*, at notes 512–35 and accompanying text.

332. Supplementary Convention on the Abolition of Slavery, *supra* note 112.

333. Convention on the Nationality of Married Women, *opened for signature and ratification* Jan. 29, 1957, G.A. Res. 1040 (XI), 309 U.N.T.S. 67 (entered into force Aug. 11, 1958).

334. Convention on the Reduction of Statelessness, *supra* note 115.

335. Convention Relating to the Status of Refugees, *supra* note 114.

The Protocol Relating to the Status of Refugees;[336]

The Convention on the Political Rights of Women;[337] and

The Convention on Consent to Marriage, Minimum Age for Marriage and Registration of Marriages.[338]

These agreements were either adopted by the General Assembly of the United Nations or adopted by special conferences of plenipotentiaries under the auspices of the United Nations, before being opened for signature, ratification, and accession.

Other important human rights prescriptions, adopted by such specialized agencies as the International Labor Organization and the United Nations Educational, Scientific, and Cultural Organization, include:

The Discrimination (Employment and Occupation) Convention;[339]

The Convention against Discrimination in Education;[340]

The Equal Remuneration Convention;[341]

The Abolition of Forced Labor Convention;[342]

The Freedom of Association and Protection of the Right to Organize Convention;[343]

The Right to Organize and Collective Bargaining Convention;[344]

---

336. Protocol Relating to the Status of Refugees, *supra* note 286.

337. Convention on the Political Rights of Women, *supra* note 113.

338. Convention on Consent to Marriage, Minimum Age for Marriage and Registration of Marriages, *opened for signature and ratification* Dec. 20, 1952, G.A. Res. 640(VII), 193 U.N.T.S. 135 (entered into force July 7, 1954).

All of the above-mentioned conventions are conveniently *reprinted in* U.N. HUMAN RIGHTS INSTRUMENTS, *supra* note 51.

339. Convention concerning Discrimination in Respect of Employment and Occupation, *adopted* June 25, 1958, 362 U.N.T.S. 31 (ILO General Conference) (entered into force June 15, 1960).

340. Convention against Discrimination in Education, *adopted* Dec. 14, 1960, 429 U.N.T.S. 93 (UNESCO General Conference) (entered into force May 22, 1962).

341. Equal Remuneration Convention, *adopted* June 29, 1951, 165 U.N.T.S. 304 (entered into force May 23, 1953).

342. Convention concerning the Abolition of Forced Labour, *adopted* June 25, 1957, 320 U.N.T.S. 292 (ILO General Conference) (entered into force Jan. 17, 1959). For a commentary, *see* C. JENKS, HUMAN RIGHTS AND INTERNATIONAL LABOUR STANDARDS 25–46 (1960).

343. Convention (No. 87) concerning Freedom of Association and Protection of the Right to Organize, *adopted* July 9, 1948, and entered into force July 4, 1950, *reprinted in* U.N. HUMAN RIGHTS INSTRUMENTS, *supra* note 51, at 82–84.

344. Convention (No. 98) concerning the Application of the Principles of the Right to Organize and to Bargain Collectively, *adopted* July 1, 1949, and entered into force July 18, 1951, *reprinted in* U.N. HUMAN RIGHTS INSTRUMENTS, *supra* note 51, at 84–86.

The Workers' Representatives Convention;[345] and

The Employment Policy Convention.[346]

These covenants, conventions, and protocols obviously encompass a wide range of values.

The least deliberate form of prescription, commonly known as the creation of customary law, involves the generation of expectations about policies, authority, and control by cooperative behavior, both official and nonofficial. The perspectives among peoples, especially among their effective decision makers, are crystallized in such a way that certain past uniformities in decision and behavior are expected to be continued in the future.

The technical requirements for establishing a customary prescription in international law are, despite considerable controversy among the commentators, generally observed to include two key elements: a "material" element in certain past uniformities in behavior and a "psychological" element, or *opinio juris,* in certain subjectivities of "oughtness" attending such uniformities in behavior.[347] Both these requirements are, however, susceptible to varying interpretations. The relevant uniformities in behavior may include the acts and utterances not only of officials (transnational and national) located at many different positions in structures of authority, but even of private individuals and representatives of nongovernmental organizations. Such acts differ greatly both in the frequency of repetition and in the duration of recurrence. The subjectivities of oughtness required to attend such uniformities of behavior may relate to many different systems of norms, such as prior authority, natural law, reason, morality, or religion. The honoring in law-creating consequences even of subjectivities asserted initially in contravention of prior authority suggests that the critical subjectivities are those of expectation of future uniformities in decision, irrespective of the norms of justification. Similarly, the evidences which decision makers may consult in order to ascertain past behavior and subjectivities include not only such familiar items as international agreements, resolutions of international governmental organizations, public utterances by international and national officials, diplomatic correspondence and

345. Convention (No. 135) concerning Protection and Facilities to Be Afforded Workers' Representatives in the Undertaking, *adopted* June 23, 1971, and entered into force June 30, 1973, *reprinted in* U.N. Human Rights Instruments, *supra* note 51, at 86–87.

346. Convention (No. 122) concerning Employment Policy, *adopted* July 9, 1964, and entered into force July 15, 1966, *reprinted in* U.N. Human Rights Instruments, *supra* note 51, at 88–89.

347. The quoted words are from Silving, *supra* note 315, at 622. *See also* A. D'Amato, *supra* note 315, at 47–72; Kopelmanas, *supra* note 315, at 129; Kunz, *supra* note 315, at 665.

instructions, and the writings of publicists, but also "every written document, every record of act or spoken word which presents an authentic picture of the practice of states in their international dealings."[348]

A frequent confusion relates to the degree of uniformity required for the establishment of customary international prescription. It may be emphasized that the uniformities in past behavior and subjectivities required are those of generality, not of universality. The explicit consent of every single state on the globe is not a prerequisite to the authority of a particular prescription. Though the Westphalian concept of international law is said to depend upon the notion of consent, it appears that the function of a concept of customary international law is precisely to eliminate any requirement of specific consent as a basis of international obligation. The honoring of the somewhat diffuse expectations created by cooperative, reciprocal behavior generally has permitted "sovereign" states to be subjected to international law without being made subservient to other particular states. By this process of accommodation, states can, without undue affront to inflated notions of sovereignty, take account of their conditions of interdependence and reciprocity, and cooperate in the pursuit of common goals and policies without explicit agreement. Hence, a customary prescription need not be unanimous; it need only be, in the words of Kunz, "applied by the overwhelming majority of states which hitherto had an opportunity to apply it."[349]

Another historic requirement relates to the length of time necessary for the development of a customary international prescription. It may be noted that this temporal requirement is a function both of general community objectives and of circumstances in context. The overriding goal of the contemporary world community in establishing certain decision makers with competence to prescribe future policies is to secure prescription in accord with contemporary demands about what such policies should be. The requirement of time is designed only to ensure that the contemporary demands and expectations of the community are accurately ascertained. Generally, of course, the paramount concern of contemporary demands and expectations is for a distribution of values, not in the past, but in the future. "Time-honored practice is not a necessary

---

348. G. Finch, *supra* note 315, at 51 (quoting Walker).

349. Kunz, *supra* note 315, at 666. In the same vein, Lauterpacht wrote:

> If universality is to be made the condition of the application of customary rules, it may become doubtful whether many rules would qualify for that purpose. For while in most fields of international law there is agreement as to broad principle, there is almost invariably a pronounced degree of divergence with regard to the application of specific rules.

H. Lauterpacht, *supra* note 39, at 370.

element in customary International Law,"[350] though it serves importantly as evidence, which may be otherwise supplied, of contemporary expectations. Thus, somewhat tautologically, Lauterpacht's Oppenheim observes: "Wherever and as soon as a line of international conduct frequently adopted by States is considered legally obligatory or legally right, the rule which may be abstracted from such conduct is a rule of customary International Law."[351] In some contexts the requisite degree of certainty about contemporary expectations has been held to have been established by reference to past behavior and subjectivities of relatively short duration.[352]

To make fully meaningful the traditional requirements of a flow of uniformities in behavior and subjectivity through time for the creation of customary international law, these requirements must be located in their larger context. The historic emphases refer only to certain features of the more comprehensive process of communication by which expectations about policy, authority, and control are created. The full exposition of how customary international law is created must require a thorough exploration of every feature of the more comprehensive process. Some of the relevant questions include: Who are the communicators and communicatees (official and nonofficial) and what is the range of participation? What are the participants' perceptions about the content of their communication and its relation to existing law? What are the institutional, geographic, temporal, and crisis features of the situation? What differing bases in knowledge, understanding, skill, and strength do the parties enjoy? What are the strategies in communication, including both the flow of words and the flow of behavior? What uniformities characterize both words and behavior? What are the detailed outcomes in shared expectations about policy, authority, and control?[353]

The prescription of law for the transnational protection of human rights by customary behavior early found expression in the broadly accepted international law about the responsibility of states for injuries to aliens. This law imposes upon states which fail to accord aliens certain minimum international standards of treatment and protection a duty of reparation for the injuries they impose or suffer to be imposed.[354] The customary law of state responsibility was developed in an era when

---

350. A. Ross, A Text-Book of International Law 89 (1947).

351. 1 L. Oppenheim, *supra* note 235, at 27.

352. *See* Briggs, *The Colombian-Peruvian Asylum Case and Proof of Customary International Law,* 45 Am. J. Int'l L. 728, 729 (1951); Silving, *supra* note 315, at 622.

353. *See* V. Raman, Prescription on International Law by Custom, 1967 (unpublished J.S.D. dissertation, Yale Law School Library); Raman, *The Role of the International Court of Justice in the Development of International Customary Law,* 1965 Proc., Am. Soc'y Int'l L. 169.

354. *See* chapter 14 *infra.*

human rights generally were regarded as largely a matter of domestic jurisdiction. Though applicable only to one category of victims, it remains an important source of international protection of human rights. The protection of human rights by customary law found further expression, as indicated above, in the remedy of humanitarian intervention, developed to cope with egregious violations of human rights by states.[355] This protection has also found expression in the law of war, in which the principle of humanity has played an ameliorating role in contraposition to the principle of military necessity.[356] More recently, the importance of the customary modality of prescription is, as will be developed below, underscored by the evolution of the Universal Declaration of Human Rights from its first status as mere common aspiration to its present wide acceptance as authoritative legal requirement.[357]

The most striking recent development in the prescribing function is in the new role of international governmental organizations. Despite the lingering myth that little direct prescriptive competence has been bestowed upon international governmental organizations, it is easily observable that such organizations, especially the United Nations and its affiliated agencies, play an increasingly important role as forums for the flow of explicit communications and acts of collaboration which create peoples' expectations about authoritative community policy. The General Assembly of the United Nations, in particular, has adopted year after year a large number of resolutions relating to various aspects of human rights, ranging from condemnations of racism and apartheid to reaffirmation of the principle of self-determination.[358] Though there continues to be considerable debate about the legal effect of these resolutions,[359] the availability of the General Assembly as a forum, combined

355. *See* notes 229–65 *supra* and accompanying text.

356. *See* note 55 *supra* and accompanying text.

357. *See* notes 558–610 *infra* and accompanying text.

358. *See* Chen, *supra* note 18, at 214–39, 250–60; chapter 7 *infra,* at notes 449–594 and accompanying text; chapter 9 *infra,* at notes 77–284 and accompanying text.

359. *See* O. Asamoah, The Legal Significance of the Declarations of the General Assembly of the United Nations (1966); J. Castaneda, Legal Effects of United Nations Resolutions (A. Amoia trans. 1969); G. Tunkin, *supra* note 315, at 160–79; Arangio-Ruiz, *The Normative Role of the General Assembly of the United Nations and the Declaration of Principles of Friendly Relations,* 137 Hague Recueil des Cours 419 (1972); Bleicher, *The Legal Significance of Recitation of General Assembly Resolutions,* 63 Am. J. Int'l L. 445 (1969); Dugard, *Legal Effect of the United Nations Resolutions on Apartheid,* 83 South African L.J. 44 (1966); Guradze, *Are Human Rights Resolutions of the United Nations General Assembly Law-Making?* 4 Human Rights J. 453 (1971); Higgins, *The Advisory Opinion on Namibia: Which UN Resolutions Are Binding under Article 25 of the Charter?* 21 Int'l & Comp. L.Q. 270 (1972); Johnson, *The Effect of Resolutions of the General Assembly of the United Nations,* 32 Brit. Y.B. Int'l L. 121 (1955–56); Manno, *Majority Decisions and Minority Responses in the United Nations General Assembly,* 10 J. Conflict Resolutions 3 (1966); Sloan, *The Binding Force of a*

with broad acceptance of the requirements for creating customary law, would appear to have established what is in effect a new modality of law making. When resolutions have the overwhelming support of the member states, including all the major powers, such resolutions would appear to be functional equivalents of legislation, whether called "instantaneous customary law,"[360] "quasi-legislation,"[361] or any other name as sweet. The important point is that the peoples of the world now have an established institutionalized process through which they can freely and unambiguously express their expectations about policy, authority, and control in relation to all problems, including those of human rights. The time requirement traditionally associated with the creation of customary law serves, as indicated above, only to ensure that such expectations really occur.[362] With the present highly institutionalized proceedings within the United Nations, any necessity for continuity through time as a means of assurance about the content of communication must recede to a minimum.

It is not our intention to suggest that all General Assembly resolutions are law. Some of them bear little resemblance to genuine legislation or to the realistic expectations of humankind. Whether a resolution coming out of the General Assembly is a genuine expression of general community expectations about authority and control must depend upon every feature of this particular process of communication. For realistic appraisal, it is necessary to examine who voted for and against the resolution, what was said about expectations of authority and control during the course of debate, the relation of the policy content of the resolution to past prescriptions and to the overriding goals of the general community, the history and deliberateness of the consideration of the resolution, the degree of participation by nongovernmental groups and individuals, the sanctioning measures contemplated or established for making the policy effective, and so on.

The present common acceptance of the Universal Declaration of Human Rights as quasi-legislation offers an excellent example of this

---

"Recommendation" of the General Assembly of the United Nations, 25 BRIT. Y.B. INT'L L. 1 (1948); Tammes, *Decisions of International Organs as a Source of International Law,* 94 HAGUE RECUEIL DES COURS 261 (1958); Vallat, *The Competence of the United Nations General Assembly,* 97 HAGUE RECUEIL DES COURS 203 (1959); Vallat, *The General Assembly and the Security Council of the United Nations,* 29 BRIT. Y.B. INT'L L. 63 (1952).

360. Cheng, *United Nations Resolutions on Outer Space: "Instant" International Customary Law?* 5 INDIAN J. INT'L L. 23 (1965),

361. Falk, *On the Quasi-Legislative Competence of the General Assembly,* 60 AM. J. INT'L L. 728 (1966), *reprinted in* R. FALK, THE STATUS OF LAW IN INTERNATIONAL SOCIETY 174–84 (1970). *Cf.* Saba, *L'Activité Quasi-Législative des Institutions Spécialisées des Nations Unies,* 111 HAGUE RECUEIL DES COURS 603 (1964).

362. *See* notes 350–52 *supra* and accompanying text.

mode of prescription. When the Universal Declaration was adopted unanimously in December 1948 by the General Assembly, the stated expectation was that it mirrored merely "a common standard of achievement," devoid of legal authority and enforceability.[363] In the nearly three decades subsequent to its adoption, however, the Universal Declaration has been affirmed and reaffirmed by numerous resolutions of United Nations entities and related agencies; invoked and reinvoked by a broad range of decision makers, national and transnational, judicial and other; and incorporated into many international agreements and national constitutions.[364] The result is that the Universal Declaration is now widely acclaimed as a Magna Carta of humankind,[365] to be complied with by all actors in the world arena. What began as mere common aspiration is now hailed both as an authoritative interpretation of the human rights provisions of the United Nations Charter and as established customary law, having the attributes of *jus cogens* and constituting the heart of a global bill of rights.[366]

The different modes of prescription offered by contemporary global constitutive process are not mutually exclusive, but rather mutually reinforcing. Depending upon context and problem, emphasis upon one mode may be more economic and effective than emphasis upon another. The crucial consideration is not so much in the precise modality of formulation and communication as in the degree to which the policies projected become a part of the working expectations of community members. As we have elsewhere suggested:

---

363. *See* N. Robinson, The Universal Declaration of Human Rights 33–35 (1958).

364. For detail, *see* United Nations Action, *supra* note 73, at 9–19.

365. On the eve of the adoption of the Universal Declaration of Human Rights, Mrs. Franklin D. Roosevelt, United States Representative to the Human Rights Commission, stated:

> We stand today at the threshold of a great event both in the life of the United Nations and in the life of mankind, that is the approval by the General Assembly of the Universal Declaration of Human Rights recommended by the Third Committee. This declaration may well become the international Magna Carta of all men everywhere. We hope its proclamation by the General Assembly will be an event comparable to the proclamation of the Declaration of the Rights of Man by the French people in 1789, the adoption of the Bill of Rights by the people of the United States, and the adoption of comparable declarations at different times in other countries.

19 Dep't State Bull. 751 (1948).

For a moving account of Mrs. Roosevelt's vital role in the adoption of the Universal Declaration, *see* J. Lash, Eleanor: The Years Alone 55–81 (1972) (the chapter is entitled "A Magna Charta for Mankind"). *See also* Whiteman, *Mrs. Franklin D. Roosevelt and the Human Rights Commission,* 62 Am. J. Int'l L. 918 (1968).

366. *See* notes 558–610 *infra* and accompanying text.

> If principles of authority are to control the flow of decision, it is ultimately essential that they be embodied in the expectations of the effective participants in the world community. At no time can it be taken for granted that human expectations, or the demands and identifications with which they interlock, are unchanging. Nor can it be validly asserted, without appropriate verification, that the words of treaties or other written documents, mirror community expectations. Since viewpoints are in flux, today's structure of expectation is open to change, and in fact is bound to change, as new conditions arise and new suggestions are put forward and assimilated.[367]

The practices of the United Nations have given a tremendous boost to the historic modes of law making, by articulated multilateral agreement and by less articulated cooperative behavior, and have added a new dimension that reflects a closer approximation to parliamentary enactment. The activities of the General Assembly, through its committees and other subsidiary entities, have greatly rationalized prescription by multilateral agreement, as witness the many important new conventions about human rights. The opportunities afforded in the General Assembly for the representatives of many different communities to state their conceptions of prevailing law and to articulate these conceptions in formal resolutions have, further, greatly eased the historic burden of identifying customary law and clarifying its content. It is this latter modality of General Assembly resolution, greatly foreshortening the time necessary for establishing customary law and affording an economic mode for articulating consensus about common interest, that increasingly bears the hallmarks of parliamentary enactment. Clearly, if existing prescriptions about the protection of human rights are inadequate, the existing prescribing process offers few impediments to their being made adequate.

The existing prescribing process would indeed appear, insofar as human rights are concerned, to exhibit an increasing inclusivity, rationality, and effectiveness. It is the great merit of the informal components in transnational prescribing processes, whereby expectations about policies, authority, and control are created by cooperative behavior, both official and nonofficial, that they foster an appropriate inclusivity. Such components represent a preferred democracy and representativeness, in that they involve a constant accommodation of the interests and behavior of all participants who are affected by the prescriptions being created. The General Assembly and other structures of authority are able to communicate to a worldwide audience, articulating and reflecting the

367. M. McDougal, H. Lasswell, & I. Vlasic, *supra* note 172, at 146.

expectations of the peoples of the world. With this salient feature of democratic participation, human rights prescriptions have generally served common rather than special interests, with an appropriate balancing of both inclusive and exclusive interests. The aggregate achievement in the formulation of transnational human rights is impressive, as witness the emerging global bill of human rights, which includes a multiplying host of specific human rights conventions and declarations. The policy content of the human rights prescription is being clarified in greater and greater detail, attendant expectations of authority are being generated and solidified, and expectations of control are gradually being affected.

It must, however, be conceded that, despite all these very encouraging developments, many difficulties remain. The global arena still lacks a well-organized, centralized institution for the purpose of prescription. In regard to the most deliberate mode of prescription, that by agreement, states are still not bound by a particular international agreement unless they express explicit consent. Until a particular agreement becomes customary law, ratification remains necessary and, as the dismal record of the United States suggests, is not always easy to achieve.[368] The

---

368. *See* J. CAREY, *supra* note 190, at 9–16; UNITED NATIONS INSTITUTE FOR TEACHING AND RESEARCH, ACCEPTANCE OF HUMAN RIGHTS TREATIES (1968); *Acceptance of Human Rights Treaties,* U.N. Doc. A/CONF.32/15 (1968) (paper prepared by UNITAR).

For the record of ratification of various human rights treaties, *see* UNITED NATIONS, MULTILATERAL TREATIES IN RESPECT OF WHICH THE SECRETARY-GENERAL PERFORMS DEPOSITORY FUNCTIONS: LIST OF SIGNATURES, RATIFICATIONS, ACCESSIONS, ETC., AS AT 31 DECEMBER 1976, U.N. Doc. ST/LEG.SER.D/10 (1977). *See also* THE WORLD ASSOCIATION OF LAWYERS, THE RATIFICATION OF INTERNATIONAL HUMAN RIGHTS TREATIES (1976) (containing ratification record up to May 1, 1976).

On the pros and cons of U.S. ratification of human rights conventions, *see* R. GARDNER, IN PURSUIT OF WORLD ORDER: U.S. FOREIGN POLICY AND INTERNATIONAL ORGANIZATIONS 245–63 (1966); Bitker, *The Constitutionality of International Agreements on Human Rights,* 12 SANTA CLARA LAWYER 279 (1972); Bitker, *Some Remarks on U.S. Policy of the Ratification of the International Human Rights Conventions,* 2 HUMAN RIGHTS J. 653 (1969); Bryant & Jones, *United States and the 1948 Genocide Convention,* 16 HARV. INT'L L.J. 683 (1975); Ferguson, *United Nations Human Rights Covenants: Problems of Ratification and Implementation,* 1968 PROC., AM. SOC'Y INT'L L. 83; Korey, *Human Rights Treaties: Why Is the U.S. Stalling?* 45 FOREIGN AFFAIRS 414 (1967); MacChesney, *Should the United States Ratify the Covenants? A Question of Merits, Not of Constitutional Law,* 62 AM. J. INT'L L. 912 (1968); Mueller & Schroth, *Racial Discrimination: The United States and the International Convention,* 4 HUMAN RIGHTS 171 (1975); Raymond, *Don't Ratify the Human Rights Conventions,* 54 A.B.A.J. 141 (1968); Tuttle, *Are the "Human Rights" Conventions Really Objectionable?* 3 INT'L LAWYER 385 (1969); *U.N. "Human Rights" Conventions,* 1 INT'L LAWYER 589 (1967); *President Supports Human Rights Stand in Speech to O.A.S.,* N.Y. Times, Apr. 15, 1977, at A1, col. 2 (city ed.); *U.S. Will Prod O.A.S. on Enforcing Rights, id.,* June 10, 1977, at A7, col. 1.

To fulfill President Carter's commitment to human rights, the Carter administration has

parliamentary mode of prescription within the United Nations is not necessarily democratic. It may be democratic in the sense of the factitious equality of all states, but not in the sense of democratic participation for individual human beings. The procedures in the General Assembly are so crude and cumbersome that prescription may still be manipulated to serve special interests rather than common interests. This is exemplified by the vivid contrast between the speedy adoption of the Declaration and the Convention on the Elimination of All Forms of Racial Discrimination and the snail-moving effort regarding the draft declaration and the draft convention on the elimination of religious discrimination and intolerance.[369] A coalition of special interests has stifled vigorous efforts toward the eradication of discrimination on the basis of religion. Other examples include inaction concerning freedom of information[370] and the reluctance to establish a United Nations High Commissioner for Human Rights, or international ombudsman.[371]

While the least deliberate mode of prescription, by uniformities in decision and behavior, admits of greater participation by groups and individuals, the process is extremely slow and fragmentary. The criteria for the identification of customary law admit of differing appreciations, and in the absence of a centralized agency empowered to make final decision, whether and when a particular customary prescription has emerged is always a matter of considerable controversy. Similarly, failures in the management of the application function have greatly hampered the establishment of expectations of control that, no less than expectations of authority, are an essential ingredient of effective law. In sum, given the realities of the contemporary global process of effective power, none of the existing modes of making international law would appear wholly adequate to the task of creating and maintaining appropriate human rights prescriptions.

---

provided new leadership toward ratification of several important human rights conventions. *See* President Carter's address before the United Nations in March 1977, *supra* note 171; *President Carter Sends Message to the Senate on the Genocide Convention,* 123 Cong. Rec. S8324 (May 23, 1977); *American Convention on Human Rights,* Weekly Compilation of Presidential Documents, Vol. 13, no. 23 (June 6, 1977) (the president's remarks upon signing the convention in a ceremony at the Pan American Union, June 1, 1977).

369. *See* chapter 11 *infra,* at notes 135–50 and accompanying text.

370. *See* H. Eek, Freedom of Information as a Project of International Legislation (1953); Final Act of the United Nations Conference on Freedom of Information (1948); J. Green, *supra* note 124, at 76–88; S. Lopez, Freedom of Information (United Nations, 1953); United Nations, Freedom of Information (1050); United Nations, 1962 Seminar on Freedom of Information (1962); Binder, *Freedom of Information and the United Nations,* 6 Int'l Org. 210 (1952).

371. *See* notes 406–23 *infra* and accompanying text.

THE INVOKING FUNCTION

The invoking function involves the provisional characterization of events in terms of community prescriptions.[372] This function is a preliminary to the applying function, which makes a more final characterization; it sets an application in motion. An invocation, when comprehensive, includes the following sequence: initiation, the exploration of facts and potential policies, the provisional characterization of the selected facts in terms of the selected authoritative policies, and the stimulation of applicative arenas. Like other claims to authority, an invocation commonly makes assertions about facts, relevant policies (prescriptions), and appropriate remedies. People who invoke make allegations about what has happened (the facts of deprivations or nonfulfillment), what policies have been violated, and what future action might remedy the wrong or nonfulfillment. Invocation thus serves as a bridge from prescription to application. Whether or not it actually sets the applying function into motion, a provisional characterization of events as deviations from prescribed norms may of itself entail significant value consequences.

The participants who engage in invocation before transnational arenas cover the whole spectrum, including states, international governmental organizations, nongovernmental organizations and groups, and individual persons. The purposes of invocation range from securing the benefits of an informal appreciation of events to setting in motion a formal application by authoritative decision makers. The situations in which invocation occurs include interactions in both the different value processes and the specialized arenas of authoritative application. In situations of a lesser degree of institutionalization, invocation is open to all effective participants; in arenas of a higher degree of institutionalization, formal access may be highly restricted. The base values of participants may vary greatly, manifesting a wide range of differences in relative strengths, abilities, skills, and resources; contrast, for example, the relative capabilities of a state invoker and of an individual invoker. The strategies employed may be in the form of private communications (letters, telegrams, etc.), the media of mass communication (editorial, reporting, letter writing, etc.), or highly stylized procedures. The outcomes may involve changing public opinion, arousing the attention of selective elites, or effectively initiating the process of application.

Broad access to and participation in the function of invocation are indispensable to a global constitutive process designed to protect human rights. Respect for and confidence in processes of authoritative decision

---

372. *See* McDougal, Lasswell, & Reisman, *supra* note 1, at 142–45.

depend in no small measure upon the ability of individuals and private groups to challenge unlawful deprivations. Similarly, an effective public order of human dignity must require that representative organs of the general community be authorized and capable of stimulating decision when injured parties are unable to do so. Though current access to invocation is far from optimum, a trend toward broader participation in this function is evident. Individuals are increasingly being accorded the competence to invoke processes of transnational decision for protection of their rights. Reference has already been made, in our discussion of arenas, to the access accorded individuals by a number of highly institutionalized, transnational arenas, including the United Nations Commission on Human Rights, the Human Rights Committee under the International Covenant on Civil and Political Rights and its Optional Protocol, the Committee on the Elimination of Racial Discrimination, the European Commission on Human Rights, and the Inter-American Commission on Human Rights.[373]

The nation-state has, for securing its power bases, been the principal protector of the human rights of its nationals abroad. The important role of state officials in invocation of the customary international law of state responsibility concerning the treatment of aliens has been noted above.[374] The extension of such protection is linked, it may be recalled, to the nationality test, and is otherwise highly discretionary. A state does not often invoke transnational decision to protect nonnationals. Even with regard to its own nationals who have sustained deprivations imposed by other governments, a state may choose not to espouse claims, because of either idiosyncratic policy considerations or ambiguous conceptions of nationality.[375] Within the contemporary human rights movement, both global and regional, the state-to-state complaint system remains, however, an important modality of invocation. As the need to seek transnational protection against deprivations imposed by one's own government becomes apparent, the state-to-state complaint procedure is increasingly being employed to protect the human rights of nonnationals.

The growing importance of the state-to-state complaint system is illustrated in the International Covenant on Civil and Political Rights,[376] the International Convention on the Elimination of All Forms of Racial Discrimination,[377] the Constitution of the International Labor Organiza-

373. *See* notes 79–108 *supra* and accompanying text.
374. *See* notes 178–84 *supra* and accompanying text.
375. *See* the appendix *infra*, at notes 4–42 and accompanying text.
376. Covenant on Civil and Political Rights, *supra* note 48, Arts. 41 and 42.
377. Convention on the Elimination of Racial Discrimination, *supra* note 97, Arts. 11–13.

tion,[378] the UNESCO Protocol Instituting a Conciliation and Good Offices Commission in Relation to the Convention against Discrimination in Education,[379] the European Convention on Human Rights,[380] and the American Convention on Human Rights,[381] all of which explicitly authorize a state party to invoke transnational prescription against defaulting parties. While the Convention of the International Labor Organization, the UNESCO Protocol, and the European Convention make the state-to-state complaint procedure mandatory, the Covenant on Civil and Political Rights and the American Convention make it optional. The utility of the state-to-state complaint procedure has been questioned in terms of its potentially harmful effects on friendly relations between states, its possible abuse from political motivation, and the likelihood of infrequent use.[382] Concerns such as these account in measure for the optional feature embodied in the Covenant on Civil and Political Rights. Article 41(1) of that Covenant reads in part:

> A State Party to the present Covenant may at any time declare under this article that it recognizes the competence of the Committee to receive and consider communications to the effect that a State Party claims that another State Party is not fulfilling its obligations under the present Covenant. Communications under this article may be received and considered only if submitted by a State Party which has made a declaration recognizing in regard to itself the competence of the Committee. No communication shall be received by the Committee if it concerns a State Party which has not made such a declaration.[383]

Experience under the European Convention on Human Rights would

---

378. The Constitution of the International Labor Organization, in Art. 26(1), provides: "Any of the Members shall have the right to file a complaint with the International Labor Office if it is not satisfied that any other Member is securing the effective observance of any Convention which both have ratified. . . ." INTERNATIONAL GOVERNMENTAL ORGANIZATIONS: CONSTITUTIONAL DOCUMENTS 994, 1003 (rev. 3d ed. A. Peaslee ed. 1974) [hereinafter cited as INTERNATIONAL GOVERNMENTAL ORGANIZATIONS]. For the actual application of this provision, *see* THE IMPACT, *supra* note 292, at 65–69.

379. Protocol Instituting a Conciliation and Good Offices Commission to Be Responsible for Seeking a Settlement of Any Disputes Which May Arise between States Parties to the Convention against Discrimination in Education, *adopted* Dec. 10, 1962, Art. 12 (entered into force Oct. 24, 1968), *reprinted in* U.N. HUMAN RIGHTS INSTRUMENTS, *supra* note 51, at 33–37.

380. European Convention, *supra* note 100, Art. 24.

381. American Convention, *supra* note 144, Arts. 45–47.

382. *See, e.g.*, Schwelb, *Civil and Political Rights: The International Measures of Implementation*, 62 AM. J. INT'L L. 827, 845–46 (1968) [hereinafter cited as Schwelb, *Civil and Political Rights*].

383. Covenant on Civil and Political Rights, *supra* note 48, Art. 41(1).

appear to document the value of the state-to-state complaint procedure. The European Convention, in Article 24, provides: "Any High Contracting Party may refer to the Commission [of Human Rights], through the Secretary-General of the Council of Europe, any alleged breach of the provisions of the Convention by another High Contracting Party."[384] As of December 1976, a dozen cases had been brought before the European Commission of Human Rights under this provision. Of these twelve cases, two were brought by Greece in 1956–57 against the United Kingdom, regarding the situation in Cyprus; one by Austria against Italy in 1960; five by Denmark, Norway, Sweden, and the Netherlands (both separately and jointly), in 1967 and in 1970, against Greece; two by Ireland against the United Kingdom, in 1971 and in 1972, regarding the situation in Northern Ireland; and two by Cyprus against Turkey in 1974 and in 1975.[385] Though complaints brought by states against other states have been infrequent in comparison with the thousands of petitions filed by individuals,[386] state complaints have generally addressed themselves to whole situations involving a mass of human rights deprivations in a particular territorial community. For instance, thanks to the availability of the state-to-state complaint procedure, the immense violations of human rights in Greece in the wake of the seizure of power by the military junta in 1967 were promptly brought before the European Commission on Human Rights, effectively exposed, condemned, and ultimately terminated.[387] This example clearly confirms Lady Gaitskell's dictum: "[T]he infrequency of complaints demonstrated the responsible attitude taken towards the procedure and its value; the procedure's very existence was a deterrent, serving to encourage a Government to remedy more quickly any abuse of human rights within its territory."[388]

Despite its usefulness, the fact remains that state elites are generally reluctant to resort to the state-to-state complaint procedure to accuse other governments of human rights violations, lest they themselves should become targets of complaints. The dynamics of reciprocity and retaliation in a decentralized world are well understood. Hence, the

---

384. European Convention, *supra* note 100, Art. 24.

385. STOCK-TAKING, *supra* note 104, at 5–12.

386. *Id.* at 4–5.

387. *See* L. SOHN & T. BUERGENTHAL, *supra* note 39, at 1059–90; Becker, *The Greek Case before the European Human Rights Commission,* 1 HUMAN RIGHTS 91 (1970); Buergenthal, *Proceedings against Greece under the European Convention on Human Rights,* 62 AM. J. INT'L L. 441 (1968); Coleman, *Greece and the Council of Europe: The International Legal Protection of Human Rights by the Political Process,* 2 ISRAEL Y.B. HUMAN RIGHTS 121 (1972); Weeramantry, *Applications before the European Commission of Human Rights against Greece,* [1969] REV. INT'L COMM'N JURISTS 37.

388. 21 U.N. GAOR, C.3 (1415th mtg) 223, U.N. Doc. A/C.3/SR.1415 (1966).

necessity of invocation by individuals and private groups cannot be overemphasized. Unless individuals and nongovernmental groups can invoke transnational authority for remedy on their own behalf or on behalf of other victims, the elaborate human rights prescriptions may become mere illusory aspiration.

The increasing access of individuals and private groups to transnational arenas of decision, such as the United Nations Commission on Human Rights and the European Commission of Human Rights, has been described above.[389] The procedures for individual petition are, however, far from simple, open, and effective. Contemporary prescriptions create an extraordinary number of obstacles to the effective exercise of the right of individual petitions, as illustrated by the procedures within the United Nations and the cumulative experience under the European Convention on Human Rights.

Under the United Nations system, as devised in 1971 by the Sub-Commission on Prevention of Discrimination and Protection of Minorities, individual petitions ("communications") must fulfill certain requirements of admissibility:[390]

1. The objective of the petition must not be inconsistent with the relevant principles of the United Nations Charter, the Universal Declaration of Human Rights, and other human rights prescriptions;
2. There must appear reasonable grounds that inquiry will "reveal a consistent pattern of gross and reliably attested violations of human rights and fundamental freedoms. . . .";[391]
3. The petition must originate from a person or group of persons who are presumably victims of the gross violations, "any person or group of persons who have direct and reliable knowledge of those violations," or "non-governmental organizations acting in good faith" and "having direct and reliable knowledge of such violations";[392]
4. The petition must indicate the facts, the purpose of the petition, and the rights allegedly violated;
5. The petition must not be abusive in its language;
6. The petition must not contain "manifestly political motivations"

389. *See* notes 79–108 *supra* and accompanying text.

390. Res. 1 (XXIV) of the Sub-Commission on Prevention of Discrimination and Protection of Minorities, Aug. 13, 1971, *Report of the Sub-Commission on Prevention of Discrimination and Protection of Minorities on Its 24th Session* 50–52, U.N. Doc. E/CN.4/1070 (1971).

391. *Id.* at 50.

392. *Id.* at 50–51.

and must not contravene "the provisions of the Charter of the United Nations";[393]

7. The petition must not be "based exclusively on reports disseminated by mass media";[394]
8. The admission of the petition must not "prejudice the functions of the specialized agencies of the United Nations system";[395]
9. The petition must not concern a matter that has already been settled by the state concerned in accordance with the Universal Declaration of Human Rights and other relevant human rights prescriptions; and
10. The petitioner must exhaust available domestic remedies and file the petition to the United Nations "within a reasonable time after the exhaustion of the domestic remedies."[396]

Unless all of these requirements are fulfilled, a petition is to be rejected as inadmissible.

Under the European Convention the conditions of admissibility for individual petitions are stipulated in Articles 25 to 27.[397] In brief:

1. The defendant state must recognize the competence of the European Commission of Human Rights to receive individual petitions (Article 25[1]);
2. The petitioner must be some "person, nongovernmental organization or group of individuals claiming to be the victim of a violation" by the defendant state "of the rights set forth" in the Convention (Article 25[1]);
3. The petitioner must exhaust "all domestic remedies" in accordance with the general principles of international law and file the

---

393. *Id.* at 51.

394. *Id.*

395. *Id.*

396. *Id.* For discussions, *see* Boyle & Hannum, *Individual Applications under the European Convention on Human Rights and the Concept of Administrative Practice: The Donnelly Case,* 68 AM. J. INT'L L. 440 (1974); Carey, *United Nations' Double Standard on Human Rights Complaints,* 60 AM. J. INT'L L. 792 (1966); Carey, *The International Legal Order on Human Rights,* in 4 THE FUTURE OF THE INTERNATIONAL LEGAL ORDER 268–90 (C. Black & R. Falk eds. 1972); Guggenheim, *Key Provisions of the New United Nations Rules Dealing with Human Rights Petitions,* 6 N.Y.U.J. INT'L L. & POLITICS 427 (1973); Humphrey, *Right of Petition in the United Nations,* 4 HUMAN RIGHTS J. 463 (1971); Lillich, *U.N. and Human Rights Complaints: U Thant as Strict Constructionist,* 64 AM. J. INT'L L. 610 (1970); Wilkoc, *Procedures to Deal with Individual Communications to International Bodies,* 1 N.Y.U.J. INT'L L. & POLITICS 277 (1968).

397. European Convention, *supra* note 100, Arts. 25–27. For commentaries, *see* J. FAWCETT, *supra* note 107, at 277–314; F. CASTBERG, *supra* note 107, at 34–67; F. JACOBS, *supra* note 107, at 218–51; A. ROBERTSON, HUMAN RIGHTS IN EUROPE 49–58 (1963).

petition "within a period of six months from the date on which the final decision was taken" (Article 26);

4. The petitioner must not be anonymous (Article 27[1] [a]);
5. The petition must not concern a matter that has already been examined by the Commission or subjected to another procedure of international investigation or settlement (Article 27[1] [b]);
6. The petition must not be "incompatible with the provisions of the present Convention, manifestly ill-founded, or an abuse of the right of petition" (Article 27[2]).

Failure to meet all these requirements renders the petition inadmissible. The high discretion accorded the Commission is obvious.

Because of these multiple requirements in the European Convention, approximately 90 percent of a total of more than 7,000 individual petitions, filed after the system of individual petitions came into operation in 1955, were declared inadmissible or struck off the list of cases by the Commission.[398] This rigorous scrutiny of individual petitions is regarded by some as having contributed to the effective functioning of the European system.[399] Yet its chilling effect upon individual invocation can scarcely be overlooked. The discretion enjoyed (or commanded) by the Commission in deciding upon the admissibility or inadmissibility of a petition is indeed considerable. The Commission's discretionary power has been especially pronounced in determining whether a petition is "incompatible with the provisions" of the Convention, or "manifestly ill-founded," or "an abuse of the right of petition," and whether "all domestic remedies" have been appropriately exhausted.[400] To make determinations on any of these grounds, the Commission inescapably finds it extremely difficult not to touch upon, in varying modalities and de-

---

398. STOCK-TAKING, *supra* note 104, at 4–5.

399. *See, e.g.*, Schwelb, *The Abuse of the Right of Petition,* 3 HUMAN RIGHTS J. 313, 329 (1970).

400. *See* F. CASTBERG, *supra* note 107, at 58–66; J. FAWCETT, *supra* note 107, at 277–314; F. JACOBS, *supra* note 107, at 234–51; Schwelb, *supra* note 399.

On the doctrine of exhaustion of local remedies, *see generally* C. AMERASINGHE, *supra* note 178, at 169–269; T. HAESLER, THE EXHAUSTION OF LOCAL REMEDIES IN THE CASE LAW OF INTERNATIONAL COURTS AND TRIBUNALS (1968); C. JENKS, INTERNATIONAL ADJUDICATION, *supra* note 15, 527–37; C. LAW, THE LOCAL REMEDIES RULE IN INTERNATIONAL LAW (1961); Amerasinghe, *The Exhaustion of Procedural Remedies in the Same Court,* 12 INT'L & COMP. L.Q. 1285 (1963); Amerasinghe, *The Rule of Exhaustion of Domestic Remedies in the Framework of International Systems for the Protection of Human Rights,* 28 ZEITSCHRIFT FÜR AUSLANDISCHES OFFENTLICHES RECHT UND VOLKERRECHT 257 (1968); Mummery, *The Content of the Duty to Exhaust Local Judicial Remedies,* 58 AM. J. INT'L L. 389 (1964); *Panel, Using a Country's Own Legal System to Cause It to Respect International Rights,* 58 PROC., AM. SOC'Y INT'L L. 100 (1964).

On the concept of abuse of rights, *see generally* Taylor, *The Content of the Rule against Abuse of Rights in International Law,* 46 BRIT. Y.B. INT'L L. 323 (1972–73).

grees, the substantive merit of a particular petition. Hence, while the concept of "admissibility" is highly technical, the deprivatory consequence of a decision of inadmissibility is unmistakable.

The conditions of admissibility regarding individual petitions, as embodied in the Optional Protocol to the International Covenant on Civil and Political Rights (Articles 1 to 5),[401] in the Regulations of the Inter-American Commission on Human Rights (Articles 37 to 40),[402] and in the American Convention on Human Rights (Articles 46 and 47),[403] are substantially the same, though with some variations, as those of the European Convention. Hence, the difficulties attending the European practice have potential significance for the application of the Optional Protocol, the Regulations, and the American Convention.

Fortunately, the provisions of Article 46 of the American Convention bring considerable clarity to the doctrine of exhaustion of domestic remedies. After indicating, in its first paragraph, the requirements that "the remedies of domestic law have been pursued and exhausted, in accordance with generally recognized principles of international law" and that "the petition is lodged within a period of six months from the date on which the party alleging violation of his rights was notified of the final decision,"[404] Article 46 further stipulates, in its second paragraph, that the above requirements would be exempted when:

> (a) the domestic legislation of the State concerned does not afford due process of law for the protection of the right or rights that have allegedly been violated;
>
> (b) the party alleging violation of his right has been denied access to the remedies of domestic jurisdiction or has been prevented from exhausting them; or
>
> (c) there has been unwarranted delay in reaching a decision on the aforementioned remedies.[405]

The facts of effective power suggest that petitions by individuals cannot at present be the most effective form of remedy for deprivations of human rights. The discrepancy in effective power between an individual petitioner and a respondent state is simply too great. It appears vital that, in addition to state-to-state complaints and individual petitions, some form of invocation, representative of the general community and

---

401. Covenant on Civil and Political Rights, *supra* note 48, Arts. 1–5.

402. Regulations of the Inter-American Commission on Human Rights, *approved* Oct. 24, 1960, with amendments to May 1967, Arts. 37–40, OAS Official Records, OEA/Ser.L/V/11.17, Doc. 26 (1967), *reprinted in* Basic Documents, *supra* note 51, at 199–209.

403. American Convention, *supra* note 144, Arts. 46 and 47.

404. *Id.*, Art. 46.

405. *Id.*

backed by its strength, be made available. The most promising expedient yet proposed would appear to be the establishment of a United Nations High Commissioner for Human Rights, a sort of international ombudsman, charged with the responsibility of invocation on behalf of both victims and the general community.[406]

The idea of creating a United Nations High Commissioner for Human Rights is traceable back to the early days of the United Nations.[407] In 1947, Professor René Cassin, French delegate on the Human Rights Commission, suggested the establishment of a United Nations Attorney-General.[408] The proposed attorney general would act as an international invoker representing individuals and groups in appellate proceedings before an international court of human rights (a special tribunal or a human rights chamber of the International Court of Jus-

---

406. In the eloquent words of Vasak:

> Because of this proliferation of [human rights] institutions, it is all the more essential that a body should be set up *capable of dealing with human rights on a world-wide scale, without reference to the level—national, regional or universal—at which these rights operate.* One may submit that this is the constructive role to be played by the *United Nations Commissioner for Human Rights,* the creation of which office has been proposed following the precedent of the protection of refugees.

Vasak, *supra* note 301, at 179 (italics original).

Regarding proposals for establishing a United Nations High Commissioner for Human Rights, *see* J. Carey, *supra* note 190, at 70–71; R. CLARK, A UNITED NATIONS HIGH COMMISSIONER FOR HUMAN RIGHTS (1972) [hereinafter cited as R. CLARK]; Etra, *International Protection of Human Rights: The Proposal for a U.N. High Commissioner,* 5 COLUM. J. TRANSNAT'L L. 150 (1966); Humphrey, *United Nations High Commissioner for Human Rights: The Birth of an Initiative,* 11 CANADIAN Y.B. INT'L L. 220 (1973); MacBride, *The Strengthening of International Machinery for the Protection of Human Rights,* in NOBEL SYMPOSIUM ON HUMAN RIGHTS, *supra* note 147, at 149, 163–65; MacDonald, *The United Nations High Commissioner for Human Rights,* 1967 CANADIAN Y.B. INT'L L. 84; Newman, *Ombudsmen and Human Rights: The New U.N. Treaty Proposals,* 34 U. CHI. L. REV. 951 (1967).

More generally, *see* OMBUDSMEN FOR AMERICAN GOVERNMENT? (S. Anderson ed. 1968); W. GELLHORN, OMBUDSMEN AND OTHERS: CITIZENS' PROTECTORS IN NINE COUNTRIES (1967); M. HIDEN, THE OMBUDSMAN IN FINLAND: THE FIRST FIFTY YEARS (A. Bell trans., D. Rowat ed. 1973); THE OMBUDSMAN: CITIZEN'S DEFENDER (2d ed. D. Rowat ed. 1968); D. ROWAT, THE OMBUDSMAN PLAN: ESSAYS ON THE WORLDWIDE SPREAD OF AN IDEA (1973); Blix, *Pattern of Effective Protection: The Ombudsman,* 11 HOW. L.J. 386 (1965); Frank, *The Ombudsman and Human Rights—Revisited,* 6 ISRAEL Y.B. HUMAN RIGHTS 122 (1976); Kutner, *World Habeas Corpus: Ombudsman for Mankind,* 24 U. MIAMI L. REV. 352 (1970); *The Ombudsman or Citizen's Defender: A Modern Institution,* 377 ANNALS (May 1968).

407. *See* R. CLARK, *supra* note 406, at 39–44.

408. *Letter from the Representative of France to the Chairman of the Working Party on Implementation of Human Rights,* U.N. Doc. E/CN.4/AC.4/1 (1947). *See also Statement by Mr. René Cassin, Representative of France, on the Implementation of Human Rights,* U.N. Doc. E/CN.4/147 (1948).

See also M. MOSKOWITZ, HUMAN RIGHTS AND WORLD ORDER 192 (1958) [hereinafter cited as M. MOSKOWITZ, 1958].

tice), while individuals and groups would be accorded the competence to initiate proceedings, through individual petitions, at the level of original jurisdiction (a special commission to be created). In 1949, the Consultative Council of Jewish Organizations submitted a memorandum to the Commission, stating that while the French proposal was made contingent upon vesting jurisdiction in an international court, it could be adapted to some other modalities to enhance the protection of human rights.[409] In 1950, at the fifth session of the General Assembly, the Uruguayan delegation formally proposed the establishment of a United Nations High Commissioner (Attorney-General) for Human Rights as a measure of implementing the proposed Covenant on Civil and Political Rights.[410] The principal thrust of the proposed functions for the high commissioner was to receive and screen petitions from individuals and private groups and to present complaints and initiate proceedings, on behalf of the individual petitioners, before a contemplated Human Rights Committee. The proposed high commissioner would represent the conscience of the general community of humankind in protecting the human rights of the individual and in defending the integrity of the contemplated Covenant, much as an attorney general in a national legal system performs the invoking function in the name of the state. Like Cassin's proposal, the Uruguayan proposal did not gain much support. Opponents characterized the proposal as premature, overambitious, ambiguous, and impractical.[411]

The idea of establishing a United Nations High Commissioner for Human Rights received a renewed interest at the Department of State in 1963 during the closing months of the Kennedy administration.[412] A group of individuals and nongovernmental organizations began new efforts. In 1965 Costa Rica formally proposed that the General Assembly establish a United Nations High Commissioner for Human Rights.[413] In

---

409. *Proposal for a United Nations Attorney General for Human Rights: Summary of a Statement Submitted by the Consultative Council of Jewish Organizations, a Non-Governmental Organization in Category B. Consultative Status,* U.N. Doc. E/CN.4/NGO/6 (1950).

See also M. Moskowitz, 1958, *supra* note 408, at 192.

410. *Bases of the Proposal to Establish a United Nations Attorney-General for Human Rights: Memorandum Submitted by Uruguay,* 6 U.N. GAOR, Annexes (Agenda Item 29) 9, U.N. Doc. A/C.3/564 (1951); *Draft First International Covenant on Human Rights and Measures of Implementation: Uruguay: Addition to the Joint Draft Resolution Submitted by Brazil, Turkey and the United States of America (A/C.3/L.76),* U.N. Doc. A/C.3/L.93 (1950).

411. *Annotations on the Text of the Draft International Covenants on Human Rights* 84–85, 10 U.N. GAOR, Annexes (Agenda Item 28, pt. 2), U.N. Doc. A/2929 (1955) (prepared by the secretary-general) [hereinafter cited as *Annotations on the Draft Covenants*].

412. *See Foreword by Richard N. Gardner,* in R. Clark, *supra* note 406, at xi-xv. *See also id.* at 45–47.

413. *Election of a United Nations High Commissioner for Human Rights: Communication from the Permanent Representative of Costa Rica to the United Nations,* U.N. Doc. E/CN.4/887 (1965);

1967 the Costa Rican proposal, having benefited from a study of a working group formed in 1966,[414] was adopted successively by the Human Rights Commission[415] and by the Economic and Social Council in its Resolution 1237 (XLII).[416] As proposed in ECOSOC Resolution 1237, the high commissioner would enjoy considerable authority in the protection of human rights. Among other functions, the high commissioner would "have access to communications concerning human rights, addressed to the United Nations, of the kind referred to in Economic and Social Council resolution 728F (XXVIII) of 30 July 1959"[417] and might, "whenever he deems it appropriate, bring them to the attention of the Government of any of the States" concerned.[418] Though this mandate would fall short of full-fledged provision of invocation, its potential importance could be far-reaching. Its adoption was no mean achievement, considering the omnipresent concern for general acceptability to a majority of governments.

By the time the ECOSOC proposal was brought before the General Assembly in the fall of 1967, however, many governments began to waver. The consideration of the agenda item entitled "Creation of the Post of United Nations High Commissioner for Human Rights" was postponed by the General Assembly again and again.[419] Finally, in 1973, at its twenty-eighth session, the General Assembly decided to transform the item from "Creation of the Post of United Nations High Commissioner for Human Rights" to "Alternative approaches and ways and means within the United Nations system for improving the effective

---

Provisional Agenda: Note by the Secretary-General, U.N. Doc. E/CN.4/879/Add. 2 (1965); *Report of the Commission on Human Rights: Letter Addressed to the President of the Council by the Permanent Representative of Costa Rica,* U.N. Doc. E/L.1080 (1965).

414. *Report of the Working Group to Study the Proposal to Create the Institution of a United Nations High Commissioner for Human Rights,* U.N. Doc. E/CN.4/934 (1967). *See also Analytical and Technical Study prepared by the Secretary-General under Paragraph 3 of Resolution 4 (XXII) of the Commission on Human Rights,* U.N. Doc. E/CN.4/AC.21/L.1 (1966).

415. Res. 14 (XXIII), COMMISSION ON HUMAN RIGHTS, REPORT ON THE TWENTY-THIRD SESSION, 42 U.M. ESCOR, Supp. (No. 6) 172, 195, U.N. Doc. E/4322 (E/CN.4/940) (1967).

416. E.S.C. Res. 1237, 42 U.N. ESCOR, Supp. (No. 1) 18, U.N. Doc. E/4393 (1967).

417. *Id.*

418. *Id.* For an excellent commentary on this resolution, see MacDonald, *supra* note 406.

419. *See* G.A. Res. 2333, 22 U.N. GAOR, Supp. (No. 16) 40, U.N. Doc. A/6716 (1967); *Creation of the Post of United Nations High Commissioner for Human Rights,* U.N. Doc. A/7170 (1968) (note by the secretary-general); *Creation of the Post of United Nations High Commissioner for Human Rights,* U.N. Doc. A/8035 (1970) (report of the secretary-general); *Creation of the Post of United Nations High Commissioner for Human Rights,* U.N. Doc. A/8231 (1970) (report of the Third Committee); *Creation of the Post of United Nations High Commissioner for Human Rights,* U.N. Doc. A/8594 (1971) (report of the Third Committee).

enjoyment of human rights and fundamental freedoms."[420] The success of this new strategy of diversion is a blow—though not fatal—to the rekindled hope for a speedy establishment of a United Nations High Commissioner for Human Rights.

The search for improved procedures for invocation has been long and tortuous. The idea of a high commissioner has been opposed "as too modest by some and too ambitious by others."[421] Despite temporary setbacks, the observation of Richard Gardner that "The High Commissioner for Human Rights is an idea whose time has come"[422] may prove prophetic. Whatever shortcomings the institution of this office might have in the beginning, the probabilities are, in the words of Humphrey, that "once the institution had been established it would grow under its own momentum."[423]

THE APPLYING FUNCTION

The applying function involves a relatively final characterization of particular events in terms of community prescription and the management of sanctioning measures to secure enforcement.[424] Conventionally, there are many different imprecise labels for describing different constituent parts of, and different approximations to, application, including "investigation," "fact-finding," "on-the-scene observation," "reporting," "negotiation," "good offices," "mediation," "commissions of enquiry," "conciliation," "arbitration," and "adjudication."[425] In its most com-

---

420. G.A. Res. 3136, 28 U.N. GAOR, Supp. (No. 30) 80, U.N. Doc. A/9030 (1973).

For an amusing account, *see* W. Buckley, United Nations Journal: A Delegate's Odyssey 221–30 (1974). *See also* Buckley, *U.N. Defers Action on Proposal for Human Rights Commissioner: Statement with Text of Resolution Adopted, December 14, 1973,* 70 Dep't State Bull. 105 (1974).

421. *Foreword by Richard N. Gardner, supra* note 412, at xv.

422. *Id.*

423. Humphrey, *The International Law of Human Rights in the Middle Twentieth Century,* in The Present State of International Law, *supra* note 32, at 75, 96 [hereinafter cited as Humphrey].

424. *See* McDougal, Lasswell, & Reisman, *supra* note 1, at 145–48.

425. It may be recalled that Art. 33(1) of the United Nations Charter provides:

> The parties to any dispute, the continuance of which is likely to endanger the maintenance of international peace and security, shall, first of all, seek a solution by negotiation, enquiry, mediation, conciliation, arbitration, judicial settlement, resort to regional agencies or arrangements, or other peaceful means of their own choice.

In addition to the sources listed in note 110 *supra, see generally* L. Bloomfield, Evolution or Revolution? The United Nations and the Problem of Peaceful Territorial Change (1957); K. Carlston, The Process of International Arbitration (1946); A. De Bustamante, The World Court (1925); F. Dunn, Peaceful Change (1937); M. Hudson,

prehensive form, application may be characterized as including the following sequential features: the exploration of potential facts, including the precipitating events and their larger factual context; the exploration of potentially relevant policies; the identification of the facts to be regarded as significant; the determination of the authoritative policies applicable; the making of the decision, including the projection of future relations between the parties; enforcement; and review.

The application of prescriptions in particular instances is of course of fundamental and crucial importance to human rights. This is the ultimate outcome sought in all human rights policies. All other functions are in a measure fashioned to assist in securing rational, uniform, effective, and constructive applications. Unless such outcomes are achieved, all the other functions are largely hortatory. As important as it is to challenge unlawful deprivations, it is equally urgent to secure applications that both put basic community policies into controlling practice and mobilize a continuing consensus, in support of prescription, toward the greater future protection and fulfillment of human rights. Applications which reflect the values of human dignity will of course be uniform, in the sense of according equal treatment to parties in equal circumstances.

The great bulk of applications of international law generally continues to be made by national officials in a process of unilateral appreciations and reciprocal responses. This process goes forward from foreign office to foreign office, in internal and external arenas. Many applications are made by internal courts, and some even by legislative bodies. National officials play important roles in application in all transnational arenas, often in collaboration with the officials of international governmental organizations. Such applications may occur in normal diplomatic activities and occasional conferences, or in the more formal parliamentary, adjudicative, and executive structures existing on the global scale. Even

---

The Permanent Court of International Justice, 1920–1942 (1943); C. Jenks, International Adjudication, *supra* note 15; M. Katz, The Relevance of International Adjudication (1968); H. Lauterpacht, The Function of Law in the International Community (1933); O. Lissitzyn, The International Court of Justice: Its Role in the Maintenance of International Peace and Security (U.N. Studies No. 6, 1951); W. Reisman, *supra* note 120; J. Scott, The Judicial Settlement of International Disputes (1927); J. Simpson & H. Fox, International Arbitration: Law and Procedure (1959); United Nations, Systematic Survey of Treaties for the Pacific Settlement of International Disputes, 1928–1948 (1949); Metzger, *Settlement of International Disputes by Non-Judicial Methods,* 48 Am. J. Int'l L. 408 (1954); Murty, *Settlement of Disputes,* in Manual of Public International Law 707–37 (M. Sorensen ed. 1968); Schachter, *The Enforcement of International Judicial and Arbitral Decisions,* 54 Am. J. Int'l L. 1 (1960); Sohn, *supra* note 118; Van Boven, *Fact-Finding in the Field of Human Rights,* 3 Israel Y.B. Human Rights 93 (1973); *Report of the Secretary-General on Methods of Fact-Finding*, 21 U.N. GAOR, Annexes (Agenda Item 87), U.N. Doc. A/6228 (1966).

nonofficials may participate, in all sectors and at all levels of social process, in a range of functional equivalents of official application. What appears to be private may be in effect a functional application of transnational prescriptions.

The principal objective in application is of course to put prescriptions into controlling practice. The demand for an application is, accordingly, a demand for performance of the entire sequence of activities constituting an application, including the exploration and characterization of facts and the exploration and choice of policies. The exploration of policies characteristically includes three interlocking subgoals: the interpretation of prescriptions (seeking the closest possible approximation to the communications made); supplementation (filling gaps and removing ambiguities), and integration (the policing and accommodation of prescriptions in terms of priorities in community demands).[426] The transnational structures of authority employed in application include all five types of arenas specified above.[427] As mentioned, diplomatic interaction is the scene of the great bulk of applications. Adjudicative arenas, including judicial and arbitral tribunals, are notably specialized to application. But even parliamentary bodies, such as the General Assembly and the Security Council, often make characterizations of particular instances in terms of prescriptions. The transnational arenas of application are increasingly open and are moving toward a modest degree of compulsoriness.[428] The base values (in terms both of authority and of effective control) at the disposal of different appliers vary immensely. An expanding body of transnational prescriptions is increasingly available to appliers in all arenas. The effective power of national officials is dependent upon the overall power of their states and perceptions of common interest, while that of international officials remains modest. Strategies of application vary according to arena and to the type of activity involved. The strategies of initiation and exploration in an adjudicative arena differ markedly from those in a diplomatic or an executive arena. In the pre-enforcement phase, various activities are undertaken by different agencies for the purposes of exploring and characterizing relevant facts and policies. The culminating outcomes of application, as expressed in a continuing flow of final characterizations of particular instances in terms of community prescriptions, affect all patterns of value allocation and of future behavior. In the case of persist-

---

426. See McDougal, *Human Rights and World Public Order: Principles of Content and Procedure for Clarifying General Community Policies,* 14 VA. J. INT'L L. 387 (1974). *See also* M. McDOUGAL, H. LASSWELL, & J. MILLER, *supra* note 324, at 35–77.

427. *See* notes 65–77 *supra* and accompanying text.

428. *See* notes 109–44 *supra* and accompanying text.

ing deviations from decision, enforcement measures may be undertaken that employ community intervention to secure the determined allocation of values or projection of future policy. Enforcement may build upon inducement as well as coercion. Particular sanctioning measures may be tailored to the different sanctioning goals of prevention, deterrence, restoration, rehabilitation, reconstruction, and correction.[429] In a fundamental sense, no decision is really final. Every application is an experiment in goal realization which is tested through time and changing context by the responses of those affected, directly and indirectly. Hence, review is often provided at many different levels and by many different modalities.[430]

The special provision made in the global constitutive process for the application of human rights prescriptions continues to be somewhat primitive. Historically, the application of prescriptions regarding state responsibility for the protection of aliens was in the beginning largely dependent upon diplomatic process, with states claiming against states for injuries to nationals.[431] As arbitration has become more popular, its procedures have been employed to secure a measure of third-party decision, with individuals and private associations having some opportunity to participate in the process of decision.[432] National courts have always served some modest role in the protection of aliens, and more recently the International Court of Justice has rendered an occasional decision.

The provision for application of the more contemporary human rights prescriptions has been quite inadequate. This inadequacy is apparent, not only in the procedures before the United Nations Human Rights Commission, which have been summarized above,[433] but also in the provisions of the two International Covenants on Human Rights and other human rights instruments. Making a fundamental distinction between civil and political rights on the one hand and economic, social, and cultural rights on the other, the two Covenants embody very different structures and procedures for application.[434]

The Covenant on Civil and Political Rights contains rudiments of a modest approach to third-party decision-making. The Covenant entrusts the function of application to the Human Rights Committee, which consists of eighteen members, chosen from nationals of the con-

---

429. *See* R. Arens & H. Lasswell, In Defense of Public Order: The Emerging Field of Sanction Law 199–204 (1961); M. McDougal & F. Feliciano, *supra* note 55, at 287–96, 309–30.

430. For a comprehensive treatment, *see* W. Reisman, *supra* note 120.

431. *See* the appendix *infra,* at notes 4–42 and accompanying text.

432. *See* notes 117–44 *supra* and accompanying text.

433. *See* notes 85–95 *supra* and accompanying text.

434. Covenant on Civil and Political Rights, *supra* note 48, Arts. 28–45; Covenant on Economic, Social, and Cultural Rights, *supra* note 47, Arts. 16–25.

tracting states, to serve in their personal capacities.[435] To perform its applying function, the Committee will receive and consider reports submitted by the state parties regarding "the measures they have adopted" to "give effect to the rights recognized in the Covenant" and "on the progress made in the enjoyment of those rights," including "the factors and difficulties, if any, affecting the implementation" of the Covenant.[436] After studying these reports, the Committee will make its own reports and "such general comments as it may consider appropriate" to the state parties.[437] The Committee may also transmit these comments to the Economic and Social Council.[438]

Another function of the Committee is to deal with complaints brought by one state against another. As mentioned above, this state-to-state complaint procedure is made optional under the Covenant—i.e., both the complainant state and respondent state must be contracting states to the Covenant and must have recognized the competence of the Committee to entertain such complaints.[439] The prescribed procedures for dealing with such complaints, as embodied in Articles 41 and 42 of the Covenant, are highly complicated and cumbersome. The procedures include three phases, as outlined below.

Bilateral Negotiations between the States Concerned

The submission of a complaint to the Human Rights Committee must be preceded by a "written communication" from the initiating state to the "receiving state," which is allegedly "not giving effect to the provisions" of the Covenant.[440] The receiving state is allowed a period of three months to furnish the initiating state "an explanation or any other statement in writing clarifying the matter," including, "to the extent possible and pertinent, reference to domestic procedures and remedies taken, pending or available in the matter."[441] If, through bilateral negotiations, "the matter is not adjusted to the satisfaction" of both states concerned "within six months after the receipt by the receiving State of the initial communication," either state is then authorized to "refer the matter to the Committee."[442] The ostensible rationale behind this requirement appears to be to base the jurisdiction of the Committee upon identifiable "disputes."[443]

---

435. Covenant on Civil and Political Rights, *supra* note 48, Art. 28.
436. *Id.*, Art. 40(1)(2).
437. *Id.*, Art. 40(4).
438. *Id.*
439. *Id.*, Art. 41(1).
440. *Id.*, Art. 41(1)(a).
441. *Id.*
442. *Id.*, Art. 41(1)(b).
443. *See* Schwelb, *Civil and Political Rights, supra* note 382, at 850–51.

Proceedings before the Human Rights Committee

The proceedings before the Human Rights Committee can be initiated only after the failure to achieve a satisfactory adjustment by the state parties concerned. Such failure may result from the noncooperation of the receiving state or from a simple lack of agreement between the two parties. While the Covenant specifies six months as the period of bilateral negotiations, it does not specify a time limit for bringing the complaint to the Committee. The Covenant does, however, require the exhaustion of domestic remedies. The principal task of the Committee is to "make available its good offices to the States Parties concerned with a view to a friendly solution of the matter on the basis of respect for human rights and fundamental freedoms as recognized" in the Covenant.[444] The Committee may call upon the parties concerned to provide any relevant information, and the state parties concerned "have the right to be represented when the matter is being considered in the Committee and to make submissions orally and/or in writing."[445]

Within twelve months after the receipt of the complaint, the Committee is to submit a report to the state parties to the proceedings.[446] If a friendly solution has been reached, the Committee "shall confine its report to a brief statement of the facts and of the solution reached."[447] Failing such a solution, the Committee is still required to "confine its report to a brief statement of the facts."[448] The Committee is not empowered to express its view as to whether any violation of the Covenant has occurred, much less make a judicial determination.

Proceedings before an Ad Hoc Conciliation Commission

The submission of the Human Rights Committee's report does not necessarily spell an end to the whole matter. With "the prior consent of the States Parties concerned"[449]—and only with their consent—the proceedings can be carried a step further before an ad hoc Conciliation Commission consisting of five persons, appointed by the Committee and "acceptable to the States Parties concerned."[450] If the state parties concerned "fail to reach agreement within three months on all or part of the composition of the Commission, the members of the Commission concerning whom no agreement has been reached shall be elected by secret ballot by a two-thirds majority vote of the Committee from among its

444. Covenant on Civil and Political Rights, *supra* note 48, Art. 41(1)(e).
445. *Id.*, Art. 41(1)(g).
446. *Id.*, Art. 41(1)(h).
447. *Id.*, Art. 41(1)(h)(i).
448. *Id.*, Art. 41(1)(h)(ii).
449. Covenant on Civil and Political Rights, *supra* note 48, Art. 42(1)(a).
450. *Id.*, Art. 42(1)(b).

members."[451] The selected members of the Commission must be nationals of states parties to the Covenant which have made declarations recognizing the state-to-state complaint procedure under Article 41, and not nationals of the disputing states. The members of the Conciliation Commission, serving in their personal capacity, are to lend their good offices toward an amicable solution. If "an amicable solution" is reached, the Commission "shall confine its report to a brief statement of the facts and of the solution reached."[452] Otherwise, "the Commission's report shall embody its findings on all questions of fact relevant to the issues between the States Parties concerned, and its views on the possibilities of an amicable solution of the matter."[453] Like the Committee, the Commission is not authorized to make a judicial determination.

Another function of the Human Rights Committee is to deal with individual petitions pursuant to the Optional Protocol to the Covenant on Civil and Political Rights. While, as previously described, the Optional Protocol contains elaborate provisions concerning the conditions of admissibility of individual petitions,[454] it says rather little about the procedure of application. The Optional Protocol contains no provision about the formation of an ad hoc conciliation commission. The Optional Protocol simply indicates that after the Committee has considered an admissible petition ("communication") "in the light of all written information made available to it by the individual and by the State Party concerned,"[455] it "shall forward its views to the State Party concerned and to the individual."[456]

It may be noted, finally, that the Human Rights Committee is required, according to Article 45 of the Covenant, to "submit to the General Assembly of the United Nations, through the Economic and Social Council, an annual report on its activities."[457] This annual report must include "a summary of its activities" under the Optional Protocol.[458] "The preparation of this summary," in the words of Humphrey, "may well prove to be one of the most important activities of the Committee under the Protocol and provide the best guarantee in the instrument; for the risk which it carries of debate in the General Assembly is a powerful deterrent."[459] Given the realities of effective power allocation, the

451. *Id.*
452. *Id.,* Art. 42(7)(b).
453. *Id.,* Art. 42(7)(c).
454. *See* notes 389–403 *supra* and accompanying text.
455. Optional Protocol, *supra* note 49, Art. 5(1).
456. *Id.,* Art. 5(4).
457. Covenant on Civil and Political Rights, *supra* note 48, Art. 45.
458. Optional Protocol, *supra* note 49, Art. 6.
459. Humphrey, *supra* note 423, at 88.

fundamental and ultimate importance of mobilizing world public opinion in the defense and fulfillment of human rights is worthy of reiteration.

The procedures for application embodied in the Covenant on Economic, Social, and Cultural Rights are even more primitive. The Covenant views economic, social, and cultural rights as "programme" rights that are to be "promoted" "progressively" rather than immediately;[460] there is no specialized institution, such as the Human Rights Committee, established for the purpose of application and also no viable procedure for application through complaints by states or by individuals. The state parties to the Covenant are obligated only to submit reports, through the secretary-general of the United Nations, to the Economic and Social Council "on the measures which they have adopted and the progress made in achieving the observance of the rights recognized" in the Covenant.[461] The Council "may submit from time to time to the General Assembly reports with recommendations of a general nature"[462] and "bring to the attention of other organs of the United Nations, their subsidiary organs and specialized agencies concerned with furnishing technical assistance any matters arising out of the reports" which "may assist such bodies in deciding, each within its field of competence, on the advisability of international measures likely to contribute to the effective progressive implementation" of the Covenant.[463] This provision appears to augment very little, if any, the existing authority of the Economic and Social Council under Article 64 of the United Nations Charter.[464]

The International Convention on the Elimination of All Forms of Racial Discrimination entrusts the applying function to the Committee on the Elimination of Racial Discrimination, which is composed of "eigh-

---

460. *See* C. JENKS, *supra* note 292, at 70–79; Humphrey, *supra* note 423, at 88–89; Schwelb, *Some Aspects, supra* note 301, at 107–10; Schwelb, *The Nature of the Obligations of the States Parties to the International Covenant on Civil and Political Rights,* in 1 RENÉ CASSIN, *supra* note 39, at 301 [hereinafter cited as Schwelb, *The Nature of the Obligations*].

In the regional context of the Council of Europe, see Smyth, *The Implementation of the European Social Charter,* in MELANGES OFFERTS À POLYS MODINOS 290–303 (1968); Tennfjord, *The European Social Charter,* 9 EUROPEAN Y.B. 71 (1961).

461. Covenant on Economic, Social, and Cultural Rights, *supra* note 47, Art. 16(1).

462. *Id.,* Art. 21.

463. *Id.,* Art. 22.

464. Art. 64 of the United Nations Charter reads:

> 1. The Economic and Social Council may take appropriate steps to obtain regular reports from the specialized agencies. It may make arrangements with the Members of the United Nations and with the specialized agencies to obtain reports on the steps taken to give effect to its own recommendations and to recommendations on matters falling within its competence made by the General Assembly.
>
> 2. It may communicate its observations on these reports to the General Assembly.

teen experts of high moral standing and acknowledged impartiality,"[465] who serve in their personal capacities. Among its other functions, the Committee is empowered to review reports on measures of compliance submitted by state parties and to make recommendations, to act upon state-to-state complaints, and to deal with petitions by individuals.[466] The detailed procedures of application stipulated have already been treated elsewhere, and will not be recounted here.[467]

The most successful model of application relates, as is well known, to the European Convention of Human Rights.[468] Its success is due in measure to features that approximate a compulsory third-party decision making. The European Convention allocates the task of application to the European Commission of Human Rights, the European Court of Human Rights, and the Committee of Ministers of the Council of Europe.

Proceedings before the European Commission of Human Rights

The overall task of the Commission, as stipulated in Article 19 of the Convention, is to "ensure the observance of the engagements undertaken" by the state parties to the Convention.[469] The Commission is composed of "a number of members equal to that of the High Contracting Parties" (eighteen in total as of 1977), who serve in their personal capacities.[470] Its proceedings are held *in camera.*[471]

The Commission, it may be recalled, is empowered to decide the admissibility or inadmissibility of complaints ("petitions," "applications") by individuals or states. Without reciting the onerous conditions of admissibility,[472] it may be noted that a decision on admissibility is final, entailing severe value consequences.

After a complaint is declared admissible, the Commission must proceed to ascertain the facts, through an investigation if necessary, and to "place itself at the disposal of the parties concerned with a view to securing a friendly settlement."[473] Even at this stage, the Commission is authorized, by Protocol No. 3, to reject by a unanimous decision an individual petition if a further examination of the facts reveals the exis-

465. Convention on the Elimination of Racial Discrimination, *supra* note 97, Art. 8(1).
466. *Id.*, Arts. 11–14.
467. *See* chapter 7 *infra.*
468. *See generally* F. Castberg, *supra* note 107; J. Fawcett, *supra* note 107; F. Jacobs, *supra* note 107; A. Robertson, *supra* note 82.
469. European Convention, *supra* note 100, Art. 19.
470. *Id.*, Art. 20.
471. *Id.*, Art. 33.
472. *See* notes 397–400 *supra* and accompanying text.
473. European Convention, *supra* note 100, Art. 28.

tence of a ground of inadmissibility specified in Article 27.[474] If a friendly settlement is secured, that is the end of the matter.

If no settlement is achieved, the Commission is to "draw up a Report on the facts and state its opinion"[475] as to whether there has been a breach of the Convention, and to submit it, with appropriate proposals, to the Committee of Ministers. The case may then be brought, within three months, to the European Court of Human Rights to decide on the issue of violation. In the absence of such referral, "the Committee of Ministers shall decide by a majority of two-thirds of the members whether there has been a violation of the Convention."[476]

It may be noted that the Commission is not authorized to examine a situation *ex officio* but may act only if a complaint is brought by a state party under Article 24[477] or by an individual or a private group under Article 25.[478] Once a complaint has been lodged, however, the Commission has both the authority and the responsibility to probe *ex officio* whether the complaint raises issues under the Convention other than those specified by the complainant.

Proceedings before the European Court of Human Rights

The Court consists of judges equal in number to the membership of the Council of Europe (eighteen), who serve in complete independence. The jurisdiction of the Court, extending to "all cases concerning the interpretation and application" of the Convention, is contingent.[479] A case may be brought before the Court only by the Commission or by a contracting state concerned, and not by an individual petitioner.[480] The Court's jurisdiction is further contingent upon the acceptance, either general or ad hoc, of its jurisdiction by the respondent state.[481] To date, fourteen states have accepted the optional competence of the Court.[482]

The Court normally sits in a chamber of seven judges; but the chamber may under certain circumstances relinquish its jurisdiction in

---

474. European Convention, *supra* note 100, Protocol No. 3 and Art. 27.

475. *Id.*, Art. 31(1).

476. *Id.*, Art 32(1).

477. *Id.*, Art. 24.

478. *Id.*, Art. 25.

479. *Id.*, Art. 45.

On the European Court of Human Rights, *see* MacBride, *European Court of Human Rights*, 3 N.Y.U.J. INT'L L. & POLITICS 1 (1970); Rolin, *Has the European Court of Human Rights a Future?* 11 How. L.J. 442 (1965).

480. European Convention, *supra* note 100, Art. 44.

481. *Id.*, Art. 46.

482. These fourteen states are Austria, Belgium, Denmark, Federal Republic of Germany, France, Iceland, Ireland, Italy, Luxembourg, the Netherlands, Norway, Sweden, Switzerland, and the United Kingdom.

favor of the plenary Court.[483] The judgment of the Court, which is final, may, "if necessary, afford just satisfaction to the injured party."[484] The contracting states have pledged to "abide by the decision of the Court in any case to which they are parties,"[485] and the Committee of Ministers undertakes to "supervise its execution."[486]

Proceedings before the Committee of Ministers

The report of the Commission, as indicated, is transmitted to the Committee of Ministers, which consists of the Ministers for Foreign Affairs (or their deputies) of the member states of the Council of Europe. Though essentially a political organ, the Committee is endowed with judicial and quasi-judicial functions. If a case reported by the Commission is not referred to the Court, the Committee of Ministers will decide, by a two-thirds majority, "whether there has been a violation of the Convention."[487] If a violation has been established, the Committee shall "prescribe a period during which the Contracting Party concerned must take the measures required" to remedy.[488] If the state concerned fails to do so, the Committee must then decide "what effect shall be given to its original decision and publish the Report."[489] The contracting parties "undertake to regard" the Committee's decision "as binding on them."[490]

The structures and procedures for both decision and enforcement in application established for the transnational protection of human rights, even with the improved model in the European Convention of Human Rights, thus remain quite obviously inadequate and afford the greatest opportunity for future improvement.

THE TERMINATING FUNCTION

By termination we refer to the function of removing the authority of prescriptions, and of arrangements effected under prescriptions, after prescriptions and arrangements have ceased to conform to demanded goals of world public order.[491] The termination of a prescription is of course itself a prescription, but it is distinguishable in that it is directed

---

483. Stock-Taking, *supra* note 104, at 3.
484. European Convention, *supra* note 100, Art. 50.
485. *Id.,* Art. 53.
486. *Id.,* Art. 54.
487. *Id.,* Art. 32(1).
488. *Id.,* Art. 32(2).
489. *Id.,* Art. 32(3).
490. *Id.,* Art. 32(4).
491. *See* McDougal, Lasswell, & Reisman, *supra* note 1, at 148–52. The discussion of termination must be found in diverse sources.

On termination of international agreements, *see* first of all Vienna Convention, *supra* note 135, Arts. 54–64. For commentaries, *see* Reports of the International Law Commission, 1966, 21 U.N. GAOR, Supp. (No. 9) 61–94, U.N. Doc. A/6309/Rev. 1 (1966)

toward changing a relatively particularized prior prescription. The communication that a termination makes, the policy it projects, is that a prior prescription or arrangement is no longer authoritative. The sequence of activities, when termination is comprehensively considered, includes the initiation of the function; the investigation of the facts about alleged obsolescence of a prescription or an arrangement; the exploration of community policy relevant to the termination of such prescription or arrangement; the cancellation or erasure of the prior prescription or arrangement; and, finally, the amelioration or minimization of the loss caused by such termination.

When performed in an effective and timely way, the terminating function encourages expectations that change can be carried on in ways compatible with human dignity and that appropriate balance can be secured between conservation and change. A public order that cherishes

---

[hereinafter cited as ILC REPORTS, 1966]; T. ELIAS, *supra* note 136, at 88–134; S. ROSENNE, *supra* note 136, at 294–333; I. SINCLAIR, *supra* note 136, at 79–109.

More generally, *see* H. BRIGGS, *supra* note 316, at 900–46; E. CARR, THE TWENTY YEARS CRISIS (1940); A. DAVID, THE STRATEGY OF TREATY TERMINATION (1975); F. DUNN, PEACEFUL CHANGE (1937); C. HILL, THE DOCTRINE OF "REBUS SIC STANTIBUS" IN INTERNATIONAL LAW (1934); Lissitzyn, *Treaties and Changed Circumstances (Rebus Sic Stantibus),* 61 AM. J. INT'L L. 895 (1967); LORD MCNAIR, THE LAW OF TREATIES 491–535 (1961); K. STRUPP, LEGAL MACHINERY FOR PEACEFUL CHANGE (1937); H. TOBIN, THE TERMINATION OF MULTIPARTITE TREATIES (1933); Garner, *The Doctrine of Rebus Sic Stantibus and the Termination of Treaties,* 21 AM. J. INT'L L. 509 (1957); *Harvard Research, "Law of Treaties,"* 29 AM. J. INT'L L. 666, 1161–73 (Supp. 1935); Kunz, *The Problem of Revision in International Law ("Peaceful Change"),* 33 AM. J. INT'L L. 33 (1939); McDougal & Lans, *Treaties and Congressional-Executive or Presidential Agreements: Interchangeable Instruments of National Policy,* in M. MCDOUGAL & ASSOCIATES, STUDIES IN WORLD PUBLIC ORDER 404, 599–611 (1960); Schwelb, *Fundamental Change of Circumstances: Notes on Article 59 of the Draft Convention on the Law of Treaties as Recommended for Adoption to the United Nations Conference on the Law of Treaties by Its Committee of the Whole in 1968,* 29 ZEITSCHRIFT FÜR AUSLÄNDISCHES ÖFFENTLICHES RECHT UND VÖLKERRECHT 39 (1969).

The process of customary development works precisely the same in termination as in prescription. Hence, the sources cited in note 315 *supra* are relevant here.

On termination of concession agreements, *see* C. AMERASINGHE, *supra* note 178; K. CARLSTON, LAW AND ORGANIZATION IN WORLD SOCIETY (1962); SOUTHWESTERN LEGAL FOUNDATIONS, SELECTED READINGS ON PROTECTION BY LAW OF PRIVATE FOREIGN INVESTMENTS (1964); Carlston, *Concession Agreements and Nationalization,* 52 AM. J. INT'L L. 260 (1958); Carlston, *International Role of Concession Agreements,* 52 NW. U.L. REV. 618 (1957); Hyde, *Economic Development Agreements,* 105 HAGUE RECUEIL DES COURS 267 (1962); Kissam & Leach, *Sovereign Expropriation of Property and Abrogation of Concession Contracts,* 28 FORDHAM L. REV. 177 (1959); Olmstead, *Economic Development Loan Agreements,* 48 CALIF. L. REV. 424 (1960); Olmstead, *Economic Development Agreements,* 49 CALIF. L. REV. 504 (1961); Olmstead, *Nationalization of Foreign Property Interests, Particularly Those Subject to Agreements with the State,* 32 N.Y.U.L. REV. 1122 (1957); M. Arsanjani, Internal Resources in World Public Order: Exclusive Uses and Inclusive Competences, 1977, at 213–423 (unpublished J.S.D. dissertation, Yale Law School Library).

human dignity will of course modify outmoded prescriptions to conform to clarified goals of human dignity, while giving appropriate deference to existing arrangements and the expectations created by such arrangements. It will seek, through contextual scrutiny of relevant facts and policies, to minimize all losses and costs likely to result from necessary change and to ameliorate potentially disruptive impact.[492] A hallmark of human dignity is sensitivity to the claims grounded in the manifold events of the past, present, and future.

The participants who play a role in termination extend, as in the other functions, to the whole spectrum of those in the effective power process, including officials of nation-states, officials of international governmental organizations, representatives of private associations and groups, and individual human beings. The fundamental demands for which this function is maintained are, first, to keep the prescriptions of the world community compatible with the goals of world public order, including minimization of unauthorized coercion and maximization of human rights protection; and, secondly, to achieve an appropriate balance between necessary change and maintenance of a constructive and humane stability. The demand for change because of the exigencies of different conditions is tempered by the demand for minimized potential deprivations and disruptions attending the obsolescence and more formal change of prescriptions, and it is disciplined by realistic expectations about the dynamics of intensifying interaction in an interdependent world.

The arenas in which decisions about change occur include all structures of authority, both transnational and national, and habitual interactions even in nonofficial processes. The base values at the disposal of different participants include, as for other functions, both authority and all the values which constitute effective power. Authority is found in a complex of prescriptions about the termination of agreements, in specified requirements for customary change (*desuetudo*),[493] and in specific provision for collective procedures; a significant base of effective power inheres in a noticeable mobilization of opinion and effort for change. The strategies of termination vary greatly with the type of prescription: multilateral agreements are terminated by new agreements, by

---

492. *See* A. David, *supra* note 491, at 239–90; G. White, Nationalisation of Foreign Property (1961); B. Wortley, Expropriation in Public International Law (1959); Weston, *Community Regulation of Foreign-Wealth Deprivations: A Tentative Framework for Inquiry,* in Essays on Expropriation 117–65 (R. Miller & R. Stanger eds. 1967).

493. *See* Judge Lauterpacht's Separate Opinion in Voting Procedure concerning the Territory of South West Africa Case, [1955] I.C.J. 67, 102; C. Allen, Law in the Making 85–86, 478–82 (7th ed. 1964); A. D'Amato, *supra* note 315, at 239–40; D. O'Connell, *supra* note 322, at 266.

unilateral denunciation upon the ground of changed conditions, and by obsolescence through customary development; customary prescriptions can be terminated either by appropriately comprehensive agreements or by the development of new and different customs; and, finally, the organized community maintains a variety of collective procedures, as in the United Nations structure. The outcomes of the function involve varying degrees of change (complete or partial), including amendment, modification, suspension, withdrawal, and termination of the particularized prescription.

The existing human rights prescriptions, happily, create certain difficulties about termination because they express the basic, most intensely demanded, policies for which the whole global constitutive process is maintained. These prescriptions have been authoritatively enshrined in the United Nations Charter (as expressed in the preamble and Articles 1[3], 13[1], 55, 56, 62[2], and 76) and given detailed specification in the Universal Declaration of Human Rights, the International Covenant on Economic, Social, and Cultural Rights, the International Covenant on Civil and Political Rights and its Optional Protocol, and a host of other ancillary conventions and expressions, including the Convention on the Prevention and Punishment of the Crime of Genocide,[494] the International Convention on the Elimination of All Forms of Racial Discrimination,[495] and the International Convention on the Suppression and Punishment of the Crime of Apartheid.[496] The authoritativeness of all these prescriptions has been affirmed by international officials of many different kinds, including the International Court of Justice and other tribunals;[497] the more fundamental policies embodied in these prescriptions, especially as formulated in the Universal Declaration of Human Rights, have, further, found repeated expressions in the national constitutions and national decisions.[498] It would appear accurate, therefore, to conclude that the basic content of all these human rights prescriptions, however differently expressed in different instruments and decisions, has become customary international law.[499]

Insofar as the human rights prescriptions in the Charter of the United Nations are concerned, change may possibly be made by the prescribed procedures of the Charter.[500] The amending procedure is stipulated in Article 108:

---

494. Genocide Convention, *supra* note 111.

495. Convention on the Elimination of Racial Discrimination, *supra* note 97.

496. Apartheid Convention, *supra* note 331.

497. *See further* notes 558–610 *infra* and accompanying text.

498. *See* notes 601–06 *infra* and accompanying text.

499. For further development *see* notes 558–610 *infra* and accompanying text.

500. *See* L. Goodrich, E. Hambro, & A. Simons, *supra* note 175, at 638–47; Zacklin, The Amendment of the Constitutive Instruments of the United Nations and the

> Amendments to the present Charter shall come into force for all Members of the United Nations when they have been adopted by a vote of two-thirds of the members of the General Assembly and ratified in accordance with their respective constitutional processes by two-thirds of the Members of the United Nations, including all the permanent members of the Security Council.

Article 109 provides for a general conference to review the Charter for the purpose of Charter revision,[501] but contains, in paragraph 2, the same amending requirement as Article 108:

> Any alteration of the present Charter recommended by a two-thirds vote of the conference shall take effect when ratified in accordance with their respective constitutional processes by two thirds of the Members of the United Nations including all the permanent members of the Security Council.

Thus, the two-thirds requirement is compounded by the requisite unanimity of the five permanent members of the Security Council. Because of this built-in veto in the amending procedure, though the United Nations has indeed undergone profound constitutive development since its establishment,[502] change of Charter prescriptions through formal amendment has been remarkably modest. The only changes through formal amendment thus far relate to the enlargement, in response to the vast expansion of the total membership of the United Nations, of the

---

SPECIALIZED AGENCIES (1968); Schwelb, *The Amending Procedure of Constitutions of International Organizations,* 31 BRIT. Y.B. INT'L L. 53 (1954). *Cf.* Schwelb, *The Process of Amending the Statute of the International Court of Justice,* 64 AM. J. INT'L L. 880 (1970).

It may be noted that, insofar as the content of Charter provisions has been incorporated into the customary international law, that law can of course be changed only in a way customary law is changed. This would require a very broad participation in the amending process.

501. Art. 109(1) of the United Nations Charter provides:

> A General Conference of the Members of the United Nations for the purpose of reviewing the present Charter may be held at a date and place to be fixed by a two-thirds vote of the members of the General Assembly and by a vote of any nine members of the Security Council. Each Member of the United Nations shall have one vote in the conference.

See Schwelb, *Entry into Force of the Amendment to Article 109 of the Charter of the United Nations,* 17 INT'L & COMP. L.Q. 1011 (1968).

502. *See, e.g.,* Uniting for Peace Resolution, G.A. Res. 377, 5 U.N. GAOR, Supp. (No. 19) 10, U.N. Doc. A/1775 (1950); I. CLAUDE, *supra* note 11, at 118–90, 261–77; Gross, *Voting in the Security Council: Abstention from Voting and Absence from Meetings,* 60 YALE L.J. 209 (1951); McDougal & Gardner, *The Veto and the Charter: An Interpretation for Survival,* 60 YALE L.J. 258 (1951), *reprinted in* M. MCDOUGAL AND ASSOCIATES, STUDIES IN WORLD PUBLIC ORDER 718–60 (1960).

membership of the Security Council and of the Economic and Social Council, and to the corresponding changes in the requisite voting in the making of decisions.[503]

Insofar as the human rights conventions are concerned, some do not, while others do, contain provisions for amendment;[504] some do not, while others do, contain denunciation provisions. The two most important treaties—i.e., the International Covenant on Civil and Political Rights (and its Optional Protocol) and the International Covenant on Economic, Social, and Cultural Rights—do not provide for denunciation. This ostensible omission is highly significant: it expresses expectations that the human rights obligations embodied in the Covenants are not expected to be unilaterally disregarded. In this connection, Article 56 of the Vienna Convention on the Law of Treaties is instructive:

> 1. A treaty which contains no provision regarding its termination and which does not provide for denunciation or withdrawal is not subject to denunciation or withdrawal unless:
>
>   (a) it is established that the parties intended to admit the possibility of denunciation or withdrawal; or
>
>   (b) a right of denunciation or withdrawal may be implied by the nature of the treaty.
>
> 2. A party shall give not less than twelve months' notice of its intention to denounce or withdraw from a treaty under paragraph 1.[505]

Given the intense demand today for a global bill of human rights that constitutes an integral part of, and expresses the fundamental authoritative policies of, the world constitutive process, and given the absence of explicit provision for denunciation, it would appear that the commitments incorporated in the two Covenants were intended neither to "admit the possibility of denunciation or withdrawal" nor to raise the implication of "a right of denunciation or withdrawal."[506]

---

503. United Nations Charter, Art. 23(1) (1965 amendment increasing the number of members of the Security Council from eleven to fifteen); *id.,* Art. 27(2)(3) (1965 amendment increasing the requisite majority in the Security Council from seven to nine); *id.,* Art. 61 (1965 amendment increasing the number of members of the Economic and Social Council from eighteen to twenty-seven); *id.,* Art. 109(1) (1968 amendment increasing the requisite Security Council majority from seven to nine).

504. *See* notes 754–66 *infra* and accompanying text.

505. Vienna Convention, *supra* note 135, Art. 56.

506. For further elaboration, *see* notes 748–67 *infra* and accompanying text.

For a rather tentative observation, *see* Weis, *The Denunciation of Human Rights Treaties,* 8 HUMAN RIGHTS J. 3, 6 (1975).

Even the human rights conventions that contain provisions for denunciation cannot easily be made effective. The conventions making provision for denunciation include the International Convention on the Elimination of All Forms of Racial Discrimination (Article 21),[507] the Convention on the Prevention and Punishment of the Crime of Genocide (Article 14),[508] the Supplementary Slavery Convention (Article 14),[509] the Convention on the Nationality of Married Women (Article 9),[510] the Convention Relating to the Status of Refugees (Article 44),[511] the Convention on the Political Rights of Women (Article 8),[512] the European Convention on Human Rights (Article 65),[513] and the American Convention on Human Rights (Article 78).[514] The denunciation clauses embodied in these and other Conventions commonly exhibit certain temporal constraints: an exercise of denunciation may be barred within a specified period (*e.g.*, ten or five years) following the effective operation of a convention;[515] the effect of a formal denunciation may, further, ensue only upon the lapse of a specified period (ordinarily twelve months) subsequent to the notification of denunciation.[516] An act of denunciation does not thus, immediately upon notification, relieve the denouncing party of the obligations contained in the denounced treaty, and the denouncing party may still be held accountable under the treaty obligations, pending the lapse of the required time following the notification of its denunciation. This was clearly illustrated in the *Greek* case under the European Convention on Human Rights.[517]

An act of denunciation does not, more importantly, exempt the de-

---

507. Convention on the Elimination of Racial Discrimination, *supra* note 97, Art. 21.

508. Genocide Convention, *supra* note 111, Art. 14.

509. Supplementary Convention on the Abolition of Slavery, *supra* note 112, Art. 14.

510. Convention on the Nationality of Married Women, *supra* note 333, Art. 9.

511. Convention Relating to the Status of Refugees, *supra* note 114, Art. 44.

512. Convention on the Political Rights of Women, *supra* note 113, Art. 8.

513. European Convention, *supra* note 100, Art. 65.

514. American Convention, *supra* note 144, Art. 78.

515. This is characteristic of human rights conventions concluded under the General Conference of the International Labor Organization. *See, e.g.*, Equal Remuneration Convention, *supra* note 343, Art. 9(1); Workers' Representatives Convention, *supra* note 345, Art. 9(1); Employment Policy Convention, *supra* note 346, Art. 6.

516. *E.g.*, Convention on the Elimination of Racial Discrimination, *supra* note 97, Art. 21; Convention on the Nationality of Married Women, *supra* note 333, Art. 9(1); Convention Relating to the Status of Refugees, *supra* note 114, Art. 44(2).

517. *See* L. Sohn & T. Buergenthal, *supra* note 39, at 1059–90; Stock-Taking, *supra* note 104, at 6–9; Becker, *The Greek Case before the European Human Rights Commission*, 1 Human Rights 91 (1970); Buergenthal, *Proceedings against Greece under the European Convention of Human Rights*, 62 Am. J. Int'l L. 441 (1968); Coleman, *Greece and the Council of Europe: The International Legal Protection of Human Rights by the Political Process*, 2 Israel Y.B. Human Rights 121 (1972).

nouncing party from obligations, which may parallel or reproduce those in the denounced convention, prevailing under general customary international law. The Vienna Convention on the Law of Treaties, in Article 43, stipulates:

> The invalidity, termination or denunciation of a treaty, the withdrawal of a party from it, or the suspension of its operation, as a result of the application of the present Convention or of the provisions of the treaty, shall not in any way impair the duty of any State to fulfil any obligation embodied in the treaty to which it would be subject under international law independently of the treaty.[518]

Similarly, it may be noted that, while the four Geneva Conventions of 1949 (the Convention for the Amelioration of the Condition of the Wounded and Sick in the Field; the Convention for the Amelioration of the Conditions of Wounded, Sick and Shipwrecked Members of Armed Forces at Sea; the Prisoners of War Convention; and the Protection of Civilian Persons Convention) all contain denunciation clauses allowing the contracting parties to denounce the Conventions, these clauses make it unequivocally clear that denunciation "shall in no way impair the obligations which the Parties to the conflict shall remain bound to fulfil by virtue of the principles of the law of nations, as they result from the usages established among civilized peoples, from the laws of humanity and the dictates of the public conscience."[519]

The content of all the preceding human rights agreements, including the United Nations Charter, can of course be changed, as even national constitutions are changed, through the development of new customary law. The development of a new custom, as described above, is a complex process of communication involving a wide range of participants in continuous interaction.[520] To ascertain whether the communications in past uniformities of behavior, with their attendant subjectivities about lawfulness, have created the expectations about content, authority, and control that constitute a new customary prescription requires a comprehensive contextual inquiry: Who are the communicators and communicatees; what demands and expectations have they expressed; what

---

518. Vienna Convention, *supra* note 135, Art. 43.

519. Geneva Convention for the Amelioration of the Condition of the Wounded and Sick in Armed Forces in the Field, Aug. 12, 1949, Art. 63, 75 U.N.T.S. 135; Geneva Convention for the Amelioration of the Condition of Wounded, Sick and Shipwrecked Members of Armed Forces at Sea, Aug. 12, 1949, Art. 62, 75 U.N.T.S. 85; Geneva Convention Relative to the Treatment of Prisoners of War, Aug. 12, 1949, Art. 142, 75 U.N.T.S. 135; Geneva Convention Relative to the Protection of Civilian Persons in Times of War, Aug. 12, 1949, Art. 158, 6 U.S.T. 3516, T.I.A.S. No. 3365, 75 U.N.T.S. 287.

520. *See* notes 347–57 *supra* and accompanying text.

does the complex matrix of interaction in terms of spatial, temporal, institutional, and crisis features suggest; what inferences may be drawn from the relative bases of power of the different participants; what signs and behavior have been employed as strategies of communication, and what is the culminating mediation of expectations about future policy, authority, and control? In the absence of the United Nations machinery, the achievement of change in prescription through customary development could be extremely slow and difficult.

Fortunately, when human rights prescriptions do require change, these difficulties can be obviated in measure by employment of the United Nations machinery and appropriately dynamic conceptions of customary development. The making of a new custom—and hence a termination through customary development—can be expedited by contemporary collective procedures. The United Nations, especially in the General Assembly, provides a unique, and an exceptionally convenient, forum in which most of the peoples of the world can be represented and their important demands and expectations articulated and communicated. The tempo of communication can be accelerated through institutional arrangements; and the certainty of peoples' expectations about policy, authority, and control can be secured without great lapse in time. Just as custom can now be "instantaneously" made through this new modality, so also change and termination of prescription, if sufficiently demanded by the peoples of the world, can now be instantaneously achieved.[521]

THE APPRAISING FUNCTION

The appraising function evaluates the process of decision in terms of the policy objectives of the larger community and seeks to identify the participants responsible for past successes and failures.[522] It focuses inquiry upon the adequacy of past decision to secure postulated goals; it applies the intelligence and promoting functions to the task of determining how well the process of decision is functioning and how it can be improved. The important sequence of activities in appraisal includes gathering the requisite information about the decision process; evaluating the economy and effectiveness of decision; and disseminating findings and recommendations to relevant audiences.

---

521. *See* notes 358–71 *supra* and accompanying text.

522. *See* Lasswell, *supra* note 268; Lasswell, *Toward Continuing Appraisal of the Impact of Law on Society,* 21 Rutgers L. Rev. 645 (1967); McDougal, Lasswell, & Reisman, *supra* note 1, at 152–54; Snyder, Hermann, & Lasswell, *A Global Monitoring System: Appraising the Effects of Government on Human Dignity*, 20 Int'l Studies Q. 221 (1976).

Cf. Farer, *The Greening of the Globe: A Preliminary Appraisal of the World Order Models Project (WOMP),* 31 Int'l Org. 129 (1977).

Appraisal must, in order to achieve its goal of the overall evaluation of constitutive process in terms of desired public order, be both comprehensive and appropriately selective. When effectively performed, it will ascertain the total achievement (successes and failures) of demanded values, probe for the factors in all phases of the different decision functions that affect successes and failures, and ascribe responsibility for such successes and failures as a strategy toward improvement. Comprehensively viewed, appraisal thus seeks to employ all the different relevant intellectual tasks (clarifying goals, examining trends, identifying conditions, projecting future probabilities, and inventing alternatives) with every feature of both constitutive process and public order. To ensure necessary independence and impartiality, appraisers must be insulated from immediate pressures of threat or inducement, and self-appraisals require subjection to the critical scrutiny of other appraisers. While intermittent appraisals may mobilize needed occasional attention and support, the effects are most sustained and creative when the appraising function is continuously performed within stable structures, capable of relating each particular detail to the whole set of community goals and the entire spectrum of conditioning factors.

Participation in the appraising function, considered generally, is highly democratic. All participants in all structures of authority, national and transnational, are in measure always engaged in self-appraisal and appraisals of others, evaluating authoritative decision in terms of its economy and indulgent or deprivational effects. All the other participants who are interested in the quality of public order (the shaping and sharing of values), including political parties, pressure groups, private associations, and individuals, are also constantly involved in appraisal, both general and particularized, as expressed in political platforms, demands of pressure groups, private views, and so on. Most importantly, on the contemporary scene, intellectuals (within and without the academic community) play a special role in performing all the difficult tasks of appraisal. The basic purpose for which the appraising function is maintained is, as indicated, to secure a continuing reform and adaptation of the decision process in the light of changing perspectives and conditions. Structures of authority may sometimes be specialized to the appraising function; more often than not, appraisal is rather incidental to structures specialized to other functions. The performance of the appraising function tends to be widely dispersed rather than concentrated, and to be more episodic than continuous. The structures have not yet been created and maintained to make systematic appraisal an important, continuing feature of the process of decision. Most of the base values which are employed to gather, process, and disseminate information and knowledge are directly relevant to appraisal. The capacities and potentialities for appraisal have vastly expanded with the proliferation of information about world social process, the acquisition of new knowledge and skills in evaluating public order effects, the development of expertise in a wide variety of fields for analyzing the past and the present and forecasting the future, and the great increase in interdisciplinary cooperation. Most of the strategies which are employed for intelligence and promotion are equally useful for the appraising function. The culminating outcomes of appraisal are in a continuing flow of information and assessment, and the ascription of responsibility, relevant to the different features of the decision process.

The appraising function is fully illustrated in the provisions of the United Nations Charter, including Articles 15, 17, 24(3), 62(1), 64, 87, 88, and 98. Article 15 empowers the General Assembly to "receive and consider annual and special reports from the Security Council" and from "the other organs of the United Nations." In dealing with budgetary matters under Article 17, the General Assembly is inevitably involved, in varying degrees and fashions, in appraising past successes and failures as a guide for priorities and allocations. The bulk of the annual report of the Economic and Social Council relates comprehensively to human rights matters. This reporting task has been greatly facilitated by the provision of Article 64:

> 1. The Economic and Social Council may take appropriate steps to obtain regular reports from the specialized agencies. It may make arrangements with the Members of the United Nations and with the specialized agencies to obtain reports on the steps taken to give effect to its own recommendations and to recommendations on matters falling within its competence made by the General Assembly.
> 2. It may communicate its observations on these reports to the General Assembly.

Worthy of special notice, finally, is the unique role played by the secretary-general in making, under Article 98, his "annual report to the General Assembly on the work of the Organization." When taken seriously and effectively performed, the secretary-general's annual report can provide not only essential information about the work of the organization, but also an important occasion for appraisal of the state of the world community, in human rights and other fields. Given his unique vantage point, his continuing and comprehensive authority, as assisted by a substantial corps of international civil servants in the Secretariat, the secretary-general can make enormous contributions through his annual report.[523] The annual report can highlight (without being polemic or strident) the past successes and failures in human rights and other fields and focus world attention on matters that deserve high priorities or require continuing follow-up efforts, thereby eliciting the timely collaboration of all parties concerned (governmental and nongovernmental sectors alike) in achieving the better protection and greater fulfillment of human rights on a global scale.

With specific reference to human rights, it may be recalled that under a reporting system instituted by the Economic and Social Council, the member states of the United Nations, specialized agencies, and certain nongovernmental organizations are required to submit periodic reports to the Commission on Human Rights.[524] While the reports submitted by governments tend to be perfunctory and self-serving, the quality and significance of reports can greatly be enhanced if the Commission and the Economic and Social Council take seriously their tasks of appraisal and do not merely serve as transmitting belts of superficial information.

The contemporary human rights conventions generally establish a reporting system, designed, beyond the purposes of intelligence and application, to afford a continuing channel of appraisal. The list, as indicated above, includes the International Covenant on Civil and Political Rights; the International Covenant on Economic, Social, and Cultural Rights; the International Convention on the Elimination of All Forms of Racial Discrimination; the Convention on the Political Rights of Women; the Convention Relating to the Status of Refugees; the European Convention on Human Rights; the European Social Charter; and the American Convention on Human Rights.[525] Though the potential of appraisal tends to be underutilized, it need not remain so.

The most successful example of appraisal through the reporting system is found in the long-standing experience of the International Labor Organization. The ILO Constitution requires a member to "make an annual report to the International Labour Office on the measures it has

523. *See generally* S. Bailey, The Secretariat of the United Nations (1964); Commission to Study the Organization of Peace, The UN Secretary-General: His Role in World Politics (1962); Public Papers of the Secretary-General of the United Nations (A. Cordier & W. Foote eds. 1969–77) (8 vols.); L. Gordenker, The United Nations Secretary-General and the Maintenance of Peace (1967); T. Lie, In the Cause of Peace (1954); A. Rovine, The First Fifty Years: The Secretary-General in World Politics, 1920–1970 (1970); S. Schwebel, The Secretary-General of the United Nations (1952); Jackson, *The Developing Role of the Secretary-General,* 11 Int'l Org. 431 (1957); Schachter, *Dag Hammarskjold, the Charter Law and the Future Role of the United Nations Secretary-General,* 56 Am. J. Int'l L. 9 (1962); Stein, *Mr. Hammarskjold, the Charter and the Future Role of the United Nations Secretary-General,* 56 Am. J. Int'l L. 9 (1962).

524. *See* notes 279–95 *supra* and accompanying text.

525. *See* notes 279–88 *supra* and accompanying text.

taken to give effect to the provisions of Conventions to which it is a party. These reports shall be made in such form and shall contain such particulars as the Governing Body may request."[526] Such reports are essential not only to application of ILO Conventions but also to realistic appraisal. To facilitate the applying and appraising functions, the director-general is required to submit a summary of the governments' reports to each session of the International Labor Conference, and the member governments are obligated to transmit copies of their annual reports to the representative organizations of employers and workers, in keeping with the unique, tripartite character of the ILO.[527] These annual reports are regularly examined by a Committee of Experts consisting of independent persons of the highest standing, whose findings are reviewed by the Conference Committee on the Application of Conventions and Recommendations.[528] The Committee of Experts sees its "essential function" as "that of criticism,"[529] and it draws up, after a thorough examination, a report. The Conference Committee makes appraisal by reference to the Summary of Reports submitted by the director-general, the Report of the Committee of Experts, and the additional information furnished by governments. At the Conference Committee, governments are afforded the opportunity of "adding, through their representatives . . . any observations they may think desirable to make, or of clearing up any obscurities to which the Committee of Experts [has] drawn attention."[530] As the Conference Committee is tripartite in composition (representing governments, employers, and workers), nongovernmental interests are well represented in the appraising process.[531] This unique character has over the years proved to be a major asset of the ILO reporting system.

In addition to the continuing channels of established structures and procedures, appraisal can also be performed through such methods as occasional international conferences, exemplified by the International Conference on Human Rights, the World Conference of the International Women's Year, the World Conference on the Environment, the

---

526. The Constitution of the International Labor Organization, Art. 22, in INTERNATIONAL GOVERNMENTAL ORGANIZATIONS: CONSTITUTIONAL DOCUMENTS 994, 1003 (rev. 3d ed. A. Peaslee ed. 1974).

527. *Id.*, Art. 23.

528. *See* E. LANDY, *supra* note 292, at 19–34; INTERNATIONAL LABOUR OFFICE, THE I.L.O. AND HUMAN RIGHTS 18–24 (1968) (report presented by the International Labor Organization to the International Conference on Human Rights, 1968).

529. 1952 REPORT OF THE COMMITTEE OF EXPERTS ON THE APPLICATION OF CONVENTIONS AND RECOMMENDATIONS 4 (*quoted in* E. LANDY, *supra* note 292, at 28).

530. 8 RECORD OF PROCEEDINGS OF THE INTERNATIONAL LABOUR CONFERENCE 402 (1926) (*quoted in* E. LANDY, *supra* note 292, at 36).

531. On the origin and features of tripartite representation of the International Labor Organization, *see* Beguin, *I.L.O. and the Tripartite System*, 523 INT'L CONCILIATION (1959).

World Population Conference, and the World Food Conference.[532] In conferences of this kind, multiple purposes are normally involved, including exchanging information and knowledge, making new proposals, and mobilizing support for action. A key objective relates to the function of appraisal. For instance, the International Conference on Human Rights, convened in Teheran in 1968, included in its agenda an item entitled the "evaluation of the effectiveness of methods and techniques employed in the field of human rights at the international and regional levels."[533] Achievements in this regard turned out, however, to be quite disappointing. As was pointed out by the Jamaican delegation, "owing to the fact that the methods used had been insufficiently examined and evaluated the Conference had failed to answer the question whether the human rights machinery should be expanded at the present stage or whether a more rational use should be made of the machinery now available."[534] The World Conference of the International Women's Year, convened in Mexico City in 1975, was fairly successful in appraising the process of decision for the protection of women. Its ultimate effects depend in a measure upon how the plans of action adopted at the Conference are carried out, in the years to come, at all community levels (global, regional, and national) and in all sectors of life (governmental and nongovernmental).[535]

On the national level, nation-states are constantly involved, in one form or another, in the appraising function in regard to events occurring within their own borders, for either internal or transnational consumption (*e.g.*, reports submitted to various international governmental entities). Increasingly, a nation-state may find it necessary to appraise the successes and failures within other nation-states in the protection of human rights. This is exemplified by the United States congressional enactment requiring the Department of State to report to the Congress on human rights situations, on a country-by-country basis. Section 502(B) of the Foreign Assistance Act, as amended, requires that "the Secretary of State transmit annually to the Congress, as part of the presentation materials for security assistance programs, a full and complete report with respect to the practices regarding the observance of a respect for internationally recognized human rights in each country proposed as a recipient of security assistance."[536] With a new administra-

---

532. *See* notes 67–72 *supra* and accompanying text.

533. FINAL ACT OF THE INTERNATIONAL CONFERENCE ON HUMAN RIGHTS, TEHERAN, 22 APRIL TO 13 MAY 1968, at 3, U.N. Doc. A/CONF.32/41 (1968).

534. 23 U.N. GAOR, C.3 (1626th mtg.) 4, U.N. Doc. A/C.3/SR.1626 (1968).

For a critical appraisal of the International Conference on Human Rights, *see* M. MOSKOWITZ, INTERNATIONAL CONCERN WITH HUMAN RIGHTS 12–23 (1974).

535. *See* notes 196–97 *supra* and accompanying text.

536. § 502(B) of the Foreign Assistance Act, *supra* note 225.

tion repeatedly affirming its commitment to human rights, the appraisals embodied in the March 1977 reports of the Department of State begin to appear more critical and more valuable.[537]

In addition to the activities of officials, transnational and national, the appraising function is, as indicated, highly open, admitting many nongovernmental participants. Requiring no special authority, nongovernmental organizations (regardless of their consultative status with the Economic and Social Council) and individuals can play an important role in appraisal, beyond the more familiar roles of intelligence and promotion. They can undertake to evaluate the efficacy of authoritative decision and the quality of public order and, hence, make provisional ascriptions of responsibility. The media of mass communication (audio, visual, or both) have constantly performed a vital function in appraisal, with varying degrees of deliberateness. The intellectual community contributes to appraisal, both individually and collectively.[538] A multiplicity of appraisers (governmental and nongovernmental) add rich diversity to the process of appraisal and serve certain policing function in the common interest. On the whole, however, the appraising function remains quite sporadic, fragmentary, and unorganized. A more centralized, systematized structure, with adequate authority and effective bases of power, is needed. Given the tremendous potentialities of modern communication and technology, a proper balance between systematic and sporadic, centralized and decentralized, and organized and unorganized appraisal would greatly enhance the quality of performance of the function, thereby contributing to the efficiency of each of the other functions and indeed of the whole global constitutive process of authoritative decision.

THE HUMAN RIGHTS PRESCRIPTIONS AS AN EMERGING GLOBAL BILL OF RIGHTS

The above survey of the major features of the contemporary global constitutive process has established, it is believed, that protection of the fundamental policies embodied in all the different human rights prescriptions has become an integral part of each of the features of that process. It remains to be demonstrated that this new protection of human rights on a global scale is beginning to take on the substance, as well as the form, of the basic bills of rights long established and maintained in the more mature national communities.[539]

---

537. Human Rights Reports, *supra* note 225.

538. *See, e.g.*, Snyder, Hermann, & Lasswell, *supra* note 522.

539. The degree to which a global bill of rights has been established was at least an underlying issue in a recent debate in the columns of the New York Times. *See Human Rights: The "Weak" U.N. Covenant*, N.Y. Times, Mar. 20, 1977, § 4, at 16, col. 3 (letter by John P. Humphrey, former director of the Division of Human Rights in the United

What distinguishes a bill of rights in factual terms, as contrasted with ascribed legal consequences, is the intensity with which the policies it expresses are demanded by community members.[540] There would appear little question that the peoples of the world, whatever their differences in cultural traditions and institutional practices, are today demanding most intensely all those basic rights commonly summarized in terms of the greater production and wider sharing of the values of human dignity.[541] This heightening intensity in demand can indeed be observed in every feature of the global process of effective power. The demands come from all participants, both official and nonofficial, and are expressed in authoritative instruments, political platforms, pressure group activities, private association activities, and individualistic proclamations. The values demanded cover the whole spectrum cherished by contemporary humankind, ranging from collective political emancipation to individual political freedom, from equality for all to personal autonomy, from group survival to individual life and safety, from a New International Economic Order[542] to a basic income for every individual, from an open and abundant flow of information and knowledge to freedom of individual expression, from high levels of skill in the management of modern technology to the acquisition and expression of individual talent, from group solidarity to individual intimacy, and from collective norms of responsible conduct to freedom of individual conscience.[543] These demands are made on behalf both of the individual self

Nations Secretariat); *On Human Rights Covenants: The Case for U.S. Ratification, id.*, Apr. 1, 1977, at A28, col. 1 (letter by Louis Henkin, President of the United States Institute of Human Rights); *On Human Rights Covenants: "A Powerful Influence," id.*, Apr. 1, 1977, at A28, col. 2 (letter by Erik Suy, Legal Counsel, Under Secretary-General, United Nations); *World Human Rights: The Binding Declaration, id.*, Apr. 7, 1977, at A24, col. 3 (letter by K. Venkata Raman, United Nations Institute for Teaching and Research).

540. *See* de Smith, *Federalism, Human Rights, and the Protection of Minorities*, in FEDERALISM AND THE NEW NATIONS OF AFRICA 279–313 (D. Currie ed. 1964); *Comprehensiveness in Conceptions of Constitutive Process, supra* note 3. *See also* CONSTITUTIONS AND CONSTITUTIONALISM (2d ed. W. Andrews ed. 1963); S. DE SMITH, THE NEW COMMONWEALTH AND ITS CONSTITUTIONS 162–215 (1964); C. FRIEDRICH, CONSTITUTIONAL GOVERNMENT AND DEMOCRACY (4th ed. 1968); F. HAYEK, THE CONSTITUTION OF LIBERTY (1960); K. LOEWENSTEIN, POLITICAL POWER AND THE GOVERNMENTAL PROCESS (1957); C. MCILWAIN, CONSTITUTIONALISM, ANCIENT AND MODERN (rev. ed. 1947); R. POUND, THE DEVELOPMENT OF CONSTITUTIONAL GUARANTEES OF LIBERTY (1957); K. WHEARE, MODERN CONSTITUTIONS (2d ed. 1966); F. WORMUTH, THE ORIGINS OF MODERN CONSTITUTIONALISM (1949); Friedrich, *Constitutions and Constitutionalism*, 3 INT'L ENCYC. SOC. SC. 318 (1968); Hamilton, *Constitutionalism*, 4 ENCYC. SOC. SC. 255 (1931); Wheeler, *Constitutionalism*, in 5 HANDBOOK OF POLITICAL SCIENCE 1–91 (F. Greenstein & N. Polsby eds. 1975).

541. Chapter 1 *supra*. Ambassador Scranton put it aptly: "The idea of human rights is not unique to certain groups at isolated points in history; the idea is a unifying thread through all of the history of man, even in darkest times." Scranton, *supra* note 94, at 746.

542. *See* notes 208–11 *supra* and accompanying text.

543. *See* chapter 1 *supra*.

and of others, and for small and large groups as well as for the whole of humanity. They are, further, asserted with increasingly realistic, shared expectations about the interdependences of all individuals everywhere for all values.

The geographic range of these demands, like the effective power process of which they are a part, embraces the entire globe. The assertion of demand is both continuous and episodic, and is made in a vast variety of institutional arrangements, both organized and unorganized. Such assertion pervades both crisis and noncrisis conditions. In pursuit of fulfillment, peoples commit enormous resources and manpower, seeking to employ not merely authority, but all the bases of effective power. The intensity of demand is expressed through all modalities of communication, and is addressed to both small and large audiences. While persuasion may, in conformity with human dignity commitment, be a preferred strategy, people often fight and sometimes die for human rights. To secure their demanded values, many different individuals (official and nonofficial alike) are continuously engaged in efforts to obtain the information essential to effective decision making; to promote, and agitate for, human rights causes; to formulate new prescriptions and refine existing prescriptions; to invoke relevant prescriptions to cope with deprivations and nonfulfillments of values; to secure the application of prescriptions through appropriate institutions and procedures; to terminate obsolete prescriptions; and to maintain an appraising function that secures a continuous improvement of decision process.

This intensity of demand for the better protection of human rights infuses every constituent community, national and regional, of the larger global community. The history of the establishment of bills of rights within many of the more mature nation-states (as, for example, within Great Britain, the United States, and France) is well known.[544] Most of the newly independent states have made clear their comparable aspirations by incorporating, or making reference to, the provisions of the Universal Declaration of Human Rights in their formal constitutions.[545] In addition, regional communities have established, or sought

---

544. *See generally* I. BRANT, THE BILL OF RIGHTS: ITS ORIGIN AND MEANING (1967); A. DICEY, AN INTRODUCTION TO THE STUDY OF THE LAW OF THE CONSTITUTION (10th ed. 1959); G. DORSEY, AMERICAN FREEDOMS: AN ESSAY ON THE BILL OF RIGHTS (1974); E. DUMBAULD, THE BILL OF RIGHTS AND WHAT IT MEANS TODAY (1957); R. RUTLAND, THE BIRTH OF THE BILL OF RIGHTS (1955); J. GOUGH, FUNDAMENTAL LAW IN ENGLISH CONSTITUTIONAL HISTORY (1955); L. HAND, THE BILL OF RIGHTS: THE OLIVER WENDELL HOLMES LECTURES, 1958 (1958); B. SCHWARTZ, THE BILL OF RIGHTS: A DOCUMENTARY HISTORY (1971); 1 & 2 DOCUMENTS ON FUNDAMENTAL HUMAN RIGHTS (Z. Chafee ed. 1963); B. SCHWARTZ, THE GREAT RIGHTS OF MANKIND: A HISTORY OF THE AMERICAN BILL OF RIGHTS (1977).

545. *See* UNITED NATIONS ACTION, *supra* note 73, at 17–19. *See also* ASIAN-AFRICAN LEGAL CONSULTATIVE COMMITTEE, CONSTITUTIONS OF AFRICAN STATES (1972); CONSTITU-

to establish, on a broader geographic basis effective bills of rights, which take account of their peculiar cultural attitudes and institutional practices. The successful model of the European Convention of Human Rights, in which the members of the Council of Europe participate, is widely admired and beginning to be emulated.[546] Within the framework of the Organization of American States, the commitment to a regional bill of rights is enunciated in the OAS Charter proclamation of "the fundamental rights of the individual without distinction as to race, nationality, creed or sex";[547] the American Declaration of the Rights and Duties of Man,[548] which antedates the Universal Declaration of Human Rights; and the American Convention on Human Rights adopted in 1969.[549] Though the American Convention did not enter into force until July 17, 1978, the Inter-American Commission on Human Rights has been in operation since 1960; with expanding authority, the Commission has been entrusted with the task of applying the provisions of the American Declaration of the Rights and Duties of Man.[550] The growing human rights concern of the League of Arab States has found expression in the establishment of the Permanent Arab Regional Commission on Human Rights, which seeks to enhance human rights by stressing the need for creating national commissions of human rights and for fostering people's predispositions in the defense and fulfillment of human

---

TIONS OF NATIONS (rev. 3d. ed. A. Peaslee ed. 1965–70); 1 CONSTITUTIONS OF NATIONS (rev. 4th ed. A. Peaslee ed. 1974).

546. *See* notes 468–90 *supra* and accompanying text.

547. Charter of the Organization of American States, Art. 3(j), in INTERNATIONAL GOVERNMENTAL ORGANIZATIONS: CONSTITUTIONAL DOCUMENTS 1182, 1183 (rev. 3d ed. A. Peaslee ed. 1974) [hereinafter cited as IGO DOCUMENTS].

548. The Declaration was adopted by the Ninth International Conference of American States, held in Bogota, Colombia, Mar. 30–May 2, 1948. For the text, *see* PAN AMERICAN UNION, FINAL ACT OF THE NINTH CONFERENCE OF AMERICAN STATES 38–45 (1948), *reprinted in* BASIC DOCUMENTS, *supra* note 51, at 187–93.

549. American Convention, *supra* note 144.

550. *See* Buergenthal, *The Revised OAS Charter and the Protection of Human Rights,* 69 AM. J. INT'L L. 828 (1975). For recent activities of the Commission, *see, e.g.,* INTER-AMERICAN COMMISSION ON HUMAN RIGHTS, ANNUAL REPORT, 1976, OEA/Ser.L/V/II.40, Doc. 5 Corr. 1 (1977).

For further background on the protection of human rights in the Americas, *see* HUMAN RIGHTS AND THE LIBERATION OF MAN IN THE AMERICAS (L. Colonnese ed. 1970); A. SCHREIBER, THE INTER-AMERICAN COMMISSION ON HUMAN RIGHTS (1970); K. VASAK, LA COMMISSION INTERAMERICAINE DES DROITS DE L'HOMME (1968); Cabranes, *The Protection of Human Rights by the Organization of American States,* 62 AM. J. INT'L L. 889 (1968); Fox, *The American Convention on Human Rights and Prospects for United States Ratification,* 3 HUMAN RIGHTS 243 (1973); Thomas & Thomas, *Human Rights and the Organization of American States,* 12 SANTA CLARA LAWYER 319 (1972); Thomas & Thomas, *The Inter-American Commission on Human Rights,* 20 SW. L.J. 282 (1966); Sandifer, *Human Rights in the Inter-American System,* 11 HOW. L.J. 508 (1965).

rights.[551] The Organization of African Unity expresses, through the OAU Charter, its aspirations for a bill of rights for Africa, by pledging to "promote international cooperation, having due regard to the Charter of the United Nations and the Universal Declaration of Human Rights."[552] Though incorporation of a bill of rights by reference to the Universal Declaration is, as indicated, not uncommon in constitutions adopted by newly independent states,[553] such explicit reference in the charter of a regional governmental organization marks a new dimension in demand.

The different communities of the world have sought, historically, to make effective their higher intensities in demand for human rights prescriptions by attaching to such prescriptions certain protective legal consequences under such technical terms as "fundamental law," "the higher law," "constitutionalism" or "constitutional limitations," "bills of rights" or "rights of man," "civil liberties," "an international bill of human rights," "*jus cogens*" or "peremptory norms," "public order" or "*ordre public*," and "public policy."[554] In all these technical terms, and their ancillary expressions, the common core of reference, beyond identification of policies demanded with the highest intensity, is specification of certain projected features of constitutive process, designed to give effect to such priorities in intensity of demand. Thus, when it is said that a prescription is a "fundamental law" or "higher law," what is meant is that it was created in certain specific, sometimes formal, ways and that it can be changed only with extraordinary difficulty or in the same way in which it was created.[555] Such a prescription may be said to be applicable to all official and nonofficial acts within a community, and even legislative acts may be required to conform to such prescriptions upon pain of being regarded as unconstitutional. When prescriptions are described as

---

551. *See* A. Robertson, Human Rights in the World 140–47 (1972).

552. Charter of the Organization of African Unity, Art. 2(1)(e), *reprinted in* IGO Documents, *supra* note 547, at 1165, 1166.

See A. Robertson, *supra* note 551, at 148–58; *A Commission on Human Rights for Africa,* 2 Human Rights J. 696 (1969); Cowen, *Human Rights in Contemporary Africa,* 9 Natural L. Forum 1 (1964); Robertson, *African Legal Process and the Individual,* 5 Human Rights J. 465 (1972).

Cf. Baldwin, *Western Constitutionalism and African Nation-Building: The Anglophonic East African Experience,* 2 Hastings Const. L.Q. 373 (1975); Paul, *Some Observations on Constitutionalism, Judicial Review, and Rule of Law in Africa,* 35 Ohio State L.J. 851 (1974); Van Boven, *Some Remarks on Special Problems Relating to Human Rights in Developing Countries,* 3 Human Rights J. 383 (1970).

553. *See* note 545 *supra.*

554. *See* note 544 *supra. See also* notes 635–99 *infra* and accompanying text.

555. *See, e.g.,* E Corwin, The "Higher Law" Background of American Constitutional Law (1955).

constituting a bill of rights, what is often meant is that the individual human being may challenge acts regarded as contravening such prescription. Sometimes judicial bodies are accorded competence to review the acts of other branches of the government for their conformity to prescriptions described as fundamental law or as constituting a bill of rights.[556] In international law, the terms "*jus cogens*" and "peremptory norms" are employed to refer to prescriptions that are inalienable and subject to termination only in the ways in which they are created.[557]

---

556. On judicial review outside the United States, *see* M. CAPPELLETTI, JUDICIAL REVIEW IN THE CONTEMPORARY WORLD (1971); Waline, *The Constitutional Council of the French Republic,* 12 AM. J. COMP. L. 483 (1963); H. ABRAHAM, THE JUDICIAL PROCESS (3d ed. 1975); Cappelletti & Adams, *Judicial Review: European Antecedents and Adaptations,* 79 HARV. L. REV. 1207 (1966); Radin, *The Judicial Review of Statutes in Continental Europe,* 41 W. VA. L.Q. 112 (1935); Deener, *Judicial Review in Modern Constitutional Systems,* 46 AM. POL. SC. REV. 1079 (1952); E. MCWHINNEY, JUDICIAL REVIEW IN THE ENGLISH-SPEAKING WORLD (2d ed. 1960); von Mehren, *The New German Constitutional Court,* 1 AM. J. COMP. L. 70 (1952); Rupp, *Judicial Review in the Federal Republic of Germany,* 9 AM. J. COMP. L. 29 (1959); Eder, *Judicial Review in Latin America,* 21 OHIO ST. L.J. 570 (1960); E. MCWHINNEY, CONSTITUTIONALISM IN GERMANY AND THE FEDERAL CONSTITUTIONAL COURT (1962); J. MAKI, COURT AND CONSTITUTION IN JAPAN (1964); Griswold, *The Demise of the High Court of Parliament in South Africa,* 66 HARV. L. REV. 864 (1953); R. JOHNSTON, THE EFFECT OF JUDICIAL REVIEW IN FEDERAL-STATE RELATIONS IN AUSTRALIA, CANADA, AND THE UNITED STATES (1970); Seidman, *Judicial Review and Fundamental Freedoms in Anglophonic Independent Africa,* 35 OHIO STATE L.J. 820 (1974).

On judicial review within the United States, *see generally* A. BICKEL, THE LEAST DANGEROUS BRANCH (1962); A. BICKEL, THE SUPREME COURT AND THE IDEA OF PROGRESS (1970); C. BLACK, PERSPECTIVES IN CONSTITUTIONAL LAW (rev. ed. 1970); C. BLACK, THE PEOPLE AND THE COURT: JUDICIAL REVIEW IN A DEMOCRACY (1960); L. BOUDIN, GOVERNMENT BY JUDICIARY (1932); SUPREME COURT AND SUPREME LAW (E. Cahn ed. 1954); A. COX, THE ROLE OF THE SUPREME COURT IN AMERICAN GOVERNMENT (1977); W. CROSSKEY, POLITICS AND THE CONSTITUTION IN THE HISTORY OF THE UNITED STATES (1953); C. HAINES, THE AMERICAN DOCTRINE OF JUDICIAL SUPREMACY (2d ed. 1959); P. KURLAND, POLITICS, THE CONSTITUTION AND THE WARREN COURT (1970); THE SUPREME COURT AND THE JUDICIAL FUNCTION (P. Kurland ed. 1975); JUDICIAL REVIEW AND THE SUPREME COURT (L. Levy ed. 1967); E. ROSTOW, THE SOVEREIGN PREROGATIVE: THE SUPREME COURT AND THE QUEST FOR LAW (1962); H. WECHSLER, PRINCIPLES, POLITICS, AND FUNDAMENTAL LAW (1961); Bork, *Neutral Principles and Some First Amendment Problems,* 47 IND. L.J. 1 (1971); Wright, *Professor Bickel, The Scholarly Tradition, and the Supreme Court,* 84 HARV. L. REV. 768 (1971).

Constitutional law case books typically begin with judicial review. *See* P. BREST, PROCESSES OF CONSTITUTIONAL DECISIONMAKING: CASES AND MATERIALS 46–87 (1975); E. BARRETT, CONSTITUTIONAL LAW: CASES AND MATERIALS 17–153 (5th ed. 1977); J. BARRON & C. DIENES, CONSTITUTIONAL LAW: PRINCIPLES AND POLICY: CASES AND MATERIALS 1–139 (1975); P. FREUND, A. SUTHERLAND, M. HOWE, & E. BROWN, CONSTITUTIONAL LAW: CASES AND OTHER PROBLEMS 1–146 (4th ed. 1977); G. GUNTHER, CASES AND MATERIALS ON CONSTITUTIONAL LAW 1–80 (9th ed. 1975); P. KAUPER, CONSTITUTIONAL LAW: CASES AND MATERIALS 1–314 (4th ed. 1972); W. LOCKHART, Y. KAMISAR, & J. CHOPER, CONSTITUTIONAL LAW: CASES—COMMENTS—QUESTIONS 1–159 (4th ed. 1975).

557. *See* notes 635–99 and 748–67 *infra* and accompanying text.

The basic features of constitutive process which are emphasized, albeit somewhat anecdotally, in the whole of these technical terms denoting "fundamental law" or "basic rights" can, it is suggested, be most conveniently summarized in terms of four of the decision functions discussed above:

1. Prescription.

The most intensely demanded constitutive prescriptions explicitly designed to protect individual rights are, like other constitutive prescriptions, established and maintained in a wide variety of communications and uniformities in behavior commonly summed up as customary law. Written instruments and charters are, however, often component items in this flow of communication, especially when the members of a community seek drastic change from past policies. Deliberate formulations of individual rights and specifications for a balancing and limitation of official power may be projected into the flow of customary communication and decision in a conscious effort to expedite and increase the protection of individual rights.

2. Application.

Provision is made for the applicability of intensely demanded prescriptions about individual rights to all decision makers and community members, whether official or nonofficial. Officials at all levels of government, from central to provincial, are required to observe and promote these rights, and nonofficials are required to respect the equal rights of others in all interactions in social process.

Prescriptions designed to protect human rights are buttressed by specialized institutions for application. Allocations of competence may be balanced so as to secure disinterested judicial review of decisions and activities by officials and others who are alleged to have imposed deprivations of human rights.

3. Invocation.

Special provision is made to enable individuals who allege that their human rights have been violated to challenge putative deprivations before authoritative decision makers.

Provision is made for specialized invocation by representatives of the community, such as ombudsmen or attorneys general.

4. Termination.

Special difficulties are placed in the way of amending or terminating intensely demanded prescriptions about human rights. It is commonly the case that such prescriptions can be changed only in the ways that they are created.

It may now be demonstrated that all these different features of constitutive process, so thoroughly tested and so highly cherished in national communities, have appeared, or are in process of appearing, in global constitutive process in relation to the protection of human rights. It is convenient, again, in recounting these developments to focus upon each of the four decision functions.

Prescription

The prescriptions about human rights range, as described above, from the most deliberate form (agreement) to the least deliberate form (customary development), with a paramount role being increasingly accorded communication emanating from the United Nations.[558]

The deliberate effort to create an international bill of human rights began even before the formal establishment of the United Nations. In recognition of the intimate relationship between human rights and peace, as vividly brought home by the atrocities of the Third Reich, a proposal to include an International Bill of Human Rights in the United Nations Charter itself was presented at the San Francisco conference.[559] While the delegates were not ready for such a proposal, the Charter, as finally adopted, did contain several significant human rights provisions;[560] and the "idea of establishing an International Bill of Rights" was, in the words of Schwelb, "treated as inherent in the Charter."[561] Appearing at the close of the San Francisco conference, President Truman stated emphatically:

> We have good reason to expect the framing of an international bill of rights, acceptable to all the nations involved. That bill of rights will be as much a part of international life as our own Bill of Rights is a part of our Constitution. The Charter is dedicated to the achievement and observance of human rights and fundamental freedoms. Unless we can attain those objectives for all men and women everywhere—without regard to race, language or religion—we cannot have permanent peace and security.[562]

---

558. *See* notes 315–67 *supra* and accompanying text.

559. *See* R. Russell, A History of the United Nations Charter 323–27 (1958); E. Schwelb, Human Rights and the International Community 31 (1964) [hereinafter cited as E. Schwelb]; U.S. Department of State, Postwar Foreign Policy Preparation, 1939–1945, at 115–16, 472, 483–85 (1949); Sohn, *A Short History of United Nations Documents on Human Rights,* in Commission to Study the Organization of Peace, The United Nations and Human Rights 39, 46–56 (1968) [hereinafter cited as Sohn, *A Short History*].

560. *See* U.N. Charter, Preamble and Arts. 1(3), 13, 55, 56, 62(2), and 76(c).

561. E. Schwelb, *supra* note 559, at 31.

562. 1 United Nations Information Organization, Documents of the United Nations Conference on International Organization 717 (1945).

Prior to the Charter's coming into force on October 24, 1945, the Preparatory Commission of the United Nations and its executive committee had recommended that the Commission on Human Rights, as provided in the Charter, accord the top priority to the "formulation of an international bill of rights" in its future work.[563] Hence, when the Commission on Human Rights was created in February 1946, "an international bill of rights" was the first item on its agenda.[564] Shortly after the Commission and a drafting committee commenced their work, it became apparent that there were differences among the members regarding the appropriate modality of the envisaged international bill of rights—whether in the form of a "declaration" or "manifesto" by the General Assembly or of an international convention.[565] While the proponents of the "declaration" route expected the proposed declaration to be reinforced by one or more conventions, the proponents of the "convention" route endorsed the adoption also of a general and comprehensive declaration. Eventually, in 1947, it was decided that the contemplated "International Bill of Human Rights" would consist of a Declaration, a Convention (Covenant), and "Measures of Implementation."[566] The first part of this international bill—the Universal Declaration of Human Rights—was adopted unanimously on December 10, 1948, by the General Assembly in the form of a resolution.[567]

Subsequent to the adoption of the Universal Declaration, the ideological controversy relating to the nature and prominence of "civil and political rights" and of "economic, social, and cultural rights" led the General Assembly to decide, in 1952, that two covenants—one on civil and political rights and the other on economic, social, and cultural rights—should be simultaneously prepared, submitted, approved, and opened for sig-

---

563. Report of the Preparatory Commission of the United Nations 28, 36 (1946).

564. G.A. Res. 7, U.N. Doc. A/64 at 12 (1946); E.S.C. Res. 5, 1 U.N. ESCOR 163 (1946).

565. See Commission on Human Rights, *Report of the Drafting Committee on an International Bill of Human Rights: First Session,* U.N. Doc. E/CN.4/21 (1 July 1947).

566. *See* Report of the Commission on Human Rights, 2d Session, 6 U.N. ESCOR, Supp. (No. 1) 5, U.N. Doc. E/600 (1947). *See also* G.A. Res. 543, 6 U.N. GAOR, Supp. (No. 20) 36, U.N. Doc. A/2119 (1952); G.A. Res. 421, 5 U.N. GAOR, Supp. (No. 20) 42, U.N. Doc. A/1775 (1950); G.A. Res. 217 F, U.N. Doc. A/810, at 79 (1948).

For accounts of this development, *see* Y.B.U.N. 1947–48, at 572–73. *See also* Schwelb, *Notes on the Early Legislative History of the Measures of Implementation of the Human Rights Covenants,* in Melanges Offerts à Polys Modinos 270–89 (1968); Sohn, *A Short History, supra* note 559, at 60–67 (1968).

567. Universal Declaration, *supra* note 45.

For its history and growth, *see N. Robinson, supra* note 363; E. Schwelb, *supra* note 559; United Nations Action, *supra* note 73, at 8–19; Cassin, *From the Ten Commandments to the Rights of Man,* in Of Law and Man: Essays in Honor of Haim H. Cohn 13–25 (S. Shoham ed. 1971); Humphrey, *The UN Charter and the Universal Declaration of Human Rights,* in E. Luard, International Protection, *supra* note 57, at 39–58.

nature, and that "measures of implementation" should be incorporated in each of the two covenants.[568] The Human Rights Commission, entrusted with the primary task of drafting, completed its work on the two draft covenants in 1954.[569] After the lapse of more than a decade, the General Assembly, on December 16, 1966, adopted unanimously the International Covenant on Economic, Social, and Cultural Rights and the International Covenant on Civil and Political Rights,[570] and, by majority vote, the Optional Protocol to the International Covenant on Civil and Political Rights (dealing with procedures for individual petitions).[571] Despite some gloomy predictions, the Covenant on Economic, Social, and Cultural Rights has been in force since January 3, 1976, while the Covenant on Civil and Political Rights and its Optional Protocol have been in force since March 23, 1976.[572] Thus, the International Bill of Human Rights, as contemplated at the founding of the United Nations, has been projected in familiar form.

This developing International Bill of Human Rights has, further, been greatly fortified by various ancillary instruments dealing with particular categories of participants (women, refugees, stateless persons, youths, children, mentally retarded persons, and so on), or particular value categories or subject matters (genocide, apartheid, discrimination, racial discrimination, sex-based discrimination, slavery, forced labor, nationality, employment, education, marriage, and so on),[573] by the decisions and recommendations of international governmental organizations (especially by the various organs and entities of the United Nations), and by customary developments in the transnational arena.

Representing a new departure from traditional preoccupation with "interstate" relations, the United Nations has projected an unmistakably new commitment toward world order, seeking to secure not only a minimum order (in the sense of minimization of unauthorized coercion)

---

568. G.A. Res. 543, 6 U.N. GAOR, Supp. (No. 20) 36, U.N. Doc. A/2119 (1952).

For a detailed account of this decision, *see Annotations on the Draft Covenants, supra* note 411, at 7–10. *See also* Schwelb, *Some Aspects, supra* note 301, at 105–07; Sohn, *A Short History, supra* note 599, at 101–07.

569. The completed work of Human Rights Commission on the draft covenants is fully incorporated in *Annotations on the Draft Covenants, supra* note 411.

570. Covenant on Economic, Social, and Cultural Rights, *supra* note 47; Covenant on Civil and Political Rights, *supra* note 48.

571. Optional Protocol, *supra* note 49. The Optional Protocol was adopted by a vote of sixty-six for, two against, and thirty-eight abstentions.

572. *See After 30 Years, an International Bill of Human Rights,* 13 UN MONTHLY CHRONICLE 50 (Apr. 1976); Schwelb, *Entry into Force of the International Covenants on Human Rights and the Optional Protocol to the International Covenant on Civil and Political Rights,* 70 AM. J. INT'L L. 511 (1976).

573. These instruments are conveniently collected in U.N. HUMAN RIGHTS INSTRUMENTS, *supra* note 51. *See also* BASIC DOCUMENTS ON HUMAN RIGHTS (I. Brownlie ed. 1971).

but also a maximum order (in the sense of the greater production and wider distribution of all values). The United Nations Charter offers multiple provisions suggesting that the protection of human rights is a coequal, even indistinguishable, goal in relation to the maintenance of peace and security. The determination of the peoples of the United Nations "to reaffirm faith in fundamental human rights, in the dignity and worth of the human person, in the equal rights of men and women," as expressed in the preamble, is immediately followed, in Article 1(3), by the enunciation of the following as a principal purpose of the United Nations:

> To achieve international co-operation in solving international problems of an economic, social, cultural, or humanitarian character, and in promoting and encouraging respect for human rights and for fundamental freedoms for all without distinction as to race, sex, language, or religion.

Toward this purpose, the General Assembly is authorized, under Article 13(1)(b), to "initiate studies and make recommendations"; the Economic and Social Council is similarly authorized, under Article 62(2), to "make recommendations"; and Article 76c makes explicit that enhancement of "respect for human rights and for fundamental freedoms" is one of the "basic objectives" of the international trusteeship system. Most importantly, Articles 55 and 56 together oblige all member states to "pledge themselves to take joint and separate action in co-operation with the Organization for the achievement of," among other things, "universal respect for, and observance of, human rights and fundamental freedoms for all without distinction as to race, sex, language, or religion."

In the light of this mass of explicit references to the protection of human rights, many scholars have, from the beginning of the United Nations, taken the position that the human rights provisions of the Charter are law in the sense of imposing definite legal obligations upon the member states and others. Dismissing the argument that the Charter provisions on human rights "are a mere declaration of principle devoid of any element of legal obligation" as "no more than a facile generalisation,"[574] Lauterpacht eloquently stated:

> For the provisions of the Charter on the subject figure prominently in the statement of the Purposes of the United Nations. Members of the United Nations are under a legal obligation to act in accordance with these Purposes. It is their legal duty to respect and observe fundamental rights and freedoms. . . .[575]

574. H. Lauterpacht, *supra* note 39, at 147.
575. *Id.*

Drawing upon other Charter provisions, he elaborated:

> There is a mandatory obligation implied in the provision of Article 55 that the United Nations "shall promote respect for, and observance of, human rights and fundamental freedoms"; or, in the terms of Article 13, that the Assembly shall make recommendations for the purpose of assisting in the realisation of human rights and freedoms. There is a distinct element of legal duty in the undertaking expressed in Article 56 in which "All Members pledge themselves to take joint and separate action in cooperation with the Organisation for the achievement of the purposes set forth in Article 55." The cumulative legal result of all these pronouncements cannot be ignored. The legal character of these obligations of the Charter would remain even if the Charter were to contain no provisions of any kind for their implementation. For the Charter fails to provide for the enforcement of its other numerous obligations the legal character of which is undoubted.[576]

The position taken by Jessup is equally emphatic: "It is already the law, at least for Members of the United Nations, that respect for human dignity and fundamental human rights is obligatory. The duty is imposed by the Charter, a treaty to which they are parties."[577]

This interpretation of the human rights provisions of the Charter, as imposing definable specific obligations upon states, has recently received authoritative confirmation from the International Court of Justice. In the *Namibia* case, in 1971, the Court held that the extension of apartheid to Namibia (South West Africa) by the government of South Africa is in contravention of the Charter of the United Nations.[578] The Court declared:

> Under the Charter of the United Nations, the former Mandatory had pledged itself to observe and respect, in a territory having an international status, human rights and fundamental freedoms for all without distinction as to race. To establish instead, and to en-

---

576. *Id.* at 148.

577. P. JESSUP, *supra* note 16, at 91. *See also* G. TUNKIN, *supra* note 315, at 80–82; Carey, *The International Legal Order on Human Rights,* in 4 THE FUTURE OF THE INTERNATIONAL LEGAL ORDER 268, 269–70 (C. Black & R. Falk eds. 1972); Newman, *Interpreting the Human Rights Clauses of the UN Charter,* 5 HUMAN RIGHTS J. 283 (1972). For other views endorsing this position, *see* Schwelb, *The International Court of Justice and the Human Rights Clauses of the Charter,* 66 AM. J. INT'L L. 337, 339–41 (1972) [hereinafter cited as Schwelb, *ICJ and Human Rights*]. Dissenting views are summarized in Schwelb, *supra*, at 338–39.

578. Advisory Opinion on Legal Consequences for States of the Continued Presence of South Africa in Namibia (South West Africa) Notwithstanding Security Council Resolution 276 (1970), [1971] I.C.J. 16 [hereinafter cited as Advisory Opinion on Namibia].

> force, distinctions, exclusions, restrictions and limitations exclusively based on grounds of race, colour, descent or national or ethnic origin which constitute a denial of fundamental human rights is a flagrant violation of the purposes and principles of the Charter.[579]

In particular application to the case before it, the Court stated emphatically that

> no factual evidence is needed for the purpose of determining whether the policy of *apartheid* as applied by South Africa in Namibia is in conformity with the international obligations assumed by South Africa under the Charter of the United Nations. In order to determine whether the laws and decrees applied by South Africa in Namibia, which are a matter of public record, constitute a violation of the purposes and principles of the Charter of the United Nations, the question of intent or governmental discretion is not relevant; nor is it necessary to investigate or determine the effects of those measures upon the welfare of the inhabitants.[580]

In his incisive analysis of the Court's opinion, Schwelb notes that "the interpretation of the human rights clauses [as imposing legal obligation upon member states] contained in the Advisory Opinion is backed by the authority of the Court as a body and of the thirteen Judges who voted for it and . . . is not challenged by one of the two dissenting Judges and not specifically objected to by the other."[581] "To sum up," Schwelb adds, "the authority of the Court is now clearly behind the interpretation of the human rights clauses of the Charter as presented almost a generation ago by Lauterpacht and others."[582]

The very general authoritative prescriptions of the Charter about human rights were shortly given somewhat more detailed specification in the Universal Declaration of Human Rights, adopted in 1948. This Declaration has acquired, as we have already described, the attributes of authority in two different ways.[583] First, it is commonly accepted as an authoritative specification of the content of the human rights provisions of the United Nations Charter. Secondly, its frequent invocation and application by officials, at all levels of government and in many different communities about the world, have conferred upon its content those crystallized expectations of future invocation and application characteristic of customary law.

---

579. *Id.* at 57.
580. *Id.*
581. Schwelb, *ICJ and Human Rights, supra* note 577, at 350.
582. *Id.*
583. *See* notes 358–67 *supra* and accompanying text.

Thus, the Montreal Statement of the Assembly for Human Rights (a world assembly attended by both officials and nonofficials in commemoration of the International Year of Human Rights) declared, in March 1968, that "The Universal Declaration of Human Rights constitutes an authoritative interpretation of the Charter of the highest order, and has over the years become a part of customary international law."[584] Similarly, in his separate opinion in the *Namibia* case, Judge Ammoun, vice-president of the Court, after observing that the Court's "Advisory Opinion takes judicial notice of the Universal Declaration of Human Rights,"[585] elaborated as follows:

> Although the affirmations of the Declaration are not binding *qua* international convention within the meaning of Article 38, paragraph 1(a), of the Statute of the Court, they can bind States on the basis of custom within the meaning of paragraph 1(b) of the same Article, whether because they constituted a codification of customary law as was said in respect of Article 6 of the Vienna Convention on the Law of Treaties, or because they have acquired the force of custom through a general practice accepted as law, in the words of Article 38, paragraph 1(b), of the Statute.[586]

In documenting a thesis that "the adoption of the [Universal] Declaration may well have been one of the greatest achievements of the United Nations,"[587] Humphrey offers relevant historical context for the Declaration:

> It provides the framework for the international recognition of those human rights and fundamental freedoms that were left undefined by the Charter. In the tradition of Magna Carta, the American Declaration of Independence, the French Declaration of the Rights of Man, and other historic statements, the Universal Declaration of Human Rights enshrines on the international level a universally accepted philosophy of freedom for the 20th century moving beyond the historic declarations by recognizing that civil and political rights can have little meaning without economic, social, and cultural rights. Its moral and political authority is equal to that of the Charter itself.[588]

---

584. Montreal Statement of the Assembly for Human Rights (1968). *See also* Sohn, *The Human Rights Law of the Charter,* 12 Texas Int'l L.J. 129, 132–34 (1977).

585. [1971] I.C.J. 67, 76.

586. *Id.* at 76.

587. Humphrey, *The International Bill of Rights: Scope and Implementation,* 17 Wm. & Mary L. Rev. 527, 529 (1976) [hereinafter cited as Humphrey, *The International Bill of Rights*].

588. *Id.*

In summarizing the use to which the Universal Declaration has been put, Humphrey concludes:

> In the more than a quarter of a century since its adoption, however, the Declaration has been invoked so many times both within and without the United Nations that lawyers now are saying that, whatever the intention of its authors may have been, the Declaration is now part of the customary law of nations and therefore is binding on all states. The Declaration has become what some nations wished it to be in 1948: the universally accepted interpretation and definition of the human rights left undefined by the Charter.[589]

The same conclusion is announced by Waldock in a much quoted passage:

> This constant and widespread recognition of the principles of the Universal Declaration clothes it, in my opinion, in the character of customary law. Be that as it may, the Declaration has acquired a status inside and outside the United Nations which gives it high authority as the accepted formulation of the common standards of human rights. Furthermore, if you look at the Declaration, you will see that it unequivocally starts from the standpoint of the rule of law—the standpoint that the function of law is not merely to regulate the conduct of the governed but also to protect them from abuses of power by the governors.[590]

The two International Covenants on Human Rights and the Optional Protocol to the Covenant on Civil and Political Rights have, as indicated, been in effect since early 1976. They are of course binding for all states that have ratified or acceded to them. Like the Universal Declaration, they are, further, authoritative interpretations of the Charter provisions on human rights, as well as vital components in the flow of communication that creates the expectations comprising customary international law. They have both given further detailed specification to the content of internationally protected human rights and provided structures and procedures (albeit with some inadequacies) for remedying deprivations, thereby contributing mightily to the stabilization of authoritative expectations about the defense and fulfillment of human rights.[591] Similarly, a

---

589. *Id.*

590. Waldock, *Human Rights in Contemporary International Law and the Significance of the European Convention,* in THE EUROPEAN CONVENTION ON HUMAN RIGHTS 1, 15 (1965) (Brit. Institute of Int'l & Comp. L., Int'l L. Series No. 5).

591. *See* notes 96, 376–83, 434–64 *supra* and accompanying text. *See also* A. ROBERTSON, *supra* note 551; Humphrey, *The International Bill of Rights, supra* note 587; Schwelb, *Civil and Political Rights, supra* note 382; Schwelb, *The Nature of the Obligations, supra* note 460; Schwelb, *Some Aspects, supra* note 301.

growing body of more particular conventions dealing with certain deprivers or various deprivations has significantly contributed to the enrichment and growth of the core content of the human rights prescriptions projected in the United Nations Charter.[592]

The authoritativeness of the Charter provisions on human rights, and of the specification of these provisions in the Universal Declaration and related instruments, has been greatly fortified by the practice of international governmental organizations, especially the various organs of the United Nations. As Schwelb observes:

> In the practice of the United Nations and of its Members neither the vagueness and generality of the human rights clauses of the Charter nor the domestic jurisdiction clause have prevented the United Nations from considering, investigating, and judging concrete human rights situations, provided there was a majority strong enough and wishing strongly enough to attempt to influence the particular development.[593]

Some of the more important aspects of this United Nations practice have already been summarized by reference to each of the seven decision functions performed.[594] Here attention may be called to a recent, somewhat more comprehensive, and conventionally organized study emanating from the United Nations, which describes the depth and wide acceptance of this practice.[595] This study summarizes in terms of:

1. "General pronouncements endorsing the Universal Declaration or calling upon Governments to live up to its provisions."[596]

   The list includes:

   General Assembly Resolution on "Essentials of Peace" of December 1, 1949;

   The "Uniting for Peace" Resolution adopted by the General Assembly on November 3, 1950;

   The Resolution on "Observance of Human Rights" adopted by the General Assembly on February 4, 1952;

   The landmark Declaration on the Granting of Independence to Colonial Countries and Peoples adopted by the Assembly on December 14, 1960;

592. *See* notes 326–46 *supra* and accompanying text.
593. Schwelb, *ICJ and Human Rights, supra* note 577, at 341.
594. *See* notes 154–68 *supra* and accompanying text.
595. United Nations Action, *supra* note 73.
596. *Id.* at 9.

The United Nations Declaration on the Elimination of All Forms of Racial Discrimination adopted on November 20, 1963;

The General Assembly Resolution on measures to accelerate the promotion of respect for human rights and fundamental freedoms adopted on December 18, 1965;

The General Assembly Resolution of December 19, 1968, endorsing the Proclamation of Teheran as "an important and timely reaffirmation of the principles embodied in the Universal Declaration and in other international instruments in the field of human rights";

The Declaration on Social Progress and Development of 1969;

The General Assembly Declaration on the Occasion of the Twenty-fifth Anniversary of the United Nations (October 24, 1970).[597]

2. "United Nations resolutions invoking the Universal Declaration in support of action on a world-wide scale for the solution of human rights problems in specific fields."[598]

These specific fields include:

Action against discrimination in general;

Action against sex-based discrimination and for the protection of women;

The right of asylum;

Administration of justice;

Freedom of information;

The protection of refugees;

The protection of the child and of the youth;

The protection of the elderly and the aged;

The protection of mentally retarded persons;

Action against the outflow of skilled personnel from developing to developed countries.[599]

3. "United Nations resolutions invoking the Universal Declaration in regard to concrete human rights situations."[600]

---

597. See *id.* at 9–11.
598. *Id.* at 11.
599. *See id.* at 11–14.
600. *Id.* at 14.

> The concrete human rights situations involved include:
>
> Respect for human rights in non-self-governing territories;
>
> The racial situation in southern Africa;
>
> The Namibia controversy;
>
> Matters relating to forced labor;
>
> The exploitation of labor through illicit and clandestine trafficking;
>
> The policy of apartheid in South Africa;
>
> The Russian wives case;
>
> The question of Tibet.[601]

The summary in the United Nations study includes also a specification of "the influence of the Universal Declaration on international treaties"[602] and of "the influence of the Universal Declaration on national constitutions, municipal laws and court decisions."[603] The first influence, that on the proliferation of human rights conventions, has already been noted.[604]

The second influence of the Universal Declaration, that on the making of national constitutions, statutes, and decisions, is of particular importance in augmenting the great historic communication—that the protection of human rights is of the highest priority—inherent in the practice of national constitutionalism during the past two hundred years. This flow of communication on the national level confirms community-wide expectations that the basic content of human rights, as specified in many relevant documents, is rapidly becoming the most fundamental law of the global community. The United Nations study offers this summation:

> Evidence of the impact of the Universal Declaration may be found in texts of various national constitutions which were enacted after the adoption of the Universal Declaration. Several of these constitutions expressly refer, either in their preambles or in their operative provisions, to the Universal Declaration. In addition, many other constitutions contain detailed provisions on a number of human rights, most of which are inspired by, or often modelled on, the text of the articles of the Declaration.[605]

---

601. *See id.* at 14–15.
602. *Id.* at 16.
603. *Id.* at 17.
604. *See* notes 326–46 *supra* and accompanying text.
605. United Nations Action, *supra* note 73, at 17.

Another important body of practice contributing to the establishment and maintenance of a global bill of rights is the customary international law of the responsibility of states about the treatment of aliens. This still vital inheritance, which afforded transnational protection to a particular category of human beings (nationals abroad) in an era when human rights matters were commonly accepted as within the domain of domestic jurisdiction, continues to serve the common interest today. In fact, as we have developed elsewhere, the customary international law of state responsibility, in constant interaction with the contemporary human rights movement and as an integral part of this movement, has greatly contributed to the sum total of the human rights protection, helping to raise the level of transnational protection of nationals as well as of aliens.[606] The conjunction of the customary protection through state responsibility and the new human rights prescriptions generated by, and radiated from, the United Nations Charter has eliminated "out-groups" in the regime of transnational protection of human rights and accorded protection to all human beings, irrespective of their nationality or their place of sojourn.

The end result of all this comprehensive and continuing prescription, ranging in modality from the most deliberate to the least deliberate, would appear to be that the core content of the various communications has, in the immemorial manner of constitutive process, been prescribed as a global bill of human rights. This global bill of rights is in form and policy content very much like those bills of rights created and maintained in the more mature national communities. The English constitution, for example, supposedly "unwritten," is in fact composed both of a series of instruments, traceable back to Magna Carta, and of customary practice.[607] Similarly, when the United States Constitution is properly understood, it is not merely a single written document, but the whole flow of communication and decision, preceding 1787 and coming down to date;[608] the Bill of Rights in this Constitution goes well beyond the

---

606. *See* chapter 14 *infra*.

607. *Cf.* A. DICEY, *supra* note 544; F. MAITLAND, THE CONSTITUTIONAL HISTORY OF ENGLAND (1908).

For more recent developments, *see* Daintith, *The Protection of Human Rights in the United Kingdom*, 1 HUMAN RIGHTS J. 275 and 407 (1968).

608. *See* H. MCBAIN, THE LIVING CONSTITUTION (1927); C. MERRIAM, THE WRITTEN CONSTITUTION AND THE UNWRITTEN ATTITUDE (1931); *Comprehensiveness in Conceptions of Constitutive Process, supra* note 3; Grey, *Do We Have an Unwritten Constitution?* 27 STAN. L. REV. 703 (1975); Miller, *Notes on the Concept of the "Living" Constitution*, 31 GEO. WASH. L. REV. 881 (1963); Reich, *The Living Constitution and the Court's Role*, in HUGO BLACK AND THE SUPREME COURT 133–62 (S. Strickland ed. 1967).

Contrast Rehnquist, *The Notion of a Living Constitution*, 54 TEXAS L. REV. 693 (1976).

confines of the first eight or ten articles of the amendments to the Constitution.[609] In any constitutive process, it is not merely a simple isolated act of communication, but a whole flow of communication and decision through time, that establishes and maintains authoritative expectations.[610]

Application

The contemporary transnational prescriptions for the protection of human rights would appear to project the same broad compass in applicability characteristic of the bills of rights of mature national communities. These prescriptions are clearly made applicable to the United Nations and its organs and other international governmental organizations, to nation-states and all their officials, and to all the nongovernmental groups and individuals active in the whole of world social process.

THE UNITED NATIONS AND ITS ORGANS

The United Nations Charter is commonly expected, as indicated in a vast flow of communication before and since 1945, to be the most fundamental law of the global community, binding all participants. For member states this made explicit in Article 103, the Charter's supremacy clause. This article stipulates: "In the event of a conflict between the obligations of the Members of the United Nations under the present Charter and their obligations under any other international agreement, their obligations under the present Charter shall prevail." It is not to be thought that the member states and their global audience could have understood by these words that the members were creating an organization or agencies with a competence to transgress the obligations, with respect to security and human rights, that they themselves were assuming. The struggle to bring kings and presidents and other agencies within the confines of the fundamental laws of national communities has left too indelible an impression upon too many peoples to make plausible any supposition that the founders of the United Nations intended to create, or have created, an organization free of its own basic principles.

In the detailed provisions of the United Nations Charter, its framers definitively expressed a fundamental constitutive feature that all grants of competence to the organization and its different organs and agencies were made subject to many limitations upon competence in favor of both the autonomy of members and the protection of individual human

---

609. For a comparable view, *see* W. Cohen & J. Kaplan, Bill of Rights: Constitutional Law for Undergraduates 1–3 (1976).

610. *See* Miller, *supra* note 608. For a comprehensive development of this theme, *see* P. Brest, *supra* note 556.

rights. The basic point is made by Brownlie, who, in writing of international organizations more generally, observes:

> The division of competence between organs and the limits to the powers of the organization as a whole may be carefully drawn, and, as in the Charter of the United Nations, the obligations set out in the relevant instrument may be expressed to apply to the organization itself, and the organs.[611]

In making explicit what would otherwise be axiomatic, the United Nations Charter, after spelling out in Article 1 major purposes that include the protection of human rights, provides in Article 2: "The Organization and its Members, in pursuit of the Purposes stated in Article 1, shall act in accordance with the following Principles. . . ."[612] Similarly, Article 24 of the Charter, while granting competence to the Security Council for the maintenance of peace and security, makes the grant subject explicitly to "the Purposes and Principles of the United Nations," which include the protection of human rights. Beyond making grants of competence subject to limitations in favor of human rights, the Charter further imposes affirmative obligations upon both members and the organization for the protection of such rights. Thus, for securing fulfillment of the human rights obligations embodied in Article 55, Article 56 requires "all Members" to "pledge themselves to take joint and separate action in co-operation with the Organization." In the light of all these provisions and the broader flow of community expectation, the conclusion would hence appear incontrovertible that any exercises of competences by the organization or its subsidiary organs must, if they are to be lawful, be in accord with the basic human rights prescriptions of the Charter.

---

611. I. Brownlie, *supra* note 172, at 677.

612. Goodrich, Hambro, and Simons point out:

> Article 2 is of fundamental importance in the total economy of the Charter. It lays down basic principles which the Organization, functioning through its various organs, and its members, must respect. Since the General Assembly, the Security Council, the Economic and Social Council, and the Trusteeship Council are composed of member states, it might be thought that—at least with respect to the activities of these organs—the inclusion of the word "Organization" is superfluous. This, of course, would not, in any case, be true of all the activities of the Organization, for example, those of the Secretariat and the Court. Furthermore, since the Organization has a separate personality and legal capacity from that of its members, its inclusion is justifiable for technical as well as more broadly political reasons. Frequent references to the "Principles of the Organization" as providing standards of conduct are to be found in the resolutions adopted by United Nations organs and in statements by members. Commonly, both principles and purposes are referred to in this connection.

L. Goodrich, E. Hambro, & A. Simons, *supra* note 175, at 36 (footnote omitted).

The conclusion that all grants of competence to the United Nations or its organs must be accommodated to the basic human rights prescriptions is reinforced by the continuing controversy about the legal consequences to be attached to resolutions of the General Assembly and other organs.[613] If a resolution of the General Assembly or other organ is not regarded as law, in any instance of conflict between such a resolution and the basic prescriptions about human rights there would appear little question that the human rights prescriptions must be held to prevail. Whether a resolution by a particular organ of the United Nations is to be regarded as law is, as we have seen, today widely regarded as a function of many variables, including the policy content of the resolution, the compatibility of that content with existing customary international law, the numbers and characteristics of the supporters and opposers of the resolution, the expectations stated about the legal character of the resolution by its supporters, and so on.[614] In a context permitting so broad a discretion, it is unlikely that many observers would ascribe the attributes of law to resolutions patently in violation of the human rights prescriptions of the Charter and its ancillary statements.

The conclusion that United Nations organs and officials are not authorized to take actions which contravene the human rights prescriptions is fortified, further, by the possibility that the organization might even be held affirmatively responsible for any particular deprivation of human rights. It will be recalled that in the *Reparations* case[615] the International Court of Justice described the United Nations as "a subject of international law," having a distinctive legal personality,[616] and capable of possessing both rights and duties. Activities, even under color of law, in deprivation of human rights might be brought within the confines of classic *excès de pouvoir.*[617]

Any action by United Nations organs or officials in contravention of the basic prescriptions about human rights can of course be expected to draw complaints from the states affected and others concerned with the common interest. In a most modest move toward judicial review, the International Court of Justice in the *Namibia* case indicated its willing-

613. *See* notes 358–71 *supra* and accompanying text.

614. *See* notes 353–67 *supra* and accompanying text.

615. Advisory Opinion on Reparation for Injuries Suffered in the Service of the United Nations, [1949] I.C.J. 174.

616. *Id.* at 178–79.

617. Some governmental organizations make explicit provisions for review of lawfulness of acts of their constituent bodies. *See* Lauterpacht, *The Legal Effect of Illegal Acts of International Organizations,* in CAMBRIDGE ESSAYS IN INTERNATIONAL LAW: ESSAYS IN HONOUR OF LORD MCNAIR 88, 94–99 (1965). For a more general discussion, *see* McRae, *Legal Obligations and International Organizations,* 1973 CANADIAN Y.B. INT'L L. 87.

ness to appraise the actions, not merely of the South African government, but also of the Security Council and the General Assembly for conformity to fundamental law.[618]

NATION-STATES AND THEIR OFFICIALS

One of the references made in the common description of the contemporary human rights prescriptions as law is that these prescriptions are applicable to all nation-state acts, whether unilateral acts or bilateral or multilateral agreements. The point may bear some further documentation for both unilateral acts and agreements.

Unilateral Acts

The applicability of the human rights prescriptions to the unilateral acts of particular states inheres in the very nature—whether viewed from monist, dualist, or eclectic perspectives—of international law as supreme over national law.[619] In the eloquent words of Mann:

> The supremacy of international law is or should be, the touchstone of any legal system which cherishes its attachment to the fundamental order of mankind and refuses to accept as law what is contrary to the elementary demands of righteousness and morality. In other words, it should be intolerable for any judge to be compelled to apply a law which is, and is known to be, contrary to international law and therefore a wrong.[620]

---

618. There are two cases in which the International Court of Justice did review the lawfulness of acts of constituent bodies of international governmental organizations: the *IMCO* case, [1960] I.C.J. 150, and *Certain Expenses of the United Nations,* [1962] I.C.J. 151. Though these cases do not bear directly upon human rights, they do offer an appropriate mode. For discussion, *see* Lauterpacht, *supra* note 617, at 100–16. *See also* D. Bowett, The Law of International Institutions 325–27 (2d ed. 1970).

619. For survey of different perspectives about the nature of international law, *see* The Relevance of International Law (K. Deutsch & S. Hoffmann eds. 1971); H. Kelsen, Principles of International Law 553–88 (2d ed. R. Tucker rev. & ed. 1966); D. O'Connell, *supra* note 323, at 38–79; Borchard, *The Relations between International Law and Municipal Law,* 27 Va. L. Rev. 137 (1940); Dickinson, *Changing Concepts and the Doctrine of Incorporation,* 26 Am. J. Int'l L. 239 (1932); McDougal, *Impact of International Law upon National Law: A Policy-Oriented Perspective,* 4 South Dakota L. Rev. 265 (1959), *reprinted in* M. McDougal & Associates, Studies in World Public Order 157–236 (1960) [hereinafter McDougal, *Impact of International Law*]; Morgenstern, *Judicial Practice and the Supremacy of International Law,* 27 Brit. Y.B. Int'l L. 42 (1950); Seidl-Hohenveldern, *Transformation or Adoption of International Law into Municipal Law,* 12 Int'l & Comp. L.Q. 88 (1963); Starke, *Monism and Dualism in the Theory of International Law,* 17 Brit. Y.B. Int'l L. 66 (1936); Van Panhuys, *Relations and Interactions between International Law and National Scenes of Law,* 112 Hague Recueil des Cours 1 (1961).

620. F. Mann, *supra* note 172, at 468.

This doctrine of the supremacy of international law was authoritatively expressed by the International Law Commission of the United Nations shortly after it commenced its work on the codification and development of international law. The Draft Declaration on Rights and Duties of States, adopted by the Commission in 1949, states in Article 13: "Every State has the duty to carry out in good faith its obligations arising from treaties and other sources of international law, and it may not invoke provisions in its constitution or its laws as an excuse for failure to perform its duty."[621] Most recently, the doctrine has been authoritatively reaffirmed by the International Law Commission in conjunction with its continuing work on state responsibility: "An act of a State may only be characterized as internationally wrongful by international law. Such characterization cannot be affected by the characterization of the same act as lawful by national law."[622] The constitutional supremacy of international law has long been evidenced in judicial decision. In its classic advisory opinion on the *Treatment of Polish Nationals in Danzig,*[623] the Permanent Court of International Justice, in concluding that the treatment of Polish nationals in Danzig was to be appraised in terms of the requirements of the Treaty of Versailles and the Convention of Paris rather than the Constitution of Danzig, offered this explanation:

> [W]hile on the one hand, according to generally accepted principles, a State cannot rely, as against another State, on the provisions of the latter's Constitution, but only on international law and international obligations duly accepted, on the other hand and conversely, a State cannot adduce as against another State its own Constitution with a view to evading obligations incumbent upon it under international law or treaties in force. Applying these principles to the present case, it results that the question of the treatment of Polish nationals . . . must be settled on the bases of the rules of international law and the treaty provisions in force between Poland and Danzig.[624]

621. The General Assembly acknowledged that the Draft Declaration was "a notable and substantial contribution towards the progressive development of international law and its codification and as such commend[ed] it to the continuing attention of Member States and of jurists of all nations." G.A. Res. 375, U.N. Doc. A/1251, at 66 (1949).

See further Preparatory Study Concerning a Draft Declaration on the Rights and Duties of States, U.N. Doc. A/CN.4/2 (1948) (memorandum submitted by the secretary-general); Kelsen, *The Draft Declaration on Rights and Duties of States,* 44 Am. J. Int'l L. 259 (1950).

The text of this draft declaration is *reprinted in* The Work of the International Law Commission, *supra* note 128, at 61–62.

622. *Report of the Commission to the General Assembly (U.N. Doc. A/9010/Rev. 1),* in [1973] 2 Y.B. Int'l L. Comm'n 161, 184, U.N. Doc. A/CN.4/SER.A/1973/Add. 1 (1975).

623. P.C.I.J., Ser. A/B, No. 44 (1932).

624. *Id.* at 24.

Similarly, in the *Greco-Bulgarian "Communities"* case, when asked whether the demanded application of a treaty or a conflicting internal law should prevail, the Permanent Court declared that local law "would not prevail as against the convention" because "the provisions of municipal law cannot prevail over those of the treaty."[625] Arbitral tribunals are equally explicit and firm in announcing the same principle. Thus, Briggs, in making broad reference to cases ranging from protection of aliens to diplomatic immunities, observes: "In thousands of decisions of international claims tribunals, allegations that a State had incurred international responsibility through denial of justice or kindred measures were tested by the standards of international law rather than by municipal law or constitutional provisions."[626]

The segment of the contemporary human rights prescriptions composed of customary international law about the responsibility of states for the protection of aliens offers, as several of the authoritative expressions above indicate, excellent example of the supremacy of international law. It is thoroughly established that a state cannot evade its international responsibility associated with injuries to aliens by invoking its internal decision processes, constitutive or otherwise. Thus, the Draft Convention on the International Responsibility of States for Injuries to Aliens, of which Sohn and Baxter were reporters, states in Article 2(2) that "A State cannot avoid international responsibility by invoking its municipal law."[627] Sohn and Baxter offer this commentary:

> That a State cannot avoid international responsibility by invoking its municipal law is a logical consequence of the primacy of international law. . . . This principle, which is one of the foundation stones of the law of nations, indicating as it does that international law and treaties occupy a higher place in the juridical order than does the domestic law of members of the international community, finds ample support in the jurisprudence of the World Court. . . .[628]

The underlying policy of this "foundation stone" is excellently elaborated by Dunn:

> Now it is obvious that if the purpose of having an international legal system at all is to obtain some measure of common standards of action for the international community as a whole, such a purpose would be defeated if each individual state were free to fix the stan-

625. P.C.I.J., Ser. B, No. 17, at 32–35 (1930).

626. H. Briggs, *supra* note 316, at 62. *See also* E. Borchard, *supra* note 178; M. Whiteman, Damages in International Law (1937–43) (3 vols.).

627. F. Garcia-Amador, L. Sohn, & R. Baxter, *supra* note 178, at 157.

628. *Id.* at 162.

> dard in accordance with its own convenience or desires. Hence the above rule is, in effect, merely a statement of the practical conditions which are necessary, in a world of diverse cultures, interests and ideas of justice, if the advantages foreseen from having a set of common standards are to be realized.[629]

With respect to that segment of the human rights prescriptions deriving from the United Nations Charter and many derivative formulations, the authoritative obligation of member and nonmember states is only formally different. Member states are bound by their many explicit commitments in the Charter and associated statements, and in Article 103 they have created their own supremacy clause in stipulating that their obligations under the Charter take priority over all other obligations. It may be recalled that many of the scholars who early found the human rights provisions to be law, rather than mere aspiration,[630] indicated that what they meant was that member states were bound to conform their activities to the content of these provisions, and that the International Court of Justice in the *Namibia* case based its decision upon the view that South Africa was violating its obligations under the Charter.[631] Nonmember states, though they may not have explicitly assumed the obligations of the Charter, are equally bound by the core content of the Charter, of the Universal Declaration of Human Rights, and of the many associated commitments through the dictates of customary international law.[632] It may be recalled that it is now practically universal opinion that this core content of the major contemporary human rights prescriptions has become customary international law.[633] The generally accepted, and inevitably required, doctrine of the supremacy of international over national law, as indicated above,[634] must make this new international law about the protection of human rights, even as it does the older law for the protection of aliens, paramount over all incompatible state practice.

Agreements

It might appear axiomatic that what states may not lawfully do by their unilateral acts in contravention of human rights prescriptions, they may

629. F. Dunn, *supra* note 178, at 119.

630. *See* notes 574–77 *supra* and accompanying text.

631. Advisory Opinion on Namibia, *supra* note 578, at 57.
For commentary *see* Schwelb, *ICJ and Human Rights, supra* note 577.

632. *Cf.* R. Falk, The Status of Law in International Society 185–241 (1970); G. Schwarzenberger, International Constitutional Law, *supra* note 15, at 31–35, 224–29; Kunz, *Revolutionary Creation of Norms of International Law,* 41 Am. J. Int'l L. 119 (1947).

633. *See* notes 558–610 *supra* and accompanying text.

634. *See* notes 619–29 *supra* and accompanying text.

not lawfully do in concert or combination through agreement, whether bilateral or multilateral. If any authoritative fortification of this commonsense inference is required, happily such fortification may readily be found both in Article 103 of the United Nations Charter and in the doctrine, newly emerging in the transnational arena, of *jus cogens.*[635] The Charter provision and this new doctrine abundantly, even supererogatorily, confirm that the contemporary human rights prescriptions are applicable, even inalienably applicable, to all the activities of nation-states and their officials.

The text of Article 103 of the Charter, already quoted, which stipulates that "the obligations of the Members of the United Nations under the present Charter" shall in cases of conflict prevail over "their obligations under any other international agreement," requires no extensive elaboration. This article clearly establishes that all agreements between members of the United Nations, and perhaps even between members and nonmembers, must be made subject, if to be regarded as lawful, to the overriding, basic human rights prescriptions of the Charter and the affiliated instruments authoritatively specifying its meaning.

The newly emphasized notion of *jus cogens* had its origin, in various roughly equivalent forms, in national legal systems.[636] In most legal systems, it is a key constitutional postulate that some policies are so

---

635. On *jus cogens, see* I. BROWNLIE, *supra* note 172, at 499–502; CONFERENCE ON INTERNATIONAL LAW, PAPERS AND PROCEEDINGS II, THE CONCEPT OF JUS COGENS IN INTERNATIONAL LAW (1967) (containing articles by Abi-Saab, Suy, Murty, & Schwarzenberger) [hereinafter cited as CONFERENCE ON JUS COGENS]; T. ELIAS, *supra* note 136, at 177–87; S. ROSENNE, THE LAW OF TREATIES, *supra* note 136, at 290–94; C. ROZAKIS, THE CONCEPT OF JUS COGENS IN THE LAW OF TREATIES (1976); I. SINCLAIR, *supra* note 136, at 110–31; G. TUNKIN, *supra* note 315, at 147–60; Domb, *Jus Cogens and Human Rights,* 6 ISRAEL Y.B. HUMAN RIGHTS 104 (1976); Mann, *The Doctrine of Jus Cogens in International Law,* in FESTSCHRIFT FÜR ULRICH SCHEUNER ZUM 70, GEBURTSTAG 399 (1973) [hereinafter cited as Mann]; Scheuner, *Conflict of Treaty Provisions with a Peremptory Norm of General International Law and Its Consequences,* 27 ZEITSCHRIFT FÜR AUSLANDISCHES OFFENTLICHES RECHT UND VOLKERRECHT 520 (1976) [hereinafter cited as Scheuner]; Schwelb, *Some Aspects of International Jus Cogens as Formulated by the International Law Commission,* 61 AM. J. INT'L L. 946 (1967) [hereinafter cited as Schwelb, *Jus Cogens*]; Schwarzenberger, *International "Jus Cogens"?* 43 TEXAS L. REV. 455 (1965); Schwarzenberger, *The Problem of International Public Policy,* 18 CURRENT LEGAL PROB. 191 (1965); Tunkin, *Jus Cogens in Contemporary International Law,* 1971 U. TOL. L. REV. 107; Verdross, *Forbidden Treaties in International Law,* 31 AM. J. INT'L L. 571 (1937) [hereinafter cited as Verdross, *Forbidden Treaties*]; Verdross, *Jus Dispositivum and Jus Cogens in International Law,* 60 AM. J. INT'L L. 55 (1966) [hereinafter cited as Verdross, *Jus Cogens*]; American Society of International Law, Study Group on the Draft Articles on the Law of Treaties, Memorandum No. 3 (Provisional Version), Feb. 1966 (unpublished) [hereinafter cited as ASIL Memorandum].

636. *See* Schwelb, *Jus Cogens, supra* note 635, at 948–49; Suy, *The Concept of Jus Cogens in Public International Law,* in CONFERENCE ON JUS COGENS, *supra* note 635, at 17, 18–22 [hereinafter cited as Suy].

intensely demanded, and so fundamental to the common interest of the community, that private parties cannot be permitted to deviate from such policies by agreement. In fact, this notion is so widespread and so common that it could be said to be part of the general principles of law regarded as authoritative source of international law.[637] Within different national communities this notion is expressed through varying technical concepts, such as *jus cogens,* public policy, public order, and so on.[638] The more fundamental policies or prescriptions brought within this mantle of inalienability or immunity to private change vary from community to community, depending upon what policies are most intensely demanded within particular communities. Thus, one community may place emphasis upon precluding landlords from exacting exorbitant and onerous agreements from tenants; another community may be more concerned to protect family life or the wages and conditions of labor. In summary of peremptory law in modern Germany, one commentator writes:

> The provisions of public law are on principle peremptory because there the general interest prevails. In private law provisions are peremptory where considerations of the common weal, moral communication, care for the family and for those who are economically weak, protection against a person's own imprudence and inexperience make this necessary, i.e., where it is necessary "to safeguard the moral and economic basis of co-existence."[639]

There is clearly little that is novel or parochial in a constitutional postulate protecting certain basic community policies from private will.

---

637. In the words of Lord McNair:

> It is difficult to imagine any society, whether of individuals or of States, whose law sets no limit whatever to freedom of contract. In every civilized community there are some rules of law and some principles of morality which individuals are not permitted by law to ignore or to modify by their agreements.

Lord McNair, The Law of Treaties 213–14 (1961).

638. *See generally* E. Bodenheimer, Jurisprudence: The Philosophy and Method of the Law 367–72 (rev. ed. 1974); W. Friedmann, Legal Theory 436–514 (5th ed. 1967); D. Lloyd, Public Policy: A Comparative Study in English and French Law (1953); E. Lorenzen, Selected Articles on the Conflict of Laws, 1–18 (1947); J. Morris, The Conflict of Laws 507–16 (1971); G. Paton, A Textbook of Jurisprudence 134–62 (4th ed. G. Paton & D. Derham eds. 1972); J. Stone, Social Dimensions of Law and Justice 182–98 (1966); Eek, *Peremptory Norms and Private International Law,* 139 Hague Recueil des Cours 1 (1973); Gellhorn, *Contracts and Public Policy,* 35 Colum. L. Rev. 679 (1935); Husserl, *Public Policy and Ordre Public,* 25 Va. L. Rev. 37 (1938); Knight, *Public Policy in English Law,* 38 Law Q. Rev. 207 (1922); Kosters, *Public Policy in Private International Law,* 29 Yale L.J. 745 (1920); Nussbaum, *Public Policy and the Political Crisis in the Conflict of Laws,* 49 Yale L.J. 1027 (1940); Winfield, *Public Policy in the English Common Law,* 42 Harv. L. Rev. 76 (1929).

639. ASIL Memorandum, *supra* note 635, at 3.

In the modern law of nations the notion of a *jus cogens,* so fundamental that it cannot be changed by agreement, begins with the great founders of the system, who distinguished between two kinds of law: first, the necessary law of nations embodying the law of nature, and, second, the positive law created by agreement and custom. The first could not be changed, and the second could be changed only in the way that it was created, by new agreement or custom. Thus Christian Wolff wrote: "The immutability of the necessary law of nations arises from the very immutability of natural law, and is finally derived from the essence and nature of man as a source whence flows the very immutability of natural law."[640] Vattel made the reasoning and conclusion somewhat more explicit:

> Since, therefore, the necessary Law of Nations consists in applying the natural law to States, and since the natural law is not subject to change, being founded on the nature of things and particularly upon the nature of man, it follows that the necessary Law of Nations is not subject to change.
>
> Since this law is not subject to change and the obligations which it imposes are necessary and indispensable, Nations can not alter it by agreement, nor individually or mutually release themselves from it.[641]

At a later date Bluntschli stated, in his book *Modern Law of Nations of Civilized States,* first published in 1867, that "treaties the contents of which violate the generally recognized human right or the binding rules of international law are invalid."[642] Among such treaties, he found, are those which "introduce, extend, or protect slavery"; which "declare that aliens have no rights"; and which "provide for persecutions on the ground of religion."[643]

Early efforts in state practice and judicial decision to identify the principles which have the character of *jus cogens* and to specify the legal consequences appropriately attached to such principles were not entirely successful. The more recent developments in the formulation of the

---

640. 2 C. Wolff, Jus Gentium Methodo Scientifica Pertractatum 10 (J. Drake trans. 1934).

Some observers reject the concept of *jus cogens* because they reject any form of natural law. It is not of course necessary to ground *jus cogens* in natural law notions. *Jus cogens* can be grounded, as we have shown, in the intensity of peoples' demands for certain fundamental policies. It is the grounding in natural law, rather than the secular fact of differing intensities in demand, that creates difficulties in the important contributions of Verdross. *See* Verdross, *Forbidden Treaties, supra* note 635; Verdross, *Jus Cogens, supra* note 635.

641. E. de Vattel, *supra* note 179, at 4.

642. *Quoted in* ASIL Memorandum, *supra* note 635, at 7.

643. *Id.*

doctrine are traceable to the work of the International Law Commission in regard to the Law of Treaties. In his First Report on the Law of Treaties of 1953, Lauterpacht suggested in Article 15 of his draft that "A treaty, or any of its provisions, is void if its performance involves an act which is illegal under international law and if it is declared so to be by the International Court of Justice."[644] The critical "test," according to his commentary, "was not inconsistency with customary international law pure and simple, but inconsistency with such overriding principles of international law which may be regarded as constituting principles of international public policy."[645] These overriding principles, Lauterpacht continued, "may be expressive of rules of international morality so cogent that an international tribunal would consider them as forming part of [the] principles of law generally recognized by civilized nations. . . ."[646]

After his succession to Lauterpacht as special rapporteur, Fitzmaurice formally introduced the term *jus cogens* in his expository code on the Law of Treaties submitted to the International Law Commission in 1958. In spelling out the "legality of the object" of a treaty, Fitzmaurice proposed in Article 16(2): "It is essential to the validity of a treaty that it should be in conformity with or not contravene, or that its execution should not involve an infraction of those principles and rules of international law which are in the nature of *jus cogens.*"[647] In his commentary, Fitzmaurice characterized *jus cogens* as "mandatory and imperative in any circumstances"[648] and *jus dispositivum* as "merely . . . a rule for application in the absence of any other agreed regime. . . ."[649] He stressed that "a feature common" to "the rules of international law that have the character of *jus cogens,*"[650] or, at least, "to a great many of them, evidently is that they involve not only legal rules but considerations of morals and of international good order."[651]

The doctrine of *jus cogens* was retained by Waldock, upon his succeeding Fitzmaurice as special rapporteur. Waldock sought to specify the content of *jus cogens* by offering illustrative itemizations. According to his proposal, "a treaty is contrary to international law and void if its object or execution involves": (1) "the use or threat of force in contravention of the principles of the Charter of the United Nations," (2) "any act or omission characterized by international law as an international

644. [1953] 2 Y.B. INT'L L. COMM'N 154.
645. *Id.* at 155.
646. *Id.*
647. [1958] 2 Y.B. INT'L L. COMM'N 20, 26.
648. *Id.* at 40.
649. *Id.*
650. *Id.* at 40–41.
651. *Id.* at 41.

crime," or (3) "any act or omission in the suppression or punishment of which every State is required by international law to co-operate."[652] Waldock's illustrative approach was rejected by the members of the International Law Commission, largely because of their shared concern that such an approach might unduly restrict the development and scope of international norms having the character of *jus cogens.*[653] The debates in the Commission clearly exhibited, however, in the words of Suy, "the unanimity with which the members of the Commission accepted the idea of *jus cogens.*"[654] The biggest difference in opinion was about the appropriate labeling of the concept, with alternatives offered in terms of "peremptory norms of general international law,"[655] "fundamental principles of international law,"[656] and "general peremptory norms of international law from which no derogation is permitted."[657] The final recommendation of the Commission was both open-ended and tautological: "A treaty is void if it conflicts with a peremptory norm of general international law from which no derogation is permitted and which can be modified only by a subsequent norm of general international law having the same character."[658]

---

652. [1963] 2 Y.B. Int'l L. Comm'n 1, 52 (Art. 13[2]).
The full text of Art. 13 of Waldock's proposed draft reads as follows:

1. A treaty is contrary to international law and void if its object or its execution involves the infringement of a general rule or principle of international law having the character of *jus cogens.*
2. In particular, a treaty is contrary to international law and void if its object or execution involves—
   (a) the use of threat of force in contravention of the principles of the Charter of the United Nations;
   (b) any act or omission characterized by international law as an international crime; or
   (c) any act or omission in the suppression or punishment of which every State is required by international law to co-operate.
3. If a provision, the object or execution of which infringes a general rule or principle of international law having the character of *jus cogens,* is not essentially connected with the principal objects of the treaty and is clearly severable from the remainder of the treaty, only that provision shall be void.
4. The provisions of this article do not apply, however, to a general multilateral treaty which abrogates or modifies a rule having the character of *jus cogens.*

Id. at 52.

653. *Id.* at 199.

654. Suy, *supra* note 636, at 50.

655. [1963] 2 Y.B. Int'l L. Comm'n 62 (Briggs's suggestion).

656. *Id.* at 69 (Tunkin's suggestion).

657. *Id.* at 66 (Ago's suggestion). For other suggestions, *see id.* at 60–72; Suy, *supra* note 636, at 50–51.

658. ILC Reports, 1966, *supra* note 491, at 76 (Art. 50). *See also* Art. 61, *id.* at 88–89.

The consensus favoring some doctrine of *jus cogens* crystallized and found more authoritative expression in the Vienna Convention on the Law of Treaties,[659] adopted in May 1969 by the United Nations Conference on the Law of Treaties, which for the first time offered some identification in empirical terms of what prescriptions might be *jus cogens.* This Convention, in dealing with "treaties conflicting with a peremptory norm of general international law *(jus cogens),*" states in Article 53:

> A treaty is void if, at the time of its conclusion, it conflicts with a peremptory norm of general international law. For the purposes of the present Convention, a peremptory norm of general international law is a norm accepted and recognized by the international community of States as a whole as a norm from which no derogation is permitted and which can be modified only by a subsequent norm of general international law having the same character.[660]

Article 64 of the Convention further provides, "If a new peremptory norm of general international law emerges, any existing treaty which is in conflict with that norm becomes void and terminates."[661]

The important contributions of the Vienna Convention are severalfold. First, the Convention puts to rest the futile controversy, raging among academics, as to whether there are any principles of transnational public order which parties with effective power cannot vary by agreement;[662] the one question left open is what in detail such principles are. Secondly, the Convention offers the beginnings of an empirical identification of those prescriptions which are *jus cogens* in terms of the high intensity with which the peoples of the world demand them. In lieu of the prior definitions, mostly in tautological terms about legal consequences,[663] the Convention makes reference to norms "accepted and recognized by the international community of states as a whole."[664] The root notion in this description is clearly that of the "general principles" common to most of the peoples of the world, traditionally regarded as a major source of international law.[665] The *travaux preparatoires* of the Convention make clear that the words "as a whole" in the Convention were not intended to require universality, thus giving one or few states a

659. Documents of the Treaty Conference, *supra* note 135, at 289.

660. *Id.* at 296.

661. *Id.* at 297.

662. *See, e.g.,* G. Tunkin, *supra* note 315, at 147–60; Schwarzenberger, *International "Jus Cogens"? supra* note 635; Suy, *supra* note 636, at 26–49.

663. *See, e.g.,* ILC Reports, 1966, *supra* note 491, at 76–77.

664. Vienna Convention, *supra* note 135, Art. 53.

665. Statute of the International Court of Justice, Art. 38(1)(c).

veto, but rather to require only the recognition and acceptance of a "very large majority" of states.[666] Thirdly, and finally, the Convention does specify the legal consequences to be attached to prescriptions identified as *jus cogens* in terms of nonderogation and modes of modification, and provides measures for the settlement of disputes.[667]

It should be no cause for surprise that the great bulk of the contemporary human rights prescriptions, so insistently demanded by so many different peoples about the world, and forming along with peace and security the basic purposes for which the contemporary global constitutive process is maintained, should be widely regarded today, by both official and nonofficial observers, as among the principles clearly identifiable as *jus cogens.* This wide recognition and acceptance of the human rights prescriptions as fundamental, nonderogable law is remarkably manifest in the long, painstaking official efforts to secure a codification of *jus cogens,* as well as in opinions from the International Court of Justice and in statements by private scholars.

Throughout the protracted official deliberations preceding the final adoption of the Vienna Convention, various human rights prescriptions figured prominently in all attempted itemizations of peremptory norms. For example, Lauterpacht included among the agreements that his draft would make void those in contravention of an alleged customary international law against slave trading.[668] Similarly, when Fitzmaurice first introduced the label *jus cogens* in his 1958 report to the International Law Commission, he illustrated the concept by reference to "cases where the position of the individual is involved, and where the rules contravened are rules instituted for the protection of the individual."[669] In his proposal to specify the content of *jus cogens* by allusive itemization, Waldock, as we have seen, included "any act or omission characterized by international law as an international crime"[670] (which would include

---

666. In the words of Mr. Yasseen, chairman of the Drafting Committee to the Committee of the Whole of the Vienna Conference:

> [By] inserting the words "as a whole" in article 50 the Drafting Committee had wished to stress that there was no question of requiring a rule to be accepted and recognized as peremptory by all States. It would be enough if a very large majority did so; that would mean that, if one State in isolation refused to accept the peremptory character of a rule, or if that State was supported by a very small number of States, the acceptance and recognition of the peremptory character of the rule by the international community as a whole would not be affected.

United Nations Conference on the Law of Treaties, Official Records, 1st Session 472, U.N. Doc. A/CONF.39/11 (1969) (80th mtg. of the Committee of the Whole).

667. *See* notes 505–20 *supra* and notes 748–67 *infra* and accompanying text.

668. [1953] 2 Y.B. Int'l L. Comm'n 154–55.

669. [1958] 2 Y.B. Int'l L. Comm'n 40.

670. [1963] 2 Y.B. Int'l L. Comm'n 52.

some violations of human rights) and "any act or omission in the suppression or punishment of which every State is required by international law to cooperate"[671] (clearly including slave trading, piracy, and genocide); but other members of the Commission rejected this itemization upon the ground that it might not include "treaties violating human rights or the principle of self-determination."[672] At the Vienna Conference the Italian delegate began a substantial itemization of rules of *jus cogens* with "the rules intended to safeguard the fundamental rights of the human person"[673] and continued to characterize these rules, along with others, as "based on the legal conscience of the whole of mankind."[674] In fitting recollection of the basic purposes of the Charter, in peace and human rights, the delegate from Cuba stated that "it was undeniable" that "the principles set forth in Article 2 of the United Nations Charter, in the Preamble, and in Article 1 were peremptory norms of general international law."[675]

Upon several occasions the International Court of Justice or individual judges have found human rights prescriptions to be within the ambit of *jus cogens.* In its early advisory opinion on *Reservations to the Convention on the Prevention and Punishment of the Crime of Genocide,* the International Court of Justice, in holding that "a State which has made and maintained a reservation which has been objected to by one or more of the parties to the Convention but not by others" could "be regarded as being a party to the Convention if the reservation is compatible with the object and purpose of the Convention,"[676] based its opinion in part upon the fact that the Genocide Convention embodied policies that were almost universally demanded with high intensity. The Court stated:

> The origins of the Convention show that it was the intention of the United Nations to condemn and punish genocide as "a crime under international law" involving a denial of the right of existence of entire human groups, a denial which shocks the conscience of mankind and results in great losses to humanity, and which is contrary to moral law and to the spirit and aims of the United Nations. . . . The first consequence arising from this conception is that the principles underlying the Convention are principles which are recognized by

---

671. *Id.*

672. *Id.* at 199.

673. United Nations Conference on the Law of Treaties, Second Session, Vienna, 9 April–22 May 1969, Official Records 104, U.N. Doc. A/CONF.39/11/Add. 1 (1970) (remarks of Mr. Maresca at the 20th plenary mtg.) [hereinafter cited as Treaty Conference Records, 2d Session].

674. *Id.*

675. *Id.* at 97 (remarks of Mr. Alvarez Tabio at the 19th plenary mtg.).

676. [1951] I.C.J. 15, 29.

> civilized nations as binding on States, even without any conventional obligation. A second consequence is the universal character both of the condemnation of genocide and of the cooperation required "in order to liberate mankind from such an odious scourge. . . ."[677]

In the *South West Africa* cases (Second Phase) of 1966,[678] in which the Court refused to deal with the substantive issues involved on the ground that the Applicants (Ethiopia and Liberia) lacked legal standing, Judge Tanaka delivered a much acclaimed and highly influential dissenting opinion (foreshadowing the opinion of the Court in the 1971 *Namibia* case). Judge Tanaka articulated in ringing words the intense and peremptory character of the human rights prescriptions:

> If a law exists independently of the will of the State and, accordingly, cannot be abolished or modified even by its constitution, because it is deeply rooted in the conscience of mankind and of any reasonable man, it may be called "natural law" in contrast to "positive law." Provisions of the constitutions of some countries characterize fundamental human rights and freedoms as "inalienable," "sacred," "eternal," "inviolate," etc. Therefore, the guarantee of fundamental human rights and freedoms possesses a super-constitutional significance.
>
> If we can introduce in the international field a category of law, namely *jus cogens,* recently examined by the International Law Commission, a kind of imperative law which constitutes the contrast to the *jus dispositivum,* capable of being changed by way of agreement between States, surely the law concerning the protection of human rights may be considered to belong to the *jus cogens.*[679]

In the *Namibia* case, in holding that members of the United Nations, and in some measure nonmembers, were under obligation to "recognize the illegality of South Africa's presence in Namibia and the invalidity of its acts on behalf of or concerning Namibia,"[680] the International Court of Justice observed that

> member States are under obligation to abstain from entering into treaty relations with South Africa in all cases in which the Government of South Africa purports to act on behalf of or concerning Namibia. With respect to existing bilateral treaties, member States must abstain from invoking or applying those treaties or provisions of treaties concluded by South Africa on behalf of or concerning

677. *Id.* at 23.
678. [1966] I.C.J. 6.
679. *Id.* at 298.
680. Advisory Opinion on Namibia, *supra* note 578, at 58.

> Namibia which involve active intergovernmental co-operation. With respect to multilateral treaties, however, the same rule cannot be applied to certain general conventions such as those of a humanitarian character, the non-performance of which may adversely affect the people of Namibia. It will be for the competent international organs to take specific measures in this respect.[681]

The view so clearly expressed in official decision and opinion that the human rights prescriptions are within *jus cogens* is amply confirmed by the opinions of private scholars. In the Lagonissi conference on *jus cogens,* held in 1966 under the auspices of the Carnegie Endowment for International Peace and attended by a group of distinguished legal experts from various parts of the world, the conclusion was somewhat cautious, but prophetic of a growing recognition:

> The interests of international society which are protected by *jus cogens* are diversely conceived. A hard-core consensus exists over the maintenance of peace by the prohibition of resort to force as well as over a minimum of humanitarian principles. While the first category transcends the interests of States as such to those of society as a whole, the second transcends them to those of the individual.[682]

Verdross, the author of a pioneering article,[683] is emphatic that "A very important group of norms having the character of *jus cogens* are all rules of general international law created for a humanitarian purpose."[684] Human rights conventions, he points out, "are not created in the interest of individual states, but in the higher interest of humanity as a whole."[685] Scheuner distinguishes "peremptory norms" which "deal with definite material questions in particular areas of international life"[686] from other inalienable rules deriving from "the legal structure of the international order"[687] and offers three categories of peremptory norms. His first

681. *Id.* at 55.
682. Conference on Jus Cogens, *supra* note 635, at 13.
683. Verdross, *Forbidden Treaties, supra* note 635.
684. Verdross, *Jus Cogens, supra* note 635, at 59.
685. *Id.*
686. Scheuner, *supra* note 635, at 525–26.
687. *Id.* at 526.

We would not make distinctions between *jus cogens* relating to "definite material questions in particular areas of international life" and that deriving from "the legal structure of the international order," as Scheuner has made. Both of these simply represent high intensities of the demand by the peoples of the world. Whatever the validity of Scheuner's distinction, human rights prescriptions can be brought within either branch of his dichotomy. The important point is that these intensities in demand are indispensable features of the contemporary global constitution.

category is composed of "the maxims of international law which protect the foundations of law, peace and humanity"[688] and includes the prohibitions of genocide and slavery. His third category of "imperative norms" relates to "the protection of humanity, especially of the most essential human rights,"[689] and includes "those rules which protect human dignity, personal and racial equality, life and personal freedom."[690] Mann builds upon Scheuner, finding the latter's categorizations "as good as any other"[691] and the norms comprised "to come within the terms of Article 53" as "'accepted and recognized' within the community of nations."[692] In his Hague lecture, Fitzmaurice offers "a primary example" of *jus cogens* by reference to "the law of war" having to do with "the treatment of the civilian population in war time, the treatment of prisoners of war, the sick and wounded in the field, civilian internees, the population in occupied territory, and so on."[693] He emphasizes that these prescriptions "are intended not so much for the benefit of the States, as directly for the benefit of the individuals concerned, as human beings and on humanitarian grounds."[694] Judge Lachs cites with approval earlier writers (*e.g.*, Bluntschli, Nippold, and Fiore) who "considered void treaties the substance of which was contrary to the laws recognized by humanity. . . ."[695] The "catalogue" of *jus cogens,* he continues, "covers not only the prohibition of such institutions as slavery, piracy, and white slave traffic, but also the essential right to peace and the inherent rights to independence of States and to self-determination of nations."[696] In somewhat different illustration, Tunkin finds that though the "norms relating to war crimes originated long ago,"[697] in comparatively recent times "they have acquired an imperative charac-

---

688. *Id.*

689. *Id.*

690. *Id.* at 526–27. It may be noted that Scheuner's second category is not relevant to our present purpose.

691. Mann, *supra* note 635, at 402.

692. *Id.*

"If there is a subject matter," in the words of Schwelb, "in present-day international law which appears to be a successful candidate for regulation by peremptory norms, it is certainly the prohibition of racial discrimination." Schwelb, *Jus Cogens, supra* note 635, at 956.

693. Fitzmaurice, *The General Principles of International Law Considered from the Standpoint of the Rule of Law,* 92 Hague Recueil des Cours 1, 125 (1957).

694. *Id.*

695. Lachs, *The Law of Treaties: Some General Reflections on the Report of the International Law Commission,* in Recueil d'Études de droit International, En Hommage a Paul Guggenheim 391, 399 (1968).

696. *Id.*

697. G. Tunkin, *supra* note 315, at 160.

ter."[698] He adds: "The norms regarding crimes against peace are relatively new imperative norms. The norms relating to crimes against humanity were until recently to some extent moral norms which now are imperative norms of international law."[699]

The evidences of general community expectation are thus overwhelming that particular states, whether or not members of the United Nations, will not today be protected by global constitutive process in the making and performance of agreements, any more than in the performance of unilateral acts, which are in contravention of the basic policies of the contemporary human rights prescriptions.

NONGOVERNMENTAL ACTORS

The contemporary human rights prescriptions would appear fully as applicable to individuals and private groups, that is, to all nongovernmental actors, as to states and international governmental organizations and their officials. Sometimes this applicability to individuals and private groups is achieved through the international prescriptions' being made part of the internal law of particular states, and sometimes it is achieved through a more direct, unmediated subjection of individuals and groups to the international prescriptions. Whether the human rights prescriptions are expressed through customary expectation or multilateral agreement, or both, states find little special difficulty in their own constitutive processes in making such prescriptions their own internal law.

Insofar as the human rights prescriptions are expressed through the expectations constituting customary international law—and we have already observed that the core content of the Universal Declaration of Human Rights and most of the contemporary agreements has become customary law[700]—many states, without employing any special constitutional procedures, indulge in a well-hallowed tradition that international law is an integral part of internal law, to be applied in appropriate cases like any other law. Even in states in which it is asserted that international norms require some special procedures of incorporation or transformation, international law seems always to be applied. The differences among "incorporation," "transformation," "adoption," and so on have been elsewhere described as differences between tweedledum and tweedledee.[701] Fortunately, it appears increasingly common for states to

698. *Id.*
699. *Id.*
700. *See* notes 315–67 and 558–610 *supra* and accompanying text.
701. McDougal, *The Impact of International Law, supra* note 619, at 212–13.

maintain explicit constitutional provisions stipulating that international law is the law of the land.[702]

When human rights prescriptions are expressed through multilateral agreements, the requirements in state constitutions about making agreements the law of the land do not appear, again, to cause any insuperable difficulty. For making agreements the law of the land, when performance requires internal application, state constitutions exhibit two modalities in form which have substantially equivalent outcomes. The first modality, of which the United States offers an example, is characterized by a constitutional provision which specifies that certain agreements, made in certain ways, automatically become the law of the land.[703] The second modality, of which the United Kingdom is an example, is characterized by a constitutional requirement that certain agreements must have special legislative or parliamentary approval before they can change internal law.[704] Upon close examination of what is required for the making and approval of agreements, and of how these requirements are applied in practice, these two assertedly different modalities take on a striking resemblance, and neither greatly impedes a

---

702. *See* Deener, *International Law Provisions in Post-World War II Constitutions,* 36 CORNELL L.Q. 505 (1951); McDougal, *The Impact of International Law, supra* note 619, at 213–14.

703. Art. VI(2) of the United States Constitution, applied in almost countless instances in all kinds of internal arenas, reads:

> [A]ll Treaties made, or which shall be made, under the Authority of the United States, shall be the supreme Law of the Land; and the Judges in every State shall be bound thereby, any Thing in the Constitution or Laws of any State to the Contrary notwithstanding.

See L. HENKIN, FOREIGN AFFAIRS AND THE CONSTITUTION 156–67 (1972); Dickinson, *The Law of Nations as Part of the National Law of the United States,* 101 U. PA. L. REV. 26 and 792 (1952–53).

704. The practice of Great Britain, prime advocate of parliamentary supremacy, has been aptly summed up by Lord McNair:

> Accordingly, if the Crown enters into a treaty which is likely to come into question in a Court of law or to require for its enforcement the assistance of a Court of law, and the application and enforcement of that treaty involves any modification of or addition to the rules of law administered by an English Court (which include the rules of international law as understood and ascertained by English Courts), the Crown must induce Parliament to pass the necessary legislation, for it is only Parliament that can change the law binding upon an English Court. This question can arise either upon a treaty which merely creates a particular obligation between the parties, or upon a treaty which purports to create new rules of international law binding upon a number of parties.

McNair, *The Method Whereby International Law Is Made to Prevail in Municipal Courts on an Issue of International Law,* 30 TR. GROTIUS SOC'Y 11, 19 (1945).

willing state in the performance of an undertaking to make a human rights agreement its internal law.[705]

One safeguard for the internal application of human rights prescriptions is that states are commonly not permitted to raise their own constitutional inadequacies in defense against performance of their international obligations. It has long been accepted international law that a state cannot escape international responsibility by interposing a constitutional provision relating to the "performance" of an agreement. In recent confirmation, the Vienna Convention on the Law of Treaties, in Article 27, provides: "A party may not invoke the provisions of its internal law as justification for its failure to perform a treaty. . . ."[706] In settling a point of some controversy, the Vienna Convention adds, further, that a state may not invoke "a provision of its internal law" about competence to make an agreement unless the "violation" is "manifest" and concerns "a rule of its internal law of fundamental importance."[707] It may be recalled, also, that all efforts to put a "federal clause" into the Vienna Convention as defense against responsibility for internal application failed.[708] A state may not, finally, by invoking its own constitutional inadequacies, escape responsibility for the failures by individuals and private groups, any more than for the failures of its officials, to conform to the international standards about the protection of aliens.[709]

Many human rights conventions have explicitly stipulated that ratifying states insure, by appropriate internal procedures, the effective application of such conventions to private individuals and groups. Thus, the International Covenant on Civil and Political Rights, in obligating each state party to undertake "to respect and to ensure to all individuals within its territory and subject to its jurisdiction the rights recognized"[710] in the Covenant, states in Article 2(2):

> Where not already provided for by existing legislative or other measures, each State Party to the present Covenant undertakes to take the necessary steps, in accordance with its constitutional processes and with the provisions of the present Covenant, to adopt such

---

705. *See MacChesney*, et al., *The Treaty Power and the Constitution: The Case Against Amendment,* 40 A.B.A.J. 203 (1954).

706. Vienna Convention, *supra* note 135, Art. 27.

707. Vienna Convention, *supra* note 135, Art. 46(1). Art. 46(2) defines what is meant by "manifest": "A violation is manifest if it would be objectively evident to any State conducting itself in the matter in accordance with normal practice and in good faith."

708. *See* T. Elias, *supra* note 136, at 18–20; Treaty Conference Records, 2d Session, *supra* note 673, at 6–15.

709. *See* notes 619–34 *supra* and accompanying text.

710. Covenant on Civil and Political Rights, *supra* note 48, Art. 2(1).

> legislative or other measures as may be necessary to give effect to the rights recognized in the present Covenant.[711]

This undertaking can only be made effective by making the provisions of the Covenant applicable to nongovernmental and governmental actors (or deprivers) alike.

The Convention on the Elimination of Racial Discrimination, designed to eradicate "radical discrimination in all its forms,"[712] is even more particularized. Article 2(1)(c) stipulates, "Each State Party shall take effective measures to review governmental, national and local policies, and to amend, rescind or nullify any laws and regulations which have the effect of creating or perpetuating racial discrimination wherever it exists."[713] Article 2(1)(d) adds, "Each State Party shall prohibit and bring to an end, by all appropriate means, including legislation as required by circumstances, racial discrimination by any persons, group or organization."[714] Within these provisions there is clear recognition that racial discrimination cannot be wiped out unless all nongovernmental actors (private individuals and groups) are brought directly within the application of the prescriptions.

The international Covenant on Economic, Social, and Cultural Rights, for example, reflecting the difference in the nature of its obligation from that of the Covenant on Civil and Political Rights,[715] in Article 2(1) provides only that

> Each State Party to the present Covenant undertakes to take steps, individually and through international assistance and co-operation, especially economic and technical, to the maximum of its available resources, with a view to achieving progressively the full realization of the rights recognized in the present Covenant by all appropriate means, including particularly the adoption of legislative measures.[716]

Even this undertaking would appear, however, to require appropriate application to private individuals and groups.

Some of the prescriptions of transnational origins in which human rights are at stake are made more directly applicable to nongovernmen-

---

711. *Id.*, Art. 2(2).
712. Convention on the Elimination of Racial Discrimination, *supra* note 97, Art. 2(1) (opening sentence).
713. *Id.*, Art. 2(1)(c).
714. *Id.*, Art. 2(1)(d).
715. *See* notes 434–64 *supra* and accompanying text.
716. Covenant on Economic, Social, and Cultural Rights, *supra* note 48, Art. 2(1).

tal as well as governmental actors, individual and group. These are largely the prescriptions identifying crimes which are regarded as of such importance to the whole community of humankind that any state which apprehends, or secures effective control over, an offender is regarded as authorized to make application of such prescriptions. The "universality" principle of jurisdiction, sometimes confused with the concept of *jus cogens* because of its application *erga omnes,*[717] authorizes any state having possession of an accused offender against specified prescriptions to try, and if appropriate, to punish such offender without regard for the geographic and temporal features of the events alleged to constitute the crime and without regard for the national identity of the offender or the victim.[718] It is upon occasion debated whether the prescriptions being so applied partake of the "true nature" of national or international law, but if the fundamental policies in the protection of common interest incorporated within the prescriptions are in fact applied, the matter of labeling would, again, appear a matter of tweedledum and tweedledee. The prescriptions most often specified, and regarded through the longest period of time, as coming within the authorization of the "universality" principle of jurisdiction are those relating to war crimes and the prohibition of piracy.[719] By multilateral agreement and supporting customary expectation the crime of slave trading has upon occasion been brought within the same principle.[720] The Charter of the Nuremberg Tribunal sought, not with entire success, to introduce "crimes against peace" and "crimes against humanity" into the same commonly abhorred categorization as war crimes.[721]

---

717. *See* notes 745–47 *infra* and accompanying text.

718. *See generally* 1 A TREATISE ON INTERNATIONAL CRIMINAL LAW (M. Bassiouni & V. Nanda eds. 1973).

719. *See* M. McDOUGAL & W. BURKE, THE PUBLIC ORDER OF THE OCEANS 805–23 (1962); M. McDOUGAL & F. FELICIANO, *supra* note 55, at 330–33. *See also* the sources listed in note 721 *infra.*

720. *See* chapter 7 *infra,* at notes 132–282 and accompanying text.

721. 1 TRIAL OF THE MAJOR WAR CRIMINALS BEFORE THE INTERNATIONAL MILITARY TRIBUNALS 10–18 (Secretariat of the Tribunal, 1947–49). *See* I. BROWNLIE, *supra* note 172, at 544–47; WOETZEL, THE NUREMBERG TRIALS IN INTERNATIONAL LAW (rev. ed. 1962); Harris, *International Human Rights and the Nuremberg Judgment,* 12 SANTA CLARA LAWYER 209 (1972).

For subsequent developments, *see* 3 THE VIETNAM WAR AND INTERNATIONAL LAW 193–485 (R. Falk ed. 1972); J. GOLDSTEIN, B. MARSHALL, & J. SCHWARTZ, THE MY LAI MASSACRE AND ITS COVER-UP: BEYOND THE REACH OF LAW? (1976) (the Peers Commission Report with a Supplement and Introductory Essay on the Limits of Law); Baade, *Individual Responsibility,* in 4 THE FUTURE OF THE INTERNATIONAL LEGAL ORDER 291–327 (C. Black & R. Falk eds. 1972); Falk, *Nuremberg: Past, Present, and Future,* 80 YALE L.J. 1456, 1501 (1971); Falk, *War Crimes and Individual Responsibility,* 1971 U. TOL. L. REV. 21; Farer, *Laws of War 25 Years after Nuremberg,* 583 INT'L CONCILIATION (May 1971); Farer & others, *Vietnam and the*

It was indeed the failure of the Nuremberg tribunal to accept jurisdiction over "crimes against humanity" in times of peace that precipitated the formulation and acceptance of the Genocide Convention, with its important provisions for the direct application of international law to offending individuals and groups.[722] In the wake of the Nazi atrocities and of the war crimes trials, the United Nations General Assembly, in 1948, adopted the Convention on the Prevention and Punishment of the Crime of Genocide,[723] in order to mobilize the conscience of humankind by outlawing, under international law, the intentional destruction of racial, ethnical, national, and religious groups.[724] The Convention extends its compass of punishment beyond acts of "genocide," to "conspiracy to commit genocide," "direct and public incitement to commit genocide," "attempt to commit genocide," and "complicity in genocide."[725] All persons, "whether they are constitutionally responsible rulers, public officials or private individuals," who commit "genocide or any of the other [related] acts" are subject to punishment,[726] and the contracting states "undertake to enact, in accordance with their respective Constitutions, the necessary legislation to give effect" to the Convention and to provide "effective penalties."[727] Trial is to be "by a competent tribunal of the State in the territory of which the act was committed, or by such international penal tribunal as may have jurisdiction with respect

---

Nuremberg Principles: A Colloquy on War Crimes, 5 RUTGERS CAMDEN L.J. 1 (1973); Mallard, *Nuremberg—A Step Forward?* 4 INT'L LAWYER 673 (1970).

722. *See* N. ROBINSON, THE GENOCIDE CONVENTION: A COMMENTARY (1960); *Genocide Convention: Hearings before a Subcommittee of the Senate Comm. on Foreign Relations,* 91st Cong., 2d Sess. (1970); Gorove, *The Problem of "Mental Harm" in the Genocide Convention,* 1951 WASH. U.L.Q. 174; McDougal & Arens, *The Genocide Convention and the Constitution,* 3 VAND. L. REV. 683 (1950); Reisman, *Responses to Crimes of Discrimination and Genocide: An Appraisal of the Convention on the Elimination of Racial Discrimination,* 1 DENVER J. INT'L L. & POLICY 29 (1971).

723. Genocide Convention, *supra* note 111.

724. Art. 2 of the Genocide Convention defines "genocide" as

> any of the following acts committed with intent to destroy, in whole or in part, a national, ethnical, racial or religious group, as such:
>
> (a) Killing members of the group;
>
> (b) Causing serious bodily or mental harm to members of the group;
>
> (c) Deliberately inflicting on the group conditions of life calculated to bring about its physical destruction in whole or in part;
>
> (d) Imposing measures intended to prevent births within the group;
>
> (e) Forcibly transferring children of the group to another group.

Id.

725. Genocide Convention, *supra* note 111, Art. 3.

726. *Id.,* Art. 4.

727. *Id.,* Art. 5.

to those Contracting Parties which shall have accepted its jurisdiction."[728] This Convention is very rapidly being invested with the authority of customary expectation and is being made to serve as a model for the prohibition of other activities regarded as affected with intense common interest.[729]

The establishment of the appropriate specialized institutions to insure the application of the human rights prescriptions is of course at its merest inception. The great bulk of the application of such prescriptions still occurs in the foreign office-to-foreign office diplomacy of nation-states. Whatever redress most individuals are able to secure for deprivations of their rights derives from this traditional remedy. There are, however, some initiatives toward more inclusive and more effective institutions and procedures. It may be recalled that the United Nations Human Rights Commission, as assisted by the Sub-Commission on Prevention of Discrimination and Protection of Minorities, is ridding itself of its self-imposed shackles in order to deal with complaints, not merely from states, but also from private groups and individuals.[730] Despite its somewhat cautious attitude, the Commission obviously constitutes a worldwide forum with authority, both extant and potential, in general community expectation to make application of the basic prescriptions to gross deprivations of human rights wherever they may occur. The Human Rights Committee, established under the International Covenant on Civil and Political Rights and its Optional Protocol, can be expected, after its initial phase of internal organization and rule making, to begin to make application of the important policies of that Covenant to a significant segment of the world's population.[731] The Committee on the Elimination of Racial Discrimination, established under the International Convention on the Elimination of All Forms of Racial Discrimination, has moved beyond its initial phase of internal organization and rule making to deal with a wide array of issues involving racial discrimination, and is quickly becoming a major institution for combatting racial discrimination, in all its forms and manifestations.[732]

In addition to these specialized institutions, the existing major organs of the United Nations, notably the General Assembly and the Security Council, are of course as available for application of human rights pre-

728. *Id.,* Art. 6.

729. *See* Apartheid Convention, *supra* note 331.

730. *See* notes 85–95 *supra* and accompanying text.

731. *See* notes 435–59 *supra* and accompanying text.

732. *See* ANNUAL REPORTS OF THE COMMITTEE ON THE ELIMINATION OF RACIAL DISCRIMINATION: 1970 Report, 25 U.N. GAOR, Supp. (No. 27), U.N. Doc. A/8027 (1970); 1971 Report, 26 U.N. GAOR, Supp. (No. 18), U.N. Doc. A/8418 (1971); 1972 Report, 27 U.N. GAOR, Supp. (No. 18), U.N. Doc. A/8718 (1972); 1973 Report, 28 U.N. GAOR, Supp.

scriptions as for other prescriptions. In appropriate contexts in which human rights are significantly at stake, these organs do apply, or make recommendations with respect to the application of, relevant human rights prescriptions.[733] The Economic and Social Council, beyond its functions as specified in the Charter, has been given new responsibility under the International Covenant on Economic, Social, and Cultural Rights. The Council is made the institution to which the contracting parties to the Covenant must submit their reports concerning their respective applications of the Covenant.[734]

On the regional level, an excellent model for the application of human rights prescriptions is, as indicated, the system establishing the European Convention on Human Rights. The application of the European Convention is carried out by a complex of specialized institutions, consisting of the European Commission on Human Rights, the European Court on Human Rights, and the Committee of Ministers of the Council of Europe.[735] Within the framework of the Organization of American States, the Inter-American Commission on Human Rights, with its expanding authority, is making serious efforts toward application.[736]

The balancing of competences among different structures of authority to secure judicial review at the global level of alleged deprivations appears still further in the future. A significant intimation of possible development comes from the 1971 *Namibia* opinion of the International Court of Justice, in which the Court, while protesting otherwise, did in fact examine the lawfulness of certain resolutions by the General Assembly and the Security Council.[737] Whether the Court may eventually be able to assume competence to review the acts of international and national officials for compatibility with human rights prescriptions remains to be seen.

Invocation

The provision afforded by global constitutive process for the invocation of human rights prescriptions is undergoing improvement in direc-

---

(No. 18), U.N. Doc. A/9018 (1973); 1974 Report, 29 U.N. GAOR, Supp. (No. 18), U.N. Doc. A/9618 (1974); 1975 Report, 30 U.N. GAOR, Supp. (No. 18), U.N. Doc. A/10018 (1975); 1976 Report, 31 U.N. GAOR, Supp. (No. 18), U.N. Doc. A/31/18 (1976); 1977 Report, 32 U.N. GAOR, Supp. (No. 18), U.N. Doc. A/32/18 (1977); 1978 Report, 33 U.N. GAOR, Supp. (No. 18), U.N. Doc. A/33/18 (1978).

733. *See* notes 154–68 *supra* and accompanying text.

734. Covenant on Economic, Social, and Cultural Rights, *supra* note 47, Arts. 16–25. *See* notes 457–64 *supra* and accompanying text.

735. *See* notes 468–90 *supra* and accompanying text.

736. *See* note 108 *supra* and accompanying text.

737. Advisory Opinion on Namibia, *supra* note 578, at para. 89.

tions appropriate to a genuine bill of rights. The most dramatic improvement is in the increasing opportunity accorded to the individual human being himself to challenge in appropriate structures of authority the lawfulness of deprivations imposed upon him. The change in authoritative interpretation permitting individuals and private groups to petition the United Nations Human Rights Commission regarding gross violations of human rights now seems thoroughly established.[738] The right of individual petition is provided in the Optional Protocol to the International Covenant on Civil and Political Rights[739] and is also provided in the International Convention on the Elimination of All Forms of Racial Discrimination.[740] The continuing importance of individual petition is clearly confirmed by cumulative experience under the European Convention on Human Rights. It may be recalled that the great bulk of the complaints brought before the European Commission on Human Rights originates from either individuals or private groups.[741]

Still further improvement in invocation derives from expansion of the historic modality of state complaint. Many of the major human rights conventions contain, as we have seen, provision for complaints by states against other states, in transnational as well as national arenas of authority, for the protection, not merely of the nationals of the challenging state, but of all victims of deprivation.[742] One knowledgeable student of human rights has observed in this growing recognition of the common interests of all states in the protection of all individuals, irrespective of nationality, the emergent outlines of an international *actio popularis,* admitting of the same readiness in application as its ancient national prototype.[743]

In recognition of the realities of effective power (and especially of the enormous discrepancy between the power of the state and that of the individual), proposals continue to be made for more effective invocation through representatives of the general community. It is often too formidable a task for the deprived individual successfully to confront, even before authoritative decision makers, the depriving state. The proposals for establishing a United Nations High Commissioner for Human Rights and other equivalents of an international ombudsman represent de-

738. *See* notes 85–95 and 389–96 *supra* and accompanying text.
739. *See* note 96 *supra* and accompanying text.
740. *See* notes 97–99 *supra* and accompanying text.
741. *See* notes 100–05 *supra* and accompanying text.
742. *See* notes 439–53 *supra* and accompanying text.
743. *See* Schwelb, *The Actio Popularis and International Law,* 2 ISRAEL Y.B. HUMAN RIGHTS 46 (1972). *See also* Judge Jessup's Separate Opinion, [1962] I.C.J. 425, 430; [1966] I.C.J. 325, 373 *et seq.* (dissenting opinion).

mands for the improvement of constitutive process which, despite the opposition of states, would appear destined to prevail.[744]

The importance of the invocation function and its bases in authority are not, unhappily, always clearly understood. Thus, in the *Barcelona Traction* case,[745] the International Court of Justice, in holding that Belgium had no standing to protect its nationals, shareholders in a Canadian company, against injuries allegedly done to the company through acts of various organs of the Spanish government, appeared to require, before it could find standing to sue, that the customary international law about the responsibility of states to aliens be invested with the attributes of universality of jurisdiction. In an often quoted passage, the Court said:

> In particular, an essential distinction should be drawn between the obligations of a State towards the international community as a whole, and those arising vis-à-vis another State in the field of diplomatic protection. By their very nature the former are the concern of all States. In view of the importance of the rights involved, all States can be held to have a legal interest in their protection; they are obligations *erga omnes.*
>
> Such obligations derive, for example, in contemporary international law, from the outlawing of acts of aggression, and of genocide, as also from the principles and rules concerning the basic rights of the human person, including protection from slavery and racial discrimination. Some of the corresponding rights of protection have entered into the body of general international law . . .; others are conferred by international instruments of a universal or quasi-universal character.
>
> Obligations the performance of which is the subject of diplomatic protection are not of the same category. It cannot be held, when one such obligation in particular is in question, in a specific case, that all States have a legal interest in its observance.[746]

One can only applaud the Court's perception that "the basic rights of the human person" are today of intense common interest and concern to the international community as a whole. Genocide and slave trading have indeed, after some difficulty, been brought within the principle of universality of jurisdiction. One is, however, a little surprised to see that protection against racial discrimination and other basic human rights,

---

744. *See* notes 406–23 *supra* and accompanying text.

745. Case concerning the Barcelona Traction, Light and Power Company, Ltd., [1970] I.C.J. 3.

746. *Id.* at 32.

and even the prohibition of acts of aggression, are described as within this principle. In any event, there would appear to be no sequitur whatever, syntactic or empirical, between the Court's proposition that the customary international law protecting the rights of aliens does not entail universality of jurisdiction and its conclusion that Belgium had no standing to espouse the claims of its nationals. Certainly, within the expectation of most of the world today, aliens (potentially including all persons) are among those entitled to basic human rights, and no rational reason would appear for denying such persons the protection of their state of nationality merely because customary international law does not yet confer upon them the benefit of all possible protectors.[747]

Termination

The difficulties that the global constitutive process presents for terminating or modifying the contemporary human rights prescriptions would appear entirely comparable to those presented by mature national constitutive processes for the change of basic, most intensely demanded policies. Certainly, under prevailing customary international law, these prescriptions—like parallel national policies—can only be changed by modalities in prescription comparable to those by which they were created. For the human rights prescriptions appropriately regarded as *jus cogens,* which as demonstrated above include the great bulk of all such prescriptions,[748] this consequence is made explicit by Article 53 of the Vienna Convention on the Law of Treaties.[749] This article, in its partially tautological definition, describes a "peremptory norm of general international law" as one which permits "no derogation" and "can be modified only by a subsequent norm of general international law having the same character."[750]

It has already been observed in some detail that the contemporary human rights prescriptions have been created through a comprehensive and complex process of continuing communication which includes both the deliberate and formal modalities of multilateral agreement and parliamentary procedures and the less deliberate and most informal modalities of customary behavior.[751] It is the cumulative, and mutually reinforcing, effect of all of these modalities of communication which establishes the core content of the human rights prescriptions as au-

747. *See* chapter 14 and the appendix *infra.*
748. *See* notes 635–99 *supra* and accompanying text.
749. Vienna Convention, *supra* note 135, Art. 53.
750. *Id.*
751. *See* notes 315–67 *supra* and accompanying text.

thoritative and controlling within the expectations of most of humankind.[752] The termination or modification of these expectations must, accordingly, require a process of communication no less comprehensive and complex, employing all the same modalities. The special difficulties that the global constitutive process places in the way of employing each of these modalities for purposes of change may be noted.

Insofar as the human rights prescriptions are grounded in the Charter of the United Nations, any formal change in these prescriptions must of course conform to the procedures established for changing the Charter. Because of the apparent difficulty stemming from the built-in veto in the amending procedure embodied in Article 108 of the Charter, formal amendment of the Charter has thus far been extremely modest, reflecting only the numerical changes in the composition and voting procedures of key organs, as necessitated by the vast enlargement of the membership of the United Nations.[753] It would not be easy for proposals to terminate or drastically alter the human rights prescriptions to escape this same difficulty.

Insofar as the human rights prescriptions are embodied in multilateral agreements, any proposals for change must confront the characteristic difficulties in changing agreements to which there are many parties.[754] The two vital pillars—the International Covenant on Civil and Political Rights (and its Optional Protocol) and the International Covenant on Economic, Social, and Cultural Rights—do not provide for denunciation; the commitments undertaken under the Covenants are so fundamental and intensely demanded that they are not expected to be altered, certainly not by unilateral action.[755] Even in human rights conventions embodying provisions for denunciation, such provisions are so hedged that they cannot, as described above, easily be made effective.[756]

Similarly, for the lesser change involved in amendment or revision, when explicit provision is made, two distinct patterns emerge: one under the auspices of the United Nations and one under the auspices of the International Labor organization. A typical United Nations formula reads as follows:

> 1. A request for the revision of this Convention may be made at any time by any State Party by means of a notification in writing addressed to the Secretary-General of the United Nations.

752. *See* notes 558–610 *supra* and accompanying text.
753. *See* notes 500–03 *supra* and accompanying text.
754. *See* Vienna Convention, *supra* note 135, Arts. 54–64.
755. *See* notes 504–06 *supra* and accompanying text.
756. *See* notes 507–20 *supra* and accompanying text.

2. The General Assembly of the United Nations shall decide upon the steps, if any, to be taken in respect of such a request.[757]

This formula is found in the International Convention on the Elimination of All Forms of Racial Discrimination (Article 23),[758] in the Convention on the Non-Applicability of Statutory Limitations to War Crimes and Crimes against Humanity (Article 9),[759] in the Convention Relating to the Status of Stateless Persons (Article 41),[760] in the Convention Relating to the Status of Refugees (Article 45),[761] and in the Convention on the International Right of Correction (Article 12).[762] Though under this formula the General Assembly is afforded a broad discretion, it is not to be expected that the General Assembly can be mobilized easily to recommend important changes.

The formula employed in several human rights conventions adopted under the auspices of the International Labor Organization suggests comparable difficulties. The standard provision reads as follows:

1. Should the [International Labor] Conference adopt a new Convention revising this Convention in whole or in part, then, unless the new Convention otherwise provides:

   (a) The ratification by a member of the new revising Convention shall *ipso jure* involve the immediate denunciation of this Convention, notwithstanding the provisions of article 16 [relating to denunciation], if and when the new revising Convention shall have come into force;

   (b) As from the date when the new revising Convention comes into force this Convention shall cease to be open to ratification by the Members.

2. This Convention shall in any case remain in force in its actual form and content for those Members which have ratified it but have not ratified the revising Convention.[763]

---

757. Convention on the Elimination of Racial Discrimination, *supra* note 97, Art. 23.

758. *Id.*

759. The Convention on the Non-Applicability of Statutory Limitations on War Crimes and Crimes against Humanity, *adopted* and *opened* for signature, ratification, and accession Nov. 26, 1968, Art. 9 (entered into force Nov. 11, 1970), *reprinted in* U.N. HUMAN RIGHTS INSTRUMENTS, *supra* note 51, at 42, 44.

760. Convention Relating to the Status of Stateless Persons, *supra* note 287, Art. 41.

761. Convention Relating to the Status of Refugees, *supra* note 114, Art. 45.

762. Convention on the International Right of Correction, *opened for signature* Dec. 16, 1952, Art. 12 (entered into force Aug. 24, 1962), *reprinted in* U.N. HUMAN RIGHTS INSTRUMENTS, *supra* note 51, at 79–81.

763. Freedom of Association and Protection of the Right to Organize Convention, *supra* note 343, Art. 20.

This provision is found, for example, in the Freedom of Association and Protection of the Right to Organize Convention (Article 20),[764] in the Right to Organize and Collective Bargaining Convention (Article 15),[765] and in the Workers' Representatives Convention (Article 13).[766]

Insofar as the human rights prescriptions are inferred from the uniformities that create customary law, any termination or modification of their content must require the development of new customary expectation. The unique difficulty in this mode of terminating the human rights prescriptions is apparent in the requirement of the subjectivities of "rightness" or "oughtness" which must attend the behavior from which customary expectations are inferred.[767] In the light of the intensities with which the basic content of the human rights prescriptions is presently demanded by the peoples of the world, it is difficult to foresee a context in which opposite content could be demanded with the requisite subjectivities of "right" to transform uniformities in behavior, in violation of the contemporary prescriptions, into acceptable bases for inferring an opposite international law. It is not intended by this to suggest that the existing human rights prescriptions cannot be changed and improved. What is being suggested is that, so long as the peoples of the world continue to express the same high intensities in demand for the basic human rights embodied in the existing prescriptions, any changes in the fundamental content of such prescriptions must confront enormous difficulties and be effected through the modalities by which the prescriptions were created.

Quod erat demonstrandum.

---

764. *Id.*

765. The Right to Organize and Collective Bargaining Convention, *supra* note 344, Art. 15.

766. The Workers' Representatives Convention, *supra* note 345, Art. 13.

767. *See* notes 347–53 *supra* and accompanying text.

II

The Clarification of General Community Policies

5. THE BASIC POLICIES OF A COMPREHENSIVE PUBLIC ORDER OF HUMAN DIGNITY

In previous discussion we have observed that there is a human rights dimension in every social interaction and that any comprehensive inquiry about human rights must locate particular instances of deprivation and nonfulfillment in the total context of a global social process.[1] We have noted also that there are human rights policies at stake in every authoritative decision, at whatever community level, and that any serious concern for improvement in the aggregate protection of human rights must extend through every phase of constitutive decision and relate to all types of public order decisions in all communities, from local to global.[2] It is, further, a matter of common knowledge, abundantly documented in many media, that contemporary global social process exhibits grave and immense disparities between the growing common demands of the peoples of the world for a greater production and wider sharing of human dignity values and the actual production and distribution of such values.[3] The task incumbent upon us now is that of exploring in some detail the intellectual procedures and institutional arrangements whereby the protection of human dignity values can be improved in particular instances of deprivation and responding decision and in the aggregate flow of social interaction and all authoritative responses.

The deliberately policy-oriented, configurative approach we recommend for inquiry about human rights problems, as for all legal problems, begins with the unequivocal establishment of an observational

1. *See* chapters 1 and 2 *supra.*

In this chapter, we draw in some measure upon our earlier formulations in M. McDougal, H. Lasswell, & I. Vlasic, Law and Public Order in Space, chapter 2 (1963) and McDougal, *Human Rights and World Public Order: Principles of Content and Procedure for Clarifying General Community Policies,* 14 Va. J. Int'l L. 387 (1974). The latter item was designed from its inception to become a part of this chapter.

2. *See* chapter 1 *supra*, at notes 218–24 and accompanying text.

3. *See id.* at notes 8–88 and accompanying text.

standpoint in identification with the whole of humankind and with the explicit postulation of a comprehensive set of preferences, formulated at necessarily high levels of abstraction, about the shaping and sharing of all human dignity values. The more detailed clarification of these postulated preferences, for guiding choices in particular instances of authoritative prescription and application or other decision, builds upon both a broad formulation of the common interests in human rights of all individuals on a global scale and the further systematic employment of a number of distinguishable, but interrelated, intellectual tasks in the necessary specification, and accommodation, of these common interests. The task of describing past trends, or historic task, is employed to make effective comparisons through time and across community boundaries of the consequences of different decisions about human rights, to ascertain where any particular community stands at any particular time in achievement or deprivation, and to draw upon inherited wisdom about successes and failures. The scientific task is designed to explore the multiple conditions, in terms of individual perspectives and of social and environmental interconnections, that affect particular deprivations and decisions, both for increased understanding of the past and more effective projection of the future. The projection of possible future developments, by disciplined employment of trend and scientific knowledge, can be made to serve both realism about emerging problems and creativity in the invention and evaluation of alternatives. Within this framework of configurative and continuing performance of the various relevant intellectual tasks, the ultimate and culminating task—that of the selection, invention, and evaluation of specific alternatives in decision—may be made much more rational in relation to the postulated, more abstract, preferences about the shaping and sharing of human dignity values. In the absence of the performance of these various intellectual tasks, neither observer nor decision maker can have any assurance that the decision alternatives chosen in any particular instance bear a rational relation to the more fundamental goals sought. The outlines and potentialities of this recommended approach to the difficult, but inescapable, problem of clarifying fundamental policies may, as a prelude to examination of a range of specific human rights problems, be indicated in somewhat more detail.

THE OBSERVATIONAL STANDPOINT: IDENTIFICATION WITH THE WHOLE OF HUMANKIND

In approaching the policy problems of human dignity on a global scale it is essential, as we have several times indicated, to make manifest the standpoint of observation and participation. The viewpoint we take is that of citizens of the world community who are identified with the future of humankind as a whole rather than with the primacy of any particular group. Our commitment is, therefore, to the comprehensive goal of realizing human dignity on the widest possible scale.

The most conspicuous fact about the contemporary structure of world social process is that the global arena is divided into rival systems of public order. No one set of decision makers is at present authorized to speak for the human congregation. Who, then, is our audience?

We have implied that the largest potential audience that we address is composed of all members of the world community. None of the basic goals and objectives that we formulate are so remote from the lives of men, women, and children of every area that they cannot be understood if sufficient care and skill are exercised to communicate with the involved and concerned individuals. Our role as scholars is not necessarily to prepare the ultimate communications that will be of the most help in enabling all individuals and groups to become aware of their fundamental interests and to perceive what policy steps, if taken, will protect and extend their value positions. Our professional responsibility is to set in motion a sequence of activities that may eventually succeed in clarifying and guiding the perspectives and operations required to remold institutional arrangements in ways that foster human dignity. All preliminary formulations of goals and alternatives must, as indicated, be disciplined by the available knowledge of past trends and conditioning factors, and of the estimated course of future development.

Within the universal audience, it is likely to be most rewarding to focus upon the most influential decision makers and their advisers, especially their legal consultants. What is said here will affect the flow of decision to the extent that it is eventually endorsed by those who wield authority and control in the bodies politic that comprise the present and future arenas of public and civic order. Our role as scholars in relation to official decision makers is essentially the same as our role in communicating with the whole body of citizens. We observe, analyze, and propose; the decision makers dispose. The goals of public policy can be clarified in terms of timing and specificity, and of the potential range of strategic action brought into relationship to the whole.

Even though no complete system of universal order has yet been achieved, a complex process of decision is, as outlined in detail above,[4] in operation throughout the world community. Authority and control are dispersed among all the elites of the separate nation-states and other lesser communities in the global arena. Elites are continually engaged in assessing their relative positions in terms of power, wealth, respect, and every other value. These elites are inventing and evaluating policies in

4. *See* chapter 4 *supra*.

search of alternatives that they expect will yield the greatest net contribution to their value positions. It is hardly necessary to acknowledge that their calculations may be true or false: they may overestimate or underestimate capabilities and intentions. We hope to affect the flow of decision in several ways, particularly by providing provisional maps of the emerging future, and by bringing into the focus of attention an interpretation of the characteristics of public order which, if attained, will maximize the value outcomes of the human beings who interact with one another in world social process.

As a means of clarifying the outcomes to be sought in the decision process, we utilize a postulational method that exploits the potential of an inclusive observational standpoint. We postulate a preferred pattern of value distribution and invite all who will to join in discovering and proposing policy principles and particular policies for the implementation of these objectives. Our overriding postulate is compatible with all formulations which accept human dignity as the common interest of all participants in the future of world social process. We propose to draw numerous implications for the changing structure of global public order.

Candor requires that we raise the question of impact. What is the likelihood, especially since it is evident that we must rely entirely upon the impact of communication, that scholarly analysis and recommendations will influence decision?

It is encouraging to take note of the fact that in various past circumstances systems of public order have been affected by scholarly communication. In general, elites are predisposed to receive clarifying advice when they find themselves in the midst of accelerating change. Members of elite groups differ from one another in significant ways, such as in degree of rigidity or adaptability of perception. The more inventive decision makers recognize that it is unwise to depend upon simple extrapolations of history into prophecy. They may be open to advice about what precedents from the past to accept as factually relevant and normatively appropriate, or even about what novelties are likely to appear and what innovative formulations are apt to yield optimum results.

As we shall have occasion to confirm in some detail, the scientific, technological, and rectitude (ethical) changes of modern times have created a context in which demands for the dissolution of static, caste societies have gained in intensity and effectiveness.[5] Whether we consider the rise of political democracy, or any other trend toward equality of value participation, we cannot fail to be impressed by the role of specialized scholarly intellectuals in the process. Systematic inquiries

5. *See* chapter 7 *infra,* at notes 303–86 and accompanying text.

have become landmarks along the path of change, both authenticating and generating popular texts for purposes of popular education and technical treatises for the sake of constitutive prescription or legal justification. Scholarly output has reached, and presumably will continue to reach, every phase of policy formation in the public and civic (private) orders.

As we pointed out in our study of public order in space, there is a direct parallel between today and another period of scholarly influence and enlarging awareness of the common physical resources of the earth.[6] During the age of discovery the elites and peoples of Europe were becoming aware of the oceans and the continental land masses. Top elite figures became acutely aware of the costs of perpetuating a state of affairs in which the major powers sought extensive control over land and sea. Losses of ships, men, and cargo affected every national participant and cut into the gains from new transportation routes. Latent demands were building up in favor of a public order that would offer greater protection for common interests in trade and production. It was in this setting that Grotius and his contemporaries performed their clarifying task. Today's parallel is expanding penetration of access to solar system and to deeper space; and the recognized dangers of acute conflict have inclined formal decision makers to give attention to scholarly analyses and proposals about the proper management of the earth's common interest in space.

We call attention to another parallel between the present time and the era in which Grotius lived. Participants in the world arena were divided by ideological no less than economical and legal barriers. The most evocative symbols of the age were theological. The challenge that confronts anyone who adopts the observational standpoint of the world community as a whole is assisting those who are identified with rivalrous and hostile systems of faith, belief, and loyalty to perceive common values, and to cooperate in consolidating an effective public order which is designed to defend and extend common values. In today's world the principal systems of political myth are secular ("liberal," "communist," etc.) rather than sacred ("Christian," "Muslim," etc.).

To affirm that we are concerned with the common interests of human beings is not to imply that we hold ourselves aloof from current strife and avoid taking a position in current controversies. The problem is to cut through present-day misconceptions and to identify the true battlefronts. Seen in one dimension, world struggles appear to conform to the boundary lines of nation-states. Nevertheless, in another perspective, the front lines crisscross boundaries and follow lines of civilization, class,

6. M. McDougal, H. Lasswell, & I. Vlasic, *supra* note 1, at chapter 2.

interest, personality, and level of crisis. Under some circumstances a national elite group is almost entirely identified at the conscious level with the past and future value position of its own state. It would, however, be a mistaken act of judgment to assume that this is a universal rule. On the contrary, such elites often deliberately associate themselves with party, religious, ethnic, and other groupings that traverse state boundaries and alter the monolithic unity of parochial units. Systems of identification provide the fundamental frameworks of self-reference in which value indulgences (advantages) and deprivations (disadvantages) are assessed. In the process, self-reference symbols influence both the specific interpretations and the relative weights that are assigned to the values sought to be maximized. An increasing identification by individuals with a global community of humankind is among the factors to be taken into account within processes of effective power.

Within the context of the innumerable battlefronts that intersect one another in the world arena of today we undertake to outline ways of specifying the value patterns and institutions of public order that are consonant with, and facilitative of, human dignity. Although the validity of this goal is seldom challenged in the polemics of contemporary politics, no competent observer is so credulous as to assume that articulated goals are scrupulously adhered to in the realities of world affairs. Current controversies turn almost exclusively upon questions of definition and evidence concerning the degree to which rival systems of public order do in fact attain behavioral conformity to proclaimed norms.

The principal objective of the present inquiry is explication of a framework within which realistic assessments can be made of the relevance of alternative policies to the public order of the global community and its component communities. The prescriber or applier or other evaluator of policy options has an obligation to make himself as conscious as possible of the full range of communities, from global to local, of which he is a member and upon which his choices will have unavoidable impact. The aspiration of a decision maker who represents a community whose basic constitutive process projects a comprehensive order of human dignity—as is increasingly sought in the contemporary emerging global "bill of human rights"[7]—and who is personally committed to this goal, should be to make his every particular decision contribute to progress toward this outcome. Such a decision maker will recognize that, in the global interdetermination of all values, there is indeed a human rights dimension to all interaction and decision, and will make every effort to insure that such dimensions are effectively taken into account in decision.

7. *See* chapter 4 *supra*.

This recommendation, it must be clearly understood, is not that a decision maker assume the license to impose his own unique, idiosyncratic preferences upon the community. It is, rather, a demand that the decision maker identify with the whole of the communities he represents, and that he undertake a systematic, disciplined effort to relate the specific choices he must make to a clarified common interest, specified in terms of overriding community goals, for which he personally can take responsibility.

The relevant perspective, that of identification with the whole of humankind engaged in a vast cooperative effort to enhance the protection of human rights, has been well stated by a contemporary author:

> More and more, the world has come to recognize the validity of the claim of the human personality to be heard in every decision affecting the fate of man and to cast its decisive vote in the council of nations. Pope John XXIII spoke for all when he postulated a set of international rules of conduct and conscience, which rests on a conception of the universe in which the recognition of the moral personality of man and his dignity and rights stand in the center. In his celebrated encyclical *Pacem in Terris* of April 10, 1963, Pope John declared:
>
> > Like the common good of individual political communities, so too the universal common good cannot be determined except by having regard to the human person. Therefore, the public authority of the world community, too, must have as its fundamental objective the recognition, respect, safeguarding and promotion of the rights of the human person. . . .
>
> Above all the clamor of differences which divide people, men and women of all continents and of all latitudes and longitudes, regardless of the diversity in their background and outlook, are united in their quest for personal dignity and for the satisfaction of their human rights and fundamental freedoms.[8]

THE PERSPECTIVES OF A COMPREHENSIVE WORLD PUBLIC ORDER: CLARIFYING POLICIES

In a world social process of ever-shifting and interactive components, there is no doubt that the current systems of public order will be continually modified. If these changes are to be compatible with the fundamental requirements of human dignity, decision makers must be prepared to seize every opportunity for the guidance of policy toward the

8. M. Moskowitz, The Politics and Dynamics of Human Rights 75–76 (1968).

invention and adoption of appropriate measures. The clarification of goals is an essential part of adequate preparation for the multiple challenges of the future, whether immediate or remote.

By the term "public order" we are referring to the pattern of preferred policy outcomes and the basic institutions protected by the legal system. If we are to assist in the process of clarification it is evident that our recommendations must explicate the patterns of value shaping and sharing which it is proposed to protect and fulfill through legal order, and further, must provide some provisional specification of the institutions to be maintained. Our position is unmistakable in reference to the preferred value pattern. In numerous publications and activities we have made it abundantly clear that we yield to no one in firm commitment to a public order of human dignity brought progressively into realization on the largest possible scale.[9] In reference to value shaping and sharing the overriding goal is to attain a social process in which values are widely, not narrowly, available throughout the world community. As we examine the global process as a whole or in particular localities and sectors, we are aware of the fact that the institutional practices whereby values are assembled and processed, accumulated or enjoyed, exhibit prodigious variation in detail. We emphasize that the test of whether legal facilities are to be made available in support of the specific practices of any institution is whether these practices do in fact harmonize with the requirements of human dignity. The recommendations that we propose for the public order of the future are comprehensive in space and in all the value sectors of the entire community.

Legal order is itself a component of public order and, besides affording a bulwark to other institutions, must also provide for its own protection. Our specialized frame of reference within the world social process is with decision, or the stream of commitment within the shaping and sharing of power. The relevant institutions must be designed to be at once authoritative and controlling. To be authoritative is to operate within the perspectives provided by the broad outlines (the formula) of community expectations about how, and for what basic policies, community decisions should be taken. Decisions are controlling when they are, in fact, effective. The problem confronted by anyone who is con-

9. *See, e.g.*, M. McDougal & Associates, Studies in World Public Order (1960); M. McDougal & F. Feliciano, Law and Minimum World Public Order: The Legal Regulation of International Coercion (1961); M. McDougal & W. Burke, The Public Order of the Oceans: A Contemporary International Law of the Sea (1962); M. McDougal, H. Lasswell, & I. Vlasic, *supra* note 1; M. McDougal, H. Lasswell, & J. Miller, The Interpretation of Agreements and World Public Order: Principles of Content and Procedure (1967); L. Chen & H. Lasswell, Formosa, China, and the United Nations (1967).

cerned with the legal order of tomorrow is that of proposing provisions for incorporation into the formula of the world community which, if made controlling, will nurture and maintain a public order of human dignity under the dynamic conjuncture of developments that comprise the human context as a whole.

If the flow of decision is to be controlled in harmony with authoritative principles of human dignity, the fundamental principles must find lodgement in the expectations entertained by the effective participants in the world political process. At no time can it be safely assumed that human expectations, or the demands and identifications with which they interlock, are unchanging. Nor can it be taken for granted, without appropriate verification, that community perspectives can unambiguously be inferred from the language of authoritative documents. Viewpoints are in perpetual flux; hence, today's structure of expectation is open to change as new conditions alter old relationships, and new or revised recommendations are put forward and assimilated.

The Postulation of the Goal Values of Human Dignity

In an interdependent world the reverberations of any policy decision permeate every geographical area and every functional component of society. A perfectionist aspiration toward total completeness is utterly unrealistic. The time and the facilities required definitively to assess particular or aggregate policy effects, or to arrive at comprehensive advance estimates of these efforts, are far beyond the assets at the disposal of individual or collective participants in decision processes. Obviously, however, this situation does not imply that it is not worth attempting to anticipate or to examine in retrospect the impact of public policy on the values and institutions of the world social process. The task of calculating the consequences of any particular decision is, as a distinguished American legal philosopher has said, an "infinite" one if the calculator does not operate with "discriminating" criteria of what consequences are "important."[10] The insistent question for every decision maker or other evaluator is to what basic policy goals he, as a representative of the larger community of humankind and of its various lesser component communities, is willing to commit himself as the primary postulates of public order for inspiring and shaping the particular choices he has to make. The defensible implications are that approximations are the appropriate targets of inquiry and that selectivity is necessary if significant results are to be achieved by the use of whatever allocations of time and facilities are at hand. Both observers and decision

10. Cohen, *Transcendental Nonsense and the Functional Approach,* 35 Colum. L. Rev. 809, 848 (1935).

makers must operate, whether consciously or unconsciously, at many different levels of abstraction, from highest to lowest.

The first step, as we have repeatedly indicated, is commitment to an inclusive map of values. The fundamental choice is in terms of human impact. Should policy aim at the realization of human dignity or indignity? Our recommended postulate of human dignity is much easier to accept and to explicate today than ever before. The contemporary image of man as capable of respecting himself and others, and of constructively participating in the shaping and sharing of all human dignity values, is the culmination of many different trends in thought, secular as well as religious, with origins extending far back into antiquity and coming down through the centuries with vast cultural and geographic reach.[11]

---

11. It is sometimes suggested that the words "human dignity" are of relatively recent origin and that there is very great difficulty in ascribing meaning to the concept. Spiegelberg, *Human Dignity: A Challenge to Contemporary Philosophy,* in HUMAN DIGNITY: THIS CENTURY AND NEXT 39 (R. Gotesky & E. Laszlo eds. 1970).

Though the words "human dignity" may not have come into common use until within the last two or three centuries, the demanded values to which we, and others, refer by use of these words are of the most ancient lineage.

Some of the difficulties philosophers find with the words may arise from their characteristic failure to indicate what intellectual tasks they seek to perform. The words "human dignity" can be used to refer to a preferred pattern in shaping and sharing of values, and the historical, scientific, and developmental tasks can be employed in inquiry about the modalities by, and the degrees to, which these values are secured, without indulging in an infinitely regressive derivational search for some true "basis" or "foundation" or "cornerstone" of an imagined "absolute" or "universal" conception. The preferred patterns in the shaping and sharing of values to which we make reference have of course throughout history been "derived" and "justified" in many different ways, religious and secular, and, as our summaries indicate, have at different times and places been sought and achieved through many different modalities and in many different degrees. The past ambiguities with which the words "human dignity" have been employed are of some, but not of overwhelming, interest to those who seek to create a more comprehensive and constructive intellectual map for future guidance.

Needless to say, the literature is vast. *See generally* H. BAKER, THE IMAGE OF MAN: A STUDY OF THE IDEA OF HUMAN DIGNITY IN CLASSICAL ANTIQUITY, THE MIDDLE AGES, AND THE RENAISSANCE (1961); A. BRECHT, POLITICAL THEORY: THE FOUNDATIONS OF TWENTIETH-CENTURY POLITICAL THOUGHT (1959); S. CLOUGH, BASIC VALUES OF WESTERN CIVILIZATION (1960); EQUALITY AND FREEDOM: INTERNATIONAL AND COMPARATIVE JURISPRUDENCE (G. Dorsey ed. 1977) (3 vols.); 2 P. GAY, THE ENLIGHTENMENT: AN INTERPRETATION (1969); F. HAYEK, THE CONSTITUTION OF LIBERTY (1960); P. KRISTELLER, RENAISSANCE CONCEPTS OF MAN (1972); H. LAUTERPACHT, INTERNATIONAL LAW AND HUMAN RIGHTS 73–141 (1950); S. LUKES, INDIVIDUALISM (1973); J. MARITAIN, THE RIGHTS OF MAN AND NATURAL LAW (D. Anson trans. 1943); I. SZABO, THE SOCIALIST CONCEPT OF HUMAN RIGHTS (1966); UNESCO, BIRTHRIGHT OF MAN (1969); Castberg, *Natural Law and Human Rights: An Idea-Historical Survey,* in INTERNATIONAL PROTECTION OF HUMAN RIGHTS 13 (A. Eide & A. Schou eds. 1968) (Nobel Symposium 7); Claude, *The Classical Model of Human Rights Development,* in COMPARATIVE HUMAN RIGHTS 6 (R. Claude ed. 1976).

See generally also J. ALFARO, THEOLOGY OF JUSTICE IN THE WORLD (1973); THE GOOD

The postulate of human dignity can no longer be regarded as the eccentric doctrine of lonely philosophers and peculiar sects.[12] This postulate, as we have defined it in terms of demands for the greater production and wider sharing of all values and a preference for persuasion over

SOCIETY: A BOOK OF READINGS (A. Arblaster & S. Lukes eds. 1972); B. BAILYN, THE IDEOLOGICAL ORIGINS OF THE AMERICAN REVOLUTION (1967); K. BARTH, THE HUMANITY OF GOD (1960); I. BERLIN, FOUR ESSAYS ON LIBERTY (1968); THE FATE OF MAN (C. Brinton ed. 1961); J. BRONOWSKI, THE ASCENT OF MAN (1973); A. CARLYLE, POLITICAL LIBERTY: A HISTORY OF THE CONCEPTION IN THE MIDDLE AGES AND MODERN TIMES (1963); E. CASSIRER, THE INDIVIDUAL AND THE COSMOS IN RENAISSANCE PHILOSOPHY (M. Domandi trans. 1972); G. COLE, A HISTORY OF SOCIALIST THOUGHT (1953–60) (5 vols.); HUMAN RIGHTS AND THE LIBERATION OF MAN IN THE AMERICAS (L. Colonnese ed. 1970); M. CRANSTON, WHAT ARE HUMAN RIGHTS? (1973); R. CUMMING, HUMAN NATURE AND HISTORY: A STUDY IN THE DEVELOPMENT OF LIBERAL POLITICAL THOUGHT (1969) (2 vols.); THE BUDDHIST TRADITION IN INDIA, CHINA AND JAPAN (W. de Bary ed. 1972); G. DE RUGGIERO, THE HISTORY OF EUROPEAN LIBERALISM (R. Collingwood trans. 1959); M. FOSS, THE IDEA OF PERFECTION IN THE WESTERN WORLD (1964); THE ENLIGHTENMENT: A COMPREHENSIVE ANTHOLOGY (P. Gay ed. 1973); D. GERMINO, MODERN WESTERN POLITICAL THOUGHT: MACHIAVELLI TO MARX (1972); G. GHURYE, GODS AND MEN (1962); L. HARTZ, THE LIBERAL TRADITION IN AMERICA (1955); L. HOBHOUSE, LIBERALISM (1964); K. JASPERS, MAN IN THE MODERN AGE (E. Paul & C. Paul trans. 1957); J. KITAGAWA, RELIGIONS OF THE EAST (1968); THE HUMAN RIGHT TO INDIVIDUAL FREEDOM (L. Kutner ed. 1970); C. LAMONT, THE PHILOSOPHY OF HUMANISM (5th ed. 1965); GREAT EXPRESSIONS OF HUMAN RIGHTS (R. MacIver ed. 1950); J. MARITAIN, APPROACHES TO GOD (1954); L. MCDONALD, WESTERN POLITICAL THEORY FROM ITS ORIGINS TO THE PRESENT (1968); THE RELIGION OF THE HINDUS (K. Morgan ed. 1953); F. MOTE, INTELLECTUAL FOUNDATIONS OF CHINA (1971); D. MUNRO, THE CONCEPT OF MAN IN EARLY CHINA (1969); R. NEVILLE, THE COSMOLOGY OF FREEDOM (1974); F. NORTHROP, THE MEETING OF EAST AND WEST (1966); F. OPPENHEIM, DIMENSIONS OF FREEDOM: AN ANALYSIS (1961); J. PASSMORE, THE PERFECTIBILITY OF MAN (1971); TWENTIETH CENTURY THEOLOGY IN THE MAKING: 3, ECUMENICITY AND RENEWAL (J. Pelikan ed. 1971); G. PICO DELLA MIRANDOLA, ORATION ON THE DIGNITY OF MAN (A. Caponigri trans. 1956); HUMAN RIGHTS (E. Pollack ed. 1971); R. POUND, THE DEVELOPMENT OF CONSTITUTIONAL GUARANTEES OF LIBERTY (1957); POLITICAL THEORY AND THE RIGHTS OF MAN (D. Raphael ed. 1967); HINDUISM (L. Renou ed. 1962); MOLDERS OF MODERN THOUGHT (B. Seligman ed. 1970); N. SMART, THE RELIGIOUS EXPERIENCE OF MANKIND (1969); L. STRAUSS, NATURAL RIGHT AND HISTORY (1953); R. TAGORE, THE RELIGION OF MAN (1931); P. TEILHARD DE CHARDIN, THE PHENOMENON OF MAN (1965); C. TRINKAUS, "IN OUR IMAGE AND LIKENESS": HUMANITY AND DIVINITY IN ITALIAN HUMANIST THOUGHT (1970); A. WATTS, THE WAY OF ZEN (1957); M. WEBER, THE RELIGION OF INDIA: THE SOCIOLOGY OF HINDUISM AND BUDDHISM (H. Gerth & D. Martindale trans. & eds. 1958); ISLAM (J. Williams ed. 1962); Caponigri & De George, *Humanism*, in 4 MARXISM, COMMUNISM, AND WESTERN SOCIETY: A COMPARATIVE ENCYCLOPEDIA 178 (C. Kernig ed. 1972); Fetscher & Muller, *Enlightenment*, in 3 *id.* 170; Germino, *The Contemporary Relevance of the Classics of Political Philosophy*, in 1 HANDBOOK OF POLITICAL SCIENCE 229 (F. Greenstein & N. Polsby eds. 1975).

12. For an impressive attempt at specification of goals in terms of "national and regional goals" and "international and transnational goals," *see* E. LASZLO, et al., GOALS FOR MANKIND (1977) (a report to the Club of Rome on the New Horizons of Global Community). It sums up the demands for human dignity in terms of "a world solidarity revolution."

See also B. MOORE, INJUSTICE: THE SOCIAL BASES OF OBEDIENCE AND REVOLT (1978).

coercion, has been incorporated, as our study of constitutive process demonstrates, with many varying degrees of completeness and precision into a great cluster of global prescriptions, both conventional and customary, and into the constitutional and legislative codes of many different national communities.[13] The prescriptions in this huge contemporary authoritative postulation are of course formulated at many different levels of abstraction and employ many different complementarities of meaning, both explicit and implicit. The opportunity is, however, open to responsible decision makers to clarify and apply prescriptions that give expression to the rising common demands of peoples throughout the globe. The relevant postulations can be differentiated and appraised value by value and institutional practice by institutional practice in relation to the principal outcomes sought individually and collectively. From an analysis of available world trends it is observable, as we have documented above, that the world community is moving toward an ever more powerful consensus on the basic components of an international bill of rights.[14] In the long run it is these demands and expectations which will provide the effective conditions for enhanced international protection of human rights.

The reader will observe that we emphasize the postulation and clarification of public order goals rather than their derivation by the exercise of logical (syntactic) skill. No one doubts that, when definitions have been introduced into a family of statements, contradictions must be noted and done away with. However, the most direct contact with empirical reality is obtained by the systematic clarification of postulated value outcomes. Starting from a postulated reference, several disciplined procedures are available to explore its empirical implications. These procedures include, we continue to emphasize, the description of past trends, the analysis of interdetermining (conditioning) factors, the projection of future developments, and the invention and evaluation of alternative policies. As these relevant events are brought to the focus of attention, the decision makers, individually or collectively, discover that different degrees of certainty confirm or modify initial commitments. The way is thereby cleared to assign probabilities and priorities to value outcomes.

POSTULATED GOAL VALUES IN SOCIAL PROCESS

Experience confirms the observation that both deprivations and fulfillments of human rights occur as integral parts of the larger community processes in which all values exhibit their interdependences. The task of decision might be aided if all evaluators operated with more

13. *See* chapter 4 *supra.*
14. *See id.*

comprehensive, cognitive maps of their presumptive preferences about the different features of the value processes comprised within the larger community processes. The decision maker does an inadequate job if he does not appraise any specific choice in the light of all relevant community policies. "Unless," as one of the authors has elsewhere written, "tentative value judgments are reviewed in the context of a total conception of the preferred form of social order, unnecessary inconsistencies and omissions occur."[15]

The more comprehensive and detailed specification of presumptive preferences might extend beyond the general postulation of higher levels of production and wide sharing in all value processes to an itemization value by value and phase by phase within each value process. The kind of detailed itemization that might be employed to put flesh and blood onto bare analytical preferences is indicated in the following list:

Outcomes

Achievement of an optimum aggregate in the shaping and sharing of the value;

Access to a fundamental share of benefits;[16]

Enjoyment of further benefits on the basis of merit and contribution;

Participation

Widest possible access compatible with other overriding community values;

Freedom from discrimination irrelevant to merit;

Freedom to form and join groups;

Perspectives

Freedom to acquire demands for the value;

Opportunity to discover latent capabilities for participation;

Opportunity to acquire capabilities;

Opportunity to exercise capabilities;

Freedom to establish and change identifications;

15. Lasswell, *Clarifying Value Judgment: Principles of Content and Procedure,* 1 INQUIRY 87 (1958).

16. We use "fundamental share" rather than "basic minimum" here and elsewhere in our recommendations because we think the word "minimum" carries unfortunate implications. The aspiration should be for securing as large a share as possible for each individual, without regard to constraints created by derivational logic. *Contrast* J. RAWLS, A THEORY OF JUSTICE (1971).

Opportunity to achieve realism in expectations;

Situations

Freedom from interference in initiating and constituting institutions;

The establishment and maintenance of specialized and nonspecialized institutions, adequate to maximize human potentials;

Freedom of access to appropriate institutions;

Compulsory access when necessary to responsibility;

Freedom from deprivations disproportionate to crises;

Optimum adjustment of institutions in space (territorially and pluralistically) and through time for the realization of purposes above;

Base Values

Access to authoritative decision to defend and fulfill all rights;

Access to controlling value processes:
  Basic minimum;
  Equal access (protection against monopolization);

Opportunity for continuing accumulation of the value;

Special assistance to overcome handicaps in achieving access;

Strategies

Freedom to employ effective strategies in the shaping and sharing of the value;

Preference for persuasive, rather than coercive, strategies;

Freedom from discriminatory strategies.

If initial presumptive preferences of this order were applied to each value process, and to each recurring claim for human rights within each value process,[17] it might be possible to create the comprehensive and detailed map that would assist in rational decision. In particular decisions the presumptive preferences with regard to each particular value process, or phase of such process, would, if basic goals in the protection of human rights were to be fulfilled, be given the utmost deference compatible with aggregate achievement. The precise delineation of the rights of any particular individual in any particular context would, however, always require—as the contemporary human rights prescriptions

17. *See* chapter 3 *supra*.

do require—an infinitely delicate accommodation with the comparable rights of other individuals and with the inclusive interests of all community members.[18]

The types of presumptive preferences that might serve the purposes of a rational clarification of community policies may be indicated systematically in relation to each of the more common claims, as outlined above, about the different phases of the major human dignity values.[19]

Preferred Policies Relating to the World Process of Value Fulfillment and Deprivation

I. Preferences relating to respect

A. Preferences relating to outcomes

1. Preferences for a basic degree of respect for every individual as a human being;[20] preferences for the widest freedom of choice compatible with the aggregate common interest; eradication of slavery and its equivalent practices; eradication of apartheid; eradication of caste
2. Preferences for an effective equality of opportunity, precluding discriminations based on race (including color; national, ethnic, or social origin; birth; descent (or other status); sex; religion; political opinion; language; or other grounds irrelevant to capability; and for establishment of a social environment affording such conditions as will enable people to enjoy a wide range of effective choice in their interactions with others[21]
3. Preferences for distinctive recognition of preeminent contribution to the common interest
4. Preferences for an aggregate pattern of social interactions in which the demands of the individual are appropriately accommodated with the aggregate interests of the community, including the comparable interests of others, and in which all individuals and groups are protected in the utmost practicable autonomy and subjected to the least possible coercion, governmental or private[22]

---

18. The familiar contraposition of "human rights" and "collective rights" would appear to be a false one. When "collective rights" are given detailed semantic reference, they can refer only to the rights of individuals. The relevant question is of the compatibility of the rights, "individual" or "collective," with criteria of human dignity. *See* chapter 16 *infra* for further elaboration.

Cf. Koblernicz, *Individual and Collective,* in 4 MARXISM, COMMUNISM, AND WESTERN SOCIETY, *supra* note 11, at 234.

19. *See* chapter 3 *supra.*

20. *See* chapter 6 *infra.*

21. *See* chapter 8 *infra.*

22. *See* chapter 16 *infra.*

B. Preferences relating to participation
   1. Preferences for wide participation[23] by both individuals and groups in the shaping of respect
   2. Preferences for wide participation by both individuals and groups in the sharing of respect
C. Preferences relating to perspectives
   1. Preferences for the fullest freedom for individuals to acquire a demand for respect, including the establishment of opportunities to discover, acquire, and exercise capabilities
   2. Preferences for freedom to establish and change identification and to maintain an appropriate balance between inclusive and exclusive identification
   3. Preferences for opportunities to achieve realism in expectations about the conditions for engaging in shared respect
D. Preferences relating to situations
   1. Relating to institutions specialized to respect
      (a) Preferences for wide freedom to initiate and constitute institutions specialized to respect
      (b) Preferences for wide freedom of access to institutions specialized to respect
   2. Relating to institutions not specialized to respect—preferences for wide freedom of access to institutions not specialized to respect
   3. Relating to crisis—preferences that derogations from respect in times of crisis be appraised in terms both of necessity and of proportionality by the criteria of the aggregate common interest[24]
E. Preferences relating to base values
   1. Authoritative—preferences that the processes of authoritative decision always be available to individuals to defend and fulfill respect
   2. Controlling
      (a) Preferences that participation in each of the other value processes be managed in a way to defend and fulfill respect
      (b) Preferences that special assistance be given to permit individuals to overcome handicaps not attributable to merit
F. Preferences relating to strategies
   1. Preferences for freedom to employ the diplomatic instrument to

---

23. For the sake of economy in expression, by "wide participation" is meant the widest possible participation in each of the value processes.

24. For general discussion of the complexities of the problems of derogation and accommodation, *see* chapter 16 *infra.* In addition to the references indicated in *id.* at note 50, *see* Higgins, *Derogation under Human Rights Treaties,* 68 BRIT. Y.B. INT'L L. 281 (1975–76); Note, *The Doctrine of Margin of Appreciation and the European Convention on Human Rights,* 53 NOTRE DAME LAWYER 90 (1977).

facilitate shared respect and for freedom from deprivations of respect by its coercive use

2. Preferences for freedom to employ the ideological instrument to facilitate shared respect and for freedom from deprivations of respect by its coercive use
3. Preferences for freedom to manage goods and services to facilitate shared respect and for freedom from deprivation of respect through coercive manipulation of goods and services
4. Preferences for the use of the military instrument, under appropriate conditions of extreme necessity, to facilitate shared respect and for freedom from deprivation of respect through the coercive use of the military instrument.

II. Preferences relating to power

A. Preferences relating to participation

1. Preferences for wide individual participation
   - (a) Preferences for recognition of all individuals as persons
   - (b) Preferences for full protection of individuals in interactions external to particular communities (preferences for human dignity in the conferment and withdrawal of nationality)[25]
   - (c) Preferences for wide participation in the internal constitutive processes of communities through office holding and voting as well as through participation in the value processes which establish effective power
   - (d) Preferences for minimizing nonparticipation based on grounds—such as race, religion, political opinion, language, etc.—irrelevant to capabilities
2. Preferences for wide freedom of association in the establishment and maintenance of groups
   - (a) Preferences for wide freedom to establish and join political parties
   - (b) Preferences for wide freedom to establish and join pressure groups
   - (c) Preferences for wide freedom to establish and join private associations directly related to values other than power
   - (d) Preferences for the fullest protection of minorities that is compatible with the aggregate interest[26]

---

25. *See* the appendix *infra.*

26. *See* Claydon, *The Transnational Protection of Ethnic Minorities: A Tentative Framework of Inquiry,* 1975 Canadian Y.B. Int'l L. 25. *See also* I. Claude, National Minorities: An International Problem (1955); Ethnicity: Theory and Experience (N. Glazer & D. Moynihan eds. 1975); H. Isaacs, Idols of the Tribe: Group Identity and Political Change (1977); J. LaPonce, The Protection of Minorities (1960); Bruegel, *A Neglected*

(e) Preferences for freedom and appropriate opportunity to change authoritative and effective rulers (a right of revolution)[27]

(f) Preferences for freedom to constitute a new entity (a right of self-determination) when impacts are not destructive of a larger public order[28]

(g) Preferences for particular communities to be free from external coercion by acts or threats of deprivation and violence by any instrument of policy, military or other[29]

B. Preferences relating to perspectives

1. Preferences for freedom, after exposure to adequate enlightenment, to acquire, or not to acquire, a demand for power; preferences for freedom to discover latent capabilities for participation, and to acquire and exercise capabilities

2. Preferences for freedom to establish and change identifications and memberships in territorial and functional groups

---

Field: The Protection of Minorities, 4 HUMAN RIGHTS J. 413 (1971); Hauser, *The International Protection of Minorities and the Right of Self-Determination,* 1 ISRAEL Y. B. HUMAN RIGHTS 92 (1971); Macartney, *League of Nations' Protection of Minority Rights,* in THE INTERNATIONAL PROTECTION OF HUMAN RIGHTS 22 (E. Luard ed. 1967).

27. *See* Suzuki, *Extraconstitutional Change and World Public Order: A Prologue to Decision-Making,* 15 HOUSTON L. REV. 23 (1977); Sumida, *The Right of Revolution: Implications for International Law,* in POWER AND LAW 130 (C. Barker ed. 1971). More generally, *see* H. ARENDT, ON REVOLUTION (1963); C. BRINTON, THE ANATOMY OF REVOLUTION (rev. ed. 1952); E. BURKE, REFLECTIONS ON THE REVOLUTION IN FRANCE (1790); C. FRIEDRICH, MAN AND HIS GOVERNMENT 634–56 (1963); REVOLUTION (C. Friedrich ed. 1966); C. JOHNSON, REVOLUTIONARY CHANGE (1966); H. LASSWELL & D. BLUMENSTOCK, WORLD REVOLUTIONARY PROPAGANDA (1939); C. LEIDEN & K. SCHMITT, THE POLITICS OF VIOLENCE: REVOLUTION IN THE MODERN WORLD (1968); J. LOCKE, SECOND TREATISE ON GOVERNMENT (1689); T. PAINE, THE RIGHTS OF MAN (1791; 1951).

28. *See* Chen, *Self-Determination as a Human Right,* in TOWARD WORLD ORDER AND HUMAN DIGNITY: ESSAYS IN HONOR OF MYRES S. MCDOUGAL 198 (W. Reisman & B. Weston eds. 1976), and many pertinent references therein. *See also* L. BUCHHEIT, SECESSION: THE LEGITIMACY OF SELF-DETERMINATION (1978); W. OFUATEY-KODJOE, THE PRINCIPLE OF SELF-DETERMINATION IN INTERNATIONAL LAW (1977); U. UMOZURIKE, SELF-DETERMINATION IN INTERNATIONAL LAW (1972); T. Mensah, Self-Determination under United Nations' Auspices, 1963 (unpublished J.S.D. dissertation, Yale Law School Library); Nanda, *Self-Determination in International Law,* 66 AM. J. INT'L L. 321 (1972); Suzuki, *Self-Determination and World Public Order: Community Response to Territorial Separation,* 16 VA. J. INT'L L. 779 (1976). *Cf.* W. REISMAN, PUERTO RICO AND THE INTERNATIONAL PROCESS: NEW ROLES IN ASSOCIATION (1975); Cabranes, *Puerto Rico: Out of the Colonial Closet,* 33 FOREIGN POLICY 66 (1978–79); *The Question of Self-Determination in Western Sahara: Hearing before the Subcomm. on International Organizations and on Africa of the House Comm. on International Relations,* 95th Cong., 1st Sess. (1977).

29. *See* M. MCDOUGAL & F. FELICIANO, *supra* note 9. *See also* L. Chen, The Legal Regulation of Minor International Coercion, 1964 (unpublished J.S.D. dissertation, Yale Law School Library).

3. Preferences for opportunity to achieve realism in expectations about how power is shaped and shared in all relevant groupings

C. Preferences relating to arenas
1. Geographical
   (a) Preferences for freedom of transnational movement, including the freedom to enter, to stay in, and to leave a particular territorial community, temporarily or permanently, for nonnationals (including ordinary aliens and refugees) as well as nationals;[30] preferences for progress toward a nonsegregated world in which people, resources, and ideas can move freely in achieving an optimum shaping and sharing of all values, with present disparities in the distribution of people in relation to resources equitably redressed around the globe[31]
   (b) Preferences for freedom of internal movement, affording all individuals (nonnationals as well as nationals) the utmost practicable freedom in the choice of places to live, work, enjoy, and retire
2. Temporal—preferences for freedom from deprivations stemming from arbitrary temporal features (such as retroactivity) in the application of law and for stability in expectations about continuation of rights
3. Authoritative institutions
   (a) Preferences for freedom to initiate and constitute institutions specialized to power, both governmental and nongovernmental
   (b) Preferences for freedom of access to all institutions specialized to power
4. Controlling institutions
   (a) Preferences for freedom to initiate and constitute institutions specialized to values other than power
   (b) Preferences for freedom of access to institutions specialized to values other than power
5. Crisis—preferences for affording individuals protection and fulfillment of rights despite crises (in security, power, respect, en-

---

30. *See* Chen, *Expulsion and Expatriation in International Law: The Right to Leave, to Stay, and to Return,* 1973 Proc., Am. Soc'y Int'l L. 122, 127–32. *See also* G. Goodwin-Gill, International Law and the Movement of Persons between States (1978); R. Plender, International Migration Law (1972); D. Turack, The Passport in International Law (1972); The Right to Leave and to Return (K. Vasak & S. Liskofsky eds. 1976); Goodwin-Gill, *The Limits of the Power of Expulsion in Public International Law,* 67 Brit. Y.B. Int'l L. 55 (1977); Higgins, *The Right in International Law of an Individual to Enter, Stay in and Leave a Country,* 1973 Int'l Affairs 341.

31. *See* Chen, *supra* note 30.

lightenment, well-being, wealth, skill, affection, and rectitude), with derogation of rights only when necessary and proportionate, by criteria of the common interest

D. Preferences relating to base values
   1. Authoritative—preferences that the processes of authoritative decision, at all community levels, be securely and economically available to individuals to defend and fulfill all rights
   2. Controlling
      (a) Preferences that participation in value processes, other than those of authoritative power, be made available to individuals to defend and fulfill all rights
      (b) Preferences for affording individuals and groups all needed special assistance to overcome handicaps in movement toward genuine equality

E. Preferences relating to strategies
   1. Preferences for freedom to employ all instruments (diplomatic, ideological, economic, military) to enhance the shaping and sharing of power
   2. Preferences for freedom from arbitrary restraints in the employment of all instruments of strategy
   3. Preferences for freedom from the coercive employment of any and all instruments

F. Preferences relating to outcomes
   1. General
      (a) Preferences for a wide domain of civic order in which interference from, or coercion by, either official or effective power is kept to a minimum[32]
      (b) Preferences for freedom from the arbitrary exercise of any power of government, especially for freedom from arbitrary seizure and confinement
      (c) Preferences for the widest possible sharing of power, in the sense of individual participation in all governmental functions
   2. Particular—preferences for the establishment and maintenance of a community that effectively, responsibly, and responsively performs all essential decision functions, i.e., intelligence, promotion, prescription, invocation, application, termination, and appraisal[33]
      (a) Intelligence: preferences for freedom to receive all information necessary to rational participation in the decision process and for freedom from subjection to coercive disclosure

---

32. For detailed development of this preference, *see* chapter 16 *infra.*

33. *See* McDougal, Lasswell, & Reisman, *The World Constitutive Process of Authoritative Decision,* in 1 The Future of the International Legal Order 73 (R. Falk & C. Black eds. 1969). *See also* chapter 4 *supra.*

(b) Promotion: preferences for freedom to formulate and propagate demands both as individuals and in groups and for freedom from coercive promotional activities; preferences for freedom to abstain from membership in political parties, pressure groups, and private associations
(c) Prescription: preferences for open opportunities to participate in law-making activities, from the most deliberate to the least deliberate, and for appropriate representation in both authoritative and effective control groups that affect prescriptions, including participation in cooperative activities that create customary expectations
(d) Invocation: preferences for freedom to challenge all alleged deprivations and nonfulfillments because of nonconformity to community policies, and for open access to authoritative arenas to stimulate processes of decision for the protection and fulfillment of human rights
(e) Application: preferences for the safeguards of due process (notice, proper hearing, adequate personal representation, etc.) in the application of authoritative prescriptions in particular instances
(f) Termination: preferences for the availability of appropriate measures for amelioration of losses and damages resulting from the termination of particular prescriptions and other arrangements
(g) Appraisal: preferences for opportunities to receive realistic appraisals of the functioning of decision processes and to participate in appraising activities, both formally (*e.g.*, through commissions of inquiry) and informally as citizens

III. Preferences relating to enlightenment

A. Preferences relating to outcomes

1. Preferences for achieving an optimum aggregate in the shaping and sharing of enlightenment i.e., in the gathering, processing, and dissemination of knowledge and information; preferences for affording individuals opportunities to acquire and employ the knowledge necessary to contribute creatively to the aggregate common interest through understanding of different social processes and their conditioning factors
2. Preferences for affording individuals a fundamental share of access to all kinds of knowledge and information for the making of choices that affect their value positions (power, wealth, etc.) at all community levels
3. Preferences for furnishing those individuals having unique capabilities for comprehending and using complex knowledge

(*e.g.*, scientific knowledge) with greater access to such knowledge in order to further the aggregate production and distribution of enlightenment and other values

B. Preferences relating to participation
   1. Preferences for affording the general opportunity for all individuals to acquire and communicate the basic knowledge and information essential to rational choice
   2. Preferences for freedom from discrimination in the acquisition, use, and communication of knowledge and information
   3. Preferences for affording groups appropriate opportunity to acquire and communicate knowledge and information

C. Preferences relating to perspectives
   1. Preferences for freedom of the individual to develop the demand for knowledge
   2. Preferences for freedom of the individual from destructive conditioning, whether from governmental or private sources, of thought processes and for the maintenance of competing, open channels of communication
   3. Preferences for freedom from distorted communication, emanating from governmental or private sources, and for general opportunities to cultivate improved maps of reality about the physical, biological, and cultural features of the earth-space community
   4. Preferences for full disclosure of special interests that may warp the making of rational choices in the common interest

D. Preferences relating to situations
   1. Institutions specialized to enlightenment
      (a) Preferences for freedom to initiate and constitute institutions specialized to the acquisition, processing, and communication of knowledge and information, with maintenance of an appropriate balance between governmental and nongovernmental institutions and of a vigorous, pluralistic network of communication[34]
      (b) Preferences for maintenance of the utmost freedom of access to institutions specialized to enlightenment
   2. Institutions not specialized to enlightenment—preferences for freedom of access to institutions other than those specialized to knowledge and information when such access affects the achievement of enlightenment
   3. Crisis—preferences that derogations from access to enlightenment, even in times of crises, be permitted only under conditions of necessity and proportionality as measured by common interest

---

34. *See* the recommendations of the Commission on Freedom of the Press, A FREE AND RESPONSIBLE PRESS: A GENERAL REPORT ON MASS COMMUNICATION (1947).

E. Preferences relating to base values
  1. Authoritative—preferences that the processes of authoritative decision be made available to defend and fulfill all features of the enlightenment process, thereby affording individuals adequate protection in the acquisition and communication of knowledge and information
  2. Controlling
    (a) Preferences that participation in each of the other value processes be made available to the extent necessary to protect enlightenment, and that monopoly of knowledge and information in any form, governmental or private, be kept as limited as possible
    (b) Preferences for affording individuals special assistance to overcome any unique or particular disadvantages, biological or cultural
    (c) Preferences for freedom to acquire and employ appropriate language to foster the widest possible participation (receiving and imparting) in the enlightenment process[35]

F. Preferences relating to strategies
  1. Singly
    (a) Preferences for freedom of communication and expression in small group settings
    (b) Preferences for freedom of access to and employment of mass communication to reach wide audiences
    (c) Preferences for freedom in assembling appropriate resources for enhancing individual enlightenment and for contributing to aggregate enlightenment
    (d) Preferences for freedom to resort to the military instrument, under conditions of genuine necessity, to preserve information and knowledge vital to the common interest of the larger community
  2. In combination—preferences for freedom from coerced deprivation and disclosure of enlightenment

IV. Preferences relating to well-being

A. Preferences relating to outcomes
  1. Preferences for an optimum aggregate in the shaping and sharing of well-being[36]

---

35. *See* chapter 13 *infra.*

36. *See* Caldwell, *Well-Being: Its Place among Human Rights,* in TOWARD WORLD ORDER AND HUMAN DIGNITY, *supra* note 28, at 169–97. *See generally also* A. CHASE, THE BIOLOGICAL IMPERATIVES: HEALTH, POLITICS, AND HUMAN SURVIVAL (1971); K. DAVIS, NATIONAL HEALTH INSURANCE: BENEFITS, COSTS, AND CONSEQUENCES 1–30 (1975); THE HEALTH OF AMERICANS (B. Jones ed. 1970); K. JONES, L. SHAINBERG, & C. BYER, A CHANGING CONCEPT

2. Preferences for fullest protection of the sanctity of life
3. Preferences for affording individuals opportunities to enjoy a fundamental share in safety, health, and comfort, maintaining a level of somatic and psychological functioning that gives expression to their greatest potentials as human beings
4. Preferences for affording individuals the widest possible range of additional choices in relation to body form, organs, sex, offspring, and so on
5. Preferences for enabling individuals to progress toward an optimum fulfillment of somatic and psychological potentials and expression through life
6. Preferences for freedom to depart life when the decision is based upon an informed, insightful, and mature choice[37]

B. Preferences relating to participation
   1. Preferences for the widest participation in the realization of bodily and mental health and development
   2. Preferences for freedom of the individual from restrictions upon the enjoyment of well-being for reasons irrelevant to capabilities and contributions
   3. Preferences for the utmost defense of group survival and development (the eradication of genocide)

C. Preferences relating to perspectives
   1. Preferences for opportunities and freedom for the individual to acquire the demand for life and its fullest development
   2. Preferences for opportunities for the individual to achieve a positive identification of the self with life
   3. Preferences for opportunities for the individual to develop realistic matter-of-fact expectations about the conditions of well-being and of threats and dangers to well-being

---

OF HEALTH (1972); E. KENNEDY, IN CRITICAL CONDITION (1972); C. LEWIS, R. FEIN, & D. MECHANIC, A RIGHT TO HEALTH: THE PROBLEM OF ACCESS TO PRIMARY MEDICAL CARE (1976); V. LOWENFELD & W. BRITAIN, CREATIVE AND MENTAL GROWTH (4th ed. 1964); R. STEVENS & R. STEVENS, WELFARE MEDICINE IN AMERICA (1974), especially at 1–56; ETHICS AND HEALTH POLICY (R. Veatch & R. Branson eds. 1976); WORLD HEALTH ORGANIZATION, HEALTH ASPECTS OF HUMAN RIGHTS (1976); Bracht, *Health Care: The Largest Human Service System,* 19 SOC. WORK 532 (1974); Ritvo, McKinney, & Chatterjee, *Health Care as a Human Right,* 10 CASE W. RES. J. INT'L L. 323 (1978).

37. *See* EUTHANASIA AND THE RIGHT TO DIE: THE CASE FOR VOLUNTARY EUTHANASIA (A. Downing ed. 1970); GROUP FOR THE ADVANCEMENT OF PSYCHIATRY, THE RIGHT TO DIE: DECISION AND DECISION MAKERS (1974); E. KLUGE, THE PRACTICE OF DEATH (1975); J. KRISHNAMURTI, THE FIRST AND LAST FREEDOM (1954); M. MANNES, LAST RIGHTS (1974); N. ST. JOHN-STEVAS, LIFE, DEATH AND THE LAW (1964); G. WILLIAMS, THE SANCTITY OF LIFE AND THE CRIMINAL LAW 248–350 (1957); Kutner, *Due Process of Euthanasia: The Living Will, A Proposal,* 44 IND. L.J. 539 (1969); Morris, *Voluntary Euthanasia,* 45 WASH. L. REV. 239 (1970).

D. Preferences relating to situations
  1. Geographical—preferences for the maintenance of a physical environment that is conducive not merely to survival, but to optimum human development[38]
  2. Institutions specialized to well-being
     (a) Preferences for the establishment and maintenance of adequate institutions specialized to well-being (hospitals, recreational facilities, etc.)
     (b) Preferences for freedom of access to institutions specialized to well-being, without discrimination for reasons irrelevant to capabilities and irrespective of wealth position
  3. Institutions not specialized to well-being—preferences for freedom of access to institutions not specialized to well-being when necessary to the protection of well-being
  4. Crisis—preferences for the effective safeguarding of life during crises; preferences for minimization of armed conflict and for conformity to the criteria of humanity when armed conflict occurs

E. Preferences relating to base values
  1. Authoritative—preferences that the processes of authoritative decision (including an effective network of constitutive, regulatory, supervisory, and enterprisory codes) be made available and adequate to defend and fulfill well-being (in medicine, in environment, in product liability, in insurance, in housing, and so on)
  2. Controlling
     (a) Preferences that participation in value processes other than well-being be made available to defend and fulfill well-being
     (b) Preferences for affording special assistance to individuals in special need (*e.g.*, because of physical or mental handicap, economic position, ignorance, indoctrination, or irrational beliefs)
     (c) Preferences for the employment of pertinent science and technology in the continuing improvement of well-being

---

38. *See* McDougal & Schneider, *The Protection of the Environment and World Public Order: Some Recent Developments,* 45 MISS. L.J. 1085 (1974). *See also* ENVIRONMENT AND SOCIETY IN TRANSITION (P. Albertson & M. Barnett eds. 1971) (Annals of the New York Academy of Sciences, Vol. 184); R. CARSON, SILENT SPRING (1962); P. EHRLICH & A. EHRLICH, POPULATION, RESOURCES, ENVIRONMENT (1970); R. FALK, THIS ENDANGERED PLANET (1971); THE ENVIRONMENTAL CRISIS: MAN'S STRUGGLE TO LIVE WITH HIMSELF (H. Helfrich ed. 1970); WORLD ECO-CRISIS: INTERNATIONAL ORGANIZATIONS IN RESPONSE (D. Kay & E. Skolnikoff eds. 1972); R. MCKENZIE, ON HUMAN ECOLOGY (A. Hawley ed. 1968); H. SPROUT & M. SPROUT, TOWARD A POLITICS OF THE PLANET EARTH (1971); B. WARD & R. DUBOS, ONLY ONE EARTH: THE CARE AND MAINTENANCE OF A SMALL PLANET (1972); WORLD HEALTH ORGANIZATION, HEALTH HAZARDS OF THE HUMAN ENVIRONMENT (1972).

F. Preferences relating to strategies
   1. Preferences for the employment of appropriate strategies in relation to health for prevention, deterrence, restoration, rehabilitation, and reconstruction:[39]
      (a) Prevention: preferences for the prevention (through inoculation, immunization, safety regulations, sterilization, and so on) of disease, injury, handicap, and unwanted births
      (b) Deterrence: preferences for appropriate measures to control epidemics, physical hazards, and nuisances
      (c) Restoration: preferences for prompt and effective treatment of the diseased, the injured, and the handicapped
      (d) Rehabilitation: preferences for appropriate measures and facilities to enable the deviant (*e.g.*, the alcoholic or drug addict) to reshape constructive participation in social process
      (e) Reconstruction: preferences for affording individuals opportunities to rebuild personal health and for consolidating and improving both general environment and medical care and facilities
   2. Preferences for freedom from coercive strategies
   3. Preferences for freedom to accept or reject medical service when the decision is based upon an informed, mature choice
   4. Preferences for freedom to accept or reject organ transplant and repair when the decision is based upon an informed, mature choice[40]
   5. Preferences for freedom to employ appropriate measures in birth control and to facilitate effective family planning[41]
   6. Preferences for freedom to employ genetic engineering (*e.g.*, artificial insemination, incubation outside the body, choice of psychophysical pattern)[42]

---

39. For articulation of these objectives in the context of criminal law, *see* R. Arens & H. Lasswell, In Defense of Public Order: The Emerging Field of Sanction Law, especially at 199–203 (1961).

40. *See* A. Watson, Legal Transplants: An Approach to Comparative Law (1974).

41. *See* D. Callahan, Abortion: Law, Choice and Morality (1970); R. Gardner, Abortion: The Personal Dilemma (1972); D. Granfield, The Abortion Decision (1969); Family Planning (J. Medawar & D. Pyke eds. 1971); The Morality of Abortion: Legal and Historical Perspectives (J. Noonan ed. 1970); Advances in Voluntary Sterilization: Proceedings of the Second International Conference, Geneva, 1973 (M. Schima, et al., eds. 1974); United Nations, Dep't of Economic and Social Affairs, Social Welfare and Family Planning, U.N. Doc. ST/ESA/27 (1976); Kutner, *Due Process of Abortion,* 53 Minn. L. Rev. 1 (1968); G. Williams, *supra* note 37, at 146–247.

42. *See* Protection of Human Rights in the Light of Scientific and Technological Progress in Biology and Medicine: Proceedings of 8th CIOMS Round Table Conference, Geneva, November 1973 (S. Btesh ed. 1974); A. Etzioni, Genetic Fix: The Next Technological Revolution (1973); J. Fletcher, The Ethics of Genetic Con-

V. Preferences relating to wealth

A. Preferences relating to outcomes
   1. Preferences for the maintenance of high levels of productivity in a rising standard of living, that is, for a productivity in goods and services that will reinforce optimum levels in the shaping and sharing of values other than wealth
   2. Preferences for establishing for all individuals a fundamental share of benefits from the wealth process, through such measures as guaranteed income, social security, and other strategies designed to abolish poverty[43]
   3. Preferences for the enjoyment by the individual of additional benefits on the basis of contribution to the common interest
B. Preferences relating to participation
   1. Preferences for general participation in the shaping and sharing of wealth, through adequate opportunities to work, to invest, to employ resources, to enjoy goods and services, and so on
   2. Preferences for freedom from restrictions and discriminations irrelevant to capabilities for contribution in the shaping and sharing of wealth
   3. Preferences for freedom of association in group shaping and sharing of wealth
C. Preferences relating to perspectives
   1. Preferences for freedom of individuals to acquire (or reject) demands upon the self (or by others) to participate in the wealth process
   2. Preferences for the maintenance of an appropriate balance be-

---

TROL: ENDING REPRODUCTIVE ROULETTE (1974); P. RAMSEY, FABRICATED MAN: THE ETHICS OF GENETIC CONTROL (1970); P. RAMSEY, THE ETHICS OF FETAL RESEARCH (1975); GENETICS AND THE FUTURE OF MAN (J. Roslansky ed. 1966); U.S. DEP'T OF HEALTH, EDUCATION AND WELFARE, PROTECTION OF HUMAN SUBJECTS: FETUSES, PREGNANT WOMEN, AND IN VITRO FERTILIZATION (1975); E. VILAR, THE MANIPULATED MAN (1972); READINGS ON ETHICAL AND SOCIAL ISSUES IN BIOMEDICINE (R. Wertz ed. 1973); G. WILLIAMS, *supra* note 37, at 112–45; WORLD HEALTH ORGANIZATION, HEALTH ASPECTS OF HUMAN RIGHTS, WITH SPECIAL REFERENCE TO DEVELOPMENTS IN BIOLOGY AND MEDICINE (1976).

43. *See generally* THE CRISIS IN SOCIAL SECURITY: PROBLEMS AND PROSPECTS (M. Boskin ed. 1977); STUDIES IN THE ECONOMICS OF INCOME MAINTENANCE (O. Eckstein ed. 1967); W. FRIEDLANDER, INTRODUCTION TO SOCIAL WELFARE (1955); H. GIRVETZ, THE EVOLUTION OF LIBERALISM (rev. ed. 1963); M. HARRINGTON, THE OTHER AMERICA: POVERTY IN THE UNITED STATES (1962); F. HIRSCH, SOCIAL LIMITS TO GROWTH (1976); J. HUBER & W. FORM, INCOME AND IDEOLOGY: AN ANALYSIS OF THE AMERICAN POLITICAL FORMULA (1973); J. MORGAN, et al., INCOME AND WELFARE IN THE UNITED STATES (1962); A. MUNNELL, THE FUTURE OF SOCIAL SECURITY (1977); G. MYRDAL, BEYOND THE WELFARE STATE (1963); ECONOMIC JUSTICE: SELECTED READINGS (E. Phelps comp. 1973); C. SCHOTTLAND, THE SOCIAL SECURITY PROGRAM IN THE UNITED STATES (2d ed. 1970); THE GUARANTEED INCOME: NEXT STEP IN ECONOMIC EVOLUTION? (R. Theobald ed. 1966); R. TITMUSS, INCOME DISTRIBUTION AND SOCIAL CHANGE: A STUDY IN CRITICISM (1962).

tween inclusive and exclusive identification in the shaping and sharing of wealth

3. Preferences for fostering realistic knowledge about the conditions affecting the shaping and sharing of wealth, individual and aggregate

D. Preferences relating to situations
   1. Institutions specialized to wealth
      (a) Preferences for freedom to initiate and constitute institutions specialized to wealth
      (b) Preferences for freedom of access to institutions specialized to wealth
   2. Institutions not specialized to wealth—preferences for freedom of access to institutions which, though not specialized to wealth, vitally affect participation in the wealth process
   3. Crises—preferences for freedom from deprivations of wealth disproportionate to crises and for the equitable sharing of the costs and burdens precipitated by crises

E. Preferences relating to base values
   1. Authoritative
      (a) Preferences that the process of authoritative decision be kept available to defend and fulfill claims to wealth as to other values
      (b) Preferences for an appropriate protection of the employment of resources in the wealth process, with minimization of the arbitrary taking of wealth from individuals and groups[44]
      (c) Preferences for the continuing individual accumulation of assets in ways that are compatible with the common interest
   2. Controlling
      (a) Preferences that participation in each of the other value processes be available to support wealth demands
      (b) Preferences for affording individuals special assistance to overcome handicaps in participation in the wealth process
      (c) Preferences for freedom to accumulate and employ resources for productive purposes and for freedom from wasteful use of resources
      (d) Preferences that resources be made open for use and development in the common interest

---

44. In addition to the references indicated in chapter 14 *infra,* at note 13, *see* B. ACKERMAN, PRIVATE PROPERTY AND THE CONSTITUTION (1977); G. DIETZE, IN DEFENSE OF PROPERTY (1963); Michelman, *Property, Utility, and Fairness: Comments on the Ethical Foundations of "Just Compensation" Law,* 80 HARV. L. REV. 1165 (1967); Sax, *Takings and the Police Power,* 74 YALE L.J. 36 (1964); Sax, *Takings, Private Property and Public Rights,* 81 YALE L.J. 149 (1971).

F. Preferences relating to strategies
   1. Preferences for freedom to employ all relevant strategies, with emphasis on innovation, in production, conservation, distribution, and consumption of wealth
   2. Preferences for freedom from coercive strategies, including freedom from enforced work, enforced production, and enforced consumption
   3. Preferences for freedom from discriminatory strategies in all features of the wealth process
   4. Preferences for freedom from capricious and arbitrary management

VI. Preferences relating to skill

A. Preferences relating to outcome
   1. Preferences for achievement of aggregate levels in acquisition and exercise of skills that promote optimum human potentials in the shaping and sharing of all values
   2. Preferences for acquisition by individuals of a fundamental share in skills relevant to effective participation in all value processes
   3. Preferences for additional acquisition of skills in accordance with talent and motivation

B. Preferences relating to participation
   1. Preferences for unrestricted opportunity to acquire and exercise socially acceptable skills
   2. Preferences for opportunities for the individual to have latent talent discovered
   3. Preferences for opportunity to acquire and exercise skill without discrimination

C. Preferences relating to perspectives—preferences for freedom for individuals to acquire a demand for, and capability of, excellence in skill expression

D. Preferences relating to situations
   1. Institutions specialized to skill
      (a) Preferences for freedom to initiate and maintain institutions specialized to skill
      (b) Preferences for freedom of access to institutions specialized to skill
   2. Institutions not specialized to skill—preferences for freedom of access to institutions not specialized to skill which condition skill acquisition and exercise
   3. Crisis—preferences that opportunities to acquire and exercise skills not be disproportionately denied because of crises

E. Preferences relating to base values
   1. Authoritative—preferences that the process of authoritative deci-

sion be available to defend and fulfill participation in the acquisition and exercise of skill

2. Controlling
   (a) Preferences that participation in each of the other value processes be made available to the extent necessary to protect the acquisition and exercise of skill
   (b) Preferences for special assistance to overcome limitations inhibiting acquisition and exercise

F. Preferences relating to strategies
   1. Preferences for affording exposure to training with a content appropriate to a culture of science and technology
   2. Preferences for exposure to strategies in training relevant to creative contributions to a culture of science and technology

VII. Preferences relating to affection

A. Preferences relating to outcomes
   1. Preferences for ample opportunities for the optimum shaping and sharing of positive sentiments and loyalty, maintaining high levels of congenial personal relations and appropriate loyalties to all groups, functional and territorial
   2. Preferences for all individuals to achieve a fundamental share of affection as human beings; preferences for the basic acceptance necessary for individuals to acquire the character and motivations to function effectively in shaping and sharing values
   3. Preferences for additional affection in accordance with capabilities and contributions

B. Preferences relating to participation
   1. Preferences for fostering the freely giving and receiving of affection on a voluntary, spontaneous basis[45]
   2. Preferences for freedom from restrictions irrelevant to capabilities
   3. Preferences for freedom to give and receive loyalty to groups of one's choice

C. Preferences relating to perspectives
   1. Preferences for freedom to acquire (or reject) a demand to participate in the affection process; preferences for fostering a demand for creativity and sensibility in personal relationships
   2. Preferences for fostering the broadest possible identifications with all groups, functional and territorial, including collective loyalty to humankind

---

45. *Cf.* Nagan, *Conflict of Laws—Group Discrimination and the Freedom to Marry: A Policy Science Prologue to Human Rights Decisions,* 21 How. L.J. 1 (1978).

3. Preferences for encouraging cultivation of realistic expectations about conditions under which congenial personal relationships can be established and maintained

D. Preferences relating to situations
  1. Institutions specialized to affection
     (a) Preferences for freedom to initiate and form intimate and congenial personal relationships
     (b) Preferences for freedom of access to institutions specialized to affection by virtue of adoption, legitimacy, choice of spouse, and so on
     (c) Preferences for recognition of membership in specialized groups
  2. Institutions not specialized to affection—preferences for freedom of access to institutions not specialized to affection in order to make voluntarism in the affection process a reality
  3. Crisis—preferences that affection not be denied in a manner disproportionate to a crisis

E. Preferences relating to base values
  1. Authoritative—preferences that the process of authoritative decision be made available to defend and facilitate affection demand
  2. Controlling
     (a) Preferences that participation in each of the other value processes be made available to defend and facilitate affection demand
     (b) Preferences for affording appropriate environments and appropriate agencies for guidance and assistance in overcoming handicaps

F. Preferences relating to strategies
  1. Preferences for freedom in the employment of persuasive strategies in the cultivation of positive sentiments and loyalty
  2. Preferences for freedom from coercive strategies, especially freedom from coercion or fraud in the formation, suspension, and dissolution of affection units[46]
  3. Preferences for freedom from discriminatory strategies

---

46. *See generally* A MODERN INTRODUCTION TO THE FAMILY (N. Bell & E. Vogel eds. 1968); J. BERNARD, THE FUTURE OF MARRIAGE (1972); HANDBOOK OF MARRIAGE AND THE FAMILY (H. Christensen ed. 1964); R. EISLER, DISSOLUTION: NO-FAULT DIVORCE, MARRIAGE, AND THE FUTURE OF WOMEN (1977); J. GOLDSTEIN & J. KATZ, THE FAMILY AND THE LAW (1965); W. GOODE, AFTER DIVORCE (1956); W. GOODE, WORLD REVOLUTION AND FAMILY PATTERNS (1963); FAMILY AND MARRIAGE (J. Mogey ed. 1962); M. RHEINSTEIN, MARRIAGE STABILITY, DIVORCE, AND THE LAW (1972); INTIMACY, FAMILY, AND SOCIETY (A. Skolnick & J. Skolnick eds. 1974); R. WINCH, MATE-SELECTION: A STUDY OF COMPLEMENTARY NEEDS (1958).

VIII. Preferences relating to rectitude

A. Preferences relating to outcomes
   1. Preferences for the maintenance of public and civic order in which individuals demand of themselves and others that they act responsibly for the common interest
   2. Preferences for ample opportunity for individuals to receive positive evaluation of rectitude, facilitating the freedom to choose a fundamental orientation toward the world
   3. Preferences for movement toward a fuller participation of all individuals in responsible conduct

B. Preferences relating to participation
   1. Preferences for freedom to participate in the formulation and application of standards, religious and secular, of responsibility, especially freedom of religious inquiry, belief, and communication
   2. Preferences for freedom from discrimination in the formulation and application of norms of responsible conduct[47]
   3. Preferences for freedom of association for rectitude purposes

C. Preferences relating to perspectives
   1. Preferences for freedom to acquire a demand on the self to act responsibly
   2. Preferences for freedom to search for, and choose among, justifications of responsible conduct (secular and religious, transempirical and empirical, etc.)

D. Preferences relating to situations
   1. Institutions specialized to rectitude
      (a) Preferences for freedom to initiate and form institutions specialized to rectitude
      (b) Preferences for freedom of access to institutions specialized to rectitude
   2. Institutions not specialized to rectitude—preferences for freedom of access to institutions not specialized to rectitude when such institutions condition the enjoyment of rectitude
   3. Crisis—preferences that rectitude not be denied disproportionately to crisis

E. Preferences relating to base values
   1. Authoritative—preferences that the processes of authoritative decision be made available to defend and facilitate freedom of choice in rectitude, to promote the fullest participation in rectitude, and to ensure conformity of rectitude norms and conduct to standards of human dignity

---

47. *See* chapter 11 *infra* and pertinent references therein.

2. Controlling
   (a) Preferences that participation in each of the other value processes (i.e., access to effective power) be made available to defend and facilitate freedom of choice in rectitude
   (b) Preferences for providing special assistance to overcome limitations in the shaping and sharing of rectitude

F. Preferences relating to strategies
   1. Preferences for freedom to employ all relevant strategies in the pursuit of rectitude
   2. Preferences for freedom from coercive strategies, especially freedom from imposition of state religion or from deprivation of religious worship
   3. Preferences for freedom from discriminatory strategies

POSTULATED GOAL VALUES IN CONSTITUTIVE PROCESS

The constitutive decisions of any community, global or lesser, are those which establish and maintain its most comprehensive process of authoritative decision: the decisions which identify the authoritative decision makers, project the basic community policies which are to be sought, establish appropriate structures of authority, allocate bases of power for sanctioning purposes, authorize procedures for the making of decisions, and secure the performance of all the different types of decision functions (intelligence, promotion, prescription, invocation, application, termination, appraisal) necessary to the making and administering of general community policy. It is these decisions which determine the freedom, security, and abundance of a community's public order, including the degree to which human rights are promoted and protected or deprived, in all the community's different value processes.[48]

The principal concern of the contemporary human rights movement in relation to constitutive process has, unfortunately, been with either too generalized a concept of "implementation" or too narrow a focus upon isolated techniques designed to protect various particular rights. Any rational effort to improve implementation would, of course, extend to comprehensive inquiry about the whole global constitutive process of authoritative decision, considering in detail how participation, the specification of goals, the establishment of structures, the allocation of bases of power, the performance of procedures, and the role of decision functions might be changed for the better promotion and securing of demanded rights. The point we would emphasize is, however, more fundamental: it is that a human rights dimension is present, not merely

---

48. Amplification of these concepts is offered in Lasswell & McDougal, *Criteria for a Theory about Law*, 44 S. CAL. L. REV. 362 (1971).

in the flow of decisions emerging from constitutive process for the protection of individual rights in all the various value processes, but also in decisions about the shaping and functioning of every feature of constitutive process. The most realistic effort to promote a better implementation of human rights must, accordingly, recommend policies appropriate to decisions about every phase of constitutive process for both the global community and its component lesser communities.

The literatures of political thought, jurisprudence, and international law offer a vast reservoir of policies relating to every phase of constitutive process potentially appropriate for the better reflection and securing of human rights.[49] In the outline that follows we present a highly impressionistic itemization, which we are in the process of developing in more detail elsewhere, of some of these inherited policies.[50] The suggestion we make is that the quality of all decision functions, and hence of the overall protection of human rights, might be greatly improved if both scholars and decision makers made explicit their own more comprehensive conceptions of this order.

Preferred Policies Relating to World Constitutive Process

The aspiration should be to achieve a constitutive process which both reflects and is effective in securing basic human dignity values. The different features of constitutive process require shaping in such a way as to establish and maintain a wide sharing of power and an appropriate production and distribution of other values. When basic human dignity goals are clarified, many varying institutional practices may be accepted in appropriate implementation of such goals. For purposes of illustration, a number of possible policies are noted with respect to each major feature of constitutive process.

PARTICIPATION IN DECISION MAKING

The overriding policy is that of universality: all who are affected by, or who can affect, authoritative decisions should, or should be made to, participate in the making of such decisions.

The complementary subgoals of this basic policy are representativeness and responsibility.

Representativeness The wide sharing of power requires both pluralism and equality.

---

49. For a brief survey of some of these policies, with references to an immense literature, *see* Lasswell & McDougal, *Trends in Theories about Law: Comprehensiveness in Conceptions of Constitutive Process,* 41 Geo. Wash. L. Rev. 1 (1972).

50. These principles were formulated in discussions which included Professor Michael Reisman and are being developed in more detail in a collaborative study with him.

All individuals and groups who are affected by decisions should be represented in such decisions, both functionally and territorially.

Participation in decision should be upon the basis of equality in interest, without discriminations irrelevant to merit and contribution and without minorities being authorized to make policies for the whole.

The individual human being should be accepted as an important participant in transnational processes of authoritative decision.

Responsibility All who can affect authoritative decision should be held accountable for responsible participation in accordance with their capabilities.

Participation may be withheld or limited in terms of capabilities and willingness to bear the burdens of shared decision.

PERSPECTIVES

The constitutive perspectives appropriate to a public order of human dignity should be directed toward the clarification and protection of common interests (significantly affecting all) and the rejection of claims of special interests (destructive of common interests).

Common interests include:

- Inclusive interests (significantly affecting more than one participant)
  - Minimum order (the prevention of unauthorized violence and coercion)
  - Optimum order (the maximum possible shaping and sharing of all values)
- Exclusive interests (predominant effects upon one participant)
  - Internal minimum order
  - Internal optimum order

The perspectives which establish the more detailed content of common interests may be described in terms of demands, identifications, and expectations.

Demands The relevant demands of community members extend to all the basic human dignity values whatever the preferred forms in categorization.

It should be observed that community members demand different values with differing degrees of intensity, and account should be taken of these differing intensities in demand. A "bill of rights" or *jus cogens,* comparable to that enjoyed in the more mature national communities, should be recognized and clarified on the global level.[51]

51. *See* chapter 4 *supra*.

Identification The identifications of established decision makers, as of community members, should be encouraged to extend to the larger community of humankind and all its component communities. For the better clarification and integration of the common interest, an appropriate balance should be sought for decision makers in terms of culture, class, group membership, and personality.

Expectations Established decision makers, again like community members, should explicitly examine their expectations, or matter-of-fact assumptions, about the conditions under which demanded values can be secured. The most realistic orientation in context requires unceasing effort to improve structures and procedures for inquiry and communication.

ARENAS

Relevant policies relate to both establishment and access.

Establishment

The creation and maintenance of authoritative structures appropriate to optimum decision may be sought in terms of certain features.

1. Institutionalization: Structures of authority should be made adequate but not over-bureaucratized, and should be balanced between those organized and unorganized and those specialized and not specialized to particular functions.
2. Geographic range: Structures of authority should be balanced between those centralized and decentralized, and integrated in a way to take into account the range and intensity of impacts within different areas.
3. Timeliness: Structures of authority should be continuous rather than sporadic, so as to facilitate timeliness in decision.
4. Responsiveness to crisis: Structures of authority should be alert and appropriately anticipatory of crises.

Access

1. Openness: Structures of authority, transnational as well as national, should be open to all individuals and governmental and private groups whose interests are affected.

   Aggrieved individuals or groups should be allowed to represent themselves and to be represented by others (including institutionalized, governmental representatives) in a wide range of structures of authority.
2. Compulsoriness: Compulsory third-party decision should be ex-

panded in matters relating to human rights as to other problems in transnational arenas.

Appropriate invocation and application should be made to run against recalcitrant parties, state and other.

BASES OF POWER

The promotion of a public order of human dignity requires a pluralistic distribution of both authority and effective control.

Authority

1. The rule of law should be extended to all interactions. There should be no honoring of "political questions." The general community should not recognize a competence in any particular community to protect special interests, destructive of the common interest.
2. The general community should determine the allocation between inclusive competence ("international concern") and exclusive competence ("domestic jurisdiction"). All aspects of human rights should be recognized as of international concern.
3. Inclusive decision makers should be accorded the competence necessary to protect inclusive interests.
4. Exclusive decision makers should be accorded the competence necessary to protect exclusive interests.
5. Conflicts between inclusive and exclusive competence, and different exercises of exclusive competence, should be resolved by a disciplined, systematic examination of the features of the context that affect interest.

Control The controlling bases of power should be allocated so as to make authority effective. A presumption should be indulged in favor of a pluralistic distribution of all values, with an appropriate balancing between different territorial communities and between functional and territorial groups.

STRATEGIES

Policies of human dignity will seek an appropriate integration of all strategies (diplomatic, ideological, economic, military), with a strong emphasis upon persuasion rather than coercion. Coercion will be authorized only as necessary and proportionate for securing public order. Procedures will be preferred which respect human dignity in detail—with no unnecessary violence, invasions of privacy, or other value deprivations. Similarly, priority will be given to procedures which are open, not covert or secret, and which have a maximum effect upon enlightenment, with an empathetic ceremonialization of the community values at stake.

Some of the policies relevant to the sequence of activities or procedures common to most types of decisions may be indicated as follows:

1. Initiation of decision process: The initiation of any of the decision functions should be prompt, nonprovocative, and fair, and should be coordinated, insofar as possible, with other related functions.
2. Exploration of potential facts and policies: The exploration of potential facts and potential community policies should, employing the best available scientific procedures, be made dependable, contextual, selective, and creative.
3. Characterization of facts and policies: The final characterization of facts and policies in prescriptive or applicative decision should be made deliberate, rational, and nonprovocative, employing contextual analysis in characterization of alternative choices.
4. Communication: The communication of the shared subjectivities indispensable to legal process should be made effective and persuasive.
5. Implementation: Measures designed to secure conformity to community prescriptions should be effective and ameliorative, emphasizing persuasive rather than coercive enforcement, through effective mobilization of a wide range of available measures.

OUTCOMES

The culminating outcomes of constitutive process include both certain aggregate consequences for public order and a continuous flow of particular types of decisions affecting public order.

Aggregate Consequences The design of a public order of human dignity should be to establish a constitutive process which will culminate in outcomes having the following characteristics:

1. Rationality: The particular decisions emerging from constitutive process should in fact integrate and secure common interests in the goal values of human dignity. Appropriate account should be taken of both short-term and long-term goals and all important community identifications.
2. Efficiency: The process should be maintained as economically as

possible in its expenditure of participants' resources in relation to goals.

3. Inclusivity: The decision outcomes should be made to embrace all participants and interactions affecting public order and should be applied equally, without discriminations irrelevant to merit and contribution.
4. Comprehensiveness and integration: The process should employ all the necessary types of decisions, appropriately integrated, in the degree necessary to secure the demanded public order.

Particular Functions (Types of Decisions) The more important policies in relation to each type of decision may be conveniently specified as follows:

1. The intelligence function (gathering, processing, and dissemination of information essential to decision making)[52]
   (a) Dependability: Information essential to decision making should be dependable in terms of content, sources, competence of analysis, and transmission.
   (b) Comprehensiveness: The flow of communications that reaches the groups or individuals who shape the world decision process should achieve inclusiveness in terms of goals, trends (both positive and negative), conditioning factors, future projections, and policy alternatives.
   (c) Selectivity: Available information should be related to perceived problems, and priorities should be indicated when a problem is imminent and important according to the values at stake.
   (d) Timeliness: Whatever information is needed for rational decision should promptly be made available whenever it is needed to whomsoever needs it.
   (e) Creativity: Efforts should be made to cultivate diversity of approach to planning problems and to institutionalize the challenging of assumptions. New and realistic objectives and strategies should be compared with older or less realistic alternatives.

52. *See* McDougal, Lasswell, & Reisman, *The Intelligence Function and World Public Order*, 46 TEMPLE L.Q. 365 (1973); Lasswell, *Research in Policy Analysis: The Intelligence and Appraisal Functions*, in 6 HANDBOOK OF POLITICAL SCIENCE 1 (F. Greenstein & N. Polsby eds. 1975).

(f) Availability (openness): The gathering and dissemination of information relevant to decision should be made open, thereby mobilizing the demand by participants for information pertinent to both immediate and long-range problems.

2. The promotional function (taking initiatives and mobilizing opinion toward particular policies)

(a) Rationality: Promotional activities should bring proposals and justifications to the focus of attention of decision makers, with sufficient fullness to permit judgments of priority and relation to be made.

(b) Integrativeness: Uncertainties and conflicts stemming from competing promotional activities should be resolved by programs that mobilize general support and represent truly integrative solutions in which there are no clear perceptions of winners or losers.

(c) Comprehensiveness: All participants in the social process should be activated with sufficient frequency to facilitate the formation of programs that reflect the full range of community interests.

(d) Effectiveness: Promotional activities should mobilize informed and outspoken judgment promptly enough to nullify propensities for endorsement of programs that, if adopted, would prove destructive. In addition, promotional activities should reach and mobilize the latent demands of groups perceiving themselves as weak and neglected.

3. The prescribing function (establishing certain policies as authoritative and controlling for community)

(a) Effectiveness: An appropriate balance should be sought in expectations about stability and change and about uniformity and relevant differentiation. Prescriptions for which there is general demand, and which are likely to continue to receive support, should be enacted promptly.

(b) Rationality: Prescriptions should be formulated to give effect to common rather than special interests and to afford a balanced protection of inclusive and exclusive interests.

(c) Inclusiveness (comprehensiveness) and prospectiveness: Prescriptions should anticipate and provide for all interactions that significantly affect common interests. Retroactivity should be indulged most sparingly.

4. The invoking function (provisional characterization of particular events in terms of community prescriptions)

(a) Timeliness: Aggrieved persons or groups should be enabled to undertake timely complaints for remedy against alleged deprivations. The lag between precipitating events, complaints, and initial action should be minimized.

(b) Dependability: Efforts should be made to ensure that a provisional characterization of facts is dependable and that discrepancies between characterization and reality are minimized.

(c) Rationality: Initiation of action should be made responsive to the common interest under circumstances in harmony with the contingencies referred to in relevant prescriptions.

(d) Nonprovocativeness: Initiatives should impose no more deprivations than are required.

(e) Effectiveness: Initiatives should be made successful in stimulating application to remedy alleged deprivations.

5. The applying function (final characterization of particular events in terms of community prescriptions and the management of sanctioning measures to secure enforcement)

   (a) Rationality and realism: The applying function should be guided by the common interest as formulated in prescriptions and supplemented by public order conceptions; application should be not merely plausibly derived, but contextually grounded in the facts of community interaction.

   (b) Uniformity: Prescriptions should be applied equally to all in equal circumstances. Application should be contextual, unbiased, independent of special interests, and free from discriminatory deprivations. Third-party participants should be mobilized to neutralize special interests.

   (c) Effectiveness: Prescriptions should be put into controlling practice. When several steps and agencies are involved, efforts should be made to supervise and review performance and to rectify nonconformity.

   (d) Constructiveness: The net effect of application should contribute to prescriptions, by mobilizing consensus toward the policies of a public order of human dignity.

6. The terminating function (putting an end to prescriptions and arrangements effected under them)

   (a) Timeliness: Obsolete prescriptions and interests should be dealt with promptly, generating the expectation that change can be facilitated in ways compatible with human dignity.

(b) Comprehensiveness and dependability: The exploration of facts and policies in connection with termination should be both comprehensive and dependable.

(c) Balance: Proper balance should be maintained between expediting and inhibiting change, and in characterization of facts and policies relevant to amelioration or imposed loss.

(d) Ameliorativeness: The destructive impacts of change should be minimized.

7. The appraising function (evaluation of decision process in terms of the policy objectives of the larger community and identification of participants responsible for past successes and failures)[53]

(a) Dependability (realism): The data upon which appraisal is based should be dependable. The explanatory analyses should be relevant and explicit; and the imputations of responsibility should be made explicit.

(b) Contextuality: Appraisal should take into account all relevant factors. Both comprehensiveness and selectivity are especially pertinent to the appraisal of total impact.

(c) Independence: Appraisers should be insulated from immediate pressures of threat or inducement. Internal appraisal should be supplemented by external appraisal.

(d) Continuity: Appraising efforts should be kept essentially continuous. While intermittent appraisals mobilize needed attention and support, the effects are greatest when appraisals are maintained through time.

The Conception of Common Interest

In previous chapters we have noted and documented the existence today of a global community in fact, in the sense of the complete interdetermination of all individual human beings, and their various groups, in the shaping and sharing of all values.[54] The interdependences that affect all contemporary human interaction we have described in two ways: first, in terms of the interdependences of all peoples transnationally within any one value process (such as respect, power, wealth, and so on); and, secondly, in terms of the interdependences of all peoples everywhere between different value processes (power as affecting

---

53. *See* Lasswell, *Research in Policy Analysis, supra* note 52; Lasswell, *Toward Continuing Appraisal of the Impact of Law on Society,* 21 Rutgers L. Rev. 645 (1967); Snyder, Hermann, & Lasswell, *A Global Monitoring System: Appraising the Effects of Government on Human Dignity,* 20 Int'l Studies Q. 221 (1976).

54. *See* chapters 1, 2, and 4 *supra.*

wealth, wealth as affecting power, and so on).[55] The inescapable outcome of this emergence of global interdependence we describe as establishing that the degree to which any particular individual, whatever his location within territorial boundaries or institutional practices, can achieve demanded values is a function of the degree to which other individuals, very differently located about the globe, can secure and maintain a corresponding enjoyment of their demanded values. One of the most obvious facts about the interactions in contemporary global social process is that all these interactions, whatever their importance or unimportance and however differentially they may affect different individuals or groups, are entirely collective or inclusive in their impacts upon subsequent interactions.

From the perspective of an anthropological observer, it is possible, further, to note that all individual human beings, whatever their territorial or functional groupings and whatever the rationality of their own perspectives, share certain common interests in the quality of the functioning of this contemporary, all-embracing, global social process as it affects the shaping and sharing of all values. By an "interest" we refer to a pattern of demands for values plus the supporting expectations about the conditions under which these demands can be fulfilled. Interests that are *common* may, in an ancient tradition, be described as those which relate in empirical reference to activities with inclusive impacts, express demands compatible with human dignity, and are supported by realistic expectations of interdetermination, as demonstrated in reciprocal tolerance and mutual accommodation. Interests may, in contrast, be described as *special* when, though relating to activities having inclusive impacts, they are destructive of common interests, as defined above, in the sense that the demands asserted are incompatible with human dignity values and the expectations entertained do not include reciprocity and mutual accommodation. It needs to be added that the common interests, manifested and sought to be protected in global public order, exhibit many differing degrees, in fact a whole continuum, of inclusivity in impact of activities, from all-embracing to relatively exclusive. It is, hence, convenient, for the clarification of policy and decision, to dichotomize common interests into two categories: *inclusive* interests and *exclusive* interests. Inclusive interests may be described as embodying demands compatible with human dignity and supported by expectations about the conditions of achievement which involve a high degree of impact upon a number of participants in global social process. Exclusive interests may be described as embodying demands for values compatible with human dignity and supported by expectations involving a predom-

55. *See* chapter 1 *supra,* at notes 117–59 and accompanying text.

inant degree of impact upon a single participant in the world social process, unaccompanied by high levels of inclusive impact.

The implication of these different conceptions of interest, for observers who define human rights comprehensively as being at stake in all interaction and decision, is of course that all individuals everywhere, whatever the differences in the institutional practices by which they seek values and however different their expectations about the conditions of fulfillment, share certain common interests, both inclusive and exclusive, in the clarification, defense, and fulfillment of human rights. These common interests, inclusive and exclusive, of all individuals may be observed to extend to certain aspects both of minimum public order and of optimum public order. By "minimum public order" we refer to an authoritatively protected social process which, in accordance with the human dignity preference for persuasion over coercion, aspires to minimize the occurrence of unauthorized coercion and violence. By "optimum public order" we refer to an authoritatively protected social process which aspires to maximize the shaping and sharing of all human dignity values.

The inclusive interests in human rights of all individuals, whoever they may be and wherever located, relating to minimum public order emphasize the close interrelationship, if not identity, of human rights and peace.[56] The task of maintaining minimum order, interpreted as freedom from both the fact and the threat of severe deprivations by unauthorized coercion and violence, has long been perceived as one of the most important, difficult, and frustrating problems confronting the world community. We have already noted that any realistic hope of movement toward minimum public order in this sense must be dependent upon maintenance of widespread expectations among individuals that the processes of authoritative and effective decision, global and local, will be responsive to their demands for a reasonable access to all the values commonly characterized as those of human dignity or of a free society.[57]

The technological revolution currently under way immensely en-

---

56. *See* McDougal & Leighton, *The Rights of Man in the World Community: Constitutional Illusions versus Rational Action,* 14 Law & Contemp. Prob. 490 (1949), *reprinted in* M. McDougal & Associates, *supra* note 10, at 335–403; Toth, *Human Rights and World Peace,* in 1 René Cassin, Amicorum Discipulorumque Liber 362 (Institut International des Droits de l'Homme ed. 1969). *Cf.* B. Moore, *supra* note 12.

57. The complementarity of fundamental policy extends so far as to contrapose the human rights prescriptions in the United Nations Charter with the proscription of the use or threat of use of force in international relations. *See* McDougal, *Foreword,* in J. Moore, Law and the Indo-China War vii–xiv (1972).

hances the difficulties of minimum public order and underscores its interrelations with human rights. The recent penetration into outer space has vastly extended the arena of potential interaction, human and perhaps other, and has resulted in the development of new instruments of violence, enormously aggravating the threats to minimum order and the obstacles in the path of creating appropriate techniques for security. Similarly, the development of new sources of energy—nuclear and other—promises sensational transformations in all social interaction, constructive and destructive. These new social forces now being released can only strengthen or weaken the demands, expectations, and institutional arrangements associated with human rights.

The inclusive interests in human rights of individuals relating to optimum public order make reference to position, potential, and expectation in the shaping and sharing of all human dignity values. It needs no elaborate documentation that the individual human being requires access to all values for fullest personal development and constructive contribution to his groups and communities; and the unmistakable lesson of the comprehensive interdependences, observable on the global or earth-space level, is that the access and constructive contribution that any particular individual can achieve is in the long run, ineluctably, a function of the access and constructive contribution that other individuals can achieve. What we have described as a global social process is but a vast cooperative enterprise by individuals, and their groups, for the creation of values, in which the share of any particular individual is dependent upon both the total creation of values and the modalities of sharing.[58]

The exclusive interests in human rights of individuals are those that pertain uniquely to the different groups, territorial and functional, that individuals employ in the shaping and sharing of values. Our concern for exclusive interests stems, not primarily from assessment of political expediency, but rather from recognition that individuals require a great diversity of territorial and functional groups for the free, abundant, and economic creation of values. To pursue human dignity as an orienting goal is to search for ways of conducting human affairs that sustain the widest possible freedom of choice, including the freedom to establish and maintain associations and groups. Many matters may concern a few individuals to a degree that motivates them actively to engage, through associations and groupings, in constructive enterprise. The problem is to

58. For a more comprehensive itemization of the principal features of an inclusive process in the shaping and sharing of particular values, *see* M. McDougal, H. Lasswell, & I. Vlasic, *supra* note 6, at 151–54.

preserve and foster such initiatives, in a public order of diversity and experimentation, for expression in ways that are compatible with the aggregate common interest.

Exclusive interests relating to minimum public order concern the security of the particular group or association against the fact and threat of unauthorized coercion and violence, external or internal (self-defense most broadly conceived). In view of the indisputable fact that the arena of world politics is still largely military, and that community-wide organization cannot be relied upon to provide timely and efficacious aid to the victims of impermissible coercion, it remains necessary to recognize that particular groups, territorial and functional, continue to have interests in measures of self-help that may upon occasion derogate from inclusive interests in human rights.[59]

The exclusive interests in human rights of individuals described in terms of optimum public order refer to opportunities for the greatest protection and widest sharing of values within particular groups or communities. The interdependences, which within the larger community of humankind bind individuals into common fate in the shaping and sharing of values, operate of course even more comprehensively and more intensely in lesser groupings and in the component communities of the larger community. It may require recall, further, that a world public order of human dignity can accommodate many diverse institutional practices or functionally equivalent means in the pursuit of particular values when overriding goals and the common interest are clarified and maintained.[60]

It has already been indicated, and certainly it is a matter of common knowledge, that the global constitutive process through its prescribing function, characteristically operating at many different levels of deliberateness and explicitness, has in response to the rising, cumulative demands of the peoples of the world transformed all these observable common interests into authoritative general community prescription.[61] There has been a vast proliferation of most deliberate and explicit prescriptions, designed both to distinguish between common and special interests by specifying the content of human rights in various value categories and to add general community expectations about authority and control to popular demand. These prescriptions include all those which we have found to constitute the central core of communication in

59. For a more comprehensive itemization of the principal features of an exclusive process in the shaping and sharing of particular values, *see id.* at 154–56.

60. *See* S. Clough, *supra* note 11; M. Olson, The Logic of Collective Action (1965).

61. *See* McDougal & Lasswell, *The Identification and Appraisal of Diverse Systems of Public Order,* 53 Am. J. Int'l L. 1 (1959), *reprinted in* M. McDougal & Associates, *supra* note 9, at 3–41, and in International Law in the Twentieth Century 169 (L. Gross ed. 1969).

a comprehensive global bill of rights, such as the United Nations Charter itself; the Universal Declaration of Human Rights; the Genocide Convention; the International Covenant on Economic, Social and Cultural Rights; and a whole host of other regional and specialized communications of varying purpose and geographic reach. On an equally fundamental level, simultaneously with all this deliberate and relatively explicit communication, the more ineluctable processes of customary prescription, with their less deliberate and less explicit formulations, have been operating through the communications from uniformities in private behavior and official decision and through the countless declarations, resolutions, and recommendations of many different bodies, governmental and nongovernmental, which have become a part of the working expectations of the peoples of the world.[62]

It will not have escaped notice that all these prescriptions, emerging as a bill of rights in global constitutive process and designed to protect the interests of individuals, are, like the broad preferences we formulated above for guiding choices by the criteria of human dignity in the shaping and sharing of values,[63] both entirely complementary in form (in terms of interests protected) and highly abstract or ambiguous in their particular formations. The necessities and potentialities of complementarity are explicitly recognized in many of the human rights prescriptions in the form of requirements, first, of the accommodation of particular rights with other rights and the aggregate common interest, and second, of permissible derogations from some rights in times of high crisis and intense threat to the common interest.[64] The necessities and potentialities of ambiguity, though less explicit, are no less inherent in the high level of abstraction with which all the human rights prescriptions, like most other prescriptions, are formulated. Thus, it may be recalled that the relevant prescriptions abound with such terms as "arbitrary," "fair hearing," "inhuman treatment of punishment," "degrading treatment," "forced or compulsory labor," "slavery or servitude," "privacy," "any obligation required by law," "compelling reasons of national security," "prejudice and interests of justice," "any propaganda for a war," "the equal protection of the law," "the protection of morals," "necessary in a democratic society," "public emergency," "threatens the life of the nation," and so on.

What may require emphasis is that all this complementarity and ambiguity in authoritative prescriptions can be, and often is, as we have sought to outline above, an accurate reflection of a corresponding com-

---

62. *See* chapter 4 *supra.*
63. *See* notes 15–47 *supra* and accompanying text.
64. For detailed elaboration, *see* chapter 16 *infra,* at notes 7–52 and accompanying text.

plementarity and ambiguity in the interests sought to be protected in social process.[65] In a pluralistic society of scarce resources it is inescapable that individuals and groups make competitive, and sometimes incompatible, demands for the same values, and that they sometimes make demands incompatible with human dignity in denial of reciprocity and mutual accommodations. Even in mature national communities, constitutive prescriptions project a wide sharing of values among many participants, through many varied institutional practices, and under conditions which cannot be anticipated in detail. Complementary formulations, framed at many different levels of abstraction, are indispensable both to express the whole range of fundamental demands and expectations and to make tentative identifications of the different factual contexts in which different distributions of values are demanded and expected. The immense flow of prescriptions embodied in the global bill of rights does in fact cover every phase of human interaction and all demanded values—whether categorized in our eight terms or as civil, political, economic, social, and cultural rights[66]—and in many particular instances of interaction such values must be in fact competitive, requiring choices among alternative prescriptions—or alternative interpretations of particular prescriptions—and among the values, or features of value processes, to be protected.

It is of course a historic mission of authoritative decision, that is, of law, to seek the accommodation of the various inclusive and exclusive interests of individuals, with rejection of all claims of special interest, through solutions that are integrative of net advantage by criteria of common interest.[67] The most effective performance of this mission has

---

65. That the complementarity in legal principle is a necessary correspondence to complementarity in social process is documented in McDougal, *The Ethics of Applying Systems of Authority: The Balanced Opposites of a Legal System,* in THE ETHIC OF POWER: THE INTERPLAY OF RELIGION, PHILOSOPHY, AND POLITICS 221 (H. Lasswell & H. Cleveland eds. 1962).

66. It may be noted that the traditional dichotomy between "civil and political rights" and "economic, social, and cultural rights" tends to pay inadequate attention to the interdependences among different rights and values. It becomes preposterous when the former are considered to represent "the Western values" and the latter "the non-Western values."

For divergent views, *see* Fetscher, *Freedom,* in 4 MARXISM, COMMUNISM, AND WESTERN SOCIETY, *supra* note 11, at 22; Pfahlberg & Brunner, *Fundamental Rights,* in *id.* at 55–65.

67. The ancient origin of this goal is indicated in E. HAVELOCK, THE LIBERAL TEMPER IN GREEK POLITICS 277, 390 (1957). A demonstration of necessity for recourse to common interest appears in McDougal & Lans, *Treaties and Congressional-Executive or Presidential Agreements: Interchangeable Instruments of National Policy,* 54 YALE L.J. 181, 534 (1945), *reprinted in* M. MCDOUGAL & ASSOCIATES, STUDIES IN WORLD PUBLIC ORDER 404, 631–34 (1960).

The challenge to create integrative rather than compromise solutions is developed in DYNAMIC ADMINISTRATION: THE COLLECTED PAPERS OF MARY PARKER FOLLETT (H. Metcalf & L. Urwich eds. 1942).

always required, and continues to require, both the careful articulation of symbols of shared demand and common expectation and the employment of all necessary intellectual procedures in a continuing exploration and assessment of potential decision outcomes for identifying those outcomes which promise greatest net advantage.[68] The basic challenge is to make *continual reference of the part to the whole* in a contextual consideration of every particular question in the light of the overriding goals and characteristics of the larger community. Experience suggests that this necessary contextual examination of every particular problem, though perhaps occasionally achievable by flashes of insight, may best be facilitated and assured by the systematic employment of a comprehensive set of principles of inquiry, both of content and procedure: principles of content for spotlighting the relevant features of the particular interaction and its community context; principles of procedure for the rational and economic identification, exploration, and appraisal of possible solutions.[69] In the pages that immediately follow we propose one possible set of such principles for the guidance of authoritative decision makers and other evaluators engaged in the application of general community prescription about human rights in particular instances. It is believed, however, that comparable formulations might serve equally for guidance of the prescribing function and of other decision functions and private choice. Though there may not be, as is often emphasized, any "natural harmony" in the various interests of the different individuals and groups about the globe, it does not follow that individuals and groups, through their authoritative representatives, cannot continuously create and recreate a common interest.

The Accommodation of Interests in Particular Instances

It should be obvious that the application in particular instances of complementary and highly abstract human rights prescriptions can be no automatic process in which the applier merely interprets the literal

---

68. For some development of this theme, *see* Lasswell, *The Public Interest: Proposing Principles of Content and Procedure,* in The Public Interest 54 (C. Friedrich ed. 1962). Helpful insights are found in M. Follett, Creative Experience (1924). *See also* W. Leys & C. Perry, Philosophy and the Public Interest (1959); Bolgar, *The Public Interest: A Jurisprudential and Comparative Overview of the Symposium of Fundamental Concepts of Public Law,* 12 J. Public L. 13 (1963); Lasswell, *supra* note 53; Lasswell, *The Political Science of Science: An Inquiry into the Possible Reconciliation of Mastery and Freedom,* 50 Am. Pol. Sc. Rev. 961 (1956); Lasswell, *The Interplay of Economic, Political and Social Criteria in Legal Policy,* 14 Vand. L. Rev. 451 (1961).

69. *See* M. McDougal, H. Lasswell, & J. Miller, *supra* note 9; McDougal, *supra* note 1; McDougal, *The Application of Constitutive Prescriptions: An Addendum to Justice Cardozo,* 33 The Record of the Association of the Bar of the City of New York 255 (1978) (Thirty-third Annual Benjamin N. Cardozo Lecture).

words of a single text and maintains a putative fidelity to that text.[70] In any particular instance an applier may be confronted with competing claims by different parties about highly complex or obscure facts and is commonly confronted not with a single prescription but with a vast body of allegedly relevant prescriptions. The responsible performance of the application function in such instances may require a whole sequence of activities or choices, including the exploration of the potential facts and their larger context; the exploration of the potential policies apparently relevant to the provisional focus upon the facts; the characterization of the facts and determination of their varying degrees of relevance; the selection from among the potential policies of those to be applied and the detailed relation of these policies to the facts regarded as relevant; and finally, the formulation and projection of the decision, with indication of measures appropriate to securing conformity.[71] For an applier genuinely dedicated to the clarification and implementation of the common interest, the necessities of an informed and rational, yet still personal, choice must stalk every act in this sequence.

The tasks of exploring and clarifying potentially relevant policies within the whole process of application are commonly recognized as especially complex and open-ended.[72] For the purpose of a more detailed examination of these tasks and of considering possible intellectual procedures for their improved performance, it is suggested that these tasks may be somewhat more discriminatingly and precisely categorized in threefold fashion.

1. Ascertaining the community expectations expressed in particular prescriptions: This task requires a genuine effort to achieve the closest possible approximation of the aggregate of effective general community expectations about the content, authority, and control of alleged prescriptive communications. No other goal could be compatible with the conception that authority comes from the members of a community and with demands for the wide sharing of power. The adequate performance of this task requires a disciplined, systematic survey and assessment of all features of the process of communication and its context which may affect expectation. The significance for community expectation of any one feature of a prescriptive process of communica-

70. The allusion is to Sir Gerald Fitzmaurice's eloquent, inspirational plea for fidelity to texts. Fitzmaurice, *Vae Victis or Woe to the Negotiators! Your Treaty or Our "Interpretation" of It?* 65 AM. J. INT'L L. 358 (1971).

71. *See* chapter 4 *supra*. *See also* McDougal, Lasswell, & Reisman, *supra* note 33.

72. This point is extensively documented in M. MCDOUGAL, H. LASSWELL, & J. MILLER, *supra* note 9.

tion is dependent upon its interrelations with all the other features of the process.

2. Supplementing incomplete and ambiguous communications: This task requires the remedying of the inevitable gaps and ambiguities in particular prescriptions by reference to more general, basic community policies about the shaping and sharing of values. In conventional presentations this task is sometimes described in terms of the exercise of "reason" or the invocation of analogies. Its adequate performance demands, however, the disciplined employment of a comprehensive set of procedures, including at least specification of each of the opposing claims about prescription in terms of the interests sought to be protected and the particular demands for authoritative decision; formulation of the different options open to the relevant decision maker or other evaluator, which may be more extensive than the options demanded by the opposing parties; estimation of the consequences of alternative choices among possible options upon the aggregate inclusive interests of the general community and the exclusive interests of the particular parties; and choice of the option which promises to promote the largest aggregate long-term common interest, inclusive and exclusive.
3. Integrating particular expectations with basic community policies: This task requires a decision maker or other evaluator, who recognizes that he is responsible for the total policy of the community which he represents or of which he is a member, to reject even the most explicit, precisely formulated expectations when they are inimical to basic, more intensely demanded community policies. The task is made authoritative with respect to international agreements by the newly formulated constitutive prescription known as *jus cogens.*[73] The considerations which prompted the making of this prescription for international agreements apply, however, no less cogently to the less deliberately formulated prescriptions of customary law. The adequate performance of this task demands procedures comparable to those recommended for supplementing expectations, with explicit specification of the more intensely demanded general community policies and the deliberate rejection of any prescriptive intimations that contravene these policies. Since the emerg-

73. Final Report of the Vienna Convention on the Law of Treaties, *opened for signature* May 23, 1969, Arts. 53, 64, U.N. Doc. A/CONF.39/27, May 22, 1969, *reprinted in* 8 INT'L LEGAL MATERIALS 679 (1969) (this treaty is not yet in force). For detailed discussion of *jus cogens, see* chapter 4 *supra*.

ing human rights prescriptions themselves largely embody our contemporary community's most intensely demanded policies, occasion for the supersession of a human rights prescription can be expected to be infrequent.

The important question now is whether it is possible to identify intellectual strategies or procedures which might be employed to minimize the arbitrariness and increase the rationality of all the various choices which an applier or other evaluator must necessarily make. Some observers find it impossible to specify goals for application, such as we have suggested above, and hence despair of introducing meaning and order into any imaginable principles of application. Other observers, underestimating the difficulties inherent in the problem, prefer to cherish the illusion that they can secure certainty by the undisciplined contemplation of the verbal texts, which, however important, are but one of the instruments of communication.[74] It is our brief that by the systematic and disciplined employment of a number of interrelated intellectual strategies it might be possible both to reduce the arbitrariness and to increase the rationality of application. The more important strategies we might recommend toward this end would include at least the following: (1) the clear establishment of an observational standpoint, in identification with the whole of humankind; (2) the explicit postulation of a comprehensive set of overriding goal values; (3) the specification of more detailed presumptive preferences with respect to all values in community process; (4) the specification of presumptive preferences about each major feature of constitutive process; and (5) the systematic employment of a comprehensive set of principles of content and procedure for the examination and appraisal of all relevant features of a problem in application in its context. What is involved in the first four of these strategies we have already specified in some detail;[75] it remains to indicate what is meant by the fifth.

The probability of maximizing the realization of the goals sought in application might, we suggest, be increased if the various established appliers employed a comprehensive set of principles, both of content and procedure, designed to guide their attention in a systematic manner to all features of the context relevant to the rational performance of the different intellectual tasks required in application. *Principles of content* could guide the choice of subject matter relevant to evaluating the alternatives in policy open to a decision maker; *principles of procedure* could offer agendas and techniques for bringing pertinent content to the focus

74. The varying views are collected in M. McDougal, H. Lasswell, & J. Miller, *supra* note 9, at 6–12.

75. *See* notes 4–53 *supra* and accompanying text.

of a decision maker's attention. The employment of such principles in application would presuppose both the careful maintenance of the observational standpoint of the community representative and continuous reference to perspectives embodying a detailed specification of the goal values of human dignity. These more detailed specifications of human dignity perspectives might include, as we sought to illustrate above, both the more general value preferences for community process as a whole and the more specific features of the constitutive process for which the applier takes responsibility.[76]

The type of principles recommended may be illustrated briefly by reference to both principles of content and principles of procedure.

PRINCIPLES OF CONTENT

The most general principle, that of contextuality, is that in performing the tasks of application, preference should be given to alternatives that have been considered and evaluated in the larger context of the processes of prescription, claim, and application and of the factors affecting such processes.

Principles Relating to the Prescribing Process

ASCERTAINING THE PRESCRIPTION

Develop principles which refer to every feature of the process of prescription, indicating the presumptive relevance of such features for shared expectations about the content, authority, and control of alleged prescriptions.

Give preference to the expectations shared by communicators and communicatees during the whole process of prescription insofar as these are compatible with the goal values of human dignity.

SUPPLEMENTING EXPECTATIONS

Observe the expectations created by prescriptive communications for gaps, ambiguities, and contradictions.

Remedy any inadequacies in prescriptive communications by reference to the postulated goal values of human dignity (both public order and constitutive).

INTEGRATING EXPECTATIONS

Observe any priorities in intensities of demand among different prescriptions and ascertain whether any alleged prescriptive communications contradict the postulated basic goal values of human dignity.

---

76. *See* notes 15–53 *supra* and accompanying text.

Give effect to ascertained priorities in intensity in demand and remove any contradictions by reference to the postulated basic goal values of human dignity.

Principles Relating to the Process of Claim

Construct principles which categorize the different types of controversies in terms of the values affected.[77]

In performing interpreting, supplementing, and integrating tasks, note the relation of different types of factual contexts to different basic community policies.

Principles Relating to the Process of Decision

Employ principles which canvass every feature of the process of decision for its potential relevance to recommended outcomes and policy effects.[78]

PRINCIPLES OF PROCEDURE

The Contextual Principle

Employ procedures appropriately calculated to bring all relevant context to the focus of attention in the order best adapted to exhibiting relevance. In appraisal of claims and in performance of all intellectual tasks, give priority to procedures which fully and systematically take the larger context into account. Avoid a fragmented approach which rigidly fixes upon a few features of the context. Although continuously engaging in evaluation, suspend final judgment until examination of the whole of the relevant context.

The Principle of Economy

Adjust the time and facilities devoted to application to the importance of the values at stake in the controversy and to community policies.

The Principle of Manifest (Provisional) Focus

For a provisional focus begin with the manifest, articulated demands of the parties themselves. For each party note the claims made about the facts (value processes affected and sought to be protected), about relevant prescriptions and other policies, and about appropriate decisions and measures in application.

77. For a comprehensive set of claims about human rights, *see* chapter 3 *supra*.

78. The principles recommended here would be comparable to those outlined in M. McDougal, H. Lasswell, & J. Miller, *supra* note 9, at 61.

On claims by states to derogate from human rights prescriptions because of public emergency, for example, contrapose the assertions of the state about necessity and proportionality with those of the individual (or his representative) about the absence of necessity and proportionality.

The Principle of Clarified Focus

Explore both asserted facts and larger context, independently of the perspectives of the parties, from the standpoint of the disinterested observer. Evaluate the different versions of potential facts and make an independent characterization. Note the whole of the potentially relevant prescriptions and the range of potential choices in decision.

With respect to claims about derogation, for example, make a systematic, disciplined examination of all features of the context of alleged crisis and of proposed (or actual) measures in derogation to achieve an independent assessment of necessity and proportionality. It does not suffice, as sometimes suggested, to regard these questions as matters of "fact," about which, in general, nothing that is useful may be said.[79]

The Principle of Observing Trends in Past Experience

Observe the successes and failures, in terms of approximations to general community policies, that have previously been achieved on comparable problems by invocation of the varying alternative prescriptions and by alternatives among the options in application.[80]

The Principle of Realistic Orientation in Factors Affecting Decision

Observe the factors in predisposition and environment that appear to have affected past applications.

Appraise the probabilities of these and other factors affecting future decisions on comparable problems.

The Principle of Observing the Constraints of Future Probabilities

Construct alternative future probabilities in decision and decision impact.

Estimate the relative costs and benefits, in terms of general community values, of the various alternatives in decision.

Calculate the probable net costs and net benefits of each option.

---

79. J. Fawcett, The Application of the European Convention on Human Rights 249 (1969), commenting on the *Lawless* case.

80. The traditional doctrine of "precedent," emphasized by so many commentators, obviously builds upon the wisdom of making the best possible use of past experience, as well as upon metaphysical notions of "binding." Past decisions alone, however, may not be adequate guides to rational future decisions.

The Principle of Evaluating and Inventing Options in Decision

Relate all options to basic general community policies and choose the option that will promote the largest net aggregate of common interest.

It is not our suggestion that any intellectual strategies, however systematically developed and carefully refined, can enable an applier to dispense with a final creative choice in the relation of human rights prescriptions, any more than of other prescriptions, to particular instances of human interaction. The necessities for such choice are inherent in the materials with which an applier must work, and the making of such a choice is his unique community responsibility. What we do suggest is that the employment of some such strategies as we have recommended, appropriately developed and elaborated, might enable an applier better to know what options are open to him and more rationally to relate his choice among such options to the fundamental general community perspectives which today infuse the human rights prescriptions. Appropriate principles of content, making reference to all the various processes of interaction, could assist by insuring the systematic examination of all the relevant features of the context in performance of the necessary intellectual tasks of specifying policies, noting degrees of achievement in past decisions, determining conditioning factors, estimating probable future developments and impacts, and appraising the costs and benefits of different options in decision. Appropriate principles of procedure, designed to make an economic use of all resources at the applier's disposal, could assist by bringing this "content" information to a central focus of attention in which every significant detail of the context is appraisable in relation to all other such details, thus affording the applier maximum opportunity for making rational choices. For appliers genuinely dedicated to the common interest, the two kinds of principles, employed in appropriate combination, might serve to minimize the arbitrariness of choice and to establish a comprehensive and coherent frame of reference for the more effective relation of particular choices in application to the overriding goal values of an increasingly universal public order of human dignity.

The degree to which this recommended mode of clarifying basic community policies builds upon the other intellectual tasks—the description of past trends, the analysis of conditioning factors, the projection of future developments, and invention and evaluation of alternatives in decision[81]—requires that we make a brief indication of the significance of each of these tasks.

---

81. For a brief summation of these intellectual tasks, *see* chapter 1 *supra,* at notes 226–27 and accompanying text. For an exposition of these tasks in the context of political de-

THE SIGNIFICANCE OF PAST TRENDS

It is basic to any realistic clarification of policies in relation to human rights that all provisional formulations of the desirable be subjected to the discipline of the possible. A first dimension of this task of estimating the possible is an examination of past trends in degrees of achievement in relation both to any particular problem and to aggregate success or failure. We need to know whence we came, where we stand now, and in what direction we are moving, if we are to have any rational hope of transforming our aspirations of the present into the facts of the future.[82]

The upsurge of common demands for the effective realization of human rights in public and civic orders, outlined in detail above,[83] is a relatively recent feature of global history. There is little difficulty in establishing the trends, however fluctuating, in the Western European or the world picture of the last two hundred years. When we look further back and undertake to penetrate to the masses of society, the situation is murky in the extreme. Through history the most numerous strata of the population were born and went to their deaths without leaving written records of their demands or expectations or identities. The literate priests or officials who sometimes reported the externalities of the lives of the poor occasionally recorded the popular songs and the folk wisdom of the anonymous many. The critical historian is far from certain that the haphazard residues of popular culture are dependable samples of the whole. Possibly they are erratic selections by idiosyncratic monks and scribes.

Historians are well aware of the probable existence at different times and places of huge reservoirs of latent discontent which broke cover and erupted from time to time in peasant revolts or urban mobs. Difficulties of interpretation persist because of the speed with which order was usually restored and the disaffected populace reverted to its customary acquiescence.

When the inquiry is pushed more deeply in a quest for causal connections, uncertainties multiply. In the absence of satisfactory information it

---

velopment and change, *see* POLITICAL DEVELOPMENT AND CHANGE: A POLICY APPROACH (G. Brewer & R. Brunner eds. 1975) (containing ample references).

82. For a very wise and incisive discussion of the relevance of past trends to future decision, *see* E. CARR, THE NEW SOCIETY (1957). *See also* C. BLACK, THE DYNAMICS OF MODERNIZATION: A STUDY IN COMPARATIVE HISTORY (1967); E. HYAMS, SOIL AND CIVILIZATION (1976); THE PHILOSOPHY OF HISTORY IN OUR TIME (H. Meyerhoff ed. 1959); J. MONTGOMERY, TECHNOLOGY AND CIVIC LIFE (1974); H. MULLER, THE USES OF THE PAST (1952); J. PLUMB, DEATH OF THE PAST (1970); THE HISTORIAN AS DETECTIVE: ESSAYS ON EVIDENCE (R. Winks ed. 1970); Deutsch, *Towards an Inventory of Basic Trends and Patterns in Comparative International Politics,* 54 AM. POL. SC. REV. 34 (1960).

83. *See* chapter 1 *supra.*

is difficult to account for the varying expressions of demand for human rights and for the ensuing failure of the public or civic order to take the steps required to give effect to demands.

The changing trends and conditions relevant to human rights are evidently connected with the culture of cities.[84] Although the past is in process of rediscovery and the story is in flux, there are grounds for asserting that urban civilizations came into existence about six thousand years ago in the valleys of the Nile, the Indus, and the Tigris–Euphrates.

Can we infer the predispositions of the leaders and the led of the early city-based empires by analyzing the characteristics of the tribes, and especially the isolated tribesmen, of today? Evidently the internal structure of folk societies was rich in contrasting detail. The fundamental tribal device for determining the position of the individual was (and is) kinship. The consequences of kinship for the shaping and sharing of values vary drastically among tribes and within tribal societies. In any case the conception of an "individual" with rights derived from some other source than kinship was a long-run consequence of the new urban environment, where the territorial state became the dominant selective factor.

The new urban environment greatly modified the traditional role of kinship without recognizing the human rights of the individual. The most prominent characteristic of urban culture was a complex division of labor which differentiated many new skills from one another and greatly increased production, exchange investment, and consumption levels. In large part the increased production was appropriated by the territorial state and empire. It was devoted to military operations and monumental public works. Great differences of wealth and income separated the social groups from one another; and these differences were crystallized and maintained by law.

Although it is convenient to distinguish the "predispositions" with which individuals or groups enter a given "environment," it is obvious on reflection that the predisposing factors continue through time and interact with significant features of the environment. The resulting adjustments are the "responses" which become interactive components of the social process as they emerge. Is it feasible to describe the significant features of the social process that elicited eventual demands for human rights? And to account for obstacles in the path of effective change?

---

84. *See* V. Childe, Man Makes Himself (1951); The Study of Urbanization (P. Hauser & L. Schnore eds. 1965); L. Mumford, The City in History: Its Origins, Its Transformations, and Its Prospects (1961); L. Mumford, The Culture of Cities (1938); L. Strauss, The City and Man (1964); A. Toynbee, Cities on the Move (1970).

For a monumental study of the history of the development of cities by region and by country, *see* E. Gutkind, International History of City Development (1964–72) (8 vols.).

Clues are to be found in the complicated set of factors that, taken together, confer distinctiveness on city culture. Since cities emerged, they have been the dynamic innovators in history. The record of civilization has become, in increasing degree, the history of competition and conflict between civilizations and surviving tribes, and among civilizations based on different regions and continents. One consequence of these competitive and conflicting relationships has been a gradual and irregular process of universalizing group demands for the rights of their members. In terms of human rights the culmination has been the modern conjoining of aspiration with faltering yet substantial levels of attainment.

The interdependence of the inhabitants of a particular urban environment is obvious enough, whether it is a question of traffic, water, garbage or more subtle matters. Intercity interdependence depends for instance on the position of the urban aggregates in the arenas of war, diplomacy, propaganda, and trade. Internal and external shifts in the power-balancing process generate coalitions of varying size and composition. If the ruling elite is divided among clashing factions and individuals, the contending elements reach out to middle and lower strata in search of support. But an expanded coalition is not necessarily permanent. An older faction may seize effective control once more and restore the temporarily suspended curbs on freedom of access to equal opportunity. Once abandoned, however, customary arrangements are not likely to be permanently restored, and the factors that favor more general participation in the shaping and sharing of values continue to affect what happens.

The significant interplay among coalitions is not restricted to intracity affairs. The competing and conflicting leaders of cities and empires seek to divide the ruling class of opposing states and to drive a wedge between rulers and ruled. The result is not necessarily to bring the masses into a permanently enlarged sphere of political and social participation. True, elite elements may struggle against one another. And yet, if the lower social formations step beyond their traditional limits, elite factions may join to protect the tacit prescriptions that keep the "great game of politics" as an elite privilege.

Despite the self-perpetuation proclivities of every system that protects the predominance of a few, the trend of much modern history has been to multiply the relative numbers of those who seek permanent equality of opportunity and who join in active, if erratic, coalitions on behalf of institutional changes that harmonize with popular demand.[85]

Many components of the urban complex have continued to grow in strength and to widen and intensify zones of interaction. Among these

---

85. *See* chapters 6 to 15 *infra* and pertinent references therein.

components we take cognizance of the changing social relations connected, for instance, with the expansion of commerce, industry, money and credit, transportation, communication, sanitation and medicare, elementary and advanced education, and scientific and technological research. Interacting with these changes has been "the respect revolution," which has cumulatively extended to the common man the patterns of self-confidence that were the traditional prerogatives of monarchs, feudal lords, high ecclesiastics, wealthy merchants, and famous physicians.[86] The division of labor in urban society has originated new skill differentiations to take the place of older modes of production. Human beings are becoming "upgraded" as a productive resource; and this carries with it greater bargaining power and self-esteem among the middle and lower classes.

Among the more crippling ideological legacies of a class- and rank-bound society has been the conception of justice as impartiality of *treatment within a group,* as distinguished from effective protection and opportunity *as a human being.* The older perspectives of justice were genuine protectors of equality among the individual members of a given class or rank. At the same time they discouraged interclass assertiveness and on the whole tended to turn classes into castes.[87]

The analyst of social inequality cannot fail to perceive the strength of factors that condition an individual or a group to contribute to social inequality as soon as he attains even a slight advantage. In a changing world community we are provided with innumerable exemplifications of the fundamental importance of *the proclivity to turn an advantage into a special interest* and to nullify or ignore, where possible, a common interest. The "proclivity toward the assertion of special interest" permeates the world of big organization, whether it is a question of officials or civic bureaucracy. The alleged "iron law of oligarchy" was first exemplified in detail by an analyst of socialist parties and trade unions. More recently, the study of developing (industrializing) countries has disclosed the same phenomenon on a formidable scale.[88] After an early phase of change in

86. *See* chapter 6 *infra.*

87. For a brief summary of varying perspectives of "justice," *see* Cahn, *Justice,* in 8 Int'l Encyc. Soc. Sc. 341 (D. Sills ed. 1968).

88. *See generally* The Politics of the Developing Areas (G. Almond & J. Coleman eds. 1960); D. Apter, Politics of Modernization (1965); Crises and Sequences in Political Development (L. Binder & L. Cindor eds. 1971); C. Black, The Dynamics of Modernization (1966); Nation-Building (K. Deutsch & W. Foltz eds. 1963); E. Eisenstadt, Modernization: Protest and Change (1966); G. Hunter, Modernizing Peasant Societies: A Comparative Study in Asia and Africa (1969); S. Huntington, Political Order in Changing Societies (1968); A. Inkeles & D. Smith, Becoming Modern: Individual Change in Six Developing Countries (1974); Bureaucracy and Political Development (2d ed. J. LaPalombara ed. 1967); Political Parties and Poli-

which "import substitution" creates a new upper and middle class of merchants, industrialists, bankers and (perhaps) trade union leaders, party managers, bureaucrats, and professionals (in science, education, medicine, for example), the motivation for more comprehensive social reconstruction is enfeebled. Society retains a structure of ineffective lower strata.

The proclivity to turn an advantage into a special interest is a result of *the apparent short-range benefits available in a situation.* It is obvious that workers who have a job at a given pay scale are apprehensive that the unemployed or lower-paid workers will undercut their advantage, or prevent a successful campaign to raise wages and improve working conditions. The small businessman who operates at a narrow margin is aware of the cost pressure from efforts to unionize the market. And so on through every group and individual in society. At any given time it is possible to discover the net value expectations of any participant and to understand why he is disposed to put a specific advantage first and to view conceptions of the common interest as applicable to somebody else.

The wonder is not that special interests are asserted and protected, but that demands and expectations relating to the longer-term or to multivalued common interest are ever effective. That perceived common interests do at times elicit joint action among the various categories of participants in society cannot be successfully denied. The "iron law of oligarchy" rusts, and new competitive businesses, unions, political parties, churches, and so on push aside the old monopolists and bring about a stable new set of effective changes. In a world of scientifically based technological change, all kinds of established interests are vulnerable. They reach out to other groups and individuals and enlarge their conceptions of interest to form and maintain successful coalitions. Every ideological affirmation of a common interest—such as the demand for international human rights—has a group of supporters who can be enlisted as coalition mates on behalf of prescriptive or other joint policy demands. Every short-range recrystallization of a new special interest remains vulnerable to assault in the name of prescriptions of the common interest. In the interdependent urbanizing globe, the continual reclustering of conditioning factors has had the net effect of moving the world community toward articulating and attaining the principles of a

---

TICAL DEVELOPMENT (J. LaPalombara & M. Weiner eds. 1966); D. LERNER, THE PASSING OF TRADITIONAL SOCIETY (1958); M. LEVY, MODERNIZATION AND THE STRUCTURE OF SOCIETIES (1966); M. LEVY, MODERNIZATION: LATECOMERS AND SURVIVORS (1972); COMMUNICATION AND POLITICAL DEVELOPMENT (L. Pye ed. 1963); POLITICAL CULTURE AND POLITICAL DEVELOPMENT (L. Pye & S. Verba eds. 1965); D. RUSTOW, A WORLD OF NATIONS: PROBLEMS OF POLITICAL MODERNIZATION (1967); MODERNIZATION: THE DYNAMICS OF GROWTH (M. Weiner ed. 1966).

respect revolution in the name of human dignity and an international public and civic order of human rights.

THE ANALYSIS OF FACTORS CONDITIONING TRENDS

By making somewhat more explicit the study of the conditions that affect the fulfillment or deprivation of human rights, one can feed back to the clarification of goals, enhance a deeper understanding of past trends, and prepare the way for the projection of probable futures and evaluation of policy options. An observer who is able to consider the factors, or constellations of factors, that sustain the pursuit of common rather than of special interests, may find it possible to examine future contingencies with a more realistic perception of the alternatives open to facilitate the optimum shaping and sharing of values.[89]

When one takes seriously the scientific task of inquiry into variables that condition trends in social process, one begins with the maximization postulate. It is possible to build upon this postulate to account for the rise or fall of systems of public order, including the degree of fulfillment or deprivation of human rights. In commonsense experience everyone is well acquainted with partial versions of the postulate. If we try to explain why consumers search for the lowest price for goods of the same quality, the obvious point to make is that they expect to be better off by paying low rather than high prices. In an ongoing process of interaction, actors participate selectively in what takes place. Most fundamentally, their selection of what activities to undertake is guided, consciously and unconsciously, by expectations about net advantage.

The maximization postulate thus asserts that people adopt one response rather than another when they expect to be better off in terms of all their values by adopting the response chosen. The postulate draws attention to the actor's own perception of alternative acts open to him in a given situation. If he considers himself as hungry, his tendency is to perceive the environment (social and physical) in terms of opportunities for food and to reach for objects that have been satisfactory in the past. Similarly, the postulate suggests that a world public order of human dignity has not yet been expected, especially by many powerful elites, to yield a more advantageous value position, potential, and expectancy for them than is yielded by more parochial and closed systems of public order. It also suggests that where effective steps have actually been taken

---

89. Concerning the scientific task of analyzing conditioning factors, *see* A. Kaplan, The Conduct of Inquiry (1964); T. Kuhn, The Structure of Scientific Revolutions (1962); E. Nagel, The Structure of Science: Problems in the Logic of Scientific Explanation (1961).

toward greater protection and fulfillment of human rights, those who have taken such steps have expected to be better off thereby.

For systematic exploration of the conditions that affect the fulfillment or deprivation of human rights, it is convenient to categorize relevant factors in terms of both predispositional and environmental variables. By predispositional variables we refer to the more fundamental demands, identifications, and expectations of the peoples of the world. By environmental variables we refer to resources (natural and technological) and to the features of the different value processes that compose the global social process. Both these two sets of variables are in constant interplay.

We note, first, the significance of predispositional variables. In a world characterized by ideological division and stark contrasts in development, many of the demands of peoples, as nurtured in differing parochial communities, tend to express special interests rather than common interests. Unable to clarify and agree upon common interests, some peoples tend to be preoccupied with short-term, immediate payoffs rather than long-term, aggregate consequences. The rising common demands of most of the peoples about the world for a wide shaping and sharing of all values, documented in detail above, would appear to be the most important variable affecting the future. As the respect revolution continues to accelerate, the demands for protection of access to all important value shaping and sharing can be expected to become more insistent. These universalizing demands for participation in the value processes making for a dignified human existence will affect all effective power decisions.

In connection with identification we note that every "ego" becomes a "self" as it is incorporated into society; that is, each individual perceives himself as "one of" or "not one of" various human groupings, functional and territorial. In the first known bands of early man there were apparently no very clear lines of demarcation between "kindred" bands and strangers. Given the struggle among both human and proto-human groupings, group members were early conditioned to incorporate the parochial syndrome. Individuals merged the primary ego with the collective identity of the kinship group, and incorporated the demand upon the self to sacrifice for, and with, the family. In a world characterized by the expectation of violence in intergroup affairs—especially among strangers—the parochial syndrome was an instrument of survival.[90] We have already taken note of the profound transformation in human soci-

---

90. *See* Lasswell, *Introduction: Universality versus Parochialism,* in M. McDougal & F. Feliciano, *supra* note 9, at xix–xxvi.

ety with the advent of cities.[91] The ties of an individual with a family or tribal group were weakened for the benefit of the systems of public order of civilized states. The transition was eased by identifications with ruling dynasties; such personifications of authority, however, were not indispensable, since "republics" could supersede personal rule. In recent times the "nation-state" has been the principal symbol around which collective identifications have been organized. In an era in which "nationalism" continues to run high, nation-states, new and old, compete to exact loyalties from their own nationals, and national identities have gained such primacy as often to stifle or impede the growth of more inclusive identities, especially those associated with common humanity.[92] This parochialism has contributed in no small measure to the further fragmentation of an already divided world.

Despite the continuing manifestations of the parochial syndrome in the contemporary world, the potentialities for forging and sustaining more inclusive identifications are strengthening. The accelerating tempo of global interaction, with the growing frequency of transfrontier movement, is making more real the increasing identifications with a universal vision of humanity. Physical mobility, as accentuated by modern means of communication and transportation, not merely allows a person to change his physical location, but affords him opportunity to change his "place" in the world through a continuing process of identifying with a multiplicity of human groupings, simultaneously or successively.[93] As interdependences, global and regional, deepen, people take one another into account more seriously and are linked to one another, in varying degrees and manner, through a complex network of territorial and functional organizations. Sharing common sets of identifying symbols in an intricate matrix of interaction and interdependence af-

---

91. *See* note 84 *supra* and accompanying text.

92. *See generally* IDEOLOGY AND DISCONTENT (D. Apter ed. 1964); G. BARCLAY, 20TH CENTURY NATIONALISM (1971); A. COBBAN, THE NATION-STATE AND NATIONAL SELF-DETERMINATION (1969); K. DEUTSCH, NATIONALISM AND ITS ALTERNATIVES (1969); K. DEUTSCH, NATIONALISM AND SOCIAL COMMUNICATION (2d ed. 1966); R. EMERSON, FROM EMPIRE TO NATION: THE RISE TO SELF-ASSERTION OF ASIAN AND AFRICAN PEOPLES (1960); L. FALLERS, THE SOCIAL ANTHROPOLOGY OF THE NATION STATE (1974); C. HAYES, ESSAYS ON NATIONALSIM (1926); F. HINSLEY, NATIONALISM AND THE INTERNATIONAL SYSTEM (1973); E. KEDOURIE, NATIONALISM (rev. ed. 1961); H. KOHN, THE IDEA OF NATIONALISM (1948); H. KOHN, NATIONALISM, ITS MEANING AND HISTORY (rev. ed. 1965); B. SHAFER, NATIONALISM: MYTH AND REALITY (1955); A. SMITH, THEORIES OF NATIONALISM (1972); L. SNYDER, THE NEW NATIONALISM (1968); L. SNYDER, VARIETIES OF NATIONALISM: A COMPARATIVE STUDY (1976); B. WARD, NATIONALISM AND IDEOLOGY (1966).

93. *See* Lerner, *Social Science: Whence and Whither?* in THE HUMAN MEANING OF THE SOCIAL SCIENCES 13, 15–19 (D. Lerner ed. 1959).

fords new opportunities for larger numbers of people to identify with one another in terms of common humanity and to act together more expeditiously than ever before in common cause.[94]

Turning to the structure of expectations of the peoples of the world, it is clear that peoples exhibit varying degrees of realism about the conditions under which human rights can be protected and fulfilled. They often fail to perceive vividly the fact and the depth of contemporary interdependences and thus fail to explore and grasp common interests. With much realism, expectations of violence remain high. Living under the perpetual threat of a balance of terror, both elites and the rank and file are highly insecure, manifesting a pervasive sense of frustration for inability to abolish armed conflict and other forms of coercion. Many measures that impose deprivations on individuals and groups, and deny them value fulfillment, are maintained, and justified, because of chronic obsession with internal and external disorder.[95]

Fortunately, because of modern education and communication, a sense of realism about the conditions of human dignity would appear to be increasing. As the network of interaction and interdependence expands, as more and more problems have impacts far beyond the frontiers of any single territorial community, it is more and more keenly perceived that common interests must be clarified and implemented. Many of the complex problems vexing humankind today (ranging from racism, through energy, inflation, unemployment, and the brain drain, to arms limitation) have impressed upon effective elites the imperatives of cooperation for mere survival. Such shared perception of common interest is a first vital condition toward better protection and richer fulfillment of human rights.

The environmental variables that constantly interplay with these predispositional factors may be explored in relation to population, resources, and institutions. It may be recalled that our most comprehensive description of social process is in terms of human beings, with varying patterns of demands, identifications, and expectations, employing resources through institutions for maximization of value outcomes.[96]

---

94. *See* Lasswell, *Future Systems of Identity in the World Community,* in 4 The Future of the International Legal Order 1 (C. Black & R. Falk eds. 1972). *See also* Erickson, *Psychological Identity,* 7 Int'l Encyc. Soc. Sc. (1968).

95. *See* R. Barnet, The Roots of War (1972); R. Falk, Legal Order in a Violent World (1968); H. Lasswell, National Security and Individual Freedom (1950); Law and Civil War in the Modern World (J. Moore ed. 1974), especially the article by Reisman, at 252–303; A. Mazrui, A World Federation of Cultures: An African Perspective 191–268 (1976).

96. *See* chapter 2 *supra.*

The relevance of population characteristics to the shaping and sharing of human rights relates to numbers, rates of growth, and distribution in relation to resources.[97] Leaders in all parts of the world are increasingly alarmed by the potentially devastating impact of the uncontrolled growth of numbers on the quality of life. As one of the authors has elsewhere written:

> Uncontrolled population growth is expected to impair the aggregate output of values in every sector of society and to sharpen inequalities of distribution everywhere. An overcrowded world can be expected to swing between extremes of political conflict and massive apathy, and between exaggerated personal hostility and indifference. The control of values such as enlightenment, wealth, skill, and respect will be concentrated in the control of a few. From shortages of food and medicare will rise crises of malnutrition, disease, and defect. As numbers multiply and competition intensifies, human conduct will grow progressively egocentric and socially irresponsible.[98]

The potential impacts of population changes may be specified in terms of the features of different values, as we have suggested in summary form above[99] and as one of the authors has described in detail, value by value:

> In relation to *power,* the relative position of a particular nation-state within the global and regional balancing of power, with varying consequences for internal power positions of individuals identified with different groups;
>
> In relation to *respect,* difficulties in achieving mutual tolerance of freedom of choice and equality in access to participation in different value processes;
>
> In relation to *enlightenment,* demand for, and distribution of, educational opportunities and mass media facilities;
>
> In relation to *well-being,* the quality of community enterprisory facilities and the prevalence of epidemics, disease, and defect;
>
> In relation to *wealth,* access to opportunities for participation in

---

97. *See* chapter 1 *supra,* at notes 90–95 and accompanying text. *See also* W. Rostow, The World Economy: History and Prospect 1–44 (1978); Fox, *Population and World Politics: A Political Science Perspective on "The World's Most Critical Problem,"* 31 J. Int'l Affairs 101 (1977).

98. Lasswell, *Population Change and Policy Sciences: Proposed Workshops on Reciprocal Impact Analysis,* in Policy Sciences and Population 117, 118 (W. Ilchman, et al., eds. 1975).

99. Chapter 1 *supra,* at note 95 and accompanying text.

productive processes, the distribution of income among different individuals and groups, and traditional practices in the production, conservation, investment, and consumption;

In relation to *skill,* access to opportunities for learning and diffusion, and differential levels in distribution;

In relation to *affection,* changes in formation and dissolution of families and other private associations, with effects upon levels of congeniality and loyalty; and

In relation to *rectitude,* difficulties in the development in communication of common standards of responsible conduct.[100]

Fortunately, population problems, like most other problems, are people-made, and can be brought under human control. Though important population choices are private choices as a part of civic order, they can be affected by authoritative decision in the name of the public order.[101]

The important resources that affect degrees in achievement of human rights appear to be diminishing in quantity, to be deteriorating in quality because of mismanagement, and to be increasingly characterized by patterns of uneven distribution, regionally and globally, in relation to population. The energy crisis and the host of problems it exacerbates (*e.g.,* inflation, monetary instability, unbalanced payment, unemployment) emphasize the potential threats of impairment of resources to the enjoyment and fulfillment of all values. Similarly, excessive military expenditures devoted to overkill or oppression and the global ecological crisis dramatize vividly the dangerous consequences of the mismanagement of resources. The problems associated with the uneven distribution of resources in relation to people are exaggerated by the arbitrariness of national boundaries.[102]

The importance of any particular resource is, however, a function of many factors, including the state of technology, available manpower, and efficiency in social organizations. The role of technology is especially crucial.[103] Thus, the technology in weaponry, justified in terms of the

---

100. Lasswell, *supra* note 98, at 131–33.

101. *Id.* at 117.

102. *See* chapter 1 *supra,* at notes 96–108 and accompanying text. *See also* W. Rostow, note 97, *supra. See especially* a series of studies under the auspices of the Club of Rome: D. Meadows, et al., The Limits to Growth (1972); M. Mesarovic & E. Pestel, Mankind at the Turning Point (1974); J. Tinbergen, et al., RIO—Reshaping the International Order (1976).

103. For incisive analyses, *see* F. Braudel, Capitalsim and Material Life 1400–1800 (M. Kochan trans. 1974); J. Ellul, Technological Society (J. Wilkinson trans. 1967). *See also* L. Berkner, The Scientific Age: The Impact of Science on Society (1964); P.

need for self-defense, has made ever more precarious the maintenance of minimum public order in the contemporary world. Yet many constraints upon resources have been, and can be, overcome by advancing technology; the relative importance of a particular resource is often changed or modified as a consequence of changing technology.

A new technology alters an established division of labor; and this sets in motion a complex chain of adjustments in the whole social equilibrium. Whatever the rate of population change, a different technology is capable of bringing profound transformations of the life of a society. A new way of doing things alters the experiences of those who are directly engaged in the innovation, or who hear about it, or are otherwise affected by its consequences. The focus of attention is differently structured as a result of substituting locomotives or turbines for horses, windmills, or waterwheels. The new attention framework brings with it a redefinition of the more enduring perspectives of individuals and groups, so that demands, expectations, and identifications undergo modifications of greater or lesser degree. The structure of the groupings which compose a given community is altered with the rise of urban as against rural-centered activities; and the suppression of nobles and peasants by such elements as merchants, manufacturers, financiers, administrators, scientists, engineers, technicians, semiskilled and unskilled machine tenders. Automation, while enhancing productivity, generates a search for answers to such questions as unemployment, reacquisition or reorientation of skills, and new modalities of enjoying leisure.[104]

Technology has of course been instrumental in making contemporary physical mobility possible. The global and regional networks of communication and transportation (on the land, in the ocean, in the air, and in space) enable people, ideas, goods, and services to move across frontiers more quickly and frequently than ever before. Frequent transfrontier mobility has removed some of the traditional barriers existing

---

Drucker, Technology, Management and Society (1970); V. Ferkiss, Technological Man: The Myth and the Reality (1969); D. Gabor, Innovations: Scientific, Technological and Social (1970); Technology and Social Change (E. Ginzberg ed. 1965); J. Montgomery, Technology and Civic Life: Making and Implementing Development Decisions (1974); H. Muller, The Children of Frankenstein: A Primer on Modern Technology and Human Values (1970); L. Mumford, Technics and Civilization (1964); L. Tribe, Channeling Technology through Law (1973); L. White, Medieval Technology and Social Change (1962).

104. *See generally* Automation and Technological Change (J. Dunlop ed. 1962); G. Friedman, Industrial Society: The Emergence of the Human Problems of Automation (H. Sheppard ed. 1955); A. Jaffe & J. Froomkin, Technology and Jobs: Automation in Perspective (1968); Automation, Alienation, and Anomie (S. Marcson comp. 1970); Technology and Social Change (W. Moore ed. 1972); Automation: Implications for the Future (M. Philipson ed. 1962).

between resources and population and assists in establishing a more efficient and economic relationship between manpower and resources.

The problems arising from the interplay of increasing population and deteriorating resources require consideration also in the light of the institutions peoples establish at different community levels (global, regional, national, and local) for the management of resources in the shaping and sharing of values. These institutional arrangements and practices, in the aggregate, condition the degree to which peoples can maximize their values. It may be recalled that existing institutions, however state-centered and tradition-bound, were created by human beings and can be changed and managed by the peoples of the world to serve their common interest, when the common interest is adequately clarified and perceived.

In a fundamental sense, the outcomes of any particular value process are a function of all the other features of that process; similarly, such outcomes are also conditioned by the outcomes and other features of all the other value processes. Hence, the character and quality of global social process, of effective power process, of world constitutive process of authoritative decision, and of protected public and civic order all operate to condition one another and, thus, the extent, character, and quality of the protection and fulfillment of human rights. For those who aspire to foster the greater protection and fulfillment of human rights, it is, accordingly, possible and necessary to work with every feature of all the relevant processes, at all different community levels. As immense as this task may appear, past changes in man's lot over the millennia would suggest that particular improvements are not beyond human ingenuity, especially when effective elites can be persuaded to see that they have more to gain than to lose by taking appropriate steps.

In examining the complex and shifting constellation of factors that have been involved in moving the world community toward the effective demand for institutions compatible with human dignity, we need not overlook the influential role that many philosophers, jurists, and other symbol specialists have played in the process. The evolution has followed a zigzag course, since one characteristic of the specialized "intellectual" or "professional" is that he or she tends to give expression to the entire range of potential views that can be derived from the changing cultural inheritance of any group whose perspectives are known.

A broad distinction can be drawn between two categories of specialists on the manipulation of symbols (whether doctrine, formula, or miranda[105]). We are aware of this distinction in the tribal societies that

105. "The *political doctrine* is the part of the political myth that formulates basic expectations and demands; the *miranda,* the part consisting of basic symbols of sentiment and identification." H. Lasswell & A. Kaplan, Power and Society 117 (1950).

preceded urban civilization, where the symbol specialists were often called "medicine men." The first category is composed of those who are acquainted with the collection of myths and rites of the tribe; it conducts the ceremonies essential, for instance, to the success of the tribe in war or in obtaining good crops. The second category includes all who in the main are oriented toward serving the individual needs of specific clients, as when treatment is given to overcome illness, infertility, or bad luck on the hunt.

In the great urban centers of antiquity we recognize the broad distinction between the two groups of specialists. Since the invention and use of writing first appeared in connection with urban life, it is easy to recognize equivalents in historic and contemporary tribes (scribes, legal counsellors, tax specialists, scientists, theologians, forecasters, teachers, authors, etc.). We take note of the specialist on public or private affairs while recognizing that the same person may serve both sets of clients.

The connection between symbol specialization and human rights is, as we remarked above, remarkably varied. Of particular importance is the development of a literary and oral tradition of respect for human dignity. True, until recent times the dominant emphasis has been on hierarchical authority and the duty of individuals to adapt themselves to customary slots of obedience. And yet the symbol specialists have had the ability and the courage to question as well as to transmit the prescriptions of the established myth. They have provided the justification for limited or general actions intended to fight discrimination and to bring symbols of group and individual identity from the shadow of indifference or contempt. The vast number of coalitions that have whittled away at traditional barriers have been able to rely upon public or private aid from sympathetic intellectuals. It is no wonder that established authority is chronically apprehensive of what "students" and "poets" and "intellectuals" may do. Such articulate proponents of human dignity are continually altering the language and the meaning of established myth, and gradually changing the boundaries among elite, mid-elite, and mass.

THE PROJECTION OF PROBABLE FUTURE DEVELOPMENTS

The projection of probable future developments, since decision making is inescapably directed toward the future, is a most important task in clarifying policies. To contemplate the future as an aid to thought is to allow the mind to assess possibilities in terms of probable occurrence. By adopting a spectator's stance, as free as possible of the distorting effects of goal commitment, a thinker may be able, by perceiving future contingencies that have been overlooked, to affect fundamental strategy. It is the broad trend, not the particular instance, that is the distinctive subject matter of projective thought. When we consider the future, the pertinent question is about a category of prospective events. The role of projective thinking is to arrive at an estimate of the probability that significant features of a social context will stay the same or change in a stated direction.[106]

A realistic projection of probable future developments cannot be in terms of "inevitability" or of simpleminded extrapolation of the past. The continuation of past events depends upon the total constellation of the many conditioning factors that may support or oppose the direction and the intensity of trend. If one is to arrive at a disciplined estimate of possible futures, it is necessary to estimate the continuing presence or absence, strength or weakness, of these various conditioning factors.

The policy makers of a community, though they can never be completely certain in their estimates about the future, may be able, by appropriate procedures, to discipline their images of possibilities in a way that increases both the realism of their projections and the inventiveness they bring to creating alternatives. One procedure is deliberately to formulate provisional maps or developmental constructs that range through a broad spectrum or continuum of possibilities, from the most optimistic to the most pessimistic. The act of considering such broad alternatives in detail may sharpen the decision makers' judgment for ultimate commitment. Favorable and unfavorable projections may be outlined on the basis of existing knowledge of past trends and conditions and of critical estimates of the interplay between such trends and conditions.[107]

The principal question for us is whether future movement will be toward or away from the practices and institutions of human dignity. The two most comprehensive constructs that might be developed present quite different images of emerging states of global public order. The optimistic construct imagines that progress toward realizing a wider

---

106. In a growing literature on future projections, *see* W. ASHER, PROPHECY AND POLICY: THE PERFORMANCE AND USE OF FORECASTING (1977); D. BELL, THE COMING OF POST-INDUSTRIAL SOCIETY: A VENTURE IN SOCIAL FORECASTING (1973); HAWAII 2000: CONTINUING EXPERIMENT IN ANTICIPATORY DEMOCRACY (G. Chaplin & G. Paige eds. 1973); B. DE JUVENEL, THE ART OF CONJECTURE (1967); WORLD FUTURES: THE GREAT DEBATE (C. Freeman & M. Jahoda eds. 1978); D. GABOR, INVENTING THE FUTURE (1964); O. HELMER, SOCIAL TECHNOLOGY (1964); E. JANTSCH, TECHNOLOGICAL FORECASTING IN PERSPECTIVE (1966); MANKIND 2000 (R. Jungk & J. Galtung eds. 1968); H. KAHN & A. WIENER, THE YEAR 2000 (1967); J. MCHALE, THE FUTURE OF THE FUTURE (1969); *Toward the Year 2000: Work in Progress,* DAEDALUS, Summer 1967.

For an inquiry employing trend, scientific, and developmental thinking of peculiar relevance to the future of human rights, *see* R. HEILBRONER, AN INQUIRY INTO THE HUMAN PROSPECT (1974).

107. For the concept of developmental constructs, *see* H. LASSWELL, WORLD POLITICS AND PERSONAL INSECURITY (1935; 1965); H. LASSWELL, A PRE-VIEW OF POLICY SCIENCES 67–69 (1971). *See also* Eulau, *H. D. Lasswell's Developmental Analysis,* 11 W. POL. Q. 229 (1958).

sharing of power and a greater production and wider sharing of all values in a world public order of human dignity will continue. The pessimistic construct hypothesizes a sequence that moves, with an increasing centralization, concentration, and militarization of power, toward a world public order of garrison-prison states in which a new order of castes is consolidated.[108]

The historical trend away from caste societies will, according to the optimistic construct, continue until a free people's commonwealth is achieved on a global scale. A free commonwealth is characterized by shared participation in both production and enjoyment of all value processes. Our study of human rights has frequently connected the contemporary movement with the expansion of interdependence throughout the global community, a process that for some purposes can be characterized as the invention and spread of urban civilization. Since the sixteenth century—to go no further back—science and technology have accelerated the tempo of change. The acceleration of tempo has increased general awareness of the interests that involve all members of the human race in a common destiny. There are no grounds for believing that science or science-based technology will be abandoned, or that interdependence will cease to be a momentous fact.

Least of all are there convincing grounds for forecasting that significant numbers of the world's intellectuals will cease to affirm and to clarify the conception of human dignity, or to evaluate the functioning of public and private institutions according to their positive or negative impacts on the realization of human rights.

In contrast, according to the pessimistic construct, the direction of history is reversing itself, with movement toward a world of militarized, garrisoned communities, controlled from the center and modeled on the prison.[109] Power and other values will be further concentrated, with a restoration of caste, in the name of providing for the common defense. We do not neglect this possibility that the world community will drift away from the course of development that gradually progresses toward a

108. These two basic developmental constructs are projected in greater detail in Lasswell, *The World Revolution of Our Time: A Framework for Basic Policy Research,* in World Revolutionary Elites 29 (H. Lasswell & D. Lerner eds. 1966).

109. One of the authors proposed the garrison-state construct some years ago. *See* Lasswell, *Sino-Japanese Crisis: The Garrison State versus the Civilian State,* 2 China Q. 643 (1937); *The Garrison State,* 46 Am. J. Sociology 455 (1941); *The Garrison-State Hypothesis Today,* in Changing Patterns of Military Politics 51 (S. Huntington ed. 1962). For a summary and critique of this construct, *see* S. Huntington, The Soldier and the State 346–50 (1957). *See also* Fox, *Harold D. Lasswell and the Study of World Politics: Configurative Analysis, Garrison State, and World Commonwealth,* in Politics, Personality, and Social Science in the Twentieth Century: Essays in Honor of Harold D. Lasswell 367 (A. Rogow ed. 1969).

public and civic order that harmonizes with the overriding goals of human dignity. The drift may well be in the direction of a comprehensive garrison state, with a system of public order that, when well entrenched, organizes the world community into a vast hierarchical pattern under the effective rule of a self-perpetuating military caste.

The "expectation of violence" may be sustained at a sufficiently high level to serve as a chronic justification for the mobilization of human resources and facilities in the name of defense from "across" or "below." The threat from "across" refers to elites that occupy territory external to the elite that considers itself endangered. The threat from "below" refers to alleged menaces from the lower strata of the elite's territorial domain. It is not to be ignored that the situation may evolve in such a way that present-day territorial elites perceive a common interest in maintaining themselves by joining in common policies to suppress and prevent the "lower orders" from erupting in defiance of the established hierarchy.

We have had occasion to take note of the fact that a common awareness of threat has often led to an expanded program of human rights. The human resources of a given area would seem to fortify the value position of a given body politic in reference to its environment. Unfortunately, it cannot be validly assumed that elite insecurities will invariably be resolved by programs of shared power. Modern science and technology would seem to contain many potential alternatives that stand in stark contradiction to the sharing of power and of other values.

The contemporary world is already acquainted with the use of technology for purposes of surveillance.[110] It is commonplace to employ novel instruments to record conversations at a distance, and to photograph gestures and other movements. Computer networks can be employed to analyze intimate as well as public information, and to penetrate conventional defenses of privacy. Chemical and other means are already available to investigators who seek to discover the inner lives of their subjects. It is also possible to look ahead to the employment of genetic engineering in ways that multiply forms of life without any potential for revolt.

As we have emphasized from time to time, we do not regard any particular version of the future as "inevitable." On the contrary, we believe that the anticipation of future contingencies is a means of increasing the likelihood that humankind can avoid the undesirable and achieve the desirable. This depends on the choice and execution of policy strategies that meet the emerging perils and opportunities of the world arena. However grim the prospects for a worldwide public order of human dignity, adverse estimates of probability cannot be permitted

---

110. *See* chapter 16 *infra,* at notes 64–80 and accompanying text.

to affect commitment to human dignity as a fundamental and enduring goal.

THE INVENTION AND EVALUATION OF ALTERNATIVES: LOOKING TOWARD AN OPTIMUM PUBLIC ORDER OF HUMAN DIGNITY

The culminating task of problem solving is, of course, the invention, evaluation, and selection of policy alternatives.[111] The previous tasks of the postulation and formulation of goals, the description of trends, the analysis of conditioning factors, and the projection of future developments are preparatory steps. The difficult question is how strategies can be devised for spanning the distance between generalized goals and the more specific objectives suitable to a problematic situation. This task involves the identification or invention of possible alternatives in institution or practice, a comparative evaluation in terms of potential short- and long-term benefits and costs, and the making of necessary final commitments. What is sought are options in institution and practice which will both facilitate the enforcement of particular applications of policy and secure a high degree of conformity to basic community policies in the aggregate flow of decision.

There are of course in any given context many functionally equivalent institutions and practices in constitutive process and public order decisions which might be employed to enhance the protection and fulfillment of human rights. Thus, contemporary discussion of the implementation of human rights is characterized by a wide variety of recommendations for change in institution and practice. These recommendations, proffered in highly conventional terms, include such items as the establishment of new human rights courts; the provision of specialized defenders of human rights, as in proposals for a United Nations High Commissioner for Human Rights; the expanded use of individual petitions in various structures of authority; reconstitution of the internal constitutive processes of states; the establishment of permanent commissions of inquiry and investigation; the strengthening of complaint procedures; educational programs in human rights; the stimulation of world public opinion by increasing roles for non-

---

111. On the invention and evaluation of policy alternatives, *see generally* D. Braybrooke & C. Lindblom, Strategy of Decision (1963); I. Bross, Design for Decision (1953); J. Brunner, et al., Contemporary Approaches to Creative Thinking (1962); C. Churchman, Prediction and Optimal Decision (1961); K. Deutsch, The Nerves of Government: Models of Political Communication and Control (2d ed. 1966); R. Lynd, Knowledge for What? (1945); D. Price, Government and Science (1954); A. Rivlin, Systematic Thinking for Social Action (1971); Lasswell, *Current Studies of the Decision Process: Automation versus Creativity,* 8 W. Pol. Q. 381 (1955).

governmental organizations (NGOs) and international officials; the development of human rights blocs; conduct of a human rights foreign policy; the requiring of human rights reports; improved survey of human rights conditions; the improvement and multiplication of regional systems for the protection of human rights; the augmentation of resources available to international governmental organizations for the protection of human rights; the further development of human rights prescriptions; the employment of economic measures (withdrawal of foreign aid, withdrawal of trade benefits, boycotts, freezing of assets, etc.); the improvement of enforcement measures by international governmental organizations and individual states; the provision of technical assistance programs, including advisory services programs; the establishment of specialized commissions and agencies to deal with particular human rights problems; and exposure of and publicity about human rights deprivations.[112]

The difficulty with most of these recommendations is that they are

---

112. *See* chapter 4 *supra*, containing many pertinent references. *See generally* HUMAN RIGHTS, INTERNATIONAL LAW AND THE HELSINKI ACCORD (T. Buergenthal ed. 1977); HUMAN RIGHTS AND AMERICAN DIPLOMACY: 1975–77 (J. Buncher ed. 1977); J. CAREY, UN PROTECTION OF CIVIL AND POLITICAL RIGHTS (1970); INTERNATIONAL PROTECTION OF HUMAN RIGHTS (A. Eide & A. Schou eds. 1968) (Nobel Symposium 7); M. GANJI, INTERNATIONAL PROTECTION OF HUMAN RIGHTS (1962); E. HAAS, HUMAN RIGHTS AND INTERNATIONAL ACTION (1970); HOUSE SUBCOMM. ON INTERNATIONAL ORGANIZATIONS AND MOVEMENTS, 93D CONG., 2D SESS., HUMAN RIGHTS IN THE WORLD COMMUNITY: A CALL FOR U.S. LEADERSHIP (Comm. Print 1974); H. LAUTERPACHT, INTERNATIONAL LAW AND HUMAN RIGHTS (1950); M. MOSKOWITZ, INTERNATIONAL CONCERN WITH HUMAN RIGHTS (1974); REPORT OF THE CONFERENCE ON IMPLEMENTING A HUMAN RIGHTS COMMITMENT IN UNITED STATES FOREIGN POLICY (Mar. 4, 1977) (sponsored by the International League for Human Rights); A. ROBERTSON, HUMAN RIGHTS IN THE WORLD (1972); HUMAN RIGHTS IN NATIONAL AND INTERNATIONAL LAW (A. Robertson ed. 1968); E. SCHWELB, HUMAN RIGHTS AND THE INTERNATIONAL COMMUNITY (1964); L. SOHN & T. BUERGENTHAL, INTERNATIONAL PROTECTION OF HUMAN RIGHTS (1973); INTERNATIONAL HUMAN RIGHTS LAW AND PRACTICE (rev. ed. J. Tuttle ed. 1978); UNITED NATIONS, UNITED NATIONS ACTION IN THE FIELD OF HUMAN RIGHTS, U.N. Doc. ST/HR/2 (1974); V. VAN DYKE, HUMAN RIGHTS, THE UNITED STATES, AND WORLD COMMUNITY (1970); *Hearings on International Protection of Human Rights before the Subcomm. on International Organization and Movements of the House Comm. on Foreign Affairs,* 93d Cong., 1st Sess. (1974); Bilder, *Rethinking International Human Rights: Some Basic Questions,* 1969 WIS. L. REV. 170; Birnbaum, *Human Rights and East-West Relations,* 55 FOREIGN AFFAIRS 783 (1977); Derian, *Human Rights and United States Foreign Relations: An Overview,* 10 CASE W. RES. J. INT'L L. 243 (1978); Fascell, *Did Human Rights Survive Belgrade?* 31 FOREIGN POLICY 104 (1978); Fraser, *Freedom and Foreign Policy,* 26 FOREIGN POLICY 140 (1977); Humphrey, *The International Law of Human Rights in the Middle Twentieth Century,* in THE PRESENT STATE OF INTERNATIONAL LAW AND OTHER ESSAYS 75 (M. Bos ed. 1973); Oda, *The Individual in International Law,* in MANUAL OF PUBLIC INTERNATIONAL LAW (M. Sorensen ed. 1968); Robertson, *Human Rights: A Global Assessment,* 53 NOTRE DAME LAW. 15 (1977); Schwelb, *Civil and Political Rights: The International Measures of Implementation,* 62 AM. J. INT'L L. 827 (1968); Vance, *Human Rights and Foreign Policy,* 7 GA. J. INT'L &

proffered in fragmented and anecdotal form, without clear and systematic relation to the comprehensive constitutive and public order decisions which they are designed to affect. Their emphasis is too much upon isolated features of rule, procedure, and structure, put forward without adequate consideration of the larger processes of authoritative decision and effective power which condition the impact of all changes in rules, procedures, and structures. What is needed, in more rational approach, is a systematic canvass of every feature both of constitutive process and of public order decision for ascertaining the entire range of possible improvements and for establishing priorities among such potential improvements in terms of temporal need, economy, effectiveness, and so on. From this perspective, one crucial measure might appear to be immediate improvement in the intelligence and appraisal functions of authoritative decision.[113] Yet, since there is a human rights dimension in all authoritative decision and social interaction and a complete interdependence between constitutive process and public order, much more comprehensive programs in improvement, involving all decision functions and placing deliberate emphasis upon the enhancement of human rights, must be required if we are even to begin to approximate a commonwealth of human dignity.

It may aid understanding of the necessities of a comprehensive approach to recall the intimate interdependences of constitutive process, public order decision, and all value processes within any particular community, global or local.[114] The degree to which any particular community can achieve desired outcomes, human dignity or other, within any particular value process is a function, not merely of the economy of the institutional features of that particular value process, but also of the outcomes and features of all other value processes, and especially of the features of the community's constitutive process and of the effective power process that maintains constitutive process. It is the constitutive process which protects and regulates the shaping and sharing of dif-

---

COMP. L. 223 (1977); Vogelgesang, *What Price Principle?—U.S. Policy on Human Rights,* 56 FOREIGN AFFAIRS 819 (1978).

Of a growing number of symposia concerned with international protection of human rights, *see* 24 N.Y.L.S.L. REV. 1 (No. 1, 1978) (including articles by Karl Carstens, Rosalyn Higgins, John P. Humphrey, Oscar Schachter, Jerome J. Shestack, John Claydon, Richard B. Lillich, Francis Wolf, & Richard P. Claude). *See also* AUSTRALIAN Y.B. INT'L L. 1970–1973 (1975); 7 GA. J. INT'L & COMP. L. 219 (Supplement, 1977); 53 NOTRE DAME LAW. 1 (Oct. 1977); 12 TEX. INT'L L.J. 129 (Spring/Summer 1977); 14 VA. J. INT'L L. 591 (Summer 1974); 10 CASE W. RES. J. INT'L L. 243 (Spring 1978).

113. *See* chapter 4 *supra. See also* notes 52 and 53 *supra.*

114. *See* chapter 1 *supra. See also* C. JENKS, LAW, FREEDOM AND WELFARE 71–82 (1963); R. KEOHANE & J. NYE, POWER AND INTERDEPENDENCE: WORLD POLITICS IN TRANSITION (1977); A. PECCEI, THE CHASM AHEAD (1969); Rosecrance, et al., *Whither Interdependence?* 31 INT'L ORG. 425 (1977).

ferent values within a community's public order, thus determining the degree of approximation or nonapproximation to the policies of human dignity; yet the kind of public order a community can achieve (in terms of wealth, enlightenment, skill, well-being, and so on) completely controls, through a grip of converse determination, the kind of constitutive process a community can maintain. The most promising and immediately responsive key to the improvement of a community's constitutive process would appear to be found in the management of its processes of effective power, which requires modification of the predispositions of the elites who maintain that process. Since effective power may be based upon participation in any or all other value processes, the most comprehensive task becomes that of generating perspectives appropriate to the enlargement and betterment of human rights protection through all of a community's different value processes.[115]

The paramount task, then, for all who are genuinely committed to the goal values of a world public order of human dignity, is that of creating in peoples of the world the perspectives necessary for accelerated movement toward such a public order. It is, as indicated above, the conflicting and disoriented perspectives of peoples—as manifested in demands for special interests, syndromes of parochial identification, and chronic expectations of violence[116]—and not the inexorable requirements of environmental variables, which perpetuate the conditions of deprivation and nonfulfillment of values. The maximization postulate suggests that the peoples of the world, through appropriate modifications in perspectives, can be encouraged to move toward the establishment of a more effective constitutive process of authoritative decision for the defense and fulfillment of human rights. It is hardly a novel insight that the factors—culture, class, interest, personality, and crisis—which importantly condition peoples' perspectives can be modified to foster constructive rather than destructive perspectives.[117] Promising alternatives in communication and collaboration designed to cultivate the perspectives vital to maintaining minimum public order and, ultimately, achieving an optimum public order of human dignity, have long been recommended by many different competent specialists, and await employment in sufficiently comprehensive, integrated, and disciplined programs.[118]

---

115. We build upon the themes developed in M. McDougal & F. Feliciano, *supra* note 9, at 261–383.

116. *See* chapter 1 *supra,* at notes 110–16 and accompanying text.

117. *See* H. Lasswell & A. Kaplan, *supra* note 105. *See also* H. Lasswell, Power and Personality (1948); H. Lasswell, Psychopathology and Politics (1960); Lasswell, *Person, Personality, Group, Culture,* 2 Psychiatry 533 (1930).

118. A whole host of recommendations is embodied in the growing literature on world order. *See generally* S. Brown, New Forces in World Politics (1974); Images of the

The distinctive types of perspectives—demands, identifications, and expectations—required for moving toward optimum shaping and sharing of values may, in the light of our previous discussion, be briefly indicated. The demands which need strengthening are, of course, those which emphasize common rather than special interests and which insist upon the greater production and wider sharing of all values compatible with human dignity. The identifications best designed to sustain a world public order of human dignity are those which most nearly embrace all humankind and achieve pluralistic expression in both functional and territorial groupings. Finally, the proponents of human dignity must establish in themselves and others credible expectations that they do accept the fundamental principle of minimum public order, precluding unauthorized coercion and violence, and that the peaceful cooperation of all peoples in the greater production and wider sharing of all values is a feasible and imperative goal. The myth of domination by violence must be exposed; so must be the myth about the indispensability of the oppression of human rights to political or economic development.[119] The reality of contemporary interdependences, in all value processes at all community levels and transcending manifold barriers, must be brought home to all inhabitants of our planet. All effective decision makers must be enabled to perceive realistically that they, and all with whom they identify, have more to gain and less to lose by genuine efforts to enhance than by efforts to stifle the protection and fulfillment of human rights.

The potentialities inherent in the planned management of the factors affecting peoples' perspectives, though infrequently employed in support of comprehensive minimum and optimum public order, have

---

FUTURE: THE TWENTY-FIRST CENTURY AND BEYOND (R. Bundy ed. 1976); PROBLEMS ON WORLD MODELING: POLITICAL AND SOCIAL IMPLICATIONS (K. Deutsch, et al., eds. 1977); R. FALK, A STUDY OF FUTURE WORLDS (1975); T. HESBURGH, THE HUMANE IMPERATIVE: A CHALLENGE FOR THE YEAR 2000 (1974); R. KOTHARI, FOOTSTEPS INTO THE FUTURE: DIAGNOSIS OF THE PRESENT AND A DESIGN OF AN ALTERNATIVE (1974); G. LAGOS & H. GODOY, REVOLUTION OF BEING: A LATIN AMERICAN VIEW OF THE FUTURE (1977); W. LEONTIEF, et al., THE FUTURE OF THE WORLD ECONOMY (1977); A. MAZRUI, A WORLD FEDERATION OF CULTURES: AN AFRICAN PERSPECTIVE (1976); M. MEAD, WORLD ENOUGH: RETHINKING THE FUTURE (1975); ON THE CREATION OF A JUST WORLD ORDER: PREFERRED WORLDS FOR THE 1990's (S. Mendlovitz ed. 1975); G. MISCHE & P. MISCHE, TOWARD A HUMAN WORLD ORDER: BEYOND THE NATIONAL SECURITY STRAITJACKET (1977); A. PECCEI, THE HUMAN QUALITY (1977); W. WAGAS, BUILDING THE CITY OF MAN: OUTLINES OF A WORLD CIVILIZATION (1971); Falk, *A New Paradigm for International Legal Studies: Prospects and Proposals,* 84 YALE L.J. 969 (1975); Falk, *Contending Approaches to World Order,* 31 J. INT'L AFFAIRS 171 (1977); Farer, *The Greening of the Globe: A Preliminary Appraisal of the World Order Models Project,* 31 INT'L ORG. 129 (1977); Lasswell, *The Promise of the World Order Modeling Movement,* 29 WORLD POLITICS 425 (1977).

119. *Cf. Economic Development and Human Rights: Brazil, Chile, and Cuba,* 1973 PROC., AM. SOC'Y INT'L L. 198.

within recent decades become widely known.[120] Techniques are available by which peoples may not merely liberate themselves from parochial and destructive biases caused by various factors but also employ such factors to cultivate appropriate inclusive and constructive perspectives. Contemporary communication media make it possible, further, for all human beings to participate in this common enterprise of emancipation and construction. The constraining biases of particular *culture* may be weakened through a deeper understanding of one's own culture and of other cultures. Cultural factors may be made to support a public order of human dignity by appropriate emphasis upon the primacy of goal values, which most cultures share, and the potential equivalence in the pursuit of basic goal values of many different institutional practices, which may fittingly vary in desirable experimentation with divergent cultural patterns. The distorting influence of *class* may be discounted by directing attention to the tendency of all classes—upper, middle, lower—to make choices in the light of their own, rather than common, interest. The class factor, when appropriately employed, may positively facilitate, in theory and in fact, a highly mobile and egalitarian society. The divisive effects of special *interests,* in different functional or territorial groups, may be minimized by candid exposure of narrow perceptions of interest and by according primacy to aggregate, long-term interests. The importance of developing multiple interests, especially through a wide range of pluralistic groups, may be stressed in positive programs to channel special interest in the direction of common interest. The harmful consequences of pathological traits in *personality* may be mitigated by the cultivation of insight, at whatever depth may be necessary, into the basic value orientations and dynamisms of the self, along with a deeper understanding of others. Positive programs relating to the personality factor could bring the tremendous resources of modern science and technology to bear upon the nurture of healthier personalities. The traumatic effects of exposure to *crisis* may be assuaged through comparable processes of awareness and insight; positive programs may include measures calculated to minimize direct confrontations in crisis situations.

The contributions which rational employment of the different in-

120. Some of these potentialities are being developed in a literature about the relevance of education. *See* T. Buergenthal & J. Torney, International Human Rights and International Education (1976); Weston, *Education for Human Survival: An Immediate World Priority,* 261 Annals of the New York Academy of Sciences 115 (1975); Weston, *Contending with a Planet in Peril and Change: The Rationale and Meaning of World Order Education* (forthcoming). *See also* M. Haavelsrud, Education for Peace—Reflection and Action (1974); Education for Peace: Focus on Mankind (G. Henderson ed. 1973); M. Montessori, Education and Peace (H. Lane trans. 1972); E. Reischauer, Toward the 21st Century: Education for a Changing World (1973).

struments of policy—diplomatic, ideological, economic, and military—might make to comprehensive programs in communication and collaboration may be briefly indicated.[121] The contributions, actual and potential, of the diplomatic instrument have been amply demonstrated not only by the long-established practice of "diplomatic" protection of nationals but by the development of a significant body of transnational human rights prescriptions which form the bulk of the emerging global bill of human rights.[122] The continuing skillful and effective use of the diplomatic instrument by both transnational and national officials has high promise. The economic instrument can be employed positively to foster fulfillment of wealth and other values and negatively as a sanctioning measure against deprivations of human rights. It has much to contribute to programs in communication and collaboration. Specialists in the management of the economic instrument are projecting comprehensive and elaborately detailed programs for promoting the development of the less developed areas of the world.[123] With some broadening of the perspectives postulated and of bases in participation, these programs could be adapted in their planning and execution to more general community purposes. While the military instrument is ordinarily associated with coercion and destruction, it may indeed be employed, by either the organized general community or individual states, to protect human rights. The constructive use of the military instrument for the maintenance of minimum public order bears directly upon the defense and fulfillment of human rights, for minimum public order is indispensable to human rights in the sense of the optimum shaping and sharing of all

---

121. *Cf.* M. McDougal & F. Feliciano, *supra* note 9, at 309–33, 380–81.

122. *See* chapter 4 *supra.*

123. *See generally* I. Adelman & C. Morris, Economic Growth and Social Equity in Developing Countries (1973); The Economics of Underdevelopment (A. Agarwala & S. Singh eds. 1963); T. Balogh, The Economics of Poverty (2d ed. 1974); P. Bauer, Dissent on Development (rev. ed. 1976); Economics and World Order: From the 1970's to the 1990's (J. Bhagwati ed. 1972); J. Bhagwati, The Economics of Underdeveloped Countries (1971); R. Dumont, Socialisms and Development (R. Cunningham trans. 1973); E. Hagen, The Economics of Development (1975); A. Hirschman, The Strategy of Economic Development (1958); G. Kay, Development and Underdevelopment: A Marxist Analysis (1975); C. Kindleberger, Economic Development (3d ed. 1977); S. Kuznets, Economic Growth of Nations (1971); W. Leontief, et al., The Future of the World Economy: A United Nations Study (1977); W. Lewis, The Theory of Economic Growth (1955); R. McNamara, One Hundred Countries, Two Billion People: The Dimensions of Development (1973); T. Morgan, Economic Development: Concept and Strategy (1975); The International Law of Development: Basic Documents (A. Mutharika comp. & ed. 1978–) (4 vols.); L. Reynolds, Image and Reality in Economic Development (1977); W. Rostow, The Stages of Economic Growth (2d ed. 1971); E. Staley, The Future of Underdeveloped Countires (rev. ed. 1961); J. Tinbergen, Development Planning (N. Smith trans. 1967).

values. Though human rights are at stake in all interaction, in armed conflict the implications for human rights are even more serious and acute. Hence, many sane voices can be heard speaking about the necessity of defending humanity and of protecting human rights during even the most destructive conflict.[124] The ideological instrument is, of course, uniquely important in promoting the defense and fulfillment of human rights. With its potentialities for instant communication about the globe and for reaching mass audiences far beyond elite groups, the ideological instrument is indispensable to forging transnational identifications and loyalties and to mobilizing world public opinion on behalf of human rights.[125] It is an instrument which, in its many modalities, lends itself to use by a wide range of participants—individuals and groups (large and small), officials (national and transnational) and nonofficials.

As we look toward the future we are aware of much uncertainty on the part of those who are estimating the potentialities of human beings. According to one strand of analysis the growth of population is likely to lead to famine, disease, disorder, and misery. In this perspective, it is no longer regarded as likely that opportunities will be available for the creative utilization of individual capability on a scale sufficient to meet human dignity requirements.

The scenarios of despair are not, however, universally accepted. We do not forget that "psychic epidemics" have exercised a profound effect on human history, and that their results have not been altogether negative. The Christian Crusades, for parochial example, stand as a prototype of remarkable mobilization of people and assets. In a world of intelligence satellites and other technologies of communication the global map is becoming more widely shared, and the possibilities of instant communication are more obvious than ever.

The task of generating and sustaining effective demands for public

---

124. *See* M. McDougal & F. Feliciano, *supra* note 9, at 384–731. *See generally* Report (to the United States Secretary of State) of the United States Delegation to the Diplomatic Conference on the Reaffirmation and Development of International Humanitarian Law Applicable in Armed Conflicts, Third Session, Geneva, Switzerland, April 21–June 11, 1976 (Oct. 15, 1976); The Laws of Armed Conflicts: A Collection of Conventions, Resolutions and Other Documents (D. Schindler & J. Toman eds. 1973); Fryer, *Applicability of International Law to Internal Armed Conflicts: Old Problems, Current Endeavors* 11 Int'l Lawyer 567 (1977); Green, *Humanitarian Law and the Man in the Field,* 14 Canadian Y.B. Int'l L. 96 (1976); Suckow, *The Development of International Humanitarian Law—Concluded,* 19 Rev. Int'l Comm'n Jurists 46 (1977).

125. *See* B. Murty, Propaganda and World Public Order (1968); W. Schramm, Mass Media and National Development: The Role of Information in the Developing Countries (1964); *The International Protection of Human Rights by the Mobilisation of Public Opinion* in International Law Association, Report of the Fifty-Seventh Conference Held at Madrid, 1976, at 524–40 (1978).

order decisions that will secure a more perfect civic order requires that all who cherish human dignity—whether scholars, advisors, active participants in decision processes at different levels, or community members—seize every opportunity to make the choices and create the public opinion that is in support of human dignity. There is, we emphasize again, a human rights dimension in every interaction and every authoritative decision, and the participants in social process are continuously engaged in redefining their expectations of net advantage. Changes in the direction of appropriate constitutive and public order decisions can be secured only if many individuals, located in many different functional and territorial structures and processes about the globe, adopt joint and parallel strategies to insure that the human rights dimension of decision is taken into account. The more simultaneous the activities in many different parts of the world, the greater the chances of major structural transformation. There is, as already suggested, a multitude of models of constitutive process and public order decisions which could be adapted to serve the values of human dignity if people have the will to render such models effective. The effective elites who establish and maintain the processes of authoritative decision must be stimulated to perceive that, even in a divided world, they will be better off by changing, rather than by continuing, the arrangements and practices that promote human *in*dignity. There is perhaps a basis for hope in the expanding, even exploding, demands of the peoples around the world for human rights and the realization that no future—however grim it may appear to be—is truly "inevitable."

The task of policy is, as we have said, to span the gap between the present and the desirable future by operating through the unfolding present in ways that bring the goal nearer.[126] In succeeding chapters we give detailed consideration to claims that have arisen, and are likely to arise, in connection with the core value of human rights, the respect value.[127] These claims are examined from the viewpoint of community decision makers whose responsibility is to achieve the effective accommodation of inclusive and exclusive interests within the common interests of the whole, and to reject claims of special interests. Trends to date are examined in the problem-solving framework that we have specified above, that is, in a policy-oriented approach that calls for the employment of all intellectual tasks pertinent to the clarification and implementation of overriding goal—the establishment of a world community of human dignity.

126. *See* pp. 436–43 *supra.*
127. *See* parts III and IV *infra.*

III

Trends in Decision and Conditioning Factors: Claims Relating to Respect

6. RESPECT AS THE CORE VALUE OF HUMAN RIGHTS

In the fundamental sense with which we are here concerned, respect is defined as an interrelation among individual human beings in which they reciprocally recognize and honor each other's freedom of choice about participation in the value processes of the world community or any of its component parts.[1] Respect includes not only the perspectives or

---

In slightly different form this chapter and chapters 7–9 *infra* first appeared as *The Protection of Respect and Human Rights: Freedom of Choice and World Public Order,* 24 AM. U.L. REV. 919 (1975).

1. The concepts of freedom and coercion with which we work are: By "freedom" we mean situations in which persons have many options, with high probabilities of gain and low probabilities of loss. By "coercion" we mean situations in which participants have few options, with low probabilities of gain and high probabilities of loss. For comparable statements, *see* Deutsch, *Strategies of Freedom: The Widening of Choices and the Change of Goals,* in LIBERTY 301 (NOMOS IV, C. Friedrich ed. 1962):

> [W]e may then define freedom as the range of effective choices open to an actor, such as an individual or a group of persons. The choices of action or policy open to a group eventually can be translated by virtue of their consequences into indirect choices for individuals.
>
> Defined as the effective range of choices for an actor, freedom has at least four major aspects or preconditions:
>
> 1. The absence of restraint, emphasized by such classical theorists as John Locke and Adam Smith.
> 2. The presence of opportunity, stressed by more recent theorists of social reform, such as T. H. Green, Karl Marx, George Bernard Shaw, and Sidney Webb.
> 3. The capacity to act, stressed by Hegel and by more recent writers on power such as Benito Mussolini.
> 4. The awareness of the reality without—including both unrestrainedness and opportunity—and of the actor's own capacity. This awareness has been stressed by Greek philosophers from Heraclitus to Socrates, and by modern depth psychologists, such as the school of Sigmund Freud.

Id. at 301–02.

Oppenheim sums up freedom of choice in these words: "Whereas social freedom refers

perceptions of worth by which the individual is characterized by himself and others, but also the translation of these perspectives into the operative facts of social process.[2] The relevant perspectives and operations extend to all the different values sought in social process and to the many distinctive institutional facilitations and deprivations by which freedom of choice is affected.

In more precise specification, respect may be said to entail four particular outcomes:

1. A fundamental freedom of choice for all individuals regarding participation in all value processes;
2. An equality of opportunity for all individuals to have experiences that enable them to enjoy the widest range of effective choice in their interactions with others and to participate in all value processes in accordance with capability, that is, without discrimination for reasons irrelevant to capability;
3. Additional rewards in deference to individuals who make preeminent contribution to common interests; and
4. An aggregate pattern of social interactions in which all individuals are protected in the utmost freedom of choice and subjected to the least possible governmental and private coercion.

It requires no detailed documentation to show that the various communities of mankind have seldom approximated, and often have not even aspired, to the full achievement of respect in terms of these four specified outcomes. Despite the increasing rhetorical acceptance in modern times of human dignity as the overriding goal for all communities, contemporary world social process continues to exhibit immense disparities between aspiration and achievement in relation to each outcome. The common assumption that slavery is a thing of the past is belied by the facts; slavery and slavelike practices are still pervasive in some parts of the world.[3] In other communities caste systems persist (with remnants of "untouchability" and rigidified discrimination); mem-

---

to two actors and their respective actions, freedom of choice signifies a relationship between one actor and a series of alternative potential actions." Oppenheim, *Freedom,* 5 INT'L ENCYC. SOC. SC. 554, 556 (1968).

2. For specification of the detailed content of the values with which we work, *see* H. LASSWELL & A. KAPLAN, POWER AND SOCIETY (1950); Lasswell & Holmberg, *Toward a General Theory of Directed Value Accumulation and Institutional Development,* in COMPARATIVE THEORIES OF SOCIAL CHANGE 12 (H. Peter ed. 1966). *Cf.* H. LASSWELL, POLITICS: WHO GETS WHAT, WHEN, HOW (1958); H. LASSWELL, WORLD POLITICS AND PERSONAL INSECURITY (1965); POLITICS, PERSONALITY, AND SOCIAL SCIENCE IN THE TWENTIETH CENTURY (A. Rogow ed. 1969).

3. *See* chapter 7 *infra,* at notes 72–78 and accompanying text.

bers of lower castes are denied access to ordinary avenues of mobility and advancement.[4] Apartheid, as imposed in South Africa and Namibia, has become a new form of caste and segregation in which the position and freedoms of individual human beings are stratified and frozen at birth on the basis of race.[5] Even where hardcore deprivations in the form of slavery and caste have decreased or disappeared, there often persists a steady denial of equality on various grounds such as race, sex, religion, culture, political opinion, and alienage.[6] The formal myth of a community may emphasize equality, yet actual conditions of deprivation and disparity may be such as to deny individuals effective choice and to render the aspiration toward equality a mockery. Aside from the ongoing "class struggles" in all mankind's differing communities, the tension generated and exacerbated by racial prejudice and discrimination, in its various manifestations, has transcended national boundaries and become a matter of intense universal concern.[7]

Too often the deliberate bestowal of honor upon individuals is abused and misused. Honor is frequently conferred upon individuals on grounds having noting to do with actual contribution to common interests. In some communities honor is still ascriptive ("hereditary"), and in others it has become simply an instrument manipulated arbitrarily by power elites for special interests.

The achievement of a comprehensive civic order, in which the aggregate pattern of social interaction accords even a minimum freedom of choice, is still far from reality. In an interdependent world, where high expectations of violence prevail and a universalizing science and technology have enormous impact, both constructive and destructive, the accelerating trend toward totalitarianism, regimentation, governmentalization, centralization, and concentration[8] culminates in many places in

---

4. *See id.* at notes 319–22 and accompanying text.

5. *See id.* at 387–598 and accompanying text.

6. *See* chapter 8 *infra,* at notes 1–29 and accompanying text.

7. *See* notes 34–52 *infra* and accompanying text; chapter 7 *infra,* at notes 1–285 and accompanying text.

8. *See generally* H. Lasswell, National Security and Individual Freedom (1950); Lasswell, *The Garrison-State Hypothesis Today,* in Changing Patterns of Military Politics 51 (S. Huntington ed. 1962); Lasswell, *The Major Trends in World Politics,* in The Ethic of Power: The Interplay of Religion, Philosophy, and Politics 343 (H. Lasswell & H. Cleveland eds. 1962); Lasswell, *The World Revolutionary Situation,* in Totalitarianism 360 (C. Friedrich ed. 1954); Lasswell, *The World Revolution of Our Time: A Framework for Basic Policy Research,* in World Revolutionary Elites 29 (H. Lasswell & D. Lerner eds. 1965); Lasswell, *Does the Garrison State Threaten Civil Rights?* 275 Annals 111 (1951); Lasswell, *The Garrison State,* 46 Am. J. Sociology 455 (1941), *reprinted in* H. Lasswell, The Analysis of Political Behavior 146 (1948); Lasswell, *The Interrelations of World Organization and Society,* 55 Yale L.J. 889 (1946). *Cf.* Reisman, *Private Armies in a Global War System,* in Law and Civil War in the Modern World 252 (J. Moore ed. 1974).

patterns of social interaction in which individuals are denied even a basic minimum of choice, and governmental encroachment into private domains expands extravagantly.

The protection of respect in any community, from the most inclusive to the smallest, is of course a function of the production and distribution of all other values. A value process of particular significance for the protection of respect is, however, that of enlightenment: many of the failures and difficulties in the protection and fulfillment of respect are monuments to sheer intellectual failure. These more particular failures include failure to identify and recognize respect as a distinct value, and failure to clarify the basic content ascribed to respect and to specify the procedures by which such content can be related to specific outcomes. Too often scholars and statesmen indulge in derivational exercises rather than in formulating procedures to facilitate empirical specification of decision in specific instances.[9] Similarly, respect is frequently defined in a negative sense only, with a focus upon the one particular outcome of nondiscrimination, rather than in a positive formulation which might foster effective equality and a rich fulfillment of human rights.[10] Even nondiscrimination is sometimes viewed so technically and narrowly, as in the European Convention on Human Rights,[11] that it relates only to preexisting legal rights with a truncation of freedoms regarding many values.[12]

The most important failure, however, has been that of not recognizing

---

9. A recent example of high indulgence in derivational exercises, without careful location in social process context, is J. Rawls, A Theory of Justice (1971) [hereinafter cited as J. Rawls].

10. *See, e.g.,* E. Vierdag, The Concept of Discrimination in International Law (1973).

11. Convention on Human Rights and Fundamental Freedoms, *adopted* Nov. 4, 1950, 1950 Europ. T.S. No. 5, 213 U.N.T.S. 221 [hereinafter cited as European Convention].

12. Art. 14 of the European Convention on Human Rights provides: "The enjoyment of *rights and freedoms set forth in this Convention* shall be secured without discrimination on any ground such as sex, race, colour, language, religion, political or other opinion, national or social origin, association with a national minority, property, birth or other status." *Id.*, Art. 14, 213 U.N.T.S. at 232 (emphasis added).

As shown by the practice of the European Commission on Human Rights, this provision is "auxiliary to" "the rights and freedoms set out" in the Convention, and does not establish "a right to non-discrimination independent of them"; hence, "there can be a breach of Article 14 only if there is a breach of such a provision of the Convention, which is also discriminatory." J. Fawcett, The Application of the European Convention on Human Rights 233–34 (1969). In the same vein, Vallat has observed: "There is a widespread tendency to regard the principle of non-discrimination as elementary, basic, self-evident and universally binding, but a moment's reflection raises serious questions as to the legal nature of the principle or the existence of a general right to be treated without discrimination." An Introduction to the Study of Human Rights x (F. Vallat ed. 1972).

the fundamental importance of respect, when appraised among all values in human motivation.[13] Among the most profound and intensely held demands of human beings in orienting themselves toward the world today is that for respect in the sense of the four outcomes specified above. It is this insistence upon basic respect that conditions people's identifications, demands, and expectations in all other value processes. It is denial of respect which most importantly conditions their willingness to engage in terror and violence to destroy established institutions and practices, and their rejection of peaceful intercourse in the shaping and sharing of wealth, power, and other values. When respect is not protected, other values cannot be securely and abundantly shaped and shared in society.[14]

The most economic route of escape from these inherited intellectual confusions is to be quite explicit, as we have sought to be above, about what is meant by respect in terms of social process outcomes and to relate these outcomes to other value processes in the larger community context of which they are a part.[15] Any rational recommendation of ways to reconstruct the process of authoritative decision the better to protect and foster respect must build upon a careful specification of the different kinds of claims that individuals, in their multifarious capacities, make upon constitutive process for the protection and fulfillment of respect.[16]

The categorization of claims with which we propose to work is as follows:

A. *Claims relating to outcomes*
   1. Claims for a basic degree of respect as individual human beings
      (a) Fundamental freedom of choice in value participation
      (b) Elimination of slavery

---

13. *Cf.* Shils, *Reflections on Deference,* in POLITICS, PERSONALITY, AND SOCIAL SCIENCE IN THE TWENTIETH CENTURY 297 (A. Rogow ed. 1969).

14. For the development of this theme *see* McDougal & Bebr, *Human Rights in the United Nations,* 58 AM. J. INT'L L. 603 (1964); McDougal & Leighton, *The Rights of Man in the World Community: Constitutional Illusions versus Rational Action,* 14 LAW & CONTEMP. PROB. 490 (1949). *See also* R. SENNETT & J. COBB, THE HIDDEN INJURIES OF CLASS (Vintage ed. 1973).

15. Recognition of the need for location in social process is long standing. In the words of Harold Laski: "[T]he idea of liberty depends upon the results of the social process at any given time; and it is against that background that its essential elements require analysis." Laski, *Liberty,* 9 ENCYC. SOC. SC. 442, 444 (1933).

16. For the development of the concept of the world constitutive process of authoritative decision, *see* McDougal, Lasswell, & Reisman, *The World Constitutive Process of Authoritative Decision,* in 1 THE FUTURE OF THE INTERNATIONAL LEGAL ORDER 73, 100 n.63 (R. Falk & C. Black eds. 1969). *See also* Lasswell & McDougal, *Trends in Theories about Law: Comprehensiveness in Conceptions of Constitutive Process,* 41 GEO. WASH. L. REV. 1 (1972); McDougal, Lasswell, & Reisman, *Theories about International Law: Prologue to a Configurative Jurisprudence,* 8 VA. J. INT'L L. 188 (1968). *See also* chapter 4 *supra.*

(c) Elimination of caste
(d) Elimination of apartheid

2. Claims relating to a basic equality of opportunity in the enjoyment of all values, that is, freedom from discrimination for reasons irrelevant to capability, in terms of:
   (a) Race (color; national, ethnic, or social origin; birth, descent, or other status)[17]
   (b) Sex
   (c) Religion
   (d) Political or other opinion
   (e) Language
   (f) Alienage
   (g) Age
   (h) Other factors
3. Claims for further rewards in respect for meritorious contribution
   (a) Recognition
   (b) Honor
   (c) Reputation
4. Claims relating to the aggregate interest in respect
   (a) Comprehensive public order
   (b) Civic order (including privacy)

B. *Claims relating to participation*
1. Claims in relation to participation in the shaping of respect
   (a) Governmental deprivations
      (i) In conformity with law
      (ii) Not in conformity with law
   (b) Nongovernmental deprivations
2. Claims in relation to participation in the sharing of respect
   (a) Individuals
   (b) Groups (minority protection)

C. *Claims relating to perspectives*
1. Claims relating to permissibility or impermissibility of purposes
   (a) Range of values included within impermissible purposes
   (b) Relevance of grounds alleged for deprivations to common interests
   (c) Discriminatory purpose per se constituting deprivation
2. Claims to be free to acquire a demand for respect—the opportunity to have experiences that will facilitate capabilities (claims to freedom from indoctrination)

---

17. In chapters 6–9 we deal only with problems through this particular claim. For continuing discussion of the general norm of nondiscrimination, *see* chapters 10–15 *infra*. The remaining claims about the respect process will be discussed in other forums.

(a) Opportunity to discover latent capabilities for participation
(b) Opportunity to acquire capabilities
(c) Opportunity to exercise capabilities
3. Claims for freedom to establish and change identification
4. Claims for opportunity to achieve realism in expectations

D. *Claims relating to situations—freedom of access to all social interactions in which respect is shaped and shared*
1. Claims relating to institutions specialized to respect
(a) Freedom to initiate and constitute institutions specialized to respect
(b) Freedom of access to institutions specialized to respect
(c) Prohibition of organizations or institutions inimical to respect (*e.g.*, racist organizations)
2. Claims relating to institutions not specialized to respect (equality in association)—freedom of access to institutions not specialized to respect (access to public accommodations, etc.)
3. Claims relating to geographic separation
4. Claims relating to crisis
(a) Impact of crises upon differentiation
(b) The accordance of respect proportionately despite crises

E. *Claims relating to base values*
1. Claims relating to authority—the availability of the process of authoritative decision to defend and fulfill respect
(a) Equality of access to authority (invocation)
(b) Impartiality in the application of law (application)
(c) Equality in law or legal interests (prescription)
2. Claims relating to control
(a) Availability of participation in each of the other value processes to defend and fulfill respect
(b) Impartial allocation of participation in value processes
3. Claims for special assistance to overcome handicaps not attributable to merit ("compensatory differentiation")

F. *Claims relating to strategies*
1. Claims for employment of the diplomatic instrument for affecting respect: enforcing agreements, prohibiting discriminatory agreements, minimizing deprivations, protecting reputation, etc.
2. Claims relating to the use of the ideological instrument for affecting respect
(a) Prohibition of race-mongering
(b) Education for the enjoyment of equality
3. Claims relating to the management of goods and services for affecting respect
(a) Prohibition of slavery, forced labor, imprisonment for debt, etc.
(b) Employment of monetary rewards

4. Claims relating to the use of the military instrument for affecting respect
   (a) Terrorist activities
   (b) Use of the military instrument for the protection of groups (martial law, etc.)

THE CLARIFICATION OF GENERAL COMMUNITY POLICIES

The commitment we make, and recommend to others, to the particular interactions we have described as respect outcomes is not dependent upon any particular mode of logical or philosophical derivation. For many centuries scholars have debated about the appropriate high-level principles and sources of authority from which outcomes comparable to those we have specified may be derived.[18] From our perspectives the method, style, and purport of derivational exercises are matters of personal choice. The more urgent questions relate to the more detailed specification of preferred outcomes in terms of empirical relations between human beings, and to how people with different modalities of derivation may cooperate in the achievement of postulated outcomes.

It may be emphasized that the most general commitment we recommend in pursuit of shared respect is broader than one of mere nondiscrimination. The core reference we make is to freedom of choice, the same core reference that has characterized most historical concepts of human dignity.[19] Even nondiscrimination we seek to define in positive terms as opportunities to discover, develop, and exercise full capabilities for constructive participation in all value processes. The rewards in honor of actual contributions to aggregate common interests that we recommend are designed to be integrative, and not incompatible, in the sense that they need not result in reducing access to values by other community members. The aggregate patterns of interaction that we specify as civic order are, further, designed to include not merely the

---

18. J. Rawls, *supra* note 9, offers some history of this debate. For a summary of Rawls's theories and an indication of the difficulties of applying these theories in specific instances, *see* Michelman, *In Pursuit of Constitutional Welfare Rights: One View of Rawls' Theory of Justice,* 121 U. Pa. L. Rev. 962 (1973). For further exposition see R. Nozick, Anarchy, State, and Utopia 183–231, 344–48 (1974); Hampshire, *A New Philosophy for the Just Society,* N.Y. Rev. Books, Feb. 24, 1972, at 34; Nagel, *Rawls on Justice,* 82 Philosophical Rev. 220 (1973).

For other surveys *see* 1 & 2 M. Adler, The Idea of Freedom (1958–61); Aspects of Liberty (M. Konvitz & C. Rossiter eds. 1958); C. Bay, The Structure of Freedom (1958); I. Berlin, Four Essays on Liberty (1969); M. Cranston, Freedom: A New Analysis (2d ed. 1954); Freedom: Its Meaning (R. Anshen ed. 1940); F. Hayek, The Constitution of Liberty (1960); Liberty (NOMOS IV, C. Friedrich ed. 1962); H. Muller, Freedom in the Modern World (1966); R. Neville, The Cosmology of Freedom (1974); F. Oppenheim, Dimensions of Freedom (1961); P. Weis, Man's Freedom (1950).

19. For an excellent brief statement on freedom of choice *see* C. Merriam, Systematic Politics 54–64 (1945). *See also* the citations in note 18 *supra.*

maximum fundamental freedom and the largest effective opportunity for the maturing of individual capability along with rational distribution of rewards for unique contributions, but also a reserved domain in which all individuals are protected in the utmost private autonomy in uncoerced choices about the value processes in which they participate and the modalities by which they participate.

Our concern extends, as noted, beyond how respect is shared to how it is shaped in the aggregate. What is known as "distributive justice," or sharing, is of course important.[20] No less important, however, is a coordinate policy of fostering a continuing development toward shaping the most ample aggregate outcomes of respect, as of other values, so that what is ultimately available to individuals is optimized.

It is, we assume, inescapable that in relation to respect, as to other values, community policies are projected and clarified in sets of complementary policies.[21] Most inherited prescriptions explicitly recognize the continuing necessity for the accommodation in particular instances of any one person's freedoms with the comparable freedoms of others and with aggregate common interests.[22] An effective method for seeking such accommodation, as has been elaborated and applied elsewhere, is a contextual method that employs adequate principles of content and procedure.[23] The proper employment of this method will, it is predicted,

---

20. The principal concern of J. RAWLS, *supra* note 9, is "distributive justice." The values available for distribution to community members, including "the least advantaged," are of course dependent upon total production.

For varying views *see* E. CAHN, THE SENSE OF INJUSTICE (1964 ed.); JUSTICE (NOMOS VI, C. Friedrich & J. Chapman eds. 1963); C. MERRIAM, SYSTEMATIC POLITICS 45–54 (1945); R. POUND, JUSTICE ACCORDING TO LAW (1951); R. STAMMLER, THE THEORY OF JUSTICE (1925); G. DEL VECCHIO, JUSTICE: AN HISTORICAL AND PHILOSOPHICAL ESSAY (A. Campbell ed. 1952).

21. *See* McDougal, *The Ethics of Applying Systems of Authority: The Balanced Opposites of a Legal System,* in THE ETHIC OF POWER: THE INTERPLAY OF RELIGION, PHILOSOPHY, AND POLITICS 221 (H. Lasswell & H. Cleveland eds. 1962).

22. *See* chapter 5 *supra.* For earlier statements, *see* McDougal, *Human Rights and World Public Order: Principles of Content and Procedure for Clarifying General Community Policies,* 14 VA. J. INT'L L. 387 (1974); McDougal, Lasswell & Chen, *Human Rights and World Public Order: A Framework for Policy-Oriented Inquiry,* 63 AM. J. INT'L L. 237, 264–69 (1969). The necessity for accommodation was underscored by Laski in these words:

> So long as it was conceived as a body of absolute rights inherent in the individual and entitled to be exerted without regard to their social consequences, liberty was divored from the ideas of both equality and justice. The individual became the antithesis of the state; and liberty itself became, as with Herbert Spencer, a principle of anarchy rather than a body of claims to be read in the context of the social process.

Laski, *Liberty,* 9 ENCYC. SOC. SC. 442, 443 (1933).

23. J. RAWLS, *supra* note 9, appears to reject the notion of a comprehensive accommodation of values, or integration of interests, in context and to search instead for transcendent

reveal that respect outcomes are often not competitive, and can be attained in many situations by genuinely integrating the interests of all.

The commitment we recommend in relation to fundamental freedom is that of community aspiration toward the widest possible range of choice for all individuals in regard to all value processes.[24] This aspiration is sometimes specified in terms of a basic minimum of freedom or liberty,[25] but the word "minimum" has unfortunate connotations: what we recommend is concern for continuing development toward an optimum shaping and sharing of values in which the participation of each individual will be as ample as possible. We recognize, of course, among the necessary constraints upon this aspiration, that the fundamental freedoms protected for any particular individual in any particular instance must perforce be measured against the comparable freedoms of others and the aggregate common interest.

The means by which the measure of this fundamental freedom, or of a basic minimum, can be established are sometimes debated.[26] This would appear, if what is sought is further high-level abstract content statements, a relatively futile quest.[27] What is needed is the specification of procedures for relating the already abundant high-level statements to the options open in any particular instance of decision. The freedoms that can be secured for any particular individual in any specific instance are a function of the values at stake and of many concomitant variables in an ongoing community process. What can be protected will vary from value to value, from problem to problem even in the same value process,

---

principles of justice. He does not, however, make clear by what criteria and procedures he would in particular instances calculate costs and benefits in determining "equality" among community members or in relating "the least advantaged" to other community members. Lasswell, *The Public Interest: Proposing Principles of Content and Procedure,* in THE PUBLIC INTEREST 54 (NOMOS V, C. Friedrich ed. 1962); Lasswell, *Clarifying Value Judgment: Principles of Content and Procedure,* 1 INQUIRY 87 (1958); McDougal, *Human Rights and World Public Order: Principles of Content and Procedure for Clarifying General Community Policies,* 14 VA. J. INT'L L. 387, 402–06 (1974).

24. *See* H. LASSWELL & A. KAPLAN, POWER AND SOCIETY (1950); Lasswell & Holmberg, *Toward a General Theory of Directed Value Accumulation and Institutional Development,* in COMPARATIVE THEORIES OF SOCIAL CHANGE 12 (H. Peter ed. 1966); McDougal, *Perspectives for an International Law of Human Dignity,* 1959 PROC., AM. SOC'Y INT'L L. 107; McDougal & Lasswell, *The Identification and Appraisal of Diverse Systems of Public Order,* 53 AM. J. INT'L L. 1 (1959). For a comparable emphasis *see* Brewster, *So the Poor Little Lambs Won't Lose Their Way,* N.Y. Times, Sept. 11, 1974, at 45, col. 1.

25. *See, e.g.,* J. RAWLS, *supra* note 9, at 265, 274–87.

26. *See* J. RAWLS, *supra* note 9, at 258–332.

27. The "original position" postulated by J. RAWLS, *supra* note 9, as a basis for his derivations would appear merely an intellectual device designed to minimize the biases and interests of an observer. It may aid objectivity, but it scarcely affords access to transcendent truth.

and from context to context. The relevant intellectual quest is for principles of procedure that will facilitate review and assessment of all the pertinent variables.[28]

The traditional philosophical justification for protecting fundamental freedom of choice has been in terms of common humanity, of protecting man as man.[29] The basic thrust of the position is that every individual should be treated as an end in himself, not as an instrument for others.[30] It may be conceded that the image that man has developed of himself as being different from animals and other forms of life has had important and beneficent historical impacts upon the acceptance and cultivation of all the values we cherish as those of human dignity.[31] More contemporary justifications toward the same ends may, however, be grounded in the findings of modern psychology, which stress the overriding importance to the individual, and to community process, of affording to every individual opportunities for the participations necessary to the development of a constructive "self," capable of respecting the self and others and therefore of sharing freedom in choice.[32]

It is apparent that all the comprehensive and systematic deprivations of freedom—slavery, caste, and apartheid—are by definition contrary to our postulated goals of human dignity. Fortunately, the rejection of all these practices, once described, can be made syntactically, as the antitheses of our basic recommendations. Thus slavery, with its complete subjection of the victim to the will of the master, would appear to represent the severest, and most intolerable, restriction of freedom of choice known to contemporary culture.[33] Similarly, caste, with its insistence

---

28. *See* notes 22–23 *supra.*

29. As Bernard Williams puts it:

> The factual statement of men's equality was seen, when pressed, to retreat in the direction of merely asserting the equality of men as men; and this was thought to be trivial. It is certainly insufficient, but not, after all, trivial. That all men are human is, if a tautology, a useful one, serving as a reminder that those who belong anatomically to the species *homo sapiens,* and can speak a language, use tools, live in societies, can interbreed despite racial differences, etc., are also alike in certain other respects more likely to be forgotten.

Williams, *The Idea of Equality,* in PHILOSOPHY, POLITICS AND SOCIETY 110, 112 (P. Laslett & W. Runciman eds. 1962).

30. For an excellent testimony to this cosmopolitan perspective, as recorded in various cultures of human history, see UNESCO, BIRTHRIGHT OF MAN (1969).

31. *See id.*

32. *See* THE SELF IN SOCIAL INTERACTION (C. Gordon & K. Gergen eds. (1968); H. SULLIVAN, CONCEPTIONS OF MODERN PSYCHIATRY (2d ed. 1953); Lasswell, *Person, Personality, Group, Culture,* 2 PSYCHIATRY 5 (1939), *reprinted in* H. LASSWELL, THE ANALYSIS OF POLITICAL BEHAVIOR 195 (1948).

33. *See* chapter 7 *infra,* at notes 27–302 and accompanying text.

upon permanent distinctions based upon the accidents of birth, would appear wholly incompatible with demands that individuals be accorded fullest opportunities to discover, mature, and exercise their latent capabilities to the highest levels of excellence for participation in social process.[34] Finally, apartheid, with its grouping and segregation of populations on the basis of race and birth and its rigid prescriptions of differential access to values, would appear to crystallize and institutionalize a system fully comparable to, and equally unacceptable as, that of a caste society.[35]

The members of a community are of course, even in the absence of legally prescribed stratifications, always classifying and reclassifying themselves in relation to one another according to their value positions, potentials, and expectancies, including a system of respect grades.[36] It is when the class system in a society is formalized as a rigidified hierarchy, in which the individual is not allowed to alter the status ascribed to him at birth, that it becomes a caste society.[37] In a less rigidified society comprised of different classes in terms of relative positions in relation to different values, though it is obviously more difficult for members of lower classes to move upward than vice versa, the mobility of people is not predetermined by status at birth, but may depend upon the capability and achievement of individual persons.[38] It is the equality of opportunity for the development of capability and for achievement that is critical.

The equality of opportunity that we specify as the second important outcome in the respect process is to be understood both positively and negatively: positively in terms of opportunities for individuals to enjoy the widest range of effective choice in their interactions with others, and negatively in terms of access to participation in all value processes without discrimination for reasons irrelevant to capability. The critical importance of a positive formulation was eloquently articulated by R. H. Tawney in his classic study *Equality,* where he insists that a genuine equality depends

> not merely on the absence of disabilities, but on the presence of abilities. It obtains in so far, and only in so far as, each member of a community, whatever his birth, or occupation, or social position,

---

34. *See id.* at notes 303–86 and accompanying text.

35. *See id.* at notes 387–439 and accompanying text.

36. *See id.* at note 305.

37. *See id.* at 303–22 and accompanying text.

38. *See* note 36 *supra. See generally* THE AMERICAN OCCUPATIONAL STRUCTURE (P. Blau & O. Duncan eds. 1967); S. LIPSET & R. BENDIX, SOCIAL MOBILITY IN INDUSTRIAL SOCIETY (1959); P. SOROKIN, SOCIAL MOBILITY (1927).

possesses in fact, and not merely in form, equal chances of using to the full his natural endowments of physique, of character, and of intelligence.[39]

It should be noted that the equality we recommend, whether the formulation be positive or negative, is an equality, not of capabilities and characteristics, but of treatment.[40] It is a commonplace that human beings differ greatly in capabilities and characteristics and in exposure to past experiences and that many such differences are indispensable to an appropriate diversity and pluralism in social process. What cannot be conceded is that some human beings should, on alleged grounds of group differences in capabilities, characteristics, and past experience, be arbitrarily treated differently from others in terms of access to social process for maturing latent talent and contributing to the aggregate common interest.

Our complex modern society, with its multiple intersecting and interacting value processes, requires many different roles and performances from individual community members. It is not to be asserted that all individuals have even comparable capabilities for all these different roles and performances. A rational community policy must honor an appropriate differentiation in opportunity, training, and recruitment. A rational policy need not, however, honor differentiations which have no basis in individual capabilities and, hence, become arbitrary discriminations.

The principal thrust of the policy we recommend is, therefore, that individuals should be accorded or denied opportunities for freedom of choice in regard to any value process only upon the basis of individual capabilities and characteristics, and not according to an alleged group capability and characteristic.[41] Permissible differentiations may be made between individuals in terms of the particular capabilities and characteristics appropriate for particular roles, but discrimination grounded

39. R. Tawney, Equality 103–04 (1964).

40. Dobzhansky has eloquently put it this way:

> Equality of opportunity neither presupposes nor promotes equality of ability. It only means that every person may, without favor or hindrance, develop whatever socially useful gifts or aptitudes he has and chooses to develop. Civilization fosters a multitude of employments and functions to be filled and served—statesmen and butchers, engineers and policemen, scientists and refuse collectors, musicians and sales clerks. Equality of opportunity stimulates the division of labor rather than sets it aside; it enables, however, a person to choose any occupation for which he is qualified by his abilities and his willingness to strive.

T. Dobzhansky, Mankind Evolving: The Evolution of the Human Species 243 (1962).

41. *See* chapters 8 and 9 *infra*.

upon alleged group characteristics is an abomination only less rigid and irrational than that of caste. All blanket assignments of individuals to allegedly different groupings with different capabilities must be condemned by a legal system whose prescriptions are compatible with human dignity. None of the historical groupings, such as race, color, sex, religion, opinion, and culture, has any invariable and uniform relevance to capability for performing roles in modern society.[42] We condemn such groupings as bases for permissible differentiation, not merely because many alleged group characteristics are beyond the effective control of the individual, but because they impose wholly unnecessary deprivations upon both individual development and fulfillment and the creation of community values. The tradition upon which we build has been well summarized by Bell:

> The principle of equality of opportunity derives from a fundamental tenet of classic liberalism: That the individual—and not the family, the community, or the state—is the basic unit of society, and that the purpose of societal arrangements is to allow the individual the freedom to fulfill his own purposes—by his labor to gain property, by exchange to satisfy his wants, by upward mobility to achieve a place commensurate with his talents. It was assumed that individuals will differ—in their natural endowments, in their energy, drive, and motivation, in their conception of what is desirable—and that the institutions of society should establish procedures for regulating fairly the competition and exchanges necessary to fulfill these diverse desires and competences.[43]

Our recommendation in reference to honor is that it be employed, not as the heritage of a class or an appendage of effective power, but in deliberate bestowal in recognition for important community achievement. We recommend that individuals who contribute conspicuously to the common interest receive honor in comparable degree. Though equality of opportunity is indispensable to the nurturing of capability, honor is properly conferred, not upon the basis of capability or potential, but in acknowledgement of actual contribution. A contribution to the common interest is a contribution to social processes where people enjoy, besides fundamental freedom, opportunities to mature their latent capabilities for participation in the shaping and sharing of values. When so conferred, honor can be integrative, not destructive; taking away from none, it may enhance the freedom of all. An incisive sum-

---

42. *See id.*

43. Bell, *On Meritocracy and Equality,* 29 The Public Interest 29, 40 (1972). *See also* D. Bell, The Coming of Post-Industrial Society 425 (1973).

mary is offered by Tawney: "[N]o one thinks it inequitable that, when a reasonable provision has been made for all, exceptional responsibilities should be compensated by exceptional rewards, as a recognition of the service performed and an inducement to perform it."[44]

The realization of appropriate respect relationships in any part of the world community depends upon achieving a vigorous civic order to interact with a public order that performs its essential tasks. The civic order we recommend is composed of aggregate patterns in a community process where coercion from any source, governmental or other, is held to a minimum. A civic order of this kind can only be the product of an effectively functioning constitutive process which both reflects human dignity values in its own features and expresses such values in the public order decisions which emanate from it.[45]

The term "civic order" is used for explicit distinction from "public order." By "public order" we refer to features of the social (value-institution) process which are established and maintained by effective power, authoritative or other, through the imposition of severe sanctions against challengers.[46] By civic order is meant the features of social process that are established and maintained by resorting to relatively mild sanctions, and which afford a maximum of autonomy, creativity, and diversity to the private choice of individuals.

Our postulated, overriding goal of human dignity favors the widest possible freedom of choice and, hence, the fewest possible coerced choices for individuals. This is part of the great liberal tradition which champions the least possible degree of politicization or governmentalization of social interactions compatible with the achievement of other goals.[47] In a totalitarian polity every sector of society is highly politicized and government swallows up society: government *is* society and society *is* government, with correlative attenuation of all zones of individual autonomy. When all the interactions occurring in a social process are encompassed by the power process, an entire society is politicized.[48] The contrasting anarchistic vision of a commonwealth of free people, in

44. R. Tawney, Equality 113 (1964).

45. *See* H. Lasswell, The Future of Political Science (1962); H. Lasswell, A Pre-View of Policy Sciences 1-2, 27-28 (1971).

46. *See* chapter 16 *infra.* For earlier presentations, *see* McDougal, Lasswell, & Reisman, *The World Constitutive Process of Authoritative Decision, supra* note 16, at 73, 100 n. 63; McDougal, *Jurisprudence for a Free Society,* 1 Ga. L. Rev. 1, 1-7 (1966); McDougal & Lasswell, *The Identification and Appraisal of Diverse Systems of Public Order,* 53 Am. J. Int'l L. 1, 6-11 (1959).

47. *See, e.g.,* F. Watkins, The Age of Ideology—Political Thought, 1750 to the Present (1964); F. Watkins, The Political Tradition of the West (1948).

48. *See* H. Lasswell, A Pre-View of Policy Sciences 28 (1971).

which power decisions have become unnecessary, is obviously a will-of-the-wisp in the contemporary world. It does, nevertheless, offer an appropriate reminder and caution to the leaders and the led of our historic period.[49]

The term "privacy" is sometimes employed, as when made equivalent to "a right to be let alone,"[50] with much the same comprehensive reference that we impute to civic order. It would appear preferable, however, to limit the reference of "privacy" to freedom of individual choice about what is to be communicated to others about oneself, and to perceive this freedom as a single example of the more comprehensive freedoms embraced within a properly functioning civic order.[51] Such a restriction on the term "privacy" could make easier and render more precise the contextual analysis that must be executed when a decision has to be made whether to limit the presumption in favor of privacy on behalf of the equal rights of others or of the aggregate common interest. Proper procedures relate different freedoms to divergent features of interaction and context.

The degree to which the four outcomes that we have specified as basic realizations of the "respect" value can be achieved in any particular social context must of course depend both upon the characteristics of the respect process and upon the management of formal authority and effective control. It is important to bear in mind the coordination of perspectives and operational behaviors that must be achieved and subsequently sustained if the requirements for shaping and sharing of respect are to be fully realized. There must be an effective process of political socialization (education) that mobilizes and particularizes the objectives and strategies included within the demand for basic human respect. Perspectives must also sustain the policies that keep the doors of opportunity open for the cultivation of individual capacities and confer distinction upon those who make exceptional contributions to common values. Crucial to the functioning of such a society is the successful transmission of demands upon the self and others to receive rewards in a form that protects the integrity of the institutions compatible with respect. For example, it would be generally understood that substantial differences in protected claims to material resources have undermined the vitality of communities whose structure at one time exhibited a high degree of equality in the control of such resources. An effective social

---

49. *Cf.* C. Jacker, The Black Flag of Anarchy (1968); G. Runkle, Anarchism: Old and New (1972).

50. *See, e.g.,* Miller, *Privacy in the Corporate State: A Constitutional Value of Dwindling Significance,* 22 J. Public L. 3 (1973).

51. *See* Lasswell, *The Threat to Privacy,* in Conflict of Loyalties 121 (R. MacIver ed. 1952).

order will remain alert to changes in resource control and will sustain effective demands to formulate prescriptions and apply procedures that reward exceptional contributions without endangering genuine access to opportunity. It is probable that forms of reward other than wealth will be emphasized and accepted by the members of a social system that is truly committed to a commonwealth of respect. Historically, it has proved dangerous to devolve titles or ranks from one person to another, especially from parent to child.

A successful program of political socialization will highlight these common problems and mobilize codes of rectitude that give support to those who refrain from attempting to institutionalize what amounts to a group-based claim to unjust enrichment in terms of social status. No specific "once and for all" set of norms can be usefully projected for these, any more than for other, dynamic human relationships. The essential challenge is to sustain a process, and especially a set of context-examining procedures, that confront long-range goals with historic, contemporary, and prospective realities. In the chapters to follow we propose to consider the strategies available for improving the institutions of the respect process in the world community. Elsewhere we focus on rearrangement of the more comprehensive features of formal and effective power that are especially relevant to the protection of respect and other human rights.[52]

52. *See* chapter 4 *supra*. *See also* note 16 *supra*.

7. CLAIMS RELATING TO FUNDAMENTAL FREEDOM OF CHOICE

The overriding importance of freedom of choice in the shaping and sharing of all values is beginning to be articulated and established as authoritative general community expectation in a wide range of formal expressions at both the transnational and the national levels. Thus, most importantly, the Charter of the United Nations reaffirms "faith in fundamental human rights, in the dignity and worth of the human person, in the equal rights of men and women," and pledges to "promote social progress and better standards of life in larger freedom" and to "employ international machinery for the promotion of the economic and social advancement of all peoples."[1] In particular, Article 55 of the Charter specifies:

> With a view to the creation of conditions of stability and well-being which are necessary for peaceful and friendly relations among nations based on respect for the principle of equal rights and self-determination of peoples, the United Nations shall promote:
>
> a. higher standards of living, full employment, and conditions of economic and social progress and development;
>
> b. solutions of international economic, social, health, and related problems; and international cultural and educational cooperation; and
>
> c. universal respect for, and observance of, human rights and fundamental freedoms for all without distinction as to race, sex, language or religion.[2]

In similar tenor, the Universal Declaration of Human Rights[3] in its Preamble recognizes "the inherent dignity" and "the equal and inalien-

1. U.N. CHARTER, Preamble.
2. *Id.*, Art. 55.
3. Universal Declaration of Human Rights, *adopted* Dec. 10, 1948, G.A. Res. 217, U.N. Doc. A/810 at 71 (1948) [hereinafter cited as Universal Declaration]. A collection of the

able rights of all members of the human family" as "the foundation of freedom, justice and peace in the world," proclaims "the advent of a world in which human beings shall enjoy freedom of speech and belief and freedom from fear and want" as "the highest aspiration of the common people," and reiterates mankind's determination "to promote social progress and better standards of life in larger freedom" and "to secure . . . universal and effective recognitions and observance" of fundamental freedoms and rights.[4] The International Covenant on Civil and Political Rights, in its Preamble, confirms that "the ideal of free human beings enjoying civil and political freedom and freedom from fear and want can only be achieved if conditions are created whereby everyone may enjoy his civil and political rights, as well as his economic, social and cultural rights."[5] The same emphasis, with practically identical formulation, is evident throughout the International Covenant on Economic, Social, and Cultural Rights.[6]

Comparable regional expression is found in the Preamble of the American Convention on Human Rights which, after stating that "the essential rights of man are not derived from one's being a national of a certain State, but are based upon attributes of the human personality," also stresses the centrality of freedom of choice.[7] The European Convention on Human Rights expresses the

> profound belief in those Fundamental Freedoms which are the foundation of justice and peace in the world and are best maintained on the one hand by an effective political democracy and on the other by a common understanding and observance of the Human Rights upon which they depend. . . .[8]

---

more important global human rights prescriptions is conveniently offered in UNITED NATIONS, HUMAN RIGHTS: A COMPILATION OF INTERNATIONAL INSTRUMENTS OF THE UNITED NATIONS, U.N. Doc. ST/HR/1 (1973). Other useful collections include BASIC DOCUMENTS ON HUMAN RIGHTS (I. Brownlie ed. 1971); BASIC DOCUMENTS ON INTERNATIONAL PROTECTION OF HUMAN RIGHTS (L. Sohn & T. Buergenthal eds. 1973).

4. Universal Declaration, *supra* note 3, Preamble, U.N. Doc. A/810 at 71–72.

5. International Covenant on Civil and Political Rights, *adopted* Dec. 16, 1966, Preamble, G.A. Res. 2200A, 21 U.N. GAOR, Supp. (No. 16) 52–53, U.N. Doc. A/6316 (1966) [hereinafter cited as Covenant on Civil and Political Rights].

6. International Covenant on Economic, Social, and Cultural Rights, *adopted* Dec. 16, 1966, G.A. Res. 2200A, 21 U.N. GAOR, Supp. (No. 16) 49 U.N. Doc. A/6316 (1966) [hereinafter cited as Covenant on Economic Rights].

7. American Convention on Human Rights, *signed* Nov. 22, 1969, Preamble, OAS Official Records OEA/Ser.K/XVI/1.1, Doc. 65, Rev. 1, Corr. 1 (Jan. 7, 1970), *reprinted in* 9 INT'L LEGAL MATERIALS 99, 101 (1970) [hereinafter cited as American Convention].

8. Convention on Human Rights and Fundamental Freedoms, *adopted* Nov. 4, 1950, Preamble, 1950 Europ. T.S. No. 5, 213 U.N.T.S. 221, 222–24 [hereinafter cited as European Convention].

In a more recent summation, the Proclamation of Teheran,[9] adopted at the International Conference on Human Rights in 1968, solemnly reaffirmed that

> The primary aim of the United Nations in the sphere of human rights is the achievement by each individual of the maximum freedom and dignity. For the realization of this objective, the laws of every country should grant each individual, irrespective of race, language, religion or political belief, freedom of expression, of information, of conscience and of religion, as well as the right to participate in the political, economic, cultural and social life of his country.[10]

It concluded by urging

> all peoples and governments to dedicate themselves to the principles enshrined in the Universal Declaration of Human Rights and to redouble their efforts to provide for all human beings a life consonant with freedom and dignity and conducive to physical, mental, social and spiritual welfare.[11]

It may be recalled, in a more comprehensive search for relevant prescription and application, that the fundamental freedom of choice with which we are here concerned is the central concept of human dignity, and that it forms the core reference of human rights in relation to all values.[12] Thus, its reference is, in relation to power, full participation as a person in the process both of effective power and of authoritative decision; in relation to enlightenment, the freedom to acquire, use, and communicate knowledge; in relation to well-being, the freedom to develop and maintain psychosomatic integrity and a healthy personality; in relation to wealth, freedom of contract and of access to goods and services; in relation to skill, the freedom to discover, mature, and exercise latent talents; in relation to affection, the freedom to establish and enjoy congenial personal relationships; and in relation to rectitude, freedom to form, maintain, and express norms of responsible conduct. This pervasiveness in reference to the central concept of freedom of choice makes relevant to its prescription and application all the more detailed prescriptions and applications about the various specific human rights relat-

9. Proclamation of Teheran, Final Act of the International Conference on Human Rights, Teheran, 22 April to 13 May 1968, U.N. Doc. A/CONF.32/41 (1968).

10. *Id.* at 4.

11. *Id.* at 6.

12. *See* chapter 6 *supra.*

ing to each of the different value processes.[13] In other words, the degree to which the claim for fundamental freedom of choice, as a generic aspiration, is protected must be confirmed by reference to the whole flow of decisions, prescriptive and other, about human rights.

The basic thrust in global community expectations toward protecting individual freedom of choice in all value processes is greatly fortified by the long history of developments within the constitutive processes of the different national communities. The continued insistence by so many peoples in different communities and cultures that authority can rightfully come only from the people is a direct expression of demand for freedom of choice in the power processes that affect all other processes.[14] It is this demand for freedom of choice, secure from arbitrary coercion, which underlies the whole historic panorama of constitutional reforms beginning with Greek and Roman liberalism and extending through the English, American, French, and Russian revolutions to the present era of the emancipation of former colonial peoples.[15] The significance of the incorporation, especially after the eighteenth century, of the long cherished doctrines of the basic human rights in formal constitutive charters has been well noted by Lauterpacht:

> The notion of human nature as a source and standard of political rights is older than the end of the eighteenth century. What was new was the formal incorporation of these rights as part of the constitutional law of States and the possibility of their consequent protection not only against the tyranny of kings but also against the intolerance of democratic majorities.[16]

The demand to clarify and enhance the protection of the fundamental freedom of the individual in the broad sense we have specified, however much aspiration may sometimes beg achievement, may be observed in every feature of contemporary national constitutive processes. For brief,

---

13. This point has been documented by a series of U.N. studies on nondiscrimination. *See, e.g.*, J. INGLES, STUDY OF DISCRIMINATION IN RESPECT OF THE RIGHT OF EVERYONE TO LEAVE ANY COUNTRY, INCLUDING HIS OWN 9–12, U.N. Doc. E/CN.4/Sub. 2/220/Rev. 1 (1963); H. SANTA CRUZ, STUDY OF DISCRIMINATION IN THE MATTER OF POLITICAL RIGHTS 15–25, U.N. Doc. E/CN.4/Sub. 2/213/Rev. 1 (1962).

14. Art. 21(3) of the Universal Declaration of Human Rights expresses this crystallized expectation: "The will of the people shall be the basis of the authority of government. . . ." Universal Declaration, *supra* note 3, Art. 21(3), U.N. Doc. A/810 at 75.

15. For an excellent summary *see* Friedrich, *Constitutions and Constitutionalism,* 3 INT'L ENCYC. SOC. SC. 318 (1968). *See also* K. LOWENSTEIN, POLITICAL POWER AND THE GOVERNMENTAL PROCESS (1957); Hamilton, *Constitutionalism,* 4 ENCYC. SOC. SC. 255 (1931).

16. H. LAUTERPACHT, INTERNATIONAL LAW AND HUMAN RIGHTS 88–89 (1950) [hereinafter cited as H. LAUTERPACHT, INTERNATIONAL LAW].

synoptic illustration, reference may be made to provision for individual as distinguished from group participation; to specification that decisions be taken by criteria of common interest, with some prescriptions—such as a "bill of rights"—being accorded priority over other prescriptions;[17] to the balancing of power, in a differentiation of competence for decision, between different branches of the government and different geographic regions;[18] to the subjection of all individuals, including officials, to authoritative decision and the pluralistic distribution of both authority and control; and to the requirement of authorized, uniform procedures in all types of decision with opportunity to challenge decisions allegedly incompatible with authority.[19] This broad sweep of contemporary demand upon constitutive processes has been well summarized by Friedrich, who finds that "the political function of a constitution," "the core objective," is "that of safeguarding each member of the political community" as "a person":[20]

> Each man is supposed to possess a sphere of genuine autonomy. The constitution is meant to protect the *self*; for the self is believed to be the (primary and ultimate) value. . . . Hence the function of a constitution may also be said to be the defining and maintaining of human rights. The constitution is to protect the individual member of the political community against interference in his personal sphere.[21]

The pervasive contemporary emphasis upon "constitutionalism" as a set of preferred prescriptions, though quite inadequate as description of the whole of constitutive process,[22] is nonetheless an eloquent and rational affirmation of the more fundamental policies which have historically underlain such process.

The special importance, in establishing transnational prescription for the protection of fundamental freedom, of the developments in national constitutive processes derives from the fact that "general principles of law" are a recognized authoritative source of international law. It is

---

17. *See* C. McIlwain, Constitutionalism, Ancient and Modern 14, 87 (rev. ed. 1947); G. Sabine, A History of Political Theory 451–54 (3d ed. 1961).

18. *See* G. Sabine, A History of Political Theory 551–60 (3d ed. 1961); M. Vile, Constitutionalism and the Separation of Powers (1967).

19. *See* K. Loewenstein, Political Power and the Governmental Process 123–63, 315–43 (1957); Lasswell & McDougal, *Trends in Theories about Law: Comprehensiveness in Conceptions of Constitutive Process,* 41 Geo. Wash. L. Rev. (1972).

20. C. Friedrich, Constitutional Government and Democracy 8 (4th ed. 1968).

21. *Id.*

22. *See* Lasswell & McDougal, *Trends in Theories about Law: Comprehensiveness in Conceptions of Constitutive Process,* 41 Geo. Wash. L. Rev. 1 (1972).

provided in a well-worn article of its statute that the International Court of Justice shall apply "the general principles of law, recognized by civilized nations,"[23] and, despite the provincialism of the wording,[24] those who apply international law habitually seek guidance for determining transnational perspectives from uniformities in national prescriptions and applications. The cumulative massing of prescriptions designed to protect the fundamental freedom of the individual in national constitutive processes must contribute significantly to the continued crystallization of global expectations that such freedom is to be protected.[25] Conversely, it may be noted that, in interaction as beneficent as cumulative, the shaping of global expectations in turn will have an important effect on the shaping of national expectations. This is most vividly illustrated in the widespread incorporation of provisions from the Universal Declaration of Human Rights in the constitutive charters of many newly independent states.[26]

SECTION 1 THE ERADICATION OF SLAVERY

Factual Background

Slavery, in all its many manifestations, and equivalences, represents the most extreme deprivation of freedom of choice about participation in value processes. Though a slave may physically participate in the shaping and sharing of values, the modality of participation is completely dictated by others. For access to and enjoyment of value processes, the slave may be in total and continuous servitude to the will of a master. His participation in community power processes will, of course, be minimal. Biologically the slave is a human being, but legally he may not be recognized as a person and may be denied any access to processes

---

23. I.C. J. Stat., Art. 38(1)(c).

24. The reference to "civilized" nations in the ICJ Statute, resented as it is by members of the African-Asian community, is a reminder that early international law was shaped largely by the European powers.

25. *See* H. Lauterpacht, International Law, *supra* note 16, at 73–93.

26. *See* United Nations, The United Nations and Human Rights 13–15 (1973); *Measures Taken within the United Nations in the Field of Human Rights* 28–30, U.N. Doc. A/Conf.32/5 (1967) (study prepared by the secretary-general).

The modalities and importance of prescription in global constitutive process are indicated in McDougal, Lasswell, & Reisman, *The World Constitutive Process of Authoritative Decision,* in 1 The Future of the International Legal Order 139–42 (R. Falk & E. Black eds. 1969). The crystallization of community expectation into authoritative policy is indispensable to the effective performance of other decision functions.

It is sometimes tragic that lawyers engaged in litigation within national constitutive processes overlook the applicability of transnational prescriptions which could be presented as the internal law of the land.

of authoritative decision.[27] He may be totally without rights or powers, or accorded participation and protection only in minor degree.

Himself an object of ownership and trade, a thing rather than a person,[28] the slave's principal participation in wealth processes is in the coerced contribution of labor and services to others. He may be sold or otherwise disposed of, either separately as a chattel (chattel slavery),[29] or together with a piece of land under an exploitative system of land tenure (serfdom, peonage).[30] He may be traded locally or transnationally.[31] He may be compelled to work for creditors practically for life because of indebtedness (debt bondage).[32] When he dies, the debt and bondage may even pass on to his heirs.[33] Members of his kin group may sometimes be taken as security for debt. He may be condemned to forced labor for the payment of debt or other reason. He may be denied the right to own property and he may have no competence to enter into any contract, for "neither his word nor his bond has any standing in law."[34]

Although their minimum health needs may be served for the security of investment, slaves may have few or no rights to well-being and per-

27. *See, e.g.,* 1 & 2 J. HURD, THE LAW OF FREEDOM AND BONDAGE IN THE UNITED STATES (1968 ed.).

28. *See, e.g.,* W. BUCKLAND, *The Slave as Res,* in THE ROMAN LAW OF SLAVERY 10 (1908) [hereinafter cited as W. BUCKLAND, ROMAN LAW]. In the words of Chief Justice Taney in the *Dred Scott* decision: "[The slave] was bought and sold, and treated as an ordinary article of merchandise and traffic, whenever a profit could be made by it." Dred Scott v. Sanford, 60 U.S. (19 How.) 393, 407 (1857). Similarly, Davis has written: "As laws governing chattel property evolved from the earliest civilizations, it was almost universally agreed that a slave could be bought, sold, traded, leased, mortgaged, bequested, presented as a gift, pledged for a debt, included in a dowry, or seized in a bankruptcy." D. DAVIS, THE PROBLEM OF SLAVERY IN WESTERN CULTURE 32 (1966) [hereinafter cited as D. DAVIS, WESTERN CULTURE].

29. *See* C. GREENIDGE, SLAVERY 36–48 (1958) [hereinafter cited as C. GREENIDGE].

30. *See id.* at 74–93; McBride, *Peonage,* 12 ENCYC. SOC. SC. 69 (1934). *See generally* J. BLUM, LORD AND PEASANT IN RUSSIA (1961).

31. On the history of the slave trade *see* E. ALPERS, THE EAST AFRICAN SLAVE TRADE (1967); L. BETHELL, THE ABOLITION OF THE BRAZILIAN SLAVE TRADE (1970); B. DAVIDSON, BLACK MOTHER: THE YEARS OF THE AFRICAN SLAVE TRADE (1961); C. GREENIDGE, *supra* note 29, at 49–57; S. O'CALLAGHAN, THE SLAVE TRADE TODAY (1961); Schakleton, *The Slave Trade Today,* in SLAVERY: A COMPARATIVE PERSPECTIVE 188 (R. Winks ed. 1972); Umdzurike, *The African Slave Trade and the Attitudes of International Law Towards It,* 16 How. L.J. 334 (1971). For a powerful description of the profound trauma visited upon victims of the slave trade *see* P. Murray, Roots of the Racial Crisis: Prologue to Policy, 1965, at 227–43 (unpublished J.S.D. dissertation, Yale Law School Library) [hereinafter cited as P. Murray].

32. *See* C. GREENIDGE, *supra* note 29, at 66–73; *Forms of Involuntary Servitude in Asia, Oceania and Australia,* U.N. Doc. E/AC.33/R.11 (1951); Gullick, *Debt-Bondage in Malaya,* in SLAVERY: A COMPARATIVE PERSPECTIVE 51–57 (R. Winks ed. 1972).

33. *See, e.g.,* N.Y. Times, Oct. 5, 1973, at 10, col. 1; *id.,* Dec. 8, 1968, at 7, col. 1.

34. C. SILBERMAN, CRISIS IN BLACK AND WHITE 89 (1964) [hereinafter cited as C. SILBERMAN].

sonal security.[35] They may be subjected to all kinds of physical abuse and torture, including castration,[36] female circumcision, branding with identification marks,[37] other types of mutilation, and sexual molestation. The effects of enslavement have been appropriately likened to those of death.[38]

The victims of servitude are commonly denied opportunity to discover, develop, and exercise their latent skills for social expression; they may be kept in a state of relative ignorance. They are often conditioned to be content with their plight—to "love their chains"—not to demand freedom to participate equally and fully in the shaping and sharing of values.[39] Denied opportunities to acquire and exercise a range of socially useful skills, they are thus condemned to manual labor.

Slaves may be denied access to the affection value and be given little opportunity to develop congenial personal relationships. They may not be permitted to mate according to their choice; although informal relationships may be tolerated, these may not be protected by the laws of marriage, parentage, and kinship.[40] Their family life, if any, is often broken and completely at the mercy of their masters, who can arbitrarily separate husband from wife, children from parents.[41] Lonely and friendless, slaves may even be forced to breed like cattle in order to supply more slave labor. Children may find themselves slaves because of their parentage. They may be sold during childhood in the guise of adoption.[42] They may become subject to "child marriage" under ar-

---

35. In the words of Kardiner and Ovesey:

> The relation of a man to a slave is quite the same as to a horse, and yet there are important differences. It is the same, insofar as the prime objective is to exploit the utility value of the slave, and to perpetuate the conditions which favor his maximum utility.

A. Kardiner & L. Ovesey, The Mark of Oppression 42 (1951).

36. *See* C. Greenidge, *supra* note 29, at 27.

37. "Slave branding provided a mark of identification, facilitated the recovery of fugitives, and satisfied the satanic claim that Negroes were less than human." D. Dumond, Antislavery 10 (1961).

38. W. Buckland, A Text-Book of Roman Law 72 (1964 ed.).

39. As Degler has put it: "In the minds of many modern Americans, the Negro is pictured as a man who was once a slave and one, moreover, who was essentially content in that status." C. Degler, Out of Our Past 168 (1959). This portrayal is, of course, but another aspect of denial of freedom to participate equally and fully in the shaping and sharing of values.

40. C. Silberman, *supra* note 34, at 89.

41. This is a consequence of paramount importance of "utility" attached to the slave. "Neither paternity nor permanent marriage could be recognized, for this would interfere with the free mobility of the slave for sale purposes." A. Kardiner & L. Ovesey, The Mark of Oppression 43 (1951).

42. *See* C. Greenidge, *supra* note 29, at 105–06.

rangements such as *Mu-tsai.*[43] They may be sold in the guise of marriage as concubines, or in exchange for a "bride price" (dowry, lobolo, or boxadi).[44] Abuses of the bride-price system lead to "prostitution, sterility and depopulation."[45]

The slave, "humbled to the condition of brutes,"[46] is deprived even of his sense of right. He is denied opportunity to develop appropriate norms of responsible conduct. In the words of Malinowski, "even his conscience is not his own."[47] Gustavus Vassa, an eighteenth-century slave, summed up his enslaved experiences this way: "When you make men slaves you deprive them of half their virtue, you set them in your own conduct, an example of fraud, rapine, and cruelty, and compel them to live with you in a state of war."[48]

The cumulative impact of enslavement is to deprive its victims of their fundamental respect for themselves as human beings. Elkins, employing insights into the behavioral patterns of prisoners in the concentration camps, suggests a comparable disintegration of adult personality in slaves.[49] Thus, he says that the slave's "relationship with his master was one of utter dependence and childlike attachment: it was indeed this childlike quality that was the very key to his being."[50] Under such conditions of infantile dependency, respect in the sense we have specified (self-esteem and deferential characterization by others) is not possible. As Kardiner and Ovesey have aptly put it, the individual's "self-esteem suffers because he is constantly receiving an unpleasant image of himself from the behavior of others to him."[51] His own sense of worth is utterly destroyed.[52]

Historically, slavery in the sense outlined above extends back to very ancient times and has existed in many cultures and many countries, with many variations in institutional manifestations and varying degrees of

---

43. *Mu-tsai,* meaning "little sister," has become a popular usage among Europeans, especially in the British colony of Hong Kong, though it has been known in China under various other names, such as *ya-tow.* It was particularly prevalent in East and Southeast Asia. *See* C. Greenidge, *supra* note 29, at 105–16; J. Gullick, Debt Bondage in Malaya (1958). In Taiwan, it is called *sim-pua,* "little daughter-in-law." *Cf.* M. Wolf, Women and the Family in Rural Taiwan (1972).

44. *See* C. Greenidge, *supra* note 29, at 94–104.

45. *Id.* at 100.

46. P. Murray, *supra* note 31, at 131 (quoting Gustavus Vassa).

47. C. Greenidge, *supra* note 29, at 21.

48. P. Murray, *supra* note 31, at 131.

49. *See* S. Elkins, Slavery 81–139 (2d ed. 1968).

50. *Id.* at 82.

51. C. Silberman, *supra* note 34, at 109 (quoting A. Kardiner).

52. *Id.* at 115.

approximation to our description.[53] The slowness of mankind's movement toward fundamental freedom is but a mirror reflection of the prevalence of slavery in its various forms. Although its origins are still controverted, it appears that slavery first emerged when tribes moved from the hunting to the pastoral stage.[54] Slavery was early associated with warfare. In the ancient Near East, captives were first killed but later spared to serve their captors. Slavery, it is said, became established in the Sumerian culture of the Babylonian area in the fourth millennium B.C.[55] In addition to capture in war, slave sale and purchase gradually became a source of supply, with victims extending to include even non-foreigners. In Egypt slavery existed from the earliest dynastic period under the pharaohs.[56]

In ancient Greece slave ownership was recognized at the time of Homer.[57] Subsequently, Aristotle, defining a slave as "a living possession," considered slavery a natural component of society in which the domination-submission relationship persists.[58] As wars were frequent

---

53. The literature on slavery is vast. It has expanded significantly in recent years because of the contemporary interest, scholarly and other, in this subject. We are indebted to our colleague Robert M. Cover for assistance in guiding us through this literature. C. GREENIDGE, *supra* note 29, is particularly useful for our present purposes. For recent outstanding historical studies on slavery *see* R. COVER, JUSTICE ACCUSED: ANTISLAVERY AND THE JUDICIAL PROCESS (1975); D. DAVIS, THE PROBLEM OF SLAVERY IN THE AGE OF REVOLUTION, 1770–1823 (1975); D. DAVIS, WESTERN CULTURE, *supra* note 80; R. FOGEL & S. ENGERMAN, TIME ON THE CROSS (1974); E. GENOVESE, ROLL, JORDAN, ROLL: THE WORLD THE SLAVES MADE (1974).

Of a growing list of anthologies, SLAVERY: A COMPARATIVE PERSPECTIVE (R. Winks ed. 1972) is especially recommended. Two concise accounts appear in Finley, *Slavery,* 14 INT'L ENCYC. SOC. SC. 307 (1968); and *Slavery*, 20 ENCYC. BRITANNICA 628 (1969) [hereinafter cited as *Slavery*]. Other useful background readings include E. COPLEY, A HISTORY OF SLAVERY AND ITS ABOLITION (1969); SLAVERY IN THE NEW WORLD (L. Foner & E. Genovese eds. 1969); J. FRANKLIN, FROM SLAVERY TO FREEDOM (2d ed. 1956); E. GENOVESE, THE POLITICAL ECONOMY OF SLAVERY (1965); J. HARRIS, SLAVERY OR "SACRED TRUST"? (1926); W. JORDAN, WHITE OVER BLACK (1968); H. KLEIN, SLAVERY IN THE AMERICAS (1967); L. LITWACK, NORTH OF SLAVERY (1961); E. MCMANUS, BLACK BONDATE IN THE NORTH (1973); H. NIEBOR, SLAVERY AS AN INDUSTRIAL SYSTEM (2d ed. 1910); AMERICAN NEGRO SLAVERY: A MODERN READER (A. Weinstein & F. Gatell eds. 1973); E. WILLIAMS, CAPITALISM & SLAVERY AND ITS ABOLITION (1969); SLAVERY IN THE NEW WORLD (L. foner & E. Genovese *Jolly Institution,* N.Y. REV. BOOKS, May 2, 1974, at 3–6.

54. *See Slavery, supra* note 105, at 629.

55. Westermann, *Slavery: Ancient,* 14 ENCYC. SOC. SC. 74 (1934).

56. *See* A. BAKIR, SLAVERY IN PHARANOIC EGYPT (1952); I. MENDELSOHN, SLAVERY IN THE ANCIENT NEAR EAST (1949).

57. Westermann, *Slavery: Ancient,* 14 ENCYC. SOC. SC. 74, 75 (1934).

58. *See* THE POLITICS OF ARISTOTLE 8–18 (E. Barker ed. & trans. 1958). *Cf.* G. MORROW, PLATO'S LAW OF SLAVERY IN ITS RELATIONS TO GREEK LAW (1939).

and piracy was rife during the Hellenistic period (323–30 B.C.), increasing numbers of captives in war fell victims of slavery. The close connection between slavery and warfare became more pronounced with the rise of the Roman Empire. As Rome's wars of conquest unfolded, large numbers of "barbarian" captives from Africa, Spain, Gaul, Greece, and Asia Minor were put upon the market.[59] The slave population of Rome increased so rapidly that by the middle of the first century it practically equalled the free population,[60] with the potential threat of insurrection. Hence, the Romans made a fine art of slavery with most elaborate and detailed legal regulation.[61] The institution of slavery became an integral part of the social structure of the Roman Empire.[62] Meanwhile, in China, India, and other parts of the East, various forms of human servitude were also widely prevalent.[63]

With the fall of the Roman Empire, slavery declined sharply but did not disappear. Throughout the Middle Ages, slavery existed in many parts of Europe, although the conditions of slavery were ameliorated by the Christian influence. Chattel slavery seems to have disappeared in Western and Central Europe in the late thirteenth century, only to be replaced by serfdom under the feudal system.[64] In Southern Europe and the Middle East, slavery continued under the Byzantine Empire and flourished with the rise of Islam.[65] The Crusades resulted in a substantial increase in the slave trade, both in Muslim lands and in Christian Europe. In the Iberian peninsula, slavery survived not only the Arabic or Moorish domination, but also the Christian reconquest of the peninsula in the fifteenth century. Having reduced the defeated Muslims to slav-

---

59. *See Slavery, supra* note 53, at 632.

60. *See* C. GREENIDGE, *supra* note 29, at 16. For a discussion of the sources and numbers of slaves in Rome see W. WESTERMANN, THE SLAVE SYSTEMS OF GREEK AND ROMAN ANTIQUITY 84–90 (1955) [hereinafter cited as W. WESTERMANN, SLAVE SYSTEMS]. *See also* R. BARROW, SLAVERY IN THE ROMAN EMPIRE 20–21 (1968 ed.).

61. *See* W. BUCKLAND, ROMAN LAW, *supra* note 28.

62. *See* R. BARROW, SLAVERY IN THE ROMAN EMPIRE (1968 ed.); W. BUCKLAND, ROMAN LAW, *supra* note 28; W. WESTERMANN, SLAVE SYSTEMS, *supra* note 60.

63. *See* D. CHANANA, SLAVERY IN ANCIENT INDIA (1960); L. HOBHOUSE, MORALS IN EVOLUTION 289–95 (1915); E. SCHAFER, THE GOLDEN PEACHES OF SAMARKAND: A STUDY OF T'ANG EXOTICS 43–47 (1963); C. WILBUR, SLAVERY IN CHINA DURING THE FORMER HAN DYNASTY (1967); Pulleyblank, *The Origins and Nature of Chattel Slavery in China,* 1 J. ECON. & SOCIAL HIST. OF THE ORIENT 201 (1958).

64. *See* W. BROWNLOW, SLAVERY AND SERFDOM IN EUROPE 42–86 (1969). In the words of Davis: "If the French serf was protected by local custom and if there was little incentive to exploit his labor for commercial or industrial profit, he enjoyed few legal rights not possessed by Roman slaves of the late Empire." D. DAVIS, WESTERN CULTURE, *supra* note 28, at 38.

65. For the perspective of Islam toward slavery *see* C. GREENIDGE, *supra* note 29, at 58–65.

ery, the Portuguese proceeded to import slaves from Africa beginning in 1444, and to set up slave trading posts on the coast of Guinea.[66] The Spaniards soon followed suit. As the Portuguese dominions extended to the East Indies and other areas, many of the natives of these regions became new victims of slavery.[67]

The discovery of the New World ushered a further epoch into the history of slavery. In the Hispanic colonies of the New World, slavery was initially confined to the aborigines (Indians). Later, Indian slaves became less significant when Negro slaves from Africa were imported on a large scale to meet the labor need of the growing plantation economy.[68] Following the Portuguese and Spaniards, the Dutch, French, and British also undertook to engage in the slave trade; all these groups scrambled for spheres of influence on the African coast, with the British playing the dominant role.[69] Of the millions of African slaves transported to America, a large number were sold in Brazil, the West Indies, and the United States.[70] The traumatic impacts of this wholesale enslavement of peoples are still being felt within both the United States and other bodies politic.[71]

---

66. *See Slavery, supra* note 53, at 634. *See also* D. DAVIS, WESTERN CULTURE, *supra* note 28, at 41–46.

67. *See* G. MACMUNN, SLAVERY THROUGH THE AGES 83–178 (1938).

68. *See* E. WILLIAMS, CAPITALISM & SLAVERY (1966). A significant interpretation is offered in E. GENOVESE, THE POLITICAL ECONOMY OF SLAVERY (1965). *Contra,* J. GRATUS, THE GREAT WHITE LIE (1973); U. PHILLIPS, AMERICAN NEGRO SLAVERY (1918). On the controversial issue of the profitability of slavery *see* DID SLAVERY PAY?: READINGS IN THE ECONOMICS OF BLACK SLAVERY IN THE UNITED STATES (H. Aitken ed. 1971); K. STAMPP, THE PECULIAR INSTITUTION 383–418 (1956); Conrad & Meyer, *The Economics of Slavery in the Ante Bellum South,* 66 J. POL. ECON. 95 (1958); Genovese, *The Slave South: An Interpretation,* 25 SCI. & SOC'Y 320 (1961); Woodman, *The Profitability of Slavery: A Historical Perspective,* 29 J. SOUTHERN HIST. 303 (1963).

69. *See* G. MACMUNN, SLAVERY THROUGH THE AGES 83–178 (1938).

70. *See generally* P. CURTIN, THE ATLANTIC SLAVE TRADE: A CENSUS (1969); DOCUMENTS ILLUSTRATIVE OF THE HISTORY OF THE SLAVE TRADE TO AMERICA (E. Donnan ed. 1930–35) (4 vols.); W. DU BOIS, THE SUPPRESSION OF THE AFRICAN SLAVE-TRADE TO THE UNITED STATES OF AMERICA, 1638–1870 (1896); D. MANNIX & M. COWLEY, BLACK CARGOES: A HISTORY OF THE ATLANTIC SLAVE TRADE, 1518–1865 (1962); O. RANSFORD, THE SLAVE TRADE (1971).

71. Originally, the fate of slavery was not confined to any particular race or ethnic group; but during the era of the European colonial expansion, the fact of the slave trade and the servile exploitation of "fellow men" from Africa appeared difficult to reconcile with the professed Christian ideal that all men are born equal before God. Hence, racism asserted itself as a new justification: the black people were condemned to slavery because of their inherent inferiority. The age-worn elitist doctrine was thus wedded to the concept of "race," the damaging impacts of which are still being felt today. This point has been repeatedly emphasized in the recent works in the field of black studies. For profound and detailed analyses *see* S. ELKINS, SLAVERY (2d ed. 1968); W. JORDAN, THE WHITE MAN'S

It is not, unhappily, to be assumed that slavery, in all its manifestations, is a mere relic of the past. In relatively recent times most states have, through their national laws, as will be described below,[72] succeeded in formally proscribing at least technical or "chattel" slavery. Yet even this most onerous form of servitude and many of its approximations—such as peonage, debt bondage, the bride price, sham adoptions, and forced labor—continue to persist in many parts of the world. Thus, Cassin has recently observed:

> Even now, after nearly two centuries of international agreements and even civil wars, the scourge of slavery has not yet been completely eradicated, and, unfortunately, millions of human beings—men, women and children—are literally still slaves, reduced to the condition of objects, or merchandise, or subjected to a regime very much like slavery.[73]

The report of the United Nations Special Rapporteur on Slavery in 1970, drawing upon a nongovernmental source, adds detail: "chattel slavery, serfdom, debt bondage, the sale of children and servile forms of marriage survive today to the extent that they constitute a recognizable element in the pattern of society in seventeen African countries, fifteen Asian countries and six Latin American countries."[74] The same report elsewhere summarizes: "A recent ILO report indicated that thousands of farm workers still live under systems of tenure entailing conditions akin to serfdom, especially in Latin America but also in other parts of the world."[75] The rapporteur's more elaborate *Report on Slavery* of 1966[76] offers country-by-country documentation. Greenidge provides a pertinent summary of the contemporary problem:

> The slavery that arose from war, and subsequently from raiding, trading and dealing, and from birth, was what is known as "classic" or chattel slavery, in which the slave was a piece of property. While

---

BURDEN: HISTORICAL ORIGINS OF RACISM IN THE UNITED STATES (1974); G. MYRDAL, AN AMERICAN DILEMMA (1944); P. Murray, *supra* note 31. *See also* M. BANTON, RACE RELATIONS (1967); Pollak, *Law and Liberty: The American Constitution and the Doctrine That All Men Are Created Equal,* 2 HUMAN RIGHTS 1 (1972).

72. *See* notes 154–78 *infra,* and accompanying text.

73. Cassin, *From the Ten Commandments to the Rights of Man,* in OF LAW AND MAN 13, 19 (S. Shoham ed. 1971).

74. *Question of Slavery and the Slave Trade in All Their Practices and Manifestations, Including the Slavery-like Practices of Apartheid and Colonialism,* U.N. Doc. E/CN.4/Sub.2/312 at 43 (1970) (progress report submitted by the special rapporteur, Mr. Mohamed Awad) [hereinafter cited as *Awad's 1970 Progress Report*].

75. *Id.* at 17.

76. M. AWAD, REPORT ON SLAVERY, U.N. Doc. E/4168/Rev. 1 (1966) [hereinafter cited as AWAD'S REPORT ON SLAVERY].

> this form still survives in Arabia, elsewhere slavery exists, as an exploitation of the weaker members of society by the stronger, and frequently maintained by social sanction, in less straightforward guises. Debt-bondage, by which a debtor may enslave himself voluntarily, or someone under his control, as security for a debt is a major cause of practical enslavement; while the system of land tenure in several parts of the world keeps millions of people in a state of near slavery under such euphemistic terms as peonage. Finally, under the pressure of economic conditions there have developed such practices as the sale of daughters into marriage without their consent, an example of which is the vexed question of the African "bride price," and the selling or giving of children to others who desire to exploit their labour under the guise of adoption, a practice particularly prevalent in the Far East.[77]

Hence, it can be no cause of surprise that the larger community of mankind continues to exhibit concern for the complete eradication both of chattel slavery and of all its approximations.[78]

Basic Community Policies

It has already been observed that slavery in all its manifestations and approximations is the antithesis of the freedom of choice essential to human dignity.[79] "The inherent contradictions of slavery," as the historian David Brion Davis has put it, resides "not in its cruelty or economic exploitation, but in the underlying conception of man as a conveyable possession with no more autonomy of will and consciousness than a domestic animal."[80] Fortunately, most of the world's great religions and secular moralities have, despite occasional tergiversations toward elitism in theory and recommendation, come to this same conclusion.[81]

The ill consequences of slavery, ramifying from its individual victims through all the communities in which they interact with others, have

---

77. C. Greenidge, *supra* note 29, at 20. Other documentations of the continued existence of slavery include Montgomery, *Slavery,* in Human Rights 59–67 (U.K. Comm. for Human Rights Year ed. 1967); *The Changing Face of Slavery,* 1973 Int'l Associations 550; *Slavery Still Plagues the Earth,* Saturday Rev., May 6, 1967, at 24; World, Dec. 19, 1972, at 4; N.Y. Times, Jan. 21, 1974, at 1, col. 7 (Paraguay); *id.,* Oct. 26, 1973, at 3, col. 1 (India); *id.,* Oct. 5, 1973, at 10, col. 1 (India); *id.,* Dec. 8, 1968, at 7, col. 1 (India); *id.,* Mar. 28, 1967, at 16, col. 3 (Saudi Arabia); *id.,* Mar. 22, 1967, at 6, col. 4 (Human Rights Comm'n).

78. For contemporary efforts toward the elimination of slavery in all its forms *see* notes 132–282 *infra* and accompanying text.

79. *See* chapter 6 *supra,* at text accompanying note 33.

80. D. Davis, Western Culture, *supra* note 28, at 62.

81. For a collection of antislavery arguments *see* The Antislavery Argument (W. Pease & J. Pease eds. 1965).

long been recognized as transnational in reach. Lincoln's dictum that a society cannot endure half slave and half free is widely, and rationally, regarded as applying equally to world society. Quoting Camus's comment, "we are all condemned to live together," Silberman observes that "man cannot deny the humanity of his fellow man without ultimately destroying his own."[82] It is not the mere amelioration of the conditions of slavery, but rather its total abolition, which is the overriding objective of general community policy today.[83]

Trends in Decision

In the ancient world, slavery was not generally regarded as unlawful under either community or transcommunity perspectives of authority.[84] The conditions of slavery were for a long time harsh and relatively unchanging. "For more than three thousand years," observes Davis, the "legal characteristics of bondage changed very little."[85] There was, however, a slow movement toward amelioration. Thus, although describing the slave "as property and economic asset rather than as human being,"[86] the Hammurabi Code accorded considerable rights to slaves. Among those rights were "the right of intermarriage with free women, the right to engage in business and to acquire property, and protection of slave concubines when they had given birth to children."[87] Similarly, under the Hebrew law a slave of Hebrew origin could be released after

---

82. C. Silberman, *supra* note 34, at 16. Slavery is, as Greenidge has put it,

> bad for the slave because it tends to make him harsh, sensual and cruel, and to grow to despise the work in which he is engaged, and to shirk it. It is bad for the master because the habit of absolute rule is corrupting. It offers constant facilities for libertinism, and the morality of the slave-owner and his sons is undermined by intimate contact with a despised and degraded class. Cruelty and lust have been its shadows wherever it has existed.

C. Greenidge, *supra* note 29, at 35.

83. The words contained in the 1848 Abolition Decree of France are worth quoting:

> Whereas slavery is an affront to human dignity, inasmuch as in destroying the free will of man it destroys the natural principles of right and duty; whereas slavery is a flagrant violation of the republican maxims of Liberty, Equality, and Fraternity . . . slavery shall be totally abolished in all French colonies and possessions.

H. Lauterpacht, An International Bill of the Rights of Man 100 n.10 (1945) (quoting the Decree) [hereinafter cited as H. Lauterpacht, An International Bill].

84. *See generally* L. Hobhouse, Morals in Evolution 270–317 (1915); Slavery in Classical Antiquity (Finley ed. 1968); W. Westermann, Slave Systems, *supra* note 60; Finley, *Between Slavery and Freedom,* 6 Comp. Studies in Soc'y & Hist. 233 (1964).

85. D. Davis, Western Culture, *supra* note 28, at 32.

86. Westermann, *Slavery: Ancient,* 14 Encyc. Soc. Sc. 74, 75 (1939).

87. *Id.*

six years of servitude, and any slave, Hebrew or not, was granted manumission upon a permanent injury by maltreatment.[88]

In ancient Greek law the slave was viewed on one hand as "a legal object" and on the other as "a legal subject"—as "a man as well as a thing."[89] Thus a slave was partly free. Establishing an elaborate set of legal regulations, the Roman law did not admit different degrees of slavery, but maintained that human beings were either free or slaves.[90] While slavery was not regarded as being in contravention of the *jus gentium,*[91] provision was made for the protection of slaves and the amelioration of their conditions. Thus, masters were forbidden to "punish slaves by making them fight with beasts";[92] a sick slave would become "free and a Latin" upon abandonment by his master;[93] masters were forbidden to "kill slaves without magisterial sanction";[94] a slave, if cruelly treated, could "take sanctuary at a temple or the statue of the Emperor";[95] and in the case of proven cruelty, the slave was not to be returned or sold to his old master.[96]

The most important amelioration related to the manumission of individual slaves. In ancient Greece, the practice of manumission was widespread, resulting in what Westermann called the "inconstancy of status and fluidity of movement from slavery to freedom."[97] Mass manumission was made possible through state and individual actions. The slave was given a manumission price, which the master could not reject.[98] Special funds, contributed by free persons, were set up so that slaves could borrow, without interest, to redeem themselves.[99] For the purpose of redemption, slaves were also allowed to work part-time for third parties to accumulate funds. And after a slave gained his freedom, no stigma was attached to him.[100] Through a long history, in deference to

---

88. *Id.*

89. *Id.* at 76. *See also* G. Morrow, Plato's Law of Slavery in Its Relation to Greek Law (1939); W. Westermann, Slave Systems, *supra* note 60, at 1–57.

90. *See* W. Buckland, Roman Law, *supra* note 28, at 1; W. Buckland, A Text-Book of Roman Law 65–67 (1964 ed.).

91. *See Slavery, supra* note 53, at 631; D. Davis, *supra* note 28, at 83; W. Westermann, Slave Systems, *supra* note 60, at 57.

92. W. Buckland, A Text-Book of Roman Law 64 (1964 ed.).

93. *Id.*

94. *Id.* at 64–65.

95. *Id.* at 65.

96. *Id.*

97. W. Westermann, Slave Systems, *supra* note 60, at 18.

98. *See* M. Konvitz & T. Leskes, A Century of Civil Rights 22 (1961).

99. W. Westermann, Slave Systems, *supra* note 60, at 23.

100. *See* R. Barrow, Slavery in the Roman Empire 173–207 (1968 ed.); W. Buckland, Roman Law, *supra* note 28, at 437–597.

natural law notions of equality, Roman law afforded procedures for facilitating manumission in large numbers.[101] Talented freedmen were commonly accepted into the "political and economic life" of the Roman community "without any manifestations of prejudice arising from their former status."[102] The liberality of Roman law set a pattern for the Middle Ages. "[I]n the Western world," Davis indicates, "it was the Roman law that gave a systematic and enduring form to the rights of masters and slaves."[103] In more recent times, manumission was apparently made relatively easy in Latin America,[104] while in the southern states of the United States "everything was done to place obstacles in the way of manumission."[105]

Because of the historic difficulties in securing the abolition of slavery and the slow progress toward amelioration of its incidents, international efforts at the turn of the nineteenth century were directed principally toward prohibiting the slave trade, so as to reduce the number of slaves.[106] Thus, in 1807, Great Britain forbade the slave trade in all its colonies.[107] In 1814, Britain and France undertook joint endeavors, through the Treaty of Paris, to suppress the slave trade.[108] This joint effort was soon translated into an eight-power declaration at the Con-

---

101. W. Westermann, Slave Systems, *supra* note 60, at 34–36.

102. *Id.* at 79.

103. D. Davis, Western Culture, *supra* note 28, at 32. "By a remarkable coincidence," Davis has noted, "a variety of laws designed to protect slaves appeared at about the same time in China, India, Ptolemaic Egypt, and Rome." *Id.* at 83 n.63. *See also* note 63 *supra.*

104. *See* M. Konvitz & T. Leskes, A Century of Civil Rights 25–36 (1961).

105. *Id.* at 33. "[T]o the Negro in Brazil, slavery was an open system; to the Negro in the South, slavery was a closed system." *Id. Cf.* C. Degler, Neither Black nor White: Slavery and Race Relations in Brazil and the United States (1971); S. Elkins, Slavery 239–53 (2d ed. 1968); H. Klein, Slavery in the Americas: A Comparative Study of Virginia and Cuba (1967); F. Tannenbaum, Slave and Citizen: The Negro in the Americas (1946); P. Murray, *supra* note 31, at 252–84.

106. The antislavery movement at the turn of the nineteenth century was most powerful in Great Britain, where William Wilberforce was the acknowledged leader. *See generally* R. Coupland, The British Anti-Slavery Movement (1933); R. Coupland, Wilberforce: A Narrative (1923); J. Harris, A Century of Emancipation 1–52 (1933); F. Klingberg, The Anti-Slavery Movement in England (1968 ed.); O. Sherrard, Freedom from Fear: The Slave and His Emancipation (1959).

For a concise and useful account of international efforts to suppress slavery and the slave trade *see* United Nations, The Suppression of Slavery, U.N. Doc. ST/SOA/4 (1951) (memorandum submitted by the secretary-general) [hereinafter cited as U.N. Memorandum on Slavery]. *See also* M. Ganji, International Protection of Human Rights 87–112 (1962); C. Greenidge, *supra* note 29, at 171–200; Nanda & Bassiouni, *Slavery and Slave Trade: Steps toward Eradication,* 12 Santa Clara Lawyer 424 (1972).

107. A. Robertson, Human Rights in the World 15 (1972).

108. *See* 1 E. Hertslet, The Map of Europe by Treaty 20 (1875) [hereinafter cited as Hertslet's Treaty Collection]; 1 Key Treaties for the Great Powers, 1814–1914, at 15–16 (M. Hurst ed. 1972) [hereinafter cited as Key Treaties]. *Additional Articles between*

gress of Vienna in 1815.[109] The Vienna Declaration characterized the slave trade "as repugnant to the principles of humanity and universal morality,"[110] and as "a scourge which has so long desolated Africa, degraded Europe, and afflicted humanity."[111] It then expressed the common desire for "prompt and effective" measures toward "the universal abolition of the Slave Trade."[112] The Declaration, however, was toned down in deference to "the interests, the habits, and even the prejudices" of the signatory states,[113] with the understanding that it could not "prejudge the period that each particular Power may consider as most advisable for the definitive abolition of the Slave Trade."[114] The Vienna Declaration of 1815 was reaffirmed by Austria, France, Great Britain, Prussia, and Russia in 1822 at Verona,[115] when those countries expressed their readiness to "concur in everything that may secure and accelerate the complete and final abolition" of the traffic in slaves.[116]

Moving from separate national action toward joint action, international measures in the middle of the nineteenth century included attempts to police the slave trade on the high seas by providing a right of visit, search, and seizure.[117] In this regard, the leading initiatives of Great Britain met with very considerable opposition, because both the United States and France were deeply suspicious of British naval power. Though it was controversial whether the right of visit and search for suppression of the slave trade was in accord with customary international law,[118] significant efforts were made to secure this right by agreement, culminating in a number of bilateral and multilateral treaties that explicitly confirmed mutual rights of visit and search. The Treaty of 1831 between France and Great Britain[119] stipulated that the "mutual

---

France and Great Britain—Paris, 30th May, 1814, in 1 BRITISH AND FOREIGN STATE PAPERS, 1812–1814, at 172 (1841).

109. *See* 3 BRITISH AND FOREIGN STATE PAPERS, 1815–1816, at 971 (1838); 1 HERTSLET'S TREATY COLLECTION, *supra* note 108, at 60. The eight declarants were Austria, France, Great Britain, Portugal, Prussia, Russia, Spain, and Sweden. For a diplomatic account *see* H. NICOLSON, THE CONGRESS OF VIENNA—A STUDY IN ALLIED UNITY: 1812–1822, at 209–14, 292–93 (Viking Compass ed. 1961).

110. 1 HERTSLET'S TREATY COLLECTION, *supra* note 108, at 60.

111. *Id.*

112. *Id.* at 61.

113. *Id.*

114. *Id.*

115. *Id.* at 695.

116. *Id.* at 696.

117. *See generally* T. LAWRENCE, VISITATION AND SEARCH (1858); H. SOULSBY, THE RIGHT OF SEARCH AND THE SLAVE TRADE IN ANGLO-AMERICAN RELATIONS, 1814–1862 (1933).

118. *See* M. MCDOUGAL & W. BURKE, THE PUBLIC ORDER OF THE OCEANS 811–82 (1962).

119. 18 BRITISH AND FOREIGN STATE PAPERS, 1830–1831, at 641 (1833). The Treaty was signed at Paris on Nov. 30, 1831.

right of search may be exercised on board the Vessels of each of the two Nations,"[120] but confined it to the waters specified in the Treaty, i.e., areas along the western coast of Africa, around Madagascar, and similar areas around Brazil, Cuba, and Puerto Rico.[121]

Modeled upon the earlier treaties between Great Britain and France, the Treaty of London of 1841,[122] signed by Austria, Great Britain, Prussia, Russia, and France, was to set a pattern for subsequent agreements. The treaty obliged the signatory states to "prohibit all trade in slaves, either by their respective subjects, or under their respective flags, or by means of capital belonging to their respective subjects; and to declare such traffic piracy."[123] "[A]ny vessel which may attempt to carry on the Slave Trade," it added, "shall, by that fact alone, lose all right to the protection of their flag."[124] Warships of any of the signatory states were empowered to visit and search such vessels. If the vessels were found to be transporting slaves, they were to be seized and handed over to the appropriate tribunals of the states to which they belonged.[125]

Prior to President Lincoln's Emancipation Proclamation,[126] the United States and Great Britain concluded the Treaty of Washington of 1862[127] conferring upon each other a reciprocal right of visit, search, and detention of ships suspected of engaging in the slave trade on the high seas.[128] The exercise of this right was, however, restricted to an area "within the distance of 200 miles from the coast of Africa, and to the southward of the 32 parallel of north latitude; and within 30 leagues from the coast of the island of Cuba."[129] Captured vessels were to be brought before a Mixed Court of Justice, "formed of an equal number of individuals of the two nations,"[130] which would employ a procedure different from

---

120. *Id.,* Art. 1, at 642.

121. *Id.*

122. 30 British and Foreign State Papers, 1841–1842, at 269 (1858). The Treaty was signed at London on Dec. 20, 1841.

123. *Id.,* Art. 1, at 272.

124. *Id.*

125. *See id.,* Arts. 2–14, at 272–84.

126. Proclamation of January 1, 1863, 12 Stat. 1268. For the background and the aftermath of the Proclamation see J. Franklin, The Emancipation Proclamation (1963); J. Franklin, From Slavery to Freedom 239–338 (1956); Dillard, *The Emancipation Proclamation in the Perspective of Time,* 23 Law in Transition Q. 95 (1963).

127. 52 British and Foreign State Papers, 1861–1862, at 50 (1868). The Treaty was signed at Washington on Apr. 7, 1862, and became effective when ratifications were exchanged at London on May 20, 1862.

128. *Id.,* Art. 1, at 50–51.

129. *Id.,* Art. 1(4), at 51.

130. *Id.,* Art. 4, at 53. These courts were located at Sierra Leone, the Cape of Good Hope, and New York. *Id. See also id.* Arts. 2–3, at 51–53.

that of the federal or state courts, and be authorized to pronounce judgment without appeal.[131]

In the late nineteenth century, important progress was made with the adoption of the General Act of the Berlin Conference on Central Africa of 1885[132] and the General Act of the Brussels Conference of 1890,[133] both of which sought to eradicate slavery and to suppress the slave trade. The General Act of Berlin of 1885, after expressing the signatories' pledge to "strive for the suppression of slavery and especially of the Negro-slave trade,"[134] affirmed that "trading in slaves is forbidden in conformity with the principles of international law as recognized by the signatory powers."[135] It further declared that the territories of the Congo basin were not to "serve as a market or way of transit for the trade in slaves of any race whatever."[136] The contracting states were to employ all means at their disposal to terminate the slave trade and to punish those engaged in it.[137]

The General Act of the Brussels Conference of 1890, called "the Magna Carta of the African slave trade,"[138] was the high point in international efforts to suppress the slave trade before World War I. Signed and ratified by seventeen states, the General Act contained one hundred articles under seven chapters, embodying a number of military, legislative, and economic measures.[139] The Act condemned slavery and the slave trade,[140] though it failed to define these terms, and prohibited the

---

131. For detail *see id.* at 58 (ANNEX B—*Regulations for the Mixed Courts of Justice*).

132. General Act of the Conference of Berlin, Relative to the Development of Trade and Civilization in Africa; the Free Navigation of the Rivers Congo, Niger, &c; the Suppression of the Slave Trade by Sea and Land; the Occupation of Territory on the African Coasts &c; Signed at Berlin, 26th February 1885, in 2 KEY TREATIES, *supra* note 108, at 880.

133. 82 BRITISH AND FOREIGN STATE PAPERS, 1889–1890, at 55 (1896). For its text in English *see* U.N. MEMORANDUM ON SLAVERY, *supra* note 106, at 46–68; 3 AM. J. INT'L L. 29 (1909).

134. U.N. MEMORANDUM ON SLAVERY, *supra* note 106, Art. 6, at 9. *Cf.* the other translated versions in 2 KEY TREATIES, *supra* note 108, at 885–86; 3 AM. J. INT'L L. Supp. 35 (1909).

135. U.N. MEMORANDUM ON SLAVERY, *supra* note 106, Art. 9, at 9.

136. *Id.*

137. *See id.*

138. C. GREENIDGE, *supra* note 29, at 176.

139. A significant fact about the General Act of Brussels was the range of its signatory states. They included not only all the major European powers and the United States, but also Turkey, Persia, and Zanzibar; the latter three still recognized slavery at the time.

140. Art. 3 of the Act provides:

> The powers exercising a sovereignty or a protectorate in Africa confirm and give precision to their former declarations, and engage to proceed gradually, as circumstances may permit, either by the means above indicated, or by any other means that

trade in arms and ammunition which had been closely linked to slave-raiding and slave-selling in Africa.[141]

Though it fell short of offering a general right to visit and search, the Brussels General Act contained detailed provisions on visit and search of vessels of less than five hundred tons within a specified maritime zone in which the slave trade still existed.[142] According to Article XLII, if officers in command of a warship had reason to believe a vessel of less than five hundred tons in the maritime zone was "engaged in the slave trade" or "guilty of the fraudulent use of a flag," they were empowered to "examine the ship's papers."[143] This latter authority was confined to examination of documents unless the flag state of the suspected ship was a party to a special convention, in which case the examining officers were authorized to call the roll of the passengers and crew.[144] If the officer was "convinced" that an act connected with the slave trade had occurred on board, the ship was escorted into the nearest port where there was "a competent magistrate of the power whose flag has been used."[145]

An important contribution of the Brussels General Act to the transnational condemnation of slavery was the institutionalization of an intelligence function,[146] a function vital to combatting both slavery and the slave trade. Two permanent agencies were established. The first was an International Maritime Office at Zanzibar, represented by a delegate from each of the contracting states, whose objective was to "centralize all documents and information of a nature to facilitate the repression of the slave trade in the maritime zone."[147] Signatory states were required to furnish the following information: instructions given to the commanders

---

> they may consider suitable, with the repression of the slave-trade, each State in its respective possessions and under its own direction. Whenever they consider it possible, they shall lend their good offices to such powers as, with a purely humanitarian object, may be engaged in Africa in the fulfillment of a similar mission.

U.N. Memorandum on Slavery, *supra* note 106, at 47–48. Art. 1(1) emphasizes that among "the most effective means of counteracting the slave-trade in the interior of Africa [is] progressive organization of the administration, judicial, religious, and military services in the African territories placed under the sovereignty or protectorate of civilized nations." *Id.* at 46.

141. *See id.*, Arts. 8–14, at 49–51.

142. *See* U.N. Memorandum on Slavery, *supra* note 106, Arts. 42–49, at 57–59. *See also* 1 United Nations Legislative Series, Laws and Regulations on the Regime of the High Seas 273–74, U.N. Doc. ST/LEG/SER.B/1 (1951).

143. U.N. Memorandum on Slavery, *supra* note 106, Art. 42, at 57.

144. *Id.*, Arts. 44–45, at 57–58.

145. *Id.*, Art. 49, at 58.

146. On the intelligence function *see* McDougal, Lasswell, & Reisman, *The Intelligence Function and World Public Order*, 46 Temple L.Q. 365 (1973).

147. U.N. Memorandum on Slavery, *supra* note 106, Art. 77, at 63.

of warships navigating the seas of the maritime zone, summaries of reports to governments regarding the grounds of seizure and of minutes indicating the results of searches, lists of "territorial or consular authorities and special delegates competent to take action as regards vessels seized,"[148] copies of judgments and condemnations of vessels, and "[a]ll information that might lead to the discovery of persons engaged in the slave trade" in the specified zone.[149] The second office was an International Bureau at Brussels, attached to the Belgian Foreign Office, whose objective was to facilitate exchange and circulation of documents and information concerning the slave trade.[150] The contracting states undertook to transmit to one another the texts of their laws and administrative regulations relating to the General Act[151] and all "[s]tatistical information concerning the slave trade, slaves arrested and liberated, and the traffic in fire arms, ammunition, and alcoholic liquors."[152] The Zanzibar Office was to submit annual reports to the Bureau at Brussels, which was to be responsible for the collection and periodic publication of relevant documents and information.[153]

The crystallization of transnational perspectives establishing the unlawfulness of slavery was accelerated by the efforts of national communities, paralleling the international efforts to suppress trade in slaves, to abolish slavery itself. Thus, in England, slavery seems to have been regarded as unlawful at least since Somerset's case in 1772.[154] In 1791 the French Assembly proclaimed that "every person is free as soon as he enters France."[155] When abolition laws were extended to colonial territories or to the "overseas territories" of the "metropolitan" powers, these laws, by sheer scope of their application, added new dimensions to transnational expectations. Thus, by the Imperial Act of 1833, Great Britain made slavery unlawful throughout the British Empire.[156] Simi-

---

148. *Id.,* Art. 77(3), at 63.

149. *Id.,* Art. 77(5).

150. *Id.,* Art. 82, at 64.

151. *Id.,* Art. 81(1).

152. *Id.,* Art. 81(2).

153. *Id.,* Arts. 83–84, at 64–65. Because of the Brussels General Act, more had been done by the international community to suppress the slave trade during the period from its enactment to the outbreak of World War I than at any other historical period.

154. Somerset v. Stewart, 98 Eng. Rep. 499 (K.B. 1772). *Cf.* A. Robertson, Human Rights in the World 15 (1972); Fisher, *The Suppression of Slavery in International Law,* 2 Int'l L.Q. 28, 31 (1950); Nadelhalft, *The Somersett [sic] Case and Slavery: Myth, Reality and Repercussions,* 51 J. Negro Hist. 193 (1966). For earlier efforts to abolish slavery in Europe *see* W. Brownlow, Slavery and Serfdom in Europe 204–43 (1969).

155. H. Lauterpacht, An International Bill, *supra* note 83, at 100.

156. *Suppression of Slavery,* 2 Geneva Special Studies No. 4, at 4 (1931) [hereinafter cited as Geneva Studies on Slavery].

larly, France in 1848,[157] the Netherlands in 1863,[158] and Portugal in 1878[159] enacted national laws to outlaw slavery in all their territories. In the United States the abolition of slavery was an important issue preceding, and coincided with, the Civil War.[160] Other instances of the abolition of slavery included Austria[161] and Chile[162] in 1811, Peru in 1821,[163] Guatemala in 1824,[164] Ceylon,[165] and the Dominican Republic[166] in 1844, Tunisia in 1846,[167] Denmark[168] and Hungary in 1848,[169] Ecuador in 1851,[170] Argentina in 1853,[171] Venezuela in 1854,[172] Brazil in 1871,[173] Cuba in 1886,[174] Egypt in 1896,[175] Siam in 1905,[176] and China in 1909.[177] The virtual universal identity in national prescription against slavery did not, however, succeed in abolishing it in fact. As has been pointed out:

> [T]o make slavery illegal and to stamp it out in practice were found to be two different matters altogether. Laws exist almost

---

157. *Id.*
158. *Id.*
159. *Id.*
160. The Thirteenth Amendment, which was ratified on Dec. 6, 1865, provides:

> SECTION 1. Neither slavery nor involuntary servitude, except as a punishment for crime whereof the party shall have been duly convicted, shall exist within the United States, or any place subject to their jurisdiction.
>
> SECTION 2. Congress shall have power to enforce this article by appropriate legislation.

U.S. CONST. amend. XIII.

See generally 2 T. EMERSON, D. HABER, & N. DORSEN, POLITICAL AND CIVIL RIGHTS IN THE UNITED STATES 1004–08 (student ed. 1967); Hamilton, *The Legislative and Judicial History of the Thirteenth Amendment* (pts. 1-2), 9 NAT'L B.J. 26 (1951) and 10 NAT'L B.J. 7 (1952); tenBroek, *The Thirteenth Amendment to the Constitution of the United States,* 39 CALIF. L. REV. 171 (1951).

161. *See* AWAD'S REPORT ON SLAVERY, *supra* note 76, at 18.
162. *Id.* at 31.
163. *Id.* at 112.
164. *Id.* at 70.
165. *Id.* at 29–30.
166. *Id.* at 55.
167. *Id.* at 134.
168. *Id.* at 53.
169. *Id.* at 73.
170. *Id.* at 55.
171. *Id.* at 16.
172. *Id.* at 161.
173. GENEVA STUDIES ON SLAVERY, *supra* note 156, at 4.
174. AWAD'S REPORT ON SLAVERY, *supra* note 76, at 49.
175. *Id.* at 139.
176. H. LAUTERPACHT, AN INTERNATIONAL BILL, *supra* note 83, at 101 n.11.
177. *Id.*

> everywhere, but practices do not conform with them. It has become increasingly clear, in recent decades, that national laws for the abolition of slavery are not enough.[178]

The more direct and explicit transnational perspectives against slavery were revived after the establishment of the League of Nations. Since activities under the Brussels General Act had been disrupted by World War I, at the end of the war it was felt among the state parties to this Act and to the General Act of Berlin of 1885 that a new convention was needed. Hence, the Convention of St. Germain-en-Laye of 1919[179] was signed and ratified by Belgium, France, Italy, Japan, the United Kingdom, and the United States. Building upon and strengthening Article 6 of the Berlin Act of 1885,[180] the contracting states pledged, according to Article 11 of the St. Germain Convention,[181] to exercise their continued vigilance "over the preservation of the native populations [in Africa] and to supervise the improvement of the conditions of their moral and material well being," and to "secure the complete suppression of slavery in all its forms," including forced labor, sham adoption of children, involuntary concubinage, and debt bondage, and "of the slave trade by land and sea."[182] In widening the concept of slavery to include its functional equivalents—"slavery in all its forms"—this Convention was a step forward. It has, however, been criticized on the grounds that it failed to embody provisions for enforcement, and that it had, according to a widely subscribed interpretation, the unfortunate effect of abrogating the Berlin Act of 1885 and the Brussels Act of 1890, at least among the immediately contracting parties.[183]

The Covenant of the League of Nations touched upon slavery in the context of the Mandates System, which was purportedly designed to fulfill "a sacred trust of civilisation" by promoting "the well-being and development" of the inhabitants of the mandated territories.[184] Article 22(5) of the Covenant proscribed practices "such as the slave trade" in these territories.[185] General international conventions governing the slave trade, existing or prospective, were made applicable to all classes of

---

178. Geneva Studies on Slavery, *supra* note 156, at 4.

179. Convention with Other Powers Revising the General Act of Berlin, Sept. 10, 1919, 49 Stat. 3027, T.S. No. 877 (effective Apr. 3, 1930).

180. *See* notes 132–37 *supra* and accompanying text; U.N. Memorandum on Slavery, *supra* note 106, at 9.

181. U.N. Memorandum on Slavery, *supra* note 106, at 12.

182. *Id.*

183. *See id.* at 11; C. Greenidge, *supra* note 29, at 178–79.

184. League of Nations Covenant, Art. 22(1). *See also* J. Harris, Slavery or "Sacred Trust"? (1926).

185. League of Nations Covenant, Art. 22(5).

Mandate. The special charters for the "C" mandates stipulated, as a rule, that "the slave trade shall be prohibited and no forced labor be permitted except for essential public work and services, and then only in return for adequate remuneration."[186] In the case of the "B" mandates, it was incumbent upon the mandatory power to facilitate the ultimate emancipation of all slaves and the elimination of slavery, domestic and other, as speedily as social conditions would permit.[187] The mandatory powers were required to submit annual reports on their administration, furnishing information relating to slavery and the slave trade and to forced labor and other forms of servitude, as well as measures taken for their suppression. These reports were first examined by the Permanent Mandates Commission, a body of experts, and then transmitted to the Council of the League for review and recommendations.[188]

In an effort to cope with the question of slavery on a wider scale, rather than merely in the mandated territories, the League of Nations in 1922 created the Temporary Slavery Commission to appraise global conditions and to make recommendations.[189] The report of the Commission in 1925[190] led to the adoption by the League Assembly, on September 25, 1926, of a most important convention which is still operative.[191] The Slavery Convention of 1926[192] contains only twelve articles.

---

186. GENEVA STUDIES ON SLAVERY, *supra* note 156, at 5.

187. *See* U.N. MEMORANDUM ON SLAVERY, *supra* note 106, at 12, 27–28.

These prescriptions about slavery were reinforced by Art. 23 of the Covenant, the applicability of which was not confined to mandated territories. Pursuant to this article, the members of the League:

> (a) will endeavour to secure and maintain fair and humane conditions of labour for men, women, and children, both in their own countries and in all countries to which their commercial and industrial relations extend, and for that purpose will establish and maintain the necessary international organizations;
>
> (b) undertake to secure just treatment of the native inhabitants of territories under their control;
>
> (c) will entrust the League with the general supervision over the execution of agreements with regard to the traffic in women and children. . . .

LEAGUE OF NATIONS COVENANT, Art. 23(a–c).

188. *See* U.N. MEMORANDUM ON SLAVERY, *supra* note 106, at 28.

189. *See id.* at 12; GENEVA STUDIES ON SLAVERY, *supra* note 156, at 7–8.

190. League of Nations Doc. A.19.1925.VI (1925). The Commission submitted the report to Sir Eric Drummond, secretary-general of the League, on July 25, 1925. *See* 5 MONTHLY SUMMARY OF THE LEAGUE OF NATIONS 180–83 (Aug. 15, 1925).

191. *See* note 228 *infra* and accompanying text.

192. International Convention to Suppress Slave Trade and Slavery, *adopted* Sept. 25, 1926, 46 Stat. 2183, T.S. No. 778, 60 L.N.T.S. 253 (entered into force Mar. 9, 1927) [hereinafter cited as Convention to Suppress Slave Trade]. For a commentary *see* A. WARNSHUIS, J. CHAMBERLAIN, & Q. WRIGHT, THE SLAVERY CONVENTION OF GENEVA, SEPTEMBER 25, 1926 (International Conciliation No. 236, 1928).

At the outset, in Article 1, it seeks to clarify the conception of the slavery that is being prohibited and to reconfirm older perspectives against the slave trade:

> (1) Slavery is the status or condition of a person over whom any or all of the powers attaching to the right of ownership are exercised.
>
> (2) The slave trade includes all acts involved in the capture, acquisition or disposal of a person with intent to reduce him to slavery; all acts involved in the acquisition of a slave with a view to selling or exchanging him; all acts of disposal by sale or exchange of a slave acquired with a view to being sold or exchanged, and, in general, every act of trade or transport in slaves.[193]

In Article 2, the contracting parties undertake to "prevent and suppress the slave trade" and "bring about, progressively and as soon as possible, the complete abolition of slavery in all its forms."[194]

Slavery, as defined in Article 1(1), could be interpreted to confine what is prohibited technically to "chattel slavery" only.[195] Similarly, the qualification, "bring about progressively and as soon as possible,"[196] obviously weakens the commitment toward the "complete abolition of slavery." The choice of words, "slavery in all its forms," is, however, of considerable significance, especially in the light of Article 5, which concerns forced labor:

> The High Contracting Parties recognize that recourse to compulsory or forced labour may have grave consequences and undertake, each in respect of the territories placed under its sovereignty, jurisdiction, protection, suzerainty or tutelage, to take all necessary measures to prevent compulsory or forced labour from developing into conditions analogous to slavery.[197]

Compulsory or forced labor, save in certain transitional circumstances, is to be exacted only for public purposes. Hence, in terms of broadening the concept of slavery to include certain functional approximations, the 1926 Convention offers some augmentation to the previous treaties con-

---

193. Convention to Suppress Slave Trade, *supra* note 192, Art. 1, 60 L.N.T.S. at 263.

194. *Id.*, Art. 2.

195. Regarding "chattel slavery" *see* C. Greenidge, *supra* note 29, at 36–48.

196. Such a gradual approach was justified on the ground that "sudden abolition would almost certainly result in social and economic disturbances which would be more prejudicial to the development and well-being of the peoples than the provisional continuation of the present state of affairs." U.N. Memorandum on Slavery, *supra* note 106, at 15.

197. Convention to Suppress Slave Trade, *supra* note 192, Art. 5, 60 L.N.T.S. at 265.

cerning slavery and the slave trade, including the General Act of Brussels of 1890.[198]

Unfortunately, the measures of implementation achieved were not adequate to support this policy. In an attempt to revive a right to visit, search, and seize vessels carrying slaves, the British government proposed before the Sixth Assembly of the League in 1925 that provision be made to treat the transport of slaves as piracy, thereby empowering public ships to exercise the same authority regarding such vessels as regarding those engaged in piracy.[199] The proposal was not accepted.[200] Instead, Article 3 of the Convention merely binds the contracting parties to "adopt all appropriate measures with a view to preventing and suppressing the embarkation, disembarkation and transport of slaves in their territorial waters and upon all vessels flying their respective flags."[201] Article 3 further states that the parties "undertake to negotiate as soon as possible a general Convention with regard to the slave trade."[202] This provision, as indicated in the United Nations Memorandum of 1951, "envisaged a revival with some modification of the maritime provisions of the General Act of Brussels 1890 as regards the Indian Ocean and Red Sea Coastal areas zone."[203] The contemplated general convention has, however, never materialized. Similarly, no continuing agencies comparable to those under the General Act of Brussels have been established.

The proscription of forced labor, which, in the words of Article 5 of the 1926 Slavery Convention, tends to develop into "conditions analogous to slavery,"[204] was given further concrete expression when the Convention concerning Forced or Compulsory Labour,[205] under the auspices of the International Labor Organization, was adopted on June 28, 1930, and came into effect on May 1, 1932. This Convention is significant in its recognition that "direct slavery cannot be overcome successfully until a way is found to deal with the variety of forms of coercive labor which in many cases become analogous to the root evil itself."[206] Article 1 of the Convention binds the contracting parties "to

198. *See* notes 107–88 *supra* and accompanying text.

199. *See* Gutteridge, *Supplementary Slavery Convention, 1956,* 6 INT'L & COMP. L.Q. 449, 454–56 (1957).

200. *Id. See also* M. MCDOUGAL & W. BURKE, THE PUBLIC ORDER OF THE OCEANS 883 (1962).

201. Convention to Suppress Slave Trade, *supra* note 192, Art. 3, 60 L.N.T.S. at 263.

202. *Id.*

203. U.N. MEMORANDUM ON SLAVERY, *supra* note 106, at 18.

204. Convention to Suppress Slave Trade, *supra* note 192, Art. 5, 60 L.N.T.S. at 265.

205. Convention concerning Forced or Compulsory Labour, *adopted* June 28, 1930, 60 L.N.T.S. 55 (ILO General Conference) (entered into force May 1, 1932).

206. GENEVA STUDIES ON SLAVERY, *supra* note 156, at 12.

suppress the use of forced or compulsory labour in all its forms within the shortest possible period."[207] "Forced or compulsory labour" is defined as "all work or service which is exacted from any person under the menace of any penalty and for which the said person has not offered himself voluntarily."[208] Article 2(2) explicitly exempts from this proscription "any work or service exacted in virtue of compulsory military service laws,"[209] "normal civic obligations,"[210] "a conviction in a court of law,"[211] emergencies,[212] and "minor communal services."[213] In sum, while the Convention forbids forced labor "for private purposes" in unequivocal terms, it adopts "a policy of gradual elimination" of forced labor "for public purposes."[214]

The establishment of the United Nations brought a new intensity to international efforts to eradicate slavery and suppress the slave trade. Though the word "slavery" is not used in the Charter of the United Nations, the provisions concerning human rights throughout the document make slavery completely incompatible with the Charter.[215]

The Charter's fundamental thrust against slavery is made more explicit in the words of the Universal Declaration of Human Rights.[216] Article 4 of this Declaration, an article acclaimed by one commentator as "the cornerstone of all human rights,"[217] states: "No one shall be held in

---

207. Convention concerning Forced or Compulsory Labour, *adopted* June 28, 1930, Art. 1(1), 60 L.N.T.S. 55, 56 (ILO General Conference) (entered into force May 1, 1932).

208. *Id.*, Art. 2(1), 60 L.N.T.S. at 58.

209. *Id.*, Art. 2(2)(a).

210. *Id.*, Art. 2(2)(b).

211. *Id.*, Art. 2(2)(c).

212. *Id.*, Art. 2(2)(d).

213. *Id.*, Art. 2(2)(e).

214. C. Jenks, Human Rights and International Labour Standards 28–29 (1960). On the question of forced labor see W. Kloosterboer, Involuntary Labour since the Abolition of Slavery (1960).

215. The Charter expresses its profound concern for human rights in its preamble and in six different articles; U.N. Charter, Arts. 1(3), 3(1)(b), 55, 56, 62, and 76. After reaffirming "faith in fundamental human rights, in the dignity and worth of the human person, in the equal rights of men and women and of nations large and small," the Preamble projects, as one of its fundamental goals, international cooperation in "promoting and encouraging respect for human rights and for fundamental freedoms for all without distinction as to race, sex, language, or religion." *Id.*, Preamble. Phrases such as "promoting and encouraging respect of human rights" and "assisting in the realization of human rights and fundamental freedoms" appear with slight variations elsewhere in the Charter. Under Art. 56, "[a]ll Members pledge themselves to take joint and separate action in cooperation with the Organization for the achievement of the purposes set forth in Article 55." *Id.*, Art. 56. Among the above-mentioned purposes of Art. 55 is "universal respect for, and observance of, human rights and fundamental freedoms for all without distinctions as to race, sex, language, or religion." *Id.*, Art. 55.

216. Universal Declaration, *supra* note 3.

217. N. Robinson, The Universal Declaration of Human Rights 107 (1958).

slavery or servitude; slavery and the slave trade shall be prohibited in all their forms."[218] The legislative history of this Article establishes that the term "servitude" was intended to be so inclusive as to embrace the various functional equivalents of slavery, such as traffic in women, forced labor, and debt bondage.[219] In an instrument stressing that "[a]ll human beings are born free and equal in dignity and rights"[220] and that "[e]veryone has the right to recognition everywhere as a person before the law,"[221] a less inclusive formulation could scarcely be accepted.

In consolidation of earlier efforts, a new Convention for the Suppression of the Traffic in Persons and the Exploitation of the Prostitution of Others[222] in 1949 proscribed an ancient form of human bondage. This Convention records the agreement of the parties to

> punish any person who, to gratify the passions of another:
> 1. Procures, entices or leads away, for purposes of prostitution, another person, even with the consent of that person;
> 2. Exploits the prostitution of another person, even with the consent of that person.[223]

The Convention also makes an offense of keeping or managing or knowingly financing "a brothel," or knowingly letting or renting "a building or other place" "for the purpose of the prostitution of others."[224] These offenses are, further, made "extraditable offenses."[225] The Convention, unfortunately, relies largely upon penal sanctions which have proved peculiarly inadequate in coping with this mode of human bondage. In the words of Nanda and Bassiouni: "[T]he emphasis was on penal sanctions without giving adequate consideration to the endemic social and psychological reasons for the existence of the problem and without any serious attempts at changing subjectivities and mores."[226]

As a result of a number of surveys requested by the General Assembly and the Economic and Social Council,[227] the United Nations has for-

---

218. Universal Declaration, *supra* note 3, Art. 4, U.N. Doc. A/810 at 73.

219. N. Robinson, The Universal Declaration of Human Rights 107–08 (1958).

220. Universal Declaration, *supra* note 3, Art. 1, U.N. Doc. A/810 at 72.

221. *Id.*, Art. 6.

222. Convention for the Suppression of the Traffic in Persons and of the Exploitation of the Prostitution of Others, *opened for signature* Mar. 21, 1950, 96 U.N.T.S. 271 (entered into force July 25, 1951).

223. *Id.*, Art. 1, 96 U.N.T.S. at 274.

224. *Id.*, Art. 2.

225. *Id.*, Art. 8, 96 U.N.T.S. at 276. We do not deal here with all aspects of this Convention. Other dimensions will be dealt with in a separate study on the affection value.

226. Nanda & Bassiouni, *Slavery and Slave Trade: Steps toward Eradication*, 12 Santa Clara Lawyer 424, 440 (1972).

227. *See* United Nations, The United Nations and Human Rights 17 (1973).

mally assumed the functions of the League of Nations under the 1926 Slavery Convention by virtue of a Protocol adopted by the General Assembly in 1953.[228] More importantly, the broad formulation of slavery in Article 4 of the Universal Declaration of Human Rights has been put into convention form. The Supplementary Convention on the Abolition of Slavery, the Slave Trade, and Institutions and Practices Similar to Slavery,[229] adopted on April 30, 1956, and entered into effect exactly a year later, seeks, as its lengthy title and Preamble show, to "supplement" and "augment," and not to "abrogate," the 1926 Slavery Convention by according prominent attention to efforts to eliminate "institutions and practices similar to slavery," i.e., all the various functional approximations to slavery.[230] Article 1 binds the contracting parties to

> take all practicable and necessary legislative and other measures to bring about progressively and as soon as possible the complete abolition or abandonment of the following institutions and practices. . . .
>
> (a) Debt bondage, that is to say, the status or condition arising from a pledge by a debtor of his personal services or of those of a person under his control as security for a debt, if the value of those services as reasonably assessed is not applied towards the liquidation of the debt or the length and nature of those services are not respectively limited and defined;
>
> (b) Serfdom, that is to say, the condition or status of a tenant who is by law, custom or agreement bound to live and labour on land belonging to another person and to render some determinate service to such other person, whether for reward or not, and is not free to change his status;
>
> (c) Any institution or practice whereby:
>
> (i) A woman, without the right to refuse, is promised or given in marriage on payment of a consideration in money or in kind to her parents, guardian, family or any other person or group; or
>
> (ii) The husband of a woman, his family, or his clan, has the right to transfer her to another person for value received or otherwise; or

---

228. Protocol Amending the Slavery Convention, *opened for signature* Dec. 7, 1953, [1956] 1 U.S.T. 479, T.I.A.S. No. 3532, 212 U.N.T.S. 17 (entered into force Dec. 7, 1953).

229. Supplementary Convention on the Abolition of Slavery, the Slave Trade, and Institutions and Practices Similar to Slavery, *done* Sept. 7, 1956, [1967] 3 U.S.T. 3201, T.I.A.S. No. 6418, 266 U.N.T.S. 3 (entered into force Apr. 30, 1957) [hereinafter cited as Supplementary Convention on Abolition of Slavery].

230. *Id.*, Preamble, [1967] 3 U.S.T. at 3204, 266 U.N.T.S. at 40–41.

(iii) A woman on the death of her husband is liable to be inherited by another person;

(d) Any institution or practice whereby a child or young person under the age of 18 years is delivered by either or both of his natural parents or by his guardian to another person, whether for reward or not, with a view to the exploitation of the child or young person or of his labour.[231]

In other provisions, in order to minimize the bondage of women, the Convention stresses the importance of "consent" in marriages, and encourages national prescription of "suitable minimum ages of marriage" and "the registration of marriages."[232] In broader reach, Article 4 provides that "[a]ny slave who takes refuge on board any vessel of a State Party to this Convention shall *ipso facto* be free."[233] Article 5 forbids "multilating, branding or otherwise marking a slave or a person of servile status."[234] While the word "slavery" is employed, as under the 1926 Convention, to designate classic "chattel" slavery, "a person of servile status" is made to refer to a victim of practices analogous to slavery, as outlined in Article 1 of the Convention.[235]

In measures toward implementation, the intelligence function is emphasized, requiring both mutual exchanges of information among the parties and active cooperation with the United Nations. The parties undertake to communicate to the U.N. secretary-general, as a clearing center, "copies of any laws, regulations and administrative measures enacted or put into effect to implement the provisions of this Convention."[236] Despite efforts to revive a right of visit and search for vessels engaged in the slave trade, equating such ships with those engaged in piracy,[237] the 1956 Supplementary Convention provides only Article 3(1), which reads:

> The act of conveying or attempting to convey slaves from one country to another by whatever means of transport, or of being accessory thereto, shall be a criminal offense under the laws of the States Parties to this Convention and persons convicted thereof shall be liable to very severe penalties.[238]

---

231. *Id.*, Art. 1, [1967] 3 U.S.T. at 3204–05, 266 U.N.T.S. at 41.

232. *Id.*, Art. 2, [1967] 3 U.S.T. at 3205, 266 U.N.T.S. at 42.

233. *Id.*, Art. 4.

234. *Id.*, Art. 5.

235. *Id.*, Art. 7, [1967] 3 U.S.T. at 3206, 266 U.N.T.S. at 43.

236. *Id.*, Art. 8(2), [1967] 3 U.S.T. at 3206, 266 U.N.T.S. at 44.

237. *See* Gutteridge, *Supplementary Slavery Convention, 1956,* 6 INT'L COMP. L.Q. 449, 454–60, 465–69 (1957).

238. Supplementary Convention on Abolition of Slavery, *supra* note 229, Art. 3(1), [1967] 3 U.S.T. at 3205, 266 U.N.T.S. at 42.

The responsibility for punishment is, by this provision, confined to the flag state. Fortunately, this gap was quickly remedied by the Convention on the High Seas concluded in 1958.[239] This Convention, in addition to incorporating the substance of the 1956 Supplementary Convention,[240] stipulates in Article 22(1) a "reasonable ground for suspecting" that "the ship is engaged in the slave trade," along with suspicion of piracy, as among the exceptional circumstances which justify a warship in boarding "a foreign merchant on the high seas."[241]

In response to the findings of the United Nations International Labour Organization *Ad Hoc* Committee on Forced Labour regarding the prevalence of "forced" or "corrective" labor used as an instrument of "political coercion" or for other purposes,[242] a new Convention concerning the Abolition of Forced Labour was unanimously adopted, on June 25, 1957, by the General Conference of the International Labour Organization.[243] Article 1 of the Convention provides:

> Each Member of the International Labour Organization which ratifies this Convention undertakes to suppress and not to make use of any form of forced or compulsory labour:
>
> (a) As a means of political coercion or education or as a punishment for holding or expressing political views or

239. Convention on the High Seas, *done* Apr. 29, 1958, [1962] 2 U.S.T. 2313, T.I.A.S. No. 5200, 450 U.N.T.S. 82.

240. Art. 13 of the High Seas Convention reads:

> Every state shall adopt effective measures to prevent and punish the transport of slaves in ships authorized to fly its flag, and to prevent the unlawful use of its flag for that purpose. Any slave taking refuge on board any ship, whatever its flag, shall *ipso facto* be free.

Id., Art. 13, [1962] 2 U.S.T. at 2316–17, 450 U.N.T.S. at 90.

Cf. Art. 4 of the 1956 Supplementary Convention: "Any slave who takes refuge on board any vessel of a State Party to this Convention shall *ipso facto* be free." Supplementary Convention on Abolition of Slavery, *supra* note 229, Art. 4, [1967] 3 U.S.T. at 3205, 266 U.N.T.S. at 42.

241. Convention on the High Seas, *done* Apr. 29, 1958, Art. 22(1), [1962] 2 U.S.T. 2318, T.I.A.S. No. 5200, 450 U.N.T.S. 82, 92.

242. *See* United Nations & International Labour Office, Report of the Ad Hoc Committee on Forced Labour, U.N. Doc. E/2431 (1953); International Labor Conference, 39th Session, Geneva, 1956, Report VI (2) (Supplement), Report of the ILO Committee on Forced Labour (1956); International Labor Conference, 40th Session, Geneva, 1957, Report IV (2) (Supplement), Report of the ILO Committee on Forced Labour (1957).

243. Convention concerning the Abolition of Forced Labour, *adopted* June 25, 1957, 320 U.N.T.S. 292 (ILO General Conference) (entered into force Jan. 17, 1959). For a commentary see C. Jenks, Human Rights and International Labour Standards 25–46 (1960).

views ideologically opposed to the established political, social or economic system;

(b) As a method of mobilising and using labour for purposes of economic development;

(c) As a means of labour discipline;

(d) As a punishment for having participated in strikes;

(e) As a means of racial, social, national, or religious discrimination.[244]

The drive toward implementation similarly took on added intensity. Unlike the familiar phrases, "within the shortest possible period" and "progressively and as soon as possible" employed in the earlier Conventions,[245] the contracting parties here pledged themselves to undertake "effective measures to secure the *immediate and complete* abolition of forced or compulsory labour."[246]

The every-growing transnational perspectives of authority outlawing slavery in all its manifestations were consolidated in the International Covenant on Civil and Political Rights adopted in 1966.[247] Thus, Article 8 of the Covenant states:

1. No one shall be held in slavery; slavery and the slave trade in all their forms shall be prohibited.
2. No one shall be held in servitude.
3. (a) No one shall be required to perform forced or compulsory labour. . . .[248]

The qualifications to this inclusiveness are that the "forced or compulsory labour" specified in paragraph 3(a) of Article 8 is not to be held "to preclude, in countries where imprisonment with hard labour may be imposed as a punishment for a crime, the performance of hard labour in pursuance of a sentence to such punishment by a competent court,"[249] and is not to include:

(i) Any work or service, not referred to in sub-paragraph *b*, normally required of a person who is under detention in consequence of a lawful order of a court, or of a person during onditional release from such detention;

---

244. Convention concerning the Abolition of Forced Labour, *supra* note 243, Art. 1, 320 U.N.T.S. at 294–96.

245. *See* notes 107–214 *supra* and accompanying text.

246. Convention concerning the Abolition of Forced Labour, *supra* note 243, Art. 2, 320 U.N.T.S. at 296 (italics added).

247. Covenant on Civil and Political Rights, *supra* note 5.

248. *Id.*, Art. 8(1)–(3)(a), U.N. GAOR, Supp. (No. 16) 54.

249. *Id.*, Art. 8(3)(b).

(ii) Any service of a military character and, in countries where conscientious objection is recognized, any national service required by law of conscientious objectors;

(iii) Any service exacted in cases of emergency or calamity threatening the life or well-being of the community;

(iv) Any work or service which forms part of normal civil obligations.[250]

The legislative history of Article 8 establishes clearly that, even if "slavery" is given a more "limited and technical" connotation,[251] "servitude" is "more general idea covering all possible forms of man's domination of man."[252] The proposed prohibition is described as extending to "servitude in any form, whether involuntary or not," so as to make it impossible "for any person to contract himself into bondage."[253]

On the regional level, comparable provisions, with the same degree of specification and with slight variations in wording, are found in Article 4 of the European Convention on Human Rights[254] and Article 6 of the American Convention on Human Rights.[255] Though Article 4 of the

---

250. *Id.*, Art. 8(3)(c).

251. *Annotations on the Text of the Draft International Covenants on Human Rights,* 10 U.N. GAOR, Annexes (Agenda Item 28) 33, U.N. Doc. A/2929 (1955) [hereinafter cited as *Annotations on the Covenants*].

252. *Id.*

253. *Id.*

254. Art. 4 of the European Convention reads:

(1) No one shall be held in slavery or servitude.

(2) No one shall be required to perform forced or compulsory labour.

(3) For the purpose of this Article the term "forced or compulsory labour" shall not include:

(a) any work required to be done in the ordinary course of detention imposed according to the provisions of Article 5 of this convention or during conditional release from such detention;

(b) any service of a military character or, in case of conscientious objectors in countries where they are recognised, service exacted instead of compulsory military service;

(c) any service exacted in case of an emergency or calamity threatening the life or well-being of the community;

(d) any work or service which forms part of normal civic obligations.

European Convention, *supra* note 8, Art. 4, 213 U.N.T.S. at 224–26.

255. Art. 6 of the American Convention on Human Rights provides:

1. No one shall be subject to slavery or to involuntary servitude, which are prohibited in all their forms, as are the slave trade and traffic in women.

2. No one shall be required to perform forced or compulsory labour. This provision shall not be interpreted to mean that, in those countries in which the

European Convention, for reasons unclear, omits specific reference to "the slave trade," it can scarcely be interpreted as making the slave trade permissible. Unlike the Covenant and the European Convention, Article 6(1) of the American Convention[256] uses the wording "involuntary servitude" instead of "servitude" and enumerates the prohibition of "traffic in women," together with that of the slave trade. The use of the additional word "involuntary" could lend support to restrictive interpretation that "voluntary" servitude is permissible. Such a reading would obviously be a misinterpretation, however, in the light of the whole development in transnational expectations of authority against slavery and servitude.[257]

The comprehensiveness with which slavery is prohibited is emphasized in Article 4(2) of the International Covenant on Civil and Political Rights[258] and in Article 15(2) of the European Convention,[259] both of which provide that under no circumstances (including even national emergencies) can there be derogation from the prohibition of slavery, the slave trade, and servitude. Regrettably, this restriction is not extended to the proscription of forced labor.[260] Such deficiency in prohibi-

---

> penalty established for certain crimes is deprivation of liberty at forced labour, the carrying out of such a sentence imposed by a competent court is prohibited. Forced labour shall not adversely affect the dignity or the physical or intellectual capacity of the prisoner.
>
> 3. For the purposes of this article the following do not constitute forced or compulsory labour:
>
> (a) work or service normally required of a person imprisoned in execution of a sentence or formal decision passed by the competent judicial authority. Such work or service shall be carried out under the supervision and control of public authorities, and any persons performing such work or service shall not be placed at the disposal of any private party, company, or juridical person;
>
> (b) military service and, in countries in which conscientious objectors are recognized, national service that the law may provide for in lieu of military service;
>
> (c) service exacted in time of danger or calamity that threatens the existence or the well-being of the community; or
>
> (d) work or service that forms part of normal civic obligations.

American Convention, *supra* note 7, Art. 6, 9 INT'L LEGAL MATERIALS at 103.

256. *Id.*, Art. 6(1).

257. *See* notes 106–253 *supra* and accompanying text.

258. Covenant on Civil and Political Rights, *supra* note 5, Art. 4(2), 21 U.N. GAOR, Supp. (No. 16) 53.

259. European Convention, *supra* note 8, Art. 15(2), 213 U.N.T.S. at 232.

260. In the *Iversen* case, brought before the European Commission on Human Rights, Iversen contended that his compulsory assignment under Norway's Provisional Act of 1956 to the public dental service in the Moskenes district in northern Norway constituted

tion is remedied in Article 27 of the American Convention,[261] which specifies immunity from derogation for the prohibition of "forced or compulsory labor," as well as that of slavery, involuntary servitude, or the slave trade.

The continuing need for more effective measures of implementation to eradicate all forms of slavery has been underscored by insistent demands within the United Nations for further study. At the request of the Economic and Social Council in July 1963, the secretary-general appointed Mohamed Awad as Special Rapporteur on Slavery.[262] Based upon the responses of the member states of the United Nations, the specialized agencies, and interested nongovernmental organizations with consultative status, the special rapporteur completed a comprehensive survey, *Report on Slavery*,[263] in 1966. After reviewing Awad's report, the Economic and Social Council, in July 1966, decided to refer the "question of slavery and the slave trade in all their practices and manifestations, including the slavery-like practices of *apartheid* and colonialism"[264] to the Commission on Human Rights for further study and specific recommendations of measures of implementation.[265] The Commission in turn entrusted this task to its Sub-Commission on Prevention of Discrimination and Protection of Minorities.[266] Thus, in 1968,

---

forced or compulsory labor in contravention of Art. 4(2) of the European Convention. Drawing upon "the provisions and application of ILO Conventions and Resolutions on Forced Labour," the Commission identified the following two elements as essential to the concept of forced or compulsory labor: (1) "the work or service is performed by the worker against his will," and (2) the work or service performed "is unjust or oppressive" or "involves avoidable hardship." Iversen Case, [1963] Y.B. EUR. CONV. ON HUMAN RIGHTS 278, 328. Applying these criteria, the Commission concluded that Iversen's service was not forced or compulsory labor under Art. 14, para. (2), of the Convention. The decision was based on the findings that the Provisional Act of 1956 imposed obligatory service, but since such service was for a short period, provided favourable remuneration, did not involve any diversion from chosen professional work, was only applied in the case of posts not filled after being duly advertised, and did not involve any discriminatory, arbitrary or punitive application, the requirement to perform that service was not unjust or oppressive; the Law of 1956 was properly applied to Iversen when he was directed to take up the post at Moskenes; further, in the particular case of the Applicant, the hardship of the post was mitigated by the reduction in the required term of his service from 2 years to 1 year. *Id.*

An additional ground of justification, based on Art. 4(3)(c), was the existence of an emergency caused by "threat of a breakdown" in the public dental service in northern Norway. *Id.* at 330.

261. American Convention, *supra* note 7, Art. 27, 9 INT'L LEGAL MATERIALS at 109.

262. ECOSOC Res. 960, 36 U.N. ECOSOC Supp. 1, at 26, U.N. Doc. E/3816 (1963).

263. AWAD'S REPORT ON SLAVERY, note 128 *supra*.

264. ECOSOC Res. 1126, 41 U.N. ECOSOC, Supp. (No. 1) 16, U.N. Doc. E/4264 (1966).

265. *Id.* at 7.

266. Commission on Human Rights, Report of the Twenty-third Session, 20 Feb.–23 March, 1967, 42 U.N. ECOSOC, Supp. (No. 6) 159–61 (1967).

Mohamed Awad was again appointed special rapporteur and was later instructed to study not only slavery but also "measures for combating the manifestations of the slavery-like practices akin to *apartheid* which exist in Southern Rhodesia and Namibia, especially the practices of forced, sweated African labour and the total denial of trade union rights to Africans in those territories."[267] After extensive consultations with the officials of many different intergovernmental organizations,[268] the special rapporteur in 1971 submitted his report,[269] which contained a number of concrete proposals toward more effective implementation of the proscriptions of slavery and the slave trade in all their forms.[270]

The culmination of these activities has been the adoption by the Economic and Social Council on June 2, 1972, of an important resolution, Resolution 1695 (LII),[271] which incorporates and reflects essentially, except in one most important point,[272] the recommendations of the special rapporteur.[273] In summary, the resolution urges the following:

1. Wider ratifications of, or accession to, the 1926 Slavery Convention and the 1956 Supplementary Convention;[274]
2. Enactment of necessary national laws "to prohibit slavery and the slave trade in all their practices and manifestations and to provide effective penal sanctions";[275]
3. Wider acceptance of the Forced Labor Convention of 1930, the Abolition of Forced Labor Convention of 1957, and other related Conventions and Recommendations adopted by the International Labor Organization;[276]

---

267. Sub-Commission Resolution 4 (XXII) Sept. 10, 1969. *See Question of Slavery and the Slave Trade in All Their Practices and Manifestations, Including the Slavery-like Practices of Apartheid and Colonialism* 5–6, U.N. Doc. E/CN.4/Sub.2/322 (1971) (report submitted by the special rapporteur, Mr. Mohamed Awad) [hereinafter cited as *Awad's 1971 Report*].

268. The most important consultations were with officials of the International Labor Organization, the Office of United Nations High Commissioner for Refugees, the Division of Narcotic Drugs, the International Criminal Police Organization (INTERPOL), and the United Nations Educational, Scientific and Cultural Organization. *See Awad's 1970 Progress Report, supra* note 74, at 11–43; *Awad's 1971 Report, supra* note 267, at 9–29. Of non-governmental organizations, the Anti-Slavery Society contributed most importantly to the special rapporteur's survey.

269. *Awad's 1971 Report, supra* note 267.

270. *See id.* at 32–50. *See also* AWAD'S REPORT ON SLAVERY, *supra* note 76, at 299–314; *Awad's 1970 Progress Report, supra* note 74, at 43–48.

271. ECOSOC Res. 1695, 52 U.N. ECOSOC, Supp. (No. 1) 21, U.N. Doc. E/5183 (1972).

272. *See* text accompanying notes 285–99 *infra.*

273. *See* note 270 *supra.*

274. ECOSOC Res. 1695, para. 1, 52 U.N. ECOSOC, Supp. (No. 1) 21, U.N. Doc. E/5183 (1972).

275. *Id.*, para. 3.

276. *Id.*, para. 4, at 22.

4. The cooperation of the International Criminal Police Organization (INTERPOL) with the United Nations, especially in furnishing information regarding "the international traffic in persons";[277]
5. Transmission by the secretary-general of relevant information to the Sub-Commission;[278]
6. Acceleration of national efforts toward "total emancipation of slaves and other persons of servile status" and absorption of such persons into "the general labor force";[279]
7. "[A]ssistance to victimized persons by all specialized agencies, intergovernmental organizations and non-governmental organizations concerned";[280]
8. Exploration by the Sub-Commission of the "possibility" of establishing "some form of permanent machinery";[281] and
9. Preparation by the secretary-general of "a survey on national legislation" and "a plan of technical co-operation," and submission of progress reports.[282]

Appraisal and Recommendations

From a perspective of many decades, there has been a conspicuous and consistent movement in transnational prescription toward the broad prohibition of servitude in all its many manifestations.[283] In substantive content, the contemporary prohibition would appear sufficiently comprehensive to meet all pertinent requirements. The more important community prescriptions most emphatically endorse and reflect basic policies consonant with our fundamental objectives and specifications honoring freedom of choice.[284]

In terms of implementation, however, achievements in the transnational arena have lagged. Undoubtedly, the adoption of the recommendations embodied in ECOSOC Resolution 1695 (LII) of 1972[285] would contribute greatly toward the elimination of slavery and the slave trade. The step most urgently required, however, is the establishment of a permanent body to oversee the application of all relevant international conventions. In this regard, it must be conceded that the response of the

277. *Id.,* para. 6.
278. *Id.,* para. 7.
279. *Id.,* para. 8.
280. *Id.,* para. 9.
281. *Id.,* para. 12.
282. *Id.,* para. 13(a-b).
283. *See* notes 84-282 *supra* and accompanying text.
284. *See* chapter 6 *supra*, at notes 18-52 and accompanying text.
285. *See* notes 271-82 *supra* and accompanying text.

Economic and Social Council has been disappointing. When the Special Rapporteur on Slavery submitted his recommendations, both in 1966[286] and in 1971,[287] he took occasion to emphasize, in the light of the earlier experience under the 1890 General Act of Brussels and the League of Nations, the overriding importance of establishing a standing committee of independent experts on slavery.[288] This, he insisted, was "the one suggestion which can be said to embrace all the other suggestions";[289] such a committee "could help in promoting and supervising all the other activities."[290] In 1966, however, the Economic and Social Council avoided responsibility by referring "the question of slavery and the slave trade in all their practices and manifestations, including the slavery-like practices of *apartheid* and colonialism" to the Commission on Human Rights.[291] The infusion of the issues of "*apartheid* and colonialism," matters of proper and continuing concern to other U.N. bodies,[292] has further had the unfortunate effect of dispersing attention from the core question of slavery. Similarly, in 1972, the Economic and Social Council, in its Resolution 1695 (LII),[293] instead of establishing appropriate permanent machinery for supervision, went no further than to order further study and exploration. For this purpose, it directed

> the Sub-Commission on Prevention of Discrimination and Protection of Minorities to examine the possibility of the establishment of some form of permanent machinery to give advice on the elimination of slavery and on the suppression of the traffic in persons and exploitation of the prostitution of others, and to make recommendations with a view to seeking the better implementation of the United Nations instruments concerned.[294]

If the world community is genuinely interested in the complete eradication of all manifestations of slavery, it is urgently necessary to go beyond further studies and to establish without more delay a permanent body of independent experts whose charter of authority follows the guidelines proposed by the special rapporteur.[295] Among the essential

---

286. AWAD'S REPORT ON SLAVERY *supra* note 76.

287. *Awad's 1971 Report, supra* note 267.

288. *See* AWAD'S REPORT ON SLAVERY, *supra* note 76, at 307–09; *Awad's 1971 Report, supra* note 267, at 49–50.

289. AWAD'S REPORT ON SLAVERY, *supra* note 76, at 307.

290. *Id.*

291. *See* text accompanying note 265 *supra.*

292. *See* notes 453–598 *infra* and accompanying text.

293. ECOSOC Res. 1695, 52 U.N. ECOSOC, Supp. (No. 1) 21, U.N. Doc. E/5183 (1972).

294. *Id.,* para. 12, at 22.

295. *See* AWAD'S REPORT ON SLAVERY, *supra* note 76, at 308–09.

activities of such a body would of course be the intelligence function—the gathering, processing, and dissemination of information relevant to decision making.[296] In a world whose crystallized community expectations so thoroughly condemn slavery and the slave trade, it is reasonable to anticipate that the authoritative exposure of offending practices would be a long step toward their eradication. The new body could also perform the promoting function by addressing action recommendations to the United Nations, to other intergovernmental organizations, and to the various states. The permanent body could also be equipped to perform an invoking function, if granted authority to bring complaints to the Commission on Human Rights[297] or other appropriate bodies. Similarly, it could be directed to submit regular reports to the Economic and Social Council,[298] in which appraisals were made of how states and intergovernmental organizations were discharging their responsibilities. Finally, the agency could design and supervise programs in education calculated to instruct and mobilize both the general public and effective elites toward more effective application of specific policies in the sphere of human rights.[299] Sustained by a vigilant world public opinion, and working in close cooperation with related entities, such as the International Labor Organization (regarding forced labor),[300] INTERPOL (regarding the traffic in persons),[301] and the Food and Agriculture Organi-

---

296. *See generally* McDougal, Lasswell, & Reisman, *The World Constitutive Process of Authoritative Decision,* in 1 THE FUTURE OF THE INTERNATIONAL LEGAL ORDER 73 (R. Falk & C. Black eds. 1969).

297. Regarding the procedures of complaints before the Commission on Human Rights *see* L. SOHN & T. BUERGENTHAL, INTERNATIONAL PROTECTION OF HUMAN RIGHTS 739–856 (1973); Carey, *Progress on Human Rights at the United Nations,* 66 AM. J. INT'L L. 107 (1972); Cassese, *The Admissibility of Communications to the United Nations on Human Rights Violations,* 5 HUMAN RIGHTS J. 375 (1972); Humphrey, *The Right of Petition in the United Nations,* 4 HUMAN RIGHTS J. 463 (1971); Newman, *The New U.N. Procedure for Human Rights Complaints: Reform, Status Quo, or Chambers of Horror?* in *Hearings on International Protection of Human Rights before the Subcomm. on International Organizations and Movements of the House Comm. on Foreign Affairs,* 93d Cong., 1st Sess. 715–22 (1973); Parsons, *The Individual Right of Petition: A Study of Methods Used by International Organizations to Utilize the Individual as a Source of Information on the Violations of Human Rights,* 13 WAYNE L. REV. 678 (1967); Schwelb, *The Abuse of the Right of Petition,* 3 HUMAN RIGHTS J. 313 (1970); Wilkoc, *Procedures to Deal with Individual Communications to International Bodies: The Subcommission on Prevention of Discrimination and Protection of Minorities,* 1 N.Y.U.J. INT'L L. & POLITICS 277 (1968).

298. For the importance of the appraising function *see* Lasswell, *Toward Continuing Appraisal of the Impact of Law on Society,* 21 RUTGERS L. REV. 645 (1967).

299. *See Awad's 1971 Report, supra* note 267, at 47–49. *See also* J. CAREY, U.N. PROTECTION OF CIVIL AND POLITICAL RIGHTS 17–21 (1970).

300. *See Awad's 1971 Report, supra* note 267, at 10–16; *Awad's 1970 Progress Report, supra* note 74, at 12–23.

301. *See Awad's 1971 Report, supra* note 267, at 22–27; *Awad's 1970 Progress Report, supra* note 74, at 32–39.

zation (regarding debt bondage and peonage),[302] such a specialized permanent body might succeed in accomplishing a great deal to make slavery in all its manifestations a thing of the past.

SECTION 2 THE ELIMINATION OF CASTE

While slavery represents the most extreme deprivation of the fundamental freedom of choice for individuals, caste is a more limited hierarchized, systematic deprivation of groups, as determined by birth (parentage).[303] In cruel paradox, the respect value itself is employed to achieve and freeze hierarchical orderings and rankings, and hence discriminations, among the designated groups, in terms not only of respect, but also of all other values. A caste system decrees and enforces an hereditary (ascriptive) transmission of incapacity for freedom of choice.[304] In most societies a class structure differentiates between individuals in terms of value position, potential, and expectancy.[305] What

---

302. A crucial task is of course land reform. *See Question of Slavery and the Slave Trade in All Their Practices and Manifestations, Including the Slave-like Practices of Apartheid and Colonialism* 9–11, U.N. Doc. E/CN.4/Sub.2/337 (1973) (note by the secretary-general).

303. For a discussion of the caste system *see* S. Anant, The Changing Concept of Caste in India (1972); A. Beteille, Castes: Old and New (1969); Social Inequality (A. Beteille ed. 1969) (especially articles by Beteille, Dumont, & Srinivas); C. Bougle, Essays on the Caste System (D. Pocock trans. 1971); O. Cox, Caste, Class, and Race (Modern Reader ed. 1970) [hereinafter cited as O. Cox]; K. Davis, The Population of India and Pakistan (1951); Japan's Invisible Race: Caste in Culture and Personality (G. De Vos & H. Wagatsuma eds. 1966) [hereinafter cited as Japan's Invisible Race]; J. Dollard, Caste and Class in a Southern Town (3d ed. 1957); L. Dumont, Homo Hierarchicus: An Essay on the Caste System (M. Sainsubry trans. 1970) [hereinafter cited as L. Dumont]; G. Ghurge, Caste and Class in India (3d ed. 1957); A. Hocart, Caste: A Comparative Study (1950); J. Hutton, Caste in India: Its Nature, Function, and Origins (4th ed. 1963) [hereinafter cited as J. Hutton]; G. Myrdal, An American Dilemma 667–705 (1964); B. Ryan, Caste in Modern Ceylon (1953); Structure and Change in Indian Society (M. Singer & B. Cohn eds. 1968); M. Srinivas, Caste in Modern India (1962) [hereinafter cited as M. Srinivas]; M. Tumin, Caste in a Peasant Society (1952) [hereinafter cited as M. Tumin]; S. Verba, B. Ahmed, & A. Bhatt, Caste, Race, and Politics: A Comparative Study of India and the United States (1971).

For a definitive historical account of castes in Indian society *see* 2 P. Kane, History of Dharmasastra (ancient and medieval religions and civil law) 19–179 (1941) [hereinafter cited as P. Kane]; 5 *id.* at 1632–43 (1962).

304. For a concise description *see* Berreman, *The Concept of Caste,* 2 Int'l Encyc. Soc. Sc. 333 (1968). *See also* Berreman, *Structure and Function of Caste Systems,* in Japan's Invisible Race, *supra* note 303, at 277–307.

305. The literature on social stratification is, of course, vast. *See generally* Class, Status, and Power: Social Stratification in Comparative Perspective (2d ed. R. Bendix & S. Lipset 1966); B. Bernard, Social Stratification: A Comparative Analysis of Structure and Process (1957); Social Inequality (A. Beteille ed. 1969); The Impact of Social Class (P. Blumberg ed. 1972); T. Bottomore, Classes in Modern Society (1965); R.

caste adds to class is the freezing, the immobilization, of these differentiations.[306] In a cognitive map of a caste society the lines between castes are relatively clear. The lines are sustained by customary community expectations and by variegated sanctioning practices, and they are transmitted with little change from generation to generation.[307] Branded as inferior at birth, members of the lower castes, especially the "untouchables" or equivalents, are condemned in perpetuity to low position, potential, and expectancy in relation to all values.[308]

Formally, participation in the community power process in terms of officeholding (elective as well as appointive) and voting may be open to all members of society. In reality, however, members of the lower castes are singularly handicapped by their lack of effective power, especially by the lack of base values such as wealth, enlightenment, and skill, whose control is necessary to effectiveness.[309] The perpetuation through the

---

DAHRENDORF, CLASSES AND CLASS CONFLICT IN INDUSTRIAL SOCIETY (rev. ed. 1959); SOCIAL MOBILITY IN BRITAIN (D. Glass ed. 1954); C. HELLER, STRUCTURED SOCIAL INEQUALITY (1968); A. HOLLINGSHEAD & F. REDLICH, SOCIAL CLASS AND MENTAL ILLNESS (1958); G. LENSKI, POWER AND PRIVILEGE: A THEORY OF SOCIAL STRATIFICATION (1966); K. MAYER & W. BUCKLEY, CLASS AND SOCIETY (3d ed. 1969); C. MILLS, WHITE COLLAR: THE AMERICAN MIDDLE CLASS (1951); M. MILNER, THE ILLUSION OF EQUALITY (1972); M. TUMIN, SOCIAL STRATIFICATION: THE FORMS AND FUNCTIONS OF INEQUALITY (1971); Parsons, *Social Classes and Class Conflict in the Light of Recent Sociological Theory,* in ESSAYS IN SOCIOLOGICAL THEORY 323 (rev. ed. 1954); *Social Stratification,* 15 INT'L ENCYC. SOC. SC. 288 (1968).

306. As Dobzhansky has put it:

> [A] person's caste is determined by that of his parents and by nothing else: one cannot be promoted to a higher caste or demoted to a lower one by any personal achievements or failures. A man of low caste could only hope that good behavior in his present life might let him be reincarnated in a higher caste. Class differentiation is, however, less rigid. Even the most rigid class society allows some individuals of humble birth to climb and others of privileged birth to slide down the social ladder.

T. DOBZHANSKY, MANKIND EVOLVING: THE EVOLUTION OF THE HUMAN SPECIES 242 (1962) [hereinafter cited as T. DOBZHANSKY]. *See also* H. LASSWELL & A. KAPLAN, POWER AND SOCIETY 62–69 (1950).

307. *See* O. COX, *supra* note 303, at 3–20.

308. Kane gave this succinct account:

> In most of the works on the castes in India a few features are pointed out as the characteristics of the caste system and as common to all castes and subcastes. They are: (1) heredity (i.e. in theory a man is assigned to a particular caste by birth in that caste); (2) endogamy and exogamy (i.e. restriction as to marrying in the same caste and not marrying certain relatives or other persons, though of the same caste); (3) restrictions as to food (i.e. what food and water may be taken or not taken and from whom); (4) occupation (i.e. members of most castes follow certain occupations and no others); (5) gradation of castes, some being at the top in the social scale and others being deemed to be so low that they are untouchable.

2 P. KANE, *supra* note 303, at 23. *Cf.* M. TUMIN, PATTERNS OF SOCIETY 91–102 (1973).

309. *See* M. SRINIVAS, *supra* note 303, 15–41; S. VERBA, B. AHMED, & A. BHATT, CASTE, RACE, AND POLITICS: A COMPARATIVE STUDY OF INDIA AND THE UNITED STATES (1971).

generations of a system of hierarchical value deprivations is characteristically sustained by severe deprivations of affection. Marriage is, as a rule, kept within the same caste so as to make crossing of caste lines virtually impossible.[310] Indeed, the whole range of an individual's permissible associations is determined by the group into which that person is born, with the barriers enforced by the myth of "pollution."[311]

Access to education and enlightenment may be formally reserved to the higher castes. Even where access is theoretically available to the lower castes, the lack of the other base values upon which the opportunity and leisure for study and inquiry depend may keep the victims of caste ignorant and content in the maintenance of a status quo of rigid stratification.[312] Members of an inferior caste are generally denied opportunity to discover and develop their latent talents or to acquire and exercise many socially useful skills. Certain highly regarded skills—those of the liberal professions, for example—may be kept within the exclusive domain of members of a superior caste, with monopolized transmission from generation to generation. The occupations open to different castes may be not only specialized but rigidly controlled, with the lower castes being permitted to perform only unskilled labor.[313] This stratified divi-

---

310. *See* L. Dumont, *supra* note 303, at 109–29; S. Anant, The Changing Concept of Caste in India 104–18 (1972). For the invalidity of intercaste marriages under the Hindu law and usage *see* N. Aiyar, Mayne's Treatise on Hindu Law and Usage 103, 164–72 (11th ed. 1950).

311. As Srinivas has put it:

> The concept of pollution governs relations between different castes. This concept is absolutely fundamental to the caste system, and along with the concepts of karma and dharma it contributes to make caste the unique institution it is. Every type of intercaste relation is governed by the concept of pollution. Contact of any kind, touching, dining, sex and other relations between castes which are structurally distant results in the higher of the two castes being polluted.

Srinivas, *The Caste System in India,* in Social Inequality 265, 267 (A. Beteille ed. 1969).

In the context of the Far East Passin has observed:

> Another common feature is that they are looked upon as inferior and polluted, and in extreme cases perhaps not even quite human. In Japan, for example, the itinerant outcastes were actually called Hinin, "nonhuman"; while the practice of calling the Eta "four," the judgment of the court that they were worth only 1/7th of ordinary people, the use of the classifier for animals in counting them—all bespeak this conception. In Korea, similarly, the *Paekchong* were considered "barbarians" who had to be domesticated. In all cases, they were considered so polluted that their very presence, not to mention their touch, was a positive danger to ordinary people.

Passin, *Untouchability in the Far East,* 11 Monumenta Nipponica 247, 260 (1955).

312. *Cf.* A. Beteille, Castes: Old and New 57–86 (1969); N.Y. Times, Apr. 23, 1973, at 17, col. 1; *id.,* Nov. 29, 1972, at 4, col. 3.

313. *See* C. Bougle, Essays on the Caste System 29–40 (D. Pocock trans. 1971); O. Cox, *supra* note 303, at 60–70.

sion of occupations and ascriptive transmission of occupational skills often result in wide disparities in the distribution of wealth, with the lower castes living in a poverty often bordering on debt bondage.[314]

Conditioned early in life to view their superior or inferior status as a "natural" or "divine" expression of God's will or as a "functional necessity" of society,[315] members of different castes are taught to be content with their respective pre-fixed stations in society. This acceptance of place and role, with its alleged avoidance of anxiety and disorder, is thought to be a key to individual well-being. Thus, life styles are made to differ significantly in terms of food, clothing, appearance, demeanor, and so on.[316] Very different considerations in social life, with expressions of respect or disrespect, are extended to the different castes.[317] The cumulative impact of these value deprivations tends to stifle even the development of appropriate norms of responsible conduct. A person's religious belief and affiliation are determined by birth; there is practically no avenue for changing one's sacred or secular orientation. Should attempts to change be made, the larger society commonly refuses to recognize or honor them. Further, enforcement is simplified since caste members are readily identifiable.[318]

Historically, the caste system in the sense we have described has existed in many different cultures throughout the history of human society with varying degrees of approximation in value impact and with highly diversified patterns of institutional detail.[319] Without questioning the often alleged "uniqueness" of each society in tradition and development, it may be observed that a caste society flourishes best under the conditions of relative noncommunication and physical immobility resulting from an underdeveloped science and technology, especially when there is a relative lack of access to communication and transportation. While accelerating developments in science and technology have in recent decades released a new drive for mobility and fostered a trend

---

314. *See* G. Myrdal, Asian Drama: An Inquiry into the Poverty of Nations 273–81, 745–49 (1971); N.Y. Times, Oct. 26, 1973, at 3, col. 1 (city ed.); *id.*, Oct 5, 1973, at 10, col. 1; *id.*, Dec. 8, 1968, at 7, col. 1.

315. For a brief summary of this theme *see* Japan's Invisible Race, *supra* note 303, at xix–xxiii. *See also* note 327 *infra.*

316. *See* S. Anant, The Changing Concept of Caste in India 73–89 (1972); L. Dumont, *supra* note 303, at 130–51; J. Hutton, *supra* note 303, at 71–91; M. Tumin, *supra* note 303, at 84–108; Beteille, *Caste in a South Indian Village,* in Social Inequality 273, 278–90 (A. Beteille ed. 1969).

317. *See* note 316 *supra.*

318. *See* J. Kitagawa, Religions of the East 99–154 (enlarged ed. 1968); M. Srinivas, *supra* note 303, at 148–60.

319. *See* Kroeber, *Caste,* 3 Encyc. Soc. Sc. 254, 254–55 (1930); 2 P. Kane, *supra* note 303, at 23; 5 *id.* at 1633.

toward universalization of equality, many communities remain in the grip of rigidly stratified barriers transmitted from the past. Though India is commonly singled out by commentators as the contemporary paradigm of a caste society,[320] that country is not alone in exhibiting indicia of high stratification and immobility.[321] In many societies, severe class differentiations approximate the hierarchical and hereditary deprivations characteristic of "caste," and the children who begin with little continue to be inordinately and permanently handicapped vis-à-vis the children who begin with much.[322]

The practices of caste are as incompatible as those of slavery with the basic policies of freedom of choice and equality of opportunity essential to human dignity.[323] To deny individuals freedom of choice on a collective basis determined by their birth is as invidious to human dignity as denial based on any other group characteristic. Such denial treats a human being as an appendage to a collectivity instead of as a person capable of self-fulfillment and contribution to society. The inherent contradiction in a system of caste is that it manipulates the value of respect in ways that institutionalize and perpetuate disrespect.[324]

---

320. *See* works cited in notes 303 and 314 *supra.*

321. *See* J. HUTTON, *supra* note 303, at 133–38; JAPAN'S INVISIBLE RACE, *supra* note 303; B. RYAN, CASTE IN MODERN CEYLON (1954); M. TUMIN, *supra* note 303; Passin, *Untouchability in the Far East,* 11 MONUMENTA NIPPONICA 247, 260 (1955). *See also* 8 PEOPLES OF THE EARTH 66–68, 79–80 (E. Evans-Pritchard ed. 1973) (regarding Hawaiian Polynesia and Tahitian Polynesia); 10 *id.* at 114–16 (Indonesian Bali); 12 *id.* at 8–36, 44–53 (India), 110–13 (Tamiland), 114–27 (Sri Lanka); 13 *id.* at 85–95 (Nepal); 15 *id.* at 92–96 (Kabul and the Pahktun Afghanistan).

322. Lenski has put it this way:

> Actually, however, there is no need to treat caste and class as separate phenomena. In the interest of conceptual parsimony one can quite legitimately define caste as a special kind of class—at least when class is defined as broadly as it has been here. Thus we may say that a class is *a caste to the degree that upward mobility into or out of it is forbidden by the mores.*

G. LENSKI, POWER AND PRIVILEGE: A THEORY OF SOCIAL STRATIFICATION 77 (1966).

323. *See* chapter 6 *supra,* at notes 18–52 and accompanying text.

324. In the words of Beteille:

> Caste has often been viewed as the prototype of all hierarchical systems. Principles of caste rank rest essentially on conceptions of social esteem. Social esteem is attached to particular styles of life, and groups are ranked as high or low according to how or whether they pursue such styles. What is highly esteemed varies from one society to another and depends ultimately on the value-system of the society. In India ritual elements (and, in particular, the ideas of purity and pollution) have historically occupied an important place in styles of life which have enjoyed high social esteem.

Beteille, *Caste in a South Indian Village,* in SOCIAL INEQUALITY 273, 290 (A. Beteille ed. 1969). *See also* notes 303–18 *supra* and accompanying text.

The same justification has been offered for caste differentiations as for racism: that some people are inherently inferior because of parentage.[325] This myth, like other elements of racism, runs afoul of modern scientific findings.[326] Additional justification of caste is sometimes grounded in a sacred mythology that purports to reward and punish people for acts committed in putative previous incarnations.[327] The ap-

---

325. De Vos and Wagatsuma state:

> In comparing systems of social segregation in various of the world's cultures, those based on alleged caste impurity and those based on alleged racial inferiority are found to be the most fixed and immutable. One can too quickly conclude that these two concepts have very different bases for the classification and separation of two or more segments of a particular society. Instead of stressing the obvious surface differences, one might do well to consider whether there is a curious similarity between these concepts, whether they are not indeed, two dissimilar faces of identical inner psychological processes that seek external expression. . . . At first glance, racism may seem to bear no direct resemblance to the social segregation found in a caste system. But it is a major proposition of this volume that the contrary is true, that from the viewpoint of comparative sociology or social anthropology, and from the viewpoint of human social psychology, racism and caste attitudes are one and the same phenomenon.

JAPAN'S INVISIBLE RACE, *supra* note 303, at xix–xx.

See also Beteille, *Caste in a South-Indian Village,* in SOCIAL INEQUALITY 273, 276–78 (A. Beteille ed. 1969); L. DUMONT, *supra* note 303, at 27–29.

326. *See* J. BAKER, RACE (1974) (contains a comprehensive bibliography); T. DOBZHANSKY, *supra* note 306; A. MONTAGU, MAN'S MOST DANGEROUS MYTH: THE FALLACY OF RACE (5th ed. 1974); A. MONTAGU, STATEMENT OF RACE (3d ed. 1972).

327. Srinivas has observed:

> A man is *born* into a sub-caste (*jati*) and this is the only way of acquiring membership. According to the traditional view, however, birth is not an accident. Certain Hindu theological notions like *karma* and *dharma* have contributed very greatly to the strengthening of the idea of hierarchy which is inherent in the caste system. The idea of *karma* teaches a Hindu that he is born in a particular sub-caste because he deserves to be born there. The actions he performed in a previous incarnation deserved such a reward or punishment, as the case might be. If he had performed better actions in his previous incarnation he would have been born in a higher caste. Thus the caste hierarchy comes to be an index of the state of an individual's soul. It also represents certain milestones on the soul's journey to God.
>
> Thus the idea of deserts is associated with birth in a particular caste. A man is born in a high caste because of the good actions performed by him in his previous life, and another is born into a low caste because of bad actions performed in his previous life.

Srinivas, *The Caste System in India*, in SOCIAL INEQUALITY 265, 266 (A. Beteille ed. 1969).

In the same vein, Passin has summarized:

> In the Hindu conception, everyone's place in the scheme of things was ordained by fate, by the endless chain of causation. Any given point in the unfolding of the universe was the effect of all preceding events. But cause and effect were not merely material; there was also an endless chain of moral cause and effect, and it was this chain of moral causation that affected the status of individuals. What one had done in previous incarnations determined one's status in the present one. The low castes were

peal of such a justification is unlikely to reach beyond the circle of "true believers," and is subject to a continuous reinterpretation of fundamental assumptions.

As further justification, it is sometimes urged that caste is necessary to the functional division of society.[328] Yet, in the contemporary world it requires no Marxist insight to recognize that, though caste may sometimes be used as a form of economic exploitation,[329] a caste system must impair, rather than facilitate, the wide shaping and sharing of wealth and other values. In a complex society, the greatest aggregate production and widest distribution of wealth and other values necessarily depends on a division of labor that lays aside the rigidification of occupational roles by inheritance, and provides individuals with ample opportunity to develop fully their varied talents in an open, mobile society. "The drawback of the caste and rigid class systems is," in the words of Dobzhansky, "precisely that they induce people to take up functions for which they are incompetent; hence so many worthless kings and barons."[330] In sum, it would appear that there is no common interest which caste can today serve in a society based upon human dignity.

In times when even slavery was still regarded as natural and lawful,[331] it could scarcely have been expected that caste might be regarded as unlawful. Beginning in the Far East and the ancient Mediterranean world, various caste systems have been sustained down through the centuries by customary expectations and practices in many different communities.[332] These range from the total and systematic stratification in India, through the "quasi-caste" systems in medieval Europe ("with aristocratic rank and privileges, sumptuary laws, feudalism, and occupation guilds in control of much of industry"[333]) and in medieval Japan (with "sharp" and elaborate "distinctions of hereditary rank"[334]) to pockets of de facto castes in recent times.[335]

---

therefore, in a sense, serving penance in this life for their past sins and shortcomings, although through virtue and good works they might be able to attain higher status in their next incarnation.

Passin, *Untouchability in the Far East,* 11 MONUMENTA NIPPONICA 247, 252 (1955).

See also J. HUTTON, *supra* note 303, at 189–91; Srinivas, *The Caste System in India,* in SOCIAL INEQUALITY 265, 269–72 (A. Beteille ed. 1969).

328. *See, e.g.,* L. DUMONT, *supra* note 303, at 92–108; J. HUTTON, *supra* note 303, at 111–32; Srinivas, *The Caste System in India,* in SOCIAL INEQUALITY 269–72 (A. Beteille ed. 1969).

329. *See* JAPAN'S INVISIBLE RACE, *supra* note 303, at xxii.

330. T. DOBZHANSKY, *supra* note 306, at 244.

331. *See* notes 84–178 *supra* and accompanying text.

332. *See* Kroeber, *Caste,* 3 ENCYC. SOC. SC. 254, 254–55 (1930).

333. *Id.* at 256.

334. *Id.*

335. *See* notes 320–22 *supra.*

In modern times, national community efforts to eradicate caste find their most striking and, of course, most important exemplification in India.[336] More than half a century of anticaste efforts culminated in the adoption of the 1949 Constitution of India, which envisages a fundamental reconstruction of the whole social structure of the country.[337] To secure "[e]quality of status and opportunity" for "all its citizens,"[338] the Indian Constitution, in section after section, includes caste as one of the impermissible grounds for differentiation in the treatment of people,[339] and strictly outlaws untouchability.[340] The prohibition of discrimination by caste extends to acts performed not only by "the State,"[341] but also by private individuals. Article 15(2) stipulates that no citizen shall on account of caste be subject to

> any disability, liability, restriction or condition with regard to:
>
> (a) access to shops, public restaurants, hotels and places of public entertainment; or
>
> (b) the use of wells, tanks, bathing *ghats,* roads and places of public resort maintained wholly or partly out of State funds or dedicated to the use of the general public.[342]

Article 16(2) further states that no citizen shall on account of caste be "ineligible for, or discriminated against in respect of, any employment or office under the State."[343] Article 17 declares the abolition of untoucha-

---

336. *See* S. ANANT, THE CHANGING CONCEPT OF CASTE IN INDIA 14–37 (1972); 1 D. BASU, COMMENTARY ON THE CONSTITUTION OF INDIA 287–543 (5th ed. 1965); C. BOUGLE, ESSAYS ON THE CASTE SYSTEM 116–42 (D. Pocock trans. 1971); Galanter, *Changing Legal Conceptions of Caste,* in STRUCTURE AND CHANGE IN INDIAN SOCIETY 299 (M. Singer & B. Cohn eds. 1968).

337. For the text of the Constitution of India, which is unusually long and detailed, *see* 2 A. PEASLEE, CONSTITUTIONS OF NATIONS 308–438 (3d ed. 1966) [hereinafter cited as A. PEASLEE]. For the provisions of the Indian Constitution relating to the protection of fundamental human rights, *see* BASIC DOCUMENTS ON HUMAN RIGHTS 29–45 (I. Brownlie ed. 1971). For an earlier attempt at reform, as symbolized by the Caste Disabilities Removal Act (XXI of 1850) *see* N. AIYAR, MAYNE'S TREATISE ON HINDU LAW AND USAGE 73, 716–18 (11th ed. 1950); 3 P. KANE, *supra* note 303, at 547 n.1021, 616, 667. *See also* 2 *id.* at 177–79.

338. CONSTITUTION, Preamble (1949, amended 1963) (India), *reprinted in* 2 A. PEASLEE, *supra* note 337, at 308.

339. *See id.,* Arts. 15–17, *reprinted in* 2 A. PEASLEE, *supra* note 337, at 312–13.

340. It reads: "'Untouchability' is abolished and its practice in any form is forbidden. The enforcement of any disability arising out of 'Untouchability' shall be an offence punishable in accordance with law." *Id.,* Art. 17.

341. Art. 15(1) provides: "The State shall not discriminate against any citizen on grounds only of religion, race, caste, sex, place of birth or any of them." *Id.,* Art. 15(1).

Art. 16(2) further states that "No citizen shall, on grounds only of . . . caste . . . be ineligible for, or discriminated against in respect of any employment or office under the State." *Id.,* Art. 16(2).

342. *Id.,* Art. 15(2).

343. *Id.,* Art. 16(2).

bility in these words: "'Untouchability' is abolished and its practice in any form is forbidden. The enforcement of any disability arising out of 'Untouchability' shall be an offence punishable in accordance with law."[344]

To carry out the prohibition of untouchability, the Untouchability (Offenses) Act was adopted in 1955.[345] The Act prescribes punishment for those who seek to impose or enforce disabilities on the ground of "untouchability" in regard to, inter alia, access to places of public worship; access to shops and restaurants and places of public accommodation; use of utensils in public places; the practice of professions, occupations, and trades; use of rivers, wells, and other water resources; access to hospitals, educational institutions, and charitable facilities; public transportation; housing; the practice of religious ceremonies and processions; and use of jewelry and finery.[346] Other measures have also been enacted to aid the "Scheduled Castes" and the "backward classes."[347] Yet, despite these heroic governmental prescriptive efforts toward the elimination of caste, the caste system, "so deeply entrenched in India's traditions,"[348] continues to persist. "The caste system," observes Gunnar Myrdal, in his monumental work *Asian Drama,* "is probably stronger today than it was at the time when India became independent."[349] Such a phenomenon, Myrdal adds, "provides a striking example of the divergence of precept and practice."[350]

Aside from India, concern for the eradication of caste has been manifested in other territorial communities. Thus, for example, Article 17(1) of the 1962 Constitution of the Islamic Republic of Pakistan states that "[n]o citizen otherwise qualified for appointment in the service of Pakistan shall be discriminated against in respect of any such appointment on the ground only of [inter alia] caste."[351] Article 10 of the 1962 Constitution of Nepal provides that "[n]o discrimination shall be made against any citizen in the application of general laws" and "in respect of appointment to the government service or any other public service" on

---

344. *Id.,* Art. 17.

345. Untouchability (Offenses) Act, No. 22 of 8 May 1955, *reprinted with commentary in* United Nations, Yearbook on Human Rights for 1955, 112, 120–22.

346. *Id.,* §§ 3–4. The act provides for up to six months imprisonment and/or a fine of 500 rupees for its violation. *Id.*

347. *See* Galanter, *Changing Legal Conceptions of Caste,* in Structure and Changes in Indian Society 299, 313–19 (M. Singer & B. Cohn eds. 1968).

348. G. Myrdal, Asian Drama: An Inquiry into the Poverty of Nations 278 (1971).

349. *Id.*

350. *Id.*

351. Constitution, Art. 17(1) (1962, amended 1964) (Pakistan), *reprinted in* 2 A. Peaslee, *supra* note 337, at 989.

account of "caste."[352] The 1948 Constitution of the Republic of Korea proclaims, in Article 9(2), that "[n]o privileged castes shall be recognized, nor be ever established in any form."[353]

The more recent trends in transnational prescription exhibit an increasing crystallization of larger community expectations that the practice of caste is unlawful. Contemporary international prescriptions have developed a peremptory norm of nondiscrimination which embodies a wide range of impermissible grounds for differentiation.[354] Though the word "caste" is not always explicitly employed in describing the impermissible grounds, the consistent condemnation of differentiation by "social origin," "birth and other status," and "descent" would appear to put beyond doubt the conclusion that caste is today prohibited on the transnational level.

The important contemporary prescription commonly construed to condemn caste derives from the United Nations Charter[355] and is clearly articulated in the Universal Declaration of Human Rights,[356] which, in Article 2, states: "Everyone is entitled to all the rights and freedoms set forth in this Declaration, without distinction of any kind, such as race, colour, sex, language, religion, political or other opinion, national or social origin, property, birth or other status."[357] This same theme is pursued in the International Covenant on Civil and Political Rights,[358] which incorporates identical or nearly indentical language in several of its provisions. Article 26 of the Covenant states:

> All persons are equal before the law and are entitled without any discrimination to the equal protection of the law. In this respect, the law shall prohibit any discrimination and guarantee to all persons equal and effective protection against discrimination on any ground such as race, colour, sex, language, religion, political or other opinion, national or social origin, property, birth or other status.[359]

Article 2(1) of the Covenant provides:

> Each State Party to the present Covenant undertakes to respect and to ensure to all individuals within its territory and subject to its

352. Constitution, Art. 10 (1962) (Nepal), *reprinted in* 2 A. Peaslee, *supra* note 337, at 774.

353. Constitution, Art. 9(2) (1948, amended 1962) (Republic of Korea), *reprinted in* 2 A. Peaslee, *supra* note 337, at 579.

354. *See* chapter 8 *infra,* at notes 1–29 and accompanying text.

355. *See* note 215 *supra.*

356. Universal Declaration, *supra* note 3.

357. *Id.,* Art. 2, U.N. Doc. A/810 at 72.

358. Covenant on Civil and Political Rights, *supra* note 5.

359. *Id.,* Art. 26, 21 U.N. GAOR, Supp. (No. 16) 55–56.

> jurisdiction the rights recognized in the present Covenant, without distinction of any kind, such as race, colour, sex, language, religion, political or other opinion, national or social origin, property, birth or other status.[360]

Other provisions of the Covenant prohibit discrimination on account of "social origin" in connection with permissible derogations;[361] discrimination against children on grounds of "social origin" or "birth";[362] and discrimination with regard to officeholding and voting on the grounds specified in Article 2.[363]

Comparable provisions appear in other important conventions. Thus, the International Covenant on Economic, Social, and Cultural Rights,[364] in Article 2(2), stipulates:

> The States Parties to the present Covenant undertake to guarantee that the rights enunciated in the present Covenant will be exercised without discrimination of any kind as to race, colour, sex, language, religion, political or other opinion, national or social origin, property, birth or other status.[365]

The Discrimination (Employment and Occupation) Convention of 1958[366] includes "social origin" among impermissible grounds of differentiation in its definition of "discrimination" in Article 1(1).[367] The Convention against Discrimination in Education of 1960 includes "birth" as well as "social origin" in its definition of discrimination in Article 1(1).[368] On the regional level, both the European Convention on Human Rights[369] and the American Convention on Human Rights[370] have included both "social origin" and "birth" in the formulation of their nondiscrimination clauses.

---

360. *Id.*, Art. 2(1), 21 U.N. GAOR, Supp. (No. 16) 53.

361. *Id.*, Art. 4(1).

362. *Id.*, Art. 24(1), 21 U.N. GAOR, Supp. (No. 16) 55.

363. *Id.*, Art. 25.

364. Covenant on Economic Rights, *supra* note 6.

365. *Id.*, Art. 2(2), 21 U.N. GAOR, Supp. (No. 16) 49–50.

366. Convention concerning Discrimination in Respect of Employment and Occupation, *adopted* June 25, 1958, 362 U.N.T.S. 31 (ILO General Conference) (entered into force June 15, 1960) [hereinafter cited as Discrimination Convention].

367. *Id.*, Art. 1(1), 362 U.N.T.S. at 32–34.

368. Convention against Discrimination in Education, *adopted* Dec. 14, 1960, Art. 1(1), 429 U.N.T.S. 93, 96 (UNESCO General Conference) (entered into force May 22, 1962) [hereinafter cited as Convention against Discrimination in Education]. "Birth," as well as "social origin," is included in its proscribed bases of discrimination.

369. European Convention, *supra* note 8, Art. 14, 213 U.N.T.S. at 232.

370. American Convention, *supra* note 7, Arts. 1 and 27, 9 INT'L LEGAL MATERIALS at 101, 109.

The legislative history of Article 2 of the Universal Declaration of Human Rights and of the similar provisions in other conventions amply establishes that the prohibition of discrimination by "social origin" and "birth and other status" indeed extends to differentiation by "caste." Thus, when the Third Committee of the General Assembly was considering Article 2 of the draft Universal Declaration, the Indian delegation proposed the substitution of "caste" for "birth,"[371] and the Soviet delegation proposed the inclusion of "class" among the impermissible grounds of differentiation.[372] Both proposals were rejected because most of the Committee members agreed that the words, "social origin" and "birth or other status," as proposed by the Informal Drafting Group, were adequate to cover discrimination by caste or class. In the course of discussion, Mr. Santa Cruz (Chile), and the Cuban representative, preferred the wording "social status" or "social condition" to "birth," but agreed that the former "expression was implied in the word 'birth.' "[373] In the view of Mr. Chang (China), "The concept of race, colour, social origin, and in most cases sex, involved the question of birth, while social origin also embraced the idea of class or caste."[374] Mr. Imperial (Philippines) felt that "[t]he words 'class' and 'caste' referred to certain specific systems while 'birth' applied to everyone."[375] The view of Mrs. Roosevelt (United States) was summarized in the Committee records in these words:

> [T]he declaration was intended for ordinary, not learned people and from that point of view, the original text seemed the most satisfactory. Although class and caste distinctions still existed, human beings were trying to outgrow the use of such words. In her opinion, the words 'property or other status' took into consideration the various new suggestions that had been made.[376]

Consequently, Mr. Appadorai (India) withdrew the Indian proposal with the following explanation: "[H]is delegation had only proposed the word 'caste' because it objected to the word 'birth.' The words 'other status' and 'social origin' were sufficiently broad to cover the whole field; the delegation of India would not, therefore, insist on its proposal."[377]

The comprehensive annotations on the draft International Covenants,

---

371. U.N. GAOR, 3D COMM. 138–39 (1948).
372. *Id.* at 126, 138.
373. *Id.* at 137–38.
374. *Id.* at 139.
375. *Id.*
376. *Id.* at 138.
377. *Id.* at 139.

as prepared by the secretary-general in 1955,[378] explicitly state that the nondiscrimination clauses in both Covenants "follow that of Article 2 of the Universal Declaration of Human Rights,"[379] and that the grounds of discrimination set forth in the Covenant provisions "are the same as those enumerated in Article 2 of the Declaration."[380] The same interpretation of other conventions influenced in their comparable provisions by the Universal Declaration would appear inescapable.

The International Convention on the Elimination of all Forms of Racial Discrimination[381] introduces still another concept—"descent"—which equally serves the function of condemning the practice of caste. This new concept originated with the Indian delegation when the Third Committee of the General Assembly was considering the adoption of the Convention.[382] As a consequence, the Convention was made to define "racial discrimination" by juxtaposing "descent" with "race, color, national or ethnic origin." Article 1(1) of the Convention, in utmost reach, states:

> In this Convention the term "racial discrimination" shall mean any distinction, exclusion, restriction or preference based on race, colour, descent, or national or ethnic origin which has the purpose or effect of nullifying or impairing the recognition, enjoyment or exercise, on an equal footing, of human rights and fundamental freedoms in the political, economic, social, cultural or any other field of public life.[383]

Although the "record gives no indication of the situations the word [descent] was intended to cover,"[384] it is "reasonable to assume," as Dr. Schwelb has observed, "that the term 'descent' includes the notion of 'caste.'"[385] The inclusion of "descent" in the specification of "racial discrimination," therefore, makes the Anti-Racial Discrimination Convention still a further prescription in condemnation of caste.[386]

---

378. *Annotations on the Covenants, supra* note 251.

379. *Id.* at 17.

380. *Id.* at 61.

381. International Convention on the Elimination of All Forms of Racial Discrimination, *opened for signature* Mar. 7, 1966, 660 U.N.T.S. 195 (entered into force Jan. 4, 1969) [hereinafter cited as Convention on the Elimination of All Forms of Racial Discrimination].

382. Schwelb, *The International Convention on the Elimination of All Forms of Racial Discrimination,* 15 Int'l & Comp. L.Q. 996, 1002–03 (1966) [hereinafter cited as Schwelb].

383. Convention on the Elimination of All Forms of Racial Discrimination, *supra* note 381, Art. 1(1), 660 U.N.T.S. at 216.

384. Schwelb, *supra* note 382, at 1003.

385. *Id.* at 1003 n.43.

386. For further elaboration *see* chapter 9 *infra,* at notes 89–284 and accompanying text.

SECTION 3 THE ELIMINATION OF APARTHEID

Factual Background

Apartheid is a comprehensive and systematic pattern of racial discrimination, containing identifiable components of both slavery and caste, which is prescribed and enforced by national law.[387] It has compo-

---

387. On apartheid *see* H. Adam, Modernizing Racial Domination: South Arica's Political Dynamics (1971) [hereinafter cited as H. Adam]; South Arica: Sociological Perspectives (H. Adam ed. 1971); African Research Group, Race to Power (1974); M. Ballinger, From Union to Apartheid (1969); E. Brookes, Apartheid: A Documentary Study of Modern SouthAfrica (1968) [hereinafter cited as E. Brookes]; Race, Peace, Law and Southern Africa (J. Carey ed. 1968); G. Carter, The Politics of Inequality: South Africa since 1948 (rev. ed. 1959); D. De Villiers, The Case for South Africa (1970); The South West Africa/Namibia Dispute (J. Dugard ed. 1973); W. Frye, In Whitest Africa: The Dynamics of Apartheid (1968); A Survey of Race Relations in South Africa (M. Horrell comp. 1973); M. Horrell, Legislation and Race Relations (rev. ed. 1971); International Comm'n of Jurists, Erosion of the Rule of Law in South Africa (1968); International Comm'n of Jurists, South Africa and the Rule of Law (1960); P. Joshi, Apartheid in South Africa (1950); L. Kuper, An African Bourgeoisie: Race, Class, and Politics in South Africa (1965); L. Kuper, Passive Resistance in South Africa (1956); Apartheid (A. La Guma ed. 1971); Apartheid and United Nations Collective Measures (A. Leiss ed. 1965); A. Mathews, Law, Order and Liberty in South Africa (1972); J. Ngubane, An African Explains Apartheid (1963); Southern Africa in Perspective (C. Potholm & R. Dale eds. 1972); P. Randall, A Taste of Power (1973); N. Rhoodie, Apartheid and Racial Partnership in Southern Africa (1969); South African Dialogue (N. Rhoodie ed. 1973); A. Sachs, Justice in South Africa (1973); S. Slonim, South West Africa and the United Nations: An International Mandate in Dispute (1973) [hereinafter cited as S. Slonim]; South Africa, Dep't of Foreign Affairs, South Africa and the Rule of Law (1968); P. Tempels, Bantu Philosophy (1971); L. Thompson, Politics in the Republic of South Africa (1966) [hereinafter cited as L. Thompson]; UNESCO, Apartheid (2d ed. 1972); P. van den Berghe, Race and Racism: A Comparative Perspective 96–111 (1967); P. van den Berghe, South Africa, A Study in Conflict (1969) [hereinafter cited as P. van den Berghe]; A. Vandenbosch, South Africa and the World (1970); Ballinger, *U.N. Action on Human Rights in Southern Africa,* in The International Protection of Human Rights 248 (E. Luard ed. 1967); Legum, *Color and Power in the South African Situation,* in Color and Race 205 (J. Franklin ed. 1968); International Comm'n of Jurists, *Apartheid in Namibia,* 6 Objective: Justice 16–25 No. 1, (1974); Landis, *South African Apartheid Legislation,* 71 Yale L.J. 1, 437 (1961) [hereinafter cited as Landis, *Apartheid Legislation*]; Mowle, *The Infringement of Human Rights in Nations of Southern Africa: The Response of the United Nations and the United States,* in *Hearings on International Protection of Human Rights before the Subcomm. on International Organization and Movements of the House Comm. on Foreign Affairs,* 93d Cong., 1st Sess. 946–64 (1974) [hereinafter cited as *Hearings*]; Suzman, *Race Classification and Definition in the Legislation of the Union of South Africa, 1910–1960,* Acta Juridica 1960, at 339–67 (1961); *U.N. and U.S. Response to Racial Discrimination in Southern Africa,* in *Hearings, supra,* at 160–86.

The United Nations, through its various subunits, has been the most important source in the gathering, processing, and dissemination of information about apartheid. Of its ever-increasing production of documents, in book form or other, useful citations include Re-

nents of slavery in that there is a complete deprivation of individual freedom of choice in regard to many values and that labor may be forced.[388] It has components of caste in that its victims are identified by birth or parentage and subjected to rigidified stratification.[389] Some descriptions of apartheid, especially those concerned with its lawfulness

---

PORT OF THE SPECIAL COMMITTEE ON THE POLICIES OF APARTHEID OF THE GOVERNMENT OF THE REPUBLIC OF SOUTH AFRICA, U.N. DOC. A/7254 (1968); H. SANTA CRUZ, RACIAL DISCRIMINATION, U.N. Doc. E/CN.4/Sub. 2/307/Rev. 1 (1971) [hereinafter cited as H. SANTA CRUZ]; UNITED NATIONS, APARTHEID AND RACIAL DISCRIMINATION IN SOUTHERN AFRICA, OPI/335 (1968) [hereinafter cited as APARTHEID IN SOUTHERN AFRICA]; UNITED NATIONS, APARTHEID IN PRACTICE, OPI/53 (1971) [hereinafter cited as APARTHEID IN PRACTICE]; UNITED NATIONS, ECONOMIC AND SOCIAL CONSEQUENCES OF RACIAL DISCRIMINATORY PRACTICES, U.N. Doc. E/CN.14/132/Rev. 1 (1963) [hereinafter cited as ECONOMIC AND SOCIAL CONSEQUENCES]; UNITED NATIONS, A PRINCIPLE IN TORMENT: 3, THE UNITED NATIONS AND NAMIBIA (1971) [hereinafter cited as UNITED NATIONS & NAMIBIA]; UNITED NATIONS, REPRESSIVE LEGISLATION OF THE REPUBLIC OF SOUTH AFRICA, U.N. DOC. ST/PSCA/SER.A/7 (1969); UNITED NATIONS, REVIEW OF UNITED NATIONS CONSIDERATION OF APARTHEID, U.N. Doc. ST/PSCA/SER.A/2(1967); *Interim Report of the Ad Hoc Working Group of Experts Prepared in Accordance with Resolution 19 (XXIX) of the Commission on Human Rights,* U.N. Doc. E/CN.4/1135 (1974); *Report of the Ad Hoc Working Group of Experts Set Up under Resolution 2 (XXIII) of the Commission on Human Rights,* U.N. Doc. E/CN.4/950 (1967); *Report of the Secretary-General on the Policies of Apartheid of South Africa,* U.N. Doc. A/9165 (1973); *Report of the Special Committee on Apartheid,* U.N. Doc. A/8422/Rev. 1 (1971); *Report of the Special Committee on Apartheid on Policies of Apartheid of the Government of South Africa,* U.N. Doc. A/9168 (1973); *Report of the Special Committee on the Policies of Apartheid of the Government of the Republic of South Africa, 1963, 18th Session,* U.N. Docs. A/5497 & Add. 1 (1963); *Report of the United Nations Commission on the Racial Situation in the Union of South Africa,* 8 U.N. GAOR, Supp. (No. 16), U.N. Docs. A/2505 & A/2505/Add. 1 (1953); *Report of the United Nations Council for Namibia,* U.N. Doc. A/9024 (1973); Rubin, *Law, Race and Colour in South Africa,* 6 OBJECTIVE: JUSTICE 29–35 (No. 1, 1974); *Study of Apartheid and Racial Discrimination in Southern Africa*, U.N. Doc. E/CN.4/949 (1967) [hereinafter cited as *Study of Apartheid*]; U.N. Doc. E/CN.4/949/Add. 1-Add. 5 (1967–68).

388. *Cf.* notes 27–78 *supra* and accompanying text. *See also* Awad, *Apartheid—A Form of Slavery,* 4 OBJECTIVE: JUSTICE 24–28 (No. 3, 1972). Apartheid, in his words, "applies [even] to death, with burial grounds racially zoned to ensure that the bodies remain as divided in death as they were in life (Group Areas Act)." *Id.* at 25.

389. *Cf.* notes 303–22 *supra* and accompanying text. Using a simple chart, Leonard Thompson has emphasized that

> the primary ingredients of South African society are a dominant white group and three subordinate nonwhite groups. Since the white group is wholly endogamous by law and the nonwhite groups are almost wholly endogamous by custom, we shall call the South African a *caste society,* and the Whites, the Coloureds, the Asians, and the Africans the four South African *castes,* even though not all the ingredients of the classic Indian caste system are present in South Africa.

L. THOMPSON, *supra* note 387, at 96. Employing "a minimum definition of 'caste' as an endogamous group, hierarchically ranked in relation to other groups, and wherein membership is determined by birth and for life," Pierre van den Berghe has reached the same conclusion. P. VAN DEN BERGHE, *supra* note 387, at 52–53.

under international law, have emphasized its racial segregation or separation features.[390] Apartheid is, however, much more than mere racial discrimination, whether that discrimination be sporadic or routine; it comprises a complex set of practices of domination and subjection, intensely hierarchized and sustained by the whole apparatus of the state, which affects the distribution of all values.[391]

In paradigm form, apartheid begins in a fundamental deprivation of respect, based upon group membership. Underlying its whole operation is a racial classification.[392] Value deprivations are linked to and imposed by formally dividing and classifying the population into various racial groups, as officially prescribed. An individual is given a racial classification that is recorded in the official population register, and is required to

---

390. *See, e.g., South West Africa Cases (Second Phase),* [1966] I.C.J. 250, 284–316 (Tanaka, J., dissenting).

391. "Individual mobility which could cut across the ascribed race barriers is legally excluded in the castelike structure." H. Adam, *supra* note 387, at 8. In a word, "the ascriptive criteria of race determine overall life chances." *Id.* at 9. A common theme about South Africa runs this way:

> What distinguishes the situation in South Africa from racial discrimination elsewhere is that *apartheid,* or racial segregation, is an official and uncompromising governmental policy. South Africa's is the only government today that makes racial discrimination the foundation of its philosophy and the separation of races the basis of its conduct.

M. Moskowitz, The Politics and Dynamics of Human Rights 177 (1968).

392. On the basis of race, the population of South Africa has officially been divided into four groups: Whites (Europeans), Bantus (Africans, Natives), Coloureds, and Asians. These categories are officially defined in these terms:

> "White person" means a person who—
>
> (a) In appearance obviously is a white person and who is not generally accepted as a coloured person; or
>
> (b) Is generally accepted as a white person and is not in appearance obviously not a white person; but does not include any person who for the purposes of his classification under the Act, freely and voluntarily admits that he is by descent a Bantu or a coloured person unless it is proved that the admission is not based on fact.
>
> "Bantu" means a person who in fact is or is generally accepted as a member of any aboriginal race or tribe of Africa.
>
> "Coloured person" means a person who is not a white person or a Bantu.
>
> "Asians" means Natives of Asia and their descendants, mainly Indians.

Quoted from H. Santa Cruz, *supra* note 387, at 149.

In 1970, the total population of South Africa was 21,448,169, of which 70.2 percent were Africans, 17.5 percent were Whites, 9.4 percent were Coloureds, and 2.9 percent were Asians. South African Institute of Race Relations, A Survey of Race Relations in South Africa, 1972, at 63 (1973) [hereinafter cited as 1972 Survey].

carry an identity card stating that classification.[393] His participation in the different value processes of the community is made to depend not upon his capability, but upon the racial label assigned to him. In the words of a recent United Nations study:

> A person's racial classification is of the utmost importance to him, for it decides, *inter alia,* where he may live, how he may live, what work he may do, what sort of education he will receive, what political rights he will have, if any, whom he may marry, the extent of the social, cultural and recreational facilities open to him, and generally, the extent of his freedom of action and movement.[394]

The basic deprivation of respect is sustained by an organization of internal power processes designed to maintain and perpetuate the domination of the ruling group.[395] Power monopolization, not power sharing, is the rule. Participation in community power processes is minimal for deprived groups, in terms of both officeholding (elective as well as appointive) and voting.[396] Membership in the representative government is open only to one ruling racial group.[397] Freedom of movement, transnational and internal, is greatly curtailed.[398] For deprived groups, movement within the national boundaries, including choice of residence,

---

393. This is required by the Population Registration Act, No. 30, of 1950. *See* E. Brookes, *supra* note 387, at 19–25; H. Santa Cruz, *supra* note 387, at 149–50.

394. Apartheid in Southern Africa, *supra* note 387, at 6.

395. Heribert Adam has observed:

> In South Africa domination is easily recognizable as direct personal exploitation. The rulers are not hidden behind a sophisticated ideology or an anonymous bureaucratic apparatus. On the contrary, they are definable as a precise group visible even to the most politically naive. In contrast to Western Countries, domination has been transformed into subtle manipulation but is experienced in daily and vivid humiliations. Consequently, there are few incentives for subordinates to identify with their rulers.

H. Adam, *supra* note 387, at 5.

He further adds:

> From the perspective of most authors in South Africa, two apparently diametrically opposed race or class castes face each other in visible polarization: white and non-white, ruler and ruled, privileged and underprivileged, exploiter and exploited, a numerical minority against a four-times stronger majority which has the support of an almost unanimous world opinion and is backed by the historical tendencies of a declining colonial era.

Id. at 9.

See also P. van den Berghe, *supra* note 387, at 73–96.

396. *See* H. Santa Cruz, *supra* note 387, at 162–68.

397. *See* Apartheid in Southern Africa, *supra* note 387, at 7; P. van den Berghe, *supra* note 387, at 75.

398. *See* Apartheid in Southern Africa, *supra* note 387, at 13–14, 37–38, 59.

is tightly controlled through an oppressive "pass system."[399] People may thus be forcibly removed from prohibited areas.[400] Members of one racial group are forbidden to participate in the activities of political parties or organizations of another racial group.[401] Individuals are subjected to arbitrary arrest and detention.[402] Differential justice in the

---

399. The "pass system" is one of the cornerstones of the apartheid in South Africa. In the words of Landis:

> "Passes," broadly defined, include all documents required, under threat of penal sanctions, to be carried on the person by adult Africans—that is, blacks over 16—and to be presented upon command to any police official. They include not only internal passports, without which Africans cannot leave their home districts, but also permits to travel, to enter a city, to seek work, to take a job, to be out after curfew, as well as identification papers, tax receipts, rent receipts, et cetera. In particular, passes determine whether Africans in the reserves can go up to the cities, where the jobs are, and can take up employment if they find work. Apartheid theory treats Africans as "transient labor units," allowed on sufferance to work a 1-year contract in a city and then forced, by operation of the pass laws, to return to their reserves, where they may apply for new permits to return to the city if their labor is still needed. Without the revenue—meager as it is—from a city job an African in the reserves who does not own a farm will be in desperate straits while even a farmowner will rarely be able to reach subsistence level.
>
> Pass raids by the police are a repeated form of harassment and source of humiliation to Africans. From time to time these raids are conducted in African "locations," where police break into homes and rouse their sleeping occupants to check on passes. Arrests for pass-related offenses have numbered from 500,000 to a million annually in recent years—this out of a population of 13 million African men, women, and children. (The number of arrests and convictions is virtually identical in pass cases.)

Landis, *Human Rights in Southern Africa and United States Policy in Relation Thereto,* in *Hearings, supra* note 387, at 164, 167. *See also* H. SANTA CRUZ, *supra* note 387, at 156–57, 168–72.

400. *See* H. SANTA CRUZ, *supra* note 387, at 169; *Interim Report of the Ad Hoc Working Group of Experts Prepared in Accordance with Resolution 19 (XIX) of the Commission on Human Rights,* 17–18, U.N. Doc. E/CN.4/1135 (1974).

401. *See* APARTHEID IN PRACTICE, *supra* note 387, at 32–33; H. SANTA CRUZ, *supra* note 387, at 166.

402. Joel Carlson, a courageous civil rights lawyer forced to exile from South Africa in 1971, has given this vivid account:

> Every single day, 365 days a year, seven days a week (Sundays included despite the super-Calvinist nature of the regime), a daily average of 2,500 Africans are arrested under the Pass Laws in South Africa. The average time for handling each of these cases is two minutes! In 1969, a parliamentarian was shocked to discover that 1,777,662 Africans had been arrested during the preceding year. On a daily average basis, the prison population is approximately 90,555 persons—two and one half times that of the United Kingdom, which has a population more than double that of South Africa. Forty-seven percent of the world's hangings take place in South Africa.

Carlson, *South Africa Today: The Security of the State vs. The Liberty of the Individual,* 2 HUMAN RIGHTS 125, 129–30 (1972). *See also* INTERNATIONAL COMM'N OF JURISTS, EROSION OF THE

courts is accorded to the various groups.[403] Accumulated deprivations in all values, finally, make impossible the participation in effective power processes necessary for change in authoritative decisions.

In education, racial segregation is pervasive at all levels; enlightenment is made separate and unequal.[404] Educational facilities are inferior for the deprived groups, whose members are educated differently for their different assigned roles in society.[405] Disproportionate levels of illiteracy are found within the deprived groups.[406] Censorship of the press is an established practice and opposing views are suppressed by coercion.[407] Similarly, members of deprived groups are commonly denied the opportunity to discover and develop their latent talents fully and to acquire and exercise a range of socially useful skills. Lack of education, job reservations, and a discriminatory apprenticeship system result in keeping skilled occupations within the domain of the ruling group and in denying deprived groups access to important skills, such as the managerial.[408]

RULE OF LAW IN SOUTH AFRICA (1968); A. MATHEWS, LAW, ORDER AND LIBERTY IN SOUTH AFRICA 53-261 (1972); A. SACHS, JUSTICE IN SOUTH AFRICA 230-63 (1973); *Report of the Ad Hoc Working Group of Experts Set Up under Resolution 2 (XXIII) of the Commission on Human Rights,* U.N. Doc. E/CN.4/950 (1967).

403. In the words of Awad's apt summary:

> Justice is placed by law firmly in the hands of the whites. Judges, juries and magistrates are always whites, as are also the prosecution. Nearly all court officials are whites. There are separate docks for white and non-white accused; separate witness boxes for white and non-white witnesses; and separate seating for white and non-white spectators.

Awad's 1971 Report, supra note 267, at 52.

See also Rubin, *Law, Race and Colour in South Africa,* 6 OBJECTIVE: JUSTICE 32-34 (No. 1, 1974).

404. *See* UNESCO, APARTHEID (2d ed. 1972); L. THOMPSON, *supra* note 387, at 98-113.

405. South Africa's official policy on education has been declared in these words:

> Education must train and teach people in accordance with their opportunities in life, according to the sphere in which they live. Good racial relations cannot exist where education is given under the control of people who create the wrong expectations on the part of the native itself. Native education should be controlled in such a way that it should be in accordance with the policy of the State. . . . Racial relations cannot improve if the result of the native education is the creation of frustrated people.

Report of the Special Committee on the Policies of Apartheid of the Government of the Republic of South Africa 90, U.N. Doc. A/5497 (1963). *See also* UNESCO, APARTHEID 37 (2d ed. 1972); International Comm'n of Jurists, *Apartheid in Namibia*, 6 OBJECTIVE: JUSTICE 16, 21 (No. 1, 1974).

406. *See* ECONOMIC AND SOCIAL CONSEQUENCES, *supra* note 387, at 63-65.

407. *See* UNESCO, APARTHEID 233-53 (2d ed. 1972); *Interim Report of the Ad Hoc Working Group of Experts Prepared in Accordance with Resolution 19 (XXIX) of the Commission on Human Rights,* U.N. Doc. E/CN.4/1135 at 38-43 (1974).

408. *See* ECONOMIC AND SOCIAL CONSEQUENCES, *supra* note 387, at 48-52; L. THOMPSON, *supra* note 389, at 55-56.

In terms of wealth, deprivation is as intense as in other sectors. Ownership of land is curtailed by racial and area restrictions.[409] Certain occupations may be reserved to a single racial group to the exclusion of others ("job reservation").[410] There are tremendous disparities in wage scales, with higher wages for "civilized labor" and outrageously lower wages for "uncivilized labor."[411] Unequal pay for equal work is the rule; race, not ability, is the determining factor.[412] For the maintenance of "a permanent, abundant and cheap labour force," individuals may be required to register for employment, and may be forced to perform "compulsory and involuntary" labor.[413] Deprived groups are forbidden to form trade unions or to engage in collective bargaining.[414] Strikes are forbidden, and when they occur they may be crushed by the police and armed forces.[415]

---

409. *See* T. VAN REENEN, LAND—ITS OWNERSHIP AND OCCUPATION IN SOUTH AFRICA (1962); APARTHEID IN PRACTICE, *supra* note 387, at 36; ECONOMIC AND SOCIAL CONSEQUENCES, *supra* note 387, at 43; H. SANTA CRUZ, *supra* note 387, at 154–55; *Study of Apartheid and Racial Discrimination in Southern Africa,* U.N. Doc. E/CN.4/949 at 55–56 (1967).

410. *See* APARTHEID IN SOUTHERN AFRICA, *supra* note 387, at 20–21; ECONOMIC AND SOCIAL CONSEQUENCES, *supra* note 387, at 48–52.

411. "In practice, 'civilized labour' meant White labour; 'uncivilized labour,' Native labour." ECONOMIC AND SOCIAL CONSEQUENCES, *supra* note 387, at 50. *See also First, Work Wages and Apartheid,* U.N. UNIT ON APARTHEID, NOTES AND DOCUMENTS, No. 22–70 (1970); Gervasi, *Poverty, Apartheid and Economic Growth,* 3 OBJECTIVE: JUSTICE 3 (No. 4, 1971); Rogers, *The Standard of Living of Africans in South Africa,* U.N. UNIT ON APARTHEID, NOTES AND COMMENTS, No. 45/71 (1971).

412. *See* ECONOMIC AND SOCIAL CONSEQUENCES, *supra* note 387, at 56–60; *Study of Apartheid and Racial Discrimination in Southern Africa,* U.N. Doc. E/CN.4/949, at 108–12; N.Y. Times, Oct. 10, 1973, at 63, col. 3.

413. UNITED NATIONS & INTERNATIONAL LABOUR OFFICE, REPORT OF THE AD HOC COMMITTEE ON FORCED LABOUR 79, U.N. Doc. E/2431 (1953). The report further stated:

> The ultimate consequence of the system is to compel the Native population to contribute, by their labour, to the implementation of the economic policies of the country, but the compulsory and involuntary nature of this contribution results from the particular status and situation created by special legislation applicable to the indigenous inhabitants alone, rather than from direct coercive measures designed to compel them to work, although such measures, which are the inevitable consequence of this status, were also found to exist.
>
> It is in this indirect sense therefore that, in the Committee's view a system of forced labor of significance to the national economy appears to exist in the Union of South Africa.

Id., at 79–80.

See also Study of Apartheid, supra note 387, at 121.

414. *See* INTERNATIONAL LABOUR OFFICE, FIGHTING DISCRIMINATION IN EMPLOYMENT AND OCCUPATION 74–75 (1968); ALLEGATIONS REGARDING INFRINGEMENTS OF TRADE UNION RIGHTS, U.N. Doc. E/5245 (1973).

415. *See* ALLEGATIONS REGARDING INFRINGEMENTS OF TRADE UNION RIGHTS, U.N. Doc. E/5245 at 15–22, 29–30 (1973).

With respect to well-being, "poverty, malnutrition and disease are widespread" among the deprived groups.[416] Torture may on occasion be used as an instrument of apartheid.[417] Poor housing conditions attend residential segregation and restrictions.[418] Health services for deprived groups are inferior, with an acute shortage of medical personnel in their groups.[419] Members of deprived groups are more exposed to demanding manual work hazardous to health.[420]

Endogamy is as much a requisite for apartheid as for caste.[421] Members of different racial groups are forbidden to intermarry, to live together, or to have any sexual contact.[422] Severe criminal penalities are imposed for violations.[423] Choice of mates within the same racial group may also be curtailed by geographical restrictions.[424] Families are forcibly split because of divergent racial classifications of family members or because of work needs.[425] Wives may not be able to live in urban areas with their working husbands.[426] Children may be required to obtain official permission in order to live with their fathers.[427] Congenial personal relationships of all kinds are stifled.[428]

The sense of responsibility and rectitude of individuals is impaired in

---

416. H. SANTA CRUZ, *supra* note 387, at 191.

417. *See* UNITED NATIONS, MALTREATMENT AND TORTURE OF PRISONERS IN SOUTH AFRICA, U.N. Doc. ST/PSCA/SER.A/13 (1973); Ahmad, *Maltreatment and Torture of Prisoners in South Africa,* 5 OBJECTIVE: JUSTICE 27–41 (No. 1, 1973).

418. *See* ECONOMIC AND SOCIAL CONSEQUENCES, *supra* note 387, at 44–46.

419. *Study of Apartheid, supra* note 387, at 133–35.

420. *Cf. Awad's 1971 Report, supra* note 267, at 57; Diggs, Jr., *Inhuman Conditions in South Africa's Gold Mines*, 5 OBJECTIVE: JUSTICE 42–47 (No. 1, 1973); N.Y. Times, Oct. 23, 1973, at 4, col. 3.

421. *Cf.* notes 310–11 *supra*, and accompanying text.

422. G. CARTER, THE POLITICS OF INEQUALITY: SOUTH AFRICA SINCE 1948, at 76–81 (rev. ed. 1959); L. THOMPSON, *supra* note 387, at 32.

423. *See* Dugard, *The Legal Framework of Apartheid,* in SOUTH AFRICAN DIALOGUE 80, 84 (N. Rhoodie ed. 1973) [hereinafter cited as Dugard].

424. *See* H. SANTA CRUZ, *supra* note 387, at 173.

425. *See* APARTHEID IN SOUTHERN AFRICA, *supra* note 387, at 12.

426. *See id.* at 12, 35–36.

427. *See* H. SANTA CRUZ, *supra* note 387, at 173.

428. In the words of Carlson:

> The degradation of police and of their victims is an inevitable result. Pass Laws and their execution act like acid corroding human relationships and destroying all respect for law. People's feelings and concern for one another, which I believe all men and women have and exhibit in all civilized society, are eaten away in South Africa's violent, primitive society.

Carlson, *South Africa Today: The Security of the State vs. The Liberty of the Individual,* 2 HUMAN RIGHTS 125, 131 (1972).

many ways. Places of public worship are racially segregated.[429] Individuals may be denied access to churches outside the designated area.[430] Traditional African religions are demeaned. The cumulative impact of apartheid tends to create a negative self-image within the deprived person, which in turn adversely affects his ability to participate effectively in community processes.[431]

Viewed in the aggregate, the practices of apartheid have created an explosive situation in which value deprivations are all-pervasive,[432] both individually and collectively. To perpetuate the domination of one race ("racial oligarchy"),[433] the deprived majority of the population is divided and fragmented by such devices as the creation of "homelands" and "group areas."[434] The wholesale practice of discriminatory deprivations is sustained by an elaborate network of oppressive laws, coercion, and "terror."[435] The victims are thus rendered powerless in managing their

---

429. *See* APARTHEID AND THE CHURCH, SPRO-CAS Pub. No. 8 (1972); Landis, *Apartheid Legislation, supra* note 387, at 452–53. *Cf.* Reeves, *"Growing Tension" between State and Church in South Africa,* 4 OBJECTIVE: JUSTICE 32–40 (No. 3, 1972).

430. *See* APARTHEID IN PRACTICE, *supra* note 387, at 37.

431. In the words of Representative Charles C. Diggs, chairman of the Subcommittee on Africa, United States House of Representatives:

> It is quite impossible to convey here the degree of suffering imposed by the system. It is not simply a matter of physical deprivation; it is a question also of the mental suffering which results from the tearing apart of the fabric of African society, just as in the days of the old slave trade.

Diggs, Jr., *Inhuman Conditions in South Africa's Gold Mines*, 5 OBJECTIVE: JUSTICE 42–47 (No. 1, 1973); N.Y. Times, Oct. 23, 1973, at 4, col. 3.

432. *See* P. VAN DEN BERGHE, RACE AND RACISM 110 (1967).

433. H. ADAM, *supra* note 387, at 42. Verwoerd officially characterized the situation in these words:

> "Reduced to its simplest form the problem is nothing else than this: We want to keep South Africa White. . . . 'Keeping it White' can only mean one thing, namely White domination, not 'leadership,' not 'guidance,' but 'control,' 'supremacy.' If we are agreed that it is the desire of the people that the White man should be able to continue to protect himself by White domination . . . we say that it can be achieved by separate development."

Reply of Ethiopia and Liberia, 4 South West Africa Cases, [1966] I.C.J. 264.

434. *See* V. HIEMSTRA, THE GROUP AREAS ACT (1953); F. ROUSSEAU, HANDBOOK ON THE GROUP AREAS ACT (1960); P. VAN DEN BERGHE, *supra* note 387, at 110–54; *Apartheid in Namibia, supra* note 387, at 22–23; Landis, *Apartheid Legislation, supra* note 387, at 16–52; Rubin, *Bantustan Policy: A Fantasy and a Fraud,* U.N. UNIT ON APARTHEID, NOTES AND COMMENTS, No. 12/71 (1971); N.Y. Times, Jan. 21, 1973, § 1, at 1, col. 6.

435. *See* Carlson, *South Africa—A Police State,* U.N. UNIT ON APARTHEID, NOTES AND DOCUMENTS, No. 16/73 (1973); Carlson, *South Africa Today: The Security of the State vs. The Liberty of the Individual,* 2 HUMAN RIGHTS 125 (1972). *But see* SOUTH AFRICA DEP'T OF FOREIGN AFFAIRS, SOUTH AFRICA AND THE RULE OF LAW (1968).

own affairs. They are deprived, in sum, of the right to shape their own destinies, of any meaningful capability of self-determination.[436]

In the sense described above, apartheid has been, and may in the future be, manifested, with varying degrees of approximation, in differing communities. The practices presently imposed in South Africa and extended to Namibia of course epitomize apartheid in the contemporary world.[437] In lesser degree, apartheid may also be taking shape in Southern Rhodesia.[438] Similar practices have existed elsewhere, as once, perhaps in more modest approximation, in the United States,[439] and potentially may occur again.

Dugard, a leading international law scholar in South Africa, has concluded:

> Apartheid is a creature of the law. Conceived in racial prejudice it is nurtured in the womb of Parliament and brought forth in legislative form. It is not merely declaratory of existing social convention; it is often constitutive of new discriminatory practices. The law is as indispensable to apartheid as is race prejudice itself. An understanding of the role of the law in South Africa is essential for an understanding of apartheid.

Dugard, *supra* note 423, at 98.

Van den Berghe has divided oppressive laws within South Africa into two kinds:

> Nationalist laws fall into two discernible categories. On the one hand, such acts as the Population Registration Act, the Prohibition of Mixed Marriages Act, the Group Areas Act, the Bantu Education Act, the Extension of University Education Act, and the Promotion of Bantu Self-Government Act all fall into an internally consistent, long premeditated, and undeviating pattern, namely the steadfast implementation of the ends of apartheid. On the other hand, laws like the Public Safety Act, the Suppression of Communism Act, the Criminal Law Amendment Act, the Riotous Assemblies Act, the Unlawful Organizations Act, the "Sabotage" Act of 1962, and the "No Trial" Act of 1963 share the character of improvised, *ad hoc,* repressive measures, hurriedly passed during, or just after, crises, to give the police powers to crush opposition.

P. van den Berghe, *supra* note 387, at 85.

436. *Cf.* Gervasi, *A Crisis of the Neo-Colonial System,* 4 Objective: Justice 21–24 (No. 3, 1972). For recent developments in South Africa *see* a series of detailed reports by Charles Mohr, a reporter for the New York Times: N.Y. Times, Nov. 20, 1974, at 18, col. 3; *id.,* Nov. 19, 1974, at 14, col. 1; *id.,* Nov. 18, 1974, at 16, col. 1; *id.,* Nov. 17, 1974, § 1, at 1, col. 6.

437. Namibia is a territory under the "illegal" occupation of the government of South Africa. In Namibia, South Africa has imposed apartheid as intensively and extensively as in South Africa. For the controversy of South Africa's continued control over Namibia, *see* notes 481–511 *infra* and accompanying text.

438. *See Study of Apartheid and Racial Discrimination in Southern Africa,* U.N. Doc. E/CN.4/949/Add. 2 (1967); *Study of Apartheid, supra* note 387, at 47–69.

439. *See, e.g.,* J. Denton, Apartheid American Style (1967). As the Kerner Commission reported in 1968, the United States "is moving toward two societies, one black, one white—separate and unequal." Report of the National Advisory Commission on Civil Disorders 1 (Bantam ed. 1968). In the view of van den Berghe, "The closest historical parallel to the South African political system is found in southern United States, and not in Nazi Germany." P. van den Berghe, *supra* note 387, at 80.

Basic Community Policies

In its aggregate patterns, apartheid would appear wholly contradictory to that fundamental freedom of individual choice which is inherent in shared respect.[440] If slavery, caste, racial discrimination, and other gross value deprivations are incompatible with human dignity when taken separately,[441] their comprehensive and systematic aggregation must *a fortiori* multiply such incompatibility.

In its origin, apartheid was sought to be justified upon the same grounds as racial discrimination; that is, some ethnic groups are by nature inferior to others.[442] It is, however, widely agreed today, as has already been noted, that there is no scientific basis for such an assumption.[443]

More recently, justifications have been offered for apartheid in terms of the richer development and ultimate independence of different ethnic groups.[444] It has not, however, been made clear that the oppres-

---

440. *See* chapter 6 *supra,* at notes 18–52 and accompanying text.

441. *See* notes 27–386 *supra* and accompanying text.

442. *See* J. Balicki, Apartheid 343 (1967); P. Joshi, Apartheid in South Africa 17–29 (1950); H. Santa Cruz, *supra* note 387, at 151.

443. *See* notes 325–26 *supra* and accompanying text; chapter 9 *infra,* at notes 54–65 and accompanying text.

444. For a recent official statement by South Africa's minister of information and minister of the interior, *see* Mulder, *South Africa's Objectives,* N.Y. Times, May 14, 1974, at 37, col. 2. In Mulder's words:

> The basic objectives of our policy include self-determination for the various nations in South Africa, protection of the identity of all ethnic groups and the elimination of domination of one people over others. This is a totally different picture from the one accepted by so many United States commentators.
>
> . . .
>
> This transition from a single South Africa state consisting of black nations and a white nation into a bloc of politically independent states, economically interdependent, is taking place systematically and peacefully.

Id.

For brief summaries of South Africa's official position *see* H. Adam, *supra* note 387, at 45–46; L. Thompson, *supra* note 387, at 13–17. For comprehensive, elaborate expositions of this position, *see* Counter Memorial of South Africa, 2 South West Africa Cases, [1966] I.C.J. 1, 457–88; Rejoinder of South Africa, 5 *id.* at 119–41, 242–47; Rejoinder of South Africa, 6 *id.* at 1, 149–65; Argument of Mr. De Villiers, 8 *id.* at 611, 653–67; Argument of Mr. De Villiers, 9 *id.* at 94–114; Address by Mr. Muller (South Africa), 12 *id.* at 67–84; Comment by Mr. De Villiers, 12 *id.* at 392–451. These complex, technical presentations have been adapted into a popular version: D. De Villiers, The Case for South Africa (1970). *See also* The Case for South Africa as Put Forth in the Public Statements of Eric H. Louw, Foreign Minister of South Africa (H. Biermann ed. 1963).

sive practices which comprise apartheid are necessary, or even contributory, to such an objective.[445]

The suggestion is sometimes made that apartheid is necessary to secure the survival of the ruling white group.[446] It is not, however, clearly established that common interest requires a single ruling group to be able to maintain its historic form through posterity, or that such maintenance is worth its costs in terms of the human rights of others.[447]

The same policies, in sum, that condemn slavery, caste, racial discrimination, and other more particular value deprivations would appear equally to condemn apartheid. In the words of a UNESCO study: "The image of man—to whatever ethnic group he belongs or is made a part of—which results from the policy of apartheid in South Africa, is an image which is clearly opposite the one to which the community of nations is ethically and legally dedicated."[448]

Trends in Decision

The prescriptions which outlaw apartheid include those relating to slavery, caste, racial discrimination, self-determination, and other more particular human rights. Increasingly, United Nations pronouncements also invoke certain prescriptions relating to crimes against humanity and threats to peace.[449] With the prescriptions relating to slavery and caste we have already dealt.[450] With the more recent crystallizations concerning racial discrimination we will deal in greater deatil below.[451] In other contexts we propose, further, to deal with the questions of self-determination and violations of more particular human rights prescriptions.[452]

The immediate focus of attention here is upon those prescriptions which, building upon and integrating all the other prescriptions, uniquely condemn apartheid as a gross violation of human rights. There has been a consistent flow of resolutions and decisions giving authoritative interpretations of the Charter of the United Nations, the Universal Declaration of Human Rights, the International Covenants of Human

---

445. For elaborate expositions of this position *see* Memorial of Ethiopia, 1 South West Africa Cases, [1966] I.C.J. 32, 108–90; Reply of Ethiopia and Liberia, 4 *id.* at 220, 476–512; Argument of Mr. Gross, 8 *id.* at 107, 111–24; Argument of Mr. Gross, 8 *id.* at 167, 258–69.

Recently, a liberal South African lawyer, Jack Unterhalter, made the observation that apartheid "sought to impose a system of 'separate development' upon a majority without its consent and to exclude it from the opportunities and benefits of the largest, best developed and richest areas of the country." N.Y. Times, Jan. 5, 1973, at 10, col. 1 (city ed.).

446. *Cf.* H. Katzew, Apartheid and Survival (1965).

447. *See* note 445 *supra.*

448. UNESCO, Apartheid 255 (2d ed. 1972).

449. *See* notes 467–531 *infra* and accompanying text.

450. *See* notes 27–386 *supra* and accompanying text.

451. *See* chapter 9 *infra.*

452. These will be treated in the chapters relating to power and other values.

Rights, and other relevant human rights prescriptions, which characterize apartheid, in the aggregate, as unlawful under international law.

The problem of apartheid has been before the United Nations ever since the first session of the General Assembly in 1946.[453] India at that time complained that South Africa had discriminated against South Africans of Indian origin.[454] From 1946 to 1952, the discussion of the Assembly was confined to the "treatment of people of Indian origin in the Union of South Africa."[455] In 1952, the larger question of apartheid was inscribed as a separate item on the Assembly agenda under the title "Question of race conflict in South Africa resulting from the policies of *apartheid* of the Government of the Union of South Africa."[456] These two items continued to be considered separately until the seventeenth session (1962), when they were combined into one item—"The policies of *apartheid* of the Government of the Republic of South Africa."[457] This composite item has been a fixture on the agenda of the General Assembly year after year.[458] Meanwhile, the Security Council, in response to the worldwide indignation aroused by the Sharpeville incident,[459] met in March and April of 1960 to discuss the policies of apartheid.[460] Subsequently, the Council took up the same questions again in 1963, 1964, 1970, and 1972.[461] In recent years, several other bodies of the United

---

453. For succinct accounts see UNITED NATIONS, ACTION AGAINST APARTHEID (1969); UNITED NATIONS, THE UNITED NATIONS AND HUMAN RIGHTS 40–45 (1973); UNITED NATIONS, REVIEW OF UNITED NATIONS CONSIDERATION OF APARTHEID, U.N. Doc. ST/PSCA/SER.A/2 (1967).

454. *See* Y.B.U.N. [1946–47] at 144–48.

455. UNITED NATIONS, REVIEW OF UNITED NATIONS CONSIDERATION OF APARTHEID, U.N. Doc. ST/PSCA/SER.A/2, at 3 (1967). *Cf.* S. MUKHERJI, INDIAN MINORITY IN SOUTH AFRICA (1959); B. PACHAI, THE INTERNATIONAL ASPECTS OF THE AFRICAN INDIAN QUESTION, 1860–1871 (1971).

456. *See* Y.B.U.N. [1952], at 297–306.

457. *See* Y.B.U.N. [1962], at 93–100.

458. *See* UNITED NATIONS, UNITED NATIONS AND HUMAN RIGHTS 40–45 (1973).

459. The incident took place on Mar. 21, 1960, in South Africa. On that day, large numbers of Africans staged peaceful protests against the new decree that all Africans carry "reference books" at all times in order to move about within their own country. The protesters left their "reference books" behind and presented themselves at various police stations to invite arrest. In Sharpeville, an African township of Vereeniging near Johannesburg, the police used armored vehicles and shot at the crowd, while jet fighter planes flew overhead to frighten the demonstrators. Sixty-nine Africans were killed and nearly 200 were wounded. The large demonstrations which followed in many cities were again met with coercive suppression by the South African government. *See* A. REEVES, SHOOTING AT SHARPEVILLE: THE AGONY OF SOUTH AFRICA (1961).

460. *See* 15 U.N. SCOR (851st–55th mtgs) (1960); Y.B.U.N. [1960], at 142–47.

461. *See* Policies of Apartheid of the Government of Africa: *Implementation by States of United Nations Resolutions on Apartheid* 2–5, 29–41 U.N. Doc. A/9168 (1973) (report of the Special Committee on Apartheid); Report of the Security Council, 1963–1964, 19 U.N.

Nations have dealt with various aspects of the apartheid question.[462]

Although the government of South Africa has consistently contended that its policy of "separate development" (apartheid) is a domestic matter outside the jurisdiction of the United Nations,[463] the U.N. organs have seen no legal difficulty in asserting their competence over this matter.[464] While the government of South Africa has exhibited continued defiance of the successive United Nations resolutions urging discontinuation of its policies and practices,[465] the numerical majority of the African-Asian members has asserted an increasing influence within the United Nations.[466] As the years have gone by, the United Nations, through various organs, has hardened and made more strident its condemnation of apartheid. The characteristic authoritative condemnations of apartheid make

---

GAOR, Supp. (No. 2) 20–43, U.N. Doc. A/5802 (1964); Report of the Security Council, 1970–71, 26 U.N. GAOR, Supp. (No. 2) 29–38, U.N. Doc. A/8402 (1971).

462. For a very useful account *see Co-ordination of United Nations Activities with Regard to Policies of Apartheid and Racial Discrimination in Southern Africa,* U.N. Doc. E/4817/Corr. 1 (1970) (report by the secretary-general). *See also* notes 555–96 *infra* and accompanying text.

463. *See* 7 U.N. GAOR 53–69 (1952); R. HIGGINS, THE DEVELOPMENT OF INTERNATIONAL LAW THROUGH THE POLITICAL ORGANS OF THE UNITED NATIONS 120–23 (1963).

464. *See* Report of the United Nations Commission on the Racial Situation in the Union of South Africa, 8 U.N. GAOR, Supp. (No. 16) 15–34, 115, U.N. Docs. A/2505 & A/2505/Add. 1 (1953). We propose to deal in detail with the problem of domestic jurisdiction in connection with human rights in chapters relating to the constitutive process of authoritative decision. Regarding the question of domestic jurisdiction *see* CORNELL LAW SCHOOL, THE STATUS OF DOMESTIC JURISDICTION (1962) (Proceedings of the Fourth Summer Conference on International Law); R. HIGGINS, THE DEVELOPMENT OF INTERNATIONAL LAW THROUGH THE POLITICAL ORGANS OF THE UNITED NATIONS 58–130 (1963); H. LAUTERPACHT, INTERNATIONAL LAW AND HUMAN RIGHTS 166–220 (1950); M. RAJAN, UNITED NATIONS AND DOMESTIC JURISDICTION (2d ed. 1961); Fawcett, *Human Rights and Domestic Jurisdiction,* in THE INTERNATIONAL PROTECTION OF HUMAN RIGHTS 286 (E. Luard ed. 1967); Ermacora, *Human Rights and Domestic Jurisdiction,* 124 Hague Recueil 371 (1968); McDougal & Reisman, *Rhodesia and the United Nations: The Lawfulness of International Concern,* 62 AM. J. INT'L L. 1 (1968). *See also* chapter 4 *supra,* at 208–15.

465. All the resolutions on South Africa, adopted up to 1972 by the General Assembly and the Security Council, are conveniently itemized in *Policies of Apartheid of the Government of Africa: Implementation by States of United Nations Resolutions on Apartheid* 29–30, U.N. Doc. A/9168 (1973) (report of the Special Committee on Apartheid).

466. For the growing influence of the African-Asian members in the United Nations *see* H. ALKER & B. RUSSETT, WORLD POLITICS IN THE GENERAL ASSEMBLY (1965); I. CLAUDE, SWORDS INTO PLOWSHARES: THE PROBLEMS AND PROGRESS OF INTERNATIONAL ORGANIZATION (4th ed. 1971); INTERNATIONAL ORGANIZATION: POLITICS & PROCESS (L. Goodrich & D. Kay eds. 1973); J. HADWEN & J. KAUFMANN, HOW UNITED NATIONS DECISIONS ARE MADE (2d ed. rev. 1962); T. HOVET, BLOC POLITICS IN THE UNITED NATIONS (1960); R. KEOHANE, POLITICAL INFLUENCE IN THE GENERAL ASSEMBLY (International Conciliation No. 557, 1966).

references to "a crime against humanity,"[467] "a crime against the conscience and dignity of mankind,"[468] "a threat to international peace and security,"[469] and a "violation" of "the Charter of the United Nations" and of "the provisions of the Universal Declaration of Human Rights."[470] Thus, General Assembly Resolution 2923F (XXVII) of Nov. 15, 1972, expresses grave concern "about the explosive situation in South Africa and in southern Africa as a whole resulting from the inhuman and aggressive policies of apartheid pursued by the Government of South Africa, a situation which constitutes a threat to international peace and security," and reaffirms that "the practice of *apartheid* constitutes a crime against humanity."[471] In a special declaration adopted on the occasion of the twenty-fifth anniversary of the United Nations, the General Assembly again proclaimed: "We strongly condemn the evil policy of *apartheid,* which is a crime against the conscience and dignity of mankind and, like nazism, is contrary to the principles of the Charter."[472] Similarly, the Security Council, in its Resolution 191 (1964) of June 18, 1964, expressed its conviction that "the situation in South Africa is continuing seriously to disturb international peace and security," and pronounced that

> the situation in South Africa arising out of the policies of *apartheid* . . . [is] contrary to the principles and purposes of the Charter

467. The formal condemnation by the General Assembly of apartheid as "a crime against humanity" first appeared in G.A. Res. 2202A, 21 U.N. GAOR, Supp. (No. 16) 20, U.N. Doc. A/6316 (1966). This characterization has been reaffirmed in subsequent years: G.A. Res. 2307, 22 U.N. GAOR, Supp. (No. 16) 19, U.N. Doc. A/6716 (1967); G.A. Res. 2396, 23 U.N. GAOR, Supp. (No. 18) 19, U.N. Doc. A/7218 (1968); G.A. Res. 2506B, 24 U.N. GAOR, Supp. (No. 30) 24, U.N. Doc. A/7630 (1969); G.A. Res. 2671F, 25 U.N. GAOR, Supp. (No. 28) 33, U.N. Doc. A/8028 (1970); G.A. Res. 2775F, 26 U.N. GAOR, Supp. (No. 29) 43, U.N. Doc. A/8429 (1971); G.A. Res. 2923E, 27 U.N. GAOR, Supp. (No. 30) 25, U.N. Doc. A/8730 (1972); G.A. Res. 3151G, 28 U.N. GAOR, Supp. (No. 30) 32, U.N. Doc. A/9030 (1973); G.A. Res. 3324E, 29 U.N. GAOR, Supp. (No. 31) 38, U.N. Doc. A/9631 (1974).

468. G.A. Res. 2627, 25 U.N. GAOR, Supp. (No. 28) 3, U.N. Doc. A/8028 (1970); G.A. Res. 2764, 26 U.N. GAOR, Supp. (No. 29) 39, U.N. Doc. A/8429 (1971).

469. *See, e.g.,* G.A. Res. 2054, 20 U.N. GAOR, Supp. (No. 14) 16, U.N. Doc. A/6014 (1965); G.A. Res. 2202A, 21 U.N. GAOR, Supp. (No. 16) 20, U.N. Doc. A/6316 (1966); G.A. Res. 2396, 23 U.N. GAOR, Supp. (No. 18) 19, U.N. Doc. A/7218 (1968); G.A. Res. 2923E, 27 U.N. GAOR, Supp. (No. 30) 25, U.N. Doc. A/8730 (1972); G.A. Res. 3151G, 28 U.N. GAOR, Supp. (No. 30) 32, U.N. Doc. A/9030 (1973).

470. *See, e.g.,* G.A. Res. 1663, 16 U.N. GAOR, Supp. (No. 17) 10, U.N. Doc. A/5100 (1961); G.A. Res. 1761, 17 U.N. GAOR, Supp. (No. 17) 9, U.N. Doc. A/5217 (1962); G.A. Res. 2671F, 25 U.N. GAOR, Supp. (No. 28) 33, U.N. Doc. A/8028 (1970).

471. G.A. Res. 2923E, 27 U.N. GAOR, Supp. (No. 30) 25, U.N. Doc. A/8730 (1972).

472. G.A. Res. 2627, 25 U.N. GAOR, Supp. (No. 28) 3, U.N. Doc. A/8028 (1970).

> of the United Nations and inconsistent with the provisions of the Universal Declaration of Human Rights as well as South Africa's obligations under the Charter.[473]

The thrust of all these authoritative condemnations, repeated again and again with only minor variations, is clearly toward the crystallization of shared general community expectations that apartheid, as an aggregate set of practices, is unlawful. Thus, as the Proclamation of Teheran in 1968 makes summary:

> Gross denials of human rights under the repugnant policy of *apartheid* is a matter of the gravest concern to the international community. This policy of *apartheid,* condemned as a crime against humanity, continues seriously to disturb international peace and security. It is therefore imperative for the international community to use every possible means to eradicate this evil. The struggle against *apartheid* is recognized as legitimate. . . .[474]

Similarly, Article 5 of the United Nations Declaration on the Elimination of All Forms of Racial Discrimination urges: "An end shall be put without delay to governmental and other public policies of racial segregation and especially policies of *apartheid,* as well as all forms of racial discrimination and separation resulting from such policies."[475] This consensus in general community expectation is codified by the enactment of the International Convention on the Elimination of All Forms of Racial Discrimination.[476] Article 3 stipulates: "States Parties particularly condemn racial segregation and *apartheid* and undertake to prevent, prohibit and eradicate all practices of this nature in territories under their jurisdiction."[477]

---

473. S.C. Res. 191 (1964), Resolutions and Decisions of the Security Council 1964, at 13 U.N. Doc. S/5773.

474. Proclamation of Teheran, Final Act of the International Conference on Human Rights, Teheran, 22 April–13 May 1968, U.N. Doc. A/CONF.32/41 at 4 (1968).

475. United Nations Declaration on the Elimination of All Forms of Racial Discrimination, *adopted* Nov. 20, 1963, Art. 5, G.A. Res. 1904, 18 U.N. GAOR, Supp. (No. 15) 35, 36, U.N. Doc. A/5515 (1963) [hereinafter cited as Declaration on the Elimination of All Forms of Racial Discrimination].

476. Convention on the Elimination of All Forms of Racial Discrimination, *supra* note 381.

477. *Id.,* Art. 3, 660 U.N.T. S. at 218. Further documentation of this expectation may be found in the Convention on the Non-Applicability of Statutory Limitations to War Crimes and Crimes against Humanity, *adopted* Nov. 26, 1968, G.A. Res. 2391, 23 U.N. GAOR Supp. (No. 18) 40, U.N. Doc. A/7218 (1968). Art. 1(b) includes "inhuman acts resulting from the policy of *apartheid*" among the crimes against humanity. *Id.,* Art. 1(b). Hence, the Convention excludes such acts from statutory limitation. For a detailed commentary *see* Miller, *The Convention of the Non-Applicability of Statutory Limitations to War Crimes and Crimes against Humanity,* 65 AM. J. INT'L L. 476 (1971).

Parallel with these developments, litigation has gone forward in the International Court of Justice testing South Africa's control over Namibia (South West Africa).[478] In this litigation, strong arguments have been made, and ultimately affirmed by the Court, that the extension of apartheid to Namibia by the Government of South Africa is incompatible with the Charter of the United Nations and, hence, with the Mandate under which South Africa holds Namibia.[479] The central position urged, and now established, is that the unlawfulness of apartheid under international law renders unlawful South Africa's continued control of Namibia.[480]

Like apartheid more generally, the dispute over South Africa's continued control over Namibia has been a regular fixture on the agenda of the General Assembly since its first session.[481] In 1946, the Assembly rejected South Africa's request to annex the mandated territory.[482] Since 1968 this dispute about Namibia has also made an annual appearance before the Security Council.[483] Concurrently, Namibia has been the subject of litigation on which the International Court of Justice has rendered judgments or advisory opinions on six different occasions—1950,[484] 1955,[485] 1956,[486] 1962,[487] 1966,[488] and 1971.[489]

Namibia, known as South West Africa until renamed by the General Assembly in 1968,[490] is the only one of seven African territories once

---

478. For a comprehensive historical and legal study *see* THE SOUTH WEST AFRICA/NAMIBIA DISPUTE (J. Dugard ed. 1973). *See also* S. SLONIM, *supra* note 387; L. SOHN & T. BUERGENTHAL, INTERNATIONAL PROTECTION OF HUMAN RIGHTS 337–504 (1973) (comprehensive bibliography on Namibia presented at 499–504) [hereinafter cited as L. SOHN & T. BUERGENTHAL]. For a brief account *see* UNITED NATIONS & NAMIBIA, *supra* note 387.

479. Advisory Opinion on Legal Consequences for States of the Continued Presence of South Africa in Namibia (South West Africa) Notwithstanding Security Council Resolution 276 (1970), [1971] I.C.J. 16, 57–58 [hereinafter cited as ICJ Advisory Opinion on Namibia].

480. *Id. See* also notes 509–11 *infra* and accompanying text.

481. *See* UNITED NATIONS & NAMIBIA, *supra* note 387.

482. *See* Y.B.U.N. [1946–47], at 205–08.

483. *See* L. SOHN & T. BUERGENTHAL, *supra* note 478, at 441–99. For the latest developments *see* REPORT OF THE UNITED NATIONS COUNCIL FOR NAMIBIA, U.N. Doc. A/9024 (1973).

484. Advisory Opinion on International Status of South-West Africa, [1950] I.C.J. 128.

485. Advisory Opinion on Voting Procedure on Questions Relating to Reports and Petitions concerning the Territory of South-West Africa, [1955] I.C.J. 67.

486. Advisory Opinion on Admissibility of Hearings of Petitioners by the Committee on South-West Africa, [1956] I.C.J. 23.

487. South West Africa Cases, [1962] I.C.J. 319 (preliminary objections).

488. South West Africa Cases (Second Phase), [1966] I.C.J. 6.

489. ICJ Advisory Opinion on Namibia, *supra* note 479.

490. The name has been changed "in accordance with the desires of its people." G.A. Res. 2372, 22 U.N. GAOR, Supp. (No. 16A) 1, U.N. Doc. A/6716/Add. 1 (1968).

under the Mandate System of the League of Nations which was not put under the United Nations Trusteeship System.[491] When the League was dissolved after World War II, no specific provision was made regarding the future of the mandated territories; it was apparently assumed that they would all be voluntarily transformed into trust territories by the Mandatory Powers.[492] South Africa, however, failed to make such transfer in regard to Namibia, and over the years has intensified its control in defiance of the resolutions of U.N. bodies and decisions of the International Court of Justice.[493]

In 1950, in *Advisory Opinion on International Status of South-West Africa,*[494] the International Court of Justice declared that South Africa, having no unilateral "competence to modify the international status of the territory,"[495] continued to be subject, in the administration of South West Africa, to international obligations expressed in the League Covenant and the Mandate,[496] and that the function of supervision was to be assumed by the United Nations.[497] This opinion laid the legal framework for subsequent United Nations action in regard to Namibia.[498]

International concern deepened as the government of South Africa extended its practices of apartheid to South West Africa.[499] Thus, in 1960, Ethiopia and Liberia, two former members of the League, instituted contentious proceedings against South Africa before the Interna-

491. The other six African mandated territories placed under the international trusteeship system were: Togoland under French administration; Togoland under British administration; Cameroons under French administration; Cameroons under British administration; Tanganyika under British administration; and Ruanda-Urundi under Belgian administration.

492. Art. 77(1)(a) of the Charter of the United Nations reads:

> The trusteeship system shall apply to such territories in the following categories as may be placed thereunder by means of trusteeship agreements:
>
> (a) territories now held under mandate.

U.N. CHARTER, Art. 77(1)(a).

This provision is traceable to the agreement reached at the Yalta Conference. For a brief legislative account *see* L. GOODRICH, E. HAMBRO & A. SIMONS, CHARTER OF THE UNITED NATIONS 478–80 (3d rev. ed. 1969). *See also* S. SLONIM, *supra* note 387, at 59–72.

493. *See* UNITED NATIONS & NAMIBIA, *supra* note 387, at 6–42. For "the Trusteeship Struggle" *see* S. SLONIM, *supra* note 387, at 75–122.

494. [1950] I.C.J. 128.

495. *Id.* at 144.

496. *Id.* at 143.

497. *Id.*

498. *See* notes 505–09 *infra* and accompanying text.

499. For the practices of apartheid in Namibia *see* APARTHEID IN SOUTHERN AFRICA, *supra* note 387, at 28–46; *Study of Apartheid and Racial Discrimination in Southern Africa,* U.N. Doc. E/CN.4/949/Add. 1 (1967).

tional Court of Justice,[500] the unlawfulness of apartheid under international law being a central theme of their argument.[501] In 1962, in *South West Africa Cases (Preliminary Objections),*[502] the Court dismissed South Africa's objections to its jurisdiction, thus clearing obstacles to a consideration of the merits.[503] Unfortunately, in July of 1966, after six long years of proceedings, the Court, patently contradicting its 1962 decision, simply held that "the Applicants cannot be considered to have established any legal right or interest appertaining to them in the subject-matter of the present claims"[504] and entirely evaded the substantive issue.

Outraged delegations within the United Nations were quick and decisive in their response.[505] On October 27, 1966, the General Assembly adopted a resolution, declaring that

---

500. Ethiopia and Liberia asked the court to require South Africa to fulfill its obligations and desist from violations of the Mandate, to abandon the policies and practices of apartheid in South Africa, and to be held accountable to the United Nations in its administration of the mandated territory.

501. Their central argument was that the policies and practices of apartheid are inherently incompatible with the obligation to "promote to the utmost the material and moral well-being and the social progress of the inhabitants," required by the Mandate. For a detailed elaboration of this theme see note 497 *supra*. For the text of the Mandate for South-West Africa *see* BASIC DOCUMENTS ON INTERNATIONAL PROTECTION OF HUMAN RIGHTS 242–44 (L. Sohn & T. Buergenthal eds. 1973).

502. [1962] I.C.J. 319.

503. *Id.* at 347.

504. South West Africa Cases (Second Phase), [1966] I.C.J. 6, 51.

505. Reactions on the part of scholars were no less emphatic. *See, e.g.,* ASIAN AFRICAN LEGAL CONSULTATIVE COMMITTEE, SOUTH WEST AFRICA CASES (1968); Alexandrowicz, *The Juridical Expression of the Sacred Trust of Civilization,* 65 AM. J. INT'L L. 149 (1971); Cheng, *The 1966 South-West Africa Judgment of the World Court,* 20 CURRENT LEGAL PROB. 181 (1967); D'Amato, *Legal and Political Strategies of the South West Africa Litigation,* 4 LAW IN TRANSITION Q. 8 (1967); Dugard, *The South West Africa Cases, Second Phase,* 83 S. AFR. L.J. 429 (1966); Falk, *The South West Africa Cases: An Appraisal,* 21 INT'L ORG. 1 (1967); Friedmann, *The Jurisprudential Implications of the South West Africa Case,* 6 COLUM. J. TRANSNAT'L L. 1 (1967); Green, *The United Nations, South West Africa and the World Court,* 7 INDIAN J. INT'L L. 491 (1967); Gross, *The South-West Africa Case,* 1 INT'L LAWYER 256 (1967); Gross, *The South-West Africa Case: What Happened?* 45 FOREIGN AFFAIRS 36 (1966); Higgins, *The International Court and South West Africa: The Implications of the Judgment,* 8 J. INT'L COMM'N JURISTS 3 (1967); Landis, *The South West African Cases: Remand to the United Nations,* 52 CORNELL L.Q. 627 (1967); Pollock, *The South West Africa Cases and the Jurisprudence of International Law,* 23 INT'L ORG. 767 (1967); Reisman, *Revision of the South West Africa Cases,* 7 VA. J. INT'L L. 1 (1966); Stone, *Reflections on Apartheid after the South West Africa Cases,* 42 WASH. L. REV. 1069 (1967); Verzijl, *The South West Africa Cases: Second Phase,* 3 INT'L RELATIONS 87 (1966); De Villiers & Grosskopf, *South West Africa Case: A Reply from South Africa,* 1 INT'L LAWYER 457 (1967); *The World Court's Decision on South West Africa: A Symposium,* 1 INT'L LAWYER 12 (1966).

> the Mandate conferred upon His Britannic Majesty to be exercised on his behalf by the Government of the Union of South Africa is therefore terminated, that South Africa has no other right to administer the Territory and that henceforth South West Africa comes under the direct responsibility of the United Nations.[506]

Subsequently, the Security Council, in its Resolution 264 (1969), stated that it

> 1. Recognize[d] that the United Nations General Assembly terminated the Mandate of South Africa over Namibia and assumed direct responsibility for the Territory until its independence;
> 2. Consider[ed] that the continued presence of South Africa in Namibia is illegal and contrary to the principles of the Charter and the previous decisions of the United Nations and is detrimental to the interests of the population of the Territory and those of the international community;
> 3. Call[ed] upon the Government of South Africa to withdraw immediately its administration from the Territory.[507]

Reiterating this resolution, the Security Council declared further, in resolution 276 (1970), that "the continued presence of the South African authorities in Namibia is illegal and that consequently all acts taken by the Government of South Africa on behalf of or concerning Namibia after the termination of the Mandate are illegal and invalid."[508] The continued defiance of the government of South Africa prompted the Security Council to submit the following question to the International Court of Justice for an advisory opinion: "What are the legal consequences for States of the continued presence of South Africa in Namibia, notwithstanding Security Council resolution 276 (1970)?"[509]

In response, in 1971 the Court at long last dealt squarely with the

---

506. G.A. Res. 2145, 21 U.N. GAOR, Supp. (No. 16) 2, U.N. Doc. A/6316 (1966).

For comments on the effect and implications of the Assembly's decision to terminate South Africa's mandate over South West Africa *see* J. DUGARD, *supra* note 387, at 396–446; S. SLONIM, *supra* note 387, at 313–46; Crawford, *South West Africa: Mandate Termination in Historical Perspective,* 6 COLUM. J. TRANSNAT'L L. 91 (1967); Dugard, *The Revocation of the Mandate for South West Africa,* 62 AM. J. INT'L L. 78 (1968); Hynning, *The Future of South West Africa: A Plebiscite?* [1971] PROC., AM. SOC'Y INT'L L. 144; Khan & Kaur, *Deadlock over South-West Africa,* 8 INDIAN J. INT'L L. 179 (1968); Monroe, *Namibia—The Quest for the Legal Status of a Mandate: An Impossible Dream?* 5 INT'L LAWYER 549 (1971).

507. S.C. Res. 264 (1969), *Resolutions and Decisions of the Security Council, 1969,* at 1–2, 24 U.N. SCOR, U.N. Doc. S/INF/24/Rev. 1.

508. S.C. Res. 276 (1970), *Resolutions and Decisions of the Security Council, 1970,* at 1, 25 U.N. SCOR, U.N. Doc. S/INF/25.

509. S.C. Res. 284 (1970), *id.* at 4.

problems of apartheid both in fact and in law. In describing the facts, the Court observed:

> It is undisputed, and is amply supported by documents annexed to South Africa's written statement in these proceedings, that the official governmental policy pursued by South Africa in Namibia is to achieve a complete physical separation of races and ethnic groups in separate areas within the Territory. The application of this policy has required, as has been conceded by South Africa, restrictive measures of control officially adopted and enforced in the Territory by the coercive power of the former Mandatory. These measures establish limitations, exclusions or restrictions for the members of the indigenous population groups in respect of their participation in certain types of activities, fields of study or of training, labour or employment and also submit them to restrictions or exclusions of residence and movement in large parts of the Territory.[510]

In clarifying the law, the Court emphatically stated that apartheid is unlawful under international law:

> Under the Charter of the United Nations, the former Mandatory had pledged itself to observe and respect, in a territory having an international status, human rights and fundamental freedoms for all without distinction as to race. To establish instead, and to enforce, distinctions, exclusions, restrictions and limitations exclusively based on grounds of race, colour, descent or national or ethnic origin which constitute a denial of fundamental human rights is a flagrant violation of the purposes and principles of the Charter.[511]

---

510. ICJ Advisory Opinion on Namibia, *supra* note 479, at 57.

511. *Id.* For Appraisals of the Advisory Opinion on Namibia *see* J. DUGARD, *supra* note 387; THE CASE FOR SOUTH WEST AFRICA (A. Lejeune ed. 1971); SOUTH AFRICA, DEP'T OF FOREIGN AFFAIRS, SOUTH WEST AFRICA ADVISORY OPINION 1971: A STUDY IN INTERNATIONAL ADJUDICATION (1972); Acheson & Marshall, *Applying Dr. Johnson's Advice*, 11 COLUM. J. TRANSNAT'L L. 193 (1972); Brown, *The 1971 ICJ Advisory Opinion on South West Africa (Namibia)*, 5 VAND. J. TRANSNAT'L L. 213 (1971); Dugard, *Namibia (South West Africa): The Court's Opinion, South Africa's Response, and Prospects for the Future*, 11 COLUM. J. TRANSNAT'L L. 14 (1972); Gordon, *Old Orthodoxies Amid New Experiences: The South West Africa (Namibia) Litigation and the Uncertain Jurisprudence of the International Court of Justice*, 1 DENVER J. INT'L L. & POLICY 65 (1971); Higgins, *The Advisory Opinion on Namibia: Which UN Resolutions Are Binding under Article 25 of the Charter?* 21 INT'L & COMP. L.Q. 270 (1972); Lissitzyn, *International Law and Advisory Opinion on Namibia*, 11 COLUM. J. TRANSNAT'L L. 50 (1972); Rovine, *The World Court Opinion on Namibia*, 11 COLUM. J. TRANSNAT'L L. 203 (1972); Schwelb, *The International Court of Justice and the Human Rights Clauses of the Charter*, 66 AM. J. INT'L L. 337 (1972).

The growing insistence that apartheid constitutes a "crime against humanity" reached a climax in the approval by the General Assembly in 1973 of the International Convention on the Suppression and Punishment of the Crime of Apartheid[512] (Apartheid Convention). This proposed agreement, building upon the Genocide Convention,[513] seeks to make apartheid a crime against humanity, subject to universal jurisdiction. Many provisions in the Apartheid Convention are comparable to, or extend beyond, those in the Genocide Convention.[514]

Article 1 of the Apartheid Convention states:

> 1. The States Parties to the present Convention declare that apartheid is a crime against humanity and that inhuman acts resulting from the policies and practices of apartheid and similar policies and practices of racial segregation and discrimination, as defined in article II of the Convention, are crimes violating the principles of international law, in particular the purposes and principles of the Charter of the United Nations, and constituting a serious threat to international peace and security.

---

512. International Convention on the Suppression and Punishment of the Crime of Apartheid, *adopted* Nov. 30, 1973, G.A. Res. 3068, 28 U.N. GAOR, Supp. (No. 30) 75, U.N. Doc. A/9030. The Convention was approved by a vote of ninety-one in favor, four against, with twenty-six abstentions. The four negative votes were cast by Portugal, South Africa, the United Kingdom, and the United States.

513. Convention on the Prevention and Punishment of the Crime of Genocide, *adopted* Dec. 9, 1948, 78 U.N.T.S. 277 (entered into force Jan. 12, 1951). For discussion of the Convention *see* Advisory Opinion on Reservations to the Convention on the Prevention and Punishment of the Crime of Genocide, [1951] I.C.J. 23; R. LEMKIN, AXIS RULE IN OCCUPIED EUROPE 79–95 (1944); N. ROBINSON, THE GENOCIDE CONVENTION (1960); *Hearings on Genocide Convention before a Subcomm. of the Senate Comm. on Foreign Relations,* 91st Cong., 2d Sess. (1970); *Study of the Question of the Prevention and Punishment of the Crime of Genocide,* U.N. Doc. E/CN.4/Sub. 2/L.565 (1972) (preliminary report by special rapporteur, N. Ruhashyankiko); Baade, *Individual Responsibility,* in 4 THE FUTURE OF THE INTERNATIONAL LEGAL ORDER 291 (R. Falk & C. Black eds. 1972); Lemkin, *Genocide as a Crime under International Law,* 41 AM. J. INT'L L. 145 (1947); Reisman, *Responses to Crimes of Discrimination and Genocide: An Appraisal of the Convention on the Elimination of Racial Discrimination,* 1 DENVER J. INT'L L. & POLICY 29 (1971) [hereinafter cited as Reisman]; Schwelb, *Crimes against Humanity,* 23 BRIT. Y.B. INT'L L. 178 (1946).

514. *See* International Convention on the Suppression and Punishment of the Crime of Apartheid, *adopted* Nov. 30, 1973, Art. 1, 28 U.N. GAOR, Supp. (No. 30) 75, U.N. Doc. A/9030 (1973); Convention on the Prevention and Punishment of the Crime of Genocide, *adopted* Dec. 9, 1948, 78 U.N.T.S. 277 (entered into force Jan. 12, 1951). *Compare* in particular the following provisions of the International Convention on the Suppression and Punishment of the Crime of Apartheid with those of the Genocide Convention respectively: Art. 1(1), *with* Art. 1; Art. 2(a)(ii), *with* Art. 2(b); Art. 2(b), *with* Art. 2(c); Art. 3, *with* Arts. 3 and 4; Art. 4, *with* Art. 5; Art. 5, *with* Art. 6. *Cf. Report of the Ad Hoc Working Group of Experts: Study Concerning the Question of Apartheid from the Point of View of International Penal Law,* U.N. Doc. E/CN.4/1075 (1972).

2. The States Parties to the present Convention declare criminal those organizations, institutions and individuals committing the crime of *apartheid*.[515]

Article 2 singles out "policies and practices of racial segregation and discrimination as practiced in southern Africa" as an acute expression of the apartheid paradigm, and defines "the crime of *apartheid*" in very wide-ranging terms.[516] The specification in definition is of designated "inhuman acts" which are "committed for the purpose of establishing and maintaining domination by one racial group of persons over any other racial group of persons and systematically oppressing them."[517] The first two types of "inhuman acts" are indicated as follows:

(a) Denial to a member or members of a racial group or groups of the right to life and liberty of person:

(i) By murder of members of a racial group or groups;

(ii) By the infliction upon the members of a racial group or groups of serious bodily or mental harm by the infringement of their freedom or dignity, or by subjecting them to torture or to cruel, inhuman or degrading treatment or punishment;

(iii) By arbitrary arrest and illegal imprisonment of the members of a racial group or groups;

(b) Deliberate imposition on a racial group or groups of living conditions calculated to cause its or their physical destruction in whole or in part.[518]

Paragraphs (a)(i), (ii) and (b) are comparable to provisions in Article 2(a)(b)(c) of the Genocide Convention.[519] "Persecution of organizations and persons, by depriving them of fundamental rights and freedoms, because they oppose apartheid" is also made a "crime of apartheid."[520] In recognition that apartheid may involve severe deprivations of all values, the definition of what constitutes a "crime of apartheid" ranges over the whole spectrum of values and many of the specific practices by which different values are shaped and shared. Thus, Article 2 of the Apartheid Convention specifies further other "inhuman acts" constituting crimes of apartheid:

515. Apartheid Convention, *supra* note 512, Art. 1, 28 U.N. GAOR, Supp. (No. 30) 75.

516. *Id.*, Art. 2, at 75–76.

517. *Id.* at 76.

518. *Id.*

519. *Compare id.*, Art. 2(a)(i–ii), (b), *with* Genocide Convention, *supra* note 513, Art. 2(a–c), 78 U.N.T.S. at 280.

520. Apartheid Convention, *supra* note 512, Art. 2(f), 28 U.N. GAOR, Supp. (No. 30) 76.

(c) Any legislative measures and other measures calculated to prevent a racial group or groups from participation in the political, social, economic and cultural life of the country and the deliberate creation of conditions preventing the full development of such a group or groups, in particular by denying to members of a racial group or groups basic human rights and freedoms, including the right to work, the right to form recognized trade unions, the right to education, the right to leave and return to their country, the right to a nationality, the right to freedom of movement and residence, the right to freedom of opinion and expression, and the right to freedom of peaceful assembly and association;

(d) Any measures, including legislative measures, designed to divide the population along racial lines by the creation of separate reserves and ghettos for the members of a racial group or groups, the prohibition of mixed marriages among members of various racial groups, the expropriation of landed property belonging to a racial group or groups or to members thereof;

(e) Exploitation of the labour of the members of a racial group or groups, in particular by submitting them to forced labour.[521]

Under Article 3 of the Convention, "[i]nternational criminal responsibility" is made to apply, "irrespective of the motive involved," to "individuals, members of organizations and institutions and representatives of the State" who "commit, participate in, directly incite or conspire," or "directly abet, encourage or cooperate" "in the commission of the crime of *apartheid*."[522] To suppress and eradicate the crime of apartheid, the contracting states are obligated to undertake "legislative, judicial and administrative," and "other measures" necessary to achieve a spectrum of sanctioning goals ranging from prevention and deterrence to prosecution, trial, and punishment.[523] Article 5 declares that the crime of apartheid imparts universal jurisdiction:

> Persons charged with the acts enumerated in article II of the present Convention may be tried by a competent tribunal of any State Party to the Convention which may acquire jurisdiction over the person of the accused or by an international penal tribunal having jurisdiction with respect to those States Parties which shall have accepted its jurisdiction.[524]

---

521. *Id.*, Arts. 2(c–e).
522. *Id.*, Art. 3.
523. *Id.*, Art. 4.
524. *Id.*, Art. 5.

The Convention further urges the contracting states to implement United Nations decisions regarding apartheid and to cooperate fully with the competent U.N. organs.[525] The contracting states are also required to "submit periodic reports"[526] for review by "a group consisting of three members of the Commission of Human Rights," to be appointed by the Commission's chairman.[527] The Commission on Human Rights is charged with additional responsibilities.[528]

Though this condemnation of apartheid has won practically universal support, doubts have been expressed about the necessity and practicability of making apartheid a crime against humanity subject to universal jurisdiction. The broad and highly general definition of the crime is seen to raise enormous difficulties, and perhaps even dangers to human rights, in applications in specific instances. Thus, when the General Assembly was considering the adoption of the Convention, Mr. Ferguson stated the official position of the United States:

> A convention establishing *apartheid* as a crime against humanity is not necessary in view of the broad, all-inclusive provisions of the International Convention on the Elimination of All Forms of Racial Discrimination. That Convention effectively outlaws all practices of racial discrimination, specifically including that of *apartheid*. Moreover, the most serious offenses which may be associated with *apartheid* are directed against racial groups and, as such, are already made criminal and punishable under the Genocide Convention.
>
> The proposed new draft convention purports to extend international criminal jurisdiction in a broad and ill-defined manner and seeks to rely upon present powers of domestic jurisdiction for its enforcement. . . .
>
> . . . Deplorable as it is, we cannot, from a legal point of view, accept that *apartheid* can in this manner be made a crime against humanity. Crimes against humanity are so grave in nature that they must be meticulously elaborated and strictly construed under existing international law, as set forth primarily in the Nuremberg charter and as applied by the Nuremberg tribunal.
>
> [T]he broad extension of international jurisdiction under this draft convention, even in cases where there are no significant contacts between the offence and the forum State, and where the offender is not a national of the forum State, makes it impossible for

525. *Id.*, Art. 6.
526. *Id.*, Art. 7(1).
527. *Id.*, Art. 9(1).
528. *Id.*, Art. 10, at 76–77.

> the United States to accept this as consistent with the basic norms of fairness, due process and notice so essential in criminal law.[529]

Similarly, Mr. MacKenzie of the United Kingdom, in voting against the adoption of the Convention, explained:

> There are a number of features of the Convention which we find entirely unsatisfactory and unacceptable. One of the most important is that it contains provisions which would violate the principles of international law concerning the proper exercise of criminal jurisdiction, principles to which we attach the highest importance. The provisions in question purport to authorize contracting States to exercise criminal jurisdiction in respect of certain matter covered by the Convention over acts done outside their jurisdiction by persons who are not their nationals. That assertion of jurisdiction would be totally inadmissible so far as my Government is concerned, and if this Convention should enter into force, my Government reserves its rights in relation to any attempt to assert such jurisdiction over United Kingdom nationals. We believe that many Governments share our position.[530]

Other delegations also voiced objections along similar lines.[531]

The important fact is, however, that whatever the merits or extravagances of the Apartheid Convention, apartheid, taken as an aggregate set of practices, violates practically every important particular prescription for the protection of specific rights embodied in the Universal Declaration of Human Rights and in the International Covenants on Human Rights. This comprehensive and systematic violation of particu-

---

529. 28 U.N. GAOR (provisional), U.N. Doc. A/PV.2185 at 12–15 (1973).

530. *Id.* at 23–25.

531. *See, e.g., Draft Convention on the Suppression and Punishment of the Crime of Apartheid* 11–14, U.N. Doc. A/8768 (1972) (note by the secretary-general) (views expressed by the delegations of Madagascar, Norway, and Sweden).

Notwithstanding these doubts and objections, it would be a mistake to discount the importance of the Apartheid Convention. It is an intense ceremonialization of the indignation that the people around the globe feel about apartheid. The characterization of apartheid as a "crime" itself promises to exert a far-reaching impact. In a comparable context, Reisman has incisively emphasized:

> On the symbolic level, the characterization "crime" should convey maximum deterrence. Hence it is no surprise that the word "crime" is reserved for that pattern of behavior which is considered either the greatest challenge to elite objectives or most deleterious to group life.

Reisman, *Responses to Crimes of Discrimination and Genocide: An Appraisal of the Convention on the Elimination of Racial Discrimination,* 1 DENVER J. INT'L L. & POLICY 34 (1971).

lar human rights prescriptions is fully documented, article by article, in the elaborate United Nations *Study of Apartheid and Racial Discrimination in Southern Africa,* conducted by Manouchehr Ganji, special rapporteur appointed by the Commission on Human Rights.[532] In the same vein, Elizabeth S. Landis, a leading expert on the matter of apartheid, has flatly stated in recent testimony before the Sub-Committee on International Organizations and Movements of the House Committee on Foreign Affairs: "Even a cursory analysis of the situation in southern Africa shows that not a single one of the rights enumerated in the Declaration is honored by the white minority regimes of southern Africa."[533] She has backed up her observation by various studies[534] and by an impressive table juxtaposing, one by one, specific provisions with specific violations.[535]

Some of the more important violations of the provisions of the Universal Declaration of Human Rights emphasized by the studies of Ganji, Landis and others[536] include:

1. The basic equality and dignity of every person protected in Article 1 and 2, violated by the deliberate systematic discriminations based on race formalized by the Population Registration Act of 1950;[537]
2. The "right to life, liberty and the security of person" under

---

532. *Study of Apartheid and Racial Discrimination in Southern Africa,* U.N. Docs. E/CN.4/949 & Add. 1–5 (1967–68) and U.N. Docs. E/CN.4/979 & Add. 1–8 (1968–69). For the summary report of the 1967–68 study *see* APARTHEID IN SOUTHERN AFRICA, *supra* note 387.

533. Landis, *Human Rights in Southern Africa and United States Policy in Relation Thereto,* in *Hearings, supra* note 387, at 164.

534. *See, e.g.,* Landis, *Apartheid Legislation, supra* note 387; Landis, *Human Rights in Southern Africa and United States Policy in Relation Thereto,* in *Hearings, supra* note 387; UNITED NATIONS, REPRESSIVE LEGISLATION OF THE REPUBLIC OF SOUTH AFRICA, U.N. Doc. ST/PSCA/SER.A/7 (1969) (a study prepared by Landis).

535. Landis, *Human Rights in Southern Africa and United States Policy in Relation Thereto,* in *Hearings, supra* note 387, at 164–66.

536. In highlighting the following itemizations, we draw heavily on the studies by Ganji, Landis, and Santa Cruz. *See* notes 532–35 *supra*; H. SANTA CRUZ, *supra* note 387, at 148–243. *See also* Advisory Opinion on Legal Consequences for States of the Continued Presence of South Africa in Namibia (South West Africa) Notwithstanding Security Council Resolution 276 (1970), [1971] I.C.J. 16, 83–84 (separate opinion of Vice-President Ammoun).

537. Population Registration Act, No. 30 of 1950, 7 STAT. REP. S. AFRICA 71 (Butterworth 1959) (effective July 7, 1950). For discussion *see* E. BROOKES, *supra* note 387, at 109–25; M. HORRELL, LEGISLATION AND RACE RELATIONS 9–12 (rev. ed. 1971) [hereinafter cited as M. HORRELL]; H. SANTA CRUZ, *supra* note 387, at 148–50.

Article 3, violated by "repressive laws," especially the Terrorism Act of 1967;[538]

3. The prohibition of "slavery or servitude" of Article 4, violated by imposition of a criminal penalty for breach of an employment contract under the Bantu Labor Act of 1964, allowing the renting of black prisoners to private employers, thus constituting practices bordering on forced labor;[539]
4. The "equal protection of the law" under Article 7, violated by separate and unequal public facilities provided in the Reservation of Separate Amenities Act of 1953;[540]
5. "The right to an effective remedy by the competent national tribunals" in Article 8, violated by exemption from judicial review "banning orders" under the Suppression of Communism Act of 1950,[541] and detention under the Terrorism Act;[542]
6. The prohibition of "arbitrary arrest, detention, or exile" of Article 9, violated by a network of terror sustained by such measures as "Terrorism Act" and 180-Day Law;[543]
7. The right to "a fair and public" trial under Article 10, violated by the regularity and prevalence of arbitrary arrest, detention, and banning orders without judicial proceedings;[544]
8. An individual's right to "privacy, family, home or correspondence," or "honor and reputation," protected under Article 12, violated by such measures as searches and seizures with-

---

538. Terrorism Act, No. 83 of 1967, 9 STAT. REP. S. AFRICA 781 (Butterworth 1959) (effective June 27, 1967). *See* REPRESSIVE LEGISLATION, *supra* note 387, for treatment of additional "repressive laws" in South Africa.

539. Bantu (Abolition of Passes and Co-ordination of Documents) Act, No. 67 of 1952, 6 STAT. REP. S. AFRICA 971 (Butterworth 1959) (effective July 11, 1952). *See* H. SANTA CRUZ, *supra* note 387, at 184–87; *Apartheid in Namibia, supra* note 387, at 20–21. *See also* notes 412–13 *supra* and accompanying text.

540. Reservation of Separate Amenities Act, No. 49 of 1953, 8 STAT. REP. S. AFRICA 311 (Butterworth 1959) (effective Oct. 9, 1953). For discussion *see* APARTHEID IN SOUTHERN AFRICA, *supra* note 387, at 26–27; M. HORRELL, *supra* note 537, at 77–83.

541. Suppression of Communism Act, No. 44 of 1950, 9 STAT. REP. S. AFRICA 71 (Butterworth 1959) (effective July 17, 1950).

542. Terrorism Act, No. 83 of 1967, 9 STAT. REP. S. AFRICA 781 (Butterworth 1959) (effective June 27, 1967). *See* REPRESSIVE LEGISLATION, *supra* note 387, at 18–43, 80–91; *"Banning Orders" Issued against Opponents of Apartheid in South Africa,* U.N. UNIT ON APARTHEID, NOTES AND DOCUMENTS, No. 3/69 (1969).

543. *See* EROSION OF THE RULE OF LAW, *supra* note 387, at 7–30; REPRESSIVE LEGISLATION, *supra* note 387; *Report of the Ad Hoc Working Group, supra* note 387, at 41–46; *Repressive Measures against Opponents of Apartheid,* U.N. Doc. A/AC.115/L.375 (1973).

544. *See* notes 402–03 *supra.*

out warrant, night raids of homes in the name of enforcing the Immorality Act prohibiting interracial sexual relations;[545]

9. The "right to freedom of movement and residence" provided in Article 13, violated by the restrictions imposed by the "pass system" and the Group Areas Act;[546]
10. The "right to marry and to found a family" protected under Article 16, violated by forbidding interracial marriages through the Prohibition of Mixed Marriages Act[547] and by the pass laws system, separating family members and restricting wives from living with husbands in a specified area;[548]
11. The "right to own property" under Article 17, violated by restrictions on land ownership and by forcible removal of Africans from "Black spots";[549]
12. The rights of "freedom of opinion and expression" of Article 19 and "freedom of peaceful assembly and association" of Article 20, violated by the Suppression of Communism, Riotous Assemblies, and Unlawful Organizations Acts;[550]

---

545. Immorality Act, No. 23 of 1957, 9 STAT. REP. S. AFRICA 611 (Butterworth 1959) (effective Apr. 12, 1957). *See* M. HORRELL, *supra* note 537, at 8; Landis, *Human Rights in Southern Africa and United States Policy in Relation Thereto,* in *Hearings on International Protection of Human Rights before the Subcomm. on International Organization and Movements of the House Comm. on Foreign Affairs,* 93d Cong., 1st Sess. 165, 167 (1974); *Study of Apartheid and Racial Discrimination in Southern Africa* 68–70, U.N. Doc. E/CN.4/949 (1967).

546. Group Areas Act, No. 36 of 1966, 15 STAT. REP. S. AFRICA 121 (Butterworth 1959) (effective Oct. 26, 1966). *See* notes 398–403 *supra*.

547. Prohibition of Mixed Marriages Act, No. 55 of 1949, 15 STAT. REP. S. AFRICA 91 (Butterworth 1959) (effective July 8, 1949).

548. *See* notes 422–27 *supra*; E. BROOKES, *supra* note 387, at 179–84; M. HORRELL, *supra* note 537, at 13.

549. *See* notes 400 and 409 *supra*.

550. Suppression of Communism Act, No. 44 of 1950, 9 STAT. REP S. AFRICA 71 (Butterworth 1959); Riotous Assemblies Act, No. 17 of 1956, *id.* at 571 (effective Mar. 16, 1956); Unlawful Organizations Act, No. 34 of 1960, *id.* at 711 (effective Apr. 7, 1960).

Section 6 of the Suppression of Communism Act provides:

> If the State President is satisfied that any periodical or other publication—
>
> (a) Professes, by its name or otherwise, to be a publication for propagating the principles or promoting the spread of communism; or
>
> (b) Is published or disseminated by or under the direction or guidance of an organization which has been declared an unlawful organization by or under section two, or was published or disseminated by or under the direction or guidance of any such organization immediately prior to the date upon which it became an unlawful organization; or
>
> (c) Serves *inter alia* as a means for expressing views propagated by any such organization, or did so serve immediately prior to the said date; or

13. The "right to take part in the government" and "the right of equal access to public service" under Article 21, violated by complete abolition of African representation in Parliament;[551]
14. The "right to work," the "right" to "just," "equal pay," and "the right to form and to join trade unions" under Article 23, violated by "job reservations," outrageously discriminatory wage differentials, and the Industrial Conciliation Act of 1956;[552]
15. The "right to education" under Article 25, violated by separate and unequal educational facilities and opportunities through such measures as the Bantu Education Act of 1953[553] and the Extension of University Education Act of 1959.[554]

The success of the general community in formulating and clarifying prescriptions designed to end apartheid has not, unfortunately, been matched by a comparable success in the application of such prescriptions. In the course of the struggle over the problems of apartheid in South Africa and Namibia, there has been a continuous flow of decisions in purported application and in performance of related functions, such as intelligence, promotion, invocation, and appraisal, in aid of application.[555] Many authoritative bodies, including the General Assembly, the

---

(d) Serves *inter alia* as a means for expressing views or conveying information, the publication of which is calculated to further the achievement of any of the objects of communism; or

(e) Is a continuation or substitution, whether or not under another name, of any periodical or other publication the printing, publication or dissemination whereof has been prohibited under this section,

he may without notice to any persons concerned, by proclamation in the Gazette prohibit the printing, publication or dissemination of such periodical, publication or the dissemination of such publication; and the State President may in like manner withdraw any such proclamation.

Suppression of Communism Act, No. 44 of 1950, *as amended by* Act. No. 50 of 1951 & Act. No. 76 of 1962, *quoted in* H. SANTA CRUZ, *supra* note 387, at 175. *See also* REPRESSIVE LEGISLATION, *supra* note 387, at 18–46, 55–59.

551. *See* E. BROOKES, *supra* note 387, at 116–29; H. SANTA CRUZ, *supra* note 387, at 162–68.

552. Industrial Conciliation Act, No. 28 of 1956, 18 STAT. REP. S. AFRICA 399 (Butterworth 1959) (effective Jan. 1, 1957). *See* notes 410–15 *supra.*

553. Bantu Education Act, No. 47 of 1953, 6 STAT. REP. S. AFRICA 1031 (Butterworth 1959) (effective Jan. 1, 1954).

554. Extension of University Education Act, No. 45 of 1959, 12 STAT. REP. S. AFRICA 693 (Butterworth 1959) (effective June 19, 1959). *See* APARTHEID IN PRACTICE, *supra* note 387, at 24–26; APARTHEID IN SOUTHERN AFRICA, *supra* note 387, at 44–45; E. BROOKES, *supra* note 387, at 41–71; M. HORRELL, *supra* note 537, at 64–73.

555. On the seven functions of decision—intelligence, promotion, prescription, invocation, application, appraisal, and termination—consult McDougal, Lasswell, & Reisman, *The World Constitutive Process of Authoritative Decision,* 19 J. LEGAL ED. 253, 261 (1967).

Security Council, the International Court of Justice, the Economic and Social Council, the secretary-general, the Secretariat (especially the Unit on Apartheid), the Commission on Human Rights, the Special Committee on Apartheid, the Special Committee on Decolonization, the Trust Fund for South Africa, the United Nations Council on Namibia, and many *ad hoc* committees of experts established under various resolutions, as well as the Specialized Agencies such as FAO, ILO, UNESCO, WHO, and the Universal Postal Union, have participated in these activities.[556] The General Assembly and the Security Council have, of course, played the most important roles. A wide range of sanctioning measures has been invoked, though without much success, in a sequence of attempts to put the prescriptions condemning apartheid into controlling practice in southern Africa.[557] These attempted enforcement measures cover the whole spectrum of the traditional instruments of policy—diplomatic, ideological, economic, and military.[558]

Prior to 1960, the General Assembly had placed most emphasis on persuasive measures by repeatedly urging a peaceful settlement through patient negotiations with the government of South Africa.[559] Since 1960, however, as persuasion proved futile and the African-Asian membership in the United Nations greatly increased, more coercive measures have been sought. The intensity of the demand of the African-Asian members for such measures is well indicated by Moskowitz:

> What makes South Africa's racial policies a matter of such urgent concern to the international community is the identification of the non-White world with the cause of the Black man there. To the overwhelming majority of the Afro-Asian nations, there is no conceivable crime greater than *apartheid.*[560]

---

556. *See* United Nations, Action against Apartheid (1969); *Co-ordination of United Nations Activities with Regard to Policies of Apartheid and Racial Discrimination in Southern Africa,* U.N. Doc. E/4817/Corr. 1 (1970) (report by the secretary-general).

557. *See generally* C. Legum & M. Legum, South Africa: Crisis for the West (1964); Apartheid and United Nations Collective Measures: An Analysis (A. Leiss ed. 1965); Sanctions against South Africa (R. Segal ed. 1964); J. Spence, Republic under Pressure: A Study of South African Foreign Policy (1965); R. Taubenfeld & H. Taubenfeld, Race, Peace, Law, and Southern Africa (1968); A. Vandenbosch, South Africa and the World (1970).

558. For a convenient summary of these proposed measures of enforcement *see Policies of Apartheid of the Government of Africa: Implementation by States of United Nations Resolutions on Apartheid* 29–41, U.N. Doc. A/9168 (1973) (report of the Special Committee on Apartheid). Concerning the four traditional instruments of policy and sanction *see* M. McDougal & F. Feliciano, Law and Minimum World Public Order 261–383 (1961).

559. *See* United Nations, Action against Apartheid 9–11 (1969); United Nations, Review of United Nations Consideration of Apartheid, U.N. Doc. ST/PSCA/SER.A/2, at 3–5 (1967).

560. M. Moskowitz, The Politics and Dynamics of Human Rights 177 (1968).

Thus, in 1962, for the first time, the General Assembly in Resolution 1761 (XVII) requested member states to undertake, "separately or collectively," the following specific measures to "bring about the abandonment" of South Africa's apartheid policies:[561]

(a) Breaking off diplomatic relations with the Government of the Republic of South Africa or refraining from establishing such relations;

(b) Closing their ports to all vessels flying the South African flag;

(c) Enacting legislation prohibiting the ships from entering South African ports;

(d) Boycotting all South African goods and refraining from exporting goods, including all arms and ammunition, to South Africa;

(e) Refusing landing and passage facilities to all aircraft belonging to the Government of South Africa and companies registered under the laws of South Africa.[562]

In the same resolution the Assembly further approved the establishment of a special committee to "keep the racial policies of the Government of South Africa under review" and to report to the Assembly and the Security Council.[563] With the expansion of its responsibilities through the years, the Special Committee on Apartheid has performed vital functions in aid of the General Assembly and the Security Council.[564]

In subsequent years, as the situation in South Africa has continued to deteriorate, the Assembly has repeatedly reaffirmed the measures recommended in Resolution 1761 (XVII) and urged fuller implementation by member states.[565] In 1969, the Assembly was more detailed and spe-

561. G.A. Res. 1761, 17 U.N. GAOR, Supp. (No. 17) 9, U.N. Doc. A/5217 (1962).

562. *Id.*, para. 4.

563. *Id.*, para. 5, 17 U.N. GAOR, Supp. (No. 17) 9–10.

564. First known as the Special Committee on the Policies of Apartheid of the Government of the Republic of South Africa, its title has been shortened, since Dec. 8, 1970, to the Special Committee on Apartheid. For its activities *see* its annual reports submitted to the General Assembly and the Security Council: *Report,* 29 U.N. GAOR, Supp. (No. 22), U.N. Doc. A/9622 (1974); *Report,* 28 U.N. GAOR, Supp. (No. 22), U.N. Doc. A/9022 (1973); *Report,* 27 U.N. GAOR, Supp. (No. 22), U.N. Doc. A/8722 (1972); *Report,* 26 U.N. GAOR, Supp. (No. 22), U.N. Doc. A/8422/Rev. 1 (1971); *Report,* 25 U.N. GAOR, Supp. (No. 22), U.N. Doc. A/8022/Rev. 1 (1970); *Report,* 24 U.N. GAOR, Supp. (No. 25), U.N. Doc. A/7625/Rev. 1 (1969); *Report,* U.N. Doc. A/7254 (1968); *Report,* U.N. Docs. A/6864 & A/6864/Add. 1–S/8196 (1967); *Report,* U.N. Doc. A/6486–S/7565 (1966); *Report,* U.N. Doc. A/5957–S/6605 (1965); *Report,* U.N. Docs. A/5825, A/5825/Add. 1–S/6073 & S/5426/Add. 1 (1964); *Report,* U.N. Docs. A/5497, A/5497/Add. 1–S/5426 & S/5426/Add. 1 (1963).

565. *See, e.g.,* G.A. Res. 2144A, 21 U.N. GAOR, Supp. (No. 16) 46, U.N. Doc. A/6316 (1966); G.A. Res. 2439, 23 U.N. GAOR, Supp. (No. 18) 47, U.N. Doc. A/7218 (1968); G.A.

cific in its recommendation of economic sanctions by urging member states

(a) To desist from collaborating with the Government of South Africa, by taking steps to prohibit financial and economic interests under their national jurisdiction from co-operating with the Government of South Africa and companies registered in South Africa;
(b) To prohibit airlines and shipping lines registered in their countries from providing services to and from South Africa and to deny all facilities to air flights and shipping services to and from South Africa;
(c) To refrain from extending loans, investments and technical assistance to the Government of South Africa and companies registered in South Africa;
(d) To take appropriate measures to dissuade the main trading partners of South Africa and economic and financial interests from collaborating with the Government of South Africa and companies registered in South Africa.[566]

Other measures that have been urged by the Assembly include coordination of efforts by the specialized agencies;[567] rendering "relief" and legal, educational, and other assistance to victims of apartheid through the United Nations Trust Fund for South Africa;[568] rendering "effective political, moral and material assistance to all those combatting the

Res. 2446, 23 U.N. GAOR, Supp. (No. 18) 51, U.N. Doc. A/7218 (1968); G.A. Res. 2547B, 24 U.N. GAOR, Supp. (No. 30) 56, U.N. Doc. A/7630 (1969); G.A. Res. 2646, 25 U.N. GAOR, Supp. (No. 28) 71, U.N. Doc. A/8028 (1970); G.A. Res. 2671F, 25 U.N. GAOR, Supp. (No. 28) 33, U.N. Doc. A/8028 (1970); G.A. Res. 2714, 25 U.N. GAOR, Supp. (No. 28) 79, U.N. Doc. A/8028 (1970).

566. G.A. Res. 2506, para. 5, 24 U.N. GAOR, Supp. (No. 30) 23, U.N. Doc. A/7630 (1969). *See also* G.A. Res. 2671F, para. 7, 25 U.N. GAOR, Supp. (No. 28) 33, U.N. Doc. A/8028 (1970); G.A. Res. 2784, 26 U.N. GAOR, Supp. (No. 29) 79, U.N. Doc. A/8429 (1971); G.A. Res. 2923E, 27 U.N. GAOR, Supp. (No. 30) 25, U.N. Doc. A/8730 (1972); G.A. Res. 3151G, 28 U.N. GAOR, Supp. (No. 30) 16–18, U.N. Doc. A/9030 (1973).

567. *See, e.g.,* G.A. Res. 2054A, para. 10, 20 U.N. GAOR, Supp. (No. 14) 16, U.N. Doc. A/6014 (1965); G.A. Res. 3151D, 28 U.N. GAOR, Supp. (No. 30) 31, U.N. Doc. A/9030 (1973).

568. G. A. Res. 2054B, para. 2, 20 U.N. GAOR, Supp. (No. 14) 17, U.N. Doc. A/6014 (1965). *See also* G.A. Res. 2144A, para. 7, 21 U.N. GAOR, Supp. (No. 16) 46, U.N. Doc. A/6316 (1966); G. A. Res. 2202B, 21 U.N. GAOR, Supp. (No. 16) 21, U.N. Doc. A/6316 (1966); G.A. Res. 2397, 23 U.N. GAOR, Supp. (No. 18) 21, U.N. Doc. A/7218 (1968); G.A. Res. 2547A, 24 U.N. GAOR, Supp. (No. 30) 55, U.N. Doc. A/7630 (1969); G.A. Res. 2671E, 25 U.N. GAOR, Supp. (No. 28) 33, U.N. Doc. A/8028 (1970); G.A. Res. 3151F, 28 U.N. GAOR, Supp. (No. 30) 32, U.N. Doc. A/9030 (1973).

policies of apartheid";[569] a massive continuing publicity campaign through the mass media, with international seminars and so on;[570] an international boycott of racially oriented sports teams;[571] discouragement of emigration to South Africa;[572] and the termination of "all cultural, educational and civic contacts and exchanges with racist institutions in South Africa."[573]

In response to the requests of the Assembly and member states, the Security Council, as indicated above, dealt with the apartheid problems in 1960, 1963, 1964, 1970, and 1972.[574] The central call on the part of the Security Council has been for an arms embargo. Thus, the Security Council in Resolution 181 (1963) called upon "all States to cease forthwith the sale and shipment of arms, ammunition of all types and military vehicles to South Africa,"[575] and further, in Resolution 182 (1963),

---

569. G.A. Res. 2202A, para. 5(c), 21 U.N. GAOR, Supp. (No. 16) 20, U.N. Doc. A/6316 (1966). *See also* G.A. Res. 2307, para. 8, 22 U.N. GAOR, Supp. (No. 16) 20, U.N. Doc. A/6716 (1967); G.A. Res. 2396, para. 7, 23 U.N. GAOR, Supp. (No. 18) 20, U.N. Doc. A/7218 (1968); G.A. Res. 2446, para. 6, 23 U.N. GAOR, Supp. (No. 18) 51, U.N. Doc. A/7218 (1968); G.A. Res. 2506B, para. 4, 24 U.N. GAOR, Supp. (No. 30) 24, U.N. Doc. A/7630 (1969); G.A. Res. 2671B, 25 U.N. GAOR, Supp. (No. 28) 32, U.N. Doc. A/8028 (1970); G.A. Res. 2775F, para. 6, 26 U.N. GAOR, Supp. (No. 29) 6, U.N. Doc. A/8429 (1971); G.A. Res. 2923E, para. 11, 27 U.N. GAOR, Supp. (No. 30) 26, U.N. Doc. A/8730 (1972).

570. G.A. Res. 2054A, 20 U.N. GAOR, Supp. (No. 14) 16, U.N. Doc. A/6014 (1965), urged all member states to "co-operate with the Secretary-General and the Special Committee" to achieve "the widest possible dissemination of information on the policies of *apartheid* of the Government of South Africa and on United Nations efforts to deal with the situation." *Id.* at 17. For reiteration of this call, see G.A. Res. 25, 47B, 24 U.N. GAOR, Supp. (No. 30) 56, U.N. Doc. A/7630 (1969); G.A. Res. 2671C, 25 U.N. GAOR, Supp. (No. 28) 32, U.N. Doc. A/8028 (1970); G.A. Res. 2775G, 26 U.N. GAOR, Supp. (No. 29) 44, U.N. Doc. A/8429 (1971); G.A. Res. 3151C, 28 U.N. GAOR, Supp. (No. 30) 30–31, U.N. Doc. A/9030 (1973).

571. *See, e.g.,* G.A. Res. 2396, para. 12, 23 U.N. GAOR, Supp. (No. 18) 20, U.N. Doc. A/7218 (1968); G.A. Res. 2671F, para. 8, 25 U.N. GAOR, Supp. (No. 28) 34, U.N. Doc. A/8028 (1970); G.A. Res. 2775D, 26 U.N. GAOR, Supp. (No. 29), 42, U.N. Doc. A/8429 (1971); G.A. Res. 2923E, para. 14, 27 U.N. GAOR, Supp. (No. 30) 26, U.N. Doc. A/8730 (1972).

572. In 1968, the General Assembly requested all member states to "discourage the flow of immigrants, particularly skilled and technical personnel, to South Africa." G.A. Res. 2396, para. 11, 23 U.N. GAOR, Supp. (No. 18) 19, U.N. Doc. A/7218 (1968). *See also* G.A. Res. 2775F, para. 9, 26 U.N. GAOR, Supp. (No. 29) 43, U.N. Doc. A/8429 (1971).

573. G.A. Res. 3151G, para. 10(d), 28 U.N. GAOR, Supp. (No. 30) 33, U.N. Doc. A/9030 (1973). *See also* G.A. Res. 2396, para. 12, 23 U.N. GAOR, Supp. (No. 18) 20, U.N. Doc. A/7218 (1968); G.A. Res. 2547B, 24 U.N. GAOR, Supp. (No. 30) 56, U.N. Doc. A/7630 (1969); G.A. Res. 2646, 25 U.N. GAOR, Supp. (No. 28) 71, U.N. Doc. A/8028 (1970); G.A. Res. 2671F, 25 U.N. GAOR, Supp. (No. 28) 33, U.N. Doc. A/8028 (1970).

574. *See* notes 459–61 *supra* and accompanying text.

575. S.C. Res. 181 (1963), *Resolutions and Decisions of the Security Council, 1963,* at 7, 18 U.N. SCOR, U.N. Doc. S/INF/Rev. 1 (1963).

called upon "all States to cease forthwith the sale and shipment of equipment and materials for the manufacture and maintenance of arms and ammunition in South Africa."[576] These resolutions calling for an arms embargo have many times been reaffirmed by the General Assembly[577] and were further strengthened by the Council itself in Resolution 282 (1970):[578]

> [This Resolution c]alls upon all States to strengthen the arms embargo
>
> (a) By implementing fully the arms embargo against South Africa unconditionally and without reservations whatsoever;
>
> (b) By withholding the supply of all vehicles and equipment for use of the armed forces and paramilitary organizations of South Africa;
>
> (c) By ceasing the supply of spare parts for all vehicles and military equipment used by the armed forces and paramilitary organizations of South Africa;
>
> (d) By revoking all licenses and military patents granted to the South African Government or to South African companies for the manufacture of arms and ammunition, aircraft and naval craft or other military vehicles and by refraining from further granting such licenses and patents;
>
> (e) By prohibiting investment in, or technical assistance for, the manufacture of arms and ammunition, aircraft, naval craft, or other military vehicles;
>
> (f) By ceasing provision of military training for members of the South African armed forces and all other forms of military co-operation with South Africa;
>
> (g) By undertaking the appropriate action to give effect to the above measures.[579]

---

576. S.C. Res. 182 (1963), *id.* at 8–10.

577. *See* G.A. Res. 1978A, 18 U.N. GAOR, Supp. (No. 15) 20, U.N. Doc. A/5515 (1963); G.A. Res. 2054A, 20 U.N. GAOR, Supp. (No. 14) 16, U.N. Doc. A/6014 (1965); G.A. Res. 2144A, 21 U.N. GAOR, Supp. (No. 16) 46, U.N. Doc. A/6316 (1966); G.A. Res. 2202A, 21 U.N. GAOR, Supp. (No. 16) 20, U.N. Doc. A/6316 (1966); G.A. Res. 2307, 22 U.N. GAOR, Supp. (No. 16) 19, U.N. Doc. A/6716 (1967); G.A. Res. 2506B, 24 U.N. GAOR, Supp. (No. 30) 24, U.N. Doc. A/7630 (1969).

578. S.C. Res. 282, *Resolutions and Decisions of the Security Council, 1970,* at 12, 25 U.N. SCOR, U.N. Doc. S/INF/25 (1970).

579. *Id.,* para. 4. In Oct. 1974, the Security Council rejected a draft resolution, sponsored by Kenya, Mauritania, Cameroon, and Iraq, which would have had the Council recommend to the General Assembly that South Africa be expelled from the United

Meanwhile, various supporting decisions were being made by the specialized agencies. On December 5, 1963, the Conference of the Food and Agriculture Organization of the United Nations decided not to invite the government of South Africa to participate in any of the Organization's activities. South Africa thereupon withdrew from FAO on December 18, 1963.[580] After repeated condemnations by the International Labor Conference, urging renunciation of the apartheid policy,[581] the government of South Africa withdrew from the International Labor Organization in March 1966.[582] In 1964, the Congress of the Universal Postal Union adopted a resolution demanding the expulsion of South Africa from the organization.[583] In April of 1955, South Africa withdrew from the United Nations Educational, Scientific, and Cultural Organization, allegedly in protest of a number of UNESCO publications condemning apartheid.[584] The World Health Assembly, in March 1964, decided to suspend the voting privileges of South Africa[585] and, in 1965, adopted an amendment to the Constitution of the World Health Organization which empowered the Health Assembly with the authority

---

Nations pursuant to Art. 6 of the Charter. Although the vote was ten in favor, three opposed, and two abstaining, the resolution was vetoed by the negative votes of France, the United Kingdom, and the United States. *See* UN MONTHLY CHRONICLE, Nov. 1974, at 9–40. Shortly afterwards, on Nov. 12, 1974, the General Assembly upheld the following ruling of its president:

> On the basis of the consistency with which the General Assembly has regularly refused to accept the credentials of the delegation of South Africa, one may legitimately infer that the General Assembly would in the same way reject the credentials of any other delegation authorized by the Government of the Republic of South Africa to represent it, which is tantamount to saying in explicit terms that the General Assembly refuses to allow the delegation of South Africa to participate in its work.

G.A. Res. 3324E, *Resolutions of the General Assembly at its Twenty-ninth Regular Session,* at 27, U.N. Press Release GA/5194 (20 Dec. 1974). South Africa was thus, in effect, suspended from the Twenty-ninth Session of the General Assembly. *See* N.Y. Times, Nov. 13, 1974, at 1, col. 2. *See also id.,* Sept. 28, 1974, at 2, col. 7; *id.,* Oct. 1, 1974, at 3, col. 1; *id.,* Oct. 7, 1974, at 6, col. 4; *id.,* Oct. 19, 1974, at 3, col. 1; *id.,* Oct. 25, 1974, at 5, col. 1; *id.,* Oct. 30, 1974, at 7, col. 1; *id.,* Oct. 31, 1974, at 1, col. 4.

580. *Report of the Special Committee on the Policies of Apartheid of the Government of the Republic of South Africa* 154, U.N. Doc. A/5825 (1964).

581. *See* notes 413–14 *supra;* INTERNATIONAL LABOUR OFFICE, FIGHTING DISCRIMINATION IN EMPLOYMENT AND OCCUPATION 72–81 (1968).

582. H. SANTA CRUZ, *supra* note 387, at 211–12.

583. *Report of the Special Committee on the Policies of Apartheid of the Government of the Republic of South Africa* 156–57, U.N. Doc. A/5825 (1964).

584. *See* H. SANTA CRUZ, *supra* note 387, at 212; UNESCO, APARTHEID (2d ed. 1972).

585. *Report of the Special Committee on the Policies of Apartheid of the Government of the Republic of South Africa* 157, U.N. Doc. A/5825 (1964).

to suspend or exclude a member "deliberately practising a policy of racial discrimination."[586]

Following the General Assembly's formal termination of South Africa's Mandate over Namibia in 1966[587] and the 1971 Advisory Opinion of the International Court of Justice on Namibia,[588] many member states of the United Nations sought sanctioning measures designed to end the "illegal occupation" of that territory by the government of South Africa.[589] As an instrument to facilitate termination of South Africa's effective control over Namibia, the United Nations Council for Namibia was established pursuant to General Assembly Resolution 2248 (S-V) of 1967.[590] The Council is empowered by the same Resolution to "administer" Namibia "until independence, with the maximum possible participation" of its people, to "promulgate" necessary "laws, decrees and administrative regulations," to establish "a constituent assembly to draw up a constitution," to maintain "law and order in the Territory," and to transfer all powers to the people of the Territory upon the declaration of independence."[591] The Council is charged by General Assembly Resolution 3031 (XXVII) of 1972[592] with additional responsibilities in conducting the foreign affairs of Namibia and in arranging for external assistance.[593] Because of the vehement opposition of the government

---

586. Art. 7(b) of the Constitution of the World Health Organization, as amended, reads:

> (b) If a Member ignores the humanitarian principles and the objectives laid down in the Constitution, by deliberately practising a policy of racial discrimination, the Health Assembly may suspend it or exclude it from the World Health Organization.
>
> Nevertheless, its rights and privileges, as well as its membership, may be restored by the Health Assembly on the proposal of the Executive Board following a detailed report proving that the State in question has renounced the policy of discrimination which gave rise to its suspension or exclusion.

CONSTITUTION OF THE WORLD HEALTH ORGANIZATION, *as amended* May 20, 1965, Art. 7(b), *reprinted in* 4 INT'L LEGAL MATERIALS 745, 746 (1965).

587. G.A. Res. 2145, 21 U.N. GAOR, Supp. (No. 16) 2, U.N. Doc. A/6316 (1966).

588. Advisory Opinion on Legal Consequences for States of the Continued Presence of South Africa in Namibia (South West Africa) Notwithstanding Security Council Resolution 276 (1970), [1971] I.C.J. 16.

589. *See* note 557, *supra.*

590. G.A. Res. 2248 (S-V), 5 U.N. GAOR, Spec. Sess., Supp. (No. 1) 1–2, U.N. Doc. A/6657 (1967).

591. *Id.*, pt. II.

592. G.A. Res. 3031, 27 U.N. GAOR, Supp. (No. 30) 88, U.N. Doc. A/8730 (1972).

593. These additional responsibilities are:

> (a) To represent Namibia in international organizations, at conferences and on any other occasion as may be required;

of South Africa, the Council has not, however, been able to assert its physical presence within Namibia.[594]

The failure of the various sanctioning measures designed to eradicate

---

> (b) To ensure the participation in an appropriate capacity of the representatives of the Namibian people in its activities;
>
> (c) To continue its consultations at the United Nations Headquarters, in Africa or elsewhere with the representatives of the Namibian people and the Organization of African Unity;
>
> (d) To continue to assume responsibility for the urgent establishment of short-term and long-term co-ordinated programmes of technical and financial assistance to Namibia in the light of the relevant provisions of resolution 2248 (S-V) and taking into account resolution 2872 (XXVI) of 20 December 1971;
>
> (e) To continue to expand the existing scheme for issuing identity certificates and travel documents to Namibians by concluding appropriate agreements with Governments of Member States;
>
> (f) To continue to promote publicity with regard to the question of Namibia and to assist the Secretary-General in the discharge of the task entrusted to him under paragraph 14 below;
>
> (g) To undertake a study of the compliance of Member States with the relevant United Nations resolutions, taking into account the advisory opinion of the International Court of Justice relating to Namibia;
>
> (h) To examine the question of foreign economic interests operating in Namibia, and to seek effective means to regulate such activities as appropriate;
>
> (i) To continue to examine the question of bilateral and multilateral treaties which explicitly or implicitly include Namibia, and to seek to replace South Africa as the party representing Namibia in all relevant bilateral and multilateral treaties.

Id., para. 9, 27 U.N. GAOR, Supp. (No. 30) 89.

594. For the recent activities of the United Nations Council for Namibia see the following reports of the Council: 24 U.N. GAOR, Supp. (No. 24), U.N. Doc. A/7624/Rev. 1 (1969); 25 U.N. GAOR, Supp. (No. 24), U.N. Doc. A/8024 (1970); 26 U.N. GAOR, Supp. (No. 24), U.N. Doc. A/8424 (1971); 27 U.N. GAOR, Supp. (No. 24), U.N. Doc. A/8724 (1972); U.N. Doc. A/9024 (1973).

In 1972, the Security Council, pursuant to its resolution 309 (1972) of Feb. 4, 1972, invited the Secretary-General

> to initiate as soon as possible contacts with all parties concerned, with a view to establishing the necessary conditions so as to enable the people of Namibia, freely and with strict regard to the principle of human equality, to exercise their right to self-determination and independence, in accordance with the Charter of the United Nations.

Resolutions of the Security Council, 1972, at 4, 27 U.N. SCOR, U.N. Doc. S/INF/28 (1972).

Hence, the secretary-general established contacts with the government of South Africa, and visited both South Africa and Namibia during Mar. 6–10, 1972. After receiving the initial encouraging report submitted by the secretary-general, U.N. Doc. S/10738 (1972),

apartheid in southern Africa is too conspicuous to require elaboration.[595] As the Special Committee on Apartheid pointed out in its 1973 Report:

> [W]hile a large number of Member States have implemented these resolutions, in some cases at great economic sacrifice, some other States (particularly a few main trading partners of South Africa) have ignored them. Some States have greatly increased their trade with and investment in South Africa during the past decade. A few States have even continued to provide military equipment to South Africa. As a result, the United Nations action on *apartheid* has remained far from effective.[596]

Such failure is perhaps but a dramatic demonstration of the characteristic weaknesses of a world arena in which both authoritative decision

---

the Security Council urged the secretary-general to continue his contacts, assisted by a special representative. S.C. Res. 319 (1972), *id.* at 5. Subsequently, the mandate of the secretary-general was further extended by S.C. Res. 323 (1972), *id.* at 6. Despite these efforts, the United Nations Council for Namibia has concluded:

> The contacts authorized by the Security Council between the Secretary-General of the United Nations and the illegal South African occupation regime have failed, clearly demonstrating the bad faith of the South African regime in refusing to accept the last offer to negotiate a peaceful transfer of power in Namibia. The failure of the contacts is due primarily to the fact that South Africa clearly entered into them with the intention of using the contacts to consolidate their domination over Namibia and to divert attention from the problem, thus arresting the increasing pressure of the international community. It is now incumbent on the Security Council, and particularly those members who argued most forcefully for offering this chance of a "dialogue" to South Africa, to adopt whatever measures may be necessary to enforce international law as defined by the International Court of Justice and the relevant resolutions of the United Nations.

Report of the United Nations Council for Namibia 73, U.N. Doc. A/9024 (1973).

595. *See* note 557 *supra.*

596. *Policies of Apartheid of the Government of Africa: Implementation by States of United Nations Resolutions on Apartheid* 5, U.N. Doc. A/9168 (1973) (report of the Special Committee on Apartheid).

See African Research Group, Race to Power (1974); D. Austin, Britain and South Africa (1966); R. First, J. Steele, & S. Gurney, The South African Connection: Western Investments in Apartheid (1972); Southern Africa and the United States (W. Hance ed. 1968); Southern Africa in Perspective (C. Potholm & R. Dale eds. 1972); United Nations, Unit on Apartheid, Foreign Investment in the Republic of South Africa, U.N. Doc. ST/PSCA/SER.A/11 (1970); Hirschmann, *Pressure on Apartheid,* 52 Foreign Affairs 168 (1973); *International Conference of Trade Unions against Apartheid,* U.N. Doc. A/9169 (1973) (report of the Special Committee on Apartheid); *Military Build-up in South Africa and Implementation of the Arms Embargo against South Africa,* U.N. Docs. A/9180 & S/11005 (1973) (report of the Special Committee on Apartheid).

making and effective power are relatively decentralized.[597] It remains for increasing global interdependence and the growing consciousness, and conscience, of mankind to change the outcome.[598]

---

597. *See generally* M. Barkun, Law without Sanctions: Order in Primitive Societies and the World Community (1968); 1 & 3 The Future of the International Legal Order (C. Black & R. Falk eds. 1969, 1971); J. Carey, UN Protection of Civil and Political Rights (1970); R. Falk, Legal Order in a Violent World (1968); R. Falk, The Status of Law in International Society (1970); W. Friedmann, The Changing Structure of International Law (1964); International Law in the Twentieth Century (L. Gross ed. 1969); O. Lissitsyn, International Law in a Divided World 1 (International Conciliation No. 543, 1963); M. McDougal & Associates, Studies in World Public Order (1960); W. Reisman, Nullity and Revision: The Review and Enforcement of International Judgments and Awards (1971); B. Roling, International Law in an Expanded World (1960).

Some of the difficulties in enforcing prescriptions about threats to the peace are illustrated by the futility of the attempts to apply sanctions in Southern Rhodesia. *See* McDougal & Reisman, *Rhodesia and the United Nations: The Lawfulness of International Concern,* 62 Am. J. Int'l L. 1 (1968).

598. There have of course been many later developments, none of which would appear to require change in the basic core of our presentation in relation to the problem discussed above. *See* J. Dugard, Human Rights and the South African Legal Order (1978); M. O'Callaghan, Namibia: The Effects of Apartheid on Culture and Education (1977); *United Nations Decade for Action to Combat Racism and Racial Discrimination,* 10 Objective: Justice 1 (No. 1, 1978); Reddy, *The United Nations and the International Campaign against Apartheid,* 9 Objective: Justice 9 (No. 4, 1977–78); Woods, *Mobilizing Effective Moral Force against Apartheid, id.* at 14–19; Minty, *Implementing the Arms Embargo against South Africa, id.* at 20–26; Richardson, *Self-Determination, International Law and the South African Bantusan Policy,* 17 Colum. J. Transn'l L. 185 (1978). *See also* Report of the Special Committee against Apartheid, 32 U.N. GAOR, Supp. (No. 22), U.N. Doc. A/32/22 (1977); 31 U.N. GAOR, Supp. (No. 22), U.N. Doc. A/31/22 (1976); 31 U.N. GAOR, Supp. (No. 22A), U.N. Doc. A/31/22/Add. 1 to 3 (1976); and Report of the United Nations Council for Namibia, 32 U.N. GAOR, Supp. (No. 24), U.N. Doc. A/32/24 (1977); 31 U.N. GAOR, Supp. (No. 24), U.N. Doc. A/31/24 (1976); *Namibia: The United Nations and U.S. Policy: Hearings before the Subcomm. on International Organizations of the House Comm. on International Relations,* 94th Cong., 2d Sess. (1976).

8. CLAIMS RELATING TO A BASIC EQUALITY OF OPPORTUNITY AND FREEDOM FROM DISCRIMINATION

The deprivations with which we are here concerned are those, whether imposed by state officials or others, which deny individuals effective freedom of choice about participation in community value processes because of alleged group characteristics which bear no rational relation to the individuals' actual potentialities for such participation. The individuals in any community may, of course, differ greatly in their potentialities for participation in different value processes or even in different phases of the same value process. These differences in potentialities for participation do not, however, vary uniformly and rationally with alleged group characteristics described in terms of race, sex, religion, political opinion, language, age, alienage, possession of property, birth, and other status. Differentiation in the treatment of individuals based upon group categorizations having no rational relation to the genuine potential of the individual for contribution to the common interest is commonly described, in both legal and popular parlance, as discrimination.[1] Thus, a basic United Nations Study of 1949 recites: "[D]iscrimina-

1. *See, e.g.*, a series of studies on discrimination undertaken under the auspices of the United Nations: C. AMMOUN, STUDY OF DISCRIMINATION IN EDUCATION, U.N. DOC. E/CN.4/Sub. 2/181/Rev. 1 (1957); J. INGLES, STUDY OF DISCRIMINATION IN RESPECT OF THE RIGHT OF EVERYONE TO LEAVE ANY COUNTRY, INCLUDING HIS OWN, AND TO RETURN TO HIS COUNTRY, U.N. DOC. E/CN.4/Sub. 2/220/Rev. 1 (1963); A. KRISHNASWAMI, STUDY OF DISCRIMINATION IN THE MATTER OF RELIGIOUS RIGHTS AND PRACTICES, U.N. DOC. E/CN.4/Sub. 2/200/Rev. 1 (1960); M. RANNAT, STUDY ON EQUALITY IN THE ADMINISTRATION OF JUSTICE, U.N. DOC. E/CN.4/Sub. 2/296/Rev. 1 (1972); V. SAARIO, STUDY OF DISCRIMINATION AGAINST PERSONS BORN OUT OF WEDLOCK, U.N. DOC. E/CN.4/Sub. 2/265/Rev. 1 (1967); H. SANTA CRUZ, RACIAL DISCRIMINATION, U.N. DOC. E/CN.4/Sub. 2/307/Rev. 1 (1971); H. SANTA CRUZ, STUDY OF DISCRIMINATION IN THE MATTER OF POLITICAL RIGHTS, U.N. DOC. E/CN.4/Sub. 2/213/Rev. 1 (1962); UNITED NATIONS, THE MAIN TYPES AND CAUSES OF DISCRIMINATION, U.N. DOC. E/CN.4/Sub. 2/40/Rev. 1 (1949) (memorandum submitted by the secretary-general).

See also E. VIERDAG, THE CONCEPT OF DISCRIMINATION IN INTERNATIONAL LAW (1973); McKean, *The Meaning of Discrimination in International and Municipal Law*, 44 BRIT. Y.B.

tion includes any conduct based on a distinction made on grounds of natural or social categories, which have no relation either to individual capacities or merits, or to the concrete behaviour of the individual person."[2] Though less extreme in its incidence than slavery,[3] and less hierarchized in its differentiations than caste[4] and apartheid,[5] discrimination may still be most comprehensive, systematic, and severe in the value deprivations it imposes.

The prevalence through history, even into contemporary life, of wide-ranging discriminations, based upon many alleged group characteristics and extending through all community value processes, is a matter of common knowledge. The horrors of comprehensive and systematic racial discrimination are matched only by the persistent and equally destructive corrosions of its less institutionalized and less routinized expression, with all such expression constituting a deep and imminent threat to contemporary world public order.[6] The damage done to

---

INT'L L. 177 (1970); Sorensen, *The Quest for Equality,* 507 INT'L CONCILIATION 289 (1956); Van Dyke, *Human Rights without Discrimination,* 67 AM. POL. SCI. REV. 1267 (1973).

For a discussion of positive programs to remove the causes of inequality and of the importance of managing all phases of the constitutive process to prevent, deter, restore, rehabilitate, and reconstruct instances of discrimination, *see* chapter 9 *infra,* at notes 239–84 and accompanying text. *See also* chapter 6 *supra,* at note 52 and accompanying text,

2. UNITED NATIONS, THE MAIN TYPES AND CAUSES OF DISCRIMINATION 9, U.N. Doc. E/CN.4/Sub. 2/40/Rev. 1 (1949) (memorandum submitted by the secretary-general). Based on the United Nations studies of various aspects of discrimination, McKean has summarized:

> It was generally agreed that the term "discrimination" is not synonymous with "differential treatment" or "distinction". Rather, in the sense used in the studies, "discrimination" means some sort of distinction made against a person according to his classification into a particular group or category rather than by taking into account his individual merits or capacities.

McKean, *The Meaning of Discrimination in International and Municipal Law,* 44 BRIT. Y.B. INT'L L. 177, 180 (1970) (footnote omitted).

3. *See* chapter 7 *supra,* at notes 27–302 and accompanying text.

4. *See id.* at notes 303–86 and accompanying text.

5. *See id.* at notes 387–598 and accompanying text.

6. The horror of racial discrimination in southern Africa, which has aroused worldwide indignation, represents, of course, the most notorious, extreme case. Racial discrimination exists elsewhere in less systematic and less routinized fashions. Discrimination is practiced against the "colored" people of Great Britain, the blacks and other minority groups of the United States, the overseas Chinese in southeast Asia, the Indian settlers in East Africa, and the Aborigines in Australia.

Drawing largely upon a series of reports published by the Minority Rights Group based in London, Dehner has given this summary account:

> Aside from South Africa, there is virtually no concern expressed about discriminatory practices of U.S.-controlled foreign companies. Yet, ethnic and racial discrimination

women, and hence to the whole community, by centuries-old practices of sex discrimination has just begun to filter into the consciousness of both women and men in a few parts of the world. The bloodiness of religious intolerance and oppression has perhaps receded in geographic range, but continues to immerse particular communities, while discriminations based upon unorthodox secular conceptions of rectitude are of abiding concern.[7] Discriminations, and even persecutions, arising from intolerance of differing political opinions are characteristic of totalitarian communities, past and present, and sometimes infect even communities which upon occasion prize the wide sharing of power.[8] Even a factor so indifferent to human potentialities as language affiliation or preference continues to give rise to varying discriminations in many different parts of the world.[9] Finally, many severe diffentiations, often amounting to discriminations and affecting access to all value processes, continue to be

---

> infests much of the world. Among the minorities which commentators have found to be victims of economic discrimination are the Burakumin (Eta) in Japan, the southern African tribes of the Sudan, the Eritreans of Ethiopia, the Crimean Tatars and the Volga Germans in the Soviet Union, the Basques of Spain and France, the Chinese in Southeast Asia, the Biharis of Bangladesh, Oriental immigrants and Druzes in Israel, the East Indians of Guyana and Trinidad, the non-white population of the United Kingdom, Albanians in Yugoslavia, Indians in Burma and Malaya, the Watusi of Rwanda, the Tamil-speaking Ceylonese of Ceylon, East Asians in Kenya, French Canadians in Canada, Walloons in Belgium, various Indian geographic and caste groups, and Arabs and Bretons in France. Even if some of these charges of discrimination are untrue, it is clear that racial prejudice is a global scourge.

Dehner, *Multinational Enterprise and Racial Non-Discrimination: United States Enforcement of an International Human Right,* 15 HARV. INT'L L. J. 71, 81–82 (1974) (footnotes omitted).

The series of reports includes G. DEVOS, JAPAN'S OUTCASTES—THE PROBLEM OF THE BURAKUMIN (Rep. No. 3, 1971); A. DZIDZIENYO, THE POSITION OF BLACKS IN BRAZILIAN SOCIETY (Rep. No. 7, 1971); Y. GHAI, THE ASIAN MINORITIES OF EAST AND CENTRAL AFRICA (Rep. No. 4, 1971); G. GRANT, THE AFRICANS' PREDICAMENT IN RHODESIA (Rep. No. 8, 1972); H. MABBETT, P. MABBETT, & C. COPPEL, THE CHINESE IN INDONESIA, THE PHILIPPINES AND MALAYSIA (Rep. No. 10, 1972); G. MORRISON, THE SOUTHERN SUDAN AND ERITREA: ASPECTS OF WIDER AFRICAN PROBLEMS (Rep. No. 5, 1971); A. SHEEHY, THE CRIMEAN TARTARS AND VOLGA GERMANS: SOVIET TREATMENT OF TWO NATIONAL MINORITIES (Rep. No. 6, 1971); B. WHITAKER, THE BIHARIS IN BANGLADESH (Rep. No. 11, 1972).

7. Long after the religious wars of the past, religious tensions have persisted. The bloodiness of the confrontation between Protestants and Catholics in Northern Ireland has been protracted. Religious friction occurs elsewhere between Buddhists and Catholics in South Vietnam, Hindus and Moslems in India and Pakistan, Arabs and Jews in Israel and the Arab countries.

8. Witness, for instance, the recent political struggles in Chile, Greece, the Philippines, South Korea, South Vietnam, and Taiwan.

9. Note, for example, India, Canada, and Belgium.

made almost everywhere in terms of such blanket categorizations as age, alienage, possession of property, birth, or other status.[10]

It has been emphasized in chapter 6 above,[11] and reiterated in our condemnations of caste and apartheid,[12] that any differentiations in the treatment of individuals based upon broad group memberships or alleged characteristics, without regard to actual individual differences in capabilities and potentialities, is highly destructive of that basic freedom of choice which shared respect requires. The most fundamental meaning of human dignity is that individuals are to be regarded and treated as total personalities having their own unique characteristics and potentialities, and are not to be manipulated and managed in mass in terms of putative characteristics assigned through group labels. The only permissible differentiations between individuals that a law of human dignity can honor for the recruitment and training of people for performance of the many different roles in our modern, complex society are very particular ones. These differentiations must be based entirely upon a careful configurative appraisal of the individual person with all his distinctive characteristics, and of the range of opportunities for participation in social processes that either are open or can be made open to him. An effective collective effort to afford every individual the utmost opportunity to develop his latent talents into socially useful skills and capabilities can only augment the aggregate production of all community values, including respect, which then become available for cumulative commitment and immediate enjoyment.

It would appear that a general norm of nondiscrimination, fully expressive of these policies, is rapidly emerging as an accepted prescription of international law. A major stated purpose of the United Nations Charter, reinforced by more detailed provisions,[13] is to "achieve international cooperation . . . in promoting and encouraging respect for human rights and for fundamental freedoms for all without distinction as to race, sex, language, or religion."[14] The Universal Declaration of Human Rights,[15] no less broad in its specification of purposes, expands the itemization of impermissible group characterizations. Article 2 states:

---

10. Deprivations based on these group characteristics extend to all the values—power, enlightenment, wealth, well-being, and so on.

11. *See* chapter 6 *supra,* at notes 18–52 and accompanying text.

12. *See* chapter 7 *supra,* at notes 303–598 and accompanying text.

13. This objective has been repeated and reinforced throughout the Charter. *See* U.N. CHARTER, Arts. 13(1), 55, 56, 62(2), 76(c).

14. *Id.,* Art. 1(3).

15. Universal Declaration of Human Rights, *adopted* Dec. 10, 1948, G.A. Res. 217, U.N. Doc. A/810 at 71 (1948) [hereinafter cited as Universal Declaration].

> Everyone is entitled to all the rights and freedoms set forth in this Declaration, without distinction of any kind, such as race, colour, sex, language, religion, political or other opinion, national or social origin, property, birth or other status.
>
> Furthermore, no distinction shall be made on the basis of the political, jurisdictional or international status of the country or territory to which a person belongs, whether it be independent, trust, non-self-governing or under any other limitation of sovereignty.[16]

The thrust toward a general principle of nondiscrimination is strengthened by Article 7: "All are equal before the law and are entitled without any discrimination to equal protection of the law. All are entitled to equal protection against any discrimination in violation of this Declaration and against any incitement to such discrimination."[17] Similarly, the International Covenants on Human Rights, though purporting to confine their protection to broadly specified particular rights, offer a broad and expandable itemization of impermissible group characterizations. Thus, the International Covenant on Civil and Political Rights states, in Article 2(1), that

> Each State Party to the present Covenant undertakes to respect and to ensure to all individuals within its territory and subject to its jurisdiction the rights recognized in the present Covenant, without distinction of any kind, such as race, colour, sex, language, religion, political or other opinion, national or social origin, property, birth or other status.[18]

It adds, in Article 26, that

> All persons are equal before the law and are entitled without any discrimination to the equal protection of the law. In this respect, the law shall prohibit any discrimination and guarantee to all persons equal and effective protection against discrimination on any ground such as race, colour, sex, language, religion, political or other opinion, national or social origin, property, birth or other status.[19]

Again, Article 2(2) of the International Covenant on Economic, Social, and Cultural Rights provides:

---

16. *Id.,* Art. 2, U.N. Doc. A/810 at 72.

17. *Id.,* Art 7, U.N. Doc. A/810 at 73.

18. International Covenant on Civil and Political Rights, *adopted* Dec. 16, 1966, Art. 2(1), G.A. Res. 2200A, 21 U.N. GAOR, Supp. (No. 16) 53.

19. *Id.,* Art. 26, 21 U.N. GAOR, Supp. (No. 16) 55–56. *Compare* the principle espoused by Art. 26 *with* Art. 7 of the Universal Declaration, *supra* note 15.

> The States Parties to the present Covenant undertake to guarantee that the rights enunciated in the present Covenant will be exercised without discrimination of any kind as to race, colour, sex, language, religion, political or other opinion, national or social origin, property, birth or other status.[20]

The increasingly explicit aspiration of authoritative prescription toward comprehensiveness, both in reference to protected rights and to impermissible group characterizations, is illustrated in the International Convention on the Elimination of All Forms of Racial Discrimination,[21] as well as in the Declaration of the same title which preceded it.[22] In practically identical terms, these influential formulations affirm that

> the Charter of the United Nations is based on the principles of dignity and equality inherent in all human beings, and that all Member States have pledged themselves to take joint and separate action, in co-operation with the Organization, for the achievement of one of the purposes of the United Nations which is to promote and encourage universal respect for and observance of human rights and fundamental freedoms for all, without distinction as to race, sex, language or religion,[23]

and that

> the Universal Declaration of Human Rights proclaims that all human beings are born free and equal in dignity and rights and that everyone is entitled to all the rights and freedoms set out therein, without distinction of any kind, in particular as to race, colour or national origin,[24]

and, further, that

> all human beings are equal before the law and are entitled to equal protection of the law against any discrimination and against any incitement to discrimination.[25]

---

20. International Covenant on Economic, Social, and Cultural Rights, *adopted* Dec. 16, 1966, Art. 2(2), G.A. Res. 2200A, 21 U.N. GAOR, Supp. (No. 16) 49–50.

21. International Convention on the Elimination of All Forms of Racial Discrimination, *opened for signature* Mar. 7, 1966, 660 U.N.T.S. 195 (entered into force Jan. 4, 1969) [hereinafter cited as Convention on the Elimination of All Forms of Racial Discrimination].

22. United Nations Declaration on the Elimination of All Forms of Racial Discrimination, *adopted* Nov. 20, 1963, G.A. Res. 1904, 18 U.N. GAOR, Supp. (No. 15) 35, 36, U.N. Doc. A/5515 (1963).

23. Convention on the Elimination of All Forms of Racial Discrimination, *supra* note 21, Preamble, 660 U.N.T.S. at 212–16.

24. *Id.* at 212–14.

25. *Id.* at 214.

The comprehensiveness of this norm of nondiscrimination is further documented and confirmed by recurring assertions in the Proclamation of Teheran issued by the International Conference on Human Rights in 1968.[26] Among its various emphases, the Proclamation solemnly states that

> It is imperative that the members of the international community fulfill their solemn obligations to promote and encourage respect for human rights and fundamental freedoms for all without distinctions of any kind such as race, colour, sex, language, religion, political or other opinions,[27]

and that

> The primary aim of the United Nations in the sphere of human rights is the achievement by each individual of the maximum freedom and dignity. For the realization of this objective, the laws of every country should grant each individual, irrespective of race, language, religion or political belief, freedom of expression, of information, of conscience and of religion, as well as the right to participate in the political, economic, cultural and social life of his country.[28]

---

26. Proclamation of Teheran, Final Act of the International Conference on Human Rights, Teheran, 22 April to 13 May 1968, U.N. Doc. A/CONF.32/41 (1968).

27. *Id.* at 4.

28. *Id.* This norm of nondiscrimination has been expressed in similar terms in other universal and regional human rights conventions and declarations. *See, e.g.,* International Convention on the Suppression and Punishment of the Crime of Apartheid, *adopted* Nov. 30, 1973, G.A. Res. 3068, 28 U.N. GAOR, Supp. (No. 30) 75, U.N. Doc. A/9233/Add. 1 (1973); American Convention on Human Rights, *signed* Nov. 22, 1969, OAS Official Records OEA/Ser.K/XVI/1.1, Doc. 65, Rev. 1, Corr. 1 (Jan. 7, 1970), *reprinted in* 9 INT'L LEGAL MATERIALS 99, 101 (1970); Declaration on Social Progress and Development, *adopted* Dec. 11, 1969, Arts. 1 and 2, G.A. Res. 2542, 24 U.N. GAOR, Supp. (No. 30) 49, U.N. Doc. A/7630 (1969); Declaration on Elimination of Discrimination against Women, *adopted* Nov. 7, 1967, G.A. Res. 2263, 22 U.N. GAOR, Supp. (No. 16) 35, U.N. Doc. A/6716 (1967); Declaration on the Promotion among Youth of the Ideals of Peace, Mutual Respect and Understanding between Peoples, *adopted* Dec. 7, 1965, Principles 1 and 3, G.A. Res. 2037, 20 U.N. GAOR, Supp. (No. 14) 40, U.N. Doc. A/6014 (1965); Employment Policy Convention, *adopted* July 9, 1964, Art. 1(2)(c), 569 U.N.T.S. 65 (entered into force July 15, 1964); Protocol to the Convention against Discrimination in Education, *adopted* Dec. 10, 1962, [1969] U.N.T.S. No. 9423 (CMD. 3894); Convention against Discrimination in Education, *adopted* Dec. 14, 1960, 429 U.N.T.S. 93, 96 (UNESCO General Conference) (entered into force May 22, 1962); Declaration on the Rights of the Child, Principle 1, *adopted* Nov. 20, 1959, G.A. Res. 1386, 14 U.N. GAOR, Supp. (No. 16) 19, U.N. Doc. A/4354 (1959); Convention concerning Discrimination in Respect of Employment and Occupation, *adopted* June 25, 1958, 362 U.N.T.S. 31 (ILO General Conference) (entered into force June 15, 1960); Convention Relating to the Status of Stateless Persons, Art 3, *adopted* Sept. 23, 1954, 360 U.N.T.S. 117 (entered into force June 6, 1960); Convention on Human Rights

It will be convenient to further document and illustrate the emergence of this general norm of nondiscrimination by reference to the development of more specific prescriptions banning discriminations based upon certain alleged particular group characteristics: race (including color, descent, national or ethnic origin), sex, religion, political opinion, language, age, alienage, possession of property, birth, and other status.[29]

---

and Fundamental Freedoms, *adopted* Nov. 4, 1950, 1950 Europ. T.S. No. 5, 213 U.N.T.S. 221; Convention Relating to the Status of Refugees, *adopted* July 25, 1951, Art. 3, 189 U.N.T.S. 137; Equal Remuneration Convention, *adopted* June 29, 1951, 165 U.N.T.S. 304 (entered into force May 23, 1953); Convention on the Prevention and Punishment of the Crime of Genocide, *adopted* Dec. 9, 1948, 78 U.N.T.S. 277 (entered into force Jan. 12, 1951).

29. The complete documentation of this thesis would explore not only expectations created by agreements, but also those created by international and other judicial authoritative decisions, as well as those created by the whole flow of decisions, constitutional and other, within national communities. In other words, the conclusion we suggest can be reached by reference to all the sources of international law itemized in Art. 38 of the Statute of the International Court of Justice: international conventions, international custom, "the general principles of law recognized by civilized nations," and "judicial decisions and the teachings of the most highly qualified publicists of the various nations." I.C.J. STAT. Art. 38. For such an approach *see* South West African Cases (Second Phase), [1966] I.C.J. 250, 284–316 (Tanaka, J., dissenting).

9. CLAIMS RELATING TO RACIAL DISCRIMINATION

FACTUAL BACKGROUND

The deprivations imposed as "racial discrimination" are made under the aegis of a group categorization which, even when "race" is supplemented by such ancillary concepts as "color," "ethnic origin," "national origin," "descent," and "birth,"[1] makes a most ambiguous and incomplete reference to empirical fact. The popular categorizations of "race," whether by officials or nonofficials when indulging in "man's most dangerous myth,"[2] are built upon vague, shifting, and erratic references to such factors as skin color, body build, eye cast or color, hair texture, nose shape, blood type, genetic affiliation, and historical or cultural association.[3] "To most people," a 1950 UNESCO statement realistically asserts, "a race is any group of people whom they choose to describe as a race."[4] The statement elaborates:

> Thus, many national, religious, geographic, linguistic or cultural groups have, in such loose usage, been called "race," when obviously Americans are not a race, nor are Englishmen, nor Frenchmen, nor any other national group. Catholics, Protestants, Moslems, and Jews are not races, nor are groups who speak English or any other language thereby definable as a race; people who live in Iceland or

1. *See* notes 113–28 *infra* and accompanying text.

2. A. Montagu, Man's Most Dangerous Myth: The Fallacy of Race (5th ed. rev. 1974).

3. For a fascinating and detailed description of the physical differences among various human groups *see* J. Baker, Race 179–417 (1974). *See also* C. Coon, The Living Races of Man (1965); C. Coon, The Origin of Races (1962).

4. A. Montagu, Statement on Race 8 (3d ed. 1972) [hereinafter cited as A. Montagu]. The Statement was prepared by a panel of distinguished scientists, representing various disciplines and regions, under the auspices of UNESCO. *See id.* at 13 for the names of these distinguished scholars. Three additional statements concerning race were subsequently issued by UNESCO: *Statement on the Nature of Race and Race Differences,* June 1951, *id.* at 137–47; *Proposals on the Biological Aspects of Race,* Aug. 1964, *id.* at 148–55; and *Statement on Race and Racial Prejudice,* Sept. 1967, *id.* at 156–64.

> England or India are not races; nor are people who are culturally Turkish or Chinese or the like thereby describable as races.[5]

Even the characterizations of "a race" offered by scientists, though displaying a somewhat more stable reference to objectively ascertainable factors, commonly admit of highly diverse application to individual human beings.[6] The core reference appears to be to subgroups within the closed species of man which are genetically open but exhibit "some distinguishing genetic variability."[7] Thus, Dobzhansky, in identifying mankind as "a complex Mendelian population, a reproductive community all members of which are connected by ties of mating and parentage,"[8] and describing a "Mendelian population" as one which possesses "a common gene pool,"[9] defines "races" as "arrays of Mendelian populations belonging to the same biological species, but differing from each other in incidence of some genetic variants."[10] He adds that the "delimitation of the Mendelian populations which are called races is always to

---

5. A. MONTAGU, *supra* note 4, at 8. Additional complications are generated by the imprecision with which these generic terms are used.

> The layman's conception of "race" is so confused and emotionally muddled that any attempt to modify it would seem to be met by the greatest obstacle of all, the term "race" itself. This is another reason why the attempt to retain the term "race" in popular parlance must fail. The term is a trigger word: utter it and a whole series of emotionally conditioned responses follow.

Id. at 65.

Hence the proposal to substitute the term "ethnic group" for "race." *See id.* at 59–71. *Cf.* C. PUTNAM, RACE AND REALITY (1967); P. ROSE, THE SUBJECT IS RACE (1968), which deals with "traditional ideologies and the teaching of race relations."

6. *See generally* A. ALLAND, HUMAN DIVERSITY (1971); T. DOBZHANSKY, MANKIND EVOLVING: THE EVOLUTION OF THE HUMAN SPECIES (1962) [hereinafter cited as T. DOBZHANSKY]; S. GARN, HUMAN RACES (3d ed. 1971); READINGS ON RACES (2d ed. S. Garn 1968); R. GOLDSBY, RACE AND RACES (1971); J. KING, THE BIOLOGY OF RACE (1971); M. KLASS & H. HELLMAN, THE KINDS OF MANKIND (1971); THE CONCEPT OF RACE (A. Montagu ed. 1964); RACE: INDIVIDUAL AND COLLECTIVE BEHAVIOR (E. Thompson & E. Hughes eds. 1958); UNESCO, RACE AND SCIENCE (1969).

7. Osborne, *The History and Nature of Race Classification,* in THE BIOLOGICAL AND SOCIAL MEANING OF RACE 159, 164 (R. Osborne ed. 1971). Similarly, the 1950 UNESCO statement on race, in identifying "race" as "one of the group of populations [capable of interbreeding] constituting the species *Homo sapiens,*" further defines it as "a group or population characterized by some concentrations relative as to frequency and distribution, of hereditary particles (genes) or physical characteristics, which appear, fluctuate, and often disappear in the course of time by reason of geographical and/or cultural isolation." A. MONTAGU, *supra* note 4, at 7–8, 36, 40–41, 46. Mankind as a whole constitutes a single biological species which is a "genetically closed system," whereas all races, whatever the usage of the word race, are "genetically open systems." T. DOBZHANSKY, *supra* note 6, at 183.

8. T. DOBZHANSKY, GENETIC DIVERSITY AND HUMAN EQUALITY 57 (1973).

9. *Id.*

10. *Id.* at 67.

some extent vague, because their gene pools are not wholly disjunct."[11] Similarly, Osborne emphasizes: "Most important is the fact that subspecies and races, unlike species, are not closed genetic or evolutionary units, but simply breeding populations within which a significant number of individuals carry a particular variant of a gene common to the species."[12] He also adds: "What is taken as a meaningful 'racial' differentiation within any given species will depend entirely upon the classifier, the circumstances, and the purposes of the classification."[13] Further, it would appear that even among scientists a diversity of references as to the core meaning of race causes difficulties. Thus, Scott observes:

> From a biological viewpoint the term race has become so encumbered with superfluous and contradictory meanings, erroneous concepts, and emotional reactions that it has almost lost its utility. Any scientist who continues to use it will run a major risk of being misunderstood, even if he rigorously limits his own definition. He will run the additional risk in his own thinking of finding it difficult to avoid past misconceptions.[14]

The value deprivations, both historical and continuing, imposed through "racial" discrimination and its equivalences, always comprehensive and intensive, may be subtle and hidden or open and horrendous.[15]

---

11. *Id.* at 59.

12. Osborne, *The History and Nature of Race Classification,* in THE BIOLOGICAL AND SOCIAL MEANING OF RACE 159, 161 (R. Osborne ed. 1971).

13. *Id.* at 164.

14. Scott, *Discussion,* in SCIENCE AND THE CONCEPT OF RACE 59 (M. Mead, T. Dobzhansky, E. Tobach, & R. Light eds. 1968). In the words of Clyde Kluckhohn, a well-known anthropologist: "Though the concept of race is genuine enough, there is perhaps no field of science in which the misunderstandings among educated people are so frequent and so serious." G. ALLPORT, THE NATURE OF PREJUDICE 106 (1958) (quoting Kluckhohn).

The vagueness of "race," it may be observed, is attributable principally to two reasons: (1) the vagueness written into the scientific definition, and (2) the bewildering diversity in the use of the word that ignores any scientific usage.

15. Some of these words are borrowed from Henkin, *National and International Perspectives in Racial Discrimination,* 4 HUMAN RIGHTS J. 263 (1971).

As Judge Ammoun, vice-president of the International Court of Justice, observed in his Separate Opinion in the Namibia case of 1971:

> The violation of human rights has not come to an end in any part of the world: to realize that fact one need only consult the archives of the European Court of Human Rights, the Human Rights Commission of the United Nations or the International Commission of Jurists, or simply read the world press. Violations of personal freedom and human dignity, the racial, social or religious discrimination which constitutes the most serious of violations of human rights since it annihilates the two-fold basis provided by equality and liberty, all still resist the currents of liberation in each of the

When racial discrimination is a systematic instrument of state policy, deprivations may begin by denying respect through official classification of populations in racial terms, such as the dichotomy of "Aryans" and "non-Aryans" under the Nazis[16] and the fourfold classification employed in South Africa today.[17] Such classifications may be reinforced by elaborate systems of identification by which members of deprived groups are required to carry identity cards and to wear specified insignia of humiliation.[18] In such regimes, the degree and scope of an individu-

---

five continents. Advisory Opinion on Legal Consequences for States of the Continued Presence of South Africa in Namibia (South West Africa) Notwithstanding Security Council Resolution 276 (1970), [1971] I.C.J. 75–76 [hereinafter cited as ICJ Advisory Opinion on Namibia].

One of the outstanding features of the contemporary world is the revival of biological traits as pseudo-biological identity symbols. In the prophetic words of Du Bois: "[T]he problem of the twentieth century is the problem of the colour line—the relation of the darker to the lighter races of men in Asia and Africa, in America and in the Islands of the sea." W. Du Bois, The Souls of Black Folk 13 (2d ed. 1903).

Similarly, Connor has given the following statistics:

> Of a total of 132 contemporary states, only 12 (9.1 percent) can be described as essentially homogeneous from an ethnic viewpoint. An additional 25 states (18.9 per cent of the sample) contain an ethnic group accounting for more than 90 per cent of the state's total population, and in still another 25 states the largest element accounts for between 75 and 89 per cent of the population. But in 31 states (23.5 per cent of the total), the largest ethnic element represents only 50 to 74 per cent of the population, and in 39 cases (29.5 per cent of all states) the largest group fails to account for even half of the state's population. Moreover, this portrait of ethnic diversity becomes more vivid when the number of distinct ethnic groups within states is considered. In some instances, the number of groups within a state runs into the hundreds, and in 53 states (40.2 per cent of the total), the population is divided into more than *five* significant groups.

Connor, *Nation-Building or Nation-Destroying?* 24 World Politics 319, 320 (1972) (footnote omitted).

16. On the atrocities associated with the racist policies of the Nazis *see* American Jewish Conference, Nazi Germany's War against the Jews (1947); H. Arendt, The Origins of Totalitarianism (2d ed. 1958); The Third Reich (M. Beaumont, J. Fried, & E. Vermeil eds. 1955); R. Hilberg, The Destruction of the European Jews (1961) [hereinafter cited as R. Hilberg]; O. Janowsky & M. Fagen, International Aspects of German Racial Policies (1937) [hereinafter cited as O. Janowsky & M. Fagen]; M. Lowenthal, The Jews of Germany (1936); Nazi Conspiracy and Aggression, Opinion and Judgment (U.S. Gov't Printing Office 1947); H. Santa Cruz, Racial Discrimination, U.N. Doc. E/CN.4/Sub. 2/307/Rev. 1 (1971).

17. This fourfold classification is as follows: white persons (Europeans); Bantus (Africans); coloured persons; and Asians. For a discussion of the wide range of severe value deprivations associated with racial discrimination in the context of apartheid see chapter 7 *supra,* at notes 392–434 and accompanying text.

18. *See* R. Hilberg, *supra* note 16, at 118–21, for a discussion of the identification system used by Nazi Germany. "The whole identification system," in the words of Hilberg, "with its personal documents, specially assigned names, and conspicuous tagging in public, was a powerful weapon in the hands of the police," facilitating the enforcement of resi-

al's participation in the different community value processes are dictated more by the arbitrary racial label attached to the individual than by his or her unique capabilities and potentialities. The degree of respect—the freedom of choice and esteem by self and others—which a person may enjoy is determined by the group to which he or she is assigned; segregation in access to public amenities and accommodations and compulsory gestures of submission may be constant reminders of disrespect.[19]

The total domination by one racial group over another may epitomize deprivations in the power process. In the name of race, individuals are often disfranchised outright or by such devices as weighted voting;[20] they also are denied access to officeholding—appointive and elective, local and national, executive and judicial, civilian and military.[21] Discriminatory measures may be taken to deprive individuals of nationality,[22] to effect banishment (expulsion),[23] or to deny emigration or travel

---

dence and movement restrictions, generating arbitrary arrests of non-Aryans, and causing "a paralyzing effect on its victims." *Id.* at 121.

19. *Cf.* J. GREENBERG, RACE RELATIONS AND AMERICAN LAW 79–114 (1959) [hereinafter cited as J. GREENBERG]; 2 G. MYRDAL, AN AMERICAN DILEMMA (1964); C. WOODWARD, THE STRANGE CAREER OF JIM CROW (2d ed. rev. 1966); Franklin, *History of Racial Segregation in the United States,* 34 ANNALS 1 (1956).

Note the vivid description by Woodward:

> The public symbols and constant reminders of his [the Negro's] inferior position were the segregation statutes, or "Jim Crow" laws. They constituted the most elaborate and formal expression of sovereign white opinion upon the subject. In bulk and detail as well as in effectiveness of enforcement the segregation codes were comparable with the black codes of the old regime, though the laxity that mitigated the harshness of the black codes was replaced by a rigidity that was more typical of the segregation code. That code lent the sanction of law to a racial ostracism that extended to churches and schools, to housing and jobs, to eating and drinking. Whether by law or by custom, that ostracism extended to virtually all forms of public transportation, to sports and recreations, to hospitals, orphanages, prisons, and asylums, and ultimately to funeral homes, morgues, and cemeteries.

C. WOODWARD, *supra* at 7 (footnote omitted).

20. According to a study prepared by the United States Commission on Civil Rights, the various devices employed to disfranchise the blacks in ten southern states of the United States include the following: "diluting the Negro vote," "preventing Negroes from becoming candidates or obtaining office," "discrimination against Negro registrants," "exclusion or an interference with Negro poll watchers," "vote fraud," "discriminatory selection of election officials," and "intimidation and economic dependence." UNITED STATES COMM'N ON CIVIL RIGHTS, POLITICAL PARTICIPATION 19–131 (1968). *See also* J. GREENBERG, *supra* note 19, at 133–53; L. LITWACK, NORTH OF SLAVERY 74–79 (1961), Comment, *Representative Government and Equal Protection,* 5 HARV. CIV. RIGHTS-CIV. LIB. L. REV. 472 (1970).

21. *See, e.g.,* O. JANOWSKY & M. FAGEN, *supra* note 16, at 134–35, 146–54; UNITED STATES COMM'N ON CIVIL RIGHTS, POLITICAL PARTICIPATION 40–59 (1968).

22. *See* O. JANOWSKY & M. FAGEN, *supra* note 16, at 60–72, 134–35, 142–45; the appendix *infra,* at notes 193–203 and accompanying text.

23. *See* R. HILBERG, *supra* note 16, at 137–44; O. JANOWSKY & M. FAGEN, *supra* note 16, at 49–60.

abroad.[24] For being or not being a member of a specified racial group, individuals may also be denied access, temporarily or permanently, to territorial communities.[25] Other measures of power deprivation include arbitrary arrest and detention,[26] police brutality and torture,[27] differential justice for various groups through perversion of the judicial process,[28] and exclusion from military training and service.[29]

Enlightenment is restricted when access to educational institutions is denied because of racial group membership. This may take the form of exclusion from higher education[30] or from elementary and secondary schools,[31] or exclusion from educational employment such as teaching and research.[32] A racial quota system may be rigidly imposed for access

---

24. *See* J. INGLES, STUDY OF DISCRIMINATION IN RESPECT OF THE RIGHT OF EVERYONE TO LEAVE ANY COUNTRY, INCLUDING HIS OWN, AND TO RETURN TO HIS COUNTRY 20–23, U.N. Doc. E/CN.4/Sub. 2/220/Rev. 1 (1963).

25. A notorious example was, of course, the essentially whites-only immigration policy in Australia. Other examples include discriminatory policies toward "coloured" immigrants in the United Kingdom and the national quota system used in the United States prior to 1965. *See generally* M. BANTON, RACE RELATIONS 368–93 (1967); P. FOOT, IMMIGRATION AND RACE IN BRITISH POLITICS (1965); I. MACDONALD, RACE RELATIONS AND IMMIGRATION LAW (1969); S. PATTERSON, IMMIGRATION AND RACE RELATIONS IN BRITAIN 1960–1967 (1969); E. ROSE, COLOUR AND CITIZENSHIP (1969); Patterson, *Immigrants and Minority Groups in British Society,* in THE PREVENTION OF RACIAL DISCRIMINATION IN BRITAIN 21 (S. Abbott ed. 1971).

See also Higham, *American Immigration Policy in Historical Perspective,* 21 LAW & CONTEMP. PROB. 213 (1956); Jaffe, *The Philosophy of Our Immigration Law,* 21 LAW & CONTEMP. PROB. 358 (1956); Scully, *Is the Door Open Again?—A Survey of Our New Immigration Law,* 13 U.C.L.A.L. Rev. 227 (1966).

26. *See* H. SANTA CRUZ, *supra* note 16, at 255.

27. *Cf. id.* at 256–57; NATIONAL ADVISORY COMM'N ON CIVIL DISORDERS, REPORT 299–336 (Bantam ed. 1968).

28. *See* O. JANOWSKY & M. FAGEN, *supra* note 16, at 192–96; H. SANTA CRUZ, *supra* note 16, at 260–63; UNITED STATES COMM'N ON CIVIL RIGHTS, JUSTICE (1961).

29. For instance, the Nazi Conscription Law provided that "Aryan descent is a presupposition for active military service." O. JANOWSKY & M. FAGEN, *supra* note 16, at 154.

Instead of being denied access to military training and service, blacks in the United States have in recent years complained that there have been proportionately too many blacks in the combat forces, especially when the United States was engaged in the Vietnam conflict. *See* Lee, *The Draft and the Negro,* in WHITE RACISM 341 (B. Schwartz & R. Disch eds. 1970).

30. *See* C. AMMOUN, STUDY OF DISCRIMINATION IN EDUCATION 10–28, U.N. Doc. E/CN.4/Sub. 2/181/Rev. 1 (1957); UNITED NATIONS, ECONOMIC AND SOCIAL CONSEQUENCES OF RACIAL DISCRIMINATORY PRACTICES, U.N. Doc. E/CN.14/132/Rev. 1 at 69–72 (1963) [hereinafter cited as ECONOMIC AND SOCIAL CONSEQUENCES]; L. LITWACK, NORTH OF SLAVERY 113–17, 120–21 (1961).

31. *See* ECONOMIC AND SOCIAL CONSEQUENCES, *supra* note 30, at 69–72; O. JANOWSKY & M. FAGEN, *supra* note 16, at 175–77.

32. O. JANOWSKY & M. FAGEN, *supra* note 16, at 158–61.

to different educational institutions.[33] Separate and unequal educational opportunities and facilities prevail where race is a critical factor in social process.[34] Other forms of privation include denial of access to the mass media and the suppression of dissent.[35] In relation to skill, members of particular groups may be denied opportunity to discover and fully develop their latent talents. By being denied access to adequate schooling, they are often deprived of the acquisition of socially significant skills.[36] Other forms include denial of the practice of the liberal professions, notably law, medicine, and dentistry,[37] and denial of pursuit of "artistic or cultural activities."[38]

In deprivations of wealth, race may be employed to limit access to resources and the enjoyment of income. Under the guise of an economic "division of labor," race discrimination may become a device for preserving an ample supply of cheap labor and perpetuating an inherited relationship of economic exploitation.[39] Because of racial groupings, individuals may be denied access to certain occupations and professions; they may be underpaid in relation to others for the same type of employment; and they may be denied job advancement.[40] The ownership, purchase, and sale of land and other property may be curtailed or forbidden because of race.[41] Practices bordering on forced labor may be visited upon deprived racial groups.[42] Other measures of wealth deprivation include expropriation of property, freezing of personal assets, and imposition of special taxes.[43]

---

33. *Cf.* W. Korey, The Soviet Cage: Anti-Semitism in Russia 52 (1973); G. Simpson & J. Yinger, Racial and Cultural Minorities 454–57 (3d ed. 1965); Braverman, *Medical School Quotas,* in Barriers: Patterns of Discrimination against Jews 74–77 (N. Belth ed. 1958).

34. *Cf.* J. Coleman, Equality of Educational Opportunity (1966); J. Greenberg, *supra* note 19, at 208–74; C. Jencks, Inequality: A Reassessment of the Effect of Family and Schooling in America (1972); G. Simpson & J. Yinger, Racial and Cultural Minorities 413–62 (3d ed. 1965).

35. R. Hilberg, *supra* note 16, at 650–53.

36. International Labour Office, Fighting Discrimination in Employment and Occupation 52–59 (1968).

37. *See, e.g.,* O. Janowsky & M. Fagen *supra* note 16, at 135, 155–58, 174–75.

38. *See, e.g., id.* at 160, 177–78.

39. *See* Economic and Social Consequences, *supra* note 30, at 48–61.

40. *See generally* B. Hepple, Race, Jobs and the Law in Great Britain 180–226 (1972); Employment, Race and Poverty (A. Ross & H. Hill eds. 1967); M. Sovern, Legal Restraints on Racial Discrimination in Employment (1966); Hepple, *Employment,* in The Prevention of Racial Discrimination in Britain 155–74 (S. Abbott ed. 1971); Jowell & Prescott-Clarke, *Racial Discrimination and White-Collar Workers in Britain,* in *id.* at 175–93.

41. H. Santa Cruz, *supra* note 16, at 174, 218, 230.

42. *Cf.* United Nations and International Labour Office, Report of the Ad Hoc Committee on Forced Labour 3–127, U.N. Doc. E/2431 (1953).

43. *See* R. Hilberg, *supra* note 16, at 54–101, 156–68.

The extremes in deprivations of well-being on grounds of race may include systematic extermination (genocide) and torture of all types.[44] Racially deprived groups, victims of poverty, suffer starvation, malnutrition, diseases, and poor health services;[45] they are often excluded from necessary health facilities and left more exposed than other groups to physical abuse and hazards. They sometimes become victims of human experimentation.[46] They suffer a higher rate of mortality, infant and adult alike, in comparison with other members of the community.[47] Racially segregated housing generally leads to the concentration of deprived groups in ghettos.[48]

The shaping and sharing of affection may be drastically impaired because of racial categorizations. Deprivations include the prohibition of interracial marriages and sexual relations between people of different races, and the termination of interracial marriages already consummated.[49] When segregated and isolated, people are handicapped in developing genuinely congenial personal relationships of any kind. Other forms of deprivation are the denial of custodian rights to parents of an allegedly inferior race[50] and the prohibition of adoption crossing racial

---

44. The most notorious example is, of course, the extermination of six million Jews under the Third Reich. For a detailed description of this destruction process see *id.* at 177-256, 555-635. More recent examples of massive extermination including the killing of Ibos in the Biafra conflict, the killing of Chinese in Indonesia, and the killing of Bengals by the Pakistanis.

45. *Id.* at 101-74; H. Santa Cruz, *supra* note 16, at 257-60; National Advisory Comm'n on Civil Disorders, Report 269-73 (Bantam ed. 1968). In Nazi Germany, for example, the government policy was to concentrate Jews in ghettos and subject them to severe food rationing, whereby many individuals died of starvation.

46. H. Santa Cruz, *supra* note 16, at 258.

Note, for instance, this brief account of the Nazis:

> The inmates were subjected to cruel experiments at Dachau in August 1942; victims were immersed in cold water until their body temperature was reduced to 28°C, when they died immediately. Other experiments included high altitude experiments in pressure chambers, experiments with how long human beings could survive in freezing water, experiments with poison bullets, experiments with contagious diseases, and experiments dealing with sterilization of men and women by X-rays and other methods.

Nazi Conspiracy and Aggression, Opinion and Judgment 81-82 (1947), *quoted in* H. Santa Cruz, *supra* note 16, at 258.

47. National Advisory Comm'n on Civil Disorders, Report 270-71 (Bantam ed. 1968).

48. For a profile of the formation of racial ghettos see *id.* at 236-47. *See also* R. Hilberg, *supra* note 16, at 106-25; 2 G. Myrdal, An American Dilemma 618-27 (1964).

49. *See* R. Sickels, Race, Marriage and the Law 10-91 (1972). *See also* O. Janowsky & M. Fagen, *supra* note 16, at 196-99.

50. *See* O. Janowsky & M. Fagen, *supra* note 16, at 199-200.

lines.[51] Under the perverse influence of the race myth, even a community's norms of rectitude are formulated and pursued under a double standard. What is permissible for one racial group may be forbidden to another. People may not be permitted to worship the same god or even to go to the same churches; places of public worship may be destroyed on account of race.[52] The cumulative impact of racial discrimination tends to foster a negative self-image among members of deprived groups, further handicapping their responsible participation in community processes.[53]

BASIC COMMUNITY POLICIES

A basic policy in any community that honors shared respect must be that of affording every individual member of the community full opportunity to discover, mature, and exercise his or her capabilities and potentialities, both for self-development and for contribution to the aggregate common interest.[54] All practices which differentiate between individuals upon the basis of alleged "racial" characteristics, whether in popular or scientific conception, would appear to be entirely destructive of this policy.

The justification commonly given for racial discrimination, as for caste differentiation and the practices of apartheid, is that some groups of people are inherently superior to other groups because of their biologi-

---

51. *See, e.g., id.* at 199–201.

52. The destruction of synagogues by the Nazis is a notorious example. R. HILBERG, *supra* note 16, at 5.

53. An inquiry into the causes of these multiple deprivations would require an extensive scientific treatise. It is simplistic to suggest that most racial discriminations are caused by prejudices, since the concept of prejudice is ill-defined and leaves open the question: what is the cause of prejudice? *See generally* G. ALLPORT, *supra* note 14; A. BURNS, COLOUR PREJUDICE (1948); D. CANTE, FRANTZ FANON (1970); F. FANON, BLACK SKIN, WHITE MASKS (1967); F. FANON, THE WRETCHED OF THE EARTH (1965); UNITED NATIONS, THE MAIN TYPES AND CAUSES OF DISCRIMINATION, U.N. Doc. E/CN.4/Sub. 2/40/Rev. 1 (1949) (memorandum submitted by the secretary-general); G. SIMPSON & J. YINGER, RACIAL AND CULTURAL MINORITIES (3d ed. 1965); *Schachter, How Effective Are Measures against Racial Discrimination?* 4 HUMAN RIGHTS J. 293 (1971).

For the importance of race in world affairs *see* RACE AMONG NATIONS: A CONCEPTUAL APPROACH (G. Shepherd & T. LeMelle eds. 1970).

Any serious investigation of the causes of racial discrimination would require a comprehensive exploration of both predispositional and environmental factors. The root causes of destructive impulses which find expression in discrimination are traceable through the whole process through which people are socialized and involve varying combinations of demands, identification, and expectations. The environmental variables are as multifaceted as the many differing features of man's social process in exploitation of the vast complex of global resources.

54. *See* chapter 6 *supra,* at notes 19, 40–44 and accompanying text.

cal inheritances.[55] Discrimination, it is argued, facilitates a more effective use of limited resources, in the aggregate common interest, if the alleged facts of inherent superiority and inferiority among groups are accepted as a basis for differential treatment and assignment of individuals' roles in ongoing social processes.

It should be obvious that none of the popular conceptions of race, based upon random combinations of physical features and cultural associations, bears any rational relation to the capabilities and potentialities of an individual for either self-development or contribution to the common interest. As Allport has observed:

> Most people do not know the difference between race and ethnic group, between race and social caste, between nurture and nature. It makes for an economy of thought to ascribe peculiarities of appearance, custom, values, to race. It is simpler to attribute differences to heredity than to juggle all the complex social grounds for differences that exist.[56]

When conceptions of this kind, of vague empirical references with no scientific basis, are employed by officials and others to make important differentiations among individuals, opportunities for arbitrary deprivation and oppression abound.

---

55. For the extreme view of Count Arthur de Gobineau, which "surpasses in scope and sinister grandeur even the pages of *Mein Kampf,*" *see* M. Biddis, Father of Racist Ideology: The Social and Political Thought of Count Gobineau (1970). In emphasizing the superiority of the Aryans, Gobineau asserted:

> Everything great, noble and fruitful in the works of man on this earth, in science, art and civilization, derives from a single starting point, is the development of a single germ and the result of a single thought; it belongs to one family alone, the different branches of which have reigned in all the civilized countries of the universe.

Id. at 113.

For a convenient summary *see* Klineberg, *Racialism in Nazi Germany,* in The Third Reich at 852–63 (M. Beaumont, J. Fried, & E. Vermeil eds. 1955). Note also the following statement by Hermann Gauch:

> The non-Nordic man occupies an intermediate position between the Nordics and the animals, just about next to the anthropoid ape. He is therefore not a complete man. He is really not a man at all in true contradistinction to animals, but a transition, an intermediate stage. Better and more apt, therefore, is the designation "subhuman" (Untermensch).

Id. at 859 (quoting Gauch).

For historical accounts of racist ideology *see* H. Arendt, The Organs of Totalitarianism 158–84 (2d ed. 1958); F. Hertz, Race and Civilization (1928).

56. G. Allport, *supra* note 13, at 107–08. "An imaginative person," he adds, "can twist the concept of race any way he wishes, and cause it to configurate and 'explain' his prejudices." *Id.* at 108.

It is scarcely less obvious that scientific conceptions of race, designed roughly to distinguish large groups for broad purposes of inquiry, can be made to differentiate individuals in terms of potentialities only with great violence to fact. When creating racial categorizations scientists are, as Osborne emphasizes, "examining a population as a whole and comparing the pattern of *gene frequencies* of that entire population with another population";[57] they are not purporting to specify the detailed characteristics or potentialities of any particular member of the group. In most scientific conceptions, further, the differences in potentialities within any particular group are greater than any of the differences between groups. In the words of Dobzhansky,

> the striking fact, which not even the racists can conceal, is that the race differences in the averages are much smaller than the variations within any race. In other words, large brains and high IQ's of persons of every race are much larger and higher than averages for their own or any other race. And conversely, the low variants in every race are much below the average for any race.[58]

Similarly, after exhaustive inquiry, Baker concludes:

> Every ethnic taxon of man includes many persons capable of living responsible and useful lives in the communities to which they belong, while even in those taxa that are best known for their contributions to the world's store of intellectual wealth, there are many so mentally deficient that they would be inadequate members of any society. It follows that no one can claim superiority simply because he or she belongs to a particular ethnic taxon.[59]

It remains unknown how such differences between individuals in capabilities and potentialities as do exist depend upon differences in heredity and environment. Dobzhansky is again an excellent witness: "The plain truth is that it is not known just how influential are the genetic variables in psychic or personality traits, or how plastic these traits might be in different environments that can be contrived by modern technology, medicine, and educational methods."[60]

---

57. Osborne, *The History and Nature of Race Classification,* in THE BIOLOGICAL AND SOCIAL MEANING OF RACE 161 (R. Osborne ed. 1971).

58. Dobzhansky, *Biological Evolution and Human Equality,* in SCIENCE AND THE MODERN WORLD 15, 28 (J. Steinhardt ed. 1966).

59. J. BAKER, RACE 534 (1974).

60. Dobzhansky, *Biological Evolution and Human Equality* in SCIENCE AND THE MODERN WORLD 15, 27 (J. Steinhardt ed. 1966). On the continuing debate of heredity versus environment (nature or nurture) *see* B. BLOOM, STABILITY AND CHANGE IN HUMAN CHARACTERISTICS (1964); J. CROW & M. KIMURA, AN INTRODUCTION TO POPULATION GE-

The continuing challenge for all dedicated to a commonwealth of human dignity is, thus, that of creating and maintaining a society which encourages and assists all individuals to develop and exercise their fullest capabilities in the shaping and sharing of all values. "The birthright of every human being," Ashley Montagu aptly asserts, "should be the recognition of his uniqueness, and the opportunity to develop that uniqueness to the optimum."[61] While extraordinary opportunities may be afforded the extraordinarily gifted, every effort should be made, in the interest both of shared respect and of the greatest aggregate production of community values, to provide every individual with the opportunity and facilities for overcoming any unique biological limitations, whether or not associated with imputed genetic deficiencies. Shared respect requires nondiscrimination for reasons irrelevant to potentialities, and shared respect is a fundamental component in any rational conception of human dignity. The important emphasis was made by Charles Darwin a century ago:

> Although the existing races of man differ in many respects, as in colour, hair, shape of skull, proportions of the body, &c., yet if their whole structure be taken into consideration they are found to resemble each other closely in a multitude of points. Many of these are of so unimportant or of so singular a nature, that it is extremely improbable that they should have been independently acquired by aboriginally distinct species or races. The same remark holds good with equal or greater force with respect to the numerous points of mental similarity between the most distinct races of man.[62]

NETICS THEORY (1970); T. DOBZHANSKY, GENETICS OF THE EVOLUTIONARY PROCESS (1970); T. DOBZHANSKY, *supra* note 6, at 51–75; R. HERRNSTEIN, I.Q. IN THE MERITOCRACY (1973); C. JENCKS, INEQUALITY: A REASSESSMENT OF THE EFFECT OF FAMILY AND SCHOOLING IN AMERICA 64–84 (1972); A. JENSEN, GENETICS AND EDUCATION (1972); Darlington, *Race, Class and Culture,* in BIOLOGY AND THE HUMAN SCIENCES 95 (J. Pringle ed. 1972); Jensen, *How Much Can We Boost IQ and Scientific Achievement?* 39 HARV. EDUCATIONAL REV. 1 (1969); Jensen, *Reducing the Heredity-Environment Uncertainty: A Reply,* 39 HARV. EDUCATIONAL REV. 449 (1969); Shockley, *Models, Mathematics, and the Moral Obligation to Diagnose the Origin of Negro IQ Deficits,* 41 REV. EDUCATIONAL RESEARCH 369 (1971).

61. A. MONTAGU, MAN'S MOST DANGEROUS MYTH: THE FALLACY OF RACE xiii (5th ed. rev. 1974). Speaking of "the man of flesh and bone," instead of "political man, social man, man in the abstract," René Dubos has observed:

> All human beings are related, biologically and mentally, but no two of them have exactly the same biological and mental constitution. Furthermore, the individuality of any person living now is different from that of anyone who has ever lived in the past or will live in the future. Each person is unique, unprecedented, and unrepeatable.

Dubos, *Biological Determinants of Individuality,* in INDIVIDUALITY AND THE NEW SOCIETY 148 (A. Kaplan ed. 1970).

62. C. DARWIN, THE DESCENT OF MAN, AND SELECTION IN RELATION TO SEX 178 (1st Ams ed. 1972).

He added:

> As man advances in civilization, and small tribes are united into larger communities, the simplest reason would tell each individual that he ought to extend his social instincts and sympathies to all members of the same nation, though personally unknown to him. This point being once reached, there is only an artificial barrier to prevent his sympathies extending to the men of all nations and races.[63]

The significance for common interest of "the self-actualization of human individuals and the fullest possible realization of their socially valuable capacities and potentialities"[64] has been well stated by Dobzhansky:

> Individuals and groups will arrange their lives differently, in accordance with their diverse notions of what form of happiness they wish to pursue. Their contributions to mankind's store of achievements will be different in kind and different in magnitude. The point is, however, that everybody should be able to contribute up to the limit of his ability. To deny the equality of opportunity to persons or groups is evil because this results in wastage of talent, ability, and aptitude, besides being contrary to the basic ethic of humanity.[65]

TRENDS IN DECISION

The concerted community effort in recent decades to combat and eradicate racial discrimination has been a driving force behind the emergence of the more general norm of nondiscrimination. Prior to the establishment of the United Nations, the global community provided individuals scant protection against discrimination on racial or other grounds. Some modest protection, "though hesitating and infrequent,"[66] was afforded by the doctrine of humanitarian intervention. The early assertions of a right of humanitarian intervention were made predominantly for the protection of oppressed religious groups,[67] yet

---

63. *Id.* at 122.

64. Dobzhansky, *Biological Evolution and Human Equality,* in SCIENCE AND THE MODERN WORLD 15, 33 (J. Steinhardt ed. 1966).

65. *Id.*

66. H. LAUTERPACHT, AN INTERNATIONAL BILL OF THE RIGHTS OF MAN 47 (1945); H. LAUTERPACHT, INTERNATIONAL LAW AND HUMAN RIGHTS 68 (1950) [hereinafter cited as H. LAUTERPACHT, INTERNATIONAL LAW].

67. *See* M. GANJI, INTERNATIONAL PROTECTION OF HUMAN RIGHTS 17–43 (1962). On humanitarian intervention *see* I. BROWNLIE, INTERNATIONAL LAW AND THE USE OF FORCE BY STATES 338–42 (1963); HUMANITARIAN INTERVENTION AND THE UNITED NATIONS (R. Lillich ed. 1973); L. SOHN & T. BUERGENTHAL, INTERNATIONAL PROTECTION OF HUMAN RIGHTS 137–211 (1973) [hereinafter cited as L. SOHN & T. BUERGENTHAL]; Bowett, *The Use of Force*

the victims for whom protection was extended upon occasion included groups of distinctive national or ethnic origin, such as the Greek people oppressed by Turkey from 1827 to 1830[68] and the Armenians oppressed by Turkey before World War I.[69]

A more substantial step was taken when, following World War I, the League of Nations was empowered to oversee an international regime for the protection of "racial, religious or linguistic minorities."[70] The victorious Principal Allied and Associated Powers, through treaty stipulations, imposed upon Poland, Czechoslovakia, the Serb-Croat-Slovene State (Yugoslavia), Romania, Greece, Austria, Bulgaria, Hungary, and Turkey special obligations to protect minority groups within their respective boundaries.[71] These states undertook to "assure full and complete protection of life and liberty" to all their inhabitants "without distinction of birth, nationality, language, race or religion."[72] Similar obligations were assumed by Albania, Estonia, Latvia, Lithuania, and Iraq upon their admissions to the League of Nations.[73] To ensure the fulfillment of these obligations, the provisions affecting "persons belonging to racial, religious, or linguistic minorities" were made "obligations of international concern,"[74] placed under the guarantee of the League of

---

in the Protection of Nationals, 43 GROTIUS SOC'Y 111 (1957); Cabranes, *Human Rights and Non-Intervention in the Inter-American System,* 65 MICH. L. REV. 1147 (1967); Claydon, *Humanitarian Intervention and International Law,* 1 QUEEN'S INTRAMURAL L.J. 36 (1969); Franck & Rodley, *After Bangladesh: The Law of Humanitarian Intervention by Military Force,* 67 AM. J. INT'L L. 275 (1973); Lillich, *Forcible Self-Help by States to Protect Human Rights,* 53 IOWA L. REV. 325 (1967); Lillich, *Intervention to Protect Human Rights,* 15 McGILL L.J. 205 (1969); Stowell, *Humanitarian Intervention,* 33 AM. J. INT'L L. 733 (1939); Wiseberg, *Humanitarian Intervention: Lessons from the Nigerian Civil War,* 7 HUMAN RIGHTS J. 61 (1974).

68. M. GANJI, INTERNATIONAL PROTECTION OF HUMAN RIGHTS 22–24 (1962); H. LAUTERPACHT, INTERNATIONAL LAW, *supra* note 66, at 120.

69. *See* L. SOHN & T. BUERGENTHAL, *supra* note 67, at 181–94.

70. We propose to deal with the question of minority protection in a later study. For pertinent references, *see* chapter 4 *supra,* at note 57.

71. These treaty stipulations were conveniently compiled in LEAGUE OF NATIONS, PROTECTION OF LINGUISTIC, RACIAL AND RELIGIOUS MINORITIES BY THE LEAGUE OF NATIONS: PROVISIONS CONTAINED IN THE VARIOUS INTERNATIONAL INSTRUMENTS AT PRESENT IN FORCE, 1927, I.B.2.

72. *Id.* at 43 (The Treaty with Poland, Art. 2). The treaty with Poland served as the model for other comparable treaties. *See also id.* at 8 (The Peace Treaty with Austria, Art. 63); *id.* at 11 (The Peace Treaty with Bulgaria, Art. 50); *id.* at 22 (The Treaty with Greece, Art. 2); *id.* at 29 (The Peace Treaty with Hungary, Art. 55); *id.* at 51 (The Treaty with Roumania, Art. 2); *id.* at 61 (The Treaty with the Serb-Croat-Slovene State, Art. 2); *id.* at 92 (The Treaty with Czechoslovakia, Art. 2); *id.* at 97 (The Peace Treaty with Turkey, Art. 38).

73. *Id.* at 4 (The Declaration Made by Albania before the Council of the League of Nations on October 2, 1921, Art. 2); *id.* at 14 (Estonia); *id.* at 32 (Latvia); *id.* at 34 (Declaration of Lithuania, dated May 12, 1922, Art. 2).

74. *See, e.g.,* The Treaty with Poland, Art. 12, *id.* at 44.

Nations," and they could not be modified "without the assent of a majority" of the League Council.[75] The Council was further authorized to "take such action and give such directions as it may deem proper and effective" when a complaint of violation was brought to its attention.[76]

The contemporary broad prescription against discriminations imposed by group categorizations of "race" has its origins in the United Nations Charter and certain authoritative ancillary expressions and commitments. The importance which most of mankind today ascribes to the prohibition of race as a ground for differentiation is clearly evidenced by the prominent place accorded race and its equivalents in all the various recent enumerations of impermissible grounds. Thus, the Charter of the United Nations, in Article 1(3), projects one of its purposes as "promoting and encouraging respect for human rights and for fundamental freedoms for all without distinction as to *race,* sex, language, or religion" and the Charter restates this concern in Articles 13(1)(b),[77] 55(c),[78] and 76(c)[79] in the chapters dealing with the functions

---

75. *Id.*

76. *Id.* at 45.

77. Art. 13(1)(b) of the U.N. Charter reads:

> 1. The General Assembly shall initiate studies and make recommendations for the purpose of:
>
> . . .
>
> b. promoting international cooperation in the economic, social, cultural, educational, and health fields, and assisting in the realization of human rights and fundamental freedoms for all without distinction as to race, sex, language, or religion.

U.N. CHARTER, Art. 13(1)(b).

78. Art. 55(c) reads:

> With a view to the creation of conditions of stability and well-being which are necessary for peaceful and friendly relations among nations based on respect for the principle of equal rights and self-determination of peoples, the United Nations shall promote:
>
> . . .
>
> c. universal respect for, and observance of, human rights and fundamental freedoms for all without distinction as to race, sex, language, or religion.

Id. Art. 55(c).

79. Art. 76(c) reads:

> The basic objectives of the trusteeship system, in accordance with the Purposes of the United Nations laid down in Article 1 of the present Charter, shall be:
>
> . . .
>
> c. to encourage respect for human rights and for fundamental freedoms for all without distinction as to race, sex, language, or religion, and to encourage recognition of the interdependence of the peoples of the world.

Id. Art. 76(c).

of the General Assembly, "International Economic and Social Co-operation," and "International Trusteeship System." Similarly, the Universal Declaration of Human Rights stipulates, in Article 2, that its protections are to be extended "without distinction of any kind, such as *race, colour,* sex, language, religion, political or other opinion, *national or social origin,* property, *birth or other status.*"[80] In Article 7 it provides for equal protection before the law "without any discrimination."[81]

This same theme is carried forward in the Discrimination (Employment and Occupation) Convention, adopted in June 1958 under the auspices of the International Labor Organization, which was designed to ensure "equality of opportunity and treatment in respect of employment and occupation. . . ."[82] This Convention specifically prohibits, in Article 1(1)(a), any discrimination "on the basis of *race, colour,* sex, religion, political opinion, *national extraction or social origin*. . . . "[83] The Convention against Discrimination in Education, adopted in December 1960 under the auspices of the United Nations Educational, Scientific, and Cultural Organization, seeks to "promote equality of opportunity and treatment for all in education."[84] This Convention prohibits, in Article 1(1), any discrimination in the field of education because of "*race, colour,* sex, language, religion, political or other opinion, *national or social origin,* economic condition or *birth*."[85]

The more recent International Covenants on Human Rights, incorporating precisely the wording and order of Article 2 of the Universal Declaration of Human Rights, also explicitly prohibit discrimination on grounds of race. Thus, the International Covenant on Civil and Political Rights, in Article 2(1), requires that a state "ensure to all individuals within its territory and subject to its jurisdiction the rights recognized in the present Covenant, without distinction of any kind, such as *race, colour,* sex, language, religion, political or other opinion, *national or social origin,* property, *birth or other status*."[86] The provision for equality before the law, in Article 26, guarantees "to all persons equal and effective protection

---

80. Universal Declaration of Human Rights, *adopted* Dec. 10, 1948, Art. 2, G.A. Res. 217, U.N. Doc. A/810 at 72 (italics added).

81. *Id.,* Art. 7, U.N. Doc. A/810 at 73.

82. Convention concerning Discrimination in Respect of Employment and Occupation, *adopted* June 25, 1958, Art. 2, 362 U.N.T.S. 34 (ILO General Conference) (entered into force June 15, 1960).

83. *Id.,* Art. 1(1)(a), 362 U.N.T.S. at 32 (italics added).

84. Convention against Discrimination in Education, *adopted* Dec. 14, 1960, Preamble, 429 U.N.T.S. 94 (UNESCO General Conference) (entered into force May 22, 1962).

85. *Id.,* Art. 1(1), 429 U.N.T.S. at 96 (italics added).

86. International Covenant on Civil and Political Rights, *adopted* Dec. 16, 1966, Art. 2(1), G.A. Res. 2200A, 21 U.N. GAOR, Supp. (No. 16) 53, U.N. Doc. A/6316 (1966) (italics added).

against discrimination on any ground such as *race, colour,* sex, language, religion, political or other opinion, *national or social origin*, property, *birth or other status*."[87] The International Covenant on Economic, Social, and Cultural Rights, in Article 2(2), imposes a comparable prohibition upon states for protection of all the rights which it enunciates.[88]

The general community prescription against racial discrimination has been further articulated and fortified by the adoption of the United Nations Declaration on the Elimination of All Forms of Racial Discrimination in November 1963,[89] and of the International Convention on the Elimination of All Forms of Racial Discrimination in December 1965.[90] In the winter of 1959–60, as "an epidemic of swastika-painting and other 'manifestations of anti-Semitism and other forms of racial and national hatred and religious and racial prejudices of a similar nature'"[91] swept through a number of states in Europe and Latin America, the Sub-Commission on Prevention of Discrimination and Protection of Minorities took the "unprecedented"[92] step of condemning these manifestations as violations of the Charter of the United Nations and the Universal Declaration of Human Rights.[93] The Sub-Commission, in gathering, processing, and studying all the relevant information, brought the matter to

---

87. *Id.*, Art. 26, 21 U.N. GAOR, Supp. (No. 16) 55–56 (italics added).

88. It reads:

> The States Parties to the present Covenant undertake to guarantee that the rights enunciated in the present Covenant will be exercised without discrimination of any kind as to race, colour, sex, language, religion, political or other opinion, national or social origin, property, birth or other status.

International Covenant on Economic, Social, and Cultural Rights, *adopted* Dec. 16, 1966, Art. 2(2), G.A. Res. 2200A, 21 U.N. GAOR, Supp. (No. 16) 49–50, U.N. Doc. A/6316 (1966).

89. United Nations Declaration on the Elimination of All Forms of Racial Discrimination, *adopted* Nov. 20, 1963, G.A. Res. 1904, 18 U.N. GAOR, Supp. (No. 15) 35, 36, U.N. Doc. A/5515 (1963) [hereinafter cited as Declaration on the Elimination of All Forms of Racial Discrimination].

90. International Convention on the Elimination of All Forms of Racial Discrimination, *opened for signature* Mar. 7, 1966, 660 U.N.T.S. 195 (entered into force Jan. 4, 1969) [hereinafter cited as Convention on the Elimination of All Forms of Racial Discrimination].

91. Schwelb, *The International Convention on the Elimination of All Forms of Racial Discrimination,* 15 INT'L & COMP. L.Q. 996, 997 (1966) [hereinafter cited as Schwelb]. *See also* Deutsch, *The 1960 Swastika-Smearings: Analysis of the Apprehended Youth,* MERRILL-PALMER Q. OF BEHAVIOR & DEV. 1 (Apr. 1962), *reprinted in* MINORITY PROBLEMS 341 (A. Rose & C. Rose eds. 1965); Moskowitz, *The Narrowing Horizons of United Nations Concern with Racial Discrimination,* 4 HUMAN RIGHTS J. 278, 282–83 (1971) [hereinafter cited as Moskowitz].

92. Humphrey, *The United Nations Sub-Commission on the Prevention of Discrimination and the Protection of Minorities,* 62 AM. J. INT'L L. 869, 882 (1968).

93. *Report of the Twelfth Session of the Sub-Commission on Prevention of Discrimination and Protection of Minorities to the Commission on Human Rights* 58, U.N. Doc. E/CN.4/800 (E/CN.4/Sub. 2/206) (1960).

the attention of its superior bodies and urged effective measures of prevention and eradication, especially the formulation of an international convention.[94] The General Assembly, at its seventeenth session in 1962, decided to prepare two separate sets of instruments: one set (a draft declaration and a draft convention) on "the elimination of all forms of racial discrimination" and the other on "the elimination of all forms of religious intolerance," with priority being accorded to the former.[95] This "compromise solution"[96] was reached largely because the Arab delegations wished to downplay the issue of anti-Semitism and because the Eastern European and other delegations insisted that the question of religious discrimination was far less important and urgent than that of racial discrimination.[97] Thereafter, on November 20, 1963, the General Assembly adopted the United Nations Declaration on the Elimination of All Forms of Racial Discrimination.[98] Meanwhile, the preparation of the draft convention on racial discrimination was under way. The Commission on Human Rights, building upon a text prepared by the Sub-Commission,[99] completed its draft in 1964,[100] and the draft was considered by the Third Committee of the General Assembly in 1965.[101] The General Assembly, on December 21, 1965, adopted the International

---

94. *Report of the Thirteenth Session of the Sub-Commission on Prevention of Discrimination and Protection of Minorities to the Commission on Human Rights* 60, 63, U.N. Doc. E/CN.4/815 (E/CN.4/Sub. 2/211) (1961).

95. G.A. Res. 1780, 17 U.N. GAOR, Supp. (No. 17) 32, U.N. Doc. A/5217 (1962); G.A. Res. 1781, *id.* at 33. It has been sharply pointed out that the decision to have two separate sets of instruments was motivated by politics rather than merits. Schwelb, *supra* note 91, at 999.

> By drawing a line of demarcation separating discrimination on religious grounds from discrimination on racial and ethnic grounds, the United Nations departed radically from well-established and widely-accepted norms which recognize that, apart from certain obvious cases, racial discrimination was usually brought about not solely by differences in race or colour, but also by cultural, religious and other differences which led to mistrust and prejudice.

Moskowitz, *supra* note 91, at 282.

96. Schwelb, *supra* note 91, at 999.

97. *See, id.;* Moskowitz, *supra* note 91, at 282–84.

98. Declaration on the Elimination of All Forms of Racial Discrimination, *supra* note 89.

99. *Report of the Sixteenth Session of the Sub-Commission on Prevention of Discrimination and Protection of Minorities to the Commission on Human Rights* 13–57, U.N. Doc. E/CN.4/873 (E/CN.4/Sub. 2/241) (1964).

100. *Report on the Twentieth Session, Commission on Human Rights,* 37 U.N. ECOSOC Supp. (No. 8) 9, U.N. Doc. E/3873 (E/CN.4/874) (1964).

101. *Report of the Third Committee, Draft International Convention on the Elimination of All Forms of Racial Discrimination,* 20 U.N. GAOR, Annexes (Agenda Item 58) 13, U.N. Doc. A/6181 (1965). For a verbatim record of the Third Committee's discussions see 20 U.N. GAOR, 3D COMM. 57–141, 147–52, 313–400, 419–66, 495–509 (1965).

Convention on the Elimination of All Forms of Racial Discrimination.[102] As of this writing, the envisaged Declaration and Convention on the Elimination of Religious Intolerance are yet to be adopted.[103]

The Declaration on the Elimination of Racial Discrimination, in solemnly affirming "the necessity of speedily eliminating racial discrimination throughout the world, in all its forms and manifestations."[104] proclaims that discrimination on the ground of "race, colour, or ethnic origin" is "an offense to human dignity," "a denial of the principles of the Charter of the United Nations," and "a violation" of the Universal Declaration of Human Rights.[105] The Declaration, extending its concern to acts of states as well as of private institutions or groups and individuals,[106] urges that special efforts be made to prevent racial discrimination, especially in "civil rights, access to citizenship, education, religion, employment, occupation, and housing,"[107] and in "equal access to any place or facility intended for use by the general public."[108] The Declaration condemns racist propaganda and organizations and urges that "all incitement to or acts of violence" against any racial group be made "punishable under law."[109] States are further urged to take steps to outlaw and prosecute racist organizations.[110] To ensure equal treatment of individuals, states are urged to "take effective measures to revise governmental and other public policies," "rescind" discriminatory "laws and regulations," and "pass" necessary legislation of protection.[111]

The International Convention on the Elimination of All Forms of Racial Discrimination, in reinforcing the preceding Declaration, represents "the most comprehensive and unambiguous codification in treaty form of the idea of the equality of race."[112] In spelling out its prohibition of discrimination, the Convention specifies in comprehensive and detailed terms the impermissible grounds for differentiation, the particular acts forbidden, and the various actors who are precluded from engaging in discrimination. Beyond the mere prohibition of activities, the bare characterization of unlawfulness, the Convention further seeks

---

102. Convention on the Elimination of All Forms of Racial Discrimination, *supra* note 90.

103. *See* chapter 11 *infra.*

104. Declaration on the Elimination of All Forms of Racial Discrimination, *supra* note 89, Preamble, 18 U.N. GAOR, Supp. (No. 15) 36.

105. *Id.,* Art. 1.

106. *Id.,* Arts. 2(1–2).

107. *Id.,* Art. 3(1).

108. *Id.,* Art. 3(2).

109. *Id.,* Art. 9(1), (2), 18 U.N. GAOR, Supp. (No. 15) 37.

110. *Id.,* Art. 9(3).

111. *Id.,* Art. 4, 18 U.N. GAOR, Supp. (No. 15) 36.

112. Schwelb, *supra* note 91, at 1057.

to cope with some of the causes of discrimination and to project procedures which may serve the purposes of preventing and deterring discrimination, as well as of restoring and rehabilitating already exacerbated situations.

The group categorization of "race," offered by the Convention in Article 1(1),[113] is as broad and generous as the group characterization commonly employed in discrimination is vague and arbitrary. In implementing its stated objective of banning racial discrimination "in all its forms and manifestations,"[114] the Convention adds to "race" the ancillary concepts of "colour, descent, or national or ethnic origin. . . . "[115] Though the *travaux preparatoires* indicate no very precise reference for "race,"[116] it appears that the framers of the Convention intended to catch all the traditional biological and cultural meanings. The UNESCO statements on race were, as several commentators have noted,[117] current at the time the Convention was prepared, and it would appear a reasonable interpretation, in light of the major purposes of the Convention, that all the biological and cultural categorizations included within these statements are among those condemned by the Convention.[118] The reach of the prohibited categorization of color—since people come in many gradations of white, black, yellow, and brown, and since almost all groups may be observed to have some uniqueness[119]—would appear to be equally broad. The concept of "national origin," specified as different from "nationality" in the sense of present membership in a state, has

---

113. Art. 1(1) of the Convention reads:

> In this Convention, the term "racial discrimination" shall mean any distinction, exclusion, restriction or preference based on race, colour, descent, or national or ethnic origin which has the purpose or effect of nullifying or impairing the recognition, enjoyment or exercise, on an equal footing, of human rights and fundamental freedoms in the political, economic, social, cultural or any other field of public life.

Convention on the Elimination of All Forms of Racial Discrimination, *supra* note 90, Art. 1(1), 660 U.N.T.S. at 216.

114. *Id.,* Preamble, 660 U.N.T.S. at 212–16.

115. *Id.,* Art. 1(1), 660 U.N.T.S. at 216.

116. The *travaux preparatoires* of the Convention are cited in notes 99–101 *supra.*

117. *See, e.g.,* N. Lerner, The U.N. Convention on the Elimination of All Forms of Racial Discrimination 41–42 (1970) [hereinafter cited as N. Lerner]; E. Vierdag, The Concept of Discrimination in International Law 89–90 (1973) [hereinafter cited as E. Vierdag]; Coleman, *The Problem of Anti-Semitism under the International Convention on the Elimination of All Forms of Racial Discrimination,* 2 Human Rights J. 609, 616–17 (1969) [hereinafter cited as Coleman]. These UNESCO statements on race are collected in A. Montagu, *supra* note 4.

118. *See* notes 1–14 *supra* and accompanying text for a discussion of the concept of race. *See also* E. Vierdag, *supra* note 117, at 87–90; Coleman, *supra* note 117, at 616–19.

119. For a detailed description of the significance and variety of color of different population groups see J. Baker, Race 149–60 (1974). *See also* E. Vierdag, *supra* note 117, at 97–99.

been said to include both "politico-legal" and "ethno-graphical" (or "historico-biological") senses.[120] Deriving its vagueness from its origin in the minorities treaties after World War I,[121] this concept apparently is intended to refer to a person's prior identifications, whether chosen or ascribed, with states and with the larger cultural groups (popularly known as nations) which transcend any particular state.[122] The words "ethnic origin," again, refer to both biological and cultural characteristics with a diversity bewildering even in scientific usage.[123] "Any discrimination," concludes one commentator, "based on an individual's cultural identification may be tantamount to discrimination on ethnic grounds."[124] The group characterization unique to this Convention, that of "descent," was, as elaborated in a previous chapter, introduced by the delegation of India to outlaw discrimination based on "caste."[125] Its ambiguities are obviously sufficiently ample to cure any inadequacies of reference that may inhere in the other concepts.

The broad sweep of prohibited grounds in the Convention—whether its categorizations are taken separately or in the aggregate—would thus appear to afford protection to a vast variety of potential victims of

---

120. *See* Coleman, *supra* note 117, at 619–22; Schwelb, *supra* note 91, at 1006–07.

121. *Cf.* notes 70–76 *supra* and accompanying text. As Claude has observed: "The basic instruments of the League minority system purported to safeguard certain rights of 'racial, religious or linguistic minorities,' but the framers of the system made it clear that they regarded this terminology as synonymous with 'national minorities.'" I. CLAUDE, NATIONAL MINORITIES: AN INTERNATIONAL PROBLEM 17 (1955).

122. During the debate before the Third Committee, Mr. Resich of Poland, in emphasizing the importance of including "national origin" as a forbidden ground in the Convention, stated:

> A "nation" was created when persons organized themselves politically on the basis of a common culture, common traditions or other factors. There were nations that were made up of different ethnic groups, such as Switzerland. But there were also situations in which a politically organized nation was included within a different State and continued to exist as a nation in the social and cultural senses even though it had no government of its own. The members of such a nation within a State might be discriminated against, not as members of a particular race or as individuals, but as members of a nation which existed in its former political form.

20 U.N. GAOR, 3D COMM. 83 (1965).

Similarly, Mr. Villgrattner of Austria indicated:

> For half a century the terms "national origin" and "nationality" had been widely used in literature and in international instruments as relating, not to persons who were citizens of or held passports issued by a given State, but to those having a certain culture, language and traditional way of life peculiar to a nation but who lived within another State.

Id. at 84.

123. *Cf.* A MONTAGU, *supra* note 4, at 59–71.

124. Coleman, *supra* note 117, at 623.

125. *See* chapter 7 *supra,* at notes 371–77 and accompanying text.

discrimination. The complex of practices known as "anti-Semitism,"[126] for example, though not mentioned in the Convention,[127] might easily be outlawed under several of the Convention's forbidden group categorizations.[128]

The inclusive, open-ended compass of the rights the Convention protects against discrimination is established both by broad generalization

---

126. On anti-Semitism *see* A. FORSTER & B. EPSTEIN, THE NEW ANTI-SEMITISM (1974); W. KOREY, THE SOVIET CAGE: ANTI-SEMITISM IN RUSSIA (1973); P. LENDVAI, ANTI-SEMITISM WITHOUT JEWS (1971); H. LUMER, SOVIET ANTI-SEMITISM—A COLD WAR MYTH (1964); ANTI-SEMITISM: A SOCIAL DISEASE (E. Simmel ed. 1946); Rogow, *Anti-Semitism*, 1 INT'L ENCYC. SOC. SC. 345 (1968).

127. In the Commission on Human Rights and at the Third Committee of the General Assembly, the United States unsuccessfully sought to incorporate a clause specifically condemning anti-Semitism in the Convention. For an account *see* Schwelb, *supra* note 91, at 1011–15. Mr. Comay of Israel, in echoing the United States proposal, emphasized that "anti-Semitism, with which the entire history and fate of every generation of the Jewish people had been tragically bound up, should be expressly mentioned in the draft Convention." 20 U.N. GAOR, 3D COMM. 115 (1965).

> The history of the Jewish people was that of a branch of the human family which had been singled out for cruel hostility and savage persecution. Anti-Semitism, which had assumed at different times religious, racial, economic and cultural aspects, was unfortunately not something which belonged to the remote past, for, after having reached its culminating horror in the twentieth century with the atrocities of the Hitler regime, the declared aim of which was to ensure the "final solution of the Jewish question" by systematically exterminating all Jews in cold blood, anti-Semitism had now become the stock-in-trade of every political group aiming to subvert democratic institutions and freedoms. It was thus precisely because anti-Semitism continued to exist in the world that it must be mentioned expressly in the Convention.

Id.

His lone voice was overshadowed, however. The Third Committee approved, instead, the Greek-Hungarian proposal "not to include in the draft International Convention on the Elimination of All Forms of Racial Discrimination any reference to specific forms of racial discrimination." *Id.* at 113, 118. Mr. Rogers of the United States, in expressing disappointment over the outcome, indicated that

> his delegation was firmly convinced that anti-Semitism, which constituted a particularly dangerous form of racial discrimination, deserved special mention just as apartheid did. Thus, in conjunction with Brazil, his delegation had submitted an amendment to include in the Convention an article condemning anti-Semitism. Anti-Semitism was one of the gravest and most persistent problems facing humanity, dating back over 2,000 years. Historically, it had been a barometer of the political health of States: where Jews had been unsafe, other minorities also soon found themselves in danger. That was what had happened in 1939.

Id. at 119.

Finally, he stressed that "it was clear that there was a general feeling condemning anti-Semitism and that anti-Semitism was covered by the terms of the Convention." *Id.*

128. *See* Coleman, *supra* note 117; Schwelb, *supra* note 91, at 1014–15. *See also* Lerner, *Anti-Semitism as Racial and Religious Discrimination under United Nations Conventions,* 1 ISRAEL Y.B. ON HUMAN RIGHTS 103 (1971).

and by detailed, illustrative specification. Thus, in Article 1(1) "racial discrimination" is defined as acts which have "the purpose or effect of nullifying or impairing the recognition, enjoyment or exercise, on an equal footing, of human rights and fundamental freedoms in the political, economic, social, cultural or any other field of public life."[129] This is followed in Article 5 by further broad generalization and a lengthy, minute itemization of protected rights, clearly intended to be illustrative, not exhaustive. The initial terms of Article 5 read:

> In compliance with the fundamental obligations laid down in Article 2 of this Convention, States Parties undertake to prohibit and to eliminate racial discrimination in all its forms and to guarantee the right of everyone, without distinction as to race, colour, or national or ethnic origin, to equality before the law, *notably* in the enjoyment of the following rights. . . .[130]

The detailed itemization of protected rights offered by Article 5 begins by indicating that all persons have the right to challenge deprivations through appropriate tribunals and the "right to security of person"; then lists political rights in general and other civil rights in particular; continues with economic, social, and cultural rights; and concludes with the right of access to public accommodations and facilities.[131] The right to challenge deprivations is recognized as fundamental to the effective realization of the norm of nondiscrimination; hence, "the right to equal treatment before the tribunals and all other organs administering justice" is accorded prominence.[132] "The right to security of person" extends to "protection by the State against violence or bodily harm, whether inflicted by government officials or by an individual group or institution."[133] Political rights include the right to voting and officeholding "at any level," elective and appointive, and "equal access to public service."[134] Other civil rights include the rights to "freedom of movement," internal and transnational,[135] to "nationality,"[136] to "marriage and choice of spouse,"[137] to "own property,"[138] to "freedom of thought" and "expression,"[139] and to "freedom of peaceful assembly and associa-

129. Convention on the Elimination of All Forms of Racial Discrimination, Art. 1(1), *supra* note 90, 660 U.N.T.S. at 216.

130. *Id.*, Art. 5, 660 U.N.T.S. at 220–22 (italics added).

131. *Id.*

132. *Id.*, Art. 5(a), 660 U.N.T.S. at 220.

133. *Id.*, Art. 5(b).

134. *Id.*, Art. 5(c).

135. *Id.*, Art. 5(d)(i, ii).

136. *Id.*, Art. 5(d)(iii).

137. *Id.*, Art. 5(d)(iv).

138. *Id.*, Art. 5(d)(v).

139. *Id.*, Art. 5(d)(vii, viii), 60 U.N.T.S. at 222.

tion."[140] "Economic, social and cultural rights" include the "right to work"; employment; "equal" and "just" remuneration;[141] the right to "form and join trade unions";[142] and the rights to "housing,"[143] health care and "social security,"[144] "education and training,"[145] and "equal participation in cultural activities."[146] Not being tied to any other particular human rights instrument, the Convention further enumerates "the right to inherit"[147] and "the right of access to any place or service intended for use by the general public, such as transport, hotels, restaurants, cafes, theatres and parks,"[148] two items ostensibly missing from the Universal Declaration of Human Rights.

That all this itemization in Article 5 is intended to be illustrative, not exhaustive, is abundantly demonstrated by the use in appropriate contexts of such terms as "notably,"[149] "in particular,"[150] and "such as."[151] The placing of "notably" in the opening paragraph, preceding any itemization, unequivocally expresses an intent for comprehensiveness in the human rights protected.[152]

It has been suggested that there might be "contradictions" between Article 1(1) and Article 5 on the grounds that while Article 1(1) employs the phrase "or any other field of *public life*" and omits a reference to "civil rights,"[153] Article 5 "lists several rights which certainly do not come within the sphere of public life."[154] The wording "any other field of

---

140. *Id.*, Art. 5(d)(ix).
141. *Id.*, Art. 5(e)(i).
142. *Id.*, Art. 5(e)(ii).
143. *Id.*, Art. 5(e)(iii).
144. *Id.*, Art. 5(e)(iv).
145. *Id.*, Art. 5(e)(v).
146. *Id.*, Art. 5(e)(vi).
147. *Id.*, Art. 5(d)(vi).
148. *Id.*, Art. 5(f).
149. *See* text accompanying note 130 *supra*.
150. This phrase is employed to illustrate "political rights," "civil rights," and "economic, social and cultural rights" in Art. 5(c–e). Thus, Art. 5(c) reads:

> Political rights, *in particular* the rights to participate in elections—to vote and to stand for election—on the basis of universal and equal suffrage, to take part in the Government as well as in the conduct of public affairs at any level and to have equal access to public service.

Convention on the Elimination of All Forms of Racial Discrimination, *supra* note 90, Art. 5(c), 660 U.N.T.S. at 220 (italics added).

151. Art. 5(f) states: "The right of access to any place or service intended for use by the general public, *such as* transport, hotels, restaurants, cafes, theatres and parks." *Id.*, Art. 5(f), 660 U.N.T.S. at 222 (italics added).
152. Lerner has pointed out that "[t]he word 'notably' was used in order to avoid a restrictive interpretation of the rights enumerated." N. Lerner, *supra* note 117, at 67.
153. *See* Schwelb, *supra* note 91, at 1005.
154. *Id.*

public life" in Article 1(1) would not appear to be used in any limiting or restrictive sense. "Public life," an innovative nontechnical term, would appear placed on the same general level as "the political, economic, social, cultural" fields so that together they might encompass all sectors of organized life of the community. The listing of many rights which would ordinarily be described as "private" in Article 5 is clear indication that "public life" in Article 1(1) is not used in contradistinction to "private" rights.[155] The reference would appear rather as a generic summation of all rights protectable by law, designed to be all inclusive in reach. This interpretation is supported not only by the major purposes of the Convention, but also by the explicit rejection of a proposal to include in Article 1(1) the modifying clause, "set forth *inter alia* in the Universal Declaration of Human Rights," as originally proposed in the Sub-Commission's draft.[156]

At the eighth session of the Committee on the Elimination of Racial Discrimination in 1973, an attempt was made to undercut the broad reach of the rights protected by the Convention by factitious interpretation of Article 5.[157] A member of the Committee[158] suggested that Article 5 of the Convention did not establish any particular human rights, even those explicitly enumerated, but only a right to be free from racial discrimination and to equality before the law.[159] "Its sole purpose," he reasoned, "was to establish the obligation of states parties to ensure that there was no racial discrimination in the enjoyment of those human rights and to 'guarantee the right of everyone . . . to equality before the law' in the enjoyment of those rights."[160] He added:

> Article 5 did not purport to be an international convention on civil, political, social, economic, cultural and other rights. Nor did it purport to virtually transform the Universal Declaration of Human Rights into an international convention, or to render the principles of that Declaration legally binding upon any State which ratified or acceded to the Convention.[161]

---

155. *See* Elkind, *Discrimination: A Guide for the Fact Finder (International Convention on the Elimination of All Forms of Racial Discrimination),* 32 U. PITT. L. REV. 307, 312–19 (1971).

156. *Report of the Sixteenth Session of the Sub-Commission on Prevention of Discrimination and Protection of Minorities to the Commission on Human Rights,* Draft Art. 1(1), at 45–46, U.N. Doc. E/CN.4/873 (E/CN.4/Sub. 2/241) (1964). *See also* N. LERNER, *supra* note 117, at 39–40, 43; Schwelb, *supra* note 91, at 1003–04.

157. *See* REPORT OF THE COMMITTEE ON THE ELIMINATION OF RACIAL DISCRIMINATION, 28 U.N. GAOR, Supp. (No. 18) 10–12, U.N. Doc. A/9018 (1973).

158. Mr. Fayez A. Sayegh of Kuwait.

159. REPORT OF THE COMMITTEE ON THE ELIMINATION OF RACIAL DISCRIMINATION, 28 U.N. GAOR, Supp. (No. 18) 12, U.N. Doc. A/9018 (1973).

160. *Id.*

161. *Id.*

The notion that a right of nondiscrimination can be established without establishing the rights protected from discrimination is about as meaningful as the notion of minting a one-sided coin. The Convention on the Elimination of All Forms of Racial Discrimination is, of course, built upon the assumption that individuals already have a wide range of human rights which are protected by the Charter of the United Nations, by many ancillary authoritative instruments and expressions, and by that consensus of general community expectations commonly known as customary international law.[162] This particular Convention is itself an important expression of this growing general community consensus; in this sense it clearly establishes the rights it purports to secure. Neither tied to, nor restricted by, any other particular human rights instrument,[163] the Convention is designed, in the words of the preamble, to eliminate "racial discrimination in all its forms and manifestations"[164] in relation to all human rights, established by whatever authority. The deliberate decision not to tie the Convention to other particular instruments, including even the much venerated Universal Declaration of Human Rights, represents a shared aspiration to make its protection as inclusive as possible of all rights, both present and prospective.[165]

The particular acts forbidden by the Convention are those which arbitrarily differentiate between individuals in the enjoyment of human rights. Article 1(1) makes the basic specification in terms of "any distinction, exclusion, restriction or preference . . . which has the purpose or effect of nullifying or impairing the recognition, enjoyment or exercise, on an equal footing, of human rights and fundamental freedoms. . . ."[166] It will be observed that this comprehensive formulation, expressed in the fourfold categories of "distinction, exclusion, restriction or preference," seeks to catch every form of deprivation that may be imposed in social process.[167] These four terms would appear to embrace

---

162. *See* chapter 8 *supra.*

163. *See* note 156 *supra* and accompanying text.

164. Convention on the Elimination of All Forms of Racial Discrimination, *supra* note 90, Preamble, 660 U.N.T.S. at 212–16.

165. When the Convention on Racial Discrimination was adopted in Dec. 1965, the two draft International Covenants on Human Rights were nearing completion in the protracted process of drafting and redrafting, which had commenced shortly after the adoption of the Universal Declaration of Human Rights in Dec. 1948. Subsequently, both draft Covenants were, on Dec. 16, 1966, adopted and opened for signature, ratification, and accession by the General Assembly.

166. Convention on the Elimination of All Forms of Racial Discrimination, *supra* note 90, Art. 1(1), 660 U.N.T.S. at 216.

167. "It was agreed finally," as Lerner has pointed out in his commentary, "that the four mentioned terms would cover all aspects of discrimination which should be taken into account." N. Lerner, *supra* note 117, at 41.

both action and inaction and coercive indulgence as well as deprivation.[168] Even attempts to discriminate appear to be included by the reference to "purpose" as an alternative to "effect." This alternative reference to purpose and effect suggests that either alone is adequate to establish unlawful discrimination: mere purpose, without proof of success, may suffice, while effects, even in the absence of deliberate intent, are clearly forbidden. This broad reach is further strengthened by the prohibition even of incitement to discrimination. Thus, Article 4 condemns "all propaganda and all organizations" preaching the "superiority" of one race and promoting "racial hatred and discrimination" and seeks the eradication of "all incitement to, or acts of," racial discrimination.[169] In promotion of this end, the Article obliges contracting states to

> declare an offence punishable by law all dissemination of ideas based on racial superiority or hatred, incitement to racial discrimination, as well as all acts of violence or incitement to such acts against any race or group of persons of another colour or ethnic origin, and also the provision of any assistance to racist activities, including the financing thereof;[170]

and, further, to

> declare illegal and prohibit organizations, and also organized and all other propaganda activities, which promote and incite racial discrimination, and [to] recognize participation in such organizations or activities as an offence punishable by law.[171]

Cognizant of the potentially intricate ramifications of such broad formulation, the Convention emphasizes at the same time that "due regard" be given to "the principles embodied in the Universal Declaration of Human Rights and the rights expressly set forth in Article 5 of this Convention,"[172] ostensibly with special reference to the rights of "freedom of opinion and expression" and "freedom of peaceful assembly and association."[173]

---

168. *Cf. id.*; Schwelb, *supra* note 91, at 1001.

169. Convention on the Elimination of All Forms of Racial Discrimination, *supra* note 90, Art. 4, 660 U.N.T.S. at 218–20.

170. *Id.*, Art. 4(a), 660 U.N.T.S. at 220.

171. *Id.*, Art. 4(b).

172. *Id.*, Art. 4.

173. *Id.*, Art. 5(d)(viii–ix), 660 U.N.T.S. at 222. Art. 4 is a very controversial provision and has provoked considerable apprehension, especially within the United States, because of its potential incompatibility with broad freedom of expression. *See, e.g.*, Hauser, *United Nations Law on Racial Discrimination*, [1970] PROC., AM. SOC'Y INT'L L. 114, 117–18; Henkin, *National and International Perspectives in Racial Discrimination*, 4 HUMAN RIGHTS J. 263,

The Convention's broad formulation of forbidden acts is not, however, intended to prescribe that all differentiations are unlawful discriminations.[174] The differentiations made impermissible are those which fail to establish a demonstrable, rational relation to individual potentialities for self-development and contribution to the aggregate common interest.[175] This basic requirement of rationality, that is, an absence of arbitrariness, is implicit in the reference in Article 1(1) to the impairment of "human rights and fundamental freedoms" and is made explicit in Articles 1(4) and 2(2).[176] Thus, these articles provide that

---

266 (1971). *But see* Bitker, *The International Treaty against Racial Discrimination,* 53 MARQ. L. REV. 68, 75–76 (1970); Ferguson, *The United Nations Convention on Racial Discrimination: Civil Rights by Treaty,* 1 LAW IN TRANSITION Q. 61, 71–75 (1964); Reisman, *Responses to Crimes of Discrimination and Genocide: An Appraisal of the Convention on the Elimination of Racial Discrimination,* 1 DENVER J. INT'L L. & POLICY 29 (1971) [hereinafter cited as Reisman].

174. McKean has aptly observed that

> in international legal usage, "discrimination" has come to acquire a special meaning. It does not mean any distinction or differentiation but only arbitrary, invidious or unjustified distinctions, unwanted by those made subject to them. Moreover, it does not forbid special measures of protection designed to aid depressed groups, classes or categories of individuals, so long as these special measures are not carried on longer than is reasonably necessary. . . .
>
> In this respect, the definition accepted in the international sphere is more advanced and sophisticated than that adopted in most municipal legal systems. This is an important instance of international law and the work of international institutions providing inspiration for municipal law, and a reversal of the usual situation whereby international law adapts principles of municipal law by analogy to deal with international problems.

McKean, *The Meaning of Discrimination in International and Municipal Law,* 44 BRIT. Y.B. INT'L L. 177, 185–86 (1970).

175. In the proceedings of the *South West Africa* cases before the International Court of Justice, the plea of Liberia and Ethiopia that a general norm of nondiscrimination existed under international law was repeatedly referred to by South Africa as alleged norms of "non-differentiation," which would obviously be untenable. "The response of Judge Tanaka in his dissenting opinion is illuminating: Briefly, a different treatment is permitted when it can be justified by the criterion of justice. One may replace justice by the concept of reasonableness generally referred to by the Anglo-American school of law." South West Africa Cases (Second Phase), [1966] I.C.J. 4, 306 (Tanaka, J., dissenting). "Justice or reasonableness," he added, "as a criterion for the different treatment logically excludes arbitrariness," *Id.* He further elaborated:

> Equal treatment is a principle but its mechanical application ignoring all concrete factors engenders injustice. Accordingly, it requires different treatment, taken into consideration, of concrete circumstances of individual cases. The different treatment is permissible and required by the considerations of justice; it does not mean a disregard of justice.

Id. at 308.

176. Art. 1(4) reads:

> Special measures taken for the sole purpose of securing adequate advancement of certain racial or ethnic groups or individuals requiring such protection as may be

appropriate measures of assistance to traditionally deprived groups undertaken for the purpose of achieving genuinely effective equality of opportunity and treatment for all members of the community do not come within the purview of the prohibition established.[177]

In its effort to secure the complete eradication of racial discrimination, the Convention brings both offical and nonofficial actors within its purview. The ban upon official discriminatory actions is extended to all levels of government. Thus, contracting states undertake, under Article 2(1)(a, b, and c),[178] to

> engage in no act or practice of racial discrimination against persons, groups of persons or institutions and to ensure that all public authorities and public institutions, national and local, shall act in conformity with this obligation . . . ; not to sponsor, defend or support racial discrimination by any persons or organizations . . . ; [and finally to] take effective measures to review governmental, national and local policies, and to amend, rescind or nullify any laws and regulations which have the effect of creating or perpetuating racial discrimination wherever it exists.[179]

This prohibition on official actors is extended also to promotion or incitement of racial discrimination. Article 4(c) obliges contracting states not to "permit public authorities or public institutions, national or local, to promote or incite racial discrimination."[180] In recognition that "racial

---

> necessary in order to ensure such groups or individuals equal enjoyment or exercise of human rights and fundamental freedoms shall not be deemed racial discrimination, provided, however, that such measures do not, as a consequence, lead to the maintenance of separate rights for different racial groups and that they shall not be continued after the objectives for which they were taken have been achieved.

Convention on the Elimination of All Forms of Racial Discrimination, *supra* note 90, Art. 1(4), 660 U.N.T.S. at 216.

Art. 2(2) reads:

> States Parties shall, when the circumstances so warrant, take, in the social, economic, cultural and other fields, special and concrete measures to ensure the adequate development and protection of certain racial groups or individuals belonging to them, for the purpose of guaranteeing them the full and equal enjoyment of human rights and fundamental freedoms. These measures shall in no case entail as a consequence the maintenance of unequal or separate rights for different racial groups after the objectives for which they were taken have been achieved.

Id., Art. 2(2), 660 U.N.T.S. at 218.

177. With the question of special assistance to deprived groups we propose to deal in some length elsewhere.

178. Convention on the Elimination of All Forms of Racial Discrimination, Arts. 2(1)(a–c), *supra* note 90, 660 U.N.T.S. at 218.

179. *Id.*

180. *Id.*, Art. 4(c), 660 U.N.T.S. at 220.

discrimination is often private discrimination,"[181] the Convention in one brief but important provision asserts a broad reach extending to private parties and associations. Article 2(1)(d) stipulates: "Each State Party shall prohibit and bring to an end, by all appropriate means, including legislation as required by circumstances, racial discrimination by any persons, group or organization."[182] In rounding out its substantive prescriptions, the Convention provides for remedies against all actors, official and nonofficial alike. Article 6 reads:

> States Parties shall assure to everyone within their jurisdiction effective protection and remedies, through the competent national tribunals and other State institutions, against any acts of racial discrimination which violate his human rights and fundamental freedoms contrary to this Convention, as well as the right to seek from such tribunals just and adequate reparation or satisfaction for any damage suffered as a result of such discrimination.[183]

The comprehensive prohibition of discrimination on grounds of race contained within this Convention is fortified by many parallel expressions emanating from various United Nations bodies. It may be recalled that in the long train of resolutions regarding apartheid, adopted both by the General Assembly and by the Security Council, there has been a recurrent, emphatic, and equally general condemnation of racial discrimination as unlawful under international law.[184] The continued exacerbation caused by racial discriminations led the General Assembly to proclaim the year 1971 as International Year for Action to Combat Racism and Racial Discrimination.[185] The intensely aroused "conscience and sense of justice of mankind" for "the total and unconditional elimination of racial discrimination and racism"[186] reached a climax with the General Assembly's decision to launch "the Decade for Action to Combat Racism and Racial Discrimination,"[187] inaugurating a wide range of concerted activities on December 10, 1973, the twenty-fifth anniversary of the Universal Declaration of Human Rights.[188] In the Programme for the Decade for Action to Combat Racism and Racial

181. Henkin, *National and International Perspectives in Racial Discrimination,* 4 HUMAN RIGHTS J. 263, 265 (1971).

182. Convention on the Elimination of All Forms of Racial Discrimination, *supra* note 90, Art. 2(1)(d), 660 U.N.T.S. at 218.

183. *Id.,* Art. 6, 660 U.N.T.S. at 222.

184. *See* chapter 7 *supra,* at note 453–73 and accompanying text.

185. G.A. Res. 2785, 26 U.N. GAOR, Supp. (No. 29) 81, U.N. Doc. A/8429 (1971).

186. G.A. Res. 2544, Preamble, 24 U.N. GAOR, Supp. (No. 30) 53, U.N. Doc. A/7630 (1969).

187. G.A. Res. 3057, 28 U.N. GAOR, Supp. (No. 30) 70, U.N. Doc. A/9030 (1973).

188. *Id.,* Preamble.

Discrimination approved by the General Assembly on November 2, 1973, it is emphatically declared that

> discrimination between human beings on the ground of race, colour or ethnic origin is an affront to humanity and shall be condemned as a violation of the principles of the Charter of the United Nations and of the human rights and fundamental freedoms proclaimed in the Universal Declaration of Human Rights, as an obstacle to friendly and peaceful relations among nations and as a factor capable of disturbing peace and security among peoples.[189]

The crystallization of contemporary prescriptions against racial discrimination is further confirmed by the International Court of Justice in the *Namibia* case.[190] One end result of the long and tortuous litigation on Namibia (South West Africa) was the unequivocal condemnation of racial discrimination by the International Court of Justice. In holding South Africa's continued occupation of Namibia to be in violation of the Mandate and the Charter of the United Nations,[191] the Court pronounced, in 1971, in language worth reiterating:

> Under the Charter of the United Nations, the former Mandatory had pledged itself to observe and respect, in a territory having an international status, human rights and fundamental freedoms for all without distinction as to race. To establish instead, and to enforce, distinctions, exclusions, restrictions and limitations exclusively based on grounds of race, colour, descent or national or ethnic origin which constitute a denial of fundamental human rights is a flagrant violation of the purposes and principles of the Charter.[192]

This conclusion had been anticipated by the profound and eloquent dissenting opinion of Judge Tanaka in the *South West Africa Cases (Second Phase)*[193] in 1966, a previous incarnation of the 1971 case. Drawing upon every source of international law authorized in the Statute of the International Court of Justice, Judge Tanaka concluded:

> From what has been said above, we consider that the norm of non-discrimination or non-separation on the basis of race has become a rule of customary international law as is contended by the Appli-

189. *Id.*, Annex at 1.
190. ICJ Advisory Opinion on Namibia, *supra* note 15.
191. *Id.* at 58.
192. *Id.* at 57.
193. South West Africa Cases (Second Phase), [1966] I.C.J. 4, 284 (Tanaka, J., dissenting).

> cants, and as a result, the Respondent's obligations as Mandatory are governed by this legal norm in its capacity as a member of the United Nations. . . .[194]

On the regional level, comparable prescription can be found in the European Convention of Human Rights and the American Convention of Human Rights. The European Convention, in Article 14, provides:

> The enjoyment of the rights and freedoms set forth in this Convention shall be secured without discrimination on any ground such as sex, *race, colour,* language, religion, political or other opinion, *national or social origin, association with a national minority,* property, *birth or other status.*[195]

Similarly, the American Convention, in Article 1(1), obliges the contracting states to

> undertake to respect the rights and freedoms recognized herein and to ensure to all persons subject to their jurisdiction the free and full exercise of those rights and freedoms, without any discrimination for reasons of *race, colour,* sex, language, religion, political or other opinion, *national or social origin,* economic status, *birth,* or any other social condition.[196]

This growing consensus in transnational expectation against racial discrimination has been further fortified by the development of new "general principles of law" as expressed in national constitutions, statutes, and judicial decisions. As Judge Tanaka observed in his condemnation of racial discrimination in the *South West Africa Cases (Second Phase)* in 1966:

> The principle of equality before the law, however, is stipulated in the list of human rights recognized by the municipal system of virtually every State no matter whether the form of government be republican or monarchical and in spite of any differences in the degree of precision of the relevant provisions. This principle has become an integral part of the constitutions of most of the civilized countries in the world. Common-law countries must be included.[197]

"There is a clear trend," in the words of Santa Cruz, "to include constitutional provisions not only guaranteeing equality before the law but spe-

---

194. *Id.* at 293.

195. Convention on Human Rights and Fundamental Freedoms, *adopted* Nov. 4, 1950, Art. 14, 1950 Europ. T.S. No. 5, 213 U.N.T.S 232 (italics added).

196. American Convention on Human Rights, *signed* Nov. 22, 1969, Art. 1(1), OAS Official Records OEA/Ser.K/XVI/1.1, Doc. 65, Rev. 1, Corr. 1 (Jan. 7, 1970), *reprinted in* 9 INT'L LEGAL MATERIALS 101 (italics added).

197. South West Africa Cases (Second Phase), [1966] I.C.J. 4, 299 (Tanaka, J., dissenting).

cifically providing against racial discrimination."[198] He further states:

> Almost all the constitutions or basic laws of States contain provisions relating to human rights and fundamental freedoms, and a great majority of States have enacted legislation or taken other measures aimed at preventing or combating racial discrimination and achieving equal rights for all without distinction. A majority of constitutions promulgated in recent years contain provisions giving effect to the human rights and fundamental freedoms set out in the Universal Declaration on Human Rights.[199]

It may be noted that the national constitutions employ, in addition to the standard terms of race, color, descent, national origin, and ethnic origin, as illustrated in the Convention on the Elimination of Racial Discrimination,[200] a wide range of other words to refer to prohibited grounds of differentiation, such as nationality,[201] racial origin,[202] origin,[203] tribe,[204] tribal affiliation,[205] family,[206] place of birth,[207] social origin and position,[208] place of origin,[209] national and racial appurtenance,[210] social extraction,[211] kinship,[212] and filiation.[213]

---

198. H. SANTA CRUZ, *supra* note 16, at 28.

199. *Id.*

200. *See* notes 112–28 *supra* and accompanying text.

201. *See, e.g.,* CONSTITUTION, Art. 20(2) (Czechoslovakia, 1960), *reprinted in* 2 A. PEASLEE, CONSTITUTIONS OF NATIONS 231 (3d ed. 1966) [hereinafter cited as A. PEASLEE]; CONSTITUTION, Arts. 123 and 135 (1936, amended 1965) (Union of Soviet Socialist Republics), *reprinted in* 2 A. PEASLEE, *supra* at 1005–06.

202. *See, e.g.,* Civil Code of Cambodia, Art. 21, *cited in* H. SANTA CRUZ, *supra* note 16, at 28 n.43.

203. *See, e.g.,* CONSTITUTION, Art. 1 (1960) (Congo [Brazzaville]), *reprinted in* 1 A. PEASLEE, *supra* note 201, at 85–86; CONSTITUTION, Arts. 2 and 3 (1958, amended 1963) (France), *reprinted in* 3 A. PEASLEE, *supra* note 201, at 312–13.

204. *See, e.g.,* CONSTITUTION, Arts. 10(2–3) (1962) (Nepal), *reprinted in* 2 A. PEASLEE, *supra* note 201, at 774.

205. *See, e.g.,* CONSTITUTION, Art. 15 (1964) (Congo [Leopoldville]), *reprinted in* 1 A. PEASLEE, *supra* note 201, at 105.

206. *See, e.g., id.*

207. *See, e.g., id.*

208. *See, e.g.,* CONSTITUTION, Art. 76 (1960) (Mongolian Peoples Republic), *reprinted in* 2 A. PEASLEE, *supra* note 201, at 762.

209. *See, e.g.,* CONSTITUTION, Art 14 (1963) (Kenya), *reprinted in* 1 A. PEASLEE, *supra* note 201, at 264; CONSTITUTION, Art. 11 (1964) (Malawi), *reprinted in* 1 A. PEASLEE, *supra* note 201, at 482; CONSTITUTION, Art. 17 (1962, amended 1963) (Uganda), *reprinted in* 1 A. PEASLEE, *supra* note 201, at 928–29; CONSTITUTION, Art. 14 (1964) (Zambia), *reprinted in* 1 A. PEASLEE, *supra* note 201, at 1031.

210. *See, e.g.,* Electoral Law of 24 Oct. 1956 (Poland), *cited in* H. SANTA CRUZ, *supra* note 16, at 30 n.69.

211. *See, e.g., id.*

212. *See, e.g.,* CONSTITUTION, Art. 11 (1951, amended 1963) (Libya), *reprinted in* 1 A. PEASLEE, *supra* note 201, at 437.

213. *See, e.g.,* CONSTITUTION, Art. 25 (1967) (Ecuador), *reprinted in* 4 A. PEASLEE, *supra*

Special national legislation, in implementation of constitutional protections, has also been enacted to prevent and eradicate racial discrimination. For example, the United States has in recent years effectively resorted to a series of civil rights enactments, notably: the Civil Rights Act of 1964, outlawing racial discrimination in public accommodations and employment and strengthening federal power to enforce school integration;[214] the Voting Rights Act of 1965 banning the use of literacy tests and related devices to deny the right to vote on account of race or color;[215] and the Fair Housing Act of 1968 abolishing discrimination in residential housing.[216] The enactment by the United Kingdom of the Race Relations Act of 1968,[217] in the wake of the growing racial tension exacerbated by the inflow of "colored" immigrants, is another notable example.

The judicial processes of states have also played a role in creating transnational expectations. The tremendous changes propelled by the Supreme Court in the law of the United States have carried a message to many parts of the world. The clear trend of the Court's decisions has been toward the elimination of racial discrimination in all its forms and manifestations.[218] In its epochal decision in *Brown* v. *Board of Educa-*

---

note 201, at 463. Art. 150, para. 1 of the Constitution of Brazil provides: "All are equal before the law, without distinction as to sex, race, occupation, religious creed, or political convictions. *Racial prejudice* shall be punished by law." CONSTITUTION, Art. 150, para. 1 (1967) (Brazil), *reprinted in* 4 A. PEASLEE, *supra* note 201, at 192 (italics added).

214. Civil Rights Act of 1964, 42 U.S.C. §§ 2000a to h-6 (1970), *as amended,* 42 U.S.C. §§ 2000c, c-6(a)(2), c-9, d-5, e to e-17, h-2 (Supp. II, 1972). For its predecessors *see* the Civil Rights Act of 1960, Pub. L. No. 86-449, 74 Stat. 90; Civil Rights Act of 1957, Pub. L. No. 85-315, 71 Stat. 634.

215. Voting Rights Act of 1965, 42 U.S.C. §§ 1973–73p (1970).

216. Fair Housing Act of 1968, 42 U.S.C. §§ 3601–31 (1970).

217. Race Relations Act of 1968, c. 71. The texts of this Act and its predecessor, the Race Relations Act of 1965, c. 71, are reprinted in A. LESTER & G. BINDMAN, RACE AND LAW IN GREAT BRITAIN 419–58 (1972). For a useful legislative background consult H. STREET, G. HOWE, & G. BINDMAN, THE STREET REPORT ON ANTI-DISCRIMINATION LEGISLATION (1967). *See also* I. MACDONALD, RACE RELATIONS AND IMMIGRATION LAW (1969); Hepple, *Race Relations Act 1968,* 32 MODERN L. REV. 181 (1969).

218. *See generally* D. BELL, RACE, RACISM AND AMERICAN LAW (1973) [hereinafter cited as D. BELL]; 2 T. EMERSON, D. HABER, & N. DORSEN, POLITICAL AND CIVIL RIGHTS IN THE UNITED STATES (stu. ed. 1967) [hereinafter cited as T. EMERSON, D. HABER, & N. DORSEN]; 2 N. DORSEN, N. CHACHKIN, & S. LAW, EMERSON, HABER & DORSEN'S POLITICAL AND CIVIL RIGHTS IN THE UNITED STATES (1973 Supp) [hereinafter cited as N. DORSEN, N. CHACHKIN, & S. LAW]; O. FISS, THE CIVIL RIGHTS INJUNCTION (1978); J. GREENBERG, *supra* note 19; M. KONVITZ, BILL OF RIGHTS READER 523–611 (5th ed. rev. 1973); J. NOWAK, R. ROTUNDA, & J. YOUNG, HANDBOOK ON CONSTITUTIONAL LAW 515–89 (1978): 2 THE CONSTITUTION AND THE SUPREME COURT: A DOCUMENTARY HISTORY 201–341 (L. Pollak ed. 1968); E. ROSTOW, THE IDEAL IN LAW 13–73 (1978); L. TRIBE, AMERICAN CONSTITUTIONAL LAW 991–1052 (1978); Gunther, *The Supreme Court, 1971 Term—Foreword: In Search of*

tion,[219] the Court held that "in the field of education the doctrine of 'separate but equal' has no place. Separate educational facilities are inherently unequal."[220] The impact of this decision has been felt not only in the educational sector,[221] but also in many other sectors of community life. In the power sector, earlier decisions invalidating "the White Primary"[222] have in recent years been fortified by a series of civil rights acts,[223] especially the Voting Rights Act of 1965[224] and the Voting Rights Act Amendments of 1970.[225] The net effect of these statutes has been to secure effectively the equal right to vote and to stand for election by outlawing the employment of obstructive devices such as literacy tests or other registration obstacles.[226] Their validity, though challenged, has been upheld by the Court.[227] Building upon a far-reaching doctrine of "state action,"[228] the Court has, further, proceeded to outlaw the separa-

---

Evolving Doctrine on a Changing Court: A Model for a Newer Equal Protection, 86 HARV. L. REV. 1 (1972); Larson, *The New Law of Race Relations,* 1969 WIS. L. REV. 470; Pollak, *Law and Liberty: The American Constitution and the Doctrine That All Men Are Created Equal,* 2 HUMAN RIGHTS 1 (1972); Scherer, *Bakke Revisited,* 7 HUMAN RIGHTS 22 (No. 2, 1978).

219. 347 U.S. 483 (1954).

220. *Id.* at 495.

221. After the first *Brown* decision of May 1954, the Supreme Court further ruled in 1955 that desegregation in public schools be effected with "all deliberate speed." Brown v. Board of Education, 349 U.S. 294, 301 (1955). Subsequently, there have been repeated attempts, through various devices, to avoid, evade, and delay compliance with the Court ruling. For a detailed description *see* A. BLAUSTEIN & C. FERGUSON, DESEGREGATION AND THE LAW (2d ed. 1962). Confronted with a flow of litigation, the Court has generally remained vigilant in barring various devices designed to sidestep the holding and spirit of the *Brown* decisions. *See, e.g.,* Swann v. Charlotte-Mecklenburg Bd. of Educ., 402 U.S. 1 (1971); Green v. County School Bd., 391 U.S. 430 (1968).

222. Terry v. Adams, 345 U.S. 461 (1953); Smith v. Allwright, 321 U.S. 649 (1944).

223. *See* D. BELL, *supra* note 218, at 129–58; 2 T. EMERSON, D. HABER, & N. DORSEN, *supra* note 218, at 1141–1219; 2 N. DORSEN, N. CHACHKIN, & S. LAW, *supra* note 218, at 39–75.

224. Voting Rights Act of 1965, 42 U.S.C. §§ 1973–73p (1970).

225. Voting Rights Act Amendments of 1970, 42 U.S.C. §§ 1973b(a), b(b), aa to bb-4 (1970).

226. *See* notes 223–25 *supra.*

227. Georgia v. United States, 411 U.S. 526 (1973); Oregon v. Mitchell, 400 U.S. 112 (1971); Gaston County v. United States, 395 U.S. 285 (1969); Hadnott v. Amos, 394 U.S. 358 (1969); Katzenbach v. Morgan, 384 U.S. 641 (1966); South Carolina v. Katzenbach, 383 U.S. 601 (1966). *See also* UNITED STATES COMM'N ON CIVIL RIGHTS, POLITICAL PARTICIPATION (1968); Avins, *Literacy Tests and the Fifteenth Amendment: The Original Understanding,* 12 SO. TEX. L.J. 24 (1970); Christopher, *The Constitutionality of the Voting Rights Act of 1965,* 18 STAN. L. REV. 1 (1965); Cox, *Constitutionality of the Proposed Voting Rights Act of 1965,* 3 HOUSTON L. REV. 1 (1965); Rice, *Voting Rights Act of 1965: Some Dissenting Observations,* 15 KAN. L. REV. 159 (1966); Note, *1965 Voting Rights Act: An Evaluation,* 3 HARV. CIV. RIGHTS-CIV. LIB. L. REV. 357 (1968).

228. *See* 2 T. EMERSON, D. HABER, & N. DORSEN, *supra* note 218, at 1645–73; 2 N.

tion of public facilities and accommodations (*e.g.*, buses, parks, beaches and bathhouses, golf courses, auditoriums, courtroom seating, hotels, restaurants, and other places of entertainment),[229] public housing,[230] employment,[231] and other areas of public concern.[232] In 1967, the Court, in holding unconstitutional a Virginia statute barring interracial marriages in *Loving* v. *Virginia*,[233] pronounced: "The clear and central purpose of the Fourteenth Amendment was to eliminate all official state sources of invidious racial discrimination in the States."[234] In *Jones* v. *Alfred H. Mayer Co.*,[235] the Court held that all racial discrimination, private as well as public, in the sale or rental of property is outlawed by the Civil Rights Act of 1866, a statute enacted in legitimate exercise of the congressional power to enforce the Thirteenth Amendment.[236] "It

---

DORSEN, N. CHACHKIN, & S. LAW, *supra* note 218, at 269–87. *See also* EDWARD S. CORWIN, THE CONSTITUTION AND WHAT IT MEANS TODAY 416–18 (13th rev. ed. H. Chase & C. Ducat eds. 1973); Avins, *Toward Freedom of Choice in Places of Public and Private Accommodation,* 48 NEB. L. REV. 21 (1968); Avins, *What Is a Place of "Public" Accommodation?* 52 MARQ. L. REV. 1 (1968).

229. *See, e.g.,* Daniel v. Paul, 395 U.S. 298 (1968) (snack bars); Heart of Atlanta Motel v. United States, 379 U.S. 241 (1964) (motels and other places of public accommodation); Watson v. Memphis, 373 U.S. 526 (1963) (parks and other recreational facilities); Wright v. Georgia, 373 U.S. 284 (1963) (parks); Gayle v. Browder, 352 U.S. 903 (1956) (buses); Holmes v. City of Atlanta, 350 U.S. 879 (1955) (golf courses); Mayor & City Council of Baltimore v. Dawson, 350 U.S. 877 (1955) (beaches).

230. *Cf.* D. BELL, *supra* note 218, at 607–710; 2 T. EMERSON, D. HABER, & N. DORSEN, *supra* note 218, at 1579–1643; 2 N. DORSEN, N. CHACHKIN, & S. LAW, *supra* note 218, at 222–68.

231. *Cf.* D. BELL, *supra* note 218, at 711–856; 2 T. EMERSON, D. HABER, & N. DORSEN, *supra* note 218, at 1467–1567; 2 N. DORSEN, N. CHACHKIN, & S. LAW, *supra* note 218, at 175–221.

232. An example is discrimination in health and welfare services. *See* 2 T. EMERSON, D. HABER, & N. DORSEN, *supra* note 218, at 1716–46; 2 N. DORSEN, N. CHACHKIN, & S. LAW, *supra* note 218, at 300–46.

233. 388 U.S. 1 (1967).

234. *Id.* at 10.

235. 392 U.S. 409 (1968).

236. *Id.* at 443–44. In the words of Justice Stewart, who delivered the opinion of the Court:

> Negro citizens, North and South, who saw in the Thirteenth Amendment a promise of freedom—freedom to "go and come at pleasure" and to "buy and sell when they please"—would be left with "a mere paper guarantee" if Congress were powerless to assure that a dollar in the hands of a Negro will purchase the same thing as a dollar in the hands of a white man. At the very least, the freedom that Congress is empowered to secure under the Thirteenth Amendment includes the freedom to buy whatever a white man can buy, the right to live wherever a white man can live. If Congress cannot say that being a free man means at least this much, then the Thirteenth Amendment made a promise the Nation cannot keep.

Id. at 443 (footnotes omitted).

may well be," in the words of Larson, "that this decision, by infusing new vitality both into the early Reconstruction statutes and into the thirteenth amendment, will prove to be the most far-reaching race relations case since the Civil War."[237] Larson adds:

> *Jones,* at one strike, supplied a broad fair housing law, and quite possibly an equally broad law banning discrimination in employment, professional services, private education, retail establishments, and service businesses of all sorts, by revitalizing the Reconstruction statutes on equal property and contract rights, as well as the thirteenth amendment abolishing slavery.[238]

In establishing structures and procedures for the application of the newly emerged basic prescription against racial discrimination, the general community has moved significantly toward more highly specialized and increasingly centralized structures and procedures. The most general goal sought in application is of course that of minimizing to the utmost degree possible the occurrence of racial discrimination. Yet, it is widely recognized that, because of the complexity residing in both the practices of racial discrimination and their causes, the broad goal of minimization must be made more specific in terms of a whole series of interrelated subgoals.[239] These subgoals may be summarized as follows: (1) *prevention,* from a long-range perspective, of the occurrence of racial discrimination by fostering appropriate predispositions in people; (2) *deterrence,* at the incipient stage, of attempts to engage in racial discrimination; (3) *restoration,* with promptness, of exacerbated situations when disruption has been caused by discriminatory acts; (4) *rehabilitation* of victims of discriminatory situations by affording appropriate remedies and compensations; (5) *reconstruction,* in a concerted long-term effort, of

---

237. Larson, *The New Law of Race Relations,* 1969 Wis. L. Rev. 470, 486.

238. *Id.* at 471. The development in the national law of the United States, entirely paralleling and supporting the Convention on Racial Discrimination, is comprehensively traced and analyzed by Professor Nathaniel Nathanson. *See* Nathanson, *International Convention on the Elimination of All Forms of Racial Discrimination: The Convention Obligations Compared with the Constitutional and Statutory Law of the United States* (paper presented to the Panel on Human Rights Law and International Implementation, American Society of International Law, February 1974). A comprehensive study would undoubtedly demonstrate the comparable trend of development in differing national communities. *Cf.* H. Santa Cruz, *supra* note 16, at 26–42; Batshaw, *A Landmark Decision against Discrimination in Canada,* 4 Human Rights J. 207 (1971); Keith, *Race Relations and the Law in New Zealand,* 6 Human Rights J. 329 (1973); Kinsella, *The Canadian Model for the Protection from Discrimination,* 4 Human Rights J. 270 (1971); Smith, *Prevention of Discrimination under Kenya Law,* 20 Int'l & Comp. L.Q. 136 (1971).

239. *Cf.* Reisman, *supra* note 173, at 51–54; Schacter, *How Effective Are Measures against Racial Discrimination,* 4 Human Rights J. 293 (1971).

the whole social environment, including the special measures necessary to ameliorate accumulated grievances and to promote the self-development of all community members; and (6) *correction* of offenders by invoking the community process of criminal sanction.[240]

Toward these ends, the Convention on the Elimination of Racial Discrimination, in recognition of the highly decentralized structure of world effective power, thrusts upon individual states the primary responsibility for achieving the major goal of minimization of racial discrimination by relating concrete undertakings to these subgoals. To secure the long-term goal of prevention, the Convention, in Article 7, stipulates:

> States Parties undertake to adopt immediate and effective measures, particularly in the fields of teaching, education, culture and information, with a view to combating prejudices which lead to racial discrimination and to promoting understanding, tolerance and friendship among nations and racial or ethnical groups, as well as to propagating the purposes and principles of the Charter of the United Nations, the Universal Declaration of Human Rights, the United Nations Declaration on the Elimination of All Forms of Racial Discrimination, and this Convention.[241]

To deter the consummation of immediately threatened discriminatory acts, the Convention, in Article 4, bans not only racist propaganda and organizations but also incitement to racial discrimination.[242] To restore the exacerbated situations caused by past discriminations, the Convention, in Article 6, requires contracting states to "assure to everyone within their jurisdiction effective protection and remedies, through the competent national tribunals and other State institutions."[243] For the purpose of rehabilitation, the Convention, again in Article 6, requires contracting states to afford victims "just and adequate reparation or satisfaction for any damage suffered. . . ."[244] For measures directed toward long-range reconstruction, the Convention stresses the importance of undertaking special programs to assist traditionally deprived groups,[245] a move vital to the attainment of genuinely effective equality

240. For detailed formulation and application of these goals, see R. Arens & H. Lasswell, In Defense of Public Order: The Emerging Field of Sanction Law 199–203 (1961); M. McDougal & F. Feliciano, Law and Minimum World Public Order 261–383 (1961).

241. Convention on the Elimination of All Forms of Racial Discrimination, *supra* note 90, Art. 7, 660 U.N.T.S. at 222.

242. *Id.*, Art. 4, 660 U.N.T.S. at 218–20.

243. *Id.*, Art. 6, 660 U.N.T.S. at 222.

244. *Id.*

245. *Id.*, Arts. 1(4) and 2(2), 660 U.N.T.S. at 216, 218.

of opportunity, and urges a continuing effort of enlightenment to change people's predispositions,[246] a task essential to the subgoal of reconstruction as well as to that of broader prevention.[247] The Convention, in Article 2(1)(e), further states: "Each State Party undertakes to encourage, where appropriate, integrationist multi-racial organizations and movements and other means of eliminating barriers between races, and to discourage anything which tends to strengthen racial division."[248] And finally, the Convention, in seeking the subgoal of correction, obliges contracting states to make certain acts criminal offenses, including dissemination of racist ideas, incitement to racial discrimination, acts of racial violence, rendering assistance to racist activities, and participation in racist organizations and activities.[249]

To supervise the degree of compliance by contracting states, the Convention on Racial Discrimination established the Committee on the Elimination of Racial Discrimination, consisting of "eighteen experts of high moral standing and acknowledged impartiality" serving "in their personal capacity."[250] The competence conferred upon the Committee is fourfold:

1. To appraise, under Article 9, reports on "the legislative, judicial, administrative or other measures" of compliance submitted by contracting states and thus to "make suggestions and general recommendations";[251]
2. To act, pursuant to Articles 11 and 13, on complaints brought by one State Party against another for failing to give effect to the provisions of the Convention;[252]
3. To deal with petitions by individuals under the conditions specified in Article 14;[253]
4. To cooperate, pursuant to Article 15, with competent United Nations bodies regarding petitions from the inhabitants of trust, non-self-governing, and other dependent territories.[254]

The reporting system is a feature characteristic of most of the transna-

---

246. *Id.*, Art. 7, 660 U.N.T.S. at 222.

247. Oriented to the long term, the subgoals of reconstruction and prevention may in many ways be overlapping; they are integrative rather than mutually exclusive.

248. Convention on the Elimination of All Forms of Racial Discrimination, *supra* note 90, Art. 2(1)(e), 660 U.N.T.S. at 218.

249. *Id.*, Arts. 4(a-b), 660 U.N.T.S. at 220.

250. *Id.*, Art. 8(1), 660 U.N.T.S. at 224.

251. *Id.*, Art. 9, 660 U.N.T.S. at 224-26.

252. *Id.*, Arts. 11-13, 660 U.N.T.S. at 226-30.

253. *Id.*, Art. 14, 660 U.N.T.S. at 230-32.

254. *Id.*, Art. 15, 660 U.N.T.S. at 232-34.

tional human rights instruments.[255] Under Article 9 of the Convention, each state party is required, except initially, to submit a biannual report, and the Committee may request further information if necessary.[256] The Committee's annual report to the General Assembly not only relays information about its activities, but may also contain both general and specific recommendations.[257] The importance of the reporting system has been underscored by Reisman in these words:

> This Committee function of appraisal and recommendation should not be underestimated. If it is carried forward impartially, a total public picture of trends in regard to the elimination of racial discrimination will be available. Trouble spots will be highlighted and publicized and priorities and tactics for action can be determined by official and private international organizations operating beyond the formal confines of the Committee. The threat of international exposure may stimulate some states to take more active measures to combat racial discrimination.[258]

Under the interstate complaint procedure provided in Articles 11 through 13, any state party may bring an alleged violation of the Convention by another party to the attention of the Committee.[259] The complaint ("communication") will be transmitted to the state party concerned, which then has three months to "submit to the Committee written explanations or statements clarifying the matter."[260] "If the matter is not adjusted to the satisfaction of both parties," either party has the right to "refer the matter again to the Committee";[261] the Committee is authorized to deal with the matter upon ascertaining that the requirements of exhaustion of "domestic remedies" are met.[262] "After the Committee has

---

255. *See* Das, *Measures of Implementation of the International Convention on the Elimination of All Forms of Racial Discrimination with Special Reference to the Provisions concerning Reports from States Parties to the Convention,* 4 HUMAN RIGHTS J. 213 (1971); Schwelb, *supra* note 91, at 1034–37. *Cf.* C. JENCKS, THE INTERNATIONAL PROTECTION OF TRADE UNION FREEDOM (1957); E. LANDY, THE EFFECTIVENESS OF INTERNATIONAL SUPERVISION: THREE DECADES OF I.L.O. EXPERIENCE (1966); Schwelb, *Civil and Political Rights: The International Measures of Implementation,* 62 AM. J. INT'L L. 827 (1968); Schwelb, *Some Aspects of the Measures of Implementation of the International Covenant on Economic, Social and Cultural Rights,* 1 HUMAN RIGHTS J. 375 (1968).

256. Convention on the Elimination of All Forms of Racial Discrimination, *supra* note 90, Art. 9(1), 660 U.N.T.S. at 224–26.

257. *Id.,* Art. 9(2), 660 U.N.T.S. at 226.

258. Reisman, *supra* note 173, at 59.

259. Convention on the Elimination of All Forms of Racial Discrimination, *supra* note 90, Arts. 11–13, 660 U.N.T.S. at 226–30.

260. *Id.,* Art. 11(1), 660 U.N.T.S. at 226.

261. *Id.,* Art. 11(2).

262. *Id.,* Art. 11(3). These requirements, as in general international law, would be dispensed with "where the application of the remedies is unreasonably prolonged." *Id.*

obtained and collated all the information it deems necessary," according to Article 12(1)(a), it is incumbent upon the Committee chairman to appoint an ad hoc conciliation commission, "comprising five persons who may or may not be members of the Committee"[263] but who are in principle "appointed with the unanimous consent of the parties to the dispute."[264] The Commission is to make available its "good offices" to the disputing parties in search of "an amicable solution" on the basis of "respect" for the Convention.[265] Failing an agreed settlement, the Commission is required to "prepare and submit to the Chairman of the Committee a report embodying its findings on all questions of fact relevant to the issue between the parties and containing such recommendations as it may think proper for the amicable solution of the dispute."[266] This report, together with the "declarations of the States Parties concerned"[267] signifying their acceptance or rejection of the report's recommendations, is to be made available to all the other contracting states after a specified period.[268]

The right of individual petition is made subject to the option of states under the Convention. "A State Party may," under Article 14(1), "at any time declare that it recognizes the competence of the Committee to receive and consider communications from individuals or groups of individuals within its jurisdiction claiming to be victims of a violation by that State Party of any of the rights set forth in this Convention."[269] The same provision, however, immediately adds: "No communication shall be received by the Committee if it concerns a State Party which has not made such a declaration."[270] Furthermore, the competence of the Committee regarding individual petitions is operative "only when at least ten States Parties" have made the requisite declarations of acceptance.[271] The Committee, guided by a set of somewhat complicated pro-

---

263. *Id.,* Art. 12(1)(a), 660 U.N.T.S. at 228.

264. *Id.* According to Art. 12(1)(b):

> If the States Parties to the dispute fail to reach agreement within three months on all or part of the composition of the Commission, the members of the Commission not agreed upon by the States Parties to the dispute shall be elected by secret ballot by a two-thirds majority vote of the Committee from among its own members.

Id., Art. 12(1)(b).

265. *Id.,* Art. 12(1)(a). Note the emphasis on "respect" for the Convention.

266. *Id.,* Art. 13(1), 660 U.N.T.S. at 230. For a technical interpretation of this provision *see* Schwelb, *supra* note 91, at 1040–41.

267. Convention on the Elimination of All Forms of Racial Discrimination, *supra* note 90, Art. 13(3), 660 U.N.T.S. at 230.

268. *Id.*

269. *Id.,* Art. 14(1).

270. *Id.*

271. *Id.,* Art. 14(9), 660 U.N.T.S. at 232.

cedures for handling such petitions,[272] especially the exhaustion of domestic remedies,[273] may engage in fact-finding and formulate "its suggestions and recommendations."[274] The Committee is required, under Article 14(8), to "include in its annual report a summary of such communications and, where appropriate, a summary of the explanations and statements of the States Parties concerned and of its own suggestions and recommendations."[275] To accord individual victims competence to invoke the prescriptions of the Convention before the Committee is indeed an immensely significant step, though achievement of the requisite number of acceptances (at least ten) seems to be delayed.[276]

Unlike Article 14(1) in the restriction it imposes on individual petitions,[277] Article 15(2)(a) authorizes the Committee to

> receive copies of the petitions from, and submit expressions of opinion and recommendations on these petitions to, the bodies of the United Nations which deal with matters directly related to the principles and objectives of this Convention in their consideration of petitions from the inhabitants of Trust and Non-Self-Governing Territories and all other territories to which General Assembly resolution 1514(XV) applies, relating to matters covered by this Convention which are before these bodies.[278]

This sharp contrast has provoked a commentator to call it another manifestation of "the UN's double standard on human rights complaints."[279]

During the first four years (1970–73) of its operation, the Committee on the Elimination of Racial Discrimination concerned itself mainly with

---

272. *Id.*, Art. 14(2–6), 660 U.N.T.S. at 230–32.

273. *Id.*, Art. 14(7)(a), 660 U.N.T.S. at 232.

274. *Id.*, Art. 14(7)(b).

275. *Id.*, Art. 14(8).

276. As of Aug. 11, 1978, only seven states—Costa Rica, Ecuador, Italy, the Netherlands, Norway, Sweden, and Uruguay—had made the required declaration. REPORT OF THE COMMITTEE ON THE ELIMINATION OF RACIAL DISCRIMINATION, 33 U.N. GAOR, Supp. (No.18) 1, 96–98, U.N. Doc. A/33/18 (1978) [hereinafter cited as 1978 REPORT].

277. *See* text accompanying note 269 *supra*.

278. Convention on the Elimination of All Forms of Racial Discrimination, Art. 15(2)(a), *supra* note 90, 660 U.N.T.S. at 232–34.

279. J. CAREY, UN PROTECTION OF CIVIL AND POLITICAL RIGHTS 151 (1970). Similarly, Mr. MacDonald of Canada, shortly after the Convention was approved by the Third Committee of the Assembly, characterized the incorporation of Art. 15 as "bad politics and worse law." 20 U.N. GAOR, 3D COMM. 504 (1965). In the words of one commentator: "It makes the Committee on the Elimination of Racial Discrimination a kind of auxiliary organ to the organs dealing with the implementation of the right to self-determination, at the present the Trusteeship Council and the Committee of Twenty-four." Schwelb, *The Implementation of the International Convention on the Elimination of All Forms of Racial Discrimination* in INTERNATIONAL LAW ASS'N, REPORT OF THE FIFTY-FIFTH CONFERENCE 605 (1974).

appraising reports submitted by the contracting states and making general recommendations,[280] and considering, pursuant to Article 15, petitions submitted by the inhabitants of various dependent territories,[281] in addition to making necessary organizational arrangements, notably its own rules of procedure.[282] The Committee was not seized of any formal interstate complaint under Article 11.[283] The procedure for individual petitions contemplated in Article 14 is yet to be set in operation, because only seven of the one hundred state parties have made the requisite declaration.[284]

---

280. The general recommendations are presented in the Committee's annual reports. *See 1973 Report,* 28 U.N. GAOR, Supp. (No. 18) 21–78, 103–07, 112–19, U.N. Doc. A/9018 (1973) [hereinafter cited as *1973 Report*]; *1972 Report,* 27 U.N. GAOR, Supp. (No. 18) 12–26, 37–39, 57–67, U.N. Doc. A/8718 (1972) [hereinafter cited as *1972 Report*]; *1971 Report,* 26 U.N. GAOR, Supp. (No. 18) 5–25, 31–34, U.N. Doc. A/8418 (1971) [hereinafter cited as *1971 Report*]; *1970 Report,* 25 U.N. GAOR, Supp. (No. 27) 9–11, 32–36, U.N. Doc. A/8027 (1970) [hereinafter cited as *1970 Report*].

281. *See 1973 Report, supra* note 280, at 79–98, 106–07, 120–22; *1972 Report, supra* note 280, at 27–29, 40–53, 68–71; *1971 Report, supra* note 280, at 26–28, 31–47, 58–61; *1970 Report, supra* note 280, at 11–14, 37–39.

282. Pursuant to Art. 10(1) of the Convention on the Elimination of All Forms of Racial Discrimination, *supra* note 90, 660 U.N.T.S. at 226, the Committee adopted its Provisional Rules of Procedure (seventy-eight rules in total) in 1970 at its first and second sessions. For its text see *1970 Report, supra* note 280, at 17–31. Prior to the adoption of the Committee's provisional Rules of Procedures, a comprehensive, detailed draft had been proposed in a law journal. *See* Newman, *The New International Tribunal,* 56 CALIF. L. REV. 1559 (1968).

For the subsequent adoption of the amendments to the Committee's Provisional Rules of Procedure *see 1971 Report, supra* note 280, at 4, 33 (Rule 35); *1972 Report, supra* note 280, at 8–11, 37 (Rules 64A and 66A); *1973 Report, supra* note 280, at 6–8, 103 (Rules 13 and 56).

283. Nevertheless, allegations arising from the reports submitted to the Committee by Panama about discrimination in the Panama Canal Zone and by Syria about discrimination in the Golan Heights took on the character, in a manner of speaking, of interstate complaints. *See 1971 Report, supra* note 280, at 13–25, 31, 34; *1973 Report, supra* note 280, at 30–31, 51–52, 104–05. *See also* L. SOHN & T. BUERGENTHAL, *supra* note 67, at 866–98; Schwelb, *supra* note 279, at 593–605.

284. 1978 REPORT, *supra* note 276, at 1, 96–98.

For more recent developments, *see* the documents cited in chapter 4 *supra,* at note 732. *See also* Buergenthal, *Implementing the UN Racial Convention,* 12 TEXAS INT'L L.J. 187 (1977); *United Nations Decade for Action to Combat Racism and Racial Discrimination,* 10 OBJECTIVE: JUSTICE 1 (No. 1, 1978).

10. THE OUTLAWING OF SEX-BASED DISCRIMINATION

During the United Nations commemoration of 1975 as "International Women's Year,"[1] in a concerted effort to "promote equality between men and women"[2] and to "ensure the full integration of women in the total development effort,"[3] the concern of the larger global community for outlawing sex-based discrimination was articulated with increased vigor. This concern both builds upon and expresses a more general norm of nondiscrimination which seeks to ban all generic differentiations among people in access to value shaping and sharing for reasons irrelevant to individual capabilities and contribution.[4] The particular norm against sex-based discrimination finds expression in many authoritative communications, at both international and national levels, and is rapidly being defined in a way to condemn all the great historic deprivations imposed upon women as a group.[5]

FACTUAL BACKGROUND

The deprivations with which we are here concerned are the discriminations based upon sex, which commonly accord women less favorable treatment than men.[6] Practices, both governmental and private, that

---

In slightly different form this chapter first appeared as *Human Rights for Women and World Public Order: The Outlawing of Sex-Based Discrimination,* 69 AM. J. INT'L L. 497 (1975).

1. G.A. Res. 3275, 29 U.N. GAOR, Supp. (No. 31) 93, U.N. Doc. A/9631 (1974); G.A. Res. 3010, 27 U.N. GAOR, Supp. (No. 30) 66, U.N. Doc. A/8730 (1972). *See also* G.A. Res. 3276, 29 U.N. GAOR, Supp. (No. 31) 93, U.N. Doc. A/9631 (1974); G.A. Res. 3277, *id.* at 94.

2. G.A. Res. 3275, *supra* note 1, at 93.

3. *Id.*

4. For detailed elaboration, *see* chapters 6–9 *supra* and chapters 11–15 *infra.*

5. *See* authorities cited in notes 96–252 *infra* and accompanying text.

6. The literature on women's rights has mushroomed in recent years. The United Nations is an important source supplying rich materials on the changing status of women around the world, as will become evident in the documentation to follow.

deny women the protection and fulfillment of human rights on an equal footing with men are "by no means relics of the past, mere historical curiosities," but continue to be "a fact of life" in the differing com-

---

On legal treatment of sex-based discriminations, with primary focus on the United States, *see generally* B. BABCOCK, A. FREEMAN, E. NORTON, & S. ROSS, SEX DISCRIMINATION AND THE LAW: CAUSES AND REMEDIES (1975); K. DAVIDSON, R. GINSBURG, & H. KAY, TEXT, CASES AND MATERIALS ON SEX-BASED DISCRIMINATIONS (1974); L. KANOWITZ, WOMEN AND THE LAW: THE UNFINISHED REVOLUTION (1969); L. KANOWITZ, SEX ROLES IN LAW AND SOCIETY: CASES AND MATERIALS (1973); S. ROSS, THE RIGHTS OF WOMEN: THE BASIC ACLU GUIDE TO A WOMAN'S RIGHTS (1973); Brown, Emerson, Falk, & Freedman, *The Equal Rights Amendment: A Constitutional Basis for Equal Rights for Women*, 80 YALE L.J. 872 (1971); Murray, *The Rights of Woman, in* THE RIGHTS OF AMERICANS 521–45 (N. Dorsen ed. 1971); Siedenberg, *The Submissive Majority: Modern Trends in the Law Concerning Women's Rights,* 55 CORNELL L. REV. 262 (1970).

For treatment from a wider comparative perspective, *see Symposium—The Status of Women,* 20 AM. J. COMP. L. 585 (1972), which deals with women in Great Britain, Sweden, Norway, France, the Soviet Union, Israel, and Senegal. A concise but useful article appears in the latest edition of Encyclopaedia Britannica: Klein, *Status of Women,* 19 ENCYC. BRITANNICA 906 (15th ed. 1974).

On the contemporary Women's Liberation Movement, see the following classic works: S. DE BEAUVOIR, THE SECOND SEX (H. Parshley trans. & ed. Bantam ed. 1961); B. FRIEDAN, THE FEMININE MYSTIQUE (1963); K. MILLETT, SEXUAL POLITICS (Avon ed. 1971). *See also* FEMINISM: THE ESSENTIAL HISTORICAL WRITINGS (M. Schneir ed. 1972); LIBERATION NOW! WRITINGS FROM THE WOMEN'S LIBERATION MOVEMENT (Laurel ed. 1971); S. ROWBOTHAM, WOMEN, RESISTANCE, AND REVOLUTION (1972); SISTERHOOD IS POWERFUL (R. Morgan ed. 1970); VOICES OF THE NEW FEMINISM (M. Thompson ed. 1970); Freeman, *The New Feminism,* THE NATION, Mar. 9, 1974, at 297-302; *Gloria Steinem,* NEWSWEEK, Aug. 16, 1971, at 51-55; *The New Woman, 1972,* TIME, Mar. 20, 1972, at 25-34. For a most recent appraisal, *see* the symposium in commemoration of International Women's Year, in SATURDAY REV., June 14, 1975.

For works on women from a socialist perspective, *see* F. ENGELS, THE ORIGIN OF THE FAMILY, PRIVATE PROPERTY AND THE STATE (1942); THE WOMAN QUESTION: SELECTIONS FROM THE WRITINGS OF KARL MARX, FREDERICK ENGELS, V. I. LENIN, JOSEPH STALIN (1951); A. BEBEL, WOMAN UNDER SOCIALISM (D. de Leon trans. Schocken ed. 1971).

For further general background readings on women, useful citations include J. BARDWICK, PSYCHOLOGY OF WOMEN: A STUDY OF BIO-CULTURAL CONFLICTS (1971); W. CHAFE, THE AMERICAN WOMAN: HER CHANGING SOCIAL, ECONOMIC, AND POLITICAL ROLES, 1920–1970 (1972); G. GREER, FEMALE EUNUCH (1970); E. JANEWAY, MAN'S WORLD, WOMAN'S PLACE: A STUDY IN SOCIAL MYTHOLOGY (1971); T. LANG, THE DIFFERENCE BETWEEN A MAN AND A WOMAN (1971); E. LEWIS, DEVELOPING WOMAN'S POTENTIAL (1968); M. MEAD, MALE AND FEMALE (Dell ed. 1949); M. MEAD, SEX AND TEMPERAMENT IN THREE PRIMITIVE SOCIETIES (1935); E. MORGAN, THE DESCENT OF WOMAN (1972); A. MYRDAL & V. KLEIN, WOMEN'S TWO ROLES: HOME AND WORK (1968); THE OTHER HALF: ROADS TO WOMEN'S EQUALITY (C. Epstein & W. Goode eds. 1971); THE POTENTIAL OF WOMAN (S. Farber & R. Wilson eds. 1963); B. ROSZAK & T. ROSZAK, MASCULINE/FEMININE (1969); C. SAFILIOS-ROTHSCHILD, TOWARD A SOCIOLOGY OF WOMEN (1972); SEX ROLES IN CHANGING SOCIETY (G. Seward & R. Williamson eds. 1970); M. TUMIN, PATTERNS OF SOCIETY 196-214 (1973); A. WATTS, NATURE, MAN AND WOMAN (Vintage ed. 1970); WOMEN OF ALL NATIONS: A RECORD OF THEIR CHARACTERISTICS, HABITS, MANNER, CUSTOMS AND INFLUENCE (T.

munities around the world.[7] Sex-based discrimination derives in large part from the "arbitrary" division of male and female roles, as culturally defined, that has always existed, in the words of Margaret Mead, "in every society of which we have any knowledge."[8] While the concept of maleness or femaleness differs among cultures, and the specific tasks and responsibilities expected of the two sexes may vary from one society to another, the existence and perpetuation of distinct sex roles, as dictated mostly by men, have characteristically resulted in male-dominated societies in which women are regarded as "the subordinate sex,"[9] "the second sex,"[10] "the weaker sex,"[11] or "the Other."[12] In its most extreme manifestation this deprivation characterizes and treats women as a form of wealth or "property," that is, as instruments of production or enjoyment. Paradoxically, the ongoing deprivations caused by sexual dif-

---

Joyce ed. 1912); THE WOMAN IN AMERICA (R. Lifton ed. 1965); WOMEN IN THE MODERN WORLD (R. Patai ed. 1967); WOMEN OF TROPICAL AFRICA (D. Paulme ed., H. Wright transl. 1963); WOMEN'S ROLE IN CONTEMPORARY SOCIETY: THE REPORT OF THE NEW YORK CITY COMMISSION ON HUMAN RIGHTS (1972); WOMEN, CULTURE, AND SOCIETY (M. Rosaldo & L. Lamphere eds. 1974); *Women around the World,* 375 ANNALS 1 (1968).

A comprehensive, up-to-date bibliography is S. JACOBS, WOMEN IN PERSPECTIVE: A GUIDE FOR CROSS-CULTURAL STUDIES (1974). *See also* A. KRICHMAR, THE WOMEN'S RIGHTS MOVEMENT IN THE UNITED STATES, 1848–1970: A BIBLIOGRAPHY AND SOURCEBOOK (1972).

7. L. KANOWITZ, WOMEN AND THE LAW: THE UNFINISHED REVOLUTION 1 (1969).

8. M. MEAD, MALE AND FEMALE, *supra* note 6, at 39.

In the words of Ralph Linton:

> All societies prescribe different attitudes and activities to men and to women. Most of them try to rationalize these prescriptions in terms of the physiological differences between the sexes or their different roles in reproduction. However, a comparative study of the statuses ascribed to women and men in different cultures seems to show that while such factors may have served as a starting point for the development of a division the actual ascriptions are almost entirely determined by culture.

R. LINTON, THE STUDY OF MAN 116 (1936).

9. V. BULLOUGH, THE SUBORDINATE SEX (Penguin ed. 1974). *But see* E. VILAR, THE MANIPULATED MAN (1972).

10. S. DE BEAUVOIR, *supra* note 6. *But see* E. DAVIS, THE FIRST SEX (1971).

11. UNITED NATIONS, EQUAL RIGHTS FOR WOMEN—A CALL FOR ACTION 6 (OPI/494, 1973) [hereinafter cited as EQUAL RIGHTS FOR WOMEN].

12. In the words of Simone de Beauvoir:

> Thus humanity is male and man defines woman not in herself but as relative to him; she is not regarded as an autonomous being. . . . And she is simply what man decrees; thus she is called "the sex," by which is meant that she appears essentially to the male as a sexual being. For him she is sex—absolute sex, no less. She is defined and differentiated with reference to man and not he with reference to her; she is the incidental, the inessential as opposed to the essential. He is the Subject, he is the Absolute—she is the Other.

S. DE BEAUVOIR, *supra* note 6, at xvi.

ferentiation have largely been accepted, consciously or unconsciously, as an inescapable fact of life by the deprivees themselves.

Despite marked improvement in status in recent decades, women around the globe still face "deep and pervasive,"[13] as well as on occasion "more subtle, discrimination."[14] The deprivations imposed on the ground of sex, both historical and continuing, are in many ways comparable to, though occasionally more pronounced than, those of racial discrimination.[15] Many severe deprivations are unique to women, especially to married women.[16]

The deprivations women suffer commence with the "second-rung" respect they receive in practically every human society. Widely viewed as "natural appendages of men,"[17] "tails wagged by the male ego,"[18] many women are conditioned early in life to look upon themselves as "the Other," whose fulfillment lies in "assisting" and "serving" men.[19] Thus perceived, women are brought up to be "contented," with a belief in "their inferiority of endowment," in a special "woman's place" ascribed at birth,[20] and are not encouraged in extravagant demands for equality and other freedoms. In the words of a recent UN study:

> Differences in sex roles begin at the moment of birth when the child is first identified as a male or female. From that moment on the child is expected to behave in accordance with the roles customarily

---

13. Brown, Emerson, Falk, & Freedman, *supra* note 6, at 872.

14. Frontiero v. Richardson, 411 U.S. 677, 686 (1973).

15. 2 G. Myrdal, An American Dilemma 1073–78 (First McGraw-Hill Paperback ed. 1964). *See also* S. Firestone, The Dialectic of Sex 119–41 (1970); C. Herton, Sex and Racism in America (1966); A. Montagu, Man's Most Dangerous Myth: The Fallacy of Race 186–89 (5th ed. 1974); Crozier, *Constitutionality of Discrimination Based on Sex,* 15 B.U.L. Rev. 723, 727–28 (1935); Hacker, *Women as a Minority Group,* 30 Social Forces 60 (1951), *reprinted in* L. Kanowitz, Sex Roles in Law and Society 1–8 (1973); Murray & Eastwood, *Jane Crow and the Law: Sex Discrimination and Title VII,* 34 Geo. Wash. L. Rev. 232, 233–35 (1965).

16. In some respects unmarried mothers suffer additional deprivations. *See* United Nations, The Status of the Unmarried Mother: Law and Practice (report of the secretary-general), U.N. Doc. E/CN.6/540/Rev. 1 (1971); *Legal and Social Status of the Unmarried Mother: Report of the Secretary-General,* U.N. Doc. E/CN.6/562 (1971).

17. H. Hays, The Dangerous Sex 11 (1964).

18. *Id.*

19. V. Bullough, *supra* note 9, at 336. Betty Friedan asserts that "the core of the problem for women today is not sexual but a problem of identity—a stunting or evasion of growth that is perpetuated by the feminine mystique." B. Friedan, *supra* note 6, at 69.

20. As in the case of the Negro, women themselves have often been brought to believe in their inferiority of endowment. As the Negro was awarded his "place" in society, so there was a "woman's place." In both cases the rationalization was strongly believed that men, in confining them to this place, did not act against the true interest of the subordinate groups. The myth of the "contented women" who did not want to have

> assigned to his or her sex. By the time the girl becomes an adult she finds that her world has been slowly but effectively restricted by the rules and expectation of others. She learns that being born female sets her apart from men and limits her rights in law and in practice.[21]

Hence, the generic status ascribed to women is sometimes compared to that of a caste.[22]

In the power process, the participation of women lags far behind that of men. In some communities women are still denied the right to vote and to hold public offices.[23] Where the right of voting and officeholding is formally recognized, there is in fact a conspicuous underrepresentation of women at all levels of government, especially in higher decision-making positions.[24] "After half a century of women's suffrage," in the words of Klein, "the number of women in higher positions of political power and influence is still small enough for them to be known by name."[25] When women do hold key public offices, they tend to be confined to such "women's spheres" as social welfare, public health, and family affairs. Women may further, where the jury system prevails, be excluded from serving on juries.[26]

> suffrage or other civil rights and equal opportunities, has the same social function as the myth of the "contented Negro."

2 G. Myrdal, *supra* note 15, at 1077.

21. Equal Rights for Women, *supra* note 11, at 6.

22. C. Andreas, Sex and Caste in America (1971). *See also* Dunbar, *Female Liberation as the Basis for Social Revolution,* in Sisterhood Is Powerful, *supra* note 6, at 477–92; Freeman, *The Legal Basis of the Sexual Caste System,* 5 Valparaiso U.L. Rev. 203 (1971). For a chart dramatizing "Castelike Status of Women and Negroes," *see* L. Kanowitz, *supra* note 15, at 7.

23. According to a recent report of the U.N. secretary-general, the following six countries still deny women the rights to vote and to be elected: Jordan, Kuwait, Liechtenstein, Nigeria, Saudi Arabia, and Yemen. *Implementation of the Declaration on the Elimination of Discrimination against Women and Related Instruments* 4, U.N. Doc. E/CN.6/571/Add. 2 (1973). *See also* Ungar, *Women in the Middle East and North Africa and Universal Suffrage,* 375 Annals 72 (1968).

24. For a dramatic demonstration of women's underrepresentation in all levels of governments, *see* U.N. Doc. E/CN.6/571/Add. 2, *supra* note 23, at 5–16. *See also* M. Duverger, The Political Role of Women (1955); P. Lanison, Few Are Chosen: American Women in Political Life Today (1968); Menon, *From Constitutional Recognition to Public Office,* 375 Annals 34 (1968). *Cf. also* Abzug, Segal, & Kelber, *Women in the Democratic Party: A Review of Affirmative Action,* 6 Colum. Human Rights L. Rev. 3 (1974).

25. Klein, *supra* note 6, at 912.

26. *See* L. Kanowitz, *supra* note 7, at 28–31; Johnston & Knapp, *Sex Discrimination by Law: A Study in Judicial Perspective,* 46 N.Y.U.L. Rev. 675, 708–21 (1971); Murray, *supra* note 6, at 522; Schulder, *Does the Law Oppress Women?* in Sisterhood Is Powerful, *supra* note 6, at 139, 140–41.

Despite occasional doubts whether serving on juries is a "right, duty, or privilege" and whether exclusion of women from jury service constitutes "benign classification or invidi-

Under the inherited doctrines that "a woman has no legal existence separate from her husband," who is "head of the family,"[27] and that "the unity of the family" is paramount, a married woman is made to suffer a host of deprivations in the legal process. To recite Blackstone's famous dictum, marriage is a declaration of "civil death" of women.[28] She is commonly required to assume her husband's name.[29] Her acquisition, change, or loss of nationality is often made to depend on the marriage relationship and automatically to follow that of her husband, in disregard of her own wishes.[30] A married woman, as Bruce has summarized, may be "unable to enter into contracts, or to sue, or be sued without the consent of her husband, or judicial authorization."[31] "The wife," she adds, "may be subject to the husband's decision concerning domicile and residence without regard to her wishes or interests; and the husband's choice may affect her exercise of important legal rights which are determined by the domicile or residence of the husband."[32]

The processes of government, national and local, are often employed to sustain and institutionalize discriminations against women. The "laws, institutions, and practices" simply "relegate women to an inferior status."[33] In the United States, for example, "[t]here exist in the various

---

ous discrimination," it would appear that involuntary exclusion is a deprivation rather than an indulgence. *Cf.* K. Davidson, R. Ginsburg, & H. Kay, *supra* note 6, at 26–35; L. Kanowitz, *supra* note 7, at 197: L. Kanowitz, *supra* note 15, at 74–89.

The recent decision of *Taylor* v. *Louisiana,* 419 U.S. 522 (1975), suggests a possible trend in a different direction. *Cf. also Case Comment, Twelve Good Persons and True: Healy* v. *Edwards and Taylor* v. *Louisiana,* 9 Harv. Civ. Rights–Civ. Lib. L., Rev. 561 (1974).

27. Bradwell v. Illinois, 83 U.S. (16 Wall.) 130, 141 (1873).

28. *Quoted in* A. Sinclair, The Better Half: The Emancipation of the American Women 83 (1965).

29. L. Kanowitz, *supra* note 7, at 41–46; Brown, Emerson, Falk, & Freedman, *supra* note 6, at 940, *Cf.* S. Ross, *supra* note 6, at 239–55; Carlsson, *Surnames of Married Women and Legitimate Children,* 17 N.Y.L. Forum 552 (1971); Hughes, *And Then There Were Two,* 23 Hastings L.J. 233 (1971); Karst, *"A Discrimination So Trivial": A Note on Law and the Symbolism of Women's Dependency,* 35 Ohio State L.J. 546 (1974).

30. *See* United Nations, Convention on the Nationality of Married Women, U.N. Doc. E/CN.6/389 (1962); United Nations, Nationality of Married Women, U.N. Doc. E/CN.6/254/Rev. 1 (1963); W. Waltz, The Nationality of Married Women (1937); the appendix *infra,* at notes 64–70, 151–55, 364–75, and accompanying text.

31. Bruce, *Work of the United Nations Relating to the Status of Women,* 4 Human Rights J. 365, 376 (1971). *See also* 1 W. Blackstone, Commentaries on the Laws of England 387–92 (4th ed. J. Andrews ed. 1899).

32. Bruce, *supra* note 31, at 377. *See also* H. Clark, The Law of Domestic Relations 149–51 (1968); L. Kanowitz, *supra* note 7, at 46–52; United Nations, Legal Status of Married Women (reports submitted by the secretary-general) 8–18, U.N. Doc. ST/SOA/35 (1958).

33. *Hearings on Equal Rights for Men and Women 1971 before Subcomm. No. 4 of the House Comm. on the Judiciary,* 92d Cong., 1st Sess., ser. 2, at 399–400 (1971) (remark of Professor Thomas I. Emerson) [hereinafter cited as *House Hearings on Equal Rights*]. Similarly, in the

States over 1,000 laws that discriminate against women."[34] In cumulative deprivation, a general lack among women of access to education, skill, wealth, and other values may handicap their participation in the effective processes of a community.[35]

In the field of enlightenment, denial of equal educational opportunity on account of sex is still widespread.[36] The access of women to education, especially higher education, is either denied or restricted, in comparison to that of men. Worldwide attendance by women at institutions of higher learning falls far behind that of men.[37] In communities of mass illiteracy, females, especially in rural areas, typically constitute the majority of the deprived.[38] In some cultures women are still deliberately kept ignorant or encouraged in frivolity, which eases the perpetuation of male domination.[39] Despite steady progress toward coeducation, it is still a commonplace in many parts of the world that boys and girls are segregated in schools, with significantly different curricula and career orientation.[40] Instead of preparing girls for "full participation in the productive life of their communities and nations,"[41] schooling is often conceived

---

words of Kanowitz, sex-based discriminations are "supported, perpetuated and often aggravated by the organized might of domestic and foreign legal system." L. KANOWITZ, *supra* note 7, at 2.

34. Faust, *Constitution Excluded Women,* in *House Hearing on Equal Rights, supra* note 33, at 106, 108. In the words of Jiagge: "The evidence of discrimination against women in private law provides enough material for several books to be written on the subject." Jiagge, *An Introduction to the Declaration on Elimination of Discrimination Against Women,* 5 UN MONTHLY CHRONICLE, 55, 58 (Mar. 1968).

35. *Cf.* UNITED NATIONS, 1965 SEMINAR ON THE PARTICIPATION OF WOMEN IN PUBLIC LIFE, U.N. Doc. ST/TAO/HR/24 (1966).

36. *See* C. AMMOUN, STUDY OF DISCRIMINATION IN EDUCATION 29–44, U.N. Doc. E/CN.4/Sub. 2/181/Rev. 1 (1957); Beasley, *Education Is the Key for Women,* 375 ANNALS 154 (1968); Friedrich, *Access to Education at All Levels, id.,* at 133.

37. *See* Klein, *supra* note 6, at 913; *House Hearings on Equal Rights, supra* note 33, at 37; K. DAVIDSON, R. GINSBURG, & H. KAY, *supra* note 6, at 869–86.

38. *Study on Equal Access of Girls and Women to Literacy* (report prepared by UNESCO), U.N. Doc. E/CN.6/538 (1970), especially at 16; Annex II, "Illiterate population and percentage of illiteracy based on censuses or surveys since 1945" in U.N. Doc. E/CN.6/538/Add. 1 (1970) (Annex II). *Study on the Equality of Access of Girls and Women to Education in the Context of Rural Development* (report prepared by UNESCO), U.N. Doc. E/CN.6/566/Rev. 1 (1973), especially at 27–29, 68–69. *See also* U.N. Doc. E/CN.6/566 (1973) under the latter title.

39. For a pertinent historical account, *cf. generally* V. BULLOUGH, *supra* note 9.

40. *International Labour Organization Activities of Special Interest in Relation to the Employment of Women* (report by the International Labour Office), at 2–3 (Annex II), U.N. Doc. E/CN.6/556 (1971) [hereinafter cited as *ILO Report on Women*]. *See also Study of Co-Education* (report prepared by UNESCO), U.N. Docs. E/CN.6/537 and Add. 1 (1969).

41. *Study of the Interrelationship of the Status of Women and Family Planning* (report of the special rapporteur) 13, U.N. Doc. E/CN.6/575 (1973) [hereinafter cited as *Report on Women and Family Planning*].

and made "just a preamble to marriage."[42] Hence, in the words of a recent ILO report, "[g]irls are given education and training in line with traditional concepts of the role of women in society which are unrelated to the needs of today. They are often discouraged from studying subjects of importance."[43] Under the adverse influence of the inherited concepts about the respective roles of both sexes, women are deprived of opportunities to acquire, develop, and exercise a range of socially useful skills. The skills women possess tend to concentrate in a small number of occupations, especially in what are known as female jobs.[44]

In regard to well-being, the physical and mental health of women is often impaired by "the burdens of involuntary childbearing."[45] Most of the women in the world are still denied freedom to control their own fertility because of either legal or religious prohibitions or the lack of relevant information, resources, and family planning services.[46] The inability to "decide freely and responsibly on the number or spacing of children (if any)"[47] has, in turn, deprived many women of benefits regarding "their health, education or employment and their roles in family and public life."[48] Sometimes women are condemned to "conditions of poverty, overwork and drudgery"[49] because child and home care, in addition to childbearing, are assumed and taken to be their exclusive domain.

Discrimination against women in the wealth sector is particularly pronounced. It appears that here "[s]ex bias takes a greater economic toll than racial bias."[50] Under the arbitrarily rigidified division of occupa-

---

42. *Id. Cf.* UNITED NATIONS, CIVIC AND POLITICAL EDUCATION OF WOMEN, U.N. DOC. E/CN.6/405/Rev. 1 (1964).

43. *ILO Report on Women, supra* note 40, at 3 (Annex II).

44. INTERNATIONAL LABOUR OFFICE, FIGHTING DISCRIMINATION IN EMPLOYMENT AND OCCUPATION 84–94 (1968); *Equal Pay for Work of Equal Value* (report by the International Labour Office) 44, U.N. Doc. E/CN.6/550 (1971); *Report on Women and Family Planning, supra* note 41, at 13; *Preliminary Research Report on Working Women in the United States* (prepared under the direction of Adele Simmons for the Twentieth Century Fund Task Force on Women and Employment, 1973), *reprinted in* N. DORSEN, N. CHACHKIN, & S. LAW, 1973 SUPPLEMENT TO VOLUME 2, EMERSON, HABER, & DORSEN'S POLITICAL AND CIVIL RIGHTS IN THE UNITED STATES 362–66 (1973). *Cf. Repercussions of Scientific and Technological Progress on the Conditions of Work and Employment of Women,* U.N. Doc. E/CN.6/539 (1970); Shelton & Berndt, *Sex Discrimination in Vocational Education: Title IX and Other Remedies,* 62 CALIF. L. REV. 1121 (1974).

45. *Report on Women and Family Planning, supra* note 41, at 12.

46. *Id.* at 10. *Cf.* J. VAN DER TAK, ABORTION, FERTILITY, AND CHANGING LEGISLATION: AN INTERNATIONAL REVIEW (1974).

47. *Report on Women and Family Planning, supra* note 41, at 10.

48. *Id.* at 20.

49. *Id.* at 21. *Cf. also* Henderson, *Impact of the World Social Situation on Women,* 375 ANNALS 26 (1968).

50. PRESIDENT'S TASK FORCE ON WOMEN'S RIGHTS AND RESPONSIBILITIES, A MATTER OF SIMPLE JUSTICE 18 (1970). *See* PRESIDENT'S COMMISSION ON THE STATUS OF WOMEN, REPORT

tions into "men's work" and "women's work," women are often confined to a narrow range of "traditionally low-paying occupations or those ranked low in prestige,"[51] and not permitted to penetrate "a wide range of occupations at all levels."[52] Women are often made to "work in jobs far below their native abilities or trained capabilities."[53] The virtually universal overrepresentation of women in the low-paying jobs, and their underrepresentation in the higher-paying jobs, especially those of managerial character, result also in wide pay differentials between men and women.[54] Even in the same employment situation, unequal pay for work of equal value generally prevails: typically, women are paid at a lower rate than men.[55] Job advancement is usually more difficult for women than for men.

In addition to these wealth deprivations common to women in general, a married woman suffers further deprivations. Marriage often entails significant effects upon the property relations of the spouses. Financially, a married woman is commonly made to depend upon her husband, because customarily she is assigned the role of a housekeeper. Taking care of "the home, the husband and children" is a task to be performed "without financial compensation during marriage."[56] Numerous restrictions, with varying degrees of severity, are widely imposed

---

OF THE COMMITTEE ON PRIVATE EMPLOYMENT (1963). *See also* B. BABCOCK, A. FREEDMAN, E. NORTON, & S. ROSS, *supra* note 6, at 191–559; K. DAVIDSON, R. GINSBURG, & H. KAY, *supra* note 6, at 419–811; K. DECROW, SEXIST JUSTICE 64–155 (1974); UNITED NATIONS, SEMINAR ON THE PARTICIPATION OF WOMEN IN THE ECONOMIC LIFE OF THEIR COUNTRIES, U.N. Doc. ST/TAO/HR/41 (1970); Johnstone, *Women in Economic Life: Rights and Opportunities,* 375 ANNALS 102 (1968); Murray, *Economic and Educational Inequality Based on Sex: An Overview,* 5 VALPARAISO U.L. REV. 237 (1971).

51. *Equal Pay for Work of Equal Value, supra* note 44, at 44.

52. *Id.*

53. REPORT OF THE COMMITTEE ON PRIVATE EMPLOYMENT, *supra* note 50, at 1.

54. *See* UNITED NATIONS, EQUAL PAY FOR EQUAL WORK (1960); *Equal Pay for Work of Equal Value* (report by the International Labour Office), U.N. Doc. E/CN.6/519 (1968); *Equal Pay for Work of Equal Value* (report by the International Labour Office), U.N. Doc. E/CN.6/550 (1971); *Note, The Rights of Working Women: An International Perspective,* 14 VA. J. INT'L L. 729 (1974). For studies directed to particular countries, *see* B. BABCOCK, A. FREEDMAN, E. NORTON, & S. ROSS, *supra* note 6, at 440–509; Berger, *Equal Pay, Equal Employment Opportunity and Equal Enforcement of the Law for Women,* 5 VALPARAISO U.L. REV. 326 (1971); *Equal Pay in New Zealand,* 105 INT'L LAB. REV. 569 (1972); *Ireland: Interim Report on Equal Pay by the Commission on the Status of Women, id.,* at 182; Simchack, *Equal Pay in the United States*, 103 INT'L LAB. REV. 541 (1971); Thalmann-Antenen, *Equal Pay: The Position in Switzerland,* 104 INT'L LAB. REV. 275 (1971); Vangsnes, *Equal Pay in Norway,* 103 INT'L LAB. REV. 379 (1971).

55. *See* authorities cited in note 54 *supra. Cf.* T. OEHMKE, SEX DISCRIMINATION IN EMPLOYMENT (1974).

56. *Legal Capacity of Married Women: Capacity to Engage in Independent Work* (progress report of the secretary-general) 4, U.N. Doc. E/CN.6/584 (1973).

on married women's "right to acquire, administer, enjoy, dispose of and inherit property, including property acquired during [and before] the marriage."[57] Thus, a married woman may be unable, without her husband's authorization or consent, to make contracts binding upon either or both of them.[58] Without his authorization or consent, she may be legally incapable of undertaking an independent work, business, profession, or other occupation, outside the home.[59] She may even be required to submit her earnings to the control, management, and disposition of her husband.[60]

With regard to the shaping and sharing of the affection value, the "partnership" between husband and wife is generally more "unequal" than "equal."[61] "In some parts of the world," as Justice Annie R. Jiagge, then chairman of the Commission on the Status of Women, sharply noted, "girls under the age of ten years are given away in marriage. Young women are forced to marry men not of their choice. In some countries, consent of the woman to marriage is not a necessary legal requirement provided the consent of her parents or guardians is obtained."[62] Women are often denied "autonomy and equality in decisions relating to marriage itself and choice of spouse, as well as decisions during marriage and at its dissolution."[63] In some parts of the world,

57. *Id.* at 14–15. *See* Kahn-Freund, *Matrimonial Property and Equality before the Law: Some Sceptical Reflections,* 4 HUMAN RIGHTS J. 493 (1971); Pedersen, *Status of Women in Private Law,* 375 ANNALS 44, 47–48 (1968). *Cf. also* H. SIMONS, AFRICAN WOMEN: THEIR LEGAL STATUS IN SOUTH AFRICA 187–210 (1968).

58. L. KANOWITZ, *supra* note 7, at 55, 197; Bradwell v. Illinois, 83 U.S. (16 Wall.) 130, 141 (1873); 1. W. BLACKSTONE, *supra* note 31, at 387–88. *See also* LEGAL STATUS OF MARRIED WOMEN, *supra* note 32, at 76–87.

59. *See Legal Capacity of Married Women, supra* note 56. This report is concerned with "[t]he capacity of wife to undertake independent work, that is, the extent to which she may freely engage in an activity of her choice, outside the home, without having to obtain her husband's authorization or consent, and the right of the wife to administer and dispose of her earnings or product of her work." *Id.* at 3.

60. *Id.* at 13–17. *Cf.* LEGAL STATUS OF WOMEN, *supra* note 32, at 89–93.

61. "The ideal of marriage generally accepted in contemporary western societies and many westernized strata of developing countries is that of partnership—that is, a sharing of interests and responsibilities between husband and wife on as nearly equal basis as possible. As was with so many other ideals, practice often falls short of precept. . . ." Klein, *supra* note 6, at 915. *See also Report on Woman and Family Planning, supra* note 41, at 15. Regarding the shaping and sharing of affection, *consult* an important sociological study: W. GOODE, WORLD REVOLUTION AND FAMILY PATTERNS (1970).

62. Jiagge, *supra* note 34, at 57. *See also* W. GOODE, *supra* note 61, at 88–101, 104–11, 174–82, 207–18, 232–36.

63. *Report on Women and Family Planning, supra* note 41, at 11. *See also* UNITED NATIONS, 1961 SEMINAR ON THE STATUS OF WOMEN IN FAMILY LIFE, U.N. Doc. ST/TAO/HR/11 (1961); UNITED NATIONS, 1962 SEMINAR ON THE STATUS OF WOMEN IN FAMILY LAW, U.N. Doc. ST/TAO/HR/14 (1962).

women are still victims of the practice of polygamy, especially where registration of marriages is not required.[64] Many communities still confer upon the father, rather than the mother, ultimate authority in matters affecting the upbringing or education of children.[65] The wife may even lack an equal voice in sexual and reproductive decisions.[66] Divorce may be effected unilaterally by the husband, but not by the wife.[67] The grounds and defenses available to men in proceedings for legal separation, divorce, or annulment of marriage may simply be denied to women.[68] Where divorce is obtainable through mutual consent, legal safeguards may be so inadequate as to render the wife's consent more apparent than real.[69] Widows, but not widowers, may be forbidden to remarry.[70]

In the formulation and application of the norms of rectitude (responsible conduct), the most distinguishing feature is of course the prevalence of double standards. What is permissible for men is often made impermissible for women. This is most conspicuous in the area of sexual morality. Chastity may be required of women, but not of men.[71] Wives may be punished for adultery, but not husbands.[72] Women may be

64. *Report on Women and Family Planning, supra* note 41, at 15; V. BULLOUGH, *supra* note 9, at 247; W. GOODE, *supra* note 61, at 101–04, 187–88, 221–25, 282–85; Pedersen, *supra* note 57, at 46–47.

65. Bruce, *supra,* note 31, at 377. *See generally* LEGAL STATUS OF MARRIED WOMEN, *supra* note 32, at 19–43; UNITED NATIONS, PARENTAL RIGHTS AND DUTIES, INCLUDING GUARDIANSHIP (report submitted by the secretary-general), U.N. Doc. E/CN.6/474/Rev. 1 (1968). "... the married father still plays a predominant role, especially in countries where he is considered to be the head of the family, whether explicitly or implicitly, while the married mother is relegated to a subsidiary role in this matter." UNITED NATIONS, THE STATUS OF THE UNMARRIED MOTHER (report of the secretary-general) 27, U.N. Doc. E/CN.6/540/Rev. 1 (1971).

66. *Report on Women and Family Planning, supra* note 41, at 13.

67. *Id.* at 15. *See* W. GOODE, *supra* note 61, at 155–62, 262–68.

68. Bruce, *supra* note 31, at 377; 1962 SEMINAR, *supra* note 63, at 21–26.

69. *Id.* In the words of Jiagge:

> Divorce laws follow the same pattern. In some countries a man can obtain a valid divorce merely by declaring three times that he has divorced his wife. Adultery is a ground of divorce available to men in some countries but not to women. Where divorce is governed by customary rules and practices, such rules are so elastic and capable of so many interpretations that it is very easy for a man to manoeuvre and obtain a divorce on practically any ground. It is significant that the same facility is not available to women.

Jiagge, *supra* note 34, at 57.

70. V. BULLOUGH, *supra* note 9, at 250; W. GOODE, *supra* note 61, at 155–62, 263–64, 376–77.

71. V. BULLOUGH, *supra* note 9, at 45.

72. In some cultures, adultery was viewed as "not a sin against morality but a trespass

penalized for prostitution, but not their male patrons.[73] Furthermore, women may be barred from participation in various religious rites and ceremonies, and denied access to the hierarchy of religious authority.[74] The cumulative impact of the various deprivations, as described above, further handicaps women's capability to participate effectively and responsibly in the social process and fosters what is called the syndrome of "social marginality," such as "withdrawal, submission, inferiority, passivity."[75]

BASIC COMMUNITY POLICIES

The group differentiation of individuals upon the basis of sex, for the purpose of allocating access to value processes, is as inimical to the fundamental policies of shared respect as group differentiation based upon alleged ethnic characteristics.[76] It cannot promote freedom of choice for the individual (or provide opportunity for an individual's discovering, maturing, and exercising of latent talent, either for self-fulfillment or for contribution to the aggregate common interest) to allocate benefits and burdens in social process upon putative qualities of "maleness" or "femaleness," rather than upon the actual characteristics and capabilities of individual persons. Sex, like race, offers no rational criterion for "classification" in "determining the legal rights of women,

---

against the husband's property. A husband had freedom to fornicate, while a wife could be put to death for doing the same thing." V. BULLOUGH, *supra* note 9, at 23.

73. Generally speaking, "prostitution is, by definition, a crime committed only by women." Brown, Emerson, Falk, & Freedman, *supra* note 6, at 963. *See* B. BABCOCK, A. FREEDMAN, E. NORTON, & S. ROSS, *supra* note 6, at 877–914; K. DAVIDSON, R. GINSBURG, & H. KAY, *supra* note 6, at 908–10. *Cf. also* V. BULLOUGH, THE HISTORY OF PROSTITUTION (1964).

74. "Traditionally, women have been barred from participation in many religious ceremonies, and from full participation in the hierarchies of authority. When this could not be accomplished legally, it was often accomplished by ridicule." C. ANDREAS, *supra* note 22, at 69. *See also* D. BAILEY, THE MAN-WOMAN RELATION IN CHRISTIAN THOUGHT (1959); M. DALY, THE CHURCH AND THE SECOND SEX (1968); G. HARKNESS, WOMEN IN CHURCH AND SOCIETY (1972).

75. *Report on Women and Family Planning*, *supra* note 41, at 9. In the same vein, Kanowitz has observed:

> Discrimination, whether social or legal or both, not only stunts the personal development of its objects, causing them to become less socially productive; it also often nurtures the development of many traits and characteristics that on any objective scale would be deemed undesirable and unworthy.

L. KANOWITZ, *supra* note 7, at 198–99.

76. For an excellent policy exposition, *see* Brown, Emerson, Falk, & Freedman, *supra* note 6, at 888–900. *Cf. also* A. MONTAGU, THE NATURAL SUPERIORITY OF WOMEN 204–16 (rev. ed. 1968).

or of men."[77] Females, no less than males, require to be treated as "persons, not statistical abstractions."[78]

The justifications offered for sex-based discrimination, subordinating women, are traditionally that it is "natural or necessary or divinely ordained."[79] Sometimes it is argued that discrimination is inherent "in the divine ordinance, as well as in the nature of things."[80] At other times it is asserted that simply out of the social necessity of functional division of activities, there exists "a wide difference in the respective spheres and destinies of man and woman."[81] The "domestic sphere," it is said, "properly belongs to the domain and functions of womanhood."[82] The boldest of discriminators may on occasion argue that women are inherently inferior to men.[83]

It would seem peculiarly difficult, in the light of contemporary knowledge and experience, to establish that there is something "divine" or "natural" about subjecting half of the human population to the domination of the other half. Nor has it been established that such a domination-subordination relationship is a "necessary" assignment of roles either for maximizing the fulfillment of the individual or for promoting the aggregate common interest. Indeed, all contemporary knowledge and experience would appear to confirm the opposite.

In a global community aspiring toward human dignity, a basic policy should, accordingly, be to make the social roles of the two sexes, with the notable exception of childbearing, as nearly interchangeable or equiva-

---

77. Brown, Emerson, Falk, & Freedman, *supra* note 6, at 889. In the words of Montagu:

> Human beings differ greatly in their abilities but practically not at all along sex lines; that is to say, abilities are not determined by sex. Abilities are functions of persons, *not* of groups or classes. Hence, so far as abilities are concerned both sexes should be afforded equal opportunities to realize their potentialities, and the judgment of their abilities should not be prejudiced by any bias of sex.

A. Montagu, *supra* note 76, at 208.

78. Brown, Emerson, Falk, & Freedman, *supra* note 6, at 889.

79. *Id.* at 872.

80. Bradwell v. Illinois, 83 U.S. (16 Wall.) 130, 141 (1873).

81. *Id.*

82. *Id.*

83. *See* authorities cited in notes 20 and 22 *supra.* For a strong attack upon the myth of women's inferiority, *see* A. Montagu, *supra* note 76. Montagu writes:

> The natural superiority of women is a biological fact, and a socially overlooked piece of knowledge. The facts have been available for half a century, but in a male-dominated world, in which the inflation of the male ego has been dependent upon the preservation of the myth of male superiority, their significance has escaped the attention merited. When the history of the subject comes to be written, this peculiar omission will no doubt serve as yet another forcible illustration that we see only what and how we want to see.

Id. at 205.

lent as possible.[84] To achieve genuine equality between the sexes, it is vital that "nobody be forced into a predetermined role on account of sex, but each person be given better possibilities to develop his or her personal talents."[85] Such a policy need not of course preclude separate consideration of matters arising from "a physical characteristic unique to one sex."[86] "So long," write recent influential authors, "as the law deals only with a characteristic found in all (or some) women but in no men, or in all (or some) men but no women, it does not ignore individual characteristics found in both sexes in favor of an average based on one sex."[87]

In sum, the most rational general community policy requires the complete emancipation of women, without countenancing the subordination of men. John Stuart Mill affirmed a mature opinion, still relevant:

> That the principle which regulates the existing social relations between the two sexes—the legal subordination of one sex to the other—is wrong in itself, and now one of the chief hindrances to human improvement; and that it ought to be replaced by a principle of perfect equality, admitting no power or privilege on the one side, nor disability on the other.[88]

TRENDS IN DECISION

The drive toward eradication of sex-based discrimination, like that designed to eliminate racial discrimination, has in recent decades been a vital component of the trend toward a more general norm of nondiscrimination. The community concern for the protection of women, antedating the broader United Nations attack upon discrimination, was evident in certain significant areas at the turn of the twentieth century. Thus, in 1902, the Hague Conventions dealt with conflicts of national laws concerning marriage, divorce, and the guardianship of minors.[89] In 1904 and 1910, conventions were adopted to combat traffic in women.[90] The Covenant of the League of Nations represented an important de-

---

84.
> From a biological viewpoint, the different parts men and women play in the reproductive function undoubtedly contribute to sex differentiation in psychological development. Thus the long period of child bearing and child rearing, which falls biologically upon the female, has far-reaching implications for sex differences in interests, attitudes, emotional traits, vocational goals, and achievement.

Anastasi, *Individual Differences: Overview,* 7 INT'L ENCYC. SOC. SC. 200, 205 (1968). *Cf. also* Tyler, *Individual Differences: Sex Differences, id.* at 207.

85. Ginsburg, *The Status of Women: Introduction,* 20 AM. J. COMP. L. 585, 589 (1972).

86. Brown, Emerson, Falk, & Freedman, *supra* note 6, at 893.

87. *Id.*

88. Mill, *The Subjection of Women,* in ESSAYS ON SEX EQUALITY: JOHN STUART MILL & HARRIET TAYLOR MILL 123, 125 (A. Rossi ed. 1970).

89. UNITED NATIONS, THE UNITED NATIONS AND THE STATUS OF WOMEN 3 (1964).

90. International Agreement for the Suppression of the White Slave Traffic, *signed* at Paris May 18, 1904 (entered into force July 18, 1905). For its text, *see* 1 L.N.T.S. 83.

velopment, calling for humane working conditions for all, irrespective of sex, and for the suppression of traffic in women.[91] Thus, employment in the League Secretariat was freed from discrimination. Article 7(3) of the Covenant of the League provided: "All positions under or in connection with the League, including the Secretariat, shall be open equally to men and women." In 1937, the League appointed an expert committee to undertake a comprehensive study on the legal status of women, the work of which was unfortunately interrupted by the outbreak of World War II. The International Labor Organization, an "autonomous partner"[92] of the League established in 1919, has continuously sought to achieve humane working conditions for all, irrespective of sex. In 1944, the purposes of ILO, as originally contained in the Preamble to its Constitution and Article 427 of the Treaty of Versailles,[93] were emphatically restated in the Declaration of Philadelphia:

> [A]ll human beings, irrespective of race, creed or *sex,* have the right to pursue both their material well-being and their spiritual development in conditions of freedom and dignity, of economic security and equal opportunity.[94]

An impressive regional effort to protect women in Latin America has been spearheaded since 1928 by the Inter-American Commission of Women.[95]

The contemporary broad prescription against sex-based discrimination has its origins in the United Nations Charter and in various ancillary expressions and commitments. The more important general prohibitions of discrimination explicitly and consistently specify sex as among the impermissible grounds of differentiation. The United Nations Charter, after reaffirming in the Preamble "faith in fundamental human rights, in the dignity and worth of the human person, in the equal rights of men

---

International Convention for the Suppression of the White Slave Traffic, *signed* at Paris May 4, 1910, Great Britain, Treaty Series No. 20 (1912). For subsequent amendments of these two treaties in 1949 through protocols, *see* 30 U.N.T.S. 23, 92 U.N.T.S. 19, 98 U.N.T.S. 101. For further details, *consult* United Nations, Multilateral Treaties in Respect of Which the Secretary-General Performs Depository Functions: List of Signatures, Ratifications, Accessions, etc. as at 31 December 1972, at 168–74, U.N. Doc. ST/LEG/SER.D/6 (1973) [hereinafter cited as Multilateral Treaties, 1972]. *See also* United Nations, Study on Traffic in Persons and Prostitution, U.N. Doc. ST/SOA/SD/8 (1959).

91. The Covenant of the League of Nations, Art. 23(a, c).

92. 1 L. Oppenheim, International Law 717 (H. Lauterpacht ed. 8th ed. 1955).

93. Treaty of Versailles, June 28, 1919, 2 Major Peace Treaties of Modern History, 1648–1967, at 1265, 1522–23 (F. Israel ed. 1967).

94. 2 International Governmental Organizations: Constitutional Documents 1246, 1247 (rev. 2d ed. A. Peaslee ed. 1961) (italics added).

95. *See* authorities cited in notes 218–27 *infra* and accompanying text.

and women," pronounces in Article 1(3) that one of its purposes is to promote and encourage "respect for human rights and for fundamental freedoms for all without distinction" on account of sex or other grounds. This theme is given further concrete expression in such provisions as Articles 13(1)(b), 55(c), 56, 62(2), and 76(c).[96] Of particular significance is Article 8, which reads: "The United Nations shall place no restrictions on the eligibility of men and women to participate in any capacity and under conditions of equality in its principal and subsidiary organs."[97] The Universal Declaration of Human Rights, in setting forth "the civil

---

96. Art. 13(1)(b) reads:

> The General Assembly shall initiate studies and make recommendations for the purpose of:
>
> . . .
>
> b. promoting international co-operation in the economic, social, cultural, educational, and health fields, and assisting in the realization of human rights and fundamental freedoms for all without distinction as to race, sex, language, or religion.

Art. 55(c) provides:

> With a view to the creation of conditions of stability and well-being which are necessary for peaceful and friendly relations among nations based on respect for the principle of equal rights and self-determination of peoples, the United Nations shall promote:
>
> . . .
>
> c. universal respect for, and observance of, human rights and fundamental freedoms for all without distinction as to race, sex, language, or religion.

Art. 56 stipulates:

> All Members pledge themselves to take joint and separate action in co-operation with the Organization for the achievement of the purposes set forth in Article 55.

Art. 62(2) states:

> It [the Economic and Social Council] may make recommendations for the purpose of promoting respect for, and observance of, human rights and fundamental freedoms for all.

Art. 76(c) reads:

> The basic objectives of the trusteeship system, in accordance with the Purposes of the United Nations laid down in Article 1 of the present Charter, shall be:
>
> . . .
>
> c. to encourage respect for human rights and for fundamental freedoms for all without distinction as to race, sex, language, or religion, and to encourage recognition of the interdependence of the peoples of the world. . . .

97. However, for a dramatic demonstration of women's underrepresentation in the higher positions within the United Nations, *see* K. Davidson, R. Ginsburg, & H. Kay, *supra* note 6, at 932–34. *See also* Szalai, *The Situation of Women in the United Nations,* UNITAR Reasearch Report No. 18 (1973); *Differential Treatment Based upon Sex under the Staff Regulations and Staff Rules* (report of the secretary-general), U.N. Doc. A/C.5/1519 (1973).

and political rights and the economic, social and cultural rights to which every individual—man or woman—is entitled,"[98] has inspired, as in other areas, much of the contemporary activity for the protection of women. In its broad formulation of the general norm of nondiscrimination, Article 2 of the Universal Declaration specifies "sex" as among the impermissible grounds of differentiation,[99] a provision further reinforced by the equal protection clause of Article 7.[100] The two International Covenants on Human Rights, incorporating and reinforcing the general norm of nondiscrimination enunciated in the Universal Declaration, emphatically forbid discrimination on account of sex. Significantly, each of the two Covenants contains, in practically identical terms, a special article on the equality of sexes. The International Covenant on Civil and Political Rights, in Article 3, provides: "The States Parties to the present Covenant undertake to ensure the equal right of men and women to the enjoyment of all civil and political rights set forth in the present Covenant."[101] Similarly, Article 3 of the International Covenant on Economic, Social, and Cultural Rights reads: "The States Parties to the present Covenant undertake to ensure the equal right of men and women to the enjoyment of all economic, social and cultural rights set forth in the present Covenant."[102] These separate articles are in addition to other pertinent nondiscrimination provisions which include "sex," along with race and other factors, among the prohibited grounds of differentiation.[103]

---

98. Bruce, *supra* note 31, at 369–70.

99. Art. 2 reads in part: "Everyone is entitled to all the rights and freedoms set forth in this Declaration, without distinction of any kind, such as race, colour, sex, language, religion, political or other opinion, national or social origin, property, birth or other status." United Nations, Human Rights: A Compilation of International Instruments of the United Nations 1, U.N. Doc. ST/HR/1 (1973) [hereinafter cited as U.N. Human Rights Instruments].

100. Art. 7 reads: "All are equal before the law and are entitled without any discrimination to equal protection of the law. All are entitled to equal protection against any discrimination in violation of this Declaration and against any incitement to such discrimination." *Id.*

101. *Id.* at 8.

102. *Id.* at 4.

103. The International Covenant on Civil and Political Rights provides in Art. 2(1) that

> Each State Party to the present Covenant undertakes to respect and to ensure to all individuals within its territory and subject to its jurisdiction the rights recognized in the present Covenant, without distinction of any kind, such as race, colour, sex, language, religion, political or other opinion, national or social origin, property, birth or other status;

and adds, in Art. 26, that

> All persons are equal before the law and are entitled without any discrimination to the equal protection of the law. In this respect, the law shall prohibit any discrimination

The general norm against sex-based discrimination, thus formulated and established, is further illustrated and reinforced by a number of conventions and other authoritative expressions oriented toward the protection of women against particular vulnerabilities or in regard to particular values.[104] Thus, in 1951, the Equal Remuneration Convention was adopted by the International Labor Organization to put into effect "the principle of equal remuneration for men and women workers for work of equal value."[105] Now operative in some seventy countries, this Convention substantially increases the protection of women in relation to wealth processes. According to Article 1, the term "equal remuneration for men and women workers for work of equal value" refers to "rates of remuneration established without discrimination based on sex,"[106] while "remuneration" embraces "the ordinary, basic or minimum wage or salary and any additional emoluments whatsoever payable directly or indirectly, whether in cash or in kind, by the employer to the worker and arising out of the workers' employment."[107] The Convention, in Article 2(1), obliges each ratifying member to "promote" and, "in so far as is consistent with" "the methods in operation for determining rates of remuneration," "ensure the application to all workers of the principle of equal remuneration for men and women workers for work of equal value."[108] The term "the methods in operation for determining rates of remuneration" was understood to mean not "the principles on which wage and salary structures are currently based" but "the procedures applicable in accordance with national law or practice for the purpose of fixing or settling wages and salaries in the various trades, industries or professions."[109] The Convention further stipulates

---

> and guarantee to all persons equal and effective protection against discrimination on any ground such as race, colour, sex, language, religion, political or other opinion, national or social origin, property, birth or other status.

Id. at 8, 11.

Similarly, the International Covenant on Economic, Social, and Cultural Rights provides in Art. 2(2) that "The States Parties to the present Covenant undertake to guarantee that the rights enunciated in the present Covenant will be exercised without discrimination of any kind as to race, colour, sex, language, religion, political or other opinion, national or social origin, property, birth or other status." *Id.* at 4.

For further elaboration, *see* chapters 6–9 *supra* and chapters 11–15 *infra.*

104. For an overview, *consult Study of Provisions in Existing Conventions That Relate to the Status of Women: Report of the Secretary-General,* U.N. Doc. E/CN.6/552 (1972). *See also The United Nations and the Advancement of Women* (study prepared by Mrs. M. K. Baxter), U.N. Doc. A/CONF.32/L.7 (1968).

105. Preamble, U.N. Human Rights Instruments, *supra* note 99, at 37.

106. U.N. Human Rights Instruments, *supra* note 99, at 37.

107. *Id.*

108. *Id.*

109. C. Jenks, Human Rights and International Labour Standards 92 (1960).

in Article 2(2), with a flexibility appropriate for different communities, that the principle of equal remuneration may be applied by means of:

(a) National laws or regulations;

(b) Legally established or recognized machinery for wage determination;

(c) Collective agreements between employers and workers; or

(d) A combination of these various means.[110]

"Where such action will assist," Article 3(1) indicates, "in giving effect to the provisions" of the Convention, "measures shall be taken to promote objective appraisal of jobs on the basis of the work to be performed."[111] "Differential rates between workers which correspond, without regard to sex, to differences as determined by such objective appraisal in the work to be performed" are, according to Article 3(3), "not" to be considered contrary to the principle of equal remuneration.[112]

Of especial importance in relation to both formal and effective power is the Convention on the Political Rights of Women, adopted by the General Assembly of the United Nations in 1952, which seeks, in implementation of "the principle of equality of rights for men and women contained in the Charter of the United Nations," to "equalize the status of men and women in the enjoyment and exercise of political rights."[113] This Convention reflected the widespread recognition that "the achievement of full status for women as *citizens* was the key to acceptance of women as equal participants in the life of the community."[114] "This Convention," in the words of a U.N. study, "is not just another treaty prepared under the auspices of an international organization—it is the first instrument of international law aiming at the granting and at the protection of women's rights on a worldwide basis."[115] The Convention declares, in Article 1, that "Women shall be entitled to vote in all elections on equal terms with men, without any discrimination";[116] and, in Article 2, that "Women shall be eligible for election to all publicly elected

110. U.N. Human Rights Instruments, *supra* note 99, at 37.

111. *Id.*

112. *Id.*

113. Preamble, *id.* at 90. Its text is printed in 193 U.N.T.S. 135. Operative since July 7, 1954, the Convention on the Political Rights of Women had, as of Dec. 31, 1972, been ratified, or acceded to, by sixty-nine states. Multilateral Treaties, 1972, *supra* note 90, at 349–50.

114. United Nations, The Convention on the Political Rights of Women: History and Commentary 1, U.N. Doc. ST/SOA/27 (1955). *Cf.* E. Flexner, Century of Struggle: The Woman's Rights Movement in the United States (1959); United Nations, The Road to Equality: Political Rights of Women, U.N. Doc. ST/SOA/13 (1953); *Political Rights of Women* (report of the secretary-general), U.N. Doc. A/8481 (1971).

115. The Convention on the Political Rights of Women, *supra* note 114, at v.

116. U.N. Human Rights Instruments, *supra* note 99, at 90.

bodies, established by national law, on equal terms with men, without any discrimination.[117] The broad reach toward voting in "all elections" and eligibility for election to "all publicly elected bodies" has obvious consequences for equality in effective power. Beyond opportunity for elective office, the Convention further affords women equal access to all appointive public posts. Article 3 reads: "Women shall be entitled to hold public office and to exercise all public functions, established by national law, on equal terms with men, without any discrimination.[118] The term "public office," as the U.S. representative emphasized before the Third Committee of the General Assembly, was meant to refer to "posts in the civil service, the foreign or diplomatic service and the judiciary branch, as well as to posts which were primarily political in nature. The number of such posts established by national law was usually large and the tasks to be performed varied widely."[119] The phrase "on equal terms with men," the representative added, "covered such questions as recruitment, exemptions, salary, old-age and retirement benefits, opportunities for promotion, and employment of married women, all of which were important matters in which women had sought equality for many years."[120]

In 1957, the Convention on the Nationality of Married Women, adopted by the General Assembly in recognition that "conflicts in law and in practice with reference to nationality arise as a result of provisions concerning the loss or acquisition of nationality by women as a result of marriage, of its dissolution or of the change of nationality by the husband during marriage,"[121] sought to remedy a special inequity often imposed upon married women. This Convention is designed to "eliminate the automatic effect on the nationality of the wife of marriage, its dissolution, or the change of nationality by the husband" and to "provide a satisfactory solution to the conflicts of law regarding the effect of marriage on the nationality of the wife."[122] The principal thrust of the Convention is to establish, in the crucial matter of married women's nationality, the principle of equality between the sexes, in discard of the anachronistic doctrine of "the unity of family" as "headed by the husband."[123] The Convention, going beyond such existing prescriptions as embodied in the 1930 Hague Convention on Certain Questions Relating

117. *Id.*

118. *Id.*

119. U.N. GAOR, 7th Sess., 3D COMM. 341 (1952).

120. *Id.*

121. U.N. HUMAN RIGHTS INSTRUMENTS, *supra* note 99, at 56. Its text is in 309 U.N.T.S. 65. Entering into effect on Aug. 11, 1958, the Convention, as of Dec. 31, 1972, had been ratified, or acceded to, by forty-four states. MULTILATERAL TREATIES, 1972, *supra* note 90, at 356–58.

122. UNITED NATIONS, CONVENTION ON THE NATIONALITY OF MARRIED WOMEN: HISTORICAL BACKGROUND AND COMMENTARY 25, U.N. Doc. E/CN.6/389 (1962).

123. *See id.* at 30–33; UNITED NATIONS, NATIONALITY OF MARRIED WOMEN 8–18, U.N. Doc. E/CN.6/254/Rev. 1 (1963).

to the Conflict of Nationality Laws,[124] stipulates emphatically in Article 1 that "neither the celebration nor the dissolution of a marriage between one of its nationals and an alien, nor the change of nationality by the husband during marriage, shall automatically affect the nationality of the wife";[125] and, in Article 2, that "neither the voluntary acquisition of the nationality of another State nor the renunciation of its nationality by one of its nationals shall prevent the retention of its nationality by the wife of such national."[126] The Convention further provides in Article 3 that "specially privileged naturalization procedures" be made available for a wife who wishes to acquire the nationality of her husband.[127]

In striking at another deprivation of broad concern, the 1958 Discrimination (Employment and Occupation) Convention prohibits in Article 1(1)(a) "any distinction, exclusion or preference" on account of sex, along with race and other grounds, which "has the effect of nullifying or impairing equality of opportunity or treatment in employment or occupation."[128] The terms "employment" and "occupation," Article 1(3) adds, include "access to vocational training, access to employment and to particular occupations, and terms and conditions of employment."[129]

Similarly, the 1960 Convention against Discrimination in Education prohibits, pursuant to Article 1(1), "any distinction, exclusion, limitation or preference," on account of sex, among others, which "has the purpose or effect of nullifying or impairing equality of treatment in education."[130] The term "education," Article 1(2) immediately adds, "refers to all types and levels of education, and includes access to education, the standard and quality of education, and the conditions under which it is given."[131]

In 1962, the Convention on Consent to Marriage, Minimum Age for Marriage and Registration of Marriages was adopted by the General Assembly seeking to ensure, in substance, "equal rights" of women and men "as to marriage, during marriage and at its dissolution" by virtue of "the principle of free consent to marriage" and prohibition of child

---

124. Art. 8, 179 L.N.T.S. 89, 101. *See* the appendix *infra,* at notes 364–75 and accompanying text.

125. U.N. Human Rights Instruments, *supra* note 99, at 56.

126. *Id.*

127. *Id.*

128. *Id.* at 29.

129. *Id. Cf. also International Labour Organization Activities of Special Interest in Relation to the Employment of Women,* U.N. Doc. E/CN.6/579 (1973).

130. U.N. Human Rights Instruments, *supra* note 99, at 31.

131. *Id.* "The establishment or maintenance of separate educational systems or institutions for pupils of the two sexes" would not be barred, provided that, pursuant to Art. 2(a), "these systems or institutions offer equivalent access to education, provide a teaching staff with qualifications of the same standard as well as school premises and equipment of the same quality, and afford the opportunity to take the same or equivalent courses of study."

marriages.[132] The Convention stipulates in Article 1(1) that "[n]o marriage shall be legally entered into without the full and free consent of both parties" and "such consent" is to be "expressed by them in person after due publicity and in the presence of the authority competent to solemnize the marriage and of witnesses, as prescribed by law."[133] Article 2 obliges contracting states to "take legislative action to specify a minimum age for marriage," though it is left to each individual state to decide that particular age.[134] In Article 3, the Convention further requires that "all marriages" be "registered in an appropriate official register by the competent authority."[135] This Convention is further strengthened and supplemented by the recommendation on the same subject adopted by the General Assembly in November 1965.[136] Instead of indulging the discretion of a contracting state, the recommendation specifies that the minimum age of marriage not be lower than "fifteen years of age."[137]

The basic framework in which community expectations against sex-based discrimination are crystallizing is indicated in the 1967 Declaration on the Elimination of Discrimination against Women[138] and in the Draft Convention on the Elimination of All Forms of Discrimination against Women prepared by the Commission on the Status of Women.[139] Unanimously adopted by the General Assembly on November 7, 1967, the Declaration, as described by a U.N. statement, "marks the culmination of efforts by the United Nations and by other organs, including non-governmental organizations, to formulate the principles of equal rights for women."[140] The Draft Convention is a consequence of a decision by

---

132. Bruce, *supra* note 31, at 375. For the text of the Convention, *see* 521 U.N.T.S. 231; U.N. HUMAN RIGHTS INSTRUMENTS, *supra* note 99, at 92. In operation since Dec. 9, 1964, the Convention, as of Dec. 31, 1972, had been ratified, or acceded to, by twenty-six states. MULTILATERAL TREATIES, 1972, *supra* note 90, at 359–60.

133. U.N. HUMAN RIGHTS INSTRUMENTS, *supra* note 99, at 92.

134. *Id.*

135. *Id.*

136. G.A. Res. 2018, U.N. GAOR, 20th Sess., Supp. (No. 14) 36, U.N. Doc. A/6014 (1965). The text of the resolution is *reprinted in* U.N. HUMAN RIGHTS INSTRUMENTS, *supra* note 99, at 93–94.

137. Principle II, U.N. HUMAN RIGHTS INSTRUMENTS, *supra* note 99, at 93.

138. G.A. Res. 2263, U.N. GAOR, 22nd Sess., Supp. (No. 16) 35, U.N. Doc. A/6716 (1967). The text is *reprinted in* U.N. HUMAN RIGHTS INSTRUMENTS, *supra* note 99, at 39–40.

139. COMMISSION ON THE STATUS OF WOMEN, REPORT ON THE TWENTY-FIFTH SESSION, ECOSOC, 56th Sess., Supp. (No. 4) 28–46, 83–84, U.N. Doc. E/5451 (E/CN.6/589) (1974) [hereinafter cited as 1974 REPORT OF THE COMMISSION ON THE STATUS OF WOMEN].

140. *Declaration on the Elimination of Discrimination against Women,* 4 UN MONTHLY CHRONICLE 113 (Dec. 1967). In 1963, the General Assembly, by a unanimous resolution, took the initiative in calling for the preparation of a Declaration on the elimination of discrimination against women. The Assembly instructed the Commission on the Status of Women to prepare a draft and invited member governments, the specialized agencies, and appropriate nongovernmental organizations to submit proposals for incorporation into

the Commission on the Status of Women, at its twenty-fifth session in January 1974, that "a single comprehensive draft convention should be prepared, without prejudice to the preparation of any future instrument or instruments which might be elaborated either by the United Nations or by the specialized agencies dealing with discrimination in specific fields."[141] The draft prepared by the Commission's Working Group was forwarded to member governments for study and comments, and the item "Consideration of a draft convention on the elimination of discrimination against women" was accorded top priority at the Commission's twenty-sixth session in 1975, the year designated as "International Women's Year."[142] Whatever final form this Convention may take, its substantive content is not likely to vary greatly from that of the version long before the Commission.

Underscoring in its Preamble the imperative need to "ensure the universal recognition in law and in fact of the principle of equality of men and women,"[143] the Declaration stresses that

---

the draft. In 1966, the General Assembly, upon receipt of the Commission's draft, decided to return it to the Commission for further work, with instructions that the suggestions made by various governments and other bodies be taken into account. The task of drafting and redrafting, though not without difficulty, came to fruition after the revised draft, completed in Mar. 1967 by the Commission, was considered by the Assembly's Third Committee in October, and unanimously approved by the General Assembly on Nov. 7, 1967.

On the legislative history of the Declaration, *see* EQUAL RIGHTS FOR WOMEN, *supra* note 11; *Draft Declaration on the Elimination of Discrimination against Women: Note by the Secretary-General,* U.N. Doc. A/6678 (1967); also under the same title, U.N. Doc. A/6349 (1966); [1967] YEARBOOK OF THE UNITED NATIONS 513–14, 518–22 [hereinafter cited as Y.B.U.N.]; Y.B.U.N. [1966] at 462–63, 466–68.

141. 1974 REPORT OF THE COMMISSION ON THE STATUS OF WOMEN, *supra* note 139, at 31. *See also* 11 UN MONTHLY CHRONICLE 26 (Feb. 1974). For the pros and cons of formulating a single comprehensive convention, *see Consideration of Proposals concerning a New Instrument or Instruments of International Law to Eliminate Discrimination against Women,* U.N. Doc. E/CN.6/573 (1973).

142. Commission Res. 1 (XXV) adopted at the 618th meeting, Jan. 25, 1974, 1974 REPORT OF THE COMMISSION ON THE STATUS OF WOMEN, *supra* note 139, at 83–84. ". . . the proposed draft Convention was broader in scope than the Declaration but, at the same time included only fundamental aspects of women's rights and avoided detailed and specific provisions which were already embodied in the International Labour Organization and UNESCO Conventions." *Consideration of Proposals concerning a New Instrument or Instruments of International Law to Eliminate Discrimination against Women* (report of the Working Group to the Commission on the Status of Women) 4, U.N. Doc. E/CN.6/574 (1974) [hereinafter cited as *Report of the Working Group*].

For subsequent developments, *see* UNITED NATIONS, REPORT OF THE WORLD CONFERENCE OF THE INTERNATIONAL WOMEN'S YEAR, MEXICO CITY, *19 June–2 July 1975,* U.N. Doc. E/CONF.66/34 (1976); *Work of the Preparatory Committee for the World Conference of the United Nations Decade for Women during Its First Session,* U.N. Doc. A/33/339 (1978) (report of the secretary-general).

143. U.N. HUMAN RIGHTS INSTRUMENTS, *supra* note 99, at 39.

> discrimination against women is incompatible with human dignity and with the welfare of the family and of society, prevents their participation, on equal terms with men, in the political, social, economic and cultural life of their countries and is an obstacle to the full development of the potentialities of women in the service of their countries and of humanity;[144]

and that

> the full and complete development of a country, the welfare of the world and the cause of peace require the maximum participation of women as well as men in all fields.[145]

The same theme is carried forward in the Draft Convention.[146]

The Declaration and the Draft Convention, drawing heavily upon the parallel formulations in relation to racial discrimination,[147] spell out in both broad and detailed terms the basic norm against discrimination, the commitment to effect necessary changes in both authoritative and effective power processes within national communities, and the content of prescription in relation to various critical sectors where women most require protection. The Declaration states the basic norm of nondiscrimination in Article 1: "Discrimination against women, denying or limiting as it does their equality of rights with men, is fundamentally unjust and constitutes an offence against human dignity."[148] The Draft Convention in its first article adds further content to the concept of discrimination:

> In this Convention the term "discrimination against women" shall mean any distinction, exclusion or restriction made on the basis of sex which has the effect of or the purpose of nullifying the recognition, enjoyment or exercise of human rights and fundamental freedoms in the political, economic, social, cultural or any field of public life.[149]

This formulation, evidently adopted from Article 1(1) of the Convention

---

144. *Id.* 145. *Id.*

146. 1974 REPORT OF THE COMMISSION ON THE STATUS OF WOMEN, *supra* note 139, at 32–34.

147. The reference is to the United Nations Declaration on the Elimination of All Forms of Racial Discrimination, G.A. Res. 1904, U.N. GAOR, 18th Sess., Supp. (No. 15) 35, U.N. Doc. A/5515 (1963), and to the International Convention on the Elimination of All Forms of Racial Discrimination, G.A. Res. 2106A, U.N. GAOR, 20th Sess., Supp. (No. 14) at 47, U.N. Doc. A-6014 (1965). The text of these two documents is *reprinted in* U.N. HUMAN RIGHTS INSTRUMENTS, *supra* note 99, at 22 and 23 respectively. For a detailed analysis, with pertinent references, *see* chapters 6–9 *supra.*

148. U.N. HUMAN RIGHTS INSTRUMENTS, *supra* note 99, at 39.

149. 1974 REPORT OF THE COMMISSION ON THE STATUS OF WOMEN, *supra* note 139, at 34.

on the Elimination of Racial Discrimination,[150] would appear to encompass at least as broad a prohibition.[151] As a means of expediting necessary changes in the processes of authoritative decision within national communities, the Declaration stipulates in Article 2:

> All appropriate measures shall be taken to abolish existing laws, customs, regulations and practices which are discriminatory against women, and to establish adequate legal protection for equal rights of men and women, in particular:
>
> (a) The principle of equality of rights shall be embodied in the constitution or otherwise guaranteed by law;
>
> (b) The international instruments of the United Nations and the specialized agencies relating to the elimination of discrimination against women shall be ratified or acceded to and fully implemented as soon as practicable.[152]

This stipulation entails positive as well as negative formulations. Negatively, all "existing laws, customs, regulations and practices" discriminatory against women are to be abolished. Positively, "adequate legal protection for equal rights of men and women" is to be established so that in all important sectors of community life women may fully develop their potentials equally and contribute to the aggregate common interest. In the course of drafting, both in the Commission and in the General Assembly, strong arguments were made in the debate against the inclusion in this provision of "customs" and "practices," along with "laws" and "regulations," on the grounds that "customs based on long-standing traditions could not be abolished overnight";[153] it would be more appropriate, according to this view, gradually to "modify" or "change" rather than "abolish," customs and practices.[154] The majority, in rejecting this view, "held it necessary to call for abolishing discriminatory customs and practices precisely because that was the very purpose of the Declaration."[155]

The Draft Convention, in addition to reiterating this broad stipula-

---

150. It may be recalled that Art. 1(1) of the International Convention on the Elimination of All Forms of Racial Discrimination reads as follows:

> In this Convention, the term "racial discrimination" shall mean any distinction, exclusion, restriction or preference based on race, colour, descent, or national or ethnic origin which has the purpose or effect of nullifying or impairing the recognition, enjoyment or exercise, on an equal footing, of human rights and fundamental freedoms in the political, economic, social, cultural or any other field of public life.

U.N. Human Rights Instruments, *supra* note 99, at 24.

151. *Cf.* chapters 6–9 *supra.*

152. U.N. Human Rights Instruments, *supra* note 99, at 39.

153. Equal Rights for Women, *supra* note 11, at 3.

154. *Id.* 155. *Id.*

tion, obliges in Article 2(b, c) a contracting state to engage in "no act or practice of discrimination against women and to ensure that public authorities and public institutions, national and local, shall act in conformity with this obligation,"[156] and "not to sponsor, defend or support discrimination against women by any person or organizations."[157] The Draft Convention further proposes in Article 5(2) to prohibit by law "[a]ny advocacy of the superiority of one sex over the other and of discrimination on the basis of sex."[158]

In attempting to promote necessary changes in effective power processes, special attention is directed to the long-range goals of prevention and reconstruction. Particular emphasis is put upon changing stereotyped community predispositions about the role of women and upon cultivating sounder perspectives that define appropriate roles for both women and men in the contemporary world. Thus, Article 3 of the Declaration reads: "All appropriate measures shall be taken to educate public opinion and to direct national aspirations towards the eradication of prejudice and the abolition of customary and all other practices which are based on the idea of the inferiority of women."[159] The Draft Convention adds a new dimension in Article 5(1) by asserting that "the protection of motherhood is a common interest of the entire society which should bear responsibilities for it."[160] The bringing up of new generations is at last acknowledged as an ongoing enterprise for the whole community.

Both the Declaration and the Draft Convention spotlight certain critical areas in which women are particularly susceptible to deprivation. Amplifying some of the prior conventions which have been noted above,[161] they offer detailed specification of a range of protected rights, embracing all important value sectors, notably power, enlightenment, wealth, well-being, and affection.

In reference to power, the Declaration stresses the equal rights of women in regard to nationality, legal capacity, freedom of movement, and voting and officeholding (elective and appointive alike). Thus, Article 4 of the Declaration states:

> All appropriate measures shall be taken to ensure to women on equal terms with men, without any discrimination:
>
> (a) The right to vote in all elections and be eligible for election to all publicly elected bodies;

---

156. 1974 Report of the Commission on the Status of Women, *supra* note 139, at 34–35.

157. *Id.* at 35.

158. *Id.* at 36.

159. U.N. Human Rights Instruments, *supra* note 99, at 39.

160. 1974 Report of the Commission on the Status of Women, *supra* note 139, at 36.

161. *See* notes 104–37 *supra* and accompanying text.

> (b) The right to vote in all public referenda;
>
> (c) The right to hold public office and to exercise all public functions.
>
> Such rights shall be guaranteed by legislation.[162]

The specification of an equal right to vote "in all public referenda," as indicated in paragraph b, is a novel feature, not included in the 1952 Convention on the Political Rights of Women.[163] The Draft Convention seeks in Article 8 to broaden and fortify this provision by urging that "all appropriate measures" be taken to "ensure to women on equal terms with men, without any discrimination, equal opportunities to participate in the political and public life of the country."[164] In illustration, the Draft Convention further underscores "equal opportunities" to "participate in the formulation of government policy and the administration thereof and to hold public office at the national and local levels"[165] and to "participate in nongovernmental organizations and associations."[166]

In the matter of nationality, the Declaration and the Draft Convention seek to protect women from the bondage and hardships caused by involuntary acquisition, change, and retention of nationality, which automatically result from marriage to an alien husband.[167] Article 5 of the Declaration reads: "Women shall have the same rights as men to acquire, change or retain their nationality. Marriage to an alien shall not automatically affect the nationality of the wife either by rendering her stateless or by forcing upon her the nationality of her husband.[168] Drawing upon the 1957 Convention on the Nationality of Married Women,[169] the Draft Convention is more detailed in its formulation. Article 9(1) reads:

> States Parties shall grant women the same rights as men to acquire, change or retain their nationality and shall require, in particular, that neither marriage of a woman to, nor dissolution of her marriage from, an alien nor the change of nationality by her alien husband during marriage shall automatically change her nationality, render her stateless or force upon her the nationality of her husband.[170]

---

162. U.N. Human Rights Instruments, *supra* note 99, at 39.
163. *See* notes 113–20 *supra* and accompanying text.
164. 1974 Report of the Commission on the Status of Women, *supra* note 139, at 36.
165. Art. 8(b), *id.*
166. Art. 8(d), *id.* at 37.
167. *Cf.* notes 121–27 *supra* and accompanying text.
168. U.N. Human Rights Instruments, *supra* note 99, at 39.
169. *Id.* at 56–57. *See also* note 167 *supra.*
170. 1974 Report of the Commission on the Status of Women, *supra* note 139, at 37.

The second paragraph of this article urges the grant of nationality to alien women married to nationals "through specially privileged naturalization procedures,"[171] as distinguished from those ordinarily applicable to aliens in general.

In further reference to shared power, the Declaration, in Article 6(1)(b, c), stipulates that "all appropriate measures, particularly legislative measures," be taken to "ensure to women, married or unmarried," the "right to equality in legal capacity and the exercise thereof"[172] and the "same rights as men with regard to the law on the movement of persons."[173] The Draft Convention, reinforcing this provision, specifies in Article 15 that women be accorded "equal civil and legal capacity with men in all stages of procedure in courts and tribunals"[174] and that "all contracts directed at restricting the legal capacity of women" be deemed "null and void."[175] Article 15(4) further includes "the freedom to choose residence" in the protection regarding the "movement of persons."[176]

In regard to the affection value, the Declaration, in Article 6(2)(b, c), stipulates that "[a]ll appropriate measures" be taken to "ensure the principle of equality of status of the husband and wife," especially that women be accorded "the same right as men to free choice of a spouse and to enter into marriage only with their free and full consent,"[177] and that women be accorded "equal rights with men during marriage and at its dissolution."[178] Emphasizing the "paramount" importance of "the interest of the children," the Declaration adds in Article 6(2)(c) that parents be accorded "equal rights and duties in matters relating to their children."[179] The adoption of this provision, despite considerable opposition based on the alleged threat to "the stability of the family as an institution,"[180] was designed to "establish the principle of sharing responsibilities between father and mother."[181] In addition, the Draft Convention specifically urges in Article 16(e) "[r]ecognition of equal rights to be guardians and trustees, and also of an equal right to adopt children."[182] In a further effort to ensure equal respect for women in

171. *Id.*

172. Art. 6(1)(b), U.N. Human Rights Instruments, *supra* note 99, at 39.

173. Art. 6(1)(c), *id.*

174. Art. 15(2), 1974 Report of the Commission on the Status of Women, *supra* note 139, at 41.

175. Art. 15(3), *id.*

176. *Id.*

177. Art. 6(2)(a), U.N. Human Rights Instruments, *supra* note 99, at 39.

178. Art. 6(2)(b), *id.*

179. *Id.* at 40.

180. Equal Rights for Women, *supra* note 11, at 11.

181. Bruce, *supra* note 31, at 388.

182. 1974 Report of the Commission on the Status of Women, *supra* note 139, at 42.

reference to the affection value, the Declaration in Article 6(3) prohibits "child marriage and betrothal of young girls before puberty,"[183] and requires states to "specify a minimum age for marriage and to make the registration of marriages in an official registry compulsory."[184] Article 8 further stipulates that "[a]ll appropriate measures, including legislation," be taken to "combat all forms of traffic in women and exploitation of prostitution of women."[185] The same provisions are embodied respectively in Article 16(2) and Article 7 of the Draft Convention.[186]

In concern for equal access to enlightenment and skill, the Declaration in Article 9 offers a variety of provisions:

> All appropriate measures shall be taken to ensure to girls and women, married or unmarried, equal rights with men in education at all levels, and in particular:
>
> (a) Equal conditions of access to, and study in, educational institutions of all types, including universities and vocational, technical and professional schools;
>
> (b) The same choice of curricula, the same examinations, teaching staff with qualifications of the same standard, and school premises and equipment of the same quality, whether the institutions are co-educational or not;
>
> (c) Equal opportunities to benefit from scholarships and other study grants;
>
> (d) Equal opportunities for access to programmes of continuing education, including adult literacy programmes;
>
> (e) Access to educational information to help in ensuring the health and well-being of families.[187]

Paragraph e, a "very carefully drafted phrase,"[188] is said to be "the first—even though very indirect—reference to certain aspects of family planning in an international instrument emanating from the Commission on the Status of Women."[189] Essentially the same provision appears in Article 10 of the Draft Convention.[190]

In an effort to "ensure to women, married or unmarried, equal rights

---

183. U.N. Human Rights Instruments, *supra* note 99, at 40.

184. *Id.*

185. *Id.*

186. 1974 Report of the commission on the Status of Women, *supra* note 139, at 42, and 36.

187. U.N. Human Rights Instruments, *supra* note 99, at 40.

188. Equal Rights for Women, *supra* note 11, at 16.

189. *Id.*

190. 1974 Report of the Commission on the Status of Women, *supra* note 139, at 37–38.

with men in the field of economic and social life," Article 10(1) of the Declaration calls for "appropriate measures" to protect certain rights:

> (a) The right, without discrimination on grounds of marital status or any other grounds, to receive vocational training, to work, to free choice of profession and employment, and to professional and vocational advancement;
> (b) The right to equal remuneration with men and to equality of treatment in respect of work of equal value;
> (c) The right to leave with pay, retirement privileges and provision for security in respect of unemployment, sickness, old age or other incapacity to work;
> (d) The right to receive family allowances on equal terms with men.[191]

The same article prescribes, in paragraph 2, certain special protection for women's "effective right to work" in requiring that measures be taken to "prevent" women from being dismissed "in the event of marriage or maternity" and to "provide paid maternity leave, with the guarantee of returning to former employment," and also to "provide the necessary social services, including childcare facilities."[192] The article further makes it clear that "measures taken to protect women in certain types of work, for reasons inherent in their physical nature," are not to be regarded as discriminatory.[193] A very explicit provision for protection of women in the wealth process appears elsewhere, in Article 6(1)(a), which ensures to "women, married or unmarried, equal rights with men" to "acquire, administer, enjoy, dispose of and inherit property, including property acquired during marriage."[194]

The Draft Convention offers more detailed protection in terms of both wealth and well-being. Thus, for example, Article 11(a) specifies that women's "right to work" includes "the right of all persons to an opportunity to earn their livelihood by work which they freely choose or to which they freely consent and the right to be employed in their field of specialization in accordance with their level of qualifications,"[195] and under Article 11(b) women are to be assured the "right to take employment and to continue their activity in the labour force and in professions irrespective of marital status or of spouse's consent."[196] Article 11(d) further specifies the right of women to

---

191. U.N. Human Rights Instruments, *supra* note 99, at 40.
192. *Id.*
193. Art. 10(3), *id.*
194. *Id.* at 39.
195. 1974 Report of the Commission on the Status of Women, *supra* note 139, at 38.
196. *Id.*

> receive equal initial or basic vocational training for preparation for employment, and advanced training on an equal footing with men for promotion and in the event of changes in the conditions of production or technical advances and, where necessary, free retraining and restoration of levels of qualification after an enforced interruption resulting from the fulfilment by women of their maternal obligations.[197]

Other measures adopted "for the protection of women" because of "their physical nature and for the promotion of the welfare of mothers," which in the words of Article 4(2) are not to be "interpreted as violating the principle of equality of rights of men and women,"[198] include the following:

1. Protection of women workers from "heavy labour and under working conditions that are physically harmful to women" (Art. 12[a]);[199]
2. Provision of "appropriate working conditions for pregnant women and nursing mothers" (Art. 12[b]);[200]
3. Grant of "adequate maternity leave with pay," "without loss of the job held" (Art. 12[c]);[201]
4. Prohibition on dismissing women on maternity leave or on account of their being "pregnant" or "nursing a child" (Art. 12[d]);[202]
5. Adequate pay leave to accommodate childcare needs (Art. 12[e, f]);[203]
6. Provision to women of "free medical care during pregnancy, confinement and the post-natal period" (Art. 12[g]);[204]
7. Provision of adequate childcare facilities and services (Art. 13).[205]

The Draft Convention makes it clear, further, that the proposed measures of protection for women in the fields of wealth and well-being are intended for wide application. Thus, Article 14 reads:

> The provisions of articles 11, 12, 13 and 14 shall apply to all women without exception, who are gainfully employed in State co-operative, public and private institutions, industrial and non-industrial enter-

197. *Id.*
198. *Id.* at 35.
199. *Id.* at 39.
200. *Id.*
201. *Id.* at 40.
202. *Id.*
203. *Id.*
204. *Id.*
205. *Id.* at 40–41.

> prises and other organizations in agriculture and on plantations, and also to women who perform for any organizations or individuals remunerated work at home or who are gainfully employed in domestic work.[206]

Finally, to eliminate double standards in relation to responsible conduct, the Declaration stipulates in Article 7 that "[a]ll provisions of penal codes which constitute discrimination against women shall be repealed."[207] This is primarily designed to protect women against prosecution for certain crimes hitherto uniquely ascribed to women or crimes in which double standards are employed in defining the crimes.[208]

The profound concern for eradicating discrimination on account of sex contained in the Declaration and the Draft Convention is fortified by many parallel expressions emanating from various United Nations and related bodies.[209] The Proclamation of Teheran, adopted by the International Conference on Human Rights in May 1968, appropriately summarizes:

> The discrimination of which women are still victims in various regions of the world must be eliminated. An inferior status for women is contrary to the Charter of the United Nations as well as the provisions of the Universal Declaration of Human Rights. The full implementation of the Declaration of the Elimination of Discrimination against Women is a necessity for the progress of mankind.[210]

The call of the Conference for "measures to promote women's rights in the modern world, including a unified long-term United Nations programme for the advancement of women"[211] was soon followed up by the General Assembly in adopting such a program in 1970.[212] In its resolution on "International Development Strategy for the Second United Na-

---

206. *Id.* at 41.

207. U.N. Human Rights Instruments, *supra* note 99, at 40.

208. Other examples include application of double standards to "such matters as adultery and even murder in certain instances, where the husband was permitted to plead reasons of personal honour to justify killing of his wife in certain circumstances." Equal Rights for Women, *supra* note 11 at 15. *See also* B. Babcock, A. Freedman, E. Norton, & S. Ross, *supra* note 6, at 819–914; Bruce, *supra* note 31, at 389.

209. *Cf.* United Nations, The United Nations and the Status of Women (1964); Bruce, *supra* note 31.

210. U.N. Human Rights Instruments, *supra* note 99, at 19; United Nations, Final Act of the International Conference on Human Rights, Teheran, 22 April to 13 May 1968, at 4, U.N. Doc. A/CONF.32/41 (1968) [hereinafter cited as Final Act of the Human Rights Conference].

211. Final Act of the Human Rights Conference, *supra* note 210, at 10–11.

212. G.A. Res. 2716, U.N. GAOR, 25th Sess., Supp. (No. 28) 81–83, U.N. Doc. A/8028 (1970).

tions Development Decade," adopted in October 1970, the General Assembly included among the "goals and objectives" of the decade the encouragement of "the full integration of women in the total development effort."[213] In order to further "strengthen universal recognition of the principle of the equality of men and women, *de jure* and *de facto*,"[214] the General Assembly, in its resolution 3010 of December 18, 1972, proclaimed "the year 1975 International Women's Year."[215] It urged "intensified action" to "promote equality between men and women" and to "ensure the full integration of women in the total development effort."[216]

On the regional level, sex is included among the impermissible grounds of differentiation in both the European Convention on Human Rights and the American Convention on Human Rights. The European Convention states in Article 14 that "the enjoyment of the rights and freedoms" provided in the Convention is to be "secured without discrimination" because of sex or other grounds.[217] The American Convention, in Article 1(1), obliges the contracting states to "undertake to respect the rights and freedoms" provided in the Convention and to "ensure to all persons subject to their jurisdiction the free and full exercise of those rights and freedoms, without any discrimination" on account of "sex" or other factors.[218] It may be noted that even before the adoption of the American Convention of Human Rights in November 1969, significant achievements for the protection of women had been made under the Inter-American System, which considerably inspired the work of the U.N. bodies in the protection of women's rights.[219] Beginning with the concern for protecting women's rights expressed in the Fifth International Conference of American States in 1923,[220] through the establishment and functioning of the Inter-American Commission of

---

213. G.A. Res. 2626, *id.*, at 39, 41.

214. G.A. Res. 3010, U.N. GAOR, 27th Sess., Supp. (No. 30) 66, U.N. Doc. A/8730 (1972).

215. *Id.* at 67.

216. *Id. See also* notes 2 and 3 *supra.*

217. Basic Documents on International Protection of Human Rights 125, 130 (L. Sohn & T. Buergenthal eds. 1973) [hereinafter cited as Basic Documents]. The Rome Treaty of 1958, establishing the European Economic Community, states, in Art. 119, that "each member State shall apply the principle of equal pay for men and women in the case of the same work."

218. Basic Documents, *supra* note 217, at 210.

219. *See* Organization of American States, General Secretariat, The Organization of American States and Human Rights, 1960–1967, at 69–79 (1972) [hereinafter cited as OAS and Human Rights]; *Report Submitted by the Organization of American States* 68–80, U.N. Doc. A/CONF.32/L.10 (1968) [hereinafter cited as *OAS Report*].

220. *See* OAS and Human Rights, *supra* note 219, at 69; *OAS Report, supra* note 219, at 68–69.

Women,[221] a number of regional prescriptions for the protection of women had come into being. Notably, the Montevideo Convention on the Nationality of Women of 1933 pioneered the principle of equality of the sexes regarding nationality: "There shall be no distinction based on sex as regards nationality in their legislation or in their practice" (Art. 1).[222] The Lima Declaration in Favor of Women's Rights, adopted at the Eighth International Conference of American States in 1938,[223] emphatically pronounced that "women have the right" to "political treatment on the basis of equality with men," to "the enjoyment of equality as to civil status," to "full protection in and opportunity for work," and to "the most ample protection as mothers."[224] In 1948, at the Ninth Conference of the Organization of American States held in Bogota, Colombia, the long years of efforts on the part of the Inter-American Commission of Women culminated in the adoption of two separate conventions: the Inter-American Convention on the Granting of Political Rights to Women, stipulating that "the right to vote and to be elected to national office shall not be denied or abridged by reason of sex";[225] and the Inter-American Convention on the Granting of Civil Rights to Women, pursuant to which the contracting states pledge to "grant to women the same civil rights that men enjoy."[226] Meanwhile, the American Declaration of the Rights and Duties of Man, adopted at the same Conference and antedating the Universal Declaration of Human Rights, also pronounced in Article 2 that "All persons are equal before the law and have the rights and duties established in this Declaration, without distinction as to race, sex, language, creed or any other factor."[227]

The accelerating movement toward the reform of national constitutions to secure equal rights for women adds substance to transnational expectations in behalf of nondiscrimination. The United States offers an excellent example. A long line of judicial decisions, slowly enlarging the rights of women[228] and changing community expectations, have culmi-

221. OAS AND HUMAN RIGHTS, *supra* note 219, at 69–70; *OAS Report, supra* note 219, at 69–70. For accounts of the recent activities of the Inter-American Commission of Women, *see Report of the Inter-American Commission of Women,* U.N. Doc. E/CN.6/558 (1972); *Programme of Concerted International Action to Promote the Advancement of Women and Their Integration in Development* (report of the Inter-American Commission of Women), U.N. Doc. E/CN.6/572 (1973).

222. NATIONALITY OF MARRIED WOMEN, *supra* note 123, at 23–24.

223. CARNEGIE ENDOWMENT FOR INTERNATIONAL PEACE, THE INTERNATIONAL CONFERENCES OF AMERICAN STATES, FIRST SUPPLEMENT, 1933–1940, at 250 (1940).

224. *Id.*

225. CONVENTION ON THE POLITICAL RIGHTS OF WOMEN, *supra* note 114, at 4.

226. *Id.* (n. 6).

227. BASIC DOCUMENTS, *supra* note 217, at 187, 188.

228. *See* N. DORSEN, N. CHACHKIN, & S. LAW, *supra* note 44, at 347–90. *Cf. also* B.

nated in a proposed Equal Rights Amendment to the Constitution, which is in the process of being ratified. The substantive sections of the proposed Equal Rights Amendment, as passed by the U.S. Congress on March 22, 1972, read as follows:

> Section 1. Equality of rights under the law shall not be denied or abridged by the United States or by any State on account of sex.
>
> Section 2. The Congress shall have the power to enforce, by appropriate legislation, the provisions of this article.[229]

From the decision in *Bradwell* v. *Illinois* (1873),[230] sanctioning the exclusion of women from the legal profession, as grounded in the anachronistic doctrine of "women's separate place" in society, the United States Supreme Court had moved a long way when, in 1971, it held unconstitutional, in *Reed* v. *Reed,*[231] an Idaho statute purporting to favor males over females in the matter of administering estates. In the words of the Court:

> To give a mandatory preference to members of either sex over members of the other, merely to accomplish the elimination of hearings on the merits, is to make the very kind of arbitrary legislative choice forbidden by the Equal Protection Clause of the Fourteenth Amendment; and whatever may be said as to the positive values of avoiding intrafamily controversy, the choice in this context may not lawfully be mandated solely on the basis of sex.[232]

The emerging prescription is further fortified by *Frontiero* v. *Richardson*

BABCOCK, A. FREEDMAN, E. NORTON, & S. ROSS, *supra* note 6; K. DAVIDSON, R. GINSBURG, & H. KAY, *supra* note 6; L. KANOWITZ, *supra* note 15.

229. As of Dec. 31, 1978, thirty-five states out of the required thirty-eight had ratified the Amendment. The initial seven-year period for ratifying the E.R.A. was extended, in October 1978, by the U.S. Congress for thirty-nine months—from Mar. 22, 1979, to June 30, 1982. For relevant constitutional law issues raised, *see* Duker, *ERA: Stretching the Deadline,* 7 HUMAN RIGHTS 20 (No. 3, 1978); Emerson, *ERA: Stretching the Deadline, id. See also* Berlow, *Senate Clears Extension of ERA Deadline*, 36 CONG. Q. 2724 (1978); Berlow, *ERA Extension Wins in House on 233-189 Vote, id.* at 2214.

The tortuous legislative history of this amendment is indicated in Brown, Emerson, Falk, & Freedman, *supra* note 6, at 981–85. *See also Hearings on S.J. Res. 61 before the Subcomm. on Constitutional Amendments of the Senate Comm. on the Judiciary,* 91st Cong., 2d Sess. (1970); *Hearings on S.J. Res. 61 and S.J. Res. 231 before the Senate Comm. on the Judiciary,* 91st Cong., 2d Sess. (1970); *House Hearings on Equal Rights, supra* note 33; WOMEN AND THE "EQUAL RIGHTS" AMENDMENT: SENATE SUBCOMMITTEE HEARINGS ON THE CONSTITUTIONAL AMENDMENT, 91ST CONGRESS (C. Stimpson ed. 1972); B. BABCOCK, A. FREEDMAN, E. NORTON, & S. ROSS, *supra* note 6, at 129–89.

230. Bradwell v. Illinois, 83 U.S. (16 Wall.) 130 (1873).

231. Reed v. Reed, 404 U.S. 71 (1971).

232. *Id.* at 76–77.

(1973),[233] in which the Supreme Court declared unconstitutional statutes which allow a serviceman to claim his wife, "for the purposes of obtaining increased quarters allowances and medical and dental benefits," "as a 'dependent' without regard to whether she is in fact dependent upon him for any part of her support,"[234] but disallow a servicewoman to "claim her husband as a 'dependent' " "unless he is in fact dependent upon her for over one-half of his support."[235] Mr. Justice Brennan, announcing the judgment of the Court and speaking for himself and three other Justices, observed that

> since sex, like race and national origin, is an immutable characteristic determined solely by the accident of birth, the imposition of special disabilities upon the members of a particular sex because of their sex would seem to violate "the basic concept of our system that legal burdens should bear some relationship to individual responsibility."[236]

"And what differentiates sex," Justice Brennan elaborated,

> from such non-suspect statuses as intelligence or physical disability, and aligns it with the recognized suspect criteria, is that the sex characteristic frequently bears no relation to ability to perform or contribute to society. As a result, statutory distinctions between the sexes often have the effect of invidiously relegating the entire class of females to inferior legal status without regard to the actual capabilities of its individual members.[237]

"[C]lassifications based upon sex," he added, "like classifications based upon race, alienage, or national origin, are inherently suspect, and must therefore be subjected to strict judicial scrutiny."[238] "Applying the analysis mandated by that stricter standard of review,"[239] Justice Brennan concluded that,

> by according differential treatment to male and female members of the uniformed services for the sole purpose of achieving administrative convenience, the challenged statutes violate the Due Process Clause of the Fifth Amendment insofar as they require a female member to prove the dependency of her husband.[240]

The *Reed* and *Frontiero* decisions undoubtedly harbinger a great potential for both the Fifth and the Fourteenth Amendments in coping with

---

233. Frontiero v. Richardson, 411 U.S. 677 (1973).
234. *Id.* at 678.
235. *Id.* at 678–79.
236. *Id.* at 686.
237. *Id.* at 686–87.
238. *Id.* at 688.
239. *Id.*
240. *Id.* at 690–91.

sex-based discriminations. Nevertheless, insistent demands continue that the Equal Rights Amendment be ratified without delay. As Emerson and his co-authors eloquently put it,

> We believe that the necessary changes in our legal structure can be accomplished effectively only by a constitutional amendment. The process of piecemeal change is long and uncertain; the prospect of judicial change through interpretation of the Fourteenth Amendment is remote and the results are likely to be inadequate. The Equal Rights Amendment provides a sound constitutional basis for carrying out the alterations which must be put into effect. It embodies a consistent theory that guarantees equal legal rights for both sexes while taking into account unique physical differences between the sexes. In the tradition of other great constitutional mandates, such as equal protection for all races, the right to freedom of expression, and the guarantee of due process, it supplies the fundamental legal framework upon which to build a coherent body of law and practice designed to achieve the specific goal of equal rights.[241]

A comprehensive comparative study, while it presumably would reveal considerable diversity in the detailed practice of different communities, would certainly confirm a trend toward prescription of equality between the sexes.[242] As noted elsewhere, it is practically a universal pattern in national constitutions to prescribe a general form of equality, which typically condemns sex, along with race and other factors, as a basis of differential treatment.[243] Many constitutions have gone further by enunciating separate provisions for equality of the sexes, explicitly highlighting equal rights for women as well as men. Thus, the 1949 Constitution of the German Federal Republic declares, in Article 3(2), that "[m]en and women shall have equal rights."[244] The 1936 Constitution of the USSR states in Article 122:

For developments subsequent to *Reed* and *Frontiero, see* Ginsburg, *From No Rights, to Half Rights, to Confusing Rights,* 7 Human Rights 12 (No. 1, 1978); *see also* Davie, *Pregnancy: A Laborious Issue,* 7 Human Rights 36 (No. 3, 1978).

241. Brown, Emerson, Falk, & Freedman, *supra* note 6, at 979. With or without appropriate constitutional amendment, lawyers engaged in litigation for the protection of human rights might make much more effective use of the transnational prescriptions outlined above. Irrespective of whether particular conventions have been ratified by the United States, the general norm of nondiscrimination could be found to be a part of the customary international law which is the law of the land of the United States.

242. *See e.g.,* United Nations, Constitutions, Electoral Laws and Other Legal Instruments Relating to the Political Rights of Women, U.N. Doc. A/6447/Rev. 1 (1968); *Symposium—The Status of Women,* 20 Am. J. Comp. L. 585 (1972).

243. *See* chapters 6–9 *supra* and chapters 11–15 *infra.*

244. Basic Documents on Human Rights 19 (I. Brownlie ed. 1971).

> Women in the U.S.S.R. are accorded equal rights with men in all spheres of economic, government, cultural, political and other public activity.
>
> The possibility of exercising these rights is ensured by women being accorded an equal right with men to work, payment for work, rest and leisure, social insurance and education, and by state protection of the interests of mother and child, state aid to mothers of large families and unmarried mothers, maternity leave with full pay, and the provision of a wide network of maternity homes, nurseries and kindergartens.[245]

Similarly, Article 96 of the Constitution of the People's Republic of China, 1954, reads:

> In the People's Republic of China women enjoy equal rights with men in all spheres—political, economic, cultural, social and domestic.
>
> The state protects marriage, the family, and the mother and child.[246]

Article 51 of the Constitution of Paraguay, 1967, provides: "This Constitution upholds the equality of the civil and political rights of men and women, whose correlative duties shall be established in the law, attending the purposes of matrimony and to the unity of the family."[247] The new Constitution of Egypt, adopted in 1972, stipulates in Article 11 that "[t]he State shall reconcile women's duties to their families and women's work in society and shall ensure the equality of women with men in the political, social, cultural and economic fields, without violating the law of the Islamic Sharia."[248]

Oftentimes protection of equal rights for women is sought through

245. *Id.* at 26. *See* Tay, *The Status of Women in the Soviet Union,* 20 AM. J. COMP. L. 662 (1972).

246. BASIC DOCUMENTS ON HUMAN RIGHTS, *supra* note 244, at 48.

247. 4 CONSTITUTIONS OF NATIONS 1067, 1074 (rev. 3d ed. A. Peaslee ed. 1970).

248. *Implementation of the Declaration on the Elimination of Discrimination against Women and Related Instruments* (report of the secretary-general) 11, U.N. Doc. E/CN.6/571 (1973).

Of course what is meant by "the law of the Islamic Sharia" is critical here. In aid of interpretation, *consult generally* 1 A. ALI, MAHOMMEDAN LAW (4th ed. 1912); 2 A. ALI, MAHOMMEDAN LAW (5th ed. 1929); A. ALI, THE SPIRIT OF ISLAM (1922), especially at 222–57; J. ANDERSON, ISLAMIC LAW IN AFRICA (1954); J. ANDERSON, ISLAMIC LAW IN THE MODERN WORLD (1959); A. MEER, THE LEGAL POSITION OF WOMEN IN ISLAM (1912); R. ROBERTS, THE SOCIAL LAWS OF THE QUORAN (1925): J. SCHACHT, INTRODUCTION TO ISLAMIC LAW (1964). *Cf. also* H. GIBB, MODERN TRENDS IN ISLAM (1947; 1972); H. GIBB, MOHAMMEDANISM: AN HISTORICAL SURVEY (2d ed. Galaxy Book ed. 1962); H. GIBB, STUDIES ON THE CIVILIZATION OF ISLAM (1962; 1968): M. QUTB, ISLAM, THE MISUNDERSTOOD RELIGION (1969); W. SMITH, ISLAM IN MODERN HISTORY (1957); THEMES OF ISLAMIC CIVILIZATION (J. Williams ed. 1971).

statutes. For instance, Israel's Woman's Equal Rights Law, 5711-1951, stipulates that "[w]ith regard to any legal act, the same law shall apply to a woman and a man, and any provision of law that discriminates against women as women shall be of no effect."[249] The General Federation of Iraqi Women Act (No. 13 of 1972) spotlighted "the need to raise the level of women by all possible means and to ensure their enjoyment of equal rights with men in all political, social, civic, economic and cultural fields, to provide them with employment opportunities, to defend their rights and interests and to abolish existing laws, customs, regulations and practices which are discriminatory against women."[250] Other examples are documented in the Reports of the U.N. secretary-general on "Implementation of the Declaration on the Elimination of Discrimination against Women and Related Instruments."[251] A report of the secretary-general points out, in sum, that "on the whole, a trend exists in those countries where full compliance in law with the provisions of the Declaration has not yet been achieved, towards the realization of a greater measure of compliance, if not total compliance in law, with the rights set forth in this international instrument."[252]

PROPOSALS FOR APPLICATION

The contemporary provision for implementation and application of the vast body of transnational prescriptions designed to secure equality of women with men is even more primitive than that designed to minimize racial discrimination.[253] In 1968, one year after the adoption of the Declaration on the Elimination of Discrimination against Women, the Economic and Social Council, acting on the recommendation of the Commission on the Status of Women, adopted a resolution, urging such "measures of implementation" as "publicity," "studies," revision of "national legislation," and, more importantly, a reporting system.[254] Needless to say, measures wholly dependent upon state cooperation, such as these, are scarcely adequate to the critical tasks of "implementation." It has increasingly been stressed that—given the decentralized character of the world arena and the complex root causes of sex-based discriminations—more comprehensive, more concerted, and more centrally directed measures are required.

The United Nations, consequently, launched a unified long-term pro-

249. *Quoted in* Albeck, *The Status of Women in Israel,* 20 Am. J. Comp. L. 693 (1972).

250. *Implementation of the Declaration, supra* note 248, at 12.

251. *See e.g.,* U.N. Doc. E/CN.6/548 (1971); U.N. Doc E/CN.6/571, *supra* note 248.

252. U.N. Doc. E/CN.6/548, *supra* note 251, at 15.

253. *Cf.* chapter 9 *supra.*

254. ECOSOC Res. 1325, ECOSOC, 44th Sess., Supp. (No. 1) 13, U.N. Doc. E/4548 (1968).

gram for the advancement of women.[255] This comprehensive program was designed, by promoting peoples' understanding, to generate changes in effective power which will make official application, national and transnational, easier.[256] The program was arranged to celebrate International Women's Year. Following the General Assembly proclamation of the year 1975 as International Women's Year,[257] the Commission on the Status of Women devoted itself to working out a comprehensive program of activities,[258] which was approved by the Economic and Social Council in May 1974.[259] Seeking to "promote equality between men and women," "ensure the full integration of women in the total development effort," and "increase the contribution of women to the development of friendly relations and co-operation among States and to the strengthening of world peace,"[260] the International Women's Year projected this central theme—"EQUALITY, DEVELOPMENT AND PEACE."[261] This program, comprehensive and detailed, was addressed, in the hope of active participation, to "Member States, the United Nations, the specialized agencies, regional intergovernmental organizations, the national and international organizations and non-governmental organizations in consultative status concerned."[262] In addition to the projected "activities at the regional and international levels,"[263] the program urged states to undertake a variety of measures, including "special acts of commemoration,"[264] mapping out national priorities and programs,[265] creation of special bodies,[266] "publicity and educational measures,"[267]

---

255. G.A. Res. 2716, U.N. GAOR, 25th Sess., Supp. (No. 28) 81–83, U.N. Doc. A/8028 (1970). *See also* note 142 *supra*.

256. *See* UNITED NATIONS, UNITED NATIONS ASSISTANCE FOR THE ADVANCEMENT OF WOMEN, U.N. Doc. E/CN.6/467 (1967); UNITED NATIONS, THE UNITED NATIONS AND HUMAN RIGHTS 66–72 (1973); Bruce, *supra* note 31, at 391–412; *Implementation of a Programme of Concerted International Action* (report of the secretary-general), U.N. Doc. E/CN.6/577 (1973); *Further Elaboration of a Programme of Concerted Action* (report of the secretary-general), U.N. Doc. E/CN.6/553 (1972). *Cf. also* UNITED NATIONS, PARTICIPATION OF WOMEN IN COMMUNITY DEVELOPMENT, U.N. Doc. E/CN.6/514/Rev. 1 (1972); UNITED NATIONS, REPORT OF THE INTERREGIONAL MEETING OF EXPERTS ON THE INTEGRATION OF WOMEN IN DEVELOPMENT, U.N. Doc. ST/SOA/120 (1972).

257. G.A. Res. 3010, *supra* note 214.

258. 1974 REPORT OF THE COMMISSION ON THE STATUS OF WOMEN, *supra* note 139, at 1–3, 20–27, 103–13. Regarding the Commission's deliberations at its twenty-fifth session, *see* U.N. Doc. E/CN.6/SR.599–612 (1974).

259. ECOSOC Res. 1849 (LVI), May 16, 1974, U.N. Doc. E/RES/1849 (1974). *See also International Women's Year: Report of the Secretary-General,* U.N. Doc. E/CN.6/576 (1973); *International Women's Year: Report of the Working Group to the Commission on the Status of Women,* U.N. Doc. E/CN.6/588 (1974); note 1 *supra*.

260. ECOSOC Res. 1849 (LVI), *supra* note 259, at 3.

261. *Id.*

262. *Id.* at 1.

263. *Id.* at 11–13.

264. *Id.* at 7.

265. *Id.* at 7–8.

266. *Id.* at 8.

267. *Id.* at 8–10.

"studies and surveys,"[268] holding conferences,[269] "exchange programs,"[270] and "ratification and implementation of international instruments."[271] With all these changes in perspectives and new activities, the prospects for a more effective application of the now widely accepted norm of nondiscrimination would appear to be substantially enhanced.[272]

It is highly probable that in future years these recent initiatives will be sustained and extended by currents that pervade the global community. The degree to which effective application of the new prescriptions forbidding sex-based discrimination can be secured will of course depend in measure upon how human rights in general, and especially all the other rights to equality projected in the more general norm of nondiscrimination, are protected and fulfilled. Since many of the deprivations imposed upon women are attributable to long-held traditions about the unique role ascribed to them in childbearing and child rearing, it is possible that the explosive growth of the biological sciences will exert a profound influence on the role separation of the sexes. It may, for example, no longer be necessary for the embryo to spend its formative months enclosed in the female body. As the biological constraints of an earlier day are transmuted into biological and cultural choices and the function of the family in social process changes, the alternatives open to world public order will be less and less constrained by yesterday's rationalizations of sexual difference as a means of justifying the subordination of women. Similarly, even some of the least welcome tendencies in the world arena, such as the persisting expectations of violence, may contribute to the elimination of discriminations that have been traditionally justified in terms of sex. In a world of universalizing science-based technology, an outstanding consequence of war and preparation for war must be the socialization of risk. No massive barrier can be made to separate danger "at the front" from the threats to which the civilian population is exposed. It may, thus, be increasingly recognized as foolhardy for a public order to maintain discriminations directed against half its population, compromising the security of the whole by failing to enlist and employ the latent capabilities of the deprived half. It is, finally, most unlikely that the insistent demands of the hitherto deprived half for equality in every nook and cranny of life will lessen in intensity.

---

268. *Id.* at 10.

269. *Id.* at 11.

270. *Id.*

271. *Id.*

272. *See* note 142 *supra. See also* G.A. Res. 32/136,32 U.N. GAOR, Supp. (No. 45) 155, U.N. Doc. A/32/45 (1977), G.A. Res. 32/137, *id.;* G.A. Res. 32/138, *id.* at 156; G.A. Res. 32/139, *id.;* G.A. Res. 32/140, *id.* at 157; G.A. Res. 32/141, *id.;* G.A. Res. 32/142, *id.* at 158. *Cf.* S. Rothman, A History of Changing Ideals and Practices, 1870 to the Present (1978); *International Women's Issues: Hearing and Briefing the Subcomms. on International Organizations and on International Development of the House Comm. on International Relations,* 95th Cong., 2d Sess. (1978).

11. CLAIMS RELATING TO FREEDOM FROM RELIGIOUS DISCRIMINATION

FACTUAL BACKGROUND

Discrimination based upon religious beliefs and expressions forms the basis for some of the most serious deprivations of civil and political rights.[1] The religious beliefs and expressions that are commonly the ground for discrimination include all of the traditional faiths and justifications from which norms of responsible conduct—that is, judgments about right and wrong—are derived. These beliefs may be theological in the sense that they refer to a personalized transempirical source of an unchallengeable message or metaphysical in the sense that they are grounded upon nonpersonalized transempirical conceptions; sometimes they are more empirical, based upon varying conceptions of science or fundamental humanity.[2] Deprivations may be imposed upon an individual because he refuses to accept the established belief system, adheres to a belief system different from the established one, attempts to create a new set of beliefs, expresses doubt about existing belief systems, or

---

In slightly different form this chapter first appeared as *The Right to Religious Freedom and World Public Order: The Emerging Norm of Nondiscrimination,* 74 MICH. L. REV. 865 (1976).

1. *See generally* M. BATES, RELIGIOUS LIBERTY: AN INQUIRY (1945); A. KRISHNASWAMI, STUDY OF DISCRIMINATION IN THE MATTER OF RELIGIOUS RIGHTS AND PRACTICES, U.N. DOC. E/CN.4/Sub. 2/200/Rev. 1 (1960): P. LANARÈS, LA LIBERTÉ RELIGIEUSE DANS LES CONVENTIONS INTERNATIONALES ET DANS LE DROIT PUBLIC GÉNÉRAL (1964); Abram, *Freedom of Thought, Conscience and Religion,* 8 J. INT'L COMM'N JURISTS 40 (No. 2, 1967); Claydon, *The Treaty Protection of Religious Rights: U.N. Draft Convention on the Elimination of All Forms of Intolerance and of Discrimination Based on Religion or Belief,* 12 SANTA CLARA LAWYER 403 (1972); Toth, *Human Dignity and Freedom of Conscience,* 10 WORLD JUSTICE 202 (1968).

2. A recent outstanding survey of religious beliefs is RELIGIOUS MOVEMENTS IN CONTEMPORARY AMERICA (I. Zaretsky & M. Leone eds. 1974) [hereinafter cited as RELIGIOUS MOVEMENTS]. For a diversity of religious perspectives, see T. DOBZHANSKY, THE BIOLOGY OF ULTIMATE CONCERN (1967); M. ELIADE, PATTERNS IN COMPARATIVE RELIGION (R. Sheed trans. 1963); M. ELIADE, THE SACRED AND THE PROFANE (W. Trash trans. 1961); S. FREUD, THE FUTURE OF AN ILLUSION (W. Robson-Scott trans 1928); J. HICK, PHILOSOPHY OF RELIGION (1963); W. KAUFMANN, CRITIQUE OF RELIGION AND PHILOSOPHY (1958); W. LESSA & E. VOGT, READER IN COMPARATIVE RELIGION (3d ed. 1972); H. LEWIS, PHILOSOPHY

explicitly challenges the validity of belief systems.[3] The individual may be deprived of rights either through formal community decision-making processes or through less obvious workings of effective power.[4]

Religious discrimination looms large in the histories of most of the world's distinctive religions. The common theme of these histories (with different religions appearing alternatively as oppressors and as victims) has been that of persecution; toleration has developed only at relatively late stages.[5] For a long time, the established mode by which many religions dealt with heretics or nonbelievers was short and quick. The ultimate deprivation was imposed upon those who failed to conform.[6] In more recent times, though toleration has become widespread, religious discrimination still abounds and is the source of repressive measures that deny individuals the most basic of human freedoms. In the words of a United Nations study:

> World-wide interest in ensuring the right to freedom of thought, conscience and religion stems from the realization that this right is

---

of Religion (1965); S. McCasland, G. Cairns, & D. Yu, Religions of the World (1969); M. Mead, Twentieth Century Faith: Hope and Survival 83–87 (1972); A. Montagu, Immortality, Religion, and Morals (1971); E. Parrinder, Comparative Religion (1962); N. Smart, The Religious Experience of Mankind (1969); J. Wach, The Comparative Study of Religions (1961); M. Weber, The Sociology of Religion (T. Parsons ed. 1963); J. Yinger, Religion, Society and the Individual (1957); J. Yinger, The Scientific Study of Religion (1970).

3. Thus, deprivees can include atheists and agnostics. *See generally* T. Altizer & W. Hamilton, Radical Theology and the Death of God (1966); C. Campbell, Toward a Sociology of Irreligion (1971); W. Clifford, The Ethics of Belief, and Other Essays (1876); J. Dewey, A Common Faith (1934); R. Robinson, An Atheist's Values (1964); G. Vahanian, The Death of God (1961).

4. Important deprivations may be imposed through the internal processes of religious groups themselves. Sometimes these deprivations have the tacit approval of government; upon occasion they become the functional equivalent of government. *Cf.* Gerlach, *Pentecostalism: Revolution or Counter-Revolution?* in Religious Movements, *supra* note 2, at 669–99; Kauper & Ellis, *Religious Corporations and the Law,* 71 Mich. L. Rev. 1499, 1557–74 (1973).

5. *See* H. Kamen, The Rise of Toleration (1967); Adeney, *Toleration,* 12 Encyc. of Religion and Ethics 360 (J. Hastings ed. 1958). *See also* J. Bigelow, Toleration and Other Essays and Studies (1927); W. Garrison, Intolerance (1934); G. Mensching, Tolerance and Truth in Religion (H. Klimkeit trans. 1971). In the words of Garrison:

> History is made up very largely of the record of man's intolerance to man. Part of that record is red with the blood of its victims and vibrant with their groans. Part of it also is warm with the glow of the faith and zeal of those who have sought, at their own peril, to turn others from the error of their ways or to break down some system which they deemed hostile to the welfare of men. But the story of intolerance is also the story of all the world's prophets and saviours, its moral leaders and social reformers, as well as its tyrants and inquisitors.

W. Garrison, *supra,* at *x.*

6. *See* text accompanying notes 28–38 *infra.*

> of primary importance. In the past, its denial has led not only to untold misery, but also to persecutions directed against entire groups of people. Wars have been waged in the name of religion or belief, either with the aim of imposing upon the vanquished the faith of the victor or as a pretext for extending economic or political domination. Although the number of such instances occurring in the second half of our century is on the decline, it must not be forgotten that mankind only recently has witnessed persecutions on a more colossal scale than ever before. And even today, notwithstanding changes in the climate of opinion, equality of treatment is not ensured for all religions and beliefs, or for their followers, in certain areas of the world.[7]

The relevant deprivations imposed upon individuals invariably involve the rectitude value itself, denying participation in the formulation and expression of moral norms. Individuals may be denied, both in form and in substance, the freedom to worship as they choose; they may be terrorized from worshipping, or they may be brainwashed or coerced into following a belief system other than that of their own choosing (*e.g.*, compulsory conversions).[8] These types of repressive measures are par-

---

7. A. Krishnaswami, *supra* note 1, at v. In the words of Claydon:

> Even a cursory survey of matters considered by the United Nations in the past twenty-five years demonstrates the extent to which religious differences continue to contribute to major and minor problems of world order. Such a list might include the following items: religious persecution in Bulgaria, Hungary, and Rumania, 1949; the Kashmir dispute between India and Pakistan; the treatment of Buddhists in South Vietnam, 1963; the actions of the People's Republic of China in Tibet, 1959–61; the Cyprus problem; the continuing Middle East crisis; and the current situation in Northern Ireland. In all of these cases the religious factor has operated in varying degrees either to precipitate or to exacerbate an international crisis; in most violence has been a component.

Claydon, *supra* note 1, at 403.

Useful contemporary area studies of the interaction of religion and politics include R. Bush, Religion in Communist China (1970); J. Coquia, Church and State Law in the Philippines (1959); G. MacEoin, Northern Ireland: Captive of History 123–44 (1974); D. MacInnis, Religious Policy and Practice in Communist China (1972); Religion, Politics, and Social Change in the Third World (D. Smith ed. 1971); D. Schmeiser, Civil Liberties in Canada 54–124 (1964); South Asian Politics and Religion (D. Smith ed. 1966).

8. *See, e.g.,* Arnold, *Persecution (Muhammadan)*, 9 Encyc. of Religion and Ethics 765, 767 (J. Hastings ed. 1960). Similar treatment is reported to occur in the Soviet Union. *See* V. Chalidze, To Defend These Rights: Human Rights and the Soviet Union 159 (G. Daniels trans. 1974). *Cf.* H. Smith, The Russians 417–38 (1976); Jancar, *Religious Dissent in the Soviet Union,* in Dissent in the USSR: Politics, Ideology, and People 191 (R. Tökés ed. 1975); Reddaway, *Freedom of Worship and the Law,* in In Quest of Justice: Protest and Dissent in the Soviet Union Today 62 (1970).

ticularly likely to occur in those communities in which an established belief system is officially sanctioned and sustained to the exclusion of other beliefs.[9] History is full of examples of religious oppression through such means as the destruction of altars, images, churches, temples, and the holy scriptures.[10]

Deprivations of power on rectitude grounds are dramatized by the

---

9. *See, e.g., Roman Catholicism, History of,* 15 ENCYC. BRITANNICA 1002, 1006–07 (15th ed. 1974).

Underscoring the central importance of "religious persecution" to Marxism. Solzhenitsyn offers this footnote: "Sergei Bulgakov showed in *Karl Marx as a Religious Type* (1906) that atheism is the chief inspirational and emotional hub of Marxism and that all the rest of the doctrine has simply been tacked on. Ferocious hostility to religion is Marxism's most persistent feature." A. SOLZHENITSYN, LETTER TO THE SOVIET LEADERS 58–59 (H. Sternberg trans. 1975). *See also* Bourdeaux, *Religions in the Soviet Union (1960–71): Introduction,* in THE FOURTH WORLD: VICTIMS OF GROUP OPPRESSION 218, 222 (B. Whitaker ed. 1972); Shararevich, *Socialism in Our Past and Future,* in A. SOLZHENITSYN, et. al., FROM UNDER THE RUBBLE 26 (M. Scammell, et al., trans. 1975), *Religious Persecution in the Soviet Union: Hearings before the Subcomms. on International Political and Military Affairs and on International Organizations of the House Comm. on International Relations,* 94th Cong., 2d Sess. (1976).

In the People's Republic of China, the Religious Affairs Bureau came into existence in the early years of the regime. The functions of the Bureau include the following:

1. To regularly investigate and study religious organizations and the activities of their personnel.
2. To control all types of religious activity.
3. To lead both Catholics and Protestants into the Three-Self Movement, and to organize Buddhists, Taoists, and Muslims for regular patriotic learning sessions.
4. To carry out thoroughly the religious policy of the central government.
5. To unceasingly teach and propagandize religious leaders and all believers concerning policies of the state with respect to current situations in order to raise their political awareness.
6. To bring church leaders closer to the government and push believers of all religions into a positive alliance for the construction of socialism.
7. To strike at politically obstinate reactionaries in churches, and cooperate with public security officers in order to tranquilize hidden counterrevolutionaries in all religions.
8. To entertain foreign religious guests.

R. BUSH, *supra* note 7, at 31 (footnote omitted). *See also* D. MACINNIS, *supra* note 7, at 373; G. PATTERSON, CHRISTIANITY IN COMMUNIST CHINA 3–4 (1969). Other works dealing with religion and communism include J. BENNETT, CHRISTIANITY AND COMMUNISM TODAY (1970); H. CHAMBRE, CHRISTIANITY AND COMMUNISM (R. Trevett trans. 1960); M. D'ARCY, COMMUNISM AND CHRISTIANITY (1957); A. GALTER, THE RED BOOK OF THE PERSECUTED CHURCH (1957); G. MACEOIN, THE COMMUNIST WAR ON RELIGION (1951).

10. *See, e.g.,* L. Dawidowicz, THE WAR AGAINST THE JEWS, 1933–1945, at 248 (1975); J. GOFF, THE PERSECUTION OF PROTESTANT CHRISTIANS IN COLOMBIA, 1948–1958, at 4/35–4/45 (1968) (SONDEOS No. 23); Adeney, *supra* note 5, at 361; Gwatkin, *Persecution (Early Church),* 9 ENCYC. OF RELIGION AND ETHICS 742, 743, 747 (J. Hastings ed. 1960).

conflicts between church and state.[11] The religiously persecuted have been forced to leave the community of which they were members and in consequence have been completely excluded from the power processes of the body politic. For many, the result has been centuries of wandering as homeless refugees and exiles in perpetual fear and jeopardy—a phenomenon that has yet to see an end.[12] The barbarity of banishment is sometimes confined within national boundaries when the persecuted are dispatched to remote, sparsely populated, and rugged frontiers.[13] Conversely, people may be denied egress, either temporarily or permanently, because of their religious background,[14] and nationals of certain religious faiths may be denied access to their own country.[15] In some notorious inquisitions, the methods employed against nonconformists have been completely arbitrary, involving no less than a total denial of due process of law.[16] Less drastically, holding or expressing particular religious beliefs may be made a criminal offense.[17] The entire arsenal of criminal sanctions, including fine, imprisonment, banishment, and capital punishment, may be mobilized to enforce religious conformity.[18] Another frequent deprivation is to forbid religious nonconformists to hold assemblies.[19]

---

11. *Cf.* G. Lewy, Religion and Revolution (1974); S. Steinberg, The Thirty Years War and the Conflict for European Hegemony, 1600–1660, at 96–99 (1966); C. Wedgwood, The Thirty Years War (1938).

12. For a comprehensive historical account, see F. Norwood, Strangers and Exiles: A History of Religious Refugees (1969).

13. Whitley, *Persecution (Modern Christian)*, 9 Encyc. of Religion and Ethics 755, 758 (J. Hastings ed. 1960).

14. For a discussion of such practices in the Soviet Union, see J. Ingles, Study of Discrimination in Respect of the Rights of Everyone to Leave Any Country, Including His Own, and to Return to His Country 25–29, U.N. Doc. E/CN.4/Sub. 2/220/Rev. 1 (1963); W. Korey, The Soviet Cage: Anti-Semitism in Russia 184–200 (1973). *See also* V. Chalidze, *supra* note 8, at 92–114; A. Sakharov, My Country and the World 51–61 (G. Daniels trans. 1975); A. Sakharov, Sakharov Speaks 159–63 (H. Salisbury ed. 1974); Shroeter, *How They Left: Varieties of Soviet Jewish Exit Experience,* 2 Soviet Jewish Affairs 9 (1972).

15. J. Ingles, *supra* note 14, at 28–29.

16. The methods employed have been said to include "[t]he spy system, delation, secrecy, torture, the union in one person of judge and accuser, the hindrances put in the way of the victim's defence, the direct interest of the tribunal in a condemnation which secured the confiscation of the property of the accused." Fawkes, *Persecution (Roman Catholic),* 9 Encyc. of Religion and Ethics 749, 753 (J. Hastings ed. 1960). For a detailed case study, *see* H. Kamen, The Spanish Inquisition 137–96 (1965).

17. *See, e.g.,* Gwatkin, *supra* note 10, at 742, 746.

18. *See, e.g.,* Nelson, *The Theory of Persecution,* in Persecution and Liberty: Essays in Honor of George Lincoln Burr 3 (1931) (Christian practices). *See generally* Labrousse, *Religious Toleration,* 4 Dictionary of the History of Ideas 112, 115 (P. Wiener ed. 1973).

19. Gwatkin, *supra* note 10, at 747.

An individual's rights to vote or to hold office may be affected by religious identification, even in communities with no established religion. "Where there is an Established Church or a State religion," according to a United Nations study, "persons who leave the officially recognized religion are sometimes deprived of their political rights, including the right to vote."[20] Sometimes, "clerics of the official religion may be regarded as officials of the Government while those of other groups do not enjoy such a status."[21] Eligibility for high governmental posts, including the head of state, may, "either by law or by tradition," be confined to those who hold the officially sanctioned religious beliefs.[22] In communities where "several religions are officially recognized," discrimination may result from the use of "quota systems" in allocating "elective and appointive posts in the public service"; such systems may stress "community membership" rather than "merit" and exclude from public service "members of religious communities not recognized by the State."[23]

In the area of educational opportunities, individuals may find access to public education, or educational resources and facilities, restricted because of their religious backgrounds. Such deprivations cannot be dismissed as historic curiosities. According to a United Nations study, "qualified candidates in some parts of the world still find their religion a barrier when they apply for admission to certain educational institutions."[24] "Although this discrimination is not overt and is in many cases contrary to the law," the study adds, "it nevertheless persists and affects a considerable number of persons."[25] The intricate relationship between religion and education, especially in regard to religious instruction, may precipitate community tension and conflict.[26] In addition, among the

---

20. H. Santa Cruz, Study of Discrimination in the Matter of Political Rights 34, U.N. Doc. E/CN.4/Sub. 2/213/Rev. 1 (1962).

21. *Id.*

22. *Id. See also* J. Laponce, The Protection of Minorities 49–50 (1960).

23. H. Santa Cruz, *supra* note 20, at 35. Difficult problems arise when an individual leaves a group in which religious process is the functional equivalent of civil process. *See, e.g.*, Zaretsky, *Jesus in Jerusalem 1973: Mission Impossible?* in Hebrew Christianity: The Thirteenth Tribe 341, 350–52 (B. Sobel ed. 1974).

24. C. Ammoun, Study of Discrimination in Education 56, U.N. Doc. E/CN.4/Sub. 2/181/Rev. 1 (1957).

25. *Id.*

26. This is most visible in cases in which proselytization is used as a form of public information. *See* Zaretsky, *supra* note 23, at 383–85. *Cf.* L. de Camp, The Great Monkey Trial (1968); Evolution and Religion: The Conflict between Science and Theology in Modern America (G. Kennedy ed. 1957); R. Morgan, The Politics of Religious Conflict (1968).

ubiquitous means of maintaining religious conformity are the policies designed to preserve an ignorant public and to stifle individual freedom of expression. Notorious examples of book burning abound in history.[27] Limited access to the means of enlightenment often results in limited opportunities for the acquisition and exercise of socially useful skills.

In a community in which discrimination takes the form of persecution, severe deprivations of well-being may ensue, ranging from the imprisonment and torture of individuals to the physical extermination of entire populations (genocide).[28] The barbarity of such deprivations has been vividly recorded: "the extirpation of heresy by fetter and by fire";[29] victims "worried by dogs, or crucified, or burned as lights for the performances" in emperor's gardens;[30] victims "left to die of famine in prison";[31] issuance of edicts requiring "all persons," including "women and boys," to be sacrificed;[32] "great massacre";[33] "public executions";[34] "wholesale burnings";[35] "the most terrible form of fire and slaughter";[36] extermination "by sword, by hurling from the summits of cliffs, by pro-

27. *See, e.g.,* Gwatkin, *supra* note 10, at 747.

In a fashion less dramatic than book burning, the Nationalist Chinese government, in January 1975, confiscated some 2,300 copies of Bibles in romanized Taiwanese (some of them in the Tayal tribal language) from the Protestant community in Taiwan. This much-protested act in violation of religious freedom is another step in a series of governmental measures designed to ban the use of the Taiwanese language and to suppress the Taiwanese (non-Chinese) identity of the Taiwanese people. *See* the Washington Post, May 2, 1975, at C7, col. 4; *The Confiscation of the Taiwanese Bibles by the Nationalist Chinese Government,* 71 MAYFLOWER 7 (July 20, 1975) (published by the Formosan Club of America, Inc.); *Joint Statement concerning the Taiwanese Bibles,* 176 TAIWAN CHENGLIAN 23 (June 1975) (published by World United Formosans for Independence); Tang, *On the Incident of Confiscating the Taiwanese Bibles,* 177 TAIWAN CHENGLIAN 34 (July 1975).

28. The Nazi Holocaust is a well-remembered example of such practices. *See* R. HILBERG, DESTRUCTION OF THE EUROPEAN JEWS (1961); H. KRAUSNICK, H. BUCHHEIM, M. BROSZHAT, & H. JACOBSEN, THE ANATOMY OF THE SS-STATE (1968); N. LEVIN, THE HOLOCAUST: THE DESTRUCTION OF THE EUROPEAN JEWRY (1968); R. MANVELL & H. FRAENKEL, THE INCOMPARABLE CRIME (1967); L. POLIAKOV, HARVEST OF HATE (1954); G. REITLINGER, THE FINAL SOLUTION (2d ed. 1968); J. TENENBAUM, RACE AND REICH (2d ed. 1956); *Holocaust,* 8 ENCYC. JUDAICA 827 (1971).

29. Labrousse, *supra* note 18, at 115.

30. Gwatkin, *supra* note 10, at 744.

31. *Id.* at 746.

32. *Id.*

33. *Id.* at 747.

34. *Id.* at 748.

35. *Id.*

36. Geden, *Persecution (Indian),* 9 ENCYC. OF RELIGION AND ETHICS 762, 764 (J. Hastings ed. 1960).

longed confinement in deadly prisons, at the stake, in the mines";[37] and survivors "sent in chains into slavery."[38]

With regard to the right to acquire and dispose of property, an individual's religious identification not infrequently becomes a source of discrimination. Nonconformists may have their property confiscated,[39] groups who profess particular religious faiths may be forbidden the right to own land,[40] public funds may be dispensed in a manner that clearly discriminates against certain religious groups,[41] and religious quotas may be imposed in employment.[42] In the words of an International Labor Office (ILO) study:

> The most numerous charges of discrimination would seem to relate to access to jobs in both the public service and the private sector. The acts of discrimination complained of appear to consist for the

37. 2 T. Lindsay, A History of the Reformation 601 (1907). Hence this observation: "But the horrors enacted in open court are a very small part of the mischiefs of persecution. We must take account of imprisonments and hardships from which even death is sometimes a relief, and of the sufferings of those who live in fear of death or yield to fear of death. Worse than this is the brutalizing of the persecutors, and worst of all the demoralization of the persecuted." Gwatkin, *supra* note 10, at 748.

38. Gwatkin, *supra* note 10, at 747.

Deprivations are sometimes inflicted by the victims themselves because of religious beliefs in the community. Such believers may deny themselves the benefits of modern medical treatment by relying on spiritual healing only, by refusing vaccination and physical examination, and by refusing blood transfusions. *See generally* C. Antieau, P. Carroll, & T. Burke, Religion under the State Constitutions 67–72 (1965); M. Cole, Jehovah's Witnesses (1955); D. Gross, The Case for Spiritual Healing (1958); J. Van Baalen, The Chaos of Cults (3d ed. 1960); Burkholder, *"The Law Knows No Heresy": Marginal Religious Movements and the Courts,* in Religious Movements, *supra* note 2, at 27, 36–41; Garrison, *Sectarianism and Psychosocial Adjustment: A Controlled Comparison of Puerto Rican Pentecostals and Catholics,* in *id.* at 298–319; Pfeffer, *The Legitimation of Marginal Religions in the United States,* in *id.* at 9, 17–20 Torrey, *Spiritualists and Shamans as Psychotherapists: An Account of Original Anthropological Sin,* in *id.* at 330–37; Cawley, *Criminal Liability in Faith Healing,* 39 Minn. L. Rev. 48 (1954); Note, *The Refused Blood Transfusion: An Ultimate Challenge for Law and Morals,* 10 Natural L. Forum 202 (1965).

39. *See, e.g.,* Gwatkin, *supra* note 10, at 747.

40. Such prohibition may take different forms: (1) only members of the state religion can own land; (2) no members of any religion may own land; and (3) members of some religions subjected to persecution may not own land. For instance, *see* the case of Emma Berger in Israel, described in Zaretsky, *supra* note 23, at 388, 398 n.27.

41. *See* P. Kauper, Religion and the Constitution 18–19 (1964); J. Laponce, *supra* note 22, at 48.

42. W. Korey, *supra* note 14, at 52.

On occasion, discrimination in employment may be imposed against people who are religiously forbidden to work on those days when the employer wants them to work. *See* Burkholder, *supra* note 38, at 33–36; Pfeffer, *supra* note 38, at 17–20.

> most part in the imposition of religious tests in selecting candidates for public appointments and the granting of preferences to members of particular faiths when engaging workers or taking on apprentices. However, discrimination may also occur in certain situations against people who belong to any religion at all, against atheists or against those who do not profess any faith whatever.[43]

Religious discrimination continues to have an important effect upon the shaping and sharing of the affection value. People of different religious backgrounds may be prohibited by legal or religious proscription from marrying one another.[44] Violators may be subjected to severe legal penalties or to social opprobrium. On a more general level, religious barriers tend to stifle the growth of congenial personal relationships.

Finally, even in the most modern societies it is not always easy for people of different religions to share a sense of mutual respect. Religious antagonists have been "[l]ikened to the poisoner of wells, the arsonist, the counterfeiter, and the murderer—the heresiarch and the votaries whom he enticed were pictured as public pests which the authorities had the solemn obligation to purge from the face of the earth."[45] At one time, religious nonconformists were simply "reduced to slavery."[46] Today, individuals may enjoy differing degrees of prestige because of differences in religious affiliations. Religion almost invariably figures significantly in the class structure of a community, especially where it is highly rigidified and hierarchical.[47]

BASIC COMMUNITY POLICIES

In a community genuinely committed to the goal of human dignity, one paramount policy should be to honor and defend the freedom of the individual to choose a fundamental orientation toward the world. One of the most distinctive acts available to man as a rational being is the continual redefinition of the self in relation to others and to the cosmos. Thus, each individual must be free to search for the basic postulates in a perspective that will unify the experiences of life. All practices that both differentiate among individuals upon the basis of religious beliefs and

---

43. International Labour Office, Fighting Discrimination in Employment and Occupation 98 (1968).

44. *See* A. Krishnaswami, *supra* note 1, at 38; 3 A. Stokes, Church and State in the United States 52–56 (1950). *Cf.* Geden, *supra* note 36, at 764–65.

45. Labrousse, *supra* note 18, at 115.

46. *See* Gwatkin, *supra* note 10, at 747.

47. *See* chapter 7 *supra,* at notes 315–18 and accompanying text. *See also* T. O'Dea, The Sociology of Religion 55–97 (1966).

expressions, whether conceived and justified in transempirical or empirical terms, and deprive the individual of the freedom to inquire and choose are wholly incompatible with preferred policy.[48]

Even so fundamental a freedom as that of religious inquiry, belief, and communication must, of course, be exercised and protected with due regard for the comparable rights of others and for the aggregate common interest in the preservation of all basic human rights.[49] Whether a particular practice is an appropriate exercise of religious freedom or is an unreasonable invasion of the rights of others may occasionally present a difficult and delicate question for community choice. The rational procedure for guiding community choice about such questions in the area of religious freedom, as in the case of other rights, is the disciplined use of a contextual analysis that investigates and assays the consequences of available options; no prior definitional exercises, however elaborate, can eliminate the need for inquiry and choice in the social process.[50]

---

48. The arbitrariness of differentiations by generic reference to religion is evident in the difficulties of defining "religion." As with the notion of "race," specialists on religion, as well as nonspecialists, can hardly agree upon a commonly acceptable definition. What are the criteria of "religious" groups: birth, devotions by one or both parents, self-definition and proclamation, conversion, conversion by group, or something else? Labeling people on the basis of religion, as on the basis of race, is easily susceptible of abuse. *See* Hollingsworth, *Constitutional Religious Protection: Antiquated Oddity or Vital Reality?* 34 OHIO STATE L.J. 15 (1973); Zaretsky, *supra* note 23.

49. The presumption against discrimination upon grounds of religion is not intended to obscure the fact that a community may have a deep interest in the quality of the rectitude standard of its members. Some religious concepts may be highly inimical to a public order of human dignity. It may on occasion be necessary to distinguish between discrimination upon religious grounds and the maintenance of an appropriate system of rectitude. The formation and proselytization of religious movements that emphasize some conceptions of pacifism may, for instance, be regarded as inimical to community security in some contexts.

See, e.g., Marnell, *Civil Disobedience and the Majority of One,* in RELIGION AND THE PUBLIC ORDER 115 (D. Giannella ed. 1969). *Cf., e.g.,* Casad, *Compulsory Education and Individual Rights,* in *id.* at 51; Coughlin, *Values and the Constitution,* in *id.* at 89.

50. *See* chapter 5 *supra*. *See also* McDougal, *Human Rights and World Public Order: Principles of Content and Procedure for Clarifying General Community Policy,* 14 VA. J. INTL. L. 387 (1974); chapter 6 *supra,* at notes 18–52 and accompanying text; chapter 8 *supra,* at note 7 and accompanying text; chapter 16 *infra,* at notes 10–15 and accompanying text.

In response to the conventional "action-belief" dichotomy for policy differentiation used in American jurisprudence, Kurland has emphasized that "this proposed distinction . . . [is] obviously not a line that can provide real assistance in resolving these knotty problems." P. KURLAND, RELIGION AND THE LAW 22 (1962). Similarly, Burkholder observes:

> If we ask just how the limits of religious freedom are set by the courts, it is clear that no one definitive rationale for adjudication has emerged. The jurists have developed a number of testing procedures—secular regulation, interest weighing, clear and present danger, compelling state interest, alternative means—but only the first of these offers a self-evident approach. In creating the possibility of carving out an exemption from existing legislation for certain kinds of religiously motivated action, and justify-

None of the arguments historically put forward to impugn the policy of religious toleration carry much weight in a complex and interactive world. Attempts have been made to justify intolerance on the ground that a single faith has unique access to revealed truth (a monopoly of truth),[51] or that intolerance is necessary for the "salvation" of individuals who are outside the mainstream of religious belief.[52] More secular and pragmatic arguments allege the necessity of achieving and maintaining community unity and cohesion against the perils of fragmentation into nonconformist groups.[53] The specious nature of claims to a monopoly of truth or exclusive access to transempirical salvation would appear amply demonstrated by the failure of any of the diverse belief systems present in the contemporary world to establish unique or exclusive successes in either empirical or transempirical inquiry.[54] Moreover, underlying all of the theories of religious intolerance is an assumption that is essentially contrary to respect for human dignity—an assumption that implies a profound distrust of the wisdom of allowing individuals to take the responsibility for their own beliefs. If human experience is a reliable

---

> ing this exemption by balancing religious conviction against public policy, the *Sherbert* formula tended to favor a case-by-case procedure. We have seen how court opinions may vary widely in their application of this balancing technique.

Burkholder, *supra* note 38, at 45.

51. In his essay on Sir James MacKintosh, Macaulay described such views: "I am in the right, and you are in the wrong. When you are the stronger, you ought to tolerate me; for it is your duty to tolerate truth. But when I am stronger, I shall persecute you; for it is my duty to persecute error." T. MACAULAY, CRITICAL AND HISTORICAL ESSAYS 336 (1870). *Cf.* N. SODERBLOM, THE LIVING GOD: BASAL FORMS OF PERSONAL RELIGION (1933); R. ZAEHNER, AT SUNDRY TIMES (1958).

52. "[A] body of truths existed, some still latent, some explicitly stated in dogmas, necessary and vital; so vital that, unless a man accepted them, he would without doubt perish everlastingly. . . ." Whitley, *supra* note 13, at 755. Augustine is said to have compared "the laws against heretics to the restraint imposed upon lunatics or persons suffering under delirium, who would otherwise destroy themselves and others." Fawkes, *supra* note 16, at 751, 752. *Cf.* S. BRANDON, HISTORY, TIME AND DEITY (1965); S. BRANDON, MAN AND HIS DESTINY IN THE GREAT RELIGIONS (1962).

53. Labrousse has aptly summarized: "If one reflects upon it, one is struck by the coherence and doctrinal consistency of the ideological justifications provided for the practice of religious intolerance. The system of justification stands up admirably on all levels, and the unavoidable sociological necessity for a minimum consensus gives it an imperative accent. This necessity for consensus has not disappeared from among us. . . ." Labrousse, *supra* note 18, at 115–16. A similar observation was offered by Fawkes: "Cohesion was the first need of primitive societies; it was more important that the group should cohere than it should progress. Innovation, therefore, was put down with a strong hand: it introduced disunion and dissipated energy—the argument is not unknown in our own time." Fawkes, *supra* note 16, at 749.

54. *See generally* W. CHRISTIAN, MEANING AND TRUTH IN RELIGION (1964); B. MITCHELL, THE JUSTIFICATION OF RELIGIOUS BELIEF (1973).

guide, it would appear that individuals will not experience an intense demand on the self to act responsibly on behalf of the common interest unless they are free to pursue their own search to relate the ego to other beings and to the universal manifold of events. The attempt to impose uniformity in such fundamental matters stifles and frustrates personal development and fulfillment. Similarly, it would appear that, in the long run, social order and individual well-being can be better achieved through open examination and choice of fundamental orientations than through regimented religious monolithism.[55]

The importance of individual freedom of inquiry and commitment to community consensus about shaping and sharing of values has been aptly summarized by Abram:

> Since that formative period of the concepts of religious liberty in the seventeenth century, differing justifications of the right to freedom of thought, conscience or belief have been advanced. Some, like Mill, have stressed the fallibility of human thought and belief; others, like Dewey, have argued the social benefits derivable from plurality of belief and freedom of inquiry; and others have calculated the comparative risks for social value of a policy of freedom, as opposed to the risks of repression. One conclusion from the number and variety of such justifications is that no single theological, secular or philosophical foundation is presupposed in the belief in the right to freedom of thought, conscience and religion. Defenders of the ideal and institutions of freedom do not and need not share metaphysical, theological or psychological beliefs; rather, they share a commitment to the value of freedom in the life of the community and an appreciation of the fruits of freedom for society and the individual.[56]

---

55. The classic exposition of this policy is J. LOCKE, LETTERS CONCERNING TOLERATION (1765). In 1689, the year the Act of Toleration was proclaimed in England, Locke's first *Letter* was anonymously published in Holland in Latin and translated into English immediately afterward. Three other *Letters* soon followed, largely in response to criticism. Emphasizing that the legitimate sphere of the state extends to external matters rather than internal matters such as religion, Locke maintained that not only the basic doctrines and articles of faith, but also the outward manifestations and rites of worship are to be kept beyond the reach of the civil authority. Not only religious toleration but also disestablishment of religion was suggested.

See R. AARON, JOHN LOCKE 24-25, 39-40, 52, 295-99 (1937); J. DUNN, THE POLITICAL THOUGHT OF JOHN LOCKE 27-40 (1969).

For an excellent contemporary exposition of the policies favoring toleration, *see* P. KAUPER, *supra* note 41, at 13-44. *Cf.* R. BAINTON, THE TRAVAIL OF RELIGIOUS LIBERTY (1951); S. HOOK, RELIGION IN A FREE SOCIETY (1967); P. MILLER, et al., RELIGION AND FREEDOM OF THOUGHT (1954); C. NORTHCOTT, RELIGIOUS LIBERTY (1948); R. POLLARD, CONSCIENCE AND LIBERTY (1940).

56. Abram, *supra* note 1, at 44-45.

TRENDS IN DECISION

The development of transnational principles of religious freedom begins within the body politic of national communities. Even within these communities, the journey toward religious tolerance has been slow and tortuous. "Ancient society," it has been noted, "was essentially intolerant."[57] Though the concepts of religious toleration and religious freedom were articulated at relatively early stages in history,[58] their transformation into national prescription and practice has been gradual. "Tolerance," observed Arcot Krishnaswami in his outstanding study, "was accorded, in the beginning, to one or a few specified religions or beliefs; and only later was it extended to all such groups. Moreover, the measure of tolerance extended to various groups was often very narrow at first, and only by a gradual expansion was full equality achieved."[59] Krishnaswami also noted that "[s]truggles for freedom of religion and conscience have occurred chiefly in Europe. For many historic non-European religions, which developed without having the feeling of possessing absolute and exclusive religious truth, the problem of toleration did not take so acute a form."[60]

In Europe, the drive toward religious toleration became significant after the Protestant Reformation.[61] The formal incorporation of the principle of religious toleration into national law first appeared in Switzerland and Transylvania, two relatively small multi-religious communities bordering the great empires.[62] In Switzerland, under the Peaces of Kappel of 1529 and 1531, each canton was empowered to decide which faith, Reformed or Catholic, its inhabitants would observe.[63] In the "common bailiwicks, ruled by Reformed and Catholic cantons in common,"[64] the Catholic minorities were allowed to adhere to

---

57. Gwatkin, *supra* note 10, at 743.

58. *See* Bainton, *Sebastian Castellio and the Toleration Controversy of the Sixteenth Century,* in PERSECUTION AND LIBERTY: ESSAYS IN HONOR OF GEORGE LINCOLN BURR 183 (1931). *Cf.* M. BATES, *supra* note 1, at 378–473; D. BURT, THE STATE AND RELIGIOUS TOLERATION: ASPECTS OF THE CHURCH-STATE THEORIES OF FOUR CHRISTIAN THINKERS (1960); Bainton, *The Parable of the Tares as the Proof Text for Religious Liberty to the End of the Sixteenth Century,* 1 CHURCH HIST. 67 (1932).

59. A. KRISHNASWAMI, *supra* note 1, at 4.

60. *Quoted in* Toth, *supra* note 1, at 208.

61. *See generally* R. BAINTON, THE REFORMATION OF THE SIXTEENTH CENTURY (1952); M. BATES, *supra* note 1, at 148–86; O. CHADWICK, THE REFORMATION (1965); G. ELTON, REFORMATION EUROPE, 1517–1599 (1964); H. GRIMM, THE REFORMATION ERA, 1500–1650, at 588–92 (1954); T. LINDSAY, *supra* note 37; R. POST, THE MODERN DEVOTION: CONFRONTATION WITH REFORMATION AND HUMANISM (1968); Bainton, *The Struggle for Religious Liberty,* 10 CHURCH HIST. 95 (1941).

62. Toth, *supra* note 1, at 209.

63. A. KRISHNASWAMI, *supra* note 1, at 4; Toth, *supra* note 1, at 209.

64. A. KRISHNASWAMI, *supra* note 1, at 4.

their faith alongside the Protestant majority.[65] In the Principality of Transylvania (then part of the Kingdom of Hungary), individuals enjoyed freedom of conscience and religion as early as 1538 under a decree by the Diet of Torda,[66] which was reaffirmed in 1571. In 1555, Germany officially justified freedom of religion in terms of "the will of the sovereignty," "the Raison d'état."[67] In France, after the religious wars of 1562 to 1598, Henry IV issued the famous Edict of Nantes, conferring upon the Calvinists (the Huguenots) specific civil liberties, including "the right to worship in specified places."[68] In England, the Toleration Act of 1689 secured personal toleration for Protestants of all sorts, although Protestant dissenters from the Church of England still remained under certain disabilities.[69]

The French and American revolutions brought with them a shift in "emphasis from the principle of mere toleration under the aegis of enlightened despotism to that of a more effective freedom and equality of worship."[70] The Declaration of the Rights of Man, issued in 1789 after the French Revolution, specified freedom of religious expression as within the scope of human rights entitled to protection: "No man is to be interfered with because of his opinions, not even because of religious opinions, provided his avowal of them does not disturb public order as established by law."[71] Many European immigrants who settled in the New World brought with them the growing expectation of religious freedom, and the principle of religious liberty gradually spread throughout the colonies. The Constitution of the United States prescribed, in Article VI, that "no religious Test shall ever be required as a Qualification to any Office or public Trust under the United States." The First Amendment, adopted in 1791, further stated that "Congress shall make no law respecting an establishment of religion or prohibiting the free exercise thereof."[72] With the passage of time, this fundamental

65. *Id.*; Toth, *supra* note 1, at 209.

66. Toth, *supra* note 1, at 209.

67. *Id.* This was based on the doctrine "*cujus regio eius religio*" embodied in the Treaty of Augsburg of 1555.

68. A. KRISHNASWAMI, *supra* note 1, at 5. Unfortunately, the Edict of Nantes of 1598 was revoked in 1685 by Louis XIV, who ordered the destruction of the Calvinist temples and forbade Calvinists to leave the country.

69. M. BATES, *supra* note 1, at 168–79.

70. De Ruggiero, *Religious Freedom,* in 13 ENCYC. SOC. SC. 239, 244 (E. Selgman & A. Johnson eds. 1934).

71. BASIC DOCUMENTS ON HUMAN RIGHTS 9 (I. Brownlie ed. 1971).

72. This part of the First Amendment contains both the establishment clause and the free-exercise clause. "The essence of the religious freedom guaranteed by our Constitution is therefore this: no religion shall either receive the state's support or incur its hostility." West Virginia Bd. of Educ. v. Barnette, 319 U.S. 624, 654 (1943) (Frankfurter, J., dissenting). Similarly, Konvitz has observed:

guarantee of religious freedom, building upon the principle of separation of church and state, has been amplified and strengthened by a series of judicial decisions.[73]

Influenced by the examples set by France and the United States, "[i]n the written constitutions of the nineteenth and twentieth centuries the guarantee of freedom of religion appears with impressive uniformity."[74]

> The Free Exercise Clause protects one against coercion to do what one does not believe or approve; the Establishment Clause protects one against coercion to do *even what one would want to do voluntarily* and what one would approve *if it were done freely.* Taken together, their purpose is not to degrade or weaken religion in any respect whatsoever, but, on the contrary, as with the other guarantees of the First Amendment, to recognize and to implement the belief that "Almighty God hath created the mind free"; and that man is not man unless his mind remains free; and that God is not served except by a mind that is free. Had God wanted a coerced worship, He would have created not man but an unfree agent; and what God did not choose to do, the government *a fortiori* may not do.

M. KONVITZ, EXPANDING LIBERTIES 29 (1966) (italics original).

73. In his recent study, Pfeffer observes that

> on the whole the American people have been faithful to the commitment that, the business of God is not that of Caesar. This does not mean that there have been no deviations and lapses. Although the national Constitution contains no reference to God, practically every State Constitution does invoke His name (usually in the preamble) and acknowledges the people's dependence on Him. Christmas is a national holiday; legislatures, national and State, open their sessions with prayer; prayer meetings are sporadically held in the White House; "In God We Trust" is to be found on the currency of the realm, and "under God" in our Pledge of Allegiance. These and similar instances of governmental religiosity are, however, marginal and of little significance. . . .

L. PFEFFER, GOD, CAESAR, AND THE CONSTITUTION 345–46 (1975).

On the general question of church and state in the United States, *see* S. COBB, THE RISE OF RELIGIOUS LIBERTY IN AMERICA (1902); T. EMERSON, D. HABER, & N. DORSEN, POLITICAL AND CIVIL RIGHTS IN THE UNITED STATES 736–854 (student ed. 1967); P. KAUPER, *supra* note 41; M. KONVITZ, *supra* note 72, at 3–47; M. KONVITZ, RELIGIOUS LIBERTY AND CONSCIENCE (1968); P. KURLAND, *supra* note 50; W. MARNELL, THE FIRST AMENDMENT: THE HISTORY OF RELIGIOUS FREEDOM IN AMERICA (1964); R. MORGAN, THE SUPREME COURT AND RELIGION (1972); L. PFEFFER, CHURCH, STATE AND FREEDOM (rev. ed. 1967); B. SCHWARTZ, RIGHTS OF THE PERSON: EQUALITY, BELIEF AND DIGNITY 649–709 (1968); A. STOKES, *supra* note 44; A. STOKES & L. PFEFFER, CHURCH AND STATE IN THE UNITED STATES (rev. ed. 1964); TORPEY, JUDICIAL DOCTRINES OF RELIGIOUS RIGHTS IN AMERICA (1948); Bittker, *Churches, Taxes and the Constitution,* 78 YALE L.J. 1285 (1969); Burkholder, *supra* note 38; Hollingsworth, *supra* note 48; Kauper, *The Supreme Court and the Establishment Clause: Back to Everson?* 25 CASE W. RES. L. REV. 107 (1974); Pfeffer, *supra,* note 38; Pfefffer, *Uneasy Trinity: Church, State, and Constitution,* 2 CIVIL LIB. REV. 138 (No. 1, 1975); Schwartz, *No Imposition of Religion: The Establishment Clause Value,* 77 YALE L.J. 692 (1968). *See also* S. AHLSTROM, A RELIGIOUS HISTORY OF THE AMERICAN PEOPLE (1972).

74. H. LAUTERPACHT, AN INTERNATIONAL BILL OF THE RIGHTS OF MAN 105 (1945). For a detailed account of those constitutional provisions for religious liberty, *see* M. BATES, *supra* note 1, at 504–41.

In the Soviet Union, for example, shortly after the February Revolution of 1917, legal protection was accorded to freedom of conscience, "including the right to profess any religion or to profess none."[75] Following the October Revolution, Lenin reaffirmed this right by proclaiming in January 1918 "the separation of the Church from the State and the School from the Church," thereby abolishing the dominance of the Orthodox Church prevailing under Czarist Russia and guaranteeing "the equality of all religions."[76] More recently, inspired by the Universal Declaration of Human Rights and other related pronouncements, the constitutions of the newly independent states have prominently incorporated religious freedom and equality into the protected sphere of human rights.[77]

The trends toward religious freedom and equality within national communities have not been isolated events. They have influenced one another and, in so doing, have brought about transnational expectations of religious liberty that, in turn, have strengthened national practice. Building upon the doctrine of natural rights as a source of transnational authority, Hugo Grotius (and other prominent international lawyers after him) emphasized that in the same sense that international law is important to the maintenance of religious toleration is religious toleration indispensable to a stable international order.[78] Thus, Krishnaswami noted that "[e]ven before the concept of freedom of thought, conscience and religion was recognized in national law—and partly because it had not been so recognized—the practice evolved of making treaty stipulations ensuring certain rights to individuals or groups professing a religion or belief different from that of the majority in the country."[79] In 1536, the King of France and the Ottoman Emperor concluded a treaty conferring various liberties, including freedom of religion, upon French subjects within the Ottoman territory;[80] these stipulations in the form of "capitulations" in peace treaties "became the model for many later treaties of this sort as the capitulation system spread during the seventeenth, eighteenth, and early nineteenth centuries."[81] The Treaty of Westphalia, concluded in 1648 after the Thirty Years' War, represented

---

75. A. Krishnaswami, *supra* note 1, at 6.

76. *Id. Cf.* H. Lauterpacht, *supra* note 74, at 106.

77. *Cf.* A. Carrillo de Albornoz, Religious Liberty 160–62 (J. Drury trans. 1967); Religious Freedom (Councilium, Vol. 18, 1966).

78. R. Bainton, *supra* note 61, at 16–17. *Cf.* M. Manton, Religious Prohibitions under the Mexican Constitution before the League of Nations and the Permanent Court of International Justice 12–28 (1934); R. Higgins, Conflict of Interests: International Law in a Divided World 17–22 (1965).

79. A. Krishnaswami, *supra* note 1, at 11.

80. *See id.;* Toth, *supra* note 1, at 210.

81. A. Krishnaswami, *supra* note 1, at 11.

an important step toward ensuring toleration both for Protestants in Catholic states and for Catholics in Protestant states, although it fell short of affording religious freedom to all individuals and groups.[82] Another landmark was the Treaty of Berlin of 1878, pursuant to which the newly established states of Bulgaria, Montenegro, Romania, Serbia, and the Sublime Porte (the Ottoman Empire) undertook to ensure religious freedom to all their inhabitants.[83] Thus, in regard to Bulgaria, the Treaty provided in Article 5:

> The difference of religious creeds and confessions shall not be alleged against any person as a ground for exclusion or incapacity in matters relating to the enjoyment of civil and political rights, admission to public employments, functions, and honours, or the exercise of the various professions and industries in any locality whatsoever. . . .
>
> The freedom and outward exercise of all forms of worship are assured to all persons belonging to Bulgaria, as well as to foreigners, and no hindrance shall be offered either to the hierarchical organization of the different communions, or to their relations with their spiritual chiefs.[84]

Similar provisions were incorporated in Article 27 (regarding Montenegro),[85] Article 35 (regarding Serbia),[86] and Article 44 (regarding Roumania).[87] Additional obligations were imposed upon the Ottoman Empire in Article 62:

> All persons shall be admitted, without distinction of religion, to give evidence before the tribunals;
>
> Ecclesiastics, pilgrims, and monks of all nationalities travelling in Turkey in Europe, or in Turkey in Asia, shall enjoy the same rights, advantages, and privileges. . . .
>
> The right of official protection by the Diplomatic and Consular Agents of the Powers in Turkey is recognized both as regards the above-mentioned persons and their religious, charitable, and other establishments in the Holy Places and elsewhere. . . .
>
> The monks of Mount Athos, of whatever country they may be natives, shall be maintained in their former possessions and advan-

---

82. *Id. See also* C. Eckhardt, The Papacy and World Affairs: As Reflected in the Secularization of Politics (1937).

83. The text of the Treaty of Berlin, *signed* July 13, 1878, is *reprinted in* 2 Key Treaties for the Great Powers, 1814–1914, at 551–77 (M. Hurst ed. 1972).

84. *Id.* at 555–56.

85. *Id.* at 564.

86. *Id.* at 567.

87. *Id.* at 570–71.

> tages, and shall enjoy, without exception, complete equality of rights and prerogatives.[88]

Those peace treaties containing provisions regarding religious freedom, from 1648 (Westphalia) to 1878 (Berlin), shared an overriding concern: the protection of religious minorities by guaranteeing freedom of conscience and religion.[89] It was this same concern that inspired the early development of the doctrines and practices of humanitarian intervention in customary international law. In the words of Ganji:

> The history of international protection of Minorities to the early part of the 20th Century is that of the international protection of religious Minorities. If not all, the greater part of the history of humanitarian intervention is the history of intervention on behalf of persecuted religious minorities. These interventions were as a rule initiated by states whose people were linked by ties of religious belief to the persecuted minorities of the state intervened against. As far back as the latter part of the 17th Century there is, in the history of international relations, evidence of international protection of religious minorities undertaken by the European Powers.[90]

In addition to inserting provisos into peace treaties, states have often inserted provisions guaranteeing religious freedom into bilateral treaties of amity, commerce, and navigation.[91] This type of protection was particularly favored by Great Britain and the United States. For example, in order to ensure religious freedom for Americans abroad, the United States included such protective clauses in the treaties of friendship and commerce with the Netherlands (1782), with Sweden (1783), and with Prussia (1785).[92] Article 9 of the treaty with Prussia stipulated: "The most perfect freedom of conscience and of worship is granted to the citizens or subjects of either party within the jurisdiction of the other, without being liable to molestation in that respect for any other cause than an insult on the religion of others."[93] Comparable protection against religious discrimination was provided for in the bilateral treaties concluded by the United States with, respectively, China, Japan, Siam, the Congo, Germany, Ecuador, Honduras, Austria, Norway, Poland,

---

88. *Id.* at 575.

89. *See* M. Bates, *supra* note 1, at 477–84.

90. M. Ganji, International Protection of Human Rights 17 (1962) (footnote omitted). For further details, see *id.* at 17–44.

91. *See* M. Bates, *supra* note 1, at 477–87, 542–43; R. Wilson, United States Commercial Treaties and International Law 244–79 (1960).

92. M. Bates, *supra* note 1, at 485.

93. *Quoted in id.* at 485–86.

Finland, Liberia, and Iraq.[94] The protection offered by these treaties was "reciprocal" and extensive, providing for "freedom of public worship, with due reservation of proper requirements, for foreigners to enjoy the same rights and benefits as nationals, including residence, travel, and the right to hold property for religious purposes, with express or implied right to conduct religious, educational, and philanthropic work."[95]

Transnational efforts toward eliminating religious discrimination were fortified with the establishment of the League of Nations. The Covenant of the League, in Article 22(5), held a Mandatory "responsible for the administration of the territory under conditions which will guarantee freedom of conscience and religion."[96] Thus, Article 1 of the French Mandate for Togoland (or the Cameroons) (Class B) stipulated:

> The Mandatory shall ensure in the territory complete freedom of conscience and the free exercise of all forms of worship, which are consonant with public order and morality; missionaries who are nationals of States Members of the League of Nations shall be free to enter the territory and to travel and reside therein, to acquire and possess property, to erect religious buildings, and to open schools throughout the territory; it being understood, however, that the Mandatory shall have the right to exercise such control as may be necessary for the maintenance of public order and good government, and to take all measures required for such control.[97]

Similarly, the South African Mandate for South-West Africa (Class C) provided:

> Subject to the provisions of any local law for the maintenance of public order and public morals, the Mandatory shall ensure in the

---

94. *Id.* at 479, 486.

95. *Id.* at 486. *Cf.* R. HIGGINS, *supra* note 78, at 23–39.

96. The Mandate System of the League was designed, at the end of World War I, to detach the territories of the defeated powers (i.e., Turkish territories and the German colonies in Africa and Oceania) and to entrust them to Mandatory Powers. For further details and subsequent development, *see* N. BENTWICH, THE MANDATES SYSTEM (1930); R. CHOWDHURI, INTERNATIONAL MANDATES AND TRUSTEESHIP SYSTEMS (1955); LEAGUE OF NATIONS, THE MANDATE SYSTEM (1945); A. MARGALITH, THE INTERNATIONAL MANDATES (1930); J. MURRAY, THE UNITED NATIONS TRUSTEESHIP SYSTEM (1957); 1 L. OPPENHEIM, INTERNATIONAL LAW 212–42 (8th ed. H. Lauterpacht 1955); L. SOHN & T. BUERGENTHAL, INTERNATIONAL PROTECTION OF HUMAN RIGHTS 337–504 (1973); C. TOUSSAINT, THE TRUSTEESHIP OF THE UNITED NATIONS (1956); E. VAN MANNEN-HELMER, THE MANDATES SYSTEM IN RELATION TO AFRICA AND THE PACIFIC ISLANDS (1929); Q. WRIGHT, MANDATES UNDER THE LEAGUE OF NATIONS (1930). *See generally* Chen, *Self-Determination as a Human Right,* in TOWARD WORLD ORDER AND HUMAN DIGNITY 198–261 (W. Reisman & B. Weston eds. 1976).

97. *Quoted in* Bates, *supra* note 1, at 488.

territory freedom of conscience and the free exercise of all forms of worship, and shall allow all missionaries, nationals of any State Member of the League of Nations, to enter into, travel and reside in the territory for the purpose of prosecuting their calling.[98]

Further important efforts to advance the goal of religious freedom were made under League auspices through the international regime of minority protection. Religious minorities were among the minority groups that the League of Nations was empowered to protect.[99] In post–World War I arrangements (effected through both treaty stipulations and League resolutions), designed by the League to shelter minority groups from discrimination and oppression, a profound concern was manifested for religious freedom. The Treaty with Poland, signed at Versailles on June 28, 1919,[100] served as a prototype for comparable arrangements with a number of other states including Czechoslovakia, the Serb-Croat-Slovene State, Roumania, Greece, Austria, Bulgaria, Hungary, and Turkey (through treaty stipulation) and Albania, Esthonia, Latvia, Lithuania, and Iraq (through League resolutions).[101]

A close examination of the provisions of the Treaty with Poland documents the deep demand existing at that time for protection against religious discrimination. Article 2 of the Treaty obliged Poland to "assure full and complete protection of life and liberty" to all of its inhabitants "without distinction" as to "religion" or other factors.[102] The same article afforded more general protection: "All inhabitants of Poland shall be entitled to the free exercise, whether public or private, of any creed, religion, or belief, whose practices are not inconsistent with public order or public morals."[103] "All Polish nationals," according to Article 7, "shall be equal before the law and shall enjoy the same civil and political rights without distinction as to race, language or religion."[104] "Differences of religion, creed or confession," the article added, "shall not prejudice any Polish national in matters relating to the enjoyment of civil or political rights, as for instance admission to public employments, functions and honours, or the exercise of professions and industries."[105] Finally, Article 8 provided:

---

98. *Reprinted in* Basic Documents on International Protection of Human Rights 242, 244 (L. Sohn & T. Buergenthal eds. 1973) [hereinafter Basic Documents] (Art. 5).

99. *See* chapter 9 *supra,* at notes 70–76 and accompanying text.

100. *Reprinted in* League of Nations, Protection of Linguistic, Racial and Religious Minorities by the League of Nations, 1927 I.B. 2, at 41–45.

101. *See id.*

102. *Id.* at 43.

103. *Id.*

104. *Id.*

105. *Id.* When people are deprived of the opportunity to become nationals because of religious beliefs, however, such a provision is futile.

> Polish nationals who belong to racial, religious or linguistic minorities shall enjoy the same treatment and security in law and in fact as the other Polish nationals. In particular they shall have an equal right to establish, manage and control at their own expense charitable, religious educational establishments, with the right to use their own language and to exercise their religion freely therein.[106]

All of these provisions were recognized under Article 1 as "fundamental laws," and hence the Treaty stipulated that "no law, regulation or official action shall conflict or interfere with these stipulations, nor shall any law, regulation or official action prevail over them."[107] Furthermore, these duties were, pursuant to Article 12, made "obligations of international concern" and placed "under the guarantee of the League of Nations."[108]

The contemporary proscription of religious discrimination, like comparable proscriptions concerning race and sex,[109] is firmly established in the Charter of the United Nations and has been further amplified in related human rights instruments. In the Charter provisions concerning discrimination, religion is consistently specified, along with race, sex, and language, as an impermissible ground of differentiation.[110] At the San Francisco Conference of 1945, it was proposed (notably by Latin American delegations) that detailed guarantees of freedom of conscience and religion be incorporated in the Charter; however, these proposals were not accepted.[111] Instead, by repeatedly employing the familiar formula of "human rights and fundamental freedoms for all, without distinction as to race, sex, language or religion,"[112] the Charter established a more general norm prohibiting discrimination. This policy was first implemented in the post-World War II peace treaties concluded in 1947 by the Allied Powers with Bulgaria, Finland, Hungary, Italy, and Roumania. Each state pledged to undertake "all measures necessary to secure to all persons under [its] jurisdiction, without distinction as to race, sex, language or religion, the enjoyment of human rights and of the fundamental freedoms, including freedom . . . of religious worship. . . ."[113]

---

106. *Id.* at 44.

107. *Id.* at 42.

108. *Id.* at 44.

109. *See* chapters 9 and 10 *supra.*

110. U.N. CHARTER, Art. 1, para. 3; Art. 13, para 1(b); Art. 55(c); Art. 62, para. 2; Art. 76(c).

111. A. KRISHNASWAMI, *supra* note 1, at 12.

112. *See* Charter provisions cited in note 110 *supra.*

113. Treaty of Peace with Bulgaria, Feb. 10, 1947, Art 2, No. 643, 41 U.N.T.S. 21; Treaty of Peace with Hungary, Feb. 10, 1947, Art. 2, No. 644, 41 U.N.T.S. 135; Treaty of Peace with Romania, Feb. 10, 1947, Art 3, No. 645, 42 U.N.T.S. 3; Treaty of Peace with Finland, Feb. 10, 1947, Art. 6, No. 746, 48 U.N.T.S. 203. *See also* Treaty of Peace with

In attempting to explicate the Charter's comprehensive prohibition of discrimination, the Universal Declaration of Human Rights, in Article 2, specifies religion as among the impermissible grounds of differentiation.[114] This general prohibition of discrimination is made more explicit in Article 18:

> Everyone has the right to freedom of thought, conscience and religion; this right includes freedom to change his religion or belief, and freedom, either alone or in community with others and in public or private, to manifest his religion or belief in teaching, practice, worship or observance.[115]

Article 1, by proclaiming that all human beings are "endowed with reason and conscience and should act towards one another in a spirit of brotherhood,"[116] further affirms the right of the individual to explore and define a personal orientation toward other persons and the universe. In order to implement this aspiration, Article 26(2) urges that education be directed to "promote understanding, tolerance and friendship among all nations, racial or religious groups."[117]

Important protection for religious groups can also be found in a number of relatively recent conventions, including the Genocide Convention of 1948.[118] This convention seeks "to prevent and to punish" certain acts "committed with intent to destroy, in whole or in part," religious groups, among others; the acts prohibited include "killing members of the group," causing members of a protected group "serious bodily or mental harm," deliberate infliction of living conditions calculated to bring about group destruction, "measures intended to prevent births within the group," and forcible transfer of children.[119] The convention also punishes "conspiracy," "incitement," "attempt to commit," and "complicity in genocide."[120] Both the Convention Relating to the Status of Refugees (1951) and the Convention Relating to the Status of

---

Italy, Feb. 10, 1947, Art. 19(4), No. 747, 49 U.N.T.S. 3 (with a slight variation in wording from the preceding provisions).

114. G.A. Res. 217A(III), U.N. GAOR, pt. 1, U.N. Doc. A/810 (1948), *reprinted in* United Nations, Human Rights: A Compilation of International Instruments of the United Nations 1, U.N. Doc. ST/HR/1 (1973) [hereinafter cited as U.N. Human Rights Instruments].

115. *Id.*

116. *Id.*

117. *Id.*

118. Convention on the Prevention and Punishment of the Crime of Genocide, *opened for signature* Dec. 9, 1948, No. 1021, 78 U.N.T.S. 277, *reprinted in* U.N. Human Rights Instruments, *supra* note 114, at 41.

119. *Id.*

120. *Id.*

Stateless Persons (1954) protect refugees and stateless persons from religious discrimination and accord them "national treatment" with regard to "freedom to practice their religion and freedom as regards the religious education of their children."[121] The Discrimination (Employment and Occupation) Convention of 1958, which aspires to bring about "equality of opportunity of treatment in employment or occupation," includes religion among the prohibited grounds of differentiation.[122] Similarly, the Convention against Discrimination in Education of 1960, designed to ensure "equality of opportunity and treatment for all in education," specifically prohibits discrimination on the basis of religion.[123]

In the International Covenant on Civil and Political Rights, adopted by the General Assembly in 1966 (taking effect on March 23, 1976), religion is included in both the general provision against discrimination in the enjoyment of all human rights under Article 2(1)[124] and in the equal protection clause under Article 26.[125] The prohibition of discrimination is regarded as of such overriding importance that states are forbidden to practice discrimination on the ground of religion (or on the ground of race, color, sex, language, or social origin) where derogations from their obligations would otherwise be justified by "public emergency" under Article 4(1).[126] In Article 18(1), the basic content of the

---

121. Art. 3 provides that "[t]he Contracting States shall apply the provisions of this Convention to refugees without discrimination as to race, religion or country of origin," and Art. 4 reads: "The Contracting States shall accord to refugees within their territories treatment at least as favourable as that accorded to their nationals with respect to freedom to practice their religion and freedom as regards the religious education of their children." Convention Relating to the Status of Stateless Persons, Sept. 9, 1954, No. 5158, 360 U.N.T.S. 130, *reprinted in* U.N. HUMAN RIGHTS INSTRUMENTS, *supra* note 114, at 61. Comparable provisions are found in Arts. 3 and 4 of the Convention Relating to the Status of Refugees, July 28, 1951, No. 254, 189 U.N.T.S. 150, *reprinted in* U.N. HUMAN RIGHTS INSTRUMENTS, *supra,* at 68.

122. Convention concerning Discrimination in Respect to Employment and Occupation, June 25, 1958, No. 5181, 362 U.N.T.S. 31, *reprinted in* U.N. HUMAN RIGHTS INSTRUMENTS, *supra* note 114, at 29.

123. Dec. 14, 1960, No. 6193, 429 U.N.T.S. 93, *reprinted in* U.N. HUMAN RIGHTS INSTRUMENTS, *supra* note 114, at 31.

124. G.A. Res. 2200, 21 U.N. GAOR, Supp. (No. 16) 52, U.N. Doc. A/6316 (1966), *reprinted in* U.N. HUMAN RIGHTS INSTRUMENTS, *supra* note 114, at 8.

125. *Id.*

126. Art. 4(1) of the International Covenant on Civil and Political Rights reads:

> In time of public emergency which threatens the life of the nation and the existence of which is officially proclaimed, the States Parties to the present Covenant may take measures derogating from their obligations under the present Covenant to the extent strictly required by the exigencies of the situation, provided that such measures are not inconsistent with their other obligations under international law and do not in-

right so emphatically protected is defined by prescribing complete freedom of choice regarding rectitude: "Everyone shall have the right to freedom of thought, conscience and religion. This right shall include freedom to have or to adopt a religion or belief of his choice, and freedom, either individually or in community with others and in public or private, to manifest his religion or belief in worship, observance, practice and teaching."[127] Article 18(2) further insulates this right by providing protection against coercion that would "impair" an individual's "freedom to have or to adopt a religion or belief of his choice."[128] Article 18(3) then expresses the recognition that this freedom, like other rights, is subject to the necessity of appropriate accommodation with the aggregate common interest.[129] In addition, Article 24(1) provides that the special protection accorded to children is to be effected without discrimination on account of religion,[130] and Article 27 specifically includes religious minorities among the protected minority groups.[131]

Similarly, the International Covenant on Economic, Social, and Cultural Rights (adopted by the General Assembly in 1966 and becoming operative on January 3, 1976) contains, in Article 2(2), a comprehensive guarantee that the rights stipulated in the Covenant will be exercised without discrimination on the ground of religion.[132] Article 13(1) amplifies this guarantee by proclaiming that education be directed to "enable all persons to participate effectively in a free society, promote understanding, tolerance and friendship among all nations and all racial, ethnic or religious groups."[133] It may be recalled, finally, that the Proclamation of Teheran of 1968 insists that it is "imperative that the members of the international community fulfill their solemn obligations

---

volve discrimination solely on the ground of race, colour, sex, language, religion or social origin.

Id.

127. *Id.*

128. *Id.*

129. Art. 18(3) reads: "Freedom to manifest one's religion or beliefs may be subject only to such limitations as are prescribed by law and are necessary to protect public safety, order, health, or morals or the fundamental rights and freedoms of others." *Id.*

130. Art. 24(1) provides: "Every child shall have, without any discrimination as to race, colour, sex, language, religion, national or social origin, property or birth, the right to such measures of protection as are required by his status as a minor, on the part of his family, society and the State." *Id.*

131. Art. 27 stipulates: "In those States in which ethnic, religious or linguistic minorities exist, persons belonging to such minorities shall not be denied the right, in community with the other members of their group, to enjoy their own culture, to profess and practice their own religion, or to use their own language." *Id.*

132. G.A. Res. 2200, 21 U.N. GAOR, Supp. (No. 16) 49, U.N. Doc. A/6316 (1966), *reprinted in* U.N. Human Rights Instruments, *supra* note 114, at 3.

133. *Id.*

to promote and encourage respect for human rights and fundamental freedoms for all without distinctions of any kind," including "religion."[134]

Both the continuing demand for more tightly articulated international prescriptions to ensure religious freedom and the difficulty involved in formulating such prescriptions are demonstrated by the efforts within the United Nations to formulate a convention and a declaration on elimination of all forms of religious intolerance. At its Seventeenth Session in 1962, the General Assembly (in response to recurring manifestations of anti-Semitism and other forms of racial and religious prejudice) decided to formulate a declaration and a convention on "the elimination of all forms of religious intolerance," paralleling a set of instruments on "the elimination of all forms of racial discrimination."[135] Although the Declaration and the Convention on the Elimination of All Forms of Racial Discrimination were successively adopted by the General Assembly in 1963 and in 1965 (the latter taking effect on January 4, 1969),[136] the contemplated Declaration and Convention on the Elimination of Religious Intolerance are yet to be completed. This "marked contrast," characterized by "the stormy course of the instruments dealing with religious intolerance,"[137] has been caused by a coalition of delegations seeking to downplay the issues of anti-Semitism and other forms of religious intolerance.[138] Religious warfare, it would appear, is not entirely an affair of the past. In 1964 (two years after the Assembly's decision to formulate a declaration and a convention), the Sub-Commission on Prevention of Discrimination and Protection of Minorities submitted a preliminary draft declaration[139] to the Commission on

134. U.N. Doc. A/CONF.32/41 (1968), *reprinted in* U.N. HUMAN RIGHTS INSTRUMENTS, *supra* note 114, at 18.

135. *See* chapter 9 *supra,* at notes 89–103 and accompanying text.

136. *Id.*

137. Liskofsky, *Eliminating Intolerance and Discrimination Based on Religion or Belief: The U.N. Role,* REPORTS ON THE FOREIGN SCENE, Feb. 1968, No. 8, at 1, 3.

138. *See* chapter 9, *supra,* at notes 89–103 and accompanying text. *See also* Liskofsky, *supra* note 137, at 3–4.

For the legislative history of the proposed declaration and the proposed convention on the elimination of religious intolerance and discrimination, see *Manifestations of Racial Prejudice and National and Religious Intolerance* (report of the secretary-general), U.N. Doc. A/6347 (1966); *Elimination of All Forms of Religious Intolerance* (note by the secretary-general), U.N. Doc. A/7177 (1968); *Elimination of All Forms of Religious Intolerance* (note by the secretary-general), U.N. Doc. A/7930 (1970); *Elimination of All Forms of Religious Intolerance* (note by the secretary-general), U.N. Doc. A/8330 (1971) [hereinafter cited as U.N. Doc. A/8330]; *Elimination of All Forms of Religious Intolerance* (report of the Third Committee), U.N. Doc. A 9322 (1973); *Draft Declaration on the Elimination of All Forms of Religious Intolerance* (working paper prepared by the Secretariat), U.N. Doc. E/CN.4/1145 (1973).

139. COMMISSION ON HUMAN RIGHTS, REPORT ON THE TWENTIETH SESSION, 37 U.N. ECOSOC, Supp. (No. 8) 69–74, U.N. Doc. E/3873 (E/CN.4/874) (1964). The full text of the

Human Rights, which, through a fifteen-member Working Group, was able to agree upon only six of the proposed articles.[140] After reporting this outcome to the Assembly through the Economic and Social Council and seeking further instructions,[141] the Commission began preparing a draft convention.

In 1965, the Sub-Commission presented a preliminary draft convention to the Commission.[142] Building upon the Sub-Commission's draft, the Commission, at its sessions from 1965 to 1967, adopted a preamble and twelve articles but was unable to consider the proposed articles on measures of implementation.[143] The Commission's draft convention, together with other related proposals not considered by the Commission, was transmitted to the General Assembly in 1967 by the Economic and Social Council; the Council also expressed the hope that the Assembly would decide on appropriate implementation provisions.[144] The Assembly considered the draft convention at its Twenty-second Session in 1967 and decided to change its title to draft International Convention on the Elimination of All Forms of Intolerance and of Discrimination based on Religion or Belief;[145] however, since the 1967 session, the Assembly has deferred consideration of the draft convention.

In December 1972, the Assembly decided to "accord priority to the completion of the Declaration on the Elimination of All Forms of Religious Intolerance before resuming consideration of the International Convention on this subject."[146] The Assembly instructed that the drafts previously prepared in 1964 by the Sub-Commission and the Working Group of the Commission on Human Rights be circulated to member states and specialized agencies for comments.[147] It further urged "the adoption, if possible, of such a Declaration as part of the observance of the twenty-fifth anniversary of the Universal Declaration of Human

---

preliminary draft of a "United Nations Declaration on the Elimination of All Forms of Religious Intolerance, Prepared by the Sub-Commission on Prevention of Discrimination and Protection of Minorities" [hereinafter cited as Sub-Commission Draft Declaration] is conveniently attached as an annex to U.N. Doc. A/8330, *supra* note 138.

140. Commission on Human Rights, *supra* note 139, at 74–81; U.N. Doc. A/8330, *supra* note 138, at 4. The text of the articles as prepared by the Working Group [hereinafter cited as Working Group Draft Declaration] is attached as an annex to U.N. Doc. A/8330, *supra*.

141. U.N. Doc. A/8330, *supra* note 138, at 4–5.

142. *Id.* at 5. The draft convention [hereinafter cited as Commission Draft Convention] is also attached as an annex to U.N. Doc. A/8330.

143. *Id.* at 6.

144. ECOSOC Res. 1233, 42 U.N. ECOSOC, Supp. (No. 1) 13, U.N. Doc. E/4393 (1967).

145. U.N. Doc. A/8330, *supra* note 138, at 7.

146. G.A. Res. 3027, 27 U.N. GAOR, Supp. (No. 30) 72, U.N. Doc. A/8730 (1972).

147. *Id.*

Rights" in 1973.[148] Yet, in 1973, the task remained unfinished and its consideration took a new turn. While reaffirming the priority accorded to the "completion of the Declaration," in December of 1973, the Assembly indicated that "the preparation of a draft Declaration" required "additional study." Accordingly, it instructed the Commission on Human Rights to "submit, if possible, a single draft Declaration to the Assembly at its twenty-ninth session" in 1974 in the light of the suggestions, comments, and amendments recently received.[149] The Commission was, however, nowhere near the completion of its newly assigned task at its thirtieth and thirty-first sessions held in 1974 and 1975.[150] In view of the slow progress within the Commission, it is unclear when the draft declaration will be completed and adopted by the General Assembly; moreover, completion of the draft convention appears to be even a more remote possibility.

Despite the delay in their completion and adoption, the contours of the proposed declaration and the proposed convention have been sufficiently articulated in the available drafts to make it possible to anticipate their ultimate form. Taken together, the respective drafts of the declara-

---

148. *Id.*

149. G.A. Res. 3069, 28 U.N. GAOR, Supp. (No. 30) 77–78, U.N. Doc. A/9030 (1973). *See also* G.A. Res. 3267, 29 U.N. GAOR, Supp. (No. 31) 88–89, U.N. Doc. a/9631 (1975); *Elimination of All Forms of Religious Intolerance* (report of the Third Committee), U.N. Doc. A/9893 (1974).

For recent comments by various governments, *see Draft Declaration on the Elimination of All Forms of Religious Intolerance* (report of the secretary-general), U.N. Doc. A/9134 (1973); *Analytical Presentation of the Observations Received from Governments concerning the Draft Declaration on the Elimination of All Forms of Religious Intolerance* (note by the secretary-general), U.N. Doc. A/9135 (1973); *Draft Declaration on the Elimination of All Forms of Religious Intolerance* (report of the secretary-general), U.N. Doc. E/CN.4/1146 (1974).

150. *Commission on Human Rights, Report on the Thirtieth Session (4 Feb.-8 March 1974),* 56 U.N. ECOSOC, Supp. (No. 5) 7, 18–22, 57, U.N. Doc. E/5464 (E/CN.4/1154) (1974). After considerable debate in its Thirtieth Session in 1974 about ways and means of accelerating the preparation of a single draft declaration, the Commission has set up "an informal Working Group open to all members of the Commission." *Id.* at 19. The informal Working Group, with Mr. Pierre Juvigny (France) serving as chairman-rapporteur, agreed to proceed on the basis of "consensus," and was able to consider only "the title and the first two preambular paragraphs of a draft Declaration" in the six meetings it held in February 1974.

For an account of the limited progress made in 1975, *see Commission on Human Rights, Report on the Thirty-First Session (3 Feb.-7 March 1975),* 58 U.N. ECOSOC, Supp. (No. 4) 4, 36–41, U.N. Doc. E/5635 (E/CN.4/1179) (1975).

For more recent developments, *see* the Commission's Reports of 1976, 1977, and 1978: 60 U.N. ECOSOC, Supp. (No. 3) 37–41, 73 (1976); 62 U.N. ECOSOC, Supp. (No. 6) 43–48, 86 (1977); 1978 U.N. ECOSOC, Supp. (No. 4) 56–65, 129 (1978). *See also Elimination of All Forms of Religious Intolerance,* U.N. Doc. A/33/474 (1978) (report of the Third Committee).

tion proposed by the Sub-Commission[151] and the Working Group of the Commission on Human Rights,[152] along with the draft convention prepared by the Commission,[153] appear to parallel the Declaration and the Convention on the Elimination of Racial Discrimination. This parallelism is observable in proposed provisions concerning the grounds of differentiation prohibited, the rights protected, the specific acts forbidden, and the actors precluded from engaging in discrimination.[154]

Discrimination on the ground of religion or belief is condemned as an "offence to human dignity," "a denial of the principles of the Charter of the United Nations," "a violation of the human rights and fundamental freedoms proclaimed in the Universal Declaration of Human Rights," and "an obstacle to friendly and peaceful relations among nations."[155] In terms as broad and inclusive as those used in the racial convention, the draft convention defines "discrimination on the ground of religion or belief" to mean "any distinction, exclusion, restriction or preference based on religion or belief which has the purpose or effect of nullifying or impairing the recognition, enjoyment or exercise, on an equal footing, of human rights and fundamental freedoms in the political, economic, social, cultural, or any other field of public life."[156] The terms "religion or belief" are defined as including "theistic, non-theistic, and atheistic beliefs."[157] In recognition of the "complexities of the issues involved in the elaboration of standards for religious liberty in a world community of diverse beliefs and institutions,"[158] Article 1(4) of the draft convention adds: "Neither the establishment of a religion nor the recognition of a religion or belief by a State nor the separation of Church from State shall by itself be considered religious intolerance or discrimination on the ground of religion or belief."[159] This provision appears to be an unfortunate departure from the conventional wisdom that the establishment or recognition of an official religion may promote intolerance of other beliefs.[160]

---

151. Sub-Commission Draft Declaration, *supra* note 139.

152. Working Group Draft Declaration, *supra* note 140.

153. Commission Draft Convention, *supra* note 142.

154. *See* chapter 9 *supra,* at notes 104–83 and accompanying text.

155. Sub-Commission Draft Declaration, *supra* note 139, Art. 1, at 2; Working Group Draft Declaration, *supra* note 140, Art. 2, at 2.

156. Commission Draft Convention, *supra* note 142, Art. 1(b), at 2.

157. *Id.,* Art. 1(a).

158. Abram, *supra* note 1, at 46.

159. Commission Draft Convention, *supra* note 142, Art. 1(d), at 2.

160. In the words of Krishnaswami:

> For centuries, a close relationship existed in almost all countries between the State and the predominant religion. This religion enjoyed a special status, either because it had been recognized as the Established Church or because it had been accepted as the

The drafts of both the convention and the declaration contemplate comprehensive protection against religious discrimination. Thus, the drafts speak in terms of protecting all of the "political, civic, economic, social and cultural rights"[161] and "human rights and fundamental freedoms" in "any other field of public life."[162] In the course of considering which rights should be protected by the proposed instruments, however, a fundamental issue has been "whether to deal only with discrimination based on religion or belief, e.g. in employment, education, housing or citizenship, or, in addition, with the 'freedom' of all to practice and manifest religion and belief."[163] The response has thus far been in favor of the latter position; this position appears to recognize that, in order to eliminate religious intolerance and discrimination, it is essential to "keep fully in the forefront the substance of the right to freedom of thought, conscience and religion."[164] "What would be the meaning of tolerance," it has been asked, "without the affirmation of the rich substance of the right, which all should be free to exercise?"[165] Hence, both the draft declaration and the draft convention make elaborate and detailed provi-

---

> State religion. Not infrequently recognition of the predominant religion led to the total exclusion of all other religions, or at least to their reduction to a subordinate position. Thus in the past the mere existence in a country of an Established Church or of a State religion usually connoted severe discrimination—and sometimes even outright persecution—directed against dissenters.

A. Krishnaswami, *supra* note 1, at 46. Commenting on this conventional wisdom, he cautioned readers today not to jump to such an inference without a thorough contextual scrutiny. *Id.* at 46–54.

In the same vein, Abram has explained:

> Member States include those in which there is complete separation of Church and State, those in which several religions are recognized by the State, and those with a single Established Church or State religion. While it has often been argued that a particular juridical relationship logically determines a potential pattern of infringement of the rights of minority religions or beliefs, it seems difficult to confirm this argument in practice. . . .
>
> The moral of these examples is easily drawn: the determinants of the religious freedom of a society include not only the juridical framework and the laws of the State but also the *mores* of the society, including the value placed upon this freedom by the major religions and ideologies within the society.

Abram, *supra* note 1, at 46–47.

161. Commission Draft Convention, *supra* note 142, Art. 5, at 4. *See also* Working Group Draft Declaration, *supra* note 140, Art. 4(1), at 2.

162. Commission Draft Convention, *supra* note 142, Art. 1(b), at 2.

163. Liskofsky, *supra* note 137, at 3.

164. Observations made by the Commission of the Churches on International Affairs to the Sub-Commission's Draft Declaration, *reprinted in* A. Carrillo de Albornoz, Religious Liberty 32, 33 (1964).

165. *Id.*

sion for "the right to freedom of thought, conscience, religion or belief" as the core freedom, indispensable to the achievement of an environment free from discrimination on account of religion or belief. This core freedom, to be extended to each person, includes:

1. Freedom to adhere or not to adhere to any religion or belief and to change his religion or belief in accordance with the dictates of his conscience. . . .
2. Freedom to manifest his religion or belief either alone or in community with others, and in public or in private. . . .
3. Freedom to express opinion on questions concerning a religion or belief.
4. Freedom to worship, to hold assemblies related to religion or belief. . . .
5. Freedom to teach, to disseminate and to learn his religion or belief. . . .
6. Freedom to practise his religion or belief by establishing and maintaining charitable and education institutions. . . .
7. Freedom to observe the rituals, dietary and other practices of his religion or belief. . . .
8. Freedom to make pilgrimages and other journeys in connection with his religion or belief. . . .
9. Equal legal protection for the places of worship or assembly, the rites, ceremonies and activities, and the places of disposal of the dead associated with his religion or belief;
10. Freedom to organize and maintain local, regional, national and international associations in connexion with his religion or belief. . . .
11. Freedom from compulsion to take an oath of a religious nature.[166]

The particular acts that would be prohibited by the draft convention

166. Commission Draft Convention, *supra* note 142, Art. 3, at 2–3. *See also* Sub-Commission Draft Declaration, *supra* note 139, Art. 6, at 3–4; Working Group Draft Declaration, *supra* note 140, Art. 6, at 3.

A further protection concerns the right of parents or legal guardians to bring up their children in the religion or belief of their choice and their responsibility to inculcate in their children tolerance for the religion of others. States would further be obliged not to discriminate "in the granting of subsidies, in taxation or in exemptions from taxation, between different religions or beliefs or their adherents." Sub-Commission Draft Declaration, *supra* note 139, Arts. 5, 12, at 2, 4. *See also* Working Group Draft Declaration, *supra* note 140, Art. 5, at 3; Commission Draft Convention, *supra* note 142, Art. 4, at 3–4.

and the draft declaration include "any distinction, exclusion, restriction or preference" that "has the purpose or effect of nullifying or impairing" equality in "recognition, enjoyment or exercise" of protected rights.[167] The fourfold characterizations of "distinction, exclusion, restriction or preference" are sufficiently broad to encompass a wide range of activities.[168] In addition, criminal sanctions would be imposed for "[a]ny act of violence against the adherents of any religion or belief or against the means used for its practice, any incitement to such acts or incitement to hatred likely to result in acts of violence against any religion or belief or its adherents,"[169] and "all propaganda designed to foster or justify" such activities.[170]

In their efforts to secure the elimination of religious intolerance and discrimination, the proposed drafts would, like the Declaration and the Convention on the Elimination of Racial Discrimination, bring both official and nonofficial actors within their authority: "No States, institution, group or individual" would be permitted to "make any discrimination in matters of human rights and fundamental freedoms in the treatment of persons on the grounds of their religion or their belief."[171] These drafts also underscore the critical importance of intranational action to bring about the necessary internal changes in both authoritative and effective power processes that would ensure the maintenance of the freedoms sought to be promoted by the drafts.[172] The drafts manifest, finally, a

---

167. Commission Draft Convention, *supra* note 142, Art. 1(b), at 2.

168. *See* chapter 9 *supra,* at notes 162–77 and accompanying text.

169. Commission Draft Convention, *supra* note 142, Art. 9, at 5.

170. Sub-Commission Draft Declaration, *supra* note 139, Art. 14(2), at 5.

171. *Id.,* Art. 2, at 2. *See also* Working Group Draft Declaration, *supra* note 140, Art. 3(1), at 2.

172. Commission Draft Convention, Art. 6, *supra* note 142, provides:

> States Parties undertake to adopt immediate and effective measures, particularly in the fields of teaching, education, culture and information, with a view to combating prejudices as, for example, anti-Semitism and other manifestations which lead to religious intolerance and to discrimination on the ground of religion or belief, and to promoting and encouraging, in the interest of universal peace, understanding, tolerance, co-operation and friendship among nations, groups and individuals, irrespective of differences in religion or belief, in accordance with the purposes and principles of the Charter of the United Nations, the Universal Declaration of Human Rights and this Convention.

Art. 7 would oblige contracting states to

> take effective measures to prevent and eliminate discrimination on the ground of religion or belief, including the enactment or abrogation of laws or regulations where necessary to prohibit such discrimination by any person, group or organization, [and not to] pursue any policy or enact or retain laws or regulations restricting or impeding freedom of conscience, religion or belief or the free and open exercise thereof, nor

deep realization of the necessity of an appropriate accommodation of the rights and freedoms to be enjoyed by individuals with the aggregate common interest.[173]

On the regional level, the principle of religious freedom is embodied both in general prescriptions banning discrimination that include religion as a prohibited ground of differentiation and in more particular prescriptions that give substance to the freedom of thought, conscience, and religion. Thus, the European Convention on Human Rights includes religion, in Article 14, as among the impermissible grounds of differentiation[174] and spells out the content of freedom of religion in Article 9.[175] Similarly, the American Declaration of the Rights and

---

> discriminate against any person, group or organization on account of membership or non-membership in, practice or non-practice of, or adherence or non-adherence to any religion or belief.

Moreover, Art. 10 reads:

> State Parties shall ensure to everyone within their jurisdiction effective protection and remedies, through the competent national tribunals and other State institutions, against any acts, including acts of discrimination on the ground of religion or belief, which violate his human rights and fundamental freedoms contrary to this Convention, as well as the right to seek from such tribunals just and adequate reparation or satisfaction for any damage suffered as a result of such acts.

See also Sub-Commission Draft Declaration, *supra* note 139, Arts. 3(2), 14, at 2, 5; Working Group Draft Declaration, *supra* note 140, Arts. 3(2), at 2.

173. The Commission Draft Convention, *supra* note 142, provides:

> 11. Nothing in this Convention shall be interpreted as giving to any person, group, organization or institution the right to engage in activities aimed at prejudicing national security, friendly relations between nations or the purposes and principles of the United Nations.
>
> 12. Nothing in this Convention shall be construed to preclude a State Party from prescribing by law such limitations as are necessary to protect public safety, order, health or moral or the individual rights and freedoms of others, or the general welfare in a democratic society.

Art. 13(2) of the Sub-Commission Draft Declaration, *supra* note 139, reads:

> The freedoms and rights set out elsewhere in this Declaration shall be subject only to the restrictions prescribed by law solely for the purpose of securing due recognition and respect for the rights and freedoms of others and of meeting the legitimate requirements of morality, health, public order and the general welfare in a democratic society. Any restrictions which may be imposed shall be consistent with the purposes and principles of the United Nations and with the rights and freedoms stated in the Universal Declaration of Human Rights. These freedoms and rights may in no case be exercised contrary to the purposes and principles of the United Nations.

174. Convention for the Protection of Human Rights and Fundamental Freedoms, Nov. 4, 1950, *reprinted in* BASIC DOCUMENTS, *supra* note 98, at 125.

175. *Id.*

Duties of Man[176] proclaims, in Article 2, that "[a]ll persons are equal before the law and have the rights and duties established in this Declaration, without distinction as to race, sex, language, creed or any other factor." Article 1(1) of the American Convention on Human Rights[177] expressly forbids discrimination on account of religion, and this general principle is reinforced by the equal protection clause of Article 24; furthermore, Article 27(1) provides that a state may not take measures that involve religious discrimination, even during a national emergency. The provision on the freedom of thought, conscience, and religion is found in Article 12, which (like Article 9 of the European Convention) employs wording essentially similar to that contained in Article 18 of the Universal Declaration and of the International Covenant on Civil and Political Rights.[178]

In addition to the prescriptions emanating from secular sources, it is relevant to note that the fundamental philosophy of the world's great religions has increasingly exhibited support (including fewer demands for religious exclusivity and intolerance) for the principle of freedom of choice about religion.[179] The principle of religious tolerance and freedom has become so deeply ingrained, in both the secular and the nonsecular worlds, that a number of the great religions have recently issued manifestos in favor of religious freedom. The thrust of this new global movement is powerfully demonstrated by the Declaration on Religious Freedom adopted by the Vatican II Council in 1965.[180] Inspired in no small measure by the Universal Declaration of Human Rights, this Declaration pronounces that "the human person has a right to religious freedom,"[181] which "has its foundation in the very dignity of the human person as this dignity is known through the revealed word of God and by reason itself."[182] Elaborating on this freedom, the Declaration states that "all men are to be immune from coercion on the part of individuals or of social groups and of any human power, in such ways that no one is to be

---

176. *Reprinted in* Basic Documents, *supra* note 98, at 187.

177. *Reprinted in id.* at 210.

178. *See* text accompanying notes 115, 127–29 *supra.*

179. *See* A. Carrillo de Albornoz, *supra* note 77; L. Janssens, Freedom of Conscience and Religious Freedom (Lorenzo trans. 1966); Religious Freedom, *supra* note 77. *Cf.* Toth, *The Churches and the New World Order,* 11 World Justice 193 (1969).

180. *Reprinted in* L. Janssens, *supra* note 179, at 145–60 *and in* A. Carrillo de Albornoz, *supra* note 77, at 169–87. *See also* A. Carrillo de Albornoz, The Basis of Religious Liberty (1963); Freedom and Man (J. Murray ed. 1965); Religious Liberty: An End and a Beginning (J. Murray ed. 1966).

181. A. Carrillo de Albornoz, *supra* note 77, at 170; L. Janssens, *supra* note 179, at 146.

182. A. Carrillo de Albornoz, *supra* note 77, at 171; L. Janssens, *supra* note 179, at 147.

forced to act in a manner contrary to his own beliefs, whether privately or publicly, whether alone or in association with others, within due limits."[183] With this Declaration—"an effort of the Church to catch up with the recognition of a right previously asserted in secular, protestant, Jewish and other religious traditions"[184]—it has been observed that "for the first time in many centuries, Christians are unanimous in formally proclaiming the universality and inviolability of religious freedom. They all agree that it is the right of every man and every religious confession."[185] A comparable trend is also observable in the non-Christian world. As Abram has put it, "In Judaism, in Islam, in Marxism, and in other religious or secular movements, there have been formulated claims of ultimate truth and of the special status that truth entails both for the believer and the non-believer, on the one hand, and arguments for the freedom of thought, conscience and religion of all men, on the other."[186]

The application of proscriptions against religious discrimination is, of course, still left to the more general enforcement machinery presently available for the protection of other human rights at varying community levels—national, regional, and global.[187] It is to be hoped that the proposed International Convention on the Elimination of All Forms of Intolerance and of Discrimination Based on Religion or Belief, when finally adopted, will incorporate provisions for implementation comparable to those built into the International Convention on the Elimination of All Forms of Racial Discrimination.[188] Meanwhile, it may be noted that, because discriminatory practices are sometimes based upon racial as well

183. A. Carrillo de Albornoz, *supra* note 77, at 170–71; L. Janssens, *supra* note 179, at 146–47.

184. Abram, *supra* note 1, at 45–46.

185. A. Carrillo de Albornoz, *supra* note 77, at 155. For the Declarations on Religious Liberty issued by the World Council of Churches in 1948 and 1961, see *id.* at 189–99. The 1948 Declaration pronounced at the outset: "The rights of religious freedom herein declared shall be recognized and observed for all persons without distinction as to race, colour, sex, language, or religion, and without imposition of disabilities by virtue of legal provision of administrative acts." *Id.* at 189–90. It then proceeded to declare that "Every person" has "the right" to "determine his own faith and creed," to "express his religious beliefs in worship, teaching and practice, and to proclaim the implications of his beliefs for relationships in a social or political community," and to "associate with others and to organize with them for religious purposes." *Id.* at 190–91. *Cf.* P. Wogaman, Protestant Faith and Religious Liberty (1967).

186. Abram, *supra* note 1, at 45. *Cf.* Judaism and Human Rights (M. Konvitz ed. 1972).

187. The general problem of implementation is treated in detail in chapter 4 *supra.*

188. *Cf.* chapter 9 *supra,* at notes 241–84 and accompanying text. *See Preliminary Draft on Additional Measures of Implementation Transmitted to the Commission on Human Rights by the Sub-Commission on Prevention of Discrimination and Protection of Minorities,* annexed to U.N. Doc. A/8330, *supra* note 139. *See also* Claydon, *supra* note 1, at 419–23.

as religious grounds (such as practices conventionally labeled "anti-Semitism"), the machinery of implementation established for racial discrimination (especially the implementation provisions of the Convention on the Elimination of Racial Discrimination) can sometimes be invoked to redress deprivations based upon religious grounds.[189]

THE INCLUSIVE CONTEXT OF RELIGIOUS AND OTHER BASIC FREEDOMS OF BELIEF

The trend of past decision in the world community regarding matters of fundamental belief has been largely confined to the task of formulating acceptable prescriptions. Thus, the world community has yet to reach a consensus as to a system of presumptively authoritative expecta-

---

189. With regard to many homogeneous groups it is difficult to tell whether characterizations of the group are by religion, ethnicity, or language (*e.g.*, the Ibo, Dinka, or Zulu). This applies in both developing and developed countries. For such groups, protection of freedom from discrimination upon religious grounds may on occasion be secured by invocation and application of the prescriptions relating to race or language. *Cf.* Coleman, *The Problem of Anti-Semitism under the International Convention on the Elimination of All Forms of Racial Discrimination,* 2 Human Rights J. 609 (1969); Lerner, *Anti-Semitism as Racial and Religious Discrimination under United Nations Conventions,* 1 Israel Y.B. Human Rights 103 (1971); chapter 9 *supra,* at notes 112–284 and accompanying text.

The ambiguities of religious and racial discrimination and other confusions are hopelessly intermingled in the controversial resolution on Zionism adopted by the United Nations General Assembly on Nov. 10, 1975, by a roll-call vote of seventy-two in favor, thirty-five against, with thirty-two abstentions. G.A. Res. 3379 (XXX), *Resolutions of the General Assembly at Its Thirtieth Regular Session (16 Sept.-17 Dec. 1975),* at 177, U.N. Press Release GA/5438 (19 Dec. 1975); 12 U.N. Monthly Chronicle 56 (No. 11, 1975). This resolution would appear more a gambit in a series of political maneuvers than an effective condemnation, or expression, of either racial or religious discrimination. For a review of the history and possible consequences of this resolution, *see* the Sixth Report of the Committee on Human Rights, the American Branch, International Law Association (Mar. 1976) (published in the 1976 Annual of the American Branch). *See also Assembly Determines Zionism Is Form of Racism as Measures against Racial Discrimination Adopted,* 12 U.N. Monthly Chronicle 37 (No. 11, 1975); El-Messiri, *Zionism and Racism,* N.Y. Times, Nov. 13, at 41, col. 2 (city ed.); Glazer, *Zionism Examined, id.* Dec. 13, 1975, at 27, col. 3; *id.* Nov. 11, 1975, at 1, col. 1.

For background readings on Zionism, *see* S. Ahlstrom, *supra* note 73, at 972–76 (1972); I. Cohen, The Zionist Movement (1945); From Haven to Conquest: Readings in Zionism and the Palestine Problem until 1948 (W. el-Khalidi ed. 1971); J. Gonen, A Psychohistory of Zionism (1975); S. Halperin, The Political World of American Zionism (1961); B. Halpern, The Idea of the Jewish State (2d ed. 1969); The Zionist Idea: A Historical Analysis and Reader (A. Hertzberg ed. 1959); T. Herzl, The Jewish State (Der Judenstaat) (H. Zohn trans. 1970); W. Laqueur, A History of Zionism (1972); 2 B. Martin, A History of Judaism 319–48 (1974); O. Rabinowicz, Arnold Toynbee on Judaism and Zionism: A Critique (1974); R. Stevens, American Zionism and U.S. Foreign Policy, 1942–1947 (1962); J. Talmon, Israel among the Nations (1970); Palestine: A Search for Truth (A. Taylor & R. Tetlie eds. 1970); D. Vital, The Origins of Zionism (1975).

tions that can be invoked or applied in the area of religious discrimination. Nevertheless, it appears that the rising volume of *national* decisions implementing national prescriptions will one day be recognized as the preliminary phase of a process that marks the eventual appearance and consolidation of an effective international law of human rights in matters of religious conviction.

The intensified demands manifested in the drafting of declarations and conventions have already exercised a profound effect upon the perceived policies of the emerging system of world public order. It is, for example, more widely understood than ever before that "religious" freedom is not ultimately to be construed as faith in any particular version of divinity. The confrontations that have taken place between spokesmen for believers in a single God and spokesmen for believers in a plurality of gods have educated many of these leaders to concede the good faith and the depth of commitment of all concerned. A similar confrontation has had a parallel effect among exponents of divinity and "atheistic" champions of an impersonal flow of determining forces in the universe. Even more striking, perhaps, is the partial acceptance of "doubters" or "searchers"—those who have chosen to withhold commitment to any theological or metaphysical body of doctrine and practice. The scientific attitude toward the world, for example, is widely interpreted to exclude other than an exploratory and tentative attitude toward the universe.

For the future it is not implausible to predict that science-based technology will continue to spread, and that the tension between tentative versus dogmatic attitudes will become one of the most polarizing forces within the world community. The conception of religious freedom will probably come to be understood to include "freedom of fundamental orientation" toward the universal manifold of events; however, considerations of political unity may be expected to interfere with the genuine acceptance of this idea. When the unity of a body politic seems to be endangered by minorities of Christians, Jews, or adherents of other religious faiths, or by those who openly profess an "atheistic" or "agnostic" position, it will often be a simple matter to single out and identify members of these groups. During crisis periods, discriminatory measures will often be leveled against those perceived as dissident individuals and groups. If the level of crisis intensifies, it is overwhelmingly probable that the demand for political unity will tend to rigidify the position of whatever systems of belief are current among the power elites.

Under circumstances of fear and anxiety, it is well known that words and emblems may be among the instruments most relied upon to maintain a tolerable level of reassurance; conversely, exposure to assertions of disbelief or doubt, or to gestures of rejection, present occasions for symbolic defense. The demand to conform typically goes beyond insistence on verbal conformity; the proper words must also be uttered in tones that are recognized modes of expressing conviction. "Tentativeness" arouses suspicions of disloyalty or treason, and the range of tolerance afforded to variety and deviation is narrowed by both public and private acts.

Thus, it can be seen that the difficulties that have retarded the evolution of a comprehensive code of rights to protect freedom of religion and belief are likely to continue for the foreseeable future. Nevertheless, arrangements designed to extend and maintain the basic freedom to worship and to choose a belief system will continue to influence the differences and apprehensions that divide the members of the world community from one another. Freedom of belief is a tenacious yet delicate achievement in the history of mankind.

12. CLAIMS FOR FREEDOM FROM DISCRIMINATION BECAUSE OF NONCONFORMING POLITICAL OPINION

In a world arena characterized by persisting expectations of violence and a concomitant trend toward politicization, there has been a deepening community concern for outlawing intolerance toward nonconformists. Expectations of violence and perceptions of crisis within a particular territorial community often lead to the mobilization of group defenses, with ruthless suppression of dissident views and discrimination against the holders of such views. The concern of the larger community both builds upon and expresses a more general norm of nondiscrimination which seeks to forbid all generic differentiations among human beings in the shaping and sharing of values for reasons irrelevant to individual capabilities and contributions.[1] The particular norm against discrimination on the ground of nonconforming opinion finds expression in many authoritative communications, at both transnational and national levels, and, under appropriate conditions, could be made an important bulwark for the protection of political freedom.

FACTUAL BACKGROUND

The deprivations to which reference is here made are those imposed upon individuals characterized in terms of their political or other opinions. Manifestations of intolerance toward "political" heretics, as toward religious, have long historical roots. In the earliest days there could of course be no distinction between discriminations on the ground of religious and political beliefs, since the organized community and the established religion were largely one and the same and little or no distinction

---

In slightly different form this chapter first appeared as *Non-Conforming Political Opinion and Human Rights: Transnational Protection against Discrimination,* 2 YALE STUDIES OF WORLD PUBLIC ORDER 1 (1975).

1. For a detailed elaboration of the general norm of nondiscrimination, *see* chapters 6–11 *supra. See also* chapters 13–15 *infra.*

was made between religion and law.[2] In more modern times, while intolerance toward religious nonconformists has waned, intolerance toward political nonconformists has significantly waxed, especially with the rise in the twentieth century of totalitarian regimes.[3] The political or other opinions that are frequently made ground for discrimination include a broad spectrum of articulated views on power and the other components of social process. As with religious discriminations, deprivations may be imposed upon an individual because he refuses to accept an established political orthodoxy, or adheres to a different set of political preferences, or expresses doubts about existing systems, or attempts peacefully to evangelize for a new set of preferences, or openly impugns the validity of prevailing systems. While dissenters in the power sector are the primary targets of deprivation, nonconformists in sectors other than power are by no means immune from discriminatory deprivations: witness the treatment accorded in recent years to the hippies, flower children, and others who have espoused counter-cultures in their search for distinct life styles and new modalities of interpersonal and social relationships.[4]

The history of deprivations imposed because of political or other opinion is vividly registered in the rise and fall of practically every known body politic. While it is true that most deprivations are imposed through community processes of authoritative decision, some measures are direct expressions of unauthorized though tolerated effective power. Impositions range from minor irritation and harassment to torture and death. The danger to a public order of human dignity of deprivations of this

---

2. *Cf.* Bertholet, *Religion,* 13 Encyc. Soc. Sc. 228, 229–31 (E. Seligman ed. 1934).

3. On totalitarianism, *see generally* H. Arendt, The Origins of Totalitarianism (1958); K. Bracher, The German Dictatorship (1970); H. Buchheim, Totalitarian Rule: Its Nature and Characteristics (R. Hein trans. 1968); B. Chapman, Police State (1970); C. Friedrich & Z. Brzezinski, Totalitarian Dictatorship and Autocracy (1961); C. Friedrich, M. Curtis, & B. Barber, Totalitarianism in Perspective: Three Views (1969); E. Fromm, Escape from Freedom (1941; 1965); F. Hayek, The Road to Serfdom (1944); S. Neumann, Permanent Revolution: Totalitarianism in the Age of International Civil War (2d ed. 1965); W. Reich, The Mass Psychology of Fascism (1946); L. Schapiro, Totalitarianism (1972); J. Talmon, The Origins of Totalitarian Democracy (1960); E. Tannenbaum, The Fascist Experience: Italian Society and Culture, 1922–1945 (1972); Totalitarianism (C. Friedrich ed. 1964); World Revolutionary Elites: Studies in Coercive Ideological Movements (H. Lasswell & D. Lerner eds. 1966).

4. Power is a function of perspectives and operations in all other value processes. Hence the preferences of elites for a general orthodoxy.

On counter-culture, *see* two contemporary classics: T. Roszak, The Making of a Counter Culture (1969); C. Reich, The Greening of America (1970). *See also* Counter Culture (J. Berke ed. 1969); R. Johnson, Counter Culture and the Vision of God (1971).

kind, which know no national or ideological boundaries, is of course immense. Characterizing the 1970s "not as a golden Space Age, but rather as a new era of political barbarism,"[5] Shelton has sharply observed:

> Most amazingly, the ninety countries known to hold political prisoners run across all socio-political lines. There is nearly as much use for the jailer of ideas in the "free world" as there is in the Communist bloc. The supposedly idealistic emergent group of Third World nations is not only not immune to the jailing fever but also is in fact heavily into the business of locking up dissenters. In many such nations, to paraphrase the German military theoretician Karl von Clausewitz, the imprisonment of dissenters is simply the continuation of state policy by other means.[6]

The analysis of political deprivations may well begin with enlightenment as a base value of power. We refer to denials of or restrictions upon individual participation in articulating and expressing opinions. Nonconformists may, when political orthodoxy is made decisive, be denied access to the media of mass communication and to institutions of higher learning, not only as channels through which to express their views, but as means of obtaining knowledge of the views of others.[7] A blanket prohibition may be levied against the formation of alternative or competing channels and institutions. Dissent may, therefore, be suppressed by monopolizing and exploiting all media of public expression, eclipsed by an educational regime of systematic indoctrination, and policed by routinized or sporadic recourse to coercion.[8] In communities exhibiting

---

5. Shelton, *The Geography of Disgrace: A World Survey of Political Prisoners*, SATURDAY REV./WORLD, June 15, 1974, at 14.

6. *Id.*

7. C. Ammoun, *Study of Discrimination in Education* 60–61, 65, U.N. Doc. E/CN.4/Sub. 2/181/Rev. 1 (1957).

8. *Cf.* T. CHEN, THOUGHT REFORM OF THE CHINESE INTELLECTUALS (1960); A. DALLIN & G. BRESLAUER, POLITICAL TERROR IN COMMUNIST SYSTEMS (1970); J. HAZARD, THE SOVIET SYSTEM OF GOVERNMENT (1957); INTERNATIONAL PRESS INSTITUTE, THE PRESS IN AUTHORITARIAN COUNTRIES (1959); R. LIFTON, THOUGHT REFORM AND THE PSYCHOLOGY OF TOTALISM: A STUDY OF "BRAINWASHING" IN CHINA (1963); S. NEUMANN, *supra* note 2, at 205–29.

> A totalitarian government will naturally organize a totalitarian educational system. In Nazi Germany, the objectives of Aryan or Nordic supremacy were applied in such a way as to deprive Jews and other non-Aryans of access to higher education, as well as to persecute them in countless ways. The authorities of Fascist Italy imposed their political credo—"Believe, obey, fight!" and "Mussolini is always right!"—upon all pupils and students and monopolized all media of public expression. The rules of the U.S.S.R. prohibit the teaching of religion, non-Marxian economics, and other doctrines deemed to be inconsistent with Communist ideology. Nations officially commit-

high degrees of political intolerance, as in a totalitarian state, it is commonplace that "[n]onconformity of opinion is treated as the equivalent of resistance or opposition to the government, and a formidable apparatus of compulsion, including various kinds of state police or secret police, is kept in being to enforce the orthodoxy of the proclaimed doctrines of the state."[9]

For political nonconformists deprivations of power are especially severe. Nonconformists are commonly denied access to appointive and elective public office, notably where one-party rule prevails.[10] In a body politic with de jure or de facto one-party rule, the party identification, party membership, and loyalty are the required credentials for governmental positions, high or low.[11] Even if nonmembers of the ruling party are allowed to compete for elective office, the opportunity is entirely nominal, since coercion, fraud, and related methods of harassment preclude any chance of success.[12] Typically, dissenters are forbidden to

---

> ted to the principles of democratic government and life tend to reveal a more pluralistic attitude toward other viewpoints and peoples.

Education, Systems of, 6 ENCYC. BRITANNICA, 417, 418 (15th ed. 1974).

9. *Political Systems,* 14 ENCYC. BRITANNICA 707, 715 (15th ed. 1974).

> [I]n a totalitarian state, in which only one party is permitted, views opposed to the policy of that party are necessarily and permanently opposed to the government and are therefore regarded as being opposed to the state. In a multiparty state, an opposition party that has a reasonable opportunity of gaining power in the future will not see its conflict with the government as a conflict with the state.

State, The, 17 ENCYC. BRITANNICA 609, 614 (15th ed. 1974).

In a nontotalitarian context, *cf.* A. WOLFE, THE SEAMY SIDE OF DEMOCRACY: REPRESSION IN AMERICA (1973); Preston, *Shadows of War and Fear,* in THE PULSE OF FREEDOM 105-53 (A. Reitman ed. 1975); Preston, *The 1940s: The Way We Really Were,* 2 CIVIL LIB. REV. 4-38 (No. 1, Winter 1975).

10. Conversely, in many one-party states, especially Communist, elections become an instrument to demonstrate the unity of the people, and to generate (or fabricate) their "unanimous" support and fortify their identification with the regime in power. As voting is thus conceived as a test of loyalty, nonvoting, though not proscribed by law, may entail severe deprivations.

11. "A single party, centrally directed and composed exclusively of loyal supporters of the regime, is the other typical feature of totalitariansim. The party is at once an instrument of social control, a vehicle for ideological indoctrination, and the body from which the ruling group recruits its members." *Political Systems, supra* note 9, at 715. *Cf. also* M. DJILAS, THE NEW CLASS: AN ANALYSIS OF THE COMMUNIST SYSTEM (1957); C. FRIEDRICH & Z. BRZEZINSKI, *supra* note 3, at 27-47; J. HAZARD, *supra* note 8, at 12-73; S. NEUMANN, *supra* note 3, at 118-41; F. SCHURMANN, IDEOLOGY AND ORGANIZATION IN COMMUNIST CHINA (2d ed. enlarged 1968); R. SOLOMON, MAO'S REVOLUTION AND THE CHINESE POLITICAL CULTURE 160-242 (1971); WORLD REVOLUTIONARY ELITES, *supra* note 3.

12. For an illustration, see the practice of the Nationalist Chinese regime in Taiwan: Axelbank, *Chiang Kai-shek's Silent Enemies,* HARPER'S MAGAZINE, Sept. 1963, at 46-53; THE ECONOMIST, May 11, 1963, at 536. *Cf.* L. CHEN & H. LASSWELL, FORMOSA, CHINA AND THE UNITED NATIONS 132-36, 151, 164-65, 170-73, 251-53, 275-82 (1967).

organize political parties and other associations.[13] They may be barred from holding meetings and assemblies.[14] They may be put into isolation or banished to remote areas. Often they are denied opportunity to go abroad, either temporarily or permanently.[15] Conversely, nonconformists may return to their own land at their peril. In extreme cases dissenters may be deprived of nationality and banished abroad.[16] To an increasing extent political refugees of today have taken the place formerly occupied by religious refugees.[17] For nonconformers in general due process of law is a luxury: arbitrary arrest, detention, trial (or nontrial), and imprisonment are the trademarks of contemporary political barbarism.[18]

---

13. *See* C. FRIEDRICH & Z. BRZEZINSKI, *supra* note 3, at 27–39; H. SANTA CRUZ, STUDY OF DISCRIMINATION IN THE MATTER OF POLITICAL RIGHTS 37–38, U.N. Doc. E/CN.4/Sub. 2/213/Rev. 1 (1962). *See also generally* AUTHORITARIAN POLITICS IN MODERN SOCIETY: THE DYNAMICS OF ESTABLISHED ONE-PARTY SYSTEMS (S. Huntington & C. Moore eds. 1970); REGIMES AND OPPOSITIONS (R. Dahl ed. 1973); and *compare* with POLITICAL OPPOSITIONS IN WESTERN DEMOCRACIES (R. Dahl ed. 1966).

Dahl has sharply observed "a self-fulfilling prophecy" of "the hegemonic regime" in these terms:

> *Since all opposition is potentially dangerous, no distinction can be made between acceptable and unacceptable opposition, between loyal and disloyal opposition, between opposition that is protected and opposition that must be repressed. Yet if all oppositions are treated as dangerous and subject to repression, opposition that would be loyal if it were tolerated becomes disloyal because it is not tolerated. Since all opposition is likely to be disloyal, all opposition must be repressed.*

Dahl, *Introduction,* in REGIMES AND OPPOSITIONS, *supra* at 1, 13.

14. *Cf.* D. BAYLEY, PUBLIC LIBERTIES IN THE NEW STATES 75–92 (1964); V. CHALIDZE, TO DEFEND THESE RIGHTS: HUMAN RIGHTS AND THE SOVIET UNION 67–91 (G. Daniels trans. 1974).

15. J. INGLES, STUDY OF DISCRIMINATION IN RESPECT OF THE RIGHT OF EVERYONE TO LEAVE ANY COUNTRY, INCLUDING HIS OWN, AND TO RETURN TO HIS COUNTRY 29–30, U.N. Doc. E/CN.4/Sub. 2/220/Rev. 1 (1963). *Cf. also* V. CHALIDZE, *supra* note 14, at 92–114; W. KOREY, THE SOVIET CAGE: ANTI-SEMITISM IN RUSSIA 184–200 (1973); A. SAKHAROV, SAKHAROV SPEAKS 159–63 (H. Salisbury ed. 1974).

16. The denationalization and banishment of Alexander I. Solzhenitsyn by the Soviet Union in February 1974 are of course the most recent dramatic illustration. For details, *see* the appendix *infra,* at note 280.

17. For a concise account of the figures of political refugees in recent history, *see Refugees,* 15 ENCYC. BRITANNICA 568, 569 (15th ed. 1974).

18. In addition to the works concerning torture cited below, *see generally* C. BELFRAGE, THE AMERICAN INQUISITION 1945–1960 (1973); A. DAVIS, IF THEY COME IN THE MORNING: VOICES OF RESISTANCE (1971); M. DJILAS, LAND WITHOUT JUSTICE (1958); C. GOODELL, POLITICAL PRISONERS IN AMERICA (1973); O. KIRCHHEIMER, POLITICAL JUSTICE: THE USE OF LEGAL PROCEDURE FOR POLITICAL ENDS (1961); J. MITFORD, THE TRIAL OF DR. SPOCK (1969); W. PRESTON, ALIENS AND DISSENTERS: FEDERAL SUPPRESSION OF RADICALS, 1903–1933 (1963); B. RUO-WANG (J. PASQUALINI) & R. CHELMINSKI, PRISONER OF MAO (1973); R. SHERRILL, MILITARY JUSTICE IS TO JUSTICE AS MILITARY MUSIC IS TO MUSIC (1970); UNITED NATIONS, FREEDOM FROM ARBITRARY ARREST, DETENTION AND EXILE (Year-

The plight of the dissenter goes far beyond the interferences mentioned above to the enduring of deprivations of well-being by jailing and torture. On every continent political dissenters are, as spotlighted in Solzhenitsyn's recent masterpiece *The Gulag Archipelago,*[19] imprisoned in large numbers in concentration camps, local jails, national prisons, or other detention centers.[20] "Conditions in these prisons," as Shelton has summarized, "are, needless to say, usually sub-human and insupportable: Torture, painful shackling, perennial semi-starvation, and carefully calculated breakdown of prisoner morale are the very grammar and rhetoric of political detention."[21] Torture, described in a recent study by Amnesty International, as a "cancer,"[22] "the most flagrant denial of man's humanity,"[23] and "the ultimate human corruption,"[24] has practically become "a worldwide phenomenon"[25] as an instrument of silencing political dissent. In crowning indignity dissenters are on occasion sent to lunatic asylums in the guise of treatment.[26]

---

book on Human Rights: First Supplementary Volume) (1959); UNITED NATIONS, STUDY OF THE RIGHT OF EVERYONE TO BE FREE FROM ARBITRARY ARREST, DETENTION AND EXILE, U.N. Doc. E/CN.4/826/Rev. 1 (1964); Inter-American Commission on Human Rights, *Report on the Status of Human Rights in Chile*, Doc. OEA/Ser.L/V/11.34/Doc.21/Corr. 1 (Oct. 25, 1974) (findings of "on-the-spot" observations in the Republic of Chile, July 22-Aug. 2, 1974); *Hearings on Human Rights in Chile before the Subcomms. on International Organizations and Movements and on Inter-American Affairs of the House Comm. on Foreign Affairs,* 93rd Cong., 2d Sess. pts. 1 & 2 (1974); *Hearings on Refugee and Humanitarian Problems in Chile before the Subcomm. to Investigate Problems Connected with Refugees and Escapees of the Senate Comm. on the Judiciary,* 93rd Cong., 1st Sess. (1973); *Hearing on Refugee and Humanitarian Problems in Chile before the Subcomm. to Investigate Problems Connected with Refugees and Escapees of the Senate Comm. on the Judiciary,* 93rd Cong., 2d Sess. (1974); *Hearings on Human Rights in South Korea: Implications for U.S. Policy before the Subcomms. on Asian and Pacific Affairs and on International Organizations and Movements of the House Comm. on Foreign Affairs,* 93rd Cong., 2d Sess. (1974); Oberdorfer, *South Korea: The Smothering of Dissent,* Washington Post, July 28, 1974, §C, at 3; Report on an Amnesty International Mission to the Republic of Korea, 27th March-9th April 1975 (unpublished paper, 1975); Fraser, *Political Repression in "Free China"* 116 CONG. REC. E7953-56; Ginsburg, *Repression in Taiwan,* THE NEW REPUBLIC, July 17, 1971, at 15-16; Peng, *Political Offences in Taiwan: Laws and Problems,* 47 CHINA Q. 471 (1971).

19. A. SOLZHENITSYN, THE GULAG ARCHIPELAGO, 1918-1956 (T. Whitney trans. 1974). For a brilliant review, *see* Lipson, *Book Review,* 84 YALE L.J. 952 (1975).

20. Shelton, *supra* note 5, at 14-19.

21. *Id.* at 14.

22. AMNESTY INTERNATIONAL, REPORT ON TORTURE 22 (1973).

23. *Id.* at 23.

24. *Id.*

25. *Id.* at 7.

26. *See* V. CHALIDZE, *supra* note 14, at 247-94; *Psychiatric Abuse of Political Prisoners in the Soviet Union—Testimony by Leonid Plyushch: Hearing before the Subcomm. on International Organizations of the House Comm. on International Relations,* 94th Cong., 2d Sess. (1976); Reddaway, *The Soviet Treatment of Dissenters and the Growth of a Civil Rights Movement,* in RIGHTS

Insofar as wealth processes are concerned, we find that deprivations against nonconformists increase correspondingly as the public sector expands. As indicated in a report of the Committee of Experts under ILO auspices: "It is in the specific field of public, or state-controlled, employment that legislative provisions or administrative practice seem most often liable to run counter to equality of employment and occupation for purely political reasons."[27] Such discrimination may be manifested in "appointments, transfers, promotion, allocation of persons to responsible or confidential positions," as well as in "access to training facilities and to special courses, conditions of employment and termination of employment."[28] Loyalty tests may be indiscriminately applied in government employment, including teaching, even in a body politic that prides itself on a tradition of democracy.[29] The invidious effect of such a program is underlined by Emerson:

> Generally speaking, cutting a person off from employment or career because of his beliefs, opinions, or associations has a grossly inhibiting effect upon the free exercise of expression by that person and by many others. Where, as in this country, loyalty qualifications are demanded for a substantial proportion of available employment, the impact is widespread and deep. Moreover, certain aspects of loyalty oaths and loyalty programs magnify the total effect.[30]

Discrimination against nonconformists is not, however, confined to the public sector. Even employers in the private sector are often reluctant to hire those who are labeled politically undesirable or those whose life styles are unconventional.[31] Confiscation of property is sometimes imposed upon dissenters. In relation to livelihood, deprivations of skill may take the form of denying "professional people and artists the right to pursue their occupations," reducing "countless scientists, historians and writers," and so on, to do "menial labor."[32]

Deprivations against political dissenters extend also to the intimate

---

AND WRONGS: SOME ESSAYS ON HUMAN RIGHTS 79, 92–97, 118–20 (C. Hill ed. 1969); Shelton, *supra* note 5, at 14.

27. INTERNATIONAL LABOUR CONFERENCE, REPORT OF THE COMMITTEE OF EXPERTS ON THE APPLICATION OF CONVENTIONS AND RECOMMENDATIONS 218 (1963).

28. INTERNATIONAL LABOUR OFFICE, FIGHTING DISCRIMINATION IN EMPLOYMENT AND OCCUPATION 108 (1968).

29. *Consult generally* R. BROWN, LOYALTY AND SECURITY (1958); T. EMERSON, THE SYSTEM OF FREEDOM OF EXPRESSION 205–46 (1970); H. HYMAN, TO TRY MEN'S SOULS: LOYALTY TESTS IN AMERICAN HISTORY (1959); D. WILLIAMS, NOT IN THE PUBLIC INTEREST (1965); Caughey, *McCarthyism Rampant,* in THE PULSE OF FREEDOM, *supra* note 9, at 154–210.

30. T. EMERSON, *supra* note 29, at 207.

31. FIGHTING DISCRIMINATION IN EMPLOYMENT AND OCCUPATION, *supra* note 28, at 112.

32. Shelton, *supra* note 5, at 14.

world of affection values and institutions. Harassed by the tactics of asserted "guilt by association," nonconformists often find themselves stifled in social isolation. They often find it impossible, for reasons beyond their control, to maintain prior congenial personal relationships or to establish new ones. Fear and anxiety are manipulated by oppressors in such a way as to frighten relatives and friends. In a prevailing atmosphere of fear and mutual suspicion, nonconformists are made social as well as political outcasts. They become public and private targets of ridicule, contempt, and shame. With the consummation of these orchestrated punishments, deprivations of respect and rectitude reach their full potential.[33]

BASIC COMMUNITY POLICIES

The differential treatment of individual human beings entirely on the basis of political and other opinions is clearly incompatible with the values of human dignity. Shared respect alone requires freedom from such discrimination. The sharing of power, further, depends upon a free exchange of opinion; a democratic society can only thrive by cultivating and testing a great pluralism of ideas and alternatives.[34] Any realization of shared enlightenment, likewise, must include broad freedom of political and other opinion. In a word, abundant production and

---

33. Friedrich and Brzezinski describe it in terms of "Islands of Separateness." *See* C. FRIEDRICH & Z. BRZEZINSKI, *supra* note 3, at 239–89. Aware of the disruptive potential that may be generated by small challenging groups, totalitarian regimes have generally sought atomization of interpersonal relations of groups below the level of the state. It may also be of interest to note that

> Apart from religion, the state sometimes imposes purely secular restrictions. The more totalitarian a government, the more likely it is to restrict or direct sexual behavior . . . sex, being a highly personal and individualistic matter, is recognized as antithetical to the whole idea of strict governmental control and supervision of the individual. This may help explain the rigid sexual censorship exerted by most totalitarian regimes. It is as though such a government, being obsessed with power, cannot tolerate the power the sexual impulse exerts on the population.

Sexual Behavior, Human, 16 ENCYC. BRITANNICA 593, 599 (15th ed. 1974). *See also* J. HAZARD, *supra* note 8, at 121–37; S. NEUMANN, *supra* note 3, at 142–204.

34. Shils offers this apt summary: "Liberalism is a system of pluralism. It is a system of many centers of power, many areas of privacy and a strong internal impulse towards the mutual adaptation of the spheres, rather than of the dominance or the submission of any one to the others." E. SHILS, THE TORMENT OF SECRECY 154 (1956). For a concise overview on pluralism, *see* Kariel, *Pluralism,* 12 INT'L ENCYC. SOC. SC. 164 (D. Sills ed. 1968). Pluralism was championed with special vigor, in reaction against the alienation and dehumanization of the individual caused by excessive capitalism, in the early part of the twentieth century by a group of writers in England, including Frederic Maitland, Harold J. Laski, R. H. Tawney, and G. D. H. Cole. *See, e.g.,* H. LASKI, AUTHORITY IN THE MODERN STATE (1919); R. TAWNEY, THE ACQUISITIVE SOCIETY (1920).

wide sharing of all values are profoundly affected by the degree to which the members of a community enjoy freedom of opinion.

The justification most commonly invoked in support of discrimination based upon political and other opinions, like that in support of religious intolerance and persecution, is phrased in terms of the necessities imposed by the need of maintaining unity, of avoiding community fragmentation in consequence of many diverging views.[35] The allegation of unity may build variously upon asserted needs of national solidarity against real or imagined external threat, upon the imperatives of pent-up nationalism, upon the task of nation building in a traditional society, upon the critical need for economic development, or, more crudely, upon the latent consolidation of power by an effective ruling elite.[36] Not infrequently, suppression of dissent is further justified in terms of governmental efficiency, or the maintenance of internal order.[37] The most dogmatic oppressors of dissent may upon occasion assert a monopoly of the truth of their proclaimed political orthodoxy, exhibiting a zeal no less intense than that of religious fanatics.[38]

The search for unity through the repression of political opinion would appear to be gravely misconceived. "There is," Emerson writes, "no fundamental conflict between freedom of expression and national unity or consensus."[39] "It would contradict," he continues, "the basic tenets of a democratic society to say that the greater the freedom of expression, the less the area of agreement among its members."[40] He elaborates:

> [A] healthy consensus is possible only where freedom of expression flourishes. Such freedom is essential to the whole process of legiti-

35. In view of the very nature of intolerance, political or religious, Maurice Cranston has observed that "the argument both for and against political toleration in the twentieth century cannot be said to have differed greatly from the debate concerning religious toleration that exercised the minds of earlier generations." Cranston, *Toleration,* 8 THE ENCYCLOPEDIA OF PHILOSOPHY 143, 146 (P. Edwards ed. 1967).

36. Excessive emphasis on this theme often leads to a misconceived dichotomy of "nation building" and "human rights"—i.e., freedoms are a luxury for a developing nation and people preoccupied with the task of nation building. The falsity of such an assertion will become clear as we deal with other value processes. Nation building is a multidimensional task that involves all aspects of national life and all important value institutions of a body politic; it can be viewed as progress toward a self-sustaining process of value accumulation and distribution. Thus, it would be a hollow exercise to talk about nation building without high regard to human rights, the core reference of which is the wide shaping and sharing of values by community members.

37. *Cf.* T. EMERSON, *supra* note 29, at 44–46, 97–399.

38. A notable example is of course claims about ultimate orthodoxy of Marxism.

39. T. EMERSON, *supra* note 28, at 44.

40. *Id.*

> mation of social decisions. Suppression not only is ineffective in promoting general agreement or stability, but hinders the process by engendering hostility, resentment, fear, and other divisive forces.[41]

Given the diversity and dynamics of the political systems prevailing in the past, present, and future of human society, any claim to monopolize truth in a particular political doctrine would appear to carry about as much persuasiveness as a comparable claim in the realm of religion. The strength of a society that honors human dignity must rest upon genuine pluralism rather than coerced monolithism.[42] The alleged "conflict" between freedom of opinion and expression and governmental efficiency would, finally, appear "more apparent than real."[43] Again the point is well made by Emerson: "In the long run, open criticism of the government's operations results in a more responsible, alert, and fair administration, and hence in more effective government."[44]

It is not being suggested that the accommodation of one individual's freedom of political opinion and expression with the comparable rights of others and the aggregate common interest, especially in the maintenance of internal public order, is an easy task. Whether the problem is formulated as a dichotomy of "expression" and "action,"[45] as "clear and

---

41. *Id.*

42. *See* note 34 *supra.*

43. T. EMERSON, *supra* note 29, at 45.

44. *Id.* at 45–46. For expositions of the policy considerations underlying freedom of expression, *see generally,* among others, C. BLACK, JR., PERSPECTIVES IN CONSTITUTIONAL LAW 83-93 (1970); Z. CHAFEE, JR., FREE SPEECH IN THE UNITED STATES (1941; 1969); T. EMERSON, *supra* note 29; H. LASKI, LIBERTY IN THE MODERN STATE (1930); H. LASSWELL, NATIONAL SECURITY AND INDIVIDUAL FREEDOM (1950); J. LOCKE, TWO TREATIES OF GOVERNMENT (2d ed. P. Laslett ed. 1967); J. MILL, ON LIBERTY (1859; 1956); J. MILTON, AREOPAGITICA (1644); A. SAKHAROV, PROGRESS, COEXISTENCE, AND INTELLECTUAL FREEDOM (The New York Times trans. 1968); D. SANDIFER & L. SCHEMAN, THE FOUNDATIONS OF FREEDOM 69–82 (1966); M. SHAPIRO, FREEDOM OF SPEECH: THE SUPREME COURT AND JUDICIAL REVIEW (1966).

45. T. EMERSON, *supra* note 29, at 8, 17. In Emerson's words:

> The central idea of a system of freedom of expression is that a fundamental distinction must be drawn between conduct which consists of "expression" and conduct which consists of "action." "Expression" must be freely allowed and encouraged. "Action" can be controlled, subject to other constitutional requirements, but not by controlling expression. A system of freedom of expression cannot exist effectively on any other foundations, and a decision to maintain such a system necessarily implies acceptance of this proposition.

Id. at 17. His expression-action theory first appeared in Emerson, *Toward a General Theory of the First Amendment,* 72 YALE L.J. 877 (1963), later published as a paperback: T. EMERSON, TOWARD A GENERAL THEORY OF THE FIRST AMENDMENT (1966).

present danger,"[46] as "bad tendency,"[47] as "incitement,"[48] or as "ad hoc balancing,"[49] it would appear that the only rational procedure for accommodation is a disciplined, contextual analysis that takes fully into account all the relevant variables and evaluates the consequences of available alternatives in the light of goals, trends, conditions, and projections. For the purposes of such an inclusive and contextual analysis, it is essential that appropriate principles of content and procedure be devised and employed to guide and assist in the making of rational decisions and in the reduction of arbitrary elements.[50]

Appropriately characterized as "the matrix, the indispensable condition of nearly every other form of freedom,"[51] freedom of opinion and expression is indeed the "touchstone of all the freedoms to which the

---

46. The famous "clear and present danger" test was formulated by Justice Holmes in Schenck v. United States, 249 U.S. 47 (1919), in which the Supreme Court of the United States unanimously sustained a conviction, under the Espionage Act of 1917, for causing insubordination in the armed forces. In the words of Justice Holmes:

> [T]he character of every act depends upon the circumstances in which it is done.... The most stringent protection of free speech would not protect a man in falsely shouting fire in a theatre and causing a panic. It does not even protect a man from an injunction against uttering words that may have all the effect of force.... The question in every case is whether the words used are used in such circumstances and are of such a nature as to create a clear and present danger that they will bring about the substantive evils that Congress has a right to prevent. It is a question of proximity and degree.

Id. at 52.

47. *E.g.*, Gitlow v. New York, 268 U.S. 652 (1925), especially at 666–72. Upholding the constitutionality of a New York statute outlawing "criminal anarchy," the U.S. Supreme Court said: "That a State in the exercise of its police power may punish those who abuse this freedom [of speech] by utterances inimical to the public welfare, tending to corrupt public morals, incite to crime, or disturb the public peace, is not open to question." *Id.* at 667.

48. *Cf.* T. Emerson, *supra* note 29, at 16, 105, 156–57, 314, 324, 717–18.

49. *See* Emerson, *Toward a General Theory of the First Amendment,* 72 Yale L.J. 877, 912–14; T. Emerson, *supra* note 29, at 116–18 *et seq.* For further analysis and comments, *see also* W. Mendelson, Justices Black and Frankfurter: Conflict in the Court (2d ed. 1966); Frantz, *The First Amendment in the Balance,* 71 Yale L.J. 1424 (1962); Meiklejohn, *The Balancing of Self-Preservation against Political Freedom,* 49 Calif. L. Rev. 4 (1961).

50. *Consult* McDougal, *Human Rights and World Public Order: Principles of Content and Procedure for Clarifying General Community Policies,* 14 Va. J. Int'l L. 387 (1974); chapter 5 *supra. See also* M. McDougal, H. Lasswell, & J. Miller, The Interpretation of Agreements and World Public Order: Principles of Content and Procedure (1967); Lasswell, *The Public Interest: Proposing Principles of Content and Procedure*, in The Public Interest 54–79 (C. Friedrich ed. 1962); Lasswell, *Clarifying Value Judgments: Principles of Content and Procedure,* 1 Inquiry 87 (1958). *See also* chapter 5 *supra.*

51. Palko v. Connecticut, 302 U.S. 319, 327 (1937) (Cardozo, J.).

United Nations is consecrated."[52] The destructive impact of deprivations of this fundamental freedom extends far beyond the direct victims themselves. In the words of John Stuart Mill:

> It is not the minds of heretics that are deteriorated most by the ban. . . . The greatest harm is done to those who are not heretics and whose whole mental development is cramped and their reason cowed by the fear of heresy. No man can be a great thinker who does not recognize that as a thinker it is his first duty to follow his intellect to whatever conclusions it may lead. Truth gains more even by the errors of one who, with due study and preparations thinks for himself than by the true opinions of those who hold them only because they do not suffer themselves to think.[53]

In comparable vein, Justice Hugo L. Black said:

> Centuries of experience testify that laws aimed at one political or religious group, however rational these laws may be in their beginnings, generate hatreds and prejudice which rapidly spread beyond control. Too often it is fear which inspires such passions, and nothing is more reckless or contagious. . . . Under such circumstances, restrictions imposed on proscribed groups are seldom static, even though the rate of expansion may not move in geometric progression.[54]

---

52. *Annotations on the Text of the Draft International Covenants on Human Rights* (prepared by the secretary-general), 10 U.N. GAOR, Annexes (Agenda Item No. 28) 50, U.N. Doc. A/2929 (1955).

53. *Quoted in* D. SANDIFER & L. SCHEMAN, *supra* note 44, at 77.

54. American Communications Association v. Douds, 339 U.S. 382, 448 (1950) (Black, J., dissenting).

On a more positive note, the importance of the freedom of expression and freedom from discrimination on account of opinions cannot be overemphasized. Justice William O. Douglas has written: "Full and free discussion keep a society from becoming stagnant and unprepared for the stresses and strains that work to tear all civilizations apart. Full and free discussion has indeed been the first article of our faith." Dennis v. U.S., 341 U.S. 494, 584 (1951) (dissenting opinion). Similarly, an Oriental philosopher writes: "In order to contribute fully to the society, each individual should have the fullest degree of self-expression. Social progress depends on each individual's freedom of expression." Lo, *Human Rights in the Chinese Tradition,* in HUMAN RIGHTS: COMMENTS AND INTERPRETATIONS 186, 189 (UNESCO ed. 1949).

Emerson summarizes:

> Maintenance of a system of free expression is necessary (1) as assuring individual self-fulfillment, (2) as a means of attaining the truth, (3) as a method of securing participation by the members of the society in social, including political, decision-making, and (4) as maintaining the balance between stability and change in the society.

Emerson, *supra* note 49, at 878–79.

TRENDS IN DECISION

Historically, it must be conceded that the transnational community has afforded individuals but meager protection against discriminations that are grounded on political or other opinions. In the rare instances in which the doctrine of humanitarian intervention has been invoked, since groups protected have in fact been characterized by a complex of religious, racial, ethnic, cultural, linguistic, or political factors, it is highly probable that some groups have exhibited highly distinctive political opinions.[55] Similarly, the transnational protection of minority groups during the era of the League of Nations could not but protect nonconformist views when the particular racial, religious, or linguistic groups held distinctive, nonconforming political opinions.[56] From a somewhat different perspective, it may be observed that freedom from discrimination on account of political or other opinion was, not insignificantly, protected in the instances in which people were given opportunity, through plebiscites or comparable arrangements, to express their political preferences and to choose their affiliations before a transfer of territory was consummated.[57]

In projecting its general norm of nondiscrimination, the United Nations Charter is relatively short in its illustrative list of impermissible grounds of differentiation: "race, sex, language, or religion."[58] The context suggests that the framers of the Charter and their audience shared the expectation that more detailed and elaborate provisions for the global protection of human rights would soon find place in a contemplated International Bill of Rights.[59] The Universal Declaration of Human Rights presently made it clear that the itemization of impermissible grounds of differentiation in the Charter was indeed illustrative, not exhaustive. In Article 2 of the Declaration the itemization is expanded as follows: "Everyone is entitled to all the rights and freedoms set forth in this Declaration, without distinction of any kind, such as race, colour, sex, language, religion, *political or other opinion*, national or social

55. *See* M. Ganji, International Protection of Human Rights 39–41 (1962); chapters 8–9, *supra* and chapters 13–14 *infra.*

56. *Cf.* chapters 8–9, 11 *supra* and chapter 13 *infra.*

57. *See* H. Johnson, Self-Determination Within the Community of Nations (1967); J. Mattern, The Employment of the Plebiscite in the Determination of Sovereignty (1920); S. Wambaugh, A Monograph on Plebiscites (1920); S. Wambaugh, Plebiscites Since the World War (1933); Chen & Reisman, *Who Owns Taiwan: A Search for International Title,* 81 Yale L.J. 599, 660–69 (1972).

58. U.N. Charter, Arts. 1(3), 13(1)(b), 55(c), and 76(c).

59. L. Goodrich, E. Hambro, & A. Simons, Charter of the United Nations: Commentary and Documents 371–74 (3d & rev. ed. 1969).

origin, property, birth or other status."[60] The comprehensiveness of this itemization is strengthened by Article 7, which accords "equal protection of the law" to "all" against "any discrimination" and "any incitement to such discrimination."[61] Further substance is added to freedom from discrimination because of political or other opinion in Article 19: "Everyone has the right to freedom of opinion and expression; this right includes freedom to hold opinions without interference and to seek, receive and impart information and ideas through any media and regardless of frontiers."[62]

The same theme is stressed in the International Covenant on Civil and Political Rights. Adopting the wording of Article 2 of the Universal Declaration, the Covenant, in Article 2(1), specifies "political or other opinion" as among the impermissible grounds of differentiation.[63] Individuals, pursuant to Article 26, are further accorded access to law to challenge any such discrimination:

> All persons are equal before the law and are entitled without any discrimination to the equal protection of the law. In this respect, the law shall prohibit any discrimination and guarantee to all persons equal and effective protection against discrimination on any ground such as race, colour, sex, language, religion, *political or other opinion,* national or social origin, property, birth or other status.[64]

As in the Universal Declaration, freedom from discrimination because of opinions, political or other, finds its deepest support in a prescribed basic freedom of opinion and expression. Article 19 of the Covenant stipulates that "Everyone shall have the right to hold opinions without interference"[65] and "the right to freedom of expression," including "freedom to seek, receive and impart information and ideas of all kinds, regardless of frontiers, either orally, in writing or in print, in the form of art, or through any other media of his choice."[66] The exercise of this right is, not inappropriately, made subject, in paragraph 3, to such "restrictions" as "provided by law and are necessary" for "respect of the rights or reputations of others" and for "the protection of national secu-

60. United Nations, Human Rights: A Compilation of International Instruments of the United Nations 1, U.N. Doc. ST/HR/1 (1973) (italics added) [hereinafter cited as U.N. Human Rights Instruments].

61. *Id.*

62. *Id.* at 2.

63. *Id.* at 8.

64. *Id.* at 11 (italics added).

65. Art. 19(1), *id.*

66. Art. 19(2), *id.*

rity or of public order (*ordre public*), or of public health or morals."[67] The International Covenant on Economic, Social, and Cultural Rights, similarly, specifically forbids, in Article 2(2), discriminations on the ground of opinions, political or other, in regard to the rights protected in the Covenant.[68]

The Proclamation of Teheran, emanating from the International Conference on Human Rights in 1968, is emphatic in its reaffirmation of freedom from discrimination on the ground of opinion. Observing that discriminations because of "expressions of opinion" "outrage the conscience of mankind and endanger the foundations of freedom, justice and peace in the world,"[69] the Proclamation considers it imperative, for "the achievement of each individual of the maximum freedom and dignity,"[70] that "the members of the international community fulfil their solemn obligations to promote and encourage respect for human rights and fundamental freedoms for all" without distinctions on such grounds as "political or other opinions."[71]

In certain human rights conventions, with more restricted focus, discrimination on the basis of political or other opinions is also proscribed. Thus, the Discrimination (Employment and Occupation) Convention prohibits, in Article 1, any "distinction, exclusion, limitation or preference" on account of "political opinion" that "has the effect of nullifying or impairing equality of opportunity or treatment in employment or occupation."[72] The Convention against Discrimination in Education prohibits, in Article 1, any "distinction, exclusion, limitation or preference" based on "political or other opinion" which "has the purpose or effect of nullifying or impairing equality of treatment in education."[73] Similarly, the Employment Policy Convention, adopted by the General Conference of the International Labor Organization in July 1964, seeks to ensure, in Article 1(2), "freedom of choice of employment and the fullest possible opportunity for each worker to qualify for, and to use his skills and endowments in, a job for which he is well suited," without distinction on such grounds as "political opinion."[74] The Genocide Convention, finally, through the protection it extends to "national, ethnical, racial or religious" groups could be made to protect groups with distinctive political opinions.[75] Group identifications under all these labels are often less than clear-cut.

67. Art. 19(3), *id.*
68. *Id.* at 4.
69. *Id.* at 19, para. 11.
70. *Id.* at 18, para. 5.
71. *Id.*, para. 1.
72. *Id.* at 29.
73. *Id.* at 31.
74. *Id.* at 88.
75. *Id.* at 41.

On the regional level, the double emphasis on freedom from discrimination because of opinions, political or other, and freedom of expression is equally evident. Thus, the European Convention on Human Rights includes "political or other opinion" among the impermissible grounds of differentiation in Article 14[76] and provides the core freedom of expression in Article 10.[77] The American Convention on Human Rights obliges the contracting parties to "respect the rights and freedoms" provided in the Convention and to "ensure to all persons subject to their jurisdiction the free and full exercise of those rights and freedoms" without any discrimination for such reasons as "political or other opinion."[78] The "right" of everyone to "freedom of thought and expression" is given detailed formulation in Article 13.[79]

The same double emphasis on freedom from discrimination on account of political or other opinions and freedom of expression is carried forward on the national level, as demonstrated in many national constitutions. The protection of freedom from discrimination because of opinions is variously sought by general incorporation of the Universal Declaration of Human Rights in the constitution,[80] by general provision of equality or nondiscrimination without specification of impermissible

76. Basic Documents on International Protection of Human Rights 130 (L. Sohn & T. Buergenthal eds. 1973).

77. Art. 10 reads:

> (1) Everyone has the right to freedom of expression. This right shall include freedom to hold opinions and to receive and impart information and ideas without interference by public authority and regardless of frontiers. This Article shall not prevent States from requiring the licensing of broadcasting, television or cinema enterprises.
>
> (2) The exercise of these freedoms, since it carries with it duties and responsibilities, may be subject to such formalities, conditions, restrictions or penalties as are prescribed by law and are necessary in a democratic society, in the interests of national security, territorial integrity or public safety, for the prevention of disorder or crime, for the protection of health or morals, for the protection of the reputation or rights of others, for preventing the disclosure of information received in confidence, or for maintaining the authority and impartiality of the judiciary.

Id. at 129.

78. Art. 1(1), *id.* at 210.

79. *Id.* at 214–15.

80. The Constitutions of the members of the French Community are especially noteworthy in this regard. For example, the Constitution of the Republic of Senegal of 1963 proclaims, in the Preamble, that "The Senegalese people hereby solemnly proclaims its independence and its attachment to the fundamental rights as defined by the Declaration of the Rights of Man and the Citizen of 1789 and by the Universal Declaration of December 10, 1948." 1 A. Peaslee, Constitutions of Nations 697, 697 (rev. 3d ed. 1965). *See also* Constitution of the Federal Republic of Cameroon, 1961, Art. 1, *id.* at 34,

grounds of differentiation,[81] or by specific inclusion of political or other opinions among the impermissible grounds of differentiation. Such specifications include the following references: "political or other opinion,"[82] "political opinions,"[83] "political belief,"[84] "opinion[s],"[85] "creed,"[86] and "political or social opinion."[87]

The comprehensiveness of these national constitutional provisions was foreshadowed in the legislative history of Article 2 (the nondiscrimination clause) of the Universal Declaration of Human Rights, which, it may be recalled, has become a prototype for the comparable provisions in many other contemporary human rights instruments.[88] This legislative history amply establishes that the term "political or other opinions" was intended to refer to views not only about the shaping and sharing of power but about other components of the social process. From the beginning, when the Sub-Commission on Prevention of Discrimination and Protection of Minorities was engaged, in November 1947, in the task of formulating a draft Universal Declaration, Mr. Masani (India) proposed that "political opinion" be included among the impermissible

34; Constitution of the Republic of Chad, 1962, Preamble, *id.* at 65, 65; Constitution of the Republic of the Congo (Brazzaville), 1963, Preamble, *id.* at 85, 85; Constitution of Dahomey, 1964, Preamble, *id.* at 151, 151; Constitution of the Republic of Gabon, 1961, Preamble, *id.* at 194, 194; Constitution of the Ivory Coast, 1960, Preamble, *id.* at 242, 242; Constitution of the Republic of Madagascar, 1959, Preamble, *id.* at 456, 456; Constitution of Niger, 1960, Preamble, *id.* at 578, 578; and Constitution of Upper Volta, 1960, Preamble, *id.* at 1012, 1012.

81. *E.g.,* Constitution of Tunisia, 1959, Art. 6, *id.* at 909, 910; Constitution of the Republic of Costa Rica, 1949, as amended to 1963, Art. 33, 4 A. PEASLEE (1970), *supra* note 80, at 328, 333; Constitution of Ecuador, 1967, Art. 4, *id.* at 460, 460.

82. *E.g.,* Constitution of Bolivia, 1967, Art. 6, 4 A. PEASLEE, *supra* note 80, at 100, 101.

83. *E.g.,* Constitution of Kenya, 1963, Art. 26(3), 1 A. PEASLEE, *supra* note 80, at 257, 276; Constitution of Malawi, 1964, Art. 23(3), *id.* at 476, 492–93; Constitution of Nigeria, 1963, Art. 28(1), *id.* at 592, 606; Constitution of Sierra Leone, 1961, Art. 11, *id.* at 715, 719; Constitution of Tanganyika, 1962, Preamble, *id.* at 860, 860; Constitution of Uganda, 1962, Art. 29(3), *id.* at 921, 938; Constitution of Zambia, 1964, Art. 25(3), *id.* at 1027, 1042; The Constitution of Barbados, 1966, Art. 23(2), 4 A. PEASLEE, *supra* note 80, at 31, 47; Constitution of the Republic of Guatemala, 1965, Art. 43, *id.* at 564, 571.

84. *E.g.,* The Constitution of the Republic of Ghana, Art. 1, 1 A. PEASLEE, *supra* note 80, at 213, 213.

85. *E.g.,* Constitution of Somalia, 1960, Art. 3, *id.* at 776, 777; Constitution of Togo, 1963, Art. 6, *id.* at 890, 891.

86. *E.g.,* Constitution of the United Arab Republic, 1964, Art. 24, *id.* at 991, 994.

87. *E.g.,* Constitution of Libya, 1951, as amended in 1962 and 1963, Art. 11, *id.* at 436, 437. In recent times some of these constitutions have been suspended or changed. In a crisis-ridden world, changes both favorable and unfavorable to the protection of political freedoms must be expected. For some of these changes, *see* 1 A. PEASLEE, CONSTITUTIONS OF NATIONS (rev. 4th ed. 1974) at 308, 433, 436, 623, 722, 926, 984, 1000.

88. *See* chapter 8 *supra.*

grounds of differentiation in the nondiscrimination clause (then draft Article 6, and ultimately Article 2).[89] His reasoning was that the future problems of discrimination "would be more in the nature of political minorities than the traditional religious minorities, which were tending to disappear."[90] Mr. Spanien (France) suggested, invoking the wording "opinions" contained in Professor René Cassin's original draft,[91] that the adjective "political" be dropped so that the very comprehensiveness of its intended reference would not be misconstrued.[92] In appreciation of this deep concern, the final wording, as suggested by Mr. McNamara (Australia), was "political or other opinion."[93]

It is worth noting that some of the older prescriptions developed by the international community about refugees and asylum can be employed to mitigate the plight of political dissenters.[94] When such dissenters find themselves the targets of discrimination and of threats of more severe deprivation they often seek security in other lands. There has been continuous transnational effort, beginning in 1921 under the League of Nations and extending through the United Nations system under the auspices of the Office of the United Nations High Commissioner for Refugees, toward improving the status and treatment of those who flee their country in fear of persecution because of political opinions or other grounds.[95] Thus, while sidestepping the prior question of whether refugees are to be accorded a right of asylum under international law, the Convention Relating to the International Status of Ref-

89. U.N. Doc. E/CN.4/Sub. 2/Sr. 4 at 2 (1947).

90. *Id.* at 6.

91. *Id.* at 5.

92. *Id.* at 5–6.

93. *Id.* at 7, 12–13.

94. *See generally* M. GARCIA-MORA, INTERNATIONAL LAW AND ASYLUM AS A HUMAN RIGHT (1956); A. GRAHL-MADSEN, THE STATUS OF REFUGEES IN INTERNATIONAL LAW (1966, 1972); L. HOLBORN, THE INTERNATIONAL REFUGEE ORGANIZATION, A SPECIALIZED AGENCY OF THE UNITED NATIONS: ITS HISTORY AND WORK, 1946–1952 (1956); F. NORWOOD, STRANGERS AND EXILES (1969); J. SCHECHTMAN, THE REFUGEE IN THE WORLD: DISPLACEMENT AND INTEGRATION (1963); S. SINHA, ASYLUM AND INTERNATIONAL LAW (1971); J. STOESSINGER, THE REFUGEES AND THE WORLD COMMUNITY (1956); UNITED NATIONS HIGH COMMISSIONER FOR REFUGEES, A MANDATE TO PROTECT AND ASSIST REFUGEES (1971); Evans, *The Political Refugee in United States Immigration Law and Practice,* 3 INT'L LAWYER 92 (1969); Krenz, *The Refugee as a Subject of International Law,* 15 INT'L & COMP. L.Q. 90 (1966); Read, *The United Nations and Refugees: Changing Concepts,* 537 INT'L CONCILIATION (1962); Rees, *Century of the Homeless Man,* 515 INT'L CONCILIATION (1957); Weis, *The Concept of the Refugee in International Law,* [1960] JOURNAL DU DROIT INTERNATIONAL 928 *et seq.;* Weis, *The International Protection of Refugees,* 48 AM. J. INT'L L. 193 (1954).

95. *See especially* A MANDATE TO PROTECT AND ASSIST REFUGEES, *supra* note 93; L. HOLBORN, *supra* note 94; Read, *supra* note 94; Van Heuven Goldhart, *The Problem of Refugees,* 82 HAGUE RECUEIL DES COURS 265 (1953).

ugees of 1933,[96] and the Convention Relating to the Status of Refugees of 1951[97]—whose scope of application has been significantly expanded by the adoption of the Protocol Relating to the Status of Refugees in 1967[98]—offer an abundance of provisions about the treatment of refugees.[99] The reluctance to confront the question of asylum has derived, understandably, from deference to the sensitivity of state elites in relation to political dissenters and refugees.

The first significant attempt to remedy this basic inadequacy in prescription was manifested in 1948 in the Universal Declaration of Human Rights, Article 14 of which provides that "Everyone has the right to seek and to enjoy in other countries asylum from persecution."[100] Although the critical wording, "enjoy" instead of "be granted," is commonly recognized as weak,[101] this prescription unmistakably signifies a deep community concern for transforming the matter of asylum from the realm of "state discretion" to that of international humanitarian concern. Regrettably, the International Covenant on Civil and Political Rights fails to

---

96. 159 L.N.T.S. 199; the Convention was signed at Geneva on Oct. 28, 1933.

97. The Convention was adopted by the United Nations Conference of Plenipotentiaries on the Status of Refugees and Stateless Persons, convened in July 1951 at Geneva under General Assembly Resolution 429(V) of Dec. 14, 1950. It has been in effect since Apr. 22, 1954. For its text *see* 189 U.N.T.S. 137; U.N. Human Rights Instruments, *supra* note 60, at 66–73. For a commentary, *see* Weis, *The International Protection of Refugees,* 48 Am. J. Int'l L. 193 (1954).

98. 606 U.N.T.S. 267; U.N. Human Rights Instruments, *supra* note 60, at 74–75. In effect since Oct. 4, 1967, the Protocol has sought wider protection of refugees by removing the temporal and geographic limitations inherent in the 1951 Refugees Convention. For a detailed treatment, *see* Weis, *The 1967 Protocol Relating to the Status of Refugees and Some Questions of the Law of Treaties,* 42 Brit. Y.B. Int'l L. 39 (1969).

99. For a comparison with the treatment accorded stateless persons, *see* the appendix *infra,* at notes 387–416 and accompanying text.

A refugee, in the popular U.N. parlance derived from the 1951 Refugee Convention, refers to "any person" who,

> owing to well-founded fear of being persecuted for reasons of race, religion, nationality, membership of a particular social group or political opinion, is outside the country of his nationality and is unable, or owing to such fear, is unwilling to avail himself of the protection of that country; or who, not having a nationality and being outside the country of his former habitual residence as a result of such events, is unable or, owing to such fear, is unwilling to return to it.

Convention Relating to the Status of Refugees, 1951, Art. 1(A)(2), U.N. Human Rights Instruments, *supra* note 60, at 67. *See also* Protocol Relating to the Status of Refugees, Art. 1, *id.* at 74.

100. U.N. Human Rights Instruments, *supra* note 60, at 2.

101. N. Robinson, The Universal Declaration of Human Rights 119–23 (2d ed., 1958); A. Verdoodt, Naissance et Signification de la Declaration Universelle des Droits de L'Homme 150–56 (1964).

incorporate even a comparable, much less a stronger, provision. This deficiency has in part been remedied by the adoption of the Declaration on Territorial Asylum by the General Assembly of the United Nations in December 1967,[102] in clear recognition of the ever-increasing importance of affording asylum to the politically persecuted. This Declaration, in Article 1(1), provides: "Asylum granted by a State, in the exercise of its sovereignty, to persons entitled to invoke article 14 of the Universal Declaration of Human Rights, including persons struggling against colonialism, shall be respected by all other States."[103] Individuals thus protected shall *not*, according to Article 3(1), be "subjected to measures such as rejection at the frontier or, if he has already entered the territory in which he seeks asylum, expulsion or compulsory return to any State where he may be subjected to persecution."[104]

It may require underlining that the effective and ultimate protection of freedom from discrimination on account of political or other opinions rests upon the realization of many related rights, which, though not directly applicable in a particular instance, have significant bearing upon aggregate protection. Notable among such rights are freedom of assembly and association,[105] freedom from torture and other inhuman treatment,[106] freedom of personal security,[107] due process of law,[108] the right to participate in the political process,[109] the right to education,[110] and the right "freely to participate in the cultural life of the community."[111] These rights, as will be elaborated in detail in appropriate contexts, are

102. G.A. Res. 2312, 22 U.N. GAOR, Supp. (No. 16) 81, U.N. Doc. A/6716 (1967). Its text is *reprinted in* U.N. HUMAN RIGHTS INSTRUMENTS, *supra* note 60, at 77–78. For a detailed analysis, *see* Weis, *Recent Developments in the Law of Territorial Asylum,* 7 CANADIAN Y.B. INT'L L. 92 (1969).

103. U.N. HUMAN RIGHTS INSTRUMENTS, *supra* note 60, at 78.

104. *Id.*

105. *E.g.,* Universal Declaration of Human Rights, Art. 20, U.N. HUMAN RIGHTS INSTRUMENTS, *supra* note 60, at 2; International Covenant on Civil and Political Rights, Arts. 21 and 22, *id.* at 11.

106. *E.g.,* Universal Declaration of Human Rights, Art. 5, *id.* at 1; International Covenant on Civil and Political Rights, Art. 7, *id.* at 9.

107. *E.g.,* Universal Declaration of Human Rights, Art. 9, *id.* at 1; International Covenant on Civil and Political Rights, Arts. 9 and 10, *id.* at 9.

108. *E.g.,* Universal Declaration of Human Rights, Arts. 8, 10, and 11, *id.* at 1–2; International Covenant on Civil and Political Rights, Arts. 14 and 15, *id.* at 10.

109. *E.g.,* Universal Declaration of Human Rights, Art. 21, *id.* at 2; International Covenant on Civil and Political Rights, Art. 25, *id.* at 11.

110. *E.g.,* Universal Declaration of Human Rights, Art. 26, *id.* at 3; International Covenant on Economic, Social and Cultural Rights, Art. 13, *id.* at 5.

111. Universal Declaration of Human Rights, Art. 27(1), *id.* at 3. *See also* International Covenant on Economic, Social, and Cultural Rights, Art. 15, *id.* at 6.

protected in numerous transnational human rights instruments, universal and regional, general and specific.[112]

It is relevant to note, finally, that there has been a conspicuous lack of demand, comparable to that in relation to the elimination of racial, sex-based, and religious discrimination, by state officials for the making of a special declaration or convention banning discrimination on account of political or other opinions. This conspicuous omission does not of course signify that this problem is unimportant for human dignity values; such importance is, as already outlined, abundantly clear. Official reluctance stems, understandably, from the very fact that the established power elites of the states simply have no desire to see their own positions weakened by subjecting themselves to elaborate prescription under which they might be obvious and primary offenders. What is at stake in needed prescription is precisely the very core of the power processes within the respective national communities. Hence there is cogency in Falk's proposal that there be established "an international committee organized along the lines of the Red Cross, to deal with the problems of political repression," designed "as a complement to the work being done by Amnesty International and other organizations."[113] Observing that "the subject of political repression is one on which governments are not to be trusted as the most reliable actors,"[114] Falk stresses the critical need of having "a nongovernmental actor with a great deal of stature in the world which is concerned not with the plight of particular individual prisoners of conscience, but with the general situation of repression, an organization which prepares authoritative reports on short notice, recommends action, and tries to gain access to the societies where these situations exist."[115] With political discrimination and persecution showing no signs of abatement, Falk's proposal merits serious consideration.

FUTURE DEVELOPMENTS

The question remains of the future of freely exchanged controversial opinion in the world community. Any disciplined expectation must rest, in part, upon an analysis of factors that have worked for or against freedom of expression in the past. Will future circumstances favor one set of conditioning factors over another and tip the changing balance of effective public policy in a predictable direction? Will new elements

---

112. *See* U.N. HUMAN RIGHTS INSTRUMENTS, *supra* note 60; BASIC DOCUMENTS ON HUMAN RIGHTS (I. Brownlie ed. 1971).

113. *Hearings on International Protection of Human Rights before the Subcomm. on International Organizations and Movements of the House Comm. on Foreign Affairs,* 93d Cong., 1st Sess., 248 (1973) (remark of Richard A. Falk).

114. *Id.* at 249.

115. *Id.* at 248–49.

enter the global arena and exert a decisive influence over the outcome?

Enough has been gleaned from a brief review of the past to emphasize the relatively recent and precarious deference and defense that have been given to opinions that contravene the doctrines, formulas, and folklore of an established order.[116] The devastation in Western Europe that accompanied the bipolar confrontation between Protestants and Catholics eventually generated an accommodation that substitutes a limited degree of toleration for outright coercion. In varying degree, secular conflicts have taken the place of religious contradictions. In the global community of the future it may be possible, we suggest, to maintain a sufficiently harmonious or ambiguous situation to permit the pluralizing diversity of world interdependence to work itself out, and incidentally to strengthen a growing unity of demand for protected freedom of opinion.

Interdependence does not, however, spread automatic acquiescence in or support for unpopular views. In the immediate future local pockets and larger regions will probably continue as battlegrounds among pro-

---

116. *See* especially a recent series of *Hearings before the Subcommittee on International Organizations of the House Committee on International Relations* on the following subjects (the subcommittee was chaired by Congressman Donald M. Fraser):

Human Rights in Cambodia, 95th Cong., 1st Sess. (1977);

Human Rights in Chile, 94th Cong., 1st Sess. (1975);

Human Rights in the Dominican Republic: The 1978 Presidential Elections, 95th Cong., 2d Sess. (1978);

Human Rights in East Timor, 95th Cong., 1st Sess. (1977);

The Recent Presidential Elections in El Salvador: Implications for U.S. Foreign Policy, 95th Cong., 1st Sess. (1977);

Human Rights in Haiti, 94th Cong., 1st Sess. (1975);

Human Rights in India, 94th Cong., 2d Sess. (1976);

Human Rights in Indonesia: A Review of the Situation with respect to the Long-Term Political Detainees, 95th Cong., 1st Sess. (1977);

Human Rights in Indonesia and the Philippines, 94th Cong. (1976);

Human Rights in Iran, 94th Cong., 2d Sess. (1976);

Human Rights in Iran, 95th Cong., 1st Sess. (1977);

Human Rights in the Philippines: Recent Developments, 95th Cong., 2d Sess. (1978);

Human Rights in South Korea and the Philippines: Implications for U.S. Policy, 94th Cong., 1st Sess. (1975);

Human Rights in Taiwan, 95th Cong., 1st Sess. (1977);

Human Rights in Thailand, 95th Cong., 1st Sess. (1977);

Human Rights in Vietnam, 95th Cong., 1st Sess. (1977); and

Human Rights in Uruguay and Paraguay, 94th Cong., 2d Sess. (1976).

grammatic groups who mobilize coercive instruments for the suppression of dissent. The critical factors may be exceptionally rapid or unequal change in political, economic, religious, and other relationships; and the dissolution of belief in the beneficial consequences of maintaining a forum for the exchange of opinions of every kind.

The implications for the policy initiatives of all members of the world community who support freedom of opinion are evident. The friends of freedom must generate and sustain unceasing activity on behalf of the theory and practice of open and diverse expression. Officials and private persons, governmental and private organizations, must be perpetual targets of praise or blame, reward and punishment, for the role that they play as defenders or assaulters of free opinion. Active assistance must go to the victims of suppression regardless of their location or social position. The channels of education and information must celebrate the contributions made to contemporary problem solving by past dissenters, and do all possible to nullify regressive manifestations of "political barbarism."

In tradition-bound societies an effective barrier exists in practice between freedom of opinion pertaining to village matters and opinions about national or transnational relations. It is frequently remarked that the old-style peasant has no conception that his business is national business. The vaguely inclusive world "up there" seems to operate on a mysterious dynamic of its own, rarely affected by the prayers or curses of the villager. In a technologically interactive global community the preconditions are ever more widely spread for the populace to acquire "pride of opinion" on issues both large and small. The expeditors of change cannot wisely assume that protected freedom of opinion will easily triumph. Nonetheless, the inference is possible that the future can be at least partially shaped in harmony with the requirements of a free forum for the dissemination and voluntary evaluation of controversial opinions in the world exchange.

13. CLAIMS FOR FREEDOM FROM DISCRIMINATION IN CHOICE OF LANGUAGE

FACTUAL BACKGROUND

The conception of human dignity is fundamentally linked to the life of the mind, which in turn is closely linked to language as a basic means of communication. Language is a rudiment of consciousness and close to the core of personality; deprivations in relation to language deeply affect identity. At this point we are concerned with the deprivations imposed upon an individual because he is a member of a group with a special language. Language is broadly understood to include all the means (signs and symbols), phonetic and phonemic, by which people communicate with one another.[1] So conceived, language is a most important in-

---

In slightly different form this chapter first appeared as *Freedom from Discrimination in Choice of Language and International Human Rights,* 1976 So. Ill. U. L. J. 151.

1. Sapir, *Language,* 9 Encyc. Soc. Sc. 155 (E. Seligman ed. 1933). On the concept and functions of language, *see generally* Advances in the Sociology of Language (J. Fishman ed. in 2 vols. 1971, 1972); L. Bloomfield, A Leonard Bloomfield Anthology (1970); L. Bloomfield, Language (1933); N. Chomsky, Language and Mind (enlarged ed. 1972); N. Chomsky, Problems of Knowledge and Freedom (1971); J. Fishman, The Sociology of Language (1972); H. Goad, Language in History (1958); J. H. Greenberg, Language, Culture, and Communication: Essays by Joseph H. Greenberg (1971); P. Henle, Language, Thought, and Culture (1958); O. Jespersen, Language: Its Nature, Development and Origin (1922); J. Katz, The Philosophy of Language (1966); Language: An Inquiry into Its Meaning and Function (R. Anshen ed. 1957); Language and Social Context (P. Giglioli ed. 1972); Language in Culture and Society: A Reader in Linguistics and Anthropology (D. Hymes ed. 1964); J. Malstrom, Language in Society (1965); New Horizons in Linguistics (J. Lyons ed. 1970); H. Paul, Principles of the History of Language (H. Strong trans. 1890; 1970); M. Pei, The Story of Language (rev. ed. 1965); Readings in the Psychology of Language (L. Jakobovits & M. Miron eds. 1967); E. Sapir, Culture, Language and Personality (1957); Social Anthropology and Language (E. Ardener ed. 1971); Universals of Language (2d ed. J. Greenberg ed. 1966); J. Whatmough, Language: A Modern Synthesis (1956); B. L. Whorf, Language, Thought, and Reality: Selected Writings of Benjamin Lee Whorf (1956).

strument of enlightenment and skill and also a significant base value for the performance of many different social roles. Further, language is commonly taken as a prime indicator of an individual's group identifications.[2] In the words of Dr. Joshua A. Fishman,

> [L]anguage is not merely a *means* of interpersonal communication and influence. It is not merely a *carrier* of content, whether latent or manifest. Language itself *is* content, a referent for loyalties and animosities, an indicator of social statuses and personal relationships, a marker of situations and topics as well as of the societal goals and the large-scale value-laden arenas of interaction that typify every speech community.[3]

Deprivations imposed in relation to language may be manifested in a variety of modes, notably denial of opportunity to acquire and employ the mother tongue,[4] the language of the national elite,[5] or world languages;[6] deprivations imposed upon individuals through group identifications and differentiations effected by language; deprivations resulting from arbitrary requirements of specified languages for access to different value processes (as for employment); the conduct of community processes and enterprises, especially of enlightenment and power, in languages alien to members of the community; and, finally, the coerced learning of specified languages other than the home language.[7]

Deprivations associated with language have deep historical roots and are more widespread than is commonly assumed. In the words of Dr. J. J. Lador-Lederer:

---

2. For the importance of language as an index of group identification, especially national groups, *see* K. DEUTSCH, NATIONALISM AND SOCIAL COMMUNICATION (2d ed. 1966); R. EMERSON, FROM EMPIRE TO NATION 132–48 (1962); J. FISHMAN, LANGUAGE AND NATIONALISM (1973); KUNIO TOYODA, MINZOKU TO GENGO NO MONDAI (The Question of Nation and Language) (1964); Deutsch, *The Trend of European Nationalism—The Language Aspect,* in READINGS IN THE SOCIOLOGY OF LANGUAGE 598–606 (J. Fishman ed. 1968); Jakobson, *The Beginning of National Self-Determination in Europe, id.,* at 585–97; Kloss, *Bilingualism and Nationalism,* 23 J. SOCIAL ISSUES, April 1967, at 39–47.

3. J. FISHMAN, THE SOCIOLOGY OF LANGUAGE 4 (1972).

4. A "mother tongue" as used in this article is one's native tongue, ordinarily the language of the home.

5. The "language of the national elite" means the language of the majority or dominant group in a country.

6. The term "world languages" is used to denote languages of relatively wide transnational use.

7. Private groups often attempt to impose language loyalty upon their members. Thus, it is sometimes difficult to accommodate demands of an individual with demands of a group which insists upon representing all its members. For instance, in the United States, some Black Power groups are said to have insisted upon teaching Swahili in certain schools while other blacks were strongly opposed to it.

> [T]he language barrier problem goes very deep and far back in history. The culture of a group depends on the reality and appropriateness of its language. Suffocation of language has always been part of policies of domination and the struggle for its maintenance was always a precondition for any political movement of liberation, whenever it might become possible.[8]

Sustained conflict between different language groups in the contemporary world continues to dramatize widespread deprivations.[9]

Deprivations in relation to language are, most importantly, deprivations of enlightenment and skill. When the processes of enlightenment (schools, other educational institutions, the mass media, etc.) are conducted exclusively in a language alien to significant numbers of the community members, the difficulties created for such members are pervasive and enduring. Denial of access to a person's mother tongue, especially at an early stage, has been shown to have an accumulative retarding effect upon the development of a child.[10] A "conscious or uncon-

---

8. J. LADOR-LEDERER, INTERNATIONAL GROUP PROTECTION 25 (1968).

9. Linguistic conflicts have taken place in a wide variety of states, including Belgium, Canada, China, Switzerland, the U.S.S.R., and Yugoslavia. For concise, global surveys, *see* 2 A. OSTROWER, LANGUAGE, LAW AND DIPLOMACY 596–664 (1965); Inglehart & Woodward, *Language Conflicts and Political Community,* in LANGUAGE AND SOCIAL CONTEXT 358–77 (P. Giglioli ed. 1972). *See also* Medina, *Spain: Regional, Linguistic and Ideological Conflict,* in 1 CASE STUDIES ON HUMAN RIGHTS AND FUNDAMENTAL FREEDOMS: A WORLD SURVEY 133 (W. Veehoven ed. 1975); Van Haegendoren, *Ethno-Linguistic Cleavage in Belgium,* in 2 *id.* at 1.

India, as well known, is a prime example. For the communal tension exacerbated by the language problem in India, *see* D. BAYLEY, PUBLIC LIBERTIES IN THE NEW STATES 95–99 (1964); P. MASON, PATTERNS OF DOMINANCE 168–71 (1970). *See also* R. GOPAL, LINGUISTIC AFFAIRS OF INDIA (1966); R. HASHMI, BRIEF FOR BAHAWALPUR PROVINCE (1972); INDIA (REPUBLIC) PUNJAB BOUNDARY COMMISSION, REPORT PRESENTED ON THE 31ST MAY, 1966 (1966); K. JOHN, THE ONLY SOLUTION TO INDIA'S LANGUAGE PROBLEM (undated); S. MAZUMDAR, MARXISM AND THE LANGUAGE PROBLEM IN INDIA (1970); C. RAJAGOPALACHARI, THE QUESTION OF ENGLISH (1962); M. RAM, HINDI AGAINST INDIA: THE MEANING OF DMK (1968); A. WADIA, THE FUTURE OF ENGLISH IN INDIA (1954); R. YADAV, THE INDIAN LANGUAGE PROBLEM (1966); Gupta, *Ethnicity, Language Demands, and National Development in India,* in ETHNICITY: THEORY AND EXPERIENCE 466–88 (N. Glazer & D. Moynihan eds. 1975).

10. In this connection, *see* an important study: UNESCO, THE USE OF VERNACULAR LANGUAGE IN EDUCATION (1953). The importance of educating children in the mother tongue is underscored in these words:

> It is axiomatic that the best medium for teaching a child is his mother tongue. Psychologically, it is the system of meaningful signs that in his mind works automatically for expression and understanding. Sociologically, it is a means of identification among the members of the community to which he belongs. Educationally, he learns more quickly through it than through an unfamiliar linguistic medium.

Id. at 11. *Cf.* T. ANDERSON & M. BOYER, BILINGUAL SCHOOLING IN THE UNITED STATES

scious policy of linguistic and cultural exclusion and alienation"[11] has often led to an "educational disaster"[12] and "dismal performance" of "bilingual" children,[13] as characterized by "low attendance, poor achievement, and high dropout rates."[14] The "difficulties encountered with being tested and given instruction in an unfamiliar language"[15] are best appreciated when experienced. Hence, in the words of Mr. Charles D. Ammoun:

> [C]ompulsory teaching in a single language, and *a fortiori,* prohibition of the teaching of the language and cultural heritage of a distinct group, have in some cases constituted a formidable instrument of oppression and discrimination, especially where the schools possessed by the group are closed, or transferred to the dominant group against the will of the members of the distinct group.[16]

Discrimination which takes the form of preventing members of a distinct group from acquiring proficiency in the language of the elite, knowledge of which may be essential for access to higher education and official position, may equally deprive those individuals of effective participation in other value processes of the larger community.[17] Another manifestation of language deprivation may be to deny individuals the opportunity

---

(1970); *Hearings on Equal Educational Opportunity before the Senate Select Comm. on Equal Educational Opportunity,* 91st Cong., 2d Sess., pt. 8 (1970); Kobrick, *A Model Act Providing for Transitional Bilingual Education Programs in Public Schools,* 9 HARV. J. LEGIS. 260 (1972); Macnamara, *The Bilingual's Linguistic Performance—A Psychological Overview,* 23 J. SOCIAL ISSUES, Apr. 1967, at 58–77; Macnamara, *The Effects of Instruction in a Weaker Language, id.* at 121–35; Note, *Linguistic Minorities and the Right to an Effective Education,* 3 CALIF. WESTERN INT'L L.J. 112, 120–23 (1972).

11. SELECT SENATE COMM. ON EQUAL EDUCATIONAL OPPORTUNITY, 92D CONG., 2D SESS., REPORT TOWARD EQUAL EDUCATIONAL OPPORTUNITY 277 (Comm. Print 1972).

12. Kobrick, *supra* note 10, at 261.

13. Note, *The Constitutional Right of Bilingual Children to an Equal Educational Opportunity,* 47 S. CAL. L. REV. 943, 953 (1974).

14. *Id.* at 950.

15. *Id.* at 953.

16. C. AMMOUN, STUDY OF DISCRIMINATION IN EDUCATION 90, U.N. Doc. E/CN.4/Sub. 2/181/Rev. 1 (1957).

17. In the words of Dr. David H. Bayley:

> Discrimination may be the product of impersonal circumstances and effectuated quite without human malice. In many of the new states large sections of the populace are unable to compete for positions in government service or even to compete effectively for national office because they have language skill only in a local, restricted dialect. This may be called "structural discrimination." It is discrimination in the sense that opportunities are uniformly limited for a group by circumstances beyond their control.

D. BAYLEY, *supra* note 9, at 94.

to acquire and utilize one or more of the world languages. Measures of this kind, whatever their motivation (for the perpetuation of a self-fulfilling castelike society for a chosen few or otherwise), may have profound, long-term deprivatory effects upon excluded individuals.

So interdependent are enlightenment and the acquisition and exercise of skill that deprivations resulting from language discrimination may be devastating for skill acquisition. Language barriers have all too often worked to frustrate and stifle the full development of latent capabilities. When people are deprived of enlightenment and skill, their capabilities for effective participation in all other value processes are correspondingly diminished.[18]

Deprivations in access to language commonly entail deprivation in access to power, both authoritative and effective. A person may be denied the right to vote for failing to "pass a literacy test in a language which is not [his] mother tongue,"[19] even though he is "highly literate in his mother tongue."[20] Handicap in a particular language is thus confused with illiteracy.[21] While "knowledge of a particular language, or even of several languages" may be reasonably "regarded as an inherent requirement of a public office,"[22] where such knowledge is not truly an inherent requirement, there does exist a certain amount of discrimination.[23] Typically, civil service examinations are given in an official language without consideration for individuals whose native tongue is other than the official language. A person may be denied naturalization for lack of proficiency in the required language.[24] Upon occasion an individual may be denied a passport to travel abroad, or be kept out of

---

18. Even when minority languages are given some recognition, discrimination may still occur. For example, a language is taught in the school, but the school board does not maintain adequate standards, or does not enforce competent training. This has upon occasion been alleged to be the case with the teaching of the Spanish language in this country.

19. H. Santa Cruz, Study of Discrimination in the Matter of Political Rights 33, U.N. Doc. E/CN.4/Sub. 2/213/Rev. 1 (1962).

20. *Id.*

21. *See* Leibowitz, *English Literacy: Legal Sanction for Discrimination,* 45 Notre Dame Law. 7 (1969), *reprinted in* 39 Revista Juridica de la Universidad de Puerto Rico 313 (1970).

22. H. Santa Cruz, *supra* note 19, at 33.

23. *Id.* at 34.

24. For instance, in the United States, naturalization is as a rule denied to those who lack proficiency in the English language.

> No person . . . shall hereafter be naturalized as a citizen of the United States upon his own petition who cannot demonstrate—
>
> (1) an understanding of the English language, including an ability to read, write, and speak words in ordinary usage in the English language. . . .

8 U.S.C. § 1423 (1970).

certain regions, if he "does not speak a widely-spoken language, or the language of the country where he intends to travel."[25] When "deprived of public enjoyment of their language,"[26] members of a language group "may feel compelled to migrate to another country (if they possess a motherland),"[27] and, hence, become refugees.

When judicial and administrative proceedings are held exclusively in an official language, deprivations may multiply. To nonspeakers of the official language, judicial and administrative notices, given in the official language, are more formalistic than real.[28] Victims of such hollow due process may extend from accused persons to witnesses.[29] Although "most legal systems attempt to provide for interpretation, free or otherwise, for persons without a sufficient knowledge of the language of the court,"[30] a litigant is sometimes required to "make his own arrangements for interpretation."[31] Linguistic difficulties arise not only in court but also out of court, for instance, in the translation of relevant documents.[32]

Handicapped by language barriers, nonspeakers of the dominant language often experience psychological difficulties, and may be subjected to severe deprivations of well-being.[33] In extreme cases, a person unable to make himself intelligible in the prevailing language of the community may even be forced to endure torture comparable to that of "the mentally retarded."[34] Such persons may upon occasion be made targets of mob violence, especially when communal conflicts are generated or exacerbated by language controversies.[35] In the wealth sector, profi-

---

25. J. Ingles, Study of Discrimination in Respect of the Right of Everyone to Leave Any Country, Including His Own, and to Return to His Country 25, U.N. Doc. E/CN.4/Sub. 2/220/Rev. 1 (1963).

26. T. Modeen, The International Protection of National Minorities in Europe 42 (1969).

27. *Id.*

28. *See* Note, *El Derecho de Aviso: Due Process and Bilingual Notice,* 83 Yale L.J. 385 (1973).

29. M. Rannat, Study of Equality in the Administration of Justice 39, U.N. Doc. E/CN.4/Sub. 2/296/Rev. 1 (1972).

30. *Id.* at 40.

31. *Id.*

32. *Id.*

33. T. Modeen, *supra* note 26, at 42.

34. Leary, *Children Who Are Tested in an Alien Language: Mentally Retarded?* 162 The New Republic, May 30, 1970, at 17–18.

35. "The intensity of linguistic antagonisms was amply demonstrated in India during the convulsive agitation for the formation of linguistic states during 1952–56. During the agitation hundreds of people lost their lives in fierce rioting between different language communities." D. Bayley, *supra* note 9, at 96.

One form of discrimination against individuals on the basis of language relates to failure to provide individuals with public services, such as medical service, from technical personnel capable in the relevant language. For example, in the United States, physicians from

ciency in a particular language may be made—arbitrarily as well as reasonably—a prerequisite for employment and for promotion.[36] In terms of affection, it is not uncommon that language barriers become, equally, barriers to establishing and cultivating congenial personal relationships. People may be prevented from making friends with, or marrying, members of an outside language group. The effort to foster "religious loyalty" by according prominence to a particular vernacular is by no means a thing of the past. Historically, "religions have rendered various languages holy or have declared them to be particularly appropriate for the expression and preservation of religious attachments."[37] Hence, unfamiliarity with a particular sacred tongue may mean a constant need to appreciate the revealed truth and receive the Divine blessing through intermediaries.

For purposes of social identification—distinguishing the self from others by the self and others—language has long served as a potent factor in social stratification, an important index for according or withholding respect.[38] In a society highly conscious of "the prestige of languages," what matters is not only the kind of language a person employs, but even the very accent of the speaker.[39] "The vocabulary of social

---

Latin American and other countries are discouraged from getting accreditation even though their linguistic skills are essential to serve some segments of the community.

36. *See* Leibowitz, *English Literacy: Legal Sanction for Discrimination,* 45 NOTRE DAME LAW. 7, 38–41 (1969).

37. J. FISHMAN, LANGUAGE IN SOCIOCULTURAL CHANGE: ESSAYS BY JOSHUA A. FISHMAN 67 (1972).

38. It has been sharply put: "To the naive monoglot, objects and ideas are identical with and inseparable from the particular words used to describe them in the one language he knows; hence he is inclined to consider speakers of other languages as something less than human, or at least foreign and hostile to the world of his own experience." M. PEI, *supra* note 1, at 259.

Regarding language as an important indicator of social stratification, *see* 1 B. BERNSTEIN, CLASS, CODES AND CONTROL (1971); 2 CLASS, CODES AND CONTROL (B. Bernstein ed. 1973); J. FISHMAN, *supra* note 3, at 64–68; O. JESPERSEN, MANKIND, NATION AND INDIVIDUAL 141–48 (1946); Bernstein, *Social Class, Language and Socialization,* in LANGUAGE AND SOCIAL CONTEXT, *supra* note 1, at 157–78; Bernstein & Henderson, *Social Class Differences in the Relevance of Language to Socialization,* in 2 ADVANCES IN THE SOCIOLOGY OF LANGUAGE 126–49 (J. Fishman ed. 1972).

For "the phonological correlates of social stratification," *see* a series of studies by Labov: W. LABOV, THE SOCIAL STRATIFICATION OF ENGLISH IN NEW YORK CITY (1966); W. LABOV, SOCIOLINGUISTIC PATTERNS (1972); Labov, *Hypercorrection by the Lower Middle Class as a Factor in Linguistic Change,* in SOCIOLINGUISTICS 84–101 (W. Bright ed. 1966); Labov, *Phonological Correlates of Social Stratification,* 66 AM. ANTHROPOLOGIST 164 (No. 6, Pt. 2, 1964); Labov, *The Effect of Social Mobility on Linguistic Behavior,* 36 SOCIOLOGICAL INQUIRY 186 (1966); Labov, *The Reflection of Social Processes in Linguistic Structures,* in READINGS IN THE SOCIOLOGY OF LANGUAGE, *supra* note 2, at 240–51.

39. For example, "'Brooklynese' and 'Cockney' English within New York and London,

intolerance," in the words of Dr. Mario Pei, "is the vocabulary of class distinction: the 'helots' of ancient Sparta, the 'plebeians' of Rome, the *eta* or 'outcasts' of Japan, the *pariah* or 'untouchables' of India."[40] Nonspeakers of the dominant language are often made to suffer a deep sense of inferiority, and all associated syndromes, because of their inadequacy in "coping" in the dominant language.[41]

BASIC COMMUNITY POLICIES

A rational conception of shared respect will include freedom of choice in regard to language. Such freedom is essential to the maturing and exercising of an individual's capabilities both for self-development and for contribution to the aggregate common interest. As a key to enlightenment and skill, language not only transmits and expresses culture but also aids overwhelmingly in the development of latent human capabilities. The fact that language is an extraordinarily important index of identities makes it equally important that no discriminations be imposed upon individuals because of such identifications. Blanket differentiations of individuals in terms of language can only be invidious and arbitrary.

In this dynamically complex and interdependent world, in which rational choice is so dependent upon intelligence and enlightenment, it is vital that individuals be accorded full protection in access to all pertinent languages, including the mother tongue, the established elite language, and world languages. Modern educational and linguistic inquiry has established the critical importance to the child of acquiring knowledge (especially at an early stage) by means of its mother tongue. Forcing children to be educated in a strange nonnative language—and denying them the opportunity to be instructed in the mother tongue—tends to retard development.[42] Similarly, access to the elite language is essential

---

respectively, do not connote foreignness or even a particular section of the city so much as lower-class status in term of income, education, or ethnicity." J. FISHMAN, SOCIOLINGUISTICS: A BRIEF INTRODUCTION 2 (1970).

40. M. PEI, *supra* note 1, at 268.

41. *See* Grubb, *Breaking the Language Barrier: The Right to Bilingual Education,* 9 HARV. CIV. RIGHTS–CIV. LIB. L. REV. 52, 55–56 (1974):

> Growing up in a family that has inherited the cycles of poverty, living in an environment that includes failures, being rejected by society, and being confronted with his own inadequacies in the school [especially because of the language barrier]—in other words, possessing all the "bad things" of our society—the disadvantaged pupil learns to look upon himself with contempt. Furthermore, his negative attitude of himself is continually reinforced.

Id.

42. *See id.* at 53–57. When the language in the home (the mother tongue) is not coterminous with the language of a particular community we are not recommending that the

for exposure to the larger culture and for effective participation in the power and other value processes of the national community. Denial of such access may generate a self-perpetuating castelike society, which offers benefits to a chosen few and which is utterly repugnant to human dignity values. The importance, finally, of having knowledge of at least one of the world languages increases concomitantly with the accelerating interdependence of the world community. Such knowledge is indispensable for giving the individual access to the cultural heritage of mankind—for orienting him to the past, present, and future of human society, and for enabling him to relate the self, the local community, and the national community to the global community and the universe. Further, knowledge of world languages is an important base for removing the artificial barriers of isolation erected by "national boundaries."[43]

Some requirements of proficiency in particular languages for participation in community value processes may of course have rational relation to the aggregate common interest. All exclusive language requirements should, however, be subjected to careful scrutiny to insure that they do not comprise arbitrary differentiation. All such requirements should be attended by procedures assuring and facilitating the acquisition of the mandatory languages. This caution applies especially to language requirements in the conduct of a community's established power processes. It is, as we have noted, all too easy to discriminate against individuals by arbitrary language requirements in processes of authoritative decision.[44] The only rational limits which a community should be able to place upon its deference to a minority language is the community's ability to finance a multilingual system with available resources.

---

language of the home be taught against the wishes of individuals if such teaching would be disadvantageous. We emphasize both freedom of choice and taking context into account.

43. In sum, to maintain a pluralistic society of rich culture, people should be afforded ample opportunity for expression in the languages of subcultures as well as in the language of the large culture, and have access to world languages as well as parochial languages. There must be no interference with private activities in cultivating any of these languages. It is recognized that community resources may be so limited as to preclude supplying alternatives to the established languages prevailing in the community.

On the importance of access to world languages, *see generally* A. GUERARD, A SHORT HISTORY OF THE INTERNATIONAL LANGUAGE MOVEMENT (1922); O. JESPERSEN, AN INTERNATIONAL LANGUAGE (1928); M. PEI, ONE LANGUAGE FOR THE WORLD (1958); I. RICHARDS, SO MUCH NEARER: ESSAYS TOWARD A WORLD ENGLISH (1968); STUDY OF THE ROLE OF SECOND LANGUAGES IN ASIA, AFRICA, AND LATIN AMERICA (F. Rice ed. 1962); J. WHATMOUGH, *supra* note 1, at 51-65; Goodman, *World State and World Language,* in READINGS IN THE SOCIOLOGY OF LANGUAGE, *supra* note 2, at 717-36; Samarin, *Lingua Francas of the World,* in READINGS IN THE SOCIOLOGY OF LANGUAGE 660-72 (J. Fishman ed. 1968).

44. *See* notes 19-32 *supra* and accompanying text.

The elements of shared respect suggest a minimum of coercion upon individuals for the compulsory learning of languages. It must be recognized, however, that community interest may upon occasion require compulsory instruction in languages other than an individual's mother tongue. The need for such instruction is sometimes justified in terms of the unity and efficient functioning of a community. "Language," in the words of Dr. Edward Sapir, "is a great force of socialization, probably the greatest that exists," and "the mere fact of a common speech serves as a peculiarly potent symbol of the social solidarity of those who speak the language."[45] Dr. Herbert C. Kelman's summary postulation that "language is a uniquely powerful instrument in unifying a diverse population and in involving individuals and subgroups in the national system"[46] is widely shared. Nevertheless, as Kelman himself has cautioned, "some of the very features of language that give it this power under some circumstances may, under other circumstances, become major sources of disintegration and internal conflict within a national system."[47] It must require a strong case to overcome the presumption in favor of persuasion and enlightenment.

TRENDS IN DECISION

Pre-United Nations Protections

The transnational community has, historically, accorded individuals scant protection against discrimination on the ground of language. As Dr. Alexander Ostrower has observed,

> Persecution of minorities by way of elimination of minorities' languages from courts, compulsory instruction in the language of the dominant political power, licensing minorities' schools on condition that the minority language be subordinated to the official form of state expression, etc., had continued in Europe until the First World War.[48]

The first significant protection came with the establishment of the

---

45. E. Sapir, Culture, Language and Personality 159 (1957).

46. Kelman, *Language as Aid and Barrier to Involvement in the National System,* in Can Language Be Planned? 21 (J. Rubin & B. Jernudd eds. 1971), *reprinted in* 2 Advances in the Sociology of Language 185 (J. Fishman ed. 1972).

47. *Id.* On the language problems confronting the territorial communities engaged in the task of nation building, *see generally* Can Language Be Planned? 46 (J. Rubin & B. Jernudd eds. 1971); Language Problems of Developing Nations (J. Fishman, C. Ferguson, & J. Das Gupta eds. 1968); R. Le Page, The National Language Question; Linguistic Problems of Newly Independent States (1964); M. Ramos, Language Policy in Certain Newly Independent States (PCLS Monograph Series No. 2, 1961).

48. 2 A. Ostrower, *supra* note 9, at 667.

League of Nations, which was empowered to protect "linguistic minorities," along with "racial, religious minorities."[49] Under the auspices of the League a network of minorities protection came into being, with the League acting as the ultimate guarantor.[50] A number of states, including Poland, Czechoslovakia, the Serb-Croat-Slovene State (Yugoslavia), Roumania, Greece, Austria, Bulgaria, Hungary, Turkey, Albania, Esthonia, Latvia, Lithuania, and Iraq, assumed special obligations to protect human rights under this international regime.[51] They undertook to "assure full and complete protection of life and liberty" to all their inhabitants "without distinction" of "language,"[52] and to assure all their nationals equality before the law and enjoyment of "the same civil and political rights" without distinction as to "language."[53]

---

49. *See* chapter 9 *supra,* at notes 70–76 and accompanying text.

50. *See id.*

51. *See id.*

52. The Treaty with Poland, June 28, 1919, Art. 2, S. Doc. No. 348, 67th Cong., 4th Sess. 3717 (1923), *reprinted in* League of Nations, Protection of Linguistic, Racial and Religious Minorities by the League of Nations 43 (1927) [hereinafter cited as Protection of Minorities by the League]. The treaty with Poland was the prototype of other comparable arrangements. *See also* The Treaty of Peace with Turkey, July 24, 1923, Art. 38, 28 L.N.T.S. 12 at 31, Protection of Minorities by the League at 97; Declaration concerning the Protection of Minorities in Lithuania, May 12, 1922, Art. 2, 22 L.N.T.S. 394 at 397, Protection of Minorities by the League at 34; Declaration concerning the Protection of Minorities in Albania, October 2, 1921, Art. 2, 9 L.N.T.S. 174 at 175, Protection of Minorities by the League at 4; Treaty concerning the Protection of Minorities in Greece, August 10, 1920, Art. 2, 28 L.N.T.S. 244 at 254, Protection of Minorities by the League at 22; The Peace Treaty with Hungary, June 4, 1920, Art. 55, S. Doc. No. 348 at 3563, Protection of Minorities by the League at 29; The Treaty with Roumania, December 9, 1919, Art. 2, *id.* at 3726, 5 L.N.T.S. 337 at 339, Protection of Minorities by the League at 51; The Peace Treaty with Bulgaria, November 27, 1919, Art. 50, Protection of Minorities by the League at 11; The Peace Treaty with Austria, September 10, 1919, Art. 63, S. Doc. No. 348 at 3176, Protection of Minorities by the League at 8; The Treaty with Czechoslovakia, September 10, 1919, Art. 2, *id.* at 3701, Protection of Minorities by the League at 92; The Treaty with the Serb-Croat-Slovene State, September 10, 1919, Art. 2, *id.* at 3733, Protection of Minorities by the League at 61; Protection of Minorities by the League at 14 (Estonia); *id.* at 32 (Latvia).

53. The Treaty with Poland, *supra* note 52, Art. 7, S. Doc. No. 348 at 3718, Protection of Minorities by the League at 43. *See also* Treaty concerning the Protection of Minorities in Greece, *supra* note 52, Art. 7, 28 L.N.T.S. 244 at 255, Protection of Minorities by the League at 22; The Peace Treaty with Hungary, *supra* note 52, Art. 58, S. Doc. No. 348 at 3564, Protection of Minorities by the League at 29; The Treaty with Roumania, *supra* note 52, Art. 8, *id.* at 3727, 5 L.N.T.S. 337 at 341, Protection of Minorities by the League at 52; The Peace Treaty with Bulgaria, *supra* note 52, Art. 53, Protection of Minorities by the League at 11; The Peace Treaty with Austria, September 10, 1919, Art. 63, S. Doc. No. 348 at 3176, Protection of Minorities by the League at 8; The Treaty with Czechoslovakia, *supra* note 52, Art. 7, *id.* at 3703, Protection of Minorities by the League at 93; The Treaty with the Serb-Croat-Slovene State, *supra* note 52, Art. 7, *id.* at 3735, Protection of Minorities by the League at 62.

In clear recognition that freedom from discrimination on account of language is practicable only when freedom of access to languages is assured, these states were made to assume special undertakings in regard to freedom of access to languages. These states explicitly agreed not to impose any restriction on "the free use" by their nationals of "any language in private intercourse, in commerce, in religion, in the press or in publications of any kind, or at public meetings."[54] Where "an official language" was established, "adequate facilities" were to be accorded nationals of the nonofficial speech "for the use of their language, either orally or in writing, before the courts."[55] Further, members of linguistic minorities were guaranteed "an equal right to establish, manage and control at their own expense charitable, religious and social institutions, schools or other educational establishments, with the right to use their own language."[56] In areas where significant numbers of nonofficial language speakers lived, the states were obligated to provide "adequate facilities" to ensure that "in the primary schools" the instruction be given to the children of such language background "through the medium of their own language,"[57] though making the teaching of the official language obligatory was not precluded.[58] As the Permanent Court of International Justice observed in *Advisory Opinion on Minority Schools in Albania,*[59] the policy underlying this detailed protection was to ensure that nationals belonging to "linguistic minorities" were "placed in every respect on a footing of perfect equality with the other nationals of the State,"[60] and to secure for the linguistic minorities "the possibility of living peaceably alongside . . . and co-operating amicably with" the population that spoke the majority language, while "preserving the characteristics which distinguish them from the majority. . . ."[61]

Protections under the United Nations

The contemporary prescription against discrimination on the ground of language was established by the Charter of the United Nations, and its ancillary expressions. In projecting the general norm of nondiscrimina-

54. *See* note 53 *supra.*
55. *See* note 53 *supra.*
56. The Treaty with Poland, *supra* note 52, Art. 8, S. Doc. No. 348 at 3718, Protection of Minorities by the League at 44. *See also* The Peace Treaty with Bulgaria, *supra* note 52, Art. 54, Protection of Minorities by the League at 11–12.
57. *E.g.,* The Treaty with Rumania, *supra* note 52, Art. 10, S. Doc. No. 348 at 3727–28, 5 L.N.T.S. 337 at 343, Protection of Minorities by the League at 53; The Treaty with Poland, *supra* note 52, Art. 9, *id.* at 3718, Protection of Minorities by the League at 44.
58. *See* note 57 *supra.*
59. [1935] P.C.I.J., Ser. A/B, No. 64.
60. *Id.* at 17.
61. *Id.*

tion, the Charter consistently enumerates "language," along with "race, sex, religion," as an impermissible ground of differentiation.[62] This broad policy was given concrete expression in the peace treaties concluded after World War II between the Allied Powers and, respectively, Italy, Bulgaria, Hungary, Roumania, and Finland.[63] These states were obligated to "take all measures necessary to secure to all persons" under their respective jurisdictions, without distinction as to "language" or other grounds, "the enjoyment of human rights and of the fundamental freedoms."[64] They further pledged to "repeal discriminatory legislation and restrictions imposed."[65]

In its further specification of the broad norm projected by the Charter, the Universal Declaration of Human Rights[66] enumerates "language" as an impermissible ground of differentiation in Article 2,[67] which is fortified by the equal protection clause of Article 7.[68] Though the Universal Declaration of Human Rights makes no explicit reference

---

62. U.N. CHARTER, Art. 1, para. 3; Art. 13, para 1(b); Art. 55(c); Art. 76(c).

63. Treaty of Peace with Italy, February 10, 1947, 61 Stat. 1245 (1947), T.I.A.S. No. 1648, 49 U.N.T.S. 3; Treaty with Bulgaria, February 10, 1947, 61 Stat. 1915 (1947), T.I.A.S. No. 1650, 41 U.N.T.S. 21; Treaty of Peace with Hungary, February 10, 1947, 61 Stat. 2065 (1947), T.I.A.S. No. 1651, 41 U.N.T.S. 135; Treaty of Peace with Roumania, February 10, 1947, 61 Stat. 1757 (1947), T.I.A.S. No. 1649, 42 U.N.T.S. 3; Treaty of Peace with Finland, February 10, 1947, 48 U.N.T.S. 203. Note, that all of the above treaties have been compiled in 4 MAJOR PEACE TREATIES OF MODERN HISTORY, 1648–1967 (F. Israel ed. 1967).

64. Treaty of Peace with Italy, *supra* note 63, Art. 15, Art. 19, para. 4, 61 Stat. at 1378, 1379, 49 U.N.T.S. at 135, 136; Treaty of Peace with Bulgaria, *supra* note 63, Art. 2, *id.* at 1955, 41 U.N.T.S. at 52; Treaty of Peace with Hungary, *supra* note 63, Art. 2, para. 1, *id.* at 2112, 41 U.N.T.S. at 172, 174; Treaty of Peace with Roumania, *supra* note 63, Art. 3, para. 1, *id.* at 1801, 42 U.N.T.S. at 36, 38; Treaty of Peace with Finland, *supra* note 63, Art. 6, 48 U.N.T.S. at 232.

65. *Cf.* Treaty of Peace with Bulgaria, *supra* note 63, Art. 3, 61 Stat. at 1955, 41 U.N.T.S. at 52; Treaty of Peace with Roumania, *supra* note 63, Art. 4, *id.* at 1801, 42 U.N.T.S. at 38, which provided that the parties to the Treaty would enact legislation to prevent imprisonment of persons due to racial origin. Since one of the predominant characteristics of racial origin is its impact upon language, these treaty requirements offer protection for minority languages. *See* text accompanying notes 96–98 *infra.*

66. G.A. Res. 217A, U.N. Doc. A/810 at 71 (1948), *reprinted in* UNITED NATIONS, HUMAN RIGHTS: A COMPILATION OF INTERNATIONAL INSTRUMENTS OF THE UNITED NATIONS 1, U.N. Doc. ST/HR/1 (1973) [hereinafter cited as U.N. HUMAN RIGHTS INSTRUMENTS].

67. Art. 2 reads in part: "Everyone is entitled to all the rights and freedoms set forth in this Declaration, without distinction of any kind, such as race, colour, sex, language, religion, political or other opinion, national or social origin, property, birth or other status." *Id.* at 72, U.N. HUMAN RIGHTS INSTRUMENTS at 1.

68. Art. 7 reads: "All are equal before the law and are entitled without any discrimination to equal protection of the law. All are entitled to equal protection against any discrimination in violation of this Declaration and against any incitement to such discrimination." *Id.* at 73, U.N. HUMAN RIGHTS INSTRUMENTS at 1.

to freedom of access to languages, such freedom would appear inherent in the policy of fundamental freedom of choice which pervades the entire Declaration, especially in those prescriptions bearing upon the right to effective remedy (Article 8),[69] the right to due process of law (Article 10),[70] the right to "privacy, family, home or correspondence" (Article 12),[71] the right to freedom of religion (Article 18),[72] the right to "freedom of opinion and expression" (Article 19)[73] the right to education (Article 26),[74] and the right to participate in the cultural life of the community (Article 27).[75] The rights to education and to freedom of expression, in particular, are intimately linked to freedom of access to language. Thus, Lador-Lederer has observed that "the right of any group to use its own language is anchored in Art. 19 of the Universal Declaration"[76] (freedom of expression), and Article 26 governing the right to education would be "non-sensical were it to exclude development of the vernacular features of the community."[77]

In the two International Covenants on Human Rights, "language" is again specified as among the impermissible grounds of differentiation in both the nondiscrimination and the equal protection clauses.[78] Address-

---

69. *Id.*
70. *Id.*
71. *Id.* at 73–74, U.N. HUMAN RIGHTS INSTRUMENTS at 2.
72. *Id.* at 74, U.N. HUMAN RIGHTS INSTRUMENTS at 2.
73. *Id.* at 74–75, U.N. HUMAN RIGHTS INSTRUMENTS at 2.
74. *Id.* at 76, U.N. HUMAN RIGHTS INSTRUMENTS at 3.
75. *Id.*
76. J. LADOR-LEDERER, *supra* note 5, at 25.
77. *Id.*
78. Art. 2, para. 1 of the International Covenant of Civil and Political Rights reads:

> Each State Party to the present Covenant undertakes to respect and to ensure to all individuals within its territory and subject to its jurisdiction the rights recognized in the present Covenant, without distinction of any kind, such as race, colour, sex, language, religion, political or other opinion, national or social origin, property, birth or other status.

G.A. Res. 2200A, 21 U.N. GAOR, Supp. (No. 16) 53, U.N. Doc. A/6316 (1966), *reprinted in* U.N. HUMAN RIGHTS INSTRUMENTS at 8.

Art. 26 of the Covenant provides:

> All persons are equal before the law and are entitled without discrimination to the equal protection of the law. In this respect, the law shall prohibit any discrimination and guarantee to all persons equal and effective protection against discrimination on any ground such as race, colour, sex, language, religion, political or other opinion, national or social origin, property, birth or other status.

Id. at 55–6, U.N. HUMAN RIGHTS INSTRUMENTS at 11.

Art. 2, para. 2 of the International Covenant on Economic, Social, and Cultural Rights stipulates:

ing the question of rights for minority groups, the International Covenant on Civil and Political Rights stipulates, in Article 27, that

> In those States in which ethnic, religious or linguistic minorities exist, persons belonging to such minorities shall not be denied the right, in community with the other members of their group, to enjoy their own culture, to profess and practice their own religion, or to use their own language.[79]

Recognizing the importance of language in due process of law, the same Covenant provides, in Article 14, paragraphs 3(a) and (f), that in connection with "any criminal charge" an accused is to be "informed promptly and in detail in a language which he understands of the nature and cause of the charge against him" and is to "have the free assistance of an interpreter if he cannot understand or speak the language used in court."[80] Beyond this, general freedom of access to languages can be inferred from a wide range of protections provided in the two Covenants, especially from the protections relating to the right of freedom of inquiry and expression,[81] the right to education,[82] and the right to participate in the cultural life of the community.[83] To achieve "the full development of the human personality,"[84] to "enable all persons to participate effectively in a free society,"[85] to facilitate participation in "cultural life"[86] and enjoyment of "the benefits of scientific progress and its

---

> The States Parties to the present Covenant undertake to guarantee that the rights enunciated in the present Covenant will be exercised without discrimination of any kind as to race, colour, sex, language, religion, political or other opinion, national or social origin, property, birth or other status.

G.A. Res. 2200A, 21 U.N. GAOR, Supp. (No. 16) 49, U.N. Doc. A/6316 (1966), *reprinted in* U.N. Human Rights Instruments at 8.

79. *Id.* at 56, U.N. Human Rights Instruments at 12.

80. *Id.* at 54, U.N. Human Rights Instruments at 10.

81. International Covenant on Civil and Political Rights, Art. 19, *id.* at 55, U.N. Human Rights Instruments at 11.

82. International Covenant on Economic, Social, and Cultural Rights, *supra* note 77, Art. 13, 21 U.N. GAOR, Supp. (No. 16) 51, U.N. Human Rights Instruments at 5.

83. International Covenant on Economic, Social, and Cultural Rights, Art. 15, *id.* at 53, U.N. Human Rights Instruments at 6.

84. Universal Declaration of Human Rights, *supra* note 66, Art. 26, para. 2. U.N. Doc. A/810 at 76, U.N. Human Rights Instruments at 3; International Covenant on Economic, Social and Cultural Rights, *supra* note 77, Art. 13, para. 1, 21 U.N. GAOR, Supp. (No. 16) 51, U.N. Human Rights Instruments at 5.

85. International Covenant on Economic, Social, and Cultural Rights, *supra* note 77, Art. 13, para. 1, *id.* at 51, U.N. Human Rights Instruments at 5.

86. Universal Declaration of Human Rights, *supra* note 66, Art. 27, para. 1. U.N. Doc. A/810 at 76, U.N. Human Rights Instruments at 3; International Covenant on Economic, Social, and Cultural Rights, *supra* note 77, Art. 15, para 1(a), 21 U.N. GAOR, Supp. (No. 16) 51, U.N. Human Rights Instruments at 6.

applications,"[87] and to ensure "the freedom indispensable for scientific research and creative activity,"[88] as stressed by both the Universal Declaration and the International Covenant on Economic, Social, and Cultural Rights, would appear to require all of that freedom of access to language, including the mother tongue, the elite language, and world languages, outlined above.[89]

In more explicit prescription, the Convention against Discrimination in Education of 1960 prohibits, under Article 1, "any distinction, exclusion, limitation or preference," on "language" or other grounds, which "has the purpose or effect of nullifying or impairing equality of treatment in education"[90] of "all types and levels."[91] Education includes "access to education, the standard and quality of education, and the conditions under which it is given."[92] In deference to the needs and wishes of different language groups, the Convention makes clear, in Article 2(b), that it would not constitute discrimination to establish or maintain, for "linguistic reasons,"

> separate educational systems or institutions offering an education which is in keeping with the wishes of the pupil's parents or legal guardians, if participation in such systems or attendance at such institutions is optional and if the education provided conforms to such standards as may be laid down or approved by the competent authorities, in particular for education of the same level.[93]

Emphasizing the importance of "the full development of the human personality,"[94] the Convention states, in Article 5, paragraph 1(c), that it is "essential" to "recognize the right of members of national minorities to carry on their own educational activities, including the maintenance of schools and, depending on the educational policy of each State, the use or the teaching of their own language," provided "this right is not exer-

---

87. International Covenant on Economic, Social, and Cultural Rights, *supra* note 77, Art. 15, para. 1(b), 21 U.N. GAOR, Supp. (No. 16) 51, U.N. HUMAN RIGHTS INSTRUMENTS at 6.

88. *Id.*, Art. 15, para. 3, 21 U.N. GAOR, Supp. (No. 16) 51, U.N. HUMAN RIGHTS INSTRUMENTS at 6.

89. *See* text accompanying notes 40–41 *supra.*

90. Convention against Discrimination in Education, Art. 1, para. 1, U.N. E.S.C.O. Res. 119, 11 U.N. E.S.C.O., U.N. Doc. CL/1462 at 1 (1960), *reprinted in* U.N. HUMAN RIGHTS INSTRUMENTS at 31.

91. *Id.*, Art. 1, para. 2, U.N. Doc. CL/1462 at 1, U.N. HUMAN RIGHTS INSTRUMENTS at 31.

92. *Id.*

93. *Id.*, Art. 2, para. b, U.N. Doc. CL/1462 at 1, U.N. HUMAN RIGHTS INSTRUMENTS at 31.

94. *Id.*, Art. 5, para. 1(a), U.N. Doc. CL/1462 at 1, U.N. HUMAN RIGHTS INSTRUMENTS at 32.

cised in a manner which prevents the members of these minorities from understanding the culture and language of the community as a whole and from participating in its activities, or which prejudices national sovereignty."[95]

In addition to all these explicit transnational prescriptions about language, it would appear, since language is often a prime indicator of a "national, ethnical or racial" group, that the various prescriptions designed for the protection of ethnic or racial groups, such as the Genocide Convention[96] and the Convention for the Elimination of Racial Discrimination,[97] might on occasion be invoked to protect groups in the enjoyment of their home language.[98]

Regional Protections: The Belgian Linguistic Cases

The two important regional prescriptions, the European Convention on Human Rights and the American Convention on Human Rights, both expressly forbid discrimination on the basis of language. The European Convention, in Article 14, recites:

> The enjoyment of the rights and freedoms set forth in this Convention shall be secured without discrimination on any ground such as sex, race, colour, *language,* religion, political or other opinion, national or social origin, association with a national minority, property, birth or other status.[99]

Article 1 of the American Convention obliges the contracting states to "respect the rights and freedoms recognized" in the Convention and to "ensure to all persons subject to their jurisdiction the free and full exercise of those rights and freedoms, without any discrimination" for "language" or other reasons.[100]

The meaning of Article 14 of the European Convention was tested in the famous *Belgian Linguistic* cases.[101] During 1962–64, the European

---

95. *Id.,* Art. 5, para. 1(c), U.N. Doc CL/1462 at 1, U.N. Human Rights Instruments at 32.

96. Convention on the Prevention and Punishment of the Crime of Genocide, G.A. Res. 260A, 3 U.N. GAOR 174–77, U.N. Doc. A/810 (1948). Its text is reprinted in U.N. Human Rights Instruments, *supra* note 66, at 41–42.

97. International Convention on the Elimination of All Forms of Racial Discrimination, G.A. Res. 2106A, 20 U.N. GAOR, Supp. (No. 14) 47–51, U.N Doc. A/6014 (1965). Its text is reprinted in U.N. Human Rights Instruments, *supra* note 66, at 23–29.

98. *Cf.* chapter 9 *supra,* at notes 89–284 and accompanying text.

99. Basic Documents on International Protection of Human Rights 130 (L. Sohn & T. Buergenthal eds. 1973) (italics added).

100. *Id.* at 210.

101. "Belgium Linguistic" Cases, 11 Y.B. Eur. Conv. on Human Rights 832 (1968) (merits).

Commission on Human Rights received a number of complaints ("applications") alleging that the linguistic system for education in Belgium under 1932 and 1963 Acts was in violation of the European Convention.[102] The petitioners ("applicants"), French-speaking Belgians living in predominantly Flemish- (Dutch-) speaking communities in the periphery of Brussels, were compelled under the Belgian law to enroll their children in the local schools, where they received instruction in Dutch, a language different from that of their parents. If these parents wished their children to be educated in their mother tongue—French—the children would have to be sent, with considerable hardship, to French-speaking schools some distance from their homes. Hence, unlike the Flemish children of the community, who received education in their mother tongue—Dutch—the children of the petitioners were alleged to have suffered discrimination in being denied education at the local schools in their mother tongue—French. Six of these petitions (with reference to more than four-hundred families) were declared admissible by the Commission, and the cases were joined.[103] In June 1965, the Commission filed a lengthy report concluding that the 1963 Acts of Belgium were in various respects incompatible with the stipulation that "[n]o person shall be denied the right to education," in Article 2 of the First Protocol, read in conjunction with the nondiscrimination clause of Article 14.[104]

Subsequently, the Commission, in view of its divided opinions on some of the complex issues involved, brought the case before the European Court on Human Rights.[105] Having dismissed a preliminary objection raised by the Belgian government, the Court rendered its judgment on the merits in July 1968.[106] The Court first addressed itself to the general question of "the meaning and scope of Article 2 of the Protocol and of Articles 8 and 14 of the Convention."[107] The Court observed that

> Article 14, even when read in conjunction with Article 2 of the [First] Protocol, does not have the effect of guaranteeing to a child or to his parent the right to obtain instruction in a language of his

102. "Belgium Linguistic" Cases, 7 Y.B. EUR. CONV. ON HUMAN RIGHTS 140–62, 252–60 (1964) (applications).

103. *See id.*

104. European Commission of Human Rights, Applications Nos. 1474/62, 1677/62, 1691/62, 1769/63, 1994/63 and 2126/64 against the Government of Belgium by Six Groups of Belgian Citizens ("Linguistic Cases"): REPORT OF THE COMMISSION (*adopted* June 25, 1965).

105. 8 Y.B. EUR. CONV. ON HUMAN RIGHTS 46 (1965).

106. *Case "Relating to certain aspects of the laws on the use of languages in education in Belgium" (Merits),* 11 Y.B. EUR. CONV. ON HUMAN RIGHTS 832 (1968).

107. *Id.* at 834.

> choice. The object of these two Articles, read in conjunction, is more limited: it is to ensure that the right to education shall be secured by each Contracting Party to everyone within its jurisdiction without discrimination on the ground, for instance, of language. This is the natural and ordinary meaning of Article 14 read in conjunction with Article 2.[108]

Only on one account did the Court come to the conclusion that there had been discrimination because of language, in violation of Article 14 of the Convention.[109] The Court found that this article, when read in conjunction with Article 2 of Protocol No. 1, established that the Belgian Act of 1963 "prevented certain children, solely on the basis of the residence of their parents, from having access to the French language schools in the six communes on the periphery of Brussels."[110]

The region covering these special communes, once a Dutch unilingual district, had seen significant influx of the French-speaking population at the turn of the 1960s. The French-speaking population in one of the six communes, for example, increased from 47 percent in 1947 to 61 percent in 1961. Consequently, a new law was enacted in 1963 to accord the six communes a special administrative status, making them bilingual in all administrative matters except education. Instruction in the public schools remained in Dutch, while a second language was permitted at the primary level when requested by a specified number of residents. The Court voiced objection, not to the retention of Dutch as a medium of instruction in the public schools, but to the residence requirements which would automatically exclude from French classes all nonresident French-speaking Belgians.

In contrast, there was no such residence requirement for enrollment in the Dutch classes. "Such a measure," the Court held, "is not justified in the light of the requirements of the Convention in that it involves elements of discriminatory treatment of certain individuals, founded even more on language than on residence."[111] "First," the Court spelled out, "this measure is not applied uniformly to families speaking one or the other national language."[112] The "residence condition," the Court further observed, "is not imposed in the interest of schools, for administrative or financial reasons: it proceeds solely, in the case of the Applicants, from considerations relating to language."[113] Accordingly, the Court concluded:

---

108. *Id.* at 866.

109. *Id.* at 922–42.

110. A. del Russo, International Protection of Human Rights 140 (1971).

111. 11 Y.B. Eur. Conv. on Human Rights 832, 940 (1968).

112. *Id.*

113. *Id.* at 942.

> The enjoyment of the right to education as the Court conceives it, and more precisely that of the right of access to existing schools, is not therefore on the point under consideration secured to everyone without discrimination on the ground, in particular, of language. In other words the measure in question is, in this respect, incompatible with the first sentence of Article 2 of the Protocol, read in conjunction with Article 14 of the Convention.[114]

National Protections

The important contribution to transnational expectation in national constitutional developments, though many "linguistic guarantees" are relatively recent,[115] has been in the achievement of a remarkable flexibility in institutions and practices designed to protect freedom of choice in regard to language and to preclude discrimination because of language. These national developments have been aptly described by Professor K. D. McRae as featured by "the diversity of means employed for implementing language rights."[116] He adds:

> Constitutional protection may be detailed and explicit, or it may be stated only in general terms or—as in the Belgian case—scarcely at all. Detailed language legislation may exist, or it may not. Language rights may be implemented through local autonomy, decentralization, and federalism, or through the pressure of a central government imposing a policy on the whole country.[117]

Professor Frank R. Scott notes that "every country that has a language problem, attempts to solve it in its own way,"[118] and summarizes that "[t]here are no universal rules, except perhaps the rule that language rights must be respected if you wish to have domestic peace."[119]

This basic flexibility has been fully documented by Ostrower in his comprehensive study *Language, Law, and Diplomacy.*[120] The following "six general patterns,"[121] he finds, have been developed by national

---

114. *Id.* For the aftermath of this decision, *see id.* at 1045–77; 12 Y.B. Eur. Conv. on Human Rights 498 (1969). For a detailed analysis of the case, *see* A. del Russo, *supra* note 109, at 134–41. *See also* McKean, *The Meaning of Discrimination in International and Municipal Law,* 44 Brit. Y.B. Int'l L. 177, 185–86 (1970).

115. McRae, *The Constitutional Protection of Linguistic Rights in Bilingual and Multilingual States,* in Human Rights, Federalism and Minorities 211, 212 (A. Gotlieb ed. 1970).

116. *Id.* at 226.

117. *Id.*

118. Scott, *Language Rights and Language Policy in Canada,* 4 Manitoba L.J. 243, 247 (1971).

119. *Id.* at 247–48.

120. 2 A. Ostrower, *supra* note 9, at 589–664.

121. *Id.* at 597.

communities to cope with "linguistic diversity in modern heterogeneous societies":[122]

1. "Legal equality of national languages for all practical and official purposes,"[123] *e.g.*, Canada, Finland, and South Africa;[124]
2. "Legal equality of all national languages, some of which are designated as official,"[125] *e.g.*, Switzerland and Belgium;[126]
3. "Formal equality of national languages (of the U.S.S.R.) conditioned upon doctrinal considerations and changing official policies";[127]
4. "Supremacy of the language of the dominant national grouping, considered as the official state language, within a system of constitutional protection of linguistic minorities,"[128] *e.g.*, Yugoslavia, Roumania, and China;[129]
5. "Recognition of a foreign idiom as an auxiliary official state language,"[130] *e.g.*, Ireland, the Philippines, and many newly independent states of Asia and Africa;[131] and
6. "Designation of one or more native tongues as the official form

---

122. *Id.* at 596.

123. *Id.* at 597.

124. *See id.* at 597–605. On the language problem in Canada, *see generally* CANADIAN CONSTITUTIONAL LAW IN A MODERN PERSPECTIVE 590–633 (J. Lyon & R. Atkey eds. 1970); COMMUNITIES AND CULTURE IN FRENCH CANADA (G. Gold & M. Tremblay eds. 1973); R. COOK, CANADA AND THE FRENCH CANADIAN QUESTION (1966); R. JONES, COMMUNITY IN CRISIS; FRENCH CANADIAN NATIONALISM IN PERSPECTIVE (1967); S. LIEBERSON, LANGUAGE AND ETHNIC RELATIONS IN CANADA (1970); LINGUISTIC DIVERSITY IN CANADA (R. Darnell ed. 1971); REPORT OF THE COMMISSION OF INQUIRY ON THE POSITION OF THE FRENCH LANGUAGE AND ON LANGUAGE RIGHTS IN QUEBEC: BOOK II, LANGUAGE RIGHTS (1972); REPORT OF THE ROYAL COMMISSION ON BILINGUALISM AND BICULTURALISM [Canada] (1967–69); C. SHEPPARD, THE LAW OF LANGUAGES IN CANADA (1971); P. TRUDEAU, FEDERALISM AND THE FRENCH CANADIANS (1968); De Mestral & Fraiberg, *Language Guarantees and the Power to Amend the Canadian Constitution,* 12 MCGILL L.J. 502 (1967); Kerr, *The Official Languages of New Brunswick Act,* 20 U. TORONTO L.J. 478 (1970); McRae, *supra* note 115; Paradis, *Language Rights in Multicultural States: A Comparative Study,* 48 CAN. B. REV. 651 (1970); Scott, *supra* note 118.

125. 2 A. OSTROWER, *supra* note 9, at 605.

126. *See id.* at 605–09. *See also* BELGIAN INFORMATION AND DOCUMENTATION INSTITUTE, THE LANGUAGE PROBLEM IN BELGIUM (1967); C. HUGHES, THE FEDERAL CONSTITUTION OF SWITZERLAND (1954); K. MCRAE, SWITZERLAND: EXAMPLE OF CULTURAL COEXISTENCE (1964); Lewis, *The Belgian Linguistic Crisis,* 208 CONTEMP. REV. 296 (1966); McRae, *supra* note 115, at 217–20; Paradis, *supra* note 124, at 652–73.

127. 2 A. OSTROWER, *supra* note 9, at 609–23.

128. *Id.* at 623.

129. *See id.* at 623–30.

130. 2 A. OSTROWER, *supra* note 9, at 630.

131. *See id.* at 630–32. *Cf.* note 47 *supra.*

of state expression,"[132] notably the countries in South and Southeast Asia.[133]

The continuing national concern for freedom from discrimination on account of language has been vividly illustrated by the reforms toward bilingualism in Canada and, with a more limited focus, the United States.

In Canada, the drive toward language reforms culminated in the adoption by the Federal Parliament in 1969 of the Official Languages Act,[134] prescribing "comprehensively for the first time in the field of public language usage."[135] The Act poclaims that "[t]he English and French languages are the official languages of Canada for all purposes of the Parliament and Government of Canada, and possess and enjoy equality of status and equal rights and privileges as to their use in all the institutions of the Parliament and Government of Canada.[136] The concluding words, "all the institutions of . . . Government of Canada," are highly significant, because they encompass all federal offices and agencies throughout the country.[137] All official acts, legislative, administrative, or judicial, are required to be promulgated in both languages.[138]

Combining "territorial bilingualism" (language "tied to the land")[139] with "personal bilingualism" (language traveling "with the person"),[140] as recommended by the Royal Commission on Bilingualism and Biculturalism,[141] the Canadian Act provides for the establishment of "federal bilingual districts" wherever the official-language minority of a "census district" or its equivalent constitutes "at least ten per cent" of the total population in the district.[142] Federal services within these districts will, hence, be made available either in English or French at the option of a citizen.[143] The Act, further, provides for the appointment of a "Commissioner of Official Languages for Canada" to oversee its implementation.[144] The net effect of the 1969 Act, as noted by McRae, "points

132. 2 A. Ostrower, *supra* note 9, at 632.

133. *See id.* at 632–64. *See also* note 9 *supra*.

134. An Act respecting the Status of the Official Language of Canada, c.54 [hereinafter cited as the Official Languages Act].

135. McRae, *supra* note 115, at 225.

136. The Official Languages Act, *supra* note 134, § 2.

137. *Id.*, §§ 9–11.

138. *Id.*, §§ 3–7.

139. Scott, *supra* note 118, at 248.

140. *Id.*

141. 1 Report of the Royal Commission on Bilingualism and Biculturalism, [Canada] (1967–69), at 71–150.

142. The Official Languages Act, *supra* note 134, §§ 12 and 1.

143. *Id.*, §§ 9–11.

144. *See id.*, §§ 19–34.

towards a widening of the principle of personality, an enlargement of the right of the citizen to obtain federal governmental services in the official language of his choice."[145]

In the United States, the Bilingual Education Act,[146] "a landmark in education legislation,"[147] was adopted in 1967 to meet "the special educational needs of the large numbers of children of limited English-speaking ability."[148] To this end, the Act, through federal financial aid, seeks to encourage local educational agencies to undertake (1) bilingual educational programs; (2) programs designed to impart to students a knowledge of the history and culture associated with their languages; and (3) efforts to establish closer cooperation between the school and the home.[149] The general trend of developments within particular national communities would, thus, appear to confirm and reflect the strong expectations against discrimination on account of language observed to be emerging at the transnational level.[150]

---

145. McRae, *supra* note 115, at 226. It may be noted that compulsory bilingualism may under certain conditions violate freedom of choice as much as compulsory unilingualism.

The Official Languages Act in its restricted application to federal purposes and agencies leaves to each province a wide area of linguistic "sovereignty." On Apr. 6, 1976, the Superior Court of Quebec, in a ninety-page judgment, rejected the complaint by the Protestant (i.e., English-language) School Boards of Quebec against Quebec's Official Language Act (Bill 22), declaring French as the sole official language of the Province. *See* The Gazette (Montreal), Apr. 7, 1976, at 1, col. 1. For the background concerning the controversy, *see* The Globe and Mail (Toronto), Sept. 2, 1975, at 6, col. 5; *id.*, Sept. 16, 1975, at 1, col. 1. For the text of Quebec's Official Language Act (Bill 22, *adopted* on July 31, 1974), *see Gazette Officielle du Québec (Québec Official Gazette),* Aug. 21, 1974, Vol. 106, No. 22, pt. 2, at 3889–3913.

146. 20 U.S.C. §§ 880b to 880b-6 (1970).

147. Kobrick, *supra* note 10, at 268.

148. 20 U.S.C. § 880b (1970). "Children of limited English-speaking ability" refer to "children who come from environments where the dominant language is other than English." *Id.*

149. T. Anderson & M. Boyer, *supra* note 10; T. Carter, Mexican Americans in School: A History of Educational Neglect (1970); Language and Poverty: Perspective on a Theme (F. Williams ed. 1970); U.S. Comm'n on Civil Rights, Mexican American Education Study (1971); *Hearings on H.R. 9840 and H.R. 10224 before the General Subcomm. on Education of the House Comm. on Education and Labor,* 90th Cong., 1st Sess. (1967); *Hearings on S. 428 before the Special Subcomm. on Bilingual Education of the Senate Comm. on Labor and Public Welfare,* 90th Cong., 1st Sess., Ser. 18, pt. 1 (1967); Fedynskyj, *State Session Laws in Non-English Languages: A Chapter of American Legal History,* 46 Ind. L.J. 463 (1971); Grubb, *supra* note 41; Montoya, *Bilingual-Bicultural Education: Making Equal Educational Opportunities Available to National Origin Minority Students,* 61 Geo. L.J. 991 (1973); Sugarman & Widess, *Equal Protection for Non-English-Speaking School Children: Lau v. Nichols,* 62 Calif. L. Rev. 157 (1974); Note, *The Constitutional Right of Bilingual Children to an Equal Educational Opportunity,* 47 S. Cal. L. Rev. 943 (1974).

150. For a detailed documentation, *see* 2 A. Ostrower, *supra* note 9, at 596–66.

FUTURE DEVELOPMENTS

The future of language discrimination depends on the relative strength of the factors that condition the demands affecting the formation and execution of language policy. The analysis of trend has demonstrated the linkage between political, economic, and other value goals and the demands for discriminatory or nondiscriminatory policies. The breakup of colonial empires brought into power the members of elites, many of whom had fought language discrimination all their lives and who were willing to support a world public order in which ancient wrongs were divested of legal support. Protests against such forms of oppression were among the strategies by which moral and other modes of assistance had been obtained from foreign allies during years of revolutionary agitation. While it is true that newly established elites were not always consistent with their professed principles, they could scarcely so quickly disavow the principle of free choice of language.

In future years it is to be expected that the world arena will be characterized by contradictory tendencies. One tendency will be for established polities to grow larger; the other will be for microstates to multiply. The result will elevate minor languages and reinstate a new set of struggles for and against language freedom. Presumably the principle of antidiscrimination will benefit. Since the economic base in microstates may be small, it may be common to plead lack of material resources to justify limits on language policy.

Technological factors have already begun to affect language access and use. Electronic instruments make it possible to expedite learning; and automatic translation and interpretation are making headway, though at a slower pace than predicted a few years ago. It is often suggested that "the languages of sentiment" (the mother tongues) will proliferate indefinitely as they are coupled with a limited number of major tongues which are acquired in aid of participation in the larger world. Motives for insisting on antidiscrimination will presumably increase. Happily, the necessary fundamental prescriptions are today reasonably well accepted in the world community. Further progress must depend on mobilizing more effective procedures of invocation and application in the global process of decision.

14. THE PROTECTION OF ALIENS FROM DISCRIMINATION: STATE RESPONSIBILITY CONJOINED WITH HUMAN RIGHTS

The deprivations with which we are here concerned are those imposed upon individuals on the ground that they do not possess the "nationality" of the imposing state. By nationality we refer to the "characterizations" states make of individuals for the purpose of controlling and protecting them for the many comprehensive concerns of states.[1] Since the larger transnational community honors states in the conferment and withdrawal of "nationality" upon many different grounds—including place of birth, blood relation, subjective identification of individuals, and various activities—these characterizations may bear little relation to the actual facts of particular community membership and, hence, to reasonable differentiations in terms of common interest in the larger community of mankind. It is our thesis that most deprivations imposed through these characterizations are made unlawful, not merely by the historic law

---

In slightly different form this chapter first appeared as *The Protection of Aliens from Discrimination and World Public Order: Responsibility of States Conjoined with Human Rights,* 70 Am. J. Int'l L 432 (1976).

1. The concept of "nationality" is often reified into a pseudoabsolute comparable to "title," with considerable normative ambiguity. For an attempt at clarification, *see* the appendix *infra,* at notes 1-3 and accompanying text, wherein relevant references are indicated. It may be recalled that stateless persons not only are aliens but may, because of the lack of a protector, be subjected to more severe deprivations. *See id.* at notes 3 and 281-94, and accompanying text.

In her recent study, the Baroness Elles employs the term "alien" to designate "an individual over whom a states [*sic*] has no jurisdiction, and no link exists between the individual and the state except in so far as the individual may be within the territory of that state." Elles, *Aliens and Activities of the United Nations in the Field of Human Rights,* 7 Human Rights J. 291, 296 (1974). This would appear inadequate and confusing. The comprehensive and continuing claims states make about individuals under the concept of "nationality" are quite different from the occasional and limited claims they make under the concept of "jurisdiction." The claims states make in relation to aliens under "jurisdiction" are, furthermore, quite extensive, and the "links" that may exist between an alien and a state may include much more than residence. *Cf.* Nottebohm case, [1955] I.C.J. 4.

of the responsibility of states, but also by a newly emerged general norm of nondiscrimination which seeks to forbid all generic differentiations among people in access to value shaping and sharing for reasons irrelevant to individual capabilities and contribution.[2]

FACTUAL BACKGROUND

Deprivations imposed upon aliens extend far back in history and have their roots deep in primitive suspicions and fears of the outsider. Dawson and Head elaborate certain traditional perspectives:

> Since ancient times foreigners have been regarded with suspicion, if not fear, either due to their nonconforming religious and social customs, their assumed inferiority, or because they were considered potential spies and agents of other nations. Thus, the Romans refused aliens the benefits of the *jus civile,* thirteenth-century England limited their recourse to the ordinary courts of justice, and imperial Spain denied them trading rights in the New World.[3]

Even in the contemporary emerging world society, with its ever-increasing personal mobility and transnational interactions, the nonnational is still often assimilated with difficulty in the minutiae of the social processes of particular communities.

Among a wide range of value deprivations still imposed upon aliens, perhaps the most important is denial of full participation in the making of community decisions. In a world largely organized by nation-states, differences in allegiance remain fundamental, and it is in the power process that the sharpest distinctions are drawn between nationals and nonnationals. Aliens are thus commonly denied access to voting and officeholding (appointive and elective alike).[4] They may be exempted from "the rights incident to citizenship, such as military service, jury service. . . ."[5] Aliens are commonly subjected to rigorous registration requirements and to harsh restrictions in regard to freedom of move-

---

2. For detailed elaboration of the general norm of nondiscrimination, *see* chapters 8–13 *supra;* chapter 15 *infra.*

3. F. Dawson & I. Head, International Law, National Tribunals and the Rights of Aliens xi (1971).

4. *See* E. Borchard, The Diplomatic Protection of Citizens Abroad or The Law of International Claims 63–64 (1922); A. Freeman, The International Responsibility of States for Denial of Justice 510–11 (1938).

In the United States, resident aliens, especially those who had formally declared their intention to become U.S. citizens, were at one time permitted to vote in twenty-two states. *See* M. Konvitz, The Alien and the Asiatic in American Law 180 (1946); Terrace v. Thompson, 263 U.S. 197 (1923).

5. E. Borchard, *supra* note 4, at 63. *See also* W. Davies, The English Law Relating to Aliens 184–210 (1931).

ment, both internally and transnationally.[6] Aliens may also be arbitrarily expelled.[7] Aliens may be hampered, for various reasons, in obtaining effective remedy for ordinary wrongs and may experience "denial of justice"[8]—including subjection to arbitrary arrest and detention, denial

6. M. Konvitz, *supra* note 4, at 1–45. *Cf. generally* J. Ingles, Study of Discrimination in Respect of the Right of Everyone to Leave Any Country, Including His Own, and to Return to His Country, U.N. Doc. E/CN.4/Sub. 2/220/Rev. 1 (1963).

7. *See* 6 A British Digest of International Law 83–241 (C. Parry ed. 1965); E. Borchard, *supra* note 4, at 48–63; I. Brownlie, Principles of Public International Law 505–07 (2d ed. 1973); 3 G. Hackworth, Digest of International Law 690–705 (1942); M. Konvitz, *supra* note 4, at 46–78; M. Konvitz, Civil Rights in Immigration 93–131 (1953); 2 D. O'Connell, International Law 706–11 (2d ed. 1970); 1 L. Oppenheim, International Law 691–95 (8th ed. H. Lauterpacht ed. 1955); United Nations, Study on Expulsion of Immigrants (1955); P. Weis, Nationality and Statelessness in International Law 49–60 (1956); 1 M. Whiteman, Damages in International Law 418–514 (1937); 8 M. Whiteman, Digest of International Law 620–22, 850–63 (1967); Puente, *Exclusion and Expulsion of Aliens in Latin America,* 36 Am. J. Int'l L. 252, 257–70 (1942).

8. The concept of "denial of justice" is of course frequently used, not primarily for its factual reference, but as a term of art to indicate a finding of state responsibility. The same cases, and their discussion in the literature, do, however, illustrate the factual deprivations imposed upon aliens. Sohn and Baxter seek to clarify this much-abused concept in these words:

> This term [denial of justice] has in the past been used in at least three different senses. In its broadest sense, this term seems to embrace the whole field of State responsibility, and has been applied to all types of wrongful conduct on the part of the State toward aliens. In its narrowest sense, this term has been limited to refusal of a State to grant an alien access to its courts or a failure of a court to pronounce a judgment. In an intermediate sense, the expression "denial of justice" is employed in connection with the improper administration of civil and criminal justice as regards an alien, including denial of access to courts, inadequate procedures, and unjust decisions. The last appears to be the most apposite usage, since the term may thus be usefully employed to describe a particular type of international wrong for which no other adequate phrase exists in the language of the law.

F. Garcia-Amador, L. Sohn, & R. Baxter, Recent Codification of the Law of State Responsibility for Injuries to Aliens 180 (1974). This book reproduces, in the first half, the draft articles on "Responsibility of the State for Injuries Caused in Its Territory to the Person or Property of Aliens" and commentary thereon, with some minor changes, as excerpted from the six reports submitted by F. V. Garcia-Amador to the International Law Commission during the period 1956–61, in his capacity as the special rapporteur on the subject of "State Responsibility." These six reports are: *First Report,* [1956] 2 Y.B. Int'l L. Comm'n 173–231, U.N. Doc. A/CN.4/96 (1956) [hereinafter cited as *Garcia-Amador's First Report*]; *Second Report,* [1957] 2 Y.B. Int'l L. Comm'n 104–30, U.N. Doc. A/CN.4/106 (1957) [hereinafter cited as *Garcia-Amador's Second Report*]; *Third Report,* [1958] 2 Y.B. Int'l L. Comm'n 47–73, U.N. Doc. A/CN.4/111 (1958); *Fourth Report,* [1959] 2 Y.B. Int'l L. Comm'n 1–36, U.N. Doc. A/CN.4/119 (1959); *Fifth Report,* [1960] 2 Y.B. Int'l L. Comm'n 41–68, U.N. Doc. A/CN.4/125 (1960); *Sixth Report,* [1961] 2 Y.B. Int'l L. Comm'n 1–54, U.N. Doc. A/CN.4/134 and Add. 1 (1961). In the second half, the book reproduces the

of access to appropriate tribunals, judicial or administrative, denial of fair hearing, and subjection to arbitrary decisions.[9]

Characteristic deprivations in the wealth process are scarcely less severe. Aliens may be restricted in the acquisition of land and other forms of property.[10] "The right to acquire immovables," wrote Borchard, "by purchase or descent, and to own and dispose of them may be forbidden to aliens."[11] Similarly, onerous restrictions may be imposed on "the property rights of aliens in certain national resources, *e.g.*, national vessels, national mines, and other kinds of property."[12] Aliens may be forbidden to engage in enumerated business enterprises. The wealth of aliens may be expropriated without adequate compensation;[13] move-

---

"Convention on the International Responsibility of States for Injuries to Aliens" (final draft with explanatory notes), prepared in 1961 by Louis B. Sohn and Richard R. Baxter, as reporters.

On denial of justice, *see generally* I. BROWNLIE, *supra* note 7, at 514–16; A. FREEMAN, note 4 *supra;* 2 C. HYDE, INTERNATIONAL LAW CHIEFLY AS INTERPRETED AND APPLIED BY THE UNITED STATES 909–17 (1945); 2 D. O'CONNELL, *supra* note 7, at 945–50; RESTATEMENT (SECOND) OF FOREIGN RELATIONS LAW OF THE UNITED STATES 502–03, 534–48 (1965) [hereinafter cited as RESTATEMENT]: De Arechaga, *International Responsibility,* in MANUAL OF PUBLIC INTERNATIONAL LAW 531, 553–57 (M. Sørensen ed. 1968); Eagleton, *Denial of Justice in International Law,* 22 AM. J. INT'L L. 538 (1928); Fitzmaurice, *The Meaning of the Term "Denial of Justice,"* 13 BRIT. Y.B. INT'L L. 93 (1932); Spiegel, *Origin and Development of Denial of Justice,* 32 AM. J. INT'L L. 63 (1938).

9. *Cf.* F. DAWSON & I. HEAD, *supra* note 3; A. FREEMAN, *supra* note 4; F. GARCIA-AMADOR, L. SOHN, & R. BAXTER, *supra* note 8, at 179–99; 2 C. HYDE, *supra* note 8, at 924–36.

10. *See* E. BORCHARD, *supra* note 4, at 87; 1 C. GORDON & H. ROSENFIELD, IMMIGRATION LAW AND PROCEDURE 1-122.1–1-123 (rev. ed. 1975); M. KONVITZ, *supra* note 4, at 148–52; McGovney, *The Anti-Japanese Land Laws,* 35 CALIF. L. REV. 61 (1947); Sullivan, *Alien Land Laws: A Re-Evaluation,* 36 TEMPLE L. Q. 15 (1962).

The Mexican laws regarding aliens' rights to acquire real property are described as "lush, barren, cragged, flat, solemn, capricious, gnarled, slashed, smoothed and painted. . . . " *Quoted in Comment, Do We Live in Alien Nations?* 3 CALIF. WESTERN INT'L L.J. 75, 83 (1972). For more details, *see id.* at 83–94.

For charts showing limitations on the acquisition of land imposed on aliens (individuals and corporations) by various states of the United States, *see id.* at 95–111.

11. E. BORCHARD, *supra* note 4, at 86.

12. *Id.* at 91.

13. For comprehensive reference, *see* Weston, *International Law and the Deprivation of Foreign Wealth: A Framework for Future Inquiry,* in 2 THE FUTURE OF THE INTERNATIONAL LEGAL ORDER 36–182 (R. Falk & C. Black eds. 1970). *Cf. generally* K. CARLSTON, LAW AND ORGANIZATION IN WORLD SOCIETY (1962); ESSAYS ON EXPROPRIATION (R. Miller & R. Stanger eds. 1967); A. FATOUROS, GOVERNMENT GUARANTEES TO FOREIGN INVESTORS (1962); I. FOIGHEL, NATIONALIZATION AND COMPENSATION (1964); W. FRIEDMANN, EXPROPRIATION IN INTERNATIONAL LAW (1953); R. LILLICH, THE PROTECTION OF FOREIGN INVESTMENT (1965); R. LILLICH, INTERNATIONAL CLAIMS: POSTWAR BRITISH PRACTICE (1967); E. MOONEY, FOREIGN SEIZURES—SABBATINO AND THE ACT OF STATE DOCTRINE (1967); RIGHTS AND DUTIES OF PRIVATE INVESTORS ABROAD (International and Comparative Law Center,

ment of their assets may be curtailed. They may even be prohibited from gainful employment, and be condemned therefore to lead a precarious existence.[14] Aliens may further be excluded from enjoying such welfare benefits as "relief, public works, public housing, old-age assistance."[15] Closely allied deprivations relate to the exercise of professional skills, as when aliens are excluded from a wide range of professions and occupations, including the practice of law, medicine, dentistry, pharmacy, public accounting, architecture, and teaching.[16]

When handicapped by a different mother tongue, aliens may enjoy limited opportunities for education, and financial aid and other assis-

---

The Southwestern Legal Foundation ed. 1965); SELECTED READINGS ON PROTECTION BY LAW OF PRIVATE FOREIGN INVESTMENTS (International and Comparative Law Center, The Southwestern Legal Foundation ed. 1964); H. STEINER & D. VAGTS, TRANSNATIONAL LEGAL PROBLEMS 408–94 (2d ed. 1976); THE VALUATION OF NATIONALIZED PROPERTY IN INTERNATIONAL LAW (Vols. 1–3) (R. Lillich ed. 1972–75); B. WESTON, INTERNATIONAL CLAIMS: POSTWAR FRENCH PRACTICE (1971); G. WHITE, NATIONALISATION OF FOREIGN PROPERTY (1961); B. WORTLEY, EXPROPRIATION IN PUBLIC INTERNATIONAL LAW (1959); Dawson & Weston, *Prompt, Adequate and Effective: A Universal Standard of Compensation,* 30 FORDHAM L. REV. 727 (1962); Lowenfeld, *Reflections on Expropriation and the Future of Investment in the Americas,* 7 INT'L LAWYER 116 (1973); MANN, *Outlines of a History of Expropriation,* 75 LAW Q. REV. 188 (1959); Metzger, *Property in International Law,* 50 VA. L. REV. 594 (1964); *Nationalization,* 14 HARV. INT'L L.J. 378 (1973).

14. As Borchard wrote: "The labor of aliens is the only exchangeable commodity they possess. To deprive them of the right to labor is to consign them to starvation." E. BORCHARD, *supra* note 4, at 186. "An alien cannot live," he added, "where he cannot work." *Id.* at 187.

Cf. W. GIBSON, ALIENS AND THE LAW 119–43 (1940); Das, *Discrimination in Employment against Aliens—The Impact of the Constitution and Federal Civil Rights Laws,* 35 U. PITT. L. REV. 499 (1974); *Comment, Equal Protection and Supremacy Clause Limitations on State Legislation Restricting Aliens,* 1970 UTAH L. REV. 136; *Note, Constitutionality of Restrictions on Aliens' Right to Work,* 57 COLUM. L. REV. 1012 (1957); *Note, Protection of Alien Rights under the Fourteenth Amendment,* 1971 DUKE L.J. 583 [hereinafter cited as *Note on Protection of Alien Rights*].

15. E. BORCHARD, *supra* note 4, at 186. *See also* UNITED NATIONS, STUDY ON ASSISTANCE TO INDIGENT ALIENS, U.N. Doc. ST/SOA/7 (1951); *Note, State Discrimination against Mexican Aliens,* 38 GEO. WASH. L. REV. 1091 (1970).

16. For a lengthy itemization of occupations that were once denied aliens in the United States, *see* M. KONVITZ, *supra* note 4, at 190–211. *Cf.* E. BORCHARD, *supra* note 4, at 80; 1 C. GORDON & H. ROSENFIELD, *supra* note 10, at 1-118–1-120; Branse, *State Laws Barring Aliens from Professions and Occupations,* 3 I.N.S. MONTHLY REV. 281 (March 1946); Cliffe, *Aliens: The Unconstitutional Classification for Admission to the Bar,* 4 ST. MARY'S L.J. 181 (1972); Sanders, *Aliens in Professions and Occupations—State Laws Restricting Participation,* 16 I.N. REPORTER 37 (1968); *Comment, Constitutional Protection of Aliens,* 40 TENN. L. REV. 235, 245–53 (1973).

Within the United States, community expectations and practices appear to be changing more favorably towards aliens. *See In re* Griffiths, 413 U.S. 717 (1973); Gordon, *The Alien and the Constitution,* 9 CALIF. WESTERN L. REV. 1 (1972); Miller & Steele, *Aliens and the Federal Government: A Newer Equal Protection,* in IMMIGRATION, ALIENAGE AND NATIONALITY 1–31 (1975) (U.C.D. L. REV. Vol. 8); *Note on Protection of Alien Rights, supra* note 14; *Recent*

tance may be withheld. Opportunities to shape enlightenment by owning and editing mass media of communication are generally restricted. Aliens may be prevented from marrying nationals because of the inhibiting consequences of involuntary acquisition or loss of nationality,[17] and are therefore handicapped in the shaping and sharing of affection. In some states, the rights of nonnationals in adoption and guardianship are curtailed.[18] The access of aliens to health facilities and services is generally less than that of nationals, and housing often presents difficult problems. Even the lives of aliens may be threatened by mob actions, inspired by xenophobia; and in many communities alienage remains a stigma of disrespect, affecting many civil liberties.[19]

BASIC COMMUNITY POLICIES

In a global society aspiring towards the utmost freedom of choice for individuals in matters of group affiliation, residence, movement, access to value processes, and so on, differentiation upon the ground of alienage is scarcely less invidious to human dignity values than discrimination based upon race, sex, and religion.[20] A unique feature of deprivations

---

Decisions—Constitutional Law—Rights of Aliens—Citizenship as a Requirement for Admission to the Bar Is a Violation of Equal Protection, 4 GA. J. INT'L & COMP. L. 206 (1974).

Cf. Christol & Bader, *Legal Rights of the Alien in Austria, with Special Reference to the United States Citizen,* 7 INT'L LAWYER 289 (1973).

17. *See* the appendix *infra,* at notes 66–70, 151–55, and 364–75, and accompanying text. *See also* UNITED NATIONS, NATIONALITY OF MARRIED WOMEN (1963); UNITED NATIONS, CONVENTION OF THE NATIONALITY OF MARRIED WOMEN (1962); W. WALTZ, THE NATIONALITY OF MARRIED WOMEN (1937).

18. E. BORCHARD, *supra* note 4, at 91.

19. In the words of Dunn: "[T]he simple fact that he is a foreigner may often be a determining factor in the kind of treatment he receives at the hands of private individuals or government officials. Prejudice against aliens as such is still a pervasive trait of human nature." F. DUNN, THE PROTECTION OF NATIONALS 36 (1932).

It may be noted that the vulnerability of the alien to severe deprivations in the host community is, of course, particularly acute at a time of high crisis, as exemplified by the extremely harsh treatment accorded "enemy aliens." The treatment of enemy aliens raises very special policy problems in relation to state security, which cannot be dealt with in this article. *See* M. DOMKE, THE CONTROL OF ALIEN PROPERTY (1947); M. DOMKE, TRADING WITH THE ENEMY IN WORLD WAR II (1943); F. LAFITTE, THE INTERNMENT OF ALIENS (1940); M. McDOUGAL & F. FELICIANO, LAW AND MINIMUM WORLD PUBLIC ORDER 89–91 (1961); 2 D. O'CONNELL, *supra* note 7, at 769–73; S. RUBIN, PRIVATE FOREIGN INVESTMENTS 57 et seq. (1956); Borchard, *The Treatment of Enemy Property,* 34 GEO. L.J. 389 (1946); Carlston, *Return of Enemy Property,* 52 A.S.I.L. PROC. 53 (1958); Jessup, *Enemy Property,* 49 AM. J. INT'L L. 57 (1955); Sommerich, *A Brief against Confiscation,* 11 LAW & CONTEMP. PROB. 152 (1945).

20. *See* note 2 *supra.*

The United States Supreme Court, in outlawing state statutes denying welfare benefits to aliens, declared in *Graham v. Richardson* that "classifications based on alienage, like those based on nationality or race, are inherently suspect and subject to close judicial scrutiny.

imposed upon the ground of alienage is, further, that they commonly involve high degrees of transnational impact. The reference of the generic label "aliens" is not to some static isolated group, but potentially to the whole of humanity. Every individual is a potential alien in relation to all the states of which he is not a national; to the extent that he moves and engages in activities across state boundaries, this potentiality becomes an actuality. It was with deep insight that many years ago Dunn characterized the problem of such deprivations as "an intricate and continuing international" one, "ultimately concerned with the possibility of maintaining a unified economic and social order for the conduct of international trade and intercourse among independent political units of diverse cultures and stages of civilization, different legal and economic systems, and varying degrees of physical power and prestige."[21]

It must be conceded that the aggregate common interest of territorially organized communities may upon occasion require some limitation of this preferred policy of the utmost individual freedom of choice in state membership and complete equality in the treatment of aliens and nationals. Insofar as the characterizations of "nationality" made by states bear some rational relation to group memberships in fact, it may be expedient for states to make appropriate differentiations for the sake of internal and external security and the optimal functioning of all internal value processes.[22] The perspective of human dignity requires that concessions to the organized interests of territorial communities should, however, be kept to a minimum. The more important differential treatments that may be held permissible upon grounds of alienage would appear to be confined to those that relate to participation in the making of community decisions (voting and officeholding). In longer-term perspective, as increasing interactions build more pluralized and regional territorial structures for the world, accompanied by the attrition of anachronistic national barriers, even such residual concessions to territoriality would presumably become functionless and unnecessary.

As a guide to the task of distinguishing deprivations imposed upon aliens that are rationally related to common interest and therefore permissible from those that are impermissible, Dunn proposed a formulation in terms of allocation of risk. He affirmed that "a workable test can only be arrived at by giving consideration to the general purpose of the notion of international responsibility in connection with injuries to foreigners" and found that purpose in maintenance of "the minimum con-

---

Aliens as a class are a prime example of a 'discrete and insular' minority . . . for whom such heightened judicial solicitude is appropriate." 403 U.S. 365, 372 (1971) (footnotes omitted).

21. F. Dunn, *supra* note 19, at 1.

22. *Cf.* the appendix *infra,* at 863–65.

ditions which are regarded as necessary for the continuance of international trade and intercourse."[23] "Normal business and social relationships"[24] were capable of bearing a certain degree of risk of "abuses of governmental power by individual officials and employees,"[25] but there was a point beyond which, Dunn found, such relationships could not carry on. Hence, he concluded, the appropriate question is:

> [D]oes the delinquency of a particular official indicate a failure on the part of the state to establish governmental organs capable of maintaining the minimum conditions necessary for the carrying on of normal social and business relations? If it does, then the state assumes the risk, otherwise not. Or the question might be put in another way. Is the delinquency of a type which, if permitted to occur generally, would make the conduct of customary social and business relations impossible? One might express this in familiar language by saying that a state is "under a duty" to provide conditions of this character, and that if it fails in this duty, then it becomes liable to make reparation.[26]

The difficulty with this test, whether confined to deprivations related to abuses of official power or extended to all legislative differentiation of aliens, is that it offers no detailed criteria for the allocation of risk or for evaluating costs and benefits in terms of the value consequences of different options in decision. When proffered and applied without guiding criteria the concept of "risk allocation" is no more than a tautologous, question-begging formula. There would appear no rational escape in relation to the problems of aliens, as of other problems, from the necessity of an explicit postulation of goals and a careful contextual analysis, with respect to every particular problem, of the inclusive interests of the larger community in a world society, the exclusive interests of the particular territorial communities in protecting their internal integrity or their nationals, and the interests of individual human beings in all basic rights.

The more fundamental policies which should be postulated, and made to infuse all decisions, for appraisal of particular instances of differentiation between aliens and nationals are of course those embodied in the contemporary human rights prescriptions, designed to reflect the common interests of the peoples of the world as individuals.[27] The fact of alienage does not change the fundamental demands and interests of the

23. F. Dunn, *supra* note 19, at 133.
24. *Id.*
25. *Id.*
26. *Id.* at 134.
27. *See* notes 93–132 *infra* and accompanying text.

individual as a human being; its only relevance must be to the organized interests of a territorial community which, in varying contexts, his activities may affect. It is widely recognized today that many, if not most, "national" boundaries are highly artificial and anachronistic from any functional perspective, impeding a rational regional organization of the world, and, as suggested above, that the grounds commonly employed by states in making their characterizations of "nationality" may bear only an accidental relation to the facts of community membership.[28] In this context, the necessities of an aggregate common interest in a global economy and society, requiring a more rational relation of peoples to resources, should be made to yield as little as possible to the demands and practices of an outmoded and destructive nationalism. A clear consciousness of interdependence offers more hope even for shared exclusive interests than the amnesia of parochialism.[29]

TRENDS IN DECISION

In ancient times the alien was commonly looked upon as an enemy and hence treated as an outlaw;[30] parochial community expectations kept him powerless and unprotected. As the Roman empire expanded, aliens were gradually accorded protection under the *jus gentium,* a law made applicable to foreigners as well as citizens, as distinguished from the *jus civile,* which applied exclusively to Roman citizens.[31] The earlier harsh treatment of aliens was further, theoretically at least, ameliorated with the spread of the Christian idea of the unity of mankind.[32] In the feudal period, "the disabilities of the alien became more clearly defined,"

---

28. *See* the appendix *infra.* The imposition of deprivations by such a flexible group label may reflect the utmost arbitrariness.

29. *Cf. id.* at 863–65, 953–58; F. Dunn, *supra* note 19.

30. In the words of Goebel:

> Very clearly, in the earliest times, the alien, as a clanless individual or outlaw, was without any of the existing personal rights. He had no "wergeld," he was not entitled to the peace and protection of the locality, and if by chance he enjoyed even liberty of person it was only by sufferance and in amelioration of the harsh laws which gave the local lord title over his person, as *ferae naturae.* How long these practices survived, we cannot say, but certainly the growth of a *Gastrecht* so common among primitive peoples was not long in superseding the ancient customs. This *Gastrecht,* or rights of hospitality, gave a certain quantum of protection to the foreigner and was exercised more particularly as a form of patronage of a lord over aliens.

Goebel, *The International Responsibility of States for Injuries Sustained by Aliens on Account of Mob Violence, Insurrection and Civil Wars,* 8 Am. J. Int'l L. 802, 803 (1914).

31. E. Borchard, *supra* note 4, at 33; A. Roth, The Minimum Standard of International Law Applied to Aliens 25–26 (1949); Head, *The Stranger in Our Midst: A Sketch of the Legal Status of the Alien in Canada,* 2 Canadian Y.B. Int'l L. 107, 108 (1964).

32. *See* A. Roth, *supra* note 31, at 26.

though such "disabilities and restrictions differed in degree in different baronies."[33] In the words of Dawson and Head:

> In the early Middle Ages international commerce was so structured that few people lived abroad. Those persons that did had few real rights. In some places they could be treated as serfs and almost everywhere they could not pass property by inheritance. As trade and commerce expanded in the later Middle Ages, the position of foreigners improved, mostly due to increased protection given them by more powerful central governments against local feudal lords, and only quite incidentally to international agreement.[34]

With the coming of the modern nation-state system, a more humanitarian attitude toward aliens began to develop. The founding fathers of contemporary international law asserted that all persons, alien or other, were entitled to certain natural rights. Francisco de Vitoria was among the first to emphasize the importance of according aliens fair treatment.[35] Taking for granted the right of free access to territorial communities, Grotius considered it "essential to make the status of the foreigner coincide as far as possible with that of the subject of the particular State."[36] It was Vattel, however, who first expounded a coherent and influential doctrine for the protection of aliens.[37] Writing more than a century after Grotius, as mercantilism was being transformed into modern capitalism and as a vast European expansion overseas was beginning, Vattel created the theoretical basis for much subsequent decision. Viewing the state as an entity composed of the sovereign and his citizens, Vattel stressed that the state had a right to protect its citizens, wherever they might be. An injury to an individual alien was asserted to be an injury to the state of his nationality. In Vattel's words:

> Whoever ill-treats a citizen indirectly injures the State, which must protect that citizen. The sovereign of the injured citizen must avenge the deed and, if possible, force the aggressor to give full satisfaction or punish him, since otherwise the citizen will not obtain the chief end of civil society, which is protection.[38]

---

33. E. Borchard, *supra* note 4, at 34.

34. F. Dawson & I. Head, *supra* note 3, at 1.

35. A. Roth, *supra* note 31, at 27.

36. *Id.* at 28. *Cf.* F. Dunn, *supra* note 19, at 46–48.

37. 3 E. de Vattel, Classics of International Law: The Law of Nations or the Principles of Natural Law (C. Fenwick trans. 1916). The book was first published in 1758. *Cf.* P. Remec, The Position of the Individual in International Law according to Grotius and Vattel (1960).

38. 3 E. de Vattel, *supra* note 37, at 136.

Vattel's doctrine was quite precisely formulated by the Permanent Court of International Justice in the *Panevezys-Saldutiskis Railway* case:

Ever since Vattel, and accompanying the spread of industrialization and European culture throughout the world, there has developed a unique customary international law for the special protection of aliens, built upon decisions from foreign office to foreign office, and in international and national tribunals, and fortified by the opinions of publicists and a vast network of relatively uniform treaties of "friendship, commerce, and navigation."[39] The identification Vattel makes of the inter-

---

> [I]n taking up the case of one of its nationals, by resorting to diplomatic action or international judicial proceedings on his behalf, a state is in reality asserting its own right, the right to ensure in the person of its nationals respect for the rules of international law. This right is necessarily limited to the intervention on behalf of its own nationals because, in the absence of a special agreement, it is the bond of nationality between the state and the individual which alone confers upon the state the right of diplomatic protection, and it is as a part of the function of diplomatic protection that the right to take up a claim and to ensure respect for the rules of international law must be envisaged. Where the injury was done to the national of some other State no claim to which such injury may give rise falls within the scope of the diplomatic protection which a State is entitled to afford nor can it give rise to a claim which that State is entitled to espouse.

[1939] P.C.I.J., Ser. A/B, No. 76, at 16.

39. On the international law of state responsibility, *see generally* C. Amerasinghe, State Responsibility for Injuries to Aliens (1967); W. Bishop, International Law: Cases and Materials 742–899 (3d ed. 1971); E. Borchard, *supra* note 4; J. Brierly, The Law of Nations 276–91 (6th ed. H. Waldock ed. 1963); The Law of Nations 601–747 (2d ed. H. Briggs ed. 1952) [hereinafter cited as H. Briggs]; I. Brownlie, *supra* note 7, at 418–581; B. Cheng, General Principles of Law as Applied by International Courts and Tribunals 161–253 (1953); F. Dawson & I. Head, *supra* note 3; C. De Visscher, Theory and Reality in Public International Law 277–94 (P. Corbett trans. 1968); F. Dunn, *supra* note 19; A. Freeman, *supra* note 4; C. Eagleton, The Responsibility of States in International Law (1928); W. Friedmann, O. Lissitzyn, & R. Pugh, Cases and Materials on International Law 745–879 (1969); F. Garcia-Amador, L. Sohn, & R. Baxter, *supra* note 8; International Law in the Twentieth Century 481–585 (L. Gross ed. 1969) [hereinafter cited as L. Gross]; W. Holder & G. Brennan, The International Legal System: Cases and Materials 629–709 (1972); P. Jessup, A Modern Law of Nations 94–122 (1968); C. Joseph, Nationality and Diplomatic Protection: The Commonwealth of Nations (1969); M. Katz & K. Brewster, The Law of International Transactions and Relations: Cases and Materials 6–398 (1960); N. Leech, C. Oliver, & J. Sweeney, Cases and Materials on the International Legal System 572–655 (1973); R. Lillich, International Claims: Their Adjudication by National Commissions (1962); R. Lillich & G. Christenson, International Claims: Their Preparation and Presentation (1962); 6 J. Moore, A Digest of International Law 605–1037 (1906); 2 D. O'Connell, *supra* note 7, at 693–719, 941–1025; 1 L. Oppenheim, *supra* note 7, at 335–69; Restatement, *supra* note 8, at 497–633; A. Roth, *supra* note 31; H. Steiner & D. Vagts, *supra* note 13, at 357–530; G. Tunkin, Theory of International Law 381–425 (W. Butler trans. 1974); Borchard, *Diplomatic Protection,* 5 Encyc. Soc. Sc. 153 (1931); Copithorne, *State Responsibility and International Claims,* in Canadian Perspectives on International Law and Organization 207–28 (R. MacDonald, G. Morris, & D. Johnston eds. 1974); De Arechaga, *supra* note 8; Garcia-Amador, *State Responsibility—Some New Problems,* 94 Hague Recueil des Cours 365 (1958); Harvard Research in International Law, *The Law of Respon-*

ests of the state and of the alien individual has often been criticized as "fiction," as in some contexts it obviously is.[40] Like other "fictions feigned," however, this identification of state and individual interests has been found, by disinterested observers as well as by claimant parties, to represent in many contexts a close approximation to social reality. People always have been, and remain, important bases of power for territorial communities.[41] The security—in the sense of a minimum freedom from external violence and coercion—and the optimum order or quality of society—in the sense of the greater production and wider sharing of all values that any community can achieve—are intimately dependent upon the numbers and characteristics of its members, including their skills, capabilities, and loyalties. The conferring of a competence upon particular states to protect their members from injuries abroad may thus, in a relatively unorganized world, serve in many contexts to protect both the interests of the state in an important base of power and the interests of the alien individual in his basic human rights. In appropriate tribute, Judge Jessup describes the "history of this branch of international law during the nineteenth and twentieth centuries"[42] as exemplifying "the way in which a body of customary international law develops in response to the need for adjustment of clashing interests."[43] He adds that it "is remarkable that in this struggle which so generally involved the relations between the strong and the weak, international law, for all its primitiveness, developed as a balance for conflict-

---

sibility of States for Damage Done in Their Territory to the Person or Property of Foreigners, 23 AM. J. INT'L L. SUPP. 131 (1929); Sweeney, *The Restatement of the Foreign Relations Law of the United States and the Responsibility of States for Injury to Aliens,* 16 SYRACUSE L. REV. 762 (1965).

For the work of the International Law Commission in regard to state responsibility, *see* Garcia-Amador's six reports, *supra* note 8, and Ago's reports, *infra* note 92.

40. *See, e.g.,* the appendix *infra,* at notes 4–42 and accompanying text; Koessler, *Government Espousal of Private Claims before International Tribunals,* 13 U. CHI. L. REV. 180 (1945).

41. As Dunn incisively observed:

> We think of the United States as an organized group of individuals occupying a particular spot of the earth's surface. Yet at any given moment, a vast number holding membership in that group are scattered all over the world, and an equally vast amount of their property, both real and personal, is situated in foreign jurisdictions. The same is true of all the other civilized nations of the world. Again, we conceive of the United States as a single economic unit. Yet if we trace the essential threads of that complicated fabric we find a surprisingly large proportion of them leading beyond the boundaries of the country to all parts of the world. If for any reason those threads should be cut, the effect upon the daily lives of all of us would be profound.

Dunn, *International Law and Private Property Rights,* 28 COLUM. L. REV. 166, 170 (1928). *See also* the appendix *infra,* at 863–66.

42. P. JESSUP, *supra* note 39, at 95.

43. *Id.*

ing interests,"[44] and concludes that, "in terms of the modernization of international law":[45]

> The function of the law of responsibility of states for injuries to aliens . . . is to provide in the general world interest, adequate protection for the stranger, to the end that travel, trade, and intercourse may be facilitated.[46]

Within the broad, historic development of this unique customary international law for the protection of aliens, two different standards about the responsibility of states, both of which purport to include a norm prohibiting discrimination against aliens, have competed for general community acceptance. One of these standards is described as the doctrine of "national treatment" or "equality of treatment" and provides that aliens should receive equal, and only equal, treatment with nationals.[47] The second standard is described as that of a "minimum international standard" and specifies that, however a state may treat its nationals, there are certain minima in humane treatment that cannot be violated in relation to aliens.[48] A review of the flow of decision and communication in development of the customary law about aliens, and especially in the recent, more general prescriptions about human rights, will establish, it is believed, that the second of these standards has become present general community expectation.[49]

It is seldom seriously asserted that states cannot differentiate between nationals and aliens in ways that bear a reasonable relation to the dif-

---

44. *Id.* at 96.

45. *Id.* at 105.

46. *Id.*

The observation of Dunn is equally illuminating:

> From a practical point of view, the foreigner, although he may be accorded full civil rights on the same basis as citizens, is often at a disadvantage in any dispute which he may have with the agents of the state of his sojourn merely by reason of the fact that he is a foreigner. Furthermore, being deprived of political rights outside of his own country, he is not at liberty to participate in the determination of the social and economic order and has not the political means for the protection of his interests that are at the disposal of the citizen. Perhaps for these reasons as much as any other, it has been found necessary, in a world of diverse cultures and heterogeneous peoples, of strong governments and weak governments, of orderly countries and disorderly countries, to work out a common code of treatment of aliens in order that there might be some basis of security and predictability upon which to build the present complex structure of international intercourse.

Dunn, *supra* note 41, at 174.

47. *See* notes 50–58 *infra* and accompanying text.

48. For an excellent historical account, *see* Borchard, *The Minimum Standard of the Treatment of Aliens,* 38 MICH. L. REV. 445 (1940). For other discussions and documentation, *see* notes 59–82 *infra* and accompanying text.

49. *See* notes 62–139 *infra* and accompanying text.

ferences in their obligations and loyalties. Thus, states reciprocally honor each other in accepting the lawfulness of a great variety of differentiations in permissible access to territory, participation in government, the ownership of important natural resources, and so on. Yet the principle would appear almost universally accepted that, with respect to participation in many important social processes, states cannot discriminate against aliens in favor of nationals in ways that have no substantial basis in the differences in their obligations and loyalties.[50] Even the Latin American states are described as having laid "claim to a peculiar virtue in placing the alien on a footing of civil equality with the national";[51] these states in fact exhibit a long history of constitutional and statutory enactment directed toward this end.[52] The perversion of this important general norm of nondiscrimination has come, as Secretary of State Hull once pointed out, from taking a principle designed for protection against inhumane treatment of the individual alien and transforming it into a formula designed to protect states from responsibility for arbitrary action.[53] One formulation of the "national treatment" doctrine propounded by many Latin Americans, and occasionally by others, is that an alien cannot expect a higher standard of treatment than a national, and hence a state cannot be held responsible under international law for any injury or damage suffered by an alien if he has been accorded the same treatment as nationals.[54] Thus, in the words of a leading proponent, Carlos Calvo: "Aliens who established themselves in a country are certainly entitled to the same rights of protection as nationals, but they cannot claim any greater measure of protection."[55]

---

50. Nondiscrimination is a principal objective of the treaties of friendship, commerce, and navigation. *See* R. WILSON, UNITED STATES COMMERCIAL TREATIES AND INTERNATIONAL LAW 6 (1960).

In its Restatement of Foreign Relations Law (§ 166), the American Law Institute characterizes "Discrimination against Alien" in these terms:

> (1) Conduct, attributable to a state and causing injury to an alien, that discriminates against aliens generally, against aliens of his nationality, or against him because he is an alien, departs from the international standard of justice specified in § 165.
>
> (2) Conduct discriminates against an alien within the meaning of Subsection (1) if it involves treating the alien differently from nationals or from aliens of a different nationality without a reasonable basis for the difference.

RESTATEMENT, *supra* note 8, at 507–08.

51. Borchard, *supra* note 47, at 55.

52. F. DAWSON & I. HEAD, *supra* note 3, at 7.

53. 3 G. HACKWORTH, *supra* note 7, at 658–60.

54. The history of the standard of national treatment is well presented in *Garcia-Amador's First Report, supra* note 8, at 201–02; F. GARCIA-AMADOR, L. SOHN, & R. BAXTER, *supra* note 8, at 3–4.

55. 6 C. CALVO, LE DROIT INTERNATIONAL 231 (5th ed. 1885), *quoted in Garcia-Amador's First Report, supra* note 8, at 201.

This formulation by Calvo was officially adopted by the First International Conference of American States held in Washington, D.C., 1889–90:

> 1. Foreigners are entitled to enjoy all the civil rights enjoyed by natives; and they shall be afforded all the benefits of said rights in all that is essential as well as in the form or procedure, and the legal remedies incident thereto, absolutely in like manner as said natives.
> 2. A nation has not, nor recognizes in favor of foreigners, any other obligations or responsibilities than those which in favor of the natives are established, in like cases, by the constitution and the laws.[56]

Similarly, the Convention on Rights and Duties of States, adopted in 1933 at the Seventh International Conference of American States held in Montevideo, proclaimed in Article 9:

> The jurisdiction of states within the limits of national territory applies to all the inhabitants.
>
> Nationals and foreigners are under the same protection of the law and the national authorities and the foreigners may not claim rights other or more extensive than those of the nationals.[57]

A comparable position has often been reiterated by Latin American statesmen and publicists.[58]

It scarcely requires argument that a principle of "national treatment" so specified, though it does not entirely repudiate international law, must leave aliens largely at the mercies of their host state. Such an interpretation of international law would, in Brierly's words, "make each state the judge of the standard required by international law and would virtually deprive aliens of the protection of their own state altogether."[59] In a world in which many states are tyrannical or totalitarian or otherwise oppressive, such an outcome is not to be desired nor lightly accepted. The absurdity inherent in such an interpretation of international law was eloquently indicated by Secretary of State Hull: "It is contended, in a word, that it is wholly justifiable to deprive an individual of his rights if all other persons are equally deprived, and if no victim is allowed to

---

56. The International Conferences of American States, 1889 to 1928, at 45 (J. Scott ed. 1931).

57. The International Conferences of American States, First Supplement, 1933–1940, at 122 (Carnegie Endowment for International Peace ed. 1940).

58. *See Garcia-Amador's First Report, supra* note 8, at 201–02; A. Roth, *supra* note 31, at 62–80; I. Brownlie, *supra* note 7, at 509–10; W. Gibson, *supra* note 14, at 19–44.

59. J. Brierly, *supra* note 39, at 278–79.

escape."[60] It is difficult not to accept the conclusion of Sohn and Baxter that "to a large extent the doctrine espousing the 'national treatment' standard is merely a reflection of a fundamental hostility on the part of some nations to the idea of accountability of States for asserted violations of the rights of aliens."[61]

The doctrine of a "minimum international standard," in sharp contradiction to that of "national treatment," insists that a state cannot escape responsibility for the inhumane treatment of aliens by the allegation that it treats its own nationals likewise. This widely and long-accepted doctrine prescribes that there is a minimum common standard in relation to many important deprivations in social process which states must observe in the treatment of aliens, irrespective of their treatment of their own nationals.[62] The classic statement of this standard, in elaboration of Vattel's thesis, is that of Elihu Root:

---

60. 3 G. Hackworth, *supra* note 7, at 659.

61. F. Garcia-Amador, L. Sohn, & R. Baxter, *supra* note 8, at 158. Similarly, in the words of Goebel:

> The Latin American states have shown considerable ingenuity in devising schemes to avoid liability for injuries to aliens. But to all appearances these have been of no avail. They have repudiated the theory of responsibility not only in their diplomatic correspondence, but in their statutes, their treaties, and even in their constitutions. From a purely political point of view, the position of the Latin American states may be regarded as a protest against indiscriminate intervention by European states. It is an effort, moreover, to maintain the privileges of equality of states and the inviolability of territorial sovereignty. From the juridical standpoint, however, we see in this attempt at repudiation of the theory of responsibility, a final effort to regulate the liability of the state by municipal legislation. This in turn may be in some measure understood as a heritage of the mother country which, in the course of development, has taken a new direction.

Goebel, *supra* note 30, at 832.

62. Borchard aptly summarized:

> Thus, while equality is the ultimate that the alien may ask of municipal law, which is by no means bound to grant equality, the body of international law developed by diplomatic practice and arbitral decision, vague and indefinite as it may be, represents the minimum which each state must accord the alien whom it admits. Whether called the fundamental, natural, or inherent rights of humanity or of man or of the alien, this minimum has acquired a permanent place in the protective ambit of international forums.

Borchard, *The "Minimum Standard" of the Treatment of Aliens*, 33 A.S.I.L. Proc. 51, 53 (1939).

On the international minimum standard, *see* C. Amerasinghe, *supra* note 39, at 278–81; E. Borchard, *supra* note 4, at 39–43; 104–09; H. Briggs, *supra* note 39, at 562–67; I. Brownlie, *supra* note 7, *at* 510–14; F. Dunn, *supra* note 19, at 113–72; C. Eagleton, *supra* note 39, at 82–87; A. Freeman, *supra* note 4, at 497–570; 1 L. Oppenheim, *supra* note 39, at 350–52; A. Roth, *supra* note 31, at 81–123; Restatement, *supra* note 8, at 501–07; H. Steiner & D. Vagts, *supra* note 13, at 360–530; 8 M. Whiteman, Digest of Interna-

> Each country is bound to give to the nationals of another country in its territory the benefit of the same laws, the same administration, the same protection, and the same redress for injury which it gives to its own citizens, and neither more nor less: provided the protection which the country gives to its own citizens conforms to the established standard of civilization.
>
> There is a standard of justice, very simple, very fundamental, and of such general acceptance by all civilized countries as to form a part of the international law of the world. The condition upon which any country is entitled to measure the justice due from it to an alien by the justice which it accords to its own citizens is that its system of law and administration shall conform to this general standard. If any country's system of law and administration does not conform to that standard, although the people of the country may be content or compelled to live under it, no other country can be compelled to accept it as furnishing a satisfactory measure of treatment to its citizens.[63]

The same formulation, echoed by many commentators, was supported by a majority of the state delegations represented at the Hague Codification Conference of 1930.[64] The Permanent Court of International Jus-

---

TIONAL LAW, *supra* note 7, at 697–704; Freeman, *Recent Aspects of the Calvo Doctrine and the Challenge to International Law,* 40 AM. J. INT'L L. 121 (1946); Garcia-Amador, *supra* note 39, at 429–31; *Garcia-Amador's First Report, supra* note 8, at 199–201; Herz, *Expropriation of Foreign Property,* 35 AM. J. INT'L L. 243, 260 (1941); Verdross, *Les Règles Internationales concernant le Traitement des Etrangers,* 37 HAGUE RECUEIL DES COURS 323, 348–88 (1931).

63. Root, *The Basis of Protection to Citizens Residing Abroad,* 4 A.S.I.L. PROC. 20–21 (1910). More recently, C. Wilfred Jenks wrote:

> The test is the "ordinary standards of civilisation"; the common denominator is the "practice of civilised nations"; the criterion is the judgment of a "reasonable and impartial man." These are all conceptions so general that their content will necessarily be determined by the policy of the times. The diplomatic protection of citizens abroad has often been associated in the past with the exercise of military, political or economic pressure by stronger against weaker States and it is therefore not a matter for surprise that a growing resistance to the concept of an international standard should have been an almost inevitable feature of a period of sharp criticism of neo-colonialism; but an international standard, fairly applied, is both so fundamental an element in the concept of internationally guaranteed basic human rights and so essential a prerequisite of any mutually beneficial international economic intercourse that the concept may be expected to reassert itself in deference to overriding considerations of international public policy which are entitled to claim, and may be expected to receive, general acceptance.

C. JENKS, THE PROSPECTS OF INTERNATIONAL ADJUDICATION 514–15 (1964) (footnotes omitted).

64. *See* Borchard, *Responsibility of States at the Hague Codification Conference,* 24 AM. J. INT'L L. 517 (1930). *See also* H. BRIGGS, *supra* note 39, at 563–64; I. BROWNLIE, *supra* note 7, at 510; A. ROTH, *supra* note 31, at 104–11.

tice, in the *Case concerning Certain German Interests in Polish Upper Silesia (Merits),* in outlining Poland's competence under a special agreement to derogate "from the rules generally applied in regard to the treatment of foreigners and the principle of respect for vested rights,"[65] referred both positively to "the limits set by the generally accepted principles of international law" and negatively to "generally accepted international law" as establishing "the only measures prohibited."[66]

The most important contribution toward the crystallization of this standard has come, however, in innumerable decisions rendered by international arbitral tribunals. The decisions of the United States–Mexican Claims Commission, established under the General Claims Convention of 1923, have been especially influential.[67] In one of its first decisions, the *Neer* case,[68] while disallowing U.S. claims that Mexican authorities did not exercise due diligence in apprehending armed murderers, this Commission affirmed that

> the propriety of governmental acts should be put to the test of international standards, and . . . the treatment of an alien, in order to constitute an international delinquency, should amount to an outrage, to bad faith, to wilful neglect of duty, or to an insufficiency of governmental action so far short of international standards that every reasonable and impartial man would readily recognize its insufficiency. Whether the insufficiency proceeds from deficient execution of an intelligent law or from the fact that the laws of the

---

65. Case concerning Certain German Interests in Polish Upper Silesia (Merits), [1926] P.C.I.J., Ser. A, No. 7, at 22.

66. *Id.*

Cf. the summary of Freeman:

> The contention that equality with nationals is the measure of a state's international obligations to aliens has been repeatedly rejected by international claims commissions as well as by the Permanent Court of International Justice itself. That court in the case concerning *Certain German Interests in Polish Upper Silesia* expressly recognized the existence of a common or generally accepted international law respecting the treatment of aliens and which is applicable to them despite municipal legislation.

Freeman, *Recent Aspects of the Calvo Doctrine and the Challenge to International Law,* 40 Am. J. Int'l L. 121, 126 (1946) (footnotes omitted).

67. *See* A. Feller, The Mexican Claims Commissions, 1923–1934 (1935); A. Roth, *supra* note 31, at 94–99; Borchard, *Decisions of the Claims Commissions, United States and Mexico,* 20 Am. J. Int'l L. 536 (1926).

68. *The United States of America on behalf of L.F.H. Neer and Pauline E. Neer, Claimants v. The United Mexican States* (Oct. 15, 1926), in Claims Commission, United States and Mexico, Opinions of Commissioners under the Convention Concluded September 8, 1923, between the United States and Mexico, February 4, 1926, to July 23, 1927, at 71 (1927) [hereinafter cited as Opinions of Commissioners]; 4 U.N.R.I.A.A. 60; [1925–26] Ann. Dig. Case No. 154, at 214.

> country do not empower the authorities to measure up to international standards is immaterial.[69]

Later, in the *Roberts* case,[70] in holding that equality of treatment of nationals was no defense to the U.S. charge that Mexican authorities had arbitrarily and illegally arrested an American citizen and subjected him to cruel and inhumane treatment for a long period of time, the Commission reaffirmed:

> Facts with respect to equality of treatment of aliens and nationals may be important in determining the merits of a complaint of mistreatment of an alien. But such equality is not the ultimate test of the propriety of the acts of authorities in the light of international law. That test is, broadly speaking, whether aliens are treated in accordance with ordinary standards of civilization.[71]

The Commission's "consistent" jurisprudence "along the lines of a well-founded and necessary postulate"[72] led Roth to observe: "The minimum standard has therewith become a reality which nobody may defy with impunity any more, and judging from its success, it certainly turned out that demand of long standing had been fulfilled with it."[73]

The doctrine of a minimum international standard found concrete expression, further, in numerous treaties, especially those of friendship, commerce, and navigation.[74] For example, the Convention respecting Conditions of Residence and Business and Jurisdiction between the British Empire, France, Italy, Japan, Greece, &c., and Turkey, signed at Lausanne on July 24, 1923, stipulated: "In Turkey the nationals of the other Contracting powers will be received and treated, both as regards their persons and property, in accordance with ordinary international law. . . ."[75] The reference to "ordinary international law" has been well understood. In Roth's words:

---

69. OPINIONS OF COMMISSIONERS, *supra* note 68, at 73.

70. *The United States of America, on behalf of Harry Roberts, Claimant, v. The United Mexican States* (November 2, 1926), in OPINIONS OF COMMISSIONERS, *supra* note 68, at 100; 4 U.N.R.I.A.A. 77; 21 AM. J. INT'L L. 357 (1927).

71. OPINIONS OF COMMISSIONERS, *supra* note 68, at 105; 21 AM. J. INT'L L. 357, 361 (1927).

72. A. ROTH, *supra* note 31, at 97.

73. *Id.*

74. *See* R. WILSON, *supra* note 50.

75. 28 L.N.T.S. 151, 157.

Another example is the Treaty of Friendship and Establishment between Egypt and Persia of 1928, which provided, in Art. 4, that "The nationals of each of the High Contracting parties . . . shall enjoy, on the same footing as nationals, the most constant protection and security for their persons, property, rights and interests, in conformity with ordinary international law." 93 L.N.T.S. 381, 397.

> Common international law provides for a special regime for the alien, largely consisting in a certain standard of treatment, which we have called the minimum standard. It is apparent therefore that any reference to the principles of common international law with regard to the treatment of the alien implies the recognition of the minimum standard.[76]

Though many of the agreements in the vast network of the treaties of friendship, commerce, and navigation that the United States has concluded with other countries provide for varying standards of treatment, including national treatment, with regard to different types of problems, they reflect an overall commitment to a minimum international standard.[77] Thus, the Treaty of Friendship, Commerce and Navigation between the United States and the Federal Republic of Germany of 1954—the prototype of such treaties in the post-World War II era—provides in Article 1:

> 1. Each Party shall at all times accord fair and equitable treatment to the nationals and companies of the other Party, and to their property, enterprises and other interests.
> 2. Between the territories of the two Parties there shall be, in accordance with the provisions of the present Treaty, freedom of commerce and navigation.[78]

The standards established in many of these treaties often go beyond national treatment in relation to particular problems, most notably in the form of "most-favored-nation treatment."[79]

---

76. A. ROTH, *supra* note 31, at 99.

77. R. WILSON, *supra* note 50, at 6–9. *Cf.* U.S. DEP'T OF STATE, TREATIES IN FORCE: A LIST OF TREATIES AND OTHER INTERNATIONAL AGREEMENTS OF THE UNITED STATES IN FORCE ON JANUARY 1, 1974 (Dep't of State Pub. 8755, 1974); R. WILSON, THE INTERNATIONAL LAW STANDARD IN TREATIES OF THE UNITED STATES 87–134 (1953). For a latest example *see* Agreement on Trade Relations between the United States of America and the Socialist Republic of Romania; TRADE AGREEMENT BETWEEN THE UNITED STATES AND ROMANIA, H.R. Doc. No. 94–114, 94th Cong., 1st Sess. (1975); 14 I.L.M. 671 (1975).

Treaties of friendship, commerce, and navigation between countries other than the United States are similar in terms. *See, e.g.,* Treaty of Friendship, Commerce and Navigation between Japan and the Argentine Republic, *signed* on Dec. 20, 1961; 613 U.N.T.S. 323.

78. [1954] 7 U.S.T. 1839, 1841; 273 U.N.T.S. 3, 4; T.I.A.S. No. 3593.

79. On most-favored nation treatment, *see generally* L. CHEN, STATE SUCCESSION RELATING TO UNEQUAL TREATIES 96–108 (1974); Schwarzenberger, *The Most-Favoured Nation Standard in British State Practice,* 22 BRIT. Y.B. INT'L L. 99 (1945); *The Most-Favored-Nation Clause in the Law of Treaties,* U.N. Doc. A/CN.4/L.127 (1968), [1968] 2 Y.B. INT'L L. COMM'N 165 (working paper submitted by Mr. Endre Ustor); Ustor, [First] *Report on the Most-Favored Nation Clause,* U.N. Doc. A/CN.4/213 (1969); *Second Report,* U.N. Doc. A/CN.4/228 & Add. 1 (1970); *Third Report,* U.N. Doc. A/CN.4/257 & Add. 1 (1972); *Fourth Report,* U.N. Doc. A/CN.4/266 (1973).

The minimum international standard for treatment of aliens, like all prescriptions which require delicate relation to the many varying features of differing contexts, has of necessity been left highly general in its empirical reference. The distinction between the lawful differentiation of the status within a country of nationals and aliens upon a reasonable basis and the discrimination against the alien which is arbitrary and unlawful must depend not only upon the values which are primarily at stake but also upon many varying features of the institutional practices by which such values are sought and shaped. The minimum international standard has, however, despite this fundamental difficulty shared by most other important prescriptions, been frequently and widely applied for the protection of aliens in many different value and institutional contexts.[80]

A most comprehensive summary is offered by Roth, though some commentators may not agree with all his characterizations:

> (1) An alien, whether natural person or corporation, is entitled by international law to have his juridical personality and legal capacity recognized by the receiving State.
>
> (2) The alien can lawfully demand respect for his life and protection for his body.
>
> (3) International law protects the alien's personal and spiritual liberty within socially bearable limits.
>
> (4) According to general international law, aliens enjoy no political rights in their State of residence, but have to fulfil such public duties as are not incompatible with allegiance to their home State.
>
> (5) General international law gives aliens no right to be economically active in foreign States. In cases where the national policies of foreign States allow aliens to undertake economic activities, however, general international law assures aliens of equality of commercial treatment among themselves.
>
> (6) According to general international law, the alien's privilege of participation in the economic life of his State of residence does not go so far as to allow him to acquire private property. The

---

80. *See* A. Roth, *supra* note 31, at 127–91; H. Steiner & D. Vagts, *supra* note 13, at 357–530. *See also* note 62 *supra.* One important contemporary mode of settling disputes about the treatment of aliens is that of lump sum settlement between states. The inherited doctrines about aliens appear to achieve a continuing viability both in the terms of settlement and in the internal decisions by which the agreed sums are apportioned. Note the wide range in types of controversies indicated in the comprehensive and insightful study R. Lillich & B. Weston, International Claims: Their Settlement by Lump Sum Agreements (1975).

State of residence is free to bar him from ownership of all certain property, whether movables or realty.

(7) Wherever the alien enjoys the privilege of ownership of property, international law protects his rights in so far as his property may not be expropriated under any pretext, except for moral or penal reasons, without adequate compensation. Property rights are to be understood as rights to tangible property which have come into concrete existence according to the municipal law of the alien's State of residence.

(8) International law grants the alien procedural rights in his State of residence as primary protection against the violation of his substantive rights. These procedural rights amount to freedom of access to court, the right to a fair, non-discriminatory and unbiased hearing, the right to full participation in any form in the procedure, the right to a just decision rendered in full compliance with the laws of the State within a reasonable time.[81]

Long before it sought generally to protect the fundamental rights of the individual against his own state, international law created, thus, an extensive and important protection for aliens in many different value processes.[82]

---

81. A. Roth, *supra* note 31, at 185–86. For a more detailed analysis of this recapitulation, *see id.* at 127–85.

82. The special protection accorded aliens under customary international law was such that Lauterpacht offered this observation:

> Although international law does not at present recognise, apart from treaty, any fundamental rights of the individual protected by international society as against the State of which he is a national, it does acknowledge some of the principal fundamental rights of the individual in one particular sphere, namely, in respect of aliens. These are entitled to treatment conforming to a minimum standard of civilisation regardless of how the State where they reside treats its own nationals. That minimum standard of civilisation comprises, in particular, the right of personal liberty and, generally, the right to equality before the law. International tribunals have repeatedly declared it to be a rule of international law. The result, which is somewhat paradoxical, is that the individual in his capacity as an alien enjoys a larger measure of protection by international law than in his character as the citizen of his own State.

H. Lauterpacht, International Law and Human Rights 121 (1950; 1968).

A specification of the exact scope of the protection thus accorded to aliens by customary international law would require a comprehensive study of past decisions, value by value. Whether a particular differentiation of aliens and nationals has a reasonable basis in the common interest of the larger community must of course depend not only upon the value primarily at stake in the differentiation but also upon many particular, and varying, features of the context in which the differentiation is made. It is this infinite complexity in the patterning of fact, as well as the failure to clarify common interest, which accounts for some of the continuing controversy over particular kinds of deprivations of aliens, such as

The new epoch in the international protection of human rights ushered in by the United Nations has, paradoxically, been attended by some unnecessary confusion about the continued protection of aliens. The rapid multiplication of newly independent states, arising from the emancipation of ex-colonial peoples, and the deepening of ideological rifts about the world have brought intense challenges to many customary prescriptions, including those about the responsibility of states.[83] The principle of the minimum international standard for the protection of aliens has been subjected to especially severe attack. Thus, Mr. Padilla Nervo (Mexico) (later judge of the International Court of Justice), in reinforcement of traditional Latin American attitudes, spoke sharply before the International Law Commission:

> The vast majority of new States had taken no part in the creation of the many institutions of international law which were consolidated and systematized in the nineteenth century. In the case of the law of the sea, for instance, though the future needs and interests of

---

in the nationalization or expropriation of property and the unilateral termination of agreements. *See* note 13 *supra.* This controversy has recently been dramatized in the adoption by the U.N. General Assembly of the Declaration on the Establishment of a New International Economic Order and its accompanying Programme of Action in May 1974 and of the Charter of Economic Rights and Duties of States in Dec. 1974. *See* G.A. Res. 3201 (S-VI), May 1, 1974, U.N. GAOR, 6 Spec. Sess., Supp. (No. 1) 3, U.N. Doc. A/9559 (1974); G.A. Res. 3202 (S-VI), May 1, 1974, *id.* at 6; G.A. Res. 3281 (XXIX), Dec. 12, 1974, U.N. Doc. A/Res./3281 (XXIX) (1975). *See also* 13 I.L.M. 715 (1974); *id.* at 720; 14 *id.* 251 (1975); 68 AM. J. INT'L L. 798 (1974); 69 *id.* 484 (1975). For further pertinent references to this development, *see Recent Developments, The General Assembly's International Economics,* 16 HARV. INT'L L.J. 670 (1975). A panorama of conflicting views is offered in 3 THE VALUATION OF NATIONALIZED PROPERTY IN INTERNATIONAL LAW (R. Lillich ed. 1975).

83. *Cf. generally* ASIAN STATES AND THE DEVELOPMENT OF UNIVERSAL INTERNATIONAL LAW (R. Anand ed. 1972); A. BOZEMAN, THE FUTURE OF LAW IN A MULTICULTURAL WORLD (1971); L. CHEN, *supra* note 79; J. COHEN & H. CHIU, PEOPLE'S CHINA AND INTERNATIONAL LAW: A DOCUMENTARY STUDY (1974); W. FRIEDMANN, THE CHANGING STRUCTURE OF INTERNATIONAL LAW (1964); R. HIGGINS, CONFLICT OF INTEREST (1964); F. OKOYE, INTERNATIONAL LAW AND THE NEW AFRICAN STATES (1972); B. ROLING, INTERNATIONAL LAW IN AN EXPANDED WORLD (1960); S. SINHA, NEW NATIONS AND THE LAW OF NATIONS (1967); J. SYATAUW, SOME NEWLY ESTABLISHED STATES AND THE DEVELOPMENT OF INTERNATIONAL LAW (1961); G. TUNKIN, *supra* note 39; Castañeda, *The Underdeveloped Nations and the Development of International Law,* 15 INT'L ORG. 38 (1961); Falk, *A New Paradigm for International Legal Studies: Prospects and Proposals,* 84 YALE L.J. 969 (1975); Falk, *The New States and International Legal Order,* 118 HAGUE RECUEIL DES COURS 1 (1966); Fatouros, *International Law and the Third World,* 50 VA. L. REV. 783 (1964); Fatouros, *The Participation of the "New" States in the International Legal Order,* in 1 THE FUTURE OF THE INTERNATIONAL LEGAL ORDER 317–71 (R. Falk & C. Black eds. 1969); Guha-Roy, *Is the Law of Responsibility of States for Injuries to Aliens a Part of Universal International Law?* AM. J. INT'L L. 863 (1961), *reprinted in* L. GROSS, *supra* note 39, at 537–65; Lissitzyn, *International Law in a Divided World,* 542 INT'L CONCILIATION (1963); McDougal & Lasswell, *The Identification and Appraisal of Diverse Systems of Public Order,* 53 AM. J. INT'L L. 1 (1959), *reprinted in* L. GROSS, *supra* note 39, at 169–97.

> newly-established small countries were not taken into account, at least the body of principles thus created was not directly inimical to them. With State responsibility, however, international rules were established, not merely without reference to small States but against them, and were based almost entirely on the unequal relations between great Powers and small States. Probably ninety-five per cent of the international disputes involving State responsibility over the last century had been between a great industrial Power and a small, newly-established State. Such inequality of strength was reflected in an inequality of rights, the vital principle of international law, *par in parem non habet imperium* being completely disregarded. . . .[84]

A more detailed attack was made by S. N. Guha-Roy, who proposed a "thorough reexamination" of the customary law about the responsibility of states for injuries to aliens, "from the standpoint of the new states" and in the interest of an "absolute justice."[85] Building upon the assumption that "a custom [is] in no way binding on other states, unless it can be shown to have had its roots in some general principles of law of a more or less universal character,"[86] Guha-Roy has no difficulty in concluding that "the law of responsibility of states for aliens" is not a "part of universal international law":[87]

> The law of responsibility then, is not founded on any universal principles of law or morality. Its sole foundation is custom, which is binding only among states where it either grew up or came to be adopted. It is thus hardly possible to maintain that it is still part of universal international law. Whatever the basis of obligation in international law in the past, when the international community was restricted to only a few states, including those, fewer still, admitted into it from time to time, the birth of a new world community has brought about a radical change which makes the traditional basis of obligation outmoded.[88]

It should be obvious that from Guha-Roy's mystical assumption about how transnational expectations of authority are created, the same, or the opposite, conclusion could be made about any asserted prescription.[89]

---

84. [1957] 1 Y.B. Int'l. L. Comm'n 155 (remarks at the 413th mtg).
85. Guha-Roy, *supra* note 83, at 537–65.
86. *Id.* at 546.
87. *Id.* at 562.
88. *Id.*
89. Guha-Roy repeatedly makes clear that he regards "custom" and "general principles" as distinct and that his "general principles" are to be found only in some brooding metaphysical or "natural law" omnipresence. *See id.* at 539, 546, 550, 555.

The more substantive arguments Guha-Roy makes for dismissing "what is ordinarily presented as the international standard of justice" are stated in the form of "five objections":

> First, a national of one state, going out to another in search of wealth or for any other purpose entirely at his own risk, may well be left to the consequences of his own ventures, even in countries known to be dangerous. For international law to concern itself with his protection in a state without that state's consent amounts to an infringement of that state's sovereignty. Secondly, a standard open only to aliens but denied to a state's own citizens inevitably widens the gulf between citizens and aliens and thus hampers, rather than helps, free intercourse among peoples of different states. Thirdly, the standard is rather vague and indefinite. Fourthly, the very introduction of an external yardstick for the internal machinery of justice is apt to be looked upon as an affront to the national system, whether or not it is below the international standard. Fifthly, a different standard of justice for aliens results in a twofold differentiation in a state where the internal standard is below the international standard. Its citizens as aliens in other states are entitled to a higher standard than their fellow citizens at home. Again, the citizens of other states as aliens in it are also entitled to a better standard than its own citizens.[90]

These "objections" may be observed to ignore the role of the international standard in the maintenance of a world economy and society, to underestimate the interests of any particular territorial community in the maintenance of such larger economy and society, to minimize the importance of the international protection of the human rights of even citizens or nationals,[91] to undercut the vast flow across state lines today of prescriptive communication about the protection of both nationals and aliens, and to aggrandize the technical concepts of sovereignty and of territorial jurisdiction.

In the context of such confusion it is understandable that the International Law Commission has made little headway in its protracted effort to clarify and codify the law of state responsibility.[92] The first special

---

90. *Id.* at 563.

91. Even in this day of the human rights movement, Guha-Roy writes, "It is, however, no concern of international law how a state discharges its responsibility to its own nationals or if it discharges that responsibility at all." *Id.* at 538.

92. *See* Baxter, *Reflections on Codification in Light of the International Law of State Responsibility for Injuries to Aliens,* 16 SYRACUSE L. REV. 745 (1965); LILLICH, *Toward the Formulation of an Acceptable Body of Law Concerning State Responsibility, id.* at 721.

For an overall review, *see Garcia-Amador's Six Reports, supra* note 8. For more recent

rapporteur of the Commission, Dr. Garcia-Amador, essayed a noble "synthesis" of the newer emerging law of human rights and the older law designed for the protection of aliens in proposing both that the newer human rights prescriptions be employed to give more precise content to the inherited minimum international standard for aliens and that the newer remedies being established for the protection of human rights generally be made to supersede certain aspects of the hallowed state interposition on behalf of its injured nationals.[93] In eloquent diagnosis of the problem he stated:

> In traditional international law the "responsibility of States for damage done in their territory to the person or property of foreigners" frequently appears closely bound up with two great doctrines or principles: the so-called "international standards of justice," and the principle of the equality of nationals and aliens. The first of these principles has been invoked in the past as the basis for the exercise of the right of States to protect their nationals abroad, while the second has been relied on for the purpose of rebutting responsibility on the part of the State of residence when the aliens concerned received the same treatment and were granted the same legal or judicial protection as its own nationals.
>
> Although, therefore, both principles had the same basic purpose, namely, the protection of the person and of his property, they appeared both in traditional theory and in past practice as mutually conflicting and irreconcilable.
>
> Yet, if the question is examined in the light of international law in its present stage of development, one obtains a very different im-

---

developments, *see First Report on State Responsibility, by Mr. Roberto Ago, Special Rapporteur,* [1969] 2 Y.B. INT'L L. COMM'N 125–56, U.N. Doc. A/CN.4/217 and Add. 1 (1969) (it deals with "Review of previous work on codification of the topic of the international responsibility of States"); *Supplement, Prepared by the Secretariat, to the "Digest of the decisions of international tribunals relating to state responsibility,"* [1969] 2 Y.B. INT'L L. COMM'N 101–13, U.N. Doc. A/CN.4/208 (1969); *Proposals Submitted to, and Decisions of, Various United Nations Organs Relating to the Question of State Responsibility: Supplement Prepared by the Secretariat to Document A/CN.4/165,* [1969] 2 Y.B. INT'L L. COMM'N 114–24, U.N. Doc. A/CN.4/209 (1969); *Second Report on State Responsibility, by Mr. Roberto Ago, Special Rapporteur,* [1970] 2 Y.B. INT'L L. COMM'N 177–97, U.N. Doc. A/CN.4/233 (1970) ("The origin of international responsibility"). For a recent discussion on the question of state responsibility before the International Law Commission, *see* [1973] 1 Y.B. INT'L L. COMM'N 5–66 (1202d mtg. to 1215th mtg.). *See also* Kearney, *The Twenty-Sixth Session of the International Law Commission,* 69 AM. J. INT'L L. 591, 602–07 (1975).

The more recent work of the Commission has been at such a high level of abstraction as to shed but a dim light upon specific controversies. The underlying assumption seems to be that state responsibility is best studied apart from particular context.

93. *See Garcia-Amador's First Report, supra* note 8, at 199–203; Garcia-Amador, *supra* note 39, at 467.

> pression. What was formerly the object of these two principles—the protection of the person and of his property—is now intended to be accomplished by the international recognition of the essential rights of man. Under this new legal doctrine, the distinction between nationals and aliens no longer has any *raison d'être,* so that both in theory and in practice these two traditional principles are henceforth inapplicable. In effect, both of these principles appear to have been outgrown by contemporary international law.[94]

His basic proposal was for equality of nationals and aliens, with both a minimum and a maximum in internationally recognized "fundamental human rights":

> 1. The State is under a duty to ensure to aliens the enjoyment of the same civil rights, and to make available to them the same individual guarantees as are enjoyed by its own nationals. These rights and guarantees shall not, however, in any case be less than the "fundamental human rights" recognized and defined in contemporary international instruments.
> 2. In consequence, in case of violation of civil rights, or disregard of individual guarantees, with respect to aliens, international responsibility will be involved only if internationally recognized "fundamental human rights" are affected.[95]

The "fundamental human rights" he specified for framing the combined contours of state responsibility were extensive:

> (a) The right to life, liberty and security of person;
> (b) The right of the person to the inviolability of his privacy, home and correspondence, and to respect for his honour and reputation;
> (c) The right to freedom of thought, conscience and religion;
> (d) The right to own property;
> (e) The right of the person to recognition everywhere as a person before the law;
> (f) The right to apply to the courts of justice or to the competent organs of the State, by means of remedies and proceedings which offer adequate and effective redress for violations of the aforesaid rights and freedoms;
> (g) The right to a public hearing, with proper safeguards, by the

94. *Id.* at 199.
95. *Garcia-Amador's Second Report, supra* note 8, at 112–13.

competent organs of the State, in the determination of rights and obligations under civil law;

(h) In criminal matters, the right of the accused to be presumed innocent until proved guilty; the right to be informed of the charge made against him in a language which he understands; the right to speak in his defense or to be defended by a counsel of his choice; the right not to be convicted of any punishable offence on account of any act or omission which did not constitute an offence, under national or international law, at the time when it was committed; the right to be tried without delay or to be released.[96]

This imaginative proposal by Dr. Garcia-Amador has not, unhappily, enjoyed wide approval from either state spokesmen or private commentators. By some his proposal is thought to extend the substantive protection of aliens much beyond what states can reasonably be expected to accept and to exacerbate the problems of cooperation between states of differing degrees of socialization.[97] By others he might be thought, perhaps justifiably, to weaken an important traditional remedy for the protection of aliens before any effective new remedy is established in replacement.[98]

The newly emerged contemporary human rights prescriptions, including both the United Nations Charter and ancillary expressions, would indeed appear, however these prescriptions may ultimately be synthesized with the older doctrines of state responsibility, to have importantly increased the transnational protection that world constitutive process affords aliens.[99] Although nowhere in the Charter or other non-

---

96. *Id.* at 113.

97. C. Amerasinghe, *supra* note 39, at 278–81, I. Brownlie, *supra* note 7, at 513–14.

98. In the words of Amerasinghe:

> There is scope, then, for the application in practice of the general non-conventional law of alien treatment, in view of the absence of any universal conventional law to replace it, whether in regard to economic interests alone or in regard to personal and social interests as well. What is more, any general convention governing the responsibility of States for injuries to aliens must take into account the existing general non-conventional law.

C. Amerasinghe, *supra* note 39, at 7.

See Lillich, *The Diplomatic Protection of Nationals Abroad: An Elementary Principle of International Law under Attack,* 69 Am. J. Int'l L. 359 (1975).

99. In the words of Sir Humphrey Waldock:

> International lawyers have already begun to speak of the assimilation of the customary law regarding the treatment of aliens with the new law of the Charter regarding "universal respect for, and observance of, human rights." The assimilation is logical enough so far as concerns the "minimum standards" of treatment, that is, the scope of

discrimination prescriptions is alienage specifically included among the impermissible grounds of differentiation,[100] it is unmistakably clear that, in the future, differentiation of treatment because of alienage will be much more strictly confined and that unlawful discrimination, with respect to many values, may be much more readily found.

> the fundamental rights and freedoms protected by international law. Human Rights, *ex hypothesi,* are rights which attach to all human beings equally, whatever their nationality. And in general, as I have said, the Universal Declaration offers aliens at least as much as the minimum standards of treatment guaranteed under customary law. To assimilate the position of aliens to that of nationals in regard to remedies would, however, be wholly unacceptable in the present state of international remedies for violations of human rights.

Waldock, *Human Rights in Contemporary International Law and the Significance of the European Convention,* in THE EUROPEAN CONVENTION ON HUMAN RIGHTS 1, 3 (1965) (The British Institute of International and Comparative Law, International Law Series No. 5) (footnote omitted).

The protection of the rights of aliens is a matter of current concern within the United Nations. Pursuant to Res. 1790 (LIV) of May 18, 1973 of the Economic and Social Council, as originated from a resolution of the Sub-Commission on Prevention of Discrimination and Protection of Minorities in Aug. 1972 that was endorsed by the Commission on Human Rights, the U.N. secretary-general conducted in 1973 a "survey of international instruments in the field of human rights concerning distinctions in the enjoyment of certain rights as between nationals and individuals who are not citizens of the States in which they live." *See The Problem of the Applicability of Existing International Provisions for the Protection of the Human Rights of Individuals Who Are Not Citizens of the Country in Which They Live,* U.N. Doc. E/CN.4/Sub. 2/335 (1973) [hereinafter cited as *Note on Aliens by the Secretary-General*]. *Cf. also* Briggs, *The "Rights of Aliens" and International Protection of Human Rights,* in ASPECTS OF LIBERTY 213–31 (M. Konvitz & C. Rossiter eds. 1958); Freeman, *Human Rights and the Rights of Aliens,* 45 A.S.I.L. PROC. 120 (1951).

The distinction made by Weis between protection of the interests of states under the customary international law of state responsibility and the interests of the larger international community under the human rights prescriptions is an utterly artificial one, which should be made to disappear. *See* Weis, *Diplomatic Protection of Nationals and International Protection of Human Rights,* 4 HUMAN RIGHTS J. 643, 675 (1971).

100. *See* U.N. Charter, Arts. 1(3), 13(1)(b), 55(c), 56, 62(2), and 76(c); chapter 8 *supra.*

It has been suggested by a reader that the Universal Declaration of Human Rights, the International Covenant on Civil and Political Rights, and the International Covenant on Economic, Social, and Cultural Rights do not protect aliens because "nationality" is not listed as a prohibited ground of differentiation. This astonishing interpretation of these various prescriptions finds no basis even in the literal words of these prescriptions.

The Universal Declaration, in the first paragraph of Art. 2, provides:

> Everyone is entitled to all the rights and freedoms set forth in this Declaration, without distinction of any kind, such as race, colour, sex, language, religion, political or other opinion, national or social origin, property, birth or other status.

UNITED NATIONS, HUMAN RIGHTS: A COMPILATION OF INTERNATIONAL INSTRUMENTS OF THE UNITED NATIONS 1, U.N. Doc. ST/HR/1 (1973) [hereinafter cited as U.N. HUMAN RIGHTS INSTRUMENTS]. It will be noted that these words stipulate that "all the rights and freedoms" are conferred upon "everyone," and begin the list of prohibited grounds with

It may be recalled that though the United Nations Charter enumerates only four specific grounds of impermissible differentiation—race, sex, language, and religion—these are intended to be illustrative and not exhaustive. The more detailed formulation in the Universal Declaration

---

"such as," clearly indicating that the list is not intended to be exhaustive. A similar formulation appears in Art. 2(1) of the International Covenant on Civil and Political Rights:

> Each State Party to the present Covenant undertakes to respect and to ensure to *all individuals* within its territory and subject to its jurisdiction the rights recognized in the present Covenant, without *distinction* of any kind, *such as* race, colour, sex, language, religion, political or other opinion, national or social origin, property, birth or other status.

U.N. Human Rights Instruments, *supra,* at 8 (italics added). It has been generally recognized that one of the major purposes of the whole panoply of human rights prescriptions has been to accord the nationals of a state the same protection previously accorded aliens and to make unnecessary, in general, any differentiation between aliens and nationals. There is nothing in the legislative history (*travaux préparatoires*) of these prescriptions to suggest any intent to exclude aliens from protection.

The one possible exception to this conclusion is in the International Covenant on Economic, Social, and Cultural Rights, which is worded somewhat differently from the Covenant on Civil and Political Rights. Art. 2(2) reads:

> The States Parties to the present Covenant undertake to guarantee that the rights enunciated in the present Covenant will be exercised without *discrimination* of any kind *as to* race, colour, sex, language, religion, political or other opinion, national or social origin, property, birth or other status.

U.N. Human Rights Instruments, *supra,* at 4 (italics added). Note the substitution of "discrimination" for "distinction" and the substitution of "as to" for "such as." Art. 2(3) adds:

> Developing countries, with due regard to human rights and their national economy, may determine to what extent they would guarantee the economic rights recognized in the present Covenant to non-nationals.

U.N. Human Rights Instruments, *supra,* at 4. These provisions could, unfortunately for the common interest, be construed as permitting some states to discriminate against aliens with respect to some economic rights. It has been recorded that Art. 2(3) was adopted by the Third Committee of the General Assembly by "41 votes to 38, with 12 abstentions," and that it was characterized by many delegates as "contrary to the spirit of universality and equality underlying the draft Covenant and likely to give rise to all kinds of discrimination alien to the intentions of the sponsors." Sohn, *Supplementary Paper: A Short History of United Nations Documents on Human Rights,* in Commission to Study the Organization of Peace, The United Nations and Human Rights 38, 116 (1968). The ambiguities in the language of Art. 2(2,3) are spelled out in *Note on Aliens by the Secretary-General, supra* note 99, at 8–11.

It may be noted, incidentally, that the International Covenant on Economic, Social, and Cultural Rights has been operative since Jan. 3, 1976. 12 U.N. Monthly Chronicle 28 (Nov. 1975). Similarly, the International Covenant on Civil and Political Rights has been operative since Mar. 23, 1976. 13 *id.* 73 (Jan. 1976).

of Human Rights makes this abundantly clear.[101] The standard formula employed by the Universal Declaration is "Everyone has the right to . . ."[102] Negatively, the formula is "No one shall be . . ."[103] "Everyone" would appear to refer to all human beings, national and alien alike. When "everyone" is given a restrictive reference to a national only, the Universal Declaration makes this explicitly clear. Thus, Article 21 provides in part:

> 1. Everyone has the right to take part in the government of his country, directly or through freely chosen representatives.
> 2. Everyone has the right of equal access to public service in his country.[104]

This is the only place in the Universal Declaration that a specified right is reserved for nationals only.[105] This provision reflects only the long-shared community expectation that differentiation on the basis of alienage is permissible in regard to participation in the making of community decisions, i.e., voting and officeholding.[106] The concern in the Universal Declaration that human rights be protected for every human being, regardless of nationality, is further manifested in the latter half of Article 2: "Furthermore, no distinction shall be made on the basis of the political, jurisdictional or international status of the country or territory to which a person belongs, whether it be independent, trust, non-self-governing or under any other limitation of sovereignty."[107]

This same concern for all human beings is even more pronounced in the International Covenant on Civil and Political Rights. This Covenant

---

101. *See Note on Aliens by the Secretary-General, supra* note 99, at 7.

102. *E.g.,* Art. 3: "Everyone has the right to life, liberty and the security of person"; Art. 10: "Everyone is entitled in full equality to a fair and public hearing by an independent and impartial tribunal, in the determination of his rights and obligations and of any criminal charge against him." U.N. HUMAN RIGHTS INSTRUMENTS, *supra* note 100, at 1. *See also* Arts. 2, 6, 8, 11(1), 13, 14, 15(1), 17(1), 18, 19, 20(1), 21, 22, 23, 24, 26(1), 27, 28, 29(1), in *id.* at 1–3.

103. *E.g.,* Art. 5: "No one shall be subjected to torture or to cruel, inhuman or degrading treatment or punishement"; Art. 17(2): "No one shall be arbitrarily deprived of his property." *Id.* at 1–2. *See also* Arts. 4, 9, 11(2), 12, 15(2), 20(2), *id.*

104. *Id.*

105. Art. 13(2) of the Universal Declaration provides that "Everyone has the right to leave any country, including his own, and to return to *his* country." The right to return thus purports to extend only to nationals. Conversely, the asylum provision, Art. 14(1) of the Universal Declaration, that "Everyone has the right to seek and to enjoy in other countries asylum from persecution" is obviously intended for nonnationals.

106. *See* H. SANTA CRUZ, STUDY OF DISCRIMINATION IN THE MATTER OF POLITICAL RIGHTS 26–27, U.N. Doc. E/CN.4/Sub. 2/213/Rev. 1 (1962).

107. U.N. HUMAN RIGHTS INSTRUMENTS, *supra* note 100, at 1.

again employs, in general, the formulae "Everyone shall have the right to . . ."[108] and "No one shall be . . ."[109] Reference is clearly to every person, national or alien. Where distinction is intended between nationals and aliens, the Covenant is explicit. Thus, Article 25 provides:

> Every citizen shall have the right and the opportunity, without any of the distinctions mentioned in article 2 and without unreasonable restrictions:
>
> (a) To take part in the conduct of public affairs, directly or through freely chosen representatives;
>
> (b) To vote and to be elected at genuine periodic elections which shall be held by secret ballot, guaranteeing the free expression of the will of the electors;
>
> (c) To have access, on general terms of equality, to public service in his country.[110]

The wording "every citizen" instead of "everyone" is significant. Again, this prescription is in deference to and expressive of the customary law that permits exclusion of aliens from participation in voting and officeholding. Similarly, Article 12(4) provides: "No one shall be arbitrarily deprived of the right to enter his own country."[111] When a prescription concerns aliens only, it is thus made clear. Article 13 reads:

> An alien lawfully in the territory of a State Party to the present Covenant may be expelled therefrom only in pursuance of a decision reached in accordance with law and shall, except where compelling reasons of national security otherwise require, be allowed to submit the reasons against his expulsion and to have his case reviewed by, and be represented for the purpose before, the competent authority or a person or persons especially designated by the competent authority.[112]

---

108. *E.g.*, Art. 19(1): "Everyone shall have the right to hold opinions without interference." *Id.* at 11. *See also* Arts. 9(1), 14(2,3,5), 16, 17(2), 18(1), 19(2), 22(1), *id.* at 9–11. In addition, the Covenant on Civil and Political Rights employs such subjects as "Every human being" (Art. 6[1]), "Anyone" (Art. 9[2–5]), and "All persons" (Arts. 10[1], 14[1], and 26). *Id.* at 9–11.

109. *E.g.*, Art. 11: "No one shall be imprisoned merely on the ground of inability to fulfil a contractual obligation." *Id.* at 9. *See also* Arts. 7, 8, 14(7), 15(1), 17(1), 18(2). *Id.* at 9–11.

110. *Id.* at 11.

111. *Id.* at 10.

112. *Id.* The overriding goal for the protection of every human being, as enunciated in the International Covenant on Civil and Political Rights, is unequivocably reiterated in the Optional Protocol to this Covenant. Thus, Art. 1 of the Optional Protocol reads:

In the International Covenant on Economic, Social, and Cultural Rights the rights protected are again designed for all human beings, irrespective of nationality.[113] Thus, the Covenant stipulates that the states parties "recognize the right of everyone to" "work,"[114] have "the enjoyment of just and favourable conditions of work,"[115] "form trade unions and join the trade union of his choice,"[116] have "social security,"[117] have "an adequate standard of living,"[118] "be free from hunger,"[119] have "the enjoyment of the highest attainable standard of physical and mental health,"[120] obtain "education,"[121] "take part in cultural life,"[122] and so on.

Even human rights conventions with a more restrictive focus are, again, formulated generally in terms of every individual human being. When alienage becomes relevant, it appears clear from each particular context.[123] Special attention may be called to Article 1(2) of the International Convention on the Elimination of Racial Discrimination, which

---

> A State Party to the Covenant that becomes a party to the present Protocol recognizes the competence of the Committee to receive and consider communications from individuals subject to its jurisdiction who claim to be victims of a violation by that State Party of any of the rights set forth in the Covenant. No communication shall be received by the Committee if it concerns a State Party to the Covenant which is not a party to the present Protocol.

Id. at 16. The protection and remedies are clearly extended to all "individuals subject to jurisdiction" of a contracting state, and not only those who possess its nationality.

113. It is clear that in this particular Covenant a state may differentiate treatment of aliens from nationals upon a reasonable basis. This is very far from providing that a state may discriminate against aliens. The reference, in Art. 2(3), that "Developing countries, with due regard to human rights and their national economy, may determine to what extent they would guarantee the economic rights recognized in the present Covenant to non-nationals" would be totally unnecessary if states may generally discriminate against aliens. For expressions of more tentative conclusions, *see Note on Aliens by the Secretary-General, supra* note 99, at 8–11; Elles, *supra* note 1, at 308–09.

114. Art 6(1), U.N. HUMAN RIGHTS INSTRUMENTS, *supra* note 100, at 4.

115. Art. 7, *id.*

116. Art. 8(1)(a), *id.*

117. Art. 9, *id.*

118. Art. 11(1), *id.* at 5.

119. Art. 11(2), *id.*

120. Art. 12, *id.*

121. Art. 13(1), *id.*

122. Art. 15(1), *id.* at 6.

123. *See, e.g.,* Art. 3(e) of the Convention against Discrimination in Education: "In order to eliminate and prevent discrimination within the meaning of this Convention, the States Parties thereto undertake: . . . (e) To give foreign nationals resident within their territory the same access to education as that given to their own nationals." *Id.* at 31–32. *Cf. also* Art. 3(c) of the same Convention, *id.* at 31; Declaration on the Elimination of Discrimination against Women, Art. 5, *id.* at 39; Convention Relating to the Status of Stateless Persons, Art. 3, *id.* at 61; Convention Relating to the Status of Refugees, Art. 3, *id.* at 68.

reads: "This Convention shall not apply to distinctions, exclusions, restrictions or preferences made by a State Party to this Convention between citizens and non-citizens."[124] In the light of the major purposes of the Convention and the relevant context, it would appear clear that this provision was intended only to reserve to states a competence to continue to make the historic differentiations between aliens and nationals established as reasonable under customary international law. It was not intended as an oblique, new prescription that alienage is in general a permissible ground of discrimination.[125] Differentiation on the basis of alienage in regard to such matters as voting and officeholding, as customarily accepted, continues to be permissible, but the standard of treatment accorded to aliens, as established under customary international law and the contemporary human rights law with respect to other values, is not to be diluted.[126]

The two regional human rights conventions—European and American—are both cast in broad language designed to protect aliens as well as nationals. The European Convention, in Article 1, provides: "The High Contracting Parties shall secure to *everyone within their jurisdiction* the rights and freedoms defined in Section I of this Convention."[127] Thus, the European Commission on Human Rights has over the years received innumerable individual petitions ("applications") brought by nonnationals resident in the member states of the Council of Europe.[128]

---

124. *Id.* at 24. The appropriate interpretation of this language in the light of the major purposes of the Convention and the absence of *travaux* to the contrary is that states may continue to differentiate between aliens and nationals on the bases that historically have been regarded as having a reasonable relation to their differences. This means, as was the principal thrust of the Convention for all individuals, that states may not discriminate against aliens on racial grounds.

It may further be noted that Art. 1(3) of this Convention provides: "Nothing in this Convention may be interpreted as affecting in any way the legal provisions of States Parties concerning nationality, citizenship or naturalization, provided that such provisions do not discriminate against any particular nationality."

125. *Cf.* Schwelb, *The International Convention on the Elimination of All Forms of Racial Discrimination,* 15 INT'L & COMP. L.Q. 996, 1006–09 (1966); *Note on Aliens by the Secretary-General, supra* note 99, at 16–17.

126. *See* Schwelb, *supra* note 125, at 1007–08. *Cf. also Note on Aliens by the Secretary-General, supra* note 99, at 16.

For an exposition of other prescriptions relevant to aliens, *see Note on Aliens by the Secretary-General, supra* at 18–35. *See also* Elles, *supra* note 1; Weis, *supra* note 99.

127. COUNCIL OF EUROPE, EUROPEAN CONVENTION ON HUMAN RIGHTS: COLLECTED TEXTS 2 (9th ed. 1974) (italics added). Its text can also be conveniently found in BASIC DOCUMENTS ON INTERNATIONAL PROTECTION OF HUMAN RIGHTS 125 (L. Sohn & T. Buergenthal eds. 1973) [hereinafter cited as BASIC DOCUMENTS]; and in BASIC DOCUMENTS ON HUMAN RIGHTS 338, 340 (I. Brownlie ed. 1971).

128. For recent statistical data, *see* McNulty, *Stock-Taking on the European Convention on Human Rights* 59–61, Doc. DH(73)8 (1973); McNulty, *Stock-Taking on the European Conven-*

The significance of this jurisprudence and practice has been underlined by Fawcett:

> This marks the great departure taken by the Convention from traditional forms of the international protection of individuals, for it dispenses with nationality as a condition of protection. Each contracting State undertakes to secure the rights and freedoms of Section I to everyone within its jurisdiction, whether he or she is an alien, a national of the State, or a stateless person, and regardless of civil status.[129]

In keeping with the human rights conventions on the global scale, the European Convention, in referring to a specified right, employs the general formulae "Everyone has the right to . . ."[130] and that "No one shall be . . ."[131]

The same interpretation would appear equally applicable to the American Convention on Human Rights. Significantly, the American Convention contains, in the Preamble, the unique proclamation that "the

---

tion on Human Rights 66–69, Doc. DH(74) 6 (Oct. 1, 1974) [hereinafter cited as *McNulty's Stock-Taking 1974*].

129. J. Fawcett, The Application of the European Convention on Human Rights 18 (1969).

130. *See, e.g.,* Arts. 5, 6, 8, 9, 10, 11, 13, Basic Documents, *supra* note 127, at 126–30.

131. *See, e.g.,* Arts. 3, 4, 7, *id.* at 126, 128.

Art. 14 of the European Convention on Human Rights reads: "The enjoyment of the rights and freedoms set forth in this Convention shall be secured without discrimination on any ground such as sex, race, colour, language, religion, political or other opinion, national or social origin, association with a national minority, property, birth or other status." *Id.* at 130. It will be noted, again, that the list of prohibited grounds begins with "such as," which clearly indicates that the list is merely illustrative. *Cf.* note 100 *supra.*

When the Convention intends to permit restrictions upon aliens, it explicitly says so. Thus, Art. 16 stipulates: "Noting in Articles 10, 11 and 14 shall be regarded as preventing the High Contracting Parties from imposing restrictions on the political activity of aliens." *Id.* at 130. Similarly, Protocol No. 4 to the Convention, in Arts. 3 and 4, makes explicit the distinction between nationals and aliens. Art. 3 reads:

> 1. No one shall be expelled, by means either of an individual or of a collective measure, from the territory of the State of which he is a national.
>
> 2. No one shall be deprived of the right to enter the territory of the State of which he is a national.

Id. at 146. Art. 4 states: "Collective expulsion of aliens is prohibited." *Id.*

The fact that an individual is an alien may of course be a relevant variable in contexts in which states engage in permissible accommodations and derogations, as provided in Arts. 8–11 and 15 of the European Convention. *Id.* at 128–30. This does not mean that alienage per se is a permissible ground for discrimination; it means only that alienage continues to be in some contexts a fact that may rationally be taken into account in determining the necessity and proportionality of a differentiation.

essential rights of man are not derived from one's being a national of a certain state, but are based upon attributes of the human personality."[132] The Convention thus specifies in Article 1:

> 1. The States Parties to this Convention undertake to respect the rights and freedoms recognized herein and to ensure to all persons subject to their jurisdiction the free and full exercise of those rights and freedoms, without any discrimination for reasons of race, color, sex, language, religion, political or other opinion, national or social origin, economic status, birth, or any other social condition.
> 2. For the purposes of this Convention, "person" means every human being.[133]

In regard to each of the specific rights to be protected, the Convention has employed the standard formulae "Every person (or "everyone") has the right to . . ."[134] and "No one shall be . . ."[135] When reference is confined to aliens, it is explicitly stated. Thus, Article 22(6) reads: "An alien lawfully in the territory of a State Party to this Convention may be expelled from it only pursuant to a decision reached in accordance with law."[136] Article 22(8) stipulates:

> In no case may an alien be deported or returned to a country, regardless of whether or not it is his country of origin, if in that country his right to life or personal freedom is in danger of being violated because of his race, nationality, religion, social status, or political opinions.[137]

Article 22(9) also reads: "The collective expulsion of aliens is prohibited."[138] In contrast, when reference is restricted to nationals, it is also clearly stated. Thus, Article 22(5) reads: "No one can be expelled from the territory of the state of which he is a national or be deprived of the right to enter it."[139] Similarly, Article 23 provides:

---

132. *Id.* at 209.

133. *Id.* at 210.

The Charter of the Organization of American States, as amended, states in Art. 3(j) that the "American States proclaim the fundamental rights of the individual without distinction as to race, nationality, creed, or sex." A. PEASLEE, INTERNATIONAL GOVERNMENTAL ORGANIZATIONS 1182, 1183 (rev. 3d ed. 1974).

134. *See, e.g.,* Arts. 3, 4(1), 5(1), 7(1), 8, 10, 11, 12(1), 13(1), 16(1), 18, 20, 21(1), 22(1)(2), 25(1), BASIC DOCUMENTS, *supra* note 127, at 210–18.

135. *See, e.g.,* Arts. 5(2), 6, 7(2)(3), 9, 11(2), 12(2), 21(2), *id.* at 211–17.

136. *Id.* at 217.

137. *Id.* at 217–18.

138. *Id.* at 218.

139. *Id.* at 217.

1. Every citizen shall enjoy the following rights and opportunities:
   a. to take part in the conduct of public affairs, directly or through freely chosen representatives;
   b. to vote and to be elected in genuine periodic elections, which shall be by universal and equal suffrage and by secret ballot that guarantees the free expression of the will of the voters; and
   c. to have access, under general conditions of equality, to the public service of his country.
2. The law may regulate the exercise of the rights and opportunities referred to in the preceding paragraph only on the basis of age, nationality, residence, language, education, civil and mental capacity, or sentencing by a competent court in criminal proceedings.[140]

In sum, the principal thrust of the contemporary human rights movement is to accord nationals the same protection formerly accorded only to aliens, while at the same time raising the standard of protection for all human beings, nationals as well as aliens, far beyond the minimum international standard developed under the earlier customary law.[141] When the new human rights prescriptions are considered in mass, they extend to all the basic human dignity values the peoples of the world today demand, and the more detailed standards specified with regard to each of these values exhibit all the precision and definiteness that rational application either permits or requires. The consequence is thus, as Dr. Garcia-Amador insisted, that continuing debate about the doctrines of the minimum international standard and equality of treatment has now become highly artificial;[142] an international standard is now authoritatively prescribed for all human beings. It does not follow, however, that these new developments in substantive prescription about human rights have rendered obsolete the protection of individuals through the traditional procedures developed by the customary law of the responsibility of states for injuries to aliens.

The notion, popularized by Vattel, that an injury to an alien individual is an injury also to the state of his nationality served as justification for

---

140. *Id.* at 218.

141. *See* notes 99–140 *supra* and accompanying text.

This conclusion might be reinforced by a comprehensive comparative study of internal constitutional developments about the world which create transnational expectations of authority. For development within the United States, *see* Gordon, *supra* note 16. *See also* the other works cited in notes 14 and 16 *supra.*

142. F. Garcia-Amador, L. Sohn, & R. Baxter, *supra* note 8, at 1–5; *Garcia-Amador's First Report, supra* note 8, at 199–203.

the protection of the interests both of the state and of an important category of individuals in an epoch when the nation-state was often regarded as "the exclusive and sole subject" of international law. Even in a time, however, when more catholic conceptions of the subjects of international law prevail and individuals are being given more direct access to authoritative arenas for their self-protection, the historic remedy of state claim for the protection of the individual would not appear to have ceased to serve the common interest.[143] Rather, the traditional channels of protection through a state,[144] together with the newly developed procedures under the contemporary human rights program of claim by individuals,[145] would appear to achieve a cumulative beneficent impact, each reinforcing the other, in the defense and fulfillment of the human rights of the individual. In recent times, individuals have in fact gained, for remedy of deprivations, either direct or derivative access to some transnational arenas of authoritative decision, such as the U.N. Commission on Human Rights (through the Sub-Commission on Prevention of Discrimination and Protection of Minorities),[146] the Commit-

---

143. The disappearance of the notion that states are the only appropriate subjects of international law need not becloud the fact of effective power that individuals sometimes need the support of their states to secure appropriate remedies against states and other entities.

For comprehensive and persuasive development of this theme, *see* Lillich, *supra* note 98. *See also* Jessup, *Non-Universal International Law,* 12 COLUM. J. TRANSNAT'L L. 415 (1973).

144. Koessler observed that "the gist of the institution of diplomatic protection" lies "in its remedial aspect rather than in the substantive character of the interest involved." "It is not," he continues, "because the protecting state feels offended by the wrong done to one of its nationals, but in order to give the latter a workable substitute for the inaccessibility of an international forum, that the strong arm of the government is extended to the private interest. . . ." Koessler, *supra* note 40, at 181.

145. *See generally* J. CAREY, U.N. PROTECTION OF CIVIL AND POLITICAL RIGHTS (1970); E. HAAS, HUMAN RIGHTS AND INTERNATIONAL ACTION (1970); M. MOSKOWITZ, INTERNATIONAL CONCERN WITH HUMAN RIGHTS (1974); C. NORGAARD, THE POSITION OF THE INDIVIDUAL IN INTERNATIONAL LAW (1962); A. ROBERTSON, HUMAN RIGHTS IN THE WORLD (1972); UNITED NATIONS, UNITED NATIONS ACTION IN THE FIELD OF HUMAN RIGHTS, U.N. Doc. ST/HR/2 (1974); V. VAN DYKE, HUMAN RIGHTS, THE UNITED STATES, AND WORLD COMMUNITY 159–254 (1970); J. Jefferies, The Individual and International Law, 1954 (unpublished J.S.D. dissertation, Yale Law School); Capotorti, *The International Measures of Implementation Included in the Covenants of Human Rights,* in INTERNATIONAL PROTECTION OF HUMAN RIGHTS 131–48 (A. Eide & A. Schou eds. 1968); Golsong, *Implementation of International Protection of Human Rights,* 110 HAGUE RECUEIL DES COURS 7 (1963); Humphrey, *The International Law of Human Rights in the Middle Twentieth Century,* in THE PRESENT STATE OF INTERNATIONAL LAW AND OTHER ESSAYS 75–105 (M. Bos ed. 1973); Korey, *The Key to Human Rights Implementation,* 570 INT'L CONCILIATION (Nov. 1968); Schwelb, *Civil and Political Rights: The International Measures of Implementation,* 62 AM. J. INT'L L. 827 (1968); Schwelb, *Notes on the Early Legislative History of the Measures of Implementation of the Human Rights Covenants,* in MÉLANGES OFFERTS À POLYS MODINOS 270–89 (1968).

146. *See* L. SOHN & T. BUERGENTHAL, INTERNATIONAL PROTECTION OF HUMAN RIGHTS 739–856 (1973); UNITED NATIONS ACTION IN THE FIELD OF HUMAN RIGHTS, *supra* note 145,

tee on the Elimination of Racial Discrimination,[147] the European Commission on Human Rights,[148] and the Inter-American Commission on

---

at 177–84; Carey, *Progress on Human Rights at the UN,* 66 AM. J. INT'L L. 107 (1972); Cassese, *The Admissibility of Communications to the UN on Human Rights Violations,* 5 HUMAN RIGHTS J. 375 (1972); Hoare, *The UN Commission on Human Rights,* in THE INTERNATIONAL PROTECTION OF HUMAN RIGHTS 59–98 (E. Luard ed. 1967); Humphrey, *The Right of Petition in the UN,* 4 HUMAN RIGHTS J. 463 (1971); Humphrey, *The United Nations Commission on Human Rights and Its Parent Body,* in 1 RENÉ CASSIN, AMICORUM DISCIPULORUMQUE LIBER 108–13 (1969); Newman, *The New U.N. Procedures for Human Rights Complaints: Reform, Status Quo, or Chambers of Horror?* in *Hearings on International Protection of Human Rights before the Subcomm. on International Organizations and Movements of the House Comm. of Foreign Affairs,* 93d Cong., 1st Sess. 715–22 (1974); Schwelb, *Complaints by Individuals to the Commission on Human Rights: 25 Years of an Uphill Struggle (1947–1971),* in THE CHANGING INTERNATIONAL COMMUNITY 119–39 (C. Boasson & M. Nurock eds. 1973); Van Boven, *The United Nations Commission on Human Rights and Violations of Human Rights and Fundamental Freedoms,* 15 NEDERLANDS TIJDSCHRIFT VOOR INTERNATIONAAL RECHT 374 (1968).

147. The International Convention on the Elimination of All Forms of Racial Discrimination provides for individual petitions in Art. 14, the first paragraph of which reads as follows:

> A State Party may at any time declare that it recognizes the competence of the Committee to receive and consider communications from individuals or groups of individuals within its jurisdiction claiming to be victims of a violation by that State Party of any of the rights set forth in this Convention. No communication shall be received by the Committee if it concerns a State Party which has not made such a declaration.

U.N. HUMAN RIGHTS INSTRUMENTS, *supra* note 100, at 23, 27. The competence of the Committee regarding individual petitions is made operative "only when at least ten States Parties" have made the requisite declarations of acceptance. Art. 14 (9), *id.* at 28. This condition has to date not been fulfilled.

See chapter 9 *supra,* at notes 250–84 and accompanying text. *See also* N. LERNER, THE UN CONVENTION ON THE ELIMINATION OF ALL FORMS OF RACIAL DISCRIMINATION 83–99 (1970); Reisman, *Responses to Crimes of Discrimination and Genocide: An Appraisal of the Convention on the Elimination of Racial Discrimination,* 1 DENVER J. INT'L L. & POLICY 29, 58–64 (1971); Schwelb, *supra* note 125, at 1031–59.

148. *See* European Convention on Human Rights, Arts. 25–32, BASIC DOCUMENTS, *supra* note 127, at 132–34.

See also R. BEDDARD, HUMAN RIGHTS AND EUROPE 50–85 (1973); F. CASTBERG, THE EUROPEAN CONVENTION ON HUMAN RIGHTS 34–67 (1974); COUNCIL OF EUROPE, THE EUROPEAN CONVENTION ON HUMAN RIGHTS 11–16 (1968); A. DEL RUSSO, INTERNATIONAL PROTECTION OF HUMAN RIGHTS 68–121 (1971); J. FAWCETT, *supra* note 129, at 277–322; C. MORRISSON, THE DEVELOPING EUROPEAN LAW OF HUMAN RIGHTS 60–98 (1967); A. ROBERTSON, HUMAN RIGHTS IN EUROPE 49–74 (1963); A. ROBERTSON, *supra* note 145, at 51–110; L. SOHN & T. BUERGENTHAL, *supra* note 146, at 1008–50, 1091–99; G. WEIL, THE EUROPEAN CONVENTION ON HUMAN RIGHTS 90–143 (1963); Golsong, *The Control Machinery of the European Convention on Human Rights,* in THE EUROPEAN CONVENTION ON HUMAN RIGHTS, *supra* note 99, at 38–69; McNulty, *The Operation and Effectiveness of the European Convention on Human Rights,* 3 U. SAN FRANCISCO L. REV. 228 (1969); *McNulty's Stock-Taking 1974,* note 128 *supra;* Schwelb, *On the Operation of the European Convention on Human Rights,* 18 INT'L ORG. 558 (1964); Waldock, *The European Convention for the Protection of Human Rights and Fundamental Freedoms,* 34 BRIT. Y.B. INT'L L. 356 (1958). *Cf. 25th Anniversary of the European Convention on Human Rights,* 8 HUMAN RIGHTS J. 325 (1975).

Human Rights;[149] and such access promises to increase significantly in the future, especially as the Optional Protocol to the International Covenant on Civil and Political Rights comes into operation.[150] Yet the prospect of further direct access by individuals to authoritative arenas, though encouraging, remains far from adequate. As long as states remain the most important and most effective participants in transnational processes of decision, espousal of claims by states for deprivations suffered by individuals would appear indispensable to full protection. Remedy through claim by a protecting state and through individual petition need not be mutually incompatible; they can be made to reinforce each other for the better defense and fulfillment of the human rights of the individual.[151]

THE FUTURE OF PROTECTION

The future development of the world community will provide the context the characteristics of which are decisive for the conception of an alien and therefore for all prescriptions that relate to "protection" or "discrimination." In political terms an alien is an outsider, a nonmember of the state whose policies are under consideration. As we have seen, it has long been regarded as permissible for state policy to erect certain

---

149. *See* A. Schreiber, The Inter-American Commission on Human Rights 41–56 (1970); Secretariat of the Inter-American Commission on Human Rights, The Organization of American States and Human Rights, 1960–1967, at 10–11, 36–39, 52–54 (1972); Buergenthal, *The Revised OAS Charter and the Protection of Human Rights,* 69 Am. J. Int'l L. 828 (1975).

150. The Optional Protocol to the International Covenant on Civil and Political Rights provides for individual petitions ("communications from individuals") and related procedures to make the protection stipulated in the Covenant more effective. It was adopted and opened for signature, ratification, and accession under U.N. General Assembly Res. 2200A (XXI) of Dec. 16, 1966, along with the two Covenants. For its text, *see* U.N. Human Rights Instruments, *supra* note 100, at 15–17. The Optional Protocol has already received more than the ten ratifications or accessions needed for becoming operative. *See* E. Schwelb, *Entry into Force of the International Covenants on Human Rights and the Optional Protocol to the International Covenant on Civil and Political Rights,* 70 Am. J. Int'l L. 511 (1976).

For detailed elaboration, *see* chapter 4 *supra,* at notes 79–144, 372–423, and accompanying text.

151. *Cf.* the appendix *infra,* at notes 474–82 and accompanying text.

It has often been alleged, perhaps with some accuracy, that the doctrine of responsibility of states has been abused. Insofar as these complaints are appropriately directed to the use of force as a means of self-help ("the gunboat policy"), they may be justified. Insofar as they relate to third-party decision making, they have no validity. In the words of Lillich: "While it is true that 'the ideas of justice and fair dealing incorporated in the accepted norms of conduct for European nations were carried over into the wider sphere of the international society of the nineteenth century,' there is no need to apologize for attempting to establish a universal consensus behind justice and fair dealing." Lillich, *Forcible Self-Help by States to Protect Human Rights,* 53 Iowa L. Rev. 325, 327–28 (1967).

barriers against nonmembers. At the same time various limitations have been applied to discriminatory activity. Sharply contrasting policies and factual circumstances have tended to sustain ambiguities of legal doctrine in regard to aliens. In preceding sections we have demonstrated how these ambiguities can be coped with on behalf of preferred policy. Questions remain about the probable future interplay of fact and doctrine in this significant area.

If we extend current trends into the future, the prediction is warranted that, after an interval in which the protection of aliens remains in jeopardy, the direction of evolution will change as many conditioning factors that sustain discrimination are weakened. We refer, for example, to the jeopardy in which individuals and corporations often find themselves in former colonial countries. Up to this time, policies of discrimination have not exhausted the reservoirs of resentment that accumulated during the period of colonial subordination and of post-colonial disappointment with the immediate fruits of independence. The initiative will continue to be taken by members of the national elite who are seeking to supplant alien interests in order to consolidate control by local capitalists. Where socialist ideology is strong, the active mobilizers of anti-alien sentiment are typically recruited from among the political elites whose members are determined to do away with and to preclude outside competition for effective control of national resources. Whether the anti-alien leaders are entirely political, or constitute a coalition of political and economic forces, their strategy will be to keep alive among the rank and file of the population the sentiments that enabled the anti-imperialist, pro-independence movement to succeed.

As time passes, many changes are likely to occur in the strength of the factors that support extremist measures against aliens. It will be increasingly evident to widening circles of leaders and the led that an unlimited anti-alien policy does not yield net advantages; that, in fact, in their own history there never was a totally anti-alien policy. Concessions are typically made at successive stages of an independence movement to foreign interests from which political, economic, and other forms of assistance were (and are) sought. These adjustments may be made to rival socialist or liberal, totalitarian or moderate, blocs. The stronger powers among former colonies also find themselves granting assistance to weaker members of the successor communities and insisting that reciprocal obligations be lived up to. In this way they reinstate the confrontations that originally led the stronger states to follow a policy inspired by Vattel (which, of course, they did not need to learn from a scholar). If the stronger among the successor powers share a common ideological orientation, synonyms will be used in order to avoid stigmatizing a fellow ideologist as an "alien." Since the external relations of every successor power are not likely to be entirely restricted to an ideological bloc, situations can be expected to arise in which the traditional language of international law will seem more effective than alternatives.

Many occasions for advancing claims on behalf of aliens will be but trivially related to economic affairs. The emerging code of human rights provides a set of standards that apply to every sector of human interaction. If we postulate that global connections will continue to gain intensity, emerging networks of association will cover more people, more localities, and more pluralization. To an increasing extent the protection of aliens will be taken for granted.

If we accept the scenario of accelerating interdependence, we must be prepared for a zigzag evolution of policies toward nonmembers of the principal bodies politic. A key problem is whether the major political divisions of the globe will contine to be perceived by enough influential members as a sufficiently important means by which net advantages can be obtained at the expense of nonmembers. It is reasonable to assume that coalitions will arise which expect to reap benefits from governmental policies that impose substantial deprivations on nonmembers. Such expectation will take advantage of the reappearance of conditioning factors that have fostered these results in the past. Lurking in the background of individuals who have not been socialized to identify fully with the world community is "fear of the stranger"; and this fear is often focused on nonmembers of the principal body politic (the state). From one situation to the other, an "alien" may be stigmatized with every identifying symbol that has a negative cathexis (racial, religious, and so on). Recent environmental circumstances may have contributed to the level of unrest generated by realized or anticipated value deprivations (political, economic, and so on). Impulses that contribute to unrest are available for displacement on such public targets as aliens. In our interactive world it is to be assumed that counterpolicies will be mobilized on behalf of the alien. In consequence, extremes of policy may be mitigated while expectations are strengthened that the prescriptive code that requires the protection of aliens is, indeed, enforceable. Barring drastic contingencies, the probability is that the code of human rights will be progressively refined in harmony with the policies necessary to protect aliens as full members of the world community.

15. THE PROTECTION OF THE AGED FROM DISCRIMINATION

FACTUAL BACKGROUND

The concept of human dignity covers the entire span of life. The deprivations to which this chapter addresses itself are those imposed upon individuals because of advanced chronological age.[1] Though the plight of the elderly varies from community to community and from culture to culture,[2] the deprivations, consciously or unconsciously imposed upon

---

In slightly different form this chapter first appeared as *The Human Rights of the Aged: An Application of the General Norm of Nondiscrimination,* 28 U. FLA. L. REV. 639 (1976).

1. The focus here is on the question of discrimination relating to advanced age. On the protection of children, *see generally* P. ADAMS, et al., CHILDREN'S RIGHTS: TOWARD THE LIBERATION OF THE CHILD (1971); D. COHEN, THE LEARNING CHILD (1972); V. DE FRANCIS, CHILD ABUSE LEGISLATION IN THE 1970'S (1970); J. GOLDSTEIN, A. FREUD, & A. SOLNIT, BEYOND THE BEST INTERESTS OF THE CHILD (1973); J. HOLT, ESCAPE FOR CHILDHOOD (1974); S. KEENY, HALF THE WORLD'S CHILDREN (1957); A. PLATT, THE CHILD SAVERS: THE INVENTION OF DELINQUENCY (1969); H. SIMMONS, PROTECTIVE SERVICES FOR CHILDREN (1968); D. ZIETZ, CHILD WELFARE: SERVICES AND PERSPECTIVES (2d ed. 1969); Coughlin, *The Rights of Children,* 47 CHILD WELFARE 133 (1968); Foster & Freed, *A Bill of Rights for Children,* 6 FAMILY L.Q. 343 (1972); Kleinfeld, *Balance of Power among Infants, Their Parents and the State,* 4 FAMILY L.Q. 410 (1970), 5 FAMILY L.Q. 64 (1971); Katz, Schroeder, & Sidman, *Emancipating Our Children—Coming of Legal Age in America,* 7 FAMILY L.Q. 211 (1973); Rezneck, *The Rights of Juveniles,* in THE RIGHTS OF AMERICANS: WHAT THEY ARE—WHAT THEY SHOULD BE 469 (N. Dorsen ed., 1970); Rodham, *Children under the Law,* 43 HARV. ED. REV. 487 (1973); Sizer & Whitten, *A Proposal for a Poor Children's Bill of Rights,* PSYCHOLOGY TODAY, Aug. 1968, at 59–63; Wald, *Making Sense out of the Rights of Youth,* 4 HUMAN RIGHTS 13 (1974); Worsfold, *A Philosophical Justification of Children's Rights,* 44 HARV. ED. REV. 142 (1974).

2. Cruelty in the treatment of the aged is by no means a modern invention, as Simone de Beauvoir has documented in her impressive study: S. DE BEAUVOIR, THE COMING OF AGE (P. O'Brian trans. 1972). Nevertheless, Cowgill and Holmes, using modernization as a central focus, have demonstrated that "the status of the aged is high in preliterate societies and is lower and more ambiguous in modern societies" and that "the status of the aged tends to be high in agricultural societies . . . [while] relatively low in urban, industrial societies." Cowgill & Holmes, *Summary and Conclusions: The Theory in Preview,* in AGING AND MODERNIZATION 305, 310, 315 (D. Cowgill & L. Holmes eds., 1972).

the elderly, have become increasingly apparent as aged segments in the community continue to expand significantly, especially in highly industrialized societies.[3]

The unique deprivation of the aged today takes the form of compulsory (involuntary) retirement from active work life, regardless of an individual's actual mental and physical capacities, as enforced by a blanket age limitation.[4] Alternatively, the deprivation may be imposed by denying employment opportunity to individuals over a specified age that may vary according to the occupation. Age-based compulsory retirement

---

3. Though community attention in the past has focused principally on early childhood, there has been a proliferation of research in the field of gerontology. This is vividly exemplified in the United States by the establishment of the National Institute on Aging (NIA) within the National Institutes of Health (NIH). In May 1974, the United States Congress enacted the Research on Aging Act of 1974, authorizing the creation of NIA. The task of NIA is to undertake and coordinate "biomedical, social, and behavioral research and training related to the aging process and the diseases and other special problems and needs of the aged." 42 U.S.C.A. §289k-2 (1974).

For a comprehensive study from a global perspective, *see Question of the Elderly and the Aged* (report of the secretary-general), U.N. Doc. A/9126 (1973) [hereinafter cited as *U.N. Study on the Aged*]. For a report on the current state of aging research, *see* Marx, *Aging Research (1): Cellular Theories of Senescence,* 186 SCIENCE 1105 (1974); Marx, *Aging Research (II): Pacemakers for Aging?* 186 SCIENCE 1196 (1974).

See also AGING AND SOCIAL POLICY (J. McKinney & F. de Vyver eds. 1966); AGING AND SOCIETY (M. Riley, J. Riley, & M. Johnson eds. 1969); Z. BLAU, OLD AGE IN A CHANGING SOCIETY (1973); J. BOTWINICK, AGING AND BEHAVIOR (1973); M. BRENNAN, P. TAFT, & M. SCHUPACK, THE ECONOMICS OF AGE (1967); M. CLARK & B. ANDERSON, CULTURE AND AGING (1967); E. CUMMING & W. HENRY, GROWING OLD (1961); J. DRAKE, THE AGED IN AMERICAN SOCIETY (1958); GROWING OLD (A. Stoller ed. 1960); HANDBOOK OF AGING AND THE INDIVIDUAL (J. Birren ed. 1959); HANDBOOK OF SOCIAL GERONTOLOGY (C. Tibbits ed. 1960); O. KNOPF, SUCCESSFUL AGING: THE FACTS AND FALLACIES OF GROWING OLD (1975); M. KOLLER, SOCIAL GERONTOLOGY (1968); A. LEVIN, THE GERIATRIC REVOLUTION (1968); MIDDLE AGE AND AGING (B. Neugarten ed. 1968); OLD AGE IN AMERICA (G. Lang ed. 1961); C. PERCY, GROWING OLD IN THE COUNTRY OF THE YOUNG (1974); RESEARCH PLANNING AND ACTION FOR THE ELDERLY: THE POWER AND POTENTIAL OF SOCIAL SCIENCE (D. Kent, R. Kastenbaum, & S. Sherwood eds. (1972); M. RILEY & A. FONER, AGING AND SOCIETY (1968); E. SMITH, HANDBOOK OF AGING (1972); SOCIAL ASPECTS OF AGING (I. Simpson & J. McKinney eds. 1966); THEORETICAL ASPECTS OF AGING (M. Rockstein ed. 1974); TOWARD AN INDUSTRIAL GERONTOLOGY (H. Sheppard ed. 1970); *Social Contribution by the Aging,* in ANNALS 279 (1952); *Symposium—Problems of the Aging,* 27 LAW & CONTEMP. PROB. 1 (1962).

4. This chapter builds upon previous studies in which the authors have sought to establish that there has emerged in the world arena a general norm that precludes the differentiation of individuals by group categorizations that have no consistent relation to individual capabilities and potentialities. *See* note 30 *infra.*

For discussions of constitutionality within the United States, *see* N. TRONCHIN-JAMES, ARBITRARY RETIREMENT (1972); Eglit, *Is Compulsory Retirement Constitutional? Another Name for Discrimination . . . ,* CIVIL LIB. REV. 89–97 (Fall 1974); *Note, Age Discrimination in Employment: Correcting a Constitutionally Infirm Legislative Judgment,* 47 S. CAL. L. REV.

tends to precipitate or accentuate the syndromes of aging, generating many value deprivations that could otherwise be avoided or mitigated. "Compulsory retirement," in the words of Eglit, "is just another name for discrimination."[5]

The traumatic impact of the sudden loss of accustomed roles, precipitated by involuntary retirement, is immense and profound. As Rosow has sharply summarized:

> *[T]he loss of roles excludes the aged from significant social participation and devalues them.* It deprives them of vital functions that underlie their sense of worth, their self-conceptions and self-esteem. In a word, they are depreciated and become marginal, alienated from the larger society. Whatever their ability, they are judged invidiously, as if they have little of value to contribute to the world's work and affairs. In a society that rewards men mainly according to their economic utility, the aged are arbitrarily stigmatized as having little marginal utility of any kind, either economic or social. On the contrary, they tend to be tolerated, patronized, ignored, rejected, or viewed as a liability. They are first excluded from the mainstream of social existence, and because of this nonparticipation, they are then penalized and denied the rewards that earlier came to them routinely.[6]

Compulsory retirement in a work-oriented society normally means drastic reduction in income, perhaps resulting in near poverty, even where there is provision for some sort of social security.[7] A drastic decrease in income compels a significant lowering of the accustomed level and style of living.

The shock of compulsory retirement may be so overwhelming as to generate a lasting state of anxiety and even depression.[8] The ordinary

---

1311 (1974) [hereinafter cited as *Age Discrimination in Employment*]; *Note, Mandatory Retirement—A Vehicle for Age Discrimination,* 51 CHI.-KENT L. REV. 116 (1974) [hereinafter cited as *Mandatory Retirement*]; *Note, Too Old to Work: The Constitutionality of Mandatory Retirement Plans,* 44 S. CAL. L. REV. 150 (1971) [hereinafter cited as *Too Old to Work*].

5. Eglit, *supra* note 4, at 87.

6. Rosow, *The Social Context of the Aging Self,* 13 THE GERONTOLOGIST 82, 82 (1973) (italics original).

7. *Cf.* S. DE BEAUVOIR, *supra* note 2, at 216–77; J. CORSON & J. MCCONNELL, ECONOMIC NEEDS OF OLDER PEOPLE (1956); EMPLOYMENT, INCOME, AND RETIREMENT PROBLEMS OF THE AGED (J. Kreps ed. 1963); SENATE SPECIAL COMM. ON AGING, 91st Cong., 2d Sess., LEGAL PROBLEMS AFFECTING OLDER AMERICANS 1–2 (1970) (a working paper); *Age Discrimination in Employment, supra* note 4; *Mandatory Retirement, supra* note 4, at 121; *Too Old to Work, supra* note 4, at 152–55.

8. S. DE BEAUVOIR, *supra* note 2, at 269. *Cf.* R. BUTLER & M. LEWIS, AGING AND MENTAL HEALTH (1973).

process of aging aside, the psychosomatic condition of the elderly may be brutally and unduly impaired and exacerbated by the shock of involuntary retirement.[9] Formerly useful skills are consigned to the scrap heap overnight. Access to the accustomed flow of information and other sources of enlightenment are lost or substantially reduced. While the power to vote may continue unaffected, eligibility for officeholding, with minor exceptions, is denied. This implies a concomitant decline in influence upon the making of effective community decisions and a sharpening sense of powerlessness. Condemning the elderly to "an idleness that hastens their decline,"[10] age-based involuntary retirement tends to affect all personal relations and to evoke "the sorrow of parting, the feeling of abandonment, solitude and uselessness."[11]

In sum, from a position as an active and useful member of society, overnight an aged person is relegated to the club of senior citizens, under a thoughtless, inconsiderate system of compulsory retirement, and becomes a target of condescension, neglect, and contempt. Instead of embarking upon a new life of enjoyable leisure in the "golden years," people who are forced to retire, except for a fortunate few, are thrust into an agonizing path of doubt, insecurity, emptiness, and futility.[12] They are bluntly "redefined," in the words of Rosow, "as old and obsolete."[13] He noted: "The norms applied to them change quickly from achievement to ascription, from criteria of performance to those of sheer age regardless of personal accomplishment. People who were formerly judged as individuals are then bewilderingly treated as members of an invidious category."[14]

BASIC COMMUNITY POLICIES

The critical policies of honoring freedom of individual choice and of fostering the utmost contribution by individuals to the aggregate common interest should protect the aged as well as other members of a community. To deny or restrict an individual's opportunity to work and to participate in other value processes, purely on the basis of an arbitrary chronological age limit, is not compatible with the overriding policy of human dignity.

Compulsory retirement on the basis of a specified age has commonly

9. It has been suggested that compulsory retirement can be an important source of disease. M. Barron, The Aging American 76 (1961); Senate Special Comm. on Aging, Developments in Aging 1969, S. Rep. No. 91-875, 91st Cong., 2nd Sess. 115 (1970).

10. S. de Beauvoir, *supra* note 2, at 273.

11. *Id.* at 269. *Cf.* C. Rosenberg, The Worker Grows Old (1970).

12. *But see e.g.,* O. Knopf, *supra* note 3.

13. Rosow, *supra* note 6, at 82.

14. *Id.* at 82–83.

been justified on several grounds. First, the elderly, on reaching a certain specified age, are said to become inefficient workers because of conspicuous deterioration both in intellectual and physical capabilities.[15] Second, it is allegedly impracticable to effect retirement ("to weed out deadwood") on a selective, individualized basis.[16] Third, mandatory retirement guided by chronological age serves the common interest by opening up avenues of advancement (promotion) and job opportunity for the young.[17] Fourth, age-based mandatory retirement enables "the prospective retiree to plan ahead with certainty,"[18] instead of being shocked by a sudden retirement that is dictated by haphazard, ad hoc criteria.

Underlying the defense of age-based compulsory retirement there is a blanket assumption, allegedly based upon statistics, about the stereotyped disabilities (mental and physical deterioration) of people reaching a certain age.[19] As gerontological studies accelerate and deepen, such an assumption encounters growing challenge.[20] In the light of contemporary knowledge it would appear that no blanket assumption about the incapacity of people over a fixed age can be accepted until it is factually demonstrated. It is obvious that a mere assertion is not an acceptable substitute for fact. The consequences are especially grave when the ends of enlightened policy are not served. Irrebuttable presumptions that preclude individualized determinations based on close contextual scru-

15. *See* HANDBOOK OF SOCIAL GERONTOLOGY, *supra* note 3, at 307–08; H. LOETHER, PROBLEMS OF AGING, SOCIOLOGICAL AND SOCIAL PSYCHOLOGICAL 59–60 (1967); *Hearings on S. 830, S. 788 before the Subcomm. on Labor of the Senate Comm. on Labor and Public Welfare,* 90th Cong., 1st Sess. 369–70 (1967); Waldman & Levine, *Is Compulsory Retirement Constitutional? . . . Serves a Valid and Legal Social Purpose,* CIVIL LIB. REV. 98–101 (Fall 1974); *Mandatory Retirement, supra* note 4, at 118; *Too Old to Work, supra* note 4, at 151.

16. *See* Waldman & Levine, *supra* note 15, at 102; Johnson, *The Superficial Aspect, When's Time to Retire?* THE NEW REPUBLIC, July 6, 1959, at 16.

17. *See* Bernstein, *The Push for Early Retirement,* THE NEW REPUBLIC, Aug. 22, 1964, at 23; Gordon, *The Older Worker and Retirement Policies,* 83 MONTHLY LAB. REV. 577, 581 (1960); Waldman & Levine, *supra* note 15, at 99.

18. MONRONEY, FEDERAL STAFF RETIREMENT SYSTEMS, S. DOC. NO. 14, 90th Cong., 1st Sess. 73 (1967).

19. Eglit, *supra* note 4, at 92–93.

20. *See* SENATE SPECIAL COMM. ON AGING, DEVELOPMENTS IN AGING: 1972 AND JANUARY–MARCH 1973, S. REP. NO. 93-147, 93d Cong., 1st Sess. 72 (1973); U.S. DEP'T OF LABOR, THE LAW AGAINST AGE DISCRIMINATION IN EMPLOYMENT (W.H. Pub. 1303, Sept. 1970); WHITE HOUSE CONFERENCE ON AGING, RETIREMENT (1971); 1971 WHITE HOUSE CONFERENCE ON AGING, TOWARD A NATIONAL POLICY ON AGING (1971); *Mandatory Retirement, supra* note 4, at 118–19; *Too Old to Work, supra* note 4, at 159–61.

For an interesting study that compares different ages at which peak performance is achieved in various professions and occupations, *see* H. LEHMAN, AGE AND ACHIEVEMENT (1953). *See also* World Health Organization, *Health Concerns of the Elderly and the Aged* in *U.N. Study on the Aged, supra* note 3, Annex III, at 6–7.

tiny cannot be tolerated. Actually, individuals both mature and decline at different rates for different capabilities; moreover, research indicates that "[g]eneral intellectual decline in old age is largely a myth."[21]

The argument as to the impossibility of administering a retirement policy on an individualized basis cannot withstand scrutiny. It is no more difficult to make decisions concerning retirement on an individualized basis than to make day-to-day decisions concerning hiring, discipline, or promotion of individual employees.[22] The appropriate criterion should be whether a person is presently capable of performing the task required, not when he or she was born.

To meet the critical job needs of the young by creating more job opportunities is of fundamental importance to sound public policy. Even granting that the absorbing capacity of the job market is limited at any given time, the policy of making room for the young at the expense of active older bread earners—completely disregarding actual capability and fitness—is nothing more than "the shifting of the problem of insufficient jobs from one age group to another."[23] The challenge of "distributive justice" remains unresolved by the body politic. Extravagant and ruthless waste of enormously useful talents and skills, seasoned by years of practical experience, is scarcely the way to augment the aggregate common interest.

It may further be observed that the knowledge that one is about to receive a declaration of instant obsolescence and uselessness on the authority imputed to the calendar is no key to a smooth, anxiety-free transition from one role or status to another.[24] If anything, a keen sense of deprivation and injustice may become so overwhelming as to engulf the involuntary retiree in a sea of nameless emptiness and chronic trauma.[25] Human beings, it may be reiterated, are not appropriately

---

21. Baltes & Schaie, *Aging and I.Q.: The Myth of the Twilight Years*, PSYCHOLOGY TODAY 35 (Mar. 1974). *See also* G. MATHIASEN, CRITERIA FOR RETIREMENT 88, 92 (1952): THE NATIONAL COUNCIL ON THE AGING, UTILIZATION OF OLDER PROFESSIONAL AND SCIENTIFIC WORKERS 9 (1961); REPORT: SEMINAR ON EMPLOYABILITY OF OLDER PERSONS 11 (J. Birren ed. 1963); U.S. DEP'T OF LABOR, BUREAU OF LABOR STATISTICS: INDUSTRIAL RETRAINING PROGRAMS FOR TECHNOLOGICAL CHANGE 6 (1963); Kutscher & Walker, *Comparative Job Performance of Office Workers by Age*, 83 MONTHLY LAB. REV. 39 (1960); Walker, *Job Performance of Federal Mail Sorters by Age*, 87 MONTHLY LAB. REV. 296 (1964); Weinberg, *Older Workers' Performance in Industrial Retraining Programs*, 86 MONTHLY LAB. REV. 935 (1963); *Too Old to Work, supra* note 4, at 159–61.

22. Eglit, *supra* note 4, at 92.

23. *Id.*

24. L. KUTNER et al., FIVE HUNDRED OVER SIXTY 88–89, 253 (1956): *Too Old to Work, supra* note 4, at 155–58.

25. "All gerontologists agree that living the last twenty years of one's life in a state of physical fitness but without any useful activity is psychologically and sociologically impos-

treated "by category" rather than as persons. Human dignity is best achieved by treating each person according to his or her unique capability and potential. Chronological age is but one of multiple indices of individual capability and potentiality. "You cannot," wrote Eglit, "consign people to the arbitrary, inflexible fate of forced retirement without at the same time offending fairness and the concept of equality which are fundamental to our society."[26] Unlike discriminations on the ground of race or sex, discrimination on the basis of advanced chronological age has keen personal implications for every member of the community because aging is a process common to everyone.

Thus, the quality of society and the degree to which human dignity values are fulfilled may be measured by the treatment accorded to the aged members of the population. The treatment of the elderly concerns not only the elderly; it involves the identity system of the self and of the whole society of which the self is a part. In primitive societies the elderly were highly prized largely because of their rarity.[27] In the contemporary world, because of advances in science and technology, the life expectancy of humankind continues to grow, and this planet is endowed with ever-increasing numbers of people living well beyond the years that were formerly thought possible.[28] As the life sciences continue to flourish, especially in gerontology, there is every indication that this trend will continue, barring unforeseeable catastrophies. Whether the longevity made possible by the cumulative heritage of humankind will become an advantage or a curse in disguise presents a critical test for modern civilization. The resulting important community task is that of devising criteria and procedures appropriate for appraising individual capabilities and potentialities at every chronological age. To maximize the self-fulfillment of individuals and their contributions to the common

---

sible. Those who live on must be given some reason for living: mere survival is worse than death." S. de Beauvoir, *supra* note 2, at 272–73.

In the words of the American Medical Association Committee on Aging: "Compulsory retirement on the basis of age will impair the health of many individuals whose job represents a major source of status, creative satisfaction, social relationships or self-respect. It will be equally disastrous for the individual who works only because he has to, and who has a minimum of meaningful goals or interests in life, job-related or otherwise. Job separation may well deprive such a person of his only source of identification, and leave him foundering in a motivational vacuum with no frame of reference whatever." *Hearings before the Senate Subcomm. on Retirement and the Individual of the Senate Special Comm. on Aging,* 90th Cong., 1st Sess., pt. 1, at 307 (1967).

26. Eglit, *supra* note 4, at 88.

27. *See* Aging and Modernization, *supra* note 2. *See also* M. Barron, *supra* note 9, at 25–26; Donahue, Orbach, & Pollak, *Retirement: The Emerging Social Pattern,* in Handbook of Social Gerontology, *supra* note 3, at 330, 334–36.

28. *See U.N. Study on the Aged, supra* note 3, at 16–28.

interest, it is imperative that individual potential receive the fullest possible expression at all stages of life.[29]

TRENDS IN DECISION

The United Nations Charter and its ancillary human rights prescriptions do not specifically include "advanced age" among the impermissible grounds of differentiation; yet, the general prescriptions on nondiscrimination are, as repeatedly indicated, designed to be illustrative rather than exhaustive.[30] The transnational prescriptions barring discrimination are broad and far-reaching. Further, the United Nations Charter, the Universal Declaration of Human Rights, the two International Covenants on Human Rights, and other related human rights prescriptions are explicitly worded to protect "everyone," presumably including every human being regardless of chronological age.[31] Recently, this general policy of nondiscrimination has been emphatically reiterated as a major objective of the Declaration on Social Progress and Development, adopted by the General Assembly in December 1969:

> Social progress and development shall aim at the continuous raising of the material and spiritual standards of living of all members of society, with respect for and in compliance with human rights and fundamental freedoms, through the attainment of the following main goals:
>
> . . . .
>
> The elimination of all forms of discrimination and exploitation and all other practices and ideologies contrary to the purposes and principles of the Charter of the United Nations. . . .[32]

---

29. Curtin observed:

> [O]ur culture does not have a concept of the whole of life. Instead, life is divided into childhood, adulthood, and old age. Instead of a cycle, a vision of unity, we have a vision of stages, in which only one—adulthood—has the possibility of being lived productively, independently, and vigorously. Old age is viewed as a childlike state, but without the charm and promise. It is as if we wanted to finally view our lives as totally devoid of meaning, where the dependency and childishness of old age wipe out the accomplishments of adulthood. The experiences of a lifetime disappear in the feeling of being useless and passed by.

S. Curtin, Nobody Ever Died of Old Age 227 (1972).

30. *See* chapters 8–14 *supra.*

31. *Id.*

32. G.A. Res. 2542, pt. 2, Art. 12(b), 24 U.N. GAOR, Supp. (No. 30) 49, 50–51, U.N. Doc. A/7630 (1969). The text of this resolution is reproduced in Human Rights: A Compilation of International Instruments of the United Nations 97, 98–99, U.N. Doc. ST/HR/1 (1973) [hereinafter cited as U.N. Human Rights Instruments].

The growing worldwide concern for the protection of the aged prompted the United Nations to undertake a timely study on the "Question of the Elderly and the Aged,"[33] culminating in the adoption by the General Assembly of a resolution on this subject in December 1973.[34] Emphasizing "respect for the dignity and worth of the human person" enunciated in the Universal Declaration,[35] reiterating that "the protection of the rights and welfare of the aged is one of the main goals of the Declaration on Social Progress and Development,"[36] and underscoring "the growing interest for developing and developed societies alike in the fuller participation of the elderly in the mainstream of national societies,"[37] the General Assembly urged member states to "enhance the contribution of the elderly to social and economic development"[38] and to "discourage, wherever and whenever the overall situation allows, discriminatory attitudes, policies and measures in employment practices based exclusively on age."[39]

Though the relevant human rights prescriptions are silent on the question of age-based mandatory retirement, it would appear that the more general norm of nondiscrimination,[40] conjoined with the protected right to work, must outlaw such an invidious practice and policy. The right to work is well protected under transnational prescriptions; the Universal Declaration of Human Rights enunciates in Article 23(1) that "[e]veryone has the right to work, to free choice of employment, to just and favourable conditions of work and to protection against unemployment."[41] The International Covenant on Economic, Social, and Cultural Rights in Article 6 fortifies the right to work in these affirmative terms:

1. The States Parties to the present Covenant recognize the right to work, which includes the right of everyone to the opportunity to gain his living by work which he freely chooses or accepts, and will take appropriate steps to safeguard this right.
2. The steps to be taken by a State Party to the present Covenant to achieve the full realization of this right shall include technical and vocational guidance and training programmes, policies and

33. *U.N. Study on the Aged, supra* note 3.
34. G.A. Res. 3137, 28 U.N. GAOR, Supp. (No. 30) 80, U.N. Doc. A/9030 (1973).
35. *Id.*
36. *Id.*
37. *Id.*
38. *Id.* at 81.
39. *Id.*
40. *See* chapters 8–14 *supra.*
41. U N. Human Rights Instruments *supra* note 32, at 2.

> techniques to achieve steady economic, social and cultural development and full and productive employment under conditions safeguarding fundamental political and economic freedoms to the individual.[42]

The contracting states not only recognize the right to work but also pledge to "take appropriate steps to safeguard" this right. Similarly, the Declaration on Social Progress and Development of 1969 in Article 6 proclaims that "[s]ocial development requires the assurance to everyone of the right to work and the free choice of employment"[43] and that "[s]ocial progress and development require the participation of all members of society in productive and socially useful labour. . . ."[44]

Prevention of discrimination is only one facet of the protection of persons of advanced age. They may have special infirmities requiring special measures of assistance.[45] This critical need is well recognized in various transnational prescriptions. For instance, the Universal Declaration of Human Rights in Article 25(1) states:

> Everyone has the right to a standard of living adequate for the health and well-being of himself and of his family, including food, clothing, housing and medical care and necessary social services, and the right to security in the event of unemployment, sickness, disability, widowhood, old *age* or lack of livelihood in circumstances beyond his control.[46]

Similarly, this concern is evident in the resolution on the "Question of the Elderly and the Aged" adopted on December 14, 1973, by the General Assembly of the United Nations.[47] More specifically, in its separate resolution on "Social Security for the Aged" adopted on the same date, the General Assembly urged member governments to provide the aged "adequate social security payments," "sufficient institutions for the care

---

42. *Id.* at 4.

43. *Id.* at 98.

44. *Id.* On the right to work, *see* INTERNATIONAL LABOUR OFFICE, THE I.L.O. AND HUMAN RIGHTS 76–84 (1968) (report presented by the International Labour Organization to the International Conference on Human Rights); C. JENKS, THE COMMON LAW OF MANKIND 255–99 (1958); C. JENKS, HUMAN RIGHTS AND INTERNATIONAL LABOUR STANDARDS 119–23 (1960); Jenks, *Work, Leisure and Social Security as Human Rights in the World Community,* 9 J. INT'L COMM'N JURISTS 49 (1968).

45. *See U.N. Study on the Aged, supra* note 3, at 38–54; STAFF OF SENATE SUBCOMM. ON AGING OF THE COMM. ON LABOR AND PUBLIC WELFARE AND THE SPECIAL COMM. ON AGING, 93d Cong., 1st Sess., POST-WHITE HOUSE CONFERENCE ON AGING REPORTS—1973 (Joint Comm. Print 1973).

46. U.N. HUMAN RIGHTS INSTRUMENTS, *supra* note 32, at 2–3 (italics added).

47. G.A. Res. 3137, *supra* note 34.

of aged persons requiring medical treatment," and adequate "architectural facilities" and "housing."[48]

The question of protecting the aged is beginning to receive increased attention within many national communities whose principal efforts relate to special assistance in terms of income (social security), housing, and medical care.[49] In addition, efforts have increasingly been directed to challenge the policy and practice of age-based mandatory retirement. Recent developments within the United States exemplify this new endeavor.[50]

After repeated attempts beginning in the 1950s, the United States Congress finally, in 1967, adopted the Age Discrimination Employment Act.[51] The act is designed to "promote employment of older persons based on their ability rather than age; to prohibit arbitrary age discrimination in employment; to help employers and workers find ways of meeting problems arising from the impact of age on employment."[52] Its proscription of discrimination extends to discharging practices as well as hiring practices, encompassing such matters as "hiring, job retention, compensation, promotions, and other conditions and privileges of employment."[53] The act bars employers, employment agencies, and labor organizations from practicing age-based discrimination against "individuals who are at least forty years of age but less than sixty-five years of

---

48. G.A. Res. 3138, 28 U.N. GAOR, Supp. (No. 30) 81, U.N. Doc. A/9030 (1973).

Worthy of special notice also is the important role played by the International Labor Organization. *See generally* E. HAAS, HUMAN RIGHTS AND INTERNATIONAL ACTION (1970); INTERNATIONAL LABOUR OFFICE, THE ILO IN THE SERVICE OF SOCIAL PROGRESS (1969); INTERNATIONAL LABOUR ORGANIZATION, CONVENTIONS AND RECOMMENDATIONS ADOPTED BY THE INTERNATIONAL LABOUR CONFERENCE, 1919–1966 (1966); C. JENKS, LAW, FREEDOM AND WELFARE 101–36 (1963); C. JENKS, SOCIAL JUSTICE IN THE LAW OF NATIONS: THE ILO IMPACT AFTER FIFTY YEARS (1970); E. LANDY, THE EFFECTIVENESS OF INTERNATIONAL SUPERVISION: THIRTY YEARS OF I.L.O. EXPERIENCE (1966); Jenks, *Human Rights, Social Justice and Peace: The Broader Significance of the I.L.O. Experience,* in INTERNATIONAL PROTECTION OF HUMAN RIGHTS 227 (A. Eide & A. Schou eds. 1968).

49. This problem is more appropriately dealt with under Claims Relating to Special Assistance. *Cf.* Goldman, *More Than a Wheelchair,* 7 HUMAN RIGHTS 40 (No. 3, 1978).

50. *See* Agatstein, *The Age Discrimination in Employment Act of 1967: A Critique,* 19 N.Y.L. FORUM 309 (1973); Brennan, *State Legislation Prohibiting Discrimination in Employment because of Age,* 18 HASTINGS L.J. 539 (1967); Halgren, *Age Discrimination in Employment Act of 1967,* 43 LAB. BULL. 361 (1968); Serwer, *Mandatory Retirement at Age 65—A Survey of the Law,* INDUSTRIAL GERONTOLOGY 11 (Winter 1974); *Age Discrimination in Employment, supra* note 4; *Mandatory Retirement, supra* note 4; *Too Old to Work, supra* note 4.

51. 29 U.S.C. §§621–34 (1970).

52. *Id.* §621(b).

53. *See* U.S. DEP'T OF LABOR, THE LAW AGAINST AGE DISCRIMINATION IN EMPLOYMENT (1970); *Improving the Age Discrimination Law, A Working Paper,* prepared for use by the Special Committee on Aging, United States Senate, 93d Cong., 1st Sess. (1973).

age."[54] The act authorizes an aggrieved individual or a group of persons under its protective umbrella to bring a civil action for "such legal or equitable relief as may be appropriate to effectuate the purposes" of the act, "including without limitation judgments compelling employment, reinstatement or promotion."[55] The right of recourse to civil action ceases, however, on the commencement of suit by the secretary of labor to enforce the right of the aggrieved party.[56] The secretary of labor is entrusted with the primary responsibility of enforcement.[57] Criminal sanctions are to be imposed upon those who "forcibly resist, oppose, impede, intimidate or interfere with a duly authorized representative of the Secretary," while he is performing his duties under the act.[58]

It is unfortunate, as commentators have repeatedly pointed out, that this act protects only those who are between ages forty and sixty-five.[59] Substantial opinion urges removal of this age limitation and the extension of protection against age-based discrimination to those who are below forty, and especially to those who are over sixty-five. Despite this shortcoming and other inadequacies, such as the limited scope of coverage in terms of employers[60] and "superficial enforcement,"[61] the Age Discrimination Employment Act represents a giant step toward protection against age-based discrimination.

Meanwhile, litigation has gone forward to challenge the constitutionality of the age sixty-five employment barrier by invoking the due process clauses of the Fifth and Fourteenth Amendments and the equal protection clause of the Fourteenth Amendment. *Weiss* v. *Walsh,*[62] decided in 1971, marked the first important challenge. The plaintiff, Paul Weiss, a renowned philosopher, complained that Fordham University had offered him the Albert Schweitzer Chair in Humanities only to withdraw the offer later simply because of the "eleventh-hour" objection[63] by the

---

54. 29 U.S.C. §631 (1970).

55. 29 U.S.C. §626(b) (1970).

56. 29 U.S.C. §626(c) (1970).

57. 29 U.S.C. §§624–28 (1970).

58. 29 U.S.C. §629 (1970).

59. *See, e.g., Age Discrimination Employment, supra* note 4, at 1331–52; *Mandatory Retirement, supra* note 4, at 135–47.

60. Initially, the act confined "employer" to "a person engaged in an industry affecting commerce who has twenty-five or more employees." 29 U.S.C. §630(b) (1970). Government employees, federal and state, did not come within the protection of the act. *Id.* Subsequently, in 1974, the act was amended to apply to government employees as well as industries with twenty or more employees. H.R. Rep. No. 93-953, 93d Cong., 2d Sess. 21–23 (1974).

61. *Mandatory Retirement, supra* note 4, at 135.

62. Weiss v. Walsh, 324 F. Supp. 75 (S.D.N.Y. 1971).

63. *Id.* at 76.

New York State Department of Education that he had passed age sixty-five. Dismissing the plaintiff's claim that the act of withdrawing the offer was in violation of the First, Fifth, and Fourteenth Amendments of the Constitution, Judge Tyler observed that: "[B]eing a classification that cuts fully across racial, religious, and economic lines, and one that generally bears some relation to mental and physical capacity, age is less likely to be an invidious distinction."[64] He added:

> Notwithstanding great advances in gerontology, the era when advanced age ceases to bear some reasonable statistical relationship to diminished capacity or longevity is still future. It cannot be said, therefore, that age ceilings upon eligibility for employment are inherently suspect, although their application will inevitably fall unjustly in the individual case.[65]

Although this reasoning was less than convincing,[66] the decision was affirmed without opinion in 1972 by the Second Circuit[67] and was denied certiorari in 1973 by the United States Supreme Court.[68]

One year later the Supreme Court addressed an equal protection challenge to school board mandatory leave regulations in an opinion that suggested parallels to mandatory retirement laws. In *Cleveland Board of Education* v. *LaFleur,*[69] the Court held unconstitutional the regulations of two school boards, one in Cleveland, Ohio, and the other in Chesterfield County, Virginia, requiring pregnant teachers to take unpaid maternity leave several months in advance of the expected childbirth. The Court outlawed these regulations as an unwarranted infringement upon "freedom of personal choice in matters of marriage and family life,"[70] which is protected by the due process clause of the Fourteenth Amendment. The two school boards contended that "firm cut off dates are necessary to maintain continuity of classroom instruction,"[71] and to allow sufficient time to find and hire qualified substitutes. Finally, the Board noted that "at least some teachers become physically incapable of adequately per-

---

64. *Id.* at 77.

65. *Id.*

66. *Cf., e.g.,* Eglit, *supra* note 4, at 92–96; *Age Discrimination in Employment, supra* note 4, at 1336–52; *Mandatory Retirement, supra* note 4, at 137–46.

67. 461 F.2d 846 (2d Cir. 1972).

68. 409 U.S. 1129 (1973). Invoking *Weiss,* a United States district court in Nebraska subsequently decided that the mandatory retirement at age sixty-five, prescribed by the Douglass County Civil Service Act, is "a permissible means of accomplishing a rational and reasonable objective" and therefore not in contravention of the United States Constitution. Armstrong v. Howell, 371 F. Supp. 48 (D. Neb. 1974).

69. Cleveland Bd. of Educ. v. LaFleur, 414 U.S. 632 (1974).

70. *Id.* at 639.

71. *Id.* at 640.

forming certain of their duties during the latter part of pregnancy."[72] Dismissing the arguments of the school boards, Mr. Justice Stewart, writing for the majority, declared that:

> [T]he provisions amount to a conclusive presumption that every pregnant teacher who reaches the fifth or sixth month of pregnancy is physically incapable of continuing. There is no individualized determination by the teacher's doctor—or the school board's—as to any particular teacher's ability to continue at her job. The rules contain an irrebuttable presumption of physical incompetency, and that presumption applies even when the medical evidence as to an individual woman's physical status might be wholly to the contrary.[73]

The Court concluded that "the mandatory termination provisions of the Cleveland and Chesterfield County maternity regulations violate the Due Process Clause of the Fourteenth Amendment, because of their use of unwarranted conclusive presumptions that seriously burden the exercise of protected constitutional liberty."[74]

The implications of the Court's holding for the outlawing of age-based mandatory retirement were keenly, and perhaps prophetically, perceived by Justice Rehnquist in his dissenting opinion. Since "the right to work for a living in the common occupations of the community," as enunciated in *Truax* v. *Raich,*[75] is "presumably on the same lofty footing as the right of choice in matters of family life,"[76] "the Court," observed Justice Rehnquist, "will have to strain valiantly in order to avoid having today's opinion lead to the invalidation of mandatory retirement statutes for governmental employees."[77]

The incisive intimation of Justice Rehnquist found expression, shortly afterwards, in *Murgia* v. *Massachusetts Board of Retirement.*[78] The case challenged the constitutionality of a Massachusetts statute prescribing mandatory retirement of state police officers at fifty years of age. In response to the argument that such age-based mandatory retirement "enhances the morale of the younger members" and facilitates "rapid promotion," the three-judge court urged that "the attractiveness of quick promotion must be weighed against the unattractiveness of early

72. *Id.* at 641.
73. *Id.* at 644.
74. *Id.* at 651.
75. Truax v. Raich, 239 U.S. 33, 41 (1915).
76. 414 U.S. at 659.
77. *Id.*
78. 376 F. Supp. 753 (D. Mass. 1974).

retirement."[79] After analyzing the objective of rapid promotion, the court concluded that this statute was simply an example of per se age discrimination.[80] The court then declared the statutory provision at issue "unconstitutional and void," holding that:

> mandatory retirement at age 50, where individualized medical screening is not only available but already required, is no more rational, and no more related to a protectable state interest, than the mandatory suspension or discharge of school teachers upon reaching their fourth or fifth month of pregnancy.[81]

On appeal, the Supreme Court reversed and held that the statute was rationally related to the state objective of protecting the public by "assuring physical preparedness of its uniformed police."[82] Recognizing that "physical ability generally declines with age,"[83] the Court concluded that mandatory retirement of police officers at age fifty removed from the service policemen "whose fitness for uniformed work presumptively has diminished with age."[84] While admitting that treatment of the aged in this country has not been "wholly free of discrimination," the Court declined to recognize age as a suspect classification.[85]

In dissent, Justice Marshall argued that previous decisions had recognized that an individual's right to work was a liberty interest guaranteed by the Fourteenth Amendment and that the State of Massachusetts must show "a reasonably substantial interest" in preserving the validity of the statute in question.[86] Since policemen over forty years of age had to undergo annual physical examinations to remain on the force, the au-

---

79. *Id.* at 754.

80. *Id.* at 755.

81. *Id.* at 756.

82. Massachusetts Bd. of Retirement v. Murgia, 96 S. Ct. 2562 (1976).

83. *Id.* at 2567. The Court, however, did note that the "testimony also recognized that particular individuals over 50 could be capable of safely performing the functions of uniformed offiers." *Id.* at 2566.

84. *Id.* at 2567–68.

85. *Id.* at 2566–67. Unlike persons discriminated against on the basis of race or national origin, the elderly "have not experienced a 'history of purposeful unequal treatment' or been subjected to unique disabilities on the basis of stereotyped characteristics not truly indicative of their abilities." *Id.* The dissenting opinion found it indisputable that the elderly constitute a class subject to "repeated and arbitrary" employment discrimination, regardless of whether the group constituted a suspect class. *Id.* at 2572 (Marshall, J., dissenting).

86. *Id.* at 2572. Mr. Justice Marshall has consistently advocated abandoning the rigid two-tier equal protection analysis still adhered to by a majority of the Court in favor of a flexible sliding scale approach that considers "the character of the classification in question, the relative importance to individuals in the class discriminated against of the gov-

tomatic termination of these officers from the force at age fifty seemed the "height of irrationality."[87]

Notably absent from either the per curiam or dissenting opinions was any reference to *LaFleur.* The failure to distinguish or to discuss this case is inexplicable, since the lower court found this analogy to be compelling.

Although noting that the problems of retirement are "beyond serious dispute,"[88] the *Murgia* Court declined to hold mandatory retirement laws for policemen unconstitutional. This decision should not, however, preclude other challenges to these laws in jobs where physical stamina is relatively unimportant.[89] As data accumulate on the relationship between aging and productivity,[90] and as the life span of the average American lengthens,[91] courts will find it increasingly difficult to find any rational basis behind mandatory retirement laws.

---

ernmental benefits that they do not receive, and the state interests asserted in support of the classification." *Id.* at 2569 (Marshall J., dissenting).

The reasons for holding the group categorization of individuals in terms of advanced age to be impermissible discrimination are eloquently stated by Justice Marshall.

> While depriving any government employee of his job is a significant deprivation, it is particularly burdensome when the person deprived is an older citizen. Once terminated, the elderly cannot readily find alternative employment. The lack of work is not only economically damaging, but emotionally and physically draining. Deprived of his status in the community and of the opportunity for meaningful activity, fearful of becoming dependent on others for his support, and lonely in his new-found isolation, the involuntarily retired person is susceptible to physical and emotional ailments as a direct consequence of his enforced idleness. Ample clinical evidence supports the conclusion that mandatory retirement poses a direct threat to the health and life expectancy of the retired person, and these consequences of termination for age are not disputed by appellant. Thus, an older person deprived of his job by the government loses not only his right to earn a living, but, too often, his health as well, in sad contradiction of Browning's promise, "The best is yet to be/The last of life, for which the first was made."

Id. at 2571–72 (footnotes omitted).

87. *Id.* at 2573 (Marshall, J., dissenting). In this situation, since annual physical examinations were required from age forty on, there would be no additional administrative burden required if physically fit officers were allowed to continue working past age fifty. *See* text accompanying note 22 *supra.*

88. 96 S. Ct. at 2568 (footnote omitted).

89. "The Court's conclusion today does not imply that all mandatory retirement laws are constitutionally valid. Here the primary state interest is in maintaining a physically fit police force, not a mentally alert or manually dexterous workforce. . . . Accordingly, a mandatory retirement law for all government employees would stand in a posture different from the law before us today." *Id.* at 2573 n.8 (Marshall, J., dissenting).

90. *See* notes 19–21 *supra* and accompanying text.

91. *See* text accompanying note 28 *supra.*

FUTURE DEVELOPMENTS

Among the policy questions that should receive greater attention in the next few years are the questions that relate to treatment of the aging. Research has stimulated decision makers to recognize the cumulative importance of the elderly. In industrializing societies the alleged resistance of the old to technical modernization has generated conflict in societies where age traditionally has been treated with great deference. In advanced industrial societies the discovery that, barring catastrophe, people will live even longer has spread confusion, uncertainty, and conflict among the policy makers in both public and civic order.

The policy of excluding the aged from significant social roles is open to so much adverse criticism that categorical declarations of obsolescence are not likely to survive. Our world is accustomed to mobilizing scientific knowledge and creative ingenuity, and it seems probable that these assets will be increasingly directed to problems connected with aging. The most fundamental approach is likely to be in terms of the overriding goal of finding social institutions that optimize the opportunities open to human beings at all levels of chronological aging. Assume, for instance, that we are on the brink of acquiring the knowledge necessary to lengthen every productive life some one-hundred years. It will be urgent that these capacities be utilized to improve the functioning of all institutions, so that value shaping activities are successfully expanded in both the material and the symbolic sectors of society. Enough has been accomplished already, though on a diminutive scale, to project the expectation that our civilization can continue to reconstruct itself in terms of its aspirations and capabilities.

Unlike problems specialized to some other forms of freedom, the immediate future of the human rights of the aged will focus on the intelligence, promotional, and prescriptive components of community decision making. The world community has not yet explicitly formulated the relevant general prescriptions or provided the structures of authority and procedures necessary to the effective application of these prescriptions. Our national community might appropriately reaffirm its commitment to the concept of human dignity.[92]

---

92. *See* chapters 8–14 *supra* for separate discussions of the claims relating to discrimination based on the grounds of race, sex, religion, political or other opinion, language, and alienage. A policy pervading so many different grounds of impermissible differentiation amply establishes that the contemporary norm of nondiscrimination is broad in reach. Studies of other grounds remain to be made. A brief itemization might include: possession of property, birth (legitimate or illegitimate child), homosexuality (sexual orientation), marital status, health (mental defect or illness), derivation of nationality (by birth or by

naturalization), moral character, behavior (criminal record), literacy, occupation (profession), nonidentification (disloyalty), and culture. Community prescriptions about these bases of differentiation are in the process of development.

More recent developments within our own national community demonstrate an increasing concern about arbitrary differentiation upon the ground of age. *See* Brickfield, *The Doors of Indifference,* 7 HUMAN RIGHTS 24 (No. 3, 1978). *See also* W. KENDIG, AGE DISCRIMINATION IN EMPLOYMENT (1978).

PART IV

Future Prospects

16. THE AGGREGATE INTEREST IN SHARED RESPECT AND HUMAN RIGHTS: THE HARMONIZATION OF PUBLIC ORDER AND CIVIC ORDER

In its most fundamental sense, respect may be defined as an interrelation among individual human beings in which they reciprocally honor each other's freedom of choice about participation in the value processes of the world community and its component parts. The central demand amidst all the rising common demands of peoples about the world today for the better clarification and securing of human rights would appear to be that of the individual for respect in this sense. The culminating achievement for a community that aspires to honor these demands and to secure human rights better may be described as that of a public and civic order in which individuals are subjected to the least possible coercion, from either public or private sources, in the making of their choices about participation in the community's various value processes.

In previous chapters we have explored the increasing protection that the global community seeks to afford individuals in their claims for a fundamental freedom of choice, for an effective equality of opportunity, and for distinctive recognition of preeminent contribution to common interest.[1] The tremendous emphasis that our contemporary society gives to the honoring of claims by individuals for these particular respect outcomes cannot, however, be permitted to blind us to the fact that every claim by individuals must be evaluated, by authoritative decision makers and others, in terms of the aggregate common interest.

By the aggregate common interest we refer to the greatest shaping and widest sharing, not only of respect, but of all the values of human

---

In slightly different form this chapter first appeared as *The Aggregate Interest in Shared Respect and Human Rights: The Harmonization of Public Order and Civic Order*, 23 N.Y.L.S.L. Rev. 183 (1977).

1. For our definition of "respect," *see* chapter 6 *supra*, at 451–52.
For further development, *see* part III *supra*.

dignity. The promotion of aggregate common interest requires an accommodation of the interests of any particular individual, in relation to respect or any other value, with those of other particular individuals and with the interests of all individuals in all other values.

The aggregate common interest need not be conceived as in antithesis to the individual interest.[2] The individual and society need not be considered as polar opposites. The aggregate interest may, however, be more than the sum total of particular individual interests, since an appropriate accommodation or integration can raise the level of value production ultimately available for all. In a properly functioning system of public order the interests of particular individuals are harmonized in a comprehensive process of shaping and sharing values which may enhance the quality of life for all.

The aggregate common interest includes both a comprehensive public order and a civic order. It encompasses the entire domain of both public decisions, constitutive and other, and private choices.[3] In the contemporary world of pluralistic and intimate interdependences, the aggregate common interest can be meaningfully and realistically postulated and achieved only in a mutually supportive integration of public order and civic order. By comprehensive public order we refer to the features of the social process which, if challenged, are established and maintained by effective power, authoritative or other, through the imposition of severe sanctions. Comprehensive public order thus includes both what we call constitutive decisions—the decisions that establish and maintain the process of authoritative decision—and the decisions which emerge from the constitutive process to regulate the shaping and sharing of all community values, such as wealth, enlightenment, well-being, and so on.[4] By civic order we refer to the features of social process that are

2. The artificiality of the dichotomy in the individual versus society was sharply indicated by Judge Lauterpacht:

> For it is clear that the distinction between the protection of the child and the protection of society is artificial. Both the laws relating to guardianship and those relating to protective upbringing are laws intended primarily for the protection of children and their interests. At the same time, the protection of children—through guardianship or protective upbringing—is preeminently in the interests of society. They are part of it—the most vulnerable and most in need of protection. All social laws are, in the last resort, laws for the protection of individuals; all laws for the protection of individuals are, in a true sense, social laws.

Guardianship of Infants Convention (1902) Case, [1958] I.C.J. 55, 85.

3. Though we contrapose choices and decisions, we recognize that the difference reflects merely a continuum in degree of severity of sanction. While decisions are severely sanctioned, choices are sustained by moderate or no sanction.

4. *See* Lasswell & McDougal, *Criteria for a Theory about Law*, 44 S. CAL. L. REV. 362, 385–88 (1971).

established and maintained by recourse to relatively mild sanctions and that afford the individual person a maximum of autonomy, creativity, and diversity in the making of private choices, with the least possible governmental or private coercion or interference.[5]

The boundaries between comprehensive public order and civic order exhibit a certain tension and are fluid and changing.[6] The difference between conventional meanings that are commonly accepted in a given setting and the functional distinctions that we adopt for purposes of valid comparison must be kept in mind. Prevailing expectations about the severity or mildness of actual or potential sanctions can be ascertained by means of contextual, empirical inquiry. It is important to note that what falls under the conventional label of government in some jurisdictions is not necessarily part of the public order. For instance, many community prescriptions are not expected to be, and are not, enforceable; many others involve only mild deprivations against offenders. On the other hand, many ecclesiastical, business and other activities, which are conventionally regarded as within the domain of civic order, may entail severe value consequences.

A major objective of contextual analysis is to exhibit value consequences within the full range of interaction in a dynamic and social process. It is, hence, of far less consequence to draw lines in a continuing gradation of events than to make certain that the whole spectrum is

5. The definition of civic order in terms both of choices maintained by mild sanction and of a maximum of autonomy in the making of private choices is designed to be self-reinforcing. When operationally defined, civic order refers to a social process in which choices are attended by a relatively small degree of expected or experienced deprivation (a minimum of coercion or constraint). All social interactions involve the application of indulgences and deprivations. Sanctions are the practices by which indulgences and deprivations are applied. Institutions labeled "governmental" may or may not maintain a monopoly of severe sanctions applied in the name of the community. Severe sanctions may in fact be applied by institutions labeled "private." For identifying choices made in the civic order, as contrasted with decisions made in the public order, it is necessary, therefore, both to pierce institutional labels for ascertaining functional realities and to consider the relative severity and mildness of sanctions. Civic order choices have the dimension of mildness in sanction, whatever the source of sanction. We do not hope or expect to operate in a social process in which choices can be free of all sanction. Autonomy connotes a wide range of choice, but not freedom from all sanction.

6. *See* notes 94–95 *infra* and accompanying text.

In the words of Theodore Lowi:

> The phrase "private life and public order" expresses two different ways of looking at the same thing: society in its effort to provide and to survive. In the real world it is impossible to separate private from public spheres. Analytically a distinction must be made between them, but only the better to assess their interconnections in the real world. "Private life and public order" is a statement of intimate relationship.

Introduction, in Private Life and Public Order vii (T. Lowi ed. 1968).

examined. The entire continuum from public through civic order poses significant policy problems for the maintenance of human rights. The freedom of choice that can be maintained with regard to any particular value process is a function both of the character and functioning of the constitutive process and of the allocations of access to all value processes.

If appropriate respect relationships are to be achieved in the inclusive world community, or in any component community, a civic order must be able to interact vigorously with a public order that performs its essential tasks. An adequate civic order is obtainable under an effectively functioning constitutive process whose structure is compatible with human dignity values and whose output of public order decisions defend and fulfill these goals. Conversely, the scope and quality of the civic order directly affect the constitutive process achievable and the flow of public order decisions.

For the development of these themes we propose to deal in sequence with, first, claims relating to comprehensive public order and, second, claims relating to the protection of civic order. Under each heading we will consider the factual background of problems, relevant policies, trends in past decision, the conditions affecting decision, and possible future alternatives.

CLAIMS RELATING TO COMPREHENSIVE PUBLIC ORDER

Factual Background

The claims relating to comprehensive public order are always complementary to the claims about more particular outcomes in relation to respect and other values. In a sense, the relevance of comprehensive public order has already been indicated in our discussions of the various claims about particular outcomes.[7] Thus, in various articles dealing with nondiscrimination we have noted the emergence of a general norm forbidding discrimination through any group label irrelevant to individual capabilities, and our central focus has always been upon whether or not a differentiation based upon a particular group categorization has a reasonable basis in relation to the common interest.[8] For purposes of clarity and emphasis, however, it may be worthwhile to reexamine the same factual settings with a more direct focus upon the aggregate common interest. The reasonableness of particular differentiations is best determined by reference to impacts upon both the comprehensive public order and the civic order which together constitute the whole of social process.

The specific events in social process with which we are concerned

---

7. *See* part III *supra.*
8. *See, e.g.,* chapter 10 *supra,* at notes 76–88 and accompanying text.

relate to incompatibilities in the demands of individuals and groups among themselves and in reference to more general claims on behalf of the aggregate common interest. In a pluralistic society it is inescapable that people make competitive, and sometimes incompatible, demands for different values and that the demands of individuals for particular values are upon occasion incompatible with community security, whether that security be conceived in the minimal sense of restraining violence and coercion or in the optimum sense of maximizing position, potential, and expectancy in the shaping and sharing of all values. The central point has been well made by Lauterpacht:

> Whatever designation of absoluteness we give to the rights of man—whether we call them fundamental, inherent, natural, or inalienable—they cannot be absolute. For they have a meaning only in relation to man living in society under the shelter of the political organization of the State. Even his fundamental rights must be exercised with due regard to the rights of others and to the safety and the welfare of the State. Freedom of speech and opinion can be recognized and protected only if it is made use of in a manner consistent with the law of libel and with public peace. Personal liberty cannot be absolute. It is subject to restraints and sanctions which the criminal law imposes for the protection of other members of the community and the common good. Even freedom of religion is conditioned by similar limitations.[9]

It is this diversity and potential for incompatibility in the demands of individuals and groups that condition the omnipresent complementarity and ambiguity in general community prescriptions, whether about respect or other values. In a world of scarce resources and enormous variations in value demands, identifications and expectations, an appropriate accommodation of common interest is a continuing necessity. Despite all the realities of diversity, it is easily observable that all manner of effective working arrangements are continuously made and maintained, through authoritative decision and otherwise, in the pursuit and furtherance of the common interest.

---

9. H. Lauterpacht, An International Bill of the Rights of Man 183–84 (1945) (footnote omitted).

For a detailed articulation of the necessity of accommodation, *see* I. Berlin, Four Essays on Liberty 118–72 (1969). As one author has stated: "To guarantee a liberty is to create an unliberty. It is to tell some people that they have a choice and others that they do not. It is to make a distinction between liberties. It is to say that some are more important than others." Frankel, *The Jurisprudence of Liberty,* 46 Miss. L.J. 561, 564 (1975). *See generally* Gorove, *The Protection of Human Rights in Constitutional Law,* in Law in the United States of America in Social and Technological Revolution 425 (J. Hazard & W. Wagner eds. 1974) [hereinafter cited as Law in the United States].

Basic Community Policies

It is as important in relation to respect outcomes as in relation to other value outcomes to recognize the critical need for, and to make appropriate provision for, the rational accommodation of any particular individual's rights with the comparable rights of others and with the aggregate common interest. The necessities for such accommodation are all-pervasive in social process and embrace ordinary noncrisis as well as crisis situations, in which the aggregate common interest is more intensely threatened.

It would not appear that new substantive policy criteria, beyond those specified in earlier discussion,[10] are required for guiding the necessary accommodations. The postulation of the basic goal values of human dignity, the more general preferences inherent in this postulation about the shaping and sharing of respect and other values, and the more general preferences about a constitutive process which both reflects and secures human dignity values—all these remain relevant.[11] It should not be difficult to formulate content principles for exploring different contexts in order to ascertain the potential impact upon basic preferences of different options in decision.[12] For evaluating decision options in situations of crisis, appropriate principles of necessity and proportionality have long been employed.[13] The underlying policy, in application of all particular principles, must of course be that of establishing a framework of community expectation and practice in which all people enjoy and exercise the utmost freedom of choice about participation in all value processes.

Similarly, the principles of procedure recommended for the application of any human rights prescription would appear equally appropriate in applications that require the accommodation of claims. It remains important to suspend judgment while exploring all features of the context, to confront the alternative versions of reality in the problem at

---

10. *See* part III *supra.*

11. *See* McDougal, *Human Rights and World Public Order: Principles of Content and Procedure for Clarifying General Community Policies*, 14 Va. J. Int'l L. 387 (1974); chapter 6 *supra*, at notes 18–52 and accompanying text.

12. *See* chapter 5 *supra;* M. McDougal, H. Lasswell, & J. Miller, The Interpretation of Agreements and World Public Order: Principles of Content and Procedure (1967); Lasswell, *Clarifying Value Judgment: Principles of Content and Procedure,* 1 Inquiry 87 (No. 2 1958); Lasswell, *The Public Interest: Proposing Principles of Content and Procedure,* in The Public Interest 54 (Friedrich ed. 1962) [hereinafter cited as *The Public Interest*]; McDougal, *supra* note 11, at 403–04.

13. *See* notes 47–50 *infra* and accompanying text. For application of the principles of necessity and proportionality in the macro-context of aggression and self-defense, see M. McDougal & F. Feliciano, Law and Minimum World Public Order 121–260 (1961).

hand, to pierce through the manifest claims about facts and policies to the genuine problems which the disinterested observer can identify, and to employ a wide range of intellectual skills—historical, scientific, developmental, and inventive—in assaying the benefits and costs to fundamental policies of different options.[14]

The overall task is that of securing the flow of applications of human rights prescriptions which best protects the rights of individuals, while simultaneously promoting the aggregate common interest. The rights that can be secured for anyone in any particular instance are a function both of the values at stake and of many relevant conditioning factors in a dynamic context. Similarly, the importance of any particular value to the claimant and others is a function of the ever-changing context. Although some values may be more intensely demanded than others by community members, there can be no absolute hierarchy of importance among different values. What can ultimately be protected must differ from value to value, from problem to problem even in the same value process, and from context to context. The most important policy concern, as we have indicated elsewhere, must be that of developing a contextual method that effectively employs adequate principles of content and procedure both to facilitate close scrutiny of all the pertinent variables and to evaluate the consequences of alternative decisions.[15]

It may require especial vigilance to insure that the claim to integrate a common interest is not abused. Power elites notoriously often confuse their special interests in power and other values with the common interest of the community as a whole. It cannot be denied that the interests of the global community and of its component communities are often not fully realized in fact and that what is proffered as common interest is sometimes spurious. Nonetheless, the urgent need for improving the harmony of particular interests in the aggregate of protected interests cannot rationally be denied or neglected.

Trends in Decision

The human rights prescriptions which affect respect, like the demands they express and protect in a pluralistic society, are both complementary in form (in terms of the rights protected) and highly abstract in their particular formulations.[16] Fortunately, many prescriptions have explicitly recognized the necessity for accommodating particular inter-

---

14. *See* M. McDougal, H. Lasswell, & J. Miller, *supra* note 12, at 65–77, 270–359; McDougal, *supra* note 11, at 404–05.

15. *See* note 12 *supra;* chapter 6 *supra,* at notes 20–32 and accompanying text.

16. *See* McDougal, *supra* note 11, at 390. For a detailed development of the complementarity in legal principle in correspondence to complementarity in social process, *see* McDougal, *The Ethics of Applying Systems of Authority: The Balanced Opposites of a Legal System,*

ests with the aggregate common interest in both ordinary and crisis situations. This recognition appears both in broad, general provisions and in the specification of particular values.

It would appear to make little difference in what form provision for accommodation is made, or whether all provisions are repetitious and cumulative in effect. Since accommodation always requires connecting particular claims in reference to different values in contexts of expanding impact and interdependence, we conclude that accommodations can rationally be made only in terms of the largest context and of impacts upon all values. Therefore, provisions that require the accommodation of any particular value outcome with other outcomes and with the aggregate common interest must of necessity go beyond any single value process and refer to all interacting processes in the larger community. Certainly, since the value "respect" is defined in terms of freedom of access to all values,[17] both the general provisions for accommodation which make explicit reference to many different values and the more particular provisions which focus primarily upon the necessities of accommodation in relation to some particular value inevitably affect the shaping and sharing of respect.

In brief exploration of how respect outcomes may be affected, it will be convenient to note, first, provisions for the accommodation of particular human rights with other human rights and the aggregate common interest, and, second, provisions for permissible derogations from some human rights in times of high crisis and intense threat to general community interest.

The explicit recognition of the necessity for rational accommodation, even in noncrisis situations, is admirably indicated in the Universal Declaration of Human Rights. After spelling out in serial detail the more important rights of the individual in its first twenty-seven articles, the Universal Declaration concludes by devoting its last three articles—28, 29, and 30—to expression of the kind of aggregate concern we recommend.

The overriding importance of the aggregate common interest is projected, in Article 28, in the most comprehensive terms: "Everyone is entitled to a social and international order in which the rights and freedoms set forth in this Declaration can be fully realized."[18] This brief

in THE ETHIC OF POWER: THE INTERPLAY OF RELIGION, PHILOSOPHY, AND POLITICS 221 (H. Lasswell & H. Cleveland eds. 1962). *See also* M. COHEN, REASON AND NATURE 165-68 (1931); Cardozo, *The Paradoxes of Legal Science,* in SELECTED WRITINGS OF BENJAMIN NATHAN CARDOZO 251, 252-70 (M. Hall ed. 1947).

17. *See* chapter 6 *supra,* at 451-52.

18. Universal Declaration of Human Rights, *adopted* Dec. 10, 1948, Art. 28, G.A. Res. 217, U.N. Doc. A/810 at 71, 76 (1948) [hereinafter cited as Universal Declaration].

provision but reflects the widely held view that, in the contemporary world of global interdependences, the human rights of the individual can be made meaningful and secure only by reference to the most inclusive context.

The inherent components of a comprehensive public order are articulated in Article 29:

> 1. Everyone has duties to the community in which alone the free and full development of his personality is possible.
> 2. In the exercise of his rights and freedoms, everyone shall be subject only to such limitations as are determined by law solely for the purpose of securing due recognition and respect for the rights and freedoms of others and of meeting the just requirements of morality, public order and the general welfare in a democratic society.
> 3. These rights and freedoms may in no case be exercised contrary to the purposes and principles of the United Nations.[19]

The provision that "everyone has duties to the community" is an indication of the relativity of the rights to be accorded to the individual; rights and duties are, indeed, regarded as two sides of the same coin. The equal emphasis upon rights and duties is made even more pronounced in the American Declaration on the Rights and Duties of Man, which is divided into two chapters: the first dealing with "Rights" and the second with "Duties."[20] Paragraph 2 of Article 29 is a key provision in its insistence that there is a comprehensive public order in which appropriate particular accommodations of conflicting claims are to be made. It provides a broad framework within which any one particular value outcome is to be reconciled with all other relevant value outcomes, aggregate or particular, in an ever-changing community context.

Exemplifying its concern for accommodations which do not unnecessarily deprive the rights of individuals, the Universal Declaration, in Article 30, provides a final safeguard and reminder: "Nothing in this Declaration may be interpreted as implying for any State, group or person any right to engage in any activity or to perform any act aimed at the destruction of any of the rights and freedoms set forth herein."[21] In

---

19. *Id.*, Art. 29, U.N. Doc. A/810, at 76–77.

20. American Declaration of the Rights and Duties of Man, Resolution XXX, *adopted* by the Ninth International Conference of American States, held at Bogota, Colombia, 30 Mar.–2 May 1948, *Pan American Union, Final Act of the Ninth Conference of American States* 38–45 (1948), *reprinted in* BASIC DOCUMENTS ON INTERNATIONAL PROTECTION OF HUMAN RIGHTS 187 (L. Sohn & T. Buergenthal eds. 1973) [hereinafter cited as American Declaration and BASIC DOCUMENTS, respectively].

21. Universal Declaration, *supra* note 18, Art. 30, U.N. Doc. A/810 at 77.

a complex world in which the rights of the individual can be affected by so many actors, official and other, in so many different ways, Article 30 serves as a significant admonition. Its message is simple and clear: the rights and freedoms protected are not to be diluted or destroyed under any pretext, even in the name of accommodation.[22]

This safeguarding theme, so manifest in the Universal Declaration, is reiterated in both Covenants on Human Rights. Thus, the International Covenant on Civil and Political Rights, in Article 5, provides:

> 1. Nothing in the present Covenant may be interpreted as implying for any State, group or person any right to engage in any activity or perform any act aimed at the destruction of any of the rights and freedoms recognized herein or at their limitation to a greater extent than is provided for in the present Covenant.
> 2. There shall be no restriction upon or derogation from any of the fundamental human rights recognized or existing in any State Party to the present Covenant pursuant to law, conventions, regulations or custom on the pretext that the present Covenant does not recognize such rights or that it recognizes them to a lesser extent.[23]

Similarly, the International Covenant on Economic, Social, and Cultural Rights, in Article 4, provides:

> The States Parties to the present Covenant recognize that, in the enjoyment of those rights provided by the State in conformity with the present Covenant, the State may subject such rights only to such limitations as are determined by law only in so far as this may be compatible with the nature of these rights and solely for the purpose of promoting the general welfare in a democratic society.[24]

Article 5 further states:

> 1. Nothing in the present Covenant may be interpreted as implying for any State, group or person any right to engage in any activity or to perform any act aimed at the destruction of any of the rights or freedoms recognized herein, or at their limitation to a greater extent than is provided for in the present Covenant.

---

22. *See* N. Robinson, The Universal Declaration of Human Rights 143 (1958).

23. International Covenant on Civil and Political Rights, *adopted* Dec. 16, 1966, Art. 5, G.A. Res. 2200A, 21 U.N. GAOR, Supp. (No. 16) 49, 53, U.N. Doc. A/6316 (1966) [hereinafter cited as Covenant on Civil and Political Rights].

24. International Covenant on Economic, Social and Cultural Rights, *adopted* Dec. 16, 1966, Art. 4, G.A. Res. 2200A, 21 U.N. GAOR, Supp. (No. 16) 49, 50, U.N. Doc. A/6316 (1966) [hereinafter cited as Covenant on Economic Rights].

2. No restriction upon or derogation from any of the fundamental human rights recognized or existing in any country in virtue of law, conventions, regulations or custom shall be admitted on the pretext that the present Covenant does not recognize such rights or that it recognizes them to a lesser extent.[25]

This same theme is given further expression in the regional human rights prescriptions. The European Convention on Human Rights states in Article 17:

> Nothing in this Convention may be interpreted as implying for any State, group or person any right to engage in any activity or perform any act aimed at the destruction of any of the rights and freedoms set forth herein or at their limitation to a greater extent than is provided for in the Convention.[26]

Article 18 of the European Convention further stipulates: "The restrictions permitted under this Convention to the said rights and freedoms shall not be applied for any purpose other than those for which they have been prescribed."[27]

The provisions in the American Convention on Human Rights are even more elaborate. Article 29 reads:

> No provision of this Convention shall be interpreted as:
>
> (a) permitting any State Party, group, or person to suppress the enjoyment or exercise of the rights and freedoms recognized in this Convention or to restrict them to a greater extent than is provided for herein;
>
> (b) restricting the enjoyment or exercise of any right or freedom recognized by virtue of the laws of any State Party or by virtue of another convention to which one of the said states is a party;
>
> (c) precluding other rights or guarantees that are inherent in the human personality or derived from representative democracy as a form of government; or
>
> (d) excluding or limiting the effect that the American Declaration

---

25. *Id.,* Art. 5, 21 U.N. GAOR, Supp. (No. 16) at 50.

26. Convention for the Protection of Human Rights and Fundamental Freedoms, *adopted* Nov. 4, 1950, Art. 17, [1950] Europ. T.S. No. 5, 213 U.N.T.S. 221, 234 [hereinafter cited as European Convention].

27. *Id.,* Art. 18, 213 U.N.T.S. at 234. The case law and problems relating to accommodations and derogations in the context of the European Convention of Human Rights are offered in EUROPEAN COMMISSION OF HUMAN RIGHTS, CASE-LAW TOPICS, NO. 4: "HUMAN RIGHTS AND THEIR LIMITATIONS" (1973) [hereinafter cited as "HUMAN RIGHTS AND THEIR LIMITATIONS"].

> of the Rights and Duties of Man and other international acts of the same nature may have.[28]

Article 30 provides:

> The restrictions that, pursuant to this Convention, may be placed on the enjoyment or exercise of the rights or freedoms recognized herein may not be applied except in accordance with laws enacted for reasons of general interest and in accordance with the purpose for which such restrictions have been established.[29]

And Article 32 states:

> 1. Every person has responsibilities to his family, his community, and mankind.
> 2. The rights of each person are limited by the rights of others, by the security of all, and by the just demands of the general welfare, in a democratic society.[30]

In addition to all these general provisions about accommodation, there are a host of more particular prescriptions, in relation to specific values, which affect the shaping and sharing of respect. Provisions which make explicit reference to respect itself, even in the more limited sense of "privacy," are infrequent. One example is found in the European Convention on Human Rights, which provides in Article 8:

> 1. Everyone has the right to respect for his private and family life, his home and his correspondence.
> 2. There shall be no interference by a public authority with the exercise of this right except such as is in accordance with the law and is necessary in a democratic society in the interests of national security, public safety or the economic well-being of the country, for the prevention of disorder or crime, for the protection of health or morals, or for the protection of the rights and freedoms of others.[31]

An excellent example of a particular provision in relation to another value which must affect respect, in its broadest sense, is found in the prescriptions concerning freedom of association. The International Covenant on Civil and Political Rights, in Article 22, provides:

---

28. American Convention on Human Rights, *signed* Nov. 22, 1969, Art. 29, OAS Official Records OEA/Ser.K/XVI/1.1, Doc. 65, Rev. 1, Corr. 1 (Jan. 7, 1970), *reprinted in* 9 INT'L LEGAL MATERIALS 99, 110 (1970) [hereinafter cited as American Convention].

29. *Id.*, Art. 30, 9 INT'L LEGAL MATERIALS at 110.

30. *Id.*, Art. 32, 9 INT'L LEGAL MATERIALS at 110.

31. European Convention, *supra* note 26, Art. 8, 213 U.N.T.S. at 230.

1. Everyone shall have the right to freedom of association with others, including the right to form and join trade unions for the protection of his interests.
2. No restrictions may be placed on the exercise of this right other than those which are prescribed by law and which are necessary in a democratic society in the interests of national security or public safety, public order (*ordre public*), the protection of public health or morals or the protection of the rights and freedoms of others. This article shall not prevent the imposition of lawful restrictions on members of the armed forces and of the police in their exercise of this right.
3. Nothing in this article shall authorize States Parties to the International Labour Organization Convention of 1948 concerning Freedom of Association and Protection of the Right to Organize to take legislative measures which would prejudice, or to apply the law in such a manner as to prejudice, the guarantees provided for in that Convention.[32]

Comparable provisions are found in Article 11 of the European Convention on Human Rights[33] and Article 16 of the American Convention on Human Rights.[34]

Other particular provisions for accommodation, which inevitably affect respect, abound. The list includes:

1. In relation to power: Articles 12(3), 13, 14(1), and 21 of the International Covenant on Civil and Political Rights (regarding

---

32. Covenant on Civil and Political Rights, *supra* note 23, Art. 22, 21 U.N. GAOR, Supp. (No. 16) at 55.

33. Art. 11 states:

> 1. Everyone has the right to . . . freedom of association with others, including the right to form and to join trade unions for the protection of his interests.
> 2. No restrictions shall be placed on the exercise of these rights other than such as are prescribed by law and are necessary in a democratic society in the interests of national security or public safety, for the prevention of disorder or crime, for the protection of health or morals or for the protection of the rights and freedoms of others. This Article shall not prevent the imposition of lawful restriction on the exercise of these rights by members of the armed forces, of the police or of the administration of the State.

European Convention, *supra* note 26, Art. 11, 213 U.N.T.S. at 232.

34. Art. 16 provides:

> 1. Everyone shall have the right to associate freely for ideological, religious, political, economic, labour, social, cultural, sports, or other purposes.
> 2. Exercise of this right shall be subject only to such restrictions established by law as may be necessary in a democratic society, in the interest of national security,

freedom of movement and residence, freedom from expulsion, "a fair and public hearing," and freedom of assembly);[35] Articles 5(1), 6, and 11 of the European Convention on Human Rights (concerning "the right to liberty and security of person," "a fair and public hearing," and freedom of assembly);[36] Article 2 of the Fourth Protocol of the European Convention (regarding freedom of movement and residence);[37] and Articles 15 and 22 of the American Convention on Human Rights (concerning freedom of assembly and freedom of movement and residence);[38]

2. In relation to enlightenment: Article 19(3) of the International Covenant on Civil and Political Rights (regarding freedom of expression);[39] Article 10 of the European Convention on Human Rights (regarding freedom of expression);[40] and Article 13 of the American Convention on Human Rights (concerning freedom of expression);[41]
3. In relation to wealth: Article 1 of the First Protocol of the European Convention on Human Rights (regarding the right to property)[42] and Article 21 of the American Convention on Human Rights (regarding the right to property);[43]
4. In relation to rectitude: Article 18(3) of the International Covenant on Civil and Political Rights (regarding "freedom to manifest one's religion and beliefs");[44] Article 9(2) of the European Con-

---

public safety, or public order, or to protect public health or morals or the rights and freedoms of others.

3. The provisions of this article do not bar the imposition of legal restrictions, including even deprivation of the exercise of the right of association, on members of the armed forces and the police.

American Convention, *supra* note 28, Art. 16, 9 INT'L LEGAL MATERIALS at 106.

35. Covenant on Civil and Political Rights, *supra* note 23, Arts. 12(3), 13, 14(1), and 21, 21 U.N. GAOR, Supp. (No. 16) at 54–55.

36. European Convention, *supra* note 26, Arts. 5(1), 6, and 11, 213 U.N.T.S. at 226–32.

37. COUNCIL OF EUROPE, EUROPEAN CONVENTION ON HUMAN RIGHTS: COLLECTED TEXTS 44 (11th ed. 1976) [hereinafter cited as COLLECTED TEXTS].

38. American Convention, *supra* note 28, Arts. 15 and 22, 9 INT'L LEGAL MATERIALS at 106–08.

39. Covenant on Civil and Political Rights, *supra* note 23, Art. 19(3), 21 U.N. GAOR, Supp. (No. 16) at 55.

40. European Convention, *supra* note 26, Art. 10, 213 U.N.T.S. at 230.

41. American Convention, *supra* note 28, Art. 13, 9 INT'L LEGAL MATERIALS at 105–06.

42. European Convention, *supra* note 26, Protocol to the Convention for the Protection of Human Rights and Fundamental Freedoms, *signed* Mar. 20, 1952, in European Convention, Protocol No. 1, Art. 1, 213 U.N.T.S. at 262.

43. American Convention, *supra* note 28, Art. 21, 9 INT'L LEGAL MATERIALS at 107.

44. Covenant on Civil and Political Rights, *supra* note 23, Art. 18(3), 21 U.N. GAOR, Supp. (No. 16) at 55.

vention on Human Rights (regarding "[f]reedom to manifest one's religion or beliefs");[45] and Article 12(3) of the American Convention on Human Rights (regarding "[f]reedom to manifest one's religion and beliefs").[46]

Provisions that authorize derogations from particular rights in times of high crisis, and which in consequence may affect the shaping and sharing of respect, are also found in all the major human rights conventions. The International Covenant on Civil and Political Rights, in Article 4, provides:

> 1. In time of public emergency which threatens the life of the nation and the existence of which is officially proclaimed, the States Parties to the present Covenant may take measures derogating from their obligations under the present Covenant to the extent strictly required by the exigencies of the situation, provided that such measures are not inconsistent with their other obligations under international law and do not involve discrimination solely on the ground of race, colour, sex, language, religion or social origin.
> 2. No derogation from articles 6, 7, 8 (paragraphs 1 and 2), 11, 15, 16 and 18 may be made under this provision.
> 3. Any State Party to the present Covenant availing itself of the right of derogation shall immediately inform the other States Parties to the present Covenant, through the intermediary of the Secretary-General of the United Nations of the provisions from which it has derogated and of the reasons by which it was actuated. A further communication shall be made, through the same intermediary on the date on which it terminates such derogation.[47]

The wording of the European Convention on Human Rights differs slightly. Article 15(1) reads:

> In time of war or other public emergency threatening the life of the nation any High Contracting Party may take measures derogating from its obligations under this Convention to the extent strictly required by the exigencies of the situation, provided that such measures are not inconsistent with its other obligations under international law.[48]

---

45. European Convention, *supra* note 26, Art. 9(2), 213 U.N.T.S. at 230.

46. American Convention, *supra* note 28, Art. 12(3), 9 INT'L LEGAL MATERIALS at 105.

47. Covenant on Civil and Political Rights, *supra* note 23, Art. 4, 21 U.N. GAOR, Supp. (No. 16) at 53.

48. European Convention, *supra* note 26, Art. 15(1), 213 U.N.T.S. at 232.

The American Convention on Human Rights, similarly, contains a derogation clause in Article 27, which reads in part:

> In time of war, public danger, or other emergency that threatens the independence or security of a State Party, it may take measures derogating from its obligations under the present Convention to the extent and for the period of time strictly required by the exigencies of the situation, provided that such measures are not inconsistent with its other obligations under international law and do not involve discrimination on the ground of race, color, sex, language, religion, or social origin.[49]

It will be noted that these prescriptions impose requirements of necessity and proportionality, the ascertainment of which must entail examination of very large factual contexts.[50]

It will be observed that all the prescriptions outlined above, whether providing for accommodation or authorizing derogation, have exhibited remarkable uniformity both in their emphasis upon the aggregate common interest and in their itemization of particular important policies. The recurring terms of reference, in quick inventory, include: "meeting the just requirements of morality, public order and the general welfare in a democratic society"; "national security"; "public safety"; "public order (*ordre public*)"; "the protection of public health"; "morals"; "the protection of the rights and freedoms of others"; "for the prevention of disorder or crime"; "the rights of others"; "the security of all"; "the just

---

49. American Convention, *supra* note 28, Art. 27, 9 INT'L LEGAL MATERIALS at 109.

50. It may be observed that the intellectual difficulties in problems of accommodation and derogation are much the same, with the latter distinguishable only by the additional fact of alleged community crisis. For general discussion of the complexities of the problems of derogation and accommodation, *see* F. CASTBERG, THE EUROPEAN CONVENTION ON HUMAN RIGHTS 165–70 (T. Opsahl & T. Ouchterlony eds. 1974); A. DEL RUSSO, INTERNATIONAL PROTECTION OF HUMAN RIGHTS 123–28, 155–59 (1971); J. FAWCETT, THE APPLICATION OF THE EUROPEAN CONVENTION ON HUMAN RIGHTS 245–50 (1969); F. JACOBS, THE EUROPEAN CONVENTION ON HUMAN RIGHTS 195–214 (1975); A. ROBERTSON, HUMAN RIGHTS IN EUROPE 112–39 (1963); Becket, *The Greek Case before the European Human Rights Commission,* 1 HUMAN RIGHTS 91 (1970); Buergenthal, *Proceedings against Greece under the European Convention of Human Rights,* 62 AM. J. INT'L L. 441 (1968); Coleman, *Greece and the Council of Europe: The International Legal Protection of Human Rights by the Political Process,* 2 ISRAEL Y.B. HUMAN RIGHTS 121 (1972); Daes, *Restrictions and Limitations on Human Rights,* in INT'L INST. OF HUMAN RIGHTS, 3 RENÉ CASSIN, AMICORUM DISCIPULORUMQUE LIBER 79 (1971); LAW IN THE UNITED STATES, *supra* note 9; *Lawless v. Ireland* (*Merits*), 4 Y.B. EUR. CONV. ON HUMAN RIGHTS 438 (1961); Morrison, *Margin of Appreciation in Human Rights Law,* 6 HUMAN RIGHTS J. 263 (1973); Schwelb, *Some Aspects of the International Covenants on Human Rights of December 1966,* in INTERNATIONAL PROTECTION OF HUMAN RIGHTS 103, 114–17 (A. Eide & A. Schou eds. 1968); Smith, *The European Convention on Human Rights and the Right of Derogation: A Solution to the Problem of Domestic Jurisdiction,* 11 HOW. L.J. 594 (1965); Van Boven, *Some Remarks on Special Problems Relating to Human Rights in Developing Countries,* 3 HUMAN RIGHTS J. 383, 391–92 (1970).

demands of the general welfare"; "in a democratic society"; "the economic well-being of the country"; "compelling reasons of national security"; "the interests of justice"; "the interest of juvenile persons"; "public interest"; and "the public interest in a democratic society."

What has been conspicuously missing from this rich body of prescriptive statement has been detailed specification of the principles of application, especially of procedure, which might be employed to increase the possibility of making rational accommodations and derogations. Exhortations to secure the balanced protection of all values and to take the aggregate common interest into account can scarcely be made effective without the specification of principles, at lower levels of abstraction, designed to facilitate the exploration of factual contexts and the assessment of the value benefits and costs of available options.

It is not adequate discharge of this particular intellectual responsibility to emphasize, as many of the prescriptions do, the importance of due process of law, in the sense that decisions about accommodation be taken in accordance with the law ("in accordance with the law," "determined by law," "prescribed by law," "in conformity with law"). This requirement for conformity with the law is of course designed to ensure that decisions are taken within structures of authority and to minimize elements of arbitrariness in the course of decision.[51] The requirement of recourse to authoritative structures for decision, though necessary, is no effective substitute for the provision of appropriate intellectual tools.[52] It is remarkable that even the literature of human rights has made so little contribution to the development of useful principles of application, either of content or of procedure.

CLAIMS RELATING TO CIVIC ORDER (INCLUDING PRIVACY)

Factual Background

By civic order, as previously indicated, we refer to the features of social process that are cultivated and sustained by recourse to relatively mild rather than severe sanctions.[53] It is the domain of social process in which the individual person is freest from coercion, governmental or other, and in which a high degree of individual autonomy and creativity prevails. Civic order thus includes all of the processes and institutions of private choice, as distinguished from public decision.[54] The core reference of civic order is, it may be reiterated, to freedom of choice for participation in each of the value processes. However, in contrast with the claims of particular individuals for a "fundamental freedom of

---

51. *See* Daes, *supra* note 50, at 82–86.
52. *See* notes 11–15 *supra* and accompanying text. *See also* chapter 5 *supra*.
53. *See* notes 4–6 *supra* and accompanying text.
54. *See* note 3 *supra*.

choice in value participation," the claims with which we dealt under the first outcome of respect,[55] the focus here is upon a freedom of choice not involving immediate and particular public decision; our concern is for the larger flow of decision protecting aggregate patterns of freedom of choice for all individuals and groups. The distinctive reference of civic order is to the totality of freedom of choice achieved or achievable in a community.

Civic order, as we define it, includes "privacy," but we give a more limited reference to privacy. The term "privacy" is, in much contemporary usage, accorded a wide range of reference.[56] Sometimes it is employed as a functional equivalent to the "right to be let alone," with practically the same broad reference that we impute to civic order.[57] It appears more appropriate, however, to restrict the reference of privacy to freedom of the individual in terms of the information that can be acquired and communicated by, and to, others about him.[58] So defined,

---

55. *See* chapter 7 *supra.*

56. Arthur R. Miller observes:

> The concept of privacy is difficult to define because it is exasperatingly vague and evanescent, often meaning strikingly different things to different people. In part this is because privacy is a notion that is emotional in its appeal and embraces a multitude of different "rights," some of which are intertwined, others often seemingly unrelated or inconsistent.

A. Miller, The Assault on Privacy: Computers, Data Banks, and Dossiers 25 (1971) (footnote omitted). Similarly, Dixon has stated: "Few concepts . . . are more vague or less amenable to definition and structural treatment than privacy." Dixon, *The Griswold Penumbra: Constitution Charter for an Expanded Law of Privacy?* 64 Mich. L. Rev. 197, 199 (1965).

On the diversity of the concept of privacy, *see* Parker, *A Definition of Privacy,* 27 Rutgers L. Rev. 275 (1974). In addition to notes 58, 144, 169, 184, and 223 *infra, see also* Report of the Committee on Privacy, Cmnd. No. 5012, at 17–22, 327–28 (Comm. Print 1972) [hereinafter cited as The Younger Report]; Can. Dep't of Com./Dep't of Just., Task Force, Privacy and Computers 12–14 (1972) [hereinafter cited as Privacy and Computers]; M. Ernst & A. Schwartz, Privacy: The Right to Be Let Alone (1962); H. Gross, Privacy—Its Legal Protection (1964); Privacy (NOMOS XIII, J. Pennock & J. Chapman eds. 1971); United States Office of Science and Technology, Privacy and Behavioral Research (1967); Christie, *The Right to Privacy and the Freedom to Know: A Comment on Professor Miller's The Assault on Privacy,* 119 U. Pa. L. Rev. 970 (1971); Gross, *The Concept of Privacy,* 42 N.Y.U.L. Rev. 34 (1967); Lusky, *Invasion of Privacy: A Clarification of Concepts,* 72 Colum. L. Rev. 693 (1972); Reubhausen & Brim, Jr., *Privacy and Behavioral Research,* 65 Colum. L. Rev. 1184 (1965); Shils, *Privacy: Its Constitution and Vicissitudes,* 31 Law & Contemp. Prob. 281 (1966); Simmel, *Privacy,* 12 Int'l Encyc. Soc. Sc. 480 (1968); *Symposium,* 4 Colum. Human Rights L. Rev. 1 (1972); *Symposium–Privacy,* 31 Law & Contemp. Prob. 251 (1966); Wagner, *The Right of Privacy and Its Limitations in the U.S.A.,* in Law in the United States of America in Social and Technological Revolution 491 (J. Hazard & W. Wagner eds. 1974).

57. The expression "the right to be let alone" is attributed to Judge Cooley. T. Cooley, The Law of Torts 29 (2d ed. 1888). *See* notes 129–223 *infra* and accompanying text.

58. Such a restrictive reference is offered by Westin: "Privacy is the claim of individuals,

the concept serves as an important component of the more comprehensive freedoms encompassed within a properly functioning civic order. Such restrictive usage may help to bring relevant policy considerations into sharper focus and to facilitate the contextual analysis essential to decision making.

The aggregate patterns of civic order are of course comprised of the particular assertions of fundamental freedoms of choice by individuals in the different value processes. It may be recalled that we described these fundamental freedoms, in relation to values other than power, as follows:

> in relation to enlightenment, the freedom to acquire, use, and communicate knowledge; in relation to well-being, the freedom to develop and maintain psychosomatic integrity and a healthy personality; in relation to wealth, freedom of contract and of access to goods and services; in relation to skill, the freedom to discover, mature, and exercise latent talents; in relation to affection, the freedom to establish and enjoy congenial personal relationships; and in relation to rectitude, freedom to form, maintain, and express norms of responsible conduct.[59]

From a global perspective, the achievement of a comprehensive civic order, in which the aggregate pattern of social interaction affords all individuals and groups a fundamental freedom of choice in the shaping and sharing of all values, is more aspiration than reality. In an interdependent yet divided world in which demands for the unity of humankind interplay with the practices of parochial fragmentation, continuing expectations of violence, external as well as internal, are widely shared by the elite and the rank and file alike.[60] Under "a global war system,"[61]

---

groups, or institutions to determine for themselves when, how, and to what extent information about them is communicated to others." A. Westin, Privacy and Freedom 7 (1968). Similarly, Arthur Miller writes: "[T]he basic attribute of an effective right of privacy is the individual's ability to control the circulation of information relating to him—a power that often is essential to maintaining social relationships and personal freedom." A. Miller, *supra* note 56, at 25. In the words of Fried: "Privacy is not simply an absence of information about us in the minds of others; rather it is the *control* we have over information about ourselves." Fried, *Privacy,* 77 Yale L.J. 475, 482 (1968).

59. Chapter 7 *supra,* at 470.

60. *See generally* R. Barnet, The Roots of War (1972); B. Cochran, The War System (1965); R. Falk, Legal Order in a Violent World (1968); R. Falk, This Endangered Planet (1971); H. Lasswell, World Politics and Personal Insecurity (1965 ed.); Law and Civil War in the Modern World (J. Moore ed. 1974); R. Nisbet, Twilight of Authority 146–93 (1975); 3 The Future of the International Legal Order (C. Black & R. Falk eds. 1971); Lasswell, *The Garrison State Hypothesis Today,* in Changing Patterns of Military Politics 51 (S. Huntington ed. 1962); Lasswell, *The Garrison State and Specialists on Violence,* in H. Lasswell, The Analysis of Political Behavior 146 (1948).

61. Reisman, *Private Armies in a Global War System: Prologue to Decision,* in Law and Civil

threats of violence and preparations for defense have generated "a pervasive anxiety for personal and group security,"[62] culminating in "a constant process of mobilization of the population under the supervision of security experts, anxiety managers, and specialists in violence."[63]

In many communities, under perpetual apprehension of violence, power considerations, as measured by aggregate fighting potential, inevitably predominate. The overriding goal of maintaining national security in the sense of freedom from external coercion and dictation necessitates the continuing appraisal and reappraisal of all social values and institutional practices with state-power considerations in view. Wealth values and institutions are drawn into the task of national defense and mobilization and are hence subordinated to power. Scientific skill and education are requisitioned for research and development. Public enlightenment is curtailed or distorted in the name of national security and defense secrecy. Public health programs are regimented in such a way as to conserve the human resources that figure in military potential. Affection and ecclesiastical institutions and practices are condoned only insofar as they interpose no ideological or behavioral obstacles to national security. Institutions and practices of social class and caste are modified and restructured to the extent that national vulnerability is believed to be at stake.

Because of obsession with the real or imagined needs of national security, resources are diverted to large-scale arms and other defense programs. Consequently, the scope of government in politics, in industry and business, in science and education, in public health, and in every other sector of life has immensely expanded. Many functions and activities, traditionally civic in nature, are either taken over or regimented by government, with its ever-burgeoning bureaucratic machinery. Expanded government leads to more centralized government, with greater concentration of power and resources in the central (federal) government, especially in a few hands in the executive branch.[64]

The degree of regimentation, governmentalization, centralization and concentration differs of course from community to community. In a totalitarian polity committed to a totalitarian ideology, society is practically subordinated to government and swallowed up by government.[65]

War in the Modern World 252 (J. Moore ed. 1974) [hereinafter cited as Reisman]; Reisman, *Private Armies in a Global War System: Prologue to Decision,* 14 Va. J. Int'l L. 1 (1973).

62. Reisman, *supra* note 61, at 263.

63. *Id.* at 264.

64. *See* M. Crozier, S Huntington, & J. Watanuki, The Crisis of Democracy (1975); Miller, *Privacy in the Corporate State: A Constitutional Value of Dwindling Significance,* 22 J. Public L. 3 (1973).

65. "The very essence of a totalitarian society," in the words of a recent Canadian

Power, which is regarded as all-pervasive and omnicompetent, tolerates little challenge. Politicization of civic activities is the catchword. "Big Brother," not the acting individual person, decides and directs. The traditional realms of private choice are extravagantly encroached upon by government. For countries preoccupied with the critical task of nation building and modernization, in a world of contending ideologies, dynamic change and insecurity, government is generally the most important, indeed the only, sector capable of undertaking this task.[66] Hence, the syndromes of governmentalization, regimentation, centralization and concentration have vigorously manifested themselves. Today, even the older liberal democratic polities are not immune from these syndromes, as they are plagued, only in lesser degree, by the chronic expectations of violence and by the complex problems of "the welfare state" and of "interdependence amid scarcity."[67]

Encroachments upon a properly functioning civic order come, increasingly, also from nongovernmental sources. Private parties may coerce through naked power and with regard to all values. The dramatic potentialities in private coercion are well illustrated in the contemporary practices of terrorism.[68] As the world community becomes a global village equipped with instantaneous communication, it is possible to focus worldwide attention simultaneously on a single spectacular event. In consequence, the terror practiced by individuals and small groups generates impact far beyond the locality in which a particular incident occurs.[69]

---

governmental report on privacy, "is that it penetrates and intrudes into these realms [of civic order]—with nearly perfect totality in Orwell's *1984*." PRIVACY AND COMPUTERS, *supra* note 56, at 12.

66. *See* L. CHEN & H. LASSWELL, FORMOSA, CHINA, AND THE UNITED NATIONS 322–32 (1967); M. JANOWITZ, THE MILITARY IN THE POLITICAL DEVELOPMENT OF NEW NATIONS (1964); THE ROLE OF THE MILITARY IN UNDERDEVELOPED COUNTRIES (J. Johnson ed. 1962).

67. Falk, *A New Paradigm for International Legal Studies: Prospects and Proposals,* 84 YALE L.J. 969, 998 (1975).

68. *See generally* INTERNATIONAL TERRORISM AND WORLD SECURITY (D. Carlton & C. Schaerf eds. 1975); Franck & Lockwood, *Preliminary Thoughts towards an International Convention on Terrorism,* 68 AM. J. INT'L L. 69 (1974); Measures to Prevent International Terrorism, Study by the Secretariat, U.N. Doc. A/C.6/418 (1972); Meron, *Some Legal Aspects of Arab Terrorists' Claims to Privileged Combatancy,* 40 NORDISK TIDSSKRIFT FOR INTERNATIONAL RET 47 (1970); Rovine, *The Contemporary International Legal Attack on Terrorism,* 3 ISRAEL Y.B. HUMAN RIGHTS 9 (1973). *See also* Abu-Lughod, *Unconventional Violence and International Politics*, 67 AM. J. INT'L L. 100–04 (1973) (No. 5, 1973 proc. AM. SOC'Y INT'L L.); Dugard, *Towards the Definition of International Terrorism, id.* at 94–100; Moore, *Toward Legal Restraints on International Terrorism, id.* at 88–94.

69. Witness, for example, the Black September at the 1972 Olympic games in Munich. The details are discussed in C. DOBSON, BLACK SEPTEMBER (1974). *See also* THE ECONOMIST, Sept. 9, 1972, at 31–34; NEWSWEEK, Sept. 18, 1972, at 24–35; TIME, Sept. 18, 1972, at 22–33; N.Y. Times, Sept. 6, 1972, at 1, col. 8; Washington Post, Sept. 6, 1972, at 1, col. 7.

Increasing threats to civic order are today most dramatically manifested in regard to privacy. This is a consequence both of the spectacular developments of modern science and technology that are capable of penetrating the traditional zones of privacy and of the intensity with which certain demands to invade privacy are propagated by governmental and private sectors alike.[70] The modalities of encroachment, as Alan Westin conveniently summarizes in his outstanding study, are threefold: (1) "physical surveillance,"[71] (2) "psychological surveillance,"[72] and (3) "data surveillance."[73]

Physical surveillance involves "the observation through optical or acoustical devices of a person's location, acts, speech, or private writing without his knowledge or against his will."[74] Such surveillance, clandestine in nature, may be carried out by a host of devices, including telephone tapping, concealed microphones of various kinds (magnetic, contact, laser, miniature, and so on, and microphone bullets), miniature transmitters, miniaturized and transistorized tape recorders, ultrared photography, hidden cameras, closed-circuit television, one-way glass, long-distance lenses, and informer infiltration.[75]

Psychological surveillance includes the use of drugs or hypnosis, singly or in combination, to induce revelation of a person's entire life history including intimate details, as well as the use of the polygraph (lie detector), personality testing (oral or written), and various other methods of enforced disclosure which extract information without knowledge or genuine informed consent of the individual concerned.[76]

---

70. For an early detection of this trend long before the contemporary burgeoning of books and articles, *see* Lasswell, *The Threat to Privacy,* in CONFLICT OF LOYALTIES 121 (R. MacIver ed. 1952).

71. A. WESTIN, *supra* note 58, at 68–69, 90.

72. *Id.* at 68, 133.

73. *Id.* at 68, 158.

74. *Id.* at 68.

75. For more details, *see* M. BRENTON, THE PRIVACY INVADERS (1964); R. BROWN, THE ELECTRONIC INVASION (1967); S. DASH, THE EAVESDROPPERS (1959); M. MAYER, RIGHTS OF PRIVACY (1972); V. PACKARD, THE NAKED SOCIETY (1964); UNCLE SAM IS WATCHING YOU (H. Barth ed. 1971); A. WESTIN, *supra* note 58, at 69–132; Donner, *Political Intelligence: Cameras, Informers and Files,* in PRIVACY IN A FREE SOCIETY 56 (Final Report–Annual Chief Justice Earl Warren Conference on Advocacy in the United States, 1974); Jones, *Some Threats of Technology to Privacy,* in PRIVACY AND HUMAN RIGHTS 139–56 (A. Robertson ed. 1973); Juvigny, *Modern Scientific and Technical Developments and Their Consequences on the Protection of the Right to Respect for a Person's Private and Family Life, His Home and Communications,* in *id.* at 132–35; Lasswell, *supra* note 70; Pyle, *Spies without Masters: The Army Still Watches Civilian Politics,* 1 CIVIL LIB. REV. 38 (Summer 1974); Schwartz, *Six Years of Tapping and Bugging, id.* at 26; Shattuck, *Tilting at the Surveillance Apparatus, id.* at 59.

76. *See* M. BRENTON, *supra* note 75, at 91–116; L. CRONBACH, ESSENTIALS OF PSYCHOLOGICAL TESTING (2d ed. 1961); F. INBAU & J. REID, LIE DETECTION AND CRIMINAL

Data surveillance, as a result of the advent of electronic data processing (primarily through the computer) and the rapid and wide application of this new technology by both governmental and nongovernmental sectors, has moved from the manual to the electronic age, from decentralization and fragmentation to centralization and concentration.[77] In a data-rich civilization, as symbolized by the mushrooming data banks, the enormous capacities (in speed, volume, and efficiency) of modern technology to gather, store, retrieve, process, and disseminate information have led to the information explosion, pregnant with menacing threats to informational privacy of individuals and groups. Under the onslaught of the escalating spiral of data gathering, dossier building and

---

INTERROGATION (3d ed. 1953); A. WESTIN, *supra* note 58, at 133–57; Dession, et al., *Drug-Induced Revelation and Criminal Investigation,* 62 YALE L.J. 315 (1953); Jones, *supra* note 75, at 156–60; Juvigny, *supra* note 75, at 137–38; Lasswell, *supra* note 70, at 125–26.

77. As Miller points out:

> Until recently, informational privacy has been relatively easy to protect: (1) large quantities of information about individuals traditionally have not been collected and therefore have not been available to others; (2) the available information generally has been maintained on a decentralized basis and typically has been widely scattered; (3) the available information has been relatively superficial in character and often has been allowed to atrophy to the point of uselessness; (4) access to the available information has not been easy to secure; (5) people in a highly mobile society have been difficult to keep track of; and (6) most people have been unable to interpret and infer revealing information from the available data.

A. MILLER, *supra* note 56, at 26. As a consequence of the "combination of greater social planning and computer capacity," "many governmental agencies are beginning to ask increasingly complex, probing, and sensitive questions." *Id.* at 21.

Characterizing the developing computer technology in terms of "digital representation," "mass storage devices," and "on-line, multi-access systems," Niblett stresses:

> These modern systems constitute a vast communication network for digital information in which the central storage devices can be interrogated and the data processed with imperceptible delays from many remote stations. By "on-line" is meant that communication is direct from the central processor to peripheral equipment such as teletype consoles and visual display screens. The systems operate in "real time"—that is to say, the result of a processing operation is available instantly or on a time scale short by comparison with the process it is controlling or monitoring. The term "multi-access" indicates that the computer is available simultaneously to many users, who may be at terminals remote from the computer itself.

Niblett, *Computers and Privacy,* in PRIVACY AND HUMAN RIGHTS 167, 169–70 (A. Robertson ed. 1973). Today, computers are employed to store not only "scientific or numerical information, or information already in the public domain," but, increasingly, sensitive information about one's personal life. *Id.* at 170–71. Such information, Niblett adds, "is increasingly being fed into the memories of computers and much of it can now be recorded and updated as it is created; we are approaching the on-line society in which our records are generated and maintained 'on line.'"

record keeping, the individual finds himself steadily losing control over personal information.[78]

As knowledge and techniques for invading privacy increase, so also do demands for encroaching upon the privacy of individuals and groups, whether for legitimate reasons or otherwise. The threats and assaults come from the private sector as well as the public. They come from actors with and without malice. "Data mania" takes on a life of its own and keeps growing.[79] The damage that the clandestine surveillances can

---

78. *See Computer Privacy, Hearings before the Subcomm. on Ad. Prac. and Proc. of the Senate Comm. on the Judiciary,* 90th Cong., 1st Sess. (Mar. 14–15, 1967); *The Computer and Invasion of Privacy: Hearings before the Special Subcomm. on Invasion of Privacy, of the House Comm. on Gov't Operations,* 89th Cong., 2d Sess. (July 26–28, 1966); RECORDS, COMPUTERS, AND THE RIGHTS OF CITIZENS (1973) (report of the secretary's Advisory Committee on Automated Personal Data Systems, U.S. Department of Health, Education & Welfare); E. ENGBERG, THE SPY IN THE CORPORATE STRUCTURE AND THE RIGHT TO PRIVACY (1967); P. HAMILTON, ESPIONAGE AND SUBVERSION IN AN INDUSTRIAL SOCIETY (1967); A. HARRISON, THE PROBLEM OF PRIVACY IN THE COMPUTER AGE: AN ANNOTATED BIBLIOGRAPHY (1970); E. LONG, THE INTRUDERS: THE INVASION OF PRIVACY BY GOVERNMENT AND INDUSTRY (1966); A. MILLER, *supra* note 56; ON RECORD: FILES AND DOSSIERS IN AMERICAN LIFE (S. Wheeler ed. 1970); PRIVACY, COMPUTERS, AND YOU (B. Rowe ed. 1972); J. ROSENBERG, THE DEATH OF PRIVACY (1969); J. RULE, PRIVATE LIVES AND PUBLIC SURVEILLANCE (1974); SECURITY AND PRIVACY IN COMPUTER SYSTEMS (L. Hoffman ed. 1973); A. WESTIN, *supra* note 58, at 158–68; A. WESTIN & M. BAKER, DATABANKS IN A FREE SOCIETY: COMPUTERS, RECORD-KEEPING AND PRIVACY (1972); *Computers, Data Banks, and Individual Privacy,* 53 MINN. L. REV. 211 (1963); INFORMATION TECHNOLOGY IN A DEMOCRACY (A. Westin ed. 1971); Lasswell, *Policy Problems of a Data-Rich Civilization,* in INFORMATION TECHNOLOGY IN A DEMOCRACY, *supra,* at 187–97; Miller, *Personal Privacy in the Computer Age: The Challenge of a New Technology in an Information-Oriented Society,* 67 MICH. L. REV. 1089 (1969); Miller, *The Right to Privacy: Data Banks and Dossiers,* in PRIVACY IN A FREE SOCIETY, *supra* note 75, at 72–85; Weisner, *The Information Revolution—and the Bill of Rights,* 5 LAW & COMPUTER TECH. 40 (No. 2, Mar.–Apr. 1972).

Thus, as Peter Drucker reminds us, "There is a great deal more to information and data processing than the computer; the computer is to the information industry roughly what the central power station is to the electrical industry." P. DRUCKER, THE AGE OF DISCONTINUITY 24 (1968).

In underscoring the threats posed by contemporary technological developments, we do not seek to minimize the constructive contribution of science-based technology to social process. The more positive contribution is described by Juvigny:

> It is easy to understand the fascination which the possible use of computers in government departments exercises on organisation and methods chiefs. In the collecting and interpreting of information, in programming, in decision-making, in improving the registration of births, marriages and deaths, in conscription, in police records, in the administration of revenue departments, staff, equipment stocks and the like, or in general or sector planning, the use of computers appears to make it possible both to run public services economically and to increase their means of action and the effectiveness of their programmes.

Juvigny, *supra* note 75, at 135.

79. As Arthur Miller has stated: "The new information technologies seem to have given birth to a new social virus—'data-mania.'" A. MILLER, *supra* note 56, at 22.

do is manifold and far-reaching. Thus, a report by the secretary-general of the United Nations summarizes:

> Wholesale invasions of privacy inhibit liberty, often purposely. This is particularly true of surreptitious invasions, like electronic eavesdropping, spies, informers, entrappers, and psychological testing, the existence of which the subject is often unaware until too late. The community becomes fear-ridden, and no one can be trusted, whether he be family, friend or associate; indeed, a person may be led to continual distrust of himself, as his efforts at individual self-fulfilment conflict with the norms of authority. This destruction of trust is one of the major dangers to a free society. A pervasive mistrust of others impairs freedom of assembly, for men fearful of spies and informers, human or mechanical, are loath to join together meaningfully. And a man's awareness that others lack faith in him seriously weakens his chance for self-fulfilment, for few men can develop adequately without the confidence of others. Thus, the detailed questionnaire for employment, housing, insurance and other matters, the hidden but suspected cameras in the washroom, the psychological tests, the lie detector and truth serum—all of these devices for ferreting out intimate and often unconscious details of our lives, produce a pervasive insecurity which suppresses individuality, discourages responsibility and encourages frightened conformity. . . .[80]

Basic Community Policies

Our postulated goal of human dignity favors the widest possible freedom of choice and, hence, the fewest possible coerced choices for the individual, whether acting singly or through groups. The projected ideal is toward a social context in which "choices," rather than "decisions," are cultivated on the largest possible scale, thereby reducing occasions for coercion to an inescapable minimum.[81] This is in keeping with the liberal tradition that seeks to minimize the politicization or governmentalization of social interactions and to maintain institutional processes compatible with human dignity values. In the words of Westin:

> Liberal democratic theory assumes that a good life for the individual

---

80. Respect for the Privacy of Individuals, U.N. Doc. E/CN.4/1116 (1973) (report of the secretary-general) [hereinafter cited as U.N. Report on Privacy].

The constellation of practices that have become known as "Watergate" of course represent the epitome of combined governmental and private invasions of civic order. For the various techniques in political surveillance and the problems they raise, *see* 1 N. Dorsen, P. Bender, & B. Neuborne, Emerson, Haber, and Dorsen's Political and Civil Rights in the United States 183–201 (4th Law School ed. 1976).

81. *See* note 3 *supra*.

> must have substantial areas of interest apart from political participation—time devoted to sports, arts, literature, and similar non-political pursuits. These areas of individual pursuit prevent the total politicizing of life and permit other models of success and happiness to serve as alternatives to the political career and the citizenship role.[82]

In more fundamental conception, he elaborates further:

> In democratic societies there is a fundamental belief in the uniqueness of the individual, in his basic dignity and worth as a creature of God and a human being, and in the need to maintain social processes that safeguard his sacred individuality. Psychologists and sociologists have linked the development and maintenance of this sense of individuality to the human need for autonomy—the desire to avoid being manipulated or dominated wholly by others.[83]

A properly functioning civic order which affords adequate protection of a large zone of personal autonomy is thus crucial for ample fulfillment of the individual and for innovation and rich diversity in community life. Personal autonomy thrives when privacy is respected. Creativity flourishes in a social environment in which voluntary participation in the life of society is affirmed and individuals are left free either to induce one another to engage in the production and accumulation of one value rather than another or to enjoy a particular value rather than to accumulate it further.

The right to privacy, in the restricted sense in which we have defined it,[84] is demonstrably indispensable to a meaningful civic order. Without substantial control over the flow of information about the private self, autonomy in an individual's personal life and private choices is unattainable. The ideal of civic order requires the least possible interference, by officials and nonofficials alike, with individual choice.[85] Such a civic order is unthinkable if the individual is under constant surveillance and indiscriminately laid bare in all matters. In summation of these interrelations, one of the authors some years ago wrote: "Respect is the deference that we give and deserve in our capacity as human beings, and on the basis of our individual merit. The presumption in favor of privacy follows from our respect for freedom of choice, for autonomy, for self-direction on the part of everyone."[86] Similarly, Clinton Rossiter has written:

---

82. A. Westin, *supra* note 58, at 24.
83. *Id.* at 33.
84. *See* note 58 *supra* and accompanying text.
85. *See* notes 53–58 *supra* and accompanying text.
86. Lasswell, *supra* note 70, at 134. For a derivational relation between privacy and affection, and philosophical grounds for the protection of privacy, *see* Fried, *supra* note 58.

> *Privacy* is a special kind of independence, which can be understood as an attempt to secure autonomy in at least a few personal and spiritual concerns, if necessary in defiance of all the pressures of modern society. It is an attempt, that is to say, to do more than maintain a posture of self-respecting independence toward other men; it seeks to erect an unbreachable wall of dignity and reserve against the entire world. The free man is the private man, the man who still keeps some of his thoughts and judgments entirely to himself, who feels no overriding compulsion to share everything of value with others, not even with those he loves and trusts.[87]

A critical function of the civic order is to foster an environment in which people can indulge in a wide range of spontaneous cultural expressions, experimentations, and innovations in ways compatible with the aggregate common interest. A rich culture and civic order intimately interact and reinforce each other. Culture flourishes when the civic order is vigorous and individuals and groups enjoy a high degree of autonomy and fulfillment in the shaping and sharing of all values. An enriched culture provides the matrix in which spontaneity, creativity, and diversity can thrive. Cultural creativity, in a wide-ranging sense, depends upon a strategic combination of innovation and the capacity to anticipate and recognize the potential significance of an innovation. In the light of historical climaxes of creativity-explosion in many groups and civilizations, it is preferable, in a search for a world community of human dignity, to rely upon the initiatives of humanity as a whole, rather than upon those of a supercaste with power permanently to domineer over their fellow beings.

To cultivate the high creativity of humanity as a whole, it is important that the range of individual choice be made as wide as possible and that effective conditions be created and sustained to stimulate awareness of the full range of personal potential. This requires that protection be

---

Fried emphasizes that privacy is not "just a defensive right"; it "forms the necessary context for the intimate relations of love and friendship." *Id.* at 490. He adds:

> [P]rivacy is not just one possible means among others to insure some other value, but . . . it is necessarily related to ends and relations of the most fundamental sort: respect, love, friendship and trust. Privacy is not merely a good technique for furthering these fundamental relations; rather without privacy they are simply inconceivable.

Id. at 477. *See also* C. FRIED, AN ANATOMY OF VALUES 137–52 (1970).

87. Rossiter, *The Pattern of Liberty,* in ASPECTS OF LIBERTY 15, 17 (M. Konvitz & C. Rossiter eds. 1958). *See also* H. ARENDT, THE HUMAN CONDITION 22–78 (1958); C. CLARKE, PRIVATE RIGHTS AND FREEDOM OF THE INDIVIDUAL (1972) (Ditchley paper No. 41); D. MADGWICK, PRIVACY UNDER ATTACK (1968); H. ROELOFS, THE TENSION OF CITIZENSHIP: PRIVATE MAN AND PUBLIC DUTY (1957); E. SHILS, THE TORMENT OF SECRECY 21–27, 201–07 (1956); Shils, *Social Inquiry and the Autonomy of the Individual,* in THE HUMAN MEANING OF THE SOCIAL SCIENCES 114 (D. Lerner ed. 1959).

extended not only to the isolated action of the individual, but also to the collective action of individuals acting in and through groups. An individual, acting qua individual, of course finds self-fulfillment and makes a contribution to the common interest in varying degrees and various ways, differing from community to community. Yet, in today's world of complex interdependences and pluralism, where an individual is often overwhelmed by a deep sense of powerlessness, individuals can ultimately find greatest self-fulfillment, and make their richest contribution to the common interest, only when they are also free to form groups of various types, identify with many different groups, and participate in group activities in the shaping and sharing of values.[88] If the aggregate freedom of choice is to be secured in a world of rich creativity and diversity, the protection of civic order must, therefore, be extended to groups as well as individuals. In the contemporary world, many people still achieve a sense of respect—self-esteem and esteem by others—only through intense group identifications. As Isaacs has said: "Some individuals derive sufficient self-esteem out of the stuff of their individual personalities alone. Others have to depend on their group associations to supply what their own individualities may often deny them."[89] It is "this need for self-esteem, the need to acquire it, feel it, assert it,"[90] that has generated the respect revolution of our time and has pointed to the critical need for affording the utmost autonomy to groups as well as individuals in ways compatible with the common interest. It may be

---

88. *See generally* B. DE JOUVENEL, SOVEREIGNTY: AN INQUIRY INTO THE POLITICAL GOOD 56–70 (J. Huntington trans. 1963); A. DE TOCQUEVILLE, DEMOCRACY IN AMERICA (J. Mayer ed. 1969); H. EHRMANN, INTEREST GROUPS ON FOUR CONTINENTS (1958); ETHNICITY: THEORY AND EXPERIENCE (N. Glazer & D. Moynihan eds. 1975) [hereinafter cited as ETHNICITY]; THE GOVERNMENT OF ASSOCIATIONS: SELECTIONS FROM THE BEHAVIORAL SCIENCES (W. Glaser & D. Sills eds. 1966); GROUP RELATIONS AND GROUP ANTAGONISMS (R. MACIVER ed. 1944); H. GUETZKOW, MULTIPLE LOYALITIES (1955); J. KLEIN, THE STUDY OF GROUPS (1956); W. KORNHAUSER, THE POLITICS OF MASS SOCIETY (1959); J. LADOR-LEDERER, INTERNATIONAL GROUP PROTECTION (1968); H. LASSWELL & A. KAPLAN, POWER AND SOCIETY 25–51 (1950); G. MCCONNELL, PRIVATE POWER AND AMERICAN DEMOCRACY (1966); M. MOSKOWITZ, THE POLITICS AND DYNAMICS OF HUMAN RIGHTS 123–73 (1968); R. NISBET, THE QUEST FOR COMMUNITY (1953); PRIVATE GOVERNMENT (S. Lakoff ed. 1973); S. SCHACHTER, THE PSYCHOLOGY OF AFFILIATION (1959); P. SECORD & C. BACKMAN, SOCIAL PSYCHOLOGY (2d ed. 1974); W. SPROTT, HUMAN GROUPS (1958); S. STOLJAR, GROUPS AND ENTITIES: AN INQUIRY INTO CORPORATE THEORY (1973); VOLUNTARY ASSOCIATIONS (NOMOS XI, J. Pennock & J. Chapman eds. 1969); Affeldt & Seney, *Group Sanctions and Personal Rights—Professions, Occupations and Labor Law,* 11 ST. LOUIS L.J. 382 (1967) and 12 ST. LOUIS L.J. 179 (1968); Cowan, *Group Interests,* 44 VA. L. REV. 331 (1958); *Interest Groups in International Perspective,* 413 ANNALS (1974).

89. Isaacs, *Basic Group Identity: The Idols of the Tribe,* in ETHNICITY, *supra* note 88, at 29, 35.

90. *Id.* at 36.

recalled that freedom of choice can be manifested in many different ways in different cultures, allowing a diversity in expression and priorities through time.

The better securing of the basic policies of civic order requires the systematic and deliberate management of effective power and authoritative decision at all community levels—global, regional, and national.[91] It is the whole matrix of decision, constitutive and public order, taken in the aggregate, that protects and maintains the civic order. It may seem somewhat visionary to suggest that a power elite be animated by the goal of aggregate freedom of choice of individuals and that power be made consciously to discipline itself.[92] Yet, a realistic aspiration for improved civic order must seek, not the unattainable goal of altogether eliminating power in the social process, but rather the conscientious employment of

---

91. *See* note 97 *infra* and accompanying text.

92. The development of the common law and of constitutionalism more generally suggests that it is not entirely utopian to seek the self-limitation of effective power. How the predispositions of effective elites may be managed to secure the establishment of appropriate constitutive process is an inquiry to which we give attention elsewhere. Some indication of the conditions that affect decision and of relevant strategies for change is made in the conclusion to this article.

The general problem of securing civic order would not appear essentially different from that involved in creating the predispositions (and institutions) necessary to the maintenance of minimum order. A comprehensive statement of the more important conditions is offered in Lasswell, *The Social and Political Framework of War and Peace,* in AGGRESSION AND DEFENSE: NEURAL MECHANISMS AND SOCIAL PATTERNS 317 (C. Clemente & D. Lindsley eds. 1967). For an outline of recommended strategies, *see* M. MCDOUGAL & F. FELICIANO, LAW AND MINIMUM WORLD PUBLIC ORDER 375–83 (1961).

In the latter reference the general problem is defined as follows:

> The task of highest priority . . . for every one genuinely committed to the goal values of a world public order of human dignity would, accordingly, appear to be that of creating in all peoples of the world the perspectives necessary both to their realistic understanding of this common interest and to their acceptance and initiation of the detailed measures in sanctioning process appropriately designed to secure such interest. It is, as we have seen, the conflicting, confused, and disoriented perspectives of peoples—such as the syndromes in expectations of violence, patterns of parochial identification, and demands for domination—and not the inexorable requirements of environmental factors, which keep alive the contention of world orders, with such appalling threat for all mankind. The maximization postulate—that men act within their capabilities to maximize their values—suggests that by appropriate modifications in perspectives the peoples of the world can be encouraged to move toward both the establishment of a more effective constitutive process and the making of more rational specific sanctioning decisions. It is common ground of both historical knowledge and contemporary science that the factors—culture, class, interest, personality, and crisis—which most directly condition peoples' perspectives can be changed and managed to promote constructive rather than destructive perspectives. Promising alternatives in communication and collaboration designed to promote the perspectives appropriate to the maintenance of minimum order and, with minimum order, opportu-

power to maximize the aggregate freedom of choice in the shaping and sharing of values.[93]

The essential requirement is that civic order interests be put under public order guarantee.[94] A dynamic society is always creating novel arrangements in the shaping and sharing of values and generating a continuum of expectations about the severity and mildness of possible sanctions. With a wide range of expectations in constant flux, some events become incorporated through decision in the body of public order, some remain within the sphere of civic order. The boundary separating the civic order from the public order is inherently fluid and

---

> nity for peaceful progress toward a more comprehensive public order of human dignity, have long been recommended by competent specialists upon different instruments of policy and different value processes, and await employment in sufficiently comprehensive, integrated, and disciplined programs.

Id. at 376.

93. Our position is thus in clear distinction to various versions of anarchism that project total abolition of power in social process. The revival of interest in anarchism is shown by the recent proliferation of literature and reproduction of classic works. *See* ANARCHISM (R. Hoffman ed. 1970); ANARCHISM TODAY (D. Apter & J. Joll eds. 1971); M. BAKUNIN, GOD AND THE STATE (Dover ed. 1970); BAKUNIN ON ANARCHY (S. Dolgoff ed. 1972); G. BALDELLI, SOCIAL ANARCHISM (1971); A. CARTER, THE POLITICAL THEORY OF ANARCHISM (1971); THE ESSENTIAL KROPOTKIN (E. Capouya & K. Tompkins eds. 1975); THE ESSENTIAL WORKS OF ANARCHISM (M. Schatz ed. 1972); W. GODWIN, AN ENQUIRY CONCERNING POLITICAL JUSTICE AND ITS INFLUENCE ON GENERAL VIRTUE AND HAPPINESS (R. Preston ed. 1926); E. GOLDMAN, ANARCHISM, AND OTHER ESSAYS (1969); D. GUERIN, ANARCHISM: FROM THEORY TO PRACTICE (1970); J. JOLL, THE ANARCHISTS (1964); A. MASTERS, BAKUNIN, THE FATHER OF ANARCHISM (1974); PATTERNS OF ANARCHY (L. Krimerman & L. Perry eds. 1966); H. READ, ANARCHY AND ORDER: ESSAYS IN POLITICS (1971); J. REIMAN, IN DEFENSE OF POLITICAL PHILOSOPHY: A REPLY TO ROBERT PAUL WOLFF'S IN DEFENSE OF ANARCHISM (1972); G. RUNKLE, ANARCHISM: OLD AND NEW (1972); B. RUSSELL, PROPOSED ROADS TO FREEDOM: SOCIALISM, ANARCHISM AND SYNDICALISM (1931); R. SCALAPINO & G. YU, THE CHINESE ANARCHIST MOVEMENT (1961); C. WARD, ANARCHY IN ACTION (1973); R. WOLFF, IN DEFENSE OF ANARCHISM (1970); G. WOODCOCK, ANARCHISM: A HISTORY OF LIBERTARIAN IDEAS AND MOVEMENTS (1962).

For a contemporary philosophical exposition espousing "the minimal state," *see* R. NOZICK, ANARCHY, STATE, AND UTOPIA (1974). Nozick, like Rawls (J. RAWLS, A THEORY OF JUSTICE [1971]), is largely concerned with establishing restraints upon the exercise of power by derivational logic. There are of course limits to the enlightenment that can be achieved by this technique.

94. The importance of public order in protecting private choice is affirmed from many philosophical perspectives. *See* Frankel, *supra* note 8; Fuller, *Freedom—A Suggested Analysis,* 68 HARV. L. REV. 1305 (1955).

One alternative Frankel does not adequately consider is the postulation of a comprehensive set of goal values without suggestion that these values have a base in any kind of natural law philosophy. Such a postulation would remove many of the difficulties Frankel finds in John Stuart Mill and others. *See generally* chapter 6 *supra,* at notes 18–52 and accompanying text.

changing in an ever-changing world. Expectations of severe sanctions attending a particular institutional practice may become weakened or disappear through time, thereby transforming a matter of public order concern to that of civic order. Conversely, when expectations of sanctions become severe within a particular conventional civic context, civic order ceases to be so in that particular context; a functional change is taking place, and the organized community steps directly into the picture. The tension generated by the fluidity of the ever-changing boundary between civic and public order is especially pronounced in the contemporary epoch of accelerating change, as characterized by fantastic gropings and innovativeness in life-style, technology, and community practice.[95]

In the light of the dynamic relationship between civic order and public order in this interdependent world of accelerating changes, it is immensely important that the whole flow of comprehensive public order decisions, including constitutive decisions, be positively managed in such a way as to promote the largest domain of civic order. This positive management must require, as has been discussed, the appropriate accommodation of different individual and community interests when they become incompatible with each other.[96] The aggregate freedom of choice of individuals and groups can only be augmented when a vigorous public order exhibits effective constitutive processes of authoritative decision and a flow of particular decisions about the shaping and sharing of values which incorporate and manifest the values of human dignity.

Trends in Decision

Since civic order entails the totality of freedom of choice of all individuals in regard to all values other than power, it is maintained and affected by the whole global constitutive process of authoritative decision and the entire flow of public order decisions which emanate from that process. The quality of civic order and the expansion or contraction of the domain of civic order in the larger community can, therefore, be realistically and fully illuminated only by reference to the functioning of the various constitutive processes of authoritative decision—global, regional, and national—and to the flow of public order decisions that emerge from such processes for the regulation of each of the different value processes.

---

95. *See* A. Toffler, Future Shock (1971), for development of the theme of accelerating change and its profoundly unsettling implications for the shaping and sharing of values.

96. *See* notes 7–52 *supra* and accompanying text.

The full impact of all these constitutive processes, including both transnational and national, upon the achievement and maintenance of an appropriate civic order depends of course upon the degree to which the important features of such processes both reflect and secure the common interest in human dignity values. The relevant decisions in any constitutive process are those which shape its more important features, such as:

The degree to which parties who are affected by decision are both represented in the making of such decision and held accountable to basic community policies;

The comprehensiveness and clarity with which the more fundamental policies, for which the process is maintained, articulate a common interest in human dignity values;

The adequacy of structures of authority and their openness in access and capabilities for insuring compulsory attendance;

The extent to which prescriptions from all communities are established and maintained for the protection of freedom of choice, with bases in effective power marshalled in support of authority;

The availability of prompt and dependable procedures in decision process, which both reflect due process and involve no unnecessary coercion or other invasion of individual rights;

And, finally, the various different outcomes in decision necessary to secure, comprehensively and economically, the common interests of all individuals and groups in the goal values of human dignity.

The different types of decision outcomes required for the better protection of civic order may be specified as including an intelligence function, which is dependable and creative, but involving no unnecessary invasions of civic order; a promotion function, which is effective and integrative, but open and nonoppressive; a prescribing function, which establishes appropriate stability in expectations about authority and control, while giving all opportunity to every individual to participate by word and deed in the clarification of common interest; an invocation function, which is responsive, timely and nonprovocative, affording full opportunity for challenge of the lawfulness of all acts, public or private; an application function, which is uniform, effective and constructive, while conducted with appropriate notice, hearing, fairness, and dispatch; a termination function, which is balanced in relation to conservation and change and appropriate amelioration of the destructive impact of change; and an appraisal function, which is independent and continuous, facilitating inquiry about the adequacy of past decision process to serve postulated goals. It scarcely needs observation that the studies necessary to evaluate the impact upon civic order of contemporary constitutive processes of authoritative decision are yet to be made.[97]

The constitutive process of authoritative decision in any community typically establishes and maintains a complex network of prescriptive codes, notably supervisory, regulatory, enterprisory, and corrective. The supervisory code relates to the private activities concerning which the community decision maker operates much in the role of umpire at the initiative of the parties. The different supervisory codes, such as those embodied in the law of agreement and the law of deprivations, establish a framework of expectations which enable members of the community to take the initiative to shape and share values by agreement (persuasion), in confidence that expectations created in their interactions will be honored and that unauthorized deprivations will be redressed. The regulatory codes of a free society are designed to defend or foster the attainment of substantive criteria and institutional routines that facilitate freedom of choice in shaping and sharing values.

The enterprisory code relates to the activities performed directly by the community acting through official, territorially inclusive institutions; it authorizes direct governmental activities and lays down the basic guides for administration. With the general growth of socializing tendencies, the scope of government management has vastly increased, going far beyond such traditional functions as national defence and the maintenance of internal order through organized military and police force. Many enterprisory activities significantly contribute to the achievement of effective and meaningful participation by all members of the community in the shaping and sharing of all values.

The distinctive task of the corrective code is to specify the criteria and measures appropriate for the maintenance of responsible, nondestructive participation in the system of public order; it is indispensable to protection of the genuine freedom of choice of individuals. In short, these different and complex codes invoke differing degrees of community interference with the individual's freedom of choice, thereby affecting the civic order in various ways and in varying degrees.[98]

The public order decisions, emanating from the constitutive processes

---

97. For some preliminary indications of the present state of the global constitutive process of authoritative decision, *see* McDougal, Lasswell, & Reisman, *The World Constitutive Process of Authoritative Decision,* in 1 THE FUTURE OF THE INTERNATIONAL LEGAL ORDER 73 (R. Falk & C. Black eds. 1969). For a brief indication of some recommended policies relating to the world constitutive process of authoritative decision, *see* McDougal, *supra* note 11, at 415–19. For more detailed development with regard to one decision function, *see* McDougal, Lasswell, & Reisman, *The Intelligence Function and World Public Order,* 46 TEMPLE L.Q. (1973).

98. *See The Public Interest, supra* note 12, at 73–76.

of authoritative decision, also importantly determine the quality of civic order achievable in global social process. These decisions include the totality of human rights decisions, both in prescription and application, both transnational and national, that permeate all value processes. It may thus be observed that the whole contemporary human rights program is designed towards ultimate attainment of a civic order in which the aggregate freedom of choice of individuals and groups is made secure, effective, and meaningful, and is sustained by the whole matrix of decision, constitutive and public order. Most of the human rights prescriptions, as embodied in the United Nations Charter, the International Bill of Rights (i.e., the Universal Declaration and the two Covenants) and their ancillary expressions, general and particular, are relevant in varying degrees to the attainment and maintenance of a global civic order.[99] Civic order is, in the sense we specify, the summation of all protection of interests in freedom of choice. This summation is a function of the kind of accommodation that is achieved in a comprehensive public order, as outlined in the preceding section.[100] Inclusive accommodation comprises an entire tapestry of particular accommodations in ever-changing contexts.

Though the human rights prescriptions make no literal reference to "civic order" as such, they do contain distinctive components which, taken in the aggregate and considered in the light of their potential development, afford promise of a closer approximation to our recommended civic order. Of foremost importance is Article 28 of the Universal Declaration of Human Rights,[101] which projects a comprehensive "social and international order" that would embrace both a comprehensive public order and civic order as we have defined them. This article, it may be recalled, reads: "Everyone is entitled to a social and international order in which the rights and freedoms set forth in this Declaration can be fully realized."[102] The "full" realization of the human rights and freedoms which are set forth in the Universal Declaration and which range through many value categories, would be possible only if people were to enjoy the protection of a comprehensive framework of public order, protecting their interests not only in all hitherto recognized rights

99. A collection of the more important global human rights prescriptions is offered in UNITED NATIONS, HUMAN RIGHTS: A COMPILATION OF INTERNATIONAL INSTRUMENTS OF THE UNITED NATIONS, U.N. Doc. ST/HR/1 (1973) [hereinafter cited as U.N. HUMAN RIGHTS INSTRUMENTS]. *See also* BASIC DOCUMENTS ON HUMAN RIGHTS (I. Brownlie ed. 1971); BASIC DOCUMENTS, *supra* note 20.

100. *See* notes 7–52 *supra* and accompanying text.

101. Universal Declaration, *supra* note 18, Art. 28, U.N. Doc. A/810 at 76.

102. *Id.*

but also in emerging interests not presently specified in the human rights instruments.

Another critically relevant provision is Article 30 of the Universal Declaration, discussed in other emphasis above, which states:

> Nothing in this Declaration may be interpreted as implying for any State, group or person any right to engage in any activity or to perform any act aimed at the destruction of any of the rights and freedoms set forth herein.[103]

This article, as will be developed, may eventually emerge as a close approximation to the Ninth Amendment of the United States Constitution, which embodies the common law presumption that choices not expressly prohibited to people are reserved as within the scope of their aggregate freedom.[104] Comparable provisions, as previously indicated, are contained in the two Covenants and the two regional human rights Conventions, European and American.[105]

The right to "participate in the cultural life of the community"[106] is an important manifestation and a critical component of civic order. Thus conceived, the cultural rights, as enunciated in the transnational human rights prescriptions, assume far greater significance than is generally recognized. In Article 22, which is authoritatively interpreted as employing the concept of social security, "not in the technical sense of social insurance and other social assistance,"[107] but more comprehensively to include "all the social and economic freedoms necessary to ensure the individual's well-being,"[108] the Universal Declaration of Human Rights stipulates:

> Everyone, as a member of society, has the right to social security and is entitled to realization, through national effort and international co-operation and in accordance with the organization and resources of each State, of the economic, social and cultural rights indispensable for his dignity and the free development of his personality.[109]

In amplification, Article 27 provides both highly general and more specific protection:

---

103. *Id.*, Art. 30, U.N. Doc. A/810 at 77.
104. *See* notes 161–65 *infra* and accompanying text.
105. *See* notes 26–30 *supra* and accompanying text.
106. Universal Declaration, *supra* note 18, Art. 27, U.N. Doc. A/810 at 76.
107. N. Robinson, *supra* note 22, at 133.
108. *Id.*
109. Universal Declaration, *supra* note 18, Art. 22, U.N. Doc. A/810 at 75.

1. Everyone has the right freely to participate in the cultural life of the community, to enjoy the arts and to share in scientific advancement and its benefits.
2. Everyone has the right to the protection of the moral and material interests resulting from any scientific, literary or artistic production of which he is the author.[110]

As befitting its title, the International Covenant on Economic, Social, and Cultural Rights[111] is more detailed in its formulation of cultural rights. Article 15 provides:

1. The States Parties to the present Covenant recognize the right of everyone:
   (a) To take part in cultural life;
   (b) To enjoy the benefits of scientific progress and its applications;
   (c) To benefit from the protection of the moral and material interests resulting from any scientific, literary or artistic production of which he is the author.
2. The steps to be taken by the States Parties to the present Covenant to achieve the full realization of this right shall include those necessary for the conservation, the development and the diffusion of science and culture.
3. The States Parties to the present Covenant undertake to respect the freedom indispensable for scientific research and creative activity.
4. The States Parties to the present Covenant recognize the benefits to be derived from the encouragement and development of international contacts and co-operation in the scientific and cultural fields.[112]

The scope and potential significance of these novel prescriptions for the protection of cultural rights were amply examined and illuminated

---

110. *Id.*, Art. 27, U.N. Doc. A/810 at 76.

111. Covenant on Economic Rights, *supra* note 24.

112. *Id.*, Art. 15, 21 U.N. GAOR, Supp. (No. 16) at 51.

On the regional level, the protection of cultural rights is enshrined in the American Declaration of the Rights and Duties of Man. Art. 13 reads:

> Every person has the right to take part in the cultural life of the community, to enjoy the arts, and to participate in the benefits that result from intellectual progress, especially scientific discoveries.
>
> He likewise has the right to the protection of his moral and material interests as

in 1970 by a panel of experts exploring the subject of "Cultural Rights as Human Rights" under the auspices of UNESCO.[113] These experts generally took a very comprehensive view of both culture and cultural rights. The "Statement on Cultural Rights as Human Rights" adopted by the panel began in broad conception: "Culture is a human experience which it is difficult to define, but we recognize it as the totality of ways by which men create designs for living. It is a process of communication between men; it is the essence of being human."[114] Encompassing "spiritual and material values,"[115] culture refers, the panel asserts, to "everything which enables man to be operative and active in his world, and to use all forms of expression more and more freely to establish communication among men."[116]

> regards his inventions or any literary, scientific or artistic works of which he is the author.

BASIC DOCUMENTS, *supra* note 20, at 189–90. The American Convention on Human Rights, in Art. 26, also provides:

> The States Parties undertake to adopt measures, both internally and through international cooperation, especially those of an economic and technical nature, with a view to achieving progressively, by legislation or other appropriate means, the full realization of the rights implicit in the economic, social, educational, scientific, and cultural standards set forth in the Charter of the Organization of American States as amended by the Protocol of Buenos Aires.

American Convention, *supra* note 28, Art. 26, 9 INT'L LEGAL MATERIALS at 109. It is unfortunate, however, that the European Convention on Human Rights, for reasons unclear, contains no comparable prescription.

113. UNESCO, *Cultural Rights as Human Rights,* 3 STUDIES AND DOCUMENTS ON CULTURAL POLICIES (1970) [hereinafter cited as *Cultural Rights*].

114. *Id.* at 105.

115. *Id.*

116. *Id.* at 105–06.

The individual experts gave "culture" a variety of definitions, including: "the essence of being human" (*id.* at 10); "everything that concerns intellectual, ethical, physical, even technical training" (*id.* at 15); "the sum of total human activities" (*id.*); "interaction" (*id.* at 39); "the sum total of material and spiritual values, created by man in the process of socio-historical practice" (*id.* at 43); "the result of man's creative activity in the material and spiritual sphere" (*id.* at 45); and "the never-ending curiosity towards the physical, the psychological and the spiritual—the unceasing wonder and reverence towards the ultimate facts of life" (*id.* at 70).

In social sciences, the classic definition of culture was that of Edward B. Tylor: "Culture . . . taken in its wide ethnographic sense, is that complex whole which includes knowledge, belief, art, morals, law, custom, and any other capabilities and habits acquired by man as a member of society." E. TYLOR, PRIMITIVE CULTURE 1 (1871). This definition has been widely adopted, with appropriate modifications, by social scientists in various disciplines.

After a comprehensive survey, Alfred L. Kroeber and Clyde Kluckhohn summed up the consensus of most social scientists in these terms: "Culture consists of patterns, explicit and implicit, of and for behavior acquired and transmitted by symbols, constituting the distinc-

The comprehensiveness with which the experts perceived culture was carried forward in their articulation and interpretation of the scope of the relevant rights. "By the right of an individual to culture," in the words of Professor Boutros-Ghali, "it is to be understood that every man has the right of access to knowledge, to the arts and literature of all peoples, to take part in scientific advancement and to enjoy its benefits, to make his contribution towards the enrichment of cultural life."[117] The panel's final "Statement on Cultural Rights as Human Rights" again

---

tive achievements of human groups, including their embodiments in artifacts; the essential core of culture consists of traditional (i.e., historically derived and selected) ideas and especially their attached values. . . ." Kroeber & Kluckhohn, *Culture: A Critical Review of Concepts and Definitions,* 47 PAPERS OF THE PEABODY MUSEUM OF AMERICAN ARCHAEOLOGY AND ETHNOLOGY 181 (1952).

Malinowski suggested an inquiry into cultures in terms of the "function" of each component of the total culture. *See* Malinowski, *Culture,* in 4 ENCYC. SOC. SC. 621 (1931). *See also* R. BENEDICT, PATTERNS OF CULTURE (1959); B. MALINOWSKI, A SCIENTIFIC THEORY OF CULTURE AND OTHER ESSAYS (1960 ed.); B. MALINOWSKI, THE SEXUAL LIFE OF SAVAGES (1932).

For our own definition, *see* H. LASSWELL & A. KAPLAN, *supra* note 88, at 47–51.

In a vast literature concerning culture, other useful citations include: S. FREUD, CHARACTER AND CULTURE (P. Rieff ed. 1962); S. FREUD, CIVILIZATION AND ITS DISCONTENTS (1930); C. GEERTZ, THE INTERPRETATION OF CULTURES: SELECTED ESSAYS (1973); E. HATCH, THEORIES OF MAN AND CULTURE (1973); J. HONIGMANN, UNDERSTANDING CULTURE (1963); A. KROEBER, CONFIGURATIONS OF CULTURAL GROWTH (1944); A. KROEBER, THE NATURE OF CULTURE (1952); LANGUAGE IN CULTURE AND SOCIETY (D. Hymes ed. 1964); C. LEVI-STRAUSS, STRUCTURAL ANTHROPOLOGY (C. Jacobson & B. Schoepf trans. 1963); R. LINTON, THE STUDY OF MAN (1936); H. MCLUHAN, CULTURE IS OUR BUSINESS (1970); K. MANNHEIM, ESSAYS ON THE SOCIOLOGY OF CULTURE (E. Mannheim & P. Kecskemeti eds. 1956); M. MEAD, CULTURE AND COMMITMENT (1970); M. MEAD, SEX AND TEMPERAMENT IN THREE PRIMITIVE SOCIETIES (1963); T. PARSONS, THE SOCIAL SYSTEM (1951); A. RADCLIFFE-BROWN, A NATURAL SCIENCE OF SOCIETY (1957); E. SAPIR, CULTURE, LANGUAGE AND PERSONALITY (D. Mandelbaum ed. 1958); SCIENCE AND CULTURE (G. Holton ed. 1965); THE SCIENCE OF MAN IN THE WORLD CRISIS (R. Linton ed. 1945); P. SOROKIN, SOCIETY, CULTURE, AND PERSONALITY (1962); A. WALLACE, CULTURE AND PERSONALITY (1961); L. WHITE, THE SCIENCE OF CULTURE: A STUDY OF MAN AND CIVILIZATION (1949); R. WILLIAMS, CULTURE AND SOCIETY (1958); Kluckhohn, *The Study of Culture,* in THE POLICY SCIENCES 86 (D. Lerner & H. Lasswell eds. 1951).

117. *Cultural Rights, supra* note 113, at 73.

The views expressed by other experts were no less comprehensive. Thus, Mshvenieradze understood "cultural rights" as

> the rights of a human being to labour and education, to free and all-round development of his or her personality, to an active participation in creating material and spiritual values as well as using them for further progress of modern civilization. These values also include science—natural, social, medical, etc.—since it is an integral part of culture.

Id. at 43–44. According to Argan:

> It is the right to create culture, or the right which every social group (and, in certain cases, even every individual) is acknowledged to possess, namely the right to play an

offered this apt summation: "The rights to culture include the possibility for each man to obtain the means of developing his personality, through his direct participation in the creation of human values, and of becoming, in this way, responsible for his situation, whether local or on a world scale."[118] In sum, it would appear that the increasing demands and aspirations for wider application of cultural rights, as articulated and repre-

---

> active part in the community, regardless of its (or his) cultural traditions, religious beliefs, scientific and technical knowledge, moral or political opinions.

Id. at 89. Thapar suggested:

> Cultural rights embrace the whole gamut of rights—economic, political, social. They cannot be studied in isolation. And the totality of rights becomes meaningless when the value system at the base is itself being made irrelevant. This is the core of the problem and cannot be overstressed.

Id. at 93. Martelanc stressed that

> [t]he aim of culture should be to free man's personality, to enable him to be creative, to enable his personality to develop to its full dimensions in order that he may take an active part in everyday life; he should not just be the object of the policy of a State.

Id. at 82.

118. *Id.* at 107.

If we turn from individual to group perspectives, it appears that Art. 27 of the International Covenant on Civil and Political Rights is relevant. This provision provides:

> In those States in which ethnic, religious or linguistic minorities exist, persons belonging to such minorities shall not be denied the right, in community with the other members of their group, to enjoy their own culture, to profess and practise their own religion, or to use their own language.

Covenant on Civil and Political Rights, *supra* note 23, Art. 27, 21 U.N. GAOR, Supp. (No. 16) at 56. The Declaration of the Principles of International Cultural Cooperation, adopted by the General Conference of UNESCO in Nov. 1966, proclaims in Art. 1:

> 1. Each culture has a dignity and value which must be respected and preserved.
> 2. Every people has the right and the duty to develop its culture.
> 3. In their rich variety and diversity, and in the reciprocal influences they exert on one another, all cultures form part of the common heritage belonging to all mankind.

U.N. HUMAN RIGHTS INSTRUMENTS, *supra* note 99, at 103; *Cultural Rights, supra* note 109, at 107. This formulation is in recognition of what some experts call "the rights of cultures," as distinguished from the rights to culture.

The director-general of UNESCO emphasized:

> In the individual nation, as in the world as a whole, any living culture is entitled to be preserved so that it may realize its full human potentialities, for a culture is essentially a certain way of living as a human being and the decline of a culture, unless it is absorbed into a new culture that takes its place, entails an impoverishment of mankind as a whole.

Report of the Director-General of UNESCO, U.N. Doc. A/9227 at 11 (1973).

sented by the panel experts, may ultimately contribute significantly to the formation of a global civic order.

The protection of civic order is appropriately extended to groups as well as individuals. As indicated above, group expression, no less than individual expression, is essential to individual self-fulfillment and to the optimalization of aggregate common interest.[119] The freedom to form voluntary groups (associations), to have access to group membership, to participate in group activities, and to maintain internal group autonomy is critical in achieving an aggregate pattern of interaction in which individual autonomy is secured. The degree to which such protection is afforded serves as one barometer of the state of civic order in a given community. Such protection has traditionally been clustered about generic freedom of association, and concomitantly, freedom of assembly.[120]

The Universal Declaration, in Article 20, provides:

> 1. Everyone has the right to freedom of peaceful assembly and association.
> 2. No one may be compelled to belong to an association.[121]

In its Article 22, with a built-in accommodation clause, the Covenant on Civil and Political Rights stipulates:

> 1. Everyone shall have the right to freedom of association with others, including the right to form and join trade unions for the protection of his interests.
> 2. No restrictions may be placed on the exercise of this right other than those which are prescribed by law and which are necessary in a democratic society in the interests of national security or public safety, public order (*ordre public*), the protection of public health or morals or the protection of the rights and freedoms of

---

119. *See* notes 88–90 *supra* and accompanying text.

120. On freedom of association, *see* G. ABERNATHY, THE RIGHT OF ASSEMBLY AND ASSOCIATION (1961); T. EMERSON, THE SYSTEM OF FREEDOM OF EXPRESSION 675–96 (1970); D. FELLMAN, THE CONSTITUTIONAL RIGHT OF ASSOCIATION (1963); R. HORN, GROUPS AND THE CONSTITUTION (AMS ed. 1971); M. KONVITZ, EXPANDING LIBERTIES 48–85 (1967); C. RICE, FREEDOM OF ASSOCIATION (1962); *A Symposium on Group Interests and the Law,* 13 RUTGERS L. REV. 427 (1959); Elias, *Freedom of Assembly and Association,* 8 J. INT'L COMM'N JURISTS 60 (1967); Emerson, *Freedom of Association and Freedom of Expression,* 74 YALE L.J. 1 (1964); Nathanson, *The Right of Association,* in THE RIGHTS OF AMERICANS 231 (N. Dorsen ed. 1971).

For an articulation of the intimate connection between freedom of association and the right to privacy, *see* Village of Belle Terre v. Boraas, 416 U.S. 1, 12 (1974) (Marshall, J., dissenting).

121. Universal Declaration, *supra* note 18, Art. 20, U.N. Doc. A/810 at 75.

> others. This Article shall not prevent the imposition of lawful restrictions on members of the armed forces and of the police in their exercise of this right.[122]

Article 11 of the European Convention on Human Rights reads, in part:

> 1. Everyone has the right to freedom of peaceful assembly and to freedom of association with others, including the right to form and to join trade unions for the protection of his interests.[123]

Comparable prescription is also found in the American Declaration of the Rights and Duties of Man[124] and the American Convention on Human Rights.[125] Article 22 of the American Declaration states: "Every person has the right to associate with others to promote, exercise and protect his *legitimate interests of a political, economic, religious, social, cultural, professional, labor union or other nature.*"[126] Article 16 of the American Convention provides:

> 1. Everyone has the right to associate freely *for ideological, religious, political, economic, labor, social, cultural, sports, or other purposes.*
> 2. The exercise of this right shall be subject only to such restrictions established by law as may be necessary in a democratic society, in the interest of national security, public safety or public order, or to protect public health or morals or the rights and freedoms of others.
> 3. The provisions of this article do not bar the imposition of legal restrictions, including even deprivation of the exercise of the

---

122. Covenant on Civil and Political Rights, *supra* note 23, Art. 22, 21 U.N. GAOR, Supp. (No. 16) at 55.

123. European Convention, *supra* note 26, Art. 11(1), 213 U.N.T.S. at 232.

Para. 2 of this article reads:

> No restrictions shall be placed on the exercise of these rights other than such as are prescribed by law and are necessary in a democratic society in the interests of national security or public safety, for the prevention of disorder or crime, for the protection of health or morals or for the protection of the rights and freedoms of others. This Article shall not prevent the imposition of lawful restrictions on the exercise of these rights by members of the armed forces, of the police or of the administration of the State.

Id.

For the application of Art. 11, *see* F. Castberg, *supra* note 50, at 152–56; J. Fawcett, *supra* note 50, at 222–24; "Human Rights and Their Limitations," *supra* note 27, at 43–46; F. Jacobs, *supra* note 50, at 157–61.

124. American Declaration, *supra* note 20.

125. American Convention, *supra* note 28.

126. American Declaration, *supra* note 20, Art. 22, Basic Documents, *supra* note 20, at 191 (italics added).

> right of association, on members of the armed forces and the police.[127]

It will be observed that these provisions make explicit, what is implicit in the other transnational prescriptions mentioned above,[128] that their protection extends to a wide range of groups specialized to the shaping and sharing of different values.

It is recognized that privacy, even in its most technical aspect, is part of civic order.[129] In its most comprehensive sense the conception of privacy can be indefinitely expanded toward the totality of civic order. In a provision, Article 12, which is broader than the technical concept of privacy and pregnant with potentiality for further expansion, the Universal Declaration stipulates: "No one shall be subjected to arbitrary interference with his privacy, family, home or correspondence, nor to attacks upon his honour and reputation. Everyone has the right to the protection of the law against such interference or attacks."[130] The International Covenant on Civil and Political Rights, in Article 17, provides:

> 1. No one shall be subjected to arbitrary or unlawful interference with his privacy, family, home or correspondence, nor to unlawful attacks on his honour and reputation.
> 2. Everyone has the right to the protection of the law against such interference or attacks.[131]

On the regional level, both the European Convention on Human Rights[132] and the American Convention on Human Rights[133] employ "private life" in lieu of "privacy." Article 8 of the European Convention, with a built-in accommodation clause, reads:

> 1. Everyone has the right to respect for his private and family life, his home and his correspondence.
> 2. There shall be no interference by a public authority with the exercise of this right except such as is in accordance with the law and is necessary in a democratic society in the interests of national security, public safety or the economic well-being of the country, for the prevention of disorder or crime, for the protec-

127. American Convention, *supra* note 28, Art. 16, 9 INT'L LEGAL MATERIALS at 106 (italics added).

128. *See* notes 120–23 *supra* and accompanying text.

129. *See* notes 56–58, 84–87 *supra* and accompanying text.

130. Universal Declaration, *supra* note 18, Art. 12, U.N. Doc. A/810 at 73–74.

131. Covenant on Civil and Political Rights, *supra* note 23, Art. 17, 21 U.N. GAOR, Supp. (No. 16) at 55.

132. European Convention, *supra* note 26.

133. American Convention, *supra* note 28.

> tion of health or morals, or for the protection of the rights and freedoms of others.[134]

Article 11 of the American Convention states:

> 1. Everyone has the right to have his honor respected and his dignity recognized.
> 2. No one may be the object of arbitrary or abusive interference with his private life, his family, his home, or his correspondence, or unlawful attacks on his honor or reputation.
> 3. Everyone has the right to the protection of the law against such interference or attacks.[135]

These provisions, it is clearly agreed, reiterate the long-cherished protections that have been extended to private life in terms of the inviolability of the home; freedom from unwarranted searches and seizures; the integrity of the family life; the secrecy of correspondence through different modalities; protection against unauthorized use of a person's name, identity, or likeness; and protection against attacks upon honor or reputation.[136] What is less clear is the potential scope of references that may appropriately be accorded the concept of "privacy" or "private life" in future application. This question has aroused growing attention and interest, as modern technology and the modern corporate machines, governmental and nongovernmental, pose increasing threats to the freedoms of individuals and groups.[137]

A number of official and nonofficial clarificatory efforts suggest that "privacy" and "private life" may admit of considerable expansion of their historic references. In his report on privacy prepared in 1973 at the request of the General Assembly,[138] the secretary-general of the United

---

134. European Convention, *supra* note 26, Art. 8, 213 U.N.T.S. at 230. For discussions of the relevant issues, *see* F. Castberg, *supra* note 50, at 138–45; J. Fawcett, *supra* note 50, at 185–97; "Human Rights and Their Limitations," *supra* note 27, at 29–33; F. Jacobs, *supra* note 50, at 125–43; Danelius, *A Survey of the Jurisprudence concerning the Rights Protected by the European Convention on Human Rights,* 8 Human Rights J. 431, 452–57 (1975); Robertson, *The Promotion of Human Rights by the Council of Europe,* 8 Human Rights J. 545, 554–65 (1975).

135. American Convention, *supra* note 28, Art. 11, 9 Int'l Legal Materials at 105.

136. *See* U.N. Report on Privacy, *supra* note 80, at 19–26. *See generally* H. Gross, Privacy—Its Legal Protection (1964); Greenawalt, *The Right of Privacy,* in The Rights of Americans 299 (N. Dorsen ed. 1971).

137. *See* notes 70–80 *supra* and accompanying text.

138. U.N. Report on Privacy, *supra* note 80. The Proclamation of Teheran, adopted by the International Conference on Human Rights in 1968, declared:

> While recent scientific discoveries and technological advances have opened vast prospects for economic, social and cultural progress, such developments may nevertheless

Nations, without attempting to elaborate "a concise international definition of privacy"[139] or to "spell out in detail the components which make up the right to privacy,"[140] makes the observation that

> the very existence of an internationally-recognized right to privacy presupposes agreement that there are certain areas of the individual's life that are outside the concern of either governmental authorities or the general public, areas which may vary in size from country to country but which do possess a common central core.[141]

Underscoring that the exercise of the right of freedom of information and of expression "must not be allowed to destroy the existence of" the

---

> endanger the rights and freedoms of individuals and will require continuing attention. . . .

United Nations, Final Act of the International Conference on Human Rights, Teheran, 22 April to 13 May 1968, at 5, U.N. Doc. A/CONF.32/41 (1968) [hereinafter cited as Final Act]. The Conference proceeded to urge the undertaking of a study on the question of human rights and scientific and technological developments. *Id.* at 12.

Acting upon the recommendation of the Conference, the General Assembly in Dec. 1968 adopted a resolution urging the secretary-general to undertake such a study and to prepare a preliminary report for the Commission on Human Rights to consider. It urged that particular attention be paid to the following:

> (a) Respect for the privacy of individuals and the integrity and sovereignty of nations in the light of advances in recording and other techniques;
>
> (b) Protection of the human personality and its physical and intellectual integrity, in the light of advances in biology, medicine and biochemistry;
>
> (c) Uses of electronics which may affect the rights of the person and the limits which should be placed on such uses in a democratic society;
>
> (d) More generally, the balance which should be established between scientific and technological progress and the intellectual, spiritual, cultural and moral advancement of humanity.

G.A. Res. 2450, 23 U.N. GAOR, Supp. (No. 18) at 54, U.N. Doc. A/7218 (1968).

Subsequently, the preliminary report prepared by the secretary-general, U.N. Docs. E/CN.4/1028, Add. 1–6 and Add. 3/Corr. 1 (1970), was considered by the Commission on Human Rights at its 27th session in 1971. In its Resolution 10 (XXVII) of Mar. 18, 1971, the Commission requested the secretary-general to continue his study on the impacts of scientific and technological developments on human rights.

The U.N. Report on Privacy, *supra* note 80, is the first of a series of reports prepared by the secretary-general under the mandate of G.A. Res. 2450, as reinforced by the Commission on Human Rights. For further details, *see* U.N. Report on Privacy, *supra* note 80, at 4–8; United Nations, United Nations Action in the Field of Human Rights 118–19, U.N. Doc. ST/HR/2 (1974). For other related documents in the series on "Human Rights and Scientific and Technological Developments," *see* U.N. Doc. E/CN.4/1141 (1973); U.N. Doc. E/CN.4/1142 (1972); U.N. Doc. E/CN.4/1142/Add. 1 (1974).

139. U.N. Report on Privacy, *supra* note 80, at 13.

140. *Id.*

141. *Id.*

right to privacy under Article 8 of the European Convention,[142] the Declaration on Mass Communication Media and Human Rights, adopted in 1970 by the Consultative Assembly of the Council of Europe, affirmed:

> The right to privacy consists essentially in the right to live one's own life with a minimum of interference. It concerns private, family and home life, physical and moral integrity, honour and reputation, avoidance of being placed in a false light, nonrevelation of irrelevant and embarrassing facts, unauthorised publication of private photographs, protection from disclosure of information given or received by the individual confidentially.[143]

In a colloquy held in 1970 by the Council of Europe and the Belgian universities to study the content of Article 8 of the European Convention, different aspects of the problem concerning respect for private and family life, home, and correspondence were thoroughly explored.[144] The participants generally took a very broad view of the sphere of private life. Henri Rolin, as president of the European Court of Human Rights, gave this summation:

> Private life has seemed to us to be a concept which covers a very wide field. Various members expressed the view that it must be taken to include protection against attacks on physical or moral integrity, moral or intellectual freedom, on honour or reputation, protection against the improper use of one's name or image, against activities for the purpose of spying or keeping a watch on or harassing persons, and against divulging information covered by professional secrecy.[145]

Professor Rolin also noted that "the colloquy achieved a very wide consensus in favour of the view"[146] that Article 8 of the Convention protects against encroachments from both governmental and nongovernmental sources.[147]

Similarly, the Nordic Conference on the Right to Privacy of 1967, attended by many jurists from different parts of the world, concluded

---

142. Eur. Consult. Ass., Res. 428 (1970), in Collected Texts, *supra* note 37, at 908, 910.

143. *Id.* at 911.

144. Privacy and Human Rights (A. Robertson ed. 1973) [hereinafter cited as Privacy and Human Rights].

145. Rolin, *Conclusions,* in *id.* at 425.

146. *Id.* at 428.

147. *Id.*

with a note that projected a relatively comprehensive view about privacy.[148] Among its "Conclusions" was this statement:

> The Right to Privacy is the right to be let alone to live one's own life with the minimum degree of interference. In expanded form, this means:
>
>> The right of the individual to lead his own life protected against: (a) interference with his private, family and home life; (b) interference with his physical or mental integrity or his moral or intellectual freedom; (c) attacks on his honour and reputation; (d) being placed in a false light; (e) the disclosure of irrelevant embarrassing facts relating to his private life; (f) the use of his name, identity or likeness; (g) spying, prying, watching and besetting; (h) interference with his correspondence; (i) misuse of his private communications, written or oral; (j) disclosure of information given or received by him in circumstances of professional confidence. . . .[149]

It would thus appear that even in the absence of "a concise international definition of privacy,"[150] existing transnational prescriptions concerning privacy or private life are undergoing an expansion in general community expectation that will permit their application to many important emerging threats to civic order.

The growing transnational concern for the protection of privacy is further manifested, and fortified, by efforts within many national communities. The intense and widespread involvement ramifies far beyond the field of informational privacy. The acute sensitivity aroused by the spread of sophisticated modes of surveillance comes at a time when people generally share an ever-deepening sense of powerlessness and of loss of individuality as they experience the grip of enormous corporate organizations, both governmental and nongovernmental.[151] Demands asserted in the name of privacy have, in fact, extended far beyond privacy in the restricted sense of control over information about oneself. "Privacy" is quickly becoming the potent catch symbol for a constellation of demands which, functionally, are demands for civic order—for the utmost practicable freedom of choice in the shaping and sharing of aggregate values. Despite the not inconsiderable controversy involved in its delimitation,[152] the contemporary renaissance of the right of "pri-

---

148. *Nordic Conference on the Right to Privacy,* 31 Bull. Int'l Comm'n Jurists 1 (1967).
149. *Id.* at 2.
150. U.N. Report on Privacy, *supra* note 80, at 13.
151. *See* notes 70–80 *supra* and accompanying text.
152. *See* notes 56–58 *supra* and accompanying text. *See also* note 169 *infra.*

vacy" has already generated a far-reaching beneficent effect upon the protection of the basic right of respect.

These developments are most dramatically exemplified by recent trends in the United States. The Supreme Court, in a series of decisions, has expounded and upheld the protection of privacy in such a degree that for all practical purposes the right of "privacy" is becoming a functional equivalent of what we call "civic order." From the well-worn article by Warren and Brandeis in 1890,[153] through Justice Brandeis's celebrated dissent espousing "the right to be let alone" in *Olmstead* v. *United States* in 1928,[154] to the decision of *Griswold* v. *Connecticut* in 1965,[155] the right to privacy has come to vigorous life.

In *Griswold,* the Supreme Court held unconstitutional, as applied to a married couple, a Connecticut statute forbidding the use of contraceptives, because it intruded upon the right of marital privacy, an aspect of a more general constitutional right of privacy. In formulating a general right of privacy, Mr. Justice Douglas, speaking for the Court, emphasized that "the zone of privacy [is] created by several fundamental constitutional guarantees,"[156] as "specific guarantees in the Bill of Rights have penumbras, formed by emanations from those guarantees that

---

153. Warren & Brandeis, *The Right to Privacy,* 4 HARV. L. REV. 193 (1890). It has become a ritual for commentators, in discussing the right to privacy, to begin by paying tribute to this pioneer article. It was of course an innovation in its time. The authors proposed freedom from unwanted communication. Their occasional reference to the right "to be let alone" (*id.* at 195) as borrowed from Judge Cooley, embodied a broader conception, close to autonomy. *Id.* at 198–214. This reference has the germ of what we mean by civic order.

At its time the article was innovative also in its suggestions for remedy—through tort or criminal law. What the contemporary observer can add is the possibility of protection and implementation as a human right. Attempts to find relevant tort and criminal law are not enough. These efforts need to be integrated in a comprehensive human rights program.

154. 277 U.S. 438, 478 (1928) (Brandeis, J., dissenting). In this case, Justice Brandeis, contrary to the opinion of the Court, took the position that wire-tapping, though involving no physical invasion, was in violation of the Fourth and Fifth Amendments of the Constitution. In his words:

> The protection guaranteed by the Amendments is much broader in scope. The makers of our Constitution undertook to secure conditions favorable to the pursuit of happiness. They recognized the significance of man's spiritual nature, of his feelings and of his intellect. They knew that only a part of the pain, pleasure and satisfactions of life are to be found in material things. They sought to protect Americans in their beliefs, their thoughts, their emotions and their sensations. They conferred, as against the Government, the right to be let alone—the most comprehensive of rights and the right most valued by civilized men. To protect that right, every unjustifiable intrusion by the Government upon the privacy of the individual, whatever the means employed, must be deemed a violation of the Fourth Amendment.

Id.

155. 381 U.S. 479 (1965).

156. *Id.* at 485.

help give them life and substance."[157] Thus conceived, the zone of privacy is, directly or peripherally, protected by the First, Third, Fourth, Fifth, Ninth, and Fourteenth Amendments.[158] Justice Douglas observed that the Court was dealing with "a right of privacy older than the Bill of Rights—older than our political parties, older than our school system."[159]

The separate opinion by Mr. Justice Goldberg, joined by Chief Justice Warren and Justice Brennan, after concurring in Justice Douglas' opinion, proceeded to an independent ground by applying and reviving the "forgotten" Ninth Amendment.[160] The Ninth Amendment provides: "The enumeration in the Constitution, of certain rights, shall not be construed to deny or disparage others retained by the people."[161] Characterizing the right of privacy as "a fundamental personal right, emanating 'from the totality of the constitutional scheme under which we live,'"[162] one that was "'retained by the people' within the meaning of the Ninth Amendment,"[163] Mr. Justice Goldberg declared that "the Ninth Amendment shows a belief of the Constitution's authors that fundamental rights exist that are not expressly enumerated in the first eight amendments and an intent that the list of rights included there not be deemed exhaustive."[164] He added:

> The Ninth Amendment to the Constitution may be regarded by some as a recent discovery and may be forgotten by others, but since 1791 it has been a basic part of the Constitution which we are sworn to uphold. To hold that a right so basic and fundamental and so deep-rooted in our society as the right of privacy in marriage may be infringed because that right is not guaranteed in so many words by the first eight amendments to the Constitution is to ignore the Ninth Amendment and to give it no effect whatsoever.[165]

---

157. *Id.* at 484.

158. *See id.* at 481–86.

159. *Id.* at 486. For an elaboration of this theme, *see* Konvitz, *Privacy and the Law: A Philosophical Prelude,* 31 LAW & CONTEMP. PROB. 272 (1966). Although "privacy" is often assumed to be "a distinctly modern notion," Westin asserts that "the modern claim to privacy derives first from man's animal origins and is shared, in quite real terms, by men and women living in primitive societies." A. WESTIN, *supra* note 58, at 7.

160. 381 U.S. at 491.

.161. U.S. CONST. amend. IX.

162. 381 U.S. at 494.

163. *Id.* at 499.

164. *Id.* at 492.

165. *Id.* at 491. Justice Goldberg sought, however, to dismiss the idea that "the Ninth Amendment constitutes an independent source of rights protected from infringement by either the States or the Federal Government." *Id.* at 492.

In contrast, Emerson observes that "Mr. Justice Goldberg discussed it [the Ninth

In their respective concurring opinions, Justices Harlan and White clearly dissociated themselves from the opinion of the Court and invalidated the Connecticut statute simply for having deprived the married couple of 'liberty' without due process of law,"[166] thereby reinvigorating the doctrine of substantive due process under the Fourteenth Amendment.[167] Justices Black and Stewart dissented on the grounds that the so-called "right of privacy" found no support in the specific guarantees of the Bill of Rights and that the Court, in interpreting the due process clause of the Fourteenth Amendment, must refrain from inventing a new right not grounded in the specific guarantees of the Constitution.[168]

Although the precise source of the right of privacy was a matter of contention among the justices and has since become a favorite subject of continuing debate among commentators,[169] the importance of the *Griswold* decision cannot be overemphasized. *Griswold* established for the

---

Amendment] at length, but his opinion seems to give it a more limited significance." Emerson, *Nine Justices in Search of a Doctrine,* 64 MICH. L. REV. 219, 227 (1965). In Emerson's view, "Mr. Justice Douglas' use of the ninth amendment carries a greater potential. Under his theory, the ninth amendment might be utilized to expand the concept of privacy or, perhaps, to guarantee other basic rights." *Id.* at 228. For vindication of Emerson's view, *see* Palmer v. Thompson, 403 U.S. 217, 233–39 (1971) (Douglas, J., dissenting).

For discussion of the potentialities of the Ninth Amendment, *see* E. CORWIN, THE "HIGHER LAW" BACKGROUND OF AMERICAN CONSTITUTIONAL LAW (1965); B. PATTERSON, THE FORGOTTON NINTH AMENDMENT (1955); Dunbar, *James Madison and the Ninth Amendment,* 42 VA. L. REV. 627 (1956); Franklin, *The Relation of the Fifth, Ninth, and Fourteenth Amendments to the Third Constitution,* 4 HOW. L.J. 170, 174–78 (1958); Kelley, *The Uncertain Renaissance of the Ninth Amendment,* 33 U. CHI. L. REV. 814 (1966); Kelsey, *The Ninth Amendment of the Federal Constitution,* 11 IND. L.J. 309 (1936); Kutner, *The Neglected Ninth Amendment: The "Other Rights" Retained by the People,* 51 MARQ. L. REV. 121 (1967); Paust, *Human Rights and the Ninth Amendment: A New Form of Guarantee,* 60 CORNELL L. REV. 231 (1975); Redlich, *Are There "Certain Rights . . . Retained by the People?"* 37 N.Y.U.L. REV. 787, 804–10 (1962); Ringold, *The History of the Enactment of the Ninth Amendment and Its Recent Development,* 8 TULSA L.J. 1 (1972); Rogge, *Unenumerated Rights,* 47 CALIF. L. REV. 787 (1959).

166. 381 U.S. at 502.

167. *See id.* at 499–502 (Harlan, J., concurring in the judgment); *id.* at 502–07 (White, J., concurring in the judgment).

168. *See id.* at 507–27 (Black, J., dissenting); *id.* at 527–31 (Stewart, J., dissenting).

169. *See* S. HUFSTEDLER, THE DIRECTIONS AND MISDIRECTIONS OF A CONSTITUTIONAL RIGHT OF PRIVACY (1971); Byrn, *An American Tragedy: The Supreme Court on Abortion,* 41 FORDHAM L. REV. 807 (1973); *Comments on the Griswold Case,* 64 MICH. L. REV. 197 (1965); Ely, *The Wages of Crying Wolf: A Comment on Roe v. Wade,* 82 YALE L.J. 920 (1973); Greenwalt, *Privacy and Its Legal Protections,* 2 HASTINGS CENTER STUDIES 45 (1974); Henkin, *Privacy and Autonomy,* 74 COLUM. L. REV. 1410 (1974); Heymann & Barzelay, *The Forest and the Trees: Roe v. Wade and Its Critics,* 53 B.U.L. REV. 765 (1973); Pollak, *Thomas I. Emerson, Lawyer and Scholar: Ipse Custodiet Custodes,* 84 YALE L.J. 638 (1975); Wellington, *Common Law Rules and Constitutional Double Standards: Some Notes on Adjudication,* 83 YALE L.J. 221 (1973) *Note, On Privacy: Constitutional Protection for Personal Liberty,* 48 N.Y.U.L. REV. 670 (1973).

first time a generic right to privacy protected under the Constitution in what had been an ambiguous situation. It matters little whether the right is derived from the First, Third, Fourth, Fifth, Ninth, or Fourteenth Amendment, or from customary expectations that have clustered around the original words. "Penumbras, peripheries, emanations, things fundamental and things forgotten,"[170] or whatever, the important fact is that the Court created constitutional protection for an important human right and stated that right in broad terms. Thus, with *Griswold,* community expectations for greater freedom of choice have been strengthened, notwithstanding the Court's initial difficulties in finding appropriate justification for the right and the absence of a clear projection of the perimeter of the zone of privacy.

In 1969, in *Stanley* v. *Georgia,*[171] the Supreme Court outlawed a Georgia statute prohibiting possession of obscene materials in one's own home. Having reaffirmed the constitutional right to "receive information and ideas" under the First Amendment,[172] Mr. Justice Marshall, delivering the opinion of the Court, hastened to add that "also fundamental is the right to be free, except in very limited circumstances, from unwanted governmental intrusions into one's privacy."[173]

In 1972, in *Eisenstadt* v. *Baird,*[174] the Supreme Court held unconstitutional a Massachusetts law which denied unmarried persons access to contraceptives but accorded married persons such access through a registered physician or through a pharmacist acting pursuant to a physician's prescription. Mr. Justice Brennan, delivering the opinion of the Court, held the Massachusetts statute in violation of the equal protection clause of the Fourteenth Amendment for having distinguished single from married persons in access to contraceptives.[175] In addition, he took the occasion to emphasize that the right to privacy enunciated in *Griswold* is not confined to the marital context. Justice Brennan stated:

> If under *Griswold* the distribution of contraceptives to married persons cannot be prohibited, a ban on distribution to unmarried persons would be equally impermissible. It is true that in *Griswold* the right of privacy in question inhered in the marital relationship. Yet the marital couple is not an independent entity with a mind and heart of its own, but an association of two individuals each with a

170. Kauper, *Penumbras, Peripheries, Emanations, Things Fundamental and Things Forgotten: The Griswold Case,* 64 Mich. L. Rev. 235 (1965). *See also* McKay, *The Right of Privacy: Emanations and Intimations, id.* at 259.

171. 394 U.S. 557 (1969).

172. *Id.* at 564.

173. *Id.*

174. 405 U.S. 438 (1972).

175. *Id.* at 446–55.

> separate intellectual and emotional makeup. If the right of privacy means anything, it is the right of the *individual,* married or single, to be free from unwarranted governmental intrusion into matters so fundamentally affecting a person as the decision whether to bear or beget a child.[176]

The creative role of the Supreme Court in *Griswold* was reaffirmed and further extended in 1973 in *Roe* v. *Wade.*[177] In *Roe* the court invalidated a Texas law banning abortion except on "'medical advice for the purpose of saving the life of the mother'"[178] on the ground that it violated the right of privacy as "founded in the Fourteenth Amendment's concept of personal liberty and restrictions upon state action."[179] The trend of decision that fortifies the Court's protection of privacy is succinctly summarized by Mr. Justice Blackmun, who spoke for the Court:

> The Constitution does not explicitly mention any right of privacy. In a line of decisions, however, going back perhaps as far as *Union Pacific R. Co.* v. *Botsford* (1891), the Court has recognized that a right of personal privacy, or a guarantee of certain areas or zones of privacy, does exist under the Constitution. In varying contexts, the

---

176. *Id.* at 453 (citation omitted).

177. 410 U.S. 113 (1973).

178. *Id.* at 118.

179. *Id.* at 153. Mr. Justice Stewart, reversing his previous position in *Griswold,* concurred that Roe's right was clearly "embraced within the personal liberty protected by the Due Process Clause of the Fourteenth Amendment." *Id.* at 170 (Stewart, J., concurring). In emphasizing the scope of "liberty," he quoted the Court's decision in Board of Regents v. Roth, 408 U.S. 564 (1971): "In a Constitution for a free people, there can be no doubt that the meaning of 'liberty' must be broad indeed." 410 U.S. at 168. He added two eloquent statements by Justices Harlan and Frankfurter:

> [T]he full scope of the liberty guaranteed by the Due Process Clause cannot be found in or limited by the precise terms of the specific guarantees elsewhere provided in the Constitution. This "liberty" is not a series of isolated points pricked out in terms of the taking of property; the freedom of speech, press, and religion; the right to keep and bear arms; the freedom from unreasonable searches and seizures; and so on. It is a rational continuum which, broadly speaking, includes a freedom from all substantial arbitrary impositions and purposeless restraints . . . and which also recognizes, what a reasonable and sensitive judgment must, that certain interests require particularly careful scrutiny of the state needs asserted to justify their abridgment.

Id. at 169 (quoting Justice Harlan's dissent from the dismissal of appeal in Poe v. Ullman, 367 U.S. 497, 543 [1960]). Justice Stewart continued: "Great concepts like. . . 'liberty' . . . were purposely left to gather meaning from experience. For they relate to the whole domain of social and economic fact, and the statesmen who founded this Nation knew too well that only a stagnant society remains unchanged." *Id.* (quoting Justice Frankfurter's dissent in National Mutual Ins. Co. v. Tidewater Transfer Co., 337 U.S. 582, 646 [1949]).

> Court or individual Justices have, indeed, found at least the roots of that right in the First Amendment, *Stanley* v. *Georgia* (1969); in the Fourth and Fifth Amendments, *Terry* v. *Ohio* (1968), *Katz* v. *United States* (1967), *Boyd* v. *United States* (1886), see *Olmstead* v. *United States* (1928) (Brandeis, J., dissenting); in the penumbras of the Bill of Rights, *Griswold* v. *Connecticut;* in the Ninth Amendment, *id.* (Goldberg, J., concurring); or in the concept of liberty guaranteed by the first section of the Fourteenth Amendment, see *Meyer* v. *Nebraska* (1923). These decisions make it clear that only personal rights that can be deemed "fundamental" or "implicit in the concept of ordered liberty," *Palko* v. *Connecticut* (1937), are included in this guarantee of personal privacy. They also make it clear that the right has some extension to activities relating to marriage, *Loving* v. *Virginia* (1967); procreation, *Skinner* v. *Oklahoma* (1942); contraception, *Eisenstadt* v. *Baird; id.* (White, J., concurring in result); family relationships, *Prince* v. *Massachusetts* (1944); and child rearing and education, *Pierce* v. *Society of Sisters* (1925), *Meyer* v. *Nebraska, supra.*[180]

With the decisive stroke of *Roe,* "it is no longer necessary," in the words of Henkin, "to eke out privacy in small pieces as aspects of other constitutional rights; there is now a Constitutional Right of Privacy."[181]

It will be observed that all these cognate terms and verbalisms about privacy reflect a struggle to secure a policy that transcends particular factual contexts and guarantees optimum freedom of choice to human beings. All decisions that protect the utmost freedom of choice in value shaping and sharing—whether justified in terms of privacy, the Bill of Rights, substantive due process, the First Amendment, the Ninth Amendment, the penumbra theory,[182] the incorporation theory,[183] or-

180. *Id.* at 152–53 (citations omitted).

181. Henkin, *supra* note 169, at 1423.

For subsequent developments, *see* J. NOWAK, R. ROTUNDA, & J. YOUNG, HANDBOOK ON CONSTITUTIONAL LAW 623–35 (1978); L. TRIBE, AMERICAN CONSTITUTIONAL LAW 886–990 (1978).

182. *See* Griswold v. Connecticut, 381 U.S. at 481–86. *See also* Dixon, *supra* note 56; McKay, *supra* note 170.

183. *See* Henkin, *"Selective Incorporation" in the Fourteenth Amendment,* 73 YALE L.J. 74 (1963). The gist of the doctrine of "selective incorporation" is that "the fourteenth amendment incorporates specific provisions of the Bill of Rights, and those that are 'absorbed' at all incorporated whole and intact, providing protections against the state exactly congruent with those against the federal government." *Id.* at 74 (footnote omitted). For an authoritative exposition of this theory, *see* Ohio ex rel. Eaton v. Price, 364 U.S. 263, 274–76 (1960). *See generally* Fairman, *Does the Fourteenth Amendment Incorporate the Bill of Rights?* 2 STAN. L. REV. 5 (1949); Morrison, *Does the Fourteenth Amendment Incorporate the Bill of Rights? id.* at 140.

dered liberty, or tort law[184]—contribute to the sum total of free choice for participating in particular value processes. The inclusive, open-ended potentialities that now exist for enlarging the scope of freedom of choice is the very essence of our preferred civic order.

This overriding accent on the freedom of choice that underlies the contemporary protection of privacy is beginning to gain recognition among commentators. Thus, Henkin writes:

> It has been insufficiently noticed that what the Court has been talking about is not at all what most people mean by privacy. None of

---

184. One of the most influential articles concerning the tort law of privacy is Prosser, *Privacy*, 48 CALIF. L. REV. 383 (1960). After a comprehensive survey, Dean Prosser concluded that

> [t]he law of privacy comprises four distinct kinds of invasion of four different interests. . . .
>
> 1. Intrusion upon [a person's] seclusion or solitude, or into his private affairs.
> 2. Public disclosure of embarrassing private facts about [a person].
> 3. Publicity which places [a person] in a false light in the public eye.
> 4. Appropriation . . . of [a person's] name or likeness.

Id. at 389. *See generally* W. PROSSER, HANDBOOK OF THE LAW OF TORTS 802–18 (4th ed. 1971). This fourfold category has been influential not only in the United States, but also in other lands.

A formidable critic of Prosser has argued that there is only one tort, not four separate torts, of privacy. Bloustein, *Privacy as an Aspect of Human Dignity: An Answer to Dean Prosser,* 39 N.Y.U.L. Rev. 962 (1964). *See also* Freund, *Privacy: One Concept or Many,* in PRIVACY, *supra* note 56, at 182–98; Green, *Continuing the Privacy Discussion: A Response to Judge Wright and Professor Bloustein,* 46 TEXAS L. REV. 750 (1968); Kalven, *Privacy in Tort Law—Were Warren and Brandeis Wrong?* 31 LAW & CONTEMP. PROB. 326 (1966). It would appear that Prosser is correct in indicating that the word "privacy" refers to many different interactions and situations which raise different policy issues. The breakdown of different interactions and situations which Prosser offers is, however, unhappily confined to the acquisition and communication of information about a person. He does not explore the broader interest of a person to be let alone in his choices as regards a wide range of values. Similarly, his concern for remedies is confined to those of tort law, with all the limitations inherent in such law. Nonetheless, Bloustein's quarrel would seem largely a matter of words. Whether one says there is only *one* tort of privacy or *four* different torts of privacy is tweedledum and tweedledee. What is important is to note significant differences in facts, relevant policies, and appropriate remedies.

Some critics reject the tort, property, and trust rationales and analogies in regard to privacy, *e.g.,* A. MILLER, *supra* note 56, at 169–201. The most effective approach would appear to be to accept any legal rationale or analogy that leads to improved human rights protection. The tort, property, and trust rationales may in some contexts afford extremely useful protection of human rights. Taken alone, however, they are not adequate. What is needed is to invoke the whole constitutive process of authoritative decision, with all different codes, for improved protection of basic human rights. There is a need, further, not only for improvement in national prescription and administration, but also for improvement in transnational prescription and application.

> the recent cases, and none of the older cases the Court cited (except those dealing with search and seizure under the fourth amendment), which the Justices have now swept together into the basket labeled "right of privacy," deals with any of the matters that are the subject of the now-massive literature on privacy.[185]

In his view, "the Court has been vindicating not a right to freedom from official intrusion, but to freedom from official regulation,"[186] that is, a right to "autonomy."[187] Elaborating, Henkin adds:

> Primarily and principally the new Right of Privacy is a zone of prima facie autonomy, of presumptive immunity from regulation, in addition to that established by the first amendment. The zone, Justice Blackmun told us, consists of "personal rights" that can be deemed "fundamental," that are "implicit in the concept of ordered liberty." The right has "some extension" to marriage, sexual relations, contraception, unwanted children, family relations and parental autonomy. But we will know which rights are and which are not within the zone only case by case, with lines drawn and redrawn, in response to individual and societal initiatives and the imaginativeness of lawyers.[188]

In the same vein, Kalven probes "the relationship of privacy to autonomy or freedom"[189] as follows:

> Do we value privacy only because it is useful to the strategy of protecting personal freedom or do we value it for its own sake independently of the practical consequences that intrusions into privacy may entail? Does privacy, absent a concern with freedom, reduce to a trivial quaint grievance? My deep personal hunch is that the topic is really freedom and that calling it privacy tends to obscure matters. In *Griswold,* for example, is the grievance really the one the Supreme Court selected, namely, the predicted intrusions by police into the bedroom in the effort to enfore the law? Or is the grievance the law's effort to limit man's freedom to decide whether and when he will breed children?[190]

---

185. Henkin, *supra* note 169, at 1424 (footnote omitted). For decisions relating to informational privacy, *see* Berger v. New York, 388 U.S. 41 (1967); Katz v. United States, 389 U.S. 347 (1967). *See also* 1 N. Dorsen, P. Bender, & B. Neuborne, *supra* note 80, at 819–45; Schwartz, *Reflections on Six Years of Legitimated Electronic Surveillance,* in Privacy in a Free Society, *supra* note 75, at 38–55; Schwartz, *The Legitimation of Electronic Eavesdropping: The Politics of "Law and Order,"* 67 Mich. L. Rev. 455 (1969).

186. Henkin, *supra* note 169, at 1424.

187. *Id.* at 1425.

188. *Id.* at 1425–26.

189. Kalvin [*sic*], "*Privacy and Freedom*"—*A Review,* 23 Rec. N.Y.C.B.A. 185, 187 (1968).

190. *Id.*

Greenawalt expresses the same insight when he stresses that "autonomy in choice of behavior is the fundamental value and that information control and freedom from intrusion are merely instrumental to autonomy."[191]

Precisely because it is freedom of choice that is at stake in issues involving privacy, Mr. Justice Douglas found it appropriate, in his concurring opinion in *Roe* and its companion case, *Doe* v. *Bolton,*[192] to reiterate that "a catalogue of" the constitutionally protected rights "includes customary, traditional, and time-honored rights, amenities, privileges, and immunities that come within the sweep of 'the Blessings of Liberty' mentioned in the preamble to the Constitution."[193] In amplification, he outlined the following comprehensive map of that "Liberty" protected under the Fourteenth Amendment:

> *First is the autonomous control over the development and expression of one's intellect, interests, tastes, and personality.*
>
> These are rights protected by the First Amendment and, in my view, they are absolute, permitting of no exceptions. . . .
>
> *Second is freedom of choice in the basic decisions of one's life respecting marriage, divorce, procreation, contraception, and the education and upbringing of children.*
>
> These rights, unlike those protected by the First Amendment, are subject to some control by the police power. . . . These rights are "fundamental," and we have held that in order to support legislative action the statute must be narrowly and precisely drawn and that a "compelling state interest" must be shown in support of the limitation. . . .
>
> . . .
>
> *Third is the freedom to care for one's health and person, freedom from bodily restraint or compulsion, freedom to walk, stroll, or loaf.*
>
> These rights, though fundamental, are likewise subject to regulation on a showing of "compelling state interest."[194]

---

191. Greenawalt, *supra* note 169, at 49.

192. 410 U.S. 179, 209 (1973) (Douglas, J., concurring).

193. *Id.* at 210.

194. *Id.* at 211–13 (citations omitted). *See also* W. DOUGLAS, THE ANATOMY OF LIBERTY 1–52 (1963).

Comparable projections of the contours of freedom of choice of course abound in earlier decisions. For example, in 1897, the Court declared:

> The liberty mentioned [in the due process clause of the Fourteenth Amendment] means not only the right of the citizen to be free from the mere physical restraint of his person, as by incarceration, but the term is deemed to embrace the right of the citizen to be free in the enjoyment of all his faculties; to be free to use them in all lawful ways; to live and work where he will; to earn his livelihood by any lawful calling; to pursue any livelihood or avocation, and for that purpose to enter into all contracts which may

While in the United States the protection of civic order finds increasingly vigorous expression through the expanding right to privacy, comparable protection has been achieved in other legal systems under a "general right of the personality."[195] The policy underlying the protection of the right to the personality is articulated by the Federal Council of Switzerland in these words:

> The right to protection of the part of a person's life which is personal and secret is an expression of the conviction that the individual cannot develop his personality unless he is assured of protection from interference with his private life, by the State or by other persons. This is among the rights which, in a liberal juridical order, are recognized as the rights to which every individual is entitled by the very act of being a person. The protection of these rights is one of the duties of the State, based on law.[196]

The development of this new right is epitomized in the Federal Republic of Germany. The long acknowledged right of the personality under the German Civil Code[197] was greatly strengthened when the Constitution of 1949 formally provided for the protection of "the free

---

> be proper, necessary and essential to his carrying out to a successful conclusion the purposes above mentioned.

Allgeyer v. Louisiana, 165 U.S. 578, 589 (1897). Similarly, in 1923, the Court stated:

> Without doubt, [liberty] denotes not merely freedom from bodily restraint but also the right of the individual to contract, to engage in any of the common occupations of life, to acquire useful knowledge, to marry, establish a home and bring up children, to worship God according to the dictates of his own conscience, and generally to enjoy those privileges long recognized at common law as essential to the orderly pursuit of happiness by free men.

Meyer v. Nebraska, 262 U.S. 390, 399 (1923).

195. *See* S. Stromholm, Right of Privacy and Rights of the Personality: A Comparative Survey (1967) (working paper prepared for the Nordic Conference on Privacy organized by the International Commission of Jurists, Stockholm, May 1967).

196. *Quoted in* U.N. Report on Privacy, *supra* note 80, at 14.

197. Two particularly relevant provisions are Articles 823 and 826, which read:

> Article 823. I. One who, intentionally or negligently, wrongfully injures the life, body, health, freedom, property or any other right of another is obligated to compensate him for damage arising therefrom.
>
> II. One who violates a provision of law intended to protect another incurs the same obligation. If the wording of the provision makes possible its violation without fault, liability for compensation arises only in the presence of fault.
>
> Article 826. One who intentionally damages another in a manner violating good morals is obligated to compensate him for such damage.

Translated and quoted in Krause, *The Right to Privacy in Germany—Pointers for American Legislation?* 1965 Duke L.J. 481, 518. *See also* S. Stromholm, *supra* note 195, at 54–58.

development of one's personality" as a fundamental right. Article 2 reads:

1. Everyone shall have the right to the free development of his personality insofar as he does not violate the rights of others or offend against the constitutional order or the moral code.
2. Everyone shall have the right to life and to inviolability of his person. The freedom of the individual shall be inviolable. These rights may only be encroached upon pursuant to a law.[198]

This doctrine, under "the energetic affirmations"[199] of judicial decisions and scholarly opinions, exhibits an "inexhaustible character,"[200] in that it is left so open-ended as to embrace a wide range of protected rights.

The rights protected under this general right of the personality have been divided into three major categories by German jurists:

1. The "right to develop one's personality":[201] "the general freedom of action, the freedom of work, the right of pursuing a professional, commercial or cultural activity, the freedoms of association, expression, religious and moral activities and education";[202]
2. The "right to defend one's personality":[203] "the protection of a person's life, body and health, the protection of intellectual property, the protection of the free will, of a person's feelings and personal relations";[204] and
3. The "right to defend one's individuality."[205] This refers to "the protection of three distinct spheres,"[206] that is, the "sphere of individuality,"[207] the "private sphere,"[208] and the "sphere of intimacy."[209] The rights protected under the first sphere include "the right to a person's name" and "likeness,"[210] the "right to a person's honour and reputation,"[211] and "the right to have one's descent established."[212] The "sphere of intimacy"[213] is distinguished from the "sphere of privacy,"[214] in that the former refers to "protection against any person trying to have access to

---

198. Basic Law of the Federal Republic of Germany, May 8, 1949, as amended to January 1, 1966, in 3 Constitutions of Nations 361–62 (A. Peaslee rev. 3d ed. 1968).
199. S. Stromholm, *supra* note 195, at 58.
200. *Id.*
201. *Id.* at 55.
202. *Id.*
203. *Id.*
204. *Id.* at 55–56.
205. *Id.* at 55.
206. *Id.* at 56.
207. *Id.*
208. *Id.*
209. *Id.*
210. *Id.* at 57.
211. *Id.*
212. *Id.*
213. *Id.*
214. *Id.*

letters, diaries, personal notes or, more generally, any facts which a person has a reasonable interest in keeping secret,"[215] and the latter refers to protection "against any prying into, surveillance of and disclosure of private facts, independently of their character."[216]

In France, it has been established that "the notion of *droits de la personnalité* is far wider than that of privacy."[217] Professor Nerson, a leading authority in the field, in urging that "the list of personal rights" be "left open,"[218] has observed that the right of the personality is designed to protect:

1. "[I]nterests in the notion of individuality":[219] "the interests relating to a person's name, domicile, status, legal capacity and profession";[220]
2. "[I]nterest" in "bodily integrity";[221]
3. Interests relating to moral elements of the personality: "the right to a person's likeness, to secrecy and honour, the moral rights of authors, rights to personal or family *souvenirs,* family tombs and the rights of family law in general."[222]

The conclusion would, thus, appear clear that the fuller protection of a civic order—in the sense of rights to the utmost freedom of choice and personal autonomy—is emerging, both transnationally and nationally.[223]

---

215. *Id.*
216. *Id.*
217. *Id.* at 49.
218. *Id.* at 51.
219. *Id.* at 50.
220. *Id.*
221. *Id.*
222. *Id.*
223. *See* THE YOUNGER REPORT, *supra* note 56, at 23–30, 308–26; U.N. Report on Privacy, *supra* note 80, at 10–54; PRIVACY AND THE LAW (1970) (a report by Justice, i.e., the British Section of the International Commission of Jurists); Brittan, *The Right of Privacy in England and the United States,* 37 TUL. L. REV. 235 (1963); Dworkin, *The Common Law Protection of Privacy,* 2 U. TASM. L. REV. 418 (1967); Gutteridge, *The Comparative Law of the Right to Privacy,* 47 LAW Q. REV. 203 (1931); Storey, *Infringement of Privacy and its Remedies,* 47 AUSTL. L.J. 498 (1973); Walton, *The Comparative Law of the Right to Privacy,* 47 LAW Q. REV. 219 (1931); Weeks, *Comparative Law of Privacy,* 12 CLEVE.-MAR. L. REV. 484 (1963); Yang, *Privacy: A Comparative Study of English and American Law,* 15 INT'L & COMP. L.Q. 175 (1966).

Although the concept of civic order or its functional equivalent could be developed to meet any particular problems associated with informational privacy, demands are insistent in many communities, especially highly industrialized ones, that more detailed prescription be formulated to deal with manifold problems arising from increasing technological and corporate threats to informational privacy. On the global level this concern is manifested in the United Nations effort to consider the question of human rights and scientific and technological development. *See* note 138 *supra.*

Regionally, it is exemplified by Res. (73) 22 on "the protection of the privacy of individuals vis-à-vis electronic data banks in the private sector," adopted by the Committee of

THE FUTURE OF HUMAN RIGHTS IN PUBLIC AND CIVIC ORDER

The degree to which effective application of the existing prescriptions for the establishment and protection of civic order can be secured will depend in large measure upon how human rights in general are protected and fulfilled, and how effectively the constitutive processes of authoritative decision are mobilized on behalf of the necessary policies. We have emphasized the mutual dependence of public and civic order throughout the world community. The institutions specialized to public order can be expected to exert a decisive impact on the freedoms of

---

Ministers of the Council of Europe on Sept. 26, 1973. COUNCIL OF EUROPE, PROTECTION OF THE PRIVACY OF INDIVIDUALS VIS-À-VIS ELECTRONIC DATA BANKS IN THE PRIVATE SECTOR (1974). Other examples include the European colloquy on privacy and the Nordic Conference on Privacy. *See* notes 144–49 *supra* and accompanying text.

On the national level, the United States offers an excellent example. Intense demands for new prescriptions protecting informational privacy are dramatized by the proliferation of privacy bills introduced before the Congress. Senator Jackson gives this summation:

> The Ninety-Third Congress, which ended in December, has been referred to as the "privacy" Congress because of the legislation it grappled with—over two hundred bills—in an attempt to regain for each person the right to privacy, the right to know what information is being kept, and thus the right to make choices about his or her life. The bills covered a wide area, including Army surveillance, government record-keeping, criminal-arrest records, federal employees' polygraphs, the Census, financial records, mailing lists, freedom of information, social-security numbers, a privacy commission, income-tax returns, and telephone communications.

Jackson, *Privacy and Society,* THE HUMANIST 30 (May/June 1975). Of the statutes that have been enacted to date, the Privacy Act of 1974, Pub. L. No. 93-579, 88 Stat. 1896, effective Dec. 31, 1974, is of paramount importance. In brief, the law provides individuals "the right to know they are the subjects of a file, to examine its contents, to challenge its contents, and to correct inaccurate, incomplete, or out-of-date information." Jackson, *supra,* at 31. Mention may also be made of the Fair Credit Reporting Act of 1970, 15 U.S.C. §§ 1681-1681t (1970), which is designed to eradicate abuses in buying and selling of personal information. To facilitate control over the flow of personal information, the Act accords individuals access to their files in consumer reporting agencies and creates a procedure for the correction of errors. *See generally Fed. Data Banks, Computers and the Bill of Rights, Hearings before the Subcomm. on Const. Rights of the Senate Comm. on the Judiciary,* 92d Cong., 1st Sess. (1971); *Computer Privacy, Hearings before the Subcomm. on Ad. Prac. and Proc. of the Senate Comm. on the Judiciary,* 90th Cong., 2d Sess. (1968); *Retail Credit Co. of Atlanta, Ga., Hearings before the Special Subcomm. on Invasion of Privacy of the House Comm. on Gov't Operations,* 90th Cong., 2d Sess. (May 16, 1968); *The Computer and Invasion of Privacy: Hearings before the Special Subcomm. on Invasion of Privacy of the House Comm. on Gov't Operations,* 89th Cong., 2d Sess. (July 26–28, 1966); Goldwater, Jr., *Bipartisan Privacy,* 1 CIVIL LIB. REV. 74–78 (Summer 1974).

On comparable efforts in other territorial communities, *see* THE YOUNGER REPORT, *supra* note 56; PRIVACY AND COMPUTERS, *supra* note 56; U.N. Report on Privacy, *supra* note 80, at 41–54; S. STROMHOLM, *supra* note 195, at 167–77; Dworkin, *The Younger Committee Report on Privacy,* 36 MODERN L. REV. 399 (1973).

ce which are exercised in the civic sector. The scope of these freeis may be wide or narrow. In turn, any commitment of public order to human rights cannot continue unless the civic order is devoted in theory and practice to these fundamental policies.

As it is often somewhat loosely phrased, the goals of a free society depend upon maintaining a vital balance between the spheres of governmental and civic activities. In previous pages we have sought to delineate these relationships with some precision, particularly the interplay between basic allocations of authorized power and the demands, expectations, and identities of the innumerable individuals and groups who comprise the world body politic. In the future is to move toward a commonwealth of human dignity it will be necessary to sustain and to extend a dynamic equilibrium of forces between public and civic order on behalf of human rights.

It is apparent from the past that a crucial factor is the expectation of violence. In our interdependent, yet divided, world, if expectations of violence continue to escalate, strong demands in support of coercive public order will persist, and the resulting expansion of government operations will in all probability restrict the scope, and cripple the vigor, of civic order. On the other hand, if expectations of large-scale violence are reduced, the scope of civic order will be relatively inclusive, differentiated, and determined to hold its own. For instance, coalitions of governmental and civic forces will modify either public or private monopolies that adversely affect the aggregate pattern of choice.

In passing, we note that although the probable future of military and police activities shows little prospect of their diminishing, no one can justifiably insist that his image of tomorrow is infallible. Common awareness of peril can be expected to sustain a sense of urgency among all who exert any significant influence on public and civic decisions and choices throughout the globe. Human rights would gain from any relaxation in the world military-police arena. Issues relating to human rights provide a cluster of programs capable of arousing intense demand for a more satisfactory quality of life.

Interwoven with the expectation of violence and with other factors influencing human rights is the evolution of science and technology. There are no sure grounds for asserting that science and technology will cease to expand, so long at least as the social process continues to function. The impacts of technological innovation on human rights are complex and contradictory. It is possible to demonstrate, for example, that the overall effect of technical change on "feudal" societies has been to generalize demands in the name of social justice based on equality of respect for basic human identity. These demands are promoted in societies where the class or caste structure is highly stratified and where social mobility is low. A new division of labor means that operations are diversified in new ways. Among groups the focus of attention is more variegated, and distinctive expectations generate novel demands and identifications. Resulting coalitions are less sanctified by tradition and more open to changes that enlarge the circle of active and effective participants in the process of decision.

These movements do not march in one direction. Some innovations increase the span of knowledge, planning, and direction on the part of top elites in governmental, economic, ecclesiastical, and other organizations. In turn, centralizing tendencies may be counteracted by decentralizing tendencies and by demands to deconcentrate control at any level of authoritative decision. The civic order may be strengthened as knowledge is more widely shared and activities are effectively executed in new places or by new groups. Tendencies toward a nondifferentiated society, in turn, may promote recentralizing, monopolistic, and regimenting trends, with adverse consequences for pluralism and individuality.

As a reminder of dynamic and structural forces, we recall the relationship between monarchy and the development of modern institutions of participatory and limited government. Monarchs were supported against other territorial magnates by expanding commercial, industrial, and financial elements of the population. They developed some of the institutions, such as parliaments and constitutional restrictions, that widened the scope of protected choice.

In the next few decades a crucial question is whether science and technology will be made available at creative centers throughout the globe, or whether, in substance, the dominance pattern of today will continue. In no trivial degree the range of choice open to the world's population will depend on shared knowledge conjoined with determination to execute population policies that harmonize with a selected level of resource utilization.

The future vitality of civic order will be deeply affected by the intelligence and strength of private organizations. Since government structures are territorially oriented, they are easily seen as comprehensive and hierarchical. By contrast, the civic order is a welter of people and projects. It is no surprise to find that the bureaucratizing tendencies of government are encouraged and that the sheer weight of public order tends to encroach on the social process as a whole. If civic order is to protect itself, it must engage in counter-organizations that mobilize prompt and intense commitment.

Recent and impending communication changes provide tools that may be used for the effective defense of civic order. The expansion of the physical, biological, and cultural sciences has already nurtured a vast and growing network of scientists, engineers, technicians, and knowledge institutions. Colleges, universities, academies, and research bureaus do not necessarily depend on government. Even in countries where these institutions are governmentalized, they usually exhibit degrees of independence that justify putting them in a relatively depoliticized sphere. In advanced industrial and pluralistic societies, knowledge institutions coexist with multiple political parties and thousands of interest groups. Specialists in the legal, social, and related policy sciences can be drawn upon to assist in formulating policy goals and strategies by every group. If research and storage facilities are accessible, the many participants located in the civic order acquire the cognitive maps necessary to influence public and private choices and decisions. The expanding sciences of culture provide an improving basis for strategies designed to attract the interest of all strata of society in the formation and execution of collective policy. The fundamental implication is that the future of human rights is interdependent with the simultaneous growth of knowledge and commitment.

APPENDIX NATIONALITY AND HUMAN RIGHTS: THE PROTECTION OF THE INDIVIDUAL IN EXTERNAL ARENAS

DELIMITATION OF THE PROBLEM

In a world of ever-increasing transnational interaction the importance to individuals of protection within transnational processes of authoritative decision correspondingly increases. The claims with which we are concerned here are those by an individual for membership in a territorial community for the purposes both of obtaining external protection against other territorial communities and of securing richer participation in the value processes of his chosen community and the world community. The traditional linkage of the individual with territorial communities for such purposes has been through the concept of nationality.[1] Individuals are said to be the "nationals" of a state when that state asserts, and the larger world community honors, claims to protect and control such individuals for all the comprehensive purposes of states, as

---

In slightly different form this appendix first appeared as *Nationality and Human Rights: The Protection of the Individual in External Arenas,* 83 YALE L.J. 900 (1974).

1. On nationality *see generally* NATIONALITY LAWS (R. Flournoy & M. Hudson eds. 1929) [hereinafter cited as R. Flournoy & M. Hudson]; United Nations Legislative Series, LAWS CONCERNING NATIONALITY, U.N. Doc. ST/LEG/SER. B/4 (1954), and SUPPLEMENT TO LAWS CONCERNING NATIONALITY, U.N. Doc. ST/LEG/SER. B/9 (1959); H. VAN PANHUYS, THE ROLE OF NATIONALITY IN INTERNATIONAL LAW (1959); P. WEIS, NATIONALITY AND STATELESSNESS IN INTERNATIONAL LAW (1956); Brownlie, *The Relations of Nationality in Public International Law,* 39 BRIT. Y.B. INT'L L. 284 (1965); Harvard Research in International Law, *The Law of Nationality,* 23 AM. J. INT'L L. SUPP. 11 (1929) [hereinafter cited as *Harvard Research*]; Hudson, *Report on Nationality, Including Statelessness,* [1952] 2 Y.B. INT'L L. COMM'N 3-24, U.N. Doc. A-CN.4/50 (1958); Silving, *Nationality in Comparative Law,* 5 AM. J. COMP. L. 410 (1956). *See also* S. Greenleigh & R. Margenau, The International Law of Nationality: A Policy-Oriented Inquiry, 1962 (unpublished student paper, Yale Law School Library); C. Liu, The Control of People as a Base of Power: International Law of Nationality and Access to Territory, 1957 (unpublished J.S.D. dissertation, Yale Law School Library). The authors have found the study by Messrs. Greenleigh and Margenau particularly helpful.

contrasted with occasional particular exercises of competence under varying principles of jurisdiction.[2]

It is, thus, of critical importance how the concept of "nationality" and all the ancillary rules about the conferment and withdrawal of nationality are managed in the allocation of competence among territorial communities to protect individual human beings against deprivations by other territorial communities and in determinations of what states are authorized to impose what burdens upon individuals in different value processes. In a world arena still largely state-organized, decisions about nationality may affect both the degree to which the individual person has access to a protector and the substantive content of his rights. It is a distinguishing characteristic of nation-states that they claim a special competence to impose upon their members unique burdens with respect, for example, to taxation, military service, and subjection to civil and criminal jurisdiction; how these burdens are distributed, and maximized or minimized, through assertion by one or more states, importantly affects the aggregate enjoyment of human rights by individuals.

The central focus of our present inquiry is upon the allocation of competence to protect individuals and the decisions which most directly affect this allocation. Given a decentralized world arena in which nation-states are still the principal official participants, if the individual human being does not have some state as a protector, the larger community aspiration for human rights is meaningless. Thus, the stateless person—the person without formal membership in any body politic—is

---

2. The concept of "nationality" is often reified into a pseudo-absolute comparable to "title." The concept, in fact, serves as a chameleonlike term for making ambiguous references to facts, claims, relevant policies, and legal consequences. The facts embrace many differing degrees of membership in one or more groups; the claims are made by both states and individuals; the relevant policies vary with a great range of practical problems; and legal consequences are commonly fashioned to serve both inclusive and exclusive policies as problems vary.

The pervasive ambiguity in the concept can be escaped only by keeping entirely distinct at least the following:

1. The facts in global social process which comprise both "group memberships" and the interactions of individuals across nation-state lines;
2. The claims that nation-states make under their varying national laws, to protect, control, and impose burdens upon individuals;
3. The policies of a transnational law which seeks to protect both the human rights of individuals and the common interests of states; and
4. The decisions taken in transnational arenas of authority in regulation of the claims of both states and individuals about protection, control, and burdens.

The flexibilities of the concept of "citizenship" are indicated in Bickel, *Citizenship in the American Constitution,* 15 ARIZ. L. REV. 369 (1973).

treated as an international outcast, an "unprotected person."[3] The possible value deprivations to which such a person may be subjected are severe and all-encompassing, far beyond those common to aliens; he has little or no access to authoritative decision, on either national or international levels. Similarly, the individual who is confronted with administrative obstacles or legal complexities in establishing a nationality, whose acknowledged state refuses to protect him, or who is denied a claim against a state of his nationality may be made equally to suffer a deprivation of human rights in the merits of his claim.

The practices of states in conferring or withholding nationality and the procedures established by states for such conferment or withholding may of course directly affect not only access to a protector but also the quantity and quality of participation in all value processes, both national and international. Hence significant inquiry about actual and potential deprivations of human rights must make detailed examination of the flow of decision about practices and procedures in the conferment and withholding of nationality.

Individuals who, in contrast with the stateless person, are claimed by more than one state—i.e., who have multiple nationality—may sometimes enjoy the advantages of greater protection. They may also, however, be held subject to greater responsibilities and be subjected to greater burdens. Thus, they may be in danger of multiple jeopardy in terms of military service, taxation, and subjection to jurisdiction.

The more detailed claims to authoritative decision with which we are here concerned may, hence, be summarized as follows:

1. Claims by the individual to a protecting state;
2. Claims relating to the conferment of nationality;
3. Claims relating to the withdrawal of nationality (including voluntary expatriation);
4. Claims relating to statelessness; and
5. Claims relating to multiple nationality.

THE CLARIFICATION OF GENERAL COMMUNITY POLICY

Historically, in the allocation of competence over peoples, the established decision makers of the transnational community have honored, in varying combinations in different contexts, two complementary policies. One policy, most preferred when expectations of large-scale violence are low, favors human rights and encourages freedom in the circulation of people and easy changes in group membership, much the same as it

---

3. For further elaboration, *see* notes 281–94 *infra* and accompanying text.

encourages freedom of movement in capital, goods, services, and ideas. The other policy, especially stressed under conditions of continuing expectations of imminent violence, concedes more to the interests of states in the exclusive protection of their bases of power, through stringent controls over people, including restrictions upon change of national membership.

The long-term policy most compatible with an international law of human dignity would be one that seeks the utmost voluntarism in affiliation, participation, and movement, with an easy assumption by states of a competence to protect such individuals as seek their protection. The individual should be able to become a member of, and to participate in the value processes of, as many bodies politic as his capabilities will permit.

It must of course be conceded that, given the present structure of the world arena, states do share some common interests which may on occasion require limitation of this preferred policy of the utmost individual voluntarism. Despite contemporary technological developments, people remain an important base of power for each of the different territorially organized communities of the world. Both the security, in the minimum sense of freedom from external violence and coercion, and the quality of society, in terms of the greater production and wider sharing of all values, that a community can achieve are intimately dependent upon the numbers and characteristics of its members, including their capabilities, skills, and loyalties. It is this intimate dependence which is reflected in the historic reciprocal honoring of the principles of *jus soli* and *jus sanguinis* in the allocation of members and of the principles of "territoriality" and "nationality" in the allocation of jurisdiction. Secondarily, territorial communities share important interests in maintaining harmonious relationships among themselves and in avoiding situations of potential conflict in their claims about members. The different communities have, finally, a common interest in a certain economy in the expenditure of resources in their practices for the allocation of members and the provision of protection in transnational processes of authoritative decision.

The task of a decision maker or other evaluator who genuinely identifies with the whole community of mankind is that of achieving an accommodation in particular instances between the complementary policies reflected in the demands of states and the demands of individuals, an accommodation which will best promote in the long run the largest net, aggregate achievement of human rights.

In search of such accommodation, a strong preference might be given policies which accord to every individual the protection of at least one state for the purpose of securing within transnational processes of authoritative decision a proper hearing upon the merits of controversies. Thus, to make certain that individuals have at least one nationality for this purpose, access to community membership upon both *jus soli* and *jus sanguinis,* and even upon the simple request of the individual, might be authorized in the most generous degree.

From broader human dignity perspectives the individual's volition should be accorded the utmost possible expression and respect in all the different decisions concerning nationality: the conferment of nationality, the procedures by which nationality is established and evidenced, the withdrawal of nationality, the minimization and amelioration of statelessness, and the regulation of multiple nationality. In particular, states should not be permitted to make arbitrary conferment (that is, upon grounds unrelated to common interest) of nationality against the wishes of the individual. Nor should states be permitted arbitrarily to deny (as for purposes of discrimination) nationality sought by the individual.

Save for conflict with the most urgent state necessities, people ought thus to be allowed freely to determine their nationality subsequent to birth. Their wishes should be made largely the decisive factor, with only a modest deference toward criteria designed to protect state interests. In support of these policies, procedures for establishing and withdrawing nationality should not be honored when they are so arbitrary as to negate whatever protection may otherwise be provided for the individual. Requirements for establishing and proving nationality need not, in order to preclude fraud, be so strict as to make compliance impossible. For the further protection of private choice, comparable policies might be recognized for the withdrawal of nationality. States should not be permitted arbitrarily (as for purposes of discrimination or punishment) to withdraw nationality, nor arbitrarily to preclude voluntary change of nationality. Statelessness should, by some one of many expedients, be abolished.

In keeping with the policy of honoring utmost voluntarism, the individual might be authorized to choose membership in all the bodies politic for which he is able and willing to assume responsibility. Such multiplicity in choice requires, of course, the right to change one's nationality. Similarly, any state of which an individual is a member should be authorized to protect him against another state, even one of which he is also a national. Multiple nationality is to be preferred in contexts in which it increases the protection available for the individual; it should be rejected when it imposes arbitrary burdens upon him. In a public order of human dignity, the whole international law of nationality should, in sum, be designed for the better protection of the individual, with minimum concessions to the organized interests of the territorial communities.

TRENDS IN DECISION AND CONDITIONING FACTORS

Decisions about every major type of claim which we have identified have, unhappily, expressed and been affected by perspectives, not of the fundamental rights of the individual, but of the paramount interests of state elites in the control of people as important bases of power.

Claims by the Individual to a Protecting State

The overwhelming trend of decision has been to permit the state of nationality, and only the state of nationality, to protect individuals.[4] Unfortunately, states are still regarded as having an option with respect to whether they will protect their nationals, for international law imposes no duty on the state to do so. Hence individuals are left to the arbitrary whim or caprice of state officials.

In addition, under the once dominant theory that states are the only "subjects" of international law, nation-states alone have been considered competent in most forums to present claims against other states.[5] Injured individuals are denied access to transnational arenas to present claims against external entities; rather, they are made to look to their own state for protection against such value deprivations.

Similarly, the principle that a state can provide protection only in cases of deprivations suffered by its own nationals is well established.[6] The

---

4. The reference we make is to direct access to processes of authoritative decision. It does not escape our notice that many nonterritorial groups—ethnic, linguistic, skill, religious, for instance—effectively engage in vast and enduring patterns of protest and appraisal for the protection of the individual.

5. On the subject of diplomatic protection, the classics are E. Borchard, The Diplomatic Protection of Citizens Abroad (1922), and F. Dunn, The Protection of Nationals (1932). *See also* L. Sohn & R. Baxter, Convention on the International Responsibility of States for Injuries to Aliens (1961); Harvard Research in International Law, *The Law of Responsibility of States for Damage Done in Their Territory to the Person or Property of Foreigners,* 23 Am. J. Int'l L. Supp. 131 (1929). Of special contemporary interest are a series of reports on international responsibility submitted to the International Law Commission, including, inter alia: *First Report on International Responsibility,* [1956] 2 Y.B. Int'l L. Comm'n 173, U.N. Doc. A/CN.4/96 (1956); *Second Report on International Responsibility,* [1957] 2 Y.B. Int'l L. Comm'n 104, U.N. Doc. A/CN.4/106 (1957); *Third Report on International Responsibility,* [1958] 2 Y.B. Int'l L. Comm'n 47, U.N. Doc. A/CN.4/111 (1958); *Sixth Report on International Responsibility,* [1961] 2 Y.B. Int'l L. Comm'n 1, U.N. Doc. A/CN.4/134 and Add. 1 (1961). More recent commentaries include F. Dawson & I. Head, International Law, National Tribunals and the Rights of Aliens (1971); C. Joseph, Nationality and Diplomatic Protection (1969); R. Lillich & G. Christenson, International Claims: Their Preparation and Presentation (1962); F. Vallat, International Law and the Practitioner (1966); Weis, *Diplomatic Protection of Nationals and International Protection of Human Rights,* 4 Human Rights J. 643 (1971).

6. The Permanent Court of International Justice declared in the Mavrommatis Palestine Concessions Case: "It is an elementary principle of international law that a State is

only "link" generally accepted for purposes of establishing standing to protect against deprivations is, thus, that of nationality.

The fiction that sustains this inhibiting practice is that an injury to the individual is an injury to the state of his nationality. The classic thesis was expounded by Vattel:

> Whoever ill-treats a citizen indirectly injures the State, which must protect that citizen. The sovereign of the injured citizen must avenge the deed and, if possible, force the aggressor to give full satisfaction or punish him, since otherwise the citizen will not obtain the chief end of civil society, which is protection.[7]

Similarly, the Permanent Court of International Justice in the *Panevezys-Saldutiskis Railway* case observed that

> in taking up the case of one of its nationals, by resorting to diplomatic action or international judicial proceedings on his behalf, a state is in reality asserting its own right, the right to ensure in the person of its nationals respect for the rules of international law. This right is necessarily limited to the intervention on behalf of its own nationals because, in the absence of a special agreement, it is the bond of nationality between the state and the individual which alone confers upon the state the right of diplomatic protection, and it is as a part of the function of diplomatic protection that the right to take up a claim and to ensure respect for the rules of international law must be envisaged. Where the injury was done to the national of some other State no claim to which such injury may give rise falls within the scope of the diplomatic protection which a State is entitled to afford nor can it give rise to a claim which that State is entitled to espouse.[8]

Under this fiction a state's right to protect is independent of the individual's interest; a state is put under no duty, but rather accorded complete discretion, to decide whether or not to press claims against external entities on behalf of its nationals. In most countries it is left to the executive branch, which may not be required to conform to judicial standards of due process, to decide. Given the overriding concern for the so-called national interest, nation-state elites tend to exaggerate, in the words of Frederick Dunn, "the importance of the political relations

---

entitled to protect its subjects, when injured by acts contrary to international law committed by another State, from whom they have been unable to obtain satisfaction through the ordinary channels." [1924] P.C.I.J., Ser. A, No. 2, at 6, 12.

7. 3 E. de Vattel, Classics of International Law: The Law of Nations or the Principles of Natural Law 136 (C. Fenwick trans. 1916).

8. Panevezys-Saldutiskis Railway Case, [1939], P.C.I.J., Ser. A/B, No. 76, at 16.

of states at the expense of the activities of men as human beings."[9] Individuals' claims are put aside when the "national" interest so dictates. At times, therefore, the state interest, asserted from perspectives of the total foreign policy of the state, may be in contravention of the wishes of the individuals concerned.

Because of its negative implications for individual human rights and its manifest incompatibility with fact, this fiction has been under increasing attack. Thus, one commentator has pointed out that a deprivation to an individual is not necessarily a deprivation to the state and that the claim of the individual, not that of the state, is basic, a reality that is implied by the requirement for the exhaustion of local remedies by the individual.[10] As stated by Umpire Parker of the United States-German Mixed Claims Commission,

> [T]he generally accepted theory formulated by Vattel, which makes the injury to the national an injury to the nation and internationally therefore the claim a national claim which may and should be espoused by the nation injured, must not be permitted to obscure the realities or blind us to the fact that the ultimate object of asserting the claim is to provide reparation for the private claimant. . . .[11]

These perspectives demand a functional, rather than fictional, concept of protection. More fundamentally, of course, in an appropriately organized world the individual would be accorded competence to protect himself.

In specific application of the "nationality" myth, the doctrine of "continuous nationality" has for over a century resulted in the rejection of innumerable claims by arbitral tribunals. As developed under customary international law, a claimant must possess the nationality of the espousing state from the moment of deprivation, through the presentation of the claim, and often to the time of settlement.[12] Thus, a claimant whose nationality is changed or lost after suffering a deprivation cannot obtain remedy. His state of nationality at the time of deprivation is precluded from espousing his claim because he is no longer its national; his new

---

9. Dunn, *The International Rights of Individuals,* [1941] PROC. AM. SOC'Y INT'L L. 14, 17.

10. "If the national State were directly injured its rights could hardly be contingent upon exhaustion of local remedies by the individual." 2 D. O'CONNELL, INTERNATIONAL LAW 1031 (2d ed. 1970). Concerning the rule of exhaustion of local remedies, *see* E. BORCHARD, *supra* note 5, at 817–32; H. BRIGGS, THE LAW OF NATIONS 620–37 (2d ed. 1952); L. SOHN & R. BAXTER, *supra* note 5, at 161–70.

11. Administrative Decision No. V (United States/Germany), 7 U.N.R.I.A.A. 119, 152–53 (1956).

12. *See* R. LILLICH & G. CHRISTENSON, *supra* note 5, at 9–12; L. SOHN & R. BAXTER, *supra* note 5, at 200–02.

state of nationality is barred because at the time of injury he was not its national. In recent years the inequities caused by this requirement have been spotlighted by the post-war measures of wealth deprivation undertaken by the Eastern European countries. Large numbers of displaced people, who fled these countries during World War II and its aftermath,[13] could derive no international succor under traditional doctrines of nationality.

The harsh effects of the doctrine are especially observable in connection with stateless persons and new immigrants, although mitigating measures are sometimes undertaken. For instance, during the nineteenth century, the United States made it a practice to afford protection to individuals on the basis of domicile plus a declaration of intent to become a United States citizen.[14] This reflected in part the positive attitude toward immigration prevailing in the United States at the time and expressed and emphasized the significant ties other than nationality that a person may have with a territorial community. Occasionally, out of explicit humanitarian considerations, protection is afforded or at least asserted for other nonnationals, such as refugees or members of minority groups. This exception reinforces contemporary concern for human rights and for protection of refugees in particular.[15]

Sometimes, in contrast, even the concept of "nationality" itself is questioned or distorted for the purpose of denying protection to individuals. Under contemporary international law, states are accorded a very broad competence for choosing among grounds for the conferment of nationality upon individuals, and the practice of states exhibits a high degree of reciprocal deference to conferments of nationality in accordance with customary criteria. Yet upon occasion individuals have been deprived of a protector and of a hearing upon the merits of their claims either by invocation of variable or spurious conceptions of nationality or by imposition of tests over and beyond any traditional conception of nationality. The destructiveness for human rights of these decisions is dramatically

---

13. *See* Kerley, *Nationality of Claims—A Vista,* [1969] PROC. AM. SOC'Y INT'L L. 35, 36.

14. *See* Copithorne, *International Claims and the Rule of Nationality,* [1969] PROC., AM. SOC'Y INT'L L. 30, 31.

15. On international protection of refugees, *see* UNITED NATIONS HIGH COMMISSIONER FOR REFUGEES, A MANDATE TO PROTECT AND ASSIST REFUGEES (1971). *See also* L. HOLBORN, THE INTERNATIONAL REFUGEE ORGANIZATION (1956); F. NORWOOD, STRANGERS AND EXILES (1969); J. SCHECHTMAN, THE REFUGEE IN THE WORLD (1963); J. STOESSINGER, THE REFUGEE AND THE WORLD COMMUNITY (1956); J. VERANANT, THE REFUGEE IN THE POST-WAR WORLD (1953); Krenz, *The Refugee as a Subject of International Law,* 15 INT'L & COMP. L.Q. 90 (1966); Read, *The United Nations and Refugees: Changing Concepts,* 537 INT'L CONCILIATION (1962); Rees, *Century of the Homeless Man,* 515 INT'L CONCILIATION (1957); Weis, *The Concept of the Refugee in International Law,* [1960] JOURNAL DU DROIT INTERNATIONAL 928; Weis, *The International Protection of Refugees,* 48 AM. J. INT'L L. 193, 195 (1954).

illustrated in such famous cases as *Nottebohm*,[16] *Flegenheimer*,[17] and the *Barcelona Traction Company*.[18] The importance to individuals of state protection in a state-organized world is such as to justify a somewhat detailed examination of these cases.

In the *Nottebohm* case,[19] involving Liechtenstein and Guatemala, the former sought restitution and compensation on behalf of one Friedrich Nottebohm for the latter country's actions allegedly in violation of international law. A German national from his birth in Germany in 1881, Nottebohm moved to Guatemala in 1905, residing and doing business there, without ever applying for Guatemalan citizenship. Thereafter, he sometimes made trips to Germany to conduct business and to Liechtenstein to visit his brother, who lived there after 1931.

While still a German national, Nottebohm applied for naturalization in Liechtenstein on October 9, 1939, shortly after the German invasion of Poland. Relieved of the three-year residence requirements, Nottebohm paid his fees and taxes to Liechtenstein and became a naturalized citizen of Liechtenstein by taking an oath of allegiance on October 20, 1939, thereby forfeiting his German nationality under the nationality law of Liechtenstein. He returned to Guatemala early in 1940 on a Liechtenstein passport to resume his business activities. At his request the Guatemalan Ministry of External Affairs changed the Nottebohm entry in its Register of Aliens from "German" to "Liechtenstein" national.

In July 1941, Nottebohm was blacklisted for trade purposes by the United States, and his assets in the United States were frozen. Shortly afterward, on December 11, 1941, a state of war came into existence between the United States and Germany and between Guatemala and Germany. Arrested in Guatemala in October 1943, Nottebohm was deported to the United States, where he was interned as an enemy alien until 1946. Upon his release Nottebohm applied for readmission to Guatemala but was refused; therefore, he took up residence in Liechtenstein. Meanwhile, the Guatemalan government, after classifying him as an enemy alien, expropriated his extensive properties without compensation.

Liechtenstein instituted proceedings against Guatemala in the International Court of Justice, asking the court to declare that Guatemala had violated international law "in arresting, detaining, expelling and refus-

---

16. Nottebohm Case, [1955] I.C.J. 4.

17. Flegenheimer Claim, 25 I.L.R. 91 (Italian-United States Conciliation Commission 1963).

18. Case concerning the Barcelona Traction, Light and Power Company, Limited, Second Phase, [1970] I.C.J. 4.

19. [1955] I.C.J. 4.

ing to readmit Mr. Nottebohm and in seizing and retaining his property."[20] Guatemala's main contention was that Liechtenstein's claim was inadmissible because of Nottebohm's nationality. Liechtenstein's competence to protect Nottebohm was challenged. Guatemala argued that

> the Principality of Liechtenstein has failed to prove that M. Nottebohm, for whose protection it is acting, properly acquired Liechtenstein nationality in accordance with the law of the Principality; because, even if such proof were provided, the legal provisions which would have been applied cannot be regarded as in conformity with international law; and because M. Nottebohm appears in any event not to have lost, or not validly to have lost, his German nationality. . . .[21]

The court rejected the Liechtenstein claim by a vote of eleven to three, declaring that Nottebohm's naturalization could not be accorded international recognition because there was no sufficient "bond of attachment" between Nottebohm and Liechtenstein. Utilizing multiple nationality cases as precedents, the court expounded a "genuine link" theory of "real and effective nationality":

> [A] State cannot claim that the rules it has thus laid down are entitled to recognition by another State unless it has acted in conformity with this general aim of making the legal bond of nationality accord with the individual's genuine connection with the State which assumes the defence of its citizens by means of protection as against other States. . . . [N]ationality is a legal bond having as its basis a social fact of attachment, a genuine connection of existence, interests and sentiments, together with the existence of reciprocal rights and duties. It may be said to constitute the juridical expression of the fact that the individual upon whom it is conferred, either directly by the law or as the result of an act of the authorities, is in fact more closely connected with the population of the State conferring nationality than with that of any other State.[22]

The court concluded:

> Naturalization was asked for not so much for the purpose of obtaining a legal recognition of Nottebohm's membership in fact in the population of Liechtenstein, as it was to enable him to substitute for his status as a national of a belligerent State that of a national of a neutral State, with the sole aim of thus coming within the protection

20. *Id.* at 6–7.
21. *Id.* at 9.
22. *Id.* at 23.

> of Liechtenstein but not of becoming wedded to its traditions, its interests, its way of life or of assuming the obligations—other than fiscal obligations—and exercising the rights pertaining to the status thus acquired.[23]

The *Nottebohm* decision has been widely criticized.[24] It has nevertheless been invoked and applied to serve different purposes in different contexts. For present purposes, the application of the "genuine link" theory, borrowed from the very different context of dual nationality problems, has the unfortunate effect of depriving an individual of a hearing on the merits and the protection by a state willing to espouse his claim in the transnational arena. The net effect is an immense loss of protection of human rights for individuals. Such a decision runs counter to contemporary community expectations emphasizing the increased protection of human rights for individuals, especially the elimination of statelessness. As Judge Guggenheim stated emphatically in his dissenting opinion,

> If the right of protection is abolished, it becomes impossible to consider the merits of certain claims alleging a violation of the rules of international law. If no other State is in a position to exercice [*sic*] diplomatic protection, as in the present case, claims put forward on behalf of an individual, whose nationality is disputed or held to be inoperative on the international level and who enjoys no other nationality, would have to be abandoned. The protection of the individual which is so precarious under existing international law would be weakened even further and I consider that this would be contrary to the basic principle embodied in Article 15(I) of the Universal Declaration of Human Rights adopted by the General Assembly of the United Nations on December 8th, 1948, according to which everyone has the right to a nationality. Furthermore, refusal to exercise protection is not in accordance with the frequent attempts made at the present time to prevent the increase in the number of cases of stateless persons and to provide protection against acts violating the fundamental human rights recognized by international law as a minimum standard, without distinction as to nationality, religion or race.[25]

In the light of the foregoing, it is unfortunate that the drafters of the 1961 Harvard draft convention on state responsibility incorporated the

---

23. *Id.* at 26.

24. *See, e.g.,* H. VAN PANHUYS, *supra* note 1, at 95–105; De Visscher, *L'Affaire Nottebohm,* 27 REVUE GENERAL DE DROIT INTERNATIONAL PUBLIC 238 (1956); Jones, *The Nottebohm Case,* 5 INT'L & COMP. L.Q. 230 (1956); Kunz, *The Nottebohm Judgment (Second Phase),* 54 AM. J. INT'L L. 536 (1960).

25. Nottebohm Case, [1955] I.C.J. 4, 63–64.

Nottebohm doctrine and proposed that a "State is not entitled to present a claim on behalf of a natural person who is its national if that person lacks a genuine connection of sentiment, residence, or other interests with that State."[26] Condoning unnecessary legalisms of imprecise policy reference, which deny individuals a hearing upon the merits of their claims, can scarcely augment human rights.

While the *Nottebohm* decision denied the competence of Liechtenstein to protect a naturalized citizen, the *Flegenheimer*[27] case involved the denial of protection to a national by birth. Paradoxically, Professor Sauser-Hall, defeated counsel for Liechtenstein in *Nottebohm*, who presided over the Italian-United States Conciliation Commission in the *Flegenheimer* case, distinguished and rejected the *Nottebohm* decision in such a way as to augment, rather than mitigate, the inequities perpetrated in *Nottbohm*.

In the *Flegenheimer* case, Albert Flegenheimer sought invalidation of the 1941 sale of his stock in an Italian company, at a nominal sum, to which he assented because of his alleged fear of prevailing Italian anti-Semitic legislation and persecution. The Commission declared the petition filed on his behalf inadmissible on the ground that he was not a "United Nations national" within the scope of Article 78 of the Peace Treaty with Italy.

Albert's father, Samuel Flegenheimer, born in Baden, Germany, had moved to the United States in the 1860s and become a naturalized American citizen in 1873. In 1874, he returned to Germany to live in the then Kingdom of Wurttemberg, where Albert was born in 1890. On August 23, 1894, Samuel Flegenheimer was naturalized in Wurttemberg; and Albert, age four, together with his brothers, was naturalized with his father. Not until 1933, when the Nazis attained power in Germany, was Albert Flegenheimer aware of his father's former American citizenship—and hence of the possibility of his own claim to such citizenship. Thereupon he approached American consulates and embassies in Europe to obtain a determination of his citizenship status, but his inquiries were answered either ambiguously or negatively.

In 1937, because of his fear of Nazi persecution, Albert Flegenheimer left Germany for Italy, Switzerland, and eventually Canada. On

26. L. Sohn & R. Baxter, *supra* note 5, at 199 (draft art. 23, para. 3).

To apply the Nottebohm doctrine to situations in which there exists only a "blood link" between a national and his state would deny hundreds of thousands of "overseas" nationals of China, France, and the United Kingdom the protection of their home governments. Goldschmidt, *Recent Applications of Domestic Nationality Laws by International Tribunals,* 28 Fordham L. Rev. 689, 695 (1960).

27. Flegenheimer Claim, 25 I.L.R. 91 (Italian-United States Conciliation Commission 1963). *See* 53 Am. J. Int'l L. 944 (1959).

November 3, 1939, he formally submitted his claim to American citizenship at the United States Consulate in Winnipeg, Canada. In response later that month, the Board of Special Inquiry of the Immigration and Naturalization Service of the United States decided (erroneously, as later appeared) that he was not an American citizen. In April 1940, he was divested of German nationality by German decree. Subsequently, he took up residence in the United States in 1941–42 on a temporary visa. In February 1942, the Immigration and Naturalization Service acknowledged that Flegenheimer was an American citizen by birth. In October 1946, the Department of State, after an earlier refusal, granted him a United States passport. Subsequent to the commencement of proceedings before the Conciliation Commission, Flegenheimer was issued, on July 10, 1952, a certificate of United States nationality by the Acting Assistant Commissioner, Inspection and Examinations Division, Immigration and Naturalization Service of the United States.

By a unanimous decision the Conciliation Commission rejected the petition on behalf of Albert Flegenheimer, stating that though he "acquired by filiation the nationality of the United States, at birth," he "acquired German and Wurttemberg nationality as the result of his naturalization in Wurttemberg on August 23, 1894, and thereby lost, after five years' residence in his new home country, his American nationality, under the Bancroft Treaty concluded on July 2, 1868, between the United States of America and Wurttemberg."[28] The Commission further found that Flegenheimer "never reacquired his American nationality after reaching majority"[29] and concluded that it was not bound by the certificate of American nationality of July 10, 1952.

In rejecting the validity of the certificate of United States nationality of July 10, 1952, the Commission substituted its own evaluation of "nationality" for that of the United States. Clearly, in order to determine its jurisdiction, an international commission may investigate the nationality of parties on whose behalf claims are presented. However, the authorized scope of investigation is confined to establishing the facts pertinent to nationality and to appraisal of whether or not a state has exceeded accepted limits in its conferment of nationality. In the absence of claims by another state to the same individual or allegations that a state accords protection on the basis of spurious, fraudulent, or impermissible grounds, the Commission is not authorized to substitute its own determination of nationality for that of a claimant state. This would appear the clear import of the Hague Convention on Nationality, which only makes customary international law explicit, when it stipulates that "[i]t is

28. 53 Am. J. Int'l L. 944, 945 (1959).
29. *Id.*

for each state to determine under its own law who are its nationals"[30] and adds that "[a]ny question as to whether a person possesses the nationality of a particular state shall be determined by the laws of that state."[31] The one constraint established upon the discretion of states in conferring nationality is that such conferment is required to be recognized by other states only insofar as it is in accord with the traditional criteria of international law.[32]

By these commonly accepted criteria of international law, the Commission might have been expected to honor the United States' authoritative determination that Flegenheimer was its national. The Commission adverted to no facts and to no policies which could give it authority to override the determination by the United States. There was no other state asserting a competing claim to Albert Flegenheimer as its national or offering to protect him. There was no suggestion, nor could one have been made, that any rule of international law would preclude the United States from recognizing Flegenheimer as its national. Even as against Wurttemberg the United States was an authoritative interpreter of any implied commitment it was alleged to have made about relinquishment of nationality. There was no suggestion that thc United States' espousal of Flegenheimer's claim was in any way fraudulent or spurious. On the contrary, the United States obviously accepted Albert Flegenheimer in the fullest degree, and imposed obligation on him in the fullest degree, as citizen and national. Indeed, it did not appear that Flegenheimer's nationality could elsewhere be denied in any forum for any purpose.

It has thus been observed that it is "an unwarranted excess of power"[33] for the Commission to pry into the authoritative decisions of a claimant state so as to appraise the facts upon which the state has based its decision, and further to substitute its own evaluation for, and in negation of, the authoritative determination of the competent state officials. The net effect, as in *Nottebohm,* is denial of protection—of the minimum right to a hearing upon the merits—to the individual concerned.

The strangling technicalities of the "nationality" myth as applied to transnational business enterprises may also be employed to deprive individuals and groups of individuals of a protector which can secure appropriate hearings upon the merits of controversies. As the role of transnational enterprises becomes increasingly important, severe strains are placed upon the traditional doctrine affirming the nationality of

30. The Convention on Certain Questions Relating to the Conflict of Nationality Laws of 1930, Art. 1, 179 L.N.T.S. 89, 99.
31. *Id.,* Art. 2.
32. *Id.,* Art 1.
33. Goldschmidt, *supra* note 26, at 714.

claims. Based more or less on the doctrine of nationality applicable to individuals, the traditional doctrine attributes the competence to protect a corporate entity to the state under the laws of which it is incorporated and in whose territory it has its registered office.[34] As with respect to individual human beings, however, the concept of the nationality of business entities is susceptible to manipulation in arbitrary ways. The *Barcelona Traction* case[35] is a dramatic recent illustration.

The Barcelona Traction, Light, and Power Company was incorporated in Toronto, Canada, in 1911, as a holding company for various wholly or substantially owned Spanish and Canadian subsidiaries, to develop and operate an electric power system in Spain. In 1948, a Spanish court declared it bankrupt and its assets were seized. As part of the company's unsuccessful efforts to resist the bankruptcy proceedings, the Belgian, British, Canadian, and United States governments made representations to Spain on behalf of the company. For reasons not of record, the Canadian government ceased its diplomatic efforts on behalf of Barcelona Traction after 1955. Since Belgian nationals owned a large majority of the stock in the company, the Belgian government, after an earlier application to the court in 1958 and its subsequent withdrawal in 1961,[36] brought this case before the International Court of Justice in 1962. The Spanish government raised four preliminary objections, two of which were rejected by the court in 1964; the other two were joined by the court on the merits. The court's final judgment, rendered in February 1970, upheld Spain's third preliminary objection, declaring that Belgium lacked standing (*jus standi*) to espouse a claim for its nationals, shareholders in a Canadian company, for damages allegedly resulting from illegal acts of various organs of the Spanish government against the company. Belgium's application was thus dismissed, and the merits of the case were not considered by the court.

The central issue was the competence of Belgium to extend protection to Belgian shareholders in a company which was a juridical entity incorporated in Canada. The actual and ultimate deprivations caused by the

---

34. Case concerning the Barcelona Traction, Light and Power Company, Limited, Second Phase, [1970] I.C.J. 4, 42.

35. *Id.* For comments on this decision, *see* Briggs, *Barcelona Traction: The Jus Standi of Belgium,* 65 AM. J. INT'L L. 327 (1971); Higgins, *Aspects of the Case concerning the Barcelona Traction, Light and Power Company, Ltd.,* 11 VA. J. INT'L L. 327 (1971); Lillich, *The Rigidity of Barcelona,* 65 AM. J. INT'L L. 522 (1971); Metzger, *Nationality of Corporate Investment under Investment Guaranty Schemes—The Relevance of Barcelona Traction,* 65 AM. J. INT'L L. 532 (1971); *Note, Protection of Shareholder Interests in Foreign Corporations—Barcelona Traction Revisited,* 41 FORDHAM L. REV. 394 (1972); 5 J. INT'L L. & ECON. DEVELOPMENT 239 (1971); *Note, Economic Internationalism vs. National Parochialism: Barcelona Traction,* 3 L. & POLICY IN INT'L BUS. 542 (1971); 3 N.Y.U.J. INT'L L. & POL. 391 (1970).

36. [1961] I.C.J. 9.

illegal treatment of the "company" were, of course, sustained by the shareholders. The court, however, building upon the traditional myth of state responsibility (state rights independent of the injured individual), phrased the issue this way: "Has a right of Belgium been violated on account of its nationals' [*sic*] having suffered infringement of their rights as shareholders in a company not of Belgian nationality?"[37] While the court conceded that individual shareholders do ultimately suffer for damage done to the company, it emphasized that the company, as a corporate entity, retains its own separate legal personality, independent of its shareholders. Though the company is "in a precarious financial situation," that condition does not constitute "the demise of the corporate entity."[38] Unless and until there is "the legal demise of the company," according to the court, there is no "independent right of action" for the shareholders and thus for their governments to espouse their claims.[39]

The court further observed that the company, endowed with the "nationality" of Canada because of its incorporation in Canada, would look only to Canada for protection. Although Canada ceased to espouse the company's claim after 1955, "[t]he Canadian Government has nonetheless retained its capacity to exercise diplomatic protection" for Barcelona Traction.[40] The Canadian government had absolute discretion to decide whether or not to exercise its right of protection:

> The state must be viewed as the sole judge to decide whether its protection will be granted, to what extent it is granted, and when it will cease. It retains in this respect a discretionary power the exercise of which may be determined by considerations of a political or other nature, unrelated to the particular case. Since the claim of the state is not identical with that of the individual or corporate person whose cause is espoused, the state enjoys complete freedom of action.[41]

The court finally cautioned that a Pandora's box would be opened if shareholders' governments were allowed to espouse their claims:

> The Court considers that the adoption of the theory of diplomatic protection of shareholders as such, by opening the door to competing diplomatic claims, could create an atmosphere of confusion and insecurity in international economic relations. The danger would be all the greater inasmuch as the shares of companies whose activity is

---

37. [1970] I.C.J. 4, 34.
38. *Id.* at 41.
39. *Id.*
40. *Id.* at 44.
41. *Id.* at 45.

> international are widely scattered and frequently change hands. . . . As the right of protection vested in the national State of the company cannot be regarded as extinguished because it is not exercised, it is not possible to accept the proposition that in case of its non-exercise the national States of the shareholders have a right of protection secondary to that of the national State of the company.[42]

In contemporary law it is thus apparent that the individual human being is almost completely dependent upon a state of nationality for securing a hearing upon the merits upon injuries done to him by other states.

Claims Relating to the Conferment of Nationality

International law accords states a high degree of discretion in the conferment of nationality. It is far from clear what limitations are imposed on the competence of states. The Hague Convention on Nationality of 1930[43] provides, somewhat ambivalently, both a grant of competence and a limitation. The grant of competence in Articles 1 and 2 stipulates that "[i]t is for each State to determine under its own law who are its nationals" and that "[a]ny question as to whether a person possesses the nationality of a particular State shall be determined in accordance with the laws of that State." The stated limitation is that the nationality law of each state "shall be recognised by other States in so far as it is consistent with international conventions, international custom, and the principles of law generally recognised with regard to nationality."[44] Unfortunately, the Convention nowhere specifies the conferment criteria that are recognized or required by international law.

Any criteria that limit states' competence to confer nationality must be inferred from customary practice. Thus, states have commonly utilized either or both of two major principles: *jus sanguinis* and *jus soli.*[45] The

42. *Id.* at 49.

43. The Convention on Certain Questions Relating to the Conflict of Nationality Laws, *signed* at the Hague, Apr. 12, 1930, 179 L.N.T.S. 89. *See* 5 M. Hudson, International Legislation 359 (1936).

44. The Convention on Certain Questions Relating to the Conflict of Nationality Laws, *supra* note 43, Art. 1.

45. *See* Sandifer, *A Comparative Study of Laws Relating to Nationality at Birth and to Loss of Nationality,* 29 Am. J. Int'l L. 248, 249–61 (1935); *cf.* Winter, *Nationality or Domicile? The Present State of Affairs,* 128 Hague Recueil des Cours 347 (1969).

"Countries of emigration," observed the *Harvard Research,* "are inclined to emphasize the *jus sanguinis* for the purpose of retaining the allegiance of descendants of their nationals who have settled in various parts of the world, while countries of immigration, including some countries of Asia and Africa, as well as those in the western hemisphere, are inclined to emphasize the *jus soli,* in order to have the allegiance of persons born within their territories of alien parents." *Harvard Research, supra* note 1, at 39.

older of the two principles, *jus sanguinis*—conferment of nationality by blood relation (descent)—is at least as old as Roman law and is preferred by the civil law countries. The principle of *jus soli*—conferment of nationality based on place of birth—is an outgrowth of the feudal system favored by the common law countries. The overwhelming trend is toward a mixed system that employs both principles in varying combinations.[46] The uniformity in exclusive reliance upon these two principles has been such as to suggest to some commentators the emergence of a customary rule that no other grounds are permissible.[47]

The important point from the perspective of human rights is that these two principles for conferment of nationality at birth disregard human volition. The individual selects neither his parents nor his place of birth. The great bulk of mankind have their nationality thrust upon them, with little effective prospect of change.[48]

With reference to grounds subsequent to birth, states have sought to confer nationality upon a finding of express consent or a variety of factors, in which consent may or may not be included.[49] Among these latter factors are marriage, recognition by affiliation, legitimation, adoption, residence (domicile), immigration *animo manendi,*[50] land ownership, paternity, appointment as a university professor,[51] and holding a public post.

Conferment upon the basis of consent is, of course, in conformity with our recommended policy of human dignity. The "general principle" underlying naturalization in its most comprehensive sense is "the voluntary choice by an individual of a particular nationality."[52]

To impose naturalization upon individual persons against their will, individually or collectively, on the other hand, is incompatible with the commonly accepted principles of international law. Thus, compulsory

---

46. "From an examination of the nationality laws of the various states," according to the often-quoted *Harvard Research,* "it appears that seventeen are based solely on *jus sanguinis,* two equally upon *jus soli* and *jus sanguinis,* twenty-five principally upon *jus sanguinis* but partly upon *jus soli* and twenty-six principally upon *jus soli* and partly upon *jus sanguinis.* The nationality law of no country is based solely upon *jus soli.* A combination of the two systems is found in the laws of most countries." *Harvard Research, supra* note 1, at 29.

47. *See, e.g.,* Article 3 of the Harvard Draft Convention on the Law of Nationality: "A state may not confer its nationality at birth upon a person except upon the basis of (a) the birth of such person within its territory or a place assimilated thereto (*jus soli*), or (b) the descent of such person from one of its nationals (*jus sanguinis*)." *Id.* at 13, 27; Hudson, *supra* note 1, at 7.

48. *See* notes 81–98 *infra* and accompanying text.

49. *See Harvard Research, supra* note 1, at 83–98; Hudson, *supra* note 1, at 8.

50. *See* Brownlie, *supra* note 1, at 308.

51. *See* Hudson, *supra* note 1, at 8.

52. J. Jones, British Nationality Law and Practice 15 (1947).

conferment upon such bases as land ownership or residence is impermissible.[53] For instance, in the nineteenth century, when certain Latin-American states (*e.g.*, Peru and Mexico) imposed nationality upon aliens who had acquired real property in the country, that practice was protested by other states and was held incompatible with international law by international tribunals. In the *Anderson and Thompson* case,[54] Mexico had objected to the jurisdiction of the United States-Mexico Mixed Claims Commission in connection with a claim of the United States on behalf of two of its nationals. Mexico argued that both Anderson and Thompson had become, under the Mexican Constitution of 1857, Mexican nationals by purchasing land in Mexico in 1863. Dismissing the Mexican demurrer, Umpire Lieber declared that, although the Mexican Constitution "clearly means to confer a benefit upon the foreign purchaser of land, . . . equity would assuredly forbid us to force this benefit upon claimants . . . merely on account of omitting a declaration of a negative."[55] Because the Mexican Nationality Law of 1886 contained the same feature, a similar issue arose subsequently in the *Rau* case before the German-Mexican Claims Commission in 1930.[56] Again, Mexico objected to the Commission's jurisdiction over the German claim on behalf of its alleged national who had acquired land in Mexico. Dismissing the Mexican objection, the Commission emphatically stated that "international law . . . does not permit compulsory change of nationality."[57] Mexico subsequently withdrew its counterclaim and the objectionable provisions were abandoned in later Mexican Nationality Laws.[58]

Imposition of nationality on the mere ground of residence is similarly impermissible. For instance, in 1889, the Provisional Government of Brazil issued a decree that all aliens residing in Brazil on November 15, 1889, would automatically be regarded as Brazilian nationals unless they should declare, within six months, a contrary intention before appropriate Brazilian officials.[59] This proclamation provoked severe condemnation and protests of nonrecognition by other states, notably Italy, Great Britain, France, Spain, Portugal, Austria-Hungary, and the United States.[60]

---

53. *See* P. Weis, *supra* note 1, at 104–16; Hudson, *supra* note 1, at 8.
54. 3 J. Moore, International Arbitrations 2479 (1898).
55. *Id.* at 2479–81.
56. *In re* Rau, [1931–32] Ann. Dig. 251 (No. 124) (German-Mexican Claims Commission 1930).
57. *Id.*
58. *See, e.g.,* The Mexican Constitution of 1917, as amended by Decree of 18 January 1934, Art. 30, Laws Concerning Nationality, *supra* note 1, at 307.
59. *See* P. Weis, *supra* note 1, at 105–06.
60. *See id.* at 106–08.

A more recent example relates to Argentina. A bill purporting to confer automatic Argentine nationality on aliens after two years' residence led to such an outburst of protests by other governments that it was finally withdrawn.[61]

Perhaps the most notorious example is the mass imposition of German nationality on nationals of territories occupied by Germany during World War II. In 1943 Hitler also purported to confer German nationality on all foreign nationals of "German origin" then serving in the German armed forces. In 1951, this matter was raised in the *Compulsory Grant of German Nationality* case[62] before a court of the German Federal Republic. The applicant, in German custody, was sought by Austria for extradition; he was a person of "German origin" serving in the German army at the time of Hitler's decree. He thus claimed nonextradition on the basis of his being a German national. The Court of Appeal of Neustadt declared Hitler's decree invalid on the ground that only the Reichstag, not the Chancellor, was empowered to prescribe naturalization matters at that point in time. The applicant was not a German national and was thus extradited to Austria. Subsequently, in 1955, the German Federal Republic undertook to enable all persons purporting to have been made German nationals under the compulsory Nazi measures to "disclaim German nationality by an explicit declaration to that effect."[63]

In the case of conferment upon such grounds as marriage, legitimation, adoption, and recognition by affiliation, inquiry may be made to ascertain the degree of volition actually present. Since, however, the activities described by these grounds are widely known to carry the consequence of nationality and often entail basic community policies about collateral problems which make nationality a desirable consequence, it is

---

61. *See* Hudson, *supra* note 1, at 8. Note, however, Art. 31 of the Constitution of the Argentine Republic:

> Foreigners who enter the country without violating the laws shall enjoy all the civil rights of Argentinians, as well as political rights, five years after having obtained Argentinian nationality. Upon their petition they may be naturalized if they have resided two consecutive years in the territory of the Nation, and they shall acquire Argentinian nationality automatically at the end of five years of continuous residence in the absence of express declaration to the contrary.

1 A. Peaslee, Constitutions of Nations 51 (2d ed. 1956).

Dean John H. Wigmore proposed that nationality be based on domicile and that two years' residence in a state automatically results in acquisition of the nationality of that state. *See* Wigmore, *Domicile, Double Allegiance, and World Citizenship,* 21 Ill. L. Rev. 761 (1927).

62. Compulsory Grant of German Nationality Case, [1951] I.L.R. 247 (Court of Appeal of Neustadt, German Federal Republic 1951).

63. Settlement of Nationality Questions Act of 1955, Art. 1, Supplement to Laws Concerning Nationality, *supra* note 1, at 116.

a common practice of decision makers to infer or assume a voluntary act on the part of the individual or those representing him. Thus, an act which has "a direct relation to nationality" may be considered to show "unquestionably the desire and intention of a person to take the nationality of a state."[64]

The classic summary is that of Hall:

> Consent no doubt may be a matter of inference: and if the individual does acts of a political, or even, possibly, of a municipal nature, without inquiry whether the law regards the performance of such acts as an expression of desire on his part to identify himself with the state, he has no ground for complaint if his consent is inferred, and if he finds himself burdened upon the state territory with obligations correlative to the privileges which he has assumed. But apart from acts which can reasonably be supposed to indicate intention, his national character may with propriety be considered to remain unaltered. It is unquestionably not within the competence of a state to impose its nationality in virtue of mere residence, of marriage with a native, of the acquisition of landed property, and other such acts, which lie wholly within the range of the personal life, or which may be necessities of commercial or industrial business.[65]

However, the element of voluntarism or consent may, as in the case of married women and minors, often be minimal or a mere fiction.

With regard to the effect of marriage on nationality, national laws differ widely.[66] Basically speaking, there are two opposing principles governing the law on the nationality of married women. The traditional principle is the unity of the family, according to which the nationality of all members of the family—mother, father, and children under age—should be the same, in order to avoid split loyalty within the family. The second principle honors the freedom of a married woman to choose her own nationality. Under the interplay of these two basic principles, municipal laws about the nationality of married women can be divided into three categories: (1) the nationality of the wife follows automatically that of the husband; (2) though marriage to a man of a different nationality affects the nationality of the wife, provisions are made to avoid the wife's statelessness or double nationality; and (3) the woman has the right to choose her own nationality and marriage will not affect the

---

64. *Harvard Research, supra* note 1, at 54.

65. W. Hall, International Law 267–68 (8th ed. 1924).

66. *See* United Nations, Nationality of Married Women (1963); United Nations, Convention on the Nationality of Married Women (1962): W. Waltz, The Nationality of Married Women (1937).

nationality of the wife. According to a recent United Nations study, an alien woman automatically acquires the nationality of her husband upon marriage under the law of twenty-eight states; under the law of sixty-eight states, the alien wife may on certain conditions acquire the nationality of the husband; and under the law of twelve states, marriage of an alien woman to a national has no effect whatever on her nationality.[67]

The United States Supreme Court once suggested that the marriage of a woman to an alien caused her to lose her nationality because it amounted to "voluntary expatriation": the woman freely contracted the marriage with notice of the consequences.[68] Because marriage is generally stipulated to affect only the wife's—not husband's—nationality, such rationalization is difficult to reconcile with the principle of the equality of the sexes.

Indeed, from the perspective of individual human rights, marriage should have no automatic effect on the nationality of either the wife or the husband. An alien woman, in marrying a national, does not necessarily signify her intention to identify with the state of which her husband is a national or to sever her ties with the state of her nationality. With the growing emphasis on the equality of the sexes, particularly in the wake of the current movement for the liberation of women, the trend is away from the principle that a married woman's nationality is automatically that of her husband.[69] Article 1 of the Convention on the Nationality of Married Women emphatically affirms this trend: "Each Contracting State agrees that neither the celebration nor the dissolution of marriage between one of its nationals and an alien, nor the change of nationality by the husband during marriage, shall automatically affect the nationality of the wife."[70]

With respect to minor children, the maintenance of family unity would seem to compel the rule that the child follows the father's nationality in the case of legitimation and adoption and that minor children are naturalized through the naturalization of their parents.[71] However, because the element of volition is absent on the part of minors, it has

---

67. NATIONALITY OF MARRIED WOMEN, *supra* note 66, at 122–25 (Annex).

68. Mackenzie v. Hare, 239 U.S. 299 (1915).

69. *See* NATIONALITY OF MARRIED WOMEN, *supra* note 66 at 7.

70. The Convention was opened for signature and ratification by General Assembly Res. 1040 (XI) of Jan. 29, 1957; it became effective on Aug. 11, 1958. UNITED NATIONS, HUMAN RIGHTS: A COMPILATION OF INTERNATIONAL INSTRUMENTS OF THE UNITED NATIONS 52 (1967) [hereinafter cited as U.N. HUMAN RIGHTS INSTRUMENTS]. For the history of and commentary on this Convention, *see* CONVENTION ON THE NATIONALITY OF MARRIED WOMEN, *supra* note 66. For its text *see* 309 U.N.T.S. 65.

71. *See* P. WEIS, *supra* note 1, at 114. There could be cases where the child's nationality ought to follow the mother's—as in cases of divorce, where the child lives with its mother in the country of her nationality.

increasingly been urged that minors be given the option to resume their original nationality when they attain adulthood.[72]

Compulsory naturalization has often been associated with territorial change.[73] For instance, when one state cedes a territory to another, the ceding state is considered competent to transfer the allegiance of the inhabitants and the transfer is deemed an automatic consequence of the cession. The acquiring state has been traditionally required, at the same time, to confer its nationality, though not the political rights of citizens, upon those persons.[74] Upon occasion, however, these harsh doctrines are modified in deference to human rights and self-determination. Sometimes a plebiscite is employed to determine whether a transfer of territory is in accord with the wishes of the majority of the inhabitants concerned.[75] More frequently, state practice—as embodied in many treaties of cession or of peace—seeks to allow individual inhabitants of the ceded territory an option on nationality, including the retention of the original nationality.[76] Thus, the Inter-American Convention on Nationality concluded at Montevideo in 1933 contains the following provision in Article 4:

> In case of the transfer of a portion of the territory on the part of one of the States signatory hereof to another of such States, the inhabi-

---

72. *See, e.g.,* the nationality laws of Australia, Belgium, Bulgaria, Canada, Ceylon, Ecuador, Great Britain, Ghana, Greece, India, Luxembourg, Malaya, Monaco, Netherlands, New Zealand, Pakistan, Syria, Sudan, Thailand, Venezuela, and Union of South Africa, in LAWS CONCERNING NATIONALITY, *supra* note 1.

73. *See* P. WEIS, *supra* note 1, at 139–64; Hudson, *supra* note 1, at 8–10; Mann, *The Effects of Changes of Sovereignty upon Nationality,* 5 MODERN L. REV. 218 (1942).

74. *See* P. JESSUP, A MODERN LAW OF NATIONS 76 (1952); *cf.* H. BRIGGS, *supra* note 10, at 501–05.

75. On plebiscites, *see generally* H. JOHNSON, SELF-DETERMINATION WITHIN THE COMMUNITY OF NATIONS (1967); J. MATTERN, THE EMPLOYMENT OF THE PLEBISCITE IN THE DETERMINATION OF SOVEREIGNTY (1920); 1 & 2 S. WAMBAUGH, PLEBISCITES SINCE THE WORLD WAR (1933); S. WAMBAUGH, A MONOGRAPH OF PLEBISCITES (1920); Chen & Reisman, *Who Owns Taiwan: A Search for International Title,* 81 YALE L.J. 599, 660–69 (1972).

76. *See* 1 L. OPPENHEIM, INTERNATIONAL LAW 551 (8th ed. H. Lauterpacht 1955) [hereinafter cited as Oppenheim-Lauterpacht]; Gettys, *The Effect of Changes of Sovereignty on Nationality,* 21 AM. J. INT'L L. 268, 271 (1927); Hudson, *supra* note 1, at 9–10; Kunz, *Nationality and the Option Clauses in the Italian Peace Treaty,* 41 AM. J. INT'L L. 622 (1947).

Lord McNair observed:

> The hardship of an involuntary change of nationality has led with increasing frequency in recent years to the adoption of one of the following forms of mitigation:
>
> (a) Plebiscite. The treaty may stipulate for the cession of particular pieces of territory to depend upon the result of a plebiscite by the nationals of the ceding State inhabiting the territory; such a provision occurs in several articles of the Peace Treaties of 1919–1920, but it was not generalized;

> tants of such transferred territory must not consider themselves as nationals of the State to which they are transferred, unless they expressly opt to change their original nationality.[77]

One harsh qualification is that "failing a stipulation expressly forbidding it, the acquiring State may expel those inhabitants who have made use of the option and retained their old citizenship, since otherwise the whole population of the ceded territory might actually consist of aliens and endanger the safety of the acquiring State."[78] It would appear vital from a human rights perspective, nevertheless, that those individual inhabitants who have chosen not to acquire the new nationality be free to reside on the ceded territory.

One important concession in favor of human rights is that states are not regarded as competent to impose nationality upon individuals who are not physically present within a territory at the time of its transfer.[79] It is said that the nationality of the successor state can be conferred upon nationals of the predecessor state only if they submit voluntarily to its jurisdiction, by virtue of an explicit declaration or voluntary return to their land of origin. This position was spotlighted in *United States ex rel. Schwarzkopf* v. *Uhl, District Director of Immigration,*[80] where the court held that an Austrian national who had been resident in the United States when Germany annexed Austria had not acquired German nationality.

With respect to the converse dimension of the naturalization problem, we must note that some of the most significant deprivations of human rights are a consequence of the denial of naturalization to people who actively seek it. Doctrine holds that naturalization is a privilege within the discretion of the state, not a right of the applicant. As the United States Supreme Court put it, "Naturalization is a privilege, to be given, qual-

---

> (b) Option of nationality. The treaty may give the nationals of the ceding State inhabiting the territory ceded an option to retain the nationality of the ceding State; if they exercise that option, the acquiring State may, in default of contrary stipulation, expel them as any aliens may be expelled;
>
> (c) Option to emigrate. The treaty may give the inhabitants an option to emigrate within a certain time and also retain their nationality.
>
> The growth of the principle of self-determination tends to favour the adoption of one or more of these palliatives. It must, however, be emphasized that the law does not enjoin them and they do not apply unless the high contracting parties choose to adopt them.

A. McNair, Legal Effects of War 388–90 (3d ed. 1948).

77. 6 M. Hudson, International Legislation 593 (1937); Laws Concerning Nationality, *supra* note 1, at 585.

78. 1 Oppenheim-Lauterpacht, *supra* note 76, at 552.

79. *See* Hudson, *supra* note 1, at 9.

80. 137 F.2d 898 (2d Cir. 1943).

ified, or withheld as Congress may determine, and which the alien may claim as of right only upon compliance with the terms which Congress imposes."[81] States differ widely in the scope and severity of limitations imposed on voluntary naturalization. These limitations may include residence, age, moral character, race, political character, health, skill, and wealth of the applicant.[82] These preconditions for naturalization, including as well administrative hurdles, are so onerous, unfortunately, that people who seek naturalization are often denied it.

For example, residence, regarded as the most significant indicator of a person's factual attachment to a territorial community, is a common precondition for naturalization. The overriding importance of the residence requirement as an inhibition upon naturalization derives from the fact that access to territory, with appropriate immigrant status, is a precondition to fulfilling the residence requirement; such access is itself subject to many difficult and arbitrary conditions.[83] States differ, moreover, in the requirements they impose with respect to length of residence and the necessity of physical presence. The length of residence required ranges from two to ten years. While there has been a trend toward greater uniformity (typically three or five years), some states still demand a longer period of residence.[84]

Some states require that an applicant for naturalization be of good character at the time his petition is filed.[85] The United States, however, insists further that the applicant demonstrate "good moral character" throughout the required "probationary period" of residence.[86] The requirement of good moral character, elusive and susceptible of arbitrary application, has proved to be the principal source of litigation concerning naturalization in the United States.[87] Though good moral character

81. United States v. Macintosh, 283 U.S. 605, 615 (1931). *See also* Fong Yue Ting v. United States, 149 U.S. 698, 707–08 (1893).

82. *Cf. Harvard Research, supra* note 1, at 83–100.

83. We will explore this problem in connection with the claims to freedom of movement, including claims of access to territory.

84. *Harvard Research, supra* note 1, at 89–91.

85. *See, e.g.*, Norway, Nationality Act No. 3 of 8 December 1950, Art. 6(3), LAWS CONCERNING NATIONALITY, *supra* note 1, at 352, 353; Japan, Nationality Law of 4 May 1950, Art. 4(3), *id.* at 271, 272; British Nationality Act of 30 July 1948, Second Schedule, § 1(c), *id.* at 468, 482.

86. 8 U.S.C. § 1427(a)(3) (1970) provides:

> No person, except as otherwise provided in this subchapter, shall be naturalized unless such petitioner . . . (3) during all the period referred to in this subsection [usually five years] has been and still is a person of good moral character, attached to the principles of the Constitution of the United States, and well disposed to the good order and happiness of the United States.

87. *See Developments in the Law—Immigration and Nationality,* 66 HARV. L. REV. 643, 710 (1953).

was made a requirement for naturalization as early as 1790,[88] the term was undefined by statute until 1952. In 1952, Congress sought to mitigate the confusing and controversial state of the law by enumerating specific grounds, such as drunkenness, adultery, polygamy, prostitution, and gambling, that would preclude a finding of good moral character.[89] Nevertheless, the good moral character test has remained a source of uncertainty for persons seeking naturalization, and the Immigration and Naturalization Service and the courts continue to enjoy wide discretion in applying it. Even if an applicant for naturalization has committed none of the proscribed acts, a court is not barred from "finding that for other reasons such person is or was not of good moral character."[90] The arbitrary and inconsistent application of this requirement is amply illustrated by the controversies concerning the sexual behavior of unmarried aliens and the suitability of homosexuals for citizenship.[91] A commentator has thus critically observed that "intelligibility is one of the finest attributes of law, if not its essence; and that on these grounds alone a statutory requirement [good moral character] destined to be empty of legal meaning for its entire legal existence should not properly be part of law."[92] The net effect, as before 1952, is significant deprivations of human rights. The requirement of good moral character has become the foremost obstacle to naturalization.

Equally susceptible of abuse are requirements relating to political activities. It has been a common practice of states to require aliens seeking naturalization to take an oath of allegiance. Some states have gone further to stipulate that the commission of certain political acts by an applicant would operate to bar his naturalization. While some states couch this requirement generally in terms of conduct detrimental to the interests of the state,[93] some have undertaken specific formulations. The United States, in particular, is most explicit in this regard. Thus, in addition to requiring adherence to the principles of the Constitution and a favorable disposition to the United States,[94] the Immigration and Nationality Act of 1952 specifically prohibits the naturalization of persons

---

88. *See Note, Good Moral Character in Naturalization Proceedings,* 48 COLUM. L. REV. 622 (1948).

89. 8 U.S.C. § 1101(f) (1970).

90. *Id.*

91. *See* Newton, *On Coherence in the Law: A Study of the "Good Moral Character" Requirement in the Naturalization Statute,* 46 TEMPLE L.Q. 40, 43–59 (1972); *Note, Naturalization and the Adjudication of Good Moral Character: An Exercise in Judicial Uncertainty,* 47 N.Y.U.L. REV. 545, 560–82 (1972).

92. Newton, *supra* note 91, at 70.

93. *See, e.g.,* Albania, Nationality Act No. 377 of 1946, Art. 7(5), LAWS CONCERNING NATIONALITY, *supra* note 1, at 4, 5; France, Nationality Code of 1945, Art. 70, *id.* at 152, 161; Hungary, Nationality Act LX of 1948, Art. 4(b), *id.* at 219, 220.

94. 8 U.S.C. § 1427 (1970).

opposed to government or law, persons who favor totalitarian forms of government,[95] and persons who have deserted from the United States Armed Forces.[96]

In sum, it is apparent that conferment of nationality at birth is not a volitional act of the individual concerned. Though states give consent greater emphasis in connection with conferment of nationality after birth, involuntary naturalization is far from a rare occurrence, and efforts toward voluntary acquisition of nationality often fail. Given the differential distribution of resources and opportunities for value shaping and sharing about the globe, the instability and fragility of the inherited organizations of territorial communities, and the ever-increasing mobility of people and frequency of transnational interactions, every individual person should be free to effect a voluntary change in his nationality and thus to identify with the political community of his own choice. The fact that a person possesses a particular nationality at birth, or after birth, should not condemn him in perpetuity to membership in a body politic which may be perceived by him to be more oppressive than protective. As a matter of human rights, every person should be free to change his nationality. Thus, the Universal Declaration of Human Rights proclaims that "[n]o one shall be arbitrarily . . . denied the right to change his nationality."[97] Similarly, the American Convention on Human Rights provides that "[n]o one shall be arbitrarily deprived . . . of the right to change [nationality]."[98] Unfortunately, however, the International Covenant on Civil and Political Rights and the European Convention on Human Rights lack comparable provisions.

Claims Relating to Withdrawal of Nationality

The nationality of an individual may be withdrawn or lost upon the initiative of the individual or of the state conferring nationality and with or without the individual's consent. When an individual takes the initiative to terminate a nationality, he is said to engage in voluntary expatriation.[99] When a state conditions its withdrawal of nationality upon the

---

95. *Id.* § 1424.

96. *Id.* § 1425.

97. Art. 15(2), U.N. Human Rights Instruments, *supra* note 70, at 2.

98. Art. 20(3), Basic Documents on International Protection of Human Rights 217 (L. Sohn & T. Buergenthal eds. 1973) [hereinafter cited as Basic Documents].

99. As Maxey has pointed out:

> [T]he word "expatriation" tends to be used indiscriminately, in both judicial discussion and popular speech, as comprehending all losses of national status, however brought about. Failure to observe sharply demarcated terminological boundaries has frequently been a source of confusion in this area of inquiry; this is especially true in the United States, where the concept of voluntary expatriation, through constant distor-

genuine consent of the individual, no problem concerning human rights arises. The difficulty is that the line between genuine consent and involuntary withdrawal is often difficult to perceive. For purposes of economy, we follow the traditional categorizations of (1) voluntary expatriation, (2) withdrawal upon consent (genuine or constructive), and (3) involuntary withdrawal, noting the difficulties as we progress.

VOLUNTARY EXPATRIATION

It has already been observed that the right to change a nationality is increasingly regarded as a fundamental human right.[100] It is only by guaranteeing this right that the world community affords individuals opportunity to escape the bondage of the effective elites of any particular community. The right to renounce nationality—"voluntary expatriation"—is of course an indispensable component of the right to change it. Similarly, just as open access to territory is a precondition to any realistic right to acquire nationality, so here a right of egress is a necessary condition to any effective right of voluntary expatriation.[101] Unless an individual can escape the bounds of a country, he may find it impossible to free himself from the shackles of its nationality. There would appear to be a slow trend toward protecting a right of voluntary expatriation.

The demand for a right of voluntary expatriation has, despite the long insistence by states upon indissoluble allegiance, a very ancient history. Its roots are deep in Greek and Roman thought. Thus, a United States Senator, citing Plato as authority, stated that "[a]t Athens it was permitted to each person upon examining the laws and customs of the republic, if there was nothing found to his charge, to retire with all of his goods, wherever else it pleased him."[102] Similarly, Hersch Lauterpacht, in making a strong case for the right of expatriation, builds upon the thought of Socrates and Cicero.[103] In the words of Socrates, "if any one does not like

---

tion, bears little, or no resemblance to the original notion, as expressed in the statutory declaration of 1868.

Maxey, *Loss of Nationality: Individual Choice or Government Fiat?* 26 ALBANY L. REV. 151, 151–52 (1962). *See also* 5 J. VERZIJL, INTERNATIONAL LAW IN HISTORICAL PERSPECTIVE 42–44 (1972). For our purposes, "expatriation" refers strictly to "voluntary expatriation" (in which a person takes initiative to terminate a nationality) and is to be distinguished from loss of nationality resulting from imputed consent and from involuntary withdrawal of nationality.

100. *See* notes 97–98 *supra* and accompanying text.

101. *See* H. LAUTERPACHT, AN INTERNATIONAL BILL OF THE RIGHTS OF MAN 129–33 (1945); H. LAUTERPACHT, INTERNATIONAL LAW AND HUMAN RIGHTS 346–50 (1950).

102. CONG. GLOBE, 40th Cong., 2d Sess. 4232 (1868) (remarks of Senator Patterson).

103. H. LAUTERPACHT, AN INTERNATIONAL BILL OF THE RIGHTS OF MAN 130–31 (1945).

the city and its constitution, there is no law to hinder or prevent him from going away whenever he likes, either to the colonies or to some foreign country and taking his property with him."[104] Notwithstanding his deference to state sovereignty, Vattel was eloquent in defense of the right of expatriation. He stated that

> every man is born free, and therefore the son of a citizen, when arrived at the age of reason, may consider whether it is well for him to join the society in which he happens to be by birth. If he does not find that it is to his advantage to remain in it, he has the right to leave it. . . . A citizen may therefore leave the State of which he is a member, provided it be not at a critical moment when his withdrawal might be greatly prejudicial to the State.[105]

The right of the individual to expatriation was incorporated in the French Constitution of September 3, 1791.[106] It is, however, the United States that has been the foremost champion of the right of voluntary expatriation. In 1868, with a view to freeing recently naturalized Americans from the allegiance demanded by the states from which they had emigrated, the United States Congress proclaimed that

> the right of expatriation is a natural and inherent right of all people, indispensable to the enjoyment of the rights of life, liberty, and the pursuit of happiness; . . .
>
> [a]ny declaration, instruction, opinion, order, or decision of any officers of this government which denies, restricts, impairs, or questions the right of expatriation, is hereby declared inconsistent with the fundamental principles of this government.[107]

The purpose of the Act of 1868, in the words of Hyde, was

> to make clear the doctrine, first, that the freedom of an alien to change his nationality through naturalization, in so far as he had any part in the matter, was not dependent upon the consent of his sovereign beyond whose control he had placed himself; secondly, that naturalization with the United States served to dissolve the tie of allegiance with respect to that sovereign; and thirdly, that by such process the individual acquired a new national character entitled to recognition upon his return to the country of origin.[108]

---

104. *Quoted in id.* at 131.

105. 3 E. DE VATTEL, *supra* note 7, at 89.

106. *See* C. DE VISSCHER, THEORY AND REALITY IN PUBLIC INTERNATIONAL LAW 185 (rev. ed. P. Corbett trans. 1968).

107. Act of July 27, 1868, ch. 249, 15 Stat. 223 (1868). The Fourteenth Amendment was passed in the same year.

108. 2 C. HYDE, INTERNATIONAL LAW: CHIEFLY AS INTERPRETED AND APPLIED BY THE UNITED STATES 1147–48 (2d rev. ed. 1945) (footnote omitted). The policy embodied in the 1868 Act found further expression in a series of treaties, known as Bancroft Treaties, the

Similarly, departing from the doctrine of "indissoluble allegiance," Great Britain acknowledged a limited right of voluntary expatriation in its Naturalisation Act of 1870, declaring: "Any British subject who has at any time . . . when in a foreign state and not under any disability voluntarily become naturalized in such state, shall . . . be deemed to have ceased to be a British subject."[109]

At the 1930 Hague Conference for the Codification of International Law, the United States Delegation made a strong plea for the incorporation of the principle of voluntary expatriation in these words:

> For a century past, it has been the policy of my country that the right of expatriation is an inherent and natural right of all persons. It is true that allegiance is a duty, but it is not a chain that holds a person in bondage and that he carries with him to a new life in a new land. It is a duty and an obligation that a free man casts off when he voluntarily assumes allegiance to the country of his new home, and takes over the duties and the rights of a national there. When he accepts the new tie, the old one is loosed and gone. This principle is not a small matter. It is not a question of language, or of formulae, or of phrases. It is a principle of the rights of man and of the liberty of the human race.[110]

Though exhibiting some ambivalence, the delegates to the Conference did not fully accept this policy. Thus, the Final Act of the Conference noted that it was desirable

> that States should apply the principle that the acquisition of a foreign nationality through naturalization involves the loss of the previous nationality,

and that,

> pending the complete realization of the above principle, States before conferring their nationality by naturalization should endeavor to ascertain that the person concerned has fulfilled, or is in a position to fulfil, the conditions required by the law of his country for the loss of its nationality.[111]

United States had concluded respectively with Baden (1868), Bavaria (1868), Hesse (1868), Belgium (1868), Sweden and Norway (1869), Austro-Hungary (1870), Great Britain (1872), Ecuador (1872), and Denmark (1872).

109. British Naturalisation Act of 1870, § 6 *reprinted in* J. JONES, BRITISH NATIONALITY LAW AND PRACTICE 88 (1947). *See* C. PARRY, NATIONALITY AND CITIZENSHIP LAWS OF THE COMMONWEALTH AND OF THE REPUBLIC OF IRELAND 78–80 (1957).

110. 2 LEAGUE OF NATIONS, ACTS OF THE CONFERENCE FOR THE CODIFICATION OF INTERNATIONAL LAW, MEETINGS OF THE COMMITTEES: NATIONALITY 80 (1930).

111. Final Act of the Conference for the Codification of International Law, Leauge of Nations Publication Series 1930.V.7 (C.228.M.115.1930.V.), at 14 [hereinafter cited as Final Act of the Hague Conference].

This same ambivalence is apparent in state practice. Many states still do not recognize that an individual has the right, without condition, voluntarily to withdraw his nationality and to sever his ties with the country which claims him.[112] So many conditions are commonly imposed that "conditional," rather than "voluntary," expatriation would appear to be the appropriate descriptive label. In a world in which people are still important bases of power, states are understandably reluctant to yield their controls.

Even where voluntary expatriation is nominally recognized, difficult barriers are erected. Notable among such barriers are the following:

1. Exacting and carefully prescribed procedures must be followed to renounce nationality. For instance, a United States national, in voluntarily renouncing his nationality "when in a foreign state," is required to make a statement before a United States diplomatic or consular officer in the form prescribed by the Secretary of State.[113] On the other hand, when the renunciation is made in the United States during a state of war, the individual must make a formal written renunciation pursuant to the form stipulated by, and before such officer as may be designated by, the Attorney General, who must determine that such renunciation is not contrary to the interests of national defense.[114]
2. An individual may not expatriate himself while he is in the territory of the state of expatriation. It is a practice for many countries, such as Germany and Switzerland, not to honor the individual's voluntary expatriation if the renunciation is made within the expatriating state.[115] That expatriation is expected to occur abroad is also suggested by the frequent discussion of the right of voluntary expatriation in terms of automatic loss of nationality upon foreign naturalization.[116] The fact that expatriation often must occur abroad also reinforces the point that the right of voluntary expatriation and the right of emigration are closely linked.
3. An individual may not expatriate himself while the expatriating state is at war. For example, Great Britain and many other Commonwealth countries specifically prohibit expatriation in a "foreign" (non-Commonwealth) state in time of war so as to pre-

---

112. *Cf. Harvard Research, supra* note 1, at 45–48, 100–06.

113. 8 U.S.C. § 1481(a)(6) (1970).

114. *Id.* § 1481(a)(7).

115. (West German) Nationality Act of 22 July 1913, §25 Laws Concerning Nationality, *supra* note 1, at 178, 183; Swiss Nationality Act of 29 September 1952, Art. 42, *id.* at 443, 449.

116. *Cf.* 2 C. Hyde, *supra* note 108, at 1143–70; P. Weis, *supra* note 1, at 131–38.

vent their nationals from evading military service.[117] Naturalization when in an enemy state may be regarded as an act of treason.[118]

4. Expatriation is conditional on release by the expatriating state. Increasingly, the achievement of expatriation is made contingent upon the grant of official permission by the expatriating state. And most states will not grant such permission unless and until the individual has fulfilled certain obligations, especially military service and payment of taxes. The "conditional expatriation" under the Soviet Union and its fraternal states is especially harsh, for the conditions to be met in order to obtain the required official permission are not publicly disclosed.[119] In Jordan, conditions of release are related to ethnic origin. Though Jordanians not of Arab origin may renounce voluntarily their Jordanian nationality without state permission, those of Arab origin are required to secure release from the Council of Ministers unless they possess the nationality of another Arab state.[120]
5. The effect of voluntary expatriation is made contingent upon acquisition of another nationality. This widespread practice is justified on the basis of protecting the individual from becoming stateless. Thus, Article 7 of the Hague Convention on Nationality provides, in part:

> In so far as the law of a State provides for the issue of an expatriation permit, such a permit shall not entail the loss of the nationality of the State which issues it, unless the person to whom it is issued possesses another nationality or unless and until he acquires another nationality. An expatriation permit shall lapse if the holder does not acquire a new nationality within the period fixed by the State which has issued the permit.[121]

---

117. *See, e.g.* Australia, Nationality and Citizenship Act No. 83 of 1948, Art. 18(5), LAWS CONCERNING NATIONALITY, *supra* note 1, at 13, 19; Canada, Citizenship Act of 1946, § 15(2), *id.* at 69, 75; Ceylon, Citizenship Act No. 18 of 1948, § 18, *id.* at 83, 86; New Zealand, British Nationality and New Zealand Citizenship Act No. 15 of 1948, Art. 21(2), *id.* at 337, 345; United Kingdom, Nationality Act of 1948, § 32(1), *id.* at 468, 480; Ghana, Nationality and Citizenship Act of 1957, § 15(1), SUPPLEMENT TO LAWS CONCERNING NATIONALITY, *supra* note 1, at 126, 129; India, Citizenship Act No. 57 of 1955, Art. 8(1), *id.* at 133, 136; Malaya, Constitution of 1957, Art. 23(2), *id.* at 36, 39.

118. *See* Rex v. Lynch, [1903] 1 K.B. 444.

119. *See, e.g.,* Decree No. 202 of October 29, 1924 of the U.S.S.R., Art. 12, in R. Flournoy & M. Hudson, *supra* note 1, at 514.

120. Jordan, Nationality Law No. 6 of 4 February 1954, Arts. 15–17, LAWS CONCERNING NATIONALITY, *supra* note 1, at 277, 279.

121. 179 L.N.T.S. 89, 101.

> Similarly, Article 7(1)(a) of the Convention on the Reduction of Statelessness provides: "If the law of a Contracting State permits renunciation of nationality, such renunciation shall not result in loss of nationality unless the person concerned possesses or acquires another nationality."[122]

The professed objective underlying these provisions seems commendable. However, given the difficulties involved in securing naturalization, as noted above, the requirement of acquiring another nationality has sometimes become more deprivatory than protective of the individual. Hence the significance of Article 7(1)(b) of the Convention on the Reduction of Statelessness:

> The provisions of sub-paragraph (a) of this paragraph shall not apply where their application would be inconsistent with the principles stated in Articles 13 and 14 of the Universal Declaration of Human Rights approved on 10 December 1948 by the General Assembly of the United Nations.[123]

Articles 13 and 14 of the Universal Declaration of Human Rights, which we will explore elsewhere, deal with the freedom of movement, transnational as well as internal, and the right of asylum.[124]

Despite the various conditions mentioned above, it appears that in increasing degree strong community expectations support the individual's right of voluntary expatriation. As may be recalled, both the Univer-

---

122. The Convention on the Reduction of Statelessness was adopted on Aug. 30, 1961, by a Conference of Plenipotentiaries which convened in 1959 and reconvened in 1961, pursuant to General Assembly Res. 896 (IX) of Dec. 4, 1954. It entered into force on Dec. 13, 1975. For its historical background and commentary, *see* Weis, *The United Nations Convention on the Reduction of Statelessness, 1961,* 11 INT'L & COMP. L.Q. 1073 (1962). For its text, *see* U.N. HUMAN RIGHTS INSTRUMENTS, *supra* note 70, at 55.

123. U.N. HUMAN RIGHTS INSTRUMENTS, *supra* note 70, at 55.

124. Art. 13 reads:

> 1. Everyone has the right to freedom of movement and residence within the borders of each State.
> 2. Everyone has the right to leave any country, including his own, and to return to his country.

And Art. 14 reads as follows:

> 1. Everyone has the right to seek and to enjoy in other countries asylum from persecution.
> 2. This right may not be invoked in the case of prosecutions genuinely arising from non-political crimes or from acts contrary to the purposes and principles of the United Nations.

Id. at 2.

sal Declaration of Human Rights and the American Convention on Human Rights provide that no one shall be "arbitrarily" denied the right to change his nationality.[125] Unhappily, both the International Covenant on Civil and Political Rights and the European Convention on Human Rights fail to protect this right. In formulating prescriptions in the future, proponents of human rights might well keep in mind Hersch Lauterpacht's admonition that the prohibition of *arbitrary* denial of change alone is not enough:[126] the right that is "inherent in the human person"[127] and gradually taking its place among "'the general principles of law recognized by civilized nations'" is more simply and comprehensively that the "right of emigration and expatriation shall not be denied."[128]

WITHDRAWAL WITH CONSENT (GENUINE OR CONSTRUCTIVE) FOR PROMOTING HARMONIOUS RELATIONS BETWEEN STATES

When withdrawal of nationality is with the genuine consent of the individual, such withdrawal may approximate voluntary expatriation and involve no problems of human rights. In the interest of promoting harmonious relations among themselves and avoiding situations of potential conflict, states may, however, disregard the question of genuine consent and impose loss of nationality upon an individual because of the "voluntary" performance of a variety of acts. The basic policy question with respect to expatriation in such contexts is whether the common interest of states in the avoidance of conflict is sufficiently substantial to justify the severe deprivations imposed upon nonconsenting individuals.

In historic practice states have, in pursuit of various policies, imposed loss of nationality upon individuals because of a wide variety of acts, ranging from the most explicit renunciation of nationality to instances in which consent is entirely fictitious. A brief itemization of this range includes execution of formal instruments of renunciation, deliberate acquisition of the nationality of another state, taking an oath of allegiance to another state, protracted residence abroad, military service in the forces of foreign governments, voting in foreign political elections, employment by foreign governments, marriage to an alien man, and the naturalization of parents by another government.

With respect to some of these acts, the withdrawal of nationality occurs under conditions which clearly approximate genuine consent and rec-

---

125. *See* notes 97–98 *supra* and accompanying text.
126. H. Lauterpacht, International Law and Human Rights 348–49, 423 (1950).
127. C. De Visscher, *supra* note 106, at 185.
128. H. Lauterpacht, *supra* note 126, at 347; H. Lauterpacht, *supra* note 103, at 129.

ognition of withdrawal in such circumstances may indeed be necessary for making effective the human rights policies intimately connected with honoring voluntary expatriation. This is certainly true with respect to the execution of formal instruments of renunciation, the deliberate acquisition of the nationality of another state, and the taking of an oath of allegiance to another state. Execution of a formal instrument of renunciation, as indicated above, is the most explicit form of accomplishing voluntary expatriation.[129] In the case of naturalization in another state, the emphasis is on deliberate choice: imposed naturalization, as mentioned above, obviously lacks voluntariness.[130] Taking an oath or other formal declaration of allegiance to a foreign state, it is said, means less than total allegiance to an individual's own state, and places him in a peculiar position where his services might be claimed by more than one state, thereby making it practically impossible for his state of nationality to provide him protection vis-à-vis that foreign state.[131] The policy consideration favoring presumption of voluntariness in regard to taking an oath of allegiance to a foreign state is understandable; the difficulty lies in ascertaining what constitutes an oath of allegiance, for the types of oath may vary from "ironbound pledges of allegiance to vague and ambiguous affirmations of fealty or obedience."[132] Criteria for ascertainment have been suggested by Secretary of State Hughes in these words:

> It is the spirit and meaning of the oath, not merely the letter, which is to determine whether it results in expatriation. It is not a mere matter of words. The test seems to be the question whether the oath taken places the person taking it in complete subjection to the state to which it is taken . . . so that it is impossible for him to perform the obligations of citizenship to [the country of nationality].[133]

Taking an oath of allegiance does not necessarily lead to naturalization. Hence, some states, such as Canada and Sudan, make taking an oath or other formal declaration of allegiance to a foreign state a ground for withdrawal of nationality only when such an oath would result in the acquisition of the foreign nationality.[134]

---

129. *See* notes 100–28 *supra* and accompanying text.

130. *See* notes 53–98 *supra* and accompanying text.

131. H.R. Doc. No. 326, 59th Cong., 2d Sess. 23 (1906).

132. Roche, *The Loss of American Nationality—The Development of Statutory Expatriation,* 99 U. Pa. L. Rev. 25, 32 (1950).

133. 3 G. Hackworth, Digest of International Law 219 (1942) (Secretary Hughes to Frank L. Polk, Mar. 17, 1924).

134. Canada, The Citizenship Act of 1952, Art. 15(1), Supplement to Laws Concerning Nationality, *supra* note 1, at 15, 21; Sudan, The Nationality Act No. 22 of 1957, Art. 12(c), *id.* at 71, 73.

Many states view military service in a foreign state as a ground for withdrawal of nationality in certain cases. Since an individual's entry into military service in a foreign state may be either voluntary or involuntary, and since the foreign state in which he serves may or may not be hostile to his state of nationality, great care should be taken in inferring voluntariness on his part. In *Nishikawa* v. *Dulles* the United States Supreme Court held that voluntariness should be proved by "clear, convincing and unequivocal evidence."[135] While voluntary service in the armed forces of a state hostile to the individual's state of nationality may be clearly inimical to his duty of loyalty, military service in a state friendly to his own is quite a different matter. Similar considerations would also apply to the case of public employment by a foreign government.[136]

Voting in a foreign political election as a ground for loss of nationality is perhaps unique to the practice of the United States.[137] Justification is sought on the ground that participation in the public affairs of another state involves a political attachment to the foreign state in a manner incompatible with continued allegiance to the United States. The constitutionality of this particular imposition, first sustained by the Supreme Court in *Perez* v. *Brownell,*[138] was rejected in *Afroyim* v. *Rusk.*[139]

In *Perez* the petitioner, Perez, was a native-born United States national who had resided in Mexico for a number of years and had voted in political elections in Mexico.[140] Upon his return to the United States, he was ordered excluded by immigration officials on the ground that he had expatriated himself. Perez sought a declaratory judgment that he was a United States national, challenging the general proposition that the United States could apply a doctrine of "constructive volition" in depriving him of his nationality. The Supreme Court, by a five-to-four vote, upheld the Congress in withdrawing nationality from a native-born national for having voted in the political elections of a foreign country.

---

135. 356 U.S. 129, 135 (1958).

136. *See S. Greenleigh & R. Margenau, supra* note 1, at 245–49; *Harvard Research, supra* note 1, at 104.

137. Section 349(a)(5) of the Immigration and Nationality Act of 1952 (as amended) provides:

> From and after the effective date of this Act a person who is a national of the United States whether by birth or naturalization, shall lose his nationality by—. . .
>
> (5) voting in a political election in a foreign state or participating in an election or plebiscite to determine the sovereignty over foreign territory. . . .

8 U.S.C. § 1481 (1970).

138. 356 U.S. 44 (1958).

139. 387 U.S. 253 (1967).

140. Perez was a dual national of both the United States and Mexico and had resided in Mexico apparently to avoid military service in the United States.

Speaking for the majority, Mr. Justice Frankfurter stated that the congressional power to control and regulate foreign affairs includes the necessary competence to expatriate any United States national for voting in foreign political elections. Because the power over foreign affairs involves more than "the maintenance of diplomatic relations . . . and the protection of American citizens," the government "must also be able to reduce to a minimum the frictions that are unavoidable in a world of sovereigns sensitive in matters touching their dignity and interests."[141] Harmonious relations with other states would be jeopardized

> when a citizen of one country chooses to participate in the political or governmental affairs of another country. The citizen may by his action unwittingly promote or encourage a course of conduct contrary to the interests of his own government; moreover, the people or government of the foreign country may regard his action to be the action of his government, or at least as a reflection if not an expression of its policy.[142]

Afroyim v. *Rusk*[143] involved a naturalized American citizen who was denied a United States passport on the ground that he had expatriated himself by voting in an Israeli legislative election. The central issue was the same as in *Perez.* In reaffirming the view that United States citizenship could be lost only "by the voluntary renunciation or abandonment by the citizen himself,"[144] Mr. Justice Black, speaking for a majority of five, rejected the notion that Congress has any general power, explicit or implicit, to denationalize, as was suggested by *Perez.* He emphasized that "the people are sovereign and the Government cannot sever its relationship to the people by taking away their citizenship."[145] Citizenship, he continued, "is no light trifle to be jeopardized any moment Congress decides to do so under the name of one of its general or implied grants

141. 356 U.S. 44, 57 (1958).
142. *Id.* at 59. Mr. Justice Frankfurter further stated:

> The critical connection between this conduct and loss of citizenship is the fact that it is the possession of American citizenship by a person committing the act that makes the act potentially embarrassing to the American Government and pregnant with the possibility of embroiling this country in disputes with other nations. The termination of citizenship terminates the problem. Moreover, the fact is not without significance that Congress has interpreted this conduct, not irrationally, as importing not only something less than complete and unswerving allegiance to the United States but also elements of allegiance to another country in some measure, at least, inconsistent with American citizenship.

Id. at 60–61.
143. 387 U.S. 253 (1967).
144. *Id.* at 266.
145. *Id.* at 257.

of power."[146] He concluded by pointing out that the decision of the Court "does no more than to give to this citizen that which is his own, a constitutional right to remain a citizen in a free country unless he voluntarily relinquishes that citizenship."[147]

Nationality is sometimes withdrawn, in an expression of policies converse to those involved in the "genuine link" requirement for naturalization, if a national has continuously resided abroad over an extended period, normally ranging from two to ten years.[148] Though it is most often made applicable to naturalized nationals, in some countries this policy applies to all nationals, by birth or naturalization.[149] As was observed decades ago:

> It is difficult to see why a person who becomes permanently established in a foreign country and identified with the life of the community in which he lives, should be allowed to continue to carry the badge of allegiance of a country with which he has little or no effective contact.[150]

Nevertheless, special care is again required in inferring consent to expatriation by the mere fact of protracted residence abroad, especially in view of the diversity in the requirements of length of stay and the growing frequency of transnational interactions.

With reference to the effect of marriage on the wife's nationality, national laws vary widely.[151] Just as a woman may automatically or by certain action acquire the nationality of her alien husband upon marriage, she may automatically or by certain action lose her original nationality as a consequence of marriage to a foreign national.[152] Historically, for the sake of family unity and undivided allegiance, in most states a woman automatically lost her original nationality and acquired instead her husband's upon marriage to a foreign national. The loss of nationality was also justified on a theory of implied consent—i.e., a woman, in marrying an alien, "consents" to abandon her original nationality. This theory of implied consent was formulated in the famous case *Mackenzie* v. *Hare,*[153] where the United States Supreme Court held that the marriage of an American woman to a British subject resulted in the loss of

---

146. *Id.* at 267–68.

147. *Id.* at 268.

148. *See Harvard Research, supra* note 1, at 104–05.

149. *See* United Nations, A Study of Statelessness 139 (1949); P. Weis, *supra* note 1, at 123; Hudson, *supra* note 1, at 18.

150. Sandifer, *supra* note 45, at 278.

151. *See* notes 66–70 *supra* and accompanying text.

152. *See* Nationality of Married Women, *supra* note 66, at 8–18, 29–125.

153. 239 U.S. 299 (1916).

her United States nationality because she "voluntarily entered into [the marriage], with notice of the consequences."[154]

More recently, however, many states have ceased imposing automatic loss of a woman's original nationality upon marriage to an alien.[155] This trend reflects in part dissatisfaction with the fiction of implied consent and in part contemporary concern about discrimination. It is in keeping with contemporary demands for the protection of the human person, as previously noted, that a woman national retain her nationality upon marriage to an alien unless she explicitly and voluntarily expatriates herself.

The nationality laws of states with respect to minor children have not been uniform. Conversely to the acquisition of nationality, a minor's nationality may be withdrawn upon the foreign naturalization of his father or widowed mother.[156] Though the primary rationale is again the unity of family allegiance, genuine consent on the minor's part, if he is capable of such consent, may be missing. This was observed in *Perkins* v. *Elg*,[157] in which the United States Supreme Court held that the American-born child of naturalized parents, who later resumed their former nationality and took her with them to Sweden, had not lost her nationality. In the words of Chief Justice Hughes,

> Expatriation is the voluntary renunciation or abandonment of nationality and allegiance. It has no application to the removal from this country of a native citizen during minority. In such a case the voluntary action which is of the essence of the right of expatriation is lacking.[158]

Hence, it appears that the trend in practice is toward the retention of the minor's nationality after the foreign naturalization of his parents, even if he may find himself in possession of multiple nationality. If, however, the minor must automatically lose his nationality upon the foreign naturalization of his parents, many commentators increasingly urge that the minor be accorded a right of option regarding his nationality upon attaining majority.[159]

WITHDRAWAL WITHOUT CONSENT AS PUNISHMENT

It is sometimes asserted that the state has the unlimited competence to withdraw nationality. In the words of Manley Hudson, "In principle, the

---

154. *Id.* at 312.

155. NATIONALITY OF MARRIED WOMEN, *supra* note 66, at 122–25.

156. *See* S. Greenleigh & R. Margenau, *supra* note 1, at 265–71; Sandifer, *supra* note 45, at 269–71; *Harvard Research, supra* note 1, at 105–06.

157. 307 U.S. 325 (1939).

158. *Id.* at 334.

159. *Cf., e.g.,* S. Greenleigh & R. Margenau, *supra* note 1, at 269–71; Sandifer, *supra* note 45, at 269–71; *Harvard Research, supra* note 1, 105–06.

power of States to cancel or withdraw nationality is, in the absence of treaty obligations, not limited by international law. . . ."[160] In practice states have acted only on certain relatively restricted grounds. Question has been raised about the permissibility of withdrawal even upon these grounds. Within the United States it is increasingly urged that the withdrawal of nationality as a sanction for inimical conduct having no particular relation to the common interests of states in the management of people may be "cruel and unusual punishment" and, hence, unconstitutional.[161] Enquiry is equally relevant whether international law does, or should, tolerate so extreme a sanction, which serves no purpose in securing the common interests of states.

The grounds upon which states seek in contemporary times to impose loss of nationality as an internal sanction may be summarized under three headings:

1. Crimes against the state, including evasion of military service or desertion from the armed forces in time of war;
2. Hostile political affiliations and activities; and
3. Possession of certain racial, ethnic, or religious characteristics.

We briefly examine each of these grounds.

It is not uncommon for states to impose loss of nationality for conviction of crimes regarded as serious attacks upon the state. Some conduct is regarded as so inimical to the security of the basic values of the community that it is incompatible with continued enjoyment of the benefits and discharge of the responsibilities of community membership.[162] The range of conduct sometimes so characterized includes treason, desertion from the armed forces, and evasion of the military draft. The Soviet Union at an early date imposed denationalization and expulsion upon individuals convicted of being "enemies of the toiling masses."[163]

Within the United States it has recently been questioned whether denationalization is an appropriate sanction for desertion or evasion of military service. In *Trop* v. *Dulles,*[164] the Supreme Court declared that depriving a citizen of nationality on the basis of a court-martial conviction for his desertion in time of war, when he had been absent from his duty less than a day and had willingly surrendered, was "cruel and unusual punishment" in violation of the Eighth Amendment. Speaking for a majority of five, Chief Justice Warren observed at the outset that

---

160. Hudson, *supra* note 1, at 10.

161. The Eighth Amendment of the Constitution provides: "Excessive bail shall not be required, nor excessive fines imposed, nor cruel and unusual punishments inflicted."

162. *See* S. Greenleigh & R. Margenau, *supra* note 1, at 218–23.

163. U.S.S.R., Decree of April 22, 1931 *reprinted in* T. Taracouzio, The Soviet Union and International Law 121 (1935).

164. 356 U.S. 86 (1958).

"[d]esertion in wartime, though it may merit the ultimate penalty, does not necessarily signify allegiance to a foreign state."[165] "Citizenship," he continued,

> is not a license that expires upon misbehavior. The duties of citizenship are numerous, and the discharge of many of these obligations is essential to the security and well-being of the nation. . . . But citizenship is not lost every time a duty of citizenship is shirked. And the deprivation of citizenship is not a weapon that the Government may use to express its displeasure at a citizen's conduct, however reprehensible that conduct may be.[166]

Emphasizing that denationalization is entirely different in character and quality from the traditional modes of criminal punishment, including even the death penalty,[167] the Chief Justice declared that denationalization as a punishment is forbidden by the Eighth Amendment and, hence, unconstitutional. He stated:

> There may be involved no physical mistreatment, no primitive torture. There is instead the total destruction of the individual's status in organized society. It is a form of punishment more primitive than torture, for it destroys for the individual the political existence that was centuries in the development.[168]

Similarly, in *Kennedy* v. *Mendoza-Martinez,*[169] the Supreme Court declared unconstitutional a statute purporting to denationalize persons who left or remained outside the United States to evade military service,[170] finding such measures to be cruel and unusual punishment.

A paradoxical case is *Kawakita* v. *United States,*[171] in which the

165. *Id.* at 92.
166. *Id.* at 92–93.
167. *Id.* at 93–100.
168. *Id.* at 101–02.
169. 372 U.S. 144 (1963).
170. Nationality Act of 1940, § 401(j), ch. 418, 58 Stat. 746 (1944), provided:

> (a) From and after the effective date of this chapter a person who is a national of the United States whether by birth or naturalization, shall lose his nationality by—
>
> . . .
>
> (10) departing from or remaining outside of the jurisdiction of the United States in time of war or during a period declared by the President to be a period of national emergency for the purpose of evading or avoiding training and service in the military, air, or naval forces of the United States. For the purposes of this paragraph failure to comply with any provision of any compulsory service laws of the United States shall raise the presumption that the departure from or absence from the United States was for the purpose of evading or avoiding training and service in the military, air, or naval forces of the United States.

171. 343 U.S. 717 (1952).

petitioner would have benefited if he could have been regarded as denationalized. He was a native-born national of the United States and a national of Japan by virtue of Japanese parentage and had been convicted of treason, with a death sentence, for having mistreated American prisoners-of-war in Japan. He contended that he could not be tried, much less convicted of treason, by the United States because he had expatriated himself from the United States, as evidenced by his use of a Japanese passport during the war, his employment by the Japanese government, his acceptance of labor papers from the Japanese government, and the entry of his name in the Japanese *Koseki* (a family census register). The Supreme Court found the implications of his alleged acts of expatriation ambiguous and insufficient.[172] The petitioner placed special emphasis on the entry of his name in the *Koseki,* but the Court held that, since he was born a dual national, this entry did not constitute a foreign naturalization signifying renunciation of his American citizenship, but "a reaffirmation of an allegiance to Japan which already exists."[173] The conviction of treason was thus sustained.

A no less paradoxical case, but with a converse twist, is *Kuhn* v. *Custodian of Enemy Property,*[174] involving a German national who had moved to Norway in 1911 and had lived there since that time. Because of his refusal to return to Germany upon the outbreak of World War I, his German nationality was withdrawn under German law. At the end of World War II he was treated as a German national and his assets were sequestered as enemy property by the Norwegian government. The Supreme Court of Norway held that, although the appellant was unable to prove conclusively his loss of German nationality, the court would certainly take judicial notice of the German draft evasion law. Accordingly, he was found to be a stateless person, rather than a German national, and the sequestration of his property was declared illegal.

Deprivation of nationality for hostile political affiliations and activities has been characterized as "a twentieth century phenomenon."[175] The affiliations and activities to which reference is here made differ from those discussed immediately above in that, though they may sometimes border on the criminal, they are not always categorized as crimes and punished by criminal sanctions. Though the ancient world knew banishment for political activities,[176] this particular form of punishment was relatively rare before World War I. After that war nationality was frequently deprived on such grounds as "disloyalty or disaffection, acts

---

172. *Id.* at 722–23.
173. *Id.* at 724.
174. [1951] I.L.R. 262 (Supreme Court, Norway 1951).
175. S. Greenleigh & R. Margenau, *supra* note 1, at 286.
176. *See* P. Weis, *supra* note 1, at 122.

prejudicial to the State or its interests, collaboration with the enemy, [and] advocacy of subversive activities."[177]

The most far-reaching denationalization measures were those undertaken in Russia, in the wake of the Bolshevik Revolution, first by the All-Russian Soviet Socialist Republic and then by the Union of Soviet Socialist Republics.[178] On December 15, 1921, the All-Russian Government issued the following decree:

> 1. Persons of the under-mentioned categories who remain outside the confines of Russia after the publication of the present decree are deprived of the rights of Russian citizenship:
>
> (a) Persons having resided abroad uninterruptedly for more than five years, and not having received before June 1, 1922, foreign passports or corresponding certificates from representatives of the Soviet Government. . . .
>
> (b) Persons who left Russia after November 7, 1917, without the authorization of the Soviet authorities.
>
> (c) Persons who have voluntarily served in armies fighting against the Soviet authority, or who have in any way participated in counter-revolutionary organizations.
>
> (d) Persons having had the right to opt for Russian citizenship and not having exercised that right within the period prescribed for option.
>
> (e) Persons not included under paragraph (a) of this section, who are residing abroad and who shall not have registered themselves at foreign representations of the R.S.F.S.R. within the period prescribed. . . .[179]

In 1924, the Soviet government adopted a new law, confirming the forfeitures of nationality under prior legislation and denationalizing all Russians abroad who failed to return upon request by competent Soviet officials.[180] These denationalization measures were obviously aimed at Russian nationals who had opposed the Bolshevik regime or were suspected to be so opposed. The net effect was an unprecedented mass denationalization of some two million people, ushering in a tragic era of refugees.[181]

---

177. *Id.* at 124.

178. For a critical comment, *see* Williams, *Denationalization,* 8 BRIT. Y.B. INT'L L. 45 (1927).

179. R. Flournoy & M. Hudson, *supra* note 1, at 511.

180. Decree No. 202 of October 29, 1924, *reprinted in id.* at 511–14.

181. *See* E. KULISCHER, EUROPE ON THE MOVE: WAR AND POPULATION CHANGES 1917–1947 (1948); 2 F. NORWOOD, *supra* note 15, at 270–75; J. SIMPSON, THE REFUGEE PROBLEM: REPORT OF A SURVEY (1939).

Following the Russian example, other states (*e.g.*, Italy, Turkey, and Germany) resorted to denationalization on political and other grounds on a wide scale.[182] After World War II several Eastern European states prescribed denationalization for any person, if abroad, committing "any act prejudicial to the national and state interests."[183] Confused by continuing expectations of violence and cold war ideological conflict, even the United States is not immune from this syndrome, as symbolized by the enactment of the Expatriation Act of 1954,[184] purporting to denationalize individuals who advocate the overthrow of the government in a manner proscribed by the Smith Act.[185] Since membership in the

182. *See* PREUSS, *International Law and Deprivation of Nationality,* 23 GEO. L.J. 250, 265–67 (1935).

183. Albania, Nationality Act No. 377 of 16 December 1946, Art. 14, LAWS CONCERNING NATIONALITY, *supra* note 1, at 4, 6. *See also* Poland, Nationality Act of 8 January 1951, Art. 12(b), *id.* at 386, 388; Yugoslavia, Nationality Act No. 370/331 of 1 July 1946, Art. 16, *id.* at 554, 557.

184. 8 U.S.C. § 1481(a)(9) (1970), provides:

> (a) From and after the effective date of this chapter a person who is a national of the United States whether by birth or naturalization, shall lose his nationality by—
>
> . . .
>
> (9) committing any act of treason against, or attempting by force to overthrow, or bearing arms against, the United States, violating or conspiring to violate any of the provisions of section 2383 of Title 18, or willfully performing any act in violation of section 2385 of Title 18, or violating section 2384 of Title 18 by engaging in a conspiracy to overthrow, put down, or to destroy by force the Government of the United States, or to levy war against them, if and when he is convicted thereof by a court martial or by a court of competent jurisdiction.

185. The Smith Act, named after its sponsor, Congressman Howard W. Smith of Virginia, was enacted by Congress in 1940, as Title I of the Alien Registration Act, ch. 439, 54 Stat. 670. Its principal substantive provisions, now incorporated in 18 U.S.C. § 2385 (1970), read as follows:

> Whoever knowingly or willfully advocates, abets, advises, or teaches the duty, necessity, desirability, or propriety of overthrowing or destroying the government of the United States or the government of any State, Territory, District or Possession, thereof, or the government of any political subdivision therein, by force or violence, or by the assassination of any officer of any such government; or
>
> Whoever, with intent to cause the overthrow or destruction of any such government, prints, publishes, edits, issues, circulates, sells, distributes, or publicly displays any written or printed matter advocating, advising, or teaching the duty, necessity, desirability, or propriety of overthrowing or destroying any government in the United States by force or violence, or attempts to do so; or
>
> Whoever organizes or helps or attempts to organize any society, group, or assembly of persons who teach, advocate, or encourage the overthrow or destruction of any such government by force or violence; or becomes or is a member of, or affiliates with, any such society, group, or assembly of persons, knowing the purposes thereof—
>
> Shall be fined not more than $20,000 or imprisoned not more than twenty years, or both, and shall be ineligible for employment by the United States or any department or agency thereof, for the five years next following his conviction.

Communist Party per se had been held to be a violation of the Smith Act,[186] the potential threat of denationalization to all American Communists was apparent. Although the constitutionality of this enactment has not yet been tested, the response to it was prompt and critical. Shortly after its passage, two students wrote a powerful Note entitled "The Expatriation Act of 1954,"[187] later acclaimed as "pioneering and remarkably prophetic" and having "an unmistakable impact on subsequent Supreme Court expressions,"[188] cogently observing that the Act's sanctions would be cruel and unusual punishments in violation of the Eighth Amendment and thus unconstitutional.[189] They further observed that the Expatriation Act "would almost undoubtedly be held void under international law,"[190] since "the use of denationalization as a punishment is diametrically opposed to the trend of international law towards a greater protection of human rights."[191] The authors concluded that

> the Act was not a sober response to the demands of national policy, but rather was enacted primarily to vent the nation's hatred of citizens who have forsaken their native country by adopting communism. Actually, democracy and anti-communism would be better strengthened by repeal of the Expatriation Act and reliance upon conventional sanctions to deter and punish subversion.[192]

Denationalization on racial, ethnic, religious, or other related grounds is particularly notorious because of its close association with Nazi and fascist atrocities.[193] In pursuit of its racial policy, the Hitler government

---

If two or more persons conspire to commit any offense named in this section, each shall be fined not more than $20,000 or imprisoned not more than twenty years, or both, and shall be ineligible for employment by the United States or any department or agency thereof, for the five years next following his conviction.

As used in this section, the terms "organizes" and "organize," with respect to any society, group, or assembly of persons, include the recruiting of new members, the forming of new units, and the regrouping or expansion of existing clubs, classes, and other units of such society, group, or assembly of persons.

186. *Cf.* 1 T. Emerson, D. Haber, & N. Dorsen, Political and Civil Rights in the United States 98–147 (student ed. 1967). *See, e.g.,* Scales v. United States, 367 U.S. 203 (1961).

187. *Note, The Expatriation Act of 1954,* 64 Yale L.J. 1164 (1955). The two students were Norbert A. Schlei and Stephen J. Pollak, each of whom was to become an assistant attorney general of the United States.

188. Gordon, *The Citizen and the State: Power of Congress to Expatriate American Citizens,* 53 Geo. L.J. 315, 344 (1965).

189. *Note, supra* note 187, at 1187–94.

190. *Id.* at 1196.

191. *Id.* at 1197.

192. *Id.* at 1200.

193. *See* H. Santa Cruz, Racial Discrimination 244–96, U.N. Doc. E/CN.4/Sub. 2/307/Rev. 1 (1971); Preuss, *supra* note 182.

first, in 1933, denaturalized a large number of naturalized citizens, primarily Jews, and then, in 1941, denationalized all German Jews residing abroad. Confiscation of property accompanied forfeiture of nationality. The measures of denationalization were undertaken as part of the National Socialist Program outlined in 1920, pursuant to which "[o]nly those who are members of the nation can be citizens of the State. Only those of German blood, irrespective of religion, can be members of the German nation. No Jews, therefore, can be a member [*sic*] of the nation. . . . All further immigration of non-Germans is to be prevented. We demand that all non-Germans who have migrated to Germany since August 2, 1914, be compelled to leave the Reich at once."[194] The underlying racist theory was that Aryans alone were capable of "heroic" deeds and hence epitomized the German nation, while non-Aryans, regarded as an alien and unassimilable race, were to be excluded from German society.[195]

On July 14, 1933, the Nazi government proclaimed that "[n]aturalizations which have taken place between November 9, 1918 and January 30, 1933 may be revoked, if the naturalization is considered undesirable."[196] Who was to be considered undesirable was made clear by a supplementary ordinance, stating that "there came especially under consideration for the revocation of naturalization: (a) Eastern Jews, unless they have fought at the front on the side of Germany during the World War, or have rendered important services to German interests. . . ."[197] Because of this and other anti-Semitic measures a mass exodus of Jews ensued, and by the fall of 1941 few Jews remained in Germany.[198] A new decree, issued on November 15, 1941, denationalized all Jews residing abroad or leaving Germany after that date and confiscated all of their assets.[199] Denationalization was extended not only to those who had emigrated from Germany during the Third Reich but also to Jews of German nationality who had never set foot in Germany. Included also were the Jewish wives and children of all such nonresident Germans.[200] The satellite countries of the Axis and those under its domination, Hungary and Roumania, for example,[201] undertook similar measures against Jews. In Italy, the fascist government revoked all naturalization certificates issued to Jews after January 1, 1919, by the decree of December 17, 1938.[202]

194. Preuss, *supra* note 182, at 251.
195. *See* H. Santa Cruz, *supra* note 193, at 247–52.
196. Preuss, *supra* note 182, at 250.
197. *Id.* at 252.
198. *See* M. Vishniak, The Legal Status of Stateless Persons 24–33 (1945).
199. *See* Abel, *Denationalization,* 6 Modern L. Rev. 57, 59–61 (1942).
200. *Id.* at 60.
201. *See* P. Meyer, et al., The Jews in the Soviet Satellites 384, 500 (1953).
202. *See* C. Roth, The History of the Jews of Italy 524–27 (1946).

Following World War II, in the wake of the Nazi holocaust, Czechoslovakia imposed loss of nationality en masse upon persons of the German and Hungarian "races"; Poland and Yugoslavia imposed similar sanctions upon persons of the German "race." Pursuant to the Potsdam Agreement, persons of the German "race" were expelled to Germany.[203]

Some states assert additional grounds or wider powers in imposing loss of nationality upon naturalized nationals, as distinguished from born nationals.[204] It is a common practice to cancel a naturalization certificate upon discovery of fraud or misrepresentation in the procurement of such certificate.[205] Extended residence abroad, where it is asserted as a ground for deprivation of nationality, is directed mostly toward naturalized nationals.[206] In the context of denationalization, states often require naturalized nationals to comply with a higher standard of loyalty.[207] Within the United States, the prohibition of involuntary withdrawal of nationality applies to naturalized citizens as well as natural-born citizens. In *Schneider* v. *Rusk,*[208] the Supreme Court declared invalid the congressional enactment that authorized denaturalization of naturalized citizens who returned for more than three years to the country of their birth or former nationality. In the words of Justice Douglas,

> This statute proceeds on the impermissible assumption that naturalized citizens as a class are less reliable and bear less allegiance

---

203. The relevant provision in the Protocol of Proceedings approved at Berlin (Potsdam) Aug. 2, 1945, reads as follows:

> The three governments [U.S., U.K., and U.S.S.R.], having considered the question in all its aspects, recognize that the transfer to Germany of German populations, or elements thereof, remaining in Poland, Czechoslovakia and Hungary, will have to be undertaken. They agree that any transfers that take place should be effected in an orderly and humane manner.

3 Treaties and Other International Agreements of the United States of America, 1776–1949, at 1207, 1220 (C. Bevans comp. 1969).

204. *See* National Legislation concerning Grounds for Deprivation of Nationality, U.N. Doc. A/CN.4/66 (1953) (memorandum prepared by Ivan S. Kerno).

205. *See* United States v. Genovese, 133 F. Supp. 820 (D.N.J. 1955); Maylott & Crystal, *The Scheiderman Case: Two Views,* 12 Geo. Wash. L. Rev. 215 (1944); *Note, Aliens: Denaturalization for Fraud,* 35 Calif. L. Rev. 449 (1947).

206. *See* National Legislation concerning Grounds for Deprivation of Nationality, *supra* note 204, at 3. As Justice Douglas stated in Schneider v. Rusk, 377 U.S. 163, 169 (1964), "Living abroad, whether the citizen be naturalized or native born, is no badge of lack of allegiance and in no way evidences a voluntary renunciation of nationality and allegiance. It may indeed be compelled by family business, or other legitimate reasons."

207. *See* National Legislation concerning Grounds for Deprivation of Nationality, *supra* note 204.

208. 377 U.S. 163 (1964). *See generally Note, Constitutional Limitations on the Naturalization Power,* 80 Yale L.J. 769 (1971).

to this country than do the native born. This is an assumption that is impossible for us to make. . . . A native-born citizen is free to reside abroad indefinitely without suffering loss of citizenship. The discrimination aimed at naturalized citizens drastically limits their rights to live and work abroad in a way that other citizens may. It creates indeed a second-class citizenship.[209]

Despite insistence by some distinguished authors, such as Manley Hudson[210] and Paul Weis,[211] that international law imposes no limitation upon the competence of states to deprive individuals of nationality, general community expectations would today appear to be moving toward restricting such allegedly "unlimited" competence. Though the views of Hudson and Weis may accurately reflect the expectations of the past, they certainly do not represent community expectations of the present and probable future. Even historically, international law would appear to have established some restraints and, as the contemporary concern for human rights becomes more intense, additional restraints on such competence will evolve. It has long been agreed that a state could not deprive individuals of nationality and then expel them to other states. The fundamental community policy of minimizing statelessness has had general and intensifying support. The emerging peremptory norm (*jus cogens*) of nondiscrimination will, as previously noted, make unlawful many types of denationalization. In sum, the whole complex of more fundamental policies for the protection of human rights, as embodied, for instance, in the United Nations Charter, the Universal Declaration of Human Rights, the International Covenants on Human Rights, and other related instruments and programs, global as well as regional, may eventually be interpreted to forbid use of denationalization as a form of "cruel, inhuman and degrading treatment or punishment."[212] Decisions

---

209. 377 U.S. at 168–69. By way of contrast, in Rogers v. Bellei, 401 U.S. 815 (1971), the Supreme Court held that Congress can provide for denationalization of a United States national who is born abroad to an American parent, who is not naturalized in the United States, and who fails to reside in the United States for five years between the ages of fourteen and twenty-eight. In the opinion of the Court, the Fourteenth Amendment is not applicable to this type of national. The Court indicated its readiness to sustain conditions that are "not unreasonable, arbitrary, or unlawful." *Id.* at 831. Four dissenting justices found no basis for distinguishing nationals who acquire their nationality by birth abroad to an American parent from those who acquire it by being born or naturalized in the United States. For comments on this decision, *see* Gordon, *The Power of Congress to Terminate United States Citizenship—A Continuing Constitutional Debate,* 4 Conn. L. Rev. 611 (1972); Ulman, *Nationality, Expatriation and Statelessness,* 25 Ad. L. Rev. 113 (1973).

210. Hudson, *supra* note 1, at 10.

211. P. Weis, *supra* note 1, at 126–29.

212. *See* The Universal Declaration of Human Rights, Art. 5: "No one shall be subjected to torture or to cruel, inhuman or degrading treatment or punishment." U.N. Human Rights Instruments, *supra* note 70, at 1.

about nationality are as much within the reference of human rights prescriptions as any other decisions.

The principle that one state could not by denationalization force individuals upon another state was established before any serious concern for human rights figured significantly in the international law about nationality. Writing nearly half a century ago, Sir John Fischer Williams stated that

> while positive international law does not forbid a state unilaterally to sever the relationship of nationality so far as the individual is concerned, even if the person affected possesses or acquires no other nationality, still a state cannot sever the tie of nationality in such a way as to release itself from the international duty, owed to other states, of receiving back a person denationalized who has acquired no other nationality, should he be expelled as an alien by the state where he happens to be.[213]

Similarly, as urged by an advocate in a famous case, "it was a universally recognized principle of international law that a State could not simply deprive of their nationality citizens who are out of sympathy with the regime and so force them on other States."[214] The perverse reasoning underlying this humane law was that a state has the sovereign competence to control and regiment people within its territory, of which "the power of expulsion" is an essential component.[215] If one state should be at liberty to render stateless its nationals residing in another state, so it was reasoned, it would encroach upon the right of the state of sojourn and interfere with the exercise of the latter's right to expel aliens. Should the parent state and other states refuse to accept denationalized persons, the state of sojourn would end up bearing the burden of accommodating them.[216] One of the participants in the International Law Commission's

---

The International Covenant on Civil and Political Rights, Art. 7, reads: "No one shall be subjected to torture or to cruel, inhuman or degrading treatment or punishment. In particular, no one shall be subjected without his free consent to medical or scientific experimentation." *Id.* at 9.

The European Convention on Human Rights, Art. 3, states: "No one shall be subjected to torture or to inhuman or degrading treatment or punishment." BASIC DOCUMENTS, *supra* note 98, at 126.

The American Convention on Human Rights, Art. 5(2), provides: "No one shall be subjected to torture or to cruel, inhuman, or degrading punishment or treatment. All persons deprived of their liberty shall be treated with respect for the inherent dignity of the human person." *Id.* at 211.

213. Williams, *supra* note 178, at 61.

214. Lempert v. Bonfol, [1933–34] Ann. Dig. 290,292 (No. 115) (Federal Tribunal, Switzerland). *See* notes 241–42 *infra* and accompanying text.

215. Preuss, *supra* note 182, at 272.

216. *Id.* at 269–76.

debate has said that "deprivation of nationality involved deprivation of protection; with the implication that the individual affected might become a charge on other states."[217] Indeed, one commentator asked bluntly, "By what right [does one treat] a foreign state as a sort of sewer into which one is entitled to discharge his social detritus?"[218] The paramount policy of this modest restraint on the state's competence was clearly more state-centered than humanistic; it was, nevertheless, a widely accepted and useful restraint.

The policy of minimizing statelessness began to gain recognition after World War I, as the transnational impact of this unfortunate status became pronounced. Before that war stateless persons were relatively few and national frontiers were usually open. The collective denationalizations executed after that war by Russia, Turkey, Germany, Austria, and Italy, however, aroused widespread community concern about the plight of stateless persons.[219] The policy for the minimization of statelessness manifested itself in the common state practice of making loss of a woman's nationality upon marriage to a foreigner contingent upon acquisition of the husband's nationality.[220] In almost every international conference on nationality there have been condemnations of denationalization measures causing statelessness.[221]

In 1896, the Institute of International Law resolved that "No one can lose his nationality or renounce it unless he shows that he has fulfilled the conditions required to obtain his admission into another state. Denationalization can never be imposed as a penalty.[222] In the wake of the mass denationalization by the Soviet Union, the International Law Association in 1924 made a broader recommendation, seeking to prohibit denationalization by executive order and thus to protect individuals from being denationalized and expelled.[223] In 1928, the Institute of International Law strengthened its earlier recommendation by urging

217. [1953] 1 Y.B. Int'l L. Comm'n 196, U.N. Doc. A/CN.4/SER.A (1959).

218. Philonenko, *Expulsion des Heimatlos,* 60 Journal de Droit International 1161, 1177 (1933), *quoted in* Preuss, *supra* note 182, at 273.

219. *See* A Study of Statelessness, *supra* note 149, at 5–7, 34–38, 75–122, 142–45; Holborn, *The Legal Status of Political Refugees,* 1920–1938, 32 Am. J. Int'l L. 680 (1938).

220. *See* notes 66–70 and 151–55 *supra* and accompanying text.

221. Commentators are no less emphatic and unanimous in denouncing denationalization measures that disregard the potential consequences of statelessness. Williams stated emphatically that it was a violation of international law for a state to denationalize any person who had not already acquired a second nationality. Williams, *supra* note 178, at 52. *See also* E. Borchard, *supra* note 5, at 591–92; C. Fenwick, International Law 263 (3d ed. 1948); Abel, *supra* note 199, at 63; Preuss, *supra* note 182, at 274.

222. J. Scott, Resolutions of the Institute of International Law 135 (1916).

223. International Law Association, Report of the Thirty-Third Conference 32 (1925).

states to refrain from actions leading to statelessness.[224] Reacting to the denationalization measures of the Nazis, the Grotius Society proposed in 1942 that no loss of nationality should be imposed by a state unless and until the individual concerned acquired another nationality.[225] At the Hague Conference for the Codification of International Law in 1930, reduction and elimination of statelessness was a major concern. Aside from efforts to eliminate provisions imposing statelessness at birth,[226] the conference adopted provisions seeking to prevent loss of nationality in cases where the individual had not acquired another nationality. The Conference considered in this connection expatriation permits;[227] the effect of marriage upon nationality;[228] the effect of naturalization of the parents on the nationality of minor children;[229] the effect of legitimation, recognition, and adoption on nationality;[230] and readmission of former nationals.[231] The Final Act of the Conference proclaimed:

> The Conference is unanimously of the opinion that it is very desirable that States should, in the exercise of their power of regulating questions of nationality, make every effort to reduce as far as possible cases of statelessness, and that the League of Nations should continue the work which it has already undertaken for the purpose of arriving at an international settlement of this important matter.[232]

This profound concern for the minimization of statelessness has found further concrete expression in the human rights programs in general; in the work of refugee organizations (especially the United Nations High Commissioner for Refugees) in particular;[233] and, above all, in the adoption of the Convention on the Reduction of Statelessness,[234] the Convention Relating to the Status of Stateless Persons,[235] the

---

224. [1928] ANNUAIRE DE L'INSTITUT DE DROIT INTERNATIONAL PUBLIC 760.

225. 28 TR. GROTIUS SOC'Y 157 (1943).

226. *See* Protocol Relating to a Certain Case of Statelessness, *signed* Apr. 12, 1930, 179 L.N.T.S. 115.

227. *See* Convention on Certain Questions Relating to the Conflict of Nationality Laws, *signed* April 12, 1930, 179 L.N.T.S. 89, 101 (Art. 7).

228. *Id.* Arts. 8–11, at 101–03.

229. *Id.* Arts. 13–15, at 103.

230. *Id.* Arts. 16–17, at 105.

231. Special Protocol concerning Statelessness, League of Nations Publications Series 1930.V.6. (C.227.M.114.1930.V.).

232. Final Act of the Hague Conference, *supra* note 111, at 14.

233. *See* the literature concerning international protection of refugees cited in note 15 *supra*. *See also* Report of the United Nations High Commissioner for Refugees, 27 U.N. GAOR, Supp. (No. 12), U.N. Doc. A/8712 (1972).

234. *See* note 122 *supra*. *See also* UNITED NATIONS, MULTILATERAL TREATIES IN RESPECT

Convention Relating to the Status of Refugees,[236] and the Protocol Relating to the Status of Refugees.[237] The detailed impact of these various conventions will be appraised in our more general discussion of statelessness.[238]

It is, however, one thing to condemn a state for acts of denationalization causing statelessness, and quite another to assuage the actual and potential consequences upon the individuals affected. Indeed, "the presumption against statelessness" may in certain circumstances work against the protection of purportedly stateless persons.[239] "It will not help the individual," Ian Brownlie has observed, "to attribute a nationality which will be nominal and leave him *de facto* stateless."[240] Thus, in ascertaining the effect of a particular denationalization measure, decision makers have not infrequently sought to interpret and apply the

---

OF WHICH THE SECRETARY-GENERAL PERFORMS DEPOSITORY FUNCTIONS: LIST OF SIGNATURES, RATIFICATIONS, ACCESSIONS, ETC. 31 DECEMBER 1977, U.N. Doc. ST/LEG/SER.D/11 at 140 (1978) [hereinafter cited as MULTILATERAL TREATIES 1977].

235. The Convention was adopted by the United Nations Conference on the Status of Stateless Persons, held in New York in Sept. 1954, pursuant to ECOSOC Res. 526A (XVII) of Apr. 26, 1954. It has been in effect since June 6, 1960. U.N. HUMAN RIGHTS INSTRUMENTS, *supra* note 70, at 57. As of Dec. 31, 1977, thirty-three states had ratified or acceded to it. MULTILATERAL TREATIES 1977, *supra* note 234, at 132. For its text, *see* 360 U.N.T.S. 117; U.N. HUMAN RIGHTS INSTRUMENTS, *supra* note 70, at 57–63.

236. The Convention was adopted by the United Nations Conference of Plenipotentiaries on the Status of Refugees and Stateless Persons, convened under General Assembly Res. 429 (V) of Dec. 14, 1950, at Geneva in July 1951. It came into force on Apr. 22, 1954. U.N. HUMAN RIGHTS INSTRUMENTS, *supra* note 70, at 63. As of Dec. 31, 1977, sixty-nine states (including the Holy See) had ratified or acceded to the Convention. MULTILATERAL TREATIES 1977, *supra* note 234, at 119–20. For its text, *see* 189 U.N.T.S. 137; U.N. HUMAN RIGHTS INSTRUMENTS, *supra* note 70, at 63–70.

237. The draft Protocol was submitted by the United Nations High Commissioner for Refugees to the General Assembly, through the Economic and Social Council, upon the recommendation of the Executive Committee of the Programme of the United Nations High Commissioner for Refugees. The Economic and Social Council noted with approval the draft Protocol in its Res. 1186 (XLI) of Nov. 18, 1966. Later, the General Assembly, noting the draft Protocol in its Res. 2198 (XXI) of Dec. 16, 1966, requested the secretary-general "to transmit the text of the Protocol to the States mentioned in article V thereof, with a view to enabling them to accede to the Protocol." It became operative on Oct. 4, 1967. U.N. HUMAN RIGHTS INSTRUMENTS, *supra* note 70, at 70. For its text, *see* 606 U.N.T.S. 267; U.N. HUMAN RIGHTS INSTRUMENTS, *supra* note 70, at 70–72. As of Dec. 31, 1977, sixty-four states (including the Holy See) had ratified or acceded to the Protocol. MULTILATERAL TREATIES 1977, *supra* note 234, at 142–43. For its legislative history, *see* Weis, *The 1967 Protocol Relating to the Status of Refugees and Some Questions of the Law of Treaties,* 42 BRIT. Y.B. INT'L L. 39 (1969).

238. *See* notes 281–416 *infra* and accompanying text.

239. *See* Brownlie, *supra* note 1, at 337–38.

240. *Id.* at 338.

measure and relevant international law in such a manner as to afford individuals "genuine" protection. For example, in *Lempert* v. *Bonfol,*[241] decided by the Swiss Federal Court, the issue was whether the child of a Swiss mother and of a father who had lost his Russian nationality under the Soviet Decree of 1921 was to be deemed a Swiss national. Swiss law provided that the child of a stateless father and a Swiss mother is a Swiss national. The court decided that the child was a Swiss national. In the words of the court,

> It is not necessary to express any opinion as to whether the fundamental sovereign right of an individual State to prescribe, according to its own discretion, the conditions of acquisition and of loss of its nationality is in any way limited by considerations of international intercourse; nor as to how far there are to be gathered from international law precise and relevant principles which would permit of the designation of a provision of this nature as inadmissible. For even if this were the case here, this would, in view of the essential nature of international law, as an ordering between States, at the most constitute a breach of duties towards other States prejudiced by the decision in question. The idea of such a breach of duties is practically meaningless if the foreign State has no legal means of compelling the former home State to revoke the deprivation of citizenship and receive back the person affected. It will not alter the fact that he is stateless according to the law which is thus criticised, that is, that his former home State does not regard him as a citizen.[242]

Similarly, in *United States ex rel. Schwarzkopf* v. *Uhl,*[243] the United States Court of Appeals for the Second Circuit decided that an Austrian national residing in the United States when Germany annexed Austria in 1938 was not to be regarded as a German national and hence sustained his application for a writ of habeas corpus against his detention as an enemy alien. The court found good reason for allowing "former nationals, who have fled from the invader and established a residence abroad, the right of voluntarily electing a new nationality and remaining 'stateless' until they can acquire it."[244] It added that "an invader cannot under international law impose its nationality upon non-residents of the subjugated country without their consent, express or tacit."[245]

In this connection, the observation made by the Supreme Court of

---

241. [1933–1934] Ann. Dig. 290 (No. 115) (Federal Tribunal, Switzerland).
242. *Id.* at 293–94.
243. 137 F.2d 898 (2d Cir. 1943).
244. *Id.* at 902.
245. *Id.*

Israel in *Casperius* v. *Casperius*[246] is particularly telling. The issue was whether the testator was a German national or a stateless person. The will would be governed by German law in the former case and by Israeli law in the latter. The answer was closely linked to the German denationalization law of 1941.[247] In response to the contention that the court could not recognize that law because of its inherent evil, the court said that

> this idea, in itself, is sound; however, it is not competent to enable our testator to acquire the nationality of the Nazi State. This is not like any other legal question. Otherwise, we would reach the ridiculous conclusion that, precisely because of the barbarism of the Nazi laws, a man in Israel will have to be regarded as a citizen of that barbarian State. It goes without saying that all the Nazi racial laws stand condemned in our eyes, but we are not prepared to rely on that invalidity in order to recognize, so far as concerns a Jew, the legal nexus with that base régime. Our opinion, therefore, is that despite the unconcealed anti-semitic motives of that law, it was capable of snapping the legal tie between the State and the citizen.[248]

The mass denationalizations upon racial, ethnic, religious, and related grounds under the Nazi and fascist regimes were so shocking that they were widely condemned. While conceding that the state had the competence to denationalize individually, commentators had no difficulty in denouncing such a wholesale discriminatory denationalization as "an abuse of rights"[249] and "a violation of international law constituting international liability."[250] In the same vein, Hannah Arendt has observed, "One is almost tempted to measure the degree of totalitarian infection by the extent to which the concerned governments use their sovereign right of denationalization. . . ."[251] Recently, the German Federal Supreme Court in a number of cases has held the Nazi denationalization decree of 1941 "null and void *ab initio*" on the theory that, because of its arbitrariness and abusiveness, it was a "non-law" lacking "the quality of law."[252] It may have been *lex,* but it was not *jus.*"[253] In 1968, the Federal Constitu-

246. [1954] I.L.R. 197.

247. *See* notes 193–202 *supra* and accompanying text.

248. [1954] I.L.R. 197, 197–98.

249. *See, e.g.* H. Lauterpacht, The Function of Law in the International Community 300 (1933); 1 L. Oppenheim, International Law 280 (6th ed. 1940).

250. Abel, *supra* note 199, at 65.

251. H. Arendt, The Origins of Totalitarianism 278 (1958).

252. Mann, *The Present Validity of Nazi Nationality Laws,* 89 Law Q. Rev. 194, 199 (1973).

253. *Id.*

tional Court of Germany emphatically declared that the 1941 decree "violated fundamental principles. It is to so intolerable a degree irreconcilable with justice that it must be considered to have been null and void ex tunc."[254]

It was in large measure in revulsion against the Nazi and fascist atrocities that the contemporary concern for human rights found concrete expression in the Charter of the United Nations.[255] Building upon the Charter provisions regarding human rights, the world community has in recent decades moved toward greater protection of human rights, including protection against deprivations of nationality. Foremost among the developing human rights prescriptions is the cardinal principle of nondiscrimination. As Judge Tanaka observed in his dissenting opinion in *South West African* cases (Second Phase), 1966, "the norm of nondiscrimination . . . on the basis of race has become a rule of customary international law."[256]

It will suffice to spotlight some of the more pertinent provisions of international documents. The Charter of the United Nations declares that promotion and encouragement of "respect for human rights and for fundamental freedoms for all without distinction as to race, sex, language, or religion" is one of the major purposes of that organization,[257] a policy in evidence elsewhere in the Charter.[258] The first paragraph of Article 2 of the Universal Declaration of Human Rights declares: "Everyone is entitled to all the rights and freedoms set forth in this Declaration, without distinction of any kind, such as race, colour, sex, language, religion, political or other opinion, national or social origin, property, birth or other status."[259] Comparable provisions can be found in the International Covenant on Civil and Political Rights,[260] the International Covenant on Economic, Social, and Cultural Rights,[261] the European Convention on Human Rights,[262] and the American Conven-

---

254. *Id.* at 199–200.

255. *See* L. Goodrich, E. Hambro, & A. Simons, Charter of the United Nations: Commentary and Documents 34–35, 370–447 (3d rev. ed. 1969); R. Russell, A History of the United Nations Charter 303–29 (1958); E. Schwelb, Human Rights and the International Community 24–29 (1964); Sohn, *A Short History of United Nations Documents on Human Rights,* in Commission to Study the Organization of Peace, the United Nations and Human Rights: 18th Report of the Commission 39, 43–59 (1968).

256. [1966] I.C.J. 284.

257. U.N. Charter, Art. 1, para. 3.

258. *Id.,* Arts. 13(1)(b), 55, 56.

259. U.N. Human Rights Instruments, *supra* note 70, at 1.

260. Arts. 2(1), 4(1), 26, *id.* at 8, 9, 12.

261. Art. 2, para. 2, *id.* at 4.

262. Art. 14, Basic Documents, *supra* note 98, at 130.

tion on Human Rights.[263] Of special relevance in the present context are the International Convention on the Elimination of All Forms of Racial Discrimination,[264] the United Nations Declaration on the Elimination of All Forms of Racial Discrimination,[265] and the Genocide Convention.[266]

According to the Convention against Racial Discrimination, "States Parties undertake to prohibit and to eliminate racial discrimination in all its forms and to guarantee the right of everyone, without distinction as to race, colour, or national or ethnic origin, to equality before the law, notably in the enjoyment of [inter alia], the right to nationality."[267] Particular efforts shall be made," pursuant to the Declaration against Racial Discrimination, "to prevent discrimination based on race, colour or ethnic origin, especially in the fields of [inter alia], access to citizenship."[268] The policies both against racial discrimination and for the protection of national affiliation deeply infuse the Genocide Convention, which provides:

> In the present Convention, genocide means any of the following acts committed with intent to destroy, in whole or in part, a national, ethnical, racial or religious group, as such:
>
> . . .
>
> (b) Causing serious bodily or mental harm to members of the group;
>
> (c) Deliberately inflicting on the group conditions of life calculated to bring about its physical destruction in whole or in part. . . .[269]

Article 9 of the Convention on the Reduction of Statelessness is particu-

---

263. Arts. 1(1), 24, 27(1), *id.* at 210, 218, 219.

264. The Convention was adopted and opened for signature and ratification by the U.N. General Assembly in its Res. 2106 (XX) of Dec. 21, 1965. It has been in effect since Jan. 4, 1969. U.N. HUMAN RIGHTS INSTRUMENTS, *supra* note 70, at 23. For its text, *see* 660 U.N.T.S. 195; U.N. HUMAN RIGHTS INSTRUMENTS, *supra* note 70, at 23.

265. The Declaration was adopted by the U.N. General Assembly in its Res. 1904 (XVIII) of Nov. 20, 1963. U.N. HUMAN RIGHTS INSTRUMENTS, *supra* note 70, at 21.

266. The Convention on the Prevention and Punishment of the Crime of Genocide was adopted by the U.N. General Assembly in its Res. 260 (III) of Dec. 9, 1948. It has been in effect since Jan. 12, 1951, U.N. HUMAN RIGHTS INSTRUMENTS, *supra* note 70, at 39. For its text, *see* 78 U.N.T.S. 277; U.N. HUMAN RIGHTS INSTRUMENTS, *supra* note 70, at 39. *See* chapters 8 and 9 *supra.*

267. Art. 5(d)(iii), U.N. HUMAN RIGHTS INSTRUMENTS, *supra* note 70, at 24.

268. Art. 3, *id.* at 22.

269. *Id.* at 39. On the Genocide Convention, *see* N. ROBINSON, THE GENOCIDE CONVENTION (1960); Reismen, *Responses to Crimes of Discrimination and Genocide: An Appraisal of the Convention on the Elimination of Racial Discrimination*, 1 DENVER J. INT'L L. & POLICY 29 (1971).

larly direct: "A Contracting State may not deprive any person or group of persons of their nationality on racial, ethnic, religious or political grounds."[270] It thus appears incontrovertible that denationalization measures based on racial, ethnic, religious, or other related grounds are impermissible under contemporary international law.

Denationalization is equally impermissible as a form of punishment. It may be recalled that both the Universal Declaration of Human Rights and the American Convention on Human Rights contain specific proscription against "arbitrary" deprivation of nationality.[271] In addition, Article 5 of the Universal Declaration of Human Rights provides that "[n]o one shall be subjected to torture or to cruel, inhuman or degrading treatment or punishment."[272] Similar provisions are embodied in the principal human rights conventions, including the International Covenant on Civil and Political Rights,[273] the European Convention on Human Rights,[274] and the American Convention on Human Rights.[275] Deprivation of nationality as a measure of punishment may easily be seen as a form of "cruel, inhuman or degrading treatment or punishment."

The policy illuminated by Chief Justice Warren in *Trop* v. *Dulles*[276] in the context of United States constitutional law is becoming equally authoritative in the international domain. Within their legal systems, states have at their disposal a whole arsenal of criminal sanctions, including fines, imprisonment, and even death, to combat criminal conduct; there is no need for their resorting to denationalization for punishment as such.[277] In the contemporary world of nation-states, the right to nationality remains in essence "the right to have rights."[278] Denationalization as

---

270. U.N. Human Rights Instruments, *supra* note 70, at 55.
271. *See* notes 97–98 *supra* and accompanying text.
272. U.N. Human Rights Instruments, *supra* note 70, at 1.
273. Art. 7, *id.* at 9.
274. Art. 3, Basic Documents, *supra* note 98, at 126.
275. Art. 5(2), *id.* at 211.
276. 356 U.S. 86 (1958).
277. *See Note, supra* note 187, at 1179–80.
278. The words of Chief Justice Warren eloquently describe what we refer to:

> The punishment strips the citizen of his status in the national and international political community. His very existence is at the sufferance of the country in which he happens to find himself. While any one country may accord him some rights, and presumably as long as he remained in this country he would enjoy the limited rights of an alien, no country need do so because he is stateless. Furthermore, his enjoyment of even the limited rights of an alien might be subject to termination at any time by reason of deportation. In short, the expatriate has lost the right to have rights.
>
> This punishment is offensive to cardinal principles for which the Constitution stands. It subjects the individual to a fate of ever-increasing fear and distress. He knows not what discriminations may be established against him, what proscriptions may be directed against him, and when and for what cause his existence in his native

a form of punishment is neither necessary nor proportionate for the purpose of criminal sanction.

In his comprehensive commentary on the application of the European Convention on Human Rights, Fawcett defines "inhuman treatment" as "the deliberate infliction of physical or mental pain or suffering, against the will of the victim, and, when forming part of criminal punishment, out of proportion to the offence."[279] Viewed in this light, the interpretation that denationalization as a punishment constitutes a cruel, inhuman treatment or punishment will in all likelihood gain increasing recognition and acceptance. Through such an interpretation and development the unfortunate omission of an explicit provision against deprivation of nationality in the International Covenant on Civil and Political Rights and European Convention on Human Rights may, fortunately, be remedied.[280]

> land may be terminated. He may be subject to banishment, a fate universally decried by civilized people. He is stateless, a condition deplored in the international community of democracies. It is no answer to suggest that all the disastrous consequences of this fate may not be brought to bear on a stateless person. The threat makes the punishment obnoxious.

Trop v. Dulles, 356 U.S. 86, 102 (1958).

279. J. Fawcett, The Application of the European Convention on Human Rights 35 (1969).

Contemporary theories about the sanctioning process raise the question whether there are any acceptable community policies in terms of which "denationalization" might be "proportionate" as a punishment; *cf.* Dession, *Sanctions, Law, and Public Order,* 1 Vand. L. Rev. 8 (1947); Dession & Lasswell, *Public Order under Law: The Role of the Advisor-Draftsman in the Formation of Code or Constitution,* 65 Yale L.J. 174 (1955); *Comment, Professor George H. Dession's Final Draft of the Code of Correction for Puerto Rico,* 71 Yale L.J. 1050 (1962).

280. The denationalization and forcible exile on Feb. 13, 1974, of Alexander I. Solzhenitsyn by the Soviet Union have focused world attention anew upon the enormous human deprivations inherent in denationalization and exile. This action by the Soviet Union was apparently precipitated by the publication in Dec. 1973 in Paris of Solzhenitsyn's latest book, *The Gulag Archipelago, 1918–1956,* a comprehensive, historical exposé of the secret police, prison camp, and terror system in the Soviet Union. The official charge against Solzhenitsyn was that of "systematically performing actions incompatible with being a citizen," a charge apparently regarded as an equivalent of treason. *See* N.Y. Times, Feb. 14, 1974, at 1, col. 8 (city ed.); *id.,* Feb. 15, 1974, at 1, col. 5 (city ed.); Washington Post, Feb. 15, 1974, at A24, col. 5.

Some question has been raised about the conformity of the Soviet edict to Soviet law; *cf.* N.Y. Times, Feb. 14, 1974, at 16, col. 1 (city ed.); *id.,* Feb. 16, 1974, at 3, col. 1 (city ed.); The Economist, Feb. 16, 1974, at 18. It is clear nonetheless that the Soviet action is in direct contravention of the emerging general community expectations that denationalization and exile are impermissible as "cruel and unusual punishment." Both the detailed circumstances attending the denationalization and forcible exile of Solzhenitsyn and their longer-term consequences indicate this conclusion. *See* Time, Feb. 25, 1974, at 34–40; Christian Science Monitor, Feb. 14, 1974, at 1, col. 1, at 2, col. 1; *id.,* Feb. 15, 1974, at 1, col. 1. In confirmation of Solzhenitsyn's own subjectivities, one of his fictional characters de-

Claims Relating to Statelessness

The status of statelessness entails a most severe and dramatic deprivation of the power of an individual. Just as, within the state, nationality is the "right to have rights," so also, on the transnational level, nationality is the right to have protection in rights. The stateless person has no state to "protect" him and lacks even the freedom of movement to find a state that is willing to protect him. His participation in the value processes of any territorial community is highly restricted. As aptly stated in the preamble of one draft convention, statelessness:

> often results in suffering and hardship shocking to conscience and offensive to the dignity of man, . . .
>
> is frequently productive of friction between States, . . .
>
> is inconsistent with the existing principle which postulates nationality as a condition of the enjoyment by the individual of certain rights recognized by international law. . . .[281]

Most importantly, nationality is commonly regarded as essential for a state to protect an individual vis-à-vis other entities in the transnational arena. In the words of Oppenheim-Lauterpacht, "Since stateless individuals do not own a nationality, the principal link by which they could derive benefits from International Law is missing, and thus they lack protection as far as this Law is concerned."[282] Thus, a stateless person has been compared to "a *res nullius,*"[283] "flotsam,"[284] a vessel "on the open sea not sailing under the flag of a State,"[285] "a *caput lupinum,*"[286] "a

---

scribes exile as "spiritual castration." A. Solzhenitsyn, The First Circle 356 (T. Whitney trans. Bantam ed. 1969). The wave of protest about the world indicates that those subjectivities are not idiosyncratic, but widely shared. It can be added that the emerging human rights norm of nondiscrimination, described above, forbids discrimination not only on grounds of race, color, religion, and sex, but also on grounds of political opinion.

The principle that one state cannot by denationalization force an individual upon other states would, paradoxically, not appear to be available here to serve the cause of humanity. Too many other states have expressed willingness to accept so redoubtable an anti-Communist into their own communities. It may be recalled that in 1929 Trotsky suffered the same fate that has now befallen Solzhenitsyn, and the press abounds with rumors of further deprivations. *See, e.g.,* N.Y. Times, Nov. 18, 1973, § 1, at 12, col. 3; *id.,* Dec. 12, 1973, at 4, col. 4 (city ed.); *id.,* Feb. 14, 1974, at 16, col. 1 (city ed.); *id.,* Feb. 19, 1974, at 3, col. 1 (city ed.); Newsweek, Feb. 25, 1974, at 38.

281. Alternative Convention on the Elimination of Present Statelessness, in Cordova, *Third Report on the Elimination or Reduction of Statelessness,* [1954] 2 Y.B. Int'l L. Comm'n 26, 36, U.N. Doc. A/CN.4/81 (1954).

282. 1 Oppenheim-Lauterpacht, *supra* note 76, at 668.

283. G. Schwarzenberger, International Law 171 (2d ed. 1949).

284. Weis, *supra* note 122, at 1073.

285. 1 Oppenheim-Lauterpacht, *supra* note 76, at 668.

286. H. Lauterpacht, *supra* note 103, at 126.

bird that flies alone,"[287] and "an international vagabond."[288] The hardship visited upon a stateless person is dramatically evident in the *Dickson Car Wheel Company* case,[289] in which the Special Claims Commission between the United States and Mexico declared in 1931: "A State . . . does not commit an international delinquency in inflicting an injury upon an individual lacking nationality, and consequently no State is empowered to intervene or complain on his behalf either before or after injury."[290] In short, statelessness means "the loss of a community willing and able to guarantee any rights whatsoever."[291]

The powerlessness of the stateless person is most apparent in the limitation upon his freedom of movement, both of egress and of return. Because of widespread, rigorous requirements for travel documents (*e.g.*, a valid passport, an entry visa), a stateless person, lacking necessary documents, usually experiences great difficulty in locating a state willing to receive him. Unable to enter the territory of a state lawfully, he is often compelled to do so clandestinely. His illegal entry continues to haunt him. "He will then," as has been observed, "lead an illegal existence, avoiding all contact with the authorities and living under the constant threat of discovery and expulsion."[292] In his presidential address in 1801, Thomas Jefferson said that "[e]very man has a right to live somewhere on the earth";[293] a stateless person, however, has no such right.

Other deprivations are visited upon the stateless individual. He is denied general participation, such as voting and officeholding, in the internal power process of any body politic. He often cannot obtain documents certifying his personal status (*e.g.*, age, relationships), because no state is in a position to give that information. He may not be properly protected by the processes of authoritative decision and may be denied access to the courts of any state. He may be subject to taxation and military service in any state where he is found.

Stateless persons are also subjected to deprivations, sometimes in common with other aliens and sometimes more severely, in value processes other than power. The stateless individual may be discriminated against in every territorial community because of his alienage; he is not properly recognized as a person and is thus denied respect. His opportunities for education are more limited; so also are his opportunities to

---

287. The description from Aristotle is quoted in C. Seckler-Hudson, Statelessness: With Special Reference to the United States 244 (1934).

288. The description is by De Lapradelle and Niboyet, *quoted in id.* at 15.

289. [1931–32] Ann. Dig. 228 (No. 115).

290. *Id.* at 230 n.l.

291. H. Arendt, *supra* note 251, at 297.

292. A Study of Statelessness, *supra* note 149, at 20.

293. *Quoted in* C. Seckler-Hudson, *supra* note 287, at 248.

shape enlightenment through the mass media of communication. He is often denied the benefits of public health and other welfare programs. His right to property, to employment, and to engage in business enterprises may be curtailed; certain professions and occupations exclude nonnationals. In the exercise of professional skills a stateless person may be denied the opportunity for fullest expression. He may encounter a great deal of difficulty in marriage because he cannot obtain authentic documents certifying his status.[294]

The important causes of statelessness quite obviously derive from the formulation and application of the nationality laws of states in contravention of human rights. The traditional myth that the regulation of nationality is a matter within the domestic jurisdiction of states[295] and the resultant diversity of nationality laws have created many gaps in the conferment of nationality both at birth and subsequent to birth.

Statelessness at birth generally arises from the inadequacy and diversity of nationality laws, which usually employ both *jus soli* and *jus sanguinis,* but different versions of *jus sanguinis* and not always *jus soli.* The main features of this problem are apparent in a "synoptic chart of possible sources of statelessness" offered by a United Nations study:[296]

Statelessness at Birth

A. Children born abroad.	1. In *jus sanguinis* country of parents of strict *jus soli* country. 2. In *jus sanguinis* country from a second or third generation of parents nationals of a *jus sanguinis* country.
B. Child born in a *jus sanguinis* country with one parent stateless.	1. Legitimate (Stateless if father stateless). 2. Illegitimate (Stateless if mother stateless).

294. For descriptions of the plight of stateless persons, *see id.* at 11–22, 244–53; A STUDY OF STATELESSNESS, *supra* note 149, at 17–31; A. Mutharika, International Regulation of Statelessness, 1970, at 12–17 (unpublished J.S.D. dissertation, Yale Law School).

295. For a general survey of such views, *see* P. WEIS, *supra* note 1, at 65–94.

In the well-known Tunis-Morocco Nationality Decrees case, a more enlightened view was intimated. The court held that nationality could be made a matter of "international concern" by agreement: "The question whether a certain matter is or is not solely within the jurisdiction of a State is an essentially relative question; it depends upon the development of international relations. Thus, in the present state of international law, questions of nationality were, in the opinion of the Court, in principle within this reserved domain." [1923] P.C.I.J., Ser. B., No. 4, at 24.

296. Cordova, *Report on the Elimination or Reduction of Statelessness,* [1953] 2 Y.B. INT'L L. COMM'N 167, 195, U.N. Doc. A/CN.4/64 (1953).

C. Born in *jus sanguinis* country of stateless father and mother or without known nationality.
D. Born in *jus sanguinis* country of unknown parents.
E. Foundlings.
F. Born on ship or aircraft.
   1. In high seas.
   2. In territorial sea.
   3. In foreign port.
   4. In air above foreign territory.
G. Born from stateless parents with diplomatic immunity.

Statelessness subsequent to birth, simply put, arises in a case when a person loses his nationality or nationalities without acquiring another. Loss of nationality may be caused by: (1) explicit, voluntary expatriation;[297] (2) withdrawal of nationality by the state upon the "constructive" and often fictitious consent of the individual;[298] (3) deprivation of nationality as punishment;[299] and (4) territorial changes.[300] The United Nations study, cited above, again offers a chart both comprehensive and economic, though using a somewhat different classification from our own, in its indication of potential causes of statelessness after birth:[301]

Statelessness Subsequent to Birth

I. Inadequacy and conflict of national legislations.
   - A. Effect of marriage on the nationality of women.
     1. Effect of marriage itself.
     2. Husband's change of nationality.
     3. Dissolution of marriage:
        (*a*) Widow of national;
        (*b*) Invalid or fictitious marriage;
        (*c*) Divorce.
   - B. Legitimation of illegitimate child.
   - C. Adoption.
   - D. Voluntary Renunciation.

297. *See* notes 100–28 *supra* and accompanying text.
298. *See* notes 129–59 *supra* and accompanying text.
299. *See* notes 160–280 *supra* and accompanying text.
300. *Cf.* 1 D. O'Connell, State Succession in Municipal Law and International Law 497–528 (1967); P. Weis, *supra* note 1, at 139–64; Hudson, *supra* note 1, at 11.
301. Cordova, *supra* note 296, at 195.

E. Change of nationality of the spouse or of a parent.

F. Naturalization of the spouse or of a parent.

II. Deprivation of nationality

(*a*) As a penalty

- (*a*) Residence abroad of nationalized citizens.
- (*b*) Service in foreign government or armed forces.
- (*c*) Departure abroad.
- (*d*) Evasion of military duties by expatriation or otherwise.
- (*e*) Disloyal attitude or activities.
- (*f*) Aid to enemies.
- (*g*) Naturalization by fraud.
- (*h*) Penal offense of naturalized citizens.

(*b*) based on: racial, religious, political grounds — Only if the State of origin deprives of its nationality; otherwise there is not a *de jure* statelessness, but only *de facto.*

III. Inadequacy of treaties on territorial settlements.

MINIMIZATION OF STATELESSNESS

In a succession of efforts since World War I, the international community has sought both to eliminate or reduce statelessness and, by mitigating hardships, to improve the position and treatment of stateless persons. During the era of the League of Nations, the landmark action was the 1930 Hague Conference for the Codification of International Law, which adopted a Convention on Certain Questions Relating to the Conflict of Nationality Laws[302] and a Protocol Relating to a Certain Case of Statelessness.[303] Convention provisions relevant to statelessness dealt with a number of matters: expatriation permits,[304] the nationality of married women,[305] the nationality of children,[306] and adoption.[307] The Protocol was concerned with the avoidance of statelessness at birth

302. Signed Apr. 12, 1930, 179 L.N.T.S. 89.
303. Signed Apr. 12, 1930, 179 L.N.T.S. 115.
304. Art. 7, 179 L.N.T.S. 101.
305. Arts. 8–9, *id.* at 101–03.
306. Arts. 13, 16, *id.* at 103–05.
307. Art. 17, *id.*

under certain circumstances.[308] The profound sense of urgency for further work in the minimization of statelessness, though expressed in the Final Act of the Conference,[309] was not followed up by the League.

Efforts to minimize statelessness were renewed after the founding of the United Nations. In 1947, the Human Rights Commission of the United Nations urged consideration of nationality questions.[310] This proposal received concrete expression in Article 15 of the Universal Declaration of Human Rights of December 1948, which proclaims:

1. Everyone has the right to a nationality.
2. No one shall be arbitrarily deprived of his nationality nor denied the right to change his nationality.[311]

As a first step in clarifying this right, in 1949 the secretary-general, at the request of the Economic and Social Council, prepared a study on statelessness.[312] This study called for the universal acceptance of the following two principles: (1) nationality is to be conferred on every child at birth; (2) no person should lose his nationality during his lifetime unless and until he has acquired a new one.[313] In August 1950, the Economic and Social Council urged the International Law Commission to prepare at the earliest possible time the necessary draft international convention or conventions for the minimization of statelessness.[314]

From its inception in 1949, the International Law Commission included "nationality, including statelessness" in its list of topics to be considered for codification.[315] It dealt with this problem from the fourth to the sixth sessions (1952–54), appointing Professors Manley O. Hudson and Roberto Cordova, successively, as special rapporteurs on the subject.[316] The Commission decided to focus its attention on the problem of

---

308. Art. 1 of the Protocol provides:

> In a State whose nationality is not conferred by the mere fact of birth in its territory, a person born in its territory of a mother possessing the nationality of that State and of a father without nationality or of unknown nationality shall have the nationality of the said State.

179 L.N.T.S. 117.

309. Final Act of the Hague Conference, *supra* note 111, at 14.

310. 6 U.N. ECOSOC, Supp. (No. 1) 13–14, U.N. Doc. E/600 (1947).

311. U.N. HUMAN RIGHTS INSTRUMENTS, *supra* note 70, at 2. For a brief commentary on this article, *see* N. ROBINSON, THE UNIVERSAL DECLARATION OF HUMAN RIGHTS 123–24 (1958); *cf.* Griffin, *The Right of a Single Nationality,* 40 TEMPLE L.Q. 57 (1966).

312. A STUDY OF STATELESSNESS, *supra* note 149.

313. *Id.* at 170.

314. ECOSOC Res. 319B III, 11 U.N. ECOSOC, Supp. (No. 1) 52, U.N. Doc. E/1849 (1950).

315. *Report to the General Assembly,* [1949] Y.B. INT'L L. COMM'N 277, 280–81.

316. For the report submitted by Professor Hudson at the Fourth Session of the International Law Commission in 1952, *see* Hudson, *supra* note 1. For the reports submitted by

statelessness. On the basis of Professor Cordova's draft Conventions on the Elimination of Future Statelessness and on the Reduction of Future Statelessness[317] and his annual reports, the Commission adopted the texts of draft Conventions on the Elimination and Reduction of Future Statelessness.[318] Both drafts were transmitted to governments for comments and, in the light of these, the Commission redrafted some of the articles in 1954.[319] These two draft conventions were designed to facilitate acquisition of the nationality of a state by virtue of birth within its territory and to avoid the loss of nationality prior to acquisition of another. When the question of statelessness came before the Sixth (Legal) Committee of the General Assembly, some delegates voiced strong objections to the draft Conventions on the ground that they encroached upon the domestic jurisdiction of states in matters of nationality.[320] Nevertheless, at the recommendation of the Sixth Committee, the General Assembly decided in December 1954, to convene an international conference of plenipotentiaries to conclude a convention for the reduction or elimination of future statelessness as soon as at least twenty states had communicated to the secretary-general their willingness to join in such an undertaking.[321]

A sufficient number of states ultimately expressed such willingness, and the Conference was finally convened in Geneva during 1959. The Conference, with thirty-five states participating, adopted provisions designed to reduce statelessness at birth but failed to reach agreement upon how to limit the competence of states to deprive an individual of nationality.[322] The Conference was reconvened in 1961, with thirty states in attendance. A compromise was reached on the controversial provision regarding deprivation of nationality, and the other provisions that had failed adoption in the previous conference were also accepted. The Conference adopted a Convention on the Reduction of Statelessness, which was open for signature in 1962.[323] The Convention came into effect on December 13, 1975.[324]

Professor Cordova, *see* Cordova, *supra* note 296; Cordova, *Second Report on the Elimination or Reduction of Statelessness,* [1953] 2 Y.B. Int'l L. Comm'n 196, U.N. Doc. A/CN.4/75 (1953); Cordova, *supra* note 281; Cordova, *Report on Multiple Nationality,* [1954] 2 Y.B. Int'l L. Comm'n 42, U.N. Doc. A/CN.4/83 (1954).

317. Cordova, *supra* note 296; Cordova, *Second Report, supra* note 316.

318. *See Report of the International Law Commission Covering the Work of Its Fifth Session,* [1953] 2 Y.B. Int'l L. Comm'n 200, 220–30, U.N. Doc. A/2456 (1953).

319. *See Report of the International Law Commission Covering the Work of Its Sixth Session,* [1954] 2 Y.B. Int'l L. Comm'n 140, 141–48, U.N. Doc. A/2693 (1954).

320. [1954] Yearbook of the United Nations 418 [hereinafter cited as Y.B.U.N.].

321. G.A. Res. 896, 9 GAOR, Supp. (No. 21) 49–50, U.N. Doc. A/2890 (1954).

322. *See* [1959] Y.B.U.N. 413–14; Weis, *supra* note 122, at 1078–80.

323. *See* note 234, *supra.* For a commentary on the Convention, *see* Weis, *supra* note 122.

324. *See* note 122 *supra.*

The Commission on the Status of Women has played a significant role in the minimization of statelessness for married women. A principal source of statelessness is marriage of women to foreign nationals.[325] As a consequence of the persistent efforts of the Commission, the General Assembly adopted the Convention on the Nationality of Married Women in January 1957. The Convention has been in operation since August 11, 1958.[326] An earlier regional convention, the Montevideo Convention on the Nationality of Women signed on December 26, 1933, was, however, the first to prescribe the principle of equality of sexes regarding nationality.[327]

The foregoing efforts, viewed in sum, are far from inconsequential. They have been directed at the various causes of statelessness and have helped to crystallize expectations for the minimization of statelessness. We briefly discuss the main features of these proposed remedies by reference to each of the causes of statelessness.

Statelessness at Birth

The important policy for the elimination of statelessness at birth has been succinctly phrased by Manley Hudson in these words: "If no other nationality is acquired at birth, the individual should acquire the nationality of the State in whose territory he is born."[328] This policy has found authoritative expression in both general and specific formulations of various conventions. The Universal Declaration of Human Rights provides, as we have seen, most generally that "everyone has the right to a nationality."[329] The International Covenant on Civil and Political Rights, though lacking a nationality provision applicable to everyone, provides that "every child has the right to acquire a nationality."[330] More specifically, the American Convention on Human Rights states that "[e]very person has the right to the nationality of the state in whose territory he was born if he does not have the right to any other nationality."[331] These recent developments were of course preceded by certain historic efforts to eradicate statelessness, efforts which attempted to make *jus soli* and *jus sanguinis* supplement and reinforce each other.[332] A provision of critical importance of the 1930 Hague Convention on Nationality, Article 15, states:

---

325. *See* notes 151–55 *supra* and accompanying text.

326. *See* note 70 *supra.*

327. 6 M. Hudson, International Legislation 589 (1937); Laws Concerning Nationality, *supra* note 1, at 584. Art. 1 of the Convention reads: "There shall be no distinction based on sex as regards nationality, in their legislation or in their practice."

328. Hudson, *supra* note 1, at 20.

329. Art 15(1), U.N. Human Rights Instruments, *supra* note 70, at 2.

330. Art. 24(3), *id.* at 12.

331. Art. 20(2), Basic Documents, *supra* note 98, at 217.

332. *See* A Study on Statelessness, *supra* note 149, at 145–60.

> Where the nationality of a State is not acquired automatically by reason of birth on its territory, a child born on the territory of that State of parents having no nationality, or of unknown nationality, may obtain the nationality of the said State. The law of that State shall determine the conditions governing the acquisition of its nationality in such cases.[333]

According to Article 14, the nationality of the state of birth is to be conferred upon a child of unknown parents; once his parentage is established, his nationality will be governed by "the rules applicable in cases where the parentage is known."[334] A foundling is "presumed to have been born on the territory of the State in which it was found." Furthermore, the Protocol Relating to a Certain Case of Statelessness (1930) provides:

> In a State whose nationality is not conferred by the mere fact of birth in its territory, a person born in its territory of a mother possessing the nationality of that State and of a father without nationality or of unknown nationality shall have the nationality of the said State.[335]

Its main purpose was to ensure the conferment of nationality upon a legitimate child or a recognized illegitimate child whose father alone is stateless.

The 1961 Convention on the Reduction of Statelessness[336] deals with the question of statelessness at birth in Articles 1–4, reflecting "a compromise between *jus soli* and *jus sanguinis* States, not a compromise between the *jus soli* and *jus sanguinis* principles."[337] A contracting state is required to "grant its nationality to a person born in its territory who would otherwise be stateless."[338] However, a contracting state may attach conditions to the conferment of such nationality, including age, residence, and absence of criminal record.[339] A "child born in wedlock in the territory of a Contracting State, whose mother has the nationality of that State, shall acquire at birth that nationality if it otherwise would be stateless."[340] A foundling present in the territory of a contracting state is

---

333. 179 L.N.T.S. 89, 103.

334. *Id.*

335. 179 L.N.T.S. 117 (Art. 1).

336. U.N. Human Rights Instruments, *supra* note 70, at 53. *See also* note 234 *supra.*

337. U.N. Doc. A/CONF.9/C.1/SR.3, at 4 (1961) (remark of the Swiss delegate).

338. Art. 1(1), U.N. Human Rights Instruments, *supra* note 70, at 54.

339. Art 1(2), *id.*

340. Art. 1(3), *id.* A comparable provision is found in a Recommendation adopted by the Consultative Assembly of the Council of Europe:

> The Assembly . . .
>
> Recommends that the Committee of Ministers:
>
> 1. Invite the Member Governments concerned to take the necessary measures so that legitimate children born in their territory of a marriage between a stateless

presumed to have been born within that territory and of parents possessing the nationality of that state.[341] This is a reaffirmation of the similar principle contained in the Hague Convention[342] and the nationality laws of numerous states. Birth "on a ship or in an aircraft" will be regarded as having occurred "in the territory of the State whose flag the ship flies or in the territory of the State in which the aircraft is registered," irrespective of the location, within territorial space or otherwise, of the ship or the aircraft at the time of birth.[343] Subject to certain conditions, a contracting state must confer its nationality on a person, not born in its territory, who would otherwise be stateless, if at the time of his birth one of his parents possessed the nationality of that state.[344]

Statelessness Subsequent to Birth

The parallel policy with respect to statelessness subsequent to birth has been stated, with equal brevity, by Hudson: "Loss of nationality subsequent to birth shall be conditional on the acquisition of another nationality."[345] The movement toward this policy in general community perspectives is made explicit in prescriptions about the consequences of voluntary renunciation of nationality. Article 7 of the Hague Convention provides that an expatriation permit issued by a state "shall not entail loss of the nationality of the State which issues it, unless the person to whom it is issued possesses another nationality or unless and until he acquires another nationality." "An expatriation permit shall lapse if the holder does not acquire a new nationality" within the prescribed period, unless he "already possesses a nationality other than that of the State" issuing the permit.[346] Similarly, the Convention on the Reduction of Statelessness provides: "If the law of a Contracting State entails loss of [*sic*] renunciation of nationality, such renunciation shall not result in loss

---

father and a mother who is a national of their country automatically acquire by right the latter's nationality;

2. Suggest that these Governments draft the legal provisions which will be adopted on this matter in such a manner that the said children, if born in a territory other than that of the mother, do not acquire dual nationality nor become stateless;

3. Keep the Assembly informed of measures which may be taken to this end by the Governments concerned.

Consultative Assembly of the Council of Europe, Recommendation 194 of Apr. 23, 1959.

341. Art. 2, U.N. Human Rights Instruments, *supra* note 70, at 54.

342. The second paragraph of Art. 14 of the Hague Convention on Nationality reads: "A foundling is, until the contrary is proved, presumed to have been born on the territory of the State in which it was found." 179 L.N.T.S. 107.

343. Art. 3, U.N. Human Rights Instruments, *supra* note 70, at 54.

344. Art. 4, *id.*

345. Hudson, *supra* note 1, at 20.

346. 179 L.N.T.S. 89, 101.

of nationality unless the person concerned possesses or acquires another nationality."[347]

Of course, the otherwise commendable policy of minimizing statelessness, embodied in these provisions, might sometimes operate to tie an individual, against his will, to a political community with which he has lost all sense of identification and loyalty and from which he expects no genuine protection. For this reason the Convention on the Reduction of Statelessness provides that enforcement of the policy of preventing statelessness should not interfere with the freedom of movement, including ingress and egress, and with the right of asylum protected by the Universal Declaration of Human Rights.[348]

One intriguing question is whether an individual should be allowed to become stateless, if he so chooses, in defiance of the ordinarily benign policy of minimizing statelessness. In keeping with the overriding policy of honoring freedom of choice, there would appear no reason why an individual should not be allowed to render himself stateless, if the decision is freely made, with full appreciation of the resultant consequences.

Of more fundamental importance, however, for the realization of the policies of voluntary expatriation and minimization of statelessness, is the liberalization of states' requirements for conferring nationality subsequent to birth. This is an area for improvement, as neglected as it is important.

Although naturalization has long been perceived as the key to reduction of existing statelessness,[349] states are notoriously reluctant to undertake the necessary humanitarian measures. At the 1930 Hague Conference for the Codification of International Law, the subject was barely considered, not because it was regarded as unimportant but because it raised serious problems arising from conflicts of nationality laws.[350] Following the 1930 Hague Conference, international efforts were directed toward improving the status and treatment of refugees (de jure and de facto stateless persons) rather than toward enabling stateless persons to acquire some nationality.[351]

Community interest in improving naturalization laws was renewed in connection with the Universal Declaration of Human Rights of 1948. To give meaning to "the right to a nationality" proclaimed in the Universal

---

347. Art 7(1)(a), U.N. HUMAN RIGHTS INSTRUMENTS, *supra* note 70, at 55.

348. Art. 7(1)(b), *id.*

349. *See* notes 81–98 *supra* and accompanying text, A. Mutharika, *supra* note 294, at 92–100.

350. This is evidenced by the official title of the Convention on Nationality adopted at the Conference, i.e., Convention on Certain Questions Relating to the Conflict of Nationality Laws, 179 L.N.T.S. 89.

351. *See* notes 387–407 *infra* and accompanying text.

Declaration, both the secretary-general of the United Nations[352] and the Economic and Social Council[353] urged governments to facilitate acquisition of nationality by stateless persons through their respective naturalization procedures. Some states have shown reluctance to discuss reforms which they regard as related to present, as contrasted with future, statelessness on the ground that naturalization is too "political" a matter.[354] Thus, the International Law Commission had initially instructed its special rapporteur on "nationality, including statelessness," Roberto Cordova, to address himself only to future statelessness, not present statelessness. He soon discovered that it was impossible to focus on one to the exclusion of the other.[355] Although he persuaded the International Law Commission to let him proceed by giving equal attention to both aspects of the problem, his proposals for reducing statelessness through naturalization were given little attention and support.[356] As a consequence, the Convention on the Reduction of Statelessness, adopted in 1961,[357] is concerned primarily with the question of future statelessness. Its limited concern for the reduction of statelessness through naturalization is expressed in Article 4, according to which a contracting state may grant its nationality, upon application in compliance with certain prescribed conditions, to a person not born in its territory "who would otherwise be stateless, if the nationality of one of his parents at the time of the person's birth was that of that State."

In this connection, a significant step is taken by Article 32 of the Convention Relating to the Status of Stateless Persons of 1954, which provides: "The Contracting States shall as far as possible facilitate the assimilation and naturalization of stateless persons. They shall in particular make every effort to expedite naturalization proceedings and to reduce as far as possible the charges and costs of such proceedings."[358] A comparable provision is found in Article 34 of the Convention Relating

---

352. A STUDY OF STATELESSNESS, *supra* note 149, at 171.

353. In its Res. 319B III of Aug. 16, 1950, the Economic and Social Council invited "States to examine sympathetically applications for naturalization submitted by stateless persons habitually resident in their territory." 11 U.N. ECOSOC 3, Supp. (No. 1) 59, U.N. Doc. E/1849 (1950).

354. *See* Cordova, *supra* note 281, at 27–28.

355. These words "future" and "present" obviously have no reference to modalities by which people become stateless. Measures such as liberalizing naturalization laws, which states refuse to consider because they could be related to existing stateless persons, may of course be of the utmost importance for alleviating future statelessness arising from the whole range of modalities by which people are made stateless.

356. *Report of the International Law Commission Covering the Work of Its Sixth Session, supra* note 319, at 147.

357. U.N. HUMAN RIGHTS INSTRUMENTS, *supra* note 70, at 53.

358. 360 U.N.T.S. 117; U.N. HUMAN RIGHTS INSTRUMENTS, *supra* note 70, at 61.

to the Status of Refugees.[359] Since both Conventions are widely accepted and have been in operation for some time, it is possible that more states will undertake serious efforts in this direction.

The general policy of making loss of one nationality contingent upon acquisition of another applies to various situations in which withdrawal of nationality is based on the individual's real or constructive consent, that is, consent inferred from such acts as deliberate acquisition of the nationality of another state, taking of an oath of allegiance to another state, protracted residence abroad, marriage to an alien man, naturalization of parents by another government, legitimation, and adoption.[360]

Thus, the Convention on the Reduction of Statelessness provides that a national seeking "naturalization in a foreign country shall not lose his nationality unless he acquires or has been accorded assurance of acquiring the nationality of that foreign country."[361] With certain limited exceptions, a national shall not be made stateless because of "departure, residence abroad, failure to register or on any similar ground."[362] The stated exceptions are meant to be exclusive. Thus, Article 7(6) of the Convention states emphatically: "Except in the circumstances mentioned in this article, a person shall not lose the nationality of a Contracting State, if such loss would render him stateless, notwithstanding that such loss is not expressly prohibited by any other provision of this Convention."[363]

The effect of marriage on the nationality of women, as noted, has been a matter of continuing interest.[364] As a manifestation of the policy of minimizing statelessness, the trend has been away from the woman's automatic loss of her nationality upon marriage to an alien.[365] Thus, the Hague Convention makes the loss of nationality of a woman married to a foreign national, by virtue either of the marriage or of her husband's change of nationality during marriage, conditional on "her acquiring the nationality of the husband."[366] Similarly, under the Convention on the Reduction of Statelessness, the loss of a woman's nationality because of marriage or her husband's loss of nationality is "conditional upon [her] possession or acquisition of another nationality."[367]

---

359. 189 U.N.T.S. 137; U.N. Human Rights Instruments, *supra* note 70, at 63, 68.
360. *See* notes 129–59 *supra* and accompanying text.
361. Art. 7(2), U.N. Human Rights Instruments, *supra* note 70, at 55.
362. Art. 7(3), *id.*
363. Art. 7(6), *id.*
364. *See* notes 66–70 and 151–55 *supra* and accompanying text.
365. *See* notes 153–55 *supra* and accompanying text.
366. Art. 8, 179 L.N.T.S. 89, 101.
367. Art. 6, U.N. Human Rights Instruments, *supra* note 70, at 55.

These prescriptions, though protective, are less than adequate, especially from the perspective of equality of men and women. Thus, a critical focus in the ongoing worldwide movement for women's liberation has been equality of the sexes in the context of nationality; the principle of equality is perceived to be the fundamental, positive answer to the question of the statelessness of married women.[368] This policy first found concrete expression in the international arena in 1933, when the Montevideo Convention on the Nationality of Women declared that "no distinction" shall be "based on sex as regards nationality,"[369] and the Montevideo Convention on Nationality of the same date further provides that "neither matrimony nor its dissolution affects the nationality of the husband or wife."[370]

More recently, the policy has been crystallized by the adoption and application of the Convention on the Nationality of Married Women of 1957,[371] which proclaims that "neither the celebration nor the dissolution of a marriage between one of its nationals and an alien, nor the change of nationality by the husband during marriage, shall automatically affect the nationality of the wife"[372] and that "neither the voluntary acquisition of the nationality of another State nor the renunciation of its nationality by one of its nationals shall prevent the retention of its nationality by the wife of such national."[373] The United Nations Declaration on Elimination of Discrimination against Women of 1967[374] reaffirms this policy in these words: "Women shall have the same rights as men to acquire, change or retain their nationality. Marriage to an alien shall not automatically affect the nationality of the wife either by rendering her stateless or by forcing upon her the nationality of her husband."[375]

The naturalization of parents, as mentioned above, ordinarily extends its effect to minor children.[376] "In cases where minor children do not acquire the nationality of their parents as the result of the naturalization

368. *See, e.g.*, NATIONALITY OF MARRIED WOMEN, *supra* note 66, at 6–7, 14–18.

369. 49 Stat. 2957, 2960; T.S. No. 875 (effective Aug. 29, 1934).

370. Art. 6, NATIONALITY OF MARRIED WOMEN, *supra* note 66, at 24.

371. 309 U.N.T.S. 65; U.N. HUMAN RIGHTS INSTRUMENTS, *supra* note 70, at 52.

372. Art. 1, U.N. HUMAN RIGHTS INSTRUMENTS, *supra* note 70, at 52.

373. Art. 2, *id.*

374. The Declaration, prepared by the Commission on the Status of Women and the Third Committee of the General Assembly, was adopted unanimously by the United Nations General Assembly on Nov. 7, 1967. G.A. Res. 2263, 22 GAOR, Supp. (No. 16) 35, U.N. Doc. A/6716 (1967). For the text *see* BASIC DOCUMENTS ON HUMAN RIGHTS 183 (I. Brownlie ed. 1971).

375. BASIC DOCUMENTS ON HUMAN RIGHTS, *supra* note 374, at 183, 185.

376. *See* notes 71–72 and 156–59 *supra* and accompanying text.

of the latter," the Hague Convention provides, "they shall retain their existing nationality."[377] A similar protection is offered by the Hague Convention in connection with legitimation of an illegitimate child and with adoption.[378] Moving beyond these provisions, the Convention on Reduction of Statelessness has formulated an all-inclusive protection clause, seeking to embrace all cases of change of personal status and to remove change of status as a cause of statelessness. Article 5(1) of the Convention states:

> If the law of a Contracting State entails loss of nationality as a consequence of any change in the personal status of a person such as marriage, termination of marriage, legitimation, recognition or adoption, such loss shall be conditional upon possession or acquisition of another nationality.[379]

The growing general community condemnation of discriminatory and punitive denationalizations[380] would appear to be establishing a comparable policy of minimizing statelessness in connection with such denationalizations. Article 8(1) of the Convention on the Reduction of Statelessness broadly pronounces that a "Contracting State shall not deprive a person of its nationality if such deprivation would render him stateless."[381] From this broad policy, unfortunately, some derogations—for acts "prejudicial to the vital interests of the State"—are permitted.[382] In light of the interpretations presently being given to the community prohibition of "cruel and inhuman punishment and treatment,"[383] these derogations could come to be regarded as impermissible.

Acquiring states have historically mitigated statelessness arising from territorial changes by conferring their nationality upon the inhabitants of the transferred territory or by giving such inhabitants the option of retaining their original nationality or accepting that of the acquiring state.[384] Some protection from statelessness in this context is now specifically afforded by Article 10 of the Convention on the Reduction of Statelessness:

> 1. Every treaty between Contracting States providing for the transfer of territory shall include provisions designed to secure that

377. Art. 13, 179 L.N.T.S. 89, 103.
378. Arts. 16–17, *id.* at 105.
379. U.N. HUMAN RIGHTS ISTRUMENTS, *supra* note 70, at 55.
380. *See* notes 160–280 *supra* and accompanying text.
381. U.N. HUMAN RIGHTS INSTRUMENTS, *supra* note 70, at 55.
382. Art. 8(3), *id.*
383. *See* notes 271–80 *supra* and accompanying text.
384. *See* A STUDY ON STATELESSNESS, *supra* note 149, at 150–53; Hudson, *supra* note 1, at 19.

no person shall become stateless as a result of the transfer. A Contracting State shall use its best endeavours to secure that any such treaty made by it with a State which is not a party to this Convention includes such provisions.

2. In the absence of such provisions the Contracting State to which territory is transferred or which otherwise acquires territory shall confer its nationality on such persons as would otherwise become stateless as a result of the transfer or acquisition.[385]

A policy of utmost voluntarism would of course afford the inhabitants the right of option as well. Unfortunately, such a proposal, though submitted by the International Law Commission, was not incorporated into the Convention.[386]

MITIGATIONS OF STATELESSNESS

Turning from efforts to avoid or reduce statelessness to those designed to mitigate or improve the treatment of stateless persons, we call attention to the fact that this subject is commonly considered in conjunction with the treatment of refugees.[387] Viewed strictly from the perspective of legal technicality, the concept of statelessness (having no nationality) and the concept of being a refugee (fleeing one's country in fear) are different.[388] Just as stateless persons may or may not be refugees, so refugees may or may not be stateless persons. In terms of lack of governmental protection, refugees who nominally have a nationality may, however, be in no better position than stateless persons. Those refugees who legally have a nationality but in fact do not enjoy the protection of the government of their country of nationality are usually called de facto stateless refugees, to distinguish them from de jure stateless refugees.[389] The majority of today's refugees are de facto rather than de jure stateless. Such refugees and stateless persons thus share one fate—they are "unprotected persons."[390] This close, though not entirely identical, relationship between stateless persons and refugees is vividly illustrated by the substantially identical provisions of two parallel conventions: the

385. U.N. Human Rights Instruments, *supra* note 70, at 56.

386. Weis, *supra* note 122, at 1084.

387. *See, e.g.,* Weis, *The Convention Relating to the Status of Stateless Persons,* 10 Int'l & Comp. L.Q. 255 (1961); A Study of Statelessness, *supra* note 149; authorities cited in note 15 *supra.*

388. *See* 1 A. Grahl-Madsen, The Status of Refugees in International Law 73–78 (1966); A Study of Statelessness, *supra* note 149, at 9–10; Van Heuven Goldhart, *The Problem of Refugees,* 82 Hague Recueil des Cours 265, 267–71 (1953).

389. A Study of Statelessness, *supra* note 149, at 8–9.

390. P. Weis, *supra* note 1, at 168.

Convention Relating to the Status of Stateless Persons[391] and the Convention Relating to the Status of Refugees.[392]

The first contemporary international effort to protect and assist stateless persons and refugees commenced in 1921 when the League of Nations created the Office of High Commissioner for Russian Refugees, responding to the critical needs of those refugees rendered stateless, as may be recalled, by the mass denationalization measures undertaken in Russia in the wake of the revolution.[393] This was followed by the conclusion of the Convention Relating to the International Status of Refugees[394] in 1933 and the establishment of the Office of the League of Nations High Commissioner for Refugees in 1938.[395] Since World War II, the need to protect and assist stateless persons and refugees has grown.[396] Under the auspices of the United Nations, the Office of the United Nations High Commissioner for Refugees (UNHCR) was created in 1950.[397] Shortly thereafter, the Convention Relating to the Status of Refugees of July 28, 1951, and the Convention Relating to the Status of Stateless Persons of September 24, 1954, successively came into existence. The scope of the 1951 Refugees Convention was greatly expanded by the adoption of the Protocol Relating to the Status of Refugees in 1967.[398]

The Convention Relating to the Status of Stateless Persons, together with the Convention Relating to the Status of Refugees (frequently called the Magna Carta of Refugees), appear to afford comprehensive protection for stateless persons and refugees. The need for a separate

---

391. 360 U.N.T.S. 117; U.N. HUMAN RIGHTS INSTRUMENTS, *supra* note 70, at 57.

392. 189 U.N.T.S. 137; U.N. HUMAN RIGHTS INSTRUMENTS, *supra* note 70, at 63.

393. *See* notes 178–81 *supra* and accompanying text.

394. Signed at Geneva on Oct. 28, 1933, the Convention defined the legal status of those refugees covered by the Convention, i.e., Russian, Armenian, and assimilated refugees. 159 L.N.T.S. 199, 201.

395. For this and subsequent developments, *see* Van Heuven Goldhart, *supra* note 388, at 271–75.

396. *See generally* L. HOLBORN, *supra* note 15; J. VERANANT, *supra* note 15.

397. The Statute of the Office of the United Nations High Commissioner for Refugees was adopted by the U.N. General Assembly in its Res. 428 (V) of Dec. 14, 1950. U.N. HUMAN RIGHTS INSTRUMENTS, *supra* note 70, at 72. For the work of the United Nations High Commissioner for Refugees, *see* A MANDATE TO PROTECT AND ASSIST REFUGEES, *supra* note 15; Report of the United Nations High Commissioner for Refugees, *supra* note 233; Weis, *The Office of the United Nations High Commissioner for Refugees and Human Rights,* 1 HUMAN RIGHTS J. 243 (1968).

398. 606 U.N.T.S. 267; U.N. HUMAN RIGHTS INSTRUMENTS, *supra* note 70, at 70. *See* note 237 *supra.* The purpose of the Protocol is to expand international protection for refugees by removing the temporal and geographical restrictions inherent in Art. 1 of the 1951 Convention Relating to the Status of Refugees. The substantive provisions (Art. 2–34 inclusive) of the 1951 Convention are made part of the Protocol in Art. 1(1).

Convention Relating to the Status of Stateless Persons was dictated by the consideration, in the words of its preamble, that "only those stateless persons who are also refugees are covered by the Convention Relating to the Status of Refugees of 28 July 1951, and that there are many stateless persons who are not covered by that Convention."[399] A major difference between the two conventions relates to the role of UNHCR: While Article 35 of the Refugees Convention explicitly entrusts to the Office of the High Commissioner the task of coordinating with the contracting states and supervising the application of the Convention,[400] there is no comparable provision in the other Convention. Otherwise, in terms of substantive protection and actual wording, the Convention Relating to the Status of Stateless Persons is essentially patterned after the Convention Relating to the Status of Refugees. Hence, an examination of treatment of stateless persons also reveals the treatment being accorded to refugees.

Under the Convention Relating to the Status of Stateless Persons, the treatment afforded for stateless persons is divided in convention terms into five broad and overlapping categories:

1. General protection: undelimited provisions for protection without specifying "national treatment," "alien treatment" and so on;[401]
2. National treatment: "treatment at least as favorable as that accorded to their nationals";[402]
3. Favorable alien treatment: "treatment as favorable as possible,

399. 360 U.N.T.S. 117, 130; U.N. Human Rights Instruments, *supra* note 70, at 57.

400. Art. 35 of the Refugee Convention reads:

> 1. The Contracting States undertake to co-operate with the Office of the United Nations High Commissioner for Refugees, or any other agency of the United Nations which may succeed it, in the exercise of its functions, and shall in particular facilitate its duty of supervising the application of the provisions of this Convention.
>
> 2. In order to enable the Office of the High Commissioner or any other agency of the United Nations which may succeed it, to make reports to the competent organs of the United Nations, the Contracting States undertake to provide them in the appropriate form with information and statistical data requested concerning:
>
> (a) The condition of refugees,
>
> (b) The implementation of this Convention, and
>
> (c) Laws, regulations and decrees which are, or may hereafter be, in force relating to refugees.

U.N. Human Rights Instruments, *supra* note 70, at 68.

401. Arts. 3, 5, 12, 16(1), 25, 27, 28, 30, 31, and 32, *id.* at 58–61.

402. Arts. 4, 14, 16(2), 20, 22(1), 23, and 24, *id.* at 58–60.

and in any event, not less favorable than that accorded to aliens generally in the same circumstances";[403]

4. Treatment accorded to nationals of the country of habitual residence: "the treatment granted to a national of the country of his habitual residence,"[404] "the same protection as is accorded to nationals" of the country of "habitual residence";[405]
5. Alien treatment: "the same treatment as is accorded to aliens generally,"[406] "subject to regulations applicable to aliens generally in the same circumstances."[407]

The following chart may indicate the kind and scope of treatment specified in different value processes:

Category of Treatment

Value Category	*1. General Protection*	*2. National Treatment*	*3. Favorable Alien Treatment*	*4. Treatment Accorded to Nationals of the Country of Habitual Residence*	*5. Alien Treatment*
Power	rights granted apart from the Convention (Art. 5)				general provision (Art. 7[1]) freedom of movement (Art. 26)
	access to courts (Art. 16 [1]) administrative assistance (Art. 25) identity papers (Art. 27) travel documents (Art. 28) nonexpulsion (Art. 31) naturalization (Art. 32)	access to courts (Art. 16[2])		access to courts (Art. 16[3])	
Respect	nondiscrimination (Art. 3)		right of nonpolitical association (Art. 15)		

403. Arts. 13, 15, 17, 18, 19, 21, and 22(2), *id.* at 59–60.
404. Art. 16(3), *id.* at 59.
405. Art. 14, *id.*
406. Art. 7(1), *id.* at 58.
407. Art. 26, *id.* at 61.

Enlightenment		elementary education (Art. 22[1])	nonelementary education (Art. 22[2])	
Well-Being		rationing (Art. 20)	housing (Art. 21)	
Wealth	transfer of assets (Art. 30)		movable and immovable property (Art. 13)	
		artistic rights and industrial property (Art. 14)		artistic rights and industrial property (Art. 14)
		public relief (Art. 23)	wage-earning employment (Art. 17)	
		labor legislation and social security (Art. 24)	self-employment (Art. 18)	
Skill			liberal professions (Art. 19)	
Affection	personal status (Art. 12)			
Rectitude		religion (Art. 4)		

This chart demonstrates that stateless persons are accorded substantial protection even in power processes.[408] Of special importance are provisions for access to courts,[409] administrative assistance,[410] identity pa-

---

408. *But see* A. Mutharika, *supra* note 294, at 159–61.

409. Art. 16 of the Convention Relating to the Status of Stateless Persons reads:

1. A stateless person shall have free access to the Courts of Law on the territory of all Contracting States.
2. A stateless person shall enjoy in the Contracting State in which he has his habitual residence the same treatment as a national in matters pertaining to access to the Courts, including legal assistance and exemption from *cautio judicatum solvi*.
3. A stateless person shall be accorded in the matters referred to in paragraph 2 in countries other than that in which he has his habitual residence the treatment granted to a national of the country of his habitual residence.

U.N. Human Rights Instruments, *supra* note 70, at 59.

410. Art. 25 of the Convention states:

1. When the exercise of a right by a stateless person would normally require the assistance of authorities of a foreign country to whom he cannot have recourse, the Contracting State in whose territory he is residing shall arrange that such assistance be afforded to him by their own authorities.
2. The authority or authorities mentioned in paragraph 1 shall deliver or cause to be delivered under their supervision to stateless persons such documents or certifica-

pers,[411] travel documents,[412] and nonexpulsion.[413] If, however, they were given full participation in the power process—with all the attendant rights and responsibilities in voting and officeholding—they would in effect be full-fledged nationals. Hence, naturalization would appear, as emphasized above and by this Convention,[414] to remain an important remedy for powerlessness.

---

tions as would normally be delivered to aliens by or through their national authorities.

3. Documents or certifications so delivered shall stand in the stead of the official instruments delivered to aliens by or through their national authorities and shall be given credence in the absence of proof to the contrary.
4. Subject to such exceptional treatments as may be granted to indigent persons, fees may be charged for the services mentioned herein, but such fees shall be moderate and commensurate with those charged to nationals for similar services.
5. The provisions of this article shall be without prejudice to articles 27 and 28.

Id. at 60–61.

411. Art. 27 of the Convention reads: "The Contracting States shall issue identity papers to any stateless person in their territory who does not possess a valid travel document." *Id.* at 61.

412. Art. 28 of the Convention provides:

> The Contracting States shall issue to stateless persons lawfully staying in their territory travel documents for the purpose of travel outside their territory, unless compelling reasons of national security or public order otherwise require, and the provisions of the Schedule to this Convention shall apply with respect to such documents. The Contracting States may issue such a travel document to any other stateless person in their territory; they shall in particular give sympathetic consideration to the issue of such a travel document to stateless persons in their territory who are unable to obtain a travel document from the country of their lawful residence.

Id.

413. Art. 31 of the Convention reads:

1. The Contracting States shall not expel a stateless person lawfully in their territory save on grounds of national security or public order.
2. The expulsion of such a stateless person shall be only in pursuance of a decision reached in accordance with due process of law. Except where compelling reasons of national security otherwise require, the stateless person shall be allowed to submit evidence to clear himself, and to appeal to and be represented for the purpose before competent authority or a person or persons specially designated by the competent authority.
3. The Contracting States shall allow such a stateless person a reasonable period within which to seek legal admission into another country. The Contracting States reserve the right to apply during that period such internal measures as they may deem necessary.

Id. In this regard, the Convention Relating to the Status of Refugees affords more comprehensive protection in its Art. 31 (refugees unlawfully in the country of refuge), Art. 32 (expulsion), and Art. 33 (prohibition of expulsion or return ["refoulement"]). *Id.* at 68.

414. Art. 32 of the Convention provides: "The Contracting States shall as far as possible facilitate the assimilation and naturalization of stateless persons. They shall in particular

All of these protections uniquely tailored for stateless persons do not preclude them from claiming the benefit of other prescriptions for protecting the rights of all human beings.[415] What is most needed for the protection of stateless and other human beings is wider acceptance and application of all of the many prescriptions already designed for such protection.[416]

Claims Relating to Multiple Nationality

The principal thrust of inherited international law relating to multiple nationality has been toward the protection of state interests rather than the protection of individual human rights. Multiple nationality differs from statelessness in that it may confer some benefits upon individuals. Thus it may provide multiple protectors in the external arena[417] or afford physical access to more than one country, with opportunities to participate in the internal value processes of all such countries.

Such benefits may, however, be accompanied, and even outweighed, by severe burdens and responsibilities. Thus, a person of multiple nationality may, like a stateless person, be deprived of all protectors in the external arena. Traditional doctrine holds that one state of nationality cannot protect an individual against another state of his nationality.[418] If the party imposing deprivations happens to be a state of his nationality, the individual having multiple nationality may never get a hearing on the merits of his claim.

A multiple national may in fact be exposed to deprivations inimical to human rights throughout all the different value processes.[419] He may be

---

make every effort to expedite naturalization proceedings and to reduce as far as possible the charges and costs of such proceedings." *Id.* at 61.

415. For compilations of human rights prescriptions, *see* U.N. Human Rights Instruments, *supra* note 70; Basic Documents on Human Rights, *supra* note 374.

416. It is especially important that wider acceptance be accorded to the Convention on the Reduction of Statelessness so that it can command wide application. As of Dec. 31, 1977, the following nine states had ratified or acceded to the Convention: Australia, Austria, Costa Rica, Denmark, Federal Republic of Germany, Ireland, Norway, Sweden, and the United Kingdom. Multilateral Treaties, 1977, *supra* note 234, at 140.

417. Vis-à-vis a third state, a person having multiple nationality enjoys multiple protectors: "But against third States each of them appears as his [dual national's] sovereign, and it is therefore possible that each of them can exercise its right of protection over him within third States." 1 Oppenheim-Lauterpacht, *supra* note 76, at 666.

418. *See* notes 433–34 *infra* and accompanying text.

419. As declared in Inouye Kanao v. The King,

> if a person possesses dual nationality . . . it does not mean that he owes any the less allegiance to this country than a person who is only a British subject. Dual nationality is not half one nationality and half another but two complete nationalities so far as our law is concerned. . . .

[1947] Ann. Dig. 103, 106 (No. 39) (Appellate Jurisdiction, Hong Kong).

subjected to the civil and criminal jurisdiction, which follows a national wherever he goes, of two or more states; he may be subject to the laws relating to treason,[420] enemy status, military service and security clearance of more than one state. More than one state may have jurisdiction to tax him, to expropriate his property, to impose restrictions on his trading activities, and to restrict disposition of his property. More than one state may discriminate against him; he may be discriminated against on different grounds in different communities. He may be subjected to physical and psychological insecurity in more than one state. He may be subjected to compulsory education in more than one state. More than one state may seek to impose restrictions on his practice of certain professions. More than one state may assert jurisdiction with respect to his family life, including marriage and children's upbringing, education, and welfare. Finally, more than one state may seek to restrict his religious affiliations and activities.

The causes of multiple nationality, as of statelessness, are to be found in the wide diversity of state laws about the conferment and withdrawal of nationality. "The most frequent case of double nationality at birth," observed Hudson, "is caused by the application of *jus soli* and *jus sanguinis* to the same individual: a person born in a country which has the *jus soli*, of parents who have the nationality of a country which employs *jus sanguinis*, becomes a double national or *sujet mixte*."[421] The same result may follow when states employ varying combinations of *jus soli* and *jus sanguinis*. Multiple nationality will also occur when an individual acquires subsequent to birth another nationality—by virtue of application, certain events (*e.g.*, marriage, naturalization of parents, legitimation, adoption), or territorial changes—without losing his original nationality.[422]

International efforts to regulate multiple nationality have, again as with statelessness, been twofold: to minimize the occurrence of multiple

---

420. As Bar-Yaacov puts it, "The legal status of an individual who happens to possess the nationalities of two belligerent States carries with it serious disadvantages. If both States require of such an individual the fulfilment of the duties of allegiance, he is likely to commit the criminal offence of treason with regard to one of them." He "may be compelled to fight against one of the belligerents; or may voluntarily adopt the cause of one country and commit acts which are treasonable as regards the other country; or he may assist one of the parties without committing acts amounting to treason against the other party." N. BAR-YAACOV, DUAL NATIONALITY 54, 57 (1961). *See also* Orfield, *The Legal Effects of Dual Nationality,* 17 GEO. WASH. L. REV. 427, 429 (1949); Vilkov, *The Settlement of Problems of Dual Nationality under International Law,* 1959 SOVIET Y.B. INT'L L. 371 (1960).

421. Hudson, *supra* note 1, at 10.

422. *See Survey of the Problem of Multiple Nationality Prepared by the Secretariat,* [1954] 2 Y.B. INT'L L. COMM'N 52, 64–85, U.N. DOC. A/CN.4/84 (1954); N. BAR-YAACOV, *supra* note 420, at 437–42.

nationality and to ameliorate the deprivations imposed upon people of multiple nationality. The Inter-American Convention on the Status of Naturalized Citizens concluded at Rio de Janeiro in 1906 dealt with naturalized persons returning to the state of their original nationality.[423] Under the terms of the Convention, a naturalized person taking up "residence in his native country without the intention of returning to the country in which he has been naturalized . . . will be considered as having reassumed his original citizenship, and as having renounced the citizenship acquired by the said naturalization."[424] Unless proved to the contrary, further, "the intention not to return will be presumed to exist when the naturalized person shall have resided in his native country for more than two years."[425] In their respective peace treaties with the Allied Powers after World War I, Germany, Austria, and Hungary undertook to recognize any new nationality acquired by their nationals pursuant to the laws of the Allied and Associated Powers, regarding "such persons as having in consequence of the acquisition of such new nationality, in all respects severed their allegiance to their country of origin."[426]

Responding to the urgent problems of multiple nationality (and also statelessness) in the aftermath of World War I, the Hague Conference for the Codification of International Law of 1930 still represents the most important effort to deal with the problem of multiple nationality. Theoretically, multiple nationality at birth could be eliminated by an outright, universal adoption of a single principle for conferment. Such a potentially promising approach, however, was obviously unacceptable to various governments, for, in the words of the Dutch delegation,

> it would be easier to obtain unanimity for a rule which admitted situations in which an individual had no nationality or two nationalities and regulated the resulting conflicts, than to establish a formula which would result in restricting to some extent the State's power of legislation.[427]

Attention was, hence, centered merely on minimizing the number of cases of multiple nationality.

---

423. *See* R. Flournoy & M. Hudson, *supra* note 1, at 645.

424. *Id.*, Art. 1.

425. *Id.*, Art. 2.

426. Treaty of Versailles, June 28, 1919, Art. 278, 2 MAJOR PEACE TREATIES OF MODERN HISTORY, 1648–1967, at 1265, 1433 (F. Israel ed. 1967); Treaty of St. Germain, September 10, 1919, Art. 230, 3 *id.* at 1535, 1647; Treaty of Trianon, June 4, 1920, Art. 213, 3 *id.* at 1863, 1971.

427. LEAGUE OF NATIONS, CONFERENCE FOR THE CODIFICATION OF INTERNATIONAL LAW: BASES OF DISCUSSION, League of Nations Publication Series 1929.V.1 (C.73. M.38. 1929.V.), at 11 [hereinafter cited as BASES OF DISCUSSION].

Though the desire for the minimization of "dual" nationality was unanimously expressed in the Final Act of the Conference,[428] solutions to the question of multiple nationality, as finally adopted, were limited in scope. Article 6 of the Hague Convention states:

> Without prejudice to the liberty of a State to accord wider rights to renounce its nationality, a person possessing two nationalities acquired without any voluntary act on his part may renounce one of them with the authorisation of the State whose nationality he desires to surrender.
>
> The authorisation may not be refused in the case of a person who has his habitual and principal residence abroad, if the conditions laid down in the law of the State whose nationality he desires to surrender are satisfied.[429]

A special provision was made with respect to children born to persons enjoying diplomatic immunities.[430]

The proposal that a person having multiple nationality at birth be afforded a right of option failed to gain support.[431] Instead the Conference recommended in its Final Act that "States should adopt legislation designed to facilitate, in the case of persons possessing two or more nationalities at birth, the renunciation of the nationality of the countries in which they are not resident, without subjecting such renunciation to unnecessary conditions. . ." and that "States should apply the principle that the acquisition of a foreign nationality through naturalisation involves the loss of the previous nationality."[432]

Recently, the Council of Europe adopted the Convention of Reduction of Cases of Multiple Nationality and Military Obligations in Cases of Multiple Nationality.[433] Article 1 of this Convention reads, in part:

---

428. Final Act of the Hague Conference, *supra* note 111, at 14.

429. 179 L.N.T.S. 89, 101.

430. Art. 12 reads:

> Rules of law which confer nationality by reason of birth on the territory of a State shall not apply automatically to children born to persons enjoying diplomatic immunities in the country where the birth occurs.
>
> The law of each State shall permit children of consuls *de carriere,* or of officials of foreign States charged with official missions by their Governments, to become divested, by repudiation or otherwise, of the nationality of the State in which they were born, in any case in which on birth they acquired dual nationality, provided that they retain the nationality of their parents.

Id. at 103.

431. The delegation of Finland proposed to "make it the *duty*" of the possessor of double nationality "to opt for one or other of the nationalities." BASES OF DISCUSSION, *supra* note 427, at 83.

432. Final Act of the Hague Conference, *supra* note 111, at 14.

433. Europ. T.S. No. 43 (1963).

1. Nationals of the Contracting Parties who are of full age and who acquire of their own free will, by means of naturalisation, option or recovery, the nationality of another Party shall lose their former nationality. They shall not be authorised to retain their former nationality.
2. Nationals of the Contracting Parties who are minors and acquire by the same means the nationality of another Party shall also lose their former nationality if, where their national law provides for the loss of nationality in such cases, they have been duly empowered or represented. They shall not be authorised to retain their former nationality.[434]

A person having "the nationality of two or more Contracting Parties may renounce one or more of these nationalities, with the consent of the Contracting Party whose nationality he desires to renounce."[435] To restrain the contracting state from arbitrarily withholding such consent, the Convention further provides:

> Such consent may not be withheld by the Contracting Party whose nationality a person of full age possesses *ipso jure,* provided that the said person has, for the past ten years, had his ordinary residence outside the territory of that Party and also provided that he has his ordinary residence in the territory of the Party whose nationality he intends to retain.

---

434. *Id.* at 2. The remainder of this article reads as follows:

> 3. Minor children, other than those who are or have been married, shall likewise lose their former nationality in the event of the acquisition *ipso jure* of the nationality of another Contracting Party upon and by reason of the naturalisation or the exercise of an option or the recovery of nationality by their father and mother. Where only one parent loses his former nationality, the law of that Contracting Party whose nationality the minor possessed shall determine from which of his parents he shall derive his nationality. In the latter case, the said law may make the loss of his nationality subject to the prior consent of the other parent or the guardian of his acquiring the new nationality.
>
> However, without prejudice to the provisions of the law of each of the Contracting Parties concerning the recovery of nationality, the Party of which the minor referred to in the foregoing paragraph possessed the nationality may lay down special conditions on which they may recover that nationality of their own free will after attaining their majority.
>
> 4. In so far as concerns the loss of nationality as provided for in the present Article, the age of majority and minority and the conditions of capacity and representation shall be determined by the law of the Contracting Party whose nationality the person concerned possesses.

Id. at 2–3.

435. Art 2(1), *id.* at 3.

> Consent may likewise not be withheld by the Contracting Party in the case of minors who fulfil the conditions stipulated in the preceding paragraph, provided that their national law allows them to give up their nationality by means of a simple declaration and provided also that they have been duly empowered or represented.[436]

In addition to such multilateral treaties,[437] a number of bilateral treaties have been concluded to minimize double nationality. Of special importance are a series of treaties, generally known as Bancroft treaties, concluded in 1868 and shortly thereafter between the United States and some of the European countries.[438] These treaties either stipulate which of the nationalities possessed is to prevail as between the contracting states or seek to facilitate revision of pertinent nationality laws to avoid instances of double nationality.

In the late 1950s the Soviet Union concluded a series of bilateral treaties with its fraternal states regarding the matter of double nationality.[439] According to these treaties, persons possessing the nationality of both contracting states and residing in the territory of one of them may opt for the single nationality of the other by filing a declaration to that effect with the latter state's embassy within one year from the effective date of the respective treaty. The declaration of option is subject to scrutiny by the competent officials to whom it has been communicated. The contracting states pledge to inform each other of the applications accepted, and, in some instances, rejected. Persons failing to exercise their right of option are regarded solely as nationals of the state of residence.[440]

The demand for further effort to solve the problem of multiple nationality, as expressed at the Hague Conference, has thus far elicited little effective response. In connection with its work on "nationality including statelessness," the International Law Commission paid only scant attention to the matter of multiple nationality.[441] In 1954, after a

---

436. Art. 2(2), *id.*

437. *See Survey of the Problem of Multiple Nationality Prepared by the Secretariat, supra* note 422, at 90–94.

438. *Id.* at 91–92. *See* note 108 *supra.*

439. *See* Sipkov, *Settlement of Dual Nationality in European Communist Countries,* 56 AM. J. INT'L L. 1010 (1962).

440. *See* treaties concluded by the Soviet Union with, respectively, Yugoslavia, May 22, 1956, 259 U.N.T.S. 155; Hungary, Aug. 24, 1957, 318 U.N.T.S. 35; Roumania, Sept. 4, 1957, 318 U.N.T.S. 89; Albania, Sept. 18, 1957, 307 U.N.T.S. 251; Czechoslovakia, Oct. 5, 1957, 320 U.N.T.S. 111; Bulgaria, Dec. 12, 1957, 302 U.N.T.S. 3; the Democratic Republic of Korea, Dec. 16, 1957, 292 U.N.T.S. 107; Poland, Jan. 21, 1958, 319 U.N.T.S. 277; and Mongolia, Aug. 25, 1958, 322 U.N.T.S. 201.

441. The Commission's special rapporteur had submitted a report, *Report on Multiple*

general debate in which divergent views were aired, the Commission decided to defer further consideration of the topic, due partly to the lack of a sense of urgency and partly to the reluctance of governments to undertake effective measures of solution.[442]

The need for amelioration of the plight of individuals having multiple nationality is well illustrated by the decisions that deny such individuals protection by one state of their nationality against the acts of another state of their nationality. This restrictive doctrine was formulated in Article 4 of the 1930 Hague Convention on Nationality in these words: "A State may not afford diplomatic protection to one of its nationals against a State whose nationality such person also possesses."[443] The International Court of Justice, in the *Reparation for Injuries* case, refers to this article as embodying an "ordinary practice whereby a State does not exercise protection on behalf of one of its nationals against a State which regards him as its own national. . . ."[444]

When an individual claimant is alleged to be a national of both the claimant state and the respondent state, an international tribunal would ordinarily decline jurisdiction pursuant to Article 4 of the Hague Convention.[445] Recently, however, this restrictive doctrine has to a considerable degree been qualified, for the benefit of individuals, by the principle of effective (i.e., active, dominant) nationality. That is to say, if the claimant state is found to be the state of the individual's effective nationality, the claim will not be dismissed for lack of jurisdiction. On the other hand, if the respondent state is found to be the state of his effective nationality, the claim will be dismissed and Article 4 applied in its pristine severity.

The substantive content of "effective nationality" is intimated in Article 5 of the Hague Convention on Nationality in its specification of the criterion to be applied by a third state in a case of dual nationality. The article reads:

> Within a third State, a person having more than one nationality shall be treated as if he had only one. Without prejudice to the application of its law in matters of personal status and of any conventions in force, a third State shall, of the nationalities which any such person possesses, recognise exclusively in its territory either the nationality

Nationality, supra note 316, and the U.N. Secretariat a memorandum, *Survey of the Problem of Multiple Nationality Prepared by the Secretariat, supra* note 422.

442. *Report of the International Law Commission Covering the Work of Its Sixth Session, supra* note 319, at 148–49.

443. Art. 4, 179 L.N.T.S. 89, 101.

444. Advisory Opinion on Reparation for Injuries Suffered in the Service of the United Nations, [1949] I.C.J. 173, 186.

445. 179 L.N.T.S. 89, 101.

> of the country in which he is habitually and principally resident, or the nationality of the country with which in the circumstances he appears to be in fact most closely connected.[446]

Considerably more detail is offered in the unfortunate *Nottebohm* case,[447] in which, though multiple nationality was not involved, the International Court of Justice attempted to build upon the analogy of dual nationality and formulated the concept of effective nationality in words which bear repetition:

> International arbitrators have decided in the same way numerous cases of dual nationality, where the question arose with regard to the exercise of protection. They have given their preference to the real and effective nationality, that which accorded with the facts, that based on stronger factual ties between the person concerned and one of the States whose nationality is involved. Different factors are taken into consideration, and their importance will vary from one case to the next: the habitual residence of the individual concerned is an important factor, but there are other factors such as the centre of his interests, his family ties, his participation in public life, attachment shown by him for a given country and inculcated in his children. . . .[448]

The most beneficent employment, from the perspective of human rights, of the concept of "effective nationality" has been in according an individual of multiple nationality a protector against deprivations by a state of his nationality. When the claimant state is proved to be the state of the claimant's effective nationality, this concept has been successfully invoked against another state of the claimant's nationality, thereby overcoming the nonprotective restriction inherent in Article 4 of the Hague Convention on Nationality and facilitating a hearing on merits of claims asserted by a multiple national claimant.

In the well-known *Apostolidis* v. *The Turkish Government,*[449] Turkey

446. *Id.*

447. Nottebohm Case, [1955] I.C.J. 4.

448. *Id.* at 22. In regard to territory and resources, the doctrine of historical use has been well established. It would appear that a comparable doctrine could be developed to serve the acquisition of nationality. Individuals should be able to acquire nationality by effective participation in the social process. When individuals have lived in a territory for a long period of time, they become effective members of that particular community. They may in effect be more active community members, in the sense of participation in value processes, than many nominal nationals of that community.

449. Franco-Turkish Mixed Arbitral Tribunal, 1928, 8 RECUEIL DES DECISIONS DES TRIBUNAUX ARBITRAUX MIXTES 373 (1929), *translated and abbreviated in* H. BRIGGS, *supra* note 10, at 513.

challenged the jurisdiction of the Franco-Turkish Mixed Arbitral Tribunal on the ground that all the claimants had retained Turkish nationality under Turkish law, which denied the validity of the foreign naturalization of Turkish nationals without Turkish authorization. The claimants had been naturalized as French nationals in 1912. The Tribunal rejected the Turkish contention, noting that

> all *other* judicial authorities, including the Mixed Arbitral Tribunal,—which, as regards public international law, is not bound by the municipal legislation of one of the contracting States—are bound to recognize the validity of the change of nationality and to recognize the claimants as French nationals.[450]

This judgment has been properly construed to mean that "the Tribunal simply disregarded the Turkish nationality for the purposes of the claim, thus attributing to the French nationality of the claimant a predominant character in order to establish jurisdiction."[451]

In the case of *Barthez de Monfort* v. *Treuhander Hauptverwaltung*[452] before the Franco-German Mixed Tribunal, the claimant possessed both French and German nationality, the latter of which she acquired through the naturalization of her husband in Germany; she had never abandoned her domicile in France. It was held that "the principle of active nationality, i.e., the determination of nationality by a combination of elements of fact and of law, must be followed by an international tribunal, and that the claimant was accordingly a French national and was entitled to judgment accordingly."[453]

In the *Georges Pinson* case,[454] decided by the French-Mexican Mixed Claims Commission in 1928, France asserted a claim on behalf of an individual alleged to be a French national *jure sanguinis* and a Mexican national *jure soli.* The individual had ties to both countries and the laws of both countries had been construed to confer nationality. In response to the Mexican contention, based on Article 4 of the Hague Convention on Nationality, the Commission held that

> even if the case were recognised as one of double nationality from the strictly legal point of view, it would be very doubtful if the claimant could not have invoked the Convention notwithstanding, owing to the fact that the Mexican government itself had always considered him, officially and exclusively, as a French subject.[455]

450. *Id.* at 514.
451. N. Bar-Yaacov, *supra* note 420, at 215.
452. [1925–26] Ann. Dig. 279 (No. 206).
453. *Id.*
454. 5 U.N.R.I.A.A. 327; [1927–28] Ann. Dig. 299 (No. 195).
455. [1927–28] Ann. Dig. 299, 300 (No. 195).

The concept of effective nationality is, unhappily, sometimes employed to deny the individual a protector on the merits when the defendant state is found to be the state of stronger ties. Thus, the *Canevaro* case,[456] brought in 1912 by Italy against Peru before the Permanent Court of Arbitration and often cited as a leading case defining the concept of effective nationality,[457] involved three brothers, two of whom were Italian nationals; the third, Rafael Canevaro, possessed Peruvian nationality *jure soli* and Italian nationality *jure sanguinis.* In response to the Peruvian contention that Rafael Canevaro could not be considered an Italian claimant, the tribunal noted that he had on several occasions acted as a Peruvian citizen: He ran as a candidate for the Senate (the membership of which was open only to Peruvian citizens) and, more importantly, he accepted the office of Consul General to the Netherlands, upon the authorization of both the Peruvian government and the Peruvian Congress. Hence, the tribunal concluded, "whatever Rafael Canevaro's status as a national may be in Italy, the Government of Peru has a right to consider him a Peruvian citizen and to deny his status as an Italian claimant."[458]

In the *Alexander Tellech* claim before the Tripartite (United States-Austro-Hungarian) Claims Commission in 1928,[459] the claimant, a United States national *jure soli* and an Austrian national *jure sanguinis,* had resided in Austria for nearly thirty years since age five, when his parents moved to live in Austria. After being interned "as an agitator engaged in propaganda in favor of Russia," he was drafted into military service by the Austrian government.[460] The Commission dismissed the United States claim for compensation on Tellech's behalf on the ground that he was a national of Austria as well as of the United States and that he had voluntarily taken "the risk incident to residing in Austrian territory and subjecting himself to the duties and obligations of an Austrian citizen arising under the municipal laws of Austria."[461]

In the *Merge* case,[462] the claimant possessed the nationality both of the claimant state, the United States, and of the respondent state, Italy. In its opinion, the Italian-United States Conciliation Commission noted the possibility of finding effective nationality in the claimant state in unequivocal terms:

---

456. 1 Hague Court Reports (Scott) 284 (Perm. Ct. Arb. 1912); 11 U.N.R.I.A.A. 397; H. Briggs, *supra* note 10, at 512.

457. *See, e.g.,* P. Weis, *supra* note 1, at 173.

458. H. Briggs, *supra* note 10, at 512.

459. 6 U.N.R.I.A.A. 248.

460. *Id.* at 249.

461. *Id.*

462. Merge Claim, [1955] I.L.R. 443 (Italian-United States Conciliation Commission 1955); 14 U.N.R.I.A.A. 236.

> The principle, based on the sovereign equality of States, which excludes diplomatic protection in the case of dual nationality, must yield before the principle of effective nationality whenever such nationality is that of the claiming State. But it must not yield when such predominance is not proved, because the first of these two principles is generally recognized and may constitute a criterion of practical application for the elimination of any possible uncertainty.[463]

After detailed examination of the facts, however, the Commission found that the claimant's family "did not have its habitual residence in the United States and the interests and the permanent professional life of the head of the family were not established there."[464] Hence, it concluded that the claimant "can in no way be considered to be dominantly a United States national."[465]

The most dramatic deprivation for a person of multiple nationality relates to the burdens of military service. Intense demands for military service have appeared to be the principal source of frictions between states in their competing claims to control individuals having multiple nationality. Hence, a paramount concern at the 1930 Hague Conference was to alleviate the burdens of "multiple" military service for people of multiple nationality and thus to help lessen frictions among states. This profound concern found concrete expression in the Protocol Relating to Military Obligations in Certain Cases of Double Nationality adopted at the Conference.[466] According to the Protocol, a person having multiple nationality "who habitually resides in one of the countries whose nationality he possesses, and who is in fact most closely connected with that country, shall be exempt from all military obligations in the other country or countries."[467] If such a person has the right, under the law of any of these states, "on attaining his majority, to renounce or decline the nationality of that State, he shall be exempt from military service in such State during his minority."[468] If he has lost one nationality and acquired another, he "shall be exempt from military obligations in the State of which he has lost the nationality."[469]

Elaborate provisions regarding military obligations are found in the European Convention on Reduction of Cases of Multiple Nationality and Military Obligations in Cases of Multiple Nationality.[470] "Persons

463. [1955] I.L.R. 443, 455.
464. *Id.* at 456.
465. *Id.* at 457.
466. The Protocol was signed at the Hague on Apr. 12, 1930. 178 L.N.T.S. 227.
467. Art. 1, *id.* at 229.
468. Art. 2, *id.* at 231.
469. Art. 3, *id.*
470. Europ. T.S. No. 43 (1963).

possessing the nationality of two or more Contracting Parties shall be required to fulfill their military obligations in relation to one of those Parties only," under special arrangements to be made between any of the contracting states.[471]

With the exception of military obligations, there is little, in terms of amelioration of value deprivations for people of multiple nationality, comparable in scope to the treatment accorded to stateless persons. Treaties are sometimes concluded to eliminate or reduce double taxation.[472] Mention may also be made of Article 3 of the European Convention on Reduction of Cases of Multiple Nationality, which states: "The Contracting Party whose nationality a person desires to renounce shall not require the payment of any special tax or charge in the event of such renunciation."[473]

---

471. *Id.* at 4. Pursuant to Art. 6, in the absence of a special agreement, the following provisions are applicable to a person possessing the nationality of two or more Contracting Parties:

1. Any such person shall be subject to military obligations in relation to the Party in whose territory he is ordinarily resident. Nevertheless, he shall be free to choose, up to the age of 19 years, to submit himself to military obligations as a volunteer in relation to any other Party of which he is also a national for a total and effective period at least equal to that of the active military service required by the former Party.
2. A person who is ordinarily resident in the territory of a Contracting Party of which he is not a national or in that of a State which is not a Party may choose to perform his military service in the territory of any Contracting Party of which he is a national.
3. A person who, in accordance with the rules laid down in paragraphs 1 and 2, shall fulfil his military obligations in relation to one Party, as prescribed by the law of that Party, shall be deemed to have fulfilled his military obligations in relation to any other Party or Parties of which he is also a national.
4. A person who, before the entry into force of this Convention between the Parties of which he is a national, has, in relation to one of those Parties, fulfilled his military obligations in accordance with the law of that Party, shall be deemed to have fulfilled the same obligations in relation to any other Party or Parties of which he is also a national.
5. A person who, in conformity with paragraph 1, has performed his active military service in relation to one of the Contracting Parties of which he is a national, and subsequently transfers his ordinary residence to the territory of the other Party of which he is a national, shall be liable to military service in the reserve only in relation to the latter Party.
6. The application of this Article shall not prejudice, in any respect, the nationality of the persons concerned.
7. In the event of mobilisation by any Party, the obligations arising under this Article shall not be binding upon that Party.

Id.

472. *See* S. Greenleigh & R. Margenau, *supra* note 1, at 412–14.

473. Europ. T.S. No. 43, at 3 (1963).

From this brief survey it can be seen that the efforts of states both to minimize the occurrence of multiple nationality and to provide ameliorations for the burdens it imposes are far from adequate. The individual is still not given full opportunity to choose between retention of multiple nationality or renunciation of nationalities which may impose burdens upon him incompatible with human rights. Multilateral conventions might be devised which would afford individuals more freedom of choice in the retention of benefits and in the renunciation of burdens, when such renunciation is not inimical to an appropriate community responsibility. Certainly the traditional doctrine that one state cannot protect an individual against another state of his nationality should be abandoned. It can only serve to deny human rights and to exaggerate state interests at the expense of the individual. The appropriate amelioration of burdens with respect to other values must of course depend upon many variables in the context in which such values are pursued.

APPRAISAL AND RECOMMENDATIONS

The fundamental problem with which we have been concerned is that of how the individual secures access to arenas of authoritative decision external to his own state for the vindication of his basic, substantive rights. Ancillary problems relate to the humanity with which the laws of nationality are shaped for affecting this access to protection and for determining which state may subject the individual to the community burdens of military service, taxation, expropriation, and criminal and civil jurisdiction. The basic, substantive rights which the individual may seek to vindicate are now importantly clarified and articulated in all the emerging human rights prescriptions. The myth, however, is still far too prevalent that the individual is not an appropriate subject of international law for the protection of these rights[474] and must have a special protector in the form of a state of nationality. It is through "nationality" only that the individual acquires much of what access he has to transnational processes of authoritative decision. Hence, it remains important to appraise trends in the degree to which the laws of nationality do afford the individual the necessary protection and other human rights and to consider alternatives for improvement in the protection of all rights.

---

474. For a general survey of views about the role of the individual in international law, *see* P. JESSUP, *supra* note 74, at 15–26; H. LAUTERPACHT, *supra* note 126, at 3–72; C. NORGAARD, THE POSITION OF THE INDIVIDUAL IN INTERNATIONAL LAW (1966); L. SOHN & T. BUERGENTHAL, INTERNATIONAL PROTECTION OF HUMAN RIGHTS 1–21 (1973); J. Jefferies, The Individual and International Law, 1954 (unpublished J.S.D. dissertation, Yale Law School); Amon, *The Individual in International Law,* 13 FAR EASTERN L. REV. 185 (1966); Manner, *The Object Theory of the Individual in International Law,* 46 AM. J. INT'L L. 428 (1952); Tucker, *Has the Individual Become the Subject of International Law?* 34 U. CIN. L. REV. 341 (1965).

Some modest movement toward human rights may be observed, as our summaries indicate, in the laws concerning conferment and withdrawal of nationality. In terms of conferment of nationality, there has been a widening use of both *jus soli* and *jus sanguinis* to ensure that an individual is born with at least one nationality. There has been some obvious loosening of rigorous requirements, at least for certain categories of people, for facilitating acquisition of nationality subsequent to birth. The imposition of nationality upon individuals without their consent is commonly regarded as contrary to international law. The right to change nationality, notably the right of voluntary expatriation, has been increasingly recognized in general community expectation as a fundamental human right. In regard to withdrawal of nationality based on imputed consent, decision makers appear increasingly to require a genuine consent or a close relation to important policies in the maintenance of harmonious relations between states. There is a growing expectation, further, that denationalization as a punishment, having no necessary relation to the maintenance of harmonious relations between states, is cruel and inhumane and, hence, unlawful. In particular, there appears to be an emerging peremptory norm of nondiscrimination which would outlaw denationalization upon racial or ethnic grounds. Many prescriptions have been enunciated both to minimize the occurrence of statelessness and to ameliorate the treatment accorded to stateless persons.[475] More limited progress has been made in measures to minimize the occurrence of multiple nationality and to lessen the burdens imposed upon people possessing multiple nationality.

The flow of state decisions about nationality and the regime of international regulation continue, however, to disregard important human rights criteria, particularly with respect to affording the individual real choice. Nationality is conferred on a person at birth by *jus soli, jus sanguinis,* or both; nationality is, further, sometimes thrust upon him subsequent to birth without his consent. States are not required to confer nationality upon any set of specified grounds, and the requirements and procedures even for accepted grounds are often arbitrary. All too often the individual is allowed to change nationality only with the consent of the state from which he seeks to escape. Conversely, the individual may still have his nationality arbitrarily taken from him. The withdrawal of nationality may be based on largely fictitious consent and may have little

475. We are aware that the mere enunciation of prescriptions may not serve to protect the human rights of people, but we do regard such enunciation as an indispensable first step toward protection. When policies are clarified and predispositions toward conformity mobilized, the potentialities for enforcement are increased. In evidence we would submit the general community experience with the Universal Declaration of Human Rights.

relation to maintaining harmonious relations between states. Deprivation of nationality is still used as a form of punishment for political or other reasons. Insufficient effort has been made to rectify the diversities in state laws that have the consequence of rendering many stateless; individuals may thus still find themselves without a nationality and unable to obtain one. Finally, the international law of multiple nationality remains largely designed to protect state, and not individual, interests; many individuals continue to find themselves subject to multiple burdens, but without protection against a most important category of deprivers, states of their nationality.[476]

The first and most fundamental recommendation we would make is that individuals be authorized to protect themselves. The substantive human rights prescriptions can never be made effective if the individual human being is not himself accorded competence to invoke them under appropriate conditions. The individual should be made a full subject of international law, with that access to all arenas, both international and national, which is necessary for him to protect himself.

Given continued state priority and domination, a second recommendation is that much greater effect be given, in the laws permitted by international law for the conferment or withdrawal of nationality, to the free choice of the individual in associating himself with a state. A most important move in this direction would be to accord the individual,

---

476. Our review of the doctrines and procedures connected with the traditional notion of nationality has spotlighted yet another sector of the vast corpus of international law that won acceptance in a historical setting where the dominant task was to find workable ways of resolving occasions for friction among members of the largely European world state system. The established myth was understood to impose no obligation on a state to act for the protection or assistance of nationals who advanced a claim on another state. By abstaining from intervention in these circumstances a state was in a position to avoid a potentially irritating confrontation with other states. At the same time, if the target state was politically weak and isolated, and especially if it sought to apply non-European prescriptions to its internal affairs, a European state could champion the claims of its nationals with great vigor, and with minimum risk of loss.

The world situation has changed and will continue to change in ways that affect the flow of transactions among states. In many parts of the globe the number of individuals whose value indulgences and deprivations are affected by transnational activities has greatly multiplied. These new participants in world community process are sensitive to the failures of their own state, or of other states, to act on behalf of the integrity of the growing system of involvement. In recent years a body of demand and expectation has steadily intensified on behalf of doctrines and procedures that might fill the conspicuous gaps that were left in the prevailing order. These new perspectives identify much more extensively than before with the rights of individual human beings. This carries with it a series of changes that are at present in full course of evolution, and to which we seek to contribute both by redefining the conceptions and operations referred to by the rubric of nationality and by suggesting new institutional practices and procedures.

contrary to the holding in the *Nottebohm* decision, a freedom of choice among potential state protectors. If the individual is able to find a state willing and able to protect him, with or without pecuniary inducement, that state should be authorized to protect him.[477] This change could easily be effected by a presumption of the validity of a certification of nationality for purposes of suit.

A third recommendation is some centralization, or organized internationalization, of the protection function on the global level. A relatively unorganized internationalization of the function would be to permit states to volunteer to protect individuals, somewhat in the fashion provided for signatories of the European Convention on Human Rights.[478] A more organized form would be a centralized international ombudsman within the framework of the United Nations.

The concept of "United Nations citizenship" might be given substance by a specialized United Nations agency for the protection of the disfranchised people of the world. The establishment "within the framework of the United Nations" of "a body" to which a stateless person "may apply for the examination of his claim and for assistance in presenting it to the appropriate authority," as envisaged in Article 11 of

---

477. The Convention on the Prevention and Punishment of Crimes against Internationally Protected Persons, including Diplomatic Agents (U.N. Doc. A/RES/3166 (XXVIII) of Feb. 5, 1974, *reprinted in* 13 I.L.M. 41 (1974)), which was adopted by the United Nations General Assembly and opened for signature on Feb. 5, 1974, would appear to make an important advance in this direction. Art. 6(2)(a) provides that an alleged offender, "if he is a stateless person," shall be entitled "to communicate without delay with the nearest appropriate representative of the State . . . which he requests and which is willing to protect his rights." 13 I.L.M. 46 (1974).

The recommendation we make for ameliorating the condition of stateless persons and persons possessing multiple nationality with respect to all values is simply that they be accorded basic human rights as formulated in contemporary prescriptions. Apart from nationality problems, their problems are the same as those of people having one nationality: they share all the same demands, identifications, and expectations and are subject to all the same finite limitations. For an excellent statement of this perspective, *see* Kellogg, *Refugees and Human Rights: The Path Ahead,* 69 DEP'T STATE BULL. 375 (1973).

478. The reference is to the state-to-state complaint system developed under Art. 24 of the European Convention on Human Rights. Under this provision a contracting state may refer to the European Commission of Human Rights alleged violations of the Convention, regarding not only its own nationals, but also nonnationals. *See* COUNCIL OF EUROPE, THE EUROPEAN CONVENTION ON HUMAN RIGHTS 12–13 (1968); EUROPEAN COMMISSION OF HUMAN RIGHTS, STOCK-TAKING ON THE EUROPEAN CONVENTION ON HUMAN RIGHTS (DH [72] 7) 4–11 (1972); A. ROBERTSON, HUMAN RIGHTS IN EUROPE 58–62 (1963); L. SOHN & T. BUERGENTHAL, *supra* note 474, at 1050–90; Fawcett, *supra* note 279, at 275–77. Also relevant are the state-to-state complaint systems embodied under Art. 11 of the International Convention on the Elimination of All Forms of Racial Discrimination and Art. 41 of the International Covenant on Civil and Political Rights. U.N. HUMAN RIGHTS INSTRUCMENTS, *supra* note 70, at 25–26 and 14 respectively.

the Convention on the Reduction of Statelessness,[479] together with the experience of the Office of the United Nations High Commissioner for Refugees (UNHCR) in protecting and assisting refugees (especially in helping them obtain identity papers and travel documents from governments concerned[480]), may suggest the rudiments of a model that could be expanded and improved. Instead of merely using its good offices to secure the cooperation of national governments and leaving the ultimate decision in these governments, as is presently the case with the Office of UNHCR,[481] the proposed U.N. agency could be empowered to confer, under its own authority, "world citizenship" (a "United Nations citizenship") upon individuals and thus itself perform the necessary protective function. Pending the achievement of a world commonwealth of free persons in open frontiers, United Nations citizenship could be made to coexist with the existing nationalities of states. All human beings should be eligible—whether out of necessity or out of choice—for such United Nations citizenship.

Nationality is a concept created in the past to promote a minimum organization of the world under past conditions. The reference and function of the concept cannot remain static: it must be as dynamic as the changing demands and identifications of peoples and the changing configuration of the world and national constitutive processes. In the words of the *Harvard Research on the Law of Nationality,*

> Nationality has no positive, immutable meaning. On the contrary its meaning and import have changed with the changing character of states. Thus nationality in the feudal period differed essentially from nationality, or what corresponded to it, in earlier times before states had become established within definite territorial limits, and it differs now from what it was in the feudal period. It may acquire a new meaning in the future as the result of further changes in the character of human society and developments in international organization.[482]

As human beings seek greater fulfillment of all values, through ever increasing transnational interactions and ever more frequent mobility, in

---

479. U.N. Human Rights Instruments, *supra* note 70, at 56.

480. *See* Arts. 27 and 28 of the Convention Relating to the Status of Refugees, U.N. Human Rights Instruments, *supra* note 70, at 67–68.

481. Identity papers and travel documents are issued by the respective governments of the contracting parties to the Refugee Convention or to the Protocol to the Refugee Convention, not by the Office of the United Nations High Commissioner for Refugees. The Office of the UNHCR is not empowered to issue such papers.

482. *Harvard Research, supra* note 1, at 21.

a world of intimate interdependences and the universalizing culture of science and technology, nationality must be made to serve the development and happiness of human beings, and not to perpetuate human bondage by anchoring people, against their will, in a particular territorial community, or alternatively casting them adrift when it is withdrawn. The time has come to make the law of nationality defend and fulfill the human rights of the individual.

TABLE OF CASES

NAME INDEX

SUBJECT INDEX